THE

AMERICAN

CENTURY

———

THE AMERICAN CENTURY

BY

HAROLD EVANS

WITH

GAIL BUCKLAND

AND

KEVIN BAKER

JONATHAN CAPE · PIMLICO
LONDON

Published by Jonathan Cape/Pimlico 1998

2 4 6 8 10 9 7 5 3 1

Copyright © Harold Evans 1998

First published in the United States of America in 1998 by Alfred A. Knopf, Inc.

First published in Great Britain in 1998 by Jonathan Cape/Pimlico
Random House, 20 Vauxhall Bridge Road, London SW1V 2SA

Random House Australia (Pty) Limited
20 Alfred Street, Milsons Point, Sydney, New South Wales 2061, Australia

Random House New Zealand Limited
18 Poland Road, Glenfield, Auckland 10, New Zealand

Random House South Africa (Pty) Limited
Endulini, 5A Jubilee Road, Parktown 2193, South Africa

Random House UK Limited Reg. No. 954009

A CIP catalogue record for this book is available from the British Library

ISBN
0-224-05217-9 (Jonathan Cape)
0-7126-6570-6 (Pimlico)

Title page **A KENNEDY LAUNCHING: Caroline Kennedy christens the world's largest conventionally powered aircraft carrier in Newport News, Virginia. It is named after her father, John F. Kennedy, four years after his death in Dallas. Her mother, her brother, John, and President Johnson approve of a sparkling performance. Photograph by George Tames.**

Endpapers **THE BIG FLAG: The unifying symbolism of the Stars and Stripes was much cherished as the wounds of the Civil War healed. The makers of this one, at the Amoskeag River Mills of Manchester, New Hampshire, put it on show on July 4, 1915. It was 95 feet long, 50 feet high, and weighed 200 pounds. Photograph by Harlan A. Marshall.**

TO GEORGE AND ISABEL,
NEW AMERICANS

GRASSROOTS DEMOCRACY: Ralph Yarborough politicking from the courthouse steps on a lazy summer day in northeast Texas, July 3, 1954.
Yarborough was to be involved in drama as a U.S. Democratic Senator from 1957 to 1970. In his first year he was one of the three southerners whose
votes Senator Lyndon Johnson secured to pass the first civil rights legislation since Reconstruction. In 1963, a feud between the liberal Yarborough
and the conservative governor John Connally was one of the reasons President John Kennedy went to Dallas. Photograph by Russell Lee.

CONTENTS

x   PREFACE

xiii   INTRODUCTION
WHY IT CAN BE CALLED
THE AMERICAN CENTURY

2   CHAPTER ONE
THE LAST FRONTIER
1889–1893

20   CHAPTER TWO
SHOWDOWN FOR DEMOCRACY
1890–1898

48   CHAPTER THREE
THE LURE OF EMPIRE
1898–1905

82   CHAPTER FOUR
OLD AND NEW AMERICANS
1880–1910

106   CHAPTER FIVE
WORKERS TAKE A STAND
1893–1916

140   CHAPTER SIX
GOOD TIMES, BAD TIMES
1914–1920

180   CHAPTER SEVEN
THE TURMOIL OF NORMALCY
1920–1929

218   CHAPTER EIGHT
THE DREAM TURNS TO DUST
1929–1939

282   CHAPTER NINE
THE ROAD TO WORLD WAR II
1936–1941

314   CHAPTER TEN
THE CITADEL OF DEMOCRACY
1941–1945

386   CHAPTER ELEVEN
AMERICA LEADS
1945–1956

452   CHAPTER TWELVE
THE DAWN OF A NEW FREEDOM
1954–1965

522   CHAPTER THIRTEEN
THE WAR OF LOST ILLUSIONS
1963–1975

566   CHAPTER FOURTEEN
THE IMPERIAL PRESIDENCY
1972–1980

612   CHAPTER FIFTEEN
PUT OUT MORE FLAGS
1981–1989

653   AFTERWORD
LET FREEDOM RING

665   ACKNOWLEDGMENTS
PHOTOGRAPHIC ACKNOWLEDGMENTS
BIBLIOGRAPHY
INDEX
ILLUSTRATION CREDITS

This book is the thanks of an immigrant to the United States, and a celebration of my becoming an American citizen. I have lived and worked in America since 1984, but I first came to this country in 1956 on the generous dollars of a Harkness Commonwealth Fund program that sought to acquaint European journalists with "the real America." I looked for it in 40 states. I imbibed at the universities of Chicago and Stanford and took 12 months to cross the country, north and south, coast to coast, driving a Plymouth, and sometimes sleeping in it. In the wake of the 1954 *Brown* school-desegregation ruling, I reported from the South, notably Mississippi, Georgia, Alabama and North Carolina, as the white backlash gained momentum and the new black leaders and white liberals gathered up their courage. I looked into the predicaments of an older minority, living for a short time among the Navajo in Arizona. In Fort Sill, Oklahoma, I spent an afternoon with the last surviving Apache who had ridden with Geronimo (and I corresponded with him and his wife until his death). In Chicago, in the middle of the crises over Suez and Hungary, I was a 1956 campaign groupie for Adlai Stevenson, but found myself unaccountably cheering for the opposition when we went to a small airport and Ike grinned and waved to us from the steps of a light plane. And back in New York I saw the Brooklyn Dodgers play where they should play.

The political experiences then and later gave me an enduring fascination with the idea of America and its unceasing struggle to achieve its ideals. I came to feel there was a need for an accessible popular political history, and I feel it more keenly today when there are so many new Americans who may not know the nature of their heritage. To that end I decided to use photography and illustration to present significant political episodes and personalities of the century. I organized these narrative pages as self-contained "modular" units, without runover, so that the casual reader can dip into any spread of pages and absorb what he or she chooses with-

out having to begin at the beginning: history for browsers. But I have also set out to give the episodes perspective and meaning by relating them to enduring themes in commentaries at the opening of each of the 15 chapters. "History as an act of inquiry," wrote Allen Weinstein, "involves putting great questions to small data, discovering general significance in small events." In these commentaries on great questions, I have tried to follow the flames of liberty and equality and to understand what saves them from extinction in the exuberant gusts of opinion characteristic of American society. I have paid consistent attention to the oppressed—to blacks, Indians, women, immigrants and others—since they are a denial of the promise of America; to America's role as a leader of nations; and throughout to individuals who made a difference. As to sources, the arguments are mine, but I have drawn most of the facts from published works—though some are also from my notes from the fifties, and some are from more recent interviews and conversations. The nature of the book suggested that footnotes would be a nuisance, but I have included a selected bibliography for each chapter as an indication of the principal published sources.

So, 40 years since I stepped off the steamship *Franconia* into a New York syncopating with the rhythms of the fifties, I offer a selective newsreel of the half century before and the half century after. I chose the year 1889 to open *The American Century* because 1889 was indeed the beginning of the second century in the life of the Republic. The year does, however, have a certain felicity for a book with 900 photographs. It was in 1889 that popular photography began with the arrival of "The Kodak Camera" from George Eastman of Rochester, New York, giving the amateur snapper equality of opportunity with the professional photographer. For this book, I like to think of the first Kodak—used to take the facing photograph—as a metaphor for America's dedication to making all men free and equal.

—Harold Evans, New York, 1998

AMERICA CELEBRATES: The New York street crowd, snapped by one of the newfangled Kodak cameras, is watching the George Washington centennial parade on April 30, 1889. It was part of the celebrations marking the first hundred years of the Republic and its entry into its second century—the century that was to become The American Century.

WHY IT CAN BE CALLED THE AMERICAN CENTURY

I N THE SPRING OF 1889 a white barge rowed by 13 sea captains, one for each of the original states, nudges into a Wall Street pier. There is a roar of gunfire from a squadron of warships in the harbor. The dainty figure who steps ashore is Benjamin Harrison, the 23rd president of the United States, and, more memorably, the first president of the United States to serve in its second century. It is 100 years to the day since President-elect George Washington landed at the same spot. Washington came ashore without the cannonade; there was no naval salute for the first president because in 1789 America had no navy to speak of. He had left his home at Mount Vernon on April 16 "with a mind oppressed with more anxious and painful sensations than I have words to express." On April 29, in New York, the new nation's first capital city, he delivered the first inaugural address and launched the United States into history: the Constitution had been ratified in 1788, the first elections had been held in January 1789 and only on that bright clear day in April did the government of the United States properly begin.

George Washington presided over a nation of nearly 4 million citizens who were concentrated on the eastern seaboard. The 23rd president prayed, with the first president's inaugural Bible in his hand, for a nation of 62 million people who had conquered a continent. One hundred years later, in April 1989, the 41st president, George Bush, spoke for almost 250 million people who had come to a preeminent position of leadership in the world. This second hundred years spans

AN AMERICAN ROUTINE: The citizens waiting for a May Day parade advertise American individualism. Jefferson's words around the flagpole remind them of American exceptionalism: "How little do my countrymen know what precious blessings they are in possession of, and which no other people on earth enjoy." The scene is New York's Union Square, 1947, the site of the last Tammany Hall, and of thousands of Democratic, Socialist, Communist, free speech, union and human rights rallies over the last century. Photograph by Jerome Liebling.

most of the twentieth century, but sheds its radiance over the whole of it. The twentieth century is the American century. The British dominated the nineteenth century, and the Chinese may cast a long shadow on the twenty-first, but the twentieth century belongs to the United States because of the triumph of its faith in its founding idea of political and economic freedom.

The political inspiration for an open and equitable society may have been the British and French philosophers of the Enlightenment, but the practical working out of the paths to individual fulfillment was principally American; and the idea of a free community of nations linked by friendship and ideals, rather than simply the mechanisms of the balance of power, was distinctly American. These are the key titles to the property. It is of note that in only the second century of its existence the United States became the world's leading economic, military and cultural power. It is remarkable that in this short period it did not merely double or triple the wealth of its citizens but increased their well-being five times over, so that they came to enjoy a standard of living and an expectation of life heretofore unknown in the history of the world. It is an intriguing commentary on style that the material pleasures of these Americans—their movies, their hamburgers and colas, their slang and their clothes—became, as *Time*'s Henry Luce put it, "the only things that every community in the world from Zanzibar to Hamburg recognizes in common." But none of this adds up to a decisive claim on the century. The glory of a people does not lie in their economic indexes, their actuarial tables or even the fame of their designer jeans: it lies in their idealism, in the use they make of their resources, in the kind of people they become amid the temptations of pride and greed.

In the twentieth century, the essentially isolationist American people did more than grow rich and expand their domestic freedoms. They sustained Western civilization by acts of courage, generosity and vision unparalleled in the history of man. They concerted the defeat of the Fascist tyranny and they contained Soviet totalitarianism until it buried itself—the fate Nikita Khrushchev had not too long before predicted for the West.

America's political system, created by and for an agricultural democracy, was exuberantly adapted in the first few decades of its second century to the complexities of an industrial society. It was a more agonizing experience for America to adapt itself to this new role as a dominant power in the world. That acute and sympathetic analyst of America,

Alexis de Tocqueville, saw much of the domestic potential of democracy, but not the capacity for creative world leadership that evolved in the American democracy. Observing America in the 1830s, he suggested that democracy would be found inferior in the conduct of foreign policy because it could not combine its measures with secrecy or await its consequences with patience: "Almost all the nations that have exercised a powerful influence upon the destinies of the world, by conceiving, following out and executing vast designs, from the Romans to the English, have been governed by aristocratic institutions." Some Americans who were prominent in later years, like Adlai Stevenson and Dean Acheson, saw the implications of American power very early, but the mass of people wanted to insulate themselves from conflicts beyond their hemisphere; they were slow to realize that they could no longer do that. The mood of the country then was well reflected in the exasperation of a leader of mass opinion normally more given to cheerleading than playing Cassandra. Luce wrote an essay in *Time* in 1941 that he called "The American Century," but the title was then more a hope than a reality. He began: "We Americans are unhappy. We are not happy about America. We are not happy about ourselves in relation to America. We are nervous—or gloomy—or apathetic." The cause, he suggested, was that Americans were unable to accommodate themselves spiritually and practically to the fact that they had become the most powerful and vital nation in the world. Luce sounded reveille. His call was for America to devote itself "in joy and gladness and vigor and enthusiasm" to become the powerhouse from which the ideals of civilization, of justice, truth and charity, "spread throughout the world and do their mysterious work of lifting the life of mankind from the levels of the beasts to what the Psalmist called a little lower than the angels."

Luce's muscular prose, reeking too much perhaps of tent pegs and clean living, did not appeal to everyone. Historian John Chamberlain spoke up for the prevailing isolationist sentiment and the grassroots distrust of doctrine of any kind. What Luce was calling for in his invocation of the "high-order abstraction" of "the American Century," said Chamberlain, was a straight-line Prometheanism. Americans, said Chamberlain, were not so heroic. Luce's program required a faith that "can only be sustained for short periods"; and since people were not normally Promethean in large numbers, Luce's program must, in ordinary times, fall into the hands of the hypocrites who were skilled in using great slogans for nefarious purposes. An interventionist America might well degenerate into "an imperialism that will fail in liberality and become something very close to the Nazi thing." The Nazi comparison (even before the Holocaust) was far-fetched, but Chamberlain was prophetic in sensing the temptations of paternalism and the presumption of promising the world more than could possibly be delivered. Ralph Waldo Emerson had put it more poetically: "The spread eagle must fold his foolish wings and be less of a peacock."

Certainly what America did for Europe and Japan, it failed to do for Latin America, too often abandoning its ideals to crush an exotic nationalism. And again in the 1960s Chamberlain's worries found justification in the ill-judged intervention in Indochina. The transition from isolationism to a benevolent internationalism was partly unintended. It owed something to the felicitous blunders of adversaries: in 1916, to the Kaiser's declaration of unrestricted submarine warfare; in 1941, to Japan's treachery at Pearl Harbor and Hitler's rashness in declaring war on the United States. It also depended to a disconcerting degree on happenstances of physical geography. Had the bullet that killed the mayor of Chicago found its intended target in Franklin Roosevelt, had the car that knocked down Winston Churchill on Park Avenue been going a little faster . . . Surely, for a start, Britain, too, without American aid and without inspired leadership, would have been overrun by the Nazis or made a deal with them. All Europe would have been Fascist by 1941, which would have been, shall we say, an awkward moment for America. Or if Hitler had lost to Stalin, Communist hegemony might have anticipated the Cold War but with grimmer geopolitics. But in the end, for all the rough edges, the 50 years that followed Luce's bugle call vindicated his faith in America. And how! as he might have written. The nationalism of the twenties and thirties was not merely tempered by a realistic self-interest. It was replaced by a vision of leading a plurality of like-minded nations, if necessary at a sacrifice. Toward the end of the twentieth century America's economic power was preeminent, and the competitive strength of the countries of Europe and the Pacific Rim was itself an American accomplishment. Wartime enemies and allies alike were joined in the new liberal international order. No design has been nobler in conception or more brilliant in execution than the complex of international organizations for economic welfare, health, education, collective security and human rights that America nourished in the second half of the century.

There were periods in the conduct of its own affairs, as in its international leadership, when America wavered and regressed in its moral vision. It is never an easy matter to hold the balance between economic individualism and social welfare, between free-for-all capitalism and the rights of labor, between states' rights and the unifying central government. Arthur Schlesinger, Jr., has elaborated the hypothesis of a cyclical pattern in American history, swings between periods of private interest and public purpose, but with continuity maintained in that conservatism and reform liberalism are both committed to individual liberty, the constitutional state and the rule of laws. But if, as he says, the two jostling strains in American thought agree more than they disagree, the velocity of the oscillations is often disturbing. In the opening decades the surge of private interest in great industrial combinations, blessed by corrupt legislatures and unimpeded by complaisant courts, left little breathing space for individualism or social equity. Americans proved to have an exceptional gift for business organization, but working men, women and children were grossly exploited and the natural resources of the country ransacked without care for tomorrow. There were times of paranoia in the twenties, forties and fifties, when good men did nothing and the values of a free society were in jeopardy. No constitution dispenses with the need for courage in its defense. The freedom promised to all was long denied to many and abused for the benefit of the few. The patriotism of the citizens was betrayed time and again by unnecessary secrecy in the guise of national security. In the prosperous 1960s and 1980s there were occasions of cruelty, intolerance and injustice that wrenched America from its true path. The "great barbecue" of materialism was ablaze in the eighties; but the inner city ghettos festered untouched, a reproach to the "American dream."

At the beginning of the second century it was open to question whether a country of such diverse stock and impossible ideals could survive its own experiment. Walt Whitman thought America might prove to be "the most tremendous failure of all time." The 24-year-old Rudyard Kipling, crossing the country for the first time in 1889, saw America as an epic archipelago of warring tribes that was bound to break up as the disgruntled factions competed for a share of diminishing natural resources. Kipling was a jealous foreigner, but in 1901 the great American historian Henry Adams predicted: "At the rate of increase of speed and momentum, the present society must break its damn neck in a definite, but remote, time, not exceeding fifty years or more." The young scholar Frederick Jackson Turner told historians at the World's Columbian Exhibition in Chicago in 1893 that the American characteristics of energy, dominant individualism and democracy must be in jeopardy because they had their roots in a frontier that had all but vanished.

H. G. Wells had the nerve to put all this skepticism to the most ebullient of presidents when he visited Theodore Roosevelt in the White House in 1905: "Does this magnificent appearance of beginnings which is America convey any clear and certain promise of permanence and fulfillment whatever? Is America a giant childhood or a giant futility?" Roosevelt could offer no effective disproof of the idea that America must presently falter, but he chose to live as if the dream could be realized. He clenched his fist with the force of his conviction: "The effort—the effort's worth it."

Roosevelt was the embodiment of the enlightened, creative will that sustained America in the dark passages of its second century. And we can now answer with experience the question that he answered with hope. America was more than merely the latest phase of a long succession of experiments in man's social history. It worked. It worked because the effort was inspired by the inner light of freedom. Democracy delivered. It honored the expectations of prosperity, the right to own land and a home, the entitlement to a free education, and to equality before the law. America is denigrated still, but it is emulated by those who criticized it the most, so that America, it is said, has a franchise on the future. The ebbs and cycles by which it reached this point will occupy historians for decades, but they may be suggested now through some of the personalities and events of America's second century, and that is the purpose of this book.

It is a fitting opening for this American century that the immigrants arriving by steamship in 1889 could see something their predecessors in earlier decades could not: that symbol of American zest and confidence, the skyscraper. New York's first skeleton steel skyscraper was finished in 1889, and Joseph Pulitzer's World Tower, with its golden dome, was rising, just 36 feet nearer the clouds than the new tower put up by the *New York Times*. The Statue of Liberty was only three years old and the Brooklyn Bridge, the first to

THE LURE OF THE WEST: Tweed's Ranch, at the head of Beaver Creek in Fremont County, Wyoming, 1903. The 13-year-old state was the scene of some of the fiercest struggles between big ranchers and homesteaders. The original populations of Shoshone and Arapaho Plains Indians were by now confined to the Wind River Reservation, but the white population at the turn of the century was only around 100,000 for the whole state. Photograph by J. E. Stimson.

use steel for cable wire, only six. The bridge was itself a soaring metaphor for what an immigrant to America might do: John Augustus Roebling, who designed it, came from Prussia. Such was the swaggering speed of growth from 1889 on that the first skyscraper was soon regarded as unremarkable, and within a decade the word "skyline" had entered the language. The ramparts of the city were suggestive of more than energy. They were emblematic of the great divide between the old and the new America. The agrarian and frontier society of the nineteenth century, characterized by smallness of scale, remoteness, regionalism and modest growth, and by settled convictions of individualism and insularity, was now about to be supplanted by a dynamic, questioning, industrial America characterized by bigness, accessibility and rapid growth. By 1890 the great new transcontinental railroads and the adventurous river steamboats had put 55 million consumers and unlimited cheap raw materials within monopolistic reach of the manufacturers and their apprentice engineers of mass production. A continental market and a national consciousness were ready to grow hand in hand.

There were still huge regional differences, physical, political and psychological. The eastern seaboard, which had the money, and the Middle West, which had the muscle, contained nearly half the population on a sixth of the land space and most of the imaginative enterprise. Chicago, "hog butcher for the world," was shouldering its way out of its boundaries, the paradigm of the new industrial metropolis. It had by 1889 come to surpass Philadelphia as America's second most populous city. With rather more than a million people, it was the fifth-largest German city of the globe, the third Swedish and the second Polish. It was to beat out New York for the honor of staging the 1893 World's Columbian Exposition, celebrating the 400th anniversary of the discovery of America by envisaging the city of the future as classical Rome with electric lighting. But, by all contemporary accounts, the gilt of what Mark Twain spoofed as "the gilded age" was a thin veneer. Of Chicago, Kipling declared: "A city—a real city. I urgently desire never to see it again. It is inhabited by savages."

Only the eastern seaboard had the appearance of a settled civilization in city and countryside. Twenty-four years after

EVER HIGHER: Skyscrapers, symbolic of America's rise to power, went up so rapidly from the start of America's second century, that "the world's tallest building" one year often lost its title the next. The 792-foot, 60-story Woolworth Building being constructed here kept the crown from 1913 to 1930, when it was displaced by the Chrysler Building, which in turn was displaced in 1931 by the 1,250-foot Empire State Building. Photograph by Brown Brothers.

the Civil War, the melancholy beauty of the South was in weedy ruins. The West had more animals than people and no political clout: the territories of Oklahoma, Arizona and New Mexico had no senators or congressmen in Washington. From the Alleghenies to the Pacific coast, according to that shrewd reporter Mark Sullivan, editor of *Collier's*, the picture of the United States at the beginning of its second century was "mainly of a country still frontier and of a people still in flux": mountain valleys raw with coal breakers, furnaces and smokestacks; western Pennsylvania and eastern Ohio erupting with wooden oil derricks; sod houses on the freshly furrowed prairies, townships of flimsy wood-frame houses and false tops, suggesting transiency, scattered at great distances along the east-west line of the Santa Fe and the Union Pacific. Robert Louis Stevenson described riding a railroad car on the long journey west. The settlers and fortune hunters packed in on narrow wooden benches. At night, as the steam engine thundered into the blackness of the plains, they lay on wooden boards stretched across the benches and paid two dollars for three straw cushions; before the sun was up the stove would be burning brightly, and at the first station "the natives would come on board with milk and eggs and coffee cakes and soon from end to end the car would be filled with little parties breakfasting upon the bed boards." The director of the U.S. Census reported in 1889 that the country's unsettled areas were so broken into isolated bodies of settlement that "there can hardly be said to be a frontier line." During 1889–90, the paraphernalia of statehood—legislatures, elections and the judiciary—came to the roustabout mining camps and cow towns of the territories of North and South Dakota, Montana, Washington, Wyoming and Idaho. It still took a hardy spirit to make the 13-day journey from New York to California. Stevenson says that as they steamed west they met equally crowded trains going east. On the plains of Nebraska and in the mountains of Wyoming, the waiting eastbound passengers ran to the station platform and cried to them through the train windows, "Come back! Come back!" But the old America would never come back.

In 1889 the country was enjoying one of four relatively good years in the middle of a long-wave depression that had begun in 1873 and would run in fits and starts to 1897. Somewhat more than 900,000 were out of work, 4 percent of the labor force, but the 6 million employed in manufacturing, construction and mining were somewhat better off than in Queen Victoria's prosperous Britain and far better off than in

mainland Europe. Working 60 hours a week, an unskilled immigrant could earn in two to three months the $100 it would take a year to earn in Italy or Hungary. Though not as skewed as Britain, wealth in America was grossly ill distributed: the wealthy and well-to-do, 12 percent of families, owned 86 percent of the real and personal property, but family income was more evenly spread. Five and a half million

PARALLELS: 1890–1990

	1890	1990
Total area in square miles	3,021,295	3,732,396
Total population	62,947,714	248,709,973
Percent black	11.9	12.3
Percent white	87.3	83.9
Percent "other"	0.8	3.8
Median age	22	32
Male life expectancy	46.3	71.8
Female life expectancy	48.3	78.8
Number of immigrants	455,132	1,536,000
Percent of population belonging to organized religious bodies	34	63
Total federal budget outlays (millions)	$318	$1,252,705
Defense expenditures (millions)*	$67	$328,400
Military personnel on active duty	38,666	2,044,000
Wine, beer and liquor consumed (gallons per capita)	15.53	39.2
Percent of population with right to vote (presidential elections) 1892–1992)†	26.9	76.0
Percent of above who voted	74.7	55.2
Gross national product (billions)	$13.1	$5,567.8
Gross national product per capita	$280	$22,276
Percent of women over age 15 (1890) or 16 (1990) who worked outside the home	18.9	57.5
Percent of infants in Massachusetts who died before age one	16.3	0.7
Number of patents issued	25,322	61,819
Miles of railroad track in operation	199,876	239,000
Miles of telephone wire (thousands)	250	1,500,000
Average number of phone calls per day nationwide (millions)	1.4	9,515
Daily newspapers in print	1,610	1,611
Total circulation (millions)	8.4	62.3
New books published	4,559	46,738

*Includes veterans' compensation and pensions
†Does not take into account Jim Crow laws

families were in the poorer classes, earning less than $500 a year, about the poverty level; but five and a half million were in the middle class ($500 to $5,000). The middle class was growing and it was already the most prosperous in the world. There were iceboxes instead of refrigerators, of course, and no vacuum cleaners yet, but some of their homes were furnished with the new telephone, and they could indulge the craze for popular music on a wind-up Gramophone from Sears, retailing at $18.75 plus $5 for 12 of its "best and loudest" records. Taxes were low. There was no income tax. (There were fewer than 200,000 federal employees to support, in contrast with 3 million in 1989.) The papers were full of enticements to join "representatives of wealth and intelligence" in buying a home in Florida, and 60,000 people paid the $100 passage for a cabin cruise to Europe.

It was the Americans who worked the land who were most in distress. The unskilled agricultural worker in the North earned about $260 a year, the southerner less than $200 (about $2,600 in 1990 dollars). Ten men could now produce the wheat it had taken 60 to produce in 1822, thanks to the gang plows, the reapers, the harvesters and threshers, but farmers and planters were caught between falling world prices and rising costs of credit and equipment. Their wives might like to thumb through the new mail-order catalogues invented by Montgomery Ward (1872) and Sears, Roebuck (1886) but they could afford little. Farmers had to pledge the bulk of their crop to borrow money for seed, feedstuffs and implements, and the suppliers in this crop-lien system charged rates of interest of 60 percent and more. The best-selling book in 1889 was Edward Bellamy's *Looking Backward,* a utopian novel about a non-Marxist socialist community in the year 2000, but the farmers were not willing to wait that long. An agrarian revolt had stirred in the South and was spreading west, seeding new political movements that would challenge and transform the two main parties. Curiously, to our generation, it was the Republicans who favored a more active government (but one at the service of surging capitalism) and the Democrats who wanted to limit intervention in the affairs of states and individuals.

The American living in the South was by far the worst off. Millions, white as well as black, were ensnared in the crop-lien system in a state of helpless peonage, ownership of the land forfeited, the indebtedness carried beyond the grave to be inherited by the sons. In the North children had seven years of free school; in the South they were lucky to get three. There was no hope of relief from conventional political action; the Civil War had left the South with a one-party monopoly that demanded white solidarity but acted for the landlord, the merchant and the industrialist. Black men and women, one tenth of the population, suffered the hatred of the South and the indifference of the North. The vote they had gained by the Civil War was exercised under duress and in starkly reduced numbers after white supremacy was restored in 1877; by 1889 Mississippi was leading the way with legal strategems to get around the Fifteenth Amendment and remove the right to vote altogether. Not all the blacks accepted their oppression meekly, despite the terror and intrigue wreaked upon them. The *Washington Post* reported the proceedings of an Afro-American convention in Chicago where the delegates replied sarcastically to those white residents of "Alabama, South Carolina, Louisiana and the other southern states" who wanted the blacks sent back to Africa. The convention resolved to "petition the honorable Congress . . . to make an appropriation of $100 million to furnish the unhappy white citizens of those states, who may wish to resettle in other and more favored states, free from Afro-American majorities, the means to do so."

The privations on the land were a principal reason that, in the last decade of the nineteenth century, for every 100 immigrants arriving 37 were going home again. Still, the pace of gross immigration was accelerating in 1889, and so was the breakneck speed of western settlement. Four times as much land was offered by the government after 1890 as before, and it was all snapped up. The half-million people who arrived in 1889—they were mainly laborers—were German, British, Irish, Italian, Scandinavian and Polish, in that order, joining the older Americans of predominantly British Protestant and Irish Catholic stock. Every nineteenth-century president, except Martin Van Buren, traced his family roots back to Britain. The white Anglo-Saxon Protestants who ran the country were beginning to worry about the new waves of immigrants from the east and south of Europe. Nearly 10 million of the population were now foreign-born, and the Roman Catholic Church, with 8 million members, had become the largest single church in the country. Three and a half million Americans were Methodists, 1.25 million Southern Baptist and 790,000 Presbyterian. Jews were only just starting to come in substantial numbers. This polyglot mass shared a common feature, noted by Henry James when he returned home after 25 years in England and rode on one of the new electric streetcars lit by Thomas Edison's incandescent light:

"The great fact . . . was that, foreign as they might be, newly inducted as they might be, they were really more at home . . . than they had ever been before." The children of the immigrants, British historian James Bryce reported, were eager to cast away their old nationality and to become in every sense Americans; such was "the educative as well as the assimilative power of the American environment."

It was not a fanciful observation. The patriotism of the new Americans was intense and extrovert enough to irritate the British Empire jingoist Kipling. He complained of their noisiness. They had a habit of boastful quantification and constant asseverations: "I was an American by birth—an American from way back." He saw it as a sign of the fragility of their connection to the land. "It must be an awful thing to live in a country where you have to explain that you really belong there." Bryce had a more genial interpretation. He was struck by how democracy had not only taught the Americans how to use liberty and how to secure equality, it had also taught them fraternity. The recognition of the duty of mutual help owed by citizen to citizen was stronger than anywhere in the Old World, and especially stronger than among the monied classes of England, France and Germany. He enthused over the relative absence of barriers of class or caste to obstruct the rise of merit. This was certainly true for both native-born and immigrant white Americans. The Scots-American steelmaster Andrew Carnegie began as a telegraph messenger; King Camp Gillette, who put his steel to such brilliant use, was a traveling hardware salesman when he invented the safety razor; America's richest man, John D. Rockefeller, had been a clerk in a commission house; the railway tycoon James J. Hill had begun as a clerk in a village store, and the genius of the department store, John Wanamaker, as a clerk in a men's clothing shop. In 1889, the great electrical engineer Charles Steinmetz was a 24-year-old immigrant who had fled Breslau because he feared persecution for his Socialist beliefs. Herbert Hoover was a 15-year-old office boy who went to night school and tried to set up a business salvaging wrecked sewing machines.

Women were not prominent in business or party politics, but they were brave and sensitive pioneers of social reform, leaders in education and religion. It was in 1889 that Jane Addams and Ellen Gates Starr set up their settlement at Hull House in Chicago, enriching the lives of poor immigrant women and training a generation of social workers. In 1890 the socialist Florence Kelley led a movement agitating for better conditions for retail saleswomen; and in 1892 the National Federation of Women's Clubs launched itself on a variety of social campaigns (though not yet for the vote). Women had only recently had access to higher education. They had no federal vote anywhere and only in Wyoming did they have a state vote. Socially, they were treated with elaborate courtesy and respect; and were expected to behave with ladylike restraint and recognize that their first place of duty was the home. It caused a sensation in 1889 in Washington, D.C., when two newly married women teachers refused to resign "as was the custom," according to the *Washington Post.* The trustees of the District of Columbia school board proclaimed that henceforth female schoolteachers would not be allowed to marry and retain their positions, and that all married teachers who refused to resign would be dismissed. The *Post* thought it prudent to ho-hum that while it could see the merits of married teachers, there was much to the custom of having a man support his wife. The trustees finally backed down in Washington, and Nellie Bly, a reporter for the *New York World,* flew a flag for liberty and equality by setting out on November 14 to better the fictional feat of Phileas Fogg in Jules Verne's *Around the World in Eighty Days:* she did it, by train and ship, in 72 days, 6 hours, 11 minutes. She was one of the 4 million women at work in 1889, out of a population of 23 million. Those who took jobs as secretaries were not known by that name: they were called typewriters, after the newfangled Remington machines. In the same year, Edward Bok, just 26 years of age, began his 30-year career as editor of a magazine that was to have a profound influence on all of them. He turned the *Ladies' Home Journal* into a bible of cooking, gardening, nursing, management and style for the American home. No more would the likes of Oscar Wilde be able to sneer at the ugliness of American interior decoration of "cast iron stoves, machine made furniture, and white walls." But the temper of the times did not tolerate Bok's campaign for sex education; 75,000 subscribers fled and he dropped it.

The position of the United States in the world in 1889 was ambiguous. Militarily it was insignificant: there were 38,666 men under arms, compared with European armies of half a million or more. But it was now the strongest industrial power and its citizens thought of their country as God's favorite. It was evidence of a condition noted by Henry Steele Commager that would confuse American politics for half a century: a dichotomy of political and economic imperialism and psychological isolationism. Walt Whitman was premature by a generation in his boastful stanza:

Have the elder races halted?
Do they droop and end their lesson,
Wearied over there beyond the seas?
We take up the task eternal.

Andrew Carnegie was also indulging in a little hyperbole when he wrote in 1886 that the upstart America now led the civilized world in population, in wealth, in annual savings, in public credit, in freedom from debt, in agriculture and in manufacture. Carnegie's pride was understandable. When he sold out to J. P. Morgan's bank in 1901, his steel company was producing more steel than the whole of Britain put together. And America had just inched out Britain for top place in the world's share of manufactures. Britain, workshop of the world, was as sensitive to "Americanization" as the Europeans were to become in the mid-1960s when Jacques Servan-Schreiber protested *le défi-americain,* or as the Americans were to become about the Japanese early in the last decade of the twentieth century. A turn-of-the-century British critic wrote an indictment of "the American Invaders" of his country:

"The average citizen wakes in the morning at the sound of an American alarum clock; rises from his New England sheets, and shaves with his New York soap, and Yankee safety razor. He pulls on a pair of Boston boots over his socks from West Carolina [*sic*], fastens his Connecticut braces, slips his Waterbury watch into his pocket and sits down to breakfast. . . . Rising from his breakfast table, the citizen rushes out, catches an electric tram, made in New York, to Shepherds Bush, where he gets into a Yankee elevator which takes him on to the American-fitted railway to the office. At his office of course everything is American. He sits on a Nebraskan swivel chair, before a Michigan roll top desk, writes his letters on a Syracuse typewriter, signing them with a New York fountain pen and drying them with a blotting sheet from New England. The letter copies are put away in files manufactured in Grand Rapids."

Still, at this precise point of the beginning of America's second century, Carnegie was wrong in his inference and in some particulars. It was one thing to exclude China, which was more populous but weak, but there were 116 million Russians to 62 million Americans; and Britain, a country the size of New Mexico, was still the dominant global power. Though Britain was increasingly challenged by Germany, united only as recently as 1870, Queen Victoria presided over a fifth of the earth's surface and a quarter of its population, the greatest empire the world had ever seen. Winston Churchill was in his second year at Harrow in 1889 and like every other English schoolboy he sang, "Rule Britannia, Britannia rules the waves / Britons never, never shall be slaves," and with good reason: the Royal Navy was stronger than the two next largest fleets put together (Russia and France). One third of all seagoing ships were British. Of every 1,000 tons of shipping passing through the Suez Canal, controlled by Britain, 700 tons were British, 95 German and only 2 American. When the financier J. P. Morgan tried to buy Cunard, the major British transatlantic carrier, the British government stepped in with a subsidy. It found this distasteful, but preferable to seeing Britain lose control of the North Atlantic. Britain was the world's banker, insurance broker and commodity dealer, and easily its leading investor. British companies and individuals owned large stakes in American mines, land and railroads: three quarters of the foreign investments in the United States, and in the world, were British. This fact provoked as much chauvinism in the United States as the fears of American penetration provoked in Britain.

But if Andrew Carnegie's exultation was a shade ahead of the facts in 1889, the Americans were going all out to make the facts catch up soon. "The old nations of the earth creep on at snail's pace, the Republic thunders past with the rush of the express," wrote Carnegie. "The United States, the growth of a single century, has already reached the foremost rank among nations, and is destined soon to outdistance all others in the race."

Industrially, he was right in more ways than even he could possibly have dreamed. It was to take all the political genius of America to reconcile this headlong materialism with the original virtues of the Republic and to figure out the responsibilities that went with world power. How would individualism survive the centralized corporate state? Would a laissez-faire philosophy doom the weak, the poor and the minorities? Would the political parties become the creatures of big money? How far should a free society limit enterprise? Could America survive as an integrated society if the door for the huddled masses remained open forever? Was there more to American life than the making of money? Perhaps we, standing on the threshold of the third century, will discern the light breaking in all directions, as Emerson did toward the end of that first century. "Trade and Government will not alone be the favored aims of mankind," he wrote, "but every useful, elegant art, every exercise of the imagination, the height of reason, the noblest affection, the purest religion, will find their home in our institutions, and write our laws for the benefit of men."

THE

AMERICAN

CENTURY

———

CHAPTER ONE

THE LAST FRONTIER
1889-1893

Land Rush

Here is the American frontier, vanishing before our eyes. One hundred and sixty acres of God's earth was the vision that drew thousands of new Americans—English, Italians, Greeks, Welsh, Poles and Russians—to the border of what is now Oklahoma, a state that gets its name from a fusion of two Choctaw Indian words, *okla,* meaning people, and *humma,* meaning red. The land was free, courtesy of the United States government, which had forced Indian tribes to sell it 2 million acres. It was one of the first acts of the new president, Benjamin Harrison, who proclaimed the lands open to settlement four years after his Democratic predecessor, Grover Cleveland, sympathetic to the Indians, had stopped settlement and warned that intruders on Indian land would be removed by troops.

The first stampede across the Indian Territory line began at high noon on April 22, 1889, when a trumpeter of the 5th Cavalry, which had been keeping back the so-called boomers, sounded the "dinner call." Many of the boomers, for all their dash, found they were beaten to it by "Sooners," who had been infiltrating since 1884 and were ready with their flags and stakes to claim prime land. The outrage of the disappointed led to more Indian land being thrown open, culminating in the second boomer invasion, pictured here, on September 6, 1893.

They are after 6 million acres of the Cherokee Outlet. All of it had been land set aside for the Indians as a permanent home "for as long as grass grows and water runs."

STAMPEDE: When the former Indian Territory was opened at the prescribed hour, horsemen galloped across the border in a tumult of buckboards, hacks, drays and covered wagons. Trains steamed across with them, so crowded that passengers traveled on the tops of the cars. Half an hour later only dust on the horizon marked the passage of the boomers. All they had to do for their free land was stake a claim, pay a small registration fee, and cultivate it for five years. In the first rush in 1889, Guthrie had a population of 15,000 by nightfall—5,000 more than it had in 1989—and Oklahoma City had 10,000. There were three rival committees planning the town map of Guthrie. A man might go to sleep at night with a plot fronting on an open square, and wake in the morning to find his entire lot covered by a new street. But Guthrie got itself organized well enough to become the capital of the Territory and then, for three years, of the state of Oklahoma, admitted in 1907.

COWBOYS AND INDIANS

When the Atchison, Topeka and Santa Fe Railroad disgorged its bursting coaches in the tent town of Guthrie, Oklahoma, in 1889, fortune hunters got an immediate taste of frontier life. The only structure was the one-room land office. The only water was from a muddy creek a mile below the depot. It sold for ten cents a drink, a dollar a bucket ($14 in modern values). Troopers guarded the water tank for the Santa Fe's steam locomotives, with orders to shoot anyone trying to get at it.

The privations were minor by comparison with what was happening to the north on the semiarid, treeless Great Plains, where it had stopped raining four years earlier. The settlers watched crops and animals shrivel under a burning sun in a cloudless steel-blue sky. "I have seen it so dry," said one of the thousands of settlers who fled back east, "that you had to prime the mourners at a funeral so they could shed tears for the departed." It was the end of the boom years. Towns proud with church steeple and schoolhouse lay like skeletons bleaching in the sun, empty of life, the bones scoured by the sirocco winds. The covered wagons rolled east, not west, from western Kansas, Nebraska and the Dakotas; in 1891 no fewer than 18,000 crossed the Missouri into Iowa, and they famously advertised their story: "In God we trusted, in Kansas we busted."

These were grim years in the West; there were only two good years for rainfall in the ten years to 1897. It makes the settlement all the more remarkable. Even looked at from the accelerated society of 100 years later, the speed of it dazzles. Just think, said a proud senator, we have populated a territory larger than that of the original 13 states in half a dozen years. He was not far wrong, though people were sparse on the northern plains of Wyoming and Montana: one body to the square mile in Montana in 1890, and 0.6 to the square mile in Wyoming. The economic base of the success in populating the West was free and cheap land, the eagerly colonizing railroads and the easy credit provided by the prosperous East. Beef, wheat, lumber, gold, silver and copper were the produce: Montana was by 1899 providing 23 percent of the world's copper supply. The railroads were given 129 million acres of public land, and what they did not need they sold off with

missionary zeal to investors across America and in Europe. They advertised the theories of Hardy Webster Campbell, evangelist of "infallible" dry-land farming: if only Campbell's plethora of words had been raindrops, nobody would have had a problem. All the communities in the West, their city councils, their banks, their newspapers, their chambers of commerce and their church societies, joined in propagating the good news of fortunes to be made, and they showed similar zeal in suppressing adverse information. Insofar as the West was settled—an air of impermanence lingers—it was not just by rugged individualism, but also by a strong instinct for the survival of the community.

The swift settlement was a typical American triumph, fired by relentless optimism and self-righteousness, and sustained by an infinite talent for gadgetry. As Walter Prescott Webb put it, the homesteaders on the Great Plains believed that rain would follow the plow. When it didn't, they found a cheap way of getting at the water 30 to 300 feet below the surface by drilling shafts for metal cylinders pumped by windmills. The railroads and cattlemen introduced the windmill to the Plains, but the farmers who followed them made hundreds of experiments with windmills hammered together at home for a few dollars. There were no trees on the High Plains, and so no wood to fence pasture, crops and wells, but from 1874 on everyone could buy Joseph Glidden's barbed wire. By 1890 H. W. Putnam's machines could produce 600 miles of finished wire a day at a sixth of its original cost. Without windmills and cheap wire, the high-risk farming of the Great Plains would have been impossible.

Of course, the farmers' barbed wire was the enemy of the first permanent white occupant of the Plains, the cowboy. It fenced him in. Some big ranchers responded to the arrival of homesteaders by throwing barbed wire around hundreds of thousands of acres of public land. The uniquely American range and ranch cattle industry, managed by a man on horseback roaming over thousands of acres, had begun in Texas before the Civil War, and in the ten years from 1876 to 1886 it had spread with phenomenal speed over 12 states/territories wherever there was grass without a farmer on it. Capitalists from the East and from Canada, England and Scotland had come into the cattle kingdom, hiring ranch managers and cowboys to raise cattle on the free grass of land they did not own. The big cattlemen did not take kindly to the small stockman (nester) who mixed his cattle with theirs or the homesteader who plowed and fenced what was once free land. When nester, sodbuster, sheepherder and hired hand stood up for themselves, the entrenched oligarchies reacted forcibly, just like the robber barons of the East. The difference in the West was that for the most part they were dealing not with downtrodden immigrants but with independent pioneers who were ready to shoot back and resist the Republican centers of power by forming Populist and Democratic alliances. (See the summary of the Johnson County cattle war, pages 8–9.)

By 1890, the years of the open range were over and with them the long drive to the cow towns and the roundup over thousands of square miles, but the romance of the Western man on horseback endured. Revisionist historians in the latter half of the twentieth century have painted the history of the West as one of failure, exploitation and despoliation. Richard Slotkin has argued that the classic novel of the West, Owen Wister's *The Virginian* (1902), was an antidemocratic defense of Social Darwinism. The cool, Anglo-Saxon hero ("smile when you say that") represented the virile elite who had to take the law into their own hands against the democratic rabble if civilization were to advance. There was certainly in the West, as in the East, a gathering concentration of power toward the end of the century, and a similar ruthlessness in maintaining it. Still, no one can debunk the role of the West in the American imagination. It has come to epitomize a spirit of freedom, equality, honor, individualism and courage: universal values but ones of central importance in America's perception of itself. And both rancher and farmer on the Plains practiced innovation in ways that went beyond the hardware of survival. They had to invent codes of behavior for the wilderness and circumvent laws that were absurd for their circumstances. If the westerners had obeyed all the laws for settling the West passed in the humid East, they would never have survived. Neither the 160-acre allotments of the Homestead Act of 1862 nor the 650 acres of the Desert Land Act of 1877 recognized that it did not rain in the West in the same way it did in the East. The 1877 act offered up to 650 acres in the desert West at 25 cents an acre, provided it was irrigated within three years; as the plainsmen saw it, the government was betting the settler 650 acres that he would starve to death on it in less than three years. To acquire the 2,500 acres that were minimally viable, the westerner had to "live a little, lie a little." Life in the West bred

contempt for the East, first given political expression by the farmers, and it also bred a more democratic spirit, exemplified by the grant of the ballot to women long before it was achieved in the East. Frederick Jackson Turner lamented the end of free land in the West because he saw it as the end of a powerful impulse for democratic independence.

The self-righteousness that, as much as self-confidence, was a characteristic of the settling of the West enabled decent and honest people to accept and even justify the cruelties by

THE MIGHTY WINDMILL: R. G. Carr, proud founder of West Union, Nebraska, named for West Union, Iowa, stands by the vital piece of technology on his Lake Downs farm. West Union, founded in 1879, reached its peak population of 90 by the turn of the century. Photograph by Soloman D. Butcher.

which the original occupants of the land were evicted and confined to smaller and smaller reservations. No Indian in 1889 had a vote (or paid taxes); none had the ear of a congressman or editor. Indians got bad press. Perceptions had not changed much since the sixties, when an editorial in the *Topeka Weekly Leader* typically characterized Indians as "a set of miserable, dirty, lousy, blanketed, thieving, lying, sneaking, murdering, graceless, faithless gut-eating skunks as the Lord ever permitted to infect the Earth, . . . whose immediate and final extermination all men, except Indian agents and traders, should pray for." In fact, as a nine-man Board of Indian Commissioners reported to President Ulysses S. Grant in 1869, the history of the border white man's connection with the Indians was "a sickening record of murder, outrage, robbery, and wrongs committed by the former, as the rule, and occasional savage outbreaks and unspeakably barbarous deeds of retaliation by the latter, as the exception."

The early Americans made an honorable enough beginning with the Native Americans. They did what the British had done, which was to treat Indian tribes as independent nations and acquire land by making treaties with their chiefs. The tenuous assumption by the U.S. was that the chiefs had the authority to sell the birthright of their tribesmen. The even more tenuous assumption by the Indians was that the U.S. would and could honor its everlasting pledge to protect the new reserves of the Indians while admitting millions of immigrants from Europe and driving railroads across the West. It was these intense pressures that doomed the Indians. West of the Mississippi was supposed to be Indian territory forever, but there were no more than 380,000 Indians of various tribes and the white population there practically doubled between 1870 and 1890, from about 2.3 million to 4.1 million. General William T. Sherman, who was caught up in frontier troubles after the Civil War, defined a reservation as "a parcel of land inhabited by Indians and surrounded by thieves." Even the friends of the Indians in the church, politics and the Army, had concluded by the eighties that it would be a fine idea for the tribes to give up their communal land so that their members could become small dirt farmers and decent Christians.

The centennial must have seemed a propitious moment to begin a new chapter. Here, early in the American century, we come upon a recurring feature: the exercise from unexpected quarters of the constitutional freedom to speak and write according to conscience. Helen Hunt Jackson, an Army officer's wife whose writings inspired the formation of the Indian Rights Association in 1882, was appalled by the perfidy, lying and murder she saw on her travels. She documented the wrongs done to the Indians in a polemic, *A Century of Dishonor* (1881), later dramatizing them in her novel *Ramona*. The Smiley brothers, a pair of Quakers who ran a picturesque resort at Lake Mohonk in the Catskills—their family was still there at the end of the twentieth century—gave focus to the movement by inviting reformers to Mohonk Mountain House. They included Carl Schurz, then editing the *New York Post,* who as secretary of the interior in the Hayes administration had campaigned against the spoils system, and Henry L. Dawes, a patrician senator from Massachusetts.

The indignation sparked by Helen Jackson and others was well founded and overdue; the remedy was questionable. It was to absorb the Indians into American society. The idea was to protect them from harassment and give them the means to survive. The principal difficulty, in the eyes of the reformers, was the communal ownership of land and the nomadic lifestyle. The friends of the Indians reasoned that if Indians were given their own individual land ownings, they would rapidly assimilate like the Polish, German and Russian farmers pouring into the country through the funnel of New York and out to the West. They rejoiced in the Indian boy who demonstrated his mastery of English at Lake Mohonk by reciting such lines as "I believe in education because I believe it will kill the Indian in me and leave the man and the citizen." The reformers were fired by a faith in Adam Smith and the doctrine of enlightened self-interest. Dawes complained that the Indians' habit of sharing everything was "communism." Or as Amherst College President Merrill Gates put it, the good Indian was an "intelligently selfish" Indian: "one best got out of the blanket and into trousers—and trousers with a pocket in them, and a pocket that aches to be filled with dollars."

The Mohonkers' vision became law when Dawes was appointed head of the Senate's Indian committee. The Dawes General Allotment (Severalty) Act of 1887 decreed that, once a tribe agreed, its land would be split up so that each Indian family got title to 160 acres of farmland, each single adult 80 acres. The land left over following this allocation was judged "surplus," for sale to white settlers at 50 cents an acre. Most chiefs, with Sitting Bull prominent among them, rejected any land deal, but on a visit to Washington in October 1888 found themselves arguing the price rather than the principle. When Benjamin Harrison succeeded Grover Cleveland, he adroitly raised the price to $1.25 an acre, in the Sioux Act of 1889, and sent General George Crook, or Three Stars as the Indians called him, to sell the new deal to the Sioux. Crook was among the greatest Indian fighters, but he was sensitive to Indian ways. He set out to get round the chiefs by exploiting a provision of the 1868 Fort Laramie treaty that allowed for a decision by three fourths of the adult males. Red Cloud and Sitting Bull stood firm for rejection. Red Cloud gave a show of power by surrounding Crook and his companions with several hundred mounted warriors. It did not faze the general. Out of uniform and with $25,000 loose change burning in the pockets of his old gray flannel suit, he worked astutely on divisions among the chiefs. He hosted huge parties of feasting and dancing. He cajoled, wheedled and bribed the half-breeds and squawmen (white husbands of Indian women), who included almost all of the tribe's real farmers. He promised the full-bloods more rations, adjusted boundaries, higher prices. He won. At the six Sioux agencies he collected 4,463 signatures out of 5,678 eligible to vote.

The Dawes plan, once it was accepted, satisfied the reformers but it also appealed to politicians with constituencies of landless voters. The 160-acre formula accounted for only two

U.S. commissioners and delegation of Sioux chiefs visiting Washington, October 15, 1888.

fifths of all Indian land, and the rest was up for grabs. By 1900 the total acreage in Indian hands had fallen from 138 million acres to 78 million; by 1934, when the Dawes policy of breaking up the tribes was reversed, Indian holdings had been reduced to 55 million acres. Many Indians were without land of their own: Dawes had made no provision for children yet unborn on the false presumption that the race would die out, and they had not been allowed to settle on land technically ceded for homesteading.

The Mohonk image of a thrifty, ambitious and Christian Indian, a small-farmer capitalist, ignored a heritage of Indian tribal culture, the harsh reality of farming the Plains and the conflicts then brewing between men who worked the land and the controllers of credit in white society. Nor was there much hope of making the Plains Indians farmers. The allotted 160 acres on the dry lands was as unviable for the red man as for the white man; and in any event nomadic hunting tribes regarded farming as women's work. So addicted were the Sioux to hunting that when they were given cattle in the government's food allotment, they let the steers go and then rode them down in pathetic imitation of a buffalo hunt.

The assimilation the centennial reformers wanted robbed the Indians of the social cohesion and disciplines of tribal life without putting anything in its place. Perhaps it would have worked if more urban and industrial skills had been stressed in the programs, since small farmers seem to be assigned to permanent ghettoes in our modern Western world. Perhaps it would have worked if there had been honest men in the Bureau of Indian Affairs instead of corrupt political appointees. Alternatively, the Indians might have been secured in a Territory of their own, where they could have preserved their culture, and the Territory matured into a state of the U.S. As it was, they became dependent on the white man's patronage, and they were betrayed time and again. The Fourteenth Amendment may have provided that "all persons born here" were citizens, but the Supreme Court in 1894 ruled that American Indians were not included. Citizenship had to wait until an act of Congress in 1924.

In the end, the Dawes Act suffered from a defect basic to the democracy that spawned it. Nobody took much notice of what the Indians really wanted. The obverse of the glorious expansion west was that for the Indian, the American dream was a nightmare: oppression instead of democracy, poverty instead of prosperity, despair instead of hope, contraction instead of expansion, confinement instead of freedom.

The Brighton ranch in Custer County, Nebraska, erected miles of barbed wire on the public land of the open range to keep out nesters (small stockmen). Settlers severed 15 miles of it. Photographer Solomon D. Butcher got them to reenact the deed, wearing masks to avoid identification.

THE GUNMEN WHO MADE THEIR OWN LAWS

In the late afternoon of April 5, 1892, a secret train of six cars with 50 armed men, their munitions and horses rolled out of Cheyenne, Wyoming, on a mission of murder. The 400 or so big ranchers in the Wyoming Stock Growers' Association had decided to liquidate the "rustlers" in Johnson County in the north-central part of the state, and had hired 23 gunfighters, all but 1 from Texas, to help them to do it. The train arrived in Casper at 4 a.m. on April 6 and the vigilantes rode off into the dark with a kill list of 70 names.

The cattle barons, who for 20 years had grazed their big herds on the free grass of the open range, hated the new small-time stock-raising settlers who ended their monopoly by claiming the same rights. The settlers were Texas cowboys who had punched cattle into Wyoming, farm boys and drifters who came in when the railroad reached east-central Wyoming. Their little bunches of cattle got mixed up with the big herds on the range and they were accused of being too swift to put their brands on orphaned calves, or mavericks, that might belong to someone else. These were the "rustlers" the vigilantes were out to kill, their excuse being that the courts of Johnson County acquitted too many of them.

The big cattlemen, educated and wealthy, ran the Republican party and the new state. They intended to seize the town of Buffalo and its militia arms. They had arranged for the telegraph line to go down, and they had an understanding with the governor, Amos W. Barber, that the state militia would not be called out to stop their killings. They got their first victims on the way to Buffalo when they surrounded a little cabin on the Powder River on April 9. One cowboy, Nick Ray, was ambushed when he came out for water in the morning. Nate Champion held out until the afternoon, writing a diary and

The city court at Guthrie, Oklahoma, soon after the land rush of 1889. Business was brisk.

THE LAWMEN WHO HELPED THEMSELVES

Every train going west, it seemed, had two lawyers aboard, one to make a claim, the other to oppose it. Their role was more significant, if less dramatic, than that of six-shooter lawmen like Wyatt Earp. Farmers, merchants and miners all needed help in the hectic complex of land deals and disputes. It took years to sort out land rights after the Oklahoma Run of 1889. There were hundreds of worthy cases where several rushees all thought they had got to a choice site first, but could not see others for trees or hills, and no one knew whose claim was truly valid. But there were thousands of challenges where land-holders were accused of having entered Oklahoma illegally and then having lied about it under oath. Many of these Soon-ers formed secret societies. They drilled themselves for courtroom appearances, and took blood oaths to testify for one another in court. The cases were fought with desperate passion. A conspiracy was discovered to dynamite the courthouse in Oklahoma City and kill Judge John G. Clark and the U.S. prosecuting attorney, W. F. Harn. A bomb was thrown at Harn's house, and a marshal saved him from being stabbed in the back as he was leaving the courtroom. In the end, so difficult was proof, a good number of Sooners got away with cheating. The lawyers fared better than anyone. They acquired a good deal of the rewards of the Run because few of the rushees had cash, and were obliged to settle their legal bills with a portion of land.

firing back. Then his cabin was set ablaze and he was shot down when he emerged, guns in hand, from the smoke. The invaders rode off again for Buffalo but the gunfight had been seen by a rancher who raced ahead of them. The town erupted, in the words of Helena Huntington Smith, "in such a wave of fury as the West has never seen before or since." Cowboys, homesteaders and ranchers flocked in from miles around with six-shooters and rifles. There were not more than 30 real rustlers in Johnson County, but on Monday morning, April 11, some 150 citizens were directing a hail of gunfire at the invaders pinned down at the TA ranch, 13 miles to the south. The besiegers' numbers grew to 400 and the plots to disrupt the telegraph and deter the state militia worked against their early rescue. It was late on Tuesday night when President Harrison was roused from his bed to order the 6th U.S. Cavalry to the rescue. All the invaders were indicted, though eventually nobody was punished. The Republicans lost the next election to a Democrat/Populist alliance.

Owen Wister took the side of the cattle barons in his classic of Western mythology, *The Virginian* (1902), but they were the villains more than half a century later in the movie *Shane,* based on Jack Schaefer's novel, and the movie *Heaven's Gate.*

LYNCHING OF CATTLE KATE

Ella Watson (Cattle Kate), a 28-year-old farmer's daughter from Kansas, had a place on Horse Creek near the Sweetwater River in Wyoming, about a mile from the roadhouse of her paramour, Jim Averell. He was a saloonkeeper, surveyor, postmaster and justice of the peace; she was a prostitute. Both had filed homestead claims that were not to the liking of the largest cattleman, Albert J. Bothwell. Averell had also proved Bothwell was holding some meadowland illegally. On July 20, 1889, Bothwell and five other men took Watson and Averell by gunpoint to a cliff fronting the Sweetwater River and strangled them both in a crude lynching from a pine tree. A brave cowboy, Frank Buchanan, tried to stop them with his six-gun. They shot at him with Winchesters, but he escaped and got the news to town. Buchanan disappeared before the grand jury could hear witnesses. Two other witnesses of the abduction vanished, another died in mysterious circumstances, and the cattlemen's tame Cheyenne press ran a campaign to blacken the names of Watson and Averell. Bothwell got Watson's and Averell's lands and lived prosperously until his death in Santa Barbara, California, in 1928. Such was Western justice.

RED MEN SHALL
BE WHITE MEN

The men in three-piece suits are Sioux and Cheyenne chiefs, the proud horsemen who 13 years before had been the primary destroyers of the hotheaded Colonel George Armstrong Custer at the battle of Little Bighorn. They are in Washington in December 1889, as 60 chiefs before them were in October 1888, because the U.S. government wanted something from them: their tribal land. These were poignant encounters, the chiefs brought to Washington on their old enemy Iron Horse, the railroad, wearing white beavers and moccasins with their suits, carrying a blanket, a stick and a tin cup for baggage, and finding themselves confronted by the agile wordsmiths of the Interior Department.

Both in 1888 and 1889 the chiefs were invited to commit tribal suicide—to endorse the division of their Great Sioux Reservation into small farms for the Sioux and the white settler. Each Sioux family was offered 160 acres of tribal land, two cows, a yoke of oxen, farm tools, $20 in cash, seed for five acres for two years and schooling for their children. It was the first step by which the Dawes Act envisaged they would become Christian American citizens. But the allocation accounted for only 12 million of the 21 million Sioux acres. The U.S. wanted the chiefs to agree that the "excess land" could be sold to whites at 50 cents an acre. By 1889 the price had risen to $1.25 an acre, and various promises had been made on which the 21 chiefs sought assurances.

The chiefs on both occasions were taken for a welcoming handshake with the president—Cleveland in '88, Harrison in '89. They were shown the National Zoo and George Catlin's Indian paintings at the Smithsonian, and introduced to the new fad, the cigarette. They sat around the hotel lobby at Belvedere House, chain-smoking with fancy holders; Sitting Bull brandished a cigar. The *Washington Post* reported that in the mornings they came "slowly and softly down the steps into the main office and sat around in the lobby for an hour or two, awaiting breakfast." Sitting Bull held a reception and ladies "gazed fondly into his classic face."

The climax came two months after the

The 21 chiefs in Washington in 1889. *Left to right, seated:* Swift Bear, Webster, Hollow Horn Bear, White Swan, John Grass, Big Mane, Fast Thunder, Wizi, Yellow Hair. *Middle row:* Lips, White Ghost, Big Head, Mad Bear, Bull Head (Sitting Bull's future assassin), Eagle Star, Charger, Swift Bird. *Top row:* Foolish Elk, Dog Bear, Crow Eagle, Straight Head. Yellow Hair presented a ball of earth to the Pine Ridge agent, saying: "We have given up nearly all of our land, and you had better take the balance now."

December powwow. General Crook having outflanked the chiefs by winning the consent of three fourths of the adult males, President Harrison on February 10, 1890, handed the "surplus" land to the boomers of the new states of North and South Dakota. Most of them were ruined within months by a drought, which also wrecked the clumsy and halfhearted attempt the Sioux made at farming. By the winter of 1890–91, they were starving and racked with whooping cough and measles. Senator Dawes said he was shocked at the speed at which his ideas of assimilation had been applied. Shoshone Chief Washakie summed up the dismay of the nomadic Indians who had given up the old hunting life to become farmers like the white man:

"God damn a potato!"

HELLO, HELLO,
IS THIS SITTING BULL?

The Pacific and Atlantic coasts were linked from the 1860s by the telegraph that so bemused the hunting Indian in Henry Farney's painting *Talking Wires* (detail left). The magic in the eighties was the telephone. General Nelson ("Bear Coat") Miles used it in his efforts to induce Sitting Bull to return to the U.S. with the 700 Sioux he had led to Canada to seek the protection of "Grandmother" (Queen Victoria) after Little Bighorn. Sit-

ting Bull sent a delegation to meet Miles, who split them between two houses, had a phone cranked up and invited the two groups to talk to one another. When they heard the voices of their friends speaking in the Dakota tongue from nowhere, said Miles, "huge drops of perspiration coursed down their bronze faces and with trembling hands they laid the instrument down." They went back to urge Sitting Bull to surrender.

THE LAST OF THE GREAT CHIEFS

By 1889 the tribes were at a low point, half-starved dependents of the Indian agencies. Many turned to Christianity, with lethal results. Missionaries had told them about Christ, and in 1890 a Paiute called Wovoka proclaimed himself the Messiah. He preached nonviolence and brotherly love, with Indian trimmings. A new springtime of sweet grass and running water was coming. The buffalo would be back, and the white man would vanish. Indians who danced the Ghost Dance would be taken into the air and set down in this Eden among the shades of their ancestors.

The Ghost Dance spread like a prairie fire through Montana, Wyoming, Nebraska and the Dakotas, Texas and Oklahoma. Hundreds and sometimes thousands of dancers shuffled hypnotically round a pole, or "tree of life." They wore Ghost Dance shirts, painted blue around the neck and adorned with brightly colored birds, suns and moons, which made them invulnerable to bullets—a belief similar to that of the Boxers in China's 1900 rebellion.

Settlers were alarmed. An experienced former agent, Dr. Valentine McGillycuddy, wisely advised that the dance should be tolerated: "If the Seventh-Day Adventists prepare their ascension robes for the second coming of the Savior, the United States Army is not put in motion to prevent them." But there was a tenderfoot agent on the reservation at Pine Ridge, South Dakota, by the white name of Daniel F. Royer and the more accurate Sioux name of Kokipa-Koshla, Young-Man-Afraid-of-the-Indians. He panicked and asked for troops. General Nelson Miles suspected that the movement was fomented by Sitting Bull and ordered his arrest.

The Sioux warrior and holy man, now about 56 years of age, was successfully farming at Grand River on the Standing Rock reservation. The agent there, James McLaughlin, regarded Sitting Bull as an obstructionist, but he would have preferred not to intervene. Hoping to avoid a clash, he arranged for the arrest to be carried out by Indian police with the Army as backup. Before sunup on December 15, 1890, 44 Indian police galloped up to Sitting Bull's log cabin. They were under the command of a former Sioux chief, Lieutenant Bull Head, who had been at Sitting

SITTING BULL (1834–1890): The Hunkpapa Sioux chief was the brains behind the coalition of tribes that defeated Custer at Little Bighorn in 1876. Many attempts were made to vilify him as a coward and wastrel. In truth he was a brave warrior condemned for holding fast to the principles of his Indian culture. Of Little Bighorn: "They tell me I murdered Custer. It's a lie.... He was a fool and rode to his death."

Bull's side in the fights at Rosebud and Little Bighorn. Bull Head and Shave Head hustled the barely dressed Sitting Bull to his cabin door with Sergeant Red Tomahawk pushing from behind with a pistol in his hand. Sitting Bull's followers were furious. One of them, Catch-the-Bear, shot Bull Head in the side. Bull Head, falling to the ground, fired his revolver into Sitting Bull's chest and Sergeant Tomahawk shot him in the back of the head. Then the police ran into Sitting Bull's cabin and murdered his 17-year-old son, Crow Foot.

At the end of the melee, four policemen and eight Sioux warriors were dead. Sitting Bull's head was smashed in and his scalp taken by the infuriated police. Several witnesses said his horse, a memento from his days with Buffalo Bill Cody's Wild West Show, took the shooting as a cue to go through a series of circus tricks. This may have been fanciful, but it epitomized the white man's murderously bizarre relations with the Indians. It was prudent for prominent Indians to fear arrest by the white men. The Apache leader Mangas Colorado was shot to death by his guards. Crazy

Horse, a leader at Little Bighorn, was bayoneted by his guard. Satanta, the Kiowa chief, "fell" headfirst from a prison hospital window. Another Bighorn leader, Chief Gall, was bayoneted but survived, only to die either of an overdose of patent medicine or a fall.

The last Apache chief, the wily Geronimo, survived to old age. The Apaches were never very numerous, probably no more than 6,000 split into bands moving between Arizona and New Mexico, and across the Rio Grande into Mexico. Subduing them, however, took 25 years of intermittent warfare, the longest and costliest of all the Indian campaigns. The attempts to keep them on reservations generally failed and not just because they were unenthusiastic farmers. General George Crook reported that the Apaches had been plundered of their government rations and agitated by "rascally agents and other unscrupulous white men." He persuaded Geronimo to return from raids in Mexico, but in May 1885 the chief got drunk and took 92 women and children, 8 well-grown boys and 34 men back into the Sierra Madre mountains. General Miles took up the pursuit. Geronimo's "army" dwindled to only 24 warriors unavailingly tracked by 5,000 soldiers, thousands of militia and the Mexican Army as well.

In the end, on September 3, 1886, Geronimo was persuaded to surrender once more with the promise that after exile in Florida his group could return to Arizona. He never saw Arizona again. The citizens of that territory refused to allow his Apaches back when they finished their hard labor sentence. Geronimo and his surviving band ended up in Fort Sill, Oklahoma, where their old enemies, the Kiowas and Comanches, offered refuge. He was briefly a Sunday school teacher in the Dutch Reformed Church, went on several tours with Buffalo Bill and rode in Teddy Roosevelt's 1905 inaugural parade at the President's request. But he was still technically a prisoner of war, growing watermelons on his little patch of Kiowa land, when he died at Fort Sill in 1909.

The Indian wars of the West, 900 engagements in 25 years, had seen brutality and gallantry on both sides. They ended in ignominy in 1890 at Wounded Knee.

THE WARNING: Sitting Bull was promised a pardon when he agreed to come back from Canada in 1881, but he was held for two years at Fort Randall in Dakota Territory as a military prisoner. Here he is with his last wife, a woman of 29, and a white female admirer. He attracted women. He had at least three wives and ten children. At Fort Randall he was befriended by Mary Clementine Collins, a missionary. A letter from another woman admirer, Mrs. Weldon of New York, was found in his cabin after his death. It warned him to take care because the government, she said, was plotting to have him killed.

Burial of the Dead
at the Battle of Wounded Knee S.D.

North Western Photo Co
Chadron Neb

14 WOUNDED KNEE, 1890

REVENGE FOR CUSTER

When Sitting Bull was killed at Standing Rock, many Sioux fled the reservation in fear. One band of about 100 joined the last of the traditional chiefs, Big Foot, in his Minneconjou camp on Cheyenne River. In the hope that the great old chief Red Cloud would protect them, Big Foot led a party of 120 men and 230 women and children south across the frozen Badlands to Pine Ridge. Four troops of cavalry came upon them on December 28, 1890, and Big Foot, hemorrhaging from pneumonia, surrendered his party. It was an eerie encounter. As he talked with his captors, Big Foot coughed up blood and it froze in the bitter cold, emblematic of the blood that had flowed in quantities 14 years before: the intercepting soldiers were in the 7th U.S. Cavalry, Custer's old regiment, and some of the men in Big Foot's party had been among the warriors that day in June 1876 at Little Bighorn. Major Samuel Whitside put Big Foot in an ambulance and at nightfall they reached the cavalry tent camp at Wounded Knee Creek.

The rest of the 7th Cavalry came into camp later that evening. Its colonel, James W. Forsyth, took command and the next morning the Sioux woke to find themselves surrounded by 500 troops, with four rapid-fire Hotchkiss machine guns trained on them from a hillside. Forsyth ranged the captives in a semicircle and ordered them to give up any weapons they had. Not satisfied with the haul of guns and knives, he sent troopers into the tents to search. The Sioux were passive, though the medicine man Yellow Bird danced a few steps of the Ghost Dance and reminded them that their sacred garments made them safe from the white man's bullets. One young Indian, Black Coyote, who was deaf, objected to giving up his Winchester. He held on to it, and it went off in a scuffle, shooting an officer.

The cavalrymen immediately opened fire on the more or less unarmed Indians. It was not a battle. It was a massacre. The Sioux men fought with knives, clubs, rocks; the women and children ran. The enraged soldiers followed them. It is certain that 200 died, and possibly as many as 300 of the 350. Big Foot was among them. Twenty-five troopers were killed, mostly by their own cross fire.

Twenty congressional Medals of Honor were awarded and the newspapers romanticized what had happened. "The members of the Seventh Cavalry have once more shown themselves to be heroes in deeds of daring," declared the *Chicago Tribune*. Even 100 years later, the *Wall Street Journal*, in its 1889–1989 edition, referred to the "battle" of Wounded Knee.

MASS GRAVE: A blizzard sprang up on December 29, 1890, and the Sioux bodies were left on the Plains for two days. "Now we have avenged Custer's death," said an unnamed officer. Crusty old Indian fighter General Miles thought the massacre "most reprehensible, most unjustifiable, and worthy of the severest condemnation." He brought charges against Forsyth, but the secretary of war blocked them.

FLASH FORWARD: 1973

STILL FIGHTING

The village of Wounded Knee was seized at gunpoint in 1973 by descendants of the Sioux in bitter protest at loss of their lands, corruption in the Bureau of Indian Affairs and dozens of uninvestigated murders. Indians and FBI men died. Ninety percent of the land that had been allocated to the Indians in 1889 was by then owned or leased by white people or people with little Indian blood. When Peter Matthiessen wrote *In the Spirit of Crazy Horse,* a book about this fight led by the American Indian Movement, he was sued by an FBI agent and a former governor of South Dakota. The cases were dismissed, but the suits effectively suppressed the book for six years.

PARADOX OF A PRESIDENT

The president who would take America into its second century was a dainty Indiana lawyer who taught bible class on Sunday and waved the bloody shirt of the Civil War in his weekday politicking. Benjamin Harrison had fought alongside Sherman in the battle for Atlanta and still raged against Democrats as "the party of the leprosy of secession." He had one foot firmly in the old, homespun, isolated America, and one toe in the new era. He held office when a president could still walk round Washington unmolested, and his staff totaled eight. But it was in his administration that America made the first moves toward becoming a world power. He bullied Chile and Canada, stood up to Britain, built steel battleships and gave his blessing to the American plotters who seized Hawaii. He has been underappreciated as a president.

His great-grandfather had signed the Declaration of Independence. His grandfather, William Henry "Tippecanoe" Harrison, was the ninth president, elected as a frontier man from a log cabin with a taste for hard cider, though in fact he was born in a Virginia mansion to a wealthy family of planters. Folklore, ethnic appeal and sectional rhetoric normally ran way ahead of policy in the campaigns of both parties. Supporters were most concerned with the "practical politics" of the spoils system, which rewarded the victors with thousands of government jobs. The campaign of 1888 was the first since 1860 in which there was an issue of real principle: tariffs. President Cleveland wanted to lower tariffs because he feared the hundred million dollars a year surplus in the Treasury vaults would lead to business stagnation and more political corruption. To Democrats inclined to argue this, he pronounced: "It is a condition, not a theory that confronts us."

Senator Matthew Quay, the Republican boss of Pennsylvania who ran Harrison's protariff campaign against Cleveland, took the practical advice of a leading protectionist to "put the manufacturers under the fire and fry the fat out of them." The chief fryer was Philadelphia's John Wanamaker, bargain king of retail shopping, founder of YMCAs and Sunday schools. He "assessed" the captains of industry, and by issuing them promises of protection from foreign

Harrison was the last of the Civil War generals to achieve the presidency, Grant, Hayes and Garfield preceding him. The next Republican president, William McKinley, had only reached the rank of major.

competition raised an estimated $3 million, at least four times the money available to the Democrats. As Harrison graciously received delegations on his home porch, votes for him were being bought for three new five-dollar gold pieces or new twenty-dollar greenbacks. The bribery was easier because the ballot papers were printed by the party organizations; the secret ballot had not yet arrived.

Cleveland had 100,000 more popular votes, but Harrison won with an electoral vote of 233 to 168. "Providence has given us victory," said the new president. "Think of the man," said Quay. "He ought to know that Providence hadn't a damn thing to do with it. He will never know how close a number of men were compelled to approach the gates of the Penitentiary to make him President."

Harrison was not a glad-hander. When his mind was full he would pass friends without a nod. His backers found him a human iceberg in the White House. He was apt not to give a visiting senator a chair and fix him with his steel-gray eyes. He had a knack of granting a favor of patronage as if he were rebuking the receiver. His handshake was "like a wilted petunia." Visitors got their own back by relaying

anecdotes about his small stature. A secretary, refusing an audience to a congressman, insisted: "The president cannot be seen," to which the visitor responded: "Can't be seen! My God, has he got as small as that?" But Harrison did have a heart. In 1893 he gave an amnesty to polygamist Mormons when the Mormon church gave up the practice as the price of statehood for Utah. He stood up for the Indians and homesteaders against aggressive railroads.

To our later eyes, Harrison is a political paradox. He was the friend of business, soft on trusts, yet he tried to persuade Andrew Carnegie to let the union back into his steel mill after the bloody confrontation of the Homestead strike in 1892. He preceded Teddy Roosevelt in trying to save the American landscape. The Land Revision Act of 1891 allowed the president to reserve national forests and Harrison used it vigorously, providing for the first reserve adjacent to Yellowstone. He appointed two reformers to the Civil Service Commission, one of them Theodore Roosevelt, but he thought T.R. something of an extremist who "wanted an end to all the evil in the world between sunrise and sunset."

The supreme paradox of Harrison was his attitude toward race. Like most Republican leaders who had fought in the Civil War, he favored black rights. He backed the young Congressman Henry Cabot Lodge in a bill to enforce civil rights in the South—it was killed by Southern filibuster—and he tried hard to get a law to stop the frequent lynchings of blacks. He was more committed to civil rights than any president until Franklin Roosevelt. Yet his appointments to the Supreme Court left a woeful legacy of reaction. One of the men he selected would write the opinion in *Plessy v. Ferguson*, which sanctioned discrimination and marked the final abandonment of American blacks to the long dark night that would not lighten until the 1950s.

This detail from Joseph Keppler's 1890 *Puck* cartoon depicts Harrison as too small for the hat of his grandfather, William Henry "Tippecanoe" Harrison, who caught a cold on the day of his inauguration as the 9th president, March 4, 1841, and died 31 days later.

STARS AND STRIPES FOREVER

It was President Harrison, celebrating the first centennial of America, who promoted a dedication to the flag that flourished through the next century. Until Harrison, the flag was respected, but neither widely displayed nor the frequent object of civilian pledges of allegiance. Harrison campaigned for the flag to fly everywhere. He asked that the centennial flags put out by New York business houses be sent to schools. He gave orders that the Stars and Stripes must fly over the executive departments and over the White House when he was in residence. "That one flag encircles us with its folds today, the unrivaled object of our loyal love." From Harrison's day on, the flag became a test of true "Americanism," waved by both sides in political and labor disputes as a sign of greater patriotism.

The centennial began a bit sourly for the Republicans. Henry Codman Potter, the Episcopal bishop of New York, went into the pulpit to denounce "practical politics" and the spoils system, a rebuke to the men of power seated in front of him. He spoke of "the growth of wealth, the prevalence of luxury, the massing of large material forces, which by their very existence are a standing menace to the freedom and integrity of the individual, the infinite swagger of our American speech and manners, mistaking bigness for greatness, and sadly confounding gain and godliness . . . All this is a contrast to the austere simplicity, the unpurchasable integrity of the first days and first men of our republic." The *New York Times* reported that Harrison, whose eyes had been wandering around the church, fixed his gaze squarely on the bishop for the rest of the sermon. As the first Republican president since Lincoln to succeed a Democrat, he was destined to have a hard time satisfying the appetite of the men around him for the spoils of office.

THE ORATOR: New York was packed and excited on April 30, 1889, when the silver-haired, silver-tongued 23rd president, Benjamin Harrison, arrived to speak at the site of Washington's inaugural on April 30, 1789. The centennial celebrations went on for three days.

CHAPTER TWO

SHOWDOWN FOR DEMOCRACY
1890–1898

Money Shouts

The power of the new money nearly gobbled up democracy as American capitalism got into its fast and furious stride from the seventies to the nineties. Mark Twain's utopian satire *The Gilded Age* (1873) gave the period its name for its worship of gold, its social ostentation and its venal politics. The young Frenchman Georges Clemenceau, who was to head France in World War I, lived in New York for a time and remarked that the United States had gone from a stage of barbarism to one of decadence without achieving any civilization between the two.

The supermen who owned the country, its steel, railways and oil, its textiles and its banks, also "rented" most of the politicians of both parties. They were seen, especially by Republicans, as captains of industry, who were making America rich by free enterprise. They were viewed as robber barons when they quashed the labor unions, set up huge monopolies and got the supine Congress to tax competitive imports. In 1890 tariffs went up from 38 to 50 percent.

Still, most white Americans, despite the frequent panics and the depression of 1893–1897, were better off than their parents. The question was whether it was possible to have the benefits of industrial concentration, and the economies of scale, without this exploitation of worker and consumer and the menace of corporate power to both liberty and equality.

CHASING UNCLE SAM: Droughboy's cover for *Life* magazine summed up the "patriotic" tariff of 1890 sponsored by Representative William McKinley and Senator Nelson Aldrich. It made coal, blankets, carpets, tableware, women's and children's dresses, fish, cabbages and oranges all suddenly more expensive.

SURVIVAL OF THE FATTEST

Texas farmers, stricken by drought in 1887, were cheered up a bit when Congress agreed they should be given $10,000 worth of seed among them. They never saw a single seed. Democratic President Grover Cleveland, in his second, nonconsecutive term, vetoed the appropriation and took the occasion to set out the conservative faith he maintained in both presidencies and throughout the depression of 1893–1897, when two out of five Americans were out of work. "I do not believe," he said, "that the power and duty of the General Government ought to be extended to the relief of individual suffering which is in no manner properly related to the public service or benefit. . . . The lesson should constantly be enforced that though the people support the Government, Government should not support the people."

Cleveland was not a cruel man. He was the most honest of presidents. He was simply being faithful to a laissez-faire philosophy with roots in Jeffersonian liberalism and pioneer individualism, but one that became fixed in the American psyche in a very particular manner in the latter decades of the nineteenth century. It has remained there ever since, sometimes submerged, sometimes coming to the surface like a log in a fast-flowing river. Herbert Hoover said much the same thing about relief for the unemployed in the early 1930s. Cleveland's sentiments on the limited duty of government might have popped up at any time during the 1980s on Ronald Reagan's teleprompter. "Government is not the solution to our problem, government is the problem," was an echo of Cleveland, of Presidents Coolidge and Hoover, and, most of all, of the English engineer and philosopher Herbert Spencer and his Yale disciple, William Graham Sumner.

The rich and powerful in America found the theories of the Social Darwinists congenial. John D. Rockefeller, Jr., explained it to a Sunday school class: "The growth of a large business is merely a survival of the fittest. . . . The American Beauty rose can be produced in the splendor and fragrance which bring cheer to its beholder only by sacrificing the early buds which grow up around it."

Herbert Spencer (1820–1903) was more acclaimed in America than England. His doctrine of the preeminence of the individual over society and of science over religion was so popular in America that, when he set sail from England in 1882 for a gala banquet in New York, Andrew Carnegie abandoned a Scottish visit and rushed to take passage on the same ship. Carnegie's faith survived the discovery that his companion was not always a celestial philosopher, but someone who could be irritatingly peevish if the wrong cheese was served at dinner. "I remember that Light came as in a flood and all was clear," Carnegie said years later of his reading of Spencer. The Light that Carnegie saw was that human society was governed by the same laws of evolution that Charles Darwin had expounded for beasts. It was Spencer, a friend of Darwin's, who gave us the phrase "the survival of the fittest"; his *Social Statics* preceded Darwin's *Origin of Species* by nine years. Life was an unceasing struggle for existence for men as for animals. Those who survived were the fittest and passed on their favorable characteristics to their offspring. Spencer believed that acquired skills, as well as physical traits, were inherited.

The perennial tension in a democratic state between liberty and equality, personal freedom and social justice, state regulation and private enterprise, barely existed for Spencer. He stood for liberty, inequality and the survival of the fittest as against "not liberty, equality, survival of the unfittest." There was no middle ground. This was a political view that had the merit of candor, but it gained momentum because it was presented as a scientific law, as immutable as the law of gravity. Most public sanitation, housing regulations, tariffs, state banking systems, the state post office and even the exposure of medical frauds and harmful patent medicines were all to be opposed because they were fruitless interferences with a scientific truth. "Private opulence, public squalor," John Kenneth Galbraith's indictment in the 1950s, was preordained.

Spencer's social theories were akin to the economic ideas of Adam Smith (1723–1790), David Ricardo (1772–1823), Thomas Robert Malthus (1766–1834) and Alfred Marshall (1842–1924), who gave America its central faith in the competition of the marketplace and, for a time, the conviction that the fecund masses could not for long rise above subsistence incomes. But Spencer differed from his gloomy countrymen in two important ways. They thought nothing could be done for the poor. He thought nothing could be done and nothing *should* be done. The iron laws of Social Darwinism doomed state aid or any other reforms that would help the poor: "The whole effort of nature is to get rid of such, to clear the world of them, and make room for better. . . . If they are sufficiently complete to live, they do live, and it is well they should live. If they are not sufficiently complete to live, they die, and it is best they should die."

Spencer's second appeal in America was that, until almost the end of his life, he was not a pessimist. The evolutionary process guaranteed progress. A state of perfection was not simply desirable, it was inevitable. "The American nation will be a long time in evolving its ultimate form, but . . . its ultimate form will be high."

Spencer was feted on his three-month trip in 1882. His own country was not even a full democracy—two out of five male adults had no vote because they did not own a house—but while England, too, was loath to accept trade unions, aristocratic paternalism was moving it away from extreme laissez-faire to the regulation of work hours and help for the poor. It already had an income tax. The new Germany was introducing social security. In the United States at the time, as Galbraith puts it, the race was still being more ruthlessly improved. Social Darwinism was just what the rich and powerful wanted to hear because it sanctified their resistance to regulation, and it was what the country got because Congress was a mere appendage of industry and the nation's judges were Social Darwinists. "The Fourteenth Amendment does not enact Mr. Herbert Spencer's *Social Statics*," declared Justice Oliver Wendell Holmes in 1905, when the Supreme Court reviewed a New York state law limiting the hours of bakers to ten a day; but he was in a minority and the law was struck down. At a banquet for Spencer at the fashionable Delmonico's in New York, the railroad baron James J. Hill spoke

YALE'S BRIGHT DOGMATIST

When Yale professor William Graham Sumner (1840–1910) heard the word "reform" he reached for his revolver. "It Is the greatest folly of which a man can be capable to sit down with a slate and pencil to plan out a new social world." He was the son of a self-educated English laborer who came to America to escape the factory system. At 45, he decided it was necessary to learn more languages, so he mastered Dutch, Spanish, Portuguese, Italian, Russian, Polish, Hebrew, Greek, Latin and two Scandinavian dialects. He preached laissez-faire in books and essays with titles like *The Absurd Effort to Make the World Over* (1895) and left a lasting imprint on American politics. His icon of "the forgotten man" would be used again and again, until finally stood on its head by Franklin Roosevelt to make the case for government intervention in the 1930s.

up to say railroad wars were indeed fought "by the law of the survival of the fittest." The business apologist Chauncey Depew applauded the "superior ability, foresight, and adaptability of the rich." John D. Rockefeller was happy to see in his own success the work of science and religion: "This is not an evil tendency in business. It is merely the working out of a law of nature and a law of God." It was preached from the pulpit, and it was sometimes denounced, but altogether it became the hot gospel at Harvard, Yale, Chicago, Columbia, Johns Hopkins and elsewhere. It was popularized by Charles A. Dana in the *New York Sun* and E. L. Godkin in *The Nation*. By 1900, Spencer's books had been bought by 350,000 Americans.

The leading American Social Darwinist, William Graham Sumner, was a powerfully built man with a voice of iron, a flair for catchy titles and a talent for seeing one side of every question. He spent most of his life promulgating a laissez-faire as deterministic as Spencer's but more tailor-made for the dominant forces in the emerging industrial society. He saw nothing wrong with monopolies of wealth. The captains of industry were simply the more benevolent evolution of war-lords in more primitive societies, men of talent, courage and fortitude. They had a duty to get rich. It was not possible that they were a danger: "Where is the rich man who is oppressing anybody? If there was one, the newspapers would ring with it." Sumner was the high priest of individualism. He was the perfect intellectual counterpoint to the novels of Horatio Alger, who sold 20 million copies of books glorifying Tom the Boot-black and his like, who left a small town as a poor boy and became rich by perseverance and hard work. Sumner's hero, "the forgotten man," was the middle-class father who brought up his children to be industrious and self-denying and hus-banded the capital by which civilization was maintained and carried on. Politics could do nothing for him except impose burdens out of greed and muddled compassion. "It is the glory of the United States, and its calling in history, that it shows what the power of personal liberty is—what self reliance, energy, enterprise, hard sense men can develop when they have room and liberty and when they are emancipated from the burden of traditions and faiths which are nothing but the accumulated follies and blunders of a hundred gener-ations of statesmen."

It was perhaps not surprising that, in an era of cynical political machines, Sumner saw "jobbery" as the greatest social evil of the time and opposed most public spending, on buildings, pensions or even on the hiring of an inspector of railroad bridges; but he also argued, in ways that foreshad-owed debates on the underclass in the 1980s, that the people in the slums and tenements preferred their misery. "They will not give up the enjoyment of the streets for any amount of rural comfort. Other classes try to help them, assuming that, to them, crowds, noise, filth, contagious diseases and narrow quarters must be painful. The evidence is that they like the life, and are indifferent to what others consider its evils and discomforts." Yet for all Sumner's academic blindness, he was not the mouthpiece of the rich. Most millionaires favored the tariff. Sumner thought it socialism. He wrote sympathetically about women garment workers suffering because the tariff raised the cost of string. At first he took a critical view of the monopoly power of labor in trade unions, but by 1889 he had modified his ideas so far as to argue that industrial war was an incident of liberty. If the workers won, they were right. If they lost, they were wrong. Yet he became increasingly skeptical about the role of democracy. It encouraged men to believe their welfare could be obtained by dogmatic assertions of rights. "Although we cannot criticize democracy profitably," he wrote in 1895, "it may be said of it with reference to our present subject that up to this time democracy never has done anything, either in politics, social affairs, or industry, to prove its power to bless mankind."

Sumner's animosity was understandable. Social Darwin-ism's flaw was that in a popular democracy the masses had to recognize their own futility and to vote, in effect, for their own selective extinction. They showed a marked disinclination to do this when politics finally began to focus on issues like prices and employment. The masses had logic on their side: If evolution was an inexorable force, why object to regulation or public spending? Wouldn't these "mistakes" be swept aside by the iron laws of science? If the robber barons could triumph by bribing legislators and hiring goons to break strikes, why should the poor not triumph by forming unions and building political machines—or, for that matter, through mob violence or the support of dictators? This is not casuistry. As Stephen Jay Gould and others have pointed out in more recent years, extrapolating faulty lessons from nature to appease one's prej-udices can have terrible consequences. A direct intellectual link runs from the Social Darwinists to Hitler and Stalin and the idea that whole populations can be annihilated as "unfit" to survive. No doubt Spencer and Sumner would have been horrified by the Nazis, but then it is not uncommon for pro-fessors and theorists not to realize their words might have real consequences.

An intellectual cavalry was riding to the rescue of the "unfit." The pragmatism expounded by William James (1842–1910) and John Dewey (1859–1952) rejected dogmatism and fatalism in favor of man's need and ability to experiment with his own destiny—just as he had been doing in the great experiment called America. The truth of any idea was not ordained. It could be discovered only by testing the conse-quences of an action, by constant trial and error. The com-mon man's experience was as relevant as anyone else's. "Pragmatism," wrote James, "is willing to take anything, to follow either logic or the senses, and to count the humblest and most personal experiences." It was a democratic, practi-cal, commonsense philosophy and when it filtered down it appealed to a restless people. The influence of James and Dewey was profound, but it was the lesser-known Lester Frank Ward (1841–1913) who gave pragmatism its social agenda. Ward was the youngest of ten children, stimulated by a mechanically inventive father and a scholarly mother, and by a boyhood living close to nature in the wilds of Illinois and Iowa. What he saw of plants and animals there led him into intense study of biology, zoology, geology, botany, anthropology, paleontology and paleobotany—he picked up Greek, Latin, French and German on the way—and scientific observation was the engine of his later theories in sociology. Even in his sixties he strode the countryside tirelessly, a big sunburned figure, sketchbook and pencil in hand. He was a reserved man. Wounded at Chancellorsville in the Union Army when he was 23, he disappeared into the federal bureaucracy for most of his life and did not have an academic chair until Brown University made him professor of sociology at the age of 65. He had been barely noticed while Sumner was being lionized, but the dogged public servant nonetheless provided a body of ideas that proved fitter to survive. They informed the nascent progressive faith in planning, social welfare and education that fired Herbert Croly (1869–1930), founder of *The New Republic,* who, in turn, had an influence on Theodore Roosevelt and Woodrow Wilson. In *Dynamic Sociology* (1883), Ward argued that even the most mediocre, properly taught, could double and triple their level of achievement. Life and liberty could be preserved and enhanced only when government freed the people to do the best they could by providing education, health and welfare. The Social Darwinist error was to overlook the human brain as a factor in

LESTER WARD: Sketches for a social agenda.

evolution or to conceive of the mind as a passive instrument. Man was not the inert figure of their gloomy dogmas. He could modify his environment as no other animal could do. Look at what man had been able to accomplish with animals. Advances in animal husbandry had outstripped nature's "wasteful" methods. It was thus that humankind had created civilization. Competition was not the law of life, it was the law of death. Look at man's inventions of medicine and surgery. They were nothing more than interferences with biological competition. By the same token, said Ward, governments had a duty to interfere with the unbridled competition that was leading to the anticompetitive domination of monopolies like Standard Oil. They were antisocial.

Ward's careful observations exposed the pseudoscience underpinning the politics of laissez-faire. Thorstein Veblen (1857–1929) deployed satire to the same end. Emerging from his isolated Norwegian community in the Middle West, he was merciless in mocking the genetic superiority of the rich and the powerful. The conspicuous idleness and consumption of the upper classes was a survival from a predatory barbarian past. They were no better than New Guinea headhunters. Henry George (1839–1897) demonstrated that many millionaires owed their wealth not to competitive enterprise but to fortuitous increases in the most fundamental monopoly, that of land. He advocated a single tax on land so that all the community would benefit: "No human being can produce or lay up land. If the Astors had all remained in Germany, or if there had never been any Astors, the land of Manhattan Island would have been here all the same."

These tributaries of pragmatism were bound to find political outlets. Paradoxically, it was the pragmatic spirit of the archetypal rugged American individual—though he himself might have called it common sense—that in the nineties led to the first great rejection of Social Darwinism and the flowering of a new agrarian politics. The name of it was Populism. The West attracted people of great courage and enterprise, the very icon of the laissez-faire philosophers, but the environmental imperative of their ordeals was cooperate or die. The rise of Populism was predicated on neighborliness, on the kind of creative cooperation and planning that was anathema to Graham Sumner. Populism in the West and South had its dark side in prejudice and paranoia, but the Populists were willing and able to rally around a set of complex issues in a way unimaginable to later generations wedded to personality-centered politics, and unimaginable, for sure, to the cold-blooded Ivy League theoreticians of their own time.

POPULIST SOIL:
John Painter, Populist leader, at his family home at Broken Bow on the plains of Nebraska.

FIGHTING MOTHER: Mrs. Mary Lease, washerwoman, mother of four, and Populist firebrand, studied for the Kansas bar by pinning sheets of notes above her washtub. She denied saying "Kansas farmers need to raise less corn and more hell," but let it stand as "a right good bit of advice." Her golden voice set the crowds hooting and hurrahing.

SOUTHERN REBEL: Redheaded Tom Watson of Georgia dreamed of uniting the Southern masses of both races against plutocracy. He got the Populist state platform to denounce the Ku Klux Klan and lynching, more frequent in Georgia than anywhere. Later, beaten and embittered by Democratic fraud and violence, he became antiblack, anti-Catholic and anti-Semitic, like all too many disillusioned Populists.

THE FARMERS START A PRAIRIE FIRE

All over the South in the seventies and eighties, thousands of farmers scrawled a sign on the nailed-shut doors of their homes: G.T.T. They had gone to Texas. A million or more crossed the Mississippi in search of new life on the Great Plains. Seventy percent of planters were tenants. They had worked on their land, but they had lost it by a cruel process. Without enough cash, they had to get their seed, equipment and food by pledging their next crop to the supply merchant. The merchant, who worked hand in hand with the landlord, and was often the same man, charged monopolistic prices for supplies and interest of 100–200 percent. The landlord/merchant set the price for the crop, too. The farmers' earnings always ended up being less than the cost of planting and harvest, so they were kept in a vicious cycle of peonage. The tenant was always in debt, providing an easy excuse for the landlord to kick him off the land if he got too "uppity." It was serfdom at a time when "backward" countries such as Russia had freed their serfs and only a few years before Charles Parnell's boycott was to end the tenant system in Ireland.

In September 1877, at a Lampasas County farm in Texas, a group of the refugees planted a miraculous seed. They formed the Southern Alliance to find ways of freeing themselves from the exactions of banks, merchants, landlords, and the railroads. Earlier attempts, like the Grange, had been defeated, but by 1890, in an evolution described by the historian Lawrence Goodwyn, the Southern Alliance had become an effective National Farmers' Alliance with 500,000 members in the South and 100,000 in Kansas. When the jute trust overnight doubled the price of bagging for cotton, the Alliance boycotted jute and placed orders with mills for cotton bags instead. They fought the monopoly that sold binding twine by erecting their own twine factory. But at the heart of the movement was a revolt about a more profound structural failure, the undemocratic and unproductive nature of the money system.

The intellectual fallacy that plagued life and politics for decades was the perception of money as a commodity with intrinsic value rather than as primarily a medium of

LETTING OFF STEAM: The Senate as the mouthpiece for the railroads, by Thomas Nast in a *Harper's Weekly* cartoon.

exchange. Bankers and hard-money politicians insisted money had to be gold or silver. At the end of the Civil War, which had been financed by $450 million of "greenbacks" (Treasury notes in green ink), unbacked by gold, they forced a return to the gold standard and effected a long contraction of the currency, with falling prices. Wheat dropped from 95 cents a bushel to 50 cents between 1880 and 1895. Cotton dropped as well. A farmer had to grow twice as much to repay a mortgage, doing so with dollars worth double what he had borrowed. Underfunded local banks had to depend on Wall Street creditors who were able to impose high interest rates.

Understanding of the causes of their calamity was carried to the farmers by the genius for communication of a 36-year-old Mississippi farmer, S. O. Daws, who had himself endured the crop-lien system. He arranged for traveling lecturers to spread the word about credit, cooperative stores and warehouses; he was the first Populist and recruited one of the most dazzling, a redheaded 34-year-old frontier farmer, William Lamb. Soon there were thousands of farmer-lecturers, striking lightning wherever they went and frightening Democrats and Republicans with their message. They reached 2 million people in 43 states in what Goodwyn describes as the most massive organizing drive by any citizen institution of nineteenth-century America.

Most of the campaigners were self-made men. "Sockless" Jerry Simpson of Kansas, so called because he derided a rich opponent's silk socks, had taken up stock raising after 20 years at sea, where he had read Henry George and got to know Dickens and Thackeray by heart. Ignatius Donnelly, a spellbinding speaker, founded a model town for artists and rural craftsmen on the west bank of the Mississippi, in Minnesota, and called it Nininger City. He was a Republican lieutenant governor at 28, a congressman at 32, a best-selling author of books "proving" there was a lost city of Atlantis and that Francis Bacon wrote Shakespeare's work. When he became a Populist, he proclaimed that politics henceforth would be a struggle "between the few who seek to grasp all power and wealth, and the many who seek to preserve their rights as American citizens and freemen." The railroad he had been promised would pass through Nininger took another route, but Donnelly lived there for 50 years amid the empty lots and tall grass.

The genius in the message carried by the Alliance campaigners was in the democratic money system devised by an Alliance lawyer-doctor, Charles W. Macune. He had seen bankers close their doors against credit for cooperatives, though backed by the produce they could see in the fields. His answer was for the federal government to store farm produce in warehouses or "subtreasuries." Farmers paying 2 percent interest could borrow up to 80 percent of the local market price in greenbacks. It was a direct, practical way of liberating the cooperative movement, but it was more. The billions of dollars that could be created in this way at harvest time would stimulate the whole economy, and they would form the basis for a new national currency, controlled by the U.S. Treasury and not by the Eastern commercial bankers.

Macune's plan was the intellectual seed for the Populist party that in 1892 came to flower from the Alliance. It is one of the most inspiring fulfillments of the ideals of American democracy that a barely literate, long oppressed people educated and organized themselves out of humiliation, and brought a new vision to the dead politics of the era.

THE WAGON TRAINS
OF MASS DEMOCRACY

Lights shone at night in 10,000 little white schoolhouse windows in Kansas in the nineties as farmers and their families gathered for supper, lectures and song. The Republican editor of the *Emporia Gazette*, William Allen White, feared what was happening. On the ebbing prairie breezes, he heard the voices of men, women and children raised in religious fervor "praising the people's will as though it were God's, cursing wealth for its iniquity." Wagon trains six miles long wound through the towns on the way to picnics where brass bands played and farmers sat on the grass earnestly listening to lectures on currency reform.

Nineteenth-century Kansas, as the historian Matthew Josephson has said, re-enacted the role of eighteenth-century Massachusetts. It was in Kansas that the National Farmers' Alliance, the great cooperative movement of the South and the West, first found spectacular political expression in 1890. Exasperated by years of Republican indolence, the farmers put up candidates and even dared to challenge the venerable Senator John J. Ingalls, after 18 years in the U.S. Senate the best-known politician in the West. Ingalls was contemptuous of the whole idea of a party dedicated to the people: "The purification of politics," he snorted, "is an iridescent dream." The dream came true. The farmers won 96 of the 125 seats in the state legislature. Sockless Jerry Simpson and four Alliance men went to Congress. Ingalls's days were numbered. In other Western states, the effect of Alliance voting was to deprive Republicans of votes. A Democratic landslide gave them control of Congress from 1891 to 1895. It lent credence to the Republican attack that the Alliance was no more than a "front" for Civil War traitors.

So the Alliance took the big leap. On July 4, 1892, in Omaha, Nebraska, 1,300 exultant delegates drew up the platform for a political party of belief, the People's Party of the U.S.A. This Populist party, as it was soon called, was not just another third party, created by a splinter group of politicians. It was the flowering of the largest democratic mass movement in American history. It demanded social justice for millions betrayed by Republican and Democratic politics debauched by the exploitation of the animosities of race, religion and Civil War. It was not socialist: individual ownership of land was a keystone of Populism. But it was radical. It demanded government ownership of railroads, telegraphs and telephones, a graduated income tax, the direct election of U.S. senators, the secret ballot, immigration restriction and laws to protect labor unions. It attacked the money system with the cash-for-crops credit plan of Charles Macune, and with calls for a national currency issued by the federal government. It also sought the unlimited coinage of silver at 16:1, a political necessity in the mining West, but a mistake in that silver was just like gold, too rigid and limited a source for the expanding nation's currency and credit needs.

The Populist campaign was a triumph, though it was not able to speak as effectively to the urban and Catholic masses as to the Protestant farmers and it was robbed in the racist South. The candidate for president, General James Weaver, carried five states and polled a million votes, approaching 10 percent. But in the South, where farmers worried that a third party might let blacks get power, the Democrats, who controlled the election machinery, met Populist candidates with a campaign of massive fraud and violence, especially in Georgia, Alabama and Texas. In the next four years the Populists gained a following of anywhere from 25–45 percent of the electorate in 20-odd states, destroying the Democratic party west of the Mississippi. It was amazing, but not enough. To gain national power the Populists came more and more to run on Populist-Democratic fusion tickets and in 1896 they were effectively absorbed by the silver Democrats. Silver, rather than cheap credit or reform, became the rallying cry; but the interventionist philosophy of Populism triumphed within the Democratic party and was the seed of the reformist Progressive movement that came to fruition in both parties at the opening of the twentieth century.

GUNS IN THE STATE HOUSE: On January 9, 1893, a jubilant parade marched through Topeka, Kansas. They were celebrating the "first People's party government on earth." The Populists, running on a joint "fusion" ticket with the small Democratic party, had won the state Senate and elected a Populist governor, Lorenzo D. Lewelling. Claiming that fraud in ten elections had robbed them of control of the state House of

Representatives, they occupied the State House with guns. The Republicans contrived to get back in, with the help of 600 assistant "sergeants at arms" (above) and 400 deputy sheriffs, whereupon the Populist Lewelling surrounded the hall with state militia. In the end, the Populists agreed to respect whatever decision the state Supreme Court made. It was dominated by Republican appointees, and the Populists lost.

TRAMPS AND MILLIONAIRES

Ignatius Donnelly (1831–1901) captured the mood of the Populists in his preamble to their 1892 program.

"We meet in the midst of a nation brought to the verge of moral, political and material ruin. Corruption dominates the ballot box, the legislatures, the Congress and even touches the ermine of the bench. . . . The newspapers are largely subsidized or muzzled; public opinion silenced; business prostrated; our homes covered with mortgages; the land concentrated in the hands of the capitalists. The urban workmen are denied the right of organization for self protection; imported pauperized labor beats down their wages; a hireling standing army, unrecognized by our laws, is established to shoot them down, and they are rapidly degenerating into European conditions. The fruits of the toil of millions are boldly stolen to build up colossal fortunes of the few. . . . From the same prolific womb of governmental injustice we breed the two great classes—tramps and millionaires."

THE DECENT
GOLDBUG

The young Mrs. Frances Cleveland kept the promise she had made on March 4, 1889, when she said good-bye to Jerry Smith, an old black servant at the White House. "Take good care of the furniture and ornaments. . . . We are coming back just four years from today." Back with a vengeance. Cleveland defeated Harrison in the most decisive Democratic victory since before the Civil War, and on March 4, 1893, the Clevelands took up residence again. It was the first, and only, time a defeated president had been returned to the White House.

Cleveland was both the 22nd and the 24th president and he had the bulldog courage and capacity for work of two men. When citizens telephoned the White House they could not be sure, as they were in his first term, that the President himself would answer; now there was a telephone operator. But once again the desk lamps on the second floor of the White House burned until 2 a.m. as he wrote letters and messages in his own hand.

He was a decent man. When he was offered the "dirt" on the private life of the Republican leader James G. Blaine, he bought the package on condition it was complete and uncopied, and without opening it, burned it on the spot. He was famous for stamping out graft, first as mayor of Buffalo, then in Washington. But he had a limited imagination for the condition of the poor, and in his four years out of office as a corporation lawyer, speculating in stocks and socializing with the magnates, he had become even more conservative. He was backed by corporate America because he was a "goldbug" determined to restore the country to the gold standard. He was right that the federal gold reserves were in danger. In 1890, horse trading between advocates of high tariffs and advocates of silver had led to the Treasury being instructed to buy more silver and issue silver certificates redeemable in gold. In the financial panic of 1893 there was a rush for gold. But Cleveland and the rest of the hard-money men were wrong that simply going back to the gold standard was wise. There was not enough gold to finance the expanding economy. An increase in the money supply, not a decrease, was required. But to Cleveland and the hard-money men the gold standard was as much a matter of morals as economics. They did not believe it was the duty of the federal government to manage money in the interests of the whole society.

On the night of his triumph, surrounded by jubilant millionaires, Cleveland had a foreboding that the path of duty—"public office is a public trust"—would be harder for the 24th president. He did wonders expanding the career civil service, but with a Democratic majority of only one in the Senate, he failed to achieve the modest reduction of tariffs he had promised. He split his party on gold. And the country was about to enter its worst-yet depression.

CLEVELAND'S 1893 CABINET: "I am dreadfully perplexed and bothered," said Cleveland in January 1894. "I cannot get the men I want to help me." His cabinet was as stodgy as it looked. Hoke Smith (back, extreme right) fought hard to protect government lands, the forests and the Indians. The dominant influence was the railroad lawyer Richard Olney (third from left), who induced Cleveland to be even more reactionary than he might have been in dealing with labor unrest.

WHERE'S MY PA?

The baby in the cartoon is Oscar Folsom Cleveland, the star of the Republican ditty: "Ma! Ma! Where's my pa? Gone to the White House. Ha! Ha! Ha!" In Buffalo when he was 37, Cleveland had fathered Oscar out of wedlock and in the 1884 election the Republicans hoped the disclosure by the *Buffalo Evening Telegraph* would cost him the presidency. Very few other newspapers, even ones hostile to him, printed the details, and Cleveland got high marks for facing the music. To friends who wanted to cover it up, he roared: "Whatever you say, tell the truth."

In truth, a male perspective has given Cleveland an overly good press about the affair. On the grounds that she was drinking, he got the local sheriff to have the mother, Maria Halpin, committed to an insane asylum and the child to an orphanage (at a fee of $5 a week). When she was allowed out and tried to regain her child, Cleveland had him adopted by "one of the best families" in Buffalo and seems to have had nothing more to do with the boy (whom the mother had mischievously named Oscar Folsom after the father of Cleveland's future bride). There is a chilly heavy-handedness to Cleveland's conduct, at one with his later response to the country's urgent social ills.

Cleveland's First Lady was Frances Folsom. He married her in 1886 when she was 22 and he was 49, in the first wedding ceremony held in the White House. Five years later Ruth Cleveland became the first baby born in the White House.

Coxey's main column in full march, 1894.

PETITIONS IN BOOTS

Thousands of unemployed marched on Washington in the second year of Cleveland's second term. They created a scare among the propertied classes as great as the financial panic of 1893, which had closed 600 banks, bankrupted 56 railroads, shut down 15,000 companies, and helped to catapult the depression that produced the armies of despair. From his fortress in St. Paul, rail tycoon James J. Hill sent an urgent warning to Cleveland that 26,000 to 30,000 men had taken over trains and were heading east. The numbers were exaggerated but out-of-work miners, farmhands and lumbermen did indeed "borrow" some 40 trains in May and June of 1894. The Attorney General, Richard Olney, pursued them with a thousand U.S. marshals and the new device of the injunction. He also planted spies in the various columns of men already marching so that Washington was ready for the invasion.

By one way or another some 17 "armies" of unemployed set out for Washington in 1894 to demand relief, totaling, by the best estimates, about 10,000. The most celebrated of the armies walked for more than a month from Massillon, Ohio, under the leadership of "General" Jacob Coxey, a successful quarry owner and Populist. Coxey's march had eccentric touches. He called it the Commonweal of Christ and rode in a carriage with his son Legal Tender. A California mystic with a sombrero on his head and silver-dollar buttons on his coat led the way, and a banner with a portrait of Christ declared, "Death to interest on Bonds!" Coxey's basic idea was that Congress should pay the unemployed to build roads at $1.25 per eight-hour day. The frightened men who ran America prevented him from entering Congress to present his petition on May 1. He was arrested for walking on the grass, and police attacked the marchers with clubs and horses. Two generations later public works programs of the kind Coxey advocated became a commonplace, but in 1894 he was derided as a crank. The armies disbanded and nothing was done. The following year unemployment rose to the highest level ever known. President Cleveland and everyone else believed there was nothing they could do about a depression except sit it out.

SECRET ORDEAL: People remarked on the thinner Cleveland. What they did not know for 25 years was that in 1894 he had gone aboard a private yacht in New York, where he was propped up in a chair against the mast and had a cancer of the mouth removed and an artificial jaw fitted.

FLASH FORWARD: 1914/1944

COXEY UNCENSORED

Twenty years after he was barred from Congress, Coxey came back to the Capitol steps to say what he would have said:

"Up these steps the lobbyists of trusts and corporations have passed unchallenged on their way to the committee rooms, access to which we, the representatives of the toiling wealth producers, have been denied. We stand here today in behalf of millions of toilers whose petitions have been buried in committee rooms, whose prayers have been unresponded to, and whose opportunities for honest, remunerative, productive labor have been taken away from them by unjust legislation which protects idlers, speculators and gamblers."

1914: Coxey finishes his speech of 1894.

1944: Coxey makes the point again—in good voice despite his 90 years.

GRADUALIST: The gentle Booker T. Washington (1856–1915) thought it folly to agitate against the ruling of the Supreme Court. He wanted blacks to emulate his own incredible rise from birth in a slave hut to founder of the Tuskegee Institute for vocational training. He counseled them to live with Jim Crow while they won economic independence by patience, thrift and the acquisition of practical skills. "In all things that are purely social," he said in a famous speech in 1895, "we can be as separate as the fingers, yet one as the hand in all things essential to mutual progress."

THE STRANGE CAREER OF JIM CROW

When he boarded a train in New Orleans on June 7, 1890, Homer Adolph Plessy was going nowhere in particular, except into history. Nor was he surprised to be arrested by Detective Christopher C. Cain. He had agreed to be the guinea pig for a challenge to a new Louisiana law requiring railroads to assign blacks to separate carriages. He took his seat in a coach for whites and it was as part of an amicable little drama arranged between black leaders in Louisiana and the railroad that he was identified and asked to leave.

Louisiana blacks were the most prosperous in the South; they had 18 legislators in the state assembly. They were sure the new law violated the Fourteenth Amendment, which in 1868 guaranteed all citizens equal protection of the law. They were right about the intention of the amendment, one of the measures taken to protect the slaves freed by the Thirteenth Amendment. But the U.S. Supreme Court, which had helped to precipitate the Civil War in the Dred Scott decision of 1857, had already shown itself to be mulish about civil equality for freedmen. It had castrated the Civil Rights Act of 1875 by saying in 1883 that individuals who owned inns, parks, railways or theaters could discriminate if they wished; only states were enjoined against discrimination. This ought to have made *Plessy v. Ferguson* an open-and-shut case when it reached the Supreme Court in 1896, since it was the state of Louisiana that was infringing rights. But now the justices fastened onto four cunning words in the Louisiana statute and used them to promulgate a new doctrine that legalized the humiliation of black Americans for 58 years. The phrase was "equal but separate accommodations." The Fourteenth Amendment, the Court ruled, guaranteed political, not social, equality. Segregation was constitutional if those segregated enjoyed equal facilities.

There was but one dissent among the nine judges. The Constitution was color-blind, said John Harlan, a former Kentucky slave owner. He protested that the

CAMPAIGNER: Ida B. Wells (1862–1931) was a black journalist who campaigned against lynching and had her office burned to the ground by a mob. She showed that most victims were successful small businessmen whose only crime was to challenge the social order; rape was alleged only against a third of them. When three black businessmen were lynched in Memphis, she used her Baptist newspaper to organize a boycott of the city's trolleys. By 1893 the city fathers had been persuaded to take such a firm stand, it was 20 years before the city saw another instance of vigilante violence.

RADICAL: Washington's leadership was attacked by William Edward Burghardt Du Bois (1868–1963), a brilliant academic. He insisted that the voteless black would never get equality by evolution. He and militant followers met at Niagara Falls, Canada, in 1905 and launched the Niagara movement to fight lynchings, disenfranchisement and discrimination. The following year the Niagara group founded the National Association for the Advancement of Colored People (NAACP). Du Bois became a black nationalist and Marxist, moved to Ghana and renounced his American citizenship.

ruling would establish a superior, dominant ruling class of citizens and stimulate aggressions more or less brutal and irritating: "The destinies of the two races are indissolubly linked together, and the interests of both require that common government of all shall not permit the seeds of race hate to be planted under the sanction of law." As for the stipulation of equal treatment, it was a transparent disguise that would not mislead anyone "or atone for the wrong this day done."

The wrong went way beyond Homer Plessy's railroad seat. It lay in the judicial blessing of racism in all aspects of American life. C. Vann Woodward suggests in his study *The Strange Career of Jim Crow* that when Union troops left the South in 1877, there was for two to three decades an interregnum that gave blacks some hope. They attended separate churches and schools, but they commonly traveled with whites in second-class rail coaches, streetcars and buses; mixed in the waiting rooms; frequented some of the same eating places; drank at the same water fountains; took their families to the same parks. And in many areas they voted and were urged to vote. Of course, it was by no means a golden age. Blacks were coerced during elections, they had to step off the

pavement to give way for whites, their schools were ramshackle or nonexistent and they lived in dread of the Ku Klux Klan. In 1892 there were 155 mob lynchings without a single case being punished; until 1913 an average of one black every week was lynched for crimes that were never committed, and their persecutors went free. Yet only in the 1890s did the South overwhelm the blacks with a plethora of segregation laws and with stratagems to take away the vote. Jim Crow laws—so called after Jim Crow, a comic jumping character in a minstrel show—ended all the mixing there had been and cemented apartheid with Jim Crow entrances and exits, Jim Crow workbenches, Jim Crow taxicabs, Jim Crow cemeteries, Jim Crow park benches and drinking fountains and Jim Crow bibles in courtrooms because a white could not be expected to hold a bible touched by a black. Disenfranchisement gathered pace. In 1896 in Louisiana 130,334 blacks voted; in 1904, the total was 1,342.

All this did not happen just from one single ruling of the Supreme Court, nor did the Court create the exploitable fears, jealousies and hatreds that tormented whites. The North let it happen and the educated South let it happen. *Plessy v. Fer-*

guson scarcely made a ripple in the Northern press. Northern liberal sentiment was anxious for reconciliation with the South. The black became a sacrifice to that desire and a casualty of the Spanish-American War, when expansionists invoked doctrines of racial superiority to justify annexing the Philippines. If the brown-skinned Filipinos were not fit to govern themselves, said the Southern racists, how could Negroes qualify to vote in America?

In the South, the black was the catalyst for a reconciliation between the competing classes of Democrat: the redneck rabble-rousers and the conservative landowners and businessmen who had previously been a moderating influence on racial passions. Both groups became alarmed at the success of the Populists in appealing to black and white voters. Josephus Daniels, editor of the *Raleigh News and Observer,* started a hate campaign following the 1894 election in North Carolina of a white-black, Populist-Republican coalition. He ended up initiating a virtual coup d'état against the legitimate Populist city government of Raleigh.

The South emerged from Reconstruction only to become hostage to one-party rule, and as Mr. Justice Harlan had predicted, both races suffered.

CARNEGIE SMASHES THE UNION

A great schism was opening up in American life, manifested with a certain romance among the Populists on the Plains but altogether grimly in the industrial areas. Andrew Carnegie took himself off to his feudal castle in Scotland in the summer of 1892, and left his great steel plant at Homestead, Pennsylvania, in the care of his general manager, Henry Clay Frick, a bitter foe of unions.

Carnegie had spoken warmly of unions. He liked his men to call him Andy. There was no excuse for a strike or lockout, he wrote in 1886, unless arbitration had been tried. "To expect that one dependent upon his daily wages for the necessaries of life will stand by peacefully and see a new man employed in his stead is to expect too much." But that is what Carnegie conspired to demand of his workers, with Frick as the hard front man. Frick had sold Carnegie the mill at Homestead and it had become the most modern in the country. They wanted to smash the Amalgamated Association of Iron, Steel and Tin Workers. With more than 24,000 members nationally, it was the strongest union in the American Federation of Labor. It had served Carnegie's purpose when it imposed equal labor costs on his competitors. Now that he had beaten most of them, the union was inconvenient. It kept up the price of labor and irritatingly demanded more money when labor-saving machinery was installed. When the union's contract ran out in June, Frick asked for wage cuts. The union rejected an ultimatum, and Frick locked out the entire labor force, the 3,000 unskilled as well as the 750 union craftsmen. It was the first confrontation between a modern corporation and a fully organized union. It led to the bloodiest labor battle the country had seen, and a reverse for unionism that lasted until Roosevelt's New Deal.

Frick built a three-mile-long fence around the factory, with barbed wire and searchlights and 200 shooting holes for rifles. He planned to replace the union members with cheaper nonunion labor brought in under the protection of 300 armed men engaged by the Pinkerton detective agency. At 3:15 a.m. on July 6, a union picket on a bridge over the Monongahela River at Pittsburgh reported to the union leaders at Homestead that the Pinkerton men, secreted in two scows enclosed by wooden ramparts, were being towed upriver by barges. The Homestead men were ready for them with guns and dynamite when they tried to land inside the plant. Who fired the first shot was long debated, but in a battle that lasted most of the day, watched by thousands, nine steelmen and seven Pinkertons died and 163 people were seriously wounded. Late in the afternoon the trapped Pinkertons raised the white flag. They were marched off up the hill to the opera house as prisoners, beaten up on the way by a mob of steelworkers and their wives.

The steelworkers won the battle but lost the war. The Democratic governor sent in 8,000 state militia, who did what the Pinkertons had failed to do. Frick was able to bring strikebreakers into the mill on July 15; many of them were blacks who were barred from membership in the Amalgamated. On July 23, Alexander Berkman, a Polish-Russian immigrant, tried to kill Frick first with a pistol and then with a dagger as he sat at his desk in Pittsburgh. Berkman was an anarchist who had nothing to do with the union or the steelworkers, but Frick's pluckiness in fighting Berkman, stopping a deputy sheriff from shooting him and then working through the rest of the day in bandages obliterated what public sympathy the Homestead workers had attracted. They were henceforth all anarchists.

With cheaper labor costs, Carnegie added hundreds of millions of dollars to his earnings throughout the nineties. His victory was complete in the riot prosecutions that followed. All the indictments were against the steelworkers. Thirty-five of their leaders were accused of treason under an 1860 statute that defined the offense as levying war against or aiding the "enemies" of the state of Pennsylvania. Since the state in those days was an alliance of business and government, the prosecutions had a certain logic, though none of these charges led to conviction. Carnegie visited Homestead in February 1893 and wrote: "I shook hands with the old men, tears in their eyes and mine." In his autobiography he said, "No pangs remain of any wound received in my business career save that of Homestead."

Andrew Carnegie's verdict on the battle of Homestead was "Life is worth living again."

THE PATERNALIST: Pullman president George M. Pullman knew what was best for his workers. He housed them in a company town where he chose the plays for the theater, supplied the books in the library and told them how to vote. He cut wages during the depression but not rents or dividends. When the workers protested, he responded: "The workers have nothing to do with the amount of wages they shall receive." *Right:* Temporary postmen, of the 15th U.S. Infantry, Blue Island, Illinois.

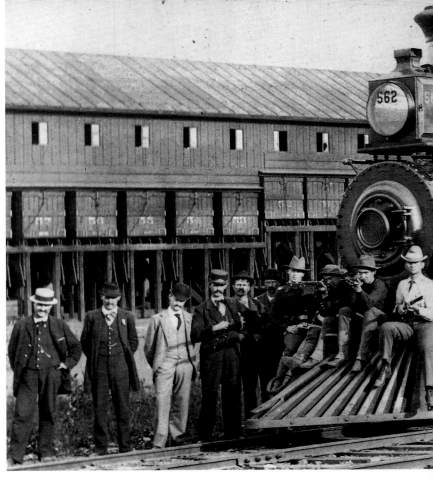

CLEVELAND'S DEVASTATING POSTCARD

Eugene Debs and George Mortimer Pullman were straight out of a Horatio Alger fable until they collided violently in the Pullman strike of 1894. Both were born poor, both left school at 14, both took menial jobs, both built great organizations. But the autocratic Pullman was business and the naively idealistic Debs was labor, and the newspapers, the government and the courts were incapable of regarding them in an equal light in the anti-labor hysteria of the nineties. The press bias is revealing of the terror aroused by a militant industrial union at a time when the business class was alarmed by the rise of the Populists and news of anarchist outrages in Europe.

The newspapers were full of paranoid falsehoods. Never once were the workers' grievances aired. To the *Washington Post* the strike was "social pestilence brought here from abroad by the criminals and outcasts of European slums." The *Chicago Tribune* said the employees in the Pullman Palace Car Company were happily at work without complaint until "dictator Debs and his dupes" came to Chicago and ordered them to strike. In fact, Debs did not seek a strike at Pullman. Having just won a strike against a wage cut by James Hill's Great Northern Railroad, he knew that the railway magnates were eager for a chance to crush his American Railway Union, one year old and the biggest in the country, with 150,000 members. It was the Pullman workers who forced the pace. After their wages had been lowered by about a third in the depression, the typical family had 76 cents a day for food and clothing. On May 11, 1894, they petitioned for relief. They were rejected, three members of the grievance committee were fired and the workers walked out. They asked the ARU convention for help in June and Jennie Curtis, a Pullman laundry worker, moved the delegates to tears with a story of destitution and the eviction her family faced from the company house on the death of her father. Debs urged arbitration. Pullman replied: "There is nothing to arbitrate about." Only then did the ARU vote for a sympathetic boycott of any train carrying Pullman cars.

Once the decision had been made, Debs threw himself into the boycott with his usual dedication. In the words of John Dos Passos, "he was a tall shamblefooted man, had a gusty sort of rhetoric that set on fire the railroad workers in their pine-boarded halls." Beginning June 21, some 120,000 railmen supported the boycott in 27 states and followed union orders to implement this by a peaceful withdrawal of labor. Chicago's new Democratic Mayor John

GOVERNOR ALTGELD: His sympathies for labor enraged conservatives.

P. Hopkins sympathized and Illinois Governor John Peter Altgeld, defender of the oppressed, refused a Pullman request for state militia. The only violence, producing damages totaling less than $6,000, came from overzealous sympathizers who interfered with trains in some cities. But all that changed in July with the intervention of Attorney General Richard Olney, a corporate lawyer who still had seats on many railway boards.

Olney was determined to crush Debs. He wanted Cleveland to send in troops. When the President demurred and demanded a fig leaf, Olney found one in the Sherman Anti-Trust Act of 1890, supposedly designed to outlaw business combinations in restraint of interstate trade. Olney asked courts across the country to declare that the union was such a combination and was interfering with delivery of the U.S. mail. The first injunction was issued on July 2, followed by others. Olney then got Cleveland to send in troops on the grounds that without them these blanket injunctions could not be enforced. Cleveland, spending sleepless nights in Washington, was a national hero when he declared: "If it takes the entire army and navy of the United States to deliver a postal card in Chicago, that card will be delivered."

Though it was right to protect the mails, the President yielded too readily to Olney. Several governors in the West protested that the troops were not needed and their imposition was a gross interference with states' rights. Two thousand soldiers arrived in Chicago, as well as 5,000 marshals backed up by 3,500 deputies who were paid by the railroads and described by the Chicago chief of police as "thugs, thieves and ex-convicts." Debs naively hoped the troops might prevent violence by the strikebreakers. Instead, they helped the strikebreakers shoot the railwaymen. Riots and fires broke out. Altogether, 34 died across the country, mostly victims of the authorities. The strike was broken, the union was broken and Debs was in jail for most of 1895 for contempt of court.

Federal force had been used when it was not necessary and with vindictiveness. The government, having failed to enforce the Sherman Anti-Trust Act against monopoly capitalism, had used it against a trade union and succeeded to the point that the right to strike had been put in question.

"DICTATOR" DEBS

In the hate campaign against the leader of the American Railway Union, Eugene Debs, the *Chicago Tribune* dubbed him Dictator Debs: "This man Debs is engaged in a conspiracy against the commerce and industries of the nation and the rights of the people. He is rushing on with the fury of a maniac." Said the *Washington Post*: "His object is the subordination of the machinery of civilization to his treasonable ambitions and his insolent and desperate arrogance."

President Cleveland's commission of inquiry later exculpated the ARU from the charge of provoking violence, criticized Pullman for selfishness and charged the rail owners with usurping powers. It was too late for Debs and the ARU.

BRYAN STIRS THE HEART OF AMERICA

In the summer of 1896 William Jennings Bryan came from Nebraska to Chicago with $100 in his pocket and a speech in his heart. He was called as the last speaker at the Democratic convention on July 9. The next day, while he was being shaved, he was told that the delegates had voted him their candidate for the presidency. He was that and more. He was their redeemer, their knight in shining armor, their Great Commoner, the keeper of America's soul.

He was 36. He knew he had it in him. One night in 1888 he had come home from a speech and awakened his wife, Mary. "I found I have power over the audience. God grant that I may use it wisely," he said, and sank to his knees to pray. In Chicago, he won the nomination without big backers or money. He won with a single speech. What happened that day stayed in the imagination of Americans for generations. It was a speech he had tried out in bits and pieces in the West and he made a variation of it 20 times a day after the convention. He traveled 18,000 miles on a great evangelical mission, carrying his own suitcases, praying each night on the floor of his sleeping car and waking to a day of rapturous acclaim. Everywhere except Babylon, as he called New York.

President Cleveland stayed away from Chicago. His party was rancorously split between his conservative followers, who believed gold must be the single basis of currency, and the "radical" Democrats, infiltrated by Populism, who wanted to inflate it with silver. They were from the West and the South and they blamed the Eastern "goldbugs" for the depression. Speaker after speaker, on either side of the question of pledging the party to bimetallism, was half heard or hissed. Then Bryan stood serenely before this mob of 20,000, a smile on his lips, waiting for his moment. There was silence, and then his calm, mellow voice resonated through the hall:

"This is not a contest between persons. The humblest citizen in all the land, when clad in the armor of a righteous cause, is stronger than all the hosts of error. I come to speak to you in defense of a cause as holy as the cause of liberty—the cause of humanity."

He spoke, he said, for the struggling masses, but it was in the depressed country folk that he found his inspiration:

"You come to us and tell us that the great cities are in favor of the gold standard; we reply that the great cities rest upon our broad and fertile prairies. Burn down your cities and leave our farms, and your cities will spring up again as if by magic; but destroy our farms and the grass will grow in the streets of every city in the country."

Then he dedicated them to a crusade:

"Having behind us the producing masses of this nation and the world, supported by the commercial interests, the laboring interests, and the toilers everywhere, we will answer their demand for a gold standard by saying to them: You shall not press down upon the brow of labor this crown of thorns, you shall not crucify mankind upon a cross of gold."

There was a great hush. Bryan thought something had gone wrong. Then there was such an explosion of cheers and yells, such a rush of state banners to the Nebraska delegation, that the hall was rocked in frenzied tumult for half an hour.

Bryan was the son of a Nebraska Baptist farmer and circuit judge and the family sang hymns around the piano on Sundays. He was not an observer. He was part of the revulsion, first dramatized by the Populists, at the consequences of laissez-faire politics and unbridled wealth. It was Bryan who in 1894, as a youthful congressman, had brilliantly attached a graduated income tax to the tariff bill so that Cleveland would not veto it, and he had seen this modest proposal (a 2 percent tax on incomes over $4,000) ruled unconstitutional, as a form of communism.

"Probably no man in civil life has succeeded in inspiring so much terror, without taking life, as Bryan," said *The Nation*. He was portrayed as an "ugly little anarchist," red in tooth and claw. The charges were absurd. The Democratic platform was merely watered-down Populism: free silver, regulation of the railroads and trusts, a lower tariff and the income tax. Bryan was calling not for revolution, but for a return to the old agrarian values; the equality he idealized was equality before the law and specifically not equality of possessions. It was tragic that his brilliance was wasted on espousing silver, rather than the full visionary Populist program for credit reform. His opponents smeared him as a hick and a naive fool, but his speeches in Congress were compellingly logical and studded with telling statistics. Of the projects he espoused, these would become law and accepted verities within the next generation: the federal income tax; women's suffrage; popular election of senators and public disclosure of campaign contributions; currency reform; more stringent railway regulation; the initiative and the referendum.

In 1896 Bryan was not able to capitalize on urban discontents. He assumed that what played in Omaha played in Boston, so he failed to put together a winning coalition. Yet there was genuine triumph in defeat. His campaign swept away much of the cynicism and apathy that had marked politics for 30 years. It made him the undisputed leader of a reformist Democratic party for the next 16 years. He reawakened an old American faith in the rights of the common man and in social justice, and in time this idealism found fulfillment in the New Deal.

POPULIST FINALE: It did not quite work out as the cartoonist suggested. It was the Democratic party that swallowed the Populist party. But Bryan infused the Democratic party with Populist ideas. The Populists merged with the Democrats because they feared that, running as a third party, they would split the silver vote with the Democrats to the benefit of Republicans.

"You shall not crucify mankind upon a cross of gold." Bryan's words rang across America. This is the great orator in Springfield, Massachusetts, in 1896.

THE
HOMETOWN SAINT

William McKinley, the Republican who beat Bryan in the watershed election of 1896, was a hometown saint who never stole a cent. The Democrats tried to make him out to be the puppet of "moneybags" Mark Hanna, a Cleveland coal, iron and newspaper tycoon who was his sponsor, because it was hard to pin anything on McKinley. He was a sweet, smiling man from small-town America, a devout, teetotaling Methodist, who sincerely believed that high tariffs built business and that business built America. It was his one political conviction. He never read a book. He was, like Dwight Eisenhower against Adlai Stevenson, a master of "common sense" consensus politics. The cynical Republican Congressman Joe Cannon snorted that he kept his ear so close to the ground that it was full of grasshoppers.

McKinley was a nationalist and a unifier; but it was his noble face that launched a thousand business combinations. His presidency was the heyday of unchecked capitalism. He was not a tool of Hanna, but he needed Hanna's political genius. Hanna invented the "steamroller," the tactic of getting a majority of state delegates irrevocably committed early on to a national figure in such a way that they could not be challenged by local bosses or party bolters. Hanna spent $100,000 on preconvention lobbying and snatched the Republican nomination from Thomas Brackett Reed of Maine, the wittily autocratic Speaker of the House. Then he staged the most razzle-dazzle, flag-waving campaign in American history. He sold McKinley, said Theodore Roosevelt, as if he were a patent medicine. He also ran a scare campaign, getting businesses to put notices in pay packets to tell workers that they would lose their jobs if Bryan won.

But McKinley was his own man. He distanced himself from Hanna by his rectitude; and Hanna idolized him. Late one night in his Cleveland den, said Hanna, as the two men sat face-to-face talking, he had "a revelation of a man of noble ideas who loved mankind much more than himself." Of one deal Hanna tried to cut with the boss of New York, McKinley proclaimed: "If I cannot be president without promising to make Tom Platt Secretary of the Treasury, I will never be president."

Bryan's energetic style launched modern presidential campaigning. The result was not a fair test of America's appetite for structural reform, but it decisively marked the boundaries of political debate for years ahead. McKinley carried only one state more than Bryan—23 to 22—but his winning coalition of the East, the Midwest and the cities yielded 271 electoral votes to 176. With 51 percent of the popular vote, he was the first president to win a popular majority since 1872. Apart from the Republican party split in 1912, it ushered in a period of Republican dominance based on the politics of business that lasted to the Great Depression of the thirties.

THE CANDIDATE: McKinley spent the campaign on his front porch. He said: "I might just as well put up a trapeze on my front lawn and compete with some professional athlete as go out speaking against Bryan." But by the end of the campaign Hanna's men had brought no fewer than 750,000 people to hear the candidate's subtle homilies on patriotism and shake his hand. Every day was a circus day in Canton—except Sunday.

MARK HANNA, THE FIXER

He was cartooned as a bullying plutocrat, and he was certainly a cynical manipulator: "It's better to be president than to be right," he tells McKinley in George Luks's caricature (left). But Hanna was not the reactionary of the Democratic cartoons. He supported labor's right to organize and said of George Pullman, "A man who won't meet his men halfway is a goddamn fool." His shakedown of business raised $7 million for McKinley's campaign: Bryan had a mere $300,000.

WILLIAM McKINLEY
25th President (Republican), 1897–1901

BORN: January 29, 1843, Niles, Ohio

DIED: September 14, 1901, Buffalo, New York

POLITICAL CAREER: Prosecuting attorney, Stark County, Ohio, 1869–1871; Congressman, 1877–1883, 1885–1891; Governor of Ohio, 1892–1896; President, 1897–1901

FIRSTS: First president of the twentieth century. First to use the telephone for campaigning. Last Union soldier to sit in the White House. Third president assassinated. Fifth to be born in Ohio and to die in office.

CHARACTER SNAPSHOT: "Those who knew McKinley best were those who most revered him."
—Biographer Margaret Leech

THE CONCILIATOR: He was 33 and had just been elected to Congress when this portrait was taken in 1876. His amiability concealed a strong character. John Hay, who had been Lincoln's assistant private secretary, later said of him: "I was more struck than ever with his mask. It is a genuine Italian ecclesiastical face of the fifteenth century, and there are idiots who think Mark Hanna will run him!" Earlier the same year he had risked public odium to defend a group of Ohio miners imprisoned for riot. Later, as the quick-footed Ways and Means chairman, he got tariffs raised to record levels in 1890, but the resulting high prices (and Democratic gerrymandering in Ohio) cost him his seat.

COUNTRY BOY: He was a country boy whose father struggled with a small iron foundry. When Fort Sumter fell at the start of the Civil War, he was clerking in the post office, trying to raise money to go back to college. As a volunteer commissary sergeant in the Union Army at Antietam in 1862, he drove his mule team to the front line with hot meat and coffee for the troops. He was adroit enough to suggest this merited a commission. He got it and showed such bravery again, as a staff officer galloping through gunfire with messages, that he was promoted to brevet major. If he fell, he wrote in his diary, it would be not only as a soldier for his country but as a Soldier of Jesus.

THE GOVERNOR: The "little rest and outing" Governor McKinley (center) took at Thomasville, Georgia, in 1895, was at the temporary winter quarters of Mark Hanna (left). They were discreetly wooing Southern Republicans to back McKinley for president. As two-term governor in Ohio he won the respect of labor and conservatives. He stood up for labor rights, but did not shrink from calling out the National Guard when his old Stark County miner clients sabotaged the railroads. He did it without bloodshed. His enemies defined his virtue. He was denounced by the anti-Catholic American Protective Association because in making appointments he did not discriminate on religious grounds. Nor did he use his office to build a fortune.

THE UNIFIER: No whistle-stopper, McKinley was simply greeting children of neighbors when his train arrived in Canton in the 1900 election. He spent most of his time there, again, on his front porch proclaiming that the Republicans had filled the workman's dinner pail. He got even more electoral votes than in 1896 (292 to Bryan's 155) and declared: "I can no longer be called the president of a party. I am now the president of a whole people."

THE MARTYR: Dinner at the home of Mark Hanna (left) in the run-up to the Republican 1896 convention with McKinley, as always, at the side of his wife, Ida Saxton (center foreground), a banker's daughter. He sat next to her so as to be able to throw a napkin over her face if she went into a convulsion, a not uncommon occurrence following the difficult birth of their second daughter. The early deaths of both their daughters strengthened their mutual devotion. When her headaches required it, they sat together in the dark of their modest house in Canton, Ohio. As governor, he stopped business at 3 p.m. every day to wave a handkerchief to Ida's facing hotel room.

The town of Dawson, a hub of the great Yukon gold rush just over the border from Alaska. Founded in 1896, it had 35,000 residents by 1898—and 3,000 by 1908. Winter brought temperatures of 70 degrees below zero and six weeks of total darkness. Saloons, gambling dens, brothels and con men abounded, but contrary to the lore that soon grew up around the Yukon, there was little violence. Canadian Mounties effectively banned all guns from the town.

THE KLONDIKE

Some 22,000 prospectors made it from Alaska over the Chilkoot, one of the two main trails into the goldfields of the Klondike in western Yukon Territory, Canada, where gold was discovered in 1896. The 35-degree climb shown here was too steep for draft animals. The prospectors had to slog it into the wilderness, carrying their mining equipment, all the tools to build a boat for the Klondike's waterways and a year's supply of food. Since few could carry more than 50 pounds at a time, this meant some 40 trips battling frostbite, blizzard and snow blindness. An avalanche on April 3, 1898, killed at least 60 men. Few found their fortune—but the strike helped to take the hottest issue out of politics. With earlier discoveries in Australia and South Africa, and a new cyanide process for extracting more gold from the ore, gold production by 1898 was twice what it had been in 1890, when its failure to keep pace with the expanding economy and population had been a central factor in the depression. Gold hardly solved the issues Populism had raised, but it was bad news for Bryan, who had tied his political fortunes to silver as the basis for expanding the money supply.

PACKERS ASCENDING SUMMIT OF CHILKOOT PASS.
COPYRIGHT 1898

THE LURE OF EMPIRE 1898–1905

War with Spain

The soldiers are pointing their weapons at the United States. They are Alphonso Guards in Puerto Rico, part of the Spanish Army of 500,000 officers and men by which Spain, discoverer of the New World, kept a grip on Puerto Rico, Cuba and the Philippines, the last outposts of its crumbling empire. In Cuba, a ten-year war against guerrillas had flared up again and by 1898 some 187,000 Spanish soldiers were fighting ferociously to put it down.

The men with their faces to the bullet-marked wall are Cuban rebels at the Spanish arsenal in Santiago, moments before execution. Some 400,000 civilians died in Cuban concentration camps. America was outraged by the cruelties of Spain in Cuba. The U.S. Army consisted of only 28,000 men, but the nation had a new navy, and it exulted in its industrial might. It went to war in Cuba for the cause of honor and humanity, but in the process it acquired an empire and found itself, in the Philippines, a colonial master like Spain.

Exerting American power outside the Western Hemisphere as well as within it became a habit. In 1900, American troops were sent to help restore order to China, and there were interventions in the Dominican Republic, Nicaragua and Haiti. In 1906 President Theodore Roosevelt used his diplomatic muscle in the most important single world event between 1900 and World War I, the Russo-Japanese War. America was discovering ambitions it had thought it never had.

Cuban rebels against Spanish rule await execution by Spain's Alphonso Guards.

ACCIDENTAL EMPIRE

In the penultimate year of the nineteenth century, America faced a crisis of identity that would reverberate throughout the twentieth. Its founding faith that people should be ruled only with their consent ran headlong into the conviction that it was the manifest destiny of America to spread the blessings of its civilization to humanity. What if humanity had other ideas? Victory in the Spanish-American War ended with America in physical possession of the Philippine Islands, Puerto Rico and Guam, as well as Cuba, the flash point of the war. What was to be done with them?

Cuba had been promised independence. No promises had been made for the other former colonies of Spain. The doctrine of rule by consent, and the precedent of Cuba, required that they should all determine their own future. But the doctrine of manifest destiny required that America should decide it for them. Self-determination would be a mere constitutional conceit if it exposed the people to anarchy or dictatorship or their domination by another power.

A precise calibration of the division of American sentiment was afforded on February 14, 1899. Twenty-nine senators voted to pledge phased independence for the Philippines, and 29 voted against making any such commitment. There were 32 abstainers. It was left to the vice president, Garret Augustus Hobart, a New Jersey lawyer, to cast the deciding vote. He voted for manifest destiny and against self-rule. By that one vote America joined the imperialist powers of the world, unequivocally imperialist in the Roman sense of seeking to exert sovereignty over large numbers of people different in blood, speech and culture. Mark Twain, in his essay "Greetings from the Nineteenth to the Twentieth Century," satirized the pretensions that were common to all the imperial powers, and he included America:

I bring you the stately nation named Christendom, returning bedraggled, besmirched, dishonored, from pirate raids into Kiao-Chou, Manchuria, South Africa, and the Philippines, with her soul full of meanness, her pocket full of boodle, and her mouth full of pious hypocrisies. Give her soap and a towel, but hide the looking glass.

Was America not so exceptional after all?

The first notable feature of American imperialism is that it was stillborn. The Panama Canal Zone (1903) and the Virgin Islands (1917) were the only subsequent acquisitions. Puerto Rico was ceded to the U.S., but the temptation to annex Cuba was resisted. U.S. troops pulled out of Cuba in 1902, and Puerto Ricans were granted U.S. citizenship in 1917. The Caribbean Sea was more or less a Yankee lake until World War I, but the American empire remained a bagatelle by comparison with "the empire on which the sun never sets": Thirty-five million Britons living on 54,000 square miles of land had by that time dominion over 16 million square miles on five continents and 322 million people. Thirty-nine million Frenchmen, having acquired the whole of Indochina as well as Morocco, Algeria, Tunisia and much of northwest Africa, had a subject population of 44 million people. Five million Dutchmen ruled 34 million people away in southeast Asia.

The eagle joined this flock but it did not soar on the same trajectory. The reasons for this are not immediately apparent. In many ways America resembled Britain at a similar point in its history. America in 1898 was rich, self-confident, preoccupied with domestic issues, content with the territories it had acquired, without much thought of empire, just as Britain had been when Queen Victoria ascended to the throne in 1837. Having lost the American colonies, and triumphed over the imperial ambitions of Napoleon, Britain was enjoying its industrial strength and the moral glow from its abolition of slavery in 1834, the foundation of the old British Empire. Yet Britain was then poised for an era of unprecedented expansion; and America, in similar circumstances, was destined to stop almost as soon as it had begun. It was powerful enough to plant the flag over vast territories to the north and south, and to push further into the Pacific, but it did not. It was fired by a sense of mission very similar to that which gave a fresh impulse to empire in the 60 years of Queen Victoria's reign. The British also believed they had a manifest destiny to civilize the world. In the words of Jan Morris, the evangelicals who had penetrated government as well as church to destroy slavery were inspired to wonder "what could not be done if the moral authority of England were distributed across the earth—to tackle the evils of slavery, ignorance and paganism at the source, to teach the simpler peoples the benefits of Steam, Free Trade and Revealed Religion, and to establish not a world empire in the bad Napoleonic sense, but a Moral Empire of loftier intent." Britain, unlike America, was a prodigious exporter of people (20 million emigrated between 1815 and 1914), but the Senate debate on the Philippines in 1899 resounded with the same moral aspirations. Bid America godspeed, said the Republican Orville H. Platt, "in its mission to relieve the oppressed, to right every wrong, and to extend the institutions of free government." See what an example is Britain, said Senator Knute Nelson. Until a few years ago the Egyptians were slaves or serfs. "Today they have the liberty and blessings of a good government such as they have never known since the days of the Pharaohs." Think of it, he said, there would have been no great Republic in the United States if England had not been a colonizing nation.

A zeal to save the world was not, of course, the sole impulse for British imperialism and it became less prominent as the empire builders developed a spectacular momentum in the second half of the nineteenth century. Geopolitics and greed, as well as God, came into the equation. Britain stayed on in Egypt after the occupation of 1882 to protect the route to India; and then it expanded into central and east Africa to secure the Upper Nile. America might well have been tempted to protect the Philippines by acquiring more bulwarks in the Pacific. But, again, the temptation was resisted.

And what of the temptations of trade? "Philanthropy plus 5 percent," was how the imperialist financier Cecil Rhodes described British policy in 1890. We would expect enterprising America to have been even more governed by the imperatives of capitalism. In his classic analysis in *Imperialism* in 1902, John Hobson suggested that capitalist states were doomed to become imperialist. They had to acquire colonies because capitalism produced more goods than its underpaid workers could consume and more capital than it could employ at home. Some U.S. historians of the so-called Open Door school identify such economics as the source of the American impulse to imperialism. "Its taproot lay in the post-1873 depressions and the need to find overseas markets for the overly productive factories and farms," say Walter LaFeber, Richard Polenberg and Nancy Woloch. If so, why did the American expansion overseas not continue into the twentieth century? The economics remained the same. In fact, it is hard to fit the Open Door analysis either to the macroeconomics—there were plenty of new customers at

home—or to what happened in Hawaii, Cuba, the Philippines and Puerto Rico.

For a start, American capitalists were not agitating for empire as a means of deploying their surplus capital. They had none. Until World War I, America spent its capital on expansion at home. Britain, by contrast, invested 9.3 billion pounds overseas in the single year of 1896, most of it in the U.S. As for American industry, it was obsessed by the home market and demanded a protective tariff, not free trade. Exports as a proportion of gross national product were only 5.8 percent between 1907 and 1911. The comparable figure for British exports was six times greater: India took 40 percent of the cotton goods exported from Lancashire.

THE MASTER RACE: America must become an empire in its second century. It was God's will and it was good for trade. The advocate of these sentiments, Senator Albert Beveridge, was a pushy lawyer of 37 from Indiana. He electrified the Senate with his soaring first speech. God had made Americans "the master organizers of the world" to rule over "savage and senile" people. America should keep the Philippines forever. The old guard walked out on his next oration. He wanted free trade for Puerto Rico.

American exports, moreover, went overwhelmingly to the developed world, not the undeveloped regions awaiting their imperial merchants. Most of America's trade was with Britain. Where, asked Senator John Daniel dryly, is the strategic island at the mouth of Liverpool harbor? Or as Arthur Schlesinger, Jr., remarks in a devastating section of *The Cycles of American History,* "The notion that poverty-stricken Samoans had the money to buy American wheat and flour, even if it were part of their diet, is absurd." The Philippine Islands in 1897 absorbed 0.55 percent of American exports. Not much hope there for the overly productive factories and farms.

THOSE DARNED ISLANDS: McKinley signed the war resolution in his dressing gown at 4 a.m. He had asked for something less than war. It was the only time in history Congress voted for war without a specific request from the president. But then the former Union major became a keen commander in chief. He set up a war room papered with maps, with white pinflags for the Spanish fleet, red for the American. He dropped in at night for a last cigar before bed. When Commodore George Dewey sailed for the Philippines, McKinley said: "I could not have told where those darned islands were within two thousand miles."

As a single explanation, manifest destiny is a more cogent explanation of the nature of American imperialism, both for its eruption and its aberrant short life. But the chronicle suggests a single generalization may not suffice. Hawaii, Cuba and the Philippines are separate cases.

Hawaii was of keen interest to certain American businesses, but not for its pitiful markets. Sugar planters, missionaries and whale hunters established a strong American presence in Hawaii, but periodic proposals that the U.S. should annex the islands got nowhere. There was just no imperial appetite for acquisitions anywhere. In 1867 the U.S. did not even bother to reply when King Cakobau offered to cede Fiji. In 1869 the Senate frustrated President Grant's wish to purchase the Virgin Islands from Denmark. In 1870 it blocked his proposed annexation of Santo Domingo. The turning point in the Pacific was 1875, and the motive was strategic, since Hawaii was now seen as vital to the defense of the Pacific coast against the rising power of Japan. In return for an understanding that Hawaii would grant territorial concessions to no other power, the United States agreed to admit Hawaiian sugar into the U.S. duty-free. In 1887 the U.S. secured the exclusive use of Pearl

(River) Harbor as a naval station. These were boom years for Hawaii, with the sons of American missionaries dominating the sugar industry. But in 1890 the McKinley tariff gave home-grown American sugar a bounty of two cents a pound, and that disaster was succeeded, in the eyes of the Americans, by another with the accession to the throne in January 1893 of Queen Liliuokalani, who promulgated a new constitution giving her autocratic powers. At the time there were only 2,000 Americans on the islands, compared with 40,000 Polynesians, 30,000 Chinese and 9,000 Portuguese. But the German-born planter Claus Spreckels, his friend Sanford Dole and the U.S. minister, John Stevens, with the aid of a few Marines, pulled off a neat little coup to depose the queen and declare Hawaii an American protectorate. That would have been that, but for the March return to the White House of Grover Cleveland, who had no time for manifest destiny. The Democrats had stalled the annexation treaty in the Senate, and he at once withdrew it. "I mistake the American people," he said, "if they favor the odious doctrine that there is no such thing as international morality, that there is one law for the strong and one for the weak." The commissioner he dispatched to Hawaii reported a big majority of the voters were strongly opposed to annexation. Cleveland would have returned Hawaii to the queen, but she alienated American opinion by her promise to behead the sugar kings who had fomented the coup. Cleveland and Congress left Hawaii to stew for four years. President McKinley signed an annexation treaty, which produced protests from Japan, but that treaty, too, was blocked by Democratic senators who had an ally in the Republican Speaker Thomas Brackett Reed of Maine: he believed that the U.S. already had too many unassimilated elements. Only the outbreak of war with Spain ended the argument. All lofty sentiment against annexation was swept aside in the rush to secure naval bases.

The real trigger for American imperialism was this decision to go to war with Spain over Cuba. Cuba made the difference because the circumstances conspired to excite national honor and appeal to the force of moral conviction. Again, the chronicle of events is instructive in illuminating the unpremeditated nature of American imperialism.

It was for many years an offense to the United States to have Spain's ramshackle colony 100 miles from its back door, an island beset by rebellion every few years. There were constant irritations—Americans in prison for running supplies to the rebels, anti-American riots in Spain, destruction of American property. But it was genuine sympathy for the oppressed that produced the momentum for intervention, together with a lot of belligerent praying from Protestant clergy. Most of the 800,000 whites and 600,000 blacks in Cuba lived lives that were short, brutish and nasty. The only part that economics played in what followed was the U.S. imposition of a 40 percent tariff on Cuban sugar—sugar again!—which put thousands out of work: the misery helped provoke yet another rebellion in 1895. If Spain had been governed by wiser heads, it would have leapt at the offer of mediation by President Cleveland, but it was unable to recognize that American outrage at the barbarisms in Cuba was not power politics masquerading as sentiment. The sentiment was real. It reached an intense pitch when General Valeriano ("Butcher") Weyler took over the job of suppressing the rebellion. He herded the rural population into *reconcentrados,* or concentration camps, where 100,000 died from disease and malnutrition. As Spain's military attaché in the Civil War, he had been on Sherman's march as an observer and was baffled by what he saw as American hypocrisy: "How do they want me to wage war? With bishops' pastorals and presents of sweets and money?" The indictment by the serious press was important in the formation of opinion in favor of intervention, but Weyler—with

his steel-blue eyes and the stern visage of his Prussian ancestry—was a perfect demon for the yellow press.

Moralizing, not greed, was the most real thing about American foreign policy in 1898. The imperialists who campaigned for liberating Cuba were not in business. They were in the Congress, the press and the church. The peacemakers were on Wall Street and in the business community. Here is arch-imperialist Teddy Roosevelt ventilating his wrath at them at the Gridiron press dinner in Washington on March 26, 1898. T.R. smacked his fist in his palm and wheeled on a fellow guest, Senator Mark Hanna, the industrialist and party boss who was opposed to intervention. "We shall have this war in Cuba," said Roosevelt. "The interests of business and of financiers might be paramount in the Senate, but not so with the American people. Now, Senator, may we please have war?"

Stock prices fell with every war scare in 1898. The business community, enjoying the revival that began with the end of the depression in 1897, was loath to disturb it by war. For this they were denounced as selfish moneymakers. As McKinley's biographer Margaret Leech notes, spokesmen for the President in 1898 did not venture to speak of peace. "It had become a symbol of obedience to avarice."

Public opinion in both countries may by this time have favored war, but neither the Spanish nor the American government did, and war was unnecessary. When McKinley became president in March 1897, he reapplied Cleveland's pressure and Spain granted autonomy to Cuba and Puerto Rico, replaced Weyler, released all American citizens from prison (mainly Cuban-born naturalized Americans) and let the U.S. send in relief supplies. Diplomacy was working; but chance was working overtime. The U.S. battleship *Maine* was sent to Havana to protect Americans, and its destruction by an explosion on February 15, 1898, drove the jingoistic yellow press into paroxysms. Spain seemed as horrified as America. The Spanish governor-general wept openly in his palace. The bishop of Havana conducted an elaborate funeral. The Madrid government and the Queen Regent suggested a joint inquiry. None of this genuine response satisfied the warmakers. Theodore Roosevelt's jibe that McKinley "has no more backbone than a chocolate éclair" was unmerited. It took backbone to resist the war hysteria, refueled with a vengeance when on March 28 the naval inquiry reported (wrongly, see page 62) that the *Maine* had been destroyed by a submarine mine. Every day the haggard McKinley, sleeping only with the aid of drugs, was confronted by the slogan of the hour: "Remember the *Maine*! To hell with Spain!" Perhaps if congressional elections had not been looming, with William Jennings Bryan calling for Cuban independence, McKinley could have resisted longer and Cuba could have had its independence without bloodshed. Spain was on the point of capitulation. America would not then have found itself in the Philippines, using tactics not unlike Weyler's to suppress a rebellion held over from the Spanish empire. There would have been no American imperialism worth talking about.

In April 1898, nobody thought much about Spain's other troubled colony, the Philippines. When Congress demanded an end to Spanish rule in Cuba, Henry Teller, the Democratic senator from Colorado, had no opposition to his rider disavowing any American designs on Cuba. The sugar interests wanted to keep Cuba outside the American tariff wall, but in any event the prevailing sentiment was idealist. The war resolution motion of April 20 said the United States disclaimed "any disposition or intention to exercise sovereignty, jurisdiction, or control" except for pacification. It went on to say that once there was peace it was determined to "leave the government and control of the island to its people." As Teller himself said later, if he had thought to add the Philippines, the vote would have been the same. Why, then, did a majority of the same body of men, including Teller himself, vote in February 1899 for something that was unthinkable in 1898? Why did McKinley denounce forcible annexation as "criminal aggression" in December 1897, and then carry it out in the Philippines in 1899? This is the key question about American imperialism. The pledge of self-rule for Cuba was kept; and nobody was asking for self-rule for Puerto Rico. It is the Philippines that provides the puzzle of American imperialism. Again, it can be understood only by looking at the unplanned convergence of people and events.

Before the national debate began, there was, of course, already a body of politicians, clergymen and promoters long committed to the expansion of American power. The politicians were mainly Republicans. They called themselves expansionists rather than imperialists and they included T.R.;

COLONIAL JUSTICE: A Spanish execution chamber and garrote in the walled city of Manila, 1898.

Henry Cabot Lodge; McKinley's secretary of state, John Hay, and his shrewd new secretary of war, Elihu Root; Whitelaw Reid, publisher of the *New York Tribune;* advocates of a larger navy such as Admiral Mahan; Republican senators like Will F. Frye of Maine and the newcomer Albert Beveridge. The muscle of the missionary element was represented by the Reverend Josiah Strong of Ohio, a Social Darwinist who called for the planting of church missions all over the world and predicted that American domination of Mexico, Latin America and Africa was inevitable, because that would represent the survival of the fittest in the coming competition of the races.

In 1895 Lodge, picking up an old American dream, asserted that there should be but one flag from the Rio Grande to the Arctic, but he was prepared to admit the remote possibility that the Filipinos might one day govern themselves. T.R., for all his jingoism, was the president who in 1902 honored the pledge to restore Cuba to self-rule to the astonishment of the European colonists. Few were as extreme as Strong, or as Senator Beveridge, who believed that America must dedicate itself to running the Philippines in perpetuity. These men were not moved by selling cotton and steel. They were moved mainly by a lofty sense of America's manifest destiny, and a down-to-earth appreciation of the strategies of defense proposed by Admiral Mahan (see page 59). They appealed to pride and prejudice, to urban masses who exulted in America's strength, but also to newly educated classes persuaded of the superiority of white Protestant Anglo-Saxons. Of course, they had allies among that minority of business groups that stood to benefit directly by empire: the importers of tropical products, the shippers, the makers of popular drinks. And it is true the imperialists themselves would from time to time extol the glittering possibilities of trade. But commerce was a rationalization rather than a justification. They never analyzed the trade figures or had any answer to the skeptics who had. In his speech on the Philippines, Lodge grumbled that the debate had been so high-minded that it had overlooked the vast benefits of easier access to the markets of China, but he spoke in the truer voice of the imperialists when he declared that a nation's honor and the advance of the Anglo-Saxon race were not to be talked of in the same breath as the trading of jackknives and the price of calico. Honor, Anglo-Saxonism, destiny, mission, civilization, power and prestige: these are the key words with which the imperialists annexed the Philippine Islands with barely a murmur about future self-rule.

The opponents of annexation gathered in the Anti-Imperialist League. There were a few Republicans like Senators

George Hoar and Eugene Hale, Speaker Reed and Carl Schurz, the German refugee who had become a Union general and then secretary of the interior under President Hayes, but they were mainly Democrats. Unlikely alliances emerged. Ex-president Grover Cleveland and William Jennings Bryan were on the same side. So were steelmaster Andrew Carnegie and Samuel Gompers of the American Federation of Labor. Carnegie paid most of the league's bills, and at one time offered to purchase the Philippines from Spain and give them back to the islanders. The philosopher of pragmatism, William James, was at one with the leading Social Darwinist, William Graham Sumner. Many of Sumner's disciples were in the imperialist camp, but he denounced them in a tract entitled "The Conquest of the United States by Spain": Annexation would ruin the U.S. as it had already ruined Spain. Militarism would lead to higher taxes, a bigger government role, and disaster for republican institutions and democracy. The literary big shots and editors were nearly all anti-imperialist—E. L. Godkin of *The Nation* and Samuel Bowles of the *Springfield Republican;* Mark Twain, William Vaughn Moody and William Dean Howells.

None of the key debaters, on either side, had been to the Philippines. The duty to Christianize the Filipinos was devoutly proclaimed by the imperialists and let pass by their critics, no one making much fuss over the small detail that

THE LIBERATORS: California troops assemble in San Francisco, next stop Manila, 1898.

nearly all the nontribal population of about 7 million were already members of the Roman Catholic Church. Like McKinley, who read it suffering from eyestrain, everyone pored over the article in *Contemporary Review* by the Englishman John Foreman, which reported that the Filipinos were incapable of anything except fighting racially among themselves. They had never known a day of self-government in 300 years of Spanish rule; and they were not Anglo-Saxons. This perception became the fulcrum of the debate. Few of the anti-imperialists, in truth, had any enthusiasm for seeing the Philippines join the Union. They agreed with the imperialists that the Filipinos were not ready for that. The Southern Democrats, who formed the core of the opposition to the treaty, were especially vehement in their racist view that the Constitution could not follow the flag. "Mongrel and semi-barbarous" tropical people could never be part of the Union, and since they were not ready for self-rule, either, the United States would be doomed to be a despotic colonizer. This was not merely a Southern view. Bananas and self-government, said South Dakota Senator Richard Pettigrew, don't grow on the same patch of ground. William Jennings Bryan's syllogism was: "The Filipinos cannot be citizens without endangering our civilization; they cannot be subjects without imperiling our form of government." But the conclusion that therefore the Filipinos should be accorded full independence was not held with much conviction by any of the anti-imperialists. It impeded their case all along, because if the Filipinos needed a

GOD'S FOUR POINTS

President McKinley had said it would be "criminal aggression" to annex the Philippines. He told the story of his conversion to a group of visiting imperialists, the missionary committee of the Methodist Episcopal Church:

"I walked the floor of the White House night after night until midnight and I am not ashamed to tell you, gentlemen, that I went down on my knees and prayed to Almighty God for light and guidance more than one night. And one night late it came to me this way—I don't know how it was, but it came. One, that we could not give the Philippines back to Spain—that would be cowardly and dishonorable. Two, that we could not turn them over to France or Germany—our commercial rivals in the Orient—that would be bad business and discreditable. Three, that we could not leave them to themselves—they were unfit for self-government—and they would soon have anarchy and misrule over there worse than Spain's was. And, four, that there was nothing left for us to do but to take them all, and to educate the Filipinos, and uplift them and civilize and Christianize them, and by God's grace do the very best we could for them, as our fellow-men for whom Christ also died. And then I went to bed, and went to sleep, and slept soundly, and the next morning I sent for the chief engineer of the War Department (our map maker), and I told him to put the Philippines on the map of the United States, and there they are, and there they will stay while I am President!"

JOHN HAY'S PLUNGE INTO BIG-POWER POLITICS

American missionaries had long dreamed of saving China's "great Niagara" of 350 million souls from passing into the dark. John D. Rockefeller's Standard Oil Company dreamed of selling oil to light all the lamps of China and started by giving away 8 million Mei Foo ("good luck") kerosene lamps.

The acquisition of the Philippines gave America a useful stepping-stone to China, but it had been carved up into bits and pieces owned by or on lease to one European power or another. So Secretary of State John Hay (right) plunged into world politics. In September 1899 he asked the powers to agree that in their spheres of influence they would not interfere with the trade of other nations. The replies were ambiguous but Hay blithely announced that this Open Door principle of commercial equality had been agreed to by all. Within months of this creative sleight of hand an aggressively antiforeign group of Chinese revolutionists known as Boxers went on the rampage. They hacked and burned to death thousands of Chinese Christians; all told, some 32,000 were murdered. The foreign legations in Peking were besieged. America swallowed its distaste for alliances and joined with the Russians, British, Japanese and French in sending a joint force of about 20,000 men to relieve the legations. They did—and then disintegrated in a riot of plunder, murder and rape. "The story is enough to sicken a Zulu," said Hay.

China seemed in danger of complete dismemberment and Hay now took the Open Door policy a big step further. He asked all the powers, in the name of morality and justice, to respect Chinese

John Hay, Secretary of State

national integrity, as well as the principle of fair trade in "all parts" of China. "Nothing so meteoric had ever been done in American diplomacy," said Henry Adams of this extension of the Open Door policy. It was high-minded, but it was also self-interested. The exposed Philippines could best be protected by preserving China as the central point of a balance of power in the East. China was indeed saved for a time, though Hay himself would not have claimed much credit. America was not ready to go to war on the issue. The policy worked principally because no power was strong enough to challenge all the others who paid lip service to the Open Door.

America did maintain good faith in one regard. It restrained the powers in their demands on China for compensation for the losses suffered in the Boxer Rebellion. When American losses were later found to have been estimated too high, Congress cut the debt in half and the Chinese put the remissions into a fund to educate Chinese students in the United States.

Thus began a long American commitment to China.

Hay was a passionate expansionist with a gift for words. The phrase "splendid little war" to describe Cuba in 1898 was his. He was sometimes called a dupe of the British—he was McKinley's ambassador in London from 1897 to 1898—because he saw great value in Anglo-American friendship. Of America's habit of lecturing the imperialist powers he said: "The talk of our preeminent moral position giving us the authority to dictate to the world is mere flapdoodle." He was secretary of state to both McKinley and Roosevelt.

---

period of tutelage, who better to provide it than America? The rebellious old Republican sage George Hoar might proclaim it "a great national crime" to rule people without their consent, but he was met with the rejoinder that no consent was sought when the United States acquired territories by the Louisiana Purchase (1803); the Adams-Onís Treaty (1819), which added Florida; the Treaty of Guadalupe-Hidalgo (1848), which added Texas, New Mexico and California; the Gadsden Purchase (1853); or the purchase of Alaska (1867); and that Arizona and New Mexico had been held for more than 50 years without admission to statehood.

In this tumult, four influences were decisive. First, pride. Its power to move men is often underrated. The country was flushed with its military triumphs. It had excited the world and it wanted to go on showing it was a power to be reckoned with. Wherever the flag has floated, said senators headily,

never shall it be hauled down. President McKinley came to favor the annexation he had condemned partly because in a midterm election swing through the country in 1898 he sensed that the mood of the people was missionary and expansionist. Mark Hanna, the stubborn opponent of foreign entanglements, finally came round to annexation for the same reason.

Secondly, preemption. The circumstances made the Philippines a prime example of what historian William Langer has called preclusive imperialism. Perhaps we should not have it, but we are hanged if the other fellow will have it. The country resented the way the Germans sailed their battleships into Manila Bay while Admiral Dewey's conquering U.S. fleet was at anchor, and into Haiti just before the American fleet off Cuba fought the battle of Santiago. The Japanese had earlier sent their warships to Hawaii. The British, who had earned America's gratitude for their support in the war, urged

McKinley that establishing a protectorate was not enough. Outright annexation of the whole archipelago was the only way to avoid the imperial powers fighting over the islands. This clinched it for McKinley. The worst solution for the Philippines would be, he said, "to fling them, a golden apple of discord, among the rival powers."

Thirdly, tactics and timing. McKinley and Hanna, once convinced, used all the powers of office to win wavering Democrats and Populists to vote for annexation. The two-thirds majority required for ratifying the treaty was secured by a single vote. The crucial final two votes were secured by inducing the Democratic Senators Samuel McEnery and John McLaurin to vote against their convictions. Not by superior eloquence or new facts, but by assisting one with an appointment to the federal bench in Louisiana, and the other with the gift of postmasterships in South Carolina. On such venality, mixed with such idealism, was the fate of the Philippines decided.

Given the tenor of the debate, it ought to have been easy for the anti-imperialists to follow up the vote for the treaty and annexation with a simple majority vote pledging the U.S. to give the Philippines self-rule in due course in all but foreign affairs. But they voted against a clear commitment and in favor of a woolly resolution that enabled the U.S. to do anything it liked. It was the outbreak of shooting in Manila in February 1899 by Filipinos seeking independence from America that made the difference. It excited the senators to frantic flag-waving. Anyone who would shoot at an American uniform did not deserve a promise of self-rule.

Fourth, idealism. The arguments for manifest destiny were not mere rhetoric. America became genuinely elated that it might civilize an alien people, a challenge and an adventure that appealed to Americans. Senator Teller, author of the anti-annexation amendment on Cuba, persuaded himself that in the Philippines a "great work of humanity" needed to be done, "doing for those people what the English flag did for us when it brought us English common law and English jurisprudence and English freedom." And Cuba? Oh, they were more ready for self-rule than Asiatics and closer to the redeeming influences of America.

In the war with the Filipinos that followed, the antis felt vindicated; the values of the republic had been put at risk. After the purchase of the islands for $20 million, Speaker Reed said: "We have bought ten million Malays at $2 a head unpicked, and nobody knows what it will cost to pick them." The answer was 4,234 Americans, along with 20,000 Filipino rebels, and 200,000 civilians dead. A larger percentage of the Filipino population died in the three years of organized resistance than did that of Vietnam in ten years of war. T.R. suppressed his discomfort with the massacres, taking refuge in a cynical use of language. He boasted that his administration had never fired a shot "against any foreign foe," by which term he and his secretaries of war excluded Filipinos, since they lived under Old Glory and could presumably be killed as a matter of domestic policy.

The antis were right also about the economics. America put in far more than it took out. All the imperialists could say was that the originating ideals prevailed in the end. When the horror of the war was over, the Philippines could be presented as a showcase—flawed by paternalism, but infinitely superior to what the Filipinos had endured under Spain and more enlightened than standard European colonialism.

"To remain a great nation or to become one, you must colonize," said the French statesman Léon Gambetta. America tried this in 1898, but the appetite did not last long when the exultations of victory were replaced with the casualty lists from Luzon. Protectorates bordering on the Caribbean Sea, that American lake, were one thing, but colonies another. The tradition of self-determination reasserted itself and was ingeniously reconciled with the duties of manifest destiny despite the temptations victory provided in two world wars.

Despite all the similarities, despite manifest destiny, America never followed the British example. The *New York World* caught the spirit in its adaptation of Rudyard Kipling:

We've taken up the white man's burden
Of ebony and brown;
Now will you kindly tell us, Rudyard,
How we may put it down?

THE WORLD'S CONSTABLE: Roosevelt wrote in 1900: "I have always been fond of the West African proverb 'Speak softly and carry a big stick.'"

58 ADMIRAL MAHAN'S DOCTRINE, 1884–1897

THE APOSTLE OF AMERICAN SEA POWER

Alfred Thayer Mahan, naval officer, leading imperialist and apostle of American naval power, hated life at sea and foreign parts. He was happier in the New York Navy Yard, counting stitches and testing thread in naval bunting to prove that hand-sewn flags were better than those produced by Isaac Singer's sewing machines. He hated the sea because he was always seasick, ships he commanded had a habit of colliding with other vessels and he found seamen profane, ignorant and unseemly. They found him aloof, sneering, cynical and priggish. He spent every minute he could in his cabin reading history books.

He wrote one himself in five months, *The Gulf and Inland Waters* (1883). It was one in a series on the Civil War, in which he had served on blockade duty. He had no grand ideas then about the Navy. He did not conceive of it as the strategic arm of a world power. He was an isolationist and became even more jaundiced about foreign involvements when he was taken from the Navy Yard the year his book was published and given command of a beat-up, wooden sailing-steam warship, the *Wachusett*, which was assigned to protect American interests in the petty turmoil of war between Chile and Peru. He was 43, pining for his wife and three children, when ten months into the sweaty two-year tour he wrote to a friend: "I dread outlying colonies, to maintain which large military establishments are necessary."

It was the last time he expressed an isolationist sentiment. A few days later he received a letter saying that there was a staff post, when he got back, at the new Navy War College. The turning point in his life, and to an extent in American and world history, came when he went ashore in Lima in November 1884 and dropped in at the English Club. He hoped the club's small library might help him bone up for the lectures he was already worrying about. He stumbled on *The History of Rome*, by Theodor Mommsen. "There dawned upon me," he wrote later, "one of those concrete perceptions which turn inward darkness into light—and give substance to shadow." The light was the idea that control of the

Admiral Mahan, in 1897, when he was 57. He died in 1914 and is buried at Quogue, Long Island.

sea was a historic factor which had never been systematically appreciated and expanded. He took the "thunder" of his great idea with him to the Navy College, endured the bureaucracy's distrust of intellectual studies and from his lectures produced his masterwork, *The Influence of Sea Power Upon History, 1660 - 1783* (1890). Taking Britain as a prime example, he demonstrated that the nation that controlled the sea controlled history. He did not initially demand colonies, but that

TROUBLESOME QUEEN: Queen Liliuokalani, the native monarch of Hawaii. Mahan irritated President Cleveland by backing the Americans who deposed her.

soon followed in the logic of his broadsides for navalism, imperialism and Social Darwinism. Mahan gave force and coherence to a body of ideas that had been around for a decade: one of his references was a small volume, written in 1881 in New York's Astor Library by a young man of 22 named Theodore Roosevelt (*The Naval War of 1812*, 1882). Roosevelt accorded *Sea Power* a rave review. In the 1890s the acclaimed author became a member of the imperialist cabal that lunched at New York's Metropolitan Club and included Roosevelt, Commodore George Dewey, Senator Henry Cabot Lodge, philosopher Brooks

Adams, John Hay, *New York Sun* editor Charles A. Dana and a jolly circuit judge named William Howard Taft. They all subscribed to Mahan's doctrine that America, home of a superior race, must penetrate world markets. It must build a merchant marine to carry the goods, and a two-ocean Navy to protect them and to defend its strategic and commercial interests in Samoa, Hawaii, the Caribbean and the Isthmus of Panama. Mahan was also convinced America must ally itself with Britain, the no. 1 naval power. America was then twelfth, its fleet a laughingstock.

But there was a less appreciative reader of Mahan in 1893, President Grover Cleveland, who was both Anglophobic and isolationist. Five days after his inauguration that March, Cleveland abruptly withdrew a treaty annexing Hawaii, just when *Forum* magazine came out with an article cogently arguing that Hawaii was vital for the defense of America's west coast. The article was by Mahan, now president of the Navy War College at Newport. His timing was off. He had been trying to do more justice to his arguments than he had in a lurid, yellow-peril letter to the *New York Times* in January, when he wrote that Hawaii must be kept because it was the "white cork in the yellow bottle." He had gotten away with being an outspoken serving officer in President Harrison's days. Now he received the punishment he feared most. He was ordered back to sea. The naval bureaucrat Francis Ramsay had no time for Mahan's plea that he could serve the Navy better by thinking. "It is not the business of a naval officer," said Ramsay, "to write books."

Mahan continued scribbling in his cabin. His influence was profound. Kaiser Wilhelm II in Berlin said he was trying to learn *Sea Power* by heart; the Japanese had it translated for the emperor, the crown prince and their officer corps; a hundred admirals and captains of the Royal Navy feted Mahan at a London banquet. Arguably, Mahan's writing had one malign result. He reinforced the Kaiser's inclination to pursue German colonies and naval domination. This, in turn, proved a stimulus to the European arms race, and to the suspicions that culminated in World War I.

HEARST FURNISHES THE WAR AND THE PICTURES:
The man taking pictures is William Randolph Hearst, black prince of yellow journalism. In June 1898 he took his Box Brownie and his staff to Cuba to report on the Spanish-American War he had helped to start. "You furnish the pictures and I'll furnish the war," he had cabled Frederic Remington in 1897, when the bored reporter-artist had said there was nothing to draw. On his expedition, Hearst did not only take pictures of the smoking wrecks of Spanish warships the morning after the battle of Santiago, he waved his pistol at some surviving Spaniards on a harbor island, hustled them back aboard his chartered steamship and delivered them to the American warship *St. Louis*, where he demanded and got a receipt: "Received of W. R. Hearst twenty-nine Spanish prisoners." One of

his *Journal* reporters with American troops storming the fortified town of El Caney was shot and opened his eyes to find his proprietor hovering over him with note-book and pencil.

Hearst was 32 when he bought the *Journal* in New York in 1895, and plunged into war on two fronts. War with Spain as soon as he could get it. War every day with Joseph Pulitzer at the *World*.

Initially, Pulitzer's paper reported events straight-forwardly, but in the battle for millions of readers, he soon became as jingoistic as Hearst. Most of the atroc-ity stories in both papers were fabrications, dreamed up by the Peanut Club, a group of Cuban exiles at 66 Broadway who fed the press both real peanuts and these "peanut" tales of rebel heroism against Spain, in the hope of inciting America to join the fight.

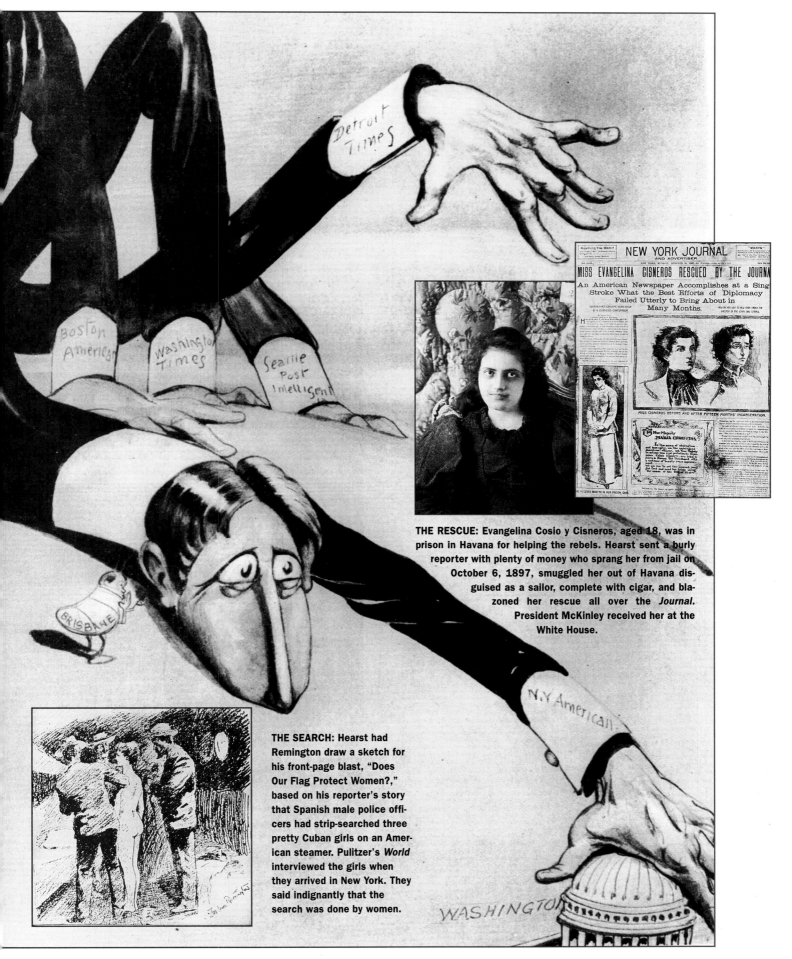

THE RESCUE: Evangelina Cosio y Cisneros, aged 18, was in prison in Havana for helping the rebels. Hearst sent a burly reporter with plenty of money who sprang her from jail on October 6, 1897, smuggled her out of Havana disguised as a sailor, complete with cigar, and blazoned her rescue all over the *Journal*. President McKinley received her at the White House.

THE SEARCH: Hearst had Remington draw a sketch for his front-page blast, "Does Our Flag Protect Women?," based on his reporter's story that Spanish male police officers had strip-searched three pretty Cuban girls on an American steamer. Pulitzer's *World* interviewed the girls when they arrived in New York. They said indignantly that the search was done by women.

THE *MAINE*
BLEW ITSELF UP

The trigger for the Spanish-American War was a false one. Spain did not plant a mine, nor did anyone else. The *Maine* was destroyed by 11,190 pounds of its own powder in a magazine for shells, ignited by fire in a coal bunker separated by a single bulkhead. It was a preventable accident. Had this been publicly known at the time, as it might have been, it is conceivable America would not have gone to war; and it might very well not have become an imperialist power.

That the Spaniards did not blow up the warship is the inescapable conclusion of a study carried out by Admiral Hyman G. Rickover in 1976 with expert testimony. The celebrated admiral's study was published by the Naval History Division of the Department of the Navy, but received surprisingly little attention. Histories still routinely refer to the *Maine*'s being sunk by a mine.

Two official inquiries, one in 1898 and another in 1911, both blamed a mine. Both are deeply flawed. Both failed to call technical experts. The evidence that induced the first board to report so devastatingly to McKinley was the divers' findings that the keel was bent into an inverted V shape (^) in the region of structural frames 18 to 22. This, the board concluded, could not have been caused by the magazine explosion and could have been brought about only by the upward force of an external explosion at this point. They were wrong. The 1911 inquiry, with the benefit of a raised wreck, found that the center of the explosion was not at frame 18 but in the magazine near frame 27. And the keel damage could, after all, be accounted for by the action of gases of low explosives in the forward magazine. It had no bearing on whether there was an external burst.

The mystery should have been cleared up there and then in 1911. But that board still concluded that the magazine was exploded by an external force. The board did so because it was puzzled that one of the four bottom sections of the *Maine* was displaced inward. Rickover's experts, Ib S. Hansen and Robert S. Price, explain this by the dynamics of the explosion on the particular design of the *Maine* and the fact

SENSATIONALISM: Hearst's *Journal* and Teddy Roosevelt were too impatient for war to wait for the facts.

that later experiments with explosions inside destroyer bulkheads have produced results just like the *Maine*. Moreover, the small section of plating folded inward showed no evidence of the deformation that would have certainly been brought about by a Spanish contact mine of the day of 100 to 200 pounds of guncotton—the size of mine that would have been needed to detonate the magazine. Other evidence also points away from a mine—no upward plume of water, no upward shock and the sheer unfeasibility of anyone being able to place a mine of sufficient size in the right location.

Of an accident, on the contrary, there is persuasive evidence. Between 1894 and 1908, more than 20 coal-bunker fires were reported on U.S. naval ships. The *Cincinnati* and *New York* nearly went the way of the *Maine*. A sad fact of the *Maine* is that while Captain Charles Sigsbee may have been a good seaman and a brave man, he was, in Rickover's words, "the victim of the new technology which was transforming the Navy . . . and perhaps it is also significant that the *Kearsarge* and *Texas* while under his command were also found

dirty." Captain Sigsbee did not know how much coal there was in the forward bunkers. The coal he had on the *Maine* was the same brand that had ignited on the *New York* in March 1897, just three and a half hours after an inspection. The explosion on the *Maine* came nearly 12 hours after the last required inspection,

ample time for a bunker fire to begin, heat the bulkheads and set fire to adjacent compartments.

Rickover's conclusion bears remembering: "In the modern technological age, the battle cry 'Remember the *Maine!*' should have a special meaning for us. With the vastness of our government and the diffi-culty of controlling it, we must make sure that those in 'high places' do not, without most careful consideration of the consequences, exert our prestige and might. Such uses of our power may result in serious international actions at great cost in lives and money—injurious to the interests and standing of the United States."

VICTIMS: The crew of the *Maine* was having a good time in Havana. The officers went to balls, dinners and bullfights. Most of them survived the explosion on February 15, 1898. The 266 dead among the 354 officers and men were mainly crew.

THE BATTLES FOR CUBA AND THE PHILIPPINES

Four hundred years of imperial dominion in the New World, the legacy of Columbus and Magellan, Cortés and de Soto, ended in ten weeks in the Spanish-American War. Supposedly fighting for the liberation of Cuba, America's first and most enduring action was thousands of miles away in the Pacific, where the Philippines became its first colony. The indolent secretary of war, Russell Alger, a match manufacturer from Michigan, had promised that on ten days' notice he could put an army of 40,000 in the field. He could not. And when 18,000 men did land in Cuba on June 22, two months after war was declared, they had antique rifles and such miserable provisions and training for the tropics that thirteen died from disease for every one of the 289 killed in the battles of El Caney and San Juan Hill (July 1), and the siege of Santiago that followed. Luckily for the Americans, the Spanish were even worse prepared. They had 200,000 soldiers in Cuba but deployed only a few thousand in battle.

The U.S. Navy was way ahead of the Army. On May 1, only a week after war was declared, Commodore George Dewey was in Manila Bay giving his famous order: "You may fire when ready, Gridley." He had sailed in with his fleet of four cruisers and two gunboats around midnight, rejecting the entreaty to let a supply ship test the wa-

HOW IT WAS: Teddy Roosevelt's Rough Riders were on foot for the charge toward San Juan Hill, as Frederic Remington's depiction suggests, because Spanish Mausers easily picked off mounted men. Only Roosevelt stayed on his horse, Little Texas, carrying a revolver salvaged from the *Maine*. He shot a defender who, he later wrote, "doubled up like a jackrabbit."

"Most everybody says this suit looks best on me." Everything after Manila Bay was anticlimactic for Admiral Dewey.

ters for mines: "I've waited for sixty years for this opportunity. Mines or no mines, I'm leading the squadron myself." The battle began at dawn, with the U.S. ships sailing up and down at six knots and pounding the Spanish fleet of ten older warships that Admiral Patricio Montojo had stationed away from Manila to spare the city from gunfire. All but one of his ships had been destroyed when he raised the white flag at 12:30 p.m. Dewey had temporarily halted the battle at 7:30 a.m. so he could check his ammunition, but fueled his legend by making a stop for breakfast. Spain lost 381 men; America had eight wounded.

The sequel for Dewey was sad. He was a national hero, eclipsing Teddy Roosevelt in his acclaim. But he did not have Roosevelt's political nose. He volunteered to be president, but got the job description wrong: "Since studying this subject I am convinced that the office of President is not such a very difficult one to fill, his duties being mainly to execute the laws of Congress. . . . I would execute the laws of Congress as faithfully as I have always executed the orders of my superiors." There were no takers.

The war made Roosevelt a national hero, and he was one, even if some artists' imaginations ran a little wild. But T.R. and his Rough Riders did not win the war all by

themselves. Roosevelt and his men were certainly equaled in valor by the less publicized black troops of the 9th and 10th Cavalry. They reached the top of San Juan ridge right along with the Rough Riders. Five black troopers won the Medal of Honor, and the 10th's commander, John J. "Black Jack" Pershing, proclaimed: "We officers could have taken our black heroes in our arms. They had again fought their way into our affections, as they had fought their way into the hearts of the American people."

Brave though all the attackers were, America won the day because Lieutenant John Parker, six years out of West Point, insisted on deploying three of his beloved Gatling machine guns, whose rapid fire unnerved the blockhouse defenders.

The Army got bogged down in Cuba, but the U.S. Navy came to the rescue in time for Independence Day. The 300-pound Major General William Shafter was thinking of withdrawing from the siege of Santiago, so starved and sick were his troops after San Juan Hill. But on July 3, an American naval squadron broke the will of the defenders by destroying all the Spanish warships in the harbor. The city surrendered on July 17. Meanwhile, Nelson Miles, the old Indian-fighting general, cakewalked it in Puerto Rico in time for the armistice on August 12.

HOW IT WASN'T: From the press, America got the idea that Teddy Roosevelt's Rough Riders made a cavalry charge at the San Juan blockhouse—and won the war all by themselves. This popular painting, in fact, borrowed its image from Lady Butler's 1881 painting of the charge of Wellington's Greys at the battle of Waterloo (1815).

THE POISONED CHALICE

The unlooked-for legacy of the high-minded war to liberate Cuba was an archipelago of 7,000 islands in the Pacific, with a population of 7 million of Malay stock and Chinese admixture, most of them Catholic and Spanish-speaking. Spain had ruled the Philippines for nearly 300 years, but under the Treaty of Paris of December 10, 1898, agreed to relinquish ownership to the victorious United States for $20 million. The Purchase cost America much in blood in the three years that followed.

The Filipinos had started their own war of liberation two years before Dewey sailed into Manila harbor on the evening of April 30, 1898. Its leader was Emilio Aguinaldo y Famy, the 29-year-old son of prosperous Chinese-Tagalog farmers, who in October 1896 proclaimed his intention of creating a government "like that of the United States." He liked to wear a sword dropped by a retreating Spanish officer in one of the skirmishes, finding it a sign from God that it was stamped "Made in Toledo 1869"—the year of his birth. For all his naive grandiloquence, he was an effective leader. He had given the Spanish Army such a hard time that late in 1897 a deal was struck: Spain would make reforms and the rebel leadership would go into exile.

Aguinaldo was in Singapore when war broke out between Spain and the U.S. in April 1898. The U.S. consul in Singapore, E. Spencer Pratt, invited him to a conspiratorial meeting at the Raffles Hotel and urged him to resume the rebellion. He was given the impression that the U.S. would support his cause, and he had no reason to disbelieve it when on May 19 he was entertained by the resplendent Dewey himself on his conquering flagship, the *Olympia,* at anchor in Manila Bay. Dewey gave Aguinaldo Spanish Mauser rifles and grandly told him, "Go ashore and start your army." Three weeks later Aguinaldo had 30,000 rebel soldiers surrounding Manila, a flag and a national anthem, and on June 12, 1898, he read a proclamation declaring an independent Philippines "under the protection of the mighty and humane United States." In August, the besieged Spaniards yielded Manila to the American Army, but Aguinaldo was left to go on with his game of government. In September, Filipino delegates in top hats

FIGHTER: Emilio Aguinaldo (1869–1964), who proclaimed a republic in June 1898. After World War II he was pardoned for broadcasting for the Japanese occupiers. In 1958 the American ambassador formally gave him back his Spanish sword.

and cutaway coats attended Aguinaldo's first national assembly to vote on a constitution. Aguinaldo's republic was the first in Asia to aspire to democratic civil liberties, though he was no radical: suffrage was limited and the propertied classes were left undisturbed in their wealth.

Dewey and everyone else in authority who had met Aguinaldo tut-tutted later at the very idea they had given him any promises of independence, but they had certainly given him hope. So had President McKinley by inaction. As America debated that summer and fall what it should do with the Philippines, and McKinley's envoys fenced with the Spaniards in Paris over the final treaty, President Aguinaldo was left to run his republic. It was natural for him to feel betrayed when in December McKinley finally sent word that the Filipinos were to be subject to "benevolent assimilation."

The reluctant warmaker-president, warmed by cheering crowds, had become an eager colonizer. He was misled into believing the Filipinos would welcome U.S. rule by General Elwell Stephen Otis, his Army commander in Manila. Otis was a Civil War hero with a bullet hole in his

head, which made him an insomniac, and he locked himself up in Malacanang Palace, fussily issuing orders sixteen hours a day on every detail. He placed his troops facing Aguinaldo's along the perimeter of Manila, with frequent incidents, but never met him. He relied for intelligence on the upper-class, propertied natives of Manila (the *illustrados*), who minimalized nationalist sentiment because they wanted to keep the friendship and protection of America. "Insurgents reported favorable to American annexation," Otis blithely cabled McKinley that December.

Aguinaldo, trying to avoid conflict with the Americans, kept hoping that the anti-imperialists in Congress would succeed in rejecting the Treaty of Paris, by which Spain ceded the Philippines to the United States, and so reopen the whole question of independence. He made passionate appeals to American idealism, seeing himself as George Washington and General Otis as George III. But on February 4 a Nebraskan volunteer shot one of Aguinaldo's men and the war was on. It clinched the Senate's cliff-hanging vote for annexation, decided a few days later on the tie-breaking vote of Vice President Hobart.

The American Army pushed into the swamps and jungles. General Otis said his 21,000 men would win in a few weeks. Then 35,000 would do fine. Victory was around the corner. The war correspondents disagreed and were branded troublemakers. Twelve months later Otis had 70,000 men and asked for another 30,000. In the spring of 1899 Aguinaldo switched from formal battles to guerrilla warfare. The war got nastier, with atrocities on both sides. In the words of Stanley Karnow, historian of both wars: "The Philippine war, like the Vietnam experience, dehumanized the U.S. troops who had volunteered out of a conviction that they were carrying America's values abroad." Villages were routinely burned and looted, prisoners shot and tortured.

A turning point came early in 1901. Aguinaldo had gone into hiding, but a courier carrying his request for reinforcements fell into the hands of Kansan volunteers serving under Brigadier General Frederick Funston, a diminutive, 35-year-old hero of the Cuban war. Funston in-

PACIFIER: William Howard Taft was a federal judge until McKinley persuaded him to run the Philippines. He called Filipinos "little brown brothers." American soldiers sang: "He may be a brother to Big Bill Taft but he ain't no brother to me." *Seated:* Taft, daughter Helen, wife Helen ("Nellie"). *Standing* (left to right): the children's German governess, Major Noble (an aide), Charles Phelps Taft II and Fred W. Carpenter (private secretary).

duced him to reveal Aguinaldo's hideout in the village of Palanan, in northeast Luzon. Aguinaldo would surely melt away if troops moved in, so Funston dreamed up a deception. Eighty Macabebes, members of an ethnic group in Pampanga province, would pose as Aguinaldo reinforcements, led by the guide and two other Tagalogs loyal to the U.S. and by a former Spanish officer, Lazaro Segovia, who had joined the rebels but been suborned by the Americans. They would take along five American "prisoners." The sham force landed by gunboat and struggled through 100 miles of jungle.

Spruce in polished black boots, Aguinaldo happily welcomed Segovia and the Tagalog officers in his house while the "prisoners" were held outside. At a signal, the Macabebes opened fire on Aguinaldo's men, Segovia shot two guards in the room, and Funston then came along to tell Aguinaldo he was a prisoner of war. "Is this not some joke?" the stunned rebel asked.

William Howard Taft, the top U.S. civil authority in the Philippines, said much the same thing when he heard that the military governor who had succeeded Otis had put up Aguinaldo at Malacanang Palace, and let him see his wife and children. General Arthur MacArthur (the father of Douglas) was sure he could get Aguinaldo to renounce the rebellion. Taft wanted execution or exile. But MacArthur proved his point. He gradually convinced Aguinaldo it was all over. On April 19, he took an oath of allegiance and issued a proclamation accepting the sovereignty of the United States: "Enough of blood, enough of tears . . . I believe I am serving thee, my beloved country. My happiness be thine!"

It was the beginning of the end, but not the end. There was a final convulsion of cruelty. In the most notorious case, supposedly loyal Filipinos on the island of Samar carried out a gruesome massacre of 54 Americans at Balangiga; then Brigadier General Jacob Smith, given command of a punitive expedition, issued the order: "Burn all and kill all. The more you burn and kill, the more you will please me." There were to be no prisoners, and every male over the age of ten was to be killed. It was a great relief to a shocked and frustrated America when President Roosevelt officially declared victory in July 1902.

Taft, who had become the first civil governor in July 1901, ran everything through the oligarchy of wealthy families. But, working to guidelines written by Secretary of War Elihu Root, he set the country on a road to an American style of self-government, realized for domestic affairs by 1916.

DEATH IN THE TEMPLE OF MUSIC

Handkerchiefs fluttered on the hot afternoon of September 6, 1901, at the Pan-American Exposition in Buffalo, where thousands waited for hours in the hope of shaking hands with the popular President McKinley. The grand marshal of the show, a Buffalo lawyer, had been disturbed at lunch by a flippant remark that it would be Vice President Roosevelt's luck to have someone shoot the President. The marshal deployed extra guards, but their position in the receiving area of the Temple of Music made it harder for the President's three Secret Service men to scrutinize every outstretched hand. The handkerchief carried by Leon Czolgosz, a short slender man in a black suit, concealed a short-barreled .32 revolver. He fired two bullets through the handkerchief. The first hit a button, the second lodged in the President's pancreas. Czolgosz was knocked to the ground. "Don't let them hurt him," said the wounded President. Moments later he turned to his secretary: "My wife, be careful how you tell her—oh, be careful."

Czolgosz, 28, was a deranged drifter who had been born to Polish immigrants and reared by his father on a threadbare Michigan farm. He said later that a lecture by the anarchist Emma Goldman "set me on fire." Anarchists in Europe had already murdered four leaders. Across the country crowds vented their anger on any anarchists they could get their hands on—and also on William Randolph Hearst. He was hanged in effigy in many cities because his newspapers had descended to viciousness in an otherwise valid campaign against McKinley as a tool of the trusts. In April 1901 Hearst's *New York Journal* said: "If bad institutions and bad men can be got rid of only by killing, then the killing must be done." And the year before, his contributor Ambrose Bierce had written a tasteless quatrain occasioned by the shooting of William Goebel, the governor-elect of Kentucky:

The bullet that pierced Goebel's
*   breast*
Can not be found in all the West;
Good reason, it is speeding here
To stretch McKinley on his bier.

Bierce later explained it was meant not as an incitement but a warning that the President should be better guarded. Few believed him.

THE EXCURSION: One hour and seventeen minutes before he was shot, McKinley rides in a carriage with John G. Milburn, president of the exposition, at Niagara Falls. The President had taken his beloved invalid wife to see the scenic gorge.
Inset: The scene of the assassination as depicted by a *Leslie's Weekly* artist at the time.

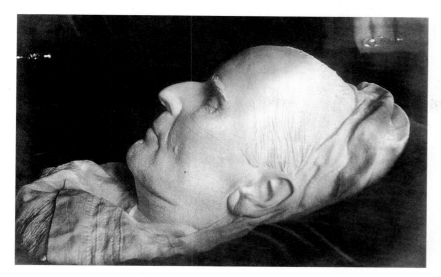

NEARER, MY GOD TO THEE . . .: The death mask of the President suggests a man at peace with himself. The doctors had been sure he would live, but they did not find the bullet, and gangrene set in. McKinley himself was well enough to ask: "How did they like my speech?," referring to an address he had given that implied he was about to change the Republican tradition of unilateral high tariffs. But late on September 13 he faded. "Good-bye, good-bye all. . . . It is God's way. His will, not ours, be done." He put his arm round his wife and began to whisper the words of his favorite hymn, "Nearer, my God to Thee, nearer to Thee." He died at 2:15 a.m. on September 14.

THE ASSASSIN: Czolgosz was tried and convicted, and electrocuted at the prison at Auburn, New York, on October 29.

WHERE'S TEDDY? The nation had no president for 12 hours. Vice President Roosevelt was camping high in the Adirondacks when a guide reached him late on September 13 with news of McKinley's relapse. He rode all night in a horse-drawn wagon to reach a special train to take him to Buffalo. Late in the afternoon of September 14 he swore the oath of office in the house where McKinley lay dead. In a letter to Henry Cabot Lodge he said, "It is a dreadful thing to come to the Presidency this way; but it would be a worse thing to be morbid about it."

THAT DAMNED COWBOY

Teddy Roosevelt personified America at the turn of the century. He was only 42, the youngest president the country has ever had. He exulted in energy and strenuous endeavor. It was not enough to grapple eight hours with senators and diplomats until he felt "like a stewed owl." He took his cabinet for skinny-dips in the icy Potomac. Twice a week in the White House he went on the mat with a pair of Japanese judo experts, and at night the corridors would resound with the yells of the President in pillow fights with his children. He was a red-blooded democrat. "The next time they don't let you in, Sylvane," he told a leathery old cowboy refused admittance to the White House, "you just shoot through the windows." Roosevelt did just that. He kept up a drumbeat of fire against the "wealthy criminal class," the "malefactors of great wealth," the "infernal thieving trusts," the "conscienceless swindlers," and, on the other side, the "cowards," "shrill eunuchs," "pin-heads and cranks of ugly radicalism." He talked loudly, but he carried a small stick. He sought to regulate big business, not to cripple it, still less destroy it. Above all, he sought to assert the rights of the people against special interests. He used the theatrical power of the presidency as no one before him to focus popular discontents in the cause of creative reform, and to fight his battles with reactionary Republican majorities in the Senate and House. The spirit of his administration is symbolic of the Progressive era, in which aggregates of local and national individuals and groups independently sought gradual reforms in social justice, city government, business and politics.

For all his jolly bluster, Roosevelt was a cultivated man and the least insular of presidents; he switched easily between French, English and German. He was a historian, naturalist and author who furnished the White House with hundreds of books. His father, one of the founders of the Chemical Bank, was a passionate philanthropist. T.R., as he was often called, was famously ashamed that this good man had bought a substitute for the Civil War (for the very good reason that his wife was a southerner), and he compensated for it with an adolescent glorification of war. It was this streak of wildness that led Mark Hanna to complain: "Now, look, that damned cowboy is president of the United States."

FAMILY MAN: Roosevelt was a devoted father. His letters to his children are full of fun and sweetness. *Left to right:* Quentin (b. 1897), who died when his plane was shot down in World War I; the President; Teddy Jr. (1887), wounded in World War I and later assistant secretary of the navy, as his father had been; Archibald (1894), wounded in the war; Alice (1884), the hell-raising daughter of Roosevelt's first wife; Kermit (1889), wounded in the war; his second wife, Edith, who kept him in check; and Ethel (1891). Alice scandalized cousin Eleanor Roosevelt: "I saw her in Bobbie Goelet's auto quite alone with three other men!"

THEODORE ROOSEVELT
26th President (Republican), 1901–1909

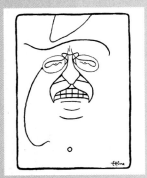

Caricature by E. Hine, 1912.

BORN: October 27, 1858, New York City

DIED: January 6, 1919, Oyster Bay, New York

POLITICAL CAREER: New York State assemblyman, 1882–1884; member, U.S. Civil Service Commission, 1889–1895; Police commissioner, New York City, 1895–1897; assistant secretary of the navy, 1897–1898; Governor of New York, 1899–1900; Vice President, 1901; President, 1901–1909

FIRSTS: First president to win the Nobel Peace Prize. First president to invite a black person to dinner at the White House (Booker T. Washington, October 16, 1901). First to intervene in dispute between capital and labor.

CHARACTER SNAPSHOT: "The man's personality was cyclonic, in that he tended to become unstable in times of low pressure. The slightest rise in the barometer outside, and his turbulence smoothed into a whirl of coordinated activity, while a stillness developed within. Under maximum pressure, Roosevelt was sunny, calm and unnaturally clear."
—Biographer Edmund Morris

WORST DAY: February 14, 1884. In the same house on East 20th Street in New York, his mother, Martha ("Mittie"), died of typhoid fever, aged 48; his wife, Alice, aged 22, died after giving birth to a daughter, Alice, on February 12. He was too grief-stricken ever to mention his wife's name again, even in his *Autobiography*.

TEEDIE: At ten, a chronic asthmatic. His father put him in a body-building gym, the beginning of a lifelong obsession with the strenuous life. On a year's grand tour of Europe at 12 he kept a diary full of detailed naturalist notes, the beginning of another lifelong passion.

HARVARD OARSMAN: He rowed, boxed as a lightweight, wrestled fiercely and was a bit of a snob. He was top in political economy and zoology—he kept a shrew in his room—and graduated with honorable mention.

COWBOY: During three years as a rancher in the Dakota Badlands in the mid-1880s, he knocked out a drunken cowboy who, with a gun in each hand, had taunted him about wearing glasses. He and two partners gave chase over 100 miles to three wild men who stole his river scow. On the six-day journey downriver to turn in their prisoners to the sheriff, T.R. read *Anna Karenina*. And then with his partners he reenacted the capture for the camera.

NAVY STRATEGIST: As assistant secretary of the navy, he intrigued to get expansionist Admiral Dewey appointed chief of the Asiatic station. Then on the afternoon of February 25, 1898, while his boss, Navy Secretary John Long, was away from his office for a massage and treatment of his corns, T.R. cabled naval commanders all over the world to be ready for war. His cable to Dewey to be ready to attack the Philippines was, said Dewey, the first step to their conquest. "The very devil seems to possess [Roosevelt]," said Long of that afternoon—but he let the historic orders stand.

BOY GOVERNOR: He was an adroit publicist. Twice every day, he perched on his desk and talked and joked with the press with unprecedented openness. As governor, he had a tough time with the Republican machine's "Easy Boss" Tom Platt, but succeeded in imposing a tax on corporations for gas, tunnel and transit franchises. He also sent a woman to the electric chair for the first time in New York State. Platt got rid of this troublemaker—he thought—by conniving at his nomination as vice president.

ROUGH RIDER: Men of the 1st U.S. Volunteer Cavalry at war in Cuba in 1898; an elaborate photograph, said Pulitzer's *World,* of the character of the regiment's founder—the only man in glasses. He and Colonel Leonard Wood handpicked the cowboys, lumberjacks, adventurers, frontiersmen, polo players, a U.S. tennis champion, a legendary Harvard quarterback, an ex-captain of the Columbia crew, two English aristocrats and soldiers from both sides of the Civil War. Nine hundred of the 1,000 survived the 133 days to the disbanding of the regiment at the end of the Spanish-American War. T.R.'s men sobbed at the Montauk farewell ceremony when they presented him with a Frederic Remington bronze of a broncobuster.

HUNTER: In Wakamba country, with a kill. Big on blood sports—he killed 296 lions, elephants, water buffaloes and other wildlife on his Africa trip—he was also passionate about preserving game species. The "Teddy Bear" was born when, hunting in Mississippi, he refused to shoot a bear cub. He was once nearly killed by a grizzly he shot; a grizzly on its hind legs, he said, was a better symbol of fearless America than the eagle.

POLICE CHIEF: He was "a man you can't cajole, can't frighten, can't buy." He tried to stem the corruption by which New York police collected $15 million for the Democratic party machine in graft from brothels, saloons, gambling and merchants. T.R. fired 200 policemen and enforced the law against Sunday drinking. He kept patrolmen on their toes by prowling the streets at night himself. He would stride through the worst slums early every morning with crusading photographer Jacob Riis—and a pistol in his pocket—discussing social reform.

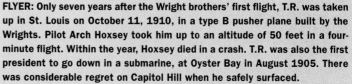

FLYER: Only seven years after the Wright brothers' first flight, T.R. was taken up in St. Louis on October 11, 1910, in a type B pusher plane built by the Wrights. Pilot Arch Hoxsey took him up to an altitude of 50 feet in a four-minute flight. Within the year, Hoxsey died in a crash. T.R. was also the first president to go down in a submarine, at Oyster Bay in August 1905. There was considerable regret on Capitol Hill when he safely surfaced.

MONEY ON PARADE

JOHN DAVISON ROCKEFELLER (1839–1937), dapper in his white wig and with his walking stick, was worth $200 million in 1900, and in 1913 became the world's first billionaire. No one had ever seen such wealth. Or such cunning, ruthless business practices. Or such philanthropy. He stopped going to his Standard Oil offices after 1897, played golf and began giving away money in earnest. He had always paid his tithe to the Baptists and given dimes to small boys on his birthday. By the time of his death at 97 in 1937, he had given away $530 million, principally to medicine, black educational institutions and the Baptist-founded University of Chicago. Striding with him, his son Junior (1874–1960), who gave away about twice as much.

HETTY GREEN (1835–1916) gave nothing away to anyone. She was the richest and meanest woman in America, and surely the richest businesswoman anywhere. She looked and smelled like a witch because she begrudged spending money on soap and clothes. She ate dry oatmeal "to give me the strength I need to fight the Wall Street wolves." At her death in 1915 she was worth $150 to $200 million, mostly made by herself from the $6 million nest egg her father left her from his whaling business. She nickeled and dimed in real estate and stocks and tried to grab her aunt's $2 million estate by fabricating her will. She cost her son his leg when she refused to pay for an operation. She left not a penny to charity.

LEGACIES OF PENSIONS AND PALACES

ANDREW CARNEGIE (1835–1919) (left), high priest of American philanthropy, was the richest man in the world when in 1901 he sold his steel company to what became U.S. Steel for $300 million. At his death in 1919, he left an estate of only $22 million, an approximation of living up to the dictum in his *Gospel of Wealth* (1889): "The man who dies thus rich dies disgraced." He believed that inherited wealth corrupted. He gave away $351 million to found 281 public libraries and to endow studies of peace and technology, but only a little over 1 percent of this amount went to his workers' pension and relief funds. He also supplied the White House with free Scotch whisky and gave pensions to widows of former presidents.

THE VANDERBILTS spent their money building palaces and breaking into society. William Kissam Vanderbilt, grandson of the great steamship and railroad king Cornelius, was one of the 32 heirs who shared in the $200 million left by his father, William Henry ("The public be damned"). He gamely tried to prove Carnegie correct that inherited wealth does not buy happiness, moodily attending the races and polo matches and lamenting that the Vanderbilt millions had left him with "nothing to hope for, with nothing definite to seek or strive for." His wife, Alva, divorced him and forced their daughter Consuelo—seen here at the races—to marry the Duke of Marlborough.

LET THEM EAT CAKE

There were nearly 4,000 millionaires in America when Teddy Roosevelt went to the White House in 1901. They represented less than one ten-thousandth of 1 percent of the population, but they had acquired 20 percent of the nation's wealth. The distortion was not as extreme as in Britain, but one half of America's wealth was owned by 1 percent of the families. The new wealthy had money to burn—and they burned it. At a great dinner in the nineties in New York, cigarettes rolled in hundred-dollar bills were given to the guests after dinner. As Thorstein Veblen noted in his penetrating and amusing *Theory of the Leisure Class* (1899), money not only had to be spent; it had to be seen to be spent.

The English moneyed classes, who into the 1880s were still more numerous than the American wealthy, often contrived to appear merely well-off, and the landed aristocracy prudently affected to be perpetually broke. Such reticence was offensive to the American ethic. The gentlemen who rode into dinner on horseback wanted to display their wealth like men. Henry Adams concluded that the American mind had been so deflected in its pursuit of money that "it could turn in no other direction. It shunned, distrusted, disliked the dangerous attraction of ideals, and stood alone in history in its ignorance of the past." Interest in the past was sanctioned only as an opportunity for ostentation. Fifth Avenue glowed with the mansions and imitation French chateaux of the glue kings, the copper kings, the railroad and banking kings; and brisk was the business done by a rubberneckers' carriage that paraded the sights for visitors. William Kissam Vanderbilt's wife, Alva, persuaded him to build a $3 million palace at 52nd Street and Fifth Avenue—$41.5 million in 1989 dollars—that was a mixture of Chateau de Blois and a fifteenth-century Renaissance mansion at Bourges. The wainscoting of carved French walnut in the great hall was torn from a French chateau, a habit that became increasingly frequent as American wealth grew. This started an all-out Vanderbilt house-building competition. By World War I, there were 17 different Vanderbilt houses around the country valued at more than $1 million each (more than $13 million in 1989). Just

along Fifth Avenue, between 51st and 58th Streets, were three palatial Vanderbilt homes. Father William Henry's was a rococo brownstone with 58 rooms, doors once owned by an Italian prince, columns four stories high made out of North African marble. Much of this building boom seems to have been due to a rivalry between Alva and Cornelius II's wife,

Alice. It bubbled over to the summer resort of Newport, where William Kissam spent $11 million ($152 million in 1989) constructing the Marble House for Alva. So Alice built an Italian palazzo of alabaster and gilt and gingerbread fantasies and called it The Breakers. Some 49 servants, complete with wigs and maroon silk breeches, were "needed" to run the place.

From the Depths, a typically melodramatic depiction of the class war in the first two decades of America's second century, drawn by William Balfour-Ker for John Ames Mitchell's *The Silent War* (1906).

The temper of the times was not wholly indulgent. The rich who were too flamboyant sometimes regretted it. The Bradley Martin family from Troy, wanting to make an impression on New York society, spent $369,000 ($4.5 million) converting the Waldorf-Astoria Hotel into a version of Versailles, and asked the 700 guests to appear in costume as courtiers of Louis XIV. Mrs. Martin, appearing incongruously as Mary Queen of Scots on the arm of Mr. Martin as the Sun King, made up for it by wearing a massive ruby necklace once owned by Marie Antoinette. The ball was staged in the middle of the depression of 1893–1897, which invited rebuke. The Bradley Martins defended it as an act of welfare promoting business for cooks, dressmakers and florists, and took themselves off to England. A similar fate awaited the most gilded youth of the period. James Hazen Hyde, who had a controlling interest in the Equitable Life Assurance Society, spent only $200,000 on his Louis XV masked ball in 1905, but Pulitzer's *World* made it so hot for him that he, too, followed the Martins overseas.

The conspicuous consumption so unforgettably nailed by Thorstein Veblen seems not to have been accompanied by the cultivation of the mind. Henry Adams found education counted for nothing, social position everything. The lives of the new rich were "no more worth living than those of their cooks." H. G. Wells, too, was depressed by a "sterile" aristocracy. H. C. Merwin in a seminal article in the *Atlantic Monthly* in 1894 commented that the upper class, with notable exceptions, was "without high aims, without sympathy, without civic pride of feeling. It has not even the personal dignity of a real aristocracy. Its sense of honor is very crude. And as this is devoted to the selfish spending, so the business class is devoted to the remorseless getting, of money." But Veblen moved beyond social comment on individuals. Between 1899 and 1923, he developed an evolutionary theory of economics on the incompatibility of making goods and making money. The filling of needs by the engineer had become subordinated to the pecuniary economy of the businessman whose behavior was a vestigial remnant from a predatory barbarian past. It

amounted to "capitalistic sabotage," and oddly, in machine-minded America, the people had come to pay deference to the

pecuniary rather than the productive. Veblen died just as his analysis seemed to be validated by the great crash of 1929.

DINNER ON HORSEBACK

The dinner on horseback was thrown at Sherry's Restaurant, New York, in 1903, by C. K. Billings, who was heir to a Chicago gas fortune.

THE RICH AND THE POOR IN 1890

This table gives an indication of the distribution of wealth and income in 1890, with 1989 values in parentheses.

Estates by annual income	Number of families	Aggregate wealth	Average wealth per family
Wealthy classes $50,000 and over ($692,000 and over)	125,000	$33,000,000,000 ($456,720,000,000)	$264,000 ($3,653,760)
Well-to-do classes $5,000 to $50,000 ($69,200–$692,000)	1,375,000	$23,000,000,000 ($318,320,000,000)	$16,000 ($221,440)
Middle classes $500 to $5,000 ($6,920–$69,200)	5,500,000	$8,200,000,000 ($113,488,000,000)	$1,500 ($20,760)
Poorer classes under $500 ($6,920)	5,500,000	$800,000,000 ($11,072,000,000)	$150 ($2,076)

Basic source: Charles B. Spahr, *An Essay on the Present Distribution of Wealth in the United States* (1896), p. 69.

THE BILLION-DOLLAR CORPORATION

The four men in the grand, mahogany-paneled library of John Pierpont Morgan at 219 Madison Avenue, New York, had been up all night. When they shook hands at dawn on January 6, 1901, they had put together the world's first billion-dollar corporation. It was U.S. Steel, a behemoth of 800 steel plants that they envisaged would mine iron ore at one end and at the other end spew out all the finished steel America needed, and more, for its machine tools and canneries, its battleships and nails, its oil rigs and bridges, the burgeoning skyscrapers of its big cities and the harvesters and barbed wire out west.

The men with Morgan in his "black library" were Andrew Carnegie's heir apparent, 38-year-old Charles Schwab, who had started with him as a dollar-a-day stake driver; John Warne ("Bet-a-million") Gates, controller of American Steel and Wire, who had begun as a barbed wire salesman in San Antonio; and Morgan's debonair partner, Robert Bacon, so athletic and handsome he was known on Wall Street as the Greek God.

It only remained to settle the small detail of a price for the Carnegie Steel Company and the smaller outfits to yield control of their businesses to the new financial holding company. The taciturn Morgan, finally satisfied that the mergers made technical sense, told Schwab: "If Andy wants to sell, I'll buy. Go and find his price." Carnegie, easily the biggest steelmaker, had been using Schwab as a propagandist for the vision of a single American company dominating the world in crude and finished steel. At 65, he wanted a new life. When Schwab asked the money question after a wintry round of golf, Carnegie scribbled figures on a slip of paper. Schwab took it to Morgan. He glanced at it and said, "I accept." It was a price of $492,556,000, of which $225,000,000 in bonds went to Carnegie himself. That was double Carnegie's own valuation a few months previously. But Morgan had a last little laugh. When they met a year later on a steamship to Europe, Carnegie said: "I made one mistake, Pierpont. I should have asked you for $100 million more than I did." Morgan, who disliked the little Scot's familiarity, replied, "Well, you would have got it if you had."

ROCKEFELLER: His grip on the oil industry he created and his ruthless way with competition made him the most unpopular of the robber barons. J. P. Flynn characterized him as having the soul of a bookkeeper.

U.S. Steel was the climax of the most massive and rapid burst of industrial concentration the world had ever seen. In the whole period from 1879 to 1897, there had been only 12 U.S. combinations (see page 80) with a total capitalization of $1 billion. In the four years 1899–1902, no fewer than 236 giant corporations were organized with a capital of more than $6 billion.

Morgan's consolidation of U.S. Steel dramatized a decisive new trend in American business. The stock promoters were taking over from the robber barons. Until the nineties, the mergers were arranged by the men who started and ran their companies—in addition to Carnegie, men like "Commodore" Cornelius Vanderbilt in railroads, Philip D. Armour and Gustavus F. Swift in meatpacking, Charles A. Pillsbury in flour milling. The pious, ulcerous John D. Rockefeller, son of a bigamist and snake-oil salesman and a straitlaced mother, was the most spectacular example of the robber baron of this earlier period. He catapulted Standard

Oil from a single refinery in 1870 to control of 85 percent of all U.S. oil production and distribution in the eighties by strangling competition. He set up the first trust combination to fix prices among 39 corporations, he gouged his rivals by making secret deals with the railroads for cheaper freight—and even finagled a percentage of the freight charges his competitors paid. He was a pirate; but, like Carnegie, he knew his business. Once, observing the production line, he counted the number of drops of solder being used to seal finished cans of oil, and suggested using 38 drops instead of 40. With 38 drops, they leaked, but with 39 they were perfect, and several thousand dollars were saved.

The new stock promoters and the longer established investment bankers, like Morgan, knew nothing of the individual industries. What they manufactured was hope. By 1893–94, nearly half of the nation's rail mileage was in receivership. Morgan would summon the despairing presidents to his library and put up cash in return for "Morganization," which meant cost cutting, route consolidation and a squeeze on creditors, who were asked to swap their bonds for ones with lower interest rates. Shareholders had little option, because in those days they could be dunned for assessments when a company lost money. Acting as proxy for the new bondholders, Morgan got control over one sixth of the country's mileage. Morgan did not want to run the railroads. He wanted order and solvency for the benefit of his shareholders first; railroad users came second. When anyone complained, he growled, "Your railroad? Your railroad belongs to my clients."

Risk taking was a popular pastime. The New York Stock Exchange, which had first transacted 2 million deals in a single day on January 7, 1901, passed the 3 million figure less than four months later, Morgan went on to put together the International Harvester Company, a huge success, and the International Merchant Marine, combining British and American shipping companies, which was not. It did not help in 1912 that one of its companies owned the *Titanic*.

J. P. MORGAN, THE LONELY ROMANTIC

John Pierpont Morgan (1837–1913) was a stuffed shirt, imperious, taciturn and moody, but he was also a romantic. "Even as he scared people away," wrote his biographer Ron Chernow, "he was a lonely man, carrying around a vast despair that he couldn't share with anyone." He married his first wife knowing she was dying of consumption and mourned her ever after. His second marriage was loveless. Anti-Semitism was but one of many prejudices. He was a snob. He despised the new rich. "You can do business with anyone," he said, "but you can only sail a boat with a gentleman." He loved yachts, elegant women, solitaire and paintings. His own *Corsaire III* was 300 feet at the waterline and carried a crew of 70. He was impulsively generous. He gave little for social welfare, but ransacked Europe for gifts to the Metropolitan Museum of Art and the American Museum of Natural History. Teddy Roosevelt crossed swords with him but remarked that "any kind of meanness and smallness were alike wholly alien to his nature." In his youth Morgan's finer qualities were less apparent. He dodged serving in the Civil War, and profited by selling defective rifles to the Union Army.

J.P. inherited $12 million ($166 million today) from his father and left ten times as much, but his power lay more in his rugged reputation than in his millions. It was the billions confidently entrusted to him that made him the world's most powerful banker. By 1912, he held 72 directorships in 47 corporations. "America," he said, "is good enough for me," to which William Jennings Bryan replied: "Whenever he doesn't like it, he can give it back to us."

WALL STREET'S CYRANO: Morgan's ferociously handsome face was marred in later life by a strawberry nose, touched up in official photographs. He was sensitive about it. He blackballed John Gates from two clubs for calling him Livernose, but he gave up trying to cure the rosacea acne. His nose, he sighed, was "part of the American business structure."

TEDDY TAKES ON EVERYONE

When Theodore Roosevelt moved into the White House in 1901, 20 men dominated American finance and industry. They flaunted a power at least as great as the president's. They decided where Americans would work and what they would pay for steel, oil, petroleum, rail freight, farm machinery, glass, rubber and tin cans; for tobacco, sugar, coal, beef, dressed meat, starch, school slates, flour, whisky, insurance, chewing gum and coffins. Hundreds of small businessmen claimed in the courts that they had been unfairly ruined by larger competitors operating through combinations, the kaleidoscopic masks, in Henry Lloyd Demarest's phrase, of monopoly power.

Combination was the process whereby great interstate corporations, or "trusts," and later holding companies, were created and centrally administered by directors answerable only to the loose laws of a local entity, such as the small states of Delaware and New Jersey. It was not an American invention. It was happening in Europe for the same reasons, but not on the same scale or with such arrogance. "I owe the public nothing," declared John Pierpont Morgan. He saw it as his duty and opportunity to bring rivals together in a "community of interest" that enabled them to cut the public's throat rather than one another's.

It was an attitude that enraged Roosevelt. He had an aristocratic concern for the people, and a disdain for the vulgarity of mere wealth. He waited five months after becoming president before shaking his fist. He did that literally, rebuking Morgan during a Washington press dinner, and on March 10, 1902, his Attorney General, Philander C. Knox, announced that the President had instructed him to prosecute Morgan's latest trust, the Northern Securities Company. Morgan and the rival banking firm Kuhn, Loeb had settled their battle for control of Northern Pacific Railroad by combining the holdings of the two biggest barons, Edward H. Harriman and James J. Hill, to form Northern Securities as a single holding company that would monopolize all transportation between the Great Lakes and the Pacific coast. Morgan hurried to the White House to say that if they had done anything wrong, "send your man [Knox] to my man [naming one of his lawyers] and we can fix it up." No laconism could more cogently express the corporate belief that politics, like business, was a mere matter of deal mak-ing. T.R. retorted: "That can't be done," and Knox explained: "We don't want to fix it up, we want to stop it."

The day after the announcement, the security markets were in a state of shock. As the *Detroit Free Press* put it, "Wall Street is paralyzed at the thought that a President of the United States should sink so low as to enforce the law." On second thoughts, big business cheered up. The prosecution was to be brought under the long neglected Sherman Anti-Trust Act of 1890, which most Americans had assumed to be a dead letter. The language of the act was fierce: "Every contract, combination, in the form of trust or otherwise, or conspiracy, in restraint of trade or commerce among the several states, or with foreign nations, is hereby declared to be illegal." But semantic weaseling by the Supreme Court had rendered it ineffective; in 1895 the Court had ruled that the act forbade only restraint of interstate "trade or commerce," and manufacturing was neither of these.

T.R. triumphed against all expectations. In 1904 the Supreme Court reversed itself, 5–4, and ordered Northern Securities broken up. To Roosevelt, it was as important a ruling in the interests of the people against monopoly as the Dred Scott case had been in the interests of the people against slavery and privilege. And the people agreed. In 1904 they elected the "trust buster" by the greatest plurality yet achieved.

Roosevelt instituted more antitrust prosecutions than Harrison, Cleveland and McKinley combined, but he was not against big business. His agenda was to reaffirm federal authority once and for all, and then allow laissez-faire to resume its course under benign regulation. In this way, he believed he would save capitalism from socialist revolution. He came to believe the law should be changed so as to prohibit only the bad trusts that gouged the consumer and operated unfairly (Standard Oil was his demon), and tolerate the good (International Harvester). He made deals with many of Morgan's companies. It brought him no thanks. When he went on a big game expedition after leaving the White House, Morgan remarked: "I hope the first lion he meets does his duty."

THE DARING MEDIATOR

There had never been such a scene in the White House: labor and capital brought face-to-face with the President as mediator. Roosevelt did it to try to end the long coal strike of 1902. The conservative press denounced him. The mine owners were furious. Their leader, George F. Baer, had refused to deal with John Mitchell's new United Mine Workers' union. "The rights and interests of the laboring man," Baer wrote, "will be protected and cared for—not by the labor agitators, but by the Christian men to whom God in his infinite wisdom has given the control of the property interests of the country." After his meeting ended in deadlock, Roosevelt sent Elihu Root to tell J. P. Morgan he was ready to send troops to seize and run the mines. Morgan persuaded Baer to go to arbitration. Even then, peace required more of T.R.'s audacity. The owners would not have a labor man on the panel. They insisted on a judge, a military officer, a mining engineer, a prominent sociologist and a coal dealer. Roosevelt solemnly announced that he was appointing one E. E. Clark as the sociologist. Heretofore Mr. Clark had not been thought of as a sociologist. He was Grand Chief of the Order of Railway Conductors, a union man. He met the definition, said Roosevelt, because he had thought deeply on social questions. Roosevelt said it gave him a glimpse into one corner of the mighty brains of these "captains of industry" that "they would heroically submit to anarchy rather than have Tweedledum, yet if I would call it Tweedledee they would accept it with rapture."

TEDDY IN HIS BULLY PULPIT:
"I have no idea what the
American people think. I only
know what they should think."

CHAPTER FOUR

OLD AND NEW AMERICANS
1880–1910

Rise of the Boss

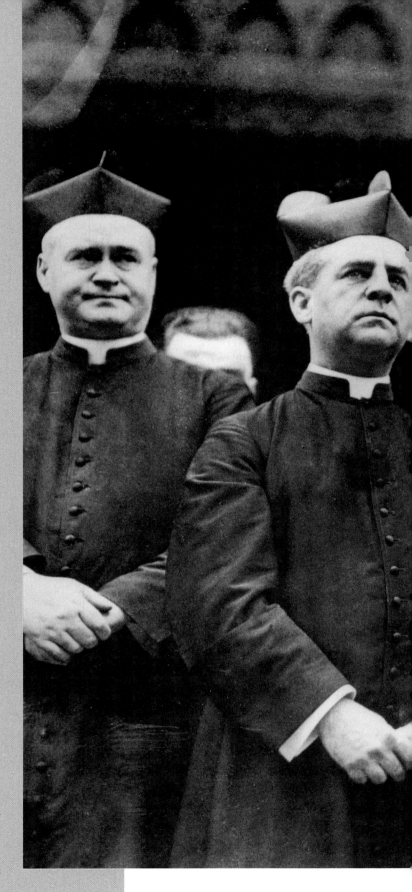

Before 1880, American cities and small towns were run mostly by men of Anglo-Saxon or Anglo-Celtic and Protestant stock. The Quakers prevailed in Philadelphia, the Puritans in Boston, the Knickerbockers in New York, but by 1894 they were all losing power to the Paddies. More than a million Irish Catholics had come to America in the ten years after the potato famine of 1845. In New York City, the single greatest center of power and wealth, they fairly rapidly took over the private organization called the Tammany Society, which dominated the Democratic party. New York had its first Catholic mayor in 1880, Boston in 1884.

More than 12 million people came between 1890 and 1910. The Irish remained politically the most significant. Three quarters of them were literate, they spoke English and their church was well organized. Even when they were in a minority, they provided leadership for the mass of immigrant Germans, Russian and Polish Jews, Slavs and Italians. As Daniel Patrick Moynihan suggested, it was the Irish who made New York the first great city in history to be ruled by men of the people. Theirs were the politics of personal obligation, rather than of political principle, and the story of city government in America is of their long battle with the "good-government" reformers of the Progressive movement—the goo-goos, as they were labeled by James Michael Curley, the archetypal Irish boss on whom Edwin O'Connor based the hero of his novel *The Last Hurrah*.

CHURCH POWER: The Catholic Church, whose power was temporal as well as spiritual, maintained its ascendancy in New York for half a century through the Irish bosses of Tammany Hall's Democratic party machine. The clergy's influence was chiefly conservative. The tough-looking priest on the far left is Francis P. Duffy, one of the more liberal priests, who went to France with the 69th Infantry, "The Fighting Irish," in 1918, and was portrayed by Pat O'Brien in a movie about that regiment. A statue of him, in full doughboy gear, stands in Father Duffy Square, a few blocks north of Times Square. The others in the party—watching the 69th from the steps of St. Patrick's Cathedral—are (from left) the Reverend John Byrne, the top-hatted Monsignor Michael Joseph Lavelle, the Reverend Bernard McQuade and, holding his boater, Monsignor Joseph P. Dineen.

CRUCIBLE OF THE CITIES

Mingling with the 1,026,499 immigrants who sailed to America in 1905 was an Englishman whose gift for prophesy had a habit of electrifying the world. H. G. Wells, already author of *The Time Machine, The War of the Worlds* and *The First Men in the Moon*, took a poor view of what his fellow voyagers to America might do to their new country. He saw "a long procession of simple-looking, sun-burned country folk from Russia, from the Carpathians, from southern Italy and Turkey and Syria," and he concluded that it would be impossible to make Americans of them. They might acquire the bare use of English and a certain patriotic persuasion, but they would remain a largely illiterate, indus-trialized peasantry. They would, he thought, sacrifice their young wives to the mills of Paterson and Fall River, their children to the Pennsylvania coal mines, but they would weaken organized labor, serve the purposes of corruption and alto-gether retard the development of an American national con-sciousness. "The immigrants are being given votes, I know, but that does not free them, it only enslaves the country." There was the disastrous possibility, Wells conjectured, of a two-nation state, a rich aristocracy of western European ori-gin, dominating a darker-haired, darker-eyed, uneducated proletariat from central and eastern Europe.

There was ample cause to be a Cassandra. The immigrants were settling in cities that were hardly academies of demo-cratic government. They were raw new metropolises in the grip of corrupt political machines, and they demeaned the people who lived in them. Despite the glitter of the Columbian Exposition in Chicago in 1893, despite the bril-liance of the creation of New York's Central Park, American cities were left to grow without any social plan. They were behind European cities in almost every department of munic-ipal administration. Pittsburgh had the world's highest mortality rate for typhoid; typhoid fever killed Theodore Roosevelt's mother in the most fashionable section of New York. Cities dumped sewage indiscriminately and were slower than European municipalities to filter their water, as indeed they were behind in other areas. London had a subway in 1886, New York, not until 1904. New York had set American cities a fine example with the creation of Central Park in the 1850s,

but most of them set aside no space for recreation—less space, in fact, than for cemeteries in the likes of Newark, Pittsburgh and Cleveland. On his visits at the turn of the century, James Bryce, a more sympathetic observer than Wells, noted in *The American Commonwealth* "evils that have scarcely showed themselves in the cities of Europe. . . . In the greatest cities there is far more dissatisfaction than exists with the munici-pal administration in such cities as Glasgow, Manchester, Dublin, Hamburg and Lyons."

There were three principal reasons for the malaise. The American cities were new to self-government. Boston, founded in 1630, received its charter as a city only in 1822, and as late as 1894 it was necessary to invent the National Municipal League to try to free cities of meddling by the states, which were dom-inated by rural interests.

The second problem was numbers. Between 1900 and 1910, 9 million people came from abroad, just about the entire population of the country in 1820, and very few spoke English. As Robert Benchley put it, "We call England the mother coun-try because most of us come from Poland or Italy." New York had more Italians than Rome, more Jews than Warsaw, more Irish than Dublin and already more blacks than any city in the world. Fully one seventh of the population of the United States in 1910 was foreign-born, and in the big cities such as Boston, Chicago, Cleveland, New York, Philadelphia, Pitts-burgh and St. Louis, the foreign-born and children of the first generation outnumbered the native stock.

Hundreds of thousands more were flooding to the cities from the rural areas. Cities were growing fast throughout the industrial world, but nowhere faster than in America. Chicago, whose population topped 1 million in the eighties, had been a frontier post only 50 years before.

America, with some 80 million people, was on the way to becoming the most powerful country in the world, but its wealth had not trickled down much, and in the biggest cities the immigrants were crowded with the poor in a squalor unsurpassed anywhere in the West. Jacob Riis estimated, in his celebrated *How the Other Half Lives* (1890), that Dickensian London had 175,816 people living on every square mile of its worst slums but New York's Lower East Side by the nineties,

THE BOSS: For William Allen White's assault on party bosses in *Collier's* in November 1906, artist Walter Appleton Clark adapted one of Thomas Nast's late-nineteenth-century caricatures of the infamous Tweed Ring that ran New York then. Allen thought the answer to bosses and demagogues was the direct primary, where every ordinary party member could vote on candidates. "Politicians have come to regard the state and all the state's affairs as their private property," wrote White. "And state central committees of the various parties, and state officers, and state bosses, form a sort of grand lodge of American politics which has its own signs and passwords. . . . Only a few of these men are actually dishonest in the sense that the thief is dishonest who makes a business of stealing. Only a few of them would accept bribes, if they knew they were being bribed. But all of them have a limited moral view, and it is a creed of the caste that the public business is theirs, and that those who seek to question their conduct of the public business is [*sic*] an enemy to society."

in contrast, had about 290,000 per square mile, making it perhaps the worst slum in the history of the Western world. And Riis's is the lowest of scholarly estimates of density, which range up to 600,000 a square mile. He records a tenement block with 1,324 Italian immigrants living in a total of 132 rooms. In one 12-by-12-foot room he found five families, 20 people, with two beds between them. One third of the entire city population—about 1.2 million—lived in 43,000 tenement houses like these, without running water or indoor flush toilets. Their streets were filthy. They subsisted on bread and potatoes. Some 40 percent of them had tuberculosis. One third of all their babies died before their first birthday. The North End of Boston, the West Side of Chicago and downtown Philadelphia were almost as grim.

The third root of the urban malaise was that neither the political machines nor their enemies the Progressives were imbued with much of a vision of what might be achieved. The reformers and campaigning newspapers were right about the plunder and incompetence associated with a city's domination by a single party machine that appointed political hacks to key positions. Crooked businessmen who bribed machine politicians for favorable franchises cost the cities millions in needed revenue. Nor was a city whose leaders were addicted to blackmail likely to be a place of order or grace. But if the reformers had the better of the argument about efficiency, and were more honorable men, they were mostly elitist, and insensitive to the needs of the immigrants in the slums. "Reformers" varied, of course. Sometimes a party machine itself would put up a "reform" candidate, usually a conservative business leader, as a means of staying in power. But the typical goo-goo equated good government with economizing on schools and public works and closing the saloons on Sunday, and as historian William Shannon noted, the majority of voters naturally disliked an administration that meddled in their public pleasures but left untouched their private burdens. The laissez-faire philosophy of Social Darwinism, with its aversion to public policy initiatives, still prevailed, and it affected many reformers active in city politics. Emphasizing character and morality in public affairs, they had no doubt that character also lay at the heart of poverty. They might be willing to deal with the symptoms of poverty, but most of them had no conception that the causes might have something to do with the resources and rhythms of the economy, with training, with dependency, with the inequitable distribution of wealth; and even if they had, they were not equipped or willing to do anything about it, for fear of being labeled radical. New York's reform mayor in the eighties, Abram S. Hewitt, spent much of his period in power denouncing his constituents.

The immigrant groups in the cities were abandoned by the formal political system. They needed decent housing. The city did not provide it. They needed food and coal when they could not find work, and medicine when they fell sick. They had to beg for them. In the 1890s and 1900s, between 23 and 30 percent of the labor force was out of work for some period of the year, but neither city nor state offered any help in providing for sickness, unemployment or old age, although Bismarck's Germany did by the last decade of the nineteenth century, and Lloyd George's England followed. Poverty in America was less prevalent than in Britain, but in 1900, by the calculation of sociologist James Patterson, there were more people below the poverty line than in the Great Depression of the thirties.

Nobody in America was advocating anything like Bismarck's "socialism," not the Progressive reformers, not even the Socialists and not many of the immigrants themselves. They expected to find their own way with the help of the network of kith, kin and church, and sometimes the Salvation Army and the newly forming settlement houses. When these failed, they had nothing else to do with their problems but to ask a favor of the precinct captain or ward boss of the dominant political party. As long as he could find them a bucket of coal, they were not much concerned about whether he had passed a civil service examination. They saw the point of New York district leader George Washington Plunkitt's defense of

Tammany Hall's practices: "When a party won, its workers got everything in sight. That was something to make a man patriotic. Now, when a party wins and its men come forward and ask for their rewards, the reply is 'Nothin' doin' unless you can answer a list of questions about Egyptian mummies and how many years it will take for a bird to wear out a mass of iron as big as the earth by steppin' on it once in a century.'"

Tammany Hall, the headquarters of New York's Democratic machine, had its Republican and Democratic counterparts in other cities, and the system was the same. Maybe the political boss could fix a job in the water works department or with the gas company that depended on the city's franchise. Maybe he could have a quiet word with the judge and get a drunk out of jail. Maybe he would find clothes and food for a family after a fire, arrange a cheerful excursion for a widow and her family, pay the rent for a mother with two children, hire counsel to prevent an eviction. The immigrants were glad to repay with their vote, to the despair of the reformers.

The political bosses who practiced this shrewd Samaritan art got into their positions of power because the party needed an organization to get out the vote, and the machine came to be the master of the party, rather than its servant. The political grafters or "boodlers" among them got the wherewithal for calculated arbitrary benevolence from the kickbacks contractors paid and by squeezing money from supposedly illegal saloons, bordellos and gambling joints. All of this qualified as "white" or "honest" graft, as distinct from the "dirty" graft of outright stealing.

The archetypal city boss was the grandson of an immigrant Irishman and the son of a saloon keeper, working his way up the party ladder from political runner to precinct captain, ward heeler and election district leader. Often he never ran for public office. New York's diamond-studded Richard Croker, who took over in 1886, was, as James Bryce remarked, rather like Lorenzo de' Medici. He held no civic office but controlled all city officials and dictated state legislation as chairman of the Tammany subcommittee on organization. On occasion, a boss might arrange things safely enough to expose himself to public ballot. George Washington Plunkitt accomplished the nifty feat of holding four positions simultaneously—state senator, alderman, magistrate and city supervisor—and drawing full salary for each. James Michael Curley, four times mayor of Boston, even won an election from jail. He was elected alderman while serving 60 days for having taken a civil service exam for a constituent who wanted to become a letter carrier, a gesture appreciated by voters as an act not of fraud but of friendliness.

The city machines were essentially an Irish feudal system grafted onto a budding democracy. Of course there were city machines run by white Anglo-Saxon Protestants, such as Mark Hanna's in Cleveland and George Cox's in Cincinnati; but the Irish were the only immigrant group until well into the twentieth century that played a significant role in organizing and manning the political machine. The ancient hierarchical customs of their village governments, their familiarity with the language and Anglo-Saxon political institutions, their clan loyalty and their energy and numbers all helped them to develop and perfect the big-city machine. Colorful Irishmen made a splash as boodlers. In Chicago, Alderman "Bathhouse John" Coughlin of the First Ward wore billiard-cloth-green suits he designed himself, and on election day, with quiet Mike "Hinky Dink" McKenna, filled up shabby bathhouses with derelicts, plied them with liquor, money, food and women, and marched them out to vote the straight ticket. The Bath and Hinky Dink threw an annual ball where they mingled their strumpet and hoodlum friends with business and civic leaders. But the top bosses, who quietly enriched themselves and stayed out of jail, were cannier than the glad-handing, stereotypical plump Irish pol. They were usually somber, teetotaling family men. New York boss Richard Croker was an Irish Protestant of English descent who joined the Catholic Church as a young man entering politics. When he temporarily "retired" to Ireland to escape an 1894 state investigation into the connections between Tammany, police graft and organized crime, he had a fortune of $8 million, his own railway car, and a $2.5 million stud farm. His successor, Charles Francis Murphy, also a saloon owner, was so wary that when an aide asked why Mr. Murphy—"Mr." even to his closest associates—did not sing the national anthem at picnics, he was told: "Maybe he doesn't want to commit himself." Tammany was big business, organized, as Daniel Moynihan remarked, in a conservative system reminiscent of feudal Ireland, in which everyone knew his place under a stern oligarchy of elders. At its height, it had a $12 million payroll at its disposal and 32,000 committeemen.

The city bosses were closer to the masses than the googoos; but they, too, failed the immigrants and on a larger scale. As Moynihan observed: "The Irish did not know what to do with power once they got it. . . . They never thought of politics as an instrument of social change—their kind of politics involved the processes of a society that was not changing." They did little to limit the overweening power of business, help the unions struggling against exploitation, challenge the slum landlords or use their local muscle to agitate for national

reforms (as Franklin Roosevelt would later when he helped to put many of the bosses out of business).

The cities slowly pulled themselves together. In some the machine was beaten not by puritan reformers but by activists with more imagination. The 1890s and early 1900s were distinguished in three Midwestern cities by self-made millionaires who saw the difference between abstract "good government" and government for the mass of the people. Cleveland's Tom Johnson read Henry George's *Progress and Poverty* in 1883, sold his streetcar lines, and got himself elected mayor in 1901. He rid the city of corrupt machine politics, which had protected businesses from paying their taxes, and in his nine-year leadership gave Cleveland pure water, well-lit streets, parks, market inspections and the public baths so essential for people without bathrooms in their homes. He was, of course, denounced as a socialist, demagogue and eccentric, and was fought with 50 court injunctions. Hazen Pingree, mayor of Detroit from 1889 to 1896, built a city-owned electric light plant. Samuel M. Jones, the "Golden Rule" mayor of Toledo, set up free kindergartens for working mothers. In New York, beginning in 1901, Seth Low improved parks and playgrounds, tightened housing laws and strengthened the city's health services for the poor. The American genius for democratic experiment asserted itself in the invention of the initiative, the referendum, the recall (adopted by Los Angeles, with a population of 300,000 in 1910) and city commissions of the type dreamed up by the citizens of Galveston (pop. 37,000) after the devastation of a tidal wave in 1900. But sometimes corruption seems endemic. Seth Low predicted in 1910 that in another decade Americans would look back on some of the scandals of that epoch in city government with as much surprise as they then regarded the earlier effort to control fires by the volunteer fire department. New York's rash of corruption in the 1980s (and its badly paved streets) would have surprised and dismayed him.

Still, Low was no more off course with his prediction than H. G. Wells was with his. The extraordinary thing—perhaps the most extraordinary thing about America—is that this generation of immigrants triumphed. They learned English, they worked hard, they taught their children, they nourished their churches and synagogues, they promoted order in their communities, they built the labor movement and got to share in the rising prosperity, they kept faith with the American dream, and eventually most of them realized it in their children. The men and women whom the Social Darwinists pointed to as weaker members of the species, ready for natural elimination, proved, if anything, to be the fittest citizens of the American republic.

Signs held by figures read: "HE IS BR... MUSCLE F... COUNTRY — UNCLE SAM", "...AWN AND ...OR MY", "HE IS A MENACE — CITIZEN", "HE ...ME LA...", "GIVES CHEAP ...BOR — CONTRACTOR", "ONE MILLION IMMIGRANTS CAME TO THE U.S. IN TWELVE MONTHS", "HE CHEAPENS MY LABOR", "WORKMAN", "STATESMAN", "HE'S A PU... TO ME"

GILLAM

COPYRIGHT 1903 BY JUDGE COMPANY OF NEW YORK

THE IMMIGRANT.

Is he an acquisition or a detriment?

NO IRISH NEED APPLY

By 1900 the midcentury image of the Irish immigrant was changing from a drunken gorilla with a stovepipe hat on his head and a big club in his hand to that of a comic leprechaun. Every accusation later made against the American blacks was made against the Irish, says their historian Andrew Greeley. Ads in the nineteenth century had often contained the notation "NINA"—No Irish Need Apply.

The animus of the "native" American now came to be focused on the Italian, the Jew and the "Oriental," in a recurrence of

the defensive nationalism known as nativism, a malign mutation of the American dream that runs a jagged course in American history from before the Civil War, through the Populist movement, and up to modern times. The numbers as much as the predominant Catholicism of the newcomers were what excited calls for exclusion. There were four times as many of them, said the Reverend Josiah Strong, as the Goths and Vandals who overwhelmed the Roman empire. Senator Henry Cabot Lodge put up a literacy test

to exclude "the most dangerous elements . . . Italians, Russians, Poles, Hungarians, Greeks and Slovaks who would wipe out the pure native breed." Cleveland thumped it with a veto.

Gillam's 1903 cartoon (above) cheerfully captures the arguments roused by the new wave of immigrants from eastern and southern Europe. Unexpected people provided a rationale for the xenophobia. Woodrow Wilson, in his 1902 *A History of the American People,* commented that the newcomers were "men of the lowest class

from the south of Italy and men of the meaner sort from Hungary and Poland, men out of the ranks where there was neither skill nor energy, nor any initiative of quick intelligence . . . sordid and hapless elements." Wilson promised during the 1912 campaign that he would omit the passage from the next edition, which he failed to do. Initially, even the small community of Jewish immigrants from Germany, 450,000 in 1889, was less than welcoming to Jewish immigrants from other countries. "What can we do with

these wild Asiatics!" said *The American Hebrew*. In 1887 the United Hebrew Charities of New York had gone so far as to persuade 1,082 Jewish immigrants to return to Russia, and talked another 3,500 out of coming by refusing to help them. The word "kike," according to the writer Andrew Feldstein, was invented by German-American Jews to deride Russian Jews whose names ended in "ki."

The Jews were commonly portrayed as unkempt anarchists. For the Italians, it proved hard to shake the shadow of the Mafia. They faced discrimination everywhere, from Irish Catholics especially but also from other minority groups. A black newspaper in Detroit declared, "The Italian . . . does not make a good American," and the Washington *Colored American* referred scathingly to the "dago"—a corruption of "day laborer," a common trade for immigrants. Worst of all was harassment by police and mob. Between 1874 and 1915, some 39 Italian Americans were lynched for alleged crimes. It was not uncommon for the police, faced with a crime, to round up as many Italians as possible. After an 1888 murder in Buffalo, New York, all of the city's 325 Italian males were arrested.

The hostility was bloodiest in New Orleans in 1891. At the height of a war between two rival Sicilian gangs, an Irish police chief, David Hennessey, who had sided with one of the gangs, was shot on the street. His last words were "The dagoes did it," so the mayor arrested every Italian he could find. Nineteen of the hundred were indicted, but when six of these were freed, an advertisement signed by prominent citizens appeared in the *New Orleans Times-Democrat* inviting "all good citizens to a mass meeting to remedy the failure of justice. . . . Come prepared for action." The mob went to the city jail, shot nine of the defendants and hanged two, one of them an Italian serving time for an unrelated minor offense.

Italy broke off diplomatic relations but the *New York Times* comment was typical of the temper of the day: "Those sneaking and cowardly Sicilians, the descendants of bandits and assassins, who have transported to this country the lawless passions, the cut throat practices, and the oath bound societies of their native country, are to us a pest without mitigation." Eventually, compensation of $25,000 was paid to the families of the victims.

G FOR GENIUS

Steinmetz in 1911 talks to a deaf Edison by tapping Morse code on his knee.

America without Albert Einstein and Irving Berlin and Andrew Carnegie and Alexander Graham Bell . . . Nativism would have imposed a high price in closing off immigration. And if Fred Austerlitz had not been admitted from Austria, what would have become of Fred Austerlitz, Jr., better known as Fred Astaire? Immigration inspectors at Castle Garden, adept at making chalk marks on the backs of the hopefuls (H for heart problem, X for feebleminded, L for limp) could have used a G for genius. Quite a number came their way. Of course, it was hard to tell. The 24-year-old frail German hunchback without money or English, who arrived in New York on June 1, 1889, would have been turned back if a Danish fellow-immigrant had not lent him money. It was a good decision for America when Charles Proteus Steinmetz was given a landing card. It was left to Thomas Edison to make the mistake the inspectors nearly made. He turned Steinmetz down for a job, saying, "It seems to me as if there is a regular epidemic of electricians coming to America."

Steinmetz was hired by another German émigré as a two-dollar-a-day draftsman. Without his solution of hundreds of scientific mysteries—he had 195 patents—the age of electricity would have come much later. He made it possible to transmit electricity more than three miles without multiple generators. Steinmetz had had to flee Germany because of his Socialist beliefs. He worked for General Electric for thirty years and remained a gentle, religious Socialist all his life.

SCHOOL FOR CITIZENS: Nine nationalities are in the class of 18 run by the Board of Education and the Bureau of Naturalization, in this photograph taken by the National Photo Company of Washington, D.C., sometime between 1919 and 1929. By 1890, more than half of the first generation of immigrants had already taken citizenship.

SAVING THE BLOOD

Becoming an American, wrote a poetic Romanian immigrant, is "a spiritual adventure of the most volcanic variety." In the history of so many American families there are countless unknown threads of heroism and sacrifice. One family today remembers its genesis in nine words spoken in Bessarabia in 1898: "Let us send the blood out of the country." The blood was a country girl of 17 and a man of 22 newly discharged from the Romanian Army. Their marriage was arranged by their parents, the life's savings of two peasant families scraped together so that the two young people, who hardly knew each other, might escape the Cossack pogroms that the parents and other children were left to endure: there was no money for everyone to go.

The Jews in eastern Europe had started to call America *goldineh medina,* the golden country, but the transition was wrenching, loved ones and homes aban-

doned, the countryside exchanged for a thrusting industrial culture. An immigrant guidebook of 1891 on surviving in the United States is urgent in its advice: "Hold fast, this is most necessary in America. Forget your customs, and your ideals. Select a goal and pursue it with all your might. . . . You will experience a bad time, but sooner or later you will achieve your goal. If you are neglectful, beware the wheel of fortune turns fast. You will lose your grip and be lost. A bit of advice for you: Do not take a moment's rest. Run." The American can-do ethic had already been absorbed by the writer: "A final virtue is needed in America—called cheek. . . . Do not say, I cannot, I do not know."

The young couple running with the blood from Bessarabia had sixteen American children, of whom nine survived to become an attorney, a celebrated hatmaker, a custom tailor, a sculptor, a legal

stenographer, a senior accountant . . . In 1986, when the 100th birthday of the Statue of Liberty was celebrated, the audio and video signals of the fireworks festival were picked up and delivered to a television network for world broadcast by a grandson of the original young immigrants—75 years to the day when they had become American citizens (July 3, 1911).

Assimilation was not the ambition of all the groups entering in the 1890s and early 1900s. The Jews were here to stay, with only 5 percent of the arrivals between 1899 and 1924 departing again, but nearly all the Chinese, 60 percent of the Hungarians and about half of the 4 million Italians were sojourners who went home again. The bulk of the Italians were men between 14 and 45, hoping to send money back to families or make a fortune and go home in splendor. Half of the southern Italians could not read or write even in their own language. They were easy prey for the *padroni*, or bosses, Italians already in America who could speak English and act as employment brokers. The *padroni* operated a form of indentured servitude. Even in the 1890s, road gangs of Italian immigrants could be seen working in the notorious Five Points neighborhood of New York City, supervised by *padroni* openly armed with rifles and pistols. It says something for these men that, despite their meager wages, they were able to send back millions of dollars—$85 million home to Italy in 1907 alone.

Of all the groups, the Jews had the most help from their own people. The initial hostility of Jews already established in America seems to have changed after attempts by gentiles in Congress to keep Jews out by imposing a language test that did not recognize Yiddish or Hebrew. The bill was defeated, and Jews began to launch wholeheartedly into forming or expanding great relief agencies that would serve so many people of all groups, not merely their own. The Jewish immigrant community was also assisted by the fact that Russia's pogroms pushed all elements of Jewish society—not simply the poorest or least learned—to emigrate together: an entire people transported nearly intact. Jews led the most effective and radical labor unions, published 150 Yiddish periodicals between 1885 and 1914, debated endlessly about socialism, anarchism, Zionism, in the Jewish "coffee saloons" on the Lower East Side and showed a passion for education unmatched by any group except the Germans. Ghetto-based libraries were first in the city in the circulation of history and science books. Some 2 percent of the New York population in 1904, Jews had 8.5 percent of all students enrolled in colleges. Lines of Jewish children waiting to use the Chatham Square library on the Lower East Side reached down two flights of stairs and out into the streets. Even the skeptical H. G. Wells was moved when he visited a school run by the Educational Alliance and saw a large class of bright-eyed Jewish children waving little American flags and singing, "God bless our native land." He wrote: "It may have been fanciful but as I watched them it seemed to me that their eyes met mine, triumphant and victorious eyes. . . . The most touching thing I had seen in America . . . Think of the flower of belief and effort that may spring from this warm sowing!"

THE RUSSIAN GERMANS: Ten of the 184,897 immigrants from Russia in 1905, the Russian German family of Jacob Mithelstadt, photographed at Ellis Island by clerk Augustus Sherman. They were on their way to Kulm, North Dakota.

THE COMING SUPERMAN

The faith (or fear) in America as a melting pot is as old as the Republic, but the phrase itself was absorbed into the bloodstream in 1908 when Israel Zangwill, in his hit play *The Melting Pot,* had David Quixano, a Russian Jewish immigrant, exult in his new country:

America is God's Crucible, the great Melting Pot where all the races of Europe are melting and reforming! Here you stand, good folk, think I, when I see them at Ellis Island, here you stand in your fifty groups with your fifty languages and histories, and your fifty blood hatreds and rivalries, but you won't be long like that, brothers, for these are the fires of God you've come to—these are the fires of God. A fig for your feuds and vendettas! German and Frenchman, Irishman and Englishman, Jews and Russians—into the Crucible with you all! God is making the American. . . . The real American has not yet arrived. He is only in the Crucible, I tell you—he will be the fusion of all the races, the coming superman.

Only eight years later Zangwill, who had become a Zionist, had lost faith himself: "Nature will return even if driven out with a pitchfork."

THE ENGLISH: Ten of the 62,824 English admitted in 1908, photographed by Augustus Sherman. About a quarter of the English went back home again.

FEMINISTS IN THE VANGUARD

Susan Anthony, severe in her gold spectacles, black dress and tight austere bob of hair, is the stereotype of the "old maid" reformer of the Gilded Age. She was, in fact, tough, canny, funny in private, difficult to shock and pungent in her rhetoric: "Women," she said, "we might as well be great Newfoundland dogs baying to the moon as to be petitioning for the passage of bills without the power to vote." And again: "For a woman to marry a man for support is a demoralizing condition. And for a man to marry a woman merely because she has a beautiful figure is a degradation." Nor have all the issues she and nineteenth- and early-twentieth-century feminists fought gone away in a hundred years. Argument has hardly ceased over a woman's right to control her reproduction, equality in the workplace, political and legal status or the right, even, to dress as she likes.

When Anthony (1820–1906) and her lifelong friend Elizabeth Cady Stanton (1815–1902) began their campaigns, traveling the states door to door with petitions, women had few rights. They could not divorce drunken or abusive men or go to college. They could not exert property rights without a husband's support. American law was still based on the jurist Blackstone's commentary that "the husband and wife are one, and that one is the husband." By 1900 most of the legal rights had been won and some of the professions had opened their doors. But suffrage was stuck, despite the success of Frances Willard (1839–1898) in persuading the Women's Christian Temperance Union (WCTU) to fight for votes as well as prohibition. Between 1896 and 1908, according to scholar Nell Irvin Painter, suffragists waged 480 separate campaigns just to get the issue on state ballots and succeeded only 17 times. Of these 17 referenda, only 2 passed—Colorado in 1893 and Utah in 1896.

Anthony was never much interested in the rising numbers of women working in factories and sweatshops, and suffragists tended to spurn the organizing efforts of black women, led by the Rev. Mary Church Terrell, for fear of losing white votes in the South. The whirlwind who came storming to the rescue of women and children in factories was Florence Kelley (1859–1932). She was the daughter

EMANCIPATOR: Susan Anthony fought for voting rights for ex-slaves, then felt betrayed when black leaders would not do the same for women.

WHIRLWIND: Florence Kelley was a Socialist and a friend and translator of Friedrich Engels.

of prosuffrage congressman William (Pig Iron) Kelley of Pennsylvania, who was constantly urged by Susan Anthony to do more "for the sake of all your women, your darling Florence included." Florence became a suffragist herself and later was one of the founders of the National Association for the Advancement of Colored People, but her true genius was to give sentiment the impetus of fact. "More than anyone else," wrote Arthur Schlesinger, Jr., "Florence Kelley devised the new techniques of social reform."

Working from the welfare and social reform of Jane Addams's Hull House in Chicago, Kelley went into the sweatshops and tenements to find out how women and children were being exploited, and documented their miseries in the seminal work *Hull-House Maps and Papers* (1895). When Illinois elected John Peter Altgeld as its progressive governor, he made her chief factory inspector. She won landmark reforms in Illinois, only to have the U.S. Supreme Court say they offended the employers' private property rights.

By 1899 she was living in New York's Henry Street settlement, and as general secretary of the new National Consumers' League flung herself into organizing middle-class boycotts of products from rogue employers. With Josephine Goldmark, she developed the "sociological" brief and devised a model statute of minimum-wage laws. They were enacted in 13 states and the District of Columbia. When they seemed in imminent peril of going the way of her Illinois reforms, she hastened to Boston to pitch a "revolutionary" new defense to attorney Louis Brandeis, that the law must consider actual working conditions and not just legal precedent. She and her colleagues backed up Brandeis's brilliant arguments with tons of hard evidence until they won the day in the 1908 case of *Muller v. Oregon*. Reform followed throughout the country; in 1912 she saw the creation of a federal Children's Bureau.

Kelley won by dedication and a blazing moral indignation. Newton Baker said of her: "Everybody was brave from the moment she came into the room." Her near anonymity today speaks to the necessity of reassessing how we have shaped our history.

RED EMMA: Emma Goldman (1869–1940) was a romantic anarchist most Americans feared and hated. She came to New York when she was 16, fleeing from czarist anti-Semitic Russia, and was deported in 1919, when she was 50, for speaking her mind about World War I. In the meantime she raised hell. Prison sentences and calls for her hanging only incited her to more wild sarcasms about the hypocrisy of private property and political parties. She was a lover of the ascetic, unbending anarchist Alexander Berkman, who tried to kill Henry Clay Frick. She crisscrossed America for 25 years in crusades for free love, birth control, homosexual rights and anyone she saw as a victim of the state. She scoffed at the suffragists, too, though she was vehement on women's rights: "I demand the independence of woman; her right to support herself; to live for herself; to love whomever she pleases, or as many as she pleases. I demand freedom for both sexes, freedom of action, freedom in love and freedom in motherhood." She seemed to delight in shocking for its own sake, whether it was praising the anarchist who assassinated the Spanish prime minister or smoking two packs of cigarettes a day in public. The assassin of President McKinley claimed to have been influenced by her. She had, in fact, rebuffed him, but while she deplored the act, she foolishly eulogized the killer as "a man with the beautiful soul of a child."

"Red" Emma was a misnomer. As an anarchist, her political color was black. She was suspicious of the masses. She was as much opposed to any Socialist idea of a central state as she was to capitalism. Unlike many American radicals in Russia, she and Berkman were appalled by the Bolsheviks' suppression of civil liberties, and fled to England. She was never allowed to settle in America again.

SCANDALS GALORE FROM THE MUCKRAKERS

IDA TARBELL, Rockefeller's nemesis. Her father was a small oil entrepreneur who had been broken by John D. Rockefeller. She exposed the coercion and spying behind Standard Oil's monopoly. The furious Rockefeller called her Miss Tarbarrel, but her sensational series in *McClure's* from 1902 to 1904 was vindicated. She was a scholar, not a campaigner. Later in life she wrote eulogies of business leaders.

LINCOLN STEFFENS indicted St. Louis, Minneapolis, Cleveland, New York, Chicago, Pittsburgh and Philadelphia in his *McClure's* series "The Shame of the Cities." In Minneapolis, he managed to photograph the ledger that recorded graft payments. He was a brilliant radical who formulated a law of municipal government: privilege controls politics. As a seer, he was less successful. In 1918, he went on an official mission to Moscow, met Lenin, and declared: "I have been over to the future and it works."

Crooks in City Hall. Opium in children's cough syrup. Rats in the meatpacking factory. Cruelty to child workers . . . Scandal followed scandal in the early 1900s as a new breed of writers investigated the evils of laissez-faire America. That high-wire artist Teddy Roosevelt was wobbling to the right for tactical reasons when, in 1906, he compared the crusaders to the muckraker in *The Pilgrim's Progress* who was so busy digging he could not see the heavens above.

The muckrakers were the heart of Progressivism, that shifting coalition of sentiment striving to make the American dream come true in the machine age. Their articles, with facts borne out by subsequent commissions, were read passionately in new national mass-circulation magazines by millions of the fast-growing aspiring white-collar middle class. Many had been to college and had absorbed the new philosophy of pragmatism. They believed that reason could promote human welfare. They held their society up to the ideals of the Constitution in its guarantees of representative government and equality of opportunity; and when the muckrakers reported that in some areas of life these guarantees were moonshine, they demanded reform. *McClure's*, founded by an ebullient Irishman, S. S. McClure, started the movement, and by 1902 its exposés were setting the pace for *Munsey's*, the *Ladies' Home Journal*, the *Saturday Evening Post* and Hearst's *Cosmopolitan*.

As Gabriel Kolko insists in his iconoclastic work *The Triumph of Conservatism* (1963), some corporate entities welcomed muckraking. The New York Stock Exchange, Chicago Board of Trade and American Medical Association endorsed exposés of fake drugs and fake stocks. But Kolko stretches his thesis too far by implying that most big corporations were pleased. They were not, and they had few allies among supposed Progressives. T.R. frequently lost his temper with the muckrakers, and both Woodrow Wilson and Herbert Croly tended to dismiss them as sentimentalists.

DAVID GRAHAM PHILLIPS had a big role in the passage of three constitutional amendments: the Sixteenth (federal income tax), Seventeenth (direct election of senators) and Nineteenth (suffrage). He depicted senators, still elected by boss-controlled state legislatures, as "the eager, resourceful, indefatigable agent of interests hostile to the American people." In 1911, he was murdered by a crazy musician who thought his family, prominent in Washington society, had been defamed by Phillips.

RAY STANNARD BAKER, third of the *McClure's* trinity, was a craftsman reporter. He showed how the *Atlanta News* had incited the 1906 race riot that ended in the deaths of 25 blacks and 1 white. He evenhandedly exposed viciousness in labor unions and malpractices on the railroads.

DYNAMITE FROM PACKINGTOWN

Jurgis Rudkus was a Lithuanian lured to America and to an inferno of exploitation. He found he had to pay graft to get his job—sweeping up guts for 17 cents an hour in a meatpacking factory where men sometimes fell into the boiling vats and went out in Durham's Pure Leaf Lard. Buying a house, he was cheated by a contract he could not read. He was victimized, went to jail and finally found salvation in the Socialist party.

This was the story told in *The Jungle*, the novel that 28-year-old Upton Sinclair (1878–1968) hoped would rouse America to active sympathy for the proletariat. It won him instant fame—but not for his cause. Eight of the 308 pages in *The Jungle* described the filth and confusion of meat processing in Packingtown (Chicago). They were intended as background but they shot to the forefront of America's concerned imagination. "I aimed at the public's heart and by accident I hit it in the stomach," said Sinclair. Despite all the headlines, it still took a lot of arm-wrestling to get government inspection extended to all stages of meat processing. Sinclair's exposé came as a climax to a long

campaign for purer food and drugs by state and federal chemists, women's clubs and muckrakers. Professor Edwin Ladd reported that 90 percent of meat had chemical preservatives; Professor James H. Shepard described Americans as breakfasting on coal-tar dye, borax and sodium sulphite.

The *Ladies' Home Journal* and *Collier's Weekly* exposed the hazardous frauds in patent medicines. The reforms proposed were modest; they still permitted fraudulent advertising and the meat law applied only to interstate commerce. But both bills ran headlong into the stone wall of a compliant House and a Republican Senate dominated by business. Senate leader Nelson Aldrich argued that a pure food law was a curtailment of the liberty of the citizen to eat what he liked. Only when the American Medical Association threatened to mobilize its 325,000 doctors against the blocking senators did they give in. Then Roosevelt got tough with the meat packers. On June 30, 1906, both the Pure Food and Drug Act and the Meat Inspection Act became law.

FLASH FORWARD: 1934

THE CALIFORNIA JUNGLE

When he was 56, Upton Sinclair won a landslide victory in the 1934 Democratic primary for governor of California. His End Poverty in California (EPIC) campaign promised to soak the rich and put the jobless to work in formerly idle factories. He looked as if he would beat Governor Frank (Old Baldy) Merriam, described by historian Greg Mitchell as "an old war-horse as out of step with trend-happy California as a silent movie." But the Republicans came to Old Baldy's rescue by inventing the modern media campaign—not just the usual dirty tricks such as faking a Communist endorsement for the anti-Communist Sinclair. Hollywood, fired up by the idea that Sinclair would make socialist movies, provided fake newsreels, the forerunners of paid commercials. Moviegoers saw armies of hoboes marching across California to join Sinclair. The images were outtakes from a recent movie, *Wild Boys of the Road*. Citizens with thick accents were filmed saying they were Sinclair's men. Quotes from villains in Sinclair's novels were put in his mouth. Sinclair was backed by Albert Einstein—they played violin duets—and by Charlie Chaplin, but the smears worked. Though EPIC candidates won 30 state assembly seats, Sinclair himself got 900,000 votes, 250,000 fewer than Merriam; some of the elements who had defeated him later recombined to send a young Richard Nixon to Washington.

SAVING AMERICA THE BEAUTIFUL

The most enduring monument to President Roosevelt and his Progressive faith is in the snowcapped mountains, sagebrush plains, rimrock canyons, rivers, lakes, wildlife and wildflowers of America. "Is there anything," he asked once, "to keep me from declaring a bird sanctuary on Pelican Island? No? Well, I so declare it." He declared 51 wild bird refuges, doubled the number of national parks from 5 to 10, set aside nearly 150 million acres of government timberland as national forest reserve and enacted National Monument protection for 16 more sites, including the redwoods of Muir Woods in California, Mount Olympus in Washington and the Grand Canyon.

No president before or since has had a better intellectual grasp of the relationship between an expanding economy and the environment, or of the subtle interactions of the natural environment. No one has had a more sublime vision of the power of nature to teach human humility.

This is not to say T.R. was proof against the blood lust considered normal for a gentleman born in the second half of the nineteenth century. He was all his life an ardent, if clumsy, hunter. But the president most often photographed with a dead beast at his feet was a passionate naturalist from an early age, and even as a child showed a reverence for life in all its forms. His father's guests were apt to find one of Teedie's snakes in the water pitcher; on one occasion he absentmindedly lifted his hat to a lady on a streetcar and several frogs leapt out. His collected letters show a president moving nimbly from warships and ambassadors to bears and fish. What could be done about the bears in Yellowstone Park who were getting their feet stuck in tin cans? Stop this nonsense of cutting down an elm tree in Lafayette Square to make way for a statue. Be sure to find ways of propagating the golden trout in Mount Whitney's Volcano Creek. His concern was democratic. The wonders of America should not be reserved "for the very rich who can control private reserves." He wanted all his fellow Americans to have a chance of enjoying the solace and satisfaction, and the replenishment of spiritual strength, he himself found in nature. This meant he was soon

at war with both parties. "Not a cent for scenery," snarled Joe Cannon, the autocratic Republican Speaker.

Conservation was a fairly new concept—indeed an unfamiliar word—when T.R. became president in 1901. The West, as James Bryce noted, was in too much of a hurry to think about the way it was squandering its splendid natural gifts. Local politics were geared to greed. There was widespread corruption in the acquisition of public land and of mineral and timber rights. T.R. moved resolutely on a broad front with his three musketeers, Frederick H. Newell, the father of reclamation; Gifford Pinchot, his chief forester; and his malleable secretary of the interior, Ethan Allen Hitchcock. The three previous presidents had set aside 50 million acres of forests for the public good; but under Harrison and McKinley these had been leased to private companies to exploit their timber and mineral resources. Roosevelt did not favor a pristine preservation of all public lands, but he did withdraw 26 million acres from private entry. He encouraged Hitch-

THE MARTYR: Gifford Pinchot (above) was a wealthy zealot of conservation who slept on a wooden pillow and had his valet wake him with buckets of icy water. T.R. made him chief of the new U.S. Forest Service. Pinchot introduced the idea of "selective cutting" to perpetuate forests (opposed by the preservationists like tree-hugging John Muir). When Taft succeeded his beloved Teddy, Pinchot accused the new interior secretary, Richard Ballinger, of turning the department into a patronage mill. Taft, who saw it as an attack on his own integrity by "a radical and a crank," fired Pinchot, who was promptly adopted by the burgeoning conservation movement as its first martyr. He went on to be a two-term governor of Pennsylvania.

cock to investigate public land frauds. More than 1,000 people in 20 states were indicted, among them several senators; 126 land sharks went to jail. In 1902, against Speaker Cannon's protests, Roosevelt supported a Democratic bill that became the great National Reclamation Act. It put an end to the piecemeal exploitation of water-power sites by private utilities, paving the way for Roosevelt Dam on the Salt River in Arizona, Hoover Dam on the Colorado, Grand Coulee on the Columbia, and Franklin Roosevelt's Tennessee Valley Authority.

The resentment in the Republican Congress at what it saw as T.R.'s usurpation of power came to a head in 1907. Oregon's Republican Senator C. W. Fulton, speaking for the timber interests, led a drive to stop the creation of any more forest reserves in Oregon, Washington, Idaho, Montana, Colorado and Wyoming. He attached a rider to an agricultural appropriations bill, declaring that future withdrawals of public lands from private exploitation in these states could only be made by an act of Congress. It was approved without even a roll call vote and T.R. seemed to be beaten. But he had ten days to sign or veto the bill and in that time he and Pinchot went to work with the gusto with which they battered each other in their boxing matches. Pinchot's young aides worked day and night drafting maps for areas where the land was wooded enough to justify the President's withdrawing it. In those ten days T.R. was able to proclaim national forests in all six states named in the rider, putting in a total of 21 new reserves and 16 million acres. When Pinchot was fired by Taft, there were 193 million acres of national forest, by comparison with 20 million in 1898.

T.R. not only saved the forests. He used his bully pulpit to sell the idea of them, and of conservation, to the American public. He appealed on pragmatic grounds of sound husbandry for future development, and on grounds of morality, for the preservation of America's heritage for future generations. It was a perfect harmonization of self-interest with idealism, manifest in most of the best American accomplishments of the century. One of his prophecies was borne out in the Dust Bowl within twenty years: "When the soil is gone, men must go; and the process does not take long."

T.R. atop Glacier Point, Yosemite National Park, in 1906 with naturalist John Muir (right).

MASTER DIPLOMAT—AND BULLY

The German Kaiser, Wilhelm II, chilled Americans. *Harper's* caught the mood with the doggerel it published in 1903:

Kaiser, Kaiser, shining bright,
You have given us a fright!
With your belts and straps and sashes,
And your skyward-turned mustaches!

Of course, no man frightened Teddy Roosevelt. He was out of office when he met the Kaiser in Germany in 1910 (right), but the Kaiser appreciated the potency of the former and possible future president. He inscribed a photograph of the two of them "When we shake hands we shake the world." The German Foreign Office tried to take the picture back because it thought the inscription undiplomatic. Roosevelt triumphantly held on to it and mounted it in his Oyster Bay home, where it can be seen to this day.

Throughout his presidency, Roosevelt was true to his prescription of 1900: "I have always been fond of the West African proverb 'Speak softly and carry a big stick and you will go far.'" He seemed ready for compromise in a 1903 dispute with Britain about the precise line of the Alaskan border with Canada. He agreed that a tribunal of three Americans and three Britons would arbitrate. But when the tribunal met in London, T.R. privately let it be known that if they did not decide in America's favor he would send in troops. He got his way. He succeeded in the same way in two major negotiations with the touchy Kaiser by keeping a cool and cunning head. In December 1902, the Kaiser sent his battleships into America's backyard, using the persuasive powers of a blockade and bombardment to collect debts owed the European powers by Venezuela. American opinion was enflamed when the Germans shelled Fort San Carlos, but T.R. publicly chose not to regard it as a breach of the Monroe Doctrine. He thought Venezuela's dictator, Cipriano Castro, was an "unspeakably villainous little monkey" who deserved a spanking. But privately and courteously Roosevelt did also let the Kaiser know he must hold his appetite in check in the Western Hemisphere. When the Kaiser seemed reluctant to go to arbitration on Venezuela,

Roosevelt reminded the German ambassador that almost the entire U.S. Navy, by accident or design, at that moment in the Caribbean. If the Kaiser did not unilaterally withdraw his forces, George F. Dewey, Admiral of the Navy, would be ordered to encourage him. T.R.'s warning was so discreet, it stayed a secret for years. In 1906 he induced the Kaiser to accept token satisfaction in a dispute with France over control of Morocco that had brought Europe to the brink of war. He wrote privately: "You will notice that while I was most suave and pleasant with the Emperor, yet when it became necessary at the end I stood him on his head with great decision."

T.R.'s greatest personal diplomatic triumph was to end the Russo-Japanese War. The conflict began in 1904. The Russians had provoked hostility by staying in Manchuria in breach of their word under the Open Door policy. Japan made a surprise attack on the Russian fleet in Port Arthur, a portent of what was to happen nearly four decades later at Pearl Harbor. T.R. had endless trouble getting the warring parties to agree even on the venue of Portsmouth, New Hampshire, for peace talks. Russia was "soddenly stupid" and Japan "entirely selfish." The Czar was a "preposterous little creature as the absolute autocrat of 150 million people. He had been unable to make war, and is now unable to make peace." But both Czar and Emperor finally came to terms on September 5, 1905, and the next year T.R. was awarded the Nobel Peace Prize.

ROOSEVELT'S LITTLE COROLLARY

Roosevelt got fed up with the "wretched republics" of Central America who did not pay their bills. After Venezuela, it was the Dominican Republic. T.R. worried that the European creditors would be so provoked they would attempt to get a foothold in the defaulting countries by armed intervention. His ingenious solution was to transform the Monroe Doctrine. Its original purpose, in 1823, was to warn European powers not to attempt to control countries in the Western Hemisphere. In 1904, T.R. invoked it to justify U.S. intervention in Central and South America. He spelled out what became known as the Roosevelt corollary in his annual message to Congress in 1904: "Chronic wrong-doing or an impotence which results in a general loosening of the ties of civilized society," he declared, "may ultimately require intervention by some civilized nation. In the Western Hemisphere the adherence of the United States to the Monroe Doctrine may force the United States, however reluctantly, in flagrant cases of such wrongdoing or impotence, to the exercise of an international police power." In practice, the corollary was applied only to Central America. South American economies continued to be dominated by Britain until World War II.

ROOSEVELT TAKES PANAMA

The dream of seven decades of linking the Atlantic and the Pacific by means of a canal across the Isthmus of Central America was finally realized by vision and heroism, and by greed and intrigue. The first step of this realization, foreshadowing a new balance of power, was the 1901 Hay-Pauncefote Treaty, by which Britain gave America a free hand on the understanding that all nations would pay the same tolls.

Nicaragua was ready to be equally helpful by offering its land for bisection. Most congressmen thought that the high, longer route through Nicaragua, linked by lakes and rivers, was preferable to cutting through the swamps of Panama, then a province of Colombia. The French had tried the Panama route for seven years under the leadership of the venerable Ferdinand de Lesseps, builder of the Suez Canal. Thousands of workmen died of disease and the canal company went bankrupt in a sensational French scandal in 1889. Enter William Nelson Cromwell.

Cromwell was that newfangled thing, a New York corporation lawyer. He was engaged by stockholders in the French company as a fast-talking lobbyist. His job was to sell to the Americans the assets of the New Panama Canal Company, principally a Colombian permit to build, which was to expire in 1904. He asked $109 million for the franchise and persuaded Senator Mark Hanna and Congress to set up an Isthmian Canal Commission to pronounce on the best route.

Enter Philippe Bunau-Varilla. The chief engineer of the French venture when he was only 26, Bunau-Varilla was a dashing Frenchman with a comically spiked moustache but the unflinching eyes, said Roosevelt, of a professional duelist. He was so passionate for "his" Panama canal, he had gone to St. Petersburg in 1894 and might have sold it to the Russians but for the death of Czar Alexander III. When the American canal commissioners arrived in Paris in 1899, Bunau-Varilla, working independently of Cromwell, lobbied its engineers incessantly. On November 16, 1901, a majority of the commissioners reported in favor of Nicaragua over the "expensive" Panamanian route, but Bunau-Varilla still

CULEBRA CUT: Cutting an eight-mile gorge through the mountain at Culebra was one of the special wonders of the canal. Six thousand men worked on it for seven years. Here, in 1913, they are cutting a drainage ditch. The first ship passed through the canal on January 7, 1914.

had hope. Commissioner George S. Morison had written a minority report for Panama, and he was, in the words of David McCullough, "a huge human bulwark." He was also the kind of strong-minded man Teddy Roosevelt liked, and that December Morison privately convinced the new president. Bunau-Varilla and Cromwell followed up by inducing the French to cut their asking price to $40 million, and in January 1902 the commission changed its mind.

It was still touch and go. In March a Senate committee voted for Nicaragua. Most senators agreed. Act II of the opéra bouffe, in April, opened with volcanic explosions. Mount Pelée's fire and lava wiped out St. Pierre on Martinique, and Mount Momotombo erupted in Nicaragua itself. The Nicaraguan minister in Washington forged a reassuring cable from his president and denied any eruption since 1835. Bunau-Varilla scurried about Washington and found 90 Nicaraguan stamps depicting Momotombo proudly in eruption. One went to each senator. On June 28, 1902, the Senate—by eight votes—decided to try Panama first, provided America could secure from Colombia perpetual sovereignty for the corridor.

Enter Theodore Roosevelt. He and his secretary of state, John Hay, pressured a Colombian envoy to grant the U.S. control of a six-mile-wide zone across the isthmus for 100 years for $10 million in gold and an annual rent of $250,000. Back in Bogotá, the Colombians reneged. They would settle only if the newly enriched French company would cough up another $10 million. Roosevelt became as active as Momotombo. The blackmailers of Bogotá, he fumed, were a corrupt pithecoid community, jackrabbits, cutthroats and bandits: "You could no more make an agreement with the rulers of Colombia than nail currant jelly to the wall." Privately, he talked of seizing Panama by force.

Act III opened quietly on September 24, 1903, in room 1162 of New York's Waldorf-Astoria Hotel, where two men invited by Cromwell plotted revolution: Bunau-Varilla and "Dr. Amador" (full name, Manuel Amador Guerrero), the 70-year-old chief physician of the Panama Railroad who mixed politics and medicine. Bunau-Varilla had just seen Roosevelt and assured Amador that if he and

his fellow conspirators rebelled, as Panamanians had been doing for 50 years, the U.S. Navy would be on hand to protect the new state. Bunau-Varilla sent Amador on his way with $100,000 for bribing the Colombian garrison, a proclamation of independence, the draft of a constitution and a flag of yellow stripes and suns stitched by Madame Bunau-Varilla.

It all worked out in the best traditions of comic opera. Dr. Amador lost his nerve when 500 Colombian soldiers arrived by gunboat in the port of Colón. His wife spurred him on. The troops were dealt with by the 77-year-old American in charge of the railway, Colonel James Shaler. He ingeniously shunted the Colombian general and his officers to Panama City—but not their men. When the Panama City plotters seized the Colombians and proclaimed the new republic of Panama the U.S. warships *Nashville* and *Dixie* were in port to shoo off the Colombian gunboat. At 11:35 a.m. on November 6, 1903, the bloodless revolution was declared a success. At 12:31 p.m., Secretary Hay accorded diplomatic recognition to the new state. To the irritation of the new Panamanians, the French citizen who had never lived in Panama signed a treaty that gave the U.S. an even better deal for a ten-mile corridor with perpetual sovereignty. Cromwell settled for his fee of $800,000.

In Europe, America earned opprobrium as a big bully, but America and the world got the canal (finished in 1914). Inside Latin America in this period, the U.S. was generally seen more as a defender of freedom against local dictators and European intruders, but the outrage in Colombia lasted a long time.

In 1908 Joseph Pulitzer's *World* reported that the $40 million paid out by the U.S. had gone not to the French government, as Roosevelt insisted, but to a mysterious American syndicate organized by J. P. Morgan and Cromwell, who had bought the rights from the French company for a mere $3.5 million. Roosevelt sued Pulitzer for criminal libel and lost. But the names of the stockholders of the New Panama Canal Company remained a secret. Roosevelt, never much interested in money matters, believed all these were details. "I took the Isthmus and let Congress debate; and while the debate goes on the Canal does also."

On August 27, 1900, in Havana, a mosquito carrying virulent yellow fever fed on army surgeon James Carroll and he fell sick with the disease. It was, for mankind, an immense benefaction. Dr. Carroll had deliberately set out to test the theory that yellow fever came from a mosquito bite. He survived, a broken man, but his bacteriologist colleague, Dr. Jesse William Lazear, who also let himself be bitten, died on September 25.

The doctors were two of a four-man yellow fever commission the American Army sent to Cuba, headed by Major Walter Reed. There is hardly a more inspiring passage in America's history of freedom than this sequel to the Spanish-American War, in which men of courage and devotion risked their lives in the hope of freeing humanity from appalling plagues. And there is hardly a more depressing footnote than the mean way they and their dependents were subsequently treated by the state. Private John R. Kissinger and other soldier volunteers in the experiments refused the $250 gratuity offered them, because they were acting in the interests of mankind. Reed touched his cap: "Gentlemen, I salute you." Kissinger, who was subsequently paralyzed, was refused a pension by the House Committee on Pensions, a scandal it took years to remedy. In 1925, the total monthly payments to the widows of Reed, Carroll and Lazear, and to Kissinger, were $475.

Yet the great American achievement of building the Panama Canal would have foundered without Major Reed's men. It was yellow fever that had ruined the French attempt. The disease killed 20,000 men—one third of the workforce—between 1881 and 1889. The idea that the mosquito was to blame for yellow fever seemed fanciful. A remarkable doctor in Cuba, Carlos Finlay, the son of a Scottish father and French mother, had been saying for 20 years that it was transmitted by a single species of mosquito, the *Stegomyia fasciata* (later called *Aëdes aegypti*). He performed 104 haphazard human experiments to prove his hunch, but they all failed.

Reed's success with his volunteers was in proving that *Stegomyia fasciata* was indeed the carrier, and that it incubated the disease to a peculiar time pattern. Reed worked out

YELLOW FEVER FIGHTERS: Dean Cornwell's imaginative painting brings together the group who conquered yellow fever. In the center, Dr. Lazear is inoculating Dr. Carroll with an infected mosquito, watched, left to right, by Dr. Finlay, the civilian; General Leonard Wood, military governor of Cuba (seated, center); and Major Reed (standing, center). Standing together on the right are Private John R. Kissinger and Acting Steward John J. Moran, who were the first two men to volunteer after the mosquito theory was accepted by the Yellow Fever Board.

that a mosquito could pick up the disease from a yellow fever victim only by drawing blood in the first three days of the sickness, and that it took another twelve days of incubation within the mosquito before its bite became virulent. Finlay's work, as Major William Crawford Gorgas said, had been the most striking example in history of "scientific clairvoyance."

Gorgas had been skeptical about mosquitoes. But to him there fell the herculean task of acting on Reed's proof, ridding Havana of all exposed standing freshwater (down to the last saucerful), where the Stegomyia might breed. He did it. By 1901, there was not a single case of yellow fever in Havana. Yet three years after Reed's discovery, Gorgas was in disgrace for trying to clean up the notorious pesthole of Panama. To the head of the Isthmian Canal Commission, Admiral John Walker, all this talk about the lethal mosquito was "balderdash." He and his fellow commissioners rejected Gorgas's plans for keeping yellow fever out of Panama. In 1905, a new chief engineer took over: John Stevens, the tough builder of James Hill's railroads. He

gave Gorgas all he wanted. Then a new chairman of the commission, Theodore P. Shonts, a Midwestern railroad executive, told Secretary of War William Howard Taft that Gorgas and his fellow mosquito fanatics should all be fired. Taft lazily endorsed the recommendation. It was only a plea from John Stevens to Roosevelt that saved Gorgas—and the canal. By 1914, thanks to the Gorgas standards of sanitation, the death rate from yellow fever in Panama was half that of the United States.

It is to the American Army that the world also owes gratitude for scientific proof that hookworm is the cause of chronic anemia and lassitude; yet again ignorance flourished. Bailey K. Ashford was only 25, an assistant army surgeon, when he landed with the troops sent to take Puerto Rico in 1898. He was appalled by the emaciated, listless condition of many of the inhabitants, and he remembered a lecture he had heard by Dr. Charles Wardell Stiles, consulting zoologist in the Federal Bureau of Animal Industry. Ashford positively identified the eggs of the parasite in the feces of victims—and promptly cured thousands with thymol and epsom salts. Stiles himself followed up, amid much medical derision, by identifying hookworm as one of the commonest diseases in the American South. The cure cost all of 50 cents, but in 1902, well before there was an income tax providing a federal revenue base, there was no chance that Congress would appropriate the money for "poor white trash" and blacks. It was not until 1908 that the American genius for philanthropy came to the rescue, and then only by chance. Walter Hines Page, the editor of *The World's Work* magazine, was sitting next to Stiles in a railway car as they traveled through the South. Someone remarked on a misshapen old man, and Page was astonished to be told by Stiles that the man could be healthy, productive citizen for the sum of 50 cents. Page arranged an introduction to John D. Rockefeller's charitable adviser, Frederick T. Gates. In November 1908 Rockefeller gave $1 million to combat hookworm—one of the finest investments in the history of philanthropy in terms of saving millions of shattered lives. It also did something for the dismal image of the donor.

VOLUNTEERS: This detachment of the Hospital Corps at Camp Columbia, Cuba, in September 1900, furnished most of the volunteers for Major Reed's experiments. Private John Kissinger is on the far left, third row up from the bottom.

Charles Wardell Stiles:
savior of the South

William Gorgas:
scourge of the mosquito

James Carroll:
the yellow-fever martyr

Walter Reed:
conqueror of yellow fever

THE GREAT WHITE FLEET SHOWS THE FLAG

Nobody in Roosevelt's cabinet, still less anyone in Congress, had any idea of the grand scheme the President was hatching in the summer of 1907. When he announced it in July, the chairman of the Senate Committee on Naval Affairs swiftly condemned it as a mad venture for which he would block funding. T.R.'s big idea was to send the entire U.S. fleet, 16 battleships in all, on a 46,000-mile voyage around the world, calling in on Japan (which ranked fifth as a naval power), China and Australia. He had anticipated the Senate's reaction. He had enough money, he retorted, to sail the fleet to San Francisco, and there it would sit indefinitely if Congress refused the funds. He got the money.

He was angrier with the "prize jingo fools," incited by William Randolph Hearst's *San Francisco Examiner,* who saw in the movement of the fleet another chance to beat their "yellow peril" drum for war with Japan. Relations were touchy. Japanese immigration was unpopular on the West Coast. Extremists in Tokyo were ready to stir up anti-American riots on any sleight. T.R. certainly wanted to impress Japan with his fleet, now second only to the Royal Navy, but he had a larger vision. It was nothing less than the future of modern civilization. He had come to believe it depended on the preservation of an East-West balance of power whereby no single nation could ever get into a position to threaten any other. This sensitivity to the dynamics of the global big-power game, central to which were the freedom and security of America and Britain, was new in an American president. With the possible exception of John Quincy Adams, T.R.'s was the first truly international mind in White House history. He was not above a racial or military power play. Before he became president, he had indiscriminately welcomed the takeover of any "backward" race by any of the "superior races": Anglo-Saxon, Teuton or Slav. By 1900, he was less an evangelist expansionist and more a calculator of the geopolitics of friendship and enmity, very much an Otto von Bismarck or a Henry Kissinger. Two books by friends, Alfred Mahan and Brooks Adams, influenced him. Both feared Russia and regarded the fate of China as crucial. Adams argued that America was endan-

PERDICARIS ALIVE OR RAISULI DEAD: T.R. sent seven warships to Tangier in the summer of 1904 when a local chieftain named Raisuli, kidnapped Ion Perdicaris, an elderly, wealthy Greek American who lived in Tangier. Secretary Hay followed up with the cable "This Government wants Perdicaris alive or Raisuli dead." Perdicaris was freed. America was thrilled. In truth, it was "Perdicaris alive" because the French, who ran Morocco, told the country's young sultan to agree to all Raisuli's demands on him. The laconic Hay commented: "It is curious how a concise impropriety hits the public."

gered by the erosion of Britain's ability to preserve the balance of power. Germany was the more immediate threat; Russia, the long-term menace because of her great landmass stretching both to Europe and to Asia.

In the Far East, T.R. looked to Japan to provide the principal bulwark against Russia, so he inclined toward the Japanese side in the Russo-Japanese War and, as mediator in 1905, leaned on Russia to give up territory. It was also the reason he sacrificed Korea to Japan in 1905. More concerned with allies and the balance of power than with business, he approved a secret understanding with the Japanese (the Taft-Katsura Memorandum) that they could make Korea their protectorate in return for recognizing American sovereignty over the Philippines. A young Korean named Syngman Rhee, who was studying at George Washington University, went to Oyster Bay to see T.R. on August 4, 1905, to plead for Korea's integrity. Forty-three years later, President Truman saw Rhee installed as the first postwar president of South Korea on

its liberation from Japan; but in 1905 Rhee got nowhere. America's national interest, T.R. believed, justified breaking America's promise to protect Korea (in the Korean-American Treaty of 1882)—something it was powerless to do in any event.

The sailing of the great white fleet from Hampton Roads on December 16, 1907, was a spectacular celebration of America's coming of age as a world power. All the German naval experts were sure the Japanese would attack it; the paranoid Kaiser sent a warning for Roosevelt's eyes only that 10,000 Japanese soldiers had been infiltrated into Mexico: they were disguised as laborers "but many of them had brass buttons on their coats." Instead, the Japanese laid on a three-day party for the U.S. Navy when it arrived. Thousands of children sang "The Star-Spangled Banner" in English.

The battle fleet returned to home port two years later, in February 1909, in time to close the Roosevelt era in a blaze of national pride. But T.R.'s Far East balance of power based on friendship with Japan did not last. His successors did not nourish it, and the very sight of the U.S. Navy may have helped the big-navy men in Japan prevail in their struggle against the pro-American peace groups. Ominously, in the very year the fleet sailed, Japan and Russia combined in a secret treaty to divide northern China between them.

Despite these unpromising sequels, Roosevelt was one of the most brilliant of twentieth-century presidents in his perceptions of a rapidly changing world. He saw vividly that isolationism could only imperil America. Standing on the Pacific Rim, at Stanford in 1903, he envisaged an age when America would have to abandon her traditional European stance and instead face west toward an East that was no longer far, but commercially and culturally near. Finally, he even saw, with an optimism and a positivism prefiguring that of Ronald Reagan, the ultimate doom of totalitarianism as democracy spread to all men. "I do not believe in the future of any race," he said, "while it is under a crushing despotism."

President Roosevelt salutes the great white fleet on its departure, December 1907.

CHAPTER FIVE

WORKERS TAKE A STAND
1893–1916

The Class Struggle in America

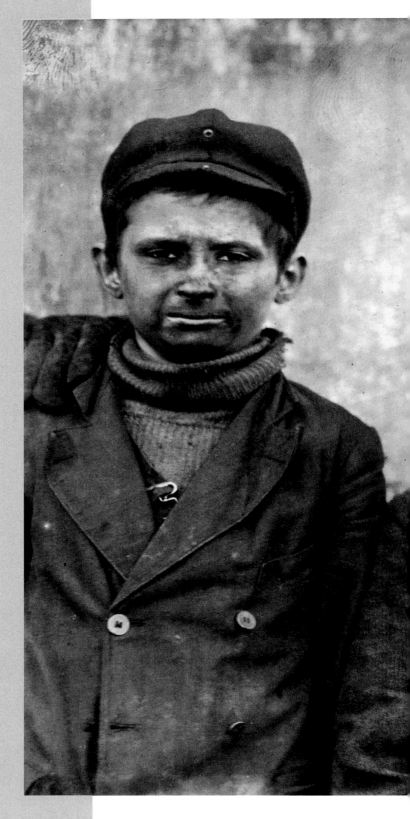

America's growing strength was rooted in the skill and energies of 37 million workers in 1910, 7 million of them women and millions no more than children. Ninety-five percent of them had no union. None of them in the early years of the century had legal protection to limit working hours, set minimum wages or compensate them for accidents. America was alone of the major nations in having no workers' compensation, yet it had the world's highest accident rate. Some 30,000 workers were killed every year and half a million injured.

The commonplace freedoms of labor today—to organize, to bargain, to strike and picket—were claimed at the risk of violence at the hands of employers' goon squads, private armies that had no parallel in other countries. England, France, Canada and Germany could not compete with America in the bloodiness of labor confrontations. Business was impatient with anything that got in the way of making America richer faster. The middle class resented immigrants and feared "socialism." The press, with the notable exception of William Randolph Hearst's empire, reflected and reinforced these emotions. There was no one in the White House to offer a different vision. In 1908, Roosevelt kept his promise to quit after two terms and handed the Republican nomination to William Howard Taft, who in the election thrashed labor's friend William Jennings Bryan.

THE ELVES: "Breaker" boys working for a Pennsylvania coal company in 1911. There were more than 15,000 boys under the age of 16 in the coal mines, picking slate out of coal from 7 a.m. to 5:30 p.m. At least 2 million children under the age of 15 were at work (understated in official figures). Edwin Markham in *Cosmopolitan* described a visit to a cigarette factory:

"One face followed me still, the gaunt face of a boy crouched like a cary-atid, pasting tiny labels on the margins of cigarette boxes. All day long he stuck little oblongs of paper marked with the runic words: 'Cork tips,' 'Cork tips,' 'Cork tips.' That was his message to the world. His pay was 25 cents a thousand; and he sat there, growing bent and haggard, and spending all his energies to promulgate to humanity this news about cork tips."

A favorite recurring analogy of owners was to liken children working ten hours a day to mythical forest creatures: "The work of these lively elves," remarked a textile owner, "seemed to resemble a sport in which habitat gave them a pleasing dexterity." Photograph by Lewis Hine.

THE STRUGGLE OF THE WORKING STIFFS

*It is we who plowed the prairies; built the
    cities where they trade;
Dug the mines and built the workshops;
    endless miles of railroad laid.
Now we stand outcasts and starving, 'mid
    the wonders we have made.*
                    —*IWW song*

Frank Little was sentenced to 30 days on the rock pile in Spokane in 1909 for reading out the Declaration of Independence. Frank Sumner Boyd was arrested in 1913 in Paterson, New Jersey, for reading aloud the free-speech clause of the state's constitution. These repressions, and many others of shocking brutality, occurred in the Progressive era because workingmen and -women tried to organize themselves into active trade unions. Some of them were radical in their politics, but if they were anticapitalist, they were very American in their passion for free speech, and their courage in defense of this freedom deserves more recognition than it conventionally receives.

The rawness of the early years of industrialization was tempered by the efforts of many reformers, though often state laws were weakly enforced. The wealth of the country increased apace, but there was a huge gulf between the guarantees of the Constitution and the daily life of millions of Americans: the dispossessed farm workers who became migratory harvest hands; miners and lumberjacks; the unskilled immigrants in the factories and sweatshops who did not speak English; blacks; and women and children. These workers lacked the homogeneity that bound the European working class together. They were divided by ethnic origin and language, religion and race, and the new immigrants had little sense of their place in society. Employers who mixed ethnic groups in the workplace found it easy to play off one group against the other. The growth of trade unions was inhibited, too, by the mobility of the workers, socially and geographically. They did not join; they moved on and often up. In the early 1880s, it had seemed the mass of farm and industrial workers might find

strength in the Noble Order of the Knights of Labor, which had grown from a secret society to a membership of 700,000 in less than 20 years. But the Knights of Labor was an uneasy hybrid of political party and labor union. Like the Populists, it had a refreshing vision of a fairer society, though it opposed immigration, but the diffusion of its aims, and especially the refusal of its leader, Terence V. Powderly, to order strikes for the eight-hour day, led to the breakaway of the unions representing skilled ironfounders, bricklayers, printers, carpenters and the like. By 1893 the Knights' membership had collapsed to 75,000. Meanwhile there was no room for the unskilled in the loose federation dedicated to collective bargaining, the American Federation of Labor (AFL), that the craft unions had established under the leadership of Samuel Gompers. Not until 1905 did the mass of American workers have an organization to fight for laborers of any origin, sex, race, color or creed, the Industrial Workers of the World (IWW) or "Wobblies."

In good times the masses shared a little in the gains made by the skilled English-speaking artisans and white-collar supervisors, but bad times, with wage cuts or unemployment, came often. There were depressions and recessions in 1893–1897, 1907–1909 and 1913–1915. These were the times when capitalism came under question, Socialists of one kind or another won office in a number of cities and states and fear revisited the business and middle classes.

The Napoleonic Gompers, canvasing the country with a black cigar between his teeth, and the craft unions that followed his lead built an enduring organization. The right to strike is the gift of their adroit good sense and determination. Despite these achievements, they were narrow in their view. Gompers claimed to speak for all the workers, but attacked the idea of industrial unions that might have organized the exploited millions in the newly developing mass production industries. Instead, steel, automobiles, public utilities, agricultural machinery, electrical manufacture, meatpacking and tobacco were without effective unions for decades, so that not only did the poorly paid industrial workers suffer but there was not the purchasing power to sustain the momentum of

RED DUO: Big Bill Haywood, the Western hard-rock miner who became a caustic crusader for the IWW, with his protégé, "Smiling Joe" Ettor, then 26. Haywood fled to the Soviet Union in 1921, where he was miserable. He died there in 1928. Half his ashes were placed in the Kremlin wall, half sent back to Chicago.

THE PAGEANT: Producer John Reed (journalist/author of *Ten Days That Shook the World*) dramatized key events of the Wobblies' battle on behalf of textile workers at Paterson, New Jersey, in 1913. The pageant was a hit. The strike failed.

national prosperity. Had the AFL joined its muscle earlier to the industrial workers, the cause of labor would have advanced more quickly. Gompers was a libertarian, which suited American society, though he built on an idea from Karl Marx that economic relationships determined everything else. If the workers could control the economic base of society, they could use it to enhance liberty and life as a whole. But he regarded socialism as "a fad of fanatics" that destroyed personal initiative. He was almost as laissez-faire as a typical mill owner, hostile to government intervention in fixing minimum wages or maximum hours, unopposed to the trusts, suspicious of social reform even to the extent of testifying against social insurance. He said it would weaken the "independence of spirit and vitality" of the mass of citizens. He was altogether confident that, free of political interference, trade union leaders and big business could make capitalism work for the benefit of both sides. He and his associates were as much products of their backgrounds as the judges whose antiunion decisions from 1908 on finally pushed the AFL into active politics, though still with limited, sectional aims.

For 40 years the judiciary sustained the employers, decades beyond the public consensus. The court's rhetoric was about liberty. The reality was an assertion of a company's property rights in its workers, with sideswipes at other "radical" ideas: when Mother Mary Harris Jones was arraigned with other United Mine Workers (UMW) organizers for picketing in 1902, the trial judge ordered her to leave West Virginia and to return to the woman's work that "the Allwise Being intended her sex should pursue." The Supreme Court deployed the Sherman Anti-Trust Act to declare strikes and boycotts an unconstitutional restraint of trade. Its use in the Pullman strike in 1894 was only a beginning. Before passage of the Clayton Act in 1914, many thousands of injunctions were issued against unions. By 1908, it was questionable whether a trade union could legally employ any sanctions at all against management. When the United Hatters' Union tried to organize a boycott against the Loewe Company in Danbury, Connecticut, that year, the Supreme Court found the union guilty of restraint of trade and fined it $175,000. The homes of the strikers that had been attached when the case began remained unoccupied and in disrepair for nearly 14 years. Samuel Gompers himself was sentenced to a year in jail in 1908, simply because he dared to keep talking about the ruling of Justice Daniel T. Wright, in the District of Columbia, prohibiting a

THE FLAG: Strikers at Lawrence, Massachusetts, marched with the Stars and Stripes to reject the charge that they were a "flag-hating conspiracy out to wreck the country." In Paterson, when the owners declared March 17, 1913, a flag day, the strikers responded with a parade behind the flag and a banner stating: "We weave the flag, we live under the flag. But damned if we'll starve under the flag." Eventually, they gained a hard-won triumph.

SAFE FLYER: Samuel Gompers, a passenger on this 1920 flight, piloted the AFL for 38 years. An emigrant from London at 13, he learned cigar making from his father and was president of his local cigar makers' union at 25. He fought hard, but on a narrow front. He rejected support from "dreamers and meddlers" who thought labor would get nowhere without political and legal reforms.

boycott against the Buck Stove and Range Company. Judge Wright called Gompers's exercise of free speech "utter, rampant, insolent defiance." As it happened, Gompers did not go to jail. After seven expensive, anxious years, the Supreme Court evaded the issue and threw the case out simply because it had been going on for so long.

The National Association of Manufacturers (NAM), formed in 1895, proclaimed the virtue of the "open shop," in which a worker in a company could join any union he chose, which sounded reasonable. In practice, this meant the right to join only a puppet "company union" or none at all. The NAM regarded all unions as criminal conspiracies, to be crushed by force under the pretense that they deprived individuals of "the free untrammeled right to earn their daily bread in such lawful manner as may seem best to them." This Arcadian view of America, palpably false in the machine age, was enforced by the courts against state and federal reforms. In 1908, the Supreme Court revoked the Erdman Act of 1898 and made it legal for an interstate railroad to discriminate against union members.

The Supreme Court used both blades of its scissors to cut off piecemeal measures of social legislation: one, it was an invasion of personal liberty for New York State, for example, to limit the hours a baker might choose to work to sixty a week; two, it was a denial of his employer's right of "due

process" guaranteed by the Fifth and Fourteenth Amendments to tell him how he could run his business. In 1916, Congress forbade the employment of children under the age of 14 in firms engaged in interstate commerce. This was ruled unconstitutional in 1918, despite the federal government's long-established authority over interstate commerce. Congress tried again, by imposing an extra 10 percent tax on factories employing young children. That, too, was thrown out. Nor could the unions expect help from other branches of government. Teddy Roosevelt had shown the striking mine workers unprecedented sympathy, but he did nothing to stop the flow of injunctions. President Taft was fearful of the union movement, and Wilson indifferent until the war forced him to reach out to it. Congress was tardy in providing any relief from the tyranny of the courts and, with rare exceptions— such as the Progressive Robert La Follette's Wisconsin—state and local governments were even more venal and deaf to the pleas of workingmen and -women.

Of course, the Wobblies who carried the red card of the IWW back across America from the West expected no better from capitalist society: they satirized it as the Iron Heel. The revolutionary industrial union was formed in 1905, when the militant Western Federation of Miners called together a bunch of radically minded "working stiffs," hard and soft socialists and anarchistic exponents of direct action. Their vision was of a utopian state run by the workers. They offered their muscle and evangelical zeal to any group of workers fighting for better conditions. As a Wobbly organizer put it: "The final aim is revolution. But for the present let's see if we can get a bed to sleep in, water enough to take a bath, and decent food to eat."

William (Big Bill) Haywood, the dynamic frontiersman with one eye who became the Wobblies' leader, defined industrial unionism as socialism with its working clothes on, but the Wobblies, unlike the mainstream Socialist party, now led by Eugene Debs, had no time for the ballot box. The millennium would arrive, at some inevitable but unknown date, after a general strike. Then the only form of government would be the administration of industry directly by the workers. It was a version of the syndicalism sweeping across the Italian, French and Scandinavian labor movements at the same time, but home-grown in the mining and lumber camps of the West, rich in its own folklore, songs and lingo: Marx with boots on. The IWW was the Big One, contemptuous of the "pork-chop unionism" of "labor fakers" like Gompers.

The Big One frightened America, straining the resilience of the founding faith in freedom. As historian Richard Hofstadter has suggested, the conflicts between Democrat and Republican, city bosses and goo-goos, muckrakers and robber barons, were, for all their sound and fury, bounded by horizons of property and enterprise. They all had faith in economic individualism. The virtues of capitalist culture were synonymous with apple pie and motherhood. The rivals for power in the Progressive era disagreed about the nature and seriousness of the abuses, but they believed they could be patched up in the common interest. But the IWW was different. In Big Bill Haywood's words, "the working class and the employing class have nothing in common."

It was this difference in philosophy that drew the white heat of suppression down on the Wobblies. Hofstadter remarks that successful societies have a kind of mute, organic consistency and shuck off ideas hostile to their fundamental working arrangements. "Such ideas may appear, but they are slowly and persistently insulated, as an oyster deposits nacre around an irritant." The rejection was rather less mellow than this elegant metaphor. Anyone who acknowledged he was a Wobbly risked club and gunshot. In 20 cities between 1909 and 1913, Wobblies were jailed just for attempting to speak in the streets. When one Wobbly was arrested in Spokane, others flooded in to demand their inalienable right to free speech.

Arresting officers beat them and crowded them into ice-cold cells. Some 334 of the 400 men held for 100 days had to be treated in hospitals. In a Fresno jail, the prisoners were blasted with 150-pound-pressure hoses for singing their revolutionary songs. Passive resistance won most of these free-speech battles, but not in San Diego in 1912, where 400 vigilantes with axe handles clubbed Wobblies arriving by train. None of the attackers was prosecuted, though a Wobbly died. America's entry into World War I was an excuse for more oppression. In 1917 the federal government charged Bill Haywood and 112 others with offenses under the espionage and sedition acts. Every one of them was found guilty, and the vehemently antiradical judge Kenesaw Mountain Landis jailed them all for long terms. Every IWW office was raided, and 2,000 Wobblies were put on trial for obstructing the war effort. In Bisbee, Arizona, armed vigilantes, with the help of the Phelps Dodge mining company, forced more than a thousand miners and other alleged subversives into railroad cattle cars and abandoned them in the New Mexico desert. The deportation was later held not to be a federal crime.

The conventional gloss on these abuses is that the Wobblies were Red loonies with sticks of dynamite in their hands. It is true that some of them talked menacingly enough, but labor historians Melvyn Dubofsky and Robert Justin Goldman independently conclude that the IWW was less an institution of violence than a victim of violence from law enforcement officials, condoned by the law-abiding. The Wobblies were not pacifists. When attacked, they might fight back, but passive resistance was their preferred tactic. The idea was to dramatize the brutality of the oppressors. As for sabotage, state and federal authorities tried hard to find evidence of it, but not a single conviction was ever obtained.

There were probably never more than 150,000 members in the IWW, and they were prone to factions, but their influence was more important than their numbers or their strikes. American workers did not like the idea of class war. Some were certainly frightened off by the repressions; more were persuaded that their true self-interest lay in class collaboration for general prosperity. But the IWW dramatized the plight of the unskilled, who eventually wound up in the Congress of Industrial Organizations (CIO), and it quickened the reform movement that led to welfare capitalism. That, of course, is not at all what the vivid legend of the Wobblies was about. It was about the freedom to be different, and by passive resistance and civic disobedience they blazed a trail that black Americans were to follow in the civil rights struggles of the sixties.

HENRY FORD MAKES HIS PEOPLE'S CAR

"Nothing has spread socialistic feeling in this country more than the use of the automobile, a picture of the arrogance of wealth," pronounced the president of Princeton University in 1907. Woodrow Wilson, a former professor of jurisprudence and political economy, had a point, and it might have remained valid for his generation but for Henry Ford, the country boy from Dearborn, Michigan. At about the same moment, Ford was sitting in a rocking chair in Detroit inventing modern America. His Model T Ford went on the market at the beginning of October 1908, conferring an egalitarian freedom of movement on a restless mass democracy.

Henry Ford was the son of an immigrant Irish farmer, and in the words of John Reed a "slight boyish figure with thin, long, sure hands incessantly moving." Compared with pioneer inventors of automobiles powered by internal combustion, he was a latecomer. French factories, building on German technology, were producing automobiles five years before Ford made his first car, the Quadricycle, in a shed at the back of his lodgings at 58 Bagley Avenue. Nor was Ford the first American maker of commercially successful cars in volume. The year before Ford's initial Model A was sold to a Chicago dentist, Dr. E. Pfenning, on July 15, 1903, Ransom Eli Olds had made 2,500 of the "Merry Oldsmobiles," which cost less than the Ford would. But in 1905, when he was 42, Ford took two big gambles. He split with the moneymen in the Ford Motor Company, who wanted to make luxury cars (at about the same time Olds was being pushed out of his company by partners who also saw the automobile as a toy for the rich). Ford emerged in absolute control of the company. Then he took the risk of transforming the company, from an assembler of components from other companies into an assembler of its own. He no longer bought engines and chassis, brakes, gears and axles from the Dodge brothers. He made them in his own factory so as to integrate them in a new effort to make a cheap car scores of thousands could afford.

Ford's technical inspiration had come earlier the same year at a U.S. automobile race. The French entered a car that crashed and Ford picked up in the wreckage a little valve-stem strip that was notably light and tough. It was made of vanadium, a steel alloy then unknown in the U.S. He persuaded a steel company in Canton, Ohio, to run its furnaces at the high temperature required to produce the alloy. They succeeded on the second attempt. By 1906 Ford had vanadium steel, to make cars stronger, lighter and faster than any built before. He put together a team to work on "a completely new job" in a locked room on the top floor of his building on Piquette Avenue. They were Edward "Spider" Huff, the electric wizard he had brought with him from the Edison Illuminating Company; an athletic Danish immigrant

THE MOONLIGHTER: By day Ford was chief engineer at Edison Illuminating Company in Detroit. He stole time and moonlighted with other Edison workers to produce his first car.

COMMON CARRIER: Almost every automobile was a Model T in Henderson, Texas, in 1926–27, but the scene was the same in every Main Street across America.

model-maker named Charles "Adonis" Sorensen, who had joined him in 1904 for $3 a day; and a young Hungarian gear-maker, Joseph Galamb. As someone who had been only a mediocre student in school, Ford always backed practical "tampering" men like himself. When he needed a man to take charge of his metallurgical laboratories, he gave the job to John Wandersee, who had recently graduated from floor sweeper to mechanic.

The Model T team worked day and night for a year. Ford would rock for hours in his mother's old chair, then draw his inspirations on a blackboard. One of them was a single casting for all four cylinders with the top sliced off—the cylinder head of modern vehicles. One day he brought in big kettles used for boiling maple syrup and he and Sorensen used them to try to insulate magnetos by cooking them in varnish. It worked. Everything did. The Model T's springs, high undercarriage and lightweight vanadium bore it triumphantly across the potholed, muddy roads of rural America; its sturdy 20-horsepower

engine could be hooked up to saw logs and grind corn. When it went on the market for $805 in October 1908, it was an instant success: 18,664 cars were sold in 1909–10 and 34,528 in 1910–11, and the following year production doubled yet again.

It was to meet this intense demand that the assembly line was perfected. Like everyone else, Ford knew that tiny savings in mass production could transform costs. Frederick "Speedy" Taylor's *Principles of Scientific Management* (1911) was a bible in Detroit. Cyrus McCormick had long made his reapers by mass production of standard parts, as had Isaac Singer with his sewing machines and Samuel Colt with his revolvers; and the Chicago beef dressers used an overhead trolley to transport carcasses. But one Sunday morning in July 1908 Sorensen and some helpers did something altogether different. They began at one end of the plant with a frame for a Model N, added axles and wheels and moved the chassis along to put together the first car ever produced on a moving line. There was a long way to go

in refining the process, but the accelerations were spectacular. By 1913 a Model T was being assembled in 12 hours and 30 minutes. The following year it took 96 minutes. For a theater show in 1916, "Speed Mechanics" did it in 2 minutes flat. Ford was able to cut the price to $440. By 1914 just about every second car in America was a Ford, yet there were only 13,000 workers at Ford, compared with 66,000 at the other plants.

In January 1914, Ford and his brilliant financial head, the flinty James Couzens, shocked Detroit and horrified the business world. They announced that Ford was doubling its basic rate of pay to the amazing figure of $5 a day. The *Wall Street Journal* called it immoral, the application of "spiritual principles where they don't belong." Adolph Ochs of the *New York Times* asked, "He's crazy, isn't he?" Not really. Apart from stopping the drift of labor from the assembly lines, Ford had created a whole new class of consumer. Now, he said, my workers will be able to buy my cars.

WILLIAM HOWARD TAFT
27th President (Republican), 1909–1913

Caricature by Oliver Herford, 1917.

BORN: September 15, 1857, Cincinnati, Ohio

DIED: March 8, 1930, Washington, D.C.

POLITICAL CAREER: Assistant prosecuting attorney, Cincinnati, Ohio, 1881–1882; Collector of internal revenue, Cincinnati, 1882–1883; Assistant county solicitor, Hamilton County, Ohio, 1885–1887; Judge, Superior Court of Ohio, 1887–1890; Solicitor general of U.S., 1890–1892; Judge, United States Circuit Court, 1892–1900; President, Philippines Commission, 1900–1901; Civilian governor, Philippines, 1901–1904; Secretary of War, 1904–1908; President, 1909–1913; Chief Justice, U.S. Supreme Court, 1921–1930

FIRSTS: First, and only, man to serve both as president and as chief justice. First president of all 48 contiguous states.

CHARACTER SNAPSHOT: "This genial, chuckling, courteous, kindly gentleman was in his heart a deep-dyed political and economic conservative, and bull-headed at that."
—William Allen White

YALIE: He was second in a class of 121 in 1878. He studied under William Graham Sumner and was a thoroughgoing Social Darwinist.

GOVERNOR: As governor of America's only real colony, he thought the Filipinos would need 50 or 100 years before they "even realize what Anglo-Saxon liberty is." He worked through the entrenched plutocracy, but he drove his team hard; he built dams, schools and sewage systems; and he established the first honest and independent judiciary. He dealt brilliantly with the problem of the Roman Catholic friars who had run the islands under Spain and fled or been killed. He went to the Vatican in June 1902 and persuaded Pope Leo XIII that the friars should not come back and their 390,000 acres should be sold to the U.S. Then he let thousands of Filipino peasants have the land on cheap mortgages.

SECRETARY OF WAR: He was Roosevelt's global troubleshooter. He supervised the building of the Panama Canal, organized relief for San Francisco after the 1906 earthquake, became temporary governor of Cuba in a civil war in 1906. He also took the opportunity to get his revenge on General Arthur MacArthur, who, as military governor of the Philippines, had refused to recognize Taft's superior civil authority. He stopped MacArthur's promotion, including his appointment as army chief of staff. Taft, said T.R. while they were still friends, is "one of the best haters I have ever known." T.R., declining a third term, fixed Taft's nomination in 1908.

SLEEPING BEAUTY: He loved his automobiles, but fell asleep in them so often, his wife called him Sleeping Beauty. He traveled 16,000 miles campaigning in the 1908 election. By the time he became president he reckoned he had been around the world twice. Note the solitary newspaperman.

THE BREAK: "Well, I guess old friends are the best," says Uncle Sam. Taft was unhappy running again in 1912, but a more radical T.R. was unhappier still when Taft beat him for the nomination. T.R. called his old friend ("one falls in love with Taft at first sight") a fathead and a standpatter. Taft wept in his private railroad car.

THE TAFTS: His wife, Helen (Nellie) Herron, a judge's daughter, pushed hard for him to be president. She became the first wife of a president to ride by her husband's side on inauguration day. Washington has her to thank for organizing the planting of 3,000 Japanese cherry trees along the Tidal Basin in 1912. Daughter Helen (left) became the official White House hostess for a year while her mother recovered from a stroke. She later became a suffragist. Son Charles (left, rear) became a Progressive mayor of Cincinnati. Son Robert held leadership roles in the Senate during his service there from 1939 to 1953. Unlike his father, he was an isolationist. Three times it cost him the Republican nomination for president, in 1940, 1948 and 1952.

CHIEF JUSTICE: He took a broad view of federal over state power. He dissented on the Court's invalidation of a law fixing a minimum wage for women. But generally he was a verbose protector of private property, which he thought "sacred." He refused to retire after a heart attack. "I must stay," he wrote in 1924, "in order to prevent the Bolsheviki from getting control." His best work was in administration. He won discretion for the Court to give precedence to cases of national significance.

THE GOLFER: A photograph Roosevelt would have censored. He told Taft he had received hundreds of letters protesting Taft's fondness for golf. "I never let my friends advertise my tennis," he advised, "and never let a photograph of me in tennis costume appear." Taft hated to be disturbed on his frequent visits to the Chevy Chase links. When once told the president of Chile was waiting, he snapped: "I'll be damned if I will give up my game of golf to see this fellow."

THE INSURGENTS TAKE ON BIG WILL TAFT

THE SENATE BOSS: Crusty Nelson Aldrich started as a wholesale grocer and made fortunes in banking, sugar, gas and electricity. In his home state of Rhode Island he organized most of the utilities into the Rhode Island Company and had it exempted from taxes and health regulations. He was the father-in-law of John D. Rockefeller, Jr.

The dancing shadow of Teddy Roosevelt, that "interesting combination of St. Paul and St. Vitus," never left the walls of the White House while Big Will Taft was the tenant. He had never wanted the job Roosevelt had bequeathed him, and never understood its theatrical nature. "When I hear someone say Mr. President," he chuckled, "I look around expecting to see Roosevelt." As a Progressive disciple, he tried hard. His record on trust-busting was better than Roosevelt's, but as a man on horseback, he was a flop. He was, in Mark Sullivan's words, "a placid man in a restless time." He fell asleep a lot, at church, at concerts, at dinners, but also when meeting senators. One suspects he fell asleep as he drafted a speech in his railroad car to Winona, Minnesota, on September 9, 1909. A few careless words there convinced an impatient public he was a traitor to the Progressive cause. "On the whole," he told the listless Winona audience, "I am bound to say that I think the Payne-Aldrich bill is the best tariff bill that the Republican party has ever passed."

In the fall of 1910, that opinion in favor of higher tariffs widened the split in the Republican party between the old guard and the new insurgents. The significance of the remark was that Taft had pledged himself in the election campaign to revise the tariff downward. The Republican party, habituated to revising it upward, fudged the wording of the party platform so that when Taft tried to carry out his promise immediately after inauguration, Nelson Aldrich, the powerful senator from Rhode Island, raised his eyebrows: "Who said anything about a revision downward?" Aldrich ran the Senate for the profit of business. He had been doing so

FIGHTING BOB: Taft thought La Follette a troublemaker. He was. He exposed fraud by the party bosses in Wisconsin, led by lumber baron Senator Philetus Sawyer. Then, as three-term governor, he forced through taxes on railroads and corporations, banned free passes for officials, conserved forests and brought in election by direct primary.

for 20 years, dominating a core group of long-tenured conservative Republicans. He did it with steely elegance. Cigar-chomping "Uncle Joe" Cannon did the same as Speaker of the House, though with a different style, more given to barnyard epithets. His motto: "This country is a hell of a success. Don't muck with it."

Roosevelt had evaded dealing with tariffs. He told Taft this was an issue of expediency, not morals. Aldrich was the expediency. He made 847 ingenious amendments to Representative Sereno E. Payne's reasonable House bill, and proceeded to railroad it through.

Aldrich ran straight into a new breed of Republican. They came from the Midwest states, where Populism had been strong— Wisconsin's Robert La Follette, Iowa's Jonathan Dolliver, Joseph Bristow of Kansas, Albert Beveridge from Indiana, Albert Cummins of Iowa and Moses Clapp of Minnesota. They were already fighting mad at the way in which reforms they made in their states were blocked at the national level by the Republican old guard. The dozen or so insurgents spoke

for a much broader American public. They stayed up night after night going through Aldrich's complex schedules and reported that the average rate on dutiable goods would be 1.5 percent higher. With this tariff, declared La Follette, the very workers who made woolens would not be able to afford them. The tariff was excoriated across the country. Taft got the blame when the bill was passed, and then at Winona seemed to be bragging about his cowardice. He was, said Dolliver, "an amiable man completely surrounded by men who know what they want." Taft's heart, in truth, was not in low tariffs. In 1910–11, when the insurgents sided with Democrats to lower tariffs on wool, steel, iron and cotton, Taft vetoed every bill.

He had a knack of attracting criticism. Roosevelt had advised him not to tangle with Cannon, the autocratic Speaker who had long exploited his powers to make key committee assignments. The friends of Roosevelt nevertheless blamed Taft when he let the 30 insurgents in the House fail in their first attempt to cut Cannon down to size. He still got no credit in 1910, when he

gave his tacit approval for a second, successful attempt by insurgents and their Democratic allies to curb the Speaker's powers.

It was Cannon who best summed up Taft's political clumsiness. If Taft were Pope, said Cannon, he'd want to appoint some Protestants to the College of Cardinals. Yet history judges Taft's record more favorably than did contemporary opinion still dazzled by Roosevelt's pyrotechnics. Taft prosecuted twice as many antitrust suits in four years as Roosevelt had in seven. He supported the adoption by Congress of an amendment to the Constitution to permit the "communistic" income tax. He overrode the objections of the banks and express companies to create a postal savings bank for average Americans and to establish parcel post. He introduced the eight-hour day for federal workers. He even declared himself in favor of transferring the election of senators from state legislatures to the people, an idea that was anathema to the old guard.

THE REBEL GIRL: ELIZABETH GURLEY FLYNN

There are women of many descriptions
In this queer world, as everyone knows.
Some are living in beautiful mansions,
And are wearing the finest of clothes.
There are blue-blooded queens and princesses,
Who have charms made of diamond and pearl;
But the only and thoroughbred lady
Is the Rebel Girl.

      —Joe Hill

THE REBEL GIRL AND THE CHILDREN'S CRUSADE

On January 20, 1912, nine days after woolen mill workers went out on strike in Lawrence, Massachusetts, police found dynamite in a shoemaker's shop next door to where Joe Ettor, a 27-year-old organizer of the Wobblies, collected his mail. The *New York Times* expressed the national indignation: "When the strikers use or prepare to use dynamite, they display a fiendish lack of humanity which ought to place them beyond the comfort of religion until they have repented."

The strikers did not repent—because they had nothing to do with the dynamite. It was wrapped in a magazine traced to John J. Breen, a former mayor and member of the school board who had been paid to place it in locations implicating the strikers by William Wood, president of the American Woolen Company, the town's principal employer. Another man admitted plotting the deception in Wood's office. He killed himself before he could testify. Breen was fined $500. Wood went unscathed.

Lawrence in 1912, as Melvyn Dubofsky writes, was America in microcosm: new and old immigrants; wealthy anti-union mill owners; a Progressive governor in the state capital; a conservative craft union representing under 10 percent of the workers; and a handful of radicals. There were 37,000 mill workers, nearly half of the city's population, earning near-starvation wages of seven to nine dollars a week, less in real terms than the English mill worker was earning. (Their chief employer, the bomb plotter Wood, liked to declare, "I never had time to count my automobiles.") Respiratory disease took the flower of their youth. On average, Massachusetts farmers lived to be 60; textile workers did not reach 40. They were mostly immigrants, English-Irish-Scotch first, and after 1895 Italian, Polish, German, Lithuanian, Armenian . . . Their wages were cut without warning when a state law reduced weekly work hours from 56 to 54. The pay cut was modest, but enough, as one striker put it, to pay for four loaves of bread. A group of Polish women left their looms first, then angry Italians rushed from mill to mill, disassembling machinery. At that point only 500 of the 20,000 strikers belonged to a union, and it was days before the IWW

arrived in the form of the debonair Ettor and Arturo Giovannitti. "Rebel girl" Elizabeth Gurley Flynn and Big Bill Haywood followed. They immediately imposed order on a Babel of different languages and interests.

Militia with fixed bayonets were soon pacing in front of the mills. Police sent to break up pickets were told to strike women on the arms and breasts, men on the head. The Wobblies taught the strikers to stand passively with folded arms. After two nonviolent weeks, police tried to block a strikers' march. A policeman was stabbed and a young Italian striker, Annie LoPezzi, shot dead. Nineteen people saw a soldier do the shooting, but Ettor and Giovannitti, who were elsewhere at the time, were arrested for her murder and held in jail for ten months. When they finally came to trial, they were kept in metal cages in the courtroom; the two were eventually acquitted.

The turning point was the children's crusade. The Italian workers proposed evacuating the children of strikers to sympathetic families outside Lawrence. Flynn organized it. The first group of strike orphans aroused great sympathy, to the rage of the town's leaders, who ordered evacuations to stop. On February 24 a group of Philadelphia women arrived to pick up 200 children. An observer later testified to what happened at the railroad station: "The police closed in on us with their clubs, beating right and left with no thought of the children, who were in desperate danger of being trampled to death. The mothers and children were thus hurled in a mass and bodily dragged to a military truck and even clubbed, irrespective of the cries of the panic-stricken mothers and children." The First Lady, Nellie Taft, who broke down in tears at the later congressional hearing. In March the public outcry persuaded the company to yield.

It was a great victory for the IWW, which saw its Lawrence membership increase to 10,000. The Wobblies redeployed to Paterson, New Jersey, where they organized a strike of silk mill workers in 1913. The IWW did not have enough money to sustain the strikers over the five months of hunger and police brutality. A hundred

were arrested every day. Men were sentenced to three years in jail just for talking. Elizabeth Gurley Flynn led the Wobblies, and again they taught the heterogeneous strikers passive resistance, but Paterson proved to be Waterloo for the Wobblies. In the early stages, they got money from the Socialist party, but while Haywood was practicing passive resistance in Paterson, his enemies got him removed from the national executive committee of the Socialist party for his theoretical advocacy of sabotage. At the end of five months, the Socialists had lost faith in industrial action. In the hope that the workers would turn to political action next, they encouraged the English-speaking skilled workers to accept a shop-by-shop settlement offered by the employers. The skilled deserted the unskilled, then the other workers stampeded back to their mills on poor terms. It was the same story in other strikes: solidarity, repression, division, defeat.

FLASH FORWARD: 1951

STILL REBELLING

1951: The rebel girl, aged 61, is shortly to face trial under the Smith Act for being a member of the Communist party, which she joined in 1937. She served 28 months at the Alderson Federal Women's Prison in West Virginia. In 1961 she was made head of the American Communist Party. She was thrown out of the American Civil Liberties Union, which she had helped to found, because of her Communist ties. She died of a heart attack on September 7, 1964, while on vacation in Russia.

THE FIRE THAT CHANGED EVERYTHING

The sight was more than New York could bear: Young women jumping to their deaths from the ninth-floor windows of the blazing Triangle Shirtwaist Company. Sometimes they join hands for their leap. A girl jumps with hair ablaze streaming around her head. Another sails her broad-brimmed hat over the crowds below, flings a few bills and coins of her pay after it and hits the pavement just after the coins. A man is seen gently handing girls onto a windowsill, "as if he were helping them onto a streetcar instead of into eternity." One of the girls turns to embrace him and she kisses him before she leaps. Then he climbs out and follows her in his fall to the pavement.

At least 46 died that way on the afternoon of March 25, 1911. Another 100 charred bodies were recovered from the building, mainly young Jewish and Italian women who sewed tailored blouses on a piecework basis. The tallest fire ladders reached only to the sixth floor, and the factory was on floors eight through ten. Altogether in New York, more than 300,000 people worked in lofts higher than ladders could reach.

It was the tragic climax to a courageous initiative the women had taken in September 1909, when 200 of them tried to join the International Ladies' Garment Workers' Union (ILGWU), founded in 1900. They were fired and staged an independent strike. Workers at another large factory joined them on the picket lines. The owners hired thugs to beat them up; the police arrested the victims. The abuses stirred a mass meeting of all the city's shirtwaist workers, and by November some 20,000 were on strike, the largest strike by women ever staged in the United States. The Uprising of the Twenty Thousand was supported by a remarkable coalition of middle-class women suffragists and members of the Women's Trade Union League.

The strikers won better hours and wages, and the right to form a local union, from which the ILGWU grew powerful; yet in the end the Triangle fire produced still greater triumphs. The stricken conscience of New York led to a state commission that investigated 1,836 factories in 20 industries, which led to the passage of 56 reform bills. They included a 54-hour work week for women and minors, safety codes, workers' compensation and a ban on night factory work for women. The sponsors were a coalition of people destined to play a powerful role in American progress, including Frances Perkins, secretary of the New York Consumers' League (later U.S. secretary of labor); state senator Robert F. Wagner (later author of the National Labor Relations Act of 1935); state legislator Al Smith (later governor of New York and Democratic presidential candidate) and a young Democratic state senator named Franklin Delano Roosevelt.

GUILTY: Firemen's nets caught only a few and some nets broke. The Triangle owners, Max Blanck and Isaac Harris, "the shirtwaist kings," kept the stairway exit doors locked to prevent theft and had ignored warnings from city inspectors—who did not follow up with enforcement. Nevertheless, with the help of a clever lawyer, Max Steuer, they were able to beat a manslaughter charge. They claimed their insurance money and after stalling for years in the courts finally paid off claimants at an estimated $75 a life. Over the next few years Blanck and Harris were repeatedly back in court for violating the new labor and fire laws. Even in their new factory, inspectors found six-foot piles of rubbish and fire doors chained shut.

JANE ADDAMS

ALICE PAUL

FEMALE CRUSADERS

An unprecedented female solidarity slowly began to emerge in the first decade of the twentieth century. Radical young women began to call themselves feminists around 1912. But even as famous a crusader as Eleanor Roosevelt (1884–1962) initially opposed female suffrage. Women like her thought they could do more good in the multitude of social organizations they formed, richer than anywhere in Europe.

JANE ADDAMS (1860—1935) launched scores of initiatives from her community house base in the slums of Chicago. She worked in the Consumers' League and the Women's Trade Union League, setting state and national agendas for reform on factory hours, sanitation, pure milk, food and water, and health care. She seconded the nomination of Teddy Roosevelt at the 1912 convention of the Progressive party, the only big party to support women's suffrage. She backed the founding of the National Association for the Advancement of Colored People (NAACP). And she crusaded for world peace. In 1931 she shared the Nobel Peace Prize.

ALICE PAUL (1885—1977) put teeth into the votes-for-women campaign when she came back from London with militant ideas from British suf-

JEANNETTE RANKIN

MARGARET SANGER

fragists, who had chained themselves to buildings and invaded Parliament. At 23 she had been in prison three times. She and her small band were attacked by passersby, jailed and beaten for going on daily sentry duty outside the White House pointing out the hypocrisy of President Wilson's fight for worldwide democracy when he would not extend it to American women. Alice Paul went on a hunger strike in prison until released.

JEANNETTE RANKIN (1880–1973) was the first and only woman elected to Congress (the 65th) in 1916, as a Republican from Montana. She got the House to pass the Nineteenth Amendment for female suffrage—by one vote. She was a dedicated pacifist, one of the 50 members of the House who voted against President Wilson's declaration of war. Later, she was the only

vote against U.S. entry into World War II, and in 1968, at the age of 87, she led 5,000 women in protest against the war in Vietnam.

MARGARET SANGER (1879–1966) was sent to the workhouse for 30 days in 1917 for opening the first U.S. birth control clinic in Brooklyn, and dragged from the platform by police when she opened the first American Birth Control Conference in New York. But the clinics thrived, and in 1936 a federal appeals court finally ruled that physicians could prescribe contraceptives—a vital first step to realizing her slogan, "Every child a wanted child." Later, she became intrigued by dubious, often racist, theories of genetics.

ROCKEFELLER'S MASSACRE

In the Rockefeller family's feudal company townships in the southern Colorado coalfields in 1913, the miners were paid $1.68 a day in scrip they could spend only at Rockefeller stores and in rent for Rockefeller shacks. Mind and body were owned by the company. No subversive thoughts (in books such as Henry George's *Social Problems* or Darwin's *Origin of Species*) were allowed into school, church or library. No union was recognized at any of the 24 mines owned by Rockefeller's Colorado Fuel and Iron Company (CFI). The workers voted as they were told. The overly trusted Rockefeller boss on the spot, a former wholesale grocer from upstate New York named LaMont Montgomery Bowers, boasted that the company registered and voted every man and woman employee, including the 70 percent who were not even naturalized citizens. "Even their mules . . . were registered if they were fortunate enough to possess names."

Organizers of the United Mine Workers of America (UMW), recognized by coal companies in 17 states, were turned away by armed guards at CFI mines. Rockefeller Senior was no longer at the 26 Broadway, New York, offices of Standard Oil—he was out on the golf course—but his 39-year-old son, John D. Rockefeller, Jr. ("Junior" or "Mr. John"), was as fierce an enemy of unions as his father. The mines lost money and he wanted to show his father he could effect a turnaround. He was so focused on finances, he had said and done nothing when an explosion killed 79 men in January 1910. The death rate in Colorado was four times greater than in Illinois, Iowa and Missouri, where unions were recognized. In 1913, 464 Colorado miners were killed or maimed. No court in Colorado, in 23 years, had given a verdict in favor of the hundreds of victims or the survivors of men killed. When reformers did manage to enact the right to join a union, a cut in the working day and mine-safety rules, the operators simply pretended it had never happened.

Junior was reinforced in his hostility to unions by the family adviser on philanthropic work, the Reverend Frederick T. Gates, a Baptist intellectual "torn between heaven and earth," in the words of Rockefeller biographer Ron Chernow. When the

"JUNIOR": belated second thoughts.

UMW called a strike on September 22, 1913, Gates declared, "The officers of the Colorado Fuel and Iron Company are standing between the country and chaos, anarchy and proscription and confiscation." Bowers rejected mediation. He hired 300 gunmen, eight machine guns and an armored car the miners came to call "the Death Special." The miners scurried around for weapons. They put up tents at a score of sites, fearing they would be evicted from their shanties and they were. Twelve thousand men, women and children trekked out in a rainstorm, their wagons piled with rickety chairs and straw bedding.

Gun battles broke out. Several strikers were killed on October 17. Junior was unfazed. Asked by a Congressional committee whether the killings were justified, he replied that "any cost" was justified to defend the great national principle, the freedom of the workers not to have a union do things for them which they and the company did not think were in their interests. His father thought it was such a good tough answer he sent him 10,000 shares of CFI stock.

When the violence intensified, the National Guard was then sent in with the Orwellian task of suppressing citizens of the state who were calling for the enforcement of state laws. At first the militia enforced the state law that barred strikebreakers from being brought in. But by December the Democratic governor, Elias Ammons, did not have enough money to meet the militia payroll. Bowers sent Mr. John a gratifying Christmas note: "We have been able to secure the cooperation of all the bankers of the city who have had three or four in-

terviews with our little cowboy governor. . . . There probably has never been such pressure brought upon any governor of this state by the strongest men in it." The bankers paid the militia, the militia were ordered to escort scabs to the mines and the scene was set for tragedy.

It was at the largest tent town, at Ludlow, where miners and militia had often clashed, that Karl Linderfelt, a militia lieutenant who was a psychopathic sadist, gave the order on April 24 for his Hotchkiss guns to open up on the miners. At the same time he launched a diversionary attack on one of the camps where miners had sent their families. Two women and eleven children hiding in a dirt bunker, suffocated when drunken militia torched the miners' tents. The miners struck back in a frenzy. The militia killed thirty miners (and lost three of their men), including strike leader Louis Tikas, who was captured, beaten and shot in the back three times. The massacre outraged more than labor and progressive circles. In Rockefeller's hometown, the *Cleveland Leader* said: "The charred bodies of two dozen women and children show that Rockefeller knows how to win!" And he did win, rejecting even President Wilson's appeal for a settlement. On April 28 President Wilson sent in federal troops. At least seventy-four people had died by the time they restored order, one of them beaten to death by Linderfelt himself. The bankrupt UMW finally abandoned the strike in December 1914.

In January 1915, the Rockefellers were firmly in the gunsights of Senator Frank Walsh, a Missouri Progressive appointed by Wilson to chair the U.S. Commission on Industrial Relations. Bowers covered his eyes as he confessed that the massacre was "a sickening, disgusting, disgraceful piece of work. . . . I wish I could forget everything about it." Nobody expected much of Junior, but with the shrewd counseling of Mackenzie King, the whizz kid of Canadian politics, he gracefully distanced himself from his father's obduracy with a public confession of error. He invited the doughty Mother Jones, 84, to his office, proposed a form of company union and made a goodwill visit to Colorado where he danced with the miners' wives. The UMW finally won recognition in 1933.

BATTLE OF BAYONNE: The striker firing a pistol is retaliating at the random fire from private guards that killed six workers at the Standard Oil refinery in Bayonne, New Jersey, in June 1915.

Of deputies like those (right) waiting for strikers at the Williamsburg Sugar Plant in July 1910, Joe Hill (inset) wrote in his poem "There Is Power in a Union":

If you like sluggers to beat off your head,
Then don't organize, all unions despise,
If you want nothing before you are dead,
Shake hands with your boss and look wise.

Swedish-born Joel Emmanuel Hägglund, alias Joe Hill, was the popular songwriter of the Wobblies. He wrote "The Preacher and the Slave" (which gave us the phrase "pie in the sky"), "Casey Jones—The Union Scab," "Nearer My Job to Thee" and "The Rebel Girl" (see page 118). He lived on the road in the West, organizing strikers. He passed into legend in November 1915, when, at about the age of 43, he was executed by a firing squad in Utah, convicted on shaky evidence of killing a Salt Lake City grocer. On the eve of his execution he wired: "Don't waste any time in mourning. *Organize.*" The mourners carrying his body to the massive funeral in Chicago (above) had, like the 30,000 others present, little doubt that he was framed for being a Wobbly.

SOCIALISM'S MILLION: Eugene Debs drew large crowds five or six times a day in his fourth run for the presidency. He won at least 901,000 votes, setting a new Socialist party record. Such was the fraud, however, that he was not credited with a single vote in his own district.

THE BULL MOOSE RUNS AMOK

Barbed wire and a thousand policemen protected Senator Elihu Root when he took the chair at the Republican convention in Chicago in 1912. What the party leaders feared was not infiltration by the Socialists, or disruption from Wobblies, but a full-blooded assault on the platform by "the Colonel." Teddy Roosevelt was now perceived by his old party as a dangerous revolutionary, and one bound to be enraged by the rulings of Chairman Root, his one-time secretary of state, that would give the nomination to Taft.

Roosevelt did want to grab a pistol and charge. "I wouldn't have wasted a bullet on a policeman," he said, "I would have got Root and got him quick." He had cause to be mad. He had become the favorite of the rank-and-file Republicans with his barnstorming Progressive speeches in the two years since his return from Africa. He won 289 delegates from states operating the new party primaries; Taft got only 71. But the system that Roosevelt had used to railroad the nomination for Taft in 1908 was still working. Despite the primaries, Taft still led 472 to 439 in total delegates. When Roosevelt's hoarse and angry supporters crowded into the Florentine Room of the Congress Hotel at 2 a.m., he jumped up on a table and declared, "Let us find out if the Republican party is the party of the plain people or the party of the bosses and the professional radicals." On August 6 in Chicago, 10,000 frenzied supporters singing "Onward Christian Soldiers" formed a new Progressive party behind Roosevelt. The candidate told the newspapers: "I'm feeling like a bull moose."

The Democratic party, which stood to benefit most from the split, was still the old coalition of rural southerners, Irish-Americans in the industrial states, city bosses, and western radicals led by Bryan, but it had an inspiring new crusader, as morally righteous as Bryan but with a colder, more analytical mind. To a friend, Woodrow Wilson described the election as between "a real, vivid person" (Roosevelt), and "a vague conjectural personality, more made up of opinions . . . than of human traits and red corpuscles" (himself). Wilson had been a laissez-faire conservative most of his life, scathing of the "crude and ignorant minds of the Populists." When he had run for governor of New Jersey in 1910 he had been opposed by labor and Progressives, but had rapidly become their darling by defiance of the bosses who had put him there as a stooge. He used the innate powers of governor as no one before in American history. In four months he turned New Jersey from a corrupt and reactionary boss-corporation state into a model of democracy and progressivism.

Wilson and Roosevelt were imbued with much the same philosophy, elaborated by Herbert Croly in *The Promises of American Life* (1909): unless the state intervened to redress the imbalance of economic power, the American people would be betrayed by their veneration of individual freedom. There were significant differences in the prescriptions for state action between Wilson's New Freedom and Roosevelt's New Nationalism, but victory for either promised the end to government in the interest of only industry, business and finance.

That was what the country wanted. More than three-quarters of the votes went to the three progressives—Wilson, Roosevelt and the Socialist Eugene Debs. Taft finished a poor third. Wilson not only won the presidency but carried the House and Senate with him.

"I WILL MAKE THIS SPEECH OR DIE"

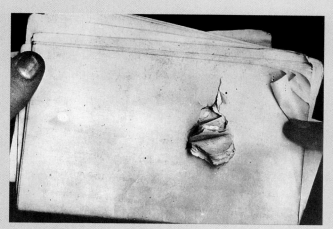

Roosevelt had roused the Bull Moosers: "We stand at Armageddon and we battle for the Lord." In Milwaukee on October 14, 1912, luck at least was on his side. Leaving his hotel to make a speech, he stood in the open car to acknowledge the cheers when a fanatic, John Schrank of New York, shot him in the chest from a distance of only six feet. Schrank said he had a dream in which the shade of McKinley appeared and told him Roosevelt was his murderer.

Roosevelt saved the would-be assassin from a mob lynching, then took the biggest risk of his life by defying the doctors and ordering the driver to go on to the hall. "I will make this speech or die," he said. "It is one thing or the other." He made the speech. The bullet, it was found, had entered his right lung, but its velocity had been spent by passing through his overcoat, a spectacle case, and the folded manuscript of his speech.

(THOMAS) WOODROW WILSON
28th President (Democrat), 1913–1921

Caricature by E. Hine, 1912.

BORN: December 29, 1856, Staunton, Virginia

DIED: February 3, 1924, Washington, D.C.

POLITICAL CAREER: Governor of New Jersey, 1911–1913; President, 1913–1921

FIRST: First, and only, leading academic to become president.

CHARACTER SNAPSHOT: "A lonely man, outwardly cold and remote, inwardly molten passion, with an unparalleled tenacity of faith, an unequaled constancy of courage." —Ray Stannard Baker

BLIND SPOT: Racism. He ordered the segregation of black and white workers in federal offices and removed Southern blacks from federal jobs.

MOST FAMOUS SAYING: "The world must be made safe for democracy" (April 2, 1917).

CHARACTERISTIC QUOTE: "I firmly believe in divine Providence. Without belief in Providence I think I should go crazy. Without God the earth would be a maze without a clue" (1919).

LATE DEVELOPER: He was so sickly, his mother kept him away from school until he was 12. He did not know the alphabet until he was 9 and could not read until he was 11, but he graduated 38th out of 105 at Princeton in 1875. Here he is at 27 at Johns Hopkins University, where he wrote his Ph.D. thesis, "Congressional Government," which compared the American system unfavorably with the British; he admired the scope Parliament gave for oratory. His heroes were the Christian Englishmen William Gladstone, Richard Cobden, John Bright, Edmund Burke and Walter Bagehot; he disliked Jefferson because he was a Deist. In 1885 he went to teach at Bryn Mawr, the new Quaker college for women, and longed to get into politics.

SOUTHERN STYLE: The Wilsons liked to think of themselves as southerners. Wilson's Ohio-born father, Dr. Joseph Ruggles Wilson, whom he revered, is in the center (third row). He was a Presbyterian pastor in Augusta, Georgia, a passionate defender of the South and slavery (the family owned slaves briefly before the Civil War). Woodrow, far left in this loose family group in Columbia, South Carolina, in 1892, was fond of saying: "The only place in the country, the only place in the world, where nothing has to be explained to me is the South." His beloved mother, Janet (Jessie), was born in Carlisle, England, and was brought to America when she was four.

THE DREAMER: He loved words. As a Princeton professor of jurisprudence and political economy from 1890 to 1902, he wrote *A History of the American People* in five volumes, a study of George Washington and two volumes of essays. Students often burst into applause at the end of a lecture. He was a star on the debate circuit. But he still carried in his heart the "deepest secret" he confided to his wife: "to strike out for myself, if I had the ability, a statesman's career."

THE GOVERNOR: With advisers at his mansion at Sea Girt, New Jersey. Within six months of humiliation at Princeton, he was governor of New Jersey and on his way to the White House. He kept his cool, astonishing the Democratic machine that got him the job, by behaving as morally as he promised he would. He stopped election fraud and bribery, regulated utilities and negotiated a viable law for compensating injured workers. He was at Sea Girt playing golf and reading aloud to his family from John Morley's *Life of Gladstone* as the 1912 Democratic convention slogged its way to nominate him on the 46th ballot. He was so poor he had to borrow to buy new clothes for the inauguration, so conscious of the sacred nature of his calling that he did not go to the inaugural ball.

LOVING HUSBAND: His family was his heartbeat. As Europe edged toward war in August 1914, he was crushed by the death of the woman he had married 29 years before, Ellen Louise Axson (seated). It was, as he said in a love letter to her a year before, a union of "wedded sweethearts." Her last thought was that someone should look after him. It was through his daughter Margaret (left) that he met and in December 1915 married the woman who did, Mrs. Norman Galt, formerly Edith Bolling. He typed out the news himself, concluding: "It is indeed the most interesting circumstance connected with the engagement just announced that the President's daughters should have picked Mrs. Galt out for their special admiration and friendship before their father did."

TRIUMPH AND DEFEAT: Princeton worshiped its president in the first four of his eight years in office (1902–1910). Other universities copied his curriculum. He raised money, put up eight buildings, borrowed the tutorial system from Oxford as a bridge between students and faculty. But his "scheme of salvation" to do away with the exclusive eating clubs in favor of something more like the dining halls of English colleges was defeated by alumni after a bitter four-year battle. It helped to radicalize him.

THE PROFESSOR
TESTS HIS
THEORIES

Woodrow Wilson, the political greenhorn with the priggish manner, swiftly fashioned the Democratic party into an instrument of national purpose. His dazzling metamorphosis, in two years, from professor to governor and then president, did not for one second turn his head. On his White House desk, and with him until the day he died, was a framed copy of the poem he had cut out of the *American Magazine* in October 1910. It was Rudyard Kipling's "If," which begins:

If you can keep your head when all about you
Are losing theirs and blaming it on you;
And if you can trust yourself when all men
. . . doubt you,
But make allowances for their doubting
too . . .

The injunction to avoid self-doubt was redundant. Wilson's faith in God's ordering of his destiny never left him. He prayed every night and morning on his knees. It was the sentiment in the last line that gave him trouble. He could not bear friends who took a different view on the big issues. They were judged morally corrupt. He did not, in any event, make friends easily. As Arthur Schlesinger, Jr., put it, no one known to history ever called him Woody. He lived an isolated life; in the evenings, when he rarely worked, he read short stories and poems aloud to his wife and daughters or went to the theater. Walter Lippmann thought his personality was chilly because he had too much feeling, not too little. Beyond the intimate family circle, he was not robust enough to withstand the strain of allowing himself to feel too deeply about other people. His confidant Colonel Edward House—his ambassador to the lower world of politics, in biographer August Heckscher's phrase—advised a friend that Wilson could be won only through his emotions: "Never begin by arguing. Discover a common hate, exploit it, get the President warmed up, then start your business." Wilson could hate people with a vengeance—Teddy Roosevelt, for instance. But generally his emotions became attached to ideas rather than to men and women. Senator John Sharp

Wilson suffered so much from neuritis and indigestion that he carried a stomach pump into the White House and used it frequently until put on a better regime by his White House physician, Admiral Cary T. Grayson.

called him "the best judge of measures and the poorest of men I ever knew."

All this makes more extraordinary his instant triumph in the personality-charged world of politics. There was such an ache for leadership. Roosevelt had been the first president since Lincoln to exploit the president's powers of national leadership. Wilson surpassed him in fusing the legislative and executive functions in his own person. "The President," he had written in his Ph.D. thesis, "is at liberty both in law and conscience to be as big as he can."

Of course, it helped that the Democrats controlled both houses of Congress, that there was an infusion of new Northern progressives, that he had the power of patronage and was unashamed to use it, that the generous William Jennings Bryan was there to coax party rebels and that the Republican party was a demoralized rump. But the real force was Wilson's inner radiance. It for a long time transcended his personal limitations. There was a synergy between his religion and a Rousseauesque faith in the moral will of the people. All men counted with him but none too much. Passion, he said, might overcome an individual's sense of right, but it could not for long overbear the people's. The American people could not govern themselves, but their representatives could rule correctly only if they heeded the people's sense of what was true and right.

This deference to the sovereign will of the people was a convenient, as well as an intoxicating, thought for Wilson, since he found that his eloquence could stir a deep response. He used the power immediately in his presidency. When Congress met in joint session on April 7, 1913, there was the erect prideful figure of the President briskly demanding a major reduction in the tariff. It was the first time a president had been seen on that rostrum since John Adams in 1797. And when lobbyists descended in droves to thwart the bill, industrial America's first venture into free trade, Wilson cowed the more protectionist senators with a ringing appeal for public opinion to resist the interest of private profit. The bill passed, and with it the first graduated federal tax on incomes, authorized by the Sixteenth Amendment, which had been ratified during Taft's presidency.

Wilson was by no means a radical reformer. His New Freedom program, articulated best by another pair of transplanted southerners, Louis D. Brandeis and William G. McAdoo, was Jeffersonian in its vision. Brandeis and McAdoo did not trust bigness in any form and believed that it must be constantly combated in the cause of preserving individual freedoms. Wilson's version was essentially passive, based on the faith that simply to remove restrictions on most American liberties was enough. Wilson's rhetoric was often populist, but his instincts remained conservative. He legislated so that labor unions could not automatically be regarded as trusts illegally in restraint of trade, but he refused to give unions the total immunity they sought for actions such as the secondary boycott. On trusts, he had given the impression in the election that he would atomize big business so as to return America to a Jeffersonian condition where small entrepreneurs engaged in free competition. Forward-looking men, as Richard Hofstadter put it, were needed for a return to the past. He had denounced Roosevelt's New Nationalism, honed and expanded by Herbert Croly, author of the

The Promise of American Life, and the former Morgan executive George W. Perkins. They argued that bigness in business was inevitable, even desirable, and that the remedy was not to try and break it up, but to regulate it in the public interest. Wilson ultimately came to believe that they were right. He came to see that the creative complexity of business made it impracticable to identify anticompetitive practices by statute. Quietly, he let the Clayton Anti-Trust Act be emasculated so that, as one senator complained, it did not have enough teeth to masticate milk toast. Instead, Wilson adopted Roosevelt's approach of regulation. On September 26, 1914, he created the Federal Trade Commission, with power to investigate and prevent unfair competition. He staffed it with conservatives.

The circumscription of reform was implicit in what was regarded at the time as most radical, his creation of the Federal Reserve banking system. Thirty years of agitation about the money system by Populists and Greenbackers had been derided. Now both big parties agreed that something had to be done. Hundreds of banks failed between 1900 and 1912. Ealier gold and banking panics in 1893 and 1895 had been resolved by J. P. Morgan acting as bankers' banker, summoning financiers to his library and sitting them down under a sixteenth-century tapestry, *The Triumph of Avarice,* while they worked out which banks they would save and how. But the panic that struck in 1907 panic was too big even for Morgan and his syndicates. He had to ask Roosevelt's Treasury to pump in federal funds. When Charles Barney of the fashionable Knickerbocker bank had come around to Morgan's library to seek help to avoid default, he could not get in to see the great man and shot himself. As John Kenneth Galbraith remarked: "A central bank would have at least let Barney in."

The obvious need was a central bank that would create money and lend reserves to the banks. Less obvious was who should run it. To bankers, the answer was axiomatic. But could America be a real democracy if a handful of men on Wall Street controlled the nation's credit? Wilson was presented with a conservative consensus in favor of a scheme for reserve banks in 15 (later 12) regions, owned and operated by the region's banks. He insisted on a "capstone" to represent the public in-

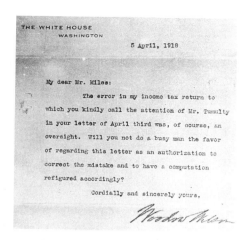

President Wilson's letter of April 5, 1918, to Joshua W. Miles of the Internal Revenue Service, asking him to clarify the already convoluted procedure of filing one's income tax.

terest, a Federal Reserve Board appointed by the president, "so that the banks may be the instruments, not the masters, of business and of individual enterprise and initiative." All hell broke loose. The *New York Sun,* speaking for Wall Street, said the Reserve Board was "covered all over with the slime of Bryanism."

Wilson kept Congress at work all through a sticky summer, and right into the Christmas recess. He signed the Federal Reserve Act on December 23, 1913. It was the most significant reform of his presidency, a unique mix of private and public control. It probably prevented a number of bank failures. It would have prevented more if conservative interests had not killed a scheme for deposit insurance, which would have discouraged panic. As it was, with thousands of banks outside the system, the failures increased in the next 20 years. The reform certainly did not bring democracy to the money system in the sense of giving citizens a real say in their economic destiny. There is force in the conclusion of William Greider, in his 1987 history, *Secrets of the Temple,* that the creation of the Fed, insulated from politics and public scrutiny, "effectively defined the permanent limits of American democracy." It remains today the most secretive and least effectively scrutinized of the public institutions.

Wilson went as far as he could. By the the end of his presidency he had achieved a record of positive legislation greater than any previous administration and equaled only twice since, Franklin Roosevelt and Lyndon Johnson.

U.S. AMBASSADOR TOASTS AN ASSASSIN

Two weeks before Woodrow Wilson was inaugurated in 1913, the American ambassador in Mexico, Henry Lane Wilson, conspired with generals who betrayed and murdered the first president of Mexico ever chosen by the people in a free election. Francisco I. Madero had been borne into office in November 1911, in the wake of the first major revolution of the twentieth century. He came from a rich mining and ranching family, but he was an ascetic young idealist whose heart bled for the peasants forced into peonage by the theft of their lands. There were 15 million Mexicans, mostly Catholics and mostly mestizo (a mix of European and Indian stock). The wealth of their country was owned by 1 percent of them—and by foreigners. American individuals or companies owned 43 percent and Europeans, principally British and Germans, owned another 25 percent; they all paid little in fees or taxes. American business interests, such as the Guggenheim, Rockefeller and Aldrich families, owned almost all the mines and smelters, as well as two thirds of the railways, and shared the oil rights with Britain's Lord Cowdray.

Ambassador Wilson saw himself as the emissary for these corporations and 40,000 Americans living in Mexico. He wanted Madero supplanted by another "strongman" like the deposed dictator Porfirio Díaz, who had run Mexico for the benefit of the few for over 34 years. The ambassador's new Díaz was General Victoriano Huerta, an old Indian fighter, described by a reporter as "an ape-like old man, of almost pure Indian blood who may almost be said to subsist on alcohol." Madero trusted Huerta enough to give him command of suppressing a half-baked coup led by a nephew of Díaz. But in ten days of battle in Mexico City, Huerta secretly went over to the rebels, then arranged for Madero to be seized. At this point, Ambassador Wilson called the capital diplomats to the American embassy, read out the names of the new cabinet members, who had been arranged in an adjoining room and introduced them to Huerta, whom he embraced and toasted. The Texas legislature and Madero's wife rushed appeals to President Taft to do something to save the de-

TRAITOR: President Madero trusted General Huerta (center), who betrayed him to a counterrevolution. President Wilson called Huerta "that desperate brute . . . that scoundrel so false and sly." The braided general (left) is the supposedly loyal Aureliano Blanquet, who seized Madero and his vice president in the National Palace.

FIXER: Henry Lane Wilson, the U.S. ambassador in Mexico City.

MARTYR: Francisco I. Madero reads a peace message during the 1911 fighting (his wife is on the step behind him).
REBEL: Fortino Samano (right) passed into legend for his nonchalance in the face of a Huerta firing squad in 1914. He refused a blindfold and gave the troops the order to fire.

posed president (Madero had lived in San Antonio for a time and was regarded as a humane man). There was no response. Huerta then sanctioned the murder of Madero ("shot while trying to escape") and set about trying to run the country from behind a cognac bottle in his favorite bar, the Café Colón.

WILSON'S EXERCISE IN MORAL IMPERIALISM

The blood on the hands of the new strongman of Mexico, Victoriano Huerta, did not deter the European governments. They promptly recognized his provisional regime. Woodrow Wilson was expected to do the same. It was the historic American practice to recognize all governments in power. He might have demurred on the grounds that Huerta's rule was not secure. The men who had backed Madero had taken up the torch again. Huerta was being fought in the north by Constitutionalists led by a stubborn old anticlerical patriot, Governor Venustiano Carranza. In the northwest there was Pancho Villa, the swaggering, unschooled outlaw and bandit. In the southwest there was the apostle of the poor, the peasant army leader Emiliano Zapata, who sheltered under the world's largest sombrero a clear head and a heart full of compassion for the landless Indians.

Wilson did not use the excuse of disorder. He announced a dramatic new doctrine of American foreign policy. Huerta's "government of butchers" would not be recognized, he said, because it did not rest on the consent of the governed. A British diplomat wearing a cutaway was received by Wilson in a gray sack suit and told: "I am going to teach the South American Republics to elect good men!" Wilson and his secretary of state, William Jennings Bryan, negotiated with Huerta for a new election in October 1913. When Carranza defeated Huerta's army in the north, Huerta panicked. On October 10, his troops surrounded the pro-Maderista Chamber of Deputies in the Mexican Congress, and 110 deputies were imprisoned. The elections went ahead all the same, with the predictable result—a tame Congress, and Huerta appointed emergency president.

The event turned Wilson the constitutional theorist into a revolutionary. Rejecting the business community's clamor that he accept Huerta for the sake of order, he retorted: "No one asks for order because order will help the masses of the people to get a portion of their rights and their land; but all demand it so that the great owners of property, the overlords, the hidalgos, the men who have exploited that rich country for their own selfish pur-

THE COUP: Wilson's pacifist secretary of state, William Jennings Bryan (right, with bodyguard), backed the idea of forcing Huerta out. A year after Huerta quit, Bryan got wind of a State Department plot to put him back. Leon J. Canova, Bryan's head adviser on Mexico, backed a pro-Huerta coup led by an exiled Mexican general, Eduardo Iturbide. The general had the support of Roman Catholic leaders in America who sought to repeal the separation of church and state enacted in Mexico 50 years before. Bryan squashed the plot. Huerta was ultimately intercepted at the border and interned in Texas for the remaining months of his life.

poses, shall be able to continue their processes undisturbed by the protests of the people from whom their wealth and power have been obtained." He revoked President Taft's veto on supplying munitions to the revolutionaries. He lay awake at night and prayed for guidance about how to depose the dictator. The answer of Providence was to arrange an incident in Tampico on April 9, 1914. American sailors landing to load supplies without permission were arrested by Mexican troops awaiting attack by Carranza. Huerta's local commander ordered their release as soon as he heard, with profuse apologies. It was not enough for the commander of the American squadron, Admiral Henry T.

Mayo. He demanded that the Stars and Stripes be raised on shore and given a 21-gun salute. Huerta said they would give the salute if given a gun-for-gun salute in return. As Huerta said, who was he, an unrecognized government, to salute anyone? It was all pantomime.

Wilson seized on the silly argument as a pretext for asking Congress to sanction armed intervention (approved by the House April 20), intending to force Huerta out. Wilson was eager to act, so consumed with emotion at being thwarted by "a desperate brute," that he misrepresented to Congress the treatment of American citizens and property in Mexico—it had been exemplary. And he did not wait for Senate approval when, on April 21, he was awakened at 2 a.m. with the news that the German steamer, the *Ypiranga*, would the following morning land ammunition for Huerta at Veracruz. He telephoned orders to seize the port. One thousand Marines and sailors went ashore at Veracruz at 11 a.m. on April 21, and 3,000 the next day. It did not work out as Wilson expected. Instead of embracing the Americans, the Mexicans defended their sacred soil. "Viva Mexico! Death to the gringos!" was the cry of Carranza's men as well as Huerta's. Nineteen Americans and 126 Mexicans died in the fighting.

World opinion saw it not as idealism but Yankee imperialism. Anti-American riots broke out in South America. At home Wilson was mocked as a hypocrite. He recoiled. "The thought haunts me," he told Admiral Grayson, "that it was I who ordered those young men to their deaths." Looking "preternaturally pale, almost parchmenty," he vetoed the Army's plans for taking Mexico City, and with alacrity accepted an offer of mediation from Argentina, Brazil and Chile. In June at Niagara Falls the U.S. agreed to accept whatever provisional government might emerge from the civil war. Huerta decided it was time for a quieter life and took the *Ypiranga* into exile in July 1914. In August Carranza rode in triumph into Mexico City. He was not grateful to Wilson. He resented the interference. But the Mexican Revolution was not over and Wilson had not given up his desire to give it constitutional guidance.

WILSON'S LITTLE WARS

This depiction of a vampirish Woodrow Wilson with an appetite for Latin American blood (right) was published in a German magazine. The viewpoint may have been chauvinistic; Germany had its own clear designs on the Caribbean. But U.S. interventions were becoming frequent. In addition to Mexico, the U.S. intervened in Cuba (1898–1902, 1906–1909); the Dominican Republic (1916–1924); Nicaragua (1912–1925, 1926–1933) and Haiti (1915–1934). The usual rationale was to protect American citizens and their property, but it was also to take control of customs so as to repay international debts the occupied countries had run up.

Haiti had been in turmoil ever since the French quit in 1804, with "full" blacks pitted against mulattoes, Creole-speaking peasantry against French-speaking aristocracy, north against south. Secretary of State Bryan found it baffling. "Dear me," he said after a briefing, "Think of it! Niggers speaking French!" U.S. warships had been compelled to sail into Haitian harbors on 12 occasions in the 50 years up to 1889 and almost every year after that, but in the anarchic violence of 1915 Wilson decided military occupation was necessary. It lasted 19 years.

The occupation was generally benign. Armed resistance, which ended in 1919, was limited to a few peasant bandit-rebel bands of Cacos. The U.S. built an infrastructure of highways, bridges, airfields, hospitals, a telephone service, lighting and an entire national health system from scratch. Haitians who protested were occasionally jailed, but in general there was more freedom of the press than at any other time in the country's history—and it was used to pour invective on the Americans. The occupation ended under Franklin Roosevelt's Good Neighbor policy, but the mere presence of 1,000 Marines and American businesses had stimulated an anti-imperialist fervor among the elite's university-educated sons and daughters. Good intentions and good works accomplished little. The U.S. had not felt it worthwhile to try to build a real democratic tradition, and after the occupation a new series of dictators, culminating with the horrific François "Papa Doc" Duvalier in 1957, returned the country to bloody despair. All the nice improvements in the infrastructure were left to crumble. In 1994, amid still more anarchy following the Haitian Army's expulsion of an elected leader, President Clinton felt he had to do what Wilson had done, and once again send in the Marines.

THE CRUCIFIXION: The Haitian rebel Charlemagne Massena Peralte, like Aguinaldo in the Philippines, was done in by perfidy. Some 18 American-trained Haitian "gendarmes," led by two Marine officers in blackface, entered his camp pretending to be a reconnaissance patrol. Once within range, Captain H. H. Hanneken shot him twice through the heart. Gendarmes placed the body on a door to be photographed for proof that he was dead (right). The picture only gave rise to the popular story that he had been crucified on the door, leading to a masterly painting by Philone Obin in 1946. Peralte's body was buried in concrete to preclude its use for voodoo, but it still became a voodoo "loa" (spirit). The painting adorns churches as part of Haiti's Catholic-nationalist tradition enshrining Charlemagne as a martyr.

"Now America is nicely in the soup!" reads the caption for this caricature drawn for a German magazine by the Norwegian caricaturist Olaf Gulbransson.

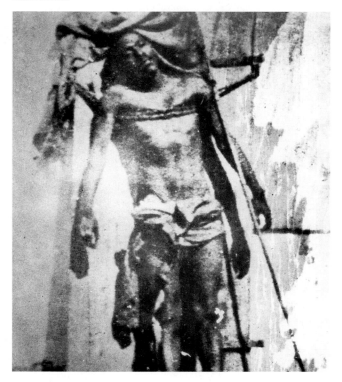

PERSHING CHASES PANCHO

Mexico's rebel patriot Pancho Villa was portrayed in American newspapers and the movies as a Robin Hood. The photograph above is a 1914 still shot by Mutual Films, which paid him $25,000 to allow its cameras at his battles. He promised to fight by daylight, and when the film crews were not ready for his attempt to take the city of Ojinaga, he delayed the attack. Ojinaga fell to Villa and film. Villa, adored by his men for his bravery and his coarse, blunt humor, was a military innovator. He

was the first Mexican to abandon the custom of taking the women and children along with the army. He made swift forced marches of bodies of cavalry, which struck terror into the enemy.

Even President Wilson joined the fan club, in midsummer 1914. When Villa started a new round of civil war against his former revolutionary ally Venustiano Carranza, following the exile of Huerta, Wilson thought Villa would win. He secretly encouraged him. He seemed a neighborly

revolutionary, on the side of the peons but also a protector of the considerable American property in the northern area he controlled. Unlike Carranza, he had even backed Wilson's seizure of Veracruz. John Reed rode with Villa and admired him, but another reporter presciently remarked that he had "the eyes of a man who will some day go crazy." He seemed to Americans to go crazy when he lost the big civil war battles and Wilson gave de facto recognition to Carranza. On January 10,

1916, Villa stopped a train at Santa Ysabel in Mexico and murdered 17 American miners and engineers on board. On March 9, he crossed the border to sack the town of Columbus, New Mexico. Nineteen Americans died before he was driven off. The madness had a cause. Villa felt betrayed by Wilson. Carranza had been able to make an end-run around Villa's forces only by getting American permission to go through U.S. territory.

Villa's intention was to provoke America into war with Mexico so that he could exploit the turmoil. He might have succeeded but for Wilson. The president or-

dered General "Black Jack" Pershing to cross the Rio Grande with a force of 5,800 men in pursuit of Villa.

Wilson's interventions in Mexico embittered relations for years, but he was, for all his mistakes, a friend of the Mexican Revolution. When Carranza became president in March 1916, Wilson, against business protests, gave Mexico full recognition, despite a new constitution that vested mineral and oil rights in the state. If Taft had been in the White House, Huerta might have been preserved in his dictatorship and the Mexican Revolution could have been even longer and bloodier.

General Pershing (right) with Pancho Villa in 1914. When he wanted him in 1916, he could not find him.

CHAPTER SIX

GOOD TIMES, BAD TIMES
1914–1920

The Last Summer of Peace

There seemed barely a storm cloud in the American sky in the summer of 1916. The country's population had just passed 100 million. The war in Europe was a long way away, but it was stimulating an export boom that gave working Americans an astonishing 13 percent increase in purchasing power in just two years. Farmworkers and the unskilled shared in the prosperity. The infant mortality rate—a key indicator of a country's well-being—had improved by 40 percent from the turn of the century. Five million automobiles were registered, a threefold increase over 1914, which meant every fifth household had wheels. The roads were still a little rough, but it was exhilarating to drive on the natural prairie tracks on a hot summer's day.

There had been a hiccup in Wilson's progressive program through 1914 and 1915. Delegations of women seeking national suffrage legislation had been turned away from the White House with the answer that it was a matter for the states. He had refused protection for women and children in factories. But in 1916 he switched back to a progressive mode. He promised a child labor law and farm credits. And his reelection campaign ("He kept us out of war") suggested that America could count on peace. But thunder was in the air. Within a year America was at war and the Russian Revolution had begun.

A fine August day in western Nebraska in 1916. The passengers were probably farmers being shown land they might buy.

SAVING THE WORLD FOR DEMOCRACY

The evolution of Woodrow Wilson from fastidious neutralist in 1914 to belligerent in April 1917 was of more lasting significance than the clash of armies in the fields of France. It was not merely that his final decision to lead America into the war on the side of Britain and France sealed the fate of Germany. If Teddy Roosevelt had still been president, he, too, would have put America's power behind the Allies; he would have declared war earlier than "Professor Wilson . . . that Byzantine logothete." To him, the issue was simpler. Germany was too powerful. It had infringed on American rights. It had to be put in its place. Roosevelt would have exploited the vengeful emotions aroused by the loss of American lives at sea, but his decision would have been rooted in a cooler calculation. He saw victory for a militarist Germany as upsetting the balance of power in Europe. A resurgent imperial Germany, unimpeded by the British fleet, would be in a position to threaten America's security and especially its national interests in South and Central America.

Roosevelt's perception of America's self-interest in the survival of the Allies was shared by many in the Wilson administration and in the country. Wilson's second secretary of state, Robert Lansing, complained to his diary in 1916: "For six months I have talked about the struggle between Autocracy and Democracy, but it does not seem that I have made any great impression." Wilson's intellectual and moral agonies were initially about how he could preserve the historic rights of American citizens to trade with the belligerents and to travel freely without at the same time compromising strict American neutrality, but this apparently narrow detachment, which so irritated Lansing and Roosevelt, was deceptive. The lofty principles that competed in the cathedral of Wilson's mind flowered as an exalted vision of America's role in the world, nothing less than a commitment to defend liberty and democracy everywhere. His decision to fight Germany was an epiphany rather than an exercise in realpolitik. He renounced self-interest. "We look for no profit. We look for no advantage. . . . We are fighting for what we believe and wish to be the rights of mankind and for the future peace and security of the world." Not content with rationalizing the immediate decision, he proposed an unprecedented doctrine for relations between states. Moral principle, rather than military power, should be the governing force in a world organization of democracies dedicated to mutual security, a league of nations. The universal interest in peace was to be superior to national interests. Roosevelt would have gone to war to remedy grievances and restore an equilibrium in the balance of power. Wilson sought nothing less than the destruction of the principle of balance of power; and he declared that America had no special grievance. It was going to war "because we have always said we were the friends and servants of mankind."

Wilson's original and stunning conception was only a faint shadow in his first foreign-policy conflicts. He justified military interventions in Haiti, Mexico, the Dominican Republic and Nicaragua by the need to uphold democratic processes (where none had existed). In a speech in Mobile, Alabama, in 1913, he envisioned a Pan-American system of mutual security between the United States and Latin American states. These were seeds for germination. His underlying imperatives were, in fact, no different from those that animated Roosevelt and Taft. European powers must not be allowed to gain preeminence in the Western Hemisphere; U.S. routes to the Panama Canal must remain invulnerable. Little of the reluctance Wilson showed over entering the European conflict was manifest in his response to these other foreign alarms. He sanctioned more military interventions than any other president before or since. Foreign policy as a moral crusade, Wilsonianism, only took shape as he wrestled over three years with the dilemmas imposed on America by the decision to stay neutral in the European war, and his yearning to seize the opportunity for reordering the universe.

His neutralism was heartfelt. Well into the First World War, in the autumn of 1915, the acting secretary of war, Henry Breckinridge, found him "trembling and white with passion" over an obscure paragraph in the *Baltimore Sun* reporting that the General Staff was preparing a plan in the event of war with Germany. Wilson ordered Breckinridge to relieve at once every officer of the General Staff and order them out out of Washington. In a cooler moment, he allowed the order to lapse, but the very idea of war games offended his sense of propriety. Hearing about the War College's continuing war games the next year, he told Secretary of War Newton Baker: "That seems to me a very dangerous occupation. I think you had better stop it." Wilson's concept of neutrality was not passive. It had a moral core and a positive purpose from the start. Keeping the peace between the millions of Americans with blood links to the warring powers was some small part of it. Supremely, he wanted to stay cool so that both sides in the conflict would turn to him for salvation as the prince of peace. In his memoir, Secretary Baker recalls: "The President thought the war had made him an instrument of Providence, but he thought it humbly."

Wilson was resisting his natural impulses in his attempt to be scrupulously neutral. He had an affinity with all things English. His idea of spiritual refreshment was a bicycling holiday in the Lake District. He was surrounded by men who wanted the Allies to win, with the sole exception of his pacifist secretary of state, William Jennings Bryan, who resigned in 1915. Lansing, the pedantic lawyer who succeeded Bryan, believed Germany a menace to America's long-term security. Wilson's ambassador to London, Walter Hines Page, was such an Anglophile he helped the British Foreign Office draft replies to awkward U.S. notes. And Colonel Edward House, Wilson's chief confidant and personal link to the British Foreign Secretary, Sir Edward Grey, was an unremitting advocate of strategies that would bring America into the war on the side of the Allies. House identified so much with the Allied cause that he allowed the head of the British secret service in the United States, Sir William Wiseman, to sit in his office in New York and read the most secret U.S. documents. But whatever the pull of Wilson's terrestrial relationships, none was as important as his citizenship, in the words of biographer Arthur Link, in another, invisible world—the world of the spirit in which a sovereign God reigned in justice and in love, an ordered universe where nations as well as men transgressed the divine ordinances at their peril. His passion to do God's work as the maker of a permanent peace overrode everything else.

Wilson's concept of an ethereal detachment from the conflict soon collided with reality. How could America stay aloof when its trading partners, now belligerents, beat a path to its door for the output of its farms and factories, and for capital? Wilson wrestled prayerfully with his feelings of revulsion about trading in munitions. It was, he wrote a critic, "one of the most perplexing things I have had to decide." On the day of Ellen Wilson's funeral in August 1914, Bryan appealed to him to stop J.P. Morgan and Company from floating a bond offering of $100 million for the French government. "Money," said Bryan, "is the worst of all contrabands—it commands all other things." Wilson agreed. He squelched it. In September he ordered the takeover of two German wireless stations in New Jersey and Long Island. In November he stopped Bethlehem Steel from selling submarines to Britain. But as the debate on complex questions of neutrality heated up late in 1914, Wilson came to realize that if he went on making case-by-case judgments guided by his conscience, he could always be accused of bias by one side or another. He found intellectual refuge in the law. If he followed the rules of international law as best he could, his conscience would be clear and his neutrality would have authority. It was of enduring significance when he made up his mind in this direction. Lansing, then Bryan's counselor at the State Department, advised the President that international law imposed no duty upon a neutral to restrict the trade in arms, three distinguished international lawyers asserted an embargo would be an "absolute violation of neutrality" and endorsement followed from an unexpected quarter. In a memorandum of December 15, 1914, the German government also affirmed that traffic in arms was entirely legal and proper. (It was nurturing such a trade with the neutrals Holland and Scandinavia.) Even Bryan, the troubador of peace and goodwill to all, came to the conclusion that an embargo would be flagrantly unneutral, and had his name hissed at rallies of the friends of the Fatherland for saying so. Those who sympathized with Germany, said Bryan, "appear to assume that some obligation rests upon this government, in the performance of its neutral duty, to prevent all trade in contraband and thus to equalize the difference due to the relative naval strengths of the belligerents. No such obligation exists; it would be an unneutral act, an act of partiality on the part of the United States to adopt such a policy if the Executive had the power to do so. If Germany and Austria-Hungary cannot import contraband from this country it is not because of that fact, the duty of the United States to close its markets to the allies. The markets of this country are open upon equal terms to all the world. . . ."

Wilson's decision, as always, was buttressed by moral rationalization. It would be injurious to the noble cause of disarmament, he said, to deny arms to the side least prepared for war (words not heeded in the nineties, when the Western powers denied arms to Bosnia); and it would be immoral to deny trade that was in the national interest. In October the French

SHIPS OF PEACE: A peace delegation aboard the liner *Noordam* en route to a women's peace congress in The Hague, April 13, 1915. The trailblazing social worker Jane Addams is fourth from the left. Later in the year a spectacular Jewish Hungarian woman, Rosika Schwimmer, took Henry Ford up on his statement that he would give half his fortune to shorten the war by a single day. On December 4, 1915, he chartered the steamship *Oscar II* and sailed for Europe with her and a party of other peace pilgrims. "We'll get the boys out of the trenches by Christmas," he said. It was a brave and generous initiative, but Wilson refused to bless the voyage, the press hooted with derision, the Dutch refused to let the group set up headquarters at The Hague and the pilgrims squabbled among themselves. Ford caught a cold in Norway and came home. He also caught a touch of paranoia that flowered unbeautifully into anti-Semitism after the war.

asked the National City Bank for $10 million, and both Bryan and Wilson let it happen, patching over the earlier objection to money-raising by declaring that this was a banking credit and not a sale of bonds to the public. Private (and later public) credit flowed freely thereafter. Germany raised $10 million soon after the French. Of course, as the war developed, the decision to trade freely with all comers was a decision to trade with the Allies. Even at the start of the war, U.S. trade with the Allies was ten times greater than with the Central Powers. By 1916 U.S.-German trade had collapsed to $1 million; trade with the Allies had grown from $824 million to $3,124 million. Much of this was in munitions, and without it the Allies would have had to surrender in 1915. When the war began, the British and French, unlike the Germans, did not have the war industries or the machine-tools industry to equip new armaments factories. Only American machine tools and know-how and American munitions could keep the Allies in the war until they had rebuilt their industries; that took until 1917.

In the thirties, revisionist historians and politicians of the left attempted to portray Wilson's decision to go to war as part of a deep-laid plot. In this scenario, Wilson is presented as a tool of the profiteering munitions makers and bankers, and a sucker of the propagandists. It is true that when Wilson tolerated the development of America as arsenal and banker, he knew it would help him with the domestic economy. But if the profit motive was a persuasive element in the decision to allow trading with belligerents, it cannot explain America's own transition from neutrality to belligerence: Why risk a good thing? Any Daddy Warbucks could calculate that America's entry into the war would sooner or later end the war, and with it the trade in its instruments.

If international law and custom gave Wilson succor in his decision on trade, he had a harder time with the consequences. The goods had to be shipped across the Atlantic. The British fleet was dominant, but the Germans had a new weapon, the U-boat, whose raison d'être cut across previous understandings of maritime law. The stars by which Wilson tried to navigate some very tricky passages from 1914 to 1917, the laws of contraband and of the sea, were a jumble of precedents. Such as it was, the law of the sea entitled belligerents to blockade enemy ports and stop and search a neutral merchant ship for contraband—practically, cargo the belligerent could demonstrate would be of use to the enemy's war effort. The law of contraband suggested it could be seized, and the ship confiscated as a prize of war, if—but only if—she was carrying more than a certain percentage of material for the enemy. An enemy merchant ship could be seized, but could not be fired on and sunk unless she resisted. Citizens of a neutral country could travel as passengers on any ship and risk the inconvenience of an inspection—but not of drowning.

Washington and Berlin and Washington and London argued endlessly about how these rules should be interpreted in the circumstances of total war. Was Germany entitled to sink enemy merchantmen without warning as a reprisal for Britain's allegedly unlawful attempt to starve the Germans to death? Who was culpable if a neutral ship was sunk by accident when British ships camouflaged themselves with neutral flags—and what about a British-owned ship legally flying the American flag under the Ship Registry Act of 1914? Was Britain legally entitled to stop a neutral ship bound for a neutral port if its cargo was continuing its journey to the enemy? Did Britain have any case at all for designating foodstuffs as contraband? Could the Royal Navy lawfully divert shipping to a British port instead of searching it on the high seas? Should America, in the interests of peace, yield the rights of unmolested travel (as William Jennings Bryan argued)? If it sought to protect them, as Wilson did, how could it do so without jeopardizing its neutrality or, at worst, getting involved in the fighting? The British and the Germans had the other side of the coin. How far dare they infringe on these rights in the cause of their own security without sacrificing the goodwill of the most powerful neutral? The admirals in both countries were ready to risk war with America; their political heads were anxious to appease America. These internal and external tensions played themselves out in a complex of dramas on the high seas, each of the incidents coolly examined by Wilson, who locked himself away for hours or days, then tapped out, on his own typewriter, the judicious results of his reflections.

The countdown to war with Germany began in February 1915, when the Kaiser, cornered in the noisy bow of a motor launch by an aggressive admiral, casually nodded to the proposal that the area around Britain should be declared a war zone where every enemy ship would be sunk without warning and neutrals might be sunk, too. But Germany had not anticipated Wilson's strong reaction that it was illegal to hazard neutral lives. Germany would be held "strictly accountable." The first big test was the sinking of the *Lusitania* without warning on May 7, 1915. The British passenger liner was carrying contraband, but 128 Americans were among the 1,198 dead. Wilson based his demand for a disavowal of the act and reparations on the law, but with a Wilsonian flourish. Germany should abandon its indiscriminate campaign, in the name of "sacred principles of justice and humanity." On June 9, 1915, he sent a second, stronger note, which provoked the resignation of Bryan, who had argued that banning Americans from sailing on vessels belonging to belligerents was a small price to pay for peace, but Wilson was not a pacifist in this sense. He believed he was making a stand not just for American rights but for all peace-loving countries. He seemed to have won when, following the deaths of two American citizens on the British passenger ship *Arabic*, the Germans announced in September 1915, that unresisting passenger liners would not be sunk without a warning and evacuation. It was a triumph for Wilson. It secured seven months without incident at sea.

The British offended Wilson often—especially in 1916, when they blacklisted American firms trading with Germany and interfered with U.S. mails—but while Foreign Secretary

DROPPING THE PILOT: William Jennings Bryan was not pushed. He jumped. He did not sleep much in June 1915 because he feared Wilson was compromising neutrality and risking war over the *Lusitania*. He resigned as secretary of state on June 9 rather than sign a tough second note to Germany. "God bless you," said Wilson and Bryan to each other when they clasped hands in farewell. The anti-Bryan press accused him of treason, but for 20 years he had been the sincerest man in politics, and he went into the wilderness with grace and courage. He led the pacifists, but when war broke out he wired Wilson offering his services as a volunteer in any capacity.

Sir Edward Grey was in control of the blockade, until January 1916, they were adroit in labyrinthine defenses of interventions as disputable breaches of law rather than calculated challenges. They could point out that what they were doing was only a slight extension of the Union Navy blockade against the Confederates in 1862–1865. Grey appreciated the workings of Wilson's mind, and the pivots of American politics. When the British added cotton to the contraband list, because of its use in gunpowder, Grey arranged to support the cotton market so as to appease the politically important South, and timed Britain's condemnation of cotton to coincide with America's preoccupation with the sinking of the *Arabic*.

Both Britain and Germany violated America's neutral rights as conventionally understood, but the British seizures by warship, while exasperating, respected the feeling at the beginning of the twentieth century that civilian life—belligerent or neutral—was sacred. The German violations, though fewer in kind, were lethal. The British interfered with American commercial rights. The Germans took American

THE 1916 ELECTION: War-hungry Teddy Roosevelt, the great Bull Moose, hoped to beat the "cowardly" Wilson as the head of a Progressive-Republican ticket. But the old guard Republicans and Eastern capitalists plucked the frosty Charles Evans Hughes from the Supreme Court. He was caricatured as the Kaiser's candidate because he accepted endorsement by the German-American and Irish-American groups that Wilson condemned as disloyal "hyphenates." Hughes was a godlike figure who had been a New York governor and investigator of insurance frauds, but he waged a poor campaign. Trapped between his party's progressive and diehard wings, he ended up appealing to bad-tempered nationalist and protectionist instincts. His wife sat behind him on the platform and pulled his coattails when she felt he had talked long enough. Roosevelt campaigned for him, but privately derided him as "the bearded lady." Wilson, smiling with his new bride, Edith, ignored Republican smears about his love life and stuck to his record of domestic reform and peace. Hughes went to bed thinking he was president, but Wilson won California by 4,000 votes and squeaked home with an electoral-vote margin of 23.

lives. They behaved recklessly. It is commonly suggested that the Germans could not follow the so-called cruiser rules of evacuating a seized ship because they had to effect their blockade by U-boat, an unsuitable vessel for stopping and searching a ship on the high seas. It was true that was risky for a U-boat captain to act as a surface policeman. An armed merchant vessel could sink a thinly plated, lightly armed U-boat, and the British invented the Q-ship, an apparently defenseless trader with concealed guns, to do just that. In August 1915 the British *Baralong,* flying an American flag, sank a U-boat honorably waiting for passengers to disembark from a prize ship. But the Germans could be effective while abiding by cruiser rules, as they showed after they fitted U-boats with deck guns in May 1915. The German Navy, itching to have no restrictions,

did not tell the Kaiser that between May and July 1915 it sank 86 percent of seized merchant ships after visit, search and evacuation. During 1915–16, of 116 German sinkings, 94 were under cruiser rules.

Had the Germans followed these cruiser rules consistently, war with America would have been avoided, but the submarine conflict was almost as much a product of Wilson's prideful insistence on neutral rights as of the failure of the German chancellor, Theobald von Bethmann-Hollweg, to defeat the militarists gaining power around the Kaiser in the deadlocked war in 1916–17. Wilson might have kept American citizens out of the war zones, as the neutrality legislation of the 1930s did. The United States could have advised its citizens against travel on armed vessels, as Texas Representative Jeff McLemore proposed in February 1916, or it could have gone further and enacted a ban on travel on any belligerent ship or neutral ship carrying contraband, as Bryan wanted to do and as the blind senator from Oklahoma, Thomas Gore, proposed in a bill.

Why Wilson did not do that is one of the puzzles of the period, but pride seems relevant. It would have been a small limitation for the sake of staying out of war, and it was one in 1915 he had told Bryan he favored if it was legal. In the spring of 1916 Wilson and Lansing themselves floated the idea of advising Americans to avoid travel on armed ships. It was part of a modus vivendi they were discussing an understanding with Germany by which the Germans would promise not to sink unarmed merchant vessels without giving time for evacuation and the British would be persuaded not to arm them. Wishful thinking! That initiative died because it was so ill received in London as to threaten Wilson's perpetual hopes of being called in as a neutral mediator, and perhaps that was still in his mind when he was faced with a rebellion within the Democratic party. The McLemore resolution would have passed, but Wilson took it as an affront to his leadership. He insisted on its rejection and strained the loyalty of Senator William Stone, the grand old man from Missouri who was an admiring chairman of the Foreign Relations Committee. Stone banged the table in a meeting with the President: The American people did not want to go to war to vindicate the right of a few people to travel or work on armed vessels. "You have no right to ask me to follow this course. It may mean war for my country." Wilson answered back in a searing public letter: "Once accept a single abatement of a right and many other humiliations would certainly follow, and the whole fine fabric of international law might crumble under our hands piece by piece." His letter put a greater value on a minor right than saving a life. He won, but he had staked out unreasonably high ground and made war more likely.

Wilson himself recognized this. He had intended to run his reelection campaign of 1916 on Americanism and Progressivism, but the Democratic convention stampeded for pacifism and he was stuck with the slogan "He kept us out of war." Wilson told Navy Secretary Josephus Daniels: "I can't keep the country out of war. They talk of me as though I were a god. Any little German lieutenant can push us into the war at any time by some calculated outrage." Wilson never pledged that he could continue to keep America at peace. He knew during the election that a new crisis was brewing. His patiently firm diplomacy had given German Chancellor Bethmann-Hollweg time and reason to induce the Kaiser to give the so-called Sussex pledge on May 4, 1916, that Germany would evacuate all captured ships, not just passenger liners but merchantmen as well. There was a rider—that America should induce Britain to relax her starvation blockade. But by October Bethmann-Hollweg had lost influence to the hero of the war in the East, Field Marshal Paul von Hindenburg. "It's a terrible thing to carry around with me," Wilson said to Walter Lippmann as he pulled out of his pocket a cable from the embassy in Berlin predicting that after the election Germany would wage ruthless U-boat warfare. Wilson was trapped by the ultimatum he had given to secure the Sussex pledge: that America would respond to any further torpedo attacks on liners or freight ships by severing diplomatic relations.

He passionately did not want war with Germany. He was by now thoroughly disenchanted with the Allies. American opinion of Britain had taken a nosedive in the wake of the brutal suppression of the Easter Rising in Ireland in April. Wilson had been so infuriated by the intensification of the British blockade, no longer administered by the dextrous Grey, that in November he encouraged the Federal Reserve Bank to cut off credit. Relations with England, he told the bank, were more strained than with Germany. But even more important than the offenses of the British fleet was Britain's reluctance to allow Wilson to set the terms of a just peace: the kind of peace Wilson envisaged had no room for honoring the secret treaties Britain had made with allies for sharing territory. There runs through these years, as a counterpoint to the dramas at sea, Wilson's subterranean efforts to become the peacemaker. With each of the initiatives there was an enlargement of his vision.

Diplomacy was the anvil on which Wilson elaborated and refined his philosophy. He was not to be satisfied with a mere ending of hostilities nor would he declare war on the issue of

THE ZIMMERMANN PLOT

On February 24, 1917, Wilson got news from Ambassador Page in London of a coup by British naval intelligence. It had intercepted a coded message that Arthur Zimmermann, Germany's foreign secretary, had sent to the German minister in Mexico on January 17, almost certainly with the Kaiser's knowledge: "It is our purpose on the 1st of February to commence the unrestricted U-boat war. The attempt will be made to keep America neutral in spite of this. In case we should not be successful in this, we propose Mexico an alliance upon the following terms: Joint conduct of the war. Joint conclusion of peace. Ample financial support and an agreement on our part that Mexico shall gain back by conquest . . . Texas, New Mexico, Arizona." The German minister was also instructed to have Mexico persuade Japan to switch sides and join with Mexico in war on the U.S. Mexico was in no state to be anybody's ally. The new president, Carranza, dropped the Germans when the bombshell burst on the American public. Zimmermann's main effect was to change opinion overnight in the pacifist West and Southwest.

U-boat outrages. He had a vision of a new world he might create. The development of Wilson's thought is intriguing. In 1912, Isaac Stockton Axson, the brother of Wilson's first wife, recorded his observing four achievements necessary to the survival of humanity: an association of nations, the guarantee of equal rights for all, absolute sanctions against aggression and removal of the manufacture of munitions from profit-making corporations to governments. He did not elaborate or develop these thoughts at the time. In September 1915, Sir Edward Grey wrote to Colonel House asking if the President would be interested in "a League of Nations binding themselves to side against any Power which broke a treaty." By December 1915, Wilson was thinking of proposing an association of democratic nations on the thesis that democracies were not innately aggressive. In his State of the Union address he linked the security of America with the security of mankind: "We insist upon security in prosecuting our self-chosen lines of national development. We do more than that. We demand it also for others. We do not confine our enthusiasm for individual liberty and free national development to the incidents and movements of affairs which affect only ourselves. We feel it wherever there is a people that tries to walk in these difficult paths of independence and right."

Throughout 1916 he tried hard to be accepted as a mediator but it seemed that whichever side thought it had a prospect of victory became deaf to his overtures. In the spring it was the Allies who let an extraordinary secret offer lapse. Colonel House and British Foreign Secretary Grey reached an understanding in London on February 22 that at a word from the Allies, Wilson would call a peace conference, and should

Germany refuse to attend, "the United States would probably enter the war against Germany." No word had come. The Allies thought they might win the war in 1916 and they did not want Wilson meddling with the settlement of victory and their secret deals. Wilson then went out on a limb on May 27 with an epitaph for isolationism. "What affects mankind," he said, "is inevitably our affair." He declared that the United States was willing to become a partner in a postwar league of nations to keep the peace. Another olive branch withered in the face of the unresponsive belligerents; but Wilson was putting into place the building blocks of a crusade. He could appeal directly to the citizens of the world, proposing terms for peace that every reasonable man might embrace.

In the dying days of the year, Wilson asked both belligerents to state the terms on which they would be willing to stop fighting, and seemed to put his assessment of both sides' war aims on such equal moral footing that King George V broke into tears. But the Germans were evasive and the Kaiser did not want Wilson at any peace conference. Undeterred, Wilson launched a secret campaign with the British and German governments to obtain their consent for his mediation. It was as part of this campaign that on January 22, 1917, he went before the Senate and called on the belligerents to make a compromise peace, "a peace without victory." He spelled out what it meant in some detail and gave "the silent mass of mankind everywhere" a vision of a new world. He brilliantly exemplified the political ideals and principles inspiring America in his outline of a just peace that the American people would help to maintain through a league of nations. It would include the freedom of the seas, the moderation of armaments, the rejection of entangling alliances and the right of national determination for all nations great and small—a "Monroe Doctrine for the world" was the way he put an ideal that has had such profound consequences. He was prophetic in his description of the consequences of the "peace after victory" that all the belligerents were seeking: "Victory would mean peace forced upon the loser, a victor's terms imposed upon the vanquished. It would be accepted in humiliation, under duress, at an intolerable sacrifice, and would leave a sting, a resentment, a bitter memory upon which terms of peace would rest, not permanently, but only as upon a quicksand. Only a peace between equals can last."

But by the time Wilson spoke, more than 100 U-boats were taking up their positions in the North Atlantic. The Kaiser, pale and excited, had on January 9 already decided at his gloomy castle near the present Polish border at Pless that he would give in to the admirals and launch a campaign of ter-

ror. Nine days after Wilson's speech, on January 31, Germany gave eight hours' notice of intent to sink any ships in the war zone around the British Isles, belligerent or neutral, warship or merchantman. Insultingly, America was told that Germany would permit one passenger vessel each week to England, provided it followed a prescribed course and was, in a critic's paraphrase, striped like a barber's pole and flew at each masthead a flag resembling a kitchen tablecloth. The Kaiser knew it would mean war with America. A little later he scrawled: "Now, once and for all, an end to negotiations with America. If Wilson wants war, let him make it, and let them then have it." He risked war with America because his admirals had guaranteed that England would be on her knees within six months—before an American soldier could set foot on the mainland of Europe. It was a reckless gamble with a nation's destiny, and bad luck, too. If Bethmann-Hollweg had been more effective in persuading the Kaiser to stick with the Sussex promise to America a little longer, his case for restraint would have been immeasurably strengthened a few months later. On March 15, 1917, the Czar's abdication eased the pressure on Germany's eastern front, and when the Bolsheviks took power they signed a separate peace with Germany at Brest-Litovsk (March 3, 1918) that ceded the Ukraine, the Baltic provinces and Poland. In those circumstances the admirals might have lost at Pless and America would have stayed out of the war.

Wilson lost all faith in Germany after the U-boat decision. Germany was "a madman that should be curbed." But he agonized over what to do. Impatient for action at a cabinet meeting on February 2, he ruminated that war had to be avoided so as "to keep the white race strong against the yellow." He seemed to be clutching at straws to avoid doing anything. When he did the next day announce the termination of diplomatic relations, he specified that "only an actual overt act" would lead to war, by which he seemed to mean only destruction of American ships and American lives. Americans traveling on belligerent ships carrying contraband—as in the *Lusitania* case—were not protected. The same day, February 3, the American *Housatonic* was sunk; on February 12, the *Lyman Law*; on February 27, the armed Italian liner *Laconia* with the loss of two American lives; and on March 12, the American steamer *Algonquin* without warning though without loss of life. Wilson responded by arming American merchant vessels. He rejoiced in the abdication of the Czar, which removed the only taint of autocracy among the Allies, but even at this eleventh hour he had no powerful sense that the Allies were right and were fighting for interests that were vital to American democracy. He told his cabinet that the Allies did not deserve to win; a draw would be more just. He worried also that war would bring a spirit of ruthless brutality into the very fiber of American life.

These were worries, but not the core of his hesitation. That lay in the recognition that if he joined the fight he would lose the authority of his qualifying halo as the independent peace-maker. It took his mind time to adjust to the reality that his halo was no longer relevant. He had for so long hoped to be the sublime referee, and it was hard to accept that nobody wanted him. He would have to impose himself. It was this sense of the futility of his peace efforts, as much as the submarine warfare itself, that made him act. Three more American ships were destroyed by U-boats from March 16 to 18, one with the loss of 15 American lives. Germany had come to be detested, but still no hysteria for war hounded Wilson as it had President McKinley in 1898. The American people in 1917 were remarkably forbearing. They had endured the revelation of sabotage and spying by Germany; the subversion of munitions workers by the Austro-Hungarian ambassador; the blowing up of the Black Tom munitions plant in New Jersey; an attempt by German agents to smuggle the deposed dictator Huerta back into Mexico; and on March 1 the sensational Zimmermann telegram (see box on page 147). It was a country with such an aptitude for peace that it was still possible for Wilson to defy the jingoes, as he called them, and keep America out.

What made Wilson finally decide on war, after all? We have little evidence of the inner workings of his complicated mind, but there are clues. There is the violent nature of his reaction to the senators who tried to frustrate his wish to arm merchantmen. He already had the power to do that, but he denounced the "little group of willful men" with venom because they had rendered the government of the United States "helpless and contemptible." It seems to have impressed him that this is how the world would view America anyway, if, after all the provocations and ultimatums, it stayed too proud to fight. Yes, by declaring war he would lose his halo, but who would want a 98-pound weakling as a mediator?

At about the time he made his decision, he spoke with Jane Addams, the peace leader. She recalled: "He said that as head of a nation participating in the war, the President of the United States would have a seat at the peace table, but that if he remained the representative of a neutral country he could at best only 'call through a crack in the door.'"

The choice for him came down to either abandoning his historic mission to change the way the world was run or going to war. But if he went to war it could not be for the narrow right of Americans to travel into dangerous areas, or indeed for any American national interest, still less for victory and the spoils of war. Belligerency, after all the fine words, had to be sanctified by a high moral purpose. So Wilson went to war to impose a peace without victory. It was more than semantics when he announced that America would support the Allies as an associate and not as an ally. It kept his distance and retained the leverage that he might use to make an independent peace. On April 2, 1917, escorted to Capitol Hill by cavalry, he made an electrifying speech to a joint session of Congress:

"The world must be made safe for democracy. Its peace must be planted upon the tested foundations of political liberty. We have no selfish ends to serve. We desire no conquest, no dominion. We seek no indemnities for ourselves, no material compensation for the sacrifices we shall freely make. We are but one of the champions of the rights of mankind. We shall fight for the things which we have always carried nearest our hearts—for democracy, for the right of those who submit to authority to have a voice in their own governments, for the rights and liberties of small nations, for a universal dominion of right by such a concert of free peoples as shall bring peace and safety to all nations and make the world itself at last free. . . . America is privileged to spend her blood and her might for the principles that gave her birth."

It was a moving address, received with a hurricane of applause and cheers, acclaimed as a triumph even by his enemies Lodge and Roosevelt, and the vote for war was approved by all but 6 of the 88 senators voting and 50 of the 423 congressmen present. Of course, for the noble objectives that exhilarated Congress, America could have joined the embattled Allies years earlier. Germany's autocracy was hardly concealed, nor her brutalities, nor her ambitions. "We shall yet be absolute masters of the world . . . all the chimerical ideas of democracy will be driven forth forever," was the way a Prussian newspaper spoke for the Germans in 1915.

Wilson had espoused neutrality at the cost of leaving the country in ignorance about the character of the belligerents and militarily quite unprepared to fight a war of the kind into which it was now plunged. For all his eloquence, the American people had only the woolliest notion of how the defense of neutral rights had turned into a great crusade for a better world, what their real security interests were and how they were to achieve them. But Wilson, patiently and with high principle, had built a case and carried the people with him. It was a triumph for the notion of American exceptionalism, and it would haunt American foreign policy for the rest of the century.

AMERICA WATCHES THE WORLD BLOW ITSELF UP

The First Lady, Ellen Axson Wilson, lay dying in midsummer 1914 as Europe prepared to tear itself to pieces after 40 years without war. The distraught president walked the lonely corridors of the White House. As the hour struck midnight, he was beseeched by his ambassador in Paris and the British foreign secretary to save the peace. He made no move. It is hardly likely he could have been effective. The heads of the rival European states that were to fight for four years at a cost of 13 million lives had gone off on vacation. America was self-contained, self-contented. "To the world, or to a nation," said the *Daily Herald* of Grand Forks, North Dakota, "an archduke more or less makes little difference." Kaiser Wilhelm II had disappeared on a three-week Norwegian cruise, having lit the fuse by assuring Austria-Hungary it would have Germany's support in punishing Serbia for the murder of Archduke Franz Ferdinand. Most of the crowned heads of Europe were related—Queen Victoria died in the arms of her grandson Kaiser Wilhelm—so they might have talked things over at the archduke's funeral. However, they did not attend because the archduke had married a commoner, and in August the interlocking alliances catapulted country after country into conflict. The lineup was Germany, Austria-Hungary, Bulgaria and Turkey (the Central Powers), opposed by Russia, France, the British empire, Japan and eventually Italy and Romania (the Allied or Entente Powers).

Wilson was emotionally drawn to the Allied cause. "Everything that I love most in the world is at stake," he told the British ambassador. There were tears in his eyes and he quoted the poetry of Wordsworth. He was aghast when the German chancellor said the Kaiser's pledge to Belgium was just "a scrap of paper." He was shocked, as millions were, when the German army put the city of Louvain to the torch and executed several thousand Belgian civilians. But, as British judge and biographer Lord Devlin put it, in the Wilsonian constitution the heart

President Wilson (opposite) holds his first granddaughter, 1915.

THE SPARK OF WORLD WAR I

The Archduke Franz Ferdinand, heir to the Austro-Hungarian throne, and his wife, Sophie, had already escaped one bomb attack when they left the town hall at Sarajevo, Bosnia, on Sunday, June 28, 1914 (top). Within minutes, they were both dead, victims of three shots fired into their open car by a Serbian terrorist, Gavrilo Princip (an accomplice under arrest, bottom), when their driver made a wrong turn on the way to the hospital to visit those injured by the bomb. Bosnia had been annexed by Austria-Hungary in 1909, yet its Slavic population then largely preferred a union with Serbia—a preference that in the 1990s would destroy the Yugoslavia created at Versailles.

was not recognized as a chamber with executive power. In public, he uttered not a word of protest, and when he proclaimed American neutrality on August 18, he meant to see it enforced.

He asked that Americans be impartial in thought as well as in name. There was no national sentiment for intervention in the first eight or nine months, though America as a whole was more in sympathy with the English cousins and the democratic French. In November 1914, the *Literary Digest* polled editors across the country. Of the 367 replies, 105 favored the Allies, 20 the Germans and 242 were neutral. Their communities favored the Allies even more: 189, against 38 towns for the Germans, and 148 divided or neutral. In part, the poll reflected ethnic geography. The Irish in Boston and New York sided with Germany out of hatred of England. In the central states there were 8 million citizens who were German-born or who had German parents. The German diplomat Arthur Zimmermann tried to play on this. He pounded the table in the face of the U.S. ambassador in Berlin, James W. Gerard, warning him that five hundred thousand German army reservists lived in America, and would rise up at a signal. "I told him," said Gerard, "that we had five hundred and one thousand lamp posts in America to hang them from." World War I was the first great test of loyalty in the new, multicultural nation, and it generally passed with flying colors.

Wilson was sensitive to the dangers of ethnic turmoil; as the *Toledo Blade* put it, "united we stand, hyphenated we fall." He even arranged for a headmasterly message to be screened in movie theaters: "It would be patriotic in the interest of the neutrality of the nation and the peace of mankind if the audience in this theater would refrain during the showing of pictures connected with the present war from expressing either approval or disapproval—Woodrow Wilson."

In 1916 he refused to accept a cutting from a rosebush that had bloomed near Verdun, where eventually more than 300,000 Frenchmen and nearly as many Germans died in an 11-month ordeal.

THE LINER THAT WAS
A SHIP OF WAR

Six days out of New York, on the sunny afternoon of May 7, 1915, passengers on the British liner *Lusitania,* bound for Liverpool, could see the low green hills of Ireland. Out of their sight below the surface of the waves and just 640 yards off the starboard bow was Unterseeboot 20. Lieutenant-Kapitan Walther Schwieger had a broadside view of the steamer in the center of the hairlines of his periscope, and at 2:07 p.m. he fired a single torpedo and sent 1,198 people to their deaths. The "unsinkable" liner sank within 18 minutes, and only 726 survived. "I submerge to 24 meters and go to sea," Schwieger noted in his log. "I could not have fired a second torpedo into this throng of humanity attempting to save themselves."

Among the dead were 270 women, 94 children and 128 American citizens. When Wilson heard in the evening that losses would be heavy, he slipped out of the White House and walked alone through the rainy streets where the newsboys were shouting. The outrage in the country was the greatest since the *Maine,* and it was inflamed by popular exultation in Germany. The head of the German Red Cross in America, Dr. Bernhard Dernburg, pronounced that the passengers had chosen to commit suicide, because they had knowingly sailed into a war zone. He was promptly sent home. Officially, Germany expressed its "deepest sympathy" to America, but did not disavow the sinking. It blamed Britain for forcing it to retaliate against the British "starvation" blockade, and for letting neutral passengers travel on a ship carrying munitions. The British denied the munitions (and still officially do) but the Germans were right. Many histories refer to "a small quantity of munitions," but the investigative journalist Colin Simp-

The *Lusitania* steams out of New York on May 1 on her last fateful voyage. *Inset:* Next to the Cunard schedule in that morning's *New York Times* and *New York Tribune* was a German embassy advertisement warning Americans of the risk of traveling on a British liner.

son, who investigated the *Lusitania* in 1973, found that nearly the whole cargo was contraband and that a false manifest had been prepared to conceal the fact. Simpson dived to the wreck in 1980 and brought up some of the explosives. The contraband included 10½ tons of explosives and 4,927 boxes of cartridges from the Remington Small Arms Company, each with 1,000 rounds of .303 bullets. There were also 1,250 cases of shrapnel, falsely franked "non explosive in bulk," and 3,813 40-pound packages labeled cheese but consigned to the Naval Experimental Establishment at Shoeburyness, whose appetite was more likely for pyroxylin, a nitrocellulose explosive highly susceptible to seawater. Probably it was the cause of the entry in the U-boat log: "An unusually heavy detonation follows with a very strong explosion cloud." The true original manifest was given to President Wilson, sealed by him and sent to the Treasury archives marked "Only to be opened by the President of the United States." In addition, the *Lusitania* had been fitted out in August 1914 to receive 12 six-inch guns, although they were not in position when it was attacked.

None of this gave the Germans a right to do what they did. According to Ambassador Gerard in Berlin the ship was flying the U.S. flag. International law gave the Germans the right to search the ship first, but they had to evacuate those aboard if they intended to sink it.

Wilson was derided in battle-bound Britain when he spoke pacifically: "There is such a thing as a man being too proud to fight. There is such a thing as a nation so right that it does not need to convince others by force." The soldiers in France named dud shells that failed to explode "Wilsons." But the President did follow up his first remarks with a campaign to make Germany pay compensation and abandon the U-boat campaign. To Teddy Roosevelt, who demanded war, he was a coward, but American opinion coalesced around the President's patient diplomacy, which was successful for a time. The country did not want war.

NEUTRAL VICTIMS: The crew slides down ropes into the ocean in a last-minute escape from a vessel torpedoed by a German U-boat: the bow has already sunk and the stern is lifting out of the water. The United States had proclaimed its neutrality, but in the three years before the U.S. entered the war 209 Americans, crew and passengers, died in the attacks by U-boats—28 of them on American ships.

All through the summer of 1915 and into 1916 the United States and Germany exchanged notes about the sinking of the *Lusitania*—a diplomatic duel punctuated by more sinkings. Two Americans were among the 44 dead when the British steamer *Arabic* was sunk without warning in August, sailing west and therefore carrying no contraband. Nine Americans died when the Italian liner *Ancona* was torpedoed in November with the loss of 200 lives.

THE YANKS ARE COMING

America was not ready for war. The German Supreme Command counted on that when they lunged for victory. Could the "doughboys" get to France before it was too late? In April 1917 the regular Army was a mere 110,000; on the scale of the carnage in Europe, they could be swallowed up in a single battle. Wilson had said in 1916 that he would be "ashamed of America" if there were not enough volunteers, but by 1917 he realized that too many men were needed: three weeks after the declaration of war only 32,000 had volunteered. Conscription was a commonplace in all the major European countries except Britain, which relied on volunteers for the first 18 months, but it was anathema to many progressives, who were sure it would destroy "democracy at home while fighting for it abroad." Wilson had a rebellion among Democrats as well as opposition by Republicans. To the men of Missouri, said the Democratic Speaker, Champ Clark, there was precious little difference between a conscript and a convict. Senator James Reed predicted that the streets would run with blood.

It was tricky, but Wilson and his astute secretary of war, Newton Baker, a former mayor of Cleveland, got the Selective Service Act through Congress and then managed the draft brilliantly. They orchestrated a mass movement of public mood in the direction they wanted, a new thing in America in its swiftness and methods. Draftees were made into heroes by parades and patriotic festivals; dissenters were pressured as "slackers." Every male between 21 and 30 was required to register at polling stations on June 5, 1917. Nearly 10 million did. On July 20, a blindfolded Secretary Baker put his hand into a goldfish bowl containing 10,500 numbers and drew out black capsule "258," the number assigned to a different draftee in each precinct. By mid-December 516,000 draftees had been sent to camp, and a Sergeant Irving Berlin at Camp Upton, New York, had written a song for them: "Oh, How I Hate to Get Up in the Morning." The most disappointed man in America was one who had to stay at home, the former commander in chief, 58-year-old Colonel Theodore Roosevelt, who had offered to recruit a division of "horse riflemen." It was the Army that vetoed the idea, not Wilson, but Wilson became even more of a hated figure to Roosevelt.

All told, nearly 24 million men from age 18 to 45 were registered in successive drafts. Despite the ripples of dissent against the war, there were only 337,649 draft dodgers. But if the operation was smooth, it was as slow a business getting a big U.S. Army into the front line as the Germans had hoped.

COME BACK SAFE: A drafted husband and father at Union Station, Kansas City, Missouri, who did not seek the exemption for men with genuine dependents. Of the nearly 1,400,000 who saw active combat, 116,516 were killed in action or died of wounds.

BLACK JACK PERSHING
TAKES CHARGE

Chasing Pancho Villa's bandits in the mountains of Mexico in 1916, Brigadier-General Black Jack Pershing fumed about the "weak, chicken-hearted, white-livered lot" in Washington who kept America from joining the Allies in the war against Germany. He got his chance a year later, when he was appointed at the age of 56 to head the American Expeditionary Force (AEF). He was then junior to five other major-generals, but he had impressed everyone with his incisive mind and strength of character.

He had fought hard against the Apaches in Arizona, the Spanish in Cuba and the Moros in the Philippines, but he had also enforced unpopular orders in restraining the punitive expedition in Mexico. He was a gruff disciplinarian. Once he kept troops waiting in the rain for hours and then complained that their boots were muddy. If necessary, he kept insubordinates in their place with sheer fist power. As a lieutenant instructor at West Point he had carried discipline to such an extreme that he was treated to the "silence," a rare rebuke in which several hundred cadets greet an unpopular officer entering the mess with absolute quiet. It was the West Point cadets who began calling him "Nigger Jack" or "Black Jack," as a term of abuse, because he had led a black regiment in the war in Cuba. The nickname came to represent his personal toughness. His lonely, driven nature was accentuated by the death of his wife and three daughters in a fire in 1915—only his son survived—while he was on active service. "About the only respite I have known," he told a friend, "is by keeping every minute occupied."

Rarely was a man better matched for the hour. Given large powers by Wilson, who disliked being commander in chief, Pershing created a disci-plined army out of thin air. In his memoirs after the war, he described it as an "inexcusable failure" that a halfhearted preparedness campaign had not yielded an army of half a million men. Such a show of strength, he argued, might have deterred Germany from challenging America in 1917, and half a million Americans ready to join the Allied front lines in 1917 would have ended the war that year at a tremendous saving in lives. He was depressed that eleven months after entry into the war he could barely field one division for combat. An American unit did not take offensive action until May 28, 1918.

The buildup accelerated throughout 1918, with more than a million Americans engaged in combat, but six months into the war America had only 86,000 men on the battlefields of France, whereas in its first six months of war in 1914–15 Britain had mobilized 354,750 men fighting. There was not a single Air Force squadron in 1917, and the eight in May 1918 were all equipped with French airplanes. American factories and machine tools had been crucial to the Allied effort, and Pershing sensibly decided to adopt the British Lee-Enfield rifle, but generally the mistake was made of trying to produce new designs of planes and guns instead of adapting British and French weapons already being churned out by American factories. Artillery, planes and machine guns had to be bought or borrowed from the French; the steel helmets the doughboys wore were British. Pershing's army received American guns just about in time to fire a salute of celebration at the armistice in November 1918.

VIVE L'AMERIQUE! The French were so excited by Pershing's arrival in Boulogne on June 13, 1917, that the band played "The Star-Spangled Banner" and the "Marseillaise" over and over again. Paris went wild when the American command party visited the grave of Lafayette, the French aristocrat who fought with the American colonists against the British in the American Revolution, and Colonel Charles Stanton announced: "Lafayette, we are here!" Inset: The King of England joined the crowds welcoming the first American troops in London in August 1917.

An army ammunition transport caught in an artillery barrage as it tries to reach the front. Location unknown. When America entered the war in 1917, the Germans were on the defensive but Allied fortunes were at low ebb. The French had already lost 2.25 million men dead and wounded. Ten days after Wilson's declaration, they flung nearly 1 million men into a disastrous offensive on a 30-mile front, and sacrificed another 200,000 men for a few miles of ground. For six weeks afterward much of the French army was in mutiny. Some units marched on Paris. In July, the British launched an offensive on the mudfields of Passchendaele and lost 265,000 men by November for a gain of seven miles. Only 86,000 American troops had arrived by then. The collapse of Russia was about to release 1 million German soldiers from that front for what the Kaiser was sure would be the decisive blow to win the war in the West before the full power of America could come to the rescue.

THE DOUGHBOYS BLOCK THE ROAD TO PARIS

Paris was in a panic at the end of May 1918. Once again, as in 1914, the German armies threatened the city. A million people fled. The dazed soldiers of seven French divisions, outnumbered two to one, cried, *"la guerre est finie!"* as they tumbled back in wild disorder. When Pershing took supper at the headquarters of the supreme Allied commander, Field Marshal Ferdinand Foch, the French generals were so demoralized "they sat through the meal scarcely speaking a word." It seemed that nothing could stop the Germans.

But there was something. On May 31, the United States Army entered the battle for Paris in a memorable way. The 3rd Division went into the line at Château-Thierry. Its 7th Machine Gun Battalion put its guns across the roads and bridges of the Marne, and the Germans got no farther. On June 1, the 2nd Division, made up of Marines and Army regulars, went into position to the west of the village across the Paris-Metz highway.

The scale of the American effort by three divisions (equal in number to six Allied divisions) was small on the vast panorama of the western front, where the Germans deployed 192 divisions, but the psychological impact of the glowing young Americans, singing "Hail! Hail! The Gang's All Here!" at the top of their voices as they marched east to battle, was quite prodigious. "We all had the impression," wrote Jean de Pierrefeu, an officer on the staff of General Henri Pétain, "that we were about to see a wonderful transfusion of blood. Life was coming in floods to re-animate the dying body of France."

There was a price. The Americans had to learn a whole new battlecraft. The Marines attacking German positions in the village of Bouresches advanced into machine gun fire in regular ranks, five yards apart, 20 yards between each rank, and fell in regular lines like wheat before a thresher. A British reporter observed: "Nothing had been seen like it, in mass innocence, in hope and at the end in unavailing heroism and self-sacrifice, since the British attack on the Somme in 1916." Only 20 Marines in the attacking battalion survived unscathed. But Belleau Wood fell on June 25 after 19 days of hell and if its strategic value was slight there was again a psychological impact,

this time on the German commanders. The Yanks were coming, they were fresh and fearless and they could win battles.

Pershing had released troops only reluctantly for combat under Foch, preferring to hold them back for integration in the American army he was assembling. He got into blazing rows with the Allied leaders because he insisted on saving shipping space for the support services and equipment to complete a full American division. "You are willing to risk our being driven back to the Loire?" challenged Foch. "Yes," responded Pershing, "I am willing to take the risk." They threatened to refer the dispute to Wilson. "Refer it to the President and be damned," retorted Pershing. French Premier Georges Clemenceau urged Foch to fire the "invincibly obstinate" Pershing; but in the end, they all compromised. The British cut down their food imports and made hundreds of ships available, Pershing agreed that 310,000 of the troops to be shipped in June and July would go into battle, with 190,000 held back for support and supply, so that he could continue to build up his integrated army. The German high command had calculated that such an acceleration was not possible. It was astonishing. Only 84,000 troops were shipped in March, but

AMERICAN ACE: Captain Eddie Rickenbacker (1890–1973), America's top flying ace, was a former auto mechanic and Indianapolis 500 racing driver. He racked up 26 "kills" in the few months he was in action. After the war he became a pioneer in civil aviation, building Eastern Air Lines. In World War II, when he was a consultant, his plane was forced down in the Pacific, but he survived 23 days in the ocean in a rubber raft.

in April 118,500 arrived, in May 246,000, in June 278,000, and in July 306,703.

There was another crisis before the integrated American Army first went into action on its own on September 12, two months before the end of the war. A force of 550,000 Americans and 110,000 Frenchmen neatly excised Foch's "hernia," the salient at St.-Mihiel, but Foch proposed a late change of plan, for good strategic reasons, that would have split up Pershing's precious army. For a mad moment, Pershing was tempted to strike the generalissimo. The quarrel was patched up, but at the cost of Pershing agreeing to disengage quickly from St.-Mihiel to launch another attack 60 miles away in the Meuse-Argonne sector. It bogged down. By this time, though, the Germans had had enough. On October 4 the new German chancellor, Prince Maximilian von Baden, asked President Wilson for peace. The Kaiser, fleeing to Holland in his pajamas, abdicated on November 9. The armistice was signed on November 11.

What was the American contribution to victory? In 1918 the British captured 188,700 prisoners and 2,840 guns; the French captured 139,000 men and 1,880 guns; the American Expeditionary Force captured 48,800 soldiers and 1,424 guns. But the American contribution must be measured more broadly—by its role as munitions maker from 1914 to 1917, without which Britain and France would have been defeated; by its part after 1917 in defeating the U-boats; by the battlefield inspiration provided by the doughboys— but above all by the gleaming potential of men and steel that the Germans could see on an endless horizon. No one country "won" the war. The French stopped Germany from winning in 1914. The Russians drained manpower. The British on land and sea made victory a possibility from 1916 on. The United States made it a certainty. Captain Liddell Hart, the British historian, summed up the achievement of Pershing and his men: "It is sufficient to say there was perhaps no other man who would or could have built the structure of the American Army on the scale he planned. And without that army the war could hardly have been saved and could not have been won."

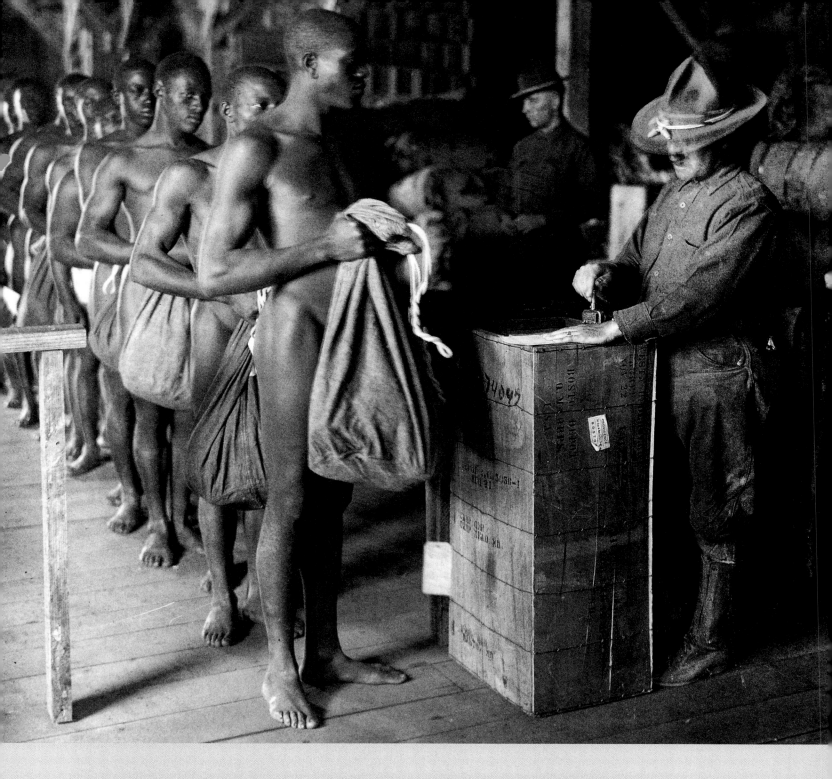

THE UNREQUITED LOYALTY OF BLACK AMERICANS

There were fears that black Americans would resist the draft after German propaganda promised that a German victory would end segregation and give them a section of the South for independent rule. But the black response to the draft was excellent. Some 2,290,000 blacks were drafted and few claimed exemptions. There were 400,000 black Americans among the 3.7 million American troops in France, and two black draft divisions, the 92nd and 93rd, served with the French. Despite their heroic performance at San Juan Hill in the Spanish-American War, blacks were mostly relegated to menial work as longshoremen, supply troops, orderlies and musicians, and no black was allowed to rise above the rank of captain.

Even so, New York's 396th Infantry, the "Harlem Hellfighters," won more than 150 Croix de Guerre decorations, and paraded proudly home through the streets of Harlem. Few black troops received such a reception. Unlike the black colonial troops of Britain and France, the black Americans were not allowed by their country to march in the victory parade in Paris. Many black soldiers were specially targeted by the white race riots that swept the country during the war and after. When black soldiers of the 24th Infantry fired into a white mob that assaulted them in Houston, Texas, in August 1917, 13 black soldiers were hurried through a trial, denied an appeal and hanged.

AMERICA'S TANGLE WITH THE BOLSHEVIKS

News of the murder of the Romanovs was brought to President Wilson at a dinner party. He abandoned the meal, declaring that "a great menace to the world has taken shape." It was the end of his last lingering hope that Bolshevism might be just a muscular form of Progressivism. Shortly afterward, Wilson sent American troops to Russia.

Five thousand, mostly Polish Americans from Michigan and Wisconsin, joined British forces already in Murmansk and Archangel, and 7,000 went to Siberia to link up with 72,000 Japanese troops in Vladivostok. Soviet history says it was an attempt by American imperialism to smash the revolution. That certainly became a motive of the British and French, but it was never Wilson's. He was confused and misinformed. He thought the Allied forces in the north were to reclaim war matériel; but the Bolsheviks had already seized most of it. He thought the troops in Siberia were helping 50,000 Czechs to get back to the war front; but

they had become allies of counterrevolutionary armies, rightist White Russians against Communist Red.

The puzzle is why these small American forces stayed long after the reason for their dispatch—the war with Germany—no longer prevailed. War Secretary Baker urged their recall in November 1918, and Wilson agreed; but he preferred not to upset the Allies on the eve of the peace conference and nobody wanted to leave Siberia to the Japanese. Nor did anybody know what was to happen in Russia, where a violent civil war raged. The Russians in the north and Vladivostok also seemed to have wanted the British and Americans to stay. And when Wilson became obsessed with the League of Nations, and sick, the anti-Bolshevists in the State Department were eager to help Whites led by Admiral A. V. Kolchak. Americans in Siberia were put to guard sections of the Trans-Siberian Railway, where they had hardly any brush with the Bolsheviks, but in the north there was

fighting in which the Americans suffered 2,845 casualties. American troops were pulled out of the north in June 1919, and the last had left Siberia by April 1920. Only constant Allied pressure got the Japanese out more than two years later.

Probably too much has been made of America's absentminded intervention as a source of the long Soviet distrust of the United States. Certainly, it was much less of a U.S. effort than the massive famine relief supervised by Herbert Hoover, which saved 10 million Russians between 1921 and 1923. "All the people inhabiting the Union of Soviet Socialist Republics," said the citation presented to Hoover by Soviet leader Lev Kamenev, "will never forget the aid rendered to them by the American people." Forever is a long time. By 1950 the Soviet encyclopedia described Hoover's workers as "saboteurs and spies," and by 1956 the entire relief effort was dismissed as "the policy of restoring German militarism." But by then Kamenev himself had long since been purged.

THE DOOMED CZAR: Nicholas II, blessing his troops before battle, was forced to abdicate on March 15, 1917, ending 300 years of rule by the Romanov dynasty. The moderate Socialist provisional government headed by Alexander Kerensky tried to continue the war, but was overthrown by the Bolsheviks in a second revolution eight months later. The Bolsheviks made a separate humiliating peace with the Germans at Brest-Litovsk in March 1918. On July 16, 1918, they murdered the Czar and his entire family in a cellar at Ekaterinburg (Sverdlovsk today). Kerensky escaped. He died in New York in 1970.

THE SECRET WAR: The bodies of 17 U.S. servicemen killed fighting the Bolsheviks at Romonofska, Siberia, begin the long journey home.

THE HERO: In jubilant London, schoolgirls scattered white carnations in the President's path as King George V took the Wilsons home to Buckingham Palace. In Paris the adoring crowds shouted *"Vive l'Amerique!"* and *"Wilson le juste,"* and showered him and Edith Wilson with cascades of violet and yellow mimosas. In Rome, the cheering masses waited six hours to see him pass.

SUMMARY OF WILSON'S FOURTEEN POINTS

1. Open covenants of peace openly arrived at
2. Freedom of the seas in peace and war
3. Removal of trade barriers
4. Disarmament
5. Impartial adjustment of all colonial claims, based on the principle that the interests of the population have equal weight with those of the power
6. Evacuation of Russia by the Germans and self-determination for the Russian people
7. Evacuation and restoration of Belgium
8. Restoration of France, with restitution of Alsace-Lorraine, taken in 1871
9. Readjustment of Italian frontiers along recognizable lines of nationality
10. Establishment of autonomy for the subject nationalities of Austria-Hungary
11. Evacuation and restoration of Romania, Serbia and Montenegro
12. Emancipation of Turkey's subject peoples
13. Establishment of an independent Poland with access to the sea
14. Formation of a general association (league) of nations to be formed under specific covenants for the purpose of affording mutual guarantees of political independence and territorial integrity to great and small states alike

EUROPE HAILS THE CONQUERING HERO

It was the sound of a bullet at Sarajevo that echoed round the world in 1914. In 1918, it was an idea espoused by an American president. Woodrow Wilson's vision of a just and permanent peace, first spelled out in his "Fourteen Points" speech on January 8, 1918, was received as a sacrament by millions of war-sick civilians and by soldiers on both sides of the trenches. It was encapsulated in 60 million pamphlets scattered all over the world. In Europe, candles were lit before poster-portraits of the new redeemer. Men clasped hands with the simple bonding word "Wilson!" Nine months after he had spoken, the speech was the basis on which the Germans sued for peace. Before the end of the year Wilson himself stood on the soil of Europe, hailed as the savior of mankind. It has been well said that no other American president had ever heard what he then heard: the voices of millions of Europeans calling his name and blessing him.

The Fourteen Points soared above the battlefields because they asked nothing for America. They were principles for the conduct of a brave new world and specific proposals for changing the boundaries of Europe to satisfy nationalist aspirations. Self-determination was not a general principle, but Wilson made it one in elaborations that added nine more principles of democratic freedom: "People," he said, "may now be dominated and governed only by their own consent." He called for the destruction of every arbitrary power and sought to restore the honor of democratic liberalism after the Bolsheviks published the secret treaties by which the Allies had pledged themselves to divide the spoils of war. He envisaged the Fourteen Points as a repudiation of that kind of Old World duplicity and an antidote to the "poison of Bolshevism."

But the president who was the idol of Europe was a wounded man when he crossed the Atlantic on the *George Washington* in December with a bevy of college professors and maps of Europe. In the November congressional elections he had called on America to reelect a Democratic majority so that he might be "your unembarrassed spokesman at home and abroad. . . . A Republican majority would be interpreted on the other side of the wa-

MIDOCEAN REHEARSAL: President Wilson addresses soldiers and crew aboard the USS *George Washington* on the Fourth of July 1919. He was preoccupied with how he would present the Versailles Treaty to the Senate, the first time a president had submitted a treaty in person. He scrapped his first draft, a rare failure, and read a second to his shipboard advisers on July 5. Mrs. Wilson insisted on taking her exhausted husband for a daily walk on deck. He despised the idea but did it meekly.

ter as a repudiation of my leadership." It was a violation of the wartime truce on party politics and an invitation to disaster. A midterm election, with all the crosscurrents of sectional, regional and national interests, could not be made into a vote of confidence on foreign policy. When the Republicans took control of the House by 237–190 and the Senate by two votes Wilson was inevitably hostage to his own partisan folly. He made matters worse when he named four yes-men as the commissioners he would take with him: Colonel House, Secretary Lansing, General Tasker H. Bliss and Henry White, an elderly diplomat. He ignored the fact that the Senate would have to ratify any

treaty. White was the only Republican.

Wilson was not without an occasional spasm of doubt. On the way over he seemed in good spirits; he laughed at Charlie Chaplin in *A Dog's Life,* joined the sailors' mess for a singalong and shook hands cheerfully with 800 sailors. But walking the deck with his propaganda chief, George Creel, he looked out on the ocean and brooded: "People will endure their tyrants for years, but they tear their deliverers to pieces if a millennium is not created immediately. Yet these ancient wrongs, these present unhappinesses, are not to be remedied in a day or with a wave of the hand. What I seem to see—I hope I am wrong—is a tragedy of disappointment."

THE BIG FOUR: Italy's weeping and raging Vittorio Orlando (second from left) went home when Wilson (at right) appealed over his head to the Italian people on possession of the port of Fiume. Wilson's pictures were torn down all over Italy. On another occasion, France's Clemenceau (third from left) accused Wilson of being pro-German, "seeking to destroy France." Britain's Lloyd George (left), having fought Wilson to make the peace harsher, tried to weasel out of their agreements when the draft treaty was criticized. A furious Wilson went to his apartment to tell him, "You make me sick."

THE ARABS: The Emir Faisal, whose father, the sharif Husajn, had proclaimed himself king of all the Arab countries, came to Versailles with his British adviser, the boyish Colonel T. E. Lawrence (second row, second from right). They appeared before the big powers on February 6, claiming title to the conquered Ottoman territories on the grounds of British promises and Wilson's Fourteen Points. They were followed on February 27 by Zionist leaders pressing the creation in Palestine of "a Jewish national home," promised by the big powers and endorsed by Wilson. Thanks to Lawrence, Faisal and the Zionists had agreed on January 3 that there should be a "Jewish commonwealth" in Palestine. In the end, there was no unified Arab state; the French won a mandate over Syria, the British over Palestine, Faisal became King of Iraq (his grandson was assassinated by Saddam Hussein's Baathists in 1958) and Jew and Arab went down the separate roads that led to a half century of hatred and bloodshed.

THE PROPHET MEETS THE TIGER AND THE WIZARD

Georges Clemenceau, the "Tiger of France," did not share the popular euphoria over President Wilson's Fourteen Points: "Even God Almighty gave us only ten—and we broke those." Clemenceau became the president of the peace conference when it opened on January 18, 1919. Twenty-seven Allied and associated powers were there, but France vetoed an invitation to revolutionary Russia and had Germany barred from the talks. Paris was packed with Czechs, Cossacks, Poles, Ukrainians, Irish Sinn Feiners, Koreans, Armenians, Kurds, Albanians and countless others from the sundered empires of Austria-Hungary, Germany and Turkey, all pressing their claims to nationhood, emboldened by Wilson's new doctrine of self-determination and autonomy for subject nationalities. It was, said Harold Nicolson, a "riot in a parrot house."

The crucial decisions were eventually fought out in private by three men—Clemenceau, aged 77; Wilson, aged 62; and the Prime Minister of Britain, the quicksilver Welsh wizard David Lloyd George, aged 56, who was catapulted to Paris on the un-Wilsonian election slogan "Hang the Kaiser!" The paunchy Clemenceau, wearing a skullcap and gray gloves for his eczemic hands, slouched drowsily through their meetings, barely concealing his disdain for Wilson's faith in man's better nature, always ready to pounce if Wilson tried to keep his promise to the Germans that it would not be a punitive peace. Clemenceau had been the young mayor of Montmartre when the Prussian Guard stamped in arrogant triumph down the Champs-Elysées in 1871. He had seen them get to the gates of Paris 43 years later. It would happen a third time, he knew, unless "the Boche" were utterly stripped of arms, territory and the sinews of war. He demanded the German Rhineland and the Saar for France, as well as Alsace-Lorraine and $200 billion in reparations.

Wilson did well in the first month. Clemenceau and Lloyd George wanted to settle the terms and only then turn to the League of Nations. Wilson insisted on priority for the league and on making it an integral part of the treaty. On St. Valentine's Day, 1919, with the adoring Edith Wilson secreted behind a curtained alcove, Wilson read out the Covenant for the league, basically a British idea he had made his own. Article X pledged every member to defend the independence of every other member. It sounded splendid, but the governing League Council could only "advise" members on actions such as sanctions or military force. And the council had to be unanimous even in giving advice. Wilson knew its limitations. He saw it primarily as leverage for the moral force of public opinion in the world. "A living thing is born," he proudly declared. Not quite. He had still to win the votes of all the delegates, and his enemies in the Senate had sharpened their daggers. On a quick trip back to Washington, he was confronted by a round-robin signed by 39 hostile senators, enough to kill the league "in the form now proposed." When he got back to Paris, he found that his advisers Colonel House and Secretary Lansing seemed to have agreed to separate league and peace treaties. Dramatically, he insisted on tying the knot again, but then to forestall his enemies in Washington he had to ask Clemenceau and Lloyd George to agree to amendments to the Covenant, such as genuflecting to the Monroe Doctrine to preserve American freedom of action in Latin America. Now they had the Sunday School teacher where they wanted him! His league amendments were hostage to their pressure for a harsh peace.

The months of March and April were an ordeal for Wilson. He found it impossible to fit the cocktail of ethnic minorities into the new states of Poland, Austria, Hungary, Czechoslovakia and Yugoslavia without violating his principle of self-determination. The new Poland acquired millions of Germans, Romania millions of Hungarians and Czechoslovakia, the cockpit of 1939, ended up with 3 million Germans, 1 million Hungarians and half a million Poles. The new small states were too weak to be part of a new balance of power in Europe and, with their captive German minorities, were at the same time a provocation to the German nationalism that in 20 years was to lead to war.

Clemenceau and Lloyd George wore Wilson down in sheer, unrelenting, daylong argument. Feeling betrayed, he abandoned the consoling conversations with House. He ignored Lansing, who whiled away the hours buying Dutch silver and drawing grotesque caricatures. He tried to do everything himself, typing his own statements, squatting on the floor to cut up maps of Europe. He worked 18 hours a day. When he resisted France's demands, ugly anti-Wilson stories appeared in the press, planted by Clemenceau, who ruled as premier by fear, using police spies and manufactured dossiers. Clemenceau, in the end, did not get his frontier on the Rhine, but he got the promise of a postwar alliance with the United States and Britain.

On April 3, Wilson collapsed with a temperature of 103 degrees. Clemenceau and Lloyd George sat in the study outside his sickroom while he passed out his answers to their proposals: No, no, no. When he emerged, his face was a death mask and he had spasms of paranoia. Every French employee was spying on him, somebody was moving the furniture, staff were using official cars for immoral purposes. He was exhausted, but his energies flowed in one channel. He must preserve the league at all costs. "Logic! Logic! I don't give a damn for logic," he flared when his experts questioned his submission on adding civilian pensions to the reparations bill. He consoled himself that when the league was in session it would remedy all the treaty's errors. "It's the best," he sighed, "that could be gotten out of a dirty past." But the treaty's terms, well summarized by Henry Kissinger as "too onerous for conciliation but not severe enough for permanent subjugation," guaranteed a dirty future.

THE GERMANS: The journey to Paris was "an overwhelming experience" for the German delegation. The French slowed their two special trains through the battle areas so that the Germans could not escape seeing the horrors. In Versailles they were confined behind barbed wire to the Hotel des Reservoirs until summoned to hear the treaty, on which no discussion was allowed—the *Diktat,* they called it. At meetings in their hotel they played the "Hungarian Rhapsody" at deafening volumes for fear of French microphones. The leader (fourth from left) was an antimilitarist diplomat, Count Ulrich von Brockdorff-Rantzau, appointed foreign minister by the new center-left president of Germany, Friedrich Ebert, a 47-year-old former saddle maker and tavern keeper.

THE VIETNAMESE: Wilson's Fourteen Points fired the imagination of a frail, 28-year-old Vietnamese called "Nguyen the Patriot" (born Nguyen That Thanh) who was working in Paris as a photo finisher. He rented a dark suit and bowler hat to haunt the corridors of Versailles Palace every day. He asked for equality of rights between the Vietnamese and the French occupiers of Indochina. Nobody would see him. But the French Socialists let him speak (above), and he turned to the Bolshevik revolution for his inspiration. Later, as Ho Chi Minh, he won more than he asked for at Versailles.

THE SIGNING: Allied officers had endured the Germans on the battlefield. Now, on June 28, 1919, they wanted to see them swallow the ignominious peace. The treaty was presented to the Germans in the Trianon Palace on May 7, 1919. The assembly rose and stood in silence as the monocled Brockdorff-Rantzau, the model of an erect Prussian diplomat, led in six of his delegation. "The hour has struck for the weighty settlement of our account," said Clemenceau, presenting a volume of 200 pages, 75,000 words, 440 clauses. The Germans were stunned by what they saw. Brockdorff-Rantzau outraged the assembly by staying seated while he denounced the treaty's opening demand that the Germans acknowledge their guilt. "Such a confession in my mouth," he said with proud venom, "would be a lie."

Only the certainty that the Allies would invade induced Germany to sign on June 28. The signing was a further humiliation, since it was staged in the Hall of Mirrors at Versailles, where

WHAT WILSON ACHIEVED

At dawn on May 7, 1919, a troubled Herbert Hoover walked the streets of Paris. Within a few blocks he met South Africa's premier, General Jan Smuts, and Britain's brilliant economist John Maynard Keynes. As if by telepathy, says Hoover, it flashed into their minds that they were all pacing the pavements for the same reason. At 4 a.m., they had received the first secret copies of the full draft peace treaty, and they were sure it spelled doom. The demand for reparations in money, ships, coal and tools would so impoverish Germany as to make it a prey for Communist insurrection and fantasies of revenge.

Wilson was attacked all over the world, either by liberals for betraying his ideals, or for his success in enforcing them against nations whose greed had not been satisfied. In his best-selling book *The Economic Consequences of the Peace* (1919), Keynes portrayed him as a slow-witted Presbyterian, bamboozled by subtle and dangerous spellbinders. Contrary to legend, Wilson achieved more of his Fourteen Points than he lost—notably the creation of Poland, Czechoslovakia and Yugoslavia; independence for Finns, Latvians, Estonians and Lithuanians; and a League of Nations as he envisaged it. But with Lloyd George he killed the French plan for carving a new buffer state out of Germany's Rhineland. He stiffened the Allies against Italy's unjust demand for Fiume. And by his relief programs, run by Hoover, hundreds of millions of Europeans were saved from famine and revolutionary chaos. (Keynes was more on the mark in advocating an all-around forgiveness of debts by the U.S. and Britain, and a rebuilding of Europe, but that kind of creative thinking was 30 years ahead of its time.)

Where Wilson conspicuously broke his word was on reparations. "If I were a German," he told Ray Stannard Baker, "I think I should never sign." The Germans were required to pay $5 billion in cash and a later sum initially fixed at $66 billion by a reparations commission (the French had asked for $200 billion and the British $120 billion). They lost 12 percent of their prewar territory, 15 percent of their arable land and 75 percent of their iron-ore deposits. Wilson's conscience had the escape clause that the league and a reparations commission could clear up all the mistakes, but he had also become more anti-German. "Justice?" he said. "Yes, justice for the dead. The German people obeyed every order however savage." For all that, the treaty would have been far less liberal if Wilson had stayed in Washington. As Hoover later wrote: "Mr. Wilson's expression of American ideals was the only spiritual expression in the Conference. At every step he fought the forces of hate."

Too much has probably been made of the economic injustice to Germany. Reparations, whatever Keynes or Adolf Hitler might say, had little adverse effect on Germany's economy in the long run. In the end, after review by American generals Charles C. Dawes and Owen Young, the Germans paid a total of just over $5 billion up to March 1937. But in the immediate postwar years the punishment didn't contribute to runaway German inflation—a catastrophe that wiped out the savings of millions, nearly toppled the fledgling Weimar Republic, and enhanced the appeal of the paramilitary organizations and fanatics at the expense of the new civilian government. The Weimar regime and the idea of democracy in general would be indelibly tainted in Germany with the belief that it was a byword for anarchy.

Perhaps the greatest hostage to fate was not that Wilson failed but that he half succeeded. Self-determination liberated millions, but the price was the creation of a string of weak states, which had to rely for their freedom on faraway powers. And within their borders were dissident groups with their nationalisms bubbling beneath the surface. Within their borders, in particular, were millions of exiled Germans, a perfect excuse for a German nationalist leader to march again.

in 1871 Wilhelm I had proclaimed himself prince emperor of Germany. *"Faites entrer les Allemandes,"* barked Clemenceau, and four officers—one British, one French, one Italian and one American—escorted in two deathly pale German officials. The ceremony took 40 minutes, crowned with the crash of cannon.

WILSON'S FIGHT TO THE DEATH

As President Wilson sailed to the peace talks in December 1918, his two most bitter enemies plotted how they would defeat his precious League of Nations. Senator Henry Cabot Lodge, Senate majority leader and chairman of the Foreign Relations Committee, traveled to Oyster Bay to see the ailing Theodore Roosevelt, his best friend for 35 years and the probable Republican candidate for the presidency in 1920. Both men realized Wilson's league was so popular it could not be defeated outright. They agreed it would have to be nibbled to death. They were not isolationist but they did not want the Democratic party to have an international diplomatic triumph on top of winning the war, and both disliked Wilson's concept of a league open to all, as the United Nations later became.

Roosevelt had been in his grave seven months by the time the exhausted Wilson returned to a hot and sticky Washington with his precious Covenant in his breast pocket. A majority of the Senate was ready, in varying degrees, to accept the league. They split into three pro-league groups. Forty-three Democrats and 1 Republican backed Wilson. Another group of 17 Republicans would ratify if mild changes were made; and 20 Republicans would vote for ratification if Lodge's more substantial changes to make the peace-keeping commitment subject to case-by-case approval by Congress were accepted: a statement of constitutional correctness but lacking Wilson's emphasis on collective security. Only 12 Republicans and 3 Democrats were irreconcilable to ratification in any circumstances.

The "irreconcilables" were led by the "Lion of Idaho," William Borah, and Hiram Johnson of California. Borah was an ornery obstructionist, but he was an honorable man who believed that the United States held freedom in trust and must always determine for itself where its duty lay. He was a cut above others like James Reed of Missouri and Joseph Medill McCormick of Illinois. "Think," said Reed, "of submitting questions involving the very life of the United States to a tribunal on which a nigger from Liberia, a nigger from Honduras, a nigger from India or an unlettered gentleman from Siam, each have [sic] votes equal to that of the great United States."

Lodge's great skill in the ensuing battle, proclaiming that he was carrying Roosevelt's torch, was to form a motley coalition of the irreconcilables and the senators with reservations. His biggest ally was Woodrow Wilson, who enabled Lodge to

William Borah and Hiram Johnson, who led the isolationists. Johnson stayed in the Senate until 1945 and from his deathbed announced his opposition to the United Nations. Calvin Coolidge caught one feature of Borah's character. On hearing that Borah had gone riding, Coolidge remarked, "How can that be? I understood horse and rider have to consent to go in the same direction."

keep mild and strong reservationists together by rejecting any reservations at all. Wilson was amiable and patient. He kept his temper in three hours of public grilling by the Foreign Relations Committee on August 19. But his elaborate answers added up to "No." He told them it had been hard enough incorporating the changes he took back to Paris in March. To go further would be to betray his promises and endanger the world; wars were already breaking out again all over Europe. The league was needed now without the delays and risks of further diplomacy.

Wilson realized by September that he did not have the two-thirds Senate majority he needed for ratification. He decided to go straight to "the men talking in the grocery stores in a thousand towns," as he once described the formers of American opinion. It was a fair gamble. All surveys of opinion in 1918, 1919 and 1920 showed that the American people wanted to join "a world organization to preserve peace." Wilson's doctors told him he was risking his health, but he was still vibrant with the emotion of his dedication at the graves of American soldiers at Suresnes: "Here stand I consecrated in spirit to the men who were once my comrades . . . who have left me under eternal bonds of fidelity."

Perhaps there has never been a more poignant testament to the American idea of democratic leadership than Wilson's odyssey. He left Washington aboard his special train, the Mayflower, on September 3, with his wife, Edith, his secretary, Joe Tumulty, and Dr. Cary T. Grayson. In murderous heat, he traveled to all but four of the states west of the Mississippi, typing his hour-long speeches as they rattled across the prairies, standing to speak night after night, a slender, lonely figure sharing his dream with anonymous thousands in hot, smoky halls, rousing them to cheers and tears by his soaring eloquence and passionate conviction. "I can predict with absolute certainty," he said in Omaha, "that within another generation there will be another world war if the nations of the world do not concert the method by which to prevent it." He made 40 speeches, and sometimes his head ached so much he saw double as he spoke. The farther west he went, the warmer his reception became. His enemies, alarmed, sent speakers to stalk him

in city after city, a "battalion of death," financed by the Republican millionaires Henry Clay Frick and Andrew W. Mellon and spearheaded by Borah and Johnson. Appealing to nativism and xenophobia, they, too, roused crowds, especially in the Midwest, where anti-British Irish and German Americans shouted at Wilson's name, "Impeach him! Impeach him!"

The climax came with Wilson's fortieth speech, in Pueblo, Colorado, on September 25. On his appearance, the crowd stood and cheered for a full ten minutes. At one point in a vibrant address he lost his thread and swayed, but struggled to a peroration recalling his day at Suresnes Cemetery. "I wish some of the men who are now opposing the settlement for which those men died could visit such a spot as that. I wish they could feel the moral obligation that rests upon us not to go back on those boys, but to see this thing through and make good their redemption of the world." He stopped, head bowed. He was sobbing. So was his wife and so were many in the audience.

That night, as the Mayflower headed east, the pain in his head prevented him from sleeping. In the hope that exercise might help, they stopped the train on the prairie and the President of the United States, the First Lady and Dr. Grayson got out and walked forlornly down a dusty lane. There happened to be a wounded soldier sitting on the porch of a house. Spontaneously Wilson climbed the fence to talk with the boy and his family. They accepted some cabbages and apples from a farmer who recognized them. But the appearance of normality was brief. Wilson could not go on. The next morning in Wichita, Kansas, the tour was canceled and the lines were cleared for the Mayflower to rush back to Washington.

The momentum was lost. The sick president was secluded in the White House in the crucial lead-up to the vote on the league. Entreaties poured in for him to meet Lodge halfway. "Let Lodge compromise!" he replied. "Let Lodge hold out the olive branch."

The Democrats did as the sick president asked. Forty-two of them voted with 13 irreconcilables to defeat Lodge's version of the treaty. When they attempted to get approval without reservations, they lost, 53 to 38. The league was dead, but twitching still. Public opinion forced the

WILSON'S ENEMY: On the stump against Wilson's league, the vinegary Boston Brahmin Henry Cabot Lodge, who hated Wilson as much as Wilson hated him. A Harvard Ph.D., he was said to have a mind like his native New England, naturally barren but highly cultivated.

Senate to reconsider. Nothing came of the rescue efforts. On March 19, 1920, the Senate voted for the Treaty of Versailles and the Covenant by 49 to 35, seven less than the two-thirds majority required of 84 votes cast (12 senators did not vote). If 7 of the 23 Democrats had rejected Wilson's advice and voted with the reservationists, America would have been in the league.

For all the league's limitations, which would have been emphasized by the Lodge amendments, it was a pity America did not enter it. In the league, America would at least have been engaged. By holding out for his sublime ideal, Wilson consigned America to the very insular nationalism that was against its vital interests. In the light of 1939, it was perhaps even more of a pity that he abandoned France. The treaty signed in Paris in June, in which America and Britain guaranteed French integrity, was never submitted to the Senate, though Lodge did not oppose it.

But Wilson in defeat was nobler than his enemies in victory. When they had won, Lodge's party sent Wilson back the actual official copy of the treaty—one of the cruelest acts in American politics.

EDITH TAKES OVER THE WHITE HOUSE

Edith Wilson was a few days from her forty-seventh birthday when she became the twenty-eighth-and-a-half president of the United States. Three days back from their trip west, on October 2, 1919, she found him unconscious on the bathroom floor. The specialists agreed that he had suffered a stroke, which had paralyzed his left side. Dr. Grayson's bulletin simply said the President was "a very sick man"; there was no mention of a stroke. The cover-up had begun.

On the day the Senate was to vote on the league, Edith Wilson made a unique personal plea to her sick husband. "For my sake, won't you accept these reservations and get this awful thing settled?" He took her hand. "Little girl, don't you desert me; that I cannot stand." It would be immoral to go against what he had signed. "Better a thousand times to go down fighting than to dip your colors in dishonorable compromise."

The next 17 months were the strangest in the history of the presidency. Wilson hung on as president but Edith controlled the conduct of business. Secretary Lansing acted promptly in summoning the cabinet together, but found the Constitution confusing. He read out the provision that when the president is incapable of discharging the power and duties of the office, "the same" devolves on the vice president. Did "the same" mean the office of presidency or the duties? And who was to pronounce on competence? They called in Grayson, who told them his patient had suffered a "nervous breakdown." It was touch and go. He must not be harassed, but he was clearheaded. From his sickbed the President had inquired, said Grayson, by what authority the cabinet was meeting.

Given Wilson's condition at the time, half blind and barely coherent, Grayson's story of Wilson's request was probably apocryphal, but it had the effect of chilling the cabinet and leaving authority in the White House. The inner circle there—the First Lady, Grayson and private secretary Joe Tumulty—all believed a semicomatose Wilson was a better president than Thomas Riley Marshall alive and well. Vice President Marshall, known to history for his proclamation, "What this country needs is a really good five-cent cigar," was a rustic yarn spinner from Indiana who did not want the job anyway. He steadfastly rejected all advice that he make a move. "I could throw this country into civil war. I am not going to seize the place."

The inner circle kept the world in ignorance of Wilson's condition and evolved a Wizard of Oz system to give the appearance of business as usual. The medical staff apart, Edith alone had access to the President. She wrote later:

"So began my stewardship. I studied every paper, sent

from the different Secretaries or Senators, and tried to digest and present in tabloid form the things that, despite my vigilance, had to go to the President. I, myself, never made a single decision regarding the disposition of public affairs. The only decision that was mine was what was important and what was not."

Edith would emerge from the sickroom with notes penciled in her big childish hand, which meandered over the careful typescript of a cabinet secretary's letter and began, "The President says . . ." or "The President wants . . ." Most of the letters to the White House went unanswered; a few bills came back with a shaky scrawl that senators speculated was a forgery of the President's signature. Edith interviewed a few men for cabinet vacancies and appointed them over tea at the White House. She kept from the President anything she thought might excite him, which was a whole range of government business, because she was not much interested in politics. She hated House and Lansing. Colonel House wrote letters on how the league might be won in the Senate that were still unopened when the President's correspondence was deposited in the Library of Congress three decades later. She had a hand in the outrageous dismissal of Lansing for the offense of holding regular cabinet meetings.

In December, the inner circle stage-managed a critical interview. Lodge used the excuse of a minor crisis over Mexico to ask the President to receive his archcritic, Senator Albert Fall, intending to use the expected refusal as evidence of chronic incompetence. But Wilson was by then good for five or ten minutes. He was coached and supplied with props for the set—a copy of Fall's resolution and the bulky report on Mexico by the Foreign Relations Committee. When Fall entered the sickroom, he found Wilson upright in bed, shaved of the long white beard he had grown and waving to Fall to take a carefully placed chair. "How are your Mexican investments getting on?" Wilson asked disconcertingly. Fall wondered if the President had seen the Mexican report, whereupon Wilson seized it in his good right hand. "You see, despite the stories going the rounds I can still use my right hand." Fall, defeated, took the President's hand as he left. "We have been praying for you, Mr. President," said Fall. Wilson shot back: "Which way, Senator?"

That ended all talk of deposing Wilson for the remaining 15 months of his term. But though he had improved, and he was later able to preside at a few painfully inept cabinet meetings, the effective Wilson presidency had ended in tears at Pueblo.

Wilson made an appearance on his doorstep on his sixty-fifth birthday in 1921. He died in 1924, outliving his successor, President Harding. Edith Bolling Galt (opposite, in 1913) was a rich and handsome widow of a jeweler when she met the newly widowed Wilson in 1915. She was a quick-witted, sunny person. Although her father was a Virginia judge, he had been short of money and she received only two years of formal education.

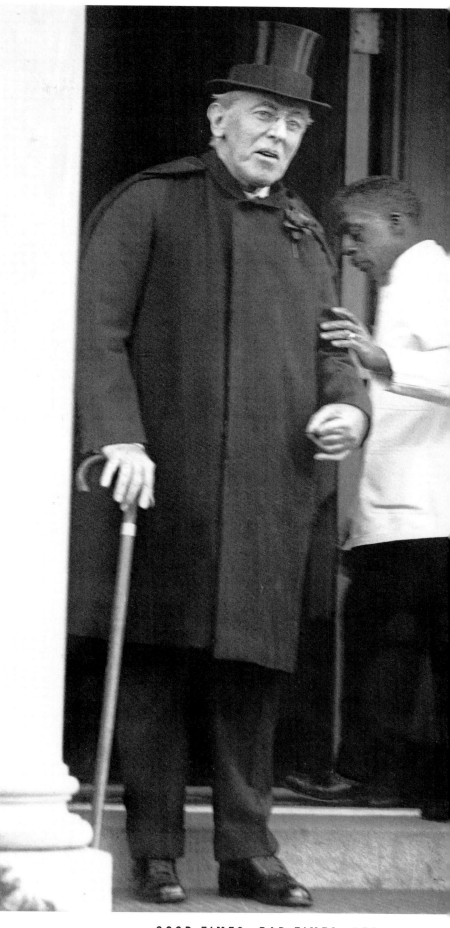

THE AMERICAN REVOLUTION THAT WASN'T

On the second anniversary of the Russian Revolution, November 7, 1919, police wielding blackjacks burst into homes and meeting places in 12 cities and bundled hundreds of bloodied and frightened people to prison. The scenes typical of Soviet terror took place in the United States. The country was convulsed by a Red scare more hysterical than anything before or since. Radicals and aliens were the targets of mob and state power. President Wilson lay paralyzed in the White House, incapable, even if he willed, of diverting the popular imagination.

There was reason for fear. Europe was in turmoil. America itself seemed to be coming apart. Four million workers, one out of every five, were on strike in 1919. In Boston, the police went on strike and looters and robbers roamed the city. Race riots erupted in 25 cities and towns: 70 blacks, some still in U.S. Army uniforms, were lynched in 1919. Anarchist pamphlets threatened a violent overthrow of society. Bombs exploded. One planted in a church in Milwaukee killed ten in April. In May, 36 packages mailed from New York to prominent Americans were found to contain bombs.

The new Attorney General, A. Mitchell Palmer, kept cool for a time. He was a 47-year-old lawyer whose ability, courage and loyalty had won him a meteoric rise in the Democratic party. As a progressive reformer, he had fought for laws to protect children, women and workers in dangerous jobs, and as a devout Quaker he refused to be secretary of war. On taking over the Justice Department in 1919, he released

Robert Minor's cartoon (1924) was just what worried the middle classes.

"Capitalism: Hey there, you're taking over one sixth of the world?

"Labor: Yes, and the job's not finished yet."

10,000 enemy aliens from parole, freed violators of wartime security, and disbanded the American Protective League of vigilantes. He spoke of America as the refuge of the oppressed and was denounced by the xenophobic *New York Times* for "pre-Adamite sentimentality." Like much of the country, the *Times* saw striking immigrant workers as "seditionaries, anarchists, plotters against the Government of the United States." It wanted them deported.

Palmer was compelled to change course. On the morning of June 3, 1919, he stood in the wreckage of his home in Washington, surrounded by congressmen demanding repression. Near midnight a bomb had exploded outside his house. It had blown its deliverer to pieces. Palmer himself had narrowly escaped death. The same night, bombs had gone off in seven cities, all hand-delivered and much more powerful than the package bombs of the May terror. Within days Palmer had worked out a strategy of mass deportation. He could not do it at will. He had to convince immigration inspectors, answerable to the Department of Labor, that an alien belonged to an organization advocating violence. He made a portentous appointment, recruiting a 24-year-old file clerk named J. Edgar Hoover.

The Palmer-Hoover raids that took place on the anniversary of the Russian Revolution in November 1919 were the beginning of a nationwide roundup of alien radicals that continued until February 1920. In December, the USS *Buford,* soon christened "the Red Ark," sailed for Finland with the first batch of 249 deportees. Hoover went down to Ellis Island to see them off. His spy system built up files on 60,000 "radically inclined" individuals, and more purges followed. Between 5,000 and 10,000 presumed alien members of radical parties were arrested, and brutally treated. Thousands turned out to be American citizens; the midnight knock on the door in Lynn, Massachusetts, netted 39 aliens plotting to set up a cooperative bakery. But the raids were popular and Palmer became an avid Red-baiter. The blaze of revolution, he said, was "eating its way into the homes of the American workman, licking at the altars of the churches, leaping into the belfry of the school house,

crawling into the sacred corners of American homes, seeking to replace the marriage vows with libertine laws, burning up the foundations of society." With his eye on the White House in 1920, he planned more raids for Easter.

The fight for American values began with Francis Fisher Kane, U.S. Attorney in Philadelphia. He resigned to protest the injustices inevitable in mass arrests. But it was an unlikely hero who stopped what he called "the deportation delirium." Louis Post, a slight 71-year-old who looked like Leon Trotsky but was a disciple of Henry George, became acting secretary of labor on the illness of Secretary William Wilson. He worked day and night on individual cases and concluded there was no basis for most of Hoover's arrests. Out of thousands of cases, he approved only 556 deportations. Congress began impeachment proceedings to remove him from office. Palmer called him a borer from within. But the spry Post convinced the House committee of injustice in case after case, and was still further vindicated when twelve of America's most illustrious lawyers, led by Felix Frankfurter and Zechariah Chafee, Jr., condemned the Department of Justice.

Palmer, egged on by Hoover, made a fatal error. He announced that the Red revolution would start on May Day 1920, with bombings and assassinations. The country went on the alert. Nothing happened. The people in the press and public life who had drummed up the hysteria were then the first to make fun of Palmer's "hallucinations." He failed to win the Democratic nomination for president. An anarchist bomb did explode in the heart of New York's financial district at Broad and Wall streets on September 16, 1920, killing 28 people and injuring more than 200. But there were no more raids.

Attorney General Mitchell Palmer (opposite), who deported hundreds, said: "Out of the sly and crafty eyes of many of them leap cupidity, cruelty, insanity and crime; from their lopsided faces, sloping brows and misshapen features may be recognized the unmistakable criminal type." Palmer, like Senator Joe McCarthy 30 years later, saw a Communist witch-hunt as a path to power.

MARTYRS OR ENEMIES OF THE AMERICAN WAY?

Nicola Sacco, shoemaker, and Bartolomeo Vanzetti, fish peddler, were young Italians who came to America with their dreams in 1908 and died in the electric chair. On April 15, 1920, a paymaster and a guard were shot dead in a robbery in South Braintree, Massachusetts, and Sacco and Vanzetti, their names linked for eternity, were convicted of the crime. For millions of people around the world the trial was a frame-up and the execution an act of judicial murder. It became an article of liberal faith that Sacco and Vanzetti were victims of a vengeful xenophobia, found guilty for their radical anarchist beliefs. Millions of words have been written portraying them as martyrs to their working-class idealism. As the eloquent Vanzetti predicted, the case has reverberated down the decades. Fifty years after their executions on August 23, 1927, Governor Michael Dukakis of Massachusetts declared the anniversary to be a memorial day. He took no position, he said, on their innocence; it was nonetheless a sensational imputation of official error.

Five men took part in the robbery, two who did the shooting and three who escaped with them in a stolen car, along with $16,000 of payroll in metal boxes. Sacco and Vanzetti were arrested three weeks later; nobody else was charged and the money was never found. Sacco had a .32 Colt pistol in his waistband with 23 loose cartridges. Vanzetti was carrying a loaded .38 Harrington and Richardson revolver, and four shotgun shells. He was also identified as the moustached man with a shotgun who had taken part in an earlier, abortive holdup. He was tried and convicted for this. Both men had alibis, and the evidence of identification had discrepancies, but they had admitted lying to the police, and the jury was impressed by the ballistics evidence. It suggested that the bullet that had killed the guard (the famous Bullet 3) could have been fired only from Sacco's Colt. There was also testimony suggesting that Vanzetti's revolver was one taken from the dead guard at the time of the robbery. On July 14, 1921, both were found guilty.

Did they have a fair trial? Many celebrated observers then and since think not.

A key witness was concealed from the defense. There was a muddle over the ballistics evidence. In 1926, Celestino Madeiros, a young killer awaiting execution, confessed that he had been a participant in the robbery and implicated the Joe Morelli gang, but Judge Webster Thayer refused a new trial. Felix Frankfurter, then a professor of law at Harvard, was enraged by Thayer's "farrago of misquotations, misrepresentations, suppressions and mutilations," and denounced Massachusetts justice in a sensational essay in the March 1927 *Atlantic Monthly:* "Outside the courtroom the Red hysteria was rampant; it was allowed to dominate within." The president of Harvard, A. Lawrence Lowell, read Frankfurter's article and expressed his misgivings to Governor Alvan Fuller. He promptly found himself appointed to a three-man commission of investigation.

The campaigners' euphoria was short-lived. The Lowell Commission concluded that both men were guilty beyond reasonable doubt. Years later, Lowell disclosed that they thought the evidence against Vanzetti weaker, being wholly circumstantial. "Our final impression was that Vanzetti was the plotter and Sacco the executioner," he wrote. Giovanni Gambere, an anarchist who helped to organize the defense, broke silence before he died in 1982 to say much the same thing.

Sacco and Vanzetti are passionate and appealing figures, but in all the years of tumult they have been consistently misrepresented. They were not wholly innocent dreamers set upon by fascists. They were not merely "philosophical anarchists," as most of the histories suggest. They led double lives. Sacco, the devoted father rising at 4 a.m. to tend his garden, was also an ultramilitant, actively engaged in the violent overthrow of capitalist society. Both men were closely associated with the anarchists who plotted some of the bomb outrages across the country in 1919. This is the conclusion of a study published in 1991 by Paul Avrich, the leading historian of anarchism. He traces how both immigrants, disillusioned by the savage political repressions and especially the 1914 Ludlow massacre, dedicated themselves to the war on the

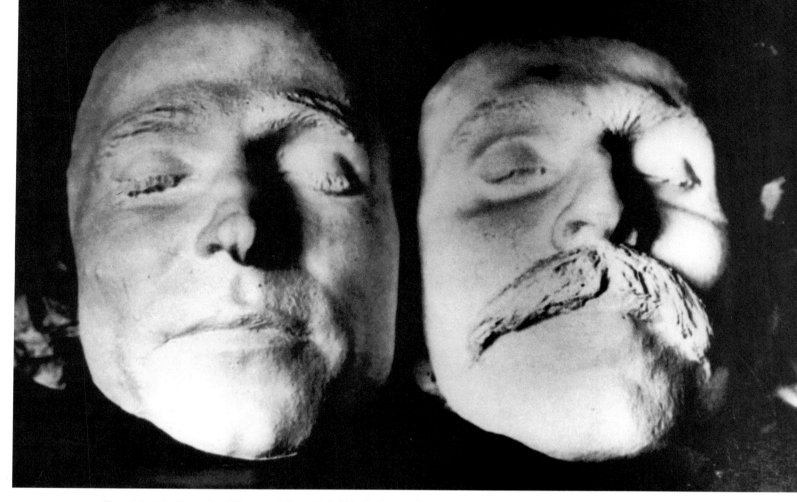

The original death masks of Sacco and Vanzetti, held in the Boston Public Library. The library also holds their ashes.

oppressors preached as a duty by the anarchist writer Luigi Galeani. When they went to Mexico in the spring of 1917 to escape the draft, they were joined by about 60 other Galeanists, and it was in Mexico that the bomb conspiracy was plotted, with Sacco and Vanzetti "almost certainly" part of it. It was almost certainly their comrade Carlo Valdinoci, who blew himself up at Palmer's house (page 176). It was probably their associate Mario Buda who planted the Wall Street bomb. And their defense counsel, Fred Moore, told Upton Sinclair that the "radical literature" they were trying to conceal on the night of their arrest was not literature but dynamite. This was the reason they lied to the police and presented an aura of guilt: but it was probably guilt of violent anarchism, not of the robbery and murder for which they were executed. "If I was arrested because of the Idea [of anarchy]," said Sacco, "I am glad to suffer. If I must, I will die for it. But they have arrested me for a gunman job."

It has the ring of truth.

Vanzetti (left) and Sacco in the Dedham courthouse. Vanzetti had a better chance of acquittal, but he told his defense counsel, "Save Nick, he has the woman and child." Vanzetti was 39 when he was executed, Sacco 36. Vanzetti's gentle last words were, "I have never done a crime, some sins, but never any crime. . . . I now wish to forgive some people for what they are doing to me." Sacco called out, "Long live anarchy!"

Their deaths provoked mass demonstrations, led by the Communists. John Dos Passos wrote a biting denunciation:

America our nation has been beaten by strangers who have turned
our language inside out who have taken the clean words our fathers
spoke and made them slimy and foul their hired men sit on the judge's
bench they sit with their feet on the tables under the dome of the
state. They are ignorant of our beliefs. They have the dollars the guns
the armed forces, the power plants. . . . We are two nations . . . we stand
defeated America.

CHAPTER SEVEN

THE TURMOIL OF NORMALCY
1920–1929

Babbitt's Day

Warren Harding, the small-town newspaper-man, was elected president on his fifty-fifth birthday, November 2, 1920, and went off to play golf. It was a gesture of relaxed confidence the country appreciated. By the end of his presidency, Harding (on the right in photograph) was lost in the woods, beset by scandals created by many of his friends in "the Ohio gang," but in 1920 he caught the mood of a country weary of Wilson's moral rebukes, the waves of strikes and Red scares, and of politics altogether. He won the largest popular victory in a century but only 49.3 percent voted, the smallest presidential election turnout in American history. He promised the people "normalcy" instead of "normality," a happy slip of the tongue that sustained the nostalgic dreams of the twenties. There was comfort, even, in the pompous alliterative style of a Harding "bloviation," as he called his purple passages: "America's present need," said Harding, "is not heroics, but healing; not nostrums, but normalcy; not revolution, but restoration; not agitation, but adjustment; not surgery, but serenity; not the dramatic, but the dispassionate; not experiment, but equipoise; not submergence in internationality, but sustainment in triumphant nationality." A Harding speech, said William McAdoo, was an army of pompous phrases moving across the landscape in search of an idea. Like Sinclair Lewis's fictional character George Babbitt, Harding embodied the spirit of the age, laissez-faire and protectionist in economics, get-rich-quick in business ideas, hypocritical in morals.

THE POLITICS OF MAIN STREET

Dawn's early light in the twenties found millions of clear-eyed citizens of the Republic fingering a piece of string with precisely twenty knots as they gazed from their bedroom windows. "Every day, in every way," they intoned at each knot, "I am getting better and better." The devotees of Emile Coué, the bearded little Frenchman who in 1923 sold Americans on the art of auto-suggestion, were more emblematic of the Jazz Age than the Charleston marathon dancers, the King Tut fetishists, the Ouija board manipulators, the mah-jongg champions and crossword fanatics and flag-pole squatters; and more numerous, we may guess, than flappers filling their bathtubs with illicit gin. Optimism, like everything else in America, was mass-produced.

The Couéists got their daily vindication in the urban areas, where good times roared on and on from 1923. The crazes of the day may have vanished but the symbols of heady energy are still rampant in every city: in New York, the Empire State and Chrysler buildings and Rockefeller Center (all conceived in the twenties), and across the continent the leading hotel, swankiest department store and tallest office block in many a downtown. Such was the exuberance of the people, manifested in spectacular bursts of invention and productivity, so fervent the cause of scientific management, so prodigious the stock of investment capital, that within a few years of the end of World War I, the United States was producing more than the other six Great Powers taken together. The economy grew by an average of 6 percent a year, productivity by 4 percent. By 1929, nearly 43.3 percent of the world's manufactures were made in America. And it was now the greatest financial and creditor nation.

A chicken for every pot? How about two cars rolling off the assembly line for every American home? Henry Ford was turning out a new car every ten seconds. The first nationwide network of dealers was selling them. In an outpouring of energy, 120 million people knitted 48 states together by nearly doubling the surfaced highways. They thronged the roads in 25 million new cars. When they weren't driving, they were talking. In the midtwenties there were 50 million telephone conversations a day: by 1927 40 percent of the homes had telephones. By 1927 every third home had a radio, two thirds had electricity. Scheduled air services had started. There was nothing like it anywhere else in the world. The employed American factory worker had a third more real purchasing power than in 1914. Nor did he have to save to buy, as his father had done. He could have his automobile, radio, refrigerator and washing machine on the new installment plan.

Naturally, the Republicans put it all down to President Coolidge's slogan that the business of America is business. "The man who builds a factory," pronounced Coolidge, "builds a temple. And the man who works there worships there." It was merely the idiom of the New Era. Business could do no wrong. It enjoyed tax cuts, high tariffs, prolific court injunctions to stem labor disputes, which declined sharply, and tolerance for a new wave of business concentration. The new generation of businessmen, usually behaving better than their fathers in the Gilded Age, genuinely believed they were revolutionaries

"The End of the Climb" by Rollin Kirby.

EMANCIPATION: On August 18, 1920, women won the national vote when Tennessee became the thirty-sixth state to yield to campaigners wearing yellow jonquils. It ratified the Nineteenth Amendment. America had been slow. Women had suffrage in 21 other countries first. Even as late as 1913, James Bryce was saying he found an "enormous majority" hostile to the idea, including women. Some thought it would lower men's respect for them. The liquor interests certainly helped the filibustering. They financed opposition because they feared, rightly, that women would vote for Prohibition.

building a new civilization: invention, not political reform, was bringing the utopia of humane capitalism.

The average American was, in fact, working ten to twelve hours a day, with no real job or health security, and while there might be a car in the driveway there was often no bathtub in the house. But the creed of the New Era was catching. The hot best-seller in 1925, *The Man Nobody Knows,* by Madison Avenue's Bruce Barton, flourished on the notion that the exemplar of modern business was Jesus Christ, "a virile go-getting he-man of business . . . a champion publicity-getter . . . the most popular dinner guest in Jerusalem . . . who picked twelve men from the bottom ranks and forged a great organization."

The prosperity certainly owed something to faith in freedom, to management skills, technology and America's emergence from the war as a creditor nation. But most of all it was due to the simple fact that America had something no other country had: the monopoly of an enormous market that could absorb the mass production; and the mass production, thanks to easy access to low-cost fuel and raw materials, was cheap enough for the millions. There was, in any event, not much argument between the Democrats and the Republicans. The country was sharply divided on cultural questions that cut across party lines, notably immigration and Pro-hibition, but on economic policy a consensus had developed. The Democrats paid the price for being pale imitations of the real thing. Warren Harding and Calvin Coolidge won by majorities of nearly two-to-one over their less colorful but equally conservative Democra-tic challengers, James M. Cox in 1920, and John W. Davis in 1924. Dissent was left to a coalition of farmers, labor unions, the remnants of Teddy Roosevelt's Bull Moose Progressives and the Socialists, who in 1924 backed Wisconsin's "Fighting Bob" La Follette in a bid for the presidency on a new Progres-sive party ticket. They campaigned for public ownership of

NICE GIRLS DON'T SMOKE: But the giddy "flapper" girls started to in the twenties and so did serious suf-fragists like Miss Anderson of Washington, D.C., puff-ing away at the Chevy Chase Club. They smoked in public places, previously thought taboo, as part of the campaign for equality with men. No advertiser until 1920 dared portray a woman smoking anywhere; by the end of the decade they were portrayed "enjoying a companionable smoke with their husbands and brothers." Cigarette production more than doubled be-tween 1918 and 1928.

the railroads and water power, a breakup of monopolies, pub-lic works in depressed times, farm relief, abolition of injunc-tions against strikes and a federal child labor amendment. Their 16 percent of the vote compared well with the Demo-cratic low point of 29 percent, but 54 percent wanted Coolidge and business as usual. After La Follette's death in 1925, politi-cal debate was dead.

The Big Money, as John Dos Passos called it, seemed to have replaced justice and freedom as the reason for America's being a country. For the writers and thinkers, and especially the pro-gressives, that was a foul dust to float in the wake of their dreams of a democracy moved by moral idealism. The disillusion was not so much with the conservatives, from whom few intellectuals had expected anything bet-ter, but with democracy itself and the low culture it seemed to have bred. Could the people possess innate virtue if they were such suckers for the bloviations of Har-ding and the insular Yankee aphorisms of Coolidge; if they tolerated crooks in gov-ernment and gangsters in business, wor-shiped movie stars and sports champions and flocked in their several millions to the antidemocratic Ku Klux Klan? And, if the state's authority to intervene was based on the enlargement of freedom, what happened when the same authority was used to deprive the worker of a beer, to disenfranchise 60,000 Socialist voters in New York State by expelling their elected assemblymen and to ban the teaching of evolution in public schools?

Disenchantment with democracy was not unique to America. The English establishment lamented that the crown-ing achievement of universal education was the vulgar new tabloid press sus-tained by millions of semiliterates. But intellectual despair was more significant in the United States because faith in the capacity of the com-mon man was the very heart of the civilization. Reformist optimism in America had been fired by conviction rather than by the aristocratic, British instinct to patronize the lower orders. Now disillusion seemed to have bred an enervating rather than an engaging empathy.

Skepticism about their native America runs through much of the creative writing of the period by Sinclair Lewis, F. Scott Fitzgerald, T. S. Eliot, Ring Lardner, Ezra Pound, and others of the so-called lost generation. The columnist H. L. Mencken, forever skewering the "homo boobus" of a hick democracy, was so morbidly antidemocratic as to be comic. Millions of Americans justified Scott Fitzgerald's judgment that "it was characteristic of the Jazz Age that it had no interest in politics at all." Less than half the eligible citizens voted in the 1920 presidential election; only 52 percent in 1924. City governments were disfigured by the psoriasis of Prohibition: the suddenly rich bootleggers bought City Hall and intimidated voters with impunity. And women, having won the vote, seemed, in the phrase of historian Geoffrey Perrett, to be pitting themselves against social conventions rather than social conditions.

The mood of the elite was most notoriously encapsulated in despairing essays by 30 young intellectuals, collected and edited by Harold Stearns in 1922 under the title *Civilization in the United States.* Only the creativity of America's new poets won acclaim in Stearns's symposium, cause enough in itself for suspicion in the America of their selective vision. It became fashionable for the better off to flee to Europe, as Stearns did, where they could excoriate the wasteland back home. The joke was that travelers observing Stearns dozing in a Paris café would remark, "There lies civilization in the United States," and they had a point. For all this disdain, the America the elite despised was developing new art forms, in the movies and jazz and the musical play and the skyscraper; it was enhancing musical appreciation among millions through the phonograph and the radio; it was founding New York's Museum of Modern Art and the Book-of-the-Month Club; it was launching new journalism, notably *The New Yorker* and *The American Mercury;* and even though there was much hand-wringing that the godless Freud stalked the land, the rise in church membership of all denominations was

"American Buddha!" by Bert Whitman. Everyone worshiped the stock market ticker tape.

faster than the rise in population. In some respects, the intellectuals had lost perspective. "There is something intrinsically absurd," wrote Bernard De Voto, "in the image of a literary man informing a hundred and twenty million people that their ideals are base, their beliefs unworthy, their ideas vulgar, their institutions corrupt, and, in sum, their civilization too trivial to engage that literary man's respect." Where there was pith to the self-indulgent lament of Stearns and his skeptics was in the conformity and intolerance they indicted. It was the mirror side of the fabled licentiousness and liberation.

The attempt to restore "normalcy" to America produced some abnormal consequences. Prohibition, which came into effect on January 16, 1920, was the most dramatic invasion of individual freedom. Aimed at closing the working-class saloons, it was at bottom an attempt by the Progressive middle classes to "Americanize" the immigrants. Immigration itself, the heartbeat of America, was attacked in quota laws in 1921 and 1924, cut back first to 357,000 a year and then 150,000, admissions being based on the composition of the population before the tidal waves of Jews and Catholics from eastern and southern Europe. Across the country, the fretful Anglo-Saxon majority followed up with numerous attempts to create new laws to suppress opinion and behavior they found abnormal. Everything from the permissible length of a skirt to the right to strike was under attack. Calvin Coolidge would not let the First Lady drive, fly, dance in public, bob her hair, wear slacks or ride a horse. Intolerance had unlikely proponents. Ernest Hemingway in his letters uses such epithets as frog, wop, jig and kike. Progressives like George Norris of Nebraska favored curtailing immigration. Wearing an academic gown, though it might as well have been a Klansman's robe, the president of Harvard sought to impose a quota on Jewish admissions; even Walter Lippmann said too many Jews were getting in there. A heroine of the women's movement, the journalist Carrie

Chapman Catt, wrote to birth control pioneer Margaret Sanger: "Your reform is too narrow to appeal to me and too sordid." Sinclair Lewis's *Main Street* (1920) immortalized this mood by portraying the sterility of small-town America. His *Babbitt* (1922) depicted the forces that turned a middle-class individual into an empty shell. The shells seemed to like it; they bought the books by the millions. Everyone seemed happy to yield his identity to a fraternal organization of his peers. The journalist Charles Merz observed: "Half the adult population now owns a fez, a scimitar, a secret code, two feet of plume, a cutlass or a pair of Anatolian breeches."

Prosperity only partly explains the dead politics of the twenties, because the good times were by no means universal. It is ironic that the laissez-faire apologist Paul Johnson, in his book *Modern Times,* calls his exultant chapter on the twenties "The Last Arcadia," for Republican politics utterly failed rural America. On the old cotton plantations and the dusty prairies and the little farms in Massachusetts, they needed all the faith they could get. Farm incomes dropped by half in a single year (1921). America had technically become an urban society, with more than half the population living in communities of more than 5,000, but there were still 30 million Americans on farms and 32 million more in communities of less than 10,000. The wartime prosperity fizzled out for most of them and did not come back for twenty years. People were migrating to the cities, but the farm machines increased output at a faster rate: the farmer in the twenties provided food for himself and three members of his family, for twelve Americans not living on farms, and for two foreigners. The Fordney-McCumber Act of Harding's presidency doubled agricultural tariffs, but for each dollar the farmer gained this way he had to spend $3.50 on the goods he needed. Farm bankruptcies multiplied fivefold; throughout the decade rural banks failed by the hundreds.

Yet a majority did keep voting for do-nothing Republicanism or, perhaps more accurately, failed to vote for the Democrats. The Democrats were hopelessly split between rural America—Klan and dry and Protestant; and urban America—wet, liberal and ethnic. The politics that thrived on Main Street were the politics of nostalgia, the "normalcy" promised by Warren Harding and epitomized in his elfin successor. The country might be on a spree by mid-decade, morality might be in ferment, but all was surely well when there was a president who took a nap on an afternoon, and a First Lady who sat in her White House parlor knitting a bedspread from ten balls of wool. The longing to retreat behind the oceans and back in time to an earlier, simpler, small-town America was a natural reaction to the disillusioning experience of the war and the disquieting revolution in morals it produced, filtering across the country from the great Eastern cities. In *The Great Gatsby* all the major characters come from the Midwest and are changed for the worse on the decadent East Coast. The narrator on the last page flees for his soul to the heartland and writes of the betrayed Gatsby: "He had come a long way to this blue lawn, and his dream must have seemed so close that he could hardly fail to grasp it. He did not know that it was already behind him, somewhere back in the vast obscurity beyond the city, where the dark fields of the republic rolled on under the night."

But nostalgia, as Spalding Gray put it, is a longing for what never was. America as Arcadia had not existed since the end of the Civil War, if then. In a fit of collective amnesia, mainstream Americans forgot that many of the previous fifty years had seen panics and depressions, bitter class, racial, ethnic, religious and urban-rural divisions; that America could not cut itself off from the rest of the world in pursuit of a mythical past, or abandon its throbbing metropolises. The disillusions led directly to the dangerous revival of the Klan as an organization of white, native-born Protestants that would do something about the Catholics, Jews, foreigners and blacks perceived as inimical to the values of the older America. The complacency nurtured the Great Depression of the 1930s. It was a frail presumption that while Coolidge dozed, the invisible hand of the marketplace was sorting everything out.

Harding had only a few months to live when J. P. Alley portrayed him with a tattered banner of "normalcy" and the plaintive "I'll have to figure out a new slogan." His hapless 882 days in office were marked by the first executive branch scandals since Grant and the worst financial scandals until the Reagan administration.

Myth meeting reality is like the meeting of two tectonic plates, a collision apt to produce a catastrophe. How did America survive and triumph as a democracy when much of Europe was succumbing to fascism and communism? There was in America a well of racial and religious hatred of the kind Hitler exploited. How did the country escape becoming an electorate manipulated in favor of a plutocratic dictatorship? There was a selfish insularity in the good times and there were politicians who were geniuses in the arts of exploitation.

Two principal reasons suggest themselves. Judged by the dismal national party politics, by the loss of 2 million in union membership, by the pocket vetoes of Coolidge, by the rulings of the Supreme Court, the 1920s were indeed a period of political reaction, ripe for convulsion. But the progressive flame, though flickering, was not extinguished. William H. Taft's reactionary Supreme Court delivered a series of majority opinions exalting property rights over civil rights, but the dissenters, Justices Oliver Wendell Holmes and Louis D. Brandeis, were educating a generation to a concept of liberty broader than liberty of contract. Zechariah Chafee, Jr., was correct when he wrote that, while the majority opinions determined the cases, "the dissenting opinions will determine the minds of the future." It is significant that for all the exhaustion with progressivism a number of dedicated, intelligent and highly talented progressives were able to retain their seats or win election to Congress. Senators Hiram Johnson, Thomas Walsh, Burton Wheeler, Robert La Follette (and his son), George Norris, Irvine Lenroot, Robert Wagner, Key Pittman, William Borah and Gerald Nye, and Congressmen Fiorello La Guardia and Sam Rayburn were among their number. Al Smith, the four-term Democratic governor of New York, stood as a jaunty champion of immigrants, free speech and progressivism.

Laissez-faire was the order of the day in business, but the genius of America has been to avoid pressing any political theory too far or too systematically. Americans rightly think of themselves as practical people. Most of them in the twenties may have disapproved of collectivist government, but business, labor, the professions, agriculture and the general public organized themselves to advance special interests. Their horizons were confined for a time to their personal destinies, as they would be in the Reagan era of the eighties. But they could agree to subsidize schools and universities and cultural institutions. A twenties cynic would say they exhibited a happy talent for hypocrisy, proclaiming a romantic individualism when it suited them and association when it paid. As for the "outs"—the farmers, large pockets of urban poor, many workers and nearly all blacks—one might lean on Fitzgerald and say they had an extraordinary gift for hope. Socialists and Communists were still firm in their belief that history was on their side. Immigrants and most blacks (massively migrating to the cities) still believed that they could someday achieve a real integration and full acceptance into the rest of America, despite the lure of Marcus Garvey's "back to Africa" movement. Social workers and urban planners still believed that poverty could be eradicated. The Great Depression was to be a keen test for the resilience of America's faith in itself.

The second and crucial portent was not so much political as social, not so much in what people said as in what they did, day to day. Americans have an instinct, among others, for democracy. It is manifest in egalitarian attitudes throughout society and in mobility, both geographical and social. These flourished in the twenties because in that decade, for all the national pressures for political conformity, for all the corruption and ineffectiveness of state and city government, this instinct was nurtured by the possibility of individual success. "Equality," as the commentator Jeffrey Madrick has remarked, "meant that we could all get ahead." Individuals and classes were not set. In Europe, by contrast, for all the political turmoil, the sharply defined permanent classes and castes held fast to privilege and aggravated social tension. The expert testimony in the 1932 federal government report "Recent Social Trends" documents in great detail the "wholly unparalleled democratization" throughout the twenties of aspects of American life: of education, with a vast multiplication of coed colleges; of transport, long an index of aristocracy, but now available to the masses with the Model T and its successors; of dress and fashion, an obliterator of traditional marks of class, especially since women wore less and less; of recreation, through the movies, the radio and the park systems; and of the marketplace. The new magazines, new national advertising and marketing now reached an audience of millions of consumers whose dollars were as good as anyone else's.

The conclusion must be that for all the reaction, for all the timidity, for all the gangsterism in the cities and the heists on Wall Street, American democracy was quietly enhanced in the twenties. Not in the clamor of Congress, or the rhetoric of politics, but as a way of life, and as a way of life that would survive the impending tectonic collision.

AN ANTI-SEMITIC BIGOT STRIKES A BLOW FOR FREEDOM

Big Mose Barnett spelled it out for Sam Shapiro. If he used his own machine in his dry cleaning shop, he would be in trouble with the price-fixing Twin Cities Cleaners and Dyers Association of Minneapolis–St. Paul. Sam, a Lithuanian immigrant who kept a shelf of constitutional law books, insisted on his rights to run his little business as he wanted. On August 20, 1927, four mobsters hit him over the head with the butts of their pistols and sprayed his customers' clothing with sulfuric acid. The police chief and county attorney took no action. City Hall was corrupt, on the take from protection racketeers, bootleggers, gamblers and brothels.

The knights who came galloping to Sam Shapiro's cause had rust on their armor. Jay Near and his partner, Howard Guilford, had just started a scandal sheet, the *Saturday Press.* There were thousands of ephemeral rags like it in America in the wide-open twenties. The trick was to excoriate the politicians while blackmailing petty crooks and prominent citizens the police might have seen in the backseat of a car in a procreative position. Near was a shrill bigot, anti-Semitic, antiblack, antilabor, anti-Red. But by comparison with the complacent big-city newspapers, which mostly closed an eye to the corruption, both men were doughty muckrakers. "A journalist," said Guilford, "is a reporter out of a job." Guilford was in the hospital when Near got Shapiro's story, the price of ignoring a warning from Big Mose that certain things were not to be reported. Gunmen in a touring car had overtaken him and shot him up. But he wrote his column and Near got the paper out, despite an attempt by the chief of police to impound every copy. Near named Big Mose, he flayed the mayor and chief of police for corruption and the county attorney for neglect. He also laid 90 percent of the crime to "Jew gangsters. . . . It is Jew, Jew, Jew, as long as one cares to comb over the records."

The officials resorted to a 1925 Minnesota statute aimed at silencing the rags. It provided for the temporary or permanent banning of "malicious, scandalous, and defamatory" publications. Truth was a defense only if "published with good motives and for justifiable ends." The action was taken by the county attorney—Floyd Olson, the golden boy of Minnesota politics, who was to become a reforming governor. Minnesota's judges rewarded him with a permanent suppression of Near and Guilford's paper.

There now emerged one of the most intriguing paradoxes in the history of American liberty. The ban was appealed to the United States Supreme Court by the American Civil Liberties Union, an opponent of anti-Semitism and the Red scare; and that appeal was financed by a manufacturer of the Red scare, Colonel Robert McCormick, the owner

READY TO RULE: The new chief justice, Charles Evans Hughes.

READY TO TESTIFY: The *Tribune*'s Colonel Robert McCormick.

of the *Chicago Tribune,* which had attacked the ACLU for "taking Bolshevick gold." Both the ACLU's Roger Baldwin and the flamboyant right-wing isolationist McCormick saw what the Minnesota judges did not: that "prior restraint" menaced freedom of speech for everyone. McCormick had already won an important First Amendment victory. His victory in a libel action brought by Chicago's mayor, Big Bill Thompson, had established the principle that every citizen had a right to criticize the government without fear of prosecution.

Near v. Minnesota looked as if it had to have a hostile reception. Six justices, including Chief Justice Taft, had taken a consistently narrow view of individual rights. One of the Court's three liberal dissenters, Oliver Wendell Holmes, might not be there much longer: he was nearing 90 and frail. But a curious quirk of fate came to play. On the day of Holmes's eighty-ninth birthday, March 8, 1930, news came of the deaths of both conservative Associate Justice Edward Sanford and Taft, who had recently resigned. Everything would depend on the attitude of their successors, the new chief justice, Charles Evans Hughes, and the new Associate Justice, Owen Roberts. On June 1, 1931, Hughes stunned the conservatives, Van Devanter, McReynolds, Sutherland and Butler, with a passionate and trenchant judgment in defense of freedom of the press. He was supported by Holmes, Brandeis, Stone and Roberts, giving a 5–4 majority for invalidating the Minnesota gag law. Butler argued that liberty could not be allowed to degenerate into the license Near practiced. But Hughes stood on higher ground, proclaiming "the rights of the best of men are secured only as the rights of the vilest and most abhorrent are protected." Reckless assaults upon public men had a baleful influence and deserved to be condemned, but government had grown so complex, the opportunities for malfeasance had so multiplied and crime so mushroomed, that a vigilant and courageous press was a primary need for public protection. The answer to a miscreant press was not prior restraint but subsequent punishment for defamation.

Near and Guilford got their paper back. In the summer of 1934 Guilford said he would run for mayor and "tell the whole story of Governor Floyd Olson's connection with the Twin Cities underworld." He did not live to do it. Gangsters in a black sedan forced his car off the road and at close range emptied a shotgun into his head. But the two men's Supreme Court triumph endured. As Fred Friendly wrote in *Minnesota Rag,* his study of the case, *Near v. Minnesota*'s defense of freedom of speech and the press withstood onslaughts from presidents, legislatures and even the judiciary for the rest of the century.

WARREN GAMALIEL HARDING
29th President (Republican), 1921–1923

Caricature by David Levine.

BORN: November 2, 1865, Blooming Grove, Ohio

DIED: August 2, 1923, San Francisco

POLITICAL CAREER: State Senator, Ohio, 1900–1904; Lieutenant Governor of Ohio, 1904–1906; U.S. Senator from Ohio, 1915–1921; President, 1921–1923

FIRSTS: First sitting senator elected to presidency. First to ride to his inaugural in an automobile. First president to be born after the end of the Civil War.

HIS HEROES: Alexander Hamilton, Napoleon, Julius Caesar

SELF-PERCEPTIONS: "I am a man of limited talents from a small town. I don't seem to grasp that I am President." "I cannot hope to be one of the great presidents, but perhaps I may be remembered as one of the best loved."

CHARACTER SNAPSHOT: "Harding was not a bad man. He was just a slob."
                                                          —Alice Roosevelt Longworth

BIRTHPLACE: The Hardings, a restless family descended from a line of English Puritans, cleared the wilderness at Blooming Grove in 1818. (*Right:* Harding revisiting the frame farmhouse in 1890 with a relative.) Harding's mother was a Seventh-Day Adventist, his vitriolic father, George Tryon, trained as a homeo-pathic doctor but also tried his hand as a Union soldier, farmer, teacher, druggist, real estate speculator and print-shop owner.

JACK OF ALL TRADES: Graduating from the local college at 17, he sold hardware, managed the People's Band in Marion and played the cornet in it, managed the baseball team, taught school and hated it, read law books and found them boring, sold insurance and got fired for selling it too cheaply.

The Marion Daily Star.

VOL. VIII. NO. 74.   MARION, OHIO, WEDNESDAY, DECEMBER 10, 1884.   PRICE 3 CENTS.

THE NEWSPAPERMAN: Ink was his adrenaline. He started a paper in college, sorted type in his father's print shop. At 18, he got a reporter's job on Marion's (Democratic) *Mirror,* and swiftly lost it for spending too much time at the Republican club. Around his nineteenth birthday, in 1884, he joined two friends in putting up $300 to buy a dying rag, the *Daily Star.* It was a struggle, selling ads and subscriptions in a town of 4,500 with two other papers. He set type, slept in the office, bluffed creditors and hedged on politics so as to win party printing and advertising. By 1890 he had bought out his original partners, one with a good poker hand. *Left:* Candidate's photo opportunity at the *Star* in 1920.

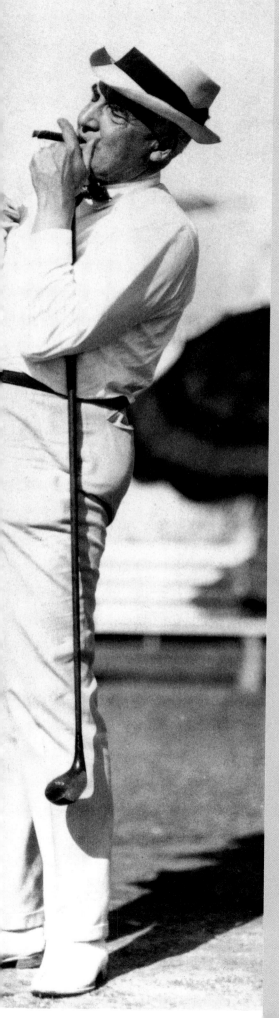

THE DUCHESS: Florence Mabel Kling, said Harding in later life, "wants to be the drum major in every band that passes." He nicknamed her the Duchess. His marriage to her in 1891 was a turning point for him. At 31, she was five years older, divorced from a drunk, and she henpecked his ambition. She was shrewish and sharp and brought a penny-pinching business flair to the *Star* that made it a financial success. She was also the daughter of Amos Kling, Marion's richest man, a banker who cut her off. He called Harding a "nigger," because of a long-standing rumor there was black blood in the family, and tried to bankrupt him.

THE DARK HORSE: Senator Harding sets off for the Republican convention in Chicago in June 1920. In the Senate, he voted with the party 95 percent of the time—when he voted. He missed more than two in five roll calls, wriggling out of voting on touchy subjects like women's suffrage. Of his 134 bills, 122 were on purely local Ohio issues, and his national bills were anodyne matters like celebrating the Pilgrims' landing. At the convention he started as a distant fourth to the better qualified General Leonard Wood, Illinois Governor Frank Lowden and Senator Hiram Johnson. He won on the tenth ballot, the night after a meeting of party bosses in suite 404 on the thirteenth floor of the Blackstone Hotel. It established the legend that the corrupt and cynical twenties had been kicked off with a deal in a "smoke-filled room." In fact, it is unclear that anything was fixed. The next day 13 of 16 senators who were delegates continued trying to block Harding until near the very end.

THE POL: Harding always had time to pet babies and dogs; but his affections were real enough. He was a genuine Mr. Nice Guy. He played golf twice a week for his health; five times in his life he confined himself to a sanatorium for his "nerves." He kept on smoking and drinking, though the Duchess stopped him chewing tobacco in public.

GENIUS CAMPS OUT

Henry Ford, Harvey Firestone and Thomas Edison, the three inventors who had done so much to create modern industrial America, took annual "back to nature" trips. They said they were escaping "fictitious civilization" and were originally guided by the great naturalist John Burroughs. Firestone relished the tours of flora and fauna. Edison spent most of his time napping and reading. Ford liked to chop firewood and challenge the other "vagabonds" to foot races. Every time he crossed a running stream he lectured his companions on the potential of water power. At night, they sat around the campfire and prodded Edison to talk about his inventions. Then they all retired to their own ten-by-ten-foot tents, complete with canvas beds and electric light.

By the time Harding joined the trio on a July weekend in 1921, at Firestone's estate near Licking Creek, Maryland, the trip had become something of an advertisement for the automobile, part of contemporary Americana, with a caravan of 50 cars, and a press party. America's new place in a speedier world was acknowledged by the presence in the undergrowth of a government cipher operator and cipher machine so the President could keep in touch with the State Department. The caution was probably excessive, but it was the first step on the road to the times when the president had to be accompanied everywhere by a man holding a briefcase with the means to blow up the world.

Harding the tippler had the more serious discomfort of being hounded to sign a total-abstinence pledge by Cincinnati's Methodist bishop, William Anderson. But the weekend suited Harding just fine. He never learned to drive but he never missed an opportunity to "boost a Booster" (one of his earliest campaign slogans back in Marion). He needed a boost to his own popularity. His fellow camper Ford was being talked of more and more as the next president. A poll of college students named Ford the third-greatest historical figure of all time, trailing only Napoleon and Jesus Christ. As the Harding scandals began to seep out, the *Wall Street Journal* pushed Ford's candidacy. Ford liked the idea. With the help of that now familiar figure the ghostwriter, he published *My Life and Work* in 1922 and saw it become an international best-seller acclaimed as an inspiration to all. He had handicaps. He could not speak in public; and his paranoid tendencies were hardening. The anti-Semitism preached in his hate sheet, the *Dearborn Independent,* had an avid reader in the up-and-coming Adolf Hitler: Ford is the only American mentioned in *Mein Kampf.* Ford's presidential hopes ended with the death of Harding and the succession of Calvin Coolidge.

The Fords and the Edisons were close. They vacationed together for 25 years, going to Florida after both men became too old for camping. In 1931, as the inventor lay dying, Ford asked Charles Edison to capture his father's last breath in a vial, which he kept at his estate for many years.

Edison is being served, Harding and Ford are to his left and Firestone is in left foreground.

THE RACIST MASTERPIECE

The lynching of Tom Shipp and Abe Smith at Marion, Indiana, August 7, 1930. Lynchings of blacks were commonplace in the postwar hysteria of hate: some of the 70 lynched in the first year after the war were still in uniform. Between 1918 and 1927, there were no fewer than 417 lynchings of blacks. In the South they were advertised beforehand. The once poor Kentucky lad D. W. Griffith did not help with his 1915 cinematic masterpiece, *The Birth of a Nation* (scene right). It glorified the Klan as standing for decency against the depredations of white carpetbaggers and freed slaves in the Reconstruction period after the Civil War. Thomas Dixon, Jr., the writer of the novel on which the film was based, *The Clansman* (1905), got Woodrow Wilson to see it, the first-ever screening in the White House. Wilson said: "It is like writing history with lightning. And my only regret is that it is all so terribly true." The professor was wrong. It was that most lethal of concoctions, a half-truth embellished by artistry.

THE SECOND KLAN

The Ku Klux Klan was revived in Georgia in 1915 and had recruited 4.5 million "white male, native-born Gentile citizens" by 1924. Its hates now were not just blacks, but Catholics, Jews, and immigrants, and it was the Midwest, rather than the South, where it was strongest. Klan governors were elected in Oklahoma and Oregon, and the Klan all but took over the state of Indiana. Imperial Wizard Hiram Evans, a dentist (first picture below), said they were proud of being "hicks, and rubes and drivers of second-hand Fords." But the more respectable members fell out when national organizer David Stephenson of Indiana (center) was convicted of a sadistic sexual murder and spilled the beans on the Klan's corruptions.

The 1921 Imperial Wizard:
Colonel William Joseph Simmons.

MARCUS GARVEY, A BLACK MOSES

Marcus Garvey was to black politics what Louis Armstrong was to the emerging jazz of the twenties, a genius who defied convention and whose themes resonated long after his heyday. The difference in their lives is that Garvey's ended in disgrace, partly because of his own character flaws, but also because his theme of black nationalism invited the hostility of both black and white power structures.

Garvey caught a swelling tide in the ghettos in the twenties. Nearly a million blacks were on the move from the South, doubling and tripling the black populations of cities like New York, Chicago, Detroit and Cleveland. In the rural areas they had been isolated. Concentrated in the cities, they developed a black consciousness imbued with the heady postwar rhetoric of self-determination and pride in their achievements in the war. The emphasis on improvisation in jazz seemed a tangible expression of the defiant creativity and resourcefulness by which black Americans had survived under the oppression of slavery and now sought their place in the modern industrial world. Jazz was but one element of a passionate renaissance of black spiritual and cultural traditions in writing, painting, poetry, photography, vaudeville, song and dance. The ferment evoked a new self-conception epitomized as "the new Negro" by Alain Locke, the first black Rhodes scholar, who in 1925 compiled an anthology by that title. The spirit of the "new Negro" was in the 1925 founding by A. Philip Randolph of the Brotherhood of Sleeping Car Porters, the most important black union in America's history. It was in the flowering of the National Association for the Advancement of Colored People (NAACP), which became, for the first time, more a black organization than an instrument of white philanthropy. It was in Garvey's achievement in building the largest secular mass movement in the history of black America.

Marcus Moziah Garvey was born in Jamaica in 1887. Experiences there as an anticolonial activist, and as a worker in Central America, awakened a sense of a world community of oppressed blacks. He read Booker T. Washington's *Up from Slavery* and absorbed the idea of separatism and self-help as a formula for survival in the South, but his vision soared beyond a regional pragmatism. He rejected integration less as a delusion and more as an insult to his race.

Paradoxically, it was the British Empire that critically shaped his program and his style. In London from 1912 as a student, Garvey sat for hours in the gallery of the House of Commons, watching the great statesmen of a white empire in action. A race without authority and power, he concluded, is a race without respect. So where was the black man's government? Where were his king and his kingdom, his president, his country, his ambassador, his army, his navy? He resolved to create a black system of power (a mass movement with newspapers, marches and shows of strength) and the appropriate symbols (uniforms, flags and a navy). He returned to Jamaica with his "brain . . . afire" and founded the Universal Negro Improvement Association (UNIA), dedicated to uniting blacks across the globe and establishing a self-rule homeland in Africa.

He arrived in New York in 1916 and climbed a Harlem stage to harangue the crowd. He gained real momentum when he founded a newspaper, the *Negro World,* in 1918. Its masthead slogan was "One Aim, One God, One Destiny." His original rallying cry, "back to Africa," soon became an ideal rather than a concrete objective. He had never visited Africa, and the Africans most likely to be invaded by his movement—the Liberians—were dismissive. But he had something more potent. He offered self-respect to a people used to measuring themselves, as W. E. B. Du Bois put it, by the tape of white America. Teach your children, he urged his disciples, to be proud of their blackness and black heritage.

Within two years of his arrival in America, Garvey had hundreds of thousands ablaze with his ideas, and a million followers worldwide. As Ralph Ellison remarked in his *Invisible Man,* "Garvey must have had something. He MUST have had something to move all those people! He moved the father of the sixties leader Malcolm X.

Not all blacks were impressed with a Jamaican who claimed to speak for the entire race. His dismissal of trade unions angered Philip Randolph. His contempt

for social equality angered the NAACP. His insistence that race was more important than class angered the Socialists. But a more important enemy watched his every move: J. Edgar Hoover was at the beginning of his long and sinister career destroying any black who spoke for social change. Hoover wrote to his superiors that "unfortunately" Garvey had not yet violated any federal laws that would permit his deportation, but perhaps they could build a fraud case.

The means were at hand. Garvey envisaged a network of black businesses as the rock on which he would build his racial

PAGEANTRY AND POWER: The heavy-set Garvey (left of sign) wears the plumage of an exiled president in this 1924 James Van Der Zee photograph of one of his parades. There was a serious purpose behind his creation of splendid uniforms for his followers and a British system of knighthoods and honors. He was largely forgotten when he died in London in 1940, but twenty years later his ideas were revived.

empire. He sold black investors thousands of shares at $5 each and set up a shipping company, the Black Star Line (BSL). It rapidly foundered. He was a victim of white businessmen who sold him decrepit vessels at inflated prices, of his own carelessness, and of dishonesty among some of his officers. When arrested in 1922 and charged with mailing material with exaggerated claims for BSL stock, he was a rare businessman federally prosecuted for such practices in those wide-open days. The majority of black leaders outside his organization cheered when his mail fraud trials ended in 1925 in a sentence of five years in prison, commuted to deportation by President Coolidge in 1927.

Garvey's philosophy was confounded by its inability to reconcile nationalism with the obvious need for blacks to get along with whites in America. It was not until the sixties that the potential for a mass movement based on both race consciousness and Americanness was to be realized. But it owed a lot to Garvey's racial pride. As he proclaimed on being led to jail in 1925, the year of the birth of Malcolm X: "If I die in Atlanta my work shall only then begin. . . . Look for me in the whirlwind or the storm, look for me all around you, for, with God's grace, I shall come and bring with me countless millions of black slaves who have died in America and the West Indies and the millions in Africa to aid you in the fight for Liberty, Freedom and Life."

THE FURNACE: Fancy lawyers and backwoodsmen shed their jackets in a courthouse averaging 100 degrees. Bryan confers with a colleague at left. Outside on the lawns, thousands listened on loudspeakers. Some 150 pressmen came, and with them the Bryan-baiter H. L. Mencken and a new breed of broadcasters from WGN in Chicago. They made it the first-ever trial carried by radio. Mencken mocked the locals as ignorant boobs, which rattled them not at all: they made a small fortune on the trial he helped publicize.

THE LAST DUEL OF WILLIAM JENNINGS BRYAN

Nineteenth-century America made its last stand in a boiling courthouse in Dayton, Tennessee. Farmers and their families, in overalls and gingham, flocked into the small mountain town in cavalcades of mule-drawn wagons and Model T flivvers, agog to hear the Great Commoner, William Jennings Bryan, defend their Bible against this newfangled notion that everyone's great-grandpappy was a monkey. Ostensibly on trial was John Thomas Scopes, a 24-year-old teacher of science and football at Dayton High School, who had agreed to be the defendant in a test case of Tennessee's new law proscribing the teaching of evolution. The boosters of Dayton hoped a show trial would put the town on the map. It did.

Scopes was simply an innocent pawn. It was his defender, the great criminal lawyer Clarence Darrow, who personified the menace of Modernity. He was Beelzebub to rural America—an agnostic, a big-city intellectual, defender of labor radicals.

DUELLIST: William Jennings Bryan, three times a candidate for president and still America's greatest orator, cooled himself in court with a palm leaf fan advertising a funeral parlor. He said the trial was "a duel to the death."

Moreover, he was notoriously fresh from saving the rich city kids Richard Loeb and Nathan Leopold from the electric chair, on the grounds that they could not help what they did when they carried out the "perfect murder" of a 14-year-old boy.

It had been 66 years since Charles Darwin's *Origin of Species* had challenged the biblical story of creation. The liberal East and the Episcopalians had long since adapted their faith to its findings, but this only deepened suspicions among the Baptists and Presbyterians in the so-called Bible Belt centered in the Southern states. They saw scientific materialism, like im-

migration, Catholics, Jews and booze, as a plot against their way of life and they took refuge in fundamentalism as well as the Klan and Prohibition. The term originated in 1910 with the publication of millions of copies of *The Fundamentals: A Testimony to Their Truth,* paid for by two wealthy laymen. The book argued the literal truth of the Protestant Bible, the Virgin birth, and the physical resurrection of Christ.

Bryan was but one of many in the fundamentalist movement campaigning against the teaching of evolution in public schools, but by 1925 his eloquence had won him its leadership. That eloquence had been considerably squandered in recent years, mostly in the cause of dubious Florida real estate deals. Seated like a pasha on a barge in the middle of a man-made lake, he would use his fine voice to sell the gullible on the benefits of buying into the Sunshine State. Yet he was still a devoutly religious man, and he was eager to help the state of Tennessee save Christianity. A lifelong opponent of Darwin's illegitimate offspring, Social Darwinism, he saw in the teaching of the "survival of the fittest" the very sort of moral neutralism that could have produced a Leopold

and Loeb. Darrow was as eager to repulse the tyranny of the majority and expose Bible Belt justice.

The two men, both Democrats, nursed an ancient rivalry and it was their personal duel that reverberated throughout America. The case itself was a foregone conclusion when Judge John T. Raulston of Fiery Gizzard, Tennessee, ruled that the issue was not the truth of evolution or the wisdom of the statute, but simply whether Scopes had broken Tennessee's law, which he admittedly had. (He was fined $100). But the real climax was on July 20, the day before the verdict, when the court moved into the open air for Darrow's cross-examination of Bryan, who volunteered himself as an expert on the Bible.

How could Bryan affirm that Jonah was swallowed by a whale? Was he aware of the size of a whale's gullet?

He had been swallowed, hedged Bryan, by a "giant fish."

Did he really believe that the serpent crawled on its belly because the Lord punished it for tempting Eve in the garden of Eden?

"I believe that," said Bryan.

Had he any idea, mocked Darrow, how the snake got about before it was cursed? Did it perhaps walk on its tail?

The huge crowd laughed. The give and take of cross-examination by a master of the art required Bryan to dance like an angel on the head of a pin. He won applause, but so did Darrow, and when Bryan wobbled he lost the support of the zealots. Did he think the Earth was made in six days? "Not six days of twenty-four hours," he answered. Once he had granted the need for interpretation, he had eliminated the fundamentalists' authority. At the end of the trial, while Darrow was surrounded in congratulations, Bryan stood alone with a solitary friend. In the press he was berated as a simpleton.

Five days later in Dayton, Bryan ate one of his enormous meals, despite the midday heat, took a nap and died in his sleep at the age of 65. The anti-evolutionists marked his death with a renewed campaign of witch-hunts and "monkey bills." But the bigotry and ignorance associated with the cause rallied liberal Christians, who believed there was no necessary conflict between the teachings of Christianity and the findings of science. There were no more prosecutions. The tide slowly ebbed.

THE OIL KING: Harry F. Sinclair arrives in his limousine at the District of Columbia jail to begin a sentence for contempt of court. In March 1927, he refused to testify to the Senate, which got him three months. In October, at his trial for conspiracy with Fall, he hired 12 operatives of the William Burns Agency to shadow the jurors in his case and see if any of them could be bribed. That got him a further six months.

SCANDALS GALORE

"THE NATIONAL GESTURE": The bribable open hand of the Harding era, caricatured by Clive Weed in *Judge*.

Albert Fall (1861–1944) went west from Kentucky as a young man. He was a cowboy in Texas, a timberman in Mexico, a hard-rock miner in New Mexico and a U.S. marshal in Texas, where once, in an El Paso saloon, he disarmed the gunfighter John Wesley Hardin. He carried a six-gun by day and read law at night. When he settled down to argue cattle rustling cases in Las Cruces, New Mexico, he became a Democrat, bought a failing newspaper and had the nerve to challenge the local Republican boss, Thomas Benton Cranton. To win, he had to raise a group of armed cowboys and risk his life in a main-street gun duel with the county's deputy sheriff. He was also a poker player who dealt Warren Harding a very bad hand.

Fall was a Republican senator, having switched back, when Harding arrived at the Capitol in 1915 and sat at the desk next to his. The future president learned the ropes from Fall and was charmed by the frontier flamboyance of the Bad Man from the Border in his big black Stetson and gambler's bow tie. When Harding became president, he made Fall secretary of the interior. Harding knew Fall reached for his six-gun when he heard the word "conservation," but he approved when Fall grabbed the naval oil reserve lands from the inept secretary of the Navy, Edwin Denby, and also when Fall leased them to private interests in deals that were kept secret. National security was cited as justification of the clandestine transactions, because the construction of oil tanks at Pearl Harbor was part of one deal. Edward Doheny of Los Angeles got his hands on the reserves at Elk Hills, California, and Harry Sinclair of New York won the oil

THE FIXER: Harry M. Daugherty, Harding's worst appointment, was in his last days as Attorney General when questioned by newsmen as he left a cabinet meeting in February 1924. In March, the Senate voted 66–1 to investigate various Daugherty malpractices. It later condemned them, but on criminal trial Daugherty escaped conviction, probably by bribing the jury. When it was suggested in a 1926 interview that he was either the most maligned man in America or the cleverest crook, he smiled, shrugged and said: "You can take your choice."

underneath Teapot Dome, a striking formation of eroded sandstone in Wyoming. What Harding did not know was that Fall had received $105,000 in cash from Doheny, a friend from Fall's early days who had struck it big since they sweated together in the Grey Eagle mine for $3.50 a day. Nor did the President know that Sinclair, another friend of Fall's and a self-made millionaire, had given Fall $304,000.

All this became known only after years of Senate investigation, spearheaded by a very different kind of self-taught lawyer, the ascetic Thomas Walsh, Democratic senator from Montana. Walsh was aroused even further when his office was ransacked, his phone tapped and his daughter warned that he should lay off. Instead, he followed the money trail and proved that Fall had lied to the Senate. In October 1929, his quarry was finally convicted and sentenced to one year in prison, the first

time a cabinet officer had been jailed for crimes committed in office.

Fall's fellow conspirators did better. Doheny, claiming that he was patriotically assisting the Navy, was acquitted of giving the bribe which Fall was convicted of receiving: the $100,000, said Doheny, was a loan, "a bagatelle to me . . . no more than $25 or $50 perhaps to the ordinary individual." He acknowledged that over the next 30 years he expected to clear a profit of $100 million from Elk Hills alone. Sinclair made $25 million off Teapot Dome just by fraudulent stock manipulation, but he was acquitted of conspiracy.

Fall emerged from jail to live in poverty in El Paso. He maintained to the end that he was not bribed and that the oil storage tanks built as a consequence of the leases he sold helped America survive Pearl Harbor. But Teapot Dome entered the language as a synonym for graft in government.

THE SURVIVOR: Albert Fall is helped into court for his trial in 1929. He was supposed to be at death's door, but he died only in 1944, outliving Doheny, Harding, Sinclair and his persecutor, Thomas Walsh.

IN THE STARS: Florence Harding, trying to get "Wurr'n" to relax on the trip west, never forgot the prediction of her astrologist Madame Marcia that he would win high office but meet "sudden, violent or peculiar death" in that office. One of the myths of his death was that Florence poisoned him.

HARDING'S UNHAPPY LAST DAYS

Warren Harding loved having his Ohio cronies round to the White House for poker and bootleg whisky. Alice Roosevelt Longworth had a displeasing glimpse of the gang in her father's old study, "the air heavy with tobacco smoke . . . a general atmosphere of waistcoat unbuttoned, feet on the desk and the spittoon alongside."

The President also dropped in for cards at the "Little Green House" on K Street (number 1625), and later the Little House on H Street (number 1509), graft headquarters of the Ohio Gang, whose liquor was delivered by armed guards, courtesy of a corrupt Prohibition commissioner. Harry Daugherty, rewarded by Harding for his work as campaign manager with the Justice Department, liked to say he took the job because he knew who the crooks were and he could protect the President from them. At the Little House, the hard little fixer Daugherty and his pulpy companion, Jess ("Whaddaya know?") Smith,

who had graduated from selling clothes, dispensed political favors in exchange for bribes. Five hundred supplicants a day came for anything from a postmaster appointment to a presidential pardon. Smith's specialty was selling "B" liquor permits, which entitled the bearer to withdraw alcohol from bonded warehouses for "pharmaceutical" purposes.

Colonel Charlie Forbes, Harding's dashing young playboy friend from the poker tables, had the same game going as head of the Veterans' Bureau. He took a cut from hospital building. With the help of a California lawyer, Charles Cramer, who sported a brushed pompadour and pince-nez, he had another roaring business shipping new hospital supplies into one end of the bureau's warehouse and literally shipping them out as surplus to his friends at the other end at the same time: Would you like to buy a million towels for three cents apiece that cost thirty-four cents apiece to make?

Harding, meanwhile, worked doggedly at the job of president, one that he knew he was not up to doing. His instincts were generous. He released Eugene Debs from jail against the entreaties of Daugherty and the nagging First Lady. But he did not have a true political philosophy. "Normalcy" was a slogan for some vague conservative impulses closely tied to political expediency. He spoke against lynching but did not back an antilynching law. He released some Wobblies in prison for speaking against the war, but refused a general amnesty of the kind Britain declared for war resisters. He let fresh air into the White House. Anyone could walk in at lunchtime and shake hands with him. "It is," he lamented, "really the only fun I have." He greeted 250,000 people, and stayed up late at night answering routine mail from citizens.

Harding was warned about Daugherty and Forbes, and Albert Fall, too. He did

LYING IN STATE: An honor guard stands by Harding's coffin in the East Room of the White House. Later, more than 30,000 filed past the open casket the afternoon it lay in the Central Rotunda of the Capitol, lying on the same black catafalque that had previously held the bodies of Lincoln, Garfield, McKinley and the Unknown Soldier.

not believe they could be so wicked. As the scandals began to leak, Cramer shot himself on March 14, 1923; two months later Jess Smith shot himself in Daugherty's apartment.

By the summer of 1923, Harding was downcast and sick. In a speaking tour sadly reminiscent of Wilson's, he set out west on a "Voyage of Understanding," and died in a hotel room in San Francisco, on August 2. Millions mourned his passing. It took years for the full extent of the scandals to be revealed and the perpetrators punished; and Daugherty escaped conviction.

The Duchess roused suspicions by burning four to six big boxes of his papers, but Harding himself was not a thief. Herbert Hoover, the only politician finally willing to make a belated dedication of the Harding Memorial tomb in Marion, summed it up when he spoke in July 1931. Warren Harding's soul was "seared by a great disillusionment." He was betrayed by men he believed were his devoted friends, and they betrayed their country.

THE DAUGHTER HE NEVER SAW

Nan Britton had been smitten by Harding's good looks when still a schoolgirl in Marion. She became his mistress, and their daughter, Elizabeth, was probably conceived in his Senate office, though other trysting sites included New York's Central Park and cheap Washington hotel rooms. Nan rejected the childless Harding's suggestion of abortion, and "Elizabeth Christian" was born in seclusion on October 22, 1919. After Harding became president, the Secret Service smuggled Nan into the White House from June 1921 through January 1923. She and the President made love, she said, in an anteroom "not more than five feet square," thereby giving rise to a persistent rumor that Harding kept a mistress in his closet. He left nothing in his will for Nan or Elizabeth, the daughter he never saw, so Nan blew the story in a book, *The President's Daughter*. It survived attempts at suppression and became a best-seller. Harding was not the first or the last president to have extramarital affairs. He was just unlucky in their documentation.

Nan Britton in October 1931 with her daughter, Elizabeth Ann, then 12.

(JOHN) CALVIN COOLIDGE
30th President (Republican), 1923–1929

IMPOSSIBLE INTERVIEW:
Greta Garbo versus Calvin Coolidge,
by *Vanity Fair*'s Miguel Covarrubias.

BORN: July 4, 1872, Plymouth, Vermont

DIED: January 5, 1933, Northampton, Massachusetts

POLITICAL CAREER: City Councilman, Northampton, Massachusetts, 1899–1900; City Solicitor, Northampton, 1901–1902; State Representative, Massachusetts, 1907–1910; Mayor, Northampton, 1910–1912; State Senator, Massachusetts, 1913–1915; Lieutenant Governor, Massachusetts, 1916–1919; Governor, Massachusetts, 1919–1921; Vice President, 1921–1923; President, 1923–1929

FIRSTS: First president to be sworn in by his father. First born on the Fourth of July. First to have his inaugural broadcast over the radio.

CHARACTER SNAPSHOT: "His frugality sanctified an age of waste, his simplicity an age of luxury, his taciturnity an age of ballyhoo. He was the moral symbol the times seemed to demand."
                                        —Arthur Schlesinger, Jr.

THE FARM BOY: He came from an old Vermont family of country squires. His father ran the local general store and his mother, who died when he was 12, was a prosperous farmer's daughter. He had a Norman Rockwell type of childhood. He split firewood, milked the cows, helped his farmer-grandfather sharpen the scythes, and went to the one-room stone schoolhouse in the isolated town of Plymouth, Vermont. Of his family he later said: "They belong to themselves, live within their income and fear no man."

FAITH AND FRUGALITY: He failed to get into a fraternity at the frat-oriented Amherst College until his senior year, when his droll wit won acclaim. He took to his heart the teachings of a Congregationalist philosopher that democracy was the climax of human institutions because the voice of the people is the voice of God. He kept cash accounts that recorded every cent of his board, his newspaper and his regular bag of peanuts. Never once did he overspend.

ON THE LADDER: The modest cum laude graduate did not tell the Northampton law firm that took him on as a clerk (or his father) that his Amherst essay, "The Principles Fought for in the American Revolution," won a $150 prize. Admitted to the bar in 1897, and elected to Northampton's city council, he spent the next 22 years slogging his way slowly up the Massachusetts political ladder. He made no money at it. "I want to be of use in the world," he told his father, "and not just get a few dollars together." His political philosophy, as historian Donald McCoy put it at the time, was "something for everybody so long as it did not cost much."

LOVE AND HEARTBREAK: Grace Goodhue was everything Coolidge was not, vivacious, sociable and outgoing. She was a teacher of the deaf when they married in 1905. "Having taught the deaf to hear," said Silent Cal, "Miss Goodhue might perhaps cause the mute to speak." Anne Morrow, Charles Lindbergh's mother-in-law, could not see "how that sulky redheaded little man ever won that pretty charming woman." In their first week of married life, he presented her with a bag containing 52 pairs of socks—all of them with holes in them. He was a testy husband, though sunk in gloom when she was away. They had two sons and were heartbroken when the younger, Calvin, died in 1924 (above, they are at his graveside). He had developed a septic blister by playing tennis in sneakers without socks. The President lamented: "The power and the glory of the presidency went with him."

PHOTO OPS: No president has been as willing as Coolidge to be photographed in improbable postures—swinging clubs in the White House basement, sporting an Indian headdress, milking cows in his grandfather's smock, pitching hay, dressing up as a cowboy. Three times a day at the White House he rode an electrically operated artificial horse, whooping as he did. When warned people might laugh at him, he replied: "Well, it's good for people to laugh."

UNLIKELY HERO: As governor of Massachusetts in 1919, he was a mild progressive unknown outside the state. In one day he vaulted into national fame, and he did it with one sentence: "There is no right to strike against the public safety by anybody, anywhere, any time." He had been slow to enforce that conviction. Boston police were on strike, claiming the right to belong to a union. There were riots and looting. Coolidge slept undisturbed. A general strike seemed imminent. For two wild days the city was turned over to criminals. The governor did nothing, saying he had no powers. On the third night he forgot his excuses. He called out the entire National Guard after the mayor had already restored order. The strike was broken and his abrupt telegram to labor leader Samuel Gompers on September 14, 1919, containing the famous phrase, turned disastrous negligence into a national triumph.

SWORN IN: On vacation at his father's home in Plymouth Notch, he had done a day's haymaking and been in bed for three hours when the news of Harding's death arrived just before midnight. He was advised to be sworn in at once with his father, a notary public, administering the oath of office. It happened in a small country sitting room, lit by a coal-oil lamp with his mother's Bible on a table. It was observed only by Grace, a stenographer, a chauffeur, a congressman and two newspapermen who were not allowed to take photographs. At 2:47 a.m. the 30th president signed the oath of office with a pen that had been in the family for fifty years.

OUTLAWING WAR: America, still paranoid about anything to do with the League of Nations, was a notable absentee when the enemies of World War I got together at the Swiss lakeside city of Locarno in 1925. Britain's monocled Austen Chamberlain (left) led the talks with Germany, France, Belgium and Italy that ended euphorically in eight treaties guaranteeing the frontiers of western (but not eastern) Europe. Benito Mussolini came by speedboat to smother the principal pact in kisses.

These and other European moves toward collective security were undermined by the prickly isolationism of the three Republican administrations of the twenties and a Senate typified by Senator William Borah's jealous nationalism. On April 6, 1927, the tenth anniversary of America's entry into world war, France's Foreign Minister Aristide Briand (far right), exported the "spirit of Locarno" by proposing a French-American pact of peace. Coolidge and his peppery new secretary of state, Frank B. Kellogg, shied away from tying the U.S. to France, but American public opinion loved the idea that war could be banished by proclamation. In a neat maneuver, the administration made the pact multilateral—and meaningless.

The Kellogg-Briand Pact outlawing war, with endless qualifications, passed the Senate 85–1 in January 1929. Nearly every country signed, but the unrecognized Soviet Union was excluded and the pact had no teeth. It simply buttressed America's illusion that with a few moral gestures it could wash its hands of world affairs. When Coolidge came to sign the pact, his pen ran dry of ink. *Inset opposite:* Marshal Foch leads Allied officers and officials on a visit to the U.S. State, War and Navy Building in Washington, D.C., during the 1921 treaty talks. All three departments could still be contained in one building.

1928: One cynical Christmas carol.

HUGHES SINKS BATTLESHIPS

God stopped the naval arms race on November 2, 1921. Or so it must have seemed to the prime ministers, diplomats, admirals, senators and editors assembled in a beautiful Washington hall for what was expected to be a protracted negotiation. There on the podium was a handsomely bearded figure making the astonishing declaration that America would junk 30 capital ships, two thirds of its battleship fleet and, in a tone that brooked no demur, asking the other great naval powers to do likewise. Charles Evans Hughes, Harding's secretary of state, swept on to name the 19 British battleships he wanted sunk, and the 17 Japanese, for a total of 66.

A tornado of joyous acclaim erupted. Hats waved, handkerchiefs fluttered, men hugged each other. In 12 days the Five-Power Naval Treaty was agreed. The reduced capital ship strength of the Big Three was fixed at a ratio of 5:5:3—500,000 tons each for the U.S. and Britain, 300,000 tons for Japan. Submarines, cruisers and destroyers were excluded, but it was a stunning measure of disarmament.

The deal gave Japan naval supremacy in the Far East, but in Washington at the same time, Hughes secured a pledge from Japan (and seven other nations) to keep the Open Door in strife-torn China: the Japanese had been trying to close it. America, Britain, Japan and France also promised to respect one another's Pacific possessions. The Republicans were proud that these two treaties did not commit America to "old-fashioned" alliances or to back words with deeds.

THE TROUBLESOME AIRMAN

Sixty miles off the Virginia coast on July 21, 1921, military men, diplomats, cabinet officers and reporters packed the USS *Henderson* to watch seven U.S. planes bomb the German battleship *Ostfriesland*, anchored at 100 fathoms. It had been turned over to the U.S. for destruction under the terms of the Treaty of Versailles and the American pilots were trying to do in peace what the British Royal Navy had failed to do in war: in the battle of Jutland the *Ostfriesland* survived 18 direct hits from 12- and 14-inch guns. At risk as much as the battleship that July morning was the reputation of the leader of the strike force, Brigadier General William Mitchell of the U.S. Army.

Billy Mitchell was a nuisance. He had the crazy idea that airpower could win a war and he believed the American ideal of free speech meant something. He would not shut up even when ordered to by his military superiors. The July test was his big chance to prove he was right and that the "hidebound, unfitted and uneducated" admirals were wrong.

Mitchell had showed early in life that he had a mind of his own. His father, a Democratic senator from Wisconsin, opposed the Spanish-American War, but Billy dropped out of college to join the 1st Wisconsin Infantry as a private, and later fought guerrillas in the Philippines. His forgiving father pulled strings to get him a Signal Corps commission.

It was a historic connection. The Army's newest toys, planes and dirigibles, were in the Signal Corps because aviation was seen as simply "the eyes of the army." Mitchell set about furiously to change all that. The airplane, he argued, was an offensive weapon to be used en masse. He even envisaged a "blitzkrieg" deploying hundreds of planes, and parachutists dropped behind enemy lines. On the General Staff by the time America entered World War I, he went to France and teamed up with Britain's Hugh Trenchard, one of the few other air radicals. Washington's brass hats found Mitchell's persistence maddening, but General John Pershing gave airpower a chance. Fifteen hundred Allied planes helped to win the battle of St. Mihiel and Mitchell was made a brigadier general, still only 38.

The bigger battle was to come. Back in Washington, he made enemies by his unceasing agitation for a separate air force. Pershing opposed it. The secretary of the Navy, Franklin D. Roosevelt, termed the idea pernicious. No one on the General Staff, not even the air chief, had flown a plane. The top admirals were angry at Mitchell's statement that their great battleships were at the mercy of flimsy flying machines. Navy Secretary Josephus Daniels offered to stand bareheaded on the bridge of any ship Mitchell tried to bomb.

The July test was a formidable challenge to Mitchell. He rushed to find the best crews from all over the U.S. and train them on mock targets. Then the Army had trouble producing six of its new 2,000-pound aerial bombs. They arrived just in time. Mitchell climbed cockily into a two-seater at Langley Field and led six Martin bombers 60 miles out to sea. With his usual flamboyance, he circled twice around the *Henderson* before the first Martin went in over the *Ostfriesland* with a 25pound ranging shot. At 12:17, the next Martin released a long, thin, cigar-shaped bomb. The four remaining planes did the same—six bombs, all they were able to carry.

The first tumbled end over end and splashed into the ocean. The other bombs were dropped two minutes apart. The *Ostfriesland* just rode the waves. Then the spectators on the *Henderson* noticed that the battleship was lower in the water. It listed slowly to port and the bow came up. There were large holes in the hull from three hits. By 12:33 the stern was underwater. By 12:38 the ship was almost perpendicular. By 12:40 it had gone.

The admirals tried to qualify the triumph. Mitchell increased his tempo. He warned that the Japanese could bomb Pearl Harbor. He accused the Army and Navy of sabotaging aviation and "possibly a falsification of evidence."

In 1925 he was demoted to his permanent rank of colonel and banished to Fort

---

JAPAN'S "MITCHELL"

The man who was to make Billy Mitchell's warnings come true was born four years after him, the seventh son of a poor village schoolmaster in Nagoka. A pilot like Mitchell, Isoroku Yamamoto also had to fight the older military brass still wedded to the battleship, but in general, expansionist Japan was more receptive than the isolationist America of the same period. Yamamoto got his torpedo planes and long-distance bombers, and at Pearl Harbor in 1941 he carried out his ideas. The most dangerous military enemy America ever faced, he was a baseball fan who studied at Harvard, knew his Bible, and played a mean game of poker and bridge. He also remained bitterly opposed to war with America; he thought it was unwinnable. He died on April 13, 1943, when the U.S., having broken the Japanese codes, ambushed his plane in the Solomon Islands.

ADMIRAL "NO": At the London Naval Conference in 1934, Vice Admiral Yamamoto denounced warship ratios between the powers as "this national degradation."

ACCUSED: The father of American airpower, Colonel Mitchell (standing left), doomed by his prophetic cussedness, listens to an assistant judge read the charges at his court-martial. The trial was held in an abandoned Army warehouse. One of his few supporters at the trial was Douglas MacArthur.

Sam Houston. It did not stop him. When the Navy bungled a three-plane mission to Hawaii and lost its dirigible *Shenandoah* on an ill-considered publicity flight, Mitchell lashed out: "These accidents are the direct result of the incompetency, criminal negligence and almost treasonable administration of the National Defense by the Navy and War Departments."

President Coolidge hated this kind of display. He also disliked raising taxes to pay for warplanes. He coped with Mitchell's popularity with the people and press by announcing on September 15 that Dwight Morrow, the presidential adviser and ambassador who was also Charles Lindbergh's father-in-law, would hold an inquiry into the state of aviation. On September 23, the War Department reported that Mitchell would be court-martialed for "conduct prejudicial to good order and military discipline." Even former supporters in the Army had become worried at Mitchell's shrillness. Pershing suggested he had caught the "Bolshevik bug" going around the country.

Ten judges tried the first major "freedom of dissent" case in American military jurisprudence. They found Mitchell guilty. He was suspended from active duty for five years without pay, though also without any official reprimand. On February 1, 1926, he resigned his commission so that he could continue his crusade.

Mitchell had effect. He died in 1936 before seeing many of his prophecies borne out in World War II, but in August 1946 his son accepted a special congressional medal in his father's honor, presented by the chief of staff of the newly created U.S. Air Force.

Mitchell (right), the first pilot in U.S. uniform to cross German lines in World War I, attempts to sell aviation to Will Rogers. Like most people, Rogers thought it was a joke.

Amerika und Nicaragua

Zeichnung von Jacobus Belsen

Gegen den Goldrausch hilft keine Trockenlegung!

YANQUI IMPERIALISM: This German cartoon attack was typical of world reaction to American intervention. Coolidge retorted: "We are not making war on Nicaragua any more than a policeman on the street is making war on passersby."

OUR MAN ON THE TIPITAPA

The impeccable Henry Stimson, who was quietly going about his business as a Wall Street trial lawyer, accepted an invitation to lunch with President Coolidge at the White House in April 1927, and in no time at all he found himself, at the age of 59, sweltering on the wild banks of the dried-up Tipitapa River in Nicaragua. He shared the lunchtime shade of a black-thorn tree with a rebel general, one José Maria Moncada, attempting to persuade him to surrender his army. They were all around, hard men in sombreros and ragged pants of white cotton, toting antique rifles and machetes. Stimson, for his part, had 500 U.S. Marines with Thompson submachine guns lining the river. He also deployed the polite menace he had used as a trust-busting U.S. Attorney in New York grilling sugar barons and bankers. "In less than 30 minutes," Stimson wrote later of Moncada, "we understood each other and had settled the matter."

Isolationism was not much in evidence in Latin America. Coolidge continued the "dollar diplomacy," or economic penetration, practiced by his Republican predecessors, Taft and Harding. It meant sending in the Marines whenever the ruling elites fought one another to the endangerment of the predominantly American businesses. This was often. Troops landed in Caribbean or Central American states on 20 occasions from 1898 to 1920. They were usually welcomed by the privileged and resisted by the nationalists. President Harding had only just brought the Marines home from Nicaragua after 13 years "keeping the peace." Within 25 days there was another coup, so Coolidge put them back on the boats. Not unlike President Reagan in the eighties, he suspected that another power was trying to export communism: in this case, Mexico, whose latest revolutionary president threatened to expropriate U.S. oil companies. Mexico backed one faction in Nicaragua, the U.S. the other. Coolidge blithely asked Stimson to "straighten the matter out."

Stimson induced the Mexican-backed Moncada to make peace with the faction the U.S. favored; and two years later Moncada was president himself. But the matter was not settled. One of Moncada's commanders declared: "We will never live in cowardly peace under a government in-

stalled by foreign power." He was Augusto Sandino, the son of a small coffee farmer and an Indian woman, immediately caricatured as a Bolshevik bandit. Sandino was a nationalist first and an ingenuous leftist second. He had the support of the countryside or he would not have survived the following six years making lightning raids on the Americans. And he kept his promise. When the last Marine left in early 1933, he submitted to the newly elected government and retired with his disarmed men to the countryside.

On February 21, 1934, Sandino was invited to dine at the president's palace. Going home, his car was flagged down by the National Guard, a supposedly nonpartisan police force trained and armed by the U.S. He was taken out and machine-gunned to death. The man who ordered the murder was the guard commander, Anastasio Somoza Garcia, the "frank, friendly and likeable" young man Stimson had engaged as an interpreter. It was the beginning of 45 years of corrupt rule by the Somoza family. They became such allies of the U.S. that Franklin Roosevelt is reported to have said: "He's a son of a bitch, but he's our son of a bitch."

PEACEMAKER STIMSON (above): In 1931, as Hoover's secretary of state, he changed his mind about the wisdom of intervening in Latin America.

GENERAL SANDINO (left, in checkered shirt) on his way to Mexico in 1928, where he got just two machine guns and 1,000 pesos. When General Moncada asked him, "Who made you a general?," he replied: "My comrades in arms, señor. I owe my rank neither to traitors nor to invaders." His ghost continues to haunt the U.S. in Latin America.

HELLO, SUCKER! The doll stepping merrily into a New York City paddy wagon is Texas Guinan, celebrated for sitting on top of a piano in her speakeasies and greeting the customers in this engagingly candid manner. Her good spirits were founded on peddling Scotch at $25 for a fifth, which netted her $700,000 in her first ten months in business, and on the knowledge that this arrest at her 300 Club in 1927 would, like all the others, not cost her a minute in jail. Her business partner, Larry Fay, had pull with Demo-

THE NOBLE EXPERIMENT

Prohibition is probably America's most misremembered deed. The movie scenes of flappers and tuxedoed beaux fleeing the cops suggest that anyone taking a drink faced jail. They did not. Private drinking was always within the law and the courts fairly soon threw out attempts to make social drinkers guilty of conspiracy. It was the suppliers, not the drinkers, that the cops went after. The Eighteenth Amendment, ratified by the vote of the thirty-sixth state, Nebraska, on January 16, 1919, prohibited the manufacture, sale or transportation of "intoxicating liquors," defined as any beverage with more than 0.5 percent alcohol (beer had 3 to 8 percent, wine 10 to 20, spirits 40). The amendment and its enforcing Volstead Act, passed over President Wilson's veto, were aimed at the liquor business and the dark, rough, all-male saloons that were seen as destructive of family life and factory discipline. They were the places where prostitutes picked up clients, wages were gambled and the ward bosses bought votes on election day. The social ills agitated the middle-class members of the Women's Christian Temperance Union (established 1874), among them the devout and much-imprisoned crusader Mrs. Carry A. Nation (1846–1911), who walked into saloons with a meat axe and chopped open the beer barrels. World War I boosted the cause. Drinkers were portrayed as draft-dodging cowards and

the beer barons as the enemy: most were German immigrants. All the Prohibitionists were gathered together in the Anti-Saloon League, founded in 1895 and brilliantly welded into an effective lobby by Ohio's Wayne B. Wheeler, an opportunist, as historian Geoffrey Perrett writes, "easily in the Lenin class." By 1916, saloons were banned in 21 states.

Enforcement of Volstead was underfinanced and halfhearted. Beer continued to be made in big breweries, with the police and agents bribed to pretend it was not happening. The federal agent Izzy Einstein reported that in most cities it took only 30 minutes to find alcohol. Chicago was 21 minutes, Atlanta 17, Pittsburgh 11—and New Orleans 35 seconds. Izzy asked the taxi driver where he could get a drink. "Right here," said the driver, producing a bottle. Two thirds of the liquor came from Canada, the rest by sea. A line of ships called "Rum Row" lay anchored outside New York's jurisdiction. Getting the liquor ashore inspired the best of American improvisation. Some came in as fruit, some was flown in and dropped in lakes, some was fired ashore in torpedoes. Similar ingenuity was shown once the hooch landed. In 1996, the old speakeasy New York's "21" on 52nd Street could still display a cellar stacked with bottles hidden behind a brick wall that slid aside at the touch of a secret button.

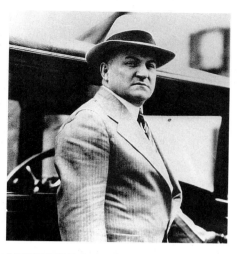

GATSBY STYLE: George Remus, on his way home to Cincinnati in 1926, after two years in jail, was a flamboyantly generous criminal lawyer turned bootlegger and one of the models for the title character in *The Great Gatsby*. At one of his debauches, 200 guests at his estate reveled around his indoor pool until morning, when servants presented each man with $25,000 worth of diamond cuff links and tie pins. The women were stunned when each was given one of 100 shiny Ford roadsters that stretched into the red Ohio dawn. Remus was jailed for bribing Jess Smith at the Department of Justice for permits to buy distilled spirits from government-bonded warehouses for "medicinal purposes." While he was in jail, his wife took up with a former Prohibition agent and squandered much of his fortune. On his release, Remus shot her down in the road, in front of their daughter. He beat the murder rap, but lived out his days in impoverished obscurity.

IZZY AND MOE GET THEIR DRINK—AND THEIR MAN

Isadore Einstein and his deputy, Moe Smith (far left), stood out among the enforcement agents. They were honest. They did not carry guns or arrive with sirens wailing. They walked into the speakeasies in elaborate disguises, ordered a drink and made an arrest—4,392 of them. Izzy preserved the evidence by pouring the whisky into his vest pocket. A funnel fed it through a rubber tube into a hidden flask. When he became famous he would just walk into a bar and announce he was Izzy Einstein and ask for a drink "for a tired Prohibition agent." The bartender would laugh, pour a shot and find himself looking at Izzy's federal badge. Speakeasies posted pictures of him framed in black crepe, captioned "Watch for this man."

Most of the other agents, all appointed through the political spoils system, could be bribed. One in 12 was dismissed for corruption. Don Chaplin ordered his 200 New York City agents into a meeting. "Put your hands on the table. Both of 'em," he ordered. "Every son of a bitch wearing a diamond is fired." Izzy and Moe were fired in 1925, but it was for being too celebrated in their work. It was said they did not behave with the dignity expected of agents; in reality it was for getting more ink than their bosses.

THE RISE OF AL CAPONE

Al Capone got his picture in the *Chicago Tribune* for the first time in May 1924, when he walked into a bar and emptied a six-shooter into the head of a gangster called Joe Howard. Three men saw him do it, but between the murder and the inquest two were overcome by amnesia and one went missing. Alphonse Capone, "antique dealer," never set foot in court. That was for years the pattern of immunity for the gangster who became the most flagrant symbol of the subversion of democracy in America's big cities by money and fear.

Capone was only 25, but he was already the strong-arm partner of John Torrio, the father of modern American gangsterism. Within a year he took over from Torrio as the Big One, chairman of the criminal syndicate that ran Chicago during the twenties. He was never out of the headlines after that.

It was Torrio who had put the syndicate together. A graduate of New York's teen gangs, he was invited to Chicago in 1909 to help his uncle, Big Jim Colosimo, defend his empire of brothels, white slavery and gambling. Prohibition arrived inconveniently for Big Jim. He was too much in love with a young opera singer to pay attention to the opportunities of great wealth Torrio saw in 1920. So Torrio had his uncle killed. Torrio used violence selectively, and always kept his own hands clean. That was why he had sent for Capone in 1919.

Diplomat and triggerman, Torrio and Capone were a perfect match of opposites. Capone was a beefy, hot-tempered bully, a vain man who covered the knife scar on his left cheek with talcum powder, flashed a $50,000 diamond ring on his middle finger, gave press conferences in monogrammed silk pajamas and got syphilis in one of his own brothels. Torrio, who stood no higher than Capone's chest, never smoked, gambled or drank, and went home every night to listen to his phonograph and play pinochle.

Torrio made bootlegging a multi-million-dollar business. He did the deals with the big brewers, bribed the cops and City Hall, and got the Chicago gangs to agree on a peaceful division of bootlegging turf. The peace lasted three years and might have lasted longer, but in 1923 the corrupt Republican mayor, William Hale

TWO CROOKED JUDGES:
Joseph Schulman swears in Emanuel Eller.

("Big Bill") Thompson, was beaten by Judge William E. Dever, a Democrat, who set out to enforce Prohibition with the help of his honest chief of police. Dever may have been the cleanest mayor Chicago ever had, but he presided over the worst outburst of machine-gunning and bombing.

It happened because Dever's Beer War cut into bootlegging profits so much that local gangs started to invade one another's territories. Dion O'Bannion, leader of the North Side Irish, broke Torrio's pact and was shot dead in his florist's shop. Then the O'Bannionites shot Torrio. He survived and promptly retreated to his native Italy, handing over to Capone breweries, speakeasies and brothels with revenues of tens of millions of dollars.

Capone had to subdue every major gang in the city and he did. He had 700 hoodlums at his call. By 1929, they had committed 300 murders (none solved) and helped his man Thompson get back in as mayor. They had judges in their pocket. When Jack Zuta, a Chicago vice lord, was shot dead at a piano player machine, he left a trail of safe-deposit boxes. Among the papers were canceled checks made out to Municipal Judge Joseph W. Schulman and former Judge Emanuel Eller for mob favors. In two months on the court Schulman summarily waived indictments against 16 different hoodlums for carrying concealed weapons.

Capone held the city in thrall. He gave flamboyant press conferences with the injured innocence of a businessman doing his best to provide a service in a wicked world.

CAPONE'S VALENTINE: He was ostentatiously away in Miami on the freezing 1929 St. Valentine's Day, when five of his men, two of them dressed as policemen, lined up seven of the Bugs Moran gang in their North Clark Street garage and blasted 100 bullets into them. They were lured there by a supposed delivery of hijacked whisky. "Only Capone kills like that," said Moran. Nobody was convicted.

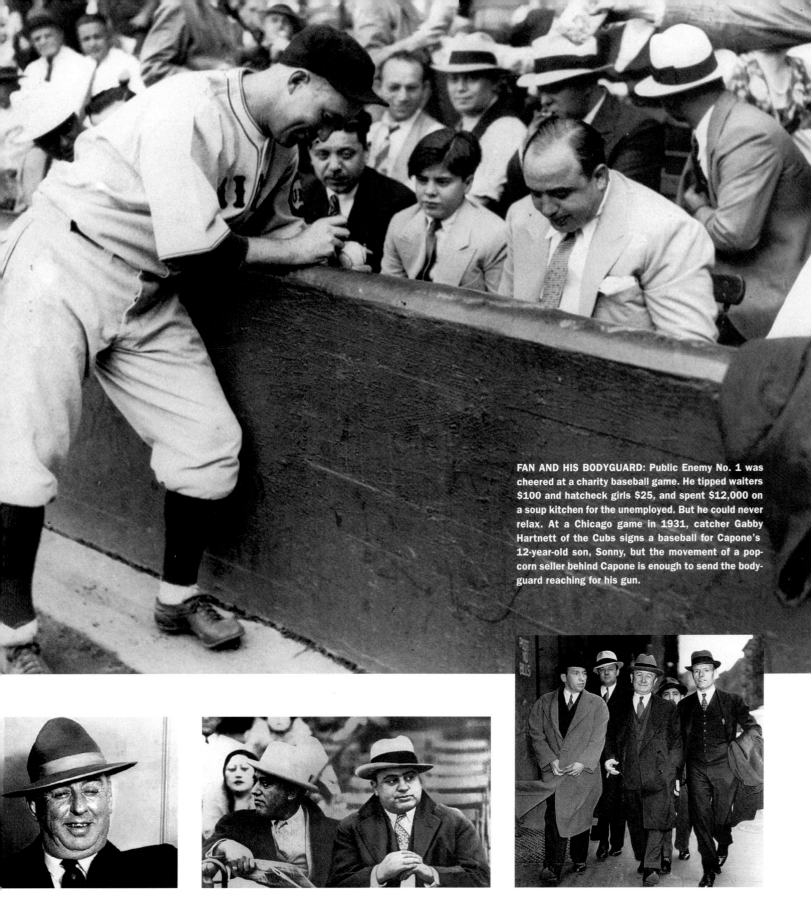

FAN AND HIS BODYGUARD: Public Enemy No. 1 was cheered at a charity baseball game. He tipped waiters $100 and hatcheck girls $25, and spent $12,000 on a soup kitchen for the unemployed. But he could never relax. At a Chicago game in 1931, catcher Gabby Hartnett of the Cubs signs a baseball for Capone's 12-year-old son, Sonny, but the movement of a popcorn seller behind Capone is enough to send the bodyguard reaching for his gun.

THE MOB'S MAYOR: Chicago was wide open under three-time Mayor William Hale Thompson (far left). "I am," he said, "wetter than the middle of the Atlantic Ocean." Capone put his triggermen and bombers at Thompson's disposal to terrorize opposition candidates, voters and election officials. Thompson was a ribald isolationist. If ever the King of England came to Chicago, said the mayor, he would punch him in the nose. *Center:* Capone takes a front row seat at a 1931 football game, with former Alderman A. J. Prinano. *Right:* John Torrio, gangland's brains, has just posted bail for $104,000 on federal charges.

This Gluyas Williams cartoon, "Crisis in Washington," is captioned "Mr. Coolidge refuses point blank to vacate the White House until his other rubber is found." Moving day was much like that. Coolidge personally supervised the packing of 150 boxes, and on inaugural day went all over the White House making sure everything was packed. He joked: "I am having rather more trouble in getting out of the White House than I had getting in."

THE HAPPY WARRIOR FIGHTS BACK

The man who halted the headlong plunge of the Democratic party in popular appeal, and the first Roman Catholic to be nominated for the presidency by a major party, grew up in a waterfront tenement on New York's Lower East Side and left school when he was 12. Alfred Smith was born into a "lace curtain" Irish family as the Brooklyn Bridge went up over their heads. His father's early death sent his mother back into an umbrella factory. Young Al sold groceries in a makeshift basement store she started. He delivered newspapers, clerked and picked up a few dollars calling out telegraph accounts of prizefights to waiting crowds. At 19, he got a sunrise-to-sunset job at the Fulton Fish Market, where he tipped off the merchants as to whether the incoming boats were heavy in the water with a good catch.

Al Smith, presidential candidate, was to find it hard understanding the fears roused by hatred for his religion. As a boy, he saw that the benign influence of his local Roman Catholic Church kept the more respectable community together. Al swam with a gang from the East Side wharves, but he also was an altar boy and pumped the organ at St. James's. Father John J. Kean patrolled the mean streets at night, kept the boys out of trouble and found them work. Al Smith was street-smart. In his early twenties, he made himself congenial in Tom Foley's saloon, where the Tammany Hall braves gathered, and got a job as an investigator for the commissioner of jurors. By the time he was 45, he was governor of New York State.

Smith was made by the city and by Tammany Hall. He looked the part, nattily suited with brown derby and bow tie, a stream of wisecracks in New Yorkese issuing between puffs of a big cigar. But he rose above both city and machine with the kind of cocky daring he had shown as a boy climbing ships' riggings at the South Street piers. He was brought up in a society where social welfare turned on the goodwill of church or machine. The surprising feature about him is that he saw the need to move beyond, to a society where the state guaranteed minimum standards

for all, irrespective of allegiance. His alliance with Senator Robert F. Wagner represented a historic grafting of social reform and machine politics. He filled the top jobs on merit. He forced William Randolph Hearst to forgo a Tammany nomination for senator. He won pensions for widows and legislated a 48-hour working week for women and children. He was also one of the few public men to stand against the prevailing Red hysteria.

In 1924 Smith was thwarted in his bid for the presidency by William G. McAdoo, an explosive Scotch-Irish lawyer out of the red hills of Georgia. McAdoo was one of the few men in the world, said Virginia's venerable senator Carter Glass, who could swear interestingly. Arriving in New York as a young man, McAdoo argued that if a tunnel could be driven ten feet under the Hudson, it could be driven a thousand. So he raised the money and built the Hudson Tubes. He ran the Treasury and the wartime railroads for Woodrow Wilson. For the Democratic nomination he dressed himself in the mantle of William Jennings Bryan. He spoke for the rural fundamentalists, for the drys and the Klan.

At the tumultuous, broiling 1924 convention in Madison Square Garden, Franklin Roosevelt forced his crippled body up to the podium to nominate Smith, "the happy warrior, the man whom strong men in arms would wish to be." But the convention deadlocked on the rural-urban hatreds, the "ape behind the mask" of the party, as pro-Klan southerners on the floor shouted insults back and forth with Tammany toughs in the galleries. After 103 ballots it ended up with the conservative banking and corporation lawyer John W. Davis, and a mealymouthed platform.

Smith won the nomination without a struggle in 1928. His success symbolized the changes in America that so many feared. He had to fight a demonic trinity of prejudices: he was a Roman Catholic, he was an Irishman from a big city (and its machine) and he was a wet. Religion, nativism and Prohibition were the key issues, rather than economic policy. Nobody questioned the boom. Within a week after his nomination, 10 million anti-Catholic handbills, leaflets and posters had been distributed. Many of the most virulent were the work of the Klan, but some bigotry was fostered by Republicans and in-

sufficiently rebuked by Herbert Hoover, the Republican candidate. For a change, the Democrats had a well-financed campaign. John J. Raskob, builder of the Empire State skyscraper, and a General Motors executive, raised a huge war chest from his fellow millionaires. He even got a hit play produced about Smith's life, *The Sidewalks of New York*, which featured Al's ebullient campaign song. But it was Smith's character that made the election memorable. He was one of those people who make a reality of American ideals. He was deeply hurt by the distrust evoked by his religion, and by mean attacks on the appearance of his wife, but he held fast to his faith in the democratic virtues. When an Alabama senator made an anti-Smith speech to a Klan rally outside Albany, Smith gave him the protection of the state police. He disdained urgent party advice to ignore the vicious campaign. If he did, "I felt deep in my heart," he wrote later, "that I would be a coward and probably unfit to be President."

He took the debate right to the heart of enemy territory in a major tour of the Midwest. On the night of September 19, as his train steamed into Oklahoma, he could see the Klan crosses burning on each side of the track. Row upon row of sullen, stony-faced farmers faced him at his meeting but, as H. L. Mencken said, not for him "the usual writhing and crawling." He answered every specific charge in a rip-roaring speech. He affirmed that he recognized no power in the institutions of his church to interfere with the operations of the Constitution. He challenged the Klan and the Republicans directly. The bigots, he said, had made "a treasonable attack upon the very foundations of American liberty."

No Democrat could have beaten Hoover in 1928. He had a smashing victory. His support for Prohibition helped him break the solid South. He took 53 percent of the popular vote, to Smith's 40.7. But Smith's popular vote was a dramatic improvement on Cox in 1920 and Davis in 1924. His background lost him votes in the West and South, but the urban masses clearly identified with him. He won the highest Democratic presidential vote total yet in the century. Even more significantly, he picked up votes in Republican cities. The Democratic majority based on a Southern-rural/Northern-urban coalition was slowly taking shape.

HERBERT HOOVER
31st President (Republican), 1929–1933

Caricature by Emilio Angelo.

BORN: August 10, 1874, West Branch, Iowa

DIED: October 21, 1964, New York City

POLITICAL CAREER: Secretary of Commerce, 1921–1928; President, 1929–1933

FIRSTS: First Quaker to be president. First president born west of the Mississippi.

ON POLITICS: "We in America have had too much experience of life to fool ourselves into pretending that all men are equal in ability, in character, in intelligence, in ambition. That was part of the claptrap of the French Revolution. We have grown to understand that all we can hope to assure to the individual through government is liberty, justice, intellectual welfare, equality of opportunity, and stimulation to service."
—*American Individualism*, 1922

ON HIMSELF: "You can't make a Teddy Roosevelt out of me." "My boyhood ambition was to be able to earn my own living, without the help of anybody, anywhere."

ORPHANS: Herbert (center) and his brother and sister in 1881, the year after their black-smith father's death at the age of 34. His mother taught school and Bible lessons and took in sewing. Two years later she, too, died at 34. Herbert was put on a train to Oregon with two dimes in his pocket, and brought up by his stern Quaker maternal uncle, a country doctor, and his aunt. He never graduated from high school. At 14, his uncle took him out of school to be an office boy in his new land sale company. Hoover learned typing and bookkeeping and polished his math in night sessions at a business school. A visit to a Cascades mine got him excited about engineering. His favorite book was *David Copperfield.* He recalled, "As gentle as are the memories of the times, I am not recommending a return to the good old days. Sadness was greater, and death came sooner."

YOUNG TYCOON: He flunked every entrance exam, except math, for the new Stanford University, but a Quaker professor got him into the "pioneer class" in 1891 and a tutor got him up to scratch. He was a student tycoon. He turned a profit on a laundry agency, a baggage service and a newspaper route, hustled for tips as a waiter, typist and handyman, made money for the baseball and football teams, and as junior treasurer cleared the entire student body of debt. He also won a campus battle against the snobbish fraternities. Studies suffered, but by 27 he was hailed as the highest salaried man of his age in the world. He earned a then phenomenal $30,000. By 1918 his worth was estimated at $4 million.

ADVENTURER: At 21, he pushed a car in the lower levels of a Nevada gold mine for $1.50 a day on a ten-hour night shift. At 23, he sweated as a manager in the Kalgoorlie goldfields in the west Australian desert. On a camel trip, he liked the look of the Sons of Gwalia prospect and bought it for his British bosses. It turned out to be fabulously wealthy. At 24, he married Lou Henry, a geologist and banker's daugher he met at Stanford University, and took her to China. They got caught in the Boxer Rebellion. Lou—photographed above with one of the big guns after it was all over—worked in a hospital with a Mauser .39 on her belt. Herbert stood night watches, built barricades under gunfire, got food and water to 600 trapped Chinese Christian refugees and saved the lives of their leaders from a hot-tempered British captain. The Hoovers were a team out of *Indiana Jones.* As First Lady, she liked to drive 90 mph down mountain roads. He added to his wealth by following ancient Chinese maps to an abandoned silver mine in Burma, complete with fresh tiger tracks inside.

BIRTHPLACE: In 1874, West Branch was a frontier settlement of 365 people.

REBUILDER: Hoover was one of the key Americans in the rebuilding of Europe. Here he is top-hatted at the King's Palace in Brussels in 1919 with Bernard Baruch, Vance McCormick and Norman Davis. Of his role at Versailles, John Maynard Keynes said: "He was the only man who emerged from the ordeal of Paris with an enhanced reputation." In 1920, Franklin Delano Roosevelt said: "He is certainly a wonder, and I wish we could make him President. There couldn't be a better one."

THE CHIEF: The mining appellation stuck to him in seven driving years as secretary of commerce. He was hot for new technology. In 1927, he had his voice and face transmitted to New York over three telephone wires in the first public demonstration of television. He pushed radio. When listeners complained of interference, he was photographed with a one-tube set he bought to find out for himself. He helped the emerging airlines and cajoled industry into standardization of everything from screws to bottle nipples. He set safety rules for railroads, automobiles, cement, elevators and much else. He wrote a manual for new homeowners and a voluntary building code.

HUMANITARIAN: "This man is not to be stopped anywhere under any circumstances." This was the order the Germans eventually wrote on Hoover's passport after he had browbeaten all the warring nations not to get in his way in saving Belgium from starvation. As head of the Commission for Relief in Belgium (CRB) from 1915, he fed 7 million Belgians and French. He took no pay, gave part of his own fortune and risked his life crisscrossing the Atlantic. Here he is arriving in New York in 1918. From 1918 to 1923 he got food to the Russians. When someone complained that it would help the Bolsheviks, he banged on the table: "Twenty million people are starving. Whatever their politics, they shall be fed!"

VISIONARY: After World War II, he raised $325 million, mostly from America, to nurture 15 million stricken children in Europe. Hoover may have saved more people from a slow and horrible death than anyone else in world history.

CHAPTER EIGHT

THE GREAT DEPRESSION
1929–1939

The Dream Turns to Dust

The winds began to blow in the spring and summer of 1929. Nobody took much notice. The stock market soared from peak to peak. The new president, the great engineer Herbert Hoover, foresaw a final triumph over poverty. But even as he entered the White House on a wet and chilly day in March 1929, a recession was gathering. Automobile sales, the heart of the twenties consumer boom, were collapsing; housing starts and manufacturing output were falling. By 1929, Americans had weathered numerous recessions and financial panics. Some could remember the wrenching depression of the 1890s. But nothing in the American past prepared its people for the catastrophe that enveloped them from 1929 right through to the midthirties, and returned in 1937–1939. When it came in the fall of 1929, the Wall Street crash helped to escalate the winds to hurricane force. Investors lost as much money on October 29 as the U.S. had spent fighting World War I. By 1932, between one quarter and one third of all American workers were unemployed. Only in one year before 1940 would unemployment dip below 8 million. National output was more than cut in half. By 1933 a quarter of all the nation's farmers had lost their land.

The American dream seemed to be blowing away with the rich Western topsoil. And more.

The entire Western world stood on the brink of abandoning its long, hard climb toward a society that would both preserve human dignity and honor the ideal of personal freedom.

Elkhart, Kansas, crouches before one of the terrifying black blizzards that struck the towns in the Dust Bowl throughout the thirties. Elkhart prided itself on being the "Broomcorn Capital of the Nation," but for ten years it harvested little but dust. By 1933, the storms had reduced the Elkhart wheat crop to only 37 percent of its normal size. Visibility was sometimes limited to 20 feet for hours. The dirt did not stop blowing until the eve of the Second World War. The photographer of this scene, taken on May 21, 1937, is unidentified.

DARKNESS AT NOON

At the very crest of the twenties, John J. Raskob decided to tear down New York's haughty old Waldorf-Astoria Hotel at 34th and Fifth and put up a skyscraper. Not any old skyscraper, but the tallest building in the world, the Empire State Building, rising 1,250 feet above the street, was destined to remain the world's tallest building for the next 42 years. It was a symbol of the thrusting ambition of America, and of the astounding capacity of its workers and business leaders: the 365,000-ton structure of beautifully streamlined steel, limestone, brick, concrete and glass was completed in just over 14 months.

Raskob himself epitomized the New Era. He was a self-made financier and business genius who reorganized General Motors and became chairman of the Democratic National Committee. He ardently believed that by buying stocks everyone in America could be a millionaire in a mere 20 years. It looked that way when a speculator need put down only 20 percent of the cost to buy industrial stocks that tripled in value between 1921 and 1928, selling sometimes for up to 50 times the annual earnings of the company per share (the traditional valuation formula then was "ten times earnings").

NO SALE: Shiny new automobiles gathered dust in showrooms throughout the Great Depression. Car sales had boomed to nearly 4.6 million by 1929. That total would not be equaled for another 20 years. The industry made continual improvements and slashed prices faster than most manufacturers, but sales dropped to less than 1.6 million by 1933. Most of the remaining small companies were wiped out.

The reality behind this boom was suggested by a discovery that came with Raskob's demolition of the Waldorf-Astoria. The fabled marbled pillars of the gilded old hotel, where robber barons, Hollywood's new stars and European royalty had promenaded down Peacock Alley, turned out to be plaster fakes. Within two months, America found out that its own prosperity was a sham. The long depression that began in 1929 took away all the fabulous gains of the twenties. Gross national product in 1933 was half what it was in 1929 and lower than in 1915. The 1929 level was not achieved again until 1941. It was the same story with average personal incomes. The collapse of output, income and employment threw into question the whole of the capitalist faith on which America had risen. Only the Soviet Union, it seemed, had the answer to the scythe of the business cycle. Undisclosed then was the full horror of the barbarisms Stalin was inflicting in his five-year plans and forcible collectivization of the peasantry. Millions were murdered and millions died of starvation, but this was the time when some young American intellectuals in government, seeing only the surface, changed their allegiance and began to work secretly for communism.

What was so wonderful about American democracy, they asked, when it could squander the skills and waste the lives of its citizens? Nearly 13 million, or one in every four of the workforce, were out of a job in early 1933, and, indirectly, perhaps half the population was affected. How could the workers who performed such miracles as the Empire State's "tower to the sun" be left to rot, when millions of Americans still needed homes and schools and electric power? Even at the end of the boom years, electricity was available only to one American farmer in ten and 75 percent of rural families had no indoor plumbing. What was the morality of a market system that could leave millions undernourished and some on the edge of starvation, when the wheat lay uncut in the fields of Iowa and dairy farmers, devastated by low prices, dumped thousands of gallons of fresh milk over the highways? James T. Patterson has calculated that in 1930 the number of Americans living below the subsistence line, then around $1,200 for urban families of four was 40 million; and 15 million of them had survived that way in the "good" years. Almost all of the country's 10 million non-whites were below the line.

The Great Depression was not simply an American phenomenon. It hit all the industrialized countries, and it devastated the subject peoples of Asia, Latin America and Africa whose very survival depended on being able to sell raw materials to the West. John A. Garraty (*The Great Depression*, 1986) has traced how all the industrialized countries suffered a period of postwar adjustment until around 1923, followed by prosperity until around 1929, and then calamity. They all responded with the traditional remedies, so they all succumbed in a similar manner in the early years of the Depression. Chancellor Heinrich Brüning of the Center Party in Germany cut government spending and raised taxes; so in Britain did Ramsay MacDonald's Labour, and later coalition, government and in France Joseph Paul-Boncour's nominally Socialist government. The result was more depression, and the marching boots of extremist politics: In Germany, Nazis and Communists leapt ahead in elections; Italy was already Fascist. From 1933, there was a spotty recovery, but it ended in the U.S. in yet another sharp recession in 1937–38 after FDR stubbornly insisted on trying to balance the budget and created a second collapse. Then in the fall of 1939, economic life was restored everywhere by the merchants of death.

THE SPECTER: The vast army of unemployed, in Robert Minor's drawing, terrified the nation's bankers.

Most people blamed President Herbert Hoover; World War I reparations, which robbed Europe of its capital; and the Wall Street crash—the famous sneeze that gave everyone else pneumonia. Hoover himself, most fully in his 1952 memoirs, insisted that the Depression did not begin in the United States. He ascribed its origins to World War I, and the creation of unviable new states by Versailles. He blamed the Europeans for living in a fool's paradise after the war and smote a smorgasbord of countries, from Bolivia to Sweden, for entering recession first. His book is an excursion into xenophobia. He criticized Presidents Harding and Coolidge for credit inflation leading to the Wall Street crash, and the chaotic U.S. banking system, but his emphasis was that America would have been out of the Depression in 1931–32 but for those Europeans again. The March 1931 agreement between Germany and Austria for a customs union was in his eyes the Sarajevo of the Great Depression. The agreement angered France and Britain, who retaliated by presenting for payment the short-term bills owed them by Austrian and German banks. The resulting financial panic led to the collapse of Austria's largest bank, and the tidal waves ripped through all of Europe and soon washed hard against the shores of America. Hoover correctly points out that true recovery never came to the United States under FDR in peacetime—there were still 10 million unemployed in 1939—but he blames the New Deal rather than the balanced budget orthodoxy he shared with FDR. Committed in his heart to an absolute individualism, Hoover castigated the New Deal policies as un-American: "There is no middle road between any breed of collectivist economy and our American system."

Hoover's solemn analysis is 500 pages of special pleading. Senator Carter Glass was pushing it only a little when he snorted that the Depression could no more be attributed to World War I than it could to the war of the Phoenicians or the conquest of Gaul by Caesar. The war certainly damaged economies worldwide, but it also created opportunities for reconstruction, and by the late twenties even Germany was booming. Postwar national rivalries in Europe were not conducive to the flowering of economic cooperation, but neither was isolationism in the U.S. "They hired the money, didn't they?" said President Coolidge, when it was suggested that the hard-pressed Europeans should be forgiven their debts in dollars because they had paid them in blood. But by 1929 World War I itself was a vestigial ache, and Hoover's thesis is belied by World War II. That war caused even more havoc to the people and industry of Europe, and yet it was followed by the greatest, longest-running boom in world history. Purchasing power was sustained, of course, in large part by injections of American capital and the Marshall Plan, but the moral of that never dawned on Hoover.

As for passing the buck to all those countries that suffered downturns before the U.S. in 1929, they never did have much influence on the American economy. By the crash, the total value of all U.S. imports and exports was less than 5 percent of gross national product. The cause-and-effect worked in the other direction. It was America, making more than 40 percent of world manufactures, that was the flywheel of the global engine. Hoover is correct that the financial panics in Europe had grave repercussions on American banks and the balance of scholarly judgment is that the international financial system aggravated the Depression. But Hoover's nationalism is misleading. American deflation was the key factor in much of the deflationary crisis in Europe in the first place. Charles P. Kindelberger has argued with some merit (*The World in Depression,* 1973) that the Depression would have been over sooner if Hoover and the Federal Reserve Board had been willing to pick up where the British left off and become the lender of last resort again, as Truman and Marshall did after World War II. Hoover deserves credit for his 1931 initiative that led to a moratorium on all intergovernmental war debts and reparations debts, a tribute to common sense that stood in enlightened contrast to Coolidge's chauvinism. Yet Hoover's vision was gravely circumscribed. A thousand economists—an event in itself—pleaded with him not to sign the Smoot-Hawley Tariff—but in 1930 he did so with a flourish of six gold pens. He thereby raised U.S. duties to the highest level in America's protectionist history, diminishing world trade and triggering retaliations. It was also the last straw for the American farmer.

Why the Depression did start, and why it lasted so long, remains a contentious subject because the issue is at the heart of our contemporary politics. The enduring questions are how much governments should intervene and how the nation's wealth should be shared out. Conservatives who believe the least government is the best have put the most emphasis on the naturalness of business cycles and the inevitability of inequality. Pauses are needed to "refresh" the economy. Inefficient businesses are wiped out and labor is given a salutary shock. Governments that interfere with nature will only make things worse, which is why, the conservatives say, the natural pause of the Depression lasted a decade. John Kenneth Galbraith has exposed how empirically thin this ice is: "No inevitable rhythm required the collapse and stagnation of 1930–40." There was no requirement for a refreshing pause. America's capital plant was not depleted. Labor was not tired. Consumers were not satiated; they might not have been able to spare a dime, but that is another matter.

We also have to look further than the Wall Street crash. The Great Depression is a complex phenomenon and in some respects it will continue to elude precision, but the common "cause and effect" recital that there was a stock market crash, followed by bank closures and then a long depression stands in need of correction. It did not happen like that. Robert Sobel, an expert on the markets of the period, may be too defensive of Wall Street when he asserts (*The Great Bull Market,* 1968) that "no causal relationship between the events of late October 1929 and the Great Depression has ever been shown through the use of empirical evidence." The crash did have a bearing on events in America. But it was certainly not the single trigger so often described.

The clouds were already there on the horizon as the great bull market roared on. There was a lull in the economy in 1928. Converting from the Model T to the Model A, Henry Ford had in 1927 shut down production for six months. Agriculture had long been depressed. All construction was in a slump in the first quarter of 1929. Wall Street was full of gas that was bound to explode—the "prestidigitation, double-shuffling, honey-fugling, hornswoggling and skulduggery" to which Professor William Z. Ripley vainly tried to draw Coolidge's attention in 1928. But it was not all downhill from October 1929, in either the markets or the economy. No major company fell in the crash. Contrary to common belief, there were no immediate bank failures. The wave of business liquidations did not take place for another year. That November, the new governor of the New York Federal Reserve Bank, George Harrison, saved the financial structure from panic. He eased interest rates and pumped $370 million into the banks through the purchase of government securities. The market did recover. It was firm from November 1929 to April 1930. Sobel concludes that, despite the crash, the economy might have escaped the tailspin in the spring of 1930 if Hoover had acted to shore up demand and if the financial system had been reformed.

Galbraith's subtly different conclusion on the role of the stock market is that had the economy been sound, the effect of the crash would have been small. But, of course, the economy was not sound. It was, as Galbraith remarks, exceedingly fragile. The crash gave a double spin to deflation. First, it worked through the financial pyramids, the hundreds of holding companies and investment trusts that had been formed one atop another simply to hold and sell stock. When

Goldman Sachs, for example, floated the Shenandoah Corporation in 1929, a third of Shenandoah's assets was stock in another investment trust, Goldman Sachs Trading Corporation. In due course, Goldman Sachs created another and larger trust, the Blue Ridge Corporation, and 80 percent of its capital was stock in the Shenandoah Corporation. Such speculative monuments of the New Era became its necropolis. Their own stock was exposed as worthless when trade slumped, and to the extent its value was maintained it was at the expense of the bottom-layer operating company, which was squeezed for every cent.

Second, the crash had a further immeasurable psychological impact, not simply on the 600,000 active investors, but on the mass of the population who had followed the Dow Jones roller coaster almost as closely as they followed Babe Ruth hitting 60 home runs in the summer of 1927. They were scared. Millions of families were in debt for the first time, buying on the installment plans: personal debt had more than doubled, from $3.1 billion in 1921 to $6.9 billion in 1929. The incipient recession in 1929 had already made consumers think twice about taking on more debt, because suddenly incomes began to look less assured. Carmakers and house builders had already felt the breeze. The crash amplified it. In 1930, even before earnings declined, and while government spending and investment were still rising, consumer spending suffered a spectacular 10 percent fall.

We should perhaps think of the crash as a fifth horseman of the Apocalypse. The first and surely the lead horseman throughout the whole decade was the skewed distribution of income. Farmers never shared in the prosperity of the twenties and were hammered by high tariffs. The urban masses were better off, but the rich got the gravy in dividends, interest, rents and profit. Industrial output from 1923 to 1929 rose 40 percent, and corporate profits 80 percent. Industrial wages, by contrast, rose only 8 percent. This lack of sustainable mass purchasing power undermined the nation's prosperity. Housing had already slumped by the time of the crash. When, in 1929, the rich started to throttle back their investment and luxury spending, it could not be replaced by consumer demand. As Galbraith puts it, the rich can buy only so much bread.

There was no one to do anything about the pattern of demand. By 1929, the union movement had been all but extinguished. Business had kept the upper hand after crushing a series of major strikes following World War I, and in the next decade it tightened its grip. The percentage of Americans in unions was tiny and many were members in name only. The old IWW had been wiped out and the AFL was a shell. The labor giants of the previous generation—Eugene Debs, Bill Haywood, Samuel Gompers—were all dead now, and no one seemed capable of taking their place. The leaders who would spring up over the next decade—John L. Lewis, Sidney Hillman and David Dubinsky—were too busy preserving their embattled organizations.

Galbraith's cogent analysis of the Depression identifies the bad banking structure as a second mischief: the image of the thirties is as much that of a line at a defaulting bank as at a soup kitchen. There were too many weak, small banks, and no deposit insurance, so the first rumor was liable to produce a disastrous run. The third horseman was the dubious state of the foreign balance. The United States had become a creditor nation. The countries with adverse balances had to either increase their exports (against an increased U.S. tariff), decrease imports, or default. All three things happened, and though foreign trade was still a small proportion of GNP, there were nasty consequences for U.S. farm exports. The fourth mischief is what Galbraith dryly calls the poor state of economic intelligence: "In the months and years following the stock market crash the

THE LIQUIDATOR: Andrew Mellon, the richest Treasury secretary in American history, advised Hoover to "liquidate labor, liquidate stocks, liquidate the farmers, liquidate real estate." Hoover eventually liquidated the liquidator, shipping him off to England when his evasions of the federal income tax became a public scandal. Mellon was the architect of the trickle-down theory. He cut taxes for the rich on the grounds that the wealth they were encouraged to create was better for everyone than redistributive taxation.

burden of reputable economic advice was invariably on the side of measures that would make things worse."

Most of the advice to Hoover was to do nothing. Bankers regarded inertia as they regarded a decent silk hat, the insignia of soundness. Albert H. Wiggin of the Chase National Bank paid obeisance to the "unconscious automatic functioning of the markets." If left alone, the markets would in due course restore normal business. This was the predominant view among the Federal Reserve governors, who had control of the money supply and interest rates. The Fed actually went to some trouble to make things worse. It was loose with money in the 1929 orgy of speculation, when it should have been tight, and erratically tight in the Depression when it should have been consistently loose. The money supply was contracted by nearly a third from 1929 to 1934. There is also evidence (Thomas Ferguson and Gerald Epstein, *Journal of Economic History,* December 1984) that in the early thirties the Reserve Bank presidents opposed increasing the money supply because they calculated it would have an adverse effect on the earnings of private commercial banks.

Hoover was critical of the Fed, which he regarded as Woodrow Wilson's mistake. He himself was neither an extreme laissez-faire ideologue nor a cold bureaucrat. In some ways, he broke the ice for Franklin Roosevelt and the New Deal by his recognition that the federal government had a duty to intervene. He was the first president to accept that the federal government must be responsible in any economic downturn. Presidents Van Buren, Grant, Cleveland and even Theodore Roosevelt had all steadfastly maintained that depressions were acts of God that must run their course: the federal government's duty was limited to keeping order and protecting the currency. This attitude was deep in the brittle bones of Hoover's own Treasury secretary, Andrew Mellon, the leading tribune of the wealthy and the very architect of the speculative craze Hoover had spent much of Coolidge's years

NO MONEY: The shuttered bank became a terrifying reality for Americans. Over 500 a year had failed even during the prosperous twenties. Thousands more closed during the first four years of the Depression. Many rural banks were too small, with assets of only $25,000 to $100,000; others had undermined their reserves by lending money for stock market speculations.

decrying. Liquidation, Mellon told Hoover, would "purge the rottenness out of the system. High costs of living and high living will come down. People will work harder, live a moral life. Values will be adjusted, and enterprising people will pick up the wrecks from the less competent people." It was the worst of the conservative verbiage surrounding the crash and also the most indicative. Economic analysts and editorial writers were full of similar bromides; the contemporary conservative historian Paul Johnson (*Modern Times,* 1984) is in this tradition in his portrayal of Hoover as a meddler who weakened the purgative effects of the Depression. In this view, it was not only natural that the good times of the twenties should be followed by the bad of the thirties. It was also right and necessary.

The most fundamental need to end the Depression was the need to put money in people's pockets, or, as the economists would prefer to say, restore aggregate demand. Looking back, it seems obvious, but it took genius and courage to elaborate the case at the time. Britain's John Maynard Keynes (1883–1946), the seminal economic thinker of the twentieth century, did not publish his book *The General Theory of Employment Interest and Money* (Keynes was economical with commas) until 1936, but he had propagated his ideas long before that. They were well matured when he wrote an open letter to FDR on December 30, 1933. A mild recession might be overcome, he argued, by stimulating business investment through lower interest rates, just as a boom might and ought to be curtailed by higher rates before the economy was fully stretched. But in a deep slump easier credit was not enough; business confidence was often too low to take advantage of cheaper money. The money supply was only a limiting factor. The operative factor was the volume of money actually spent. Relying solely on an increase in the money supply in a slump was "like trying to get fat by buying a bigger belt." So it was vital that governments should directly intervene to replace the lost purchasing power of the unemployed by cutting taxes, and by substantial spending on public works and welfare. Government spending was the key in the thirties, since so few Americans were required to pay taxes; a tax cut could not, by itself, generate much buying power.

Keynes was advocating a heresy: that the federal government should spend substantially more than it took in in taxes, i.e., run a big deficit by borrowing or printing money. "In the past orthodox finance has regarded a war as the only legitimate excuse for creating employment by government expenditure. You, Mr. President, having cast off such fetters, are free to engage in the interests of peace and prosperity the technique which hitherto has only been allowed to serve the purposes of war and destruction." He recognized the risks that so obsessed Interior Secretary Harold Ickes, that a quick program of public works invited waste, inefficiency and corruption. But Ickes, said Keynes, should weigh the risks of less speed against those of more haste: "He must get across the crevasses before it is dark."

Hoover had created the country's first significant federal works projects. But even in rock-bottom 1932—when there was no inflationary pressure whatever—he was calling for increases in taxes to balance the budget. His public works programs were conceived as sparks to restart private business, rather than as engines in themselves, and even these were frustrated by a vast gap between intent and deed—remarkable for a man who had always been a paragon of efficiency in both government and the private sector. The spending was delayed because the projects were not ready (even though such projects had been one of his tasks as commerce secretary), and the states had no money. In 1932, despite Hoover's initiatives, public construction was nearly a billion dollars less than in 1930.

Hoover was not alone in his attitude to what is now called

THE SPENDER: Britain's elegant and witty John Maynard Keynes, drawn by David Low, became the most influential economist of the century. Governments around the world followed his advice and spent their way out of the Depression. Americans proved the most reluctant Keynesians.

Keynesian thinking. Keynes wrote his letter to FDR because he saw the new president making the same mistake. The soon-to-be Treasury Secretary Henry Morgenthau, Congress and the great majority of the Democratic party leaders were against "the dole" and in favor of budgets balanced year in and year out, even in a slump when prices were falling and there was no danger of rapid inflation. So was public opinion, as it manifested itself in the new polls and in the newspaper editorials. The common intuition was that unbalanced household budgets invited catastrophe, and so would unbalanced government budgets. But common sense can be wrong. Science is a journey of the unexpected. Those who clung to the homely metaphor of kitchen budgets were like beginners at skiing who find it hard to take the expert advice to lean away from the mountainside and into the void when making a turn to reduce speed. Every instinct screams at the novice to do the opposite, to hug the slope, and every ski slope is littered with the triumph of physics over psychology.

So it was throughout the thirties. The members of the economic establishment followed their cautionary instincts, and contributed greatly to the free fall of the economy. Cheap money made no difference—the Federal discount rate was never more than 1.5 percent after 1935—but they kept on hoping that "confidence" would return. There is a myth that the New Deal was based on Keynesian economics and the New Deal failed to end mass unemployment, and therefore Keynesian remedies did not work. The New Deal did indeed fail to produce full employment, but the reason for the failure is that the one thing FDR did not really try was full-blown deficit financing. FDR was a very orthodox "sound money" man. It has to be acknowledged that it would have taken a very bold leader to commit to the level of deficit spending called for to restore full employment. The grudging New Deal deficits ran only around $3 billion. The wartime deficits, the trigger of full employment, averaged over $40 billion. It is also easy to forget how much more limited was the scope of government activity in those days. Federal spending was less than 3 percent of the gross national product, compared with 25 percent in the 1990s. FDR would have had to have been even more imaginative than he was to be a full-blown Keynesian.

The emperor of empiricism never learned the lesson Keynes tried to teach. The two men did not hit it off when they met in May 1934. FDR grumbled that "he left a whole rigmarole of figures. He must be a mathematician rather than a political economist." Keynes, for his part, was disappointed that the President was not "more literate, economically speaking." FDR also failed the Keynes hand test: the great economist had the odd notion that a person's hands revealed character and he found Roosevelt's suggestive of firmness "but not clever." But it was not just a failure of personal chemistry. In 1936 a personality utterly different from the languid Keynes's tried to educate the President. Marriner S. Eccles was a small peppery Mormon banker from Utah who had reached the same conclusions as Keynes, but from personal observation in the 1929 crash. By 1936 he had the powerful position of chairman of the Federal Reserve and he was horrified that Roosevelt was still pursuing the chimera of a balanced budget, promising it for 1939, though recovery had barely started. Unemployment had come down from the near 13 million in 1933, and would fall to just under 8 million in 1937. Eccles followed up his verbal assault with a cogent memorandum, nailing the false analogy used by FDR (and many latter-day politicians) between the debt of an individual and the debt of a nation. "The crucial consideration is not the size of the deficit, but the level of national income." Federal spending should not be cut until private enterprise had expanded enough to take up the slack in employment. Deficit expenditures were necessary in the meantime as a form of investment. A new wave of deflation, said Eccles, "would spell the doom of the Democratic party, perhaps even pave the way for totalitarianism." Roosevelt seemed to be shaken and gave Eccles the impression he was converted. It was merely adroitness. At the same time, he encouraged Treasury Secretary Morgenthau to wield the axe on relief and public works and raise social security taxes. A surplus of $66 million was achieved in the first nine months of 1937, but Eccles's warning was soon proved prescient. Between September 15 and December 15, 1937, about 1.8 million people lost their jobs.

There was a spectacular stock market crash on October 19, Black Tuesday. In 1938 the budget was balanced but unemployment was back over 10 million. In March 1938, FDR tried to escape "the Roosevelt recession" by relaxing his squeeze on the public sector—the deficit ran at $2.9 billion in 1939—but only after the wartime deficits of $19 billion (1942) and $53 billion (1943) did unemployment come down to under 1 million, in 1944. It was a belated vindication of Keynes. The war gave the economist Thorstein Veblen his vindication, too. The engineers were in control, rather than the financiers, and the result was a spectacular success. The curious thing, as the historian Henry Steele Commager points out, is the decisiveness with which the experiment was abandoned after the war, but Veblen had anticipated that, too: "This sentimental deference of the American people to the sagacity of its business men is massive, profound and alert."

At the end of the century, despite the persuasive testimony of the thirties, the balanced annual budget, come what may, is still an article of faith across a wide political spectrum. Efforts are continually made to make a simple balanced budget part of the Constitution. This is twenty-five years after Richard Nixon's confession "We're all Keynesians now" and less than a decade after Reagan's orgy of public deficit spending spurred the boom in consumption in the 1980s. Keynes remarked that it takes a generation for today's heresy to become the conventional wisdom. He was too sanguine by half.

America was not unique in clinging to a formal accountancy rather than a dynamic economic policy. Each European country tried with suicidal rectitude to balance its budget. But despite a similar initial skepticism, the Europeans were quicker to adopt Keynesian solutions and were quicker to emerge from the Depression. Socialist Sweden, where one in three had been out of work in 1932–33, was back to full employment by 1939. Germany's unemployment was down to 2.1 percent in 1938, Britain's to 9.3 percent. American unemployment meanwhile was back at 19 percent. By 1938, national incomes in Germany and Britain had exceeded those of 1929. It took until 1941 for that to happen in America. In both Germany and Britain, public spending had risen sharply—it was 35 percent of national income in Germany and 23.8 percent in Britain. By then it was only 10.7 percent in the U.S. In *Modern Times*, in his eagerness to attack affirmative government, Paul Johnson attributes the relative swiftness of Nazi Germany's escape from the Great Depression to the intrinsic strength of German industry, and the fact that Hitler "did not tinker with the economy by systematic public works programs." On the contrary, that is precisely what Hitler did. On assuming power in 1933, he went ahead with huge public works programs, most planned under the Weimar Republic. They included railroad and navigation projects, the building and repair of private homes, the construction of public buildings and the autobahns, where the spending was very heavy after 1935. And rearmament. As Hitler put it to his economics minister, Hjalmar Schacht: "If we win, the debt won't matter, and if we lose, the debt won't matter."

In America, it seems, a severe penalty was paid for the twenties' lack of intellectual curiosity, the narrowness of party differences, the erosion of progressivism and the general pressure for conformity of opinion. But the democratic habit vigorously reasserted itself at the ballot box and in the uplifting public debate that it was the particular genius of FDR to inspire. In Germany (but not France and Britain) economic recovery came at the cost of civil liberties. In the words of one historian, that state was a gigantic prison in which the Nazis locked up workers and bosses and made them cooperate with one another. The extremes of left and right had shallow roots in American soil, but as the Depression worsened any number of dubious plans emerged to alter the American system of government. Hoover and FDR rejected all of them out of hand, to their everlasting credit. When the U.S. Chamber of Commerce suggested that the country be run by a national economic council, Hoover denounced it as "an attempt to smuggle fascism into America through the back door." As vociferously as he attacked President Roosevelt's "collectivist" New Deal out of office, he never joined many of his conservative friends in the American Liberty League.

RIDING THE FREIGHT: One of the millions on the move in the thirties. By 1935 a million Plains people had left their farms, mainly for the cities and California, and another 2.5 million left from 1935 to 1940. But in 1932 the flow was actually reversed—back to the country in what one sociologist described as "a great, uncontrolled mass movement to the succoring breast of Mother Earth"—more prosaically, an effort by destitute Americans to get back to the food source. Woody Guthrie sang it: "If you ain't got the DO RE MI, boys, better go back to beautiful Texas, Oklahoma, Kansas, Georgia, Tennessee."

But the transcendent accomplishment was FDR's.

When Keynes gave his economics tutorial through the press in 1933, he began his letter to FDR: "You have made yourself the trustee for those in every country who seek to mend the evils of our condition by reasoned experiment within the framework of the existing social system. If you fail, rational choice will be gravely prejudiced throughout the world, leaving orthodoxy and revolution to fight it out." Statistically, the New Deal did no more than soften the worst impact of the Great Depression, before the war bore everything before it. But FDR did not fail his trust. He did not become a dictator. He took less executive power than Congress was willing to cede to him. He steered straight into the turbulent currents of democratic debate. The doors of the White House were open to opinion of nearly every stripe. FDR listened and he took the nation with him as he revolutionized the role of the federal government, the structure of American society and the attitudes toward poverty and sickness.

The new United States forged during the Great Depression would not prove immune to demagoguery, corruption, complacency, class and racial hatred and the other eternal problems that afflict every major society. It would prove, however, that democratic solutions were not merely possible in a great crisis, but inescapable.

Americans had abdicated much of their political power in the twenties to the business establishment and party hacks. They took it back and in free debate found a way through the darkness. What they so painfully built has endured longer than the palaces of the Gilded Age.

WALL STREET LAYS AN EGG

At high noon on Black Thursday, October 24, 1929, all eyes on Wall Street were turned imploringly to the House of Morgan. Inside the massive white building on the corner of Wall and Broad, the "Big Six"—six leading Wall Street bankers—were trying to work out a way to save the great bull market of the twenties. It was crumbling around them: by 11 a.m. that day some $9 billion had been knocked off the value of shares. Reporter Kenneth Campbell described the traders on the floor: "It was as though the bear had become a living, visible thing. Some stood with feet apart and shoulders hunched forward as though to brace themselves against the gusts of selling orders which drove them about the floor like autumn leaves in a gale." Great crowds surged up and down the street. The Stock Exchange gallery was closed to prevent a riot by hysterical investors.

The bankers at the House of Morgan were meeting coincidentally on the twenty-second anniversary of the memorable occasion when J.P. Senior had convened a similar group to stop the 1907 panic. Things looked as hopeful in 1929. When the bankers reemerged, led by a jaunty Charles Mitchell, president of the National City Bank, then the largest in the country, the cry rang out: "It's going to be all right!" A few minutes later Richard Whitney, vice president of the Exchange, walked up to Trading Post Number Two with a broad smile and bought 10,000 shares of U.S. Steel. He went around the floor, and spent $20 million buying 200,000 shares. The Big Six had pooled their assets to save the market. The Exchange rallied in the last two hours of trading, cutting losses on the day to $3 billion.

The next day President Hoover publicly reaffirmed the soundness of the economy and the market held steady on Friday and Saturday.

It was the last hurrah of old-fashioned, laissez-faire capitalism. The stock market, trading in a billion shares by 1929 and wildly overvalued, had moved beyond the control of any small group of bankers. On Monday, stocks plunged from the opening bell and now many of the truly solid investments were among them. General Electric dropped 48 points; Eastman Kodak, 42; Westinghouse and AT&T, each 34; U.S. Steel, 18. An estimated $10 to $14 billion was lost.

Hopes were raised briefly again when Mitchell was seen entering Morgan's at 1 p.m. He came out smiling, and the market staged a brief rally. Actually, Mitchell had been securing a personal loan to cover his own dubious business practices. The Big Six and their friends had decided to sell quietly, and actually made a profit. Tuesday, October 29, was, in the words of John Kenneth Galbraith, "the most devastating day in the history of the New York stock market and it may have been the most devastating day in the history of markets." Some 650,000 shares of U.S. Steel were sold in the first three minutes. Before the day was over more than 16.4 million shares had changed hands, a record that would stand until 1968. Some $32 billion had been lost.

The public turned on the former titans of Wall Street with a wrath that would last throughout the next decade. It was not unfounded. The crash found Charles Mitchell in the midst of trying to drive up his bank's stock by surreptitiously buying large amounts of it. He then tried to recoup by selling stocks he did not own to his wife, then writing it off as a tax loss. It also came out that he had loaned over $2.4 million of stockholders' money to his fellow bank officers without bothering to secure either collateral or interest. He was indicted for tax evasion by an up-and-coming young prosecutor named Thomas Dewey. He beat the rap but agreed to pay over $1 million in back taxes.

Richard Whitney, one of the other "saviors of the market," eventually went to prison for three years. He ran out of money investing in peat humus, mineral colloids and applejack liquor, so he invested about a million dollars by stealing bonds from the New York Yacht Club, Harvard, St. Paul's School—and some $667,000 from the Stock Exchange Gratuity Fund, set up for the widows and families of dead brokers. At Sing-Sing his fellow convicts treated him like a gentleman. They always let him get a hit in prison baseball games.

THE MYTHICAL JUMPERS

Legend has it that Wall Street, 1929, was lined with brokers jumping out of their windows. A 51-year-old woman who was chief clerk of the bond department at a brokerage house, Hulda Browaski, did throw herself from the forty-fourth-story roof of the Equitable Building at 120 Broadway on the morning of November 7, 1929, but she was the only one who jumped from a Wall Street window because of the crash—and she was not a player. Her own modest savings were tucked away in federal or municipal bonds, the safest of Depression investments, but she was disoriented by long days and nights sorting out the trading orders that engulfed every house.

The rumors of mass jumpings may have been started by the appearance of a workman on the roof of a Wall Street building on Black Thursday, or by the fall of a large piece of masonry from 40 Wall Street that almost killed several passersby. Suicides were actually lower in October and November than during the summer months of the bull market, but the crash did drive some to kill themselves.

The most spectacular suicide was that of John Schwitzgebel, a Kansas City insurance salesman. Sitting in his club, he dropped the financial page he was reading, shouted, "Tell the boys I can't pay them what I owe them" and shot himself twice in the chest.

ON THE RUN (above): Samuel Insull, checking in for a brief spell in jail, was a brilliant English immigrant who designed the world's first large steam-engine turbine and studied promotion under P. T. Barnum. He was a vital link between Edison's inventions and electrical power in home and factory. In the crash his Chicago utility empire, controlled through a pyramid of holding companies, began to come apart and he fled to Greece. The U.S. got him back, but he was quickly acquitted on charges of mail fraud, embezzlement and violation of bankruptcy laws. He had recklessly overextended his holdings, but juries could not find any law he had specifically violated. He was more a daring businessman than a swindler, and he was also a generous philanthropist.

INDICTED: Richard Whitney (bottom right), a former president of the Stock Exchange, pleaded guilty to two charges of grand larceny.

On Margin.

ON THE MARGIN: The crash ruined families overnight. The hardest hit were those who had played the market by putting down 10 percent in cash and borrowing the rest—buying "on margin," as dramatized in this 1929 Life cartoon.

JAMES MONTGOMERY FLAGG

FROM RICHES
TO RAGS

There were nothing like as many speculators as in pop-ular folklore. In a population of 120 million, there was a total of 1.5 million investors, and only around 600,000 speculators—those who borrowed to gamble. But how they gambled! And what didn't they believe!

In 1920, brokers lent about $1 billion to speculators buying on the margin in the expectation that the mar-ket would rise. By October 1929, margin buyers were borrowing more than $8.5 billion, about half that year's entire public debt of the United States. There was at least one new class of plunger: women. Women held more than a third of U.S. Steel and General Motors, 44 percent of the B & O Railroad and over 50 percent of the Penn-sylvania Railroad, known on Wall Street as "the Petticoat Line." The *New York Sun* described them as "lady bulls . . . dressmakers, hairdressers, stenographers, clerks, pri-vate secretaries, department store saleswomen, milliners and milliners' employees, and even cooks and house-maids." But no woman was allowed to trade on the floor of the Stock Exchange.

Any theory seemed to work in the great bull market that followed Calvin Coolidge to the White House. Thousands swore by a code for hot shares hidden in the dialogue of a popular comic strip. More than 100,000 had faith in the tips of palm-and-crystal-ball reader Evangeline Adams. She told them "the Dow Jones could climb to Heaven." Followers of sunspots and oyster sea-sons seemed to do as well, and no worse than those who relied on the financial "experts" in the media, many of whom were bribed.

BIG-TIME LOSERS

Some celebrated figures were burned. Among them:

The Vanderbilt family lost $40 million in railroads alone.

J. P. Morgan, Jr., lost between $20 million and $60 million.

The Rockefeller family lost four fifths of its fortune.

New York World editor Herbert Bayard Swope lost $16 million.

Winston Churchill lost £100,000 to £200,000, approach-ing $500,000.

Eddie Cantor: $2 million

Theodore Dreiser: $75,000

Alexander Woollcott: $200,000

Clarence Darrow was left "almost penniless."

Jerome Kern was wiped out.

Fanny Brice: $500,000

Flo Ziegfeld: $2 million

Groucho Marx: $240,000

Harpo Marx: $250,000

Rex Stout lost everything, but more than recouped by dreaming up the detective Nero Wolfe.

THE GRAPES OF WRATH

Gigantic billowing clouds of dust up to 10,000 feet high swept across the parched western Plains throughout the thirties. Sometimes they came with lightning and booming thunder but often they were eerily silent, blackening everything in their path. All human activity ground to a halt. Planes were grounded, buses and trains stalled. The clouds could move at speeds of more than 100 miles an hour: the infamous storm of Black Sunday, April 14, 1935, outraced fleeing cars and shorted their ignitions with static electricity.

It was terrifying to see, hell to live through. "This is ultimate darkness. So must come the end of the world," one Kansas woman wrote in her journal. And another: "The doors and windows were all tightly shut, yet those tiny particles seemed to seep through the very walls. It got into cupboards and clothes closets; our faces were as dirty as if we had rolled in the dirt; our hair was gray and stiff and we ground dirt between our teeth. . . ."

On the morning of May 9, 1934, the wind began to blow up the topsoil of Montana and Wyoming, and some 350 million tons were soon sweeping eastward. By late afternoon, 12 million tons had been deposited in Chicago—four pounds of prime topsoil for every man, woman and child in the Windy City. By noon the next day, Buffalo, New York, was dark with dust. On May 11, it settled over Boston, New York, Washington and Atlanta. The storm kept moving south, hazing the skies of Savannah, Georgia, on the

twelfth. Even the Atlantic was no barrier. Ships 300 miles out to sea found dust on their decks. In 1935, there were over 40 dusters that reduced visibility to less than one mile: parts of Kansas, Oklahoma and Texas went six weeks without seeing one entire day of clear sky. There were 68 more storms in 1936, 72 in 1937, 61 in 1938.

Primarily, it was Oklahoma, Texas, Kansas, Colorado and New Mexico that were blowing away, a vast oval of land 400 miles north to south and 300 miles east to west that became known as the Dust Bowl. The concept probably came from the notion of America as a vast, fruited plain between two sheltering mountain ranges, but it was an AP reporter named Robert Geiger who minted the term. Traveling in the area after Black Sunday, he wrote: "Three little words, achingly familiar on a Western farmer's tongue, rule life in the dust bowl of the continent—if it rains."

Heat and drought triggered the storms. Temperatures reached 118 degrees in Nebraska in the summer of 1934, 115 in Iowa. The average rainfall in some counties was by 1934 as low as nine inches. The farmers regarded it all as an act of God. But nature's wrath was provoked by Man, who had attempted to impose on a semiarid region farming only suitable for a humid region. Drought had long limited prehistoric and Indian culture on the southern Plains, even before the arrival of the white man. Drought and harsh winters had combined to destroy the great cattle empires of the 1870s and 1880s. By the 1890s,

millions of homesteaders had replaced the cattle barons, picking up 160 acres from the U.S. and putting it under the plow.

Wheat was the temptation. It needed little rain and even fewer hired hands, but even overgrazed native grass was a better check against wind erosion. Over 32 million new acres of sod went under the plow between 1909 and 1929, over 5 million of it after 1925. Between 1920 and 1930 U.S. wheat output went up 300 percent. Farmers were now planting land that was extremely unstable. To save time, they often burned their wheat stubble after the harvest or let their cattle eat it to the ground,

ON THE ROAD: The typical migrant family of the thirties was a young married couple with a single child. This penniless family on Highway 99, California, had been working the fields in Imperial Valley.

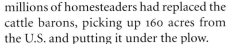

ABANDONED: Farm machinery buried by the dust in a barn lot in Dallas, South Dakota, in May 1936. On the High Plains, 10,000 houses were simply abandoned, and 9 million acres of farm turned back to nature. Banks offered mortgaged properties for as little as $25 for 160 acres—and found no takers.

leaving the thin topsoil all the more vulnerable to wind.

At their height in 1935, the dusters destroyed one half of the wheat crop in Kansas, one quarter of it in Oklahoma, and all 5 million acres of it in Nebraska. In the entire Dust Bowl, less than two bushels of wheat an acre were produced in 1937. By 1938, 10 million acres had lost at least the top five inches of their soil. Some 408 tons of soil had blown away from the average

Dust Bowl acre. In that year alone, over 850 million tons of soil had blown away— soil that contained ten times as much organic matter and nitrogen as the sand dunes left behind.

Still proud and heroic, the wheat farmers of the Dust Bowl, the sharecroppers of the South and countless others everywhere did not wait for the government to save them. They struck out yet again to find better land, or factory jobs.

As Donald Worster has written, the last frontier telescoped into a single generation all the environmental experience of the agricultural West: "From a spirited home on the range where no discouraging words were heard, to a Sante Fe Chief carrying bounteous heaps of grain to Chicago, and, finally, to an empty shack where the dust had drifted as high as the eaves."

OKIES HIT THE ROAD

They were called "Okies," or "Arkies," or the more biblical "exodusters." By 1940, some 3.5 million of them had left the Plains. They filled the roads with worn old Model Ts and rickety trucks. They fled by bus or by riding the rails—hitching illicit rides in freight cars. Forced off their land by drought and mechanization, they were looking for work or some piece of land to farm. Most were already destitute, and each of their journeys was a minor unrecorded epic. The smallest mishap—a blown tire, a cracked carburetor, a child's illness—could take every cent and leave them stranded and friendless.

The spectacular migration inspired artists. Dorothea Lange, Arthur Rothstein, Margaret Bourke-White, Walker Evans, Ben Shahn and John Vachon all produced memorable photographs. Woody Guthrie's folk songs ("This Land Is Your Land") both sympathized with the Okies' ordeal and tried to galvanize them to fight for their rights. John Steinbeck's novel *The Grapes of Wrath* burned into the American imagination. John Ford made it into a film, starring Henry Fonda, that depicted the quietly heroic Joad family seeking the promised land in California and finding it a hell on earth.

That was a fair picture. The Depression began a revival of community values against the selfishness of the twenties, but the million or so migrants who chose to complete their forefathers' manifest destiny and push on to the Golden State often got a brutal reception. Like the Joads, they were likely to be stopped by "bum blockades," set up by the state police, and turned back if they did not have much cash. If they got a job picking and boxing fruit and baling cotton, they rarely earned more than $350–$400 a year, or one half of what the state of California reckoned to be a subsistence income.

Most of the picker camps were squalid. Migrant workers were treated roughly (and there has not been much improvement). Cotton growers in the Central Valley lowered the old picking rate of $1 per hundred pounds of cotton to 40 cents, then abducted strikers. In a raid on a union office, eleven workers were shot and two killed. Lawyers who tried to defend strikers were beaten up by vigilantes. One victim was told: "You red son of a bitch, arguing constitutional law. We'll give you a taste of constitutional law." The vigilantes had a better understanding of local realities. The only people to spend any time in jail were the strike organizers.

Those who stayed on their dusty land did not have it much easier. The New Deal offered extensive federal relief, but the sharecroppers and tenant farmers of the South, who made up one fourth of its population, had a hard time getting their fair share of the money from the plantation owners.

THE PROMISED LAND: A Texas family of seven, drought refugees, camps out in Exeter, California, in 1936. One of Dorothea Lange's remarkable photographs.

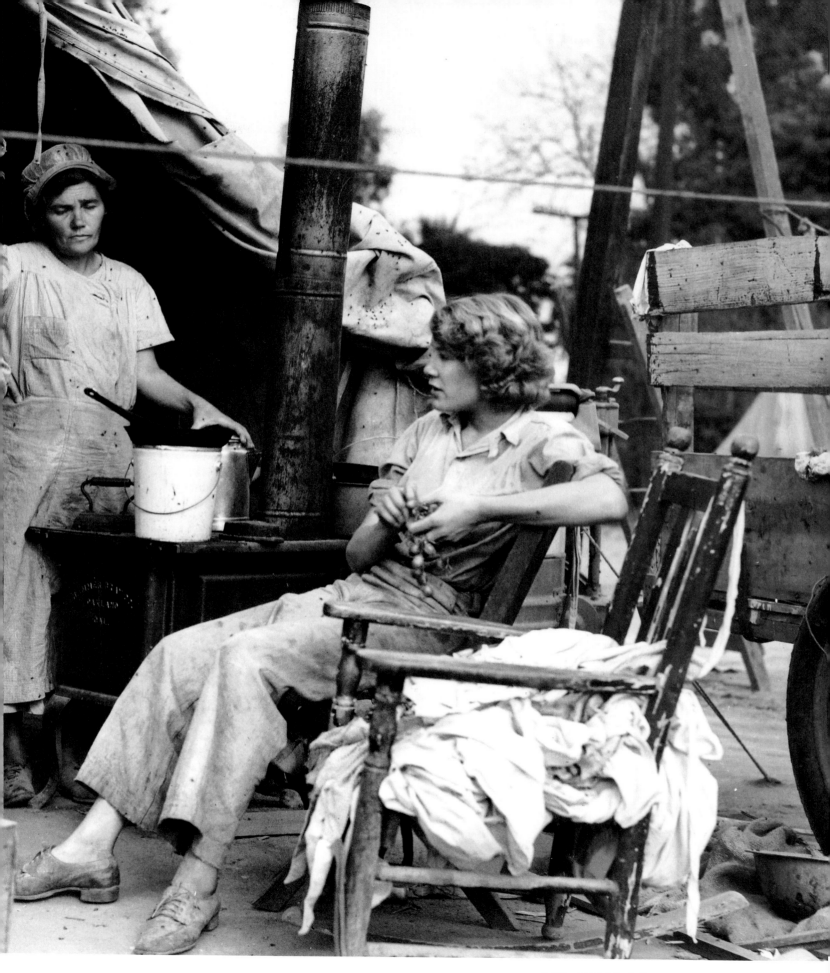

BELEAGUERED: Hoover worked 18 hours a day, and in this March 1932 photograph by Dr. Erich Salomon the strain shows. It was at a Gridiron Club dinner such as this one that the President first tried using the term "depression" instead of "panic" or "crisis," in the hope that it sounded less frightening. The term took hold—just as the Depression did.

THE TRAGEDY OF HERBERT HOOVER

Poor Herbert Hoover! Never has a president seemed more fitted for his destiny. The great Quaker humanitarian who saved Belgium and Russia from starvation; the brilliant progressive technocrat at the Commerce Department; the "Great Engineer" who stood on the tottering Mississippi levee and directed the work that saved hundreds of thousands of people in the 1927 floods; the "wonder boy" of Coolidge's bitter epithet, who had warned the President that his bull market was madly out of control—here in 1929, on the ramparts of civilization, must be his final triumph. It was not to be.

On the eve of the Wall Street crash, he and his wife had attended the last game of the World Series in Philadelphia. They received a standing ovation. In October 1931, he went back to see another of Connie Mack's great teams in the Series and was booed unmercifully. It was one of the greatest public embarrassments yet visited on an American president. The Depression had by then become Hoover's Depression. The rapidly multiplying hobo jungles around the country were called "Hoovervilles." The sacks in which the homeless carried their possessions were "Hoover bags"; the newspapers they draped on the park benches at night were "Hoover blankets"; "Hoover flags" were empty pockets turned inside

out; and the fast diminishing ranks of his defenders were "Hoovercrats."

It might more fairly have been called Coolidge's Depression. As H. L. Mencken wrote of Hoover's predecessor: "There was a volcano boiling under him, but he did not know, and was not singed. When it burst forth at last, it was Hoover who got its blast, and was fried, boiled, roasted and fricasseed." Some of the hatred of Hoover was inspired by a prodigious smear campaign, the largest between elections to that point in American history, conducted for the Democrats by the "flack" Michelson Mills and financed by Raskob, the du Ponts, Herbert Lehman, Vincent Astor and other men of immense wealth. But much of it was Hoover's own fault. He was as stiff as his old-fashioned collars. He was personally generous, but publicly callous. He frequently told the story of a hobo who had eaten ten meals in one day by waiting on all the different breadlines in town. Of the men selling apples in the streets, the symbol of the Depression, he said "many persons left their jobs for the more profitable one of selling apples." It was not a joke. Hoover did not make jokes or admit errors. The presidency was his first elected office and he resented having to deal with argumentative senators and congressmen. In a telling comparison, Richard Norton Smith writes:

"Like Jimmy Carter, another engineer, he failed to understand the fragile ego of subordinate elected officials." He got most of what he wanted in legislation, but he developed something approaching paranoia: people who disagreed with him were dolts. He showed a skill for self-delusion. He refused to believe that 500 farmers and their wives had descended on England, Arkansas, to demand food at gunpoint. It was a Communist invention. "No one," he told the press, "is actually starving." It was untrue. New York City alone had reported 46 starvation-related deaths in 1931.

His most sustained self-delusion was that he was winning. When a delegation of bishops and bankers in June 1930 urged him to expand public works, he said, "Gentlemen, you have come sixty days too late. The depression is over." Four months later, when it was manifestly worse, he was unrepentant. He denounced "economic fatalists." The Depression was being solved by "the genius of modern business." The only thing he accomplished was to convince the American people he was lying to them.

Hoover's unshakable public optimism was sired in part by his belief that restoring "business confidence" was the key to ending the Depression. He put to the test the great faith of 1920s America: voluntarism. Within a month of the crash he had called major industrial and business leaders to the White House. He got them to promise not to cut wages or to fire workers, and to provide relief for the unemployed. He got the unions to agree not to strike or to make excessive wage demands. A few of the country's businesses did what they promised, and the unions were too weak to argue. But the limits of voluntarism were soon exposed. Henry Ford made a dramatic pledge to raise the top assembly-line daily wage from $6 to $7; then it was discovered he was firing senior workers and rehiring them at lower "starting" wages. The last remnants of the agreement fell apart in 1931, when U.S. Steel, the pacesetter, cut its wages (and its dividends) by 10 percent.

As the Depression deepened, it was Hoover's attitude to the new poverty that finally poisoned his relationships with the American people. At first, his determination not to provide federal relief for the unemployed was a true reflection of public opinion. Americans had a loathing for what they saw as the stigma of "the dole." They wanted work. As an accountant on a work project put it, "I'd rather stay out there in that ditch for the rest of my life than take one cent of direct relief." But as they huddled together on the breadlines, the new poor came to feel less ashamed and to express their anger more openly. And even those who would rather die than take relief saw the suffering as a rebuke to a civilized society. Hoover clung to the last second to the illusion that the states and the community chest could cope. Even as late as June 1932, he vetoed the Garner-Wagner relief bill providing $2.1 billion for public works and direct relief to individuals (this came at a time when there was hardly a city or town that was not broke). In July, he agreed to a relief fund of $300 million, but strangled it with red tape: less than $20 million had been disbursed by March 1933.

Once Hoover finally realized that all his hopes had failed, he moved faster than many politicians of both parties wanted. In four months in 1932, he revolutionized the whole idea of a government's role. He signed a bill banning injunctions against unions and strikes. He set up a mechanism to pump capital into failing banks and businesses. He asked for money to save tens of thousands of farm mortgages and co-ops. He seemed at last to be taking decisive action. Yet beneath the surface lurked a faintheartedness that fatally undermined his efforts. As with relief, the money just did not get through. It was as if Hoover did not quite trust the American people. He himself had grown up penniless, working tirelessly for everything he got. Now he seemed incurably suspicious that if his fellow countrymen were given a helping hand they would turn into sloths. With the Depression still raging and relief money coming only in a trickle, the American people were ready in 1932 to repay his mistrust.

BEFUDDLED: Oregon's Congressman Willis Hawley and Utah's Senator Reed Smoot shake hands on the June 1930 passage of their tariff bill, which was meant to help but deepened the Depression by damaging world trade.

BEFORE AND AFTER: In this 1933 *Vanity Fair* cover, a fat 1929 stock prices cutout greets his emaciated brother of 1933. General Electric stock, for example, was worth just 8 percent of what it had been before the crash.

THE VIGIL: Veterans from California camping out on the Capitol lawn in summer 1932 in a vigil to mark the imminent adjournment of Congress and the death of the bonus bill for that session. They took turns walking round the building day and night in a slow, eerie single file soon dubbed "the death march."

GENERAL MACARTHUR
DEFIES THE PRESIDENT

Ten thousand veterans of World War I laid siege to the Capitol on June 17, 1932. Inside, senators debated whether to make 3.5 million old soldiers wait until 1945 for their $1,000 war-service bonus. The House had already approved an immediate cash offer of $500, but President Hoover had threatened a veto: "The urgent question today is the prompt balancing of the budget."

The senators argued into the night. One slipped out to whisper the result to an unemployed Oregon cannery worker, Walter W. Walters, who was the leader of the Bonus Expeditionary Force (BEF); he had fought as a sergeant under Pershing in Mexico and France. The Senate had voted 62–18 against the cash bonus, with 16 abstentions. It was a moment when the "bonus army" might have become a mob. They and their hungry families, 20,000 in all, had camped in hope all summer. There was a thunderous burst of booing and then an ominous silence. Walters called out: "Let's sing 'America,' men!" In a poignant display of patriotism, for which they were soon to be ill rewarded, the veterans obeyed. Standing at attention, heads bared, they hurled the words "My country, 'tis of thee" back into the halls of Congress. Then they formed ranks by states and marched back to their billets, some in deserted federal buildings downtown, most of them to the shantytown they had built across the Potomac on the Anacostia flats.

Hoover had all along refused to meet the veterans, but he had shown some sympathy. He had the Washington police chief provide beds and medicine and Army food. But as thousands lingered after the vote, he came to view them as a revolutionary mob requiring dispersal. His aim was reasonable, the execution outrageous. Hoover's first blunder was to entrust negotiations with the veterans to the military, blurring the subtle constitutional line between making policy and executing it. The second blunder was that the men he appointed, Secretary of War Patrick Hurley and General Douglas MacArthur, had come to believe the vets were Communists and criminals. The talks predictably failed. Then police efforts to evacuate the downtown encampments ended in violence: gunfire from a policeman caught up in a

scuffle mortally wounded two vets, both of whom had been gassed in France.

MacArthur's orders from the President were to clear the downtown area while making sure women and children received "every kindness and courtesy." They did not get it. Everyone, including onlookers, was scattered screaming by Major George Patton's troops of cavalry charging with naked sabers. It is remarkable that the reported injuries were only three wounded. On the heels of the horsemen came masked infantrymen, firing tear gas grenades through a residential area and burning the BEF's downtown encampment. That should have been the end of it. But MacArthur's blood was up. He defied Hoover's explicit orders not to cross the Eleventh Street Bridge and attack the main Anacostia camp. He told his aide, Major Dwight Eisenhower, who tried to dissuade him, "I will not permit my men to bivouac under the guns of traitors." This was fantasy. There were almost no Communists at Anacostia, they certainly did not control the camp and there was no gunfire that night when the troops went in with tear gas and set fire to everything. Two babies died from the gas, and a seven-year-old boy was bayoneted through the leg trying to save his pet rabbit. The veterans wept, shook their fists and finally ran. To Eisenhower it was "a pitiful scene."

By midnight the BEF had been routed. It was then that MacArthur executed his most adroit maneuver. He called a press conference and praised Hoover for facing a grave situation bravely. Hoover was appalled, but he was boxed in. If he fired MacArthur he would seem to have lost control, and he feared identifying himself with men he considered subversive. It is a measure of how reduced he was by the Depression that he tolerated the insubordination. More pathetically, by the time he wrote his memoirs 20 years later, he quietly passed the blame to Hurley, because MacArthur had become a national hero in World War II. He even quoted MacArthur's claim that fewer than 10 percent of the men he attacked were really veterans and claimed that "through government agencies" they learned that only "about 5,000 mixed hoodlums, ex-convicts, Communists and a minority of

ON PARADE: General MacArthur, right, did not move against the bonus army until he had changed into full dress uniform. Major Dwight Eisenhower (at left) suggested it was inapppropriate, but he, too, was ordered into boots and breeches.

veterans were left by the time of the attack." This was untrue, and Hoover had been expressly told it was false by the FBI's J. Edgar Hoover and Colonel Edmund Sterling, chief of the Secret Service. Sterling reported: "Generally speaking there were few Communists and they had little effect on the men's thinking." The records showed 94 percent had Army or Navy records, 67 percent had served overseas and 20 percent had been disabled.

To read this section of Hoover's memoir is to witness a great and kind man staining his own integrity. As a veterans' ballad put it: "In a cage that is fit for a lion/ He moves with the soul of a mouse."

A democracy is at risk when the head of the army can defy the civilian head of government with impunity. Had Hoover's successor also proven inadequate, MacArthur might have considered further how easily he had won the day on the Anacostia flats, when for the first time in American history federal troops were summoned by a president to attack American citizens in their own national capital. Franklin Roosevelt, then in the governor's mansion in Albany, concluded that MacArthur was one of the two most dangerous men in America, the other being Huey Long. MacArthur would live to disobey another president and undermine his administration. But the debacle was the end of Hoover's presidency.

HERE COMES THE NEW DEAL

Campaign buttons in the 1932 presidential election said "Anybody but Hoover." A sadly diminished Al Smith went to the Democratic convention in Chicago that June inspired by the feelings of his rich backers: "Anybody but Roosevelt." Franklin Roosevelt had worried them as two-term governor of New York. He was so open-minded. He had been the first to create a comprehensive relief program. He had brought in cheap public power.

On the first ballot, FDR had 666 votes, Smith 204, and the poker-playing Texan "Cactus" Jack Garner, 90. Roosevelt needed another 104 to win the nomination. Joseph Kennedy, having made millions in stock market speculation and movies, was backing FDR. He called William Randolph Hearst at San Simeon to say a deadlocked convention might pick Newton Baker, loathed by Hearst for his Wilsonian internationalism. For this reason and others, Hearst urged Garner to give his votes to FDR. Garner obliged his patron for the sake of the party, knowing it would mean he had to be vice president, a job he described as "not worth a pitcher of warm piss." William McAdoo, another Hearst ally, swung California and FDR had 942 votes.

Then the crippled candidate did an electric thing. He broke precedent to make an immediate acceptance speech. It meant a valiant, nine-hour plane ride to Chicago. In a moment of high drama that night in the convention stadium, he made a promise: "I pledge you, I pledge myself to a new deal for the American people." It was not a new phrase. It had been written by Sam Rosenman, munching frankfurters, when they were back in Albany. It seemed to be stolen from T.R.'s Square Deal. It was so casually born, FDR did not even use the words in a national radio broadcast a month later when he set out the Democratic national platform. But cartoonist Rollin Kirby inscribed "New Deal" on the wings of FDR's plane heading for Chicago with the image of a farmer leaning on his hoe and looking hopefully up at it. The New Deal caught on.

"HAPPY DAYS ARE HERE AGAIN": His campaign song and everything about him was upbeat. The picture was taken in 1939, but it epitomizes the sparkling sunshine he brought to dispel the swamp gases of the Depression.

His advisers wanted FDR to run a front-porch campaign. He refused, and made a 13,000-mile whistle-stop trip to the Pacific coast. He gave 16 major speeches and 67 minor ones off the back of the train. They were high on emotion, low on specifics. When they were specific, they were not of a piece. He promised to reduce federal spending by 25 percent at the same time that he promised to spend any amount for relief. But he had realized that what the country yearned for was a new system of activist government, so he promised them one "that builds from the bottom up and not from the top down, that puts faith once more in the forgotten man at the bottom of the economic pyramid."

Hoover saw nothing more in FDR than a shifty politician who would say anything to get elected. In his own belated campaign, he would point to a slight upturn in some economic index and say the economy was about to recover. All over the country the Republicans put up signs and billboards that read "Wasn't the Depression terrible?" They didn't play. In Detroit, mobs greeted the President with shouts of "Hang him!" Various tentative plots to kill him were exposed. Most of his fellow Republicans refused to pose with him when he visited their states. Hoover began making scurrilous charges about the "sinister" plans of his ever smiling opponent.

The election was the landslide everyone expected. Hoover lost by more than 7 million votes and carried only six states. FDR won every section of the country and carried huge Democratic congressional majorities into office on his coattails. The Democrats had established themselves as a powerful national party for the first time since the Civil War. A shattered Hoover asked a friend, "Why?" He told his wife: "Nobody knows the heart of a president"; and in a poignant farewell address to Congress he added: "I at least meant well for my country."

FDR's personal style was exhilarating. In Miami on February 15, 1933, in the interregnum a few weeks before he took office, he remained calm, concerned only for others, when the gunshots of an unemployed bricklayer, Joe Zangara, narrowly missed killing him. The bullets mortally wounded Mayor Anton Cermak of Chicago.

BROTHER, CAN YOU SPARE A DIME?

When Rudy Vallee visited the White House in the spring of 1932, Hoover said: "If you can sing a song that would make people forget the Depression, I'll give you a medal." Vallee turned up with an unhelpful dime, Yip Harburg's haunting lament:

They used to tell me I was building a dream
And so I followed the mob
When there was earth to plough or guns to bear
I was always right there on the job....

They used to tell me I was building a dream
With peace and glory ahead
Why should I be standing in line just waiting for bread?

Once I built a railroad, made it run
Made it race against time.
Once I built a railroad, now it's done.
Brother, can you spare a dime?

Once I built a tower, to the sun.
Brick and rivet and lime,
Once I built a tower,
Now it's done.
Brother, can you spare a dime?

Once in khaki suits
Gee, we looked swell
Full of that Yankee Doodle-de-dum.
Half a million boots went sloggin' thru Hell,
I was the kid with the drum.

Say, don't you remember, they called me Al
It was Al all the time
Say, don't you remember I was your pal!
Buddy, can you spare a dime?

But that is not why FDR's head adorns the dime. When he died, the U.S. Mint received many requests to honor the late president. The dime was selected because of FDR's March of Dimes campaign for infantile paralysis, initiated on his birthday each year. The Roosevelt dime was released in 1946 on his birthday, January 30.

FRANKLIN DELANO ROOSEVELT
32nd President (Democrat), 1933–1945

Caricature by
Miguel Covarrubias.

BORN: January 30, 1882, Hyde Park, New York

DIED: April 12, 1945, Warm Springs, Georgia

POLITICAL CAREER: State Senator, New York, 1911–1913; Assistant Secretary of the Navy, 1913–1920; Governor of New York, 1929–1933; President, 1933–1945

FIRSTS: First and only president to serve more than eight years. First handicapped president—and first handicapped person elected head of any major democracy.

CHARACTER SNAPSHOT: "Make no mistake, he is a force—a man of superior but impenetrable mind, but perfectly ruthless, a highly versatile mind which you cannot foresee."   —Carl Jung

"He must have been psychoanalyzed by God." —Anonymous

THE YOUNG SQUIRE: He was the darling only child of Hudson River gentry, leading a cloistered life on their Springwood, Hyde Park, estate. The Roosevelts had arrived in America from Holland before 1648—T.R. was an admired distant cousin of FDR's father, James. FDR's mother, Sara Delano, married James when she was 26 and he was 52. She nearly died giving FDR birth, at 10 pounds, in 24 hours of labor. She breast-fed him for a year, and they were bonded for life. She was intelligent and fearless, but a snob out of an Edith Wharton novel. She kept her beloved boy in long curls and dresses until he was nearly six, and told his governess never to let him play with the village children. The locals touched their caps to him as if he were an English lord. James wore a silk hat, but unlike most men of his wealth, he was a Democratic sympathizer. He raised money for Grover Cleveland.

THE FEATHER DUSTER: Aged 18, in his last year at Groton. He thrived on four years of cold showers and the "rugged Christianity" of Anglophile rector Endicott Peabody. He was in the top quarter of his class and won the Latin prize. At Harvard, he scored a low B to C average, but, as at Groton, he tried hardest at being popular. He "worked like a dog" on the *Crimson,* the college newspaper, and to get elected president, but never forgot his rejection by the exclusive Porcellian fraternity. He had a reputation for being two-faced and telling tall tales. He was labeled "feather duster," a play on his initials, and derided as a "mama's boy" when Sara moved to Cambridge.

CALL ME FRANKLIN: He crossed the divide from patrician to politician in 1910. "Call me Franklin," he told an astonished housepainter on his mother's estate. "I want to enter politics." The man held one of three key votes for the nomination for state senator. It was a safe Republican seat, but Franklin won. He quickly made a name for himself in Albany by successfully leading the opposition to Tammany's candidate for the U.S. Senate, "Blue-Eyed" Billy Sheehan. Most surprised of all were the fellow clerks in FDR's Wall Street law firm. They regarded him as "a harmless bust," but he had outlined to them his plan to become president by the same route T.R. had followed—election to the New York State legislature, appointment as assistant secretary of the Navy, election as governor of New York. Exhorting a Washington crowd to buy Victory Loan bonds in 1919 (above), he had already climbed two of the rungs. President Wilson had made him assistant secretary of the Navy in 1913.

NAVY MAN: He ran the Navy yards for Secretary Josephus Daniels. He was in the crow's nest (left) and everywhere else, cutting through red tape. Joseph Kennedy had a taste of his toughness in 1915. He called on FDR to say his boss, steel magnate Charles Schwab, would not turn over battleships built for Argentina unless he got the money first. FDR genially threatened to seize the ships. Kennedy called "this youngster's" bluff and was sorry he had. Four Navy tugboats with armed Marines commandeered the ships. FDR's vigorous record was marred by his habit of exaggerating his contributions. He was deviously disloyal to Daniels—who forgave him. He suffered greatly in the Newport vice scandal of 1919–20, when Republicans accused him of knowing that enlisted Navy men had been ordered to solicit homosexuals for entrapment.

NATIONAL TICKET: Tammany boss Charlie Murphy promoted FDR's candidacy for the vice presidency in 1920 for much the same reason Republican bosses had put T.R. on the national ticket: to get him out of New York politics. FDR ran against Harding and Coolidge with Ohio's three-time governor, James Cox (left). They visited the dying President Wilson and pledged themselves to the League of Nations. He took his defeat easily, describing himself to friends as "Franklin Roosevelt, Ex. VP., Canned (Erroneously reported dead)."

ELEANOR: Eleanor Roosevelt, the daughter of T.R.'s alcoholic brother, was orphaned at ten. She and her cousin FDR, now a flirtatious law student at Columbia, were emotional opposites, but they married in March 1905 and honeymooned in Europe. It was rocky from the start. FDR, so externally cool, began walking in his sleep. Eleanor feuded with his mother, Sara, who moved in next door and interfered with the raising of the children. Eleanor bore him six within ten years, but advised her daughter, Anna, that sex was "an ordeal to be borne." The idea of birth control was alien to her and the couple had separate bedrooms after 1916. In 1918, she was devastated to discover he was having an affair with her social secretary, Lucy Mercer, a Maryland beauty. It was formally ended at Sara's insistence; the marriage survived as an effective political partnership, but Gore Vidal recalls that many of her stories about life with FDR would end: "And then I fled from the table in tears!" Lucy (now the widowed Mrs. Winthrop Rutherford) started seeing him again secretly in the last years of his life, with the connivance of Anna.

THE CRUCIBLE: From the age of 39 on, when he was stricken by the polio virus, FDR was able to stand only with the aid of heavy metal braces locked round his legs, and could "walk" only with the aid of a cane or crutch and by laboriously swinging each leg forward. His mother wanted him to retire from public life when he was paralyzed in 1921, but he allowed Eleanor and his political wizard, Louis Howe, to persuade him he should stay on. Much of the next seven years was devoted to finding exercises or other cures to restore his leg muscles. His labors were in vain. Backstage, he had to be carried in the locked arms of his aides. But the ordeal matured him spiritually. Frances Perkins thought it brought out a completely humane sympathy for his fellow men. Few of them knew how crippled he was. The press respected his privacy. The public did not see pictures like this.

They are drinking to the end of Prohibition: Hollywood's Michael Jarmer, Gloria Swanson, Jeanette MacDonald and, most likely, Alice Brady.

WHOOPEE!

Prohibition died on December 5, 1933, when Utah's vote for the Twenty-first Amendment provided the required two-thirds majority to repeal the Eighteenth Amendment. An amendment to the Constitution had never before been repealed.

Prohibition spawned modern organized crime, which became a menace to the rule of law in most cities, but it was not quite the outright failure conventionally depicted. Public drunkenness all but vanished. Some people died and some went blind from bad hooch, but altogether diseases and deaths from alcohol went down. The consumption of alcohol per head did not return to pre-Prohibition levels until 1975. Martha Bensley Bruere surveyed social workers and said the early consensus was represented by the head of the Hudson Guild in New York, who told her: "A great number of men who always stopped in at the saloon on the way home and almost emptied their pay packets now bring their wages home. They and their families are living more peaceably than they did before."

The pattern of drinking changed. Surreptitious speakeasies flourished in the cities and attracted more of democracy's newest voters, the women. By 1933, women, who had been the most fervent drys, were now organizing by the millions for repeal on the grounds of individual freedom. Until about 1923–24 public sentiment, broadly, favored enforcement. Thereafter, shocked by the crime and corruption, people changed their minds. A poll of nearly 5 million by the *Literary Digest* in 1930 showed 10.5 percent for enforcement; 29.1 percent in favor of permitting light wines and beer; and 40.4 percent for repeal. Even such fervent drys as William Randolph Hearst, John D. Rockefeller, Jr., and William McAdoo had changed their minds.

In his 1928 presidential campaign, Herbert Hoover called Prohibition "a great social and economic experiment, noble in motive and far-reaching in purpose." At the time, he favored revision rather than repeal. By 1932 both parties were agreed federal Prohibition must go. Bootlegging was over—but the mobs had grown rich and arrogant. The young prosecutor Thomas E. Dewey found there was "scarcely a business in New York" that did not somehow pay its tribute to the underworld—"a tribute levied by force and collected by fear."

HAPPY DAYS ARE HERE AGAIN

On the morning of Monday, March 6, 1933, at the beginning of FDR's first week as president, his valet, Irvin McDuffie, wheeled him from the White House to the executive wing and the office Herbert Hoover had vacated just 36 hours before. McDuffie retreated, and the 32nd president found himself helplessly alone at a bare desk bereft of pen or paper, immobile in a large, bleak chamber. He could find no buzzer to summon his staff, who had thought he would like some prayerful solitude, and he sat in blank-minded fear, as paralyzed in mind as in body. It was a parable of the national predicament. And then he yelled and his beloved secretary, Missy Le Hand, came running from one side and his appointments secretary, Marvin McIntyre, from the other.

And that, too, was a parable. "This nation asks for action, and action now," he had said in his inaugural address on the slate gray day of March 4, 1933. "The only thing we have to fear is fear itself." Of all the many achievements of FDR in those early days, the most sensational was the change he wrought in the national mood. Fear, cynicism and despair yielded to hope, trust and courage. But the nation's nervous breakdown was too advanced for example or exhortation alone to suffice. Action! The day after he took the oath, FDR called Congress into emergency session for March 9.

His priority was to save the banking system. Throughout the bitter four-month interregnum, President Hoover had tried to get FDR to endorse joint policy statements. There was no love lost between the two men. When FDR had begun to wheel himself out of the room at the end of a briefing in November, Hoover curtly told him: "Nobody leaves before the president." The banking crisis had become acute by February 14, when Michigan closed all state banks. Hoover was frantic. He wrote in his own hand to FDR, urging him to make a joint statement to stem the panic. Hoover's mistake was to think this could be achieved by promising, yet again, to balance the budget, and expecting FDR to abandon 90 percent of the New Deal to that aim. FDR evaded commitment. Hoover was enraged. Roosevelt, he told Stimson, was "a madman . . . perhaps they want a breakdown. That is always the technique of revolution."

By March 2, banking had been suspended in 33 states. FDR and Eleanor paid a courtesy call on Hoover that day, two days before the inauguration, and Hoover angrily asked him: "Will you join me in signing a joint proclamation tonight, closing all the banks?" According to Eleanor, FDR replied, "Like hell, I will. If you haven't got the guts to do it yourself, I'll wait until I am president to do it!"

In the early morning hours of Tuesday, March 7, FDR proclaimed a four-day bank holiday. American citizens awoke that Tuesday to find themselves without any money other than what they had in their pockets. They cheerfully managed with barter and IOUs. The emergency session of Congress, opening on March 9, passed the Emergency Banking Act within hours.

On Sunday night, March 12, the day before the reorganized banks were to reopen, FDR spoke to the American people in the first of his radio "fireside chats." An estimated 60 million hung on his every word as he explained the banking system in warm and friendly tones and with a candor and thoroughness no recent American politician would dare to attempt. The next day everything went well when the banks reopened; there were no more frantic lines of depositors.

As the first leader of Roosevelt's "brains trust," Ray Moley, summed it up: "Capitalism was saved in eight days."

By May 18, FDR had fulfilled the dream of Senator George Norris (above) to harness Tennessee Valley water power for the people. Norris had stopped the rights from being given away piecemeal to Henry Ford and others, then had seen Coolidge and Hoover veto his public scheme.

THE HUNDRED DAYS: MILLIONS PUT TO WORK

In the famous hundred days that followed the emergency session of Congress on March 9, to its adjournment on June 16, FDR signed 15 historic bills. All the ideas had been talked about for years, but improvization, not ideology, was the engine of this First New Deal.

Try it and see, was FDR's rule. And if it does not work, try something else.

The changes were breathtaking. With the eager help of a Congress dominated by Democrats and progressive Republicans, FDR completed the rescue of the banking system with deposit insurance. He regulated the stock exchanges; coordinated the faltering rail system; went off the gold

LET THE DESERT BLOOM: FDR at the Grand Coulee Dam site on the Columbia, in Washington State, 1934. Many in the 20,000-strong crowd had driven 200–300 miles to cheer the creator of the project.

standard to raise prices; sent $500 million to the states for direct relief; saved a fifth of all home owners from foreclosure and refinanced farm mortgages. The Agricultural Adjustment Act rescued farmers. It paid them not to produce above a certain quota. Three years later farmers were 50 percent better off.

Two swift triumphs reflected FDR's long interest in conservation and public power. By the summer, 250,000 young men were at work for a dollar a day in the parks and forests: 2.5 million would serve in FDR's Civilian Conservation Corps (CCC). They planted 2 billion trees. The vaultingly ambitious Tennessee Valley Authority transformed life for 2 million people in seven states. It gave cheap power to people who had only gas engines, horses and kerosene lanterns. Floods were controlled, land reclaimed and industry developed.

The last great act of the hundred days, the Industrial Recovery Act, envisaged business and labor in a partnership with the state, represented by the National Recovery Administration (NRA). Government would waive antitrust laws and allow trade associations to draw up "fair practices" codes that would set "fair" production levels, prices and working conditions. The NRA seal of approval was a blue eagle, a stylized depiction of a Navajo thunderbird, which clutched a cogwheel in one talon and six lightning bolts in the other, above the slogan "We do our part." A frenzy of popular support was drummed up for the blue eagle; more than 1,000 cities and towns held parades; 250,000 marched in New York and 2 million cheered them on as the bands played "Happy Days Are Here Again."

This part of the NRA was the New Deal's major flop. It came to be dominated by big business, which kept neither its bargain to recognize unions nor its promise of fair play for the consumer. Prices went up beyond wage increases, so there was no stimulation of purchasing power. Its practical problems and limitations on liberties Americans had always taken for granted soon became evident. What was "unfair" competition? How detailed did the codes have to be? The ones for bowling alleys, for instance, originally went on for hundreds of pages.

But much good, albeit slowly, flowed from the second wing of the NRA, the Public Works Administration (PWA), funded with $3.3 billion. It put 140,000 directly to work each year, created more than 600,000 other jobs and left an enduring legacy: the mammoth bridges spanning the San Francisco Bay and Florida Keys; the Triborough Bridge and the Lincoln and Midtown tunnels in New York; a host of levees, floodways and dams to harness the Mississippi; the Hoover Dam; the massive Grand Coulee and Bonneville Dams to tame the wild waters of the West; the electrified Pennsylvania Railroad; and everywhere schools, public swimming pools, athletic fields, power plants, jails, waterworks, post offices, town halls and highways beyond the scope of private enterprise.

"Anybody else?" Daniel Fitzpatrick on Ickes in the *St. Louis Post-Dispatch*.

MAKERS OF THE NEW DEAL

Washington buzzed. Not even Kennedy's Camelot was to match the array of talent that was drawn by the magnetism and promise of Roosevelt and the New Deal. Legions of bright, ambitious and idealistic men and women swarmed in from the campuses, law offices, country towns and city halls. More than ever before they were women, though even New Dealers had their prejudices, as Eleanor Roosevelt acknowledged in sympathizing with Frances Perkins's difficulties: "How men hate a woman in a position of real power."

All the "uplifters," AAA administrator George Peek grumbled, were chain talkers. But without their open minds, energy and honesty, the intricate initiatives of the New Deal would have been strangled in red tape and corruption.

They justified the discretion they were given. Many of them left poorer than they came. Billions of dollars passed through their hands, but there were no financial scandals. Conservative critics portrayed them as ivory tower dreamers or scheming Reds. A small set were Communist sympathizers or spies, but the leading New Dealers were Democrats, tested in the political trenches. They had battled both corrupt machine bosses and indifferent conservative elites, and still maintained their faith that government, acting as the collective will of the people, could get things done. American public servants would never again accomplish as much.

They embraced the grand idealism Roosevelt gave voice to in 1936: "There is a mysterious cycle in human events. To some generations much is given. Of other generations much is expected. This generation of Americans has a rendezvous with destiny."

HAROLD ICKES, Secretary of the Interior, 1933–1946, long a key figure in the Progressive party, rejoiced in his nickname, Old Curmudgeon. FDR's epithet for him was "Donald Duck," because he squawked a lot—but he squawked sublimely. He was, to take the title of the biography by T. H. Watkins, a righteous pilgrim. As the longest reigning interior secretary, he did more to protect America's heritage in land than any other. He doubled the acreage of the National Park system; he beat off ranchers and farmers who tried to overgraze and plow under fragile Western lands. He directed vast public works programs with rigorous honesty: his hatred for corruption was so virulent that he wiretapped his own employees. He was also a voice of conscience. He hired blacks, he fought anti-Semitism and he transformed Indian policy. For the first time in American history, Indians were seriously consulted about what *they* wanted. He remained an enemy of special interests to the end, fighting attempts by oilmen to use the demands of World War II to make their own fortunes.

DAVID LILIENTHAL (right), a protégé of Felix Frankfurter's at Harvard, was only 34 when FDR made him one of the TVA's three bosses. Fresh from regulating utilities in the Midwest, he rejoiced in bringing cheap electric power to the Deep South: here in 1934 he excites towns-people in Corinth, Mississippi, about the first countrywide rural electricity cooperative. Critics tried to undermine the TVA by calling it "socialism." FDR typically asserted: "I'll tell them it's neither fish nor fowl, but whatever it is, it will taste awfully good to the people of the Tennessee Valley." Lilienthal was the TVA's chairman from 1941 to 1946, then he took over the Atomic Energy Commission, where he brilliantly deflected McCarthyist charges from Senate Republicans. His copious diaries give a valuable insight into the New Deal.

HARRY HOPKINS (left) and Ickes back from a cruise with FDR, whose ambiguities encouraged their rivalry for control of federal works. They were at each other's throats constantly, though they shared a determination to ensure the programs enriched ordinary Americans. Hopkins distributed $10 billion, but hated the dole and tried to make sure recipients worked for the money. In 1933–34, as head of the Civil Works Administration, he put 2 million to work in under a month. "He had the purity of St. Francis of Assisi," said Joseph E. Davis, ambassador to the USSR, "combined with the sharp shrewdness of a racetrack tout." He loved puncturing the stereotype of a social worker by playing poker and going to the racetrack, where he said he did some of his best thinking. He was a whirlwind, working 18 hours a day, who never made more than $15,000 a year.

REXFORD G. TUGWELL (resettlement administrator, 1935–1937). The bare-headed man sitting on parched grass with drought-stricken farmers in Springfield, Colorado, was an economics professor from Columbia, one of the professors FDR recruited into his "brains trust." Tugwell had written a verse while still in school: "I have gathered my tools and my charts; My plans are fashioned and practical; I shall roll up my sleeves—make America over!" He helped. He led the effort to rescue tenant farmers and sharecroppers evicted from land they farmed but did not own. He built three model "greenbelt" cities (Tugwell Towns). He backed Marriner Eccles in favor of deficit spending. Because he had visited the Soviet Union, campaigned for the poor and blacks, and was outspoken for consumer rights, he was the most traduced of all the New Dealers. *Time* called him Rex the Red. Congress investigated charges that he was a master Soviet agent. He was not even a Socialist and thought the Communists "stupid." But the media would not let up, because his demands for truth in advertising threatened their revenues; he was forced out of the Agriculture Department in 1937.

GENERAL HUGH JOHNSON (NRA, 1933–1934). The cavalrymen he led called him Old Ironpants for his fierce ways and his ability to stay in the saddle for hours. He was a great showman, with a taste for the bottle and a talent for invective. Asked what would happen if businessmen refused to go along with the NRA, he shouted, "Then they'll get a sock right in the nose." Critics were "perfumed guys from the State Department." He did not stay long in the NRA saddle. It was probably an impossible job reconciling business and labor, but his failure to resolve the myriad disputes sped the NRA's demise. As labor historian Irving Bernstein put it, "he imposed upon the strained coal negotiations his own particular blend of bluster, bombast, Bourbon and baloney."

HENRY A. WALLACE (secretary of agriculture, 1933–1940). Almost overnight the farmers under Wallace achieved everything they had sought for generations. A brilliant plant geneticist who created the world's first hybrid corn suitable for commercial use, Wallace followed his grandfather and father (Coolidge's agriculture secretary) in campaigning for farm reform and editing *Wallace's Farmer,* a populist journal. He had been an early champion of the New Deal plan to pay farmers who agreed to restrict production. Despite problems in the early years, such as having to slaughter 6 million piglets, it brought steady prosperity to the American farmer. He pushed through programs to conserve soil, assist tenant farmers and provide government warehouses and silos for surplus, and invented the federal food stamp for needy people.

THE MEN WHO BEAT CAPONE

Michael Malone, a swarthy agent of the Internal Revenue Service, passed himself off as Michael Lepito, a Philadelphia burglar, and got invited to the Capone gang's poker table. Frank Wilson, the top Revenue agent, identified a onetime Capone cashier by matching signatures on bank slips, traced him to a Florida dog track and then induced the terrified man to testify about Capone's illicit gains. Robert Isham Randolph formed "the Secret Six," an alliance of Chicago's businessmen dedicated to spending any amount of money to save their city. Eliot Ness, aged 26, led his youthful shotgun squad of uniquely unbribable Prohibition agents—"the Untouchables"—to batter down the steel doors of Capone's secret beer breweries and amass evidence of 5,000 offenses. President Hoover told his cabinet: "I want that man in jail."

All these forces converged on Capone. He put out a contract for $25,000 on Wilson and imported five New York gunmen to carry it out. Three times he tried to assassinate Ness, and he did murder his bodyguard.

The big break was a point of law rather than the point of a pistol—a Supreme Court ruling in 1927 that income from illegal transactions was taxable. Elmer L. Irey, chief of the Enforcement Branch of the U.S. Treasury, loosed agents to ferret out Capone's finances (and turned aside a Capone bribe of $1,500,000). It took until 1931 to prove that Capone had cheated the IRS. One other man then made the final, decisive difference: Federal Judge James H. Wilkerson. When the federal grand jury returned with its 22 indictments, which could yield a sentence of 34 years, Capone's canny lawyers offered a deal. Their client would plead guilty if assured of a light sentence.

The U.S. Attorney agreed to recommend 2½ years; the federal government was worried that witnesses would be intimidated and that some of the cases might exceed the statute of limitations.

Capone came cheerfully to court in a banana-yellow summer suit. But Judge Wilkerson was angry at the deal. "The parties to a criminal case may not stipulate as to the judgment to be entered. . . . It is time for somebody to impress upon the defense that it is utterly impossible to bargain with a federal court." The deal was off.

Capone elected to plead not guilty, and lost. On October 24, 1931, a week after his conviction, Wilkerson sentenced him to 11 years in jail. On May 4, 1932, Eliot Ness escorted him to the night train to Atlanta Penitentiary. He ended up in Alcatraz, suffering from the brain disease paresis, which had been brought on by untreated syphilis. When he was released in 1939, he was, in the words of gang accountant Jake Guzik, "nutty as a fruitcake." He died on January 25, 1947, at the age of 48.

FAITHFUL: Mae Capone, his Irish wife, on a visit to Alcatraz. Capone was never in the Mafia, but in the tradition of the don he confined his wife to a kind of purdah. She stayed with him to the end: "I will always love him."

RELENTLESS: Eliot Ness, the leader of "the Untouchables," nine men in their twenties who won the nickname because they could not be bribed. After Capone, he was ordered to clean up the dangerous "Moonshine Mountains" of Kentucky. "Those mountain men and their squirrel rifles," he said later, "gave me almost as many chills as the Capone mob." From 1935 to 1941, he was director of public safety in Cleveland, Ohio, where he cleaned up the police force, forcing 200 officers to resign and sending a dozen top men to prison.

THE FBI GETS ITS MAN—AND
ITS POLITICAL MISSION

The sardonic, sightless face of the dead John Dillinger, the most notorious desperado of the thirties, greeted people who called on J. Edgar Hoover at the Federal Bureau of Investigation in the summer of 1934. Hoover put the white plaster death mask on display a few weeks after his agents shot Dillinger as he went for his gun coming out of a movie at the Biograph in Chicago on the night of July 22. With the mask, Hoover displayed the straw hat Dillinger was wearing that summer night, the silver-rimmed glasses he affected to heighten his disguise, his unsmoked La Corona–Belvedere cigar and, from his trousers pocket, a wrinkled snapshot of a woman.

Hoover kept the display in the anteroom of his Washington office for 38 years, to the end of his reign as director. It was typical of his developing taste for showmanship, heralding Hoover's emergence as a celebrity in his own right. He was at the beginning of a long period of secret relationships that made him the most powerful official in the history of American government. During his career at the Bureau he worked for ten presidents, and the power he wielded lay in his willingness to break the law, notably those statutes against wiretapping and bugging, so as covertly to gather the political intelligence most of them craved. The enduring myth of J. Edgar Hoover (1895–1972) is that he intimidated presidents with his hoard of scandalous information, but the truth is more that he suborned them as their willing helpmate in political chicanery.

It began with Roosevelt. In the year Dillinger was shot FDR asked Hoover to spy on Huey Long, a possible presidential rival. In 1936, he signed a secret directive giving Hoover authority for intelligence gathering in the United States. The fear of subversion by domestic and foreign Fascists and Communists in the run-up to war was the justification, but patriotism blurred into politics. By the 1940 campaign, Hoover had the FBI investigating 200 of Roosevelt's political enemies and tapping phones to check on Communist tendencies in the CIO, to the disgust of John L. Lewis.

ALL PALS TOGETHER: Hoover was understandably enraged by this picture from Crown Point Jail, Indiana. Dillinger, awaiting trial in January 1934 for killing a policeman, drapes his arm over the shoulder of public prosecutor Robert Estill. On the night of March 4, he produced a gun and made his getaway by stealing the sheriff's car. The gun was long said to be one he carved from a washboard, but the story was circulated to conceal the bribery and corruption whereby he obtained a real weapon.

Hoover was a cold, lonely bully who was also an organizational genius. He grew up in middle-class Washington, D.C., the son of a federal official, and absorbed into his bloodstream the prejudices against blacks, Catholics and Jews common to the day. He was a boy wonder of 29, still living with his widowed mother, when he took over the wildly corrupt Bureau in 1924. He swiftly fashioned it into a model of progressive engineering, scientific and disciplined. He created centralized fingerprinting (1925), the crime laboratory (1932) and the National Police Academy (1935). He transformed the quality of the investigative agents—the Feds, or Government-men. His G-men ended an epidemic of kidnapping.

Hoover's passion for rooting out dissent, manifest in his planning of Attorney General Palmer's Red scare raids of 1919 and 1920, was inhibited in the early years, but not suppressed, by the guidelines laid down by the man who appointed him, Harlan Stone, President Coolidge's Attor-

ney General. Stone, later the twelfth Chief Justice, had a clear vision that a secret political police might set itself above the law and become a menace to free government. The Bureau, said Stone, should henceforth be concerned not with the opinions of individuals, only with their conduct and then only with conduct forbidden by law. In the twenties, Hoover convinced Roger

Baldwin and the American Civil Liberties Union (ACLU) that he was following Stone's rules. The ACLU itself, he said, had never been the subject of investigation. He was lying. He lied with his conscience clear that he was protecting the American way of life from filthy radicals, "cominists," perverts and cream-puff liberals. Hoover's Bureau continued to monitor opinion; it never stopped filing information on alleged radicals and he kept the ACLU and its members under intensive surveillance for the entire period he had power. Later, he wooed and won over Morris Ernst, the counsel of the ACLU from 1930 to 1954. Ernst was a libertarian fiercely hostile to the Communist Party, which made him sympathetic to Hoover, but Hoover also played on Ernst's love of New York nightlife and celebrities. The result, as Hoover biographer Curt Gentry remarks, was that "for nearly 25 years the one organization in the American Left which had the resources, prestige, and independence to investigate and expose the many illegal acts committed by the FBI . . . chose not criticism or silent acquiescence but blind advocacy."

Hoover was ultimately protected in his abuses of power and in his numerous petty corruptions by the presidents he served, and by the national popularity he began to enjoy. He was lucky that when Hollywood in 1934 promised to eliminate films of violent crime, it exempted films showing the government fighting crime. Scores of movies glamorized FBI agents as clean, upstanding American crusaders in Brooks Brothers suits and fedoras, climaxing in Jimmy Cagney's G-man. Hoover became Public Hero No. 1 and was swift to exploit any opportunity to mythologize himself as the fearless enemy of every criminal by feeding this image to radio dramas, magazines, books and comic strips. It was not quite so. Dillinger, Pretty Boy Floyd and Baby Face Nelson, for all their notoriety, were far less of a public menace than the conspiracy of big-city mobsters, labor racketeers and crooked politicians but Hoover ignored them: for decades he refused to acknowledge the existence of the Mafia. Even as late as 1959, he had 400 agents in his New York office investigating Communists and only 4 on organized crime. It was heresy for anybody in the Bureau to challenge his judgment.

FRIENDS: Hoover (center) and Clyde Tolson (right), who joined the Bureau in 1928, were inseparable friends, giving rise to Washington gossip that they were lovers. In a nineties biography it was claimed, on tendentious evidence, that Hoover occasionally wore a dress. He was almost certainly a repressed homosexual, a fact that may account for his near obsession with other people's sex lives. But it is possible he never slept with a man and unlikely he ever took the risk of dressing as a woman.

YOUNG TOM DEWEY GOES FOR THE TOP MOBSTERS

In the fall of 1935 the extortionist and killer Dutch Schultz (real name Arthur Flegenheimer) had it all worked out to assassinate Thomas E. Dewey, New York's special prosecutor of organized crime. Dewey was only 33, a country boy from Owosso, Michigan, but his fierce integrity was making it hot for the city's top mobsters: in the two-year period from 1935 to 1937, Dewey would win 72 convictions out of 73 racket-busting cases.

Schultz had Dewey tailed and found that every morning he walked from his apartment to a quiet little drugstore nearby. Dewey, not wanting to disturb his wife, took breakfast there and phoned his office while his two bodyguards waited outside. It was all set that on October 25, 1935, a drugstore "customer" arriving just before Dewey would shoot him as he sat in the phone booth. But on the night of October 23 it was Schultz who was gunned down, at the Palace Chop House in Newark. Two triggermen sent by Charles "Lucky" Luciano's men did it.

The Man who Gets Things Done

DEWEY

Dewey's campaign poster for governor.

Charlie "the Bug" Workman shot Schultz with a .45 as he emerged from the lavatory.

Luciano, the top Mafia leader in New York, had Schultz killed because he figured the murder of Dewey would only intensify the war on the gangs; and he was not adverse to adding Schultz's gambling and restaurant shakedowns to his drug-running and industrial rackets. In 1936, Dewey plucked the lethally suave Luciano from his grand double life (as Mr. Charles Ross, he had a suite at the Waldorf Towers) and after a sensational trial had him and his whole mob jailed for long terms for mass prostitution.

Ten years later, as governor of New York, Dewey fumed as the federal government commuted Luciano's 15- to 30-year sentence because during World War II he gave intelligence agents advice that supposedly helped keep the waterfront free of enemy infiltration and labor troubles. But no more Waldorf Towers. Luciano was deported to Sicily and died in exile.

SUMMER (left): On August 2, 1935, Dutch Schultz emerges "not guilty" from a tax trial in Malone, New York. He bought the small town with parties and gifts.

FALL (right): On October 23 he is shot down in a restaurant. He lingered for 22 hours, murmuring a mystifying stream of words: "A boy has never wept, nor dashed a thousand kim . . . Mother is the best bet and don't let Satan draw you too fast . . . French-Canadian bean soup. I want to pay. George, don't make no bull moves . . . Oh, mama, mama, mama." But he did say he was shot by "the boss himself."

FIORELLO LA GUARDIA (1882–1947) leads a Yankee Stadium crowd in the National Anthem, 1943. Too often, the Little Flower once told a friend, "life in New York is merely a squalid succession of days; whereas in fact it can be a great living adventure." He tried harder than anyone to make it so.

Thousands of "poll watchers" swarmed out of political clubhouses to shadow the voting booths in New York's 1933 mayoral election. They carried not lists of registered voters, but brass knuckles, blackjacks and sections of lead pipe. Having lost Gentleman Jimmy Walker to the law the year before, Tammany and its allies in the mob were ready to do anything to keep control of City Hall for the Democratic party.

As it turned out, the oldest and largest political machine the world had known had met its match in a volatile, pudgy lit-

tle man with a penchant for baggy suits and cowboy hats. On election night, Fiorello La Guardia, running on a Fusion slate, led out his "Ghibboni," his own dedicated legion of young reformers. "The Little Flower" walked right up to a burly Tammany lout in an East Harlem polling place and tore his "official" poll-watcher badge off his chest. "You're a thug," La Guardia told him. "Now get out of here and keep away." He turned to the rest of the gang: "I know you. You're thugs. You get out of here and keep moving." He told

his Ghibboni: "These fellows are yellow. They're a lot of punks, and I'm going to run them out of the city."

He was as good as his word. La Guardia won by over a quarter of a million votes, and was mayor for three legendary terms. He was the vivid embodiment of the melting pot. Part Italian, part Eastern European, he was raised as an Episcopalian by a Jewish mother and a Catholic father. He had lived everywhere from Trieste to Arizona. Dashing here and there every day, he made the city's government responsive to its people. He chose city workers more than anyone had before on their merits instead of their political connections. He took the gangsters head on. He built public housing, refurbished parks, put up bridges and set as many New Yorkers to work as he could. When there was a newspaper strike, he read the comics over the radio to the children. He gave public band concerts he conducted himself. He also made the first real attempts to treat Harlem's crowded black population as human beings. With the backing of New Deal dollars and federal prosecutors, he made New York a modern, honest and humane city. As biographer Thomas Kessner put it, he created "a wonderful paradox: a huge, expanding bureaucracy with a furious, tireless, incorruptible human heart beating at its core."

By 1932, the political machines, mainly Democratic, had reached a dead end in American cities. A new era began with the near simultaneous ascension of Roosevelt in Washington and his ally La Guardia in New York. FDR was not always consistent in curbing the worst excesses of the machines, but his New Deal was a death blow. It replaced the "favors" of jobs, legal aid, food and shelter, which the machine dispensed in return for control, with genuine rights and opportunities. In so doing it broke their power and brought American democracy to fuller fruition.

THE MOB'S FIXER: James J. Hines was a sunny but ruthless Tammany ward heeler who protected a slew of New York's most notorious mobsters, including Lucky Luciano, Dutch Schultz, Frank Costello and Joe Adonis, by bribing police and judges he controlled. Thomas Dewey finally linked him to the rackets, and in 1939 he was sent up the river for several years.

WOMEN REACH THE WHITE HOUSE

LIKE MOM: Frances Perkins began wearing her black, tricornered hat because it made the tough Irish ward politicians she worked with think of their mothers. She overcame an innate shyness and intense distaste for publicity, to the point where she could stand up against the roughest attacks. While doing social work in Philadelphia, she once faced down a pimp by brandishing her umbrella. She chastised GM President Alfred P. Sloan, Jr., during the great sit-down strike in his plants in 1937 until he exclaimed, "You can't talk like that to me! I'm worth seventy million dollars, and I made it all myself." Unimpressed, Perkins told him he was still a moral "rotter" and that all his money would not save his soul.

"The best man in the Cabinet," in the judgment of "Old Ironpants" General Hugh Johnson, was Frances Perkins—the first woman ever to attain a cabinet rank. FDR made her secretary of labor when he entered the White House in 1933, encouraged by the new, very different kind of First Lady, Eleanor Roosevelt. Women had won more positions in academia, the workplace and even government, but they were still treated as second-class citizens. Al Smith, as governor of New York, had relied on Perkins to push through landmark legislation on factory safety and conditions, but for all his pride in her work Smith fought against her elevation to the cabinet. "Men," he told FDR, "will take advice from a woman, but it is hard for them to take orders from a woman." The unions, too, opposed her appointment.

Perkins had no trouble giving orders to great effect. She made the young Labor Department a force to be reckoned with for the first time. She fired 59 of its corrupt employees for shaking down illegal immigrants. Working late one night, she had discovered a bunch of them trying to steal incriminating documents. She chased them out herself, and stood guard over the files. She fought doggedly for the workers' right to organize. She pushed through a statute mandating 40-hour weeks for firms doing business with the government. She was a major architect of laws setting a minimum wage, banning child labor and establishing social security. No woman played a greater part in building the social welfare system that was so soon taken for granted. Through it all, she was mercilessly pilloried. Right-wing demagogues in Congress tried to impeach her for not deporting Harry Bridges, the radical leader of the Pacific coast's longshoremen. Male newspaper columnists claimed she was tearful and hysterical, and excluded her from the annual Gridiron dinner, to which every other cabinet member was invited. Even her fellow cabinet members generally left her to talk with their wives at dinner parties while they went off to discuss serious matters among themselves. Constant rumors were spread about her by hate groups. Perkins, said their pamphlets, was really a Soviet agent named Matilda Watski. She was secretly married to Bridges, and was another Jew in the "Jew Deal."

Perkins, in fact, came from old Yankee stock. She was an ascetic Episcopalian, who tithed and spent many weekends in prayer. She paid out another 40 percent of her $15,000 salary to keep her manic-depressive husband in a private mental institution in New York and divided her free moments between him and their daughter. She was so passionate a believer in the family with the mother at home that she parted company with Eleanor Roosevelt's campaign for day care centers. She called it "a most unfortunate reaction to the hysterical propaganda about recruiting women workers."

Perkins held the highest ranking of an unprecedented

number of women in the Roosevelt administration. It would not be a lasting trend. After Perkins resigned in 1945, there would be only two more women cabinet members until Jimmy Carter became president in 1976.

Eleanor Roosevelt was FDR's eyes and ears. When he was governor she learned to look for the details he craved from her tours of state schools, asylums, prisons and homes for the aged and the blind. She lifted the cover on the stewing pot to see if the food was as good as the official menu suggested; she noticed the state of the clothes on the washlines. As the First Lady, her sensitive insights and her passion for the downtrodden helped to shape the New Deal. She talked in the Deep South to sharecroppers in their tar-paper shacks and received them in the White House. When she found discrimination against blacks in New Deal programs, she worked tirelessly to stop it. She resigned from the Daughters of the American Revolution when they barred the great black contralto Marian Anderson from singing in their hall.

The pressures of war changed her subtle relationship with FDR. She became less of a partner, more of a campaigner. If, as Joseph Lash puts it, there was always some prayer in her purse to recall her to her Christian vocation, the President's pocket always had the latest public opinion poll. She called for tolerance for the Nisei; he interned them. She spoke up for a federal antilynching bill; he let it die. She agitated for asylum for Jewish refugees; he was more concerned with the infiltration of Nazi agents. He had to worry about Congress and getting laws "to save America" past the entrenched Southern committee chairmen there. As historian Doris Kearns Goodwin wrote, he thought in terms of what could be done; she thought only of what should be done. She tried not to embarrass him by attacking Congress, but rarely refrained from putting on pressure in private. Rexford Tugwell says she turned government in new directions on innumerable occasions when, sitting down opposite FDR, she fixed him with "that devastatingly simple honest look" and began, "Franklin, surely you will not . . ." She was far ahead of her husband in seeing that the doctrine of separate but equal was a sham.

In 1942, she became the first First Lady ever to accept a government post, when she became the unpaid assistant director of the Office of Civil Defense under Fiorello La Guardia. Her vision was more exalted than the recruitment of aircraft spotters and firefighters. She set out to organize volunteers to give a people at war "better nutrition, better day by day medical care, better education, better recreation for every age," and ran smack into departmental rivalries and the hatred of all those who, eight years into the New Deal, still smoldered over social change. Southern Democrats were stirred up by the integration of blacks into civil defense work. Republicans seized on her $4,600 appointment of Mayris Chaney, a dancer and friend, to a physical fitness program. She resigned. She had much to offer, but the ambiguities of the position of First Lady got in the way. It was a dilemma that was to torment Hillary Clinton in the nineties.

EARTH AND STARS: Eleanor Roosevelt faced the same vicious smears and rumors that Perkins endured. They claimed she was a Jewish Soviet agent, a "nigger lover," a lesbian; they made fun of her protruding teeth, her way of talking, her general piety. But she was, as Arthur Schlesinger, Jr., put it, a tough old bird who saw earth as well as stars. She knew how to play rough. She never forgave Theodore Roosevelt, Jr., for going out of his way to campaign against Franklin during his run for the vice presidency in 1920. Four years later, when cousin Teddy ran for governor of New York, she followed him around the state with a giant teapot, reminding voters of the minor part he had played in the Teapot Dome scandal. Near the end of her life, she helped to bring down the last Tammany Hall machine, after its sachem, Carmine de Sapio, had denied one of her sons the nomination for governor of New York. "I told Carmine I would get him," she gloated, like an old-fashioned ward heeler, "and get him I did!"

SHOTGUN JUSTICE IN THE SOUTH

It all started because Haywood Patterson, 18, was tired of being stepped on. It was a trivial incident. Patterson had jumped a ride on a freight train winding its way from Chattanooga to Memphis, on March 25, 1931. Dozens of other young people were on the train, black and white, male and female. They were semiliterate, jobless mill hands, displaced tenant farmers, day laborers, all in search of work in the dark days of the Depression. Patterson, clutching the side of a tank car, objected to white youths stepping on his hands as they passed back and forth. A brawl broke out. Patterson and other blacks aboard were able to force most of the whites off the train. The whites reported the fight and when the train reached the depot in Paint Rock, Alabama, a large, armed sheriff's posse pulled nine black youths from the freight cars. They also approached two young, white female mill workers dressed in men's overalls, Victoria Price and Ruby Bates, who had recently been jailed for offenses ranging from vagrancy to fornication and adultery. Afraid that she was facing more jail time, Price, the older one, quickly cobbled together a story about how they had been raped by all the arrested black youths. Bates mumbled her agreement. The nine young men were trundled off to jail in nearby Scottsboro, protected from a lynch mob by the National Guard. Twelve days after their arrest, before cheering white audiences, they were sentenced to the electric chair.

As with Rosa Parks nearly 25 years later, the case of the Scottsboro "boys" came to expose the Southern system of racial injustice because an ordinary black southerner happened to make a stand. James Allen and Helen Marcy, proprietors of a Communist Party newspaper in Chattanooga, spread the news of the shot-

Haywood Patterson sits next to defense attorney Samuel Leibowitz in a Decatur, Alabama, jail. The other eight Scottsboro boys are (left to right) Olen Montgomery, Clarence Norris, Willie Roberson, Andy Wright (behind Roberson), Ozie Powell, Eugene Williams, Charlie Weems, and Roy Wright, who was spared the death penalty because he was not yet 13. Leibowitz later became a judge on the highest court in New York State.

THE HANGING TREE: Russell Lee, who took this photograph in New Madrid County, Missouri, in May 1938, noted: "Several Negroes have been hanged from this tree."

gun justice throughout the North. Within weeks, the Communist-backed International Labor Defense (ILD), sensing another Sacco and Vanzetti case, had whipped up public indignation throughout the country. In November 1932 the U.S. Supreme Court ruled that the defendants had not had proper defense counsel and ordered a new trial. The ILD surprised everyone by having the case taken by the eminent New York defense attorney Samuel Leibowitz, who was decidedly not a Communist; he had a romantic view of the South, which was shortly disabused. Death threats poured in. He and his team had to be kept under armed guard. In court, he demolished the prosecution's case. The examining doctors had found no physical evidence of rape. Ruby Bates recanted her testimony. But in the atmosphere of the South there was little hope of finding an Alabama jury capable of rising above sectional and racial prejudice. There was only one answer to the question put by the prosecution's assistant, Wade Wright, "Is justice in the case going to be bought and sold in Alabama with Jew money from New York?"

In April 1935, the U.S. Supreme Court reversed the second set of death-penalty convictions, on the ground that the defendants had been denied due process by the practice of excluding blacks from juries. In 1936, Alabama finally decided it had no case after all against four of the boys; the other five were again found guilty. Patterson escaped from a prison farm in 1947 and made his way to Michigan, where Governor G. Mennen Williams refused to extradite him. The last Scottsboro boy was not paroled until 1950. Their youths, ambitions, and much of their sanity destroyed by long, brutal years in jail, few of the Scottsboro nine adjusted well to life outside jail. Clarence Norris, who did manage to make a modest living for himself, returned in 1976 to meet with Governor George Wallace, who had finally pardoned him. Norris recounted that Wallace, who had been a boy when he had first been convicted, grabbed his hand and "just held it for a while." Then he told him how glad he was to see him free, and how much Alabama had changed. A peace of sorts had been reached, but at the time, the Scottsboro case confronted the nation with a disillusionment. There was no "new South," gradually but steadily bringing hope and opportunity to the black masses and healing the wounds left by Reconstruction. Racism had become the tie binding white southerners of all classes and incomes. It had all but become the Southern identity.

CHARLIE GUARDIPEE

"Allottee No. 644; Age: 33; Degree: 11/16; Status: Fee Pat.; Family: Wife, 3 children;
Home on Two Medicine river. Has about twenty head of horses, ten head of cattle, no chickens. No wheat, oats, or garden.
No sickness in the family. Picture shows Charlie Guardipee and family taken near Owlchild Lake." Date of survey: May 18, 1921.

THE TRIBES FIGHT BACK

The "vanishing race" of Indians—documented in these remarkable 1921 photographs with their official captions—refused to vanish in the first decades of the twentieth century. This was despite all the official efforts to make imitation white men of the Sioux and the Cherokee, the Iroquois and the Navajo, and to brainwash the 22,000 Indian children in boot-camp boarding schools. It was easier to take away Indian land than make them forget their heritage and culture. By 1931 some 90 million acres of the original 138 million supposedly secured for the Indians had passed to white title in the land grab sanctioned by the Dawes Act. The pace was such that in three generations, each tribe might be landless. It was worst in Oklahoma, where oil was discovered. The Indians were shamelessly robbed by rings of judges, guardians, lawyers, bankers and merchants; even the undertakers got in on the act. Tactics went so low as the systematic marrying and then poisoning of Indian women who had inherited land.

Reforming Commissioner John Collier, in 1938, welcomes a survivor of the Wounded Knee massacre, Dewey Beard, who has come to Washington in full tribal regalia to testify to a claim for compensation.

The scandals were documented in 1928 by a Brookings Institution commission headed by Lewis Meriam and including the Indian leader Henry Roe Cloud; afterward President Hoover stopped the worst abuses. But the cavalry did not ride to the rescue until Roosevelt's secretary of the interior, Harold Ickes, made John Collier commissioner of Indian affairs in 1932. Collier had organized immigrant communities and schools in New York and California, where his praise of cooperatives and communism in Russia got him trailed by the FBI. Then he had moved to Taos, New Mexico, and become enraptured by the Indian way of life. It was by his efforts that Congress in 1934 passed the Indian Reorganization Act, which ended the whole Dawes system of seizing "surplus" land, and offered substantial self-government to tribes who wanted it. He also tried to give the Indians rights to sue the government for past wrongs, but it was to take 16 years to get Congress to agree.

PHILIP FLATTAIL

"Allottee No. 828; Age: 45; Degree: Full;
Status: Ward; Family: Wife, 4 children;
Home on Two Medicine. Has six horses, no
cattle, no chickens. Six acres wheat,
no oats, plans garden. Planting squaw corn.
Tuberculosis in the family.
Picture shows Philip Flattail with shovel
irrigating his wheat."
Date of survey: May 17, 1921.

WILLIAM EDWARDS

"Allottee No. 622; Age: 22; Degree: 1/2;
Status: Fee Pat.; Family: Unmarried;
Home on Birch Creek but lives in Oregon and
does not intend to live on the reservation in
the future. Has no horses, cattle or chickens.
No wheat, oats or garden. Is in good health.
Picture shows William Edwards and his
mother at his mother's home on Birch Creek."
Date of survey: May 25, 1921.

MARY EAGLEHEAD

"Allottee No. 576; Age: 31; Degree: Full;
Status: Ward; Family: Div. husb.;
Home on Badger Creek. Has no horses, cattle
or chickens. No farming or gardening
activities. Is in good health.
Picture shows Mary Eaglehead and two
children belonging to Albert Fast
Buffalo Horse."
Date of survey: May 26, 1921.

FLASH FORWARD: 1956

THE LAST APACHE

Jason Betzinez was the last surviving member of Geronimo's Apache band when I photographed him and his wife, Anna, a former missionary teacher of the Dutch Reformed Church, in 1956. He called her Lady in all our conversations. He was 93, he told me, and when I arrived at his home in Fort Sill, Oklahoma, he was trying to push his old Ford out of the mud.

He was a humble, friendly man, but of a fiery, independent spirit. In 1900 he risked odium when he denounced a medicine man who started all-night dances, with liquor, as a cure for tuberculosis: the dances killed more than they cured. In the thirties, he voted against the provision in John Collier's 1934 act giving Indians the opportunity to return to communal life. He saw it as a conspiracy by the government to rob him of his allotted land. It would, he said, make the still proud Fort Sill Apaches no different from "reservation" Indians.

When the Apache common property was being disposed, he refused an officer's offer to let him take away the blacksmith tools and forge he had been using to practice the trade taught him as a prisoner of war in Florida. Geronimo had been a second cousin, and Jason had been an apprentice warrior. From 1900 to 1914, he was in the U.S. Army as a sergeant in the Indian Scouts. He died in 1960 after a car crash. The press report said he was "100."

DEATH OF GERMAN DEMOCRACY

Adolf Hitler had become Chancellor of the German Reich on January 30, 1933, just over a month before FDR was sworn in as president. By the end of the summer German democracy was dead. The Nazis were the only legal political party. Freedom of speech and independent trade unions had been destroyed. There was an orgy of burning books written by the likes of Thomas Mann, Erich Maria Remarque, Albert Einstein, Jack London, Upton Sinclair, Helen Keller, H. G. Wells, Freud, Proust and Zola. The Army was bound by an oath of personal loyalty to Hitler. Every civil liberty was subject to the will of the Führer. Compulsory sterilization was de-

creed for disabled Germans. Jews, the perennially burning focus of Hitler's paranoia, were subjected to barbaric persecution, their businesses boycotted and vandalized, and within two years they were deprived of citizenship. As early as March 22, 1933, some 4,821 Communists and Social Democrats were incarcerated in the first concentration camp at Dachau, near Munich.

Hitler had help in bringing down the Weimar Republic of Germany, set up with such high hopes after the exile of the Kaiser at the end of World War I. The worldwide depression was aggravated in Germany by reparations and the curtailment of loans

from America. Hitler exploited these miseries and the nationalist resentments of the reparations, disarmament and territorial losses imposed by the Versailles treaty. In October 1933 he took Germany out of the League of Nations in symbolic repudiation of the treaty, and he defied its disarmament terms by announcing plans to build an army of half a million men and an air force. He made it clear he was bent on reuniting the German-speaking people separated in different states by Versailles. America, though not in the league, was very much enmeshed in German affairs. It was a signatory at Versailles, and two plans to settle the German debt question were by

Hitler lunches with top Nazis in the Chancellor's garden in 1934, the summer he executed the man who launched him on his political career, Ernst Röhm, chief of the storm troopers. On his left are Madame Goebbels and Propaganda Minister Joseph Goebbels. Photograph by Heinrich Hoffmann.

Americans—the Dawes Plan and the Young Plan. FDR had campaigned hard for the League of Nations in 1920. In 1932, to placate Hearst Democrats, he renounced his belief in it. FDR briefly toyed with the idea of forcing Germany to disarm by proposing an international blockade. He told Treasury Secretary Henry Morgenthau, Jr., that without disarmament "the chances are we will have a world war." He had a more sanguine view of Benito Mussolini. He called him "the admirable Italian gentleman" and wrote him letters.

There was a good deal of ignorance. The Wisconsin millionaire diplomat John Cudahy reported benignly from Europe

that the Brown Shirt thugs were "merely an expression of the unique German gregarious instinct, accountable on the same grounds that our Elks . . . are accountable." Later he opined that the treatment of the Jews was as much a domestic matter as "our handling of the negro minority if a race war between blacks and whites occurred in the United States."

FDR knew better, but his priority was saving American democracy with the New Deal. He could not get anything past conservative opposition without the support of progressives of both parties, and most of them happened to be isolationists. America would restrict itself to moralizing.

A Berliner suspected of being Jewish has his nose measured, one of the absurdities perpetrated by the "master race" in the wake of the 1934 Nuremberg laws depriving Jews of their German citizenship.

THE MUKDEN INCIDENT

At 10:20 on the night of September 18, 1931, an agent of the Japanese Army's secret service in Manchuria pushed a plunger and exploded 42 charges of dynamite. They had been carefully planted to hurtle debris onto railroad tracks north of Mukden that had been ceded by China first to Russia and then to Japan. The next day the world woke to hear that the Japanese Army was seizing key positions in South Manchuria because the Chinese Nationalist Army had dynamited its railway at Mukden. It was a lie, of course, the culmination of a plot by Japanese militarists to create a pretext for grabbing all of Manchuria (which they renamed Manchukuo) and at the same time forcing the "Western-minded" politicians in Tokyo to be more expansionist. It worked. The Japanese Army did not stop at Mukden. The railway line led straight to Pearl Harbor.

Few at the time appreciated the significance of the incident at Mukden. Japan was hard to read. In 50 years the Japanese had catapulted themselves from medieval feudalism into a modern industrial state with democratic aspirations. But the political democracy copied from Britain's constitutional monarchy had a chromosome missing. It was a neurotic mix of the authoritarian and the anarchic. There was no real system of law. Under the silken trappings, press and unions were controlled. Factions proliferated based on clans and regions and ancient rivalries. Violence was exalted. Nationalist resentment festered on insults real and supposed. The American, British and French refusal at Versailles to reward their World War I ally with a declaration of racial equality was exacerbated in 1924 by the shutdown on Japanese immigration into America.

Mukden was not an impulse. It was the result of a long planned counterrevolution to repudiate the West. Ten years before, three young military intelligence agents had met in the Turkish bath at Baden-Baden in Germany. With Hideki Tōjō (who was to be Japan's World War II prime minister), they formed the secret Double Leaf Society. Its purpose was to restore Japanese honor by winning power at home and then empire in Asia by means of conspiracy, assassination and war.

Japanese marines in street fighting in Shanghai in 1937.

WARLORD: Baron Giichi Tanaka dreamt of a Japanese empire in Siberia and China. When the Western powers intervened against the Bolsheviks in Siberia in 1918, he plotted to send in more Japanese troops than agreed. In the twenties he campaigned for holding on to southern Manchuria.

Prime Minister Osachi Hamaguchi was assassinated because he accepted the London naval treaty of 1930. Three other prime ministers were assassinated between 1926 and 1945. Many rabidly nationalist secret societies burrowed into Japanese life. When the antimilitarist Foreign Minister Kijuro Shidehara got a whisper of the Mukden plot on September 15, 1931, he sent an order to the army commander in Manchuria prohibiting any "incident." It got there too late: the War Office message had been entrusted to one of the founding members of the expansionist Society of the Cherry.

By its seizure of Manchuria Japan breached the Nine-Power Act of 1922 and the Kellogg-Briand Pact of 1928, to both of which the U.S. was a party, and the League Covenant, to which it was not. Manchuria was the first test case of collective security and the democracies failed it. British Tories soft-pedaled because they regarded their old ally Japan as a bulwark against Chinese or Soviet communism. America, under both Hoover and FDR, did not lift a finger, for all its long patronage of China. It was crippled by paranoia about the league. Congress howled in fury when Secretary of State Henry Stimson reluctantly allowed the U.S. consul in Geneva to sit for a single day to hear the league discuss what might be done to apply the Kellogg-Briand Pact.

In 1933 the league finally condemned Japan as the aggressor. Japan promptly quit the league. America confined itself to diplomatic huffing and puffing. But all that moral obloquy did was stiffen militarist resentments. In 1937, Japan began a full-scale war against China, but FDR was howled down by the isolationists for canvassing the idea that international gangsters "should be quarantined." Even when the Japanese, in an orgy of killing in Nanking, deliberately bombed a U.S. gunboat, the *Panay*, that same year, it made no difference to American opinion. A poll found 70 percent of the American people favored a complete withdrawal of U.S. citizens from China. "The American people," said the *Philadelphia Record*, "don't give a hoot in a rain barrel who controls North China."

OSAKA, DECEMBER 1932: Emperor Hirohito inspects the latest auditory devices that warn of air attack.

EMPEROR: Hirohito was 25 when he ascended the imperial throne in 1926. He called his reign *Showa* (bright peace) but it was marked by growing militarism. William Sharp reflected the Japanese drive for naval power in his 1938 cartoon "A Pause for Reflection—A New Top."

REIGN OF THE KINGFISH

Huey Pierce Long (1893–1935), the hillbilly who might have been president, was the first genuine homespun American dictator. He came out of the red-clay country and piney woods of north-central Louisiana, where gallused small-time farmers, like his father, thrived on Baptist revivalism and political cussedness; his home territory, Winn Parish, had been a hotbed of populism and socialism.

Straight out of school he took his silver tongue on the road, selling soap, cooking oil and patent medicines. As soon as he had enough money for law school he did a three-year course in a brilliant eight months. At 21, curly-headed and snub-nosed, with a face that was, as writer Jonathan Daniels noted, a puffy caricature of a cherub, he hung up his 50-cent tin shingle in Winnfield. By the time he was 35 he was governor of the state and four years later he was performing his stunts simultaneously in Louisiana's capital and the U.S. Senate. He ran the state as a personal fiefdom. He would drop into Baton Rouge from Washington, summon a special session of legislators and strut the floor dictating new laws to them. Between August 1934 and September 1935 they passed 463 of his bills; once he whipped them on to pass 44 bills in 22 minutes.

He bribed and terrorized. He fixed his enemies with unflagging vindictiveness. He got away with it because the root of his strength was his appeal to the people of a benighted state in the most backward region of the country. The country people whooped at his assaults on the sordid alliance between the planters and robber barons led by Standard Oil and the corrupt New Orleans politicians in the Choctaw Club. His insults were vivid, but he could also speak with a rare grace and power. Under torchlight in Martinville he stood on a cotton bale and mesmerized his audience with the invocation of a state myth:

"And it is here, under this oak, where Evangeline waited for her lover Gabriel, who never came. This oak is an immortal spot, made so by Longfellow's poem, but Evangeline is not the only one who has waited here in disappointment. Where are the schools that you have waited for your children to have, that have never come? Where are the roads and the highways that

Roosevelt, Long ranted, is a liar and a faker! Officeholders are "dime a dozen punks." He called himself the Kingfish, after a character in an *Amos 'n' Andy* show, and the allusion was fitting.

"I can buy legislators like sacks of potatoes. . . ." The redneck crowds of northern Louisiana loved his feverish, flailing invective as much as the Senate hated it.

you send your money to build, that are no nearer now than ever before? Where are the institutions to care for the sick and the disabled? Evangeline wept bitter tears in her disappointment, but it lasted through only one lifetime. Your tears in this country, around this oak, have lasted for generations. Give me the chance to dry the tears of those who still weep here."

They did and they were not disappointed. The state's giant, monopolistic corporations were consistently taxed and regulated for the first time. He used the money to build highways and bridges, hospitals and rest homes, and to enhance the state university. The children got their promised free textbooks. Free night schools taught reading and writing to over 100,000 illiterate adults—of both races. Long was distinctive among Southern demagogues. He treated blacks nearly as equals. When he was denounced by Hiram Evans, the Imperial Wizard of the Klan, he

told reporters: "Quote me as saying that the Imperial bastard will never set foot in Louisiana, and that when I call him a son of a bitch I am not using profanity, but am referring to the circumstances of his birth." It was not that he was a civil rights leader; he did nothing to enfranchise blacks. "Don't say I'm working for niggers," he told Roy Wilkins, then a reporter. "I'm not. I'm for the poor man—all poor men. Black and white, they all gotta have a chance." Nor was he a social reformer. He did not stop child labor, give relief to the unemployed or support trade unions. But he did have a "folk vision" and FDR worried as his appeal spread far beyond Louisiana.

Long's support was crucial to FDR's nomination in 1932. A year later the Kingfish was disenchanted with the bureaucracy of the New Deal. When FDR called him to the White House in June 1933 he insolently kept on his straw hat during their talk. He was punished by the revival of an investigation of his taxes. Long's weapon of war was a national organization called Share Our Wealth. It was launched in 1934 as a series of clubs with the slogan "Every man a king, but no man wears a crown!" Share Our Wealth promised every American family an upper-middle-class fortune of at least $5,000–$6,000, an annual income of at least $2,000, pensions for everyone over 60, washing machines and radios and an abundance of cheap food. It was all supposed to be paid for by reducing all fortunes to around $3 million and taking away all income over $1 million a year.

By 1935 Long's 27,000 clubs claimed an active national membership of nearly 4.7 million. A Democratic poll showed that he might command enough votes to swing the electoral college to the Republicans. This seems to have been Long's intention. He told a friend that this would open his own way to the White House in 1940. He put a ghostwriter to work on a book called *My First Days in the White House,* but they were Long's last days alive.

Long was more of a banana republic bully than a Hitler or a Mussolini, an opportunist rather than an ideologue. But his lightning rise showed that the institutions of American democracy were vulnerable to a totalitarian who could identify with the yearnings of the common people.

ALL THE KING'S MEN: Long is sandwiched by his buddies, public service commissioner James O'Connor (left) and Governor Oscar K. "O.K."
Allen. When Long was wounded he fell into O'Connor's arms, and Allen, seizing a pistol, dashed about shouting, "If there's a shooting I want to be in on it."
Allen was governor by Long's grace. When Long won the U.S. Senate race in 1930, with 18 months of his governorship to go, the man who was
his lieutenant governor claimed the job. Long called out the National Guard, ran him out of office, and installed Allen as his stooge.
It was said of Allen that if a leaf blew in on his desk, he would sign it.

SHOT DOWN IN THE STATE CAPITOL

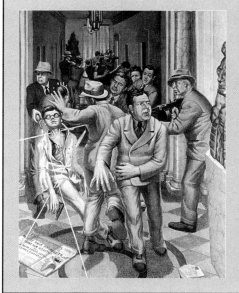

An anti-Long leader, Mason Spence, said in 1935: "I can see blood on the polished marble of this capitol, for if you ride this thing through, you will travel with the white horse of death." On the night of September 8, Long burst out of a legislative session ahead of his bodyguards. Dr. Carl Weiss (right) slipped from behind a pillar in the state capitol with a .32 caliber pistol and fired one bullet just under his ribs. Long screamed, "I'm shot!" and ran downstairs while the bodyguards pumped at least 32 bullets into Weiss, as graphically depicted in John McCrady's painting. Weiss, a brilliant, highly strung physician, was incensed that Long was gerrymandering his father-in-law, Judge Benjamin Davy, out of his seat on the bench and spreading rumors that Davy had black blood. The bullet in Long caused little damage, but a botched operation by an inexperienced surgeon failed to detect a punctured kidney. He died within two days, supposedly whispering, "God, don't let me die. I have so much to do." He was just a week past his forty-second birthday.

FAN CLUB: The vast majority of newspaper and magazine publishers were bitterly hostile, but FDR captivated their reporters as much as this *New Yorker* cartoon suggests by his charm, the seriousness of his briefings, his leaks. Joe Alsop wrote in 1982: "Instead of the preening media personalities of today, those present were only the most seasoned professional reporters, all of whom knew one another and did not wish to make asses of themselves either in front of their colleagues or in front of a president they much liked and admired."

"THAT MAN" COMES OUT ON TOP

By the spring of 1935 the talk in the clubs and the boardrooms, in Park Avenue dinner parties, in the railway parlor cars and on the blue lawns of the rich had come to be focused on "that man." Roosevelt, having saved capitalism, was rewarded with an unsurpassed measure of hatred by its elite. Among the upper and upper-middle classes, the revulsion was as much psychological as political. FDR was not merely a politician with disagreeable ideas; he was a traitor to his class. A venomous whispering campaign polluted the land. His disability was not really caused by polio, but some form of venereal disease. He had contracted it from Eleanor. She had got it from her do-gooding among the "niggers" and unemployed miners; or she had picked it up in Russia, where she met her secret masters in the Kremlin. Of course, FDR's real name was "Rosenfeld." He was really a New York kike, descended from Dutch sheenies who changed their names, and he was filling the government with fellow Jews, most of them Communists, too.

The cream of the Roosevelt-haters were in the American Liberty League, an organization of millionaires, led by the du Pont family, with one odd bedfellow. Al Smith, the happy warrior from the Lower East Side, had traded in his brown derby to stand before a league banquet in white tie and tails and revile FDR as a Bolshevik. On April 29, members of the U.S. Chamber of Commerce, who had previously backed the New Deal, assembled in Washington and denounced it as an attempt to "Sovietize America."

FDR had spent nearly nine months out of the limelight. His fireside chat the day before the businessmen deserted him had been his first all year. His populist enemies—Huey Long, Father Charles E. Coughlin and Dr. Francis Townsend—had been tearing up the pea patch. He seemed demoralized, unsure what to do next. Three million more Americans were at work; but the recovery lagged behind western Europe's. The steam had run out of the New Deal as a partnership of business and government in national planning. It was clearly time for something else.

The decisive moment, the true beginning of the Second New Deal, has been traced by biographer Kenneth Davis to the

THE EMPEROR: At his fifty-second birthday party on January 30, 1934, Roosevelt enjoyed himself by mocking the conservatives who charged that he was becoming a dictator. He put on a toga of imperial purple for a costume sketch with his women aides and relatives dressed as vestal virgins or Roman matrons. Seated on his lap is his daughter, Anna; Eleanor stands at the back.

night of Tuesday, May 14. At the urging of the liberal scholar David K. Niles and the jurist Felix Frankfurter, FDR gave a private dinner at the White House to hear the criticisms of a handful of doughty liberals— Senators Norris, Borah, Johnson, Edward Costigan, Wheeler and Robert La Follette, Jr. Cabinet members Ickes and Wallace and Frankfurter and Niles joined them. They pitched into him for trying to appease business. They invoked his idealism for the good of the American people as a whole. And FDR responded with a dramatic pledge to take a progressive stand.

On June 14, he summoned congressional leaders to the Oval Office. They were on the verge of adjourning to escape Washington's tropical summer. Instead, they found themselves handed a list of legislations that the President, with much banging on his desktop, insisted be passed that session. He demanded bills to recognize and support labor unions; to wrench power over the Federal Reserve from Wall Street's bankers; to break up the greedy power utilities; to institute a progressive tax code; and, for the first time in the nation's history, to create a system of social security for all Americans. He then flashed a big grin and left the capital to attend the Harvard-Yale rowing meet. On August 27, Congress ended its longest session since 1922 with the bulk of the Second New Deal complete. A new competitive balance of power was in the making. The ideal of har-

monious cooperation between all elements of the economy was replaced with the aim of creating a more even playing field for business and labor, with government as a highly involved referee.

In the presidential election of 1936, the Republicans, and William Randolph Hearst, put up Alf Landon, a fiscal conservative who had been a moderately progressive governor: he had driven the Klan out of Kansas. They outspent the Democrats and spread scares and anti-Semitic smears. Landon, a decent man who panicked, suggested FDR was a Communist who would set up a guillotine to behead his enemies. Republican employers stuffed pay packets with warnings that the workers might never again see the contributions they made for their new social security benefits.

A furious FDR abandoned the role of honest broker. He took up the rhetoric of class warfare. On the eve of voting, before a jubilant crowd at Madison Square Garden, he struck out in one of the most brilliantly partisan speeches in American presidential history: "For twelve years this nation was afflicted with hear-nothing, see-nothing, do-nothing government. The nation looked to government but government looked away. Nine mocking years with the golden calf and three long years of the scourge! Nine crazy years at the ticker and three long years in the breadlines! Nine mad years of mirage and three long years of despair! Powerful influences strive today to restore that kind of government with its doctrine that government is best which is most indifferent. . . . We know now that government by organized money is just as dangerous as government by organized mob."

In a deep, resonant voice, he turned on "the desperate men" and their calumnies: "Never before in all our history have these forces been so united against one candidate as they stand today. They are unanimous in their hate of me—and I welcome their hatred."

America shouted its answer. Some 83 percent of the electorate voted, and they gave Roosevelt every state save Maine and Vermont. He won by one of the greatest-ever percentages of popular vote, beating Landon by 60.8 to 36.5. The Democrats dominated House and Senate.

THE SUPREME COURT KILLS THE BLUE EAGLE

The Schechter brothers of Brooklyn sold diseased chickens for human consumption, filed false sales claims, exploited their workers and threatened government inspectors. They were convicted in New York on 16 counts of violating NRA "fair practices" regulations. But on "Black Monday," May 27, 1935, the Supreme Court ruled that the federal government had no right to prosecute them in the first place because the law the Schechters violated was itself unconstitutional. In setting up the National Recovery Administration with its codes and boards, said a vehement Chief Justice Charles Evans Hughes, Congress had delegated too much to the Executive. And it had usurped states' rights.

FDR seemed to take it in his stride. After dinner that night, he sat up in bed fuss-

ing happily with his stamp collection. "I think perhaps NRA has done all it can," he later told Labor Secretary Frances Perkins. "I don't want to impose a system on this country that will set aside the antitrust laws on any permanent basis." They both blamed an NRA labor code for the great textile strike of 1934, and FDR was already in the process of replacing the blue eagle with his Second New Deal. But, if the NRA was not much lamented by FDR, the reasons for its judicial murder were shocking to the New Dealers and bewildering to millions who had benefited from New Deal programs. It seemed that the Court was not merely adjudicating a single case, but marching out as counterrevolutionaries to replant the flag of laissez-faire capitalism. The Chief Justice based the ruling

on a definition of interstate commerce so narrow as to menace the ability of the federal government to regulate practices across most of the country's major industries (including construction, mining, manufacturing and agriculture), and clearly imperil impending legislation on wages and conditions. Only goods in actual transit across state lines qualified for federal scrutiny. (The wretched chickens had crossed state lines on the way to the slaughterhouse, but it was reasoned that when they got to New York they were intrastate because they were eaten there.)

Worse, the Court had voted 9–0. The New Dealers expected nothing but reactionary rulings in defense of business from the so-called Four Horsemen: Pierce Butler, Willis Van Devanter, George Suther-

Chief Justice Charles Evans Hughes is an impressive figure (bearded, center) leading Supreme Court justices to pay their respects to President Hoover, in 1930. He usually voted conservative but could be persuaded to keep an open mind. From left: Attorney General William D. Mitchell; Justices Harlan Fiske Stone (liberal); George Sutherland (conservative); Oliver Wendell Holmes (the great liberal judge who retired when he was 90, in 1932); Hughes; Willis Van Devanter (conservative); Louis Brandeis (liberal); Pierce Butler (conservative); Owen J. Roberts (swing vote); and Solicitor General Thomas Thacher. Benjamin Cardozo succeeded Holmes. James C. McReynolds was the other conservative justice. It was Roberts who reversed himself on minimum wage laws. "You may have saved the country," Hughes told him.

land and James McReynolds, assisted by the swing vote of Owen Roberts. A few weeks earlier, these justices had combined to deny the right of Congress to enact any compulsory pension plan for railroad employees. But in the sick chicken case, even the liberals—Louis Brandeis, Benjamin Cardozo and Harlan Fiske Stone—had deserted them. Brandeis had gone so far as to summon FDR's aide Tom Corcoran to the robing room. The gaunt, 78-year-old justice looked to Corcoran like a black-winged angel of destruction as he held his arms aloft for a page to take off his gown. "The President," said Brandeis in great excitement, "has been living in a fool's paradise. . . . This is the end of this business of centralization, and I want you to go back and tell the President that we're not going to let this government centralize everything. It's come to an end. As for your young men, you call them together and

tell them to get out of Washington—tell them to go home, back to the states. That is where they must do their work."

Brandeis was no reactionary. He was a fervent supporter of unions, a convinced advocate of progressive taxation and massive public works projects. He believed in government strong enough to combat the great business combines. It was bigness he abhorred—the curse of bigness, he called it, and he hated it in government as much as in business, preferring state and local action over federal. The NRA was anathema to him because it sanctified bigness. FDR was getting an urgent warning to abandon the New Nationalism creed of the first New Dealers.

His immediate response was a brilliant, 90-minute briefing in a press conference. He gestured elegantly with his long ivory cigarette holder, and Eleanor knitted away at a blue sock, as he eviscerated the Court's

reasoning with humor and irony. He called the Chief Justice's logic a horse-and-buggy definition of the commerce clause.

In January 1936, the diehard justices on the Court killed the Agricultural Administration 5–4, the Securities and Exchange Act 6–3, and nine other New Deal laws. In June, by a broad interpretation of the freedom of contract in the Fourteenth Amendment, they even ruled a New York minimum wage law unconstitutional, on the absurd reasoning that a 15-year-old girl in a sweatshop should not be denied the freedom to work for slave wages. Neither state nor federal government, it seemed, was to be allowed to advance on the citadel of laissez-faire. But behind his mask of affability FDR had been plotting. The climax came in the great constitutional crisis of 1937.

FDR'S GREAT BLUNDER

Something was amiss at the grand dinner FDR gave at the White House on Tuesday, February 2, 1937, in honor of the justices of the Supreme Court. Beneath the good humor and banter typical of Roosevelt's parties, everyone sensed the fuses running out on the conflict over the Court's insistent vetoing of New Deal reforms. Four men in particular were uneasy—Homer Cummings, the lean, dry Yankee who was Attorney General; Solicitor General Stanley Reed; special counsel Donald Richberg; and speechwriter Sam Rosenman. They felt like conspirators. And they were. They were the only people in the world who knew what FDR had plotted for the Court's humiliation.

FDR and Cummings had hatched it together and revealed it to the other three at a secluded lunch on the President's fifty-fifth birthday on January 30. Congress would be asked to pass a bill enabling the president to expand the Court by adding one new judge, up to a maximum of six, for every current judge over the age of 70. Cummings and FDR had winked and beamed about the origins of the idea. It dated back to 1913 and Woodrow Wilson's Attorney General, one James C. McReynolds, the same Justice McReynolds who was the implacable enemy of the New Deal and the dourest guest by far at the White House dinner (he was also an anti-Semite who refused to sit or stand next to Justice Brandeis). How delicious to take his concept of supplanting 70-year-old federal judges with younger men and extend it to the recalcitrant Supreme Court. "The cleverness, the too much cleverness," of FDR and Cummings shocked Rosenman, Reed and Richberg, but they went along and kept the secret.

Two days after the dinner, cabinet members and congressional leaders were peremptorily summoned to the White House. FDR was wheeled in and presented them with his bombshell. He gave them no time for questions. The bill went to Congress at noon. Such a crude show of arrogance and force was contrary to the way the master tactician had always taken care to step only on ice he had made sure was firm. Walter Lippmann, who led the universally hostile press, accused him of

being "drunk with power." Biographer Kenneth S. Davis suggests a more subtle explanation: that when he triumphed in 1936 against the ferociously personalized hatreds and implacable selfishness of the business community he felt his mandate was not only popular but Divine.

The move was the biggest political blunder of FDR's career. Many had come to believe the Court was exceeding its authority, but restraining an institution popularly revered as sacred to the Constitution required a reformer with his halo intact. FDR threw his away, not just by his secrecy but by the slyness of Senate Bill No. 1392. The defensible intent to end the Court's frustration of the people's will was camouflaged by the indefensible equation of age with incompetence and intolerance (the most liberal judge, Brandeis, was nearly 80) and the pretense that it was all because the Court had fallen behind in its work. Popular opinion, according to the Gallup poll, was split equally in the first two weeks, but it moved against FDR and even a brilliant fireside chat failed to do more than restore the balance. In Congress an ominous new coalition of conservative Southern Democrats and Republicans moved against him, more credible because it formed up behind the blazing liberal banner of Montana's Burton K. Wheeler.

Chief Justice Hughes, in his determination to save his Court, proved himself as tricky as FDR. Supposedly above politics and confined to silence, he managed, through Brandeis, to suggest that Wheeler ask him a question. On March 22, Wheeler stunned the country by reading to the Judiciary Committee a letter from the Chief Justice cogently refuting the idea that more judges would mean quicker decisions. Hughes had also had a quiet word with the "swing" justice, Owen Roberts, shortly after FDR's election victory. In private, on December 19, 1936, Roberts

THE ROCK: The reactionary "Four Horsemen" on the Supreme Court were opposed by a trio of progressive associate justices—Louis Brandeis (1856–1941), Benjamin N. Cardozo and Harlan F. Stone. Brandeis, photographed with his wife, Alice, on the eve of his eighty-second birthday, played a seminal role in American history as a defender of the people's rights and an enemy of bigness in government and business. Wilson caused a sensation when he appointed Brandeis, the first Jew to sit on the Court, in 1916.

THE SUPREME COURT IN SESSION (left to right): Associate Justices Owen Roberts, Pierce Butler, Louis Brandeis, Willis Van Devanter; Chief Justice Charles Evans Hughes; Associate Justices George Sutherland, Harlan Fiske Stone, Benjamin Cardozo. Associate Justice James McReynolds is not pictured.

THE GO-BETWEEN: Majority Leader Joseph Robinson of Arkansas did his best to settle the court-packing fight for FDR. He wore himself out doing it and died of a heart attack on July 14, 1937.

had done an obliging somersault. He had joined the liberals in upholding a State of Washington minimum wage law for women and children—the same kind of law he had considered unconstitutional in the New York case six months before. Because the announcement was delayed pending the vote of Justice Harlan Fiske Stone, who was sick, Roberts did not do his somersault in public until March 29, 1937, making it appear that "court packing" had frightened the justices. Then the Court kept reversing itself. In April, Hughes reversed himself to write the 5–4 opinion upholding the pro-labor Wagner Act and then the Social Security Act.

FDR persisted with his bill. On May 18, he had more good-bad news. Good in that the reactionary Justice Van Devanter announced his intention to retire at the end of the current session. Bad, because it made FDR's bill look even more gratuitous and, worse, it meant he had to fulfill his promise to fill the first Court vacancy by nominating Joe Robinson, who was fighting faithfully for the bill in the Senate but was as conservative as any of the Four Horsemen. FDR cruelly kept Robinson waiting. Under terrible strain, and suffering badly in the heat of Washington—no air conditioning in those

days—Robinson had a fatal heart attack in his room, clutching a copy of the *Congressional Record*. FDR did not go to the funeral.

Finally, FDR nominated Hugo Black, who was then revealed to have been a member of the Klan years before, though he would become one of history's most liberal and notable justices.

Against all advice FDR persisted with S. 1392. Over and over again to visitors to the Oval Office he exclaimed, "The people are with me! I know it!" They were not and the Senate was united in its detestation. On July 22, 1937, he had the humiliation of seeing S. 1392 voted down 70–20. It was Roosevelt's first major Senate defeat in his 4½ years in office. A spell had been broken. It was confirmed the next year. He attempted to unseat key conservatives in the primaries so as to draw all the nation's progressives into a new, wholly liberal Democratic party. He was almost completely unsuccessful and remained dependent on some of the most regressive—and racist—forces in the country. Still, he was the first president since James Monroe whose party controlled both houses of Congress through his second term, and those who felt his electoral appeal had run its course would soon be disillusioned.

WORKERS TAKE TO THE BARRICADES

The phony peace between capital and labor ended in open class warfare in 1934. Auto workers in Toledo, truckers in Minneapolis, longshoremen in San Francisco and mill hands from Maine to Alabama fought company goons, police, the National Guard and vigilantes in battles that often ended in gunfire. Farm workers seeking to unionize in the South and California were routinely shot, gassed, beaten or jailed. For all the reforming zeal of the New Deal, many of the rights that Americans now take for granted had to be won at the barricades in the thirties.

After 1929, millions of unemployed had been willing to do almost anything for work. Migrant farm workers begged to be given picking jobs on California's miserable factory farms. Everywhere the unions had collapsed and wages had fallen below subsistence level. Women in Chicago were making as little as a dime a day. The workers seemed cowed. More than 2,500 American companies employed armed gangs and spies supplied by Pinkerton National Detective Agency or Pearl Bergoff Services to keep them that way. A mass union movement seemed out of the question. Even the right to belong to a union, which Samuel Gompers thought he had patched up with Woodrow Wilson, had all but vanished.

The revolt that began in 1933 was rooted in desperation, but the twin catalysts were a unique generation of labor leaders and Section 7a of the National Industrial Recovery Act. By envisaging unions as part of a business-government partnership for national recovery, the NRA gave labor leaders like John L. Lewis, Sidney Hillman, David Dubinsky, Walter and Victor Reuther, and A. Philip Randolph the chance to recruit hundreds of thousands under the banner of patriotism: in the twenties it had been "un-American" to join a union; now it was endorsed by the federal government. Many of these leaders did have radical left backgrounds, but unlike the IWW leaders, all of them had slipped their former dogmas. For the most part, they did not believe revolution was coming any longer, nor did they particularly yearn for it. They constituted a pragmatic yet largely unselfish midpoint between labor's early idealistic martyrs, such as Debs and Haywood, and later conservative leaders. They were not above fighting violence with violence, defying unreasonable court orders or even seizing company property in sit-down strikes. At times they were willing to accept the help of Communists and gangsters alike.

In February 1935, a federal district court ruled that Section 7a was unconstitutional. Senator Robert Wagner of New York and Congressman William P. Connery, Jr., of Massachusetts immediately introduced a bill to give clear legal standing to unions and collective bargaining. Roosevelt stalled. He feared a wave of strikes, he did not want to hazard the congressional support of the conservative South, and the spirit of paternalism still beat within his breast. Only when it was about to pass both houses did he endorse it.

A massive campaign of defiance was begun by the National Association of Manufacturers and the American Liberty League, founded by John J. Raskob, Pierre du Pont and GM President Alfred Sloan. Even after the Supreme Court upheld the Wagner Act in 1937, most companies still refused to recognize unions and continued to terrorize those who tried to join them.

To Lewis, the response was obvious. Big business must be confronted by big labor. This meant opening the unions to everyone, not just the white craftsmen acceptable to the elite leadership of the American Federation of Labor. The issue came to a head at an angry AFL convention in Atlantic City in October 1935. The Bourbons of the AFL rejected Lewis's impassioned plea for recognition of industrial unions organizing millions of workers by workplace and product rather than splintering them by skill. When Big Bill Hutcheson of the Carpenters' Union called him a bastard, Lewis put his 220 pounds into a quick right jab that knocked Big Bill to the floor.

Lewis walked out of the convention and out of the AFL. His United Mine Workers joined with the International Ladies' Garment Workers Union, the Amalgamated Clothing Workers and some smaller unions to establish a rival complex of unions, the Committee for Industrial Organization (later, the Congress of Industrial Organizations). By 1936 ten unions representing at least one quarter of the AFL's 3.3 million members had walked out to join the CIO.

JOHN LEWIS PLAYS THE ROLE OF OGRE

John Llewellyn Lewis, founder of the CIO, cast himself as the ogre of the labor movement. He looked like an Old Testament prophet. He had a massive head and bushy eyebrows that converged in a terrifying scowl. "Madame Secretary," he confided to Labor Secretary Frances Perkins, "that scowl is worth a million dollars." There was method in Lewis's florid style beyond the compulsions of his colossal ego. He judged the average union worker wanted a man who could stand toe to toe with the big business tycoons. He was ruthless, cunning, opportunistic. He led bitter strikes of his United Mine Workers' Union shortly after World War I. When they failed to achieve much, he purged the radicals from his ranks and endorsed Coolidge and Hoover. Opponents were squashed by violence and vote

rigging. He became the most widely hated man in the coalfields. In the Depression, he swung back behind FDR, and cut deals with Socialists and Communists in the drive for industrial unions. Along the way he picked up a fancy car and chauffeur, domestic servants, several grand houses and cozy union jobs for unqualified relatives. He made a great show of reading Shakespeare, Machiavelli and the *Panchatantra*. When his longtime ally David Dubinsky (right) hesitated about leaving the AFL, it was typical of Lewis to compare his indecision to scenes in both the Bible and *Uncle Tom's Cabin*: "Mr. Dubinsky, whom I highly esteem, is apparently giving an imitation of Eliza crossing the ice. Like Lot's wife he is looking backward. He must decide for himself whether he is fish, fowl or good red herring."

WOMAN POWER: A wife expresses solidarity in a 1937 New York dock strike. The CIO embraced women though, like the AFL, its leadership was dominated by men. Even the International Ladies' Garment Workers Union had only one woman on its board of 24.

THE CHICAGO MARTYRS: It was supposed to be a happy day of picnics and rousing speeches at a union rally in the meadowlands around Republic Steel on Chicago's South Side, but that Memorial Day, 1937, over a thousand men, women and children found themselves fleeing a police force gone berserk. Mayor Edward Kelly had publicly assured the Steel Workers Organizing Committee (SWOC) of official respect for their right to picket in support of a weeklong strike. His police outside Republic Steel's front gates had another view. When the union leaders marched up with an American flag to argue their right to set up a picket line, the nervous, angry cops yelled,

"You got no rights. You Red bastards. You got no rights." Someone tossed a tree branch at the cops. They opened fire on the defenseless mass. There were 264 policemen, and they fired an estimated 200 rounds into the crowd at point-blank range. By the time it was over, 10 of the crowd had been shot dead, 7 of them in the back. Another 30, including a woman and 3 boys, suffered gunshot wounds. Nine people were permanently disabled. Another 28 had serious head injuries from police clubbing.

Mayor Kelly did nothing to discipline his police. A coroner's jury declared the killings to be "justifiable homicide." The press mostly called it a labor

or Red riot. And it was not FDR's finest hour. He responded to a union plea with the weasel words: "The majority of people are saying just one thing, 'A plague on both your houses.'"

It was altogether a huge victory for Tom Girdler, the ruthless head of Republic, who led all the steel companies except for the giant U.S. Steel in forcibly resisting union recognition. Carnegie and Morgan's old concern had accepted the union with surprising tolerance, but the "Little Steel" owners rallied round Girdler. He hired a private army of goons with shotguns and gas grenades.

It took years for Phil Murray of SWOC and CIO counsel Lee Pressman to fight back. But they did. Patiently, they documented all the unfair labor practices of Little Steel before the National Labor Relations Board (NLRB), created by the Wagner Act. On October 18, 1938, the board issued a sweeping decision in the union's favor. Some 7,000 fired Republic unionists were ordered reinstated with full back pay. The verdict was sustained in two years of court battles. On August 13, 1942, just over five years after the massacre, Girdler signed a contract with the new United Steelworkers of America.

END OF THE FORD HONEYMOON

Three strong men in Detroit were dams against the union movement sweeping across America: Alfred Sloan, head of General Motors; Walter Chrysler; and Henry Ford. Henry Ford had lost his halo by the end of the thirties. Hate had come to fill his life—hatred of Jews, hatred of Catholics, hatred of unions, hatred of his gentle son, Edsel. His company had fallen from dominating the industry to third, behind General Motors and Chrysler. He had abandoned what his biographer Robert Lacey calls his bid for utopia in Detroit. Ford factories remained spotlessly clean, their safety record was superb and company nutritionists still made sure that Ford box lunches contained at least 800 calories. But wages had dropped and fear had replaced the spirit of adventure. The man who once cared for every aspect of his empire abandoned its labor relations to Harry Bennett, a short, redheaded thug with ties to the mob who ran a "Service Department" of spies and goons. He fixed things for Ford, paying off servant girls he slept with and beating up "troublemakers." Workers on the assembly line developed the "Ford whisper," a surreptitious way of speaking with their heads down so that they could not be reported by Bennett's

Near the end of his life and nearly mad, Ford in 1942, on the steps of his home.

spies. Violence was the Bennett-Ford answer to any expression of grievance. In 1932 they crushed a Communist demonstration in a fracas at Dearborn's River Rouge plant, in which four were shot dead.

Their methods were exposed by the photographs below, which they tried to destroy in May 1937. Walter Reuther, leader of the fledgling United Automobile Workers union, went to River Rouge to hand out pamphlets. Bennett's thugs (at left) attacked unionists Robert Kanter, Reuther, Richard Frankensteen. In the center photo, Frankensteen has his coat pulled over his head while he is punched. Reuther was struck on the back of the head and kicked mercilessly as he lay on the concrete. Then

the men were thrown down the 39 steps of an overpass.

Bennett's men turned on the press and seized the camera of photographer James R. Kilpatrick of the *Detroit News.* He handed over unexposed film. The pictures he saved helped convince the courts that Ford was breaking the law. Thereafter every time Bennett and his men fired or beat up another union man, the UAW carefully documented it and filed a complaint before the National Labor Relations Board. Eventually Ford felt compelled to accept an appeal from Edsel, who was dying, that the workers be allowed to vote. On May 21, 1941, nearly 70 percent of Ford workers voted to be represented by the UAW in the CIO, and the rest chose a rival union. Almost no one voted for Ford's own moribund company union.

Ford turned somersaults. He negotiated a historically generous contract with the UAW. Then he changed his mind. At the last minute he shouted that he would rather close the plant than sign. His wife, Clara, threatened to leave him if he did not keep his word, and in the end he did. Later he said: "I'm glad that I did see it her way. Don't ever discredit the power of a woman."

1936: THE BATTLE OF THE RUNNING BULLS; DAWN OF THE SIT-DOWN STRIKE

Alfred Sloan, head of General Motors, controlled a behemoth that employed 250,000 in 110 plants in 14 states and 18 countries, controlled 45 percent of the American market and had profits of $196 million. He was so anti-union, he would move a plant to a new location rather than acknowledge a union. He fired any division head who did not meet the company standard of a 20 percent return per month, the very archetype of the most short-sighted American business practice. It impelled his plant managers not to improve their products or service so much as to squeeze their workers through constant, wracking speedups of the production lines combined with pay cuts.

The harassed GM workers rebelled. On December 28, 1936, some 7,000 workers seized control of the Fisher Body plant in Cleveland. Two days later 5,000 took over the massive Fisher One and the smaller Fisher Two plants in GM's nerve center at Flint, Michigan. This new tactic, soon called the sit-down strike, was an assault on private property rights, but for labor it was superior to the conventional walkout followed by hazardous picketing: it forestalled the replacement of strikers by scabs.

The United Automobile Workers followed its rank and file. Union sit-downs shut more and more GM plants. The spirit and discipline of the workers was remarkable. Sustained by wives and daughters shuttling in food and coffee, they settled in for a long siege. Hillbilly music over the public speaker system supplanted the racket of the machinery, but the men were kept busy. Every 15 workers were under the command of a strike captain, who organized factory patrols and safety checks, with time out for poker and Ping-Pong and classes on labor history. "They made a palace of what had been their prison," wrote the journalist Paul Gallico. There was no sabotage.

On the night of January 11, at GM's request, sheriff's deputies and police (known as bulls) stormed Fisher Two with tear gas and clubs. They were repelled by fire hoses and volleys of two-pound car hinges. They came back with gunfire, wounding 14 strikers, but the "bulls" were again forced to run. Michigan's new governor, Frank Murphy, was a pious and enigmatic man. He called out 3,500 National Guards, as GM wanted, but refused to assault the plant. "I'm not going down in history as 'Bloody Murphy,'" he exclaimed.

"My God, it seems an awful thing to shoot people for trespass." In the stalemate, the UAW devised a plan to force GM to the bargaining table. They set out to seize Flint's No. 4 plant, which was still producing engines for every Chevrolet. It was heavily guarded, but the union spread the word that it would attempt to occupy a different Chevrolet plant on the night of February 1. It hoped to be betrayed by company spies and it was. The guards were diverted by a feint attack on No. 1, while thousands of workers seized the crucial No. 4 without a fight.

On February 11, after six weeks of the great sit-down strike, GM gave in. It agreed to bargain with the UAW, and soon so did Chrysler. By October 1937, UAW membership had increased more than tenfold in just one year, to over 400,000 workers. The sit-down strike went on to enjoy a brief but effective popularity among American workers everywhere. Even counter waitresses at Woolworth's sat down at their stations, and recruited their friends to occupy counter stools. Then in 1939 the Supreme Court stepped in and banned sit-down strikes as a violation of property rights.

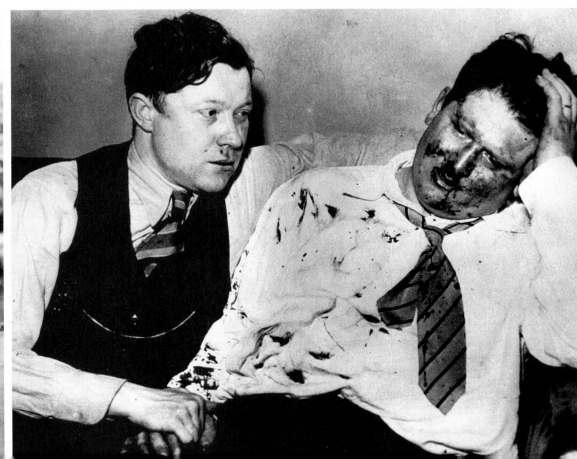

CHAPTER NINE

THE ROAD TO WORLD WAR II
1936–1941

Isolationism

At dawn on March 7, 1936, German soldiers, with drums beating and flags flying, marched into the Rhineland, the buffer zone between Germany and France demilitarized for an indefinite period by the Treaty of Versailles. Hitler sent them in just seven days after FDR had signed the second Neutrality Act. Reoccupation of the Rhineland was a violation not only of Versailles but of America's separate peace with Germany of 1921, and of the Locarno Pact of 1925, but FDR's secretary of state, Cordell Hull, did not even send a note of protest and FDR went fishing. The French and British protested, but did not move a soldier. Many European leaders were paralyzed by a quiet shame over what they now thought of as the overly harsh terms of Versailles.

It was a fateful moment. The French army, then more powerful than the German, could have easily ejected the three battalions making the ceremonial reoccupation. The Rhineland coup reinforced Hitler's contempt for the democracies. He had a distorted view of America as a materialistic society that had lost its will. He came to believe it was genetically damaged, half Judaized, half negrified. "What is America," he asked, "but millionaires, beauty queens, stupid phonograph records and Hollywood?" He hated one answer he got later, when Jesse Owens and other "inferior" blacks won Olympic gold medals in 1936 in Berlin. He left the stadium hastily. But by then he was sure he had a pact with destiny, and, unimpeded by isolationist America, he was on his way to the domination of Europe.

THE GAMBLE: Hitler's treaty-breaking soldiers riding into Düsseldorf, photographed by Stanley Devon, were a bluff. If opposed, they had been ordered not to shoot. Devon noticed that the men had down-at-heels boots. Hitler could put up only two squadrons of planes, and between flights their markings were changed to give the impression of greater numbers. Only ten were armed. Hitler himself later said it was the most nerve-wracking moment of his life: "If the French had marched into the Rhineland we would have had to withdraw with our tail between our legs."

THE AMERICANS WHO WANTED TO STAY OUT OF "EUROPE'S WAR"

Rick: I stick out my neck for nobody.
Louis: What a wise foreign policy!
(dialogue from *Casablanca*, Warner Bros., 1943)

The world war that began in Europe and Asia in the thirties was the greatest single tragedy in the history of mankind. Death and suffering, hatred and terror, consumed the souls of millions of people. The cost is beyond calculation; the arithmetic is stupefying, but the neatness of the round figures defames the chaos and the agony. We can merely note that more than 50 million people lost their lives, perhaps 20 million of them civilians. Up to 6 million Jews were murdered. Whole populations were uprooted from their homes and countries, millions of families wrenched apart. Future generations are forever culturally impoverished by the destruction, dismemberment and pillage of irreplaceable treasures of art, religion and history in ancient cities, libraries, monasteries, churches and cathedrals; in five years much of the history and heritage of Europe was lost. And the end of it all was hardly a new era of peace and justice. With Hiroshima and Nagasaki, the world became a more dangerous place. With Soviet armies at the heart of Europe, millions of survivors of the war passed into a grim new totalitarian servitude that lasted for 40 years.

It need not have happened this way.

The roots of the tragedy lay in moral cowardice and political miscalculation in the face of the rampant new imperialisms of Germany, Japan and Italy. The dictators in Europe and the militarists in Japan could have been deterred and contained by a defensive alliance without the universal destruction. In the early days, when Germany was relatively weak, a combination of Britain and France could have stopped Hitler at the Rhineland. The French, who believed in containment, did not have the nerve for it, and the British leadership of the day thought appeasement would buy peace. In these early days, the two great naval powers of Britain and the United States could have stopped Japan in its full-scale war on China, begun on July 7, 1937, but FDR would not make any kind of joint stand

with the British and the British felt unable to act on their own. American public opinion, traditionally sympathetic to China, was only narrowly opposed to such a step: in a poll in February 1938, a naval alliance was supported by 39 percent, with 50 percent against. At any time before March 1939, when Hitler swallowed the remnants of Czechoslovakia, the combination of Britain, France and the United States could have imposed peace, or defeated him in a much shorter war. So could a combination of Britain, France and the Soviet Union. Isolationism prevented the possibility of an Atlantic coalition until the aggressors were gorged on conquest and could be stopped only by a life-or-death alliance of the United States, Russia and the British Commonwealth.

Isolationism, it has to be said, was no more an American monopoly than appeasement was a British one. Before Winston Churchill took power, the rulers of the Western countries did not seek or welcome American involvement in Europe. They behaved, in A. J. P. Taylor's phrase, as though they were living in the days of Metternich or Bismarck, when Europe was still the center of the world. American isolationists behaved, in turn, as if Europe was as remote as it was in George Washington's day. Secretary of State Cordell Hull said they reminded him of a somnambulist who walks within an inch of a thousand-foot precipice without batting an eye.

American appeasement took principally an economic

INCREASING PRESSURE.

form. No distinction was made between trade with Germany and Japan and trade with the democracies. As the dictatorships grew ever more menacing, American industry blithely supplied them all with materials essential for their war machines. "Political beliefs," said Alfred Sloan of General Motors, "are irrelevant in business." Between 1936 and 1940 American investment in Germany increased by 40 percent.

Both Japan and Germany could have been boxed in by a Western understanding with the Soviet Union. This second combination that would have prevented the full horror of World War II was explored by Stalin but frustrated by mistrust on both sides. Fear of the wild, wild Reds delayed U.S. recognition of the USSR until 1933, and held up the Soviets' admittance to the League of Nations until 1934. The legitimate detestation of Stalinism among the democracies was compounded by a misreading of both Communist ambition and capacity for worldwide revolution. In the end, when they most wanted an alliance, the British and French were betrayed by the obduracy of Foreign Minister Vyacheslav Molotov and the greediness of Stalin; he sold out to the higher bidder.

But hindsight is not history. Judgment on the generation that allowed the catastrophe of World War II has to begin with Frederic Maitland's dictum: "It is very hard to remember that events now long in the past were once in the future." Appeasement seemed to many an honorable policy to repair what they saw as the injustices of the Versailles treaty, which took one tenth of Germany's population, and one eighth of its territory, and imposed an unpayable level of reparations. Appeasement was not then a dirty word. It was thought to represent the highest morality, unsullied by balance-of-power considerations. Of course, if Britain and France had exerted themselves to save strongly armed Czechoslovakia, they would have served their own national security interests as well as having the moral satisfaction of defending the only democracy between Germany and Russia. The appeasers in the British Conservative party, the Foreign Office and the *Times* of London looked back, rather than forward—back to Versailles and back to the horrors of the trenches. So did the isolationists in the American Congress, the church, the press and the public. They recoiled from getting embroiled in another conflict in Europe that would "plow under every fourth American boy." They resented the unpaid debts of the 15 countries allied with the U.S. in World War I. Britain was the object of the darkest suspicions within the State Department. Cordell Hull and his Under Secretary, Sumner Welles, were convinced that the crafty British were getting an unfair share of the diminished

THE ISMS: The politics of the thirties by John Mackey. In all the polls communism was disliked more than fascism. Asked to choose in 1938, 31 percent of the American people thought communism worse, 22 percent fascism—and 47 percent had no opinion. The national Communist vote fell throughout the decade, from 103,000 in 1932 to 46,000 in 1940. But the Communists made a lot of noise, especially after 1935, when they got orders from Moscow to form a Popular Front against fascism with the "depraved" parties of the left. A riddle of the time: "Why is the American Communist Party like the Brooklyn Bridge? Because it is suspended on cables."

world trade. They believed, like the Marxists, that imperialism impelled Britain to seize foreign markets and even that it would gang up with Hitler in economic warfare against America. "The whole history of British imperial preference," said Welles, "is a history of economic aggression against America."

All these attitudes, and more, united Americans in support of nonintervention. They weighed heavily against an effective alliance of the democracies and they encouraged Hitler in the belief that he could ignore American power. They inhibited FDR from campaigning for collective security with the consistent moral and strategic vision of Winston Churchill. In the years leading to war, FDR was less the lion of freedom than the Fred Astaire of the public opinion polls. Legislatively, these attitudes spawned the Neutrality Acts of 1935, 1936 and 1937, strait-jackets that prevented America from helping victims of aggression. Isolationism, or noninterventionism, was thus both a sentiment and a policy that made war more certain. Its strength was that it was composed of very many interwoven strands.

Politically in the twenties and thirties, isolationism was one expression of a tangle of other isms—nationalism, socialism, fascism, defeatism, anti-Semitism. It was more consistently directed against involvement in Europe than in Asia. Some nationalist isolationists, like Senator Hiram Johnson of California, were isolationist toward Europe, interventionist against Japan. Some of the principal isolationists, such as Ambassador Joseph Kennedy, were animated by hostility to Britain and France rather than a fastidious neutrality. Interventionism ranged from a desire for gestures of solidarity with western Europe to a willingness to send guns and, at the extreme, to join the fight. Many isolationists were pacifists, but a number, like Colonel Lindbergh, were as eager for rearmament as any interventionist. Isolationism was as diverse in its origins as it was in its manifestations. It was a product of history and a complex of geographic, cultural, religious, social and political influences.

Isolationism was at the very heart of America's sense of identity. The natural foreign policy of the young Republic, it was built on a strategic fact and a moral perception. America was a City Upon a Hill, superior to the decadent Old World and secured by the Atlantic Ocean from "the toils of European ambition, rivalship, interest, humor or caprice" (Washington). When President Monroe warned the European powers to stay out of the Western Hemisphere in 1823, he promised that America would stay out of the Old World. The moral superiority that distinguished American from European imperialism was cheerfully used to justify the civilizing expansion of American power in the Western Hemisphere and elsewhere, particularly in the colonies of such a decaying European power as Spain. Indeed, "isolationist" reentered the political vocabulary not with the rejection of the League of Nations but as a term of abuse for critics of expansion like William Jennings Bryan.

Isolationism was thus, in the eighteenth and nineteenth centuries, a practical means to the ends of peace and prosperity and not a delusive end in itself. It was reasonable, in 1839, for the young Abraham Lincoln to declare that "all the armies of Europe, Asia and Africa, with all the treasure of the Earth, and with a Bonaparte for a commander, could not by force take a drink from the Ohio or make a track on the Blue Ridge in a trail of a thousand years." One hundred years later, ex-

president Herbert Hoover, Major General Johnson Hawgood, General Hugh Johnson, Senator Robert Taft, the militant steel labor leader John L. Lewis and George Fielding Eliot (in his book *The Ramparts We Watch*) were saying much the same thing—pinning their isolationist faith in the Atlantic as an impenetrable barrier. It was reasonable for them to believe that Fortress America could be secured from seaborne invasion. Many of the isolationists were in favor of naval rearmament, tacit recognition though it was of the fact that for a century America had enjoyed freedom of the seas because of the British Royal Navy. But strategic airpower figured hardly at all in isolationist conceptions of strategy. And it was myopic not to see that America in the thirties was no longer self-sufficient and semi-isolated. Its future, like it or not, was as part of a prosperous and open global economy and it mattered a lot which ideas prevailed in Europe and Asia. Tradition and history were unreliable guides for the crises of the thirties.

World War I was the decisive experience. How President Woodrow Wilson took America into the war against the central isolationist axiom of her foreign policy has been sketched earlier. It was an experience that did not so much break the isolationist impulses as reinforce them. The idealism that had been roused for the war to end all wars recoiled with doubled velocity from the territorial cynicisms of Versailles. Suspicion mounted that the heroism of the trenches had been betrayed. There was so much slaughter and so little to show for it that the futility of war became a common theme of popular culture. Here is Ernest Hemingway, most macho of authors, writing in *Esquire* in September 1935: "They wrote in the old days that it is sweet and fitting to die for one's country. But in modern war there is nothing sweet nor fitting in your dying. You will die like a dog for no good reason. . . . No European country is our friend nor has been since the last war and no country but one's own is worth fighting for." All in the same vein, John Dos Passos wrote two novels, *One Man's Initiation—1917* and *Three Soldiers;* Laurence Stallings and Maxwell Anderson presented *What Price Glory?;* Faulkner wrote *Soldier's Pay;* William March, *Company K;* e. e. cummings, *The Enormous Room;* and Dalton Trumbo, *Johnny Got His Gun.* The same antiwar theme surfaced in movies like Chaplin's *Shoulder Arms,* King Vidor's silent classic *The Big Parade* and the adaptation of *All Quiet on the Western Front.* Jimmy Cagney's gangster picture *The Roaring Twenties* suggested that the despair of the trenches could lead to a wasted life of crime. Walter Millis, in 1935, successfully linked the various influences in his revisionist narrative of the tragedy, *Road to War: America 1914–17.*

SURRENDER TO THE DICTATORS

The Italian dictator Benito Mussolini, dreaming of the glories of the Roman Empire in Africa, invaded tiny Ethiopia on October 3, 1935. He was thought of as a goose-stepping buffoon, but his action exposed the cowardice of all the democracies. Ethiopia was a member of the League of Nations. If ever there was an opportunity to strike a blow in a generous cause with a minimum of risk, in the words of Winston Churchill, it was here and now. The league imposed sanctions, and threatened to include oil if America would follow the embargo. FDR would have liked to limit war supplies to the victim, but the Neutrality Act stood in the way. The most he felt he could do was warn American business that shipping war materials to either side was against the general spirit of the Neutrality Act. The isolationists howled anyway and tightened the act to forbid the President's having any discretion. Mussolini, having conquered Ethiopia with mustard gas, sent his thanks to the isolationists. The Neutrality Act, he said, was "a service to world peace." He was the first of the dictators, coming to power in 1922, and the least disliked. Even in 1938, after Ethiopia, Mussolini scored a U.S. popularity rating of 53 percent. Stalin scored 34 percent, Hitler 13 percent.

There was even less excuse for the democracies in Spain. It had been on the brink of civil war for years, riven by purely Spanish animosities of religion, language and region. In February 1936, the Spanish voters elected an anticlerical Popular Front coalition of liberal republicans, Socialists, syndicalists and Communists. The election over, the coalition fell apart in disorder, the extremists undermining the moderates just

SALUTE: The Church sided with the Fascists in Spain. A priest at Burgos Cathedral joins the Spanish dictator General Franco in the Fascist salute, November 1938.

as in Germany's Weimar Republic. On July 17, army officers with the military support of Hitler and Mussolini rebelled against the government. This civil war of Nationalist conspirators against Republican Loyalists became the ideological battlefield of Europe: Fascist order versus Communist fanaticism versus democratic liberty. Thousands of young idealist volunteers in the International Brigades, including 3,000 Americans, flung themselves into battle for the Republic. Fear of communism and a general war sapped the will of their governments. In the U.S., the Hearst

papers always referred to the Loyalists as Reds.

The British Conservatives and the French led 27 nations in a hands-off policy. Effectively, they sided with the rebel leader General Francisco Franco, since it was the legitimate government that needed help against Franco's army. The Soviet Union sent tanks and planes to the Loyalists. Mussolini sent Franco 50,000 troops and Hitler sent 16,000, including the air force Condor Legion that bombed the village of Guernica (April 26, 1937). In the words of the isolationist Senator Borah, that was "the most revolting instance of mass murder in all history." But words were all that the Loyalists got from the fretful leaders of the democracies. By tradition and international law, America had an obligation to continue trade with the Loyalist government, with which it maintained diplomatic relations, and no obligation to sell to the insurrectionists. The Neutrality Act was irrelevant: it did not apply to normal trade with a government under attack from within. But on January 7, 1937, FDR, egged on by his State Department, steamrollered a special act embargoing trade with either side.

The unfortunate truth was written in Secretary of the Interior Harold Ickes's diary on May 12, 1938, after a meeting with FDR. Behind the embargo, FDR told him, was the fear of the "jittery" congressional leadership that he would "lose every Catholic" in the upcoming election. "This was the cat that was actually in the bag," wrote Ickes, "and it is the mangiest, scabbiest cat ever." Six months later, FDR told Ickes he now realized he had made a grave mistake and he would never do such a thing again. It was too late.

Most of these pacifist persuasions were at work in Britain and France, which had shed over 2 million more lives than the U.S. during the war. The international aspect of isolationism was that the various peace movements reinforced one another. Women and students were prominent on both sides of the Atlantic. When the Oxford Union vowed in 1933 that it would not fight for King and Country, thousands of American students joined them by signing the Oxford peace pledge. At Princeton students dressed themselves up as war wounded and disturbed the tranquillity of Nassau Street by parading and demanding their medals and disability pensions now, while they were young and alive and able to enjoy them. At universities such as Harvard, Chicago and Columbia, the faculty was interventionist but the students had read e. e. cummings:

the bigness of cannon
is skilful,

but i have seen
death's clever enormous voice
which hides in a fragility of poppies. . . .

When Hitler's troops marched into Holland, Harvard students published a pacifist text entitled "Credemus" ("We Believe"). "Given a choice between on the one hand the sure and immediate horrors and costs of war, to ourselves as individuals and to our nation as a social democracy, and on the other hand the possibility of a German victory and some future threat to the United States as a result, we choose the latter alternative. And we think that here stands the vast army of Americans."

By the midthirties, however, America had also created a conspiratorial demonology out of World War I. It featured Wily Wilson, Daddy Warbucks and Perfidious Albion, and there was enough raw material to inflame popular opinion. Woodrow Wilson had indeed created an ecstasy of patriotism through George Creel's Committee on Public Information; the munitions industry and bankers did make a lot of money from the war; and British propaganda had been diabolically clever. The image of Wilson as a scheming president fueled in the thirties a new variation on the old Populist theme of the evils of an unchecked executive. Thirties neutrality legislation gained much of its momentum from this incentive to shackle another president thought to be too clever by half; and the image of Wilson's failure with the League of Nations increased Roosevelt's inclination not to get too far ahead of public opinion. Wilson preyed on his mind so much that viewing a movie of his predecessor's life even in 1944 sent his blood pressure soaring to 240 over 130.

Wilson, in the paranoia of the thirties, was seen as conspiring with bankers such as J. P. Morgan, who had effectively underwritten the British war effort, and with war profiteers. The vested interest of the munitions industry in bloodshed took off as a theme for the decade in the wake of an investigation of the arms industry by North Dakota Senator Gerald Nye's committee. As Senator Homer Bone of Washington put it: "For the sake of profits, for dollars to protect the loans of certain commercial interests in this country, 50,000 boys now lie buried in France." A book on the subject, *The Merchants of Death* by Helmuth C. Engelbrecht and F. C. Hanigan, was popularized by condensation in the *Readers' Digest,* and Daddy Warbucks surfaced in *Little Orphan Annie.* General Charteris, Britain's wartime intelligence chief in France, added to the mischief by regaling the National Club with tales of how he had fabricated stories of German atrocities. Although Britain overcompensated for such wartime excesses by shutting down its propaganda in the interwar years, its enemies were active. Three isolationist groups that stirred up resentment over Europe's unpaid war debts were creations of George Sylvester Viereck, a Nazi agent. He contrived to post tons of hate mail for free by using the franking privileges of Senators Ernest Lundeen and Robert Reynolds and Congressmen Martin L. Sweeney, Stephen A. Day and arch Roosevelt-hater Hamilton Fish.

ISOLATIONISTS: Three Senate giants who in 1939 opposed FDR's bid to loosen the handcuffs of the Neutrality Act: Robert La Follette, Jr., of Wisconsin, Hiram Johnson of California, and Arthur Vandenberg of Michigan. They had been members of Gerald Nye's committee, which blamed America's entry into World War I on greedy munitions makers. Johnson, the old Bull Mooser, had helped defeat the League of Nations and never wavered. Vandenberg later became an internationalist.

All these "lessons" of World War I were absorbed and regurgitated in different degrees by the constituents of isolationism, though they did not add up to a satisfactory explanation of how and why America had gone to war in 1917. One thinks of Mark Twain's advice: "Remember to learn no more from a situation than is in it. A cat that sits on a hot stove will not sit on a hot stove again. But he won't sit on a cold one either." To Lippmann, looking back, it was tragic that the postwar generation had never been educated to the reality of Wilson's intervention as a rejection of Germany's right to wage unrestricted submarine warfare. Instead, the American public had been "duped by a falsification of history . . . miseducated by a swarm of innocent but ignorant historians and reckless demagogues." But the deception of the well-meaning man on Main Street is also insufficient to account for the isolationist sentiment that restrained Roosevelt in his responses to aggression. As well as the cultural and intellectual environment, we have to look to regional and social influences.

To think of isolationism as a Midwest right-wing phenomenon bred by the propaganda of the *Chicago Tribune,* as so many in Europe did at the time, is to understate it regionally and wholly misstate it politically. It was a national phenomenon, given voice in the press by *Time* as well as the *Tribune* and all the Hearst newspapers, but it is true there was a distinct geographic concentration that provided the power base for legislative isolationism. As manifested by congressional voting and consistent returns in the opinion polls, a

VOYAGE OF THE DAMNED

LIFE AND DEATH: Refugees Walter and Ruth Karliner leaving Hamburg in 1939. Walter survived; Ruth perished in a concentration camp.

Send me your refugees—and I'll send them back.

The Statue of Liberty turned a basilisk eye on Walter Karliner and his sister Ruth (above). They were but two among the millions of European Jews caught in the Holocaust. The special poignancy of the story of Walter and Ruth is that it epitomizes what might have been. As the Nazi persecution intensified, the Karliner family—mother, father, two boys, two girls—fled from Peiskretscham in eastern Silesia, where they had a little grocery store. In Hamburg, they boarded the German liner *St. Louis,* whose owners were selling passages to Cuba with Cuban "immigration permits" included. The Nazis, having confiscated the Jews' property, were allowing the *St. Louis* to take them out of Germany. It was largely for propaganda, but also in part because a steward on board was a courier picking up the results of espionage in the United States.

There were 937 men, women and children on board when the *St. Louis* departed from Hamburg on May 13, 1939. It anchored in Havana harbor at 4 a.m. on May 27, but here began the nightmare. The president of Cuba had been excluded from the little racket selling immigration permits. He revoked them. Only a handful of immigrants were allowed to land. On June 2, the *St. Louis* left Havana. On June 3–4, it was off Miami, but the American government, too, would not admit the

refugees. In the end, Britain, France, Holland and Belgium took them in, but exclusion from the New World was a death sentence for most of them. The best estimate is that of the 907 who were returned to Europe only 240 lived. The others became part of the "final solution." When Vichy France was occupied by the Germans in 1942, four of the Karliners—mother, father, Ruth and older sister, Ilse—were taken by the Gestapo. Walter and his brother, Herbert, escaped with false identity papers. In 1947, eight years too late, they were accepted into America. Walter set up an antiques and gift shop in Westbrook, Connecticut. Herbert became the owner of a bakery in North Miami. Walter told me: "Today, I am glad to be in America, but I am still *very bitter* of [sic] the Roosevelt administration in 1939. They could have saved my parents, sisters and hundreds from the horrible gas chambers in Poland."

The plight of the passengers on the "Voyage of the Damned," as it came to be called, dramatizes one of the crueler consequences of the fearful mood of America in the thirties. No one was entitled to optimism about the fate of Jews turned away. Hitler had spectacularly advertised his intentions in an orgy of anti-Semitic violence two months after the Munich accords. On November 9, 1938—known as Kristallnacht (Night of the Broken Glass)—7,000 Jewish shops were wrecked. That was the least of it. Scores of Jews were

murdered on the streets, hundreds of synagogues burned, and untold thousands shipped to Dachau and Buchenwald.

FDR recalled the American ambassador. The American press cried foul. But there was no groundswell to modify immigration policy. The *New Republic* and John L. Lewis were almost alone in urging sanctuary for refugees. Congress was hostile to increasing any of the quotas: the entire German quota was only 25,957. Organized labor, the American Legion, and the Veterans of Foreign Wars were also opposed. Nativism, anti-Semitism, and anxiety about jobs in a depression were all influences for reaction (though from 1931 to 1938 there was a net migration from America of nearly 300,000). Some 67 percent of Americans in a 1938 poll said that, "with conditions as they are," the U.S. should try to keep out political refugees—a stark contrast to embattled Britain, where 70 percent said they should be welcomed.

It was not one of FDR's more glorious episodes. He never attempted to summon a higher vision of America's original ideals. He let die in committee a bill from Senator Robert Wagner to admit 200,000 German refugees. He was sensitive to the smear of his racist enemies that his was a "Jew Deal"; and he would do nothing that jeopardized his fragile congressional coalition. For the same reason, he watched Southern senators filibuster an antilynching bill to death. There was also an ugly strain of nativism and anti-Semitism in the State Department leadership, which FDR tolerated. In his cabinet only Treasury Secretary Henry Morgenthau pressed him. Cordell Hull's assistant at State, Breckenridge Long, who dealt with immigration, thought Jews were subversive. He wrote in his diary that large numbers of Jews were "entirely unfit to become citizens . . . they are lawless, scheming, deficient . . . just the same as the criminal Jews who crowd our police court docks in New York." Long would spend much of World War II repressing reports of the Holocaust leaking out of Europe and quashing schemes to save as many of its victims as possible.

My personal thoughts and memories after returning to Europe in June 1939 and not beeing admitted to America was,Thank god we ditn go back to Germany; (Not knowing what lays ahead of us.)
Today I am glad to be in America and a US Citizen but I am still _VERY BITTER_ of the Rosevelt administration in 1939, They could have saved my Parents, Sisters and hundreds from the horrible Gas Chambers in Poland.

Karliner writing to the author in 1992.

region of isolationism extended from the Midwest well into the states of the West and mountains. It stretched from the Ohio to the Rockies, and its center was not Chicago but farther west, in Kansas, Nebraska and the Dakotas. Graham Hutton, the head of Britain's wartime propaganda office, became convinced isolationism owed more to the physical insularity of this region than political perversity. He had a point. If Chamberlain could console the British people after Munich that Czechoslovakia was a faraway place, what did it look like from a farm in Nebraska? It was a long, long way from the wheatfields to the nearest town; and a whole day's journey to a big city. To a farmer overwhelmed by the immensity of his landscape, sometimes catching on his crackling radio fragments of inexplicable foreign events and unknown personalities, Europe was another planet. It was hard to imagine a city being bombed; it was inconceivable that something like that could ever happen in America. The dramatic conversion to internationalism of Michigan Senator Arthur Vandenberg was not unrelated to the shock he experienced when he had to crouch in a London air-raid shelter as German V1 "doodlebug" missiles shook the ground: "How can there be immunity or isolation," he asked, "when man can devise weapons like that?"

Europe was not only remote to the people of the American interior. It was alien, with seemingly very different values. In agrarian communities, where failure to meet interest payments on the money borrowed for seed and machinery threatened foreclosure, the Europeans' unpaid debts from World War I were a matter of disgust. Perceptions of American exceptionalism, exaggerated by distance and tradition, fused with the traditional politics of the prairies. The Populist and Progressive movements had always made hay with the exploitation of the farmer by the makers of farm machinery, the operators of the grain elevators, the merchants, the railways and the Eastern bankers who mortgaged the land back to the farmer once he had been broken on the wheel of capitalism. Beyond Wall Street were seen the shadowy figures of British bankers and Jewish financial interests. It was natural, especially in the wake of Senator Nye's investigations, that the agrarian mistrust should be synthesized in Congress as isolationism. Roosevelt's agrarian constituency had all but evaporated by the time of his October 1937 speech calling for aggressors to be quarantined. He was faced with a solid regional block of isolationists in the Senate who were Republican progressives: Hiram Johnson of California; Nye of North Dakota; George William Norris of Nebraska, the hero of TVA;

William E. Borah of Idaho; and Robert M. La Follette, Jr., of Wisconsin. They formed an isolationist alliance with the Democrat Burton K. Wheeler and the Farm-Labor representative Henrik Shipstead, both from Montana.

Ethnic allegiances and perceptions were subsidiary to the politics of land, but they were a significant layer in the complex overlapping of the traditional and cultural influences at the root of isolationism. Britain was the focus of a lot of the vestigial resentments of immigrants from Central Europe. In the early years of the war, when British officials intercepted mail from the American interior to people in Britain, they noted that each of the ethnic groups had their own pet hate among the imperialist European great powers. When the different ethnic groups gathered in communities, they tended to find a common identity, in part, by a solidarity of sympathy. The political manifestation was a reciprocity of dislike for one's neighbor's national enemy. The greatest of these perceived persecutors, the Austrian Empire, had vanished at Versailles, and the German and Russian Empires had been broken up. Britain remained for much of the period the sole obvious survivor and perpetuator of the system that had driven these populations to the New World in the first place. So the British became the residuary legatees of this collective opprobrium. It was not confined to ethnic groups. Eastern urban populations, including even intellectual and establishment pillars of English descent, had their own emotions. Throughout the thirties the *New Republic* and the *Nation* vied to attain new heights of revisionism, denouncing the league and its supposed friends in Wall Street, and characterizing Britain as the oppressor of the working people. Some Eastern liberals, as well as immigrants of Irish stock, found it hard to reconcile the British Empire and the defense of Western civilization. This was probably more important than the direct enmity of German Americans and Italian Americans who had relatives on the other side of the battlefields.

The overt fascism of Fritz Kuhn's Amerika Deutsches Volksbund (German-American Bund), which took Hitler's uniforms and hatreds onto the streets of New York, was certainly only a small excrescence. The tendency among German Americans, and Italian Americans, was not to side with the Nazis, but to join isolationist groups as a way of advertising their Americanism. For those of German ancestry, in particular, this was a response to the hostility they had faced on every street corner in the First World War, when Creel's propaganda machine portrayed Germans as Prussian brutes. People of German extraction kissed the flag, changed their names from Muller to Miller and conspicuously bought Liberty Bonds, but they were hounded all the same. Montana saw some of the worst scenes and its Sedition Act of 1918 was a model for the discredited Federal Sedition Act. Somebody who saw it all at first hand as a young district attorney, and remembered what war had done to civil liberties, was the hard-line isolationist Senator Wheeler.

The Irish-American folk memory was of persecution by the British. Their homeland espoused a rigid official neutrality and they were Catholic, like the Italian Americans. Catholic America, a key constituency for Roosevelt, was more vocally antiwar than Protestant America, excepting the Lutherans: The opposition of these groups was pacifist, but it was also political. Scandinavian Americans, strongly Populist in their politics, rejected the Old World with such decisiveness that, even in the face of the German invasion of Norway and Denmark, 95 percent of them did not want America to make a stand. In the eyes of the Catholics, the real threat to the world was not nazism but communism, and until 1940 it was a view that had the blessing of the Pope.

Left and right converged in supporting the legislative fulfillment of isolationism, the Neutrality Acts, though there were important exceptions, and each group had its own reasoning. The Socialist leader Norman Thomas was moved by the horror of war, the internationalist feeling that a bayonet had a worker on either end, and by a fear of what war might do to civil liberties in America. Henry Ford hated Jews. The Communist Party organized the Lincoln Brigade to fight for the Spanish Republic, but turned its back on democracy when its masters signed the Nazi-Soviet pact and returned to an interventionist posture only after Hitler invaded the Soviet Union.

The most striking political feature of isolationism was the focus it gave for the flowering of the militant right. In this, America was part of a wave of radical nationalist movements throughout the world. Every European state had its own Fascist groups, marching to a raggedy drumbeat of Darwin and Nietzsche, promising to destroy the cancer of Bolshevism within and without, restore the greatness of the state, control the economy, build links between workers, industry and the party, and drive out the Jews. The Fascist right in America was united on staying out of the European war and opposing communism; but it was never a cohesive or sizable group. Its capacity to cause trouble was muted by the happy American habit of free competition. There were scores of rival factions united only in their nuttiness and taste for fancy names—the German-American Bund coexisting with the Yankee Freemen, the Ethiopian Pacific

Movement, Paul Revere Sentinels, the Ra-Con Club, the Committee of One Million, the Christian Mobilizer, the National Workers League, the Gray Shirts, Cross and the Flag, Phalanx Pax (a secret gun club) and others.

The isolationist policy articulated in the Neutrality Acts of the thirties split parties, unions, churches and families: in the most famous American family, Alice Roosevelt Longworth was a vehement isolationist; her three brothers could not wait to join the fight. Charles Lindbergh and his wife, Anne Morrow Lindbergh, thought a worldwide Nazi victory inevitable; but Anne's mother, Elizabeth, worked on William Allen White's committee to help Britain. Under the pressure of events, isolationism led to the mass production of second thoughts. But it also had the capacity to divide the mind of an individual. The columns of the celebrated commentator Walter Lippmann are testimony to a not uncommon schizophrenia; he wanted Britain and France to stand up to the dictators. He saw clearly that if they failed, America would become the last stronghold of Western civilization—"the citadel of law and liberty, of mercy and charity, of justice among men and of love and goodwill." All his analysis pointed to America allying itself with the democracies. Yet at key times he argued for neutrality, as at key times FDR shrank from collective security.

Lippmann's ambivalence is evident in his columns and broadcasts, but something similar must have happened with others we think of as Atlanticists from birth. John Foster Dulles was an internationalist as a New York lawyer but in the pulpit as a Protestant lay preacher he was a passionate isolationist. And the young John F. Kennedy, who publicly supported the interventionist president of Harvard and wrote a plea for American rearming called *While England Slept,* had earlier secretly sent money to the Committee to Defend America First. Of course, the central ambiguous figure is Franklin Roosevelt. He eventually led America in an inspiring and resolute alliance with the democracies; but only after the Japanese had attacked at Pearl Harbor on December 7, 1941, and Hitler had declared war on America. The powers of his leadership were muted in the years leading up to war. Unlike the somnambulists, he was never in doubt about the nature of fascism and the threat to America's national security if the Axis powers were victorious, but in his second administration (1937–1941) he was as much concerned with his own political security and, with it, the New Deal.

It was a maladroit political maneuver by FDR that yoked America with the Neutrality Acts. In March 1935 he met the members of the Nye committee because he was worried they were about to recommend nationalizing and emasculating the arms industry they had demonized. He tried to divert their attention to the problem of maintaining American neutrality if war broke out. The argument backfired. They seized on the idea that America might drift into war and sponsored the first Neutrality Act. FDR, signing it on August 31, 1935, characterized it as "more likely to drag us into war than keep us out." FDR was sometimes more of a chameleon than a strategist. His revulsion for war moved him at times into the isolationist-pacifist camp. In the 1936 campaign, his "I hate war" speech at Chautauqua, New York, surpassed the most eloquent pacifist rhetoric. Yet he was ready, whenever the Senate would let him, to repair America's military weakness, which was manifest: Henry Ford had more men in his factories than Uncle Sam had under arms. FDR detested nazism, but sometimes in the midthirties he rationalized his own caution by drawing on a dislike bordering on contempt for the wayward democracies of Britain and France. It was bewilderingly his style to take a bold step forward and a brisk step back. He reneged on his first attempts to win power for discretionary trade sanctions in 1933. He did it again in 1937 with his quarantine speech, discussed below, and again in January 1939 after trying to persuade the Military Affairs Committee that America's frontier was on the Rhine. He did it overnight on May 27, 1941, declaring a national emergency, then backing away from the brink. U.S. Ambassador William Bullitt explained it to France's prime minister, "It sometimes happens that the President, whose impulsive temperament you recognize, expresses himself in terms which exceed his thought. . . ."

FDR's infrequent initiatives in foreign policy were marked by the traditional American preference for moral gestures, for adjectives rather than verbs. This was the spirit in which, in January 1938, to the derision of Hitler and the despair of Chamberlain, he proposed a great summit meeting where people could look one another in the eye and create a new world order. Such public initiatives that he took, as the storm gathered in the last two years of peace, were more as a mediator than as the standard-bearer of freedom against dictatorship. Privately, he did more. In October 1938, he sent a secret message to Chamberlain that if there was war he would do all he could as president to supply war matériel. It was good for the morale of the British cabinet, but the necessity to conceal the promise from the isolationists reduced its international effectiveness. And on the most famous occasion when he did give a lead toward collective security, in the wake of Japan's renewal of war on China, he began to retreat the very next day. The occasion was his speech in Chicago on October 5, 1937, calling for a quarantine of lawless aggressors. The speech, for all its ambiguities, envisaged the United States breaking out of its neutrality to commit to collective security. As a result, the assembly of the League of Nations was the next day emboldened to adopt reports condemning Japanese aggression in China. Britain talked tough. Sanctions were in the air. The first collective action against aggression seemed to be in the making. But FDR downplayed his speech at a press conference on October 6, and on October 12, in his fireside chat, he backed away from strong collective action in favor of more talk. America was still talking when the Japanese bombed and sank the United States gunboat *Panay* in the Yangtze River near Nanking.

FDR justified his retreat by the isolationist outcry. "It's a terrible thing," he told an aide, "to look over your shoulder when you are trying to lead." But how hard did he try? It is true that no Democrats spoke in support of his tentative China stand and a poll in Congress suggested two-to-one opposition to sanctions. But among American citizens there was widespread national support for the denunciation of aggressors and an influential minority endorsed sanctions. The historian William E. Leuchtenberg has reviewed scholarly research on the subject and concludes that among the minority in favor of collective action were some of the most influential people in the country, "perhaps the majority of those well informed on world affairs and some of the powerful members of Congress as well." The chairman of the Senate Foreign Relations Committee, Nevada's Key Pittman, went so far as to declare that "an economic quarantine" would end Japan's aggression against China within 30 days. There was the basis on which a sea change might have been wrought in majority public opinion. Biographer Kenneth Davis concludes: "It was not primarily for lack of followers, it was for lack of the requisite resolve, nerve, energy and clarity of mind in the aftermath of his lost court battle, that Roosevelt, nursing with desperate hope isolationist sentiments of his own, failed at this crucial point to lead."

Popular opinion remembers FDR differently, as the great educator who saw the Fascist dangers early and set out patiently to win public opinion to resist the menace. By this analysis, he could not have moved a step quicker to rearmament and war without losing the public and his congressional support for beating the continuing Depression. This is too generous. Congress was a real obstacle. It remained isolationist right up to Pearl Harbor, but the people emerged more rapidly from the shell of pacifist isolationism, and the question is whether FDR could have made more of that popular movement. It was there, at least as indicated by the polls. They were an imperfect tool, and politicians were not yet so enthralled by them, feeling themselves to be pretty good judges of public opinion. Still, a preponderance of the polls showed the people consistently more resolute than the noisy isolationists in Congress. The people were often ahead of FDR. They rejected war, but they were consistent in supporting every measure to help Britain, and every poll from as early as fall 1935 was heavily in favor of enlarging U.S. national defenses. The people were ready in 1938 for an embargo on war goods to Japan, ready in June 1940 for the first peacetime conscription, three months before Congress voted the Burke-Wadsworth Selective Service Act, which in August 1941 was renewed by only 203–202 in the House. That FDR had judged the public mood better than the isolationists in Congress was made clear in the 1940 election. His policy of "all aid short of war" for Britain and France was too popular for the Republicans to oppose him with a dedicated isolationist like Robert Taft. The curious feature of the last year before Pearl Harbor, however, is that even when elected for an unprecedented third term, FDR was restrained in his leadership. He sustained Britain by getting congressional agreement for supplies under the Lend-Lease Act, but he refused to protect British convoys or respond to German attacks on American shipping. After proclaiming the emergency in the speech of May 27, 1941, he robbed it of substance the next day, though he had attracted telegrams 95 percent in his favor. He refused to issue follow-up orders, and denied that he planned to protect shipping or change the Neutrality Act. Nobody could understand why.

By May 1941, with Britain alone against the Axis powers, 73 percent of Americans were in favor of fighting if that was the price of continuing to help Britain. But FDR prevaricated, to the exasperation of his cabinet. "Go see the isolationist over in the White House," said Henry Stimson, his Republican secretary of war, when pressed in May on the passivity of America. FDR was torn between idealism and prudence, between a desire to keep his promise not to let our boys fight in a foreign war, and his growing realization that Hitler would win if America stayed out.

Of course, FDR's dilemma was real enough, and the political judgment of the only man elected president four times merits a certain respect. In his second administration, he needed the votes of the "progressive" isolationists and pacifists to get his New Deal through Congress. For a bolder foreign policy, he needed the votes of opponents of the New Deal. Should he risk domestic reform for the sake of pursuing collective security? Or should he risk collective security to get his domestic program through? As Kenneth Davis says, this necessity to choose between equally unpalatable alternatives was especially paralyzing to "one of Roosevelt's temporizing, compromising, pragmatic disposition and aversion to rigorously logical thought." The narrowness of his congressional base was always on his mind. Even after Hitler had provoked widespread revulsion in America by the seizure of Prague on March 15, 1939, both houses of Congress decisively rejected FDR's efforts to amend the Neutrality Acts so that help could be given to the democracies.

Still, there is force in the assessment that FDR's caution veered on the fastidious. When fascism was on the rise he could have pushed harder and more consistently for an interventionist mind-set. That might have made a difference to the balance of power and Hitler's propensity to gamble. When fascism had triumphed on the mainland of Europe, FDR could have been bolder in devising a grand strategy drawing on all sources of American power, in the interests of American long-term security. But if FDR moved haltingly, and sometimes with faint heart, toward the harsh reality, he still managed to get there before most of his contemporaries, and when he did he acted with vigor.

The long debates of the thirties and early forties reflected divisions about the nature of America that remain. Does its special position, as an exemplary democracy and the greatest power, give it a moral duty to defend human rights beyond its borders and where there is no obvious national security interest? If so, with what authority and at what cost? The end of the war thrust America center stage as the only power capable of resisting the spread of Communist aggression. On this central foreign-policy issue, everybody seemed to change places. Key isolationists became cold warriors against the Soviet Union. Leading interventionists of the thirties became the prudent conciliators. Paradoxically, neutralism became a dirty word on the right: in the fifties it was advanced as the reason to deny wheat to starving India, because that new nation preached neutralism in the Cold War.

Isolationism with specific foreign-policy goals withered after Pearl Harbor, but no one can say it has vanished. On the contrary, toward the end of the century, America, as the remaining superpower, was attracting burdens that were sure to impose strains on its strength and the goodwill of its people.

THE DUPING OF A HERO

AMERICA'S MUSSOLINI

Father Coughlin, his father and dog, Pal, 1932.

Every Sunday afternoon in the thirties, 45 million Americans sat by the radio to hear the sonorous voice of Father Charles E. Coughlin peddling a fascism very similar to Mussolini's. The natural harmony of labor and capital. The immorality of usury. The sanctity of private property. The state's duty to provide social justice.

Roosevelt received Coughlin in secret in his early days in the White House. Joseph Kennedy took John Kennedy to see him at the Shrine of the Little Flower in Royal Oak, outside Detroit. Coughlin received a million letters a week in the Depression, and by the midthirties claimed 7 million members in his National Union for Social Justice. He led the isolationist campaign that kept the U.S. out of the World Court. As the crisis of the thirties deepened, and Roosevelt backed the Allies, Coughlin's ratings flagged and he got wilder. In 1936, he moved to the fascist right after his nascent third party won only 2 percent of the national vote that year against "Franklin Double Crossing Roosevelt." He became anti-Semitic. The New Deal was a Jew Deal. The Jews, the British, the President and all the East were in a vast plot. It was the Jews who started the American Civil War.

He reviewed young, unemployed Irish Americans in his associated Christian Front as if they were an army, looking on as platoons of them hunted Jews and daubed obscenities on shop windows in downtown Chicago. His publication *Social Justice*, was banned from the mails in 1942 under the Espionage Act, and the Church ordered him off the radio.

The isolationists who hobbled Roosevelt and persuaded Hitler that the United States was irrelevant ranged from pacifist left to fascist right. They included President Kennedy's father, Joseph P. Kennedy, and Henry Ford; the chairman of Sears, Roebuck, General Robert E. Wood, and John L. Lewis; the demagogic priest Father Charles E. Coughlin; high-powered senators both Democratic and Republican; and the young John Foster Dulles, who a month before Pearl Harbor declared that only hysterics believed Japan contemplated war on America. But in 1940, when all these disparate elements formed up behind the lavishly financed Committee to Defend America First, the star performer was the genuine American hero Charles A. Lindbergh, "the Lone Eagle" of the first solo nonstop flight across the Atlantic in 1927.

Isolationism was in Lindbergh's blood. His Republican father was one of the handful of congressmen to vote against the declaration of war in 1917. Having retreated to Europe for three years to escape the anguish of the kidnapping and murder of his infant son and the gross intrusions of the press (for instance, photographers broke into the morgue), Lindbergh had become convinced that the Nazis were a good thing because they were a bulwark against Soviet communism. As a Social Darwinist, he was also attracted by their doctrines of racial purity, a feeling strengthened by his work with a scientist full of dubious genetic theories. Lindbergh was thoroughly duped during three separate visits to the Reich. At a state dinner in Berlin, two weeks before the Munich crisis, he let Hitler's air chief, Hermann Göring, award him the Service Cross of the German Eagle, against the entreaty of his wife, Anne, who called it "the albatross." Göring also made him a victim of his elaborate deception schemes to convince visitors that the Luftwaffe was much more powerful than it was. For foreign visitors like Lindbergh, Göring's men would fill the skies with planes, but they were actually the same ones flown in circles to multiply the illusion of numbers. When Lindbergh visited Germany in 1937, Göring stage-managed visits to a few showcase factories. Lindbergh assumed they were typical and reported, wrongly, that Germany was mass-producing warplanes at a vastly faster rate than Britain, France or America.

He was so defeatist that, even after the battle of Britain had proved him wrong, he urged Congress to reject Lend-Lease because Germany, he felt, could not be beaten even with American intervention. He was a sincere but stubborn man who read little, and he was blind to Hitler's villainies. The climax of his career as a campaigner came at Des Moines, Iowa, in October 1941. In a departure from his earlier, reasoned speeches, he railed against Jews in press, radio and government. If war came, they would be to blame. It was the wrong note and support ebbed. After Pearl Harbor, two months later, when he was 39, he tried to take up his army commission, but Roosevelt blocked him, reportedly telling adviser Harry Hopkins, "If I die tomorrow, remember Lindbergh is a Nazi."

All his life, he felt wronged by his exclusion from the ranks. In 1941 he took a job in a Ford plant making bombers and, as a civilian, snuck in 50 flying missions against the Japanese, one of which resulted in the shooting down of an enemy plane. He devoted the later years of his life to conservation. When I talked with him in 1970, it was in the remote forests of Mindanao in the Philippines, where loggers and ranchers, aided by corrupt policemen and gunplay, were grabbing the untitled virgin land from minority groups. This time he was on the side of the victims.

CONFRONTATION: J. P. Morgan, Jr. (right), tries to make a point to isolationist Senator Nye during the hearings on war profits. Nye's chief counsel was Alger Hiss.

"Democracy is sand driven by the wind," said Italy's dictator, Mussolini. It looked that way to cartoonist David Low and others as Hitler marched unopposed into the Rhineland (1936), Austria (1938) and Czechoslovakia (1938–39). Mussolini gobbled up little Albania.

THE MAN WITH THE UMBRELLA

Roosevelt thought British Prime Minister Neville Chamberlain (opposite) had done well when he took tea with Adolf Hitler at his Berchtesgaden hideaway in September 1938 and agreed to Germany's absorption of the Sudetenland part of Czechoslovakia. "Good man," cabled FDR. Roosevelt's ambassador to London, Joseph Kennedy, concurred. He could not for the life of him, he said, see how anyone would fight to save the Czechs. Hitler did have a case in the grievances of the 3.5 million Germans in the Sudetenland. The Versailles principle of self-determination had been breached when they were deposited in the new state of Czechoslovakia, a federation of nationalities. Still, the apparently reasonable compromise of letting Hitler occupy some areas of the country and hold a referendum in others was effectively the end of the first democracy Central Europe had known. Chamberlain had to fly to Germany twice

more that month to conclude the negotiations. Each time, Hitler turned the screws. Berchtesgaden gave him the Sudetenland; the meetings in Bad Godesberg and Munich gave him immediate military occupation of the region before the report of a border commission. "This is," said Hitler, "the last territorial claim I have to make in Europe." He joined in guaranteeing the independence of the remainder of Czechoslovakia.

Chamberlain thought he had nailed Hitler down in a final meeting in the Führer's apartment. "Here is a paper which bears his name," the prime minister exulted in London, waving a note he had got Hitler to sign. It pledged that Germany and Britain would never go to war again. "I believe it is peace in our time," Chamberlain told the rapturous crowds. Hitler knew otherwise. The night before signing he told Mussolini they would sooner or later have to fight Britain. He was furious

with "that senile old rascal" who had deprived him of a triumphal march into Prague. Later, eating Viennese cream cakes at a lunch with his cronies, he fumed: "If ever that silly old man comes interfering here again with his umbrella, I'll kick him downstairs and jump on his stomach in front of photographers. . . . I will destroy them! The French, too! Latin curs and lickspittles! Jew-ridden scum!"

On March 15, 1939, Hitler took over the whole of Czechoslovakia, breaking his promise to respect the independence of the non-German areas, and destroying his excuse that he sought only to rescue a German minority. It was no longer a question of undoing Versailles. Winston Churchill, who had called for a grand alliance with France and Russia to stop Hitler, had predicted it all: "Do not suppose this is the end," he said of Munich. "This is only the beginning of the reckoning."

HITLER'S MAN: Count Joachim von Ribbentrop (in trench coat), arriving in Moscow to tie the ribbon on the 1939 Nazi-Soviet Pact, was a former champagne salesman nicknamed Germany's No. 1 parrot by Göring for endlessly repeating Hitler. *Inset:* Ribbentrop was the first to be hanged in 1946 in the executions ordered by the Nuremberg war crimes tribunal. As the hood was placed on his head, he called out: "I wish peace to the world."

THE NEW IMPERIALISTS GET TOGETHER

FDR hoped to "put the dictators on the spot" with a message he sent to Hitler and Mussolini on April 15, 1939. Would they promise, he asked, not to attack some 31 independent European and Asian states for ten years? The telegram was ill judged. Hitler promptly asked all the states if they felt threatened. All felt it was more prudent to say they did not. Hitler mocked FDR in a brilliantly sardonic speech, as if he were responding to a slow pupil. Yes, he would guarantee this state and that, and yes, he would guarantee not to invade America if Mr. Roosevelt was anxious. The party faithful rocked with laughter.

The telegram may have helped FDR with domestic opinion, but the diplomatic ploy was irrelevant to the struggles in Europe. Following Hitler's seizure of Czechoslovakia, Britain had guaranteed Poland's borders, and the Soviet Union had said it was willing to form a "Triple Alliance" with Britain and France to protect Poland and the Baltic states. It was the best hope of containing Hitler, but Britain and France dithered. While they did, Stalin opened secret talks with Germany for a nonaggression pact. Hitler had more to offer, and he saw a pact with Stalin as a way of scaring Britain from keeping its pledge to Poland. In his mountain retreat of Berchtesgaden, on August 23–24, he finally got a 3 a.m. call from his emissary to the Kremlin, Count Joachim von Ribbentrop. The deal was done. "This will strike like a bomb," Hitler exulted. He hammered both fists on the wall and shouted: "Now Europe is mine. The others can have Asia." In a secret protocol to the pact, Stalin had won a free hand to grab the part of Poland that Russia had lost at the end of World War I, plus Latvia, Estonia, Lithuania, Finland and Bessarabia.

It was FDR's turn to have a 3 a.m. phone call. On September 1, it rang in his bedroom. On the other end was William C. Bullitt, ambassador to France, telling him that a German bomb had landed in the garden of the U.S. envoy in Poland. "It's come at last," FDR told him. "God help us all."

In a fireside chat, FDR said: "This nation will remain a neutral nation, but I cannot ask that every American remain neutral in thought as well." It was a sharp contrast with Wilson's attitude in 1914. FDR asked for a revision of the Neutrality Act so that American factories could sell arms to Britain and France on a "cash-and-carry" basis. The debate was tumultuous. Herbert Hoover led a national campaign for strict neutrality. The American Communists, somersaulting without shame, joined the isolationists in opposing aid to the democracies. FDR at this point conceded that American ships and citizens should be banned from sailing into the European war zone, but by November both houses had agreed that Britain and France could be assisted as they fought for their lives.

WOOED: Hitler's men gave Yōsuke Matsuoka, Japan's foreign minister (left), a tour of Potsdam in 1940.

HITLER'S FATEFUL PROMISE

By mid-1940, Hitler was the master of mainland Europe, isolating Britain. In Japan, even the moderates wanted to gobble up the remnants of the French and Dutch empires in Indochina and the East Indies, and, with Britain itself besieged, Burma, Malaya and even India seemed vulnerable. The moderate Yonai ministry gave way to a more militarist group headed by Prince Konoe.

At this critical juncture, Japan's foreign policy was entrusted to a brash graduate of the University of Oregon Law School, Yōsuke Matsuoka, whose family had immigrated to the United States in 1893. Alas, the turn of the century in America, when Matsuoka had put himself through college by working as a hotel busboy, had been a time of intense paranoia about "the yellow peril." It was an embittered Matsuoka, with a love-hate of the West, who eventually took up a career in Japan. His first act as foreign minister, in 1940, was to line up Japan with Germany and Italy in the Tripartite Pact, the mutual-help treaty by which the Berlin-Rome-Tokyo Axis planned to divide the world among them.

Hitler's plan was for Japan to enter the war, not against America nor against his new "ally" Russia, which he was about to stab in the back, but against the British Empire in Asia. He hoped that America would stay on the sidelines. He planned to deal "severely" with America, but only when he was ready. Matsuoka was invited to Berlin and egged on to attack Britain at once by both Ribbentrop and Hitler. "Never in human imagination," Hitler told him, was there a better opportunity for the Japanese to strike in the Pacific. Matsuoka agreed. He would do his best against the weak intellectuals, businessmen and court circles in Tokyo. On April 4, 1941, Hitler worked on Matsuoka again. He pressed him to tell the fainthearted in Tokyo they need not worry about how America might respond. The U-boats, the Luftwaffe and the "superior" German soldiers would be more than a match for America, said Hitler. And then he made a reckless promise: If Japan got into conflict with the United States, Germany on her part would take "the necessary steps at once." When Matsuoka blinked, Hitler said it again. It was one of his biggest blunders.

"THIS . . . IS LONDON": AMERICA LIVES THE BLITZ

FDR sent half a million World War I rifles to Britain in June 1940. These and other arms went some way to reequip the 338,226 British soldiers plucked from French beaches in the Miracle of Dunkirk. In August, he sent three American generals to plan air, sea and land cooperation. They immediately contradicted the reports of Ambassador Joseph Kennedy that Britain was finished. But more significant than even these early military moves was the steely voice of the young Edward R. Murrow speaking to America from embattled Britain.

Murrow (1908–1965), an intense, chain-smoking perfectionist of a reporter, was chief of the Columbia Broadcasting Bureau in London in the summer months of 1940, when Hitler tried first to destroy British airpower and then to bomb its cities into submission in the Blitz, which continued at full ferocity to May 1941. He happened also to be an artist in the new medium of radio, and a man of moral fiber who had a clear vision of what was at stake in Britain's survival. He focused on the ordinary people, "the unsung heroes," he called them. "Those black-faced men with bloodshot eyes fighting fires . . . the girls who cradle the steering wheel of a heavy ambulance in their arms, the policeman who stands guard over that unexploded bomb."

Murrow's first live report, which stimulated so much excitement in America, caught the war by chance. He was a guest contributor to a BBC portrait of London at night, with a scripted talk. Just as he went on the air on August 24, 1940, from the steps of St. Martin-in-the-Fields, Trafalgar Square, the sirens sounded. Murrow ad-libbed a description of the raid, which the censors let through and which CBS rebroadcast. Regular live broadcasts were permitted from September 21. The war entered the homes of America in the sound of sirens, the whine of aircraft, the footfalls of people hurrying for shelter, the hollow clang of the shelter door, the crack of anti-aircraft fire, the thunder of bomb bursts.

Archibald MacLeish summed up how it felt to be an American listening to Murrow: "You burned the city of London in our houses and we felt the flames that burned it. You laid the dead of London at our doors and we knew the dead were our dead—all men's dead—were mankind's dead and ours. Without rhetoric, without dramatics, without more emotion than needed be, you destroyed the superstition of distance and of time."

The British people and the Royal Air Force won the battle of Britain. From July 1940 to the end of October the Germans lost 1,733 aircraft, the British, 915. The battle was a critical event in the war; and so was the admiration Murrow evoked in America for Britain's stand.

THE HALF-AMERICAN WHO SPOKE FOR BRITAIN

Winston Churchill (right), aged about 15, with his brother, Jack, and Lady Randolph, circa 1889.

Winston Churchill, the savior of Britain, was half-American. His Brooklyn-born mother, Jennie Jerome (1854–1921), was the daughter of Leonard Jerome, a New York financier and horse fancier. She was a dazzling beauty of 19 when she met the dashing 24-year-old Lord Randolph Churchill, the third son of the seventh Duke of Marlborough, in the romantic setting of Cowes Week, the yachting regatta on the Isle of Wight. They fell in love at once and pledged their troth under the stars on only the third night of their acquaintance. Randolph had a hard time overcoming the objections of his father, who took a poor view of Jennie's father. "I have heard," said the Duke, "this Mr. J. seems to be a sporting, and I should think, a vulgar sort of man."

The marriage took place in Paris on April 15, 1874. Winston was born prematurely, at Blenheim Palace, on November 30, 1874. He was neglected. His father detested him for his "stupidity." His mother was sexually promiscuous. He was brought up by his nanny, "Woom." But there was an early flowering of his genius. He was a national hero of the Boer War by the time he was 26.

He had long warned of the perils of appeasing the dictators. He was 65 when, on May 10, 1940, he succeeded Neville Chamberlain as prime minister and began so magnificently to call the free world to arms. He was proud of his American ancestry. "What kind of a people do they think we are?" he said, speaking for the Anglo-American allies just after the Japanese had attacked Pearl Harbor. He was addressing a joint session of Congress on December 26, 1941, and spoke about his ancestry: "I cannot help reflecting that if my father had been American and my mother British, instead of the other way round, I might have got here on my own. In that case, this would not have been the first time you would have heard my voice. In that case, I should not have needed an invitation; but if I had, it is hardly likely it would have been unanimous. So perhaps things are better as they are."

A CALL TO THE NEW WORLD

Just before the final fall of France, in June 1940, Churchill spoke to a cheering Parliament in words that resonated with his American cousins:

"We shall not flag or fail. We shall go on to the end, we shall fight in France, we shall fight on the seas and oceans, we shall fight with growing confidence and growing strength in the air, we shall defend our island, whatever the cost may be, we shall fight on the beaches, we shall fight on the landing grounds, we shall fight in the fields and in the streets, we shall fight in the hills; we shall never surrender, and even if, which I do not for a moment believe, this island or a large part of it were subjugated and starving, then our Empire beyond the seas, armed and guarded by the British Fleet, would carry on the struggle, until, in God's good time, the New World, with all its power and might, steps forth to the rescue and the liberation of the Old."

He stands in the gutted House of Commons after the "Full Moon Blitz" of May 10–11, 1941, which killed 1,212 people.

THE BOOM FOR WENDELL WILLKIE

Hollywood, all through the Depression, created movies where the hero was an honest, plainspoken citizen who emerged from the people to shake things up in Washington: *Gabriel Over the White House, Mr. Deeds Goes to Town* and *Mr. Smith Goes to Washington*. In 1940 the Republicans cast Wendell Willkie (1892–1944) in the role in an attempt to get FDR out of the White House.

Willkie had an unlikely résumé for a folk hero. He had made a small fortune as a Wall Street lawyer and utility executive at a time when both were despised. He had fought against the popular TVA. He did hail from the small town of Elwood, Indiana, and he did take his degree at Indiana University, but by 1929 he was living the life of a big businessman in a plush New York apartment and the only time he got back to Indiana was to look over five farms he owned. It was his character and his convictions that made the difference.

Willkie was a friendly bear of a man, engagingly rumpled: he "could make any Brooks Brothers suit look like it was bought in Macy's basement." The warmth was real. He had a genuine passion for equal rights for all men. He never shed the moral values absorbed from his crusading mother and father, both pillars of the local Methodist church but free spirits. His mother had been the first woman in Elwood to smoke cigarettes and the first to wear French high heels. Willkie cared enough for the underdog to support the New Deal's welfare, labor and job creation programs. He argued that social security should cover all citizens. He voted for FDR in 1932. What turned him into a tepid Republican in 1936 was his perception that FDR was concentrating too much power in the presidency and the bureaucracy.

Willkie became the favorite of such generally conservative publications as *Fortune, Time, Life,* the *Saturday Evening Post* and the *New York Herald Tribune.* Their editors connived at playing up his folksy qualities: "Wendell Willkie is the Mississippi Yankee, the clever bumpkin, the homespun, rail-splitting, cracker-barrel simplifier of national issues," wrote *Fortune.* Much of this effort was transparent. Harold Ickes derided Willkie as "a simple barefoot Wall Street lawyer." Told he repre-sented a grassroots movement, Alice Roosevelt cracked: "Yes, the grassroots of a thousand country clubs." Yet for all the media boosting, Willkie had a real following. It did include the monied interests who had always loathed the New Deal. But there were also plenty of old, Teddy Roosevelt progressives—professional people and small businessmen—who, like Willkie, supported much of the New Deal but felt government had got too big. He plunged into a barnstorming campaign for 51 days, trying to land a punch on FDR, who throughout the summer affected disdain for party politics, even for running again.

The most remarkable fact was that the Republican party, the citadel of isolationism, had nominated a man committed to all-out U.S. aid (short of war) for the Allies. Willkie soon found himself in a moral dilemma. Roosevelt privately sought his support for the Selective Service Act, bitterly opposed by the isolationists, and then for an agreement to trade 50 old destroyers to Britain in return for naval bases in the Americas. Willkie was faced with the choice of abandoning his convictions or becoming a de facto supporter of his opponent. He put his convictions first. His general support of both initiatives was one of the most courageous, selfless and responsible stands in the history of American politics.

Willkie had a reasonable objection on procedure. When FDR pushed the destroyer deal through in August without congressional approval, he was in breach of the Senate's constitutional right to advise and consent to treaties with foreign powers. That, said Willkie, was "regrettable." Under pressure from Republican stalwarts, he hotted up his language. FDR's deal was "the most arbitrary and dictatorial action ever taken by any president." The pressure increased as Willkie trailed. He began to shout that FDR was a warmonger who had made "secret agreements" to involve America in war by April 1941. There was a rise in his ratings and it worried FDR's men. Late in October, they urged him to get out of the White House and into the campaign. In the last days Roosevelt, too, yielded in the competition of reckless promises to the "mothers of America." In Boston he omitted the platform provision "except in case of attack"

and said flatly, "Your boys are not going to be sent into any foreign wars."

FDR had one bad moment on election night. He sat in his shirtsleeves in the family dining room at Hyde Park totting up his scores from the radio and teletype. Willkie seemed to be running stronger than he ought in New York. Suddenly, FDR ordered, "I don't want to see anybody in here." He sat in solitude for 40 minutes. The misgivings were false. Willkie did run much better than Landon in 1936 or Hoover in 1932. He had more votes than any Republican candidate in history—but he still lost by nearly 5 million. With 449 electoral votes to Willkie's 82, FDR became the first president ever elected to a third term.

HOMETOWN BOY: Elwood, Indiana, lays it on for its favorite son, Wendell Willkie, on a hot, dusty day in August 1940. That afternoon the Republican challenger to FDR's third term spoke to 200,000, the biggest political rally America had ever seen. On election night, FDR told his son: "I'm happy I've won, but I'm sorry Wendell lost." Within months they had become fast friends. Willkie would go on to support the war effort, and join the fight for black civil rights. Roosevelt sent him on a worldwide diplomatic mission during the war.

THE ROOSEVELT TAPES

The Democrats toyed with the idea of making mischief out of Wendell Willkie's barely concealed relationship with a New York divorcée, Irita Van Doren, the intellectual book review editor of the *New York Herald Tribune*. We know how it was to be done because FDR, frustrated with what he considered newspaper inaccuracies, had been experimenting with a recording device in his office. It was abandoned after a few months, but it did record his casual discussions with aides on how to use the Van Doren information. "Awful nice gal, writes for the magazine and so forth, a book reviewer. But nevertheless there is the fact. . . . We can't have any of our principal speakers refer to it, but the people down the line can get it out. I mean the Congress speakers, and state speaker and so forth. They can use the raw material."

The whispering campaign was planned as a riposte to an imminent right-wing attack on vice presidential candidate Henry Wallace by Westbrook Pegler, a right-wing columnist. Pegler had acquired some letters Wallace had written to the Russian mystic Nicholas Roerich. Wallace had years before come to consider Roerich a fake, but in the old letters he referred to Roerich as his "guru," and assigned mystical names to other members of the administration. Pegler was silenced by Democratic threats to reveal Willkie's affair.

ONWARD, CHRISTIAN SOLDIERS: The Big Two conferred on the *Augusta,* but on Sunday, August 10, 1941, FDR joined Churchill for a religious service on the quarterdeck of the *Prince of Wales.* "It was a great hour to live," Churchill wrote later. "Nearly half of those who sang were soon to die." The *Prince of Wales* was sunk in the Pacific by Japanese bombers on May 10, 1942.

FDR LENDS BRITAIN A GARDEN HOSE

Sailing in the sunlight of the Caribbean Sea soon after his election triumph, FDR sat in his deck chair and over two days read and reread a long, chilling letter from Winston Churchill. Britain was in "mortal danger." It had for the time being won the air battle against Germany, but it was losing too many merchant ships to U-boats and now it was running out of cash to pay for munitions and planes from America. The day after he got back to Washington

FDR called a press conference. "Suppose my neighbor's house catches fire and I have a length of garden hose. . . . I don't say to him, . . . 'Neighbor, my garden hose cost me 15 dollars; you have to pay me 15 dollars for it.' No! . . . I don't want 15 dollars—I want my garden hose back after the fire is over." The homely metaphor for enlightened self-interest was the introduction to Lend-Lease—a vast program to sell, transfer, exchange, lease or lend war items. The isolationists fought fiercely, but in March 1941 it passed the Senate 60–31, and the House 317–71. America had become, in FDR's phrase, the arsenal of democracy. Churchill called it the most unsordid act in the history of any nation.

By the end of the war, Lend-Lease aid amounted to $50 billion and all Allied countries benefited.

That August, FDR went sailing again. But this time the "Cape Cod" fishing was a deception. With the utmost secrecy, he transshipped from his yacht to the U.S. cruiser *Augusta* and sailed 800 miles northeast to lonely Placentia Bay, off the coast of Newfoundland. On August 9, the British battleship *Prince of Wales* anchored across from the *Augusta.* Churchill was aboard. The two men had met only once, in World War I, when Churchill was First Lord of the Admiralty and had dealt brusquely with FDR, a mere assistant Navy secretary. It was a meeting FDR had

HARRY HOPKINS, THE MODEST GLADIATOR FOR FREEDOM

The pale civilian in the third row of the photo to the left, directly behind Churchill, the only man wearing an overcoat in the August sunshine, is Harry Hopkins (1890–1946), social worker and New Dealer transmuted into gladiator for freedom. He was FDR's shadow, so close that he and his daughter had bedrooms in the White House on the same floor as the President and dined every night with FDR, Eleanor or both.

He ran Lend-Lease, presiding over a group of American and British generals and admirals. He was FDR's personal envoy to Stalin in the summer of 1941 and made the critical judgment that the Soviet Union would survive. He was at FDR's right hand at almost all the war conferences. He persuaded FDR to make two of his best appointments, George Marshall as army chief of staff, and Donald Nelson as head of the War Production Board. He forged the close and informal links between FDR and Churchill. "I am," he said, "a catalytic agent between two prima donnas."

He had a mind of his own, intuitive, idealistic, politically shrewd; so direct that Churchill called him Lord Root of the Matter, but he was indispensable to FDR as an envoy who would reflect every nuance of the President's subtle and shifting reasoning. He lived in the White House because FDR refused to let him die: Hopkins was a sick man, living on pills and injections for a wasting nutritional disease, hemochromatosis, after a bout with cancer in 1938 that necessitated the removal of most of his stomach. He liked to say, "I've taken a leave of absence from death," and drove himself relentlessly. The day and night journeys in the unheated bellies of army planes on five missions to London and two to Moscow were ordeals. His first air trip to England took three days and left him so exhausted he could not unbuckle his seat belt. On his mission to Stalin, he flew into Archangel in the back of a six-man British plane. Having replaced one of the crew, he sat beside the tail machine gun keeping an eye out for Nazi aircraft. Had any been spotted, he would have had to man the gun. Rushing from Moscow to meet Churchill on the *Prince of Wales* on the way to Placentia Bay, his plane was accidentally fired on by a Soviet warship. He got to the British base at Scapa Flow to meet the convoy, but choppy seas made it impossible for a launch to pull up. Hopkins jumped to the boat over several yards of open water; his vital diplomatic dispatches were tossed after him. His British hosts on the *Prince of Wales* thought he would not survive the trip: in the rush, he had left his pills in Moscow. His soul, said Churchill, "flamed out of a frail and failing body." He was one of the most selfless public servants in America's history, sacrificing his life without material reward, yet he was the victim of endless slanders by the right-wing press, led by the *Los Angeles Times*.

Harry Hopkins knew what the war was about. On his first visit to London in early 1941, when the U.S. was not yet in the war and Britain was still holding out alone against Hitler, he spoke out at a state dinner: "I suppose you wish to know what I am going to say to President Roosevelt on my return. Well, I am going to quote you one verse from that Book of Books. . . . 'Whither thou goest, I will go; and where thou lodgest, I will lodge: thy people shall be my people, and thy God my God.'" He paused and then added very quietly, "Even to the end." Churchill was moved to tears.

always remembered. Churchill had forgotten, but pretended to recall it with warmth. At FDR's instigation, the two men had been writing to each other since 1939. This first full meeting of the two as leaders, the precursor of summit diplomacy, was also FDR's idea. It was the beginning of a momentous friendship.

Churchill hoped to persuade America to enter the war. FDR offered, instead, a statement of war aims comparable to Woodrow Wilson's Fourteen Points. The Atlantic Charter that resulted from their three days of talks was a ringing compromise. Churchill accepted pledges on self-government and free trade that after the war could hazard the continuance of the British Empire and its system of preferential trading; later, in the fine print of Lend-Lease, FDR insisted on a British pledge to end trade discrimination. But Churchill did return to London with an American commitment to help end the Nazi tyranny. It was soon translated into deeds. On September 4 the American destroyer *Greer*, en route to Iceland, helped a British convoy; for this, it was attacked by a U-boat. FDR seized the occasion to announce that American warships would escort British and Canadian convoys up to three quarters of the way across the Atlantic and "shoot on sight" any Axis raiders.

THE EMPEROR'S POEM FOR PEACE

The clocks began to run at dangerously different speeds in Tokyo and Washington in the summer of 1941. The countdown to war began on July 24, when the impotent Vichy government of defeated France surrendered to Japanese domination of all of Indochina, and Washington finally got tough.

For 12 fretful months the United States had been trying by a mix of persuasion and the pressure of restricting trade to get Japan to pull out of northern Indochina. The move of 40,000 Japanese troops into southern Indochina in July 1941, in the wake of Hitler's June invasion of Russia, was further proof to America and Britain that the three "gangster" countries were conspiring to conquer the world.

FDR froze Japanese assets in the U.S. and imposed licenses on the export of all crucial products. It was FDR's intention to impose only a partial embargo, letting Japan have just enough oil and low-octane grades for normal life so that it would not be provoked into attacking the oil-rich Dutch East Indies. Harold Ickes and the hawkish Henry Stimson, secretary of war, did not go along. FDR, said Ickes, had slipped a noose round Japan's neck, but was unwilling to pull it tight. Ickes was in a position to give the rope a tug, as petroleum coordinator for the national defense, and so was Dean Acheson, assistant secretary of state, who was frustrated by FDR's caution. Between them, helped by FDR's ambivalence, they gummed up the works for Japanese licenses and financing, and other Western powers followed. The prospect of hanging concentrated Japanese minds on war more rapidly than most people realized—certainly more rapidly than the American people realized, since FDR did not dwell on the risks. Japan imported about 88 percent of its oil and most of its zinc, iron ore, bauxite, manganese, cotton and wheat. It could not survive a year of a thorough embargo—unless it seized British and Dutch possessions in Asia.

Washington was on an altogether more leisurely timetable. FDR and his crusty secretary of state, Cordell Hull, wanted to wave a reasonably big stick but avoid war

PEACEMAKER: Joseph Grew, America's dedicated, longtime ambassador to Tokyo. His forebodings were realized.

in the Pacific, when every day clashes in the Atlantic made war with Germany seem imminent. They attempted to walk a tightrope over a volcano. They played for time they did not have and invoked moral precepts their adversary regarded as coded insults. Asking the Japanese to bow to Wilsonian principles of territorial integrity and "equality" of commercial opportunity was asking them to accept the status quo of Western economic domination of the Pacific that the Japanese New Order had vowed to abolish. To the Japanese (and not just the militarists), the long subjugation of China by Western powers, and Western control of the raw materials of Southeast Asia, was infinitely more immoral than Japan's ambition for its "Greater East Asia Co-Prosperity Sphere."

By the time of the crisis of 1941, the United States knew what Tokyo was telling its diplomats around the world, because U.S. cryptographers had broken the Japanese diplomatic code. But the "Magic" code-breaking machine did not reveal how a well-intentioned but ham-fisted democracy should deal with a schizophrenic oligarchy of inordinate sensitivity that was also singularly inept in the arts of negotiation. The 100 or so hours of dialogue between Hull and the Japanese ambassador, Admiral Kichisaburo Nomura,

were a miasma of misunderstandings. Here were a pious Tennessee judge with an impeded Southern drawl, ramrod with principle, and a bluff old Japanese sailor with limited English and imperfect hearing. Nomura was a decent man, committed to peace, who had opposed the move into Indochina, but good intentions were not enough. His one glass eye was a metaphor for the way he behaved. Like Horatio Nelson, he had a knack, when confronted with something he did not want to see, of applying the telescope to his blind eye. In one notable mix-up, Hull rewrote an unofficial Japanese draft presented to him by Nomura, who then sent it to Tokyo as an American initiative, which it was not. The sequel was that when Tokyo tried to ride this donkey and America started quibbling, Tokyo was convinced Washington had been acting in bad faith all along.

Given all this, given the popularity of the Chinese cause among the American public and business community, and given the Japanese predicament, a collision was probably inevitable. But there was one opportunity that was missed in the month before the Japanese set the clock for war; and a second was forfeited in the last week of peace.

On August 17, 1941, his first day back in Washington after his high seas rendezvous with Churchill, Roosevelt sat in the White House as a lion in his lair. He was going to give a dressing-down to Nomura, an acquaintance from his Navy days in World War I. FDR had promised Churchill he would follow up on the oil embargo with a solemn warning, but the admiral, when he appeared, fished a conciliatory piece of paper out of his pocket. It was a follow-up to an earlier Japanese proposal that FDR and Japanese prime minister, Prince Fumimaro Konoe should meet in the Pacific. Konoe had rid himself of the bellicose Matsuoka on July 16. Now, for a summit he offered to sail anywhere with his admirals and generals on the liner *Nitta Maru*. He indicated a willingness to withdraw from Indochina as soon as the war with China could be settled.

The summit proposal was a dramatic move, and radical for a Japanese leader. It put Konoe at risk of assassination by the extremists who wanted war. America's shrewd and fair-minded ambassador in Tokyo, Joseph Grew, cabled Washington "with all the force at his command" that Konoe's proposal should not be turned aside without "very prayerful consideration."

FDR was tempted. He relished personal diplomacy. Hull saw ominous precedents. "I was opposed to the first Munich and still more opposed to a second Munich." He was angered that Magic showed a Japanese troop buildup in Southeast Asia. In September, FDR yielded to Hull's insistence that Japan should prove its sincerity by making concessions in advance of any meeting—especially a committal to withdraw from China and Indochina.

In Tokyo, the delay had strengthened the militarists over Konoe. On September 3, a liaison conference of the Japanese cabinet and military chiefs decided to seek the approval of Emperor Hirohito for a two-track quickstep. The idea was that in the next six weeks Japan would try to make a deal with America "by every possible diplomatic means," but if that deadline passed, the military would be ready two weeks later to strike south at the U.S., Britain and the Netherlands. On September 6, they went to the Imperial Palace to secure Emperor Hirohito's endorsement; the remarkable fact is that, even though FDR's formal rebuff had by then been received, the Emperor insisted that diplomacy should have priority. In a stunningly direct intervention, he rebuked the impatient military men by reading out a poem composed by his grandfather, Emperor Meiji:

Throughout the world
Everywhere we are brothers,
Why then do the winds and waves
Rage so turbulently?

That night, Konoe invited Ambassador Grew to an unprecedented meeting, a dinner served by Konoe's geisha mistress. Grew was convinced Konoe was utterly sincere in his wish to compromise. If the summit did not take place, he warned FDR, new men would come to power and launch a do-or-die effort to take over all of Southeast Asia. But Hull had FDR's ear; Grew was ignored.

On October 12, with a deadlock in the Hull-Nomura talks and the Tokyo deadline imminent, Prince Konoe went even further. He beseeched his generals and admirals to agree to the U.S. demand for a withdrawal from China. War Minister Hideki "the Razor" Tōjō was adamant.

ARISTOCRAT: Prince Fumimaro Konoe, the prime minister who tried, in the cause of peace, to meet FDR in 1941 and Stalin in 1945. He poisoned himself rather than face an Allied war crimes tribunal. His grandson became prime minister of a vastly different Japan 50 years later.

Japan would lose face; and anyway they would win a war with America. On October 16, Konoe resigned and the Emperor appointed Tōjō, as Grew had feared.

Even so, the notorious Tōjō did not abandon the two-track approach. Nimbler men were sent to help Nomura. Leading them as special envoy was a diplomat who liked America and had an American wife: Ambassador Saburo Kurusu. It cut no ice with Hull. He saw only a small man with a moustache who had been a signatory to the Tripartite Pact. Hull had also seen a Magic intercept telling Nomura that November 29 was the deadline and that "after that things are automatically going to happen." He peremptorily rejected Japan's best offer—to move troops out of southern Indochina immediately and out of China once general peace was restored, in return for a million tons of aviation gasoline.

Roosevelt himself rightly saw a glimmer of hope in all this. He scribbled his own modus vivendi to Hull, which Hull translated into the draft of an offer of a three-month truce. America would partially resume trade and not insist on an early Japanese withdrawal from China, if Japan would stop troop movements and

stay neutral in the event that America got into a war in Europe. Chiang Kai-shek, the China lobby and Churchill objected that it was a sellout of China, and then the Japanese military finished it off. On November 26, they began shipping troops south from Formosa. FDR, Stimson noted, "jumped into the air" at the news. Later in the day, Hull presented Nomura and Kurusu not with the modus vivendi but a tough ten-point note, asking for not only evacuation of China but recognition of Chiang's government. It happened to be the day the Japanese fleet secretly set sail for Hawaii.

At this eleventh hour, the Japanese, too, were playing for time, "acting like a cunning dragon seemingly asleep," as the new foreign minister, Admiral Teijiro Toyoda, had put it in an intercepted August cable. FDR made one last effort on December 6, writing an eloquent appeal to Hirohito in his own hand. The decision for war had already been taken on December 1, and December 8, Tokyo time, confirmed as X-day. A Japanese bureaucracy, conniving with the military, managed to keep this message from the Emperor until well after the bombs had dropped in Hawaii.

A more flexible and imaginative American diplomacy might have bought time, as Grew envisaged, by bartering increments of retreat, but the main responsibility for war lay with Japan's skewed conception of reality. None of the Japanese leaders saw that in the thirties the time was ripe for an inclusive, beneficial trade agreement with the United States. Even without such an overture to the West, Japan missed the perfect opportunity to achieve real hegemony over the East. A genuine, mass liberation movement spearheaded by Japan might well have succeeded in kicking out the Western powers. In fact, Japan simply offered to exchange one form of imperialism for another, with the disincentive that the Japanese army was capable of paroxysms of viciousness on a scale unknown even to the old imperialism.

It was, in any event, a fatal blunder for Japan to outrage a nation as immeasurably strong as America. It was done in a tumult of samurai pride. As General Tōjō had once lethally advised Prince Konoe: "Sometimes it is necessary to jump with one's eyes closed from the veranda of the Kiyomizu Temple."

THE COUNTDOWN TO PEARL HARBOR

Tokyo: December 6, 10 p.m.
Pearl Harbor: December 6, 2:30 a.m.
Washington: December 6, 8 a.m.

Tokyo begins transmitting to its Washington embassy the first thirteen parts of a long coded message breaking off negotiations with the U.S. The U.S. Navy Department has the message, by interception, almost as soon as the Japanese embassy. Late in the afternoon the embassy cipher staff stops work for a party. They have decoded about eight parts.

It is Saturday morning in Pearl Harbor, 24 hours before the attack. Shortly after breakfast, Admiral Husband Kimmel, commander in chief of the Pacific Fleet, and his staff confer. Lieutenant Colonel George W. Bicknell of Army Intelligence reports that the Japanese consulate is burning its papers, something he considers "very significant in view of the present situation." General Walter Short, the Army commander, is informed, but neither he nor anyone else is concerned.

It is 11 a.m. in Pearl Harbor (4:30 p.m. in Washington) when the Japanese Carrier Striking Force (Kido Butai) reaches the meridian of Oahu, at a point about 490 miles north. Commander Chuichi Nagumo breaks out the Z flag that had flown from the Japanese flagship in Japan's historic victory over Russia at Tsushima in 1905, and signals a message from Yamamoto: "The rise and fall of the Empire depends upon this battle. Every man will do his duty."

At 2 p.m. the FBI in Hawaii taps into a suspicious call from a Tokyo journalist to the Japanese-American wife of a Honolulu dentist. They discuss the number of sailors and planes around Pearl Harbor, then incongruously discuss "what kind of flowers are in bloom in Hawaii at present."

Washington is still trying to find a formula for peace. At 9 p.m. the State Department dispatches FDR's personal appeal to Emperor Hirohito. It is received an hour later by the Tokyo post office (which is at noon, December 7, Tokyo time). In Washington, Lieutenant Commander Alvin Kramer begins to drive around delivering copies of the decoded, thirteen-part message intercepted from Japan (no part of it yet received from the

PEACE ENVOYS: Japanese Ambassador Kichisaburo Nomura (right) and Special Envoy Saburo Kurusu escorted from the State Department after delivering a note to Cordell Hull on Friday, December 5, 1941.

Japanese embassy). FDR tells Harry Hopkins, "This means war"—but rejects the idea of launching a preemptive strike: "No, we can't do that. We are a democracy and a peaceful people."

The same calm prevails at Pearl Harbor. At 7 p.m. on Saturday, five hours after the suspicious "flowers" call the FBI picked up, General Short is alerted. He discusses it with his aides for 45 minutes. They all consider it "very suspicious, very fishy," but Short does nothing.

Japanese two-man midget submarines have been in the water for 30 minutes on their way to Pearl Harbor when, at 10:30 p.m., General Short drives home from a charity dinner with his chief intelligence officer and their wives. As they pass the brightly lit Pearl Harbor, Short remarks, "What a target that would make!" At about the same time, the Army contracts with

station KGMB to play music all night to help guide in twelve B-17s due from San Francisco early the next morning.

Tokyo: December 7, 9:20 p.m.
Pearl Harbor: December 7, 1:50 a.m.
Washington: December 7, 7:20 a.m.

The code breakers give Admiral Harold Stark, chief of naval operations, the fourteenth part of the Japanese note, which concludes "it is impossible to reach agreement through negotiations." An hour and a half later, the U.S. interceptors pick up an "urgent, very important" message from Tokyo to its ambassador in Washington ordering him to submit the fourteen-part message to Secretary Hull "at 1 p.m. your time"—in four hours.

Colonel Rufus Bratton of Army Intelligence runs in alarm to alert Generals Miles and Marshall. The chief of staff has left for his Sunday morning horseback ride. The same intercept reaches Admiral Stark. An intelligence man suggests he call Admiral Kimmel in Hawaii, but Stark decides an alert sent on November 27 is enough.

In Tokyo, Ambassador Grew has only just received the President's handwritten appeal to the Emperor—10½ hours after its receipt by the Tokyo post office. Grew immediately asks to see the new foreign minister, Shigenori Togo. The appointment is fixed two hours later, at 12:30 a.m., when he presents Roosevelt's peace appeal.

In Washington the Japanese are still decoding and typing the cable from Tokyo. First Secretary Katzuo Okumura is trying to type a clean copy of his 11-page transcript with another amateur typist. With the fourteenth part, he begins typing the whole message over to correct all the mistakes.

Off Oahu, Ensign R. C. McCloy, aboard a minesweeper, spots the periscope of a midget sub less than two miles outside a Pearl Harbor entrance buoy. He flashes the patrolling destroyer *Ward*. The destroyer fails to make contact and the incident goes unreported, assumed to be one of the many unsubstantiated sub sightings at this time.

The Japanese in Washington are still retyping the final message when, at 6:10 a.m. in the Pacific, Commander Shigeru Itaya's Zero takes off from the carrier *Akagi*, delayed for 20 minutes by heavy seas. Within 15 minutes, 183 of the 185 planes designated for the first attack are in the air. One hour, 24 minutes to the attack. At 6:30 a.m. the U.S. supply ship *Antares* spots a Japanese midget submarine, which the *Ward* sinks at 0645. At 0654, *Ward* radios the sinking, but the message is not decoded at Pearl Harbor until 0712.

Marshall has just reached his office, 11:25 a.m. in Washington. He is jolted to hear the Japanese have set themselves a 1 p.m. deadline. Marshall writes out a warning for Army bases in the Philippines, Panama, the Pacific coast and Hawaii. Stark asks him to tell the Army people "to inform their naval opposites" and offers the "very fast" naval transmission facilities. Marshall says he will use the Army's.

At 11:58 a.m. Marshall's "First Priority–Secret" message reaches the War Department Signal Center. It says: "Japanese are presenting at one p.m. eastern standard time today what amounts to an ulti-matum. Also they are under orders to destroy their code machines immediately. Just what significance the hour set may have we do not know but be on alert accordingly. Inform naval authorities of this communication." Atmospheric conditions block any transmission to Hawaii from the mainland. The warning is sent to Western Union at 12:17 p.m. and transmitted from the RCA facilities there.

One hour, two minutes to the attack.

In the Pacific the first wave of attacking planes is detected. It is 7 a.m., 49 minutes before the first bombing. The detection of at least 50 planes headed for Oahu is by radar operated by Private George Elliott, Jr., and Private Joseph Lockard, at the Opana Mobile Radar Station. They report the finding to the Army's information center at Fort Shafter, where Kermit Tyler, the only officer on duty, assumes that the planes are the B-17s due in from the mainland. He tells the privates to head for morning chow: "Don't worry about it."

It is 12:30 p.m. in Washington. At the Japanese embassy, Ambassador Nomura is frantic that Okumura and an assistant, coping with late corrections from Tokyo, are still typing half an hour before his 1 p.m. appointment with Hull. He asks for a delay.

At 12:45 p.m. Washington time, 7:15 a.m. in the Pacific, Kido Butai launches its second attack wave—167 of 168 scheduled warplanes. A total of 350 planes is now on course for Oahu. They zero in on music from KGMB intended to guide the B-17s.

Sixteen minutes before the attack, Marshall's warning message arrives at the RCA station in Honolulu. Not marked priority, it is given to a motorcycle messenger, Tadao Fuchikami, along with the rest of the day's cables for Short's headquarters at Fort Shafter. At about the same time, Admiral Kimmel is informed of the *Ward*'s sinking of a submarine and says he will go to Navy headquarters.

Pearl Harbor:	December 7, 7:49 a.m.
Washington:	December 7, 1:19 p.m.
Tokyo:	December 8, 3:19 a.m.

Commander Mitsuo Fuchida reaches Lahilahi Point and signals his fellow pilots, "*to, to, to*"—the first syllable of *totsu-gekiseyo*, or "charge." The first wave begins its bombing run and four minutes later Fuchida signals, "*Tora! Tora! Tora!*" ("Tiger! Tiger! Tiger!")—the signal that the U.S. Fleet has been caught by surprise. An incredulous Kimmel witnesses the start of the attack from the front lawn of his home.

At 2:20 p.m. Hull and Japan expert Joseph W. Ballantine receive Nomura and Kurusu—who are still unaware of the Pearl Harbor plan, still less that the attack has begun. Hull greets them coldly, and does not invite them to sit down. Nomura apologizes for not having delivered the message at 1 p.m. Hull pretends to read it and says: "In all my 50 years of public service I have never seen a document that was more crowded with infamous falsehoods and distortions—infamous falsehoods and distortions on a scale so huge that I never imagined until today that any government on this planet was capable of uttering them." Hull then ushers out a distraught Nomura and Kurusu, calling them under his breath "scoundrels and pissants!"

Japanese Imperial Headquarters announces that a state of war exists between Japan and the United States and the British Empire—over 2½ hours after the bombing of Oahu. A hostile crowd gathers outside the Japanese embassy in Washington and the diplomats are removed to a hotel. There, Nomura seeks to kill himself but is denied access to a samurai sword.

It is only now, nearly three hours after the attack, that the RCA messenger delivers Marshall's warning to Fort Shafter.

Washington:	December 8, 1 p.m.
Pearl Harbor:	December 8, 7:30 a.m.
Tokyo:	December 9, 3 a.m.

President Roosevelt makes a short speech to both houses of Congress, the Supreme Court and cabinet, all of whom assembled in the chamber of the House. He begins: "Yesterday, December 7, 1941— a date which will live in infamy—the United States of America was suddenly and deliberately attacked by naval and air forces of the Empire of Japan," and concludes, "I ask that the Congress declare that since the unprovoked and dastardly attack by Japan on Sunday, December 7, 1941, a state of war has existed between the United States and the Japanese Empire." The resolution passes with only one dissenting vote.

NOT QUITE A
GRAND SLAM

AIR DISASTER: Navy planes burn on the ground. Half of all of Pearl Harbor's aircraft were destroyed, many of them within minutes. Very few Army, Navy or Marine planes got into the air. Altogether, the U.S. lost 188 fighter planes, bombers and patrol aircraft, a greater relative loss than the ship sinkings. None of the U.S. anti-aircraft batteries had ready ammunition when the attack began.

EXULTATION: That fine Sunday morning of December 7, 1941, the Japanese put 350 bombers, dive bombers, torpedo bombers and fighter planes into the surprise attack on Pearl Harbor. They lost only 29. Lieutenant Commander Shigezaku Shimazaki (above) led the second wave. He was a fervent admirer of Adolf Hitler, imitating his poses and his moustache. He was killed in action in January 1945. The pilot who led the first wave, Mitsuo Fuchida, survived the war to become a Christian evangelist and a friend of Billy Graham's.

BATTLESHIP ROW: Captured Japanese film shows Ford Island from the attacker's point of view, in the opening minutes. A torpedo plane can be seen veering to the right of the water geyser in top center, after hitting the *Oklahoma*. Moments later, another torpedo tore a huge hole in the *Arizona*. Over 1,200 men were killed or trapped below by one bomb that hit the forward magazine; they lie entombed in the memorial made of the wreck. Seven of America's most powerful battleships were either sunk or seriously damaged, three light cruisers and three destroyers damaged beyond repair and 2,335 servicemen and 68 civilians were killed. But Pearl Harbor remained viable because they neglected to knock out the power station, fuel depot and repair stations—and three crucial aircraft carriers were safely at sea. The architect of the strategy, Admiral Isoroku Yamamoto, wrote on his flagship in Hiroshima Bay:

*What I have achieved
Is less than a grand slam.*

WOMEN IN THE FRONT LINE: Battleships and the very waters were ablaze with exploding oil. Flames shot 500 feet into the air from the *Arizona.* Rescue crews swarmed over bulkheads, following taps from trapped crewmen inside. Amid the turmoil, a group of Asian-American women firefighters earned the accolade "the first women defense workers of America."

THE *WEST VIRGINIA:* She was hit hard by two bombs and six or seven torpedoes. Crew discipline and prompt action limited deaths to 105 (including Captain Mervyn S. Bennion) out of 1,541 on board. Only five died on the *Tennessee,* just behind, which was hit by two bombs. Both were repaired and eventually rejoined the Pacific Fleet.

BLUNDERS, BUT
NOT CONSPIRACIES

A spent bullet from a Japanese plane attacking Pearl Harbor on December 7, 1941, pierced a window and plopped harmlessly off the chest of Admiral Husband Kimmel, the commander of the Pacific Fleet. "It would have been merciful," he murmured to a subordinate, "had it killed me." Ten days later he was relieved of his command. On January 23, 1942, a presidential commission headed by Supreme Court Justice Owen J. Roberts judged him to have lost his fleet by "dereliction of duty."

Over the next five years, Kimmel's rage at this preliminary finding caused him to lose most of his perspective, and good sense as well. He refused to accept the slightest measure of responsibility. The honest mistakes made by him, by Hawaii's Army commander, General Walter Short, and by their superiors in Washington were transformed into one of America's most enduring conspiracy theories. Millions of Americans came to believe that President Roosevelt knew of the attack, but withheld information because they wanted an excuse to get the United States into World War II.

A cottage industry grew up around this Pearl Harbor plot. Even five decades after the raid and nine official investigations, *Life* magazine felt obliged in a fiftieth-anniversary issue to give conspiracy as much credibility as foul-up.

The plots are myth without logic. If FDR wanted a disaster at Pearl Harbor to inflame public opinion, why did Hawaii receive any warnings at all? Why did FDR and his aides, under the guise of security, hush up the actual losses at Pearl Harbor? The logistics of the conspiracy theories are equally flawed. Like all great conspiracy theories, the Pearl Harbor plot is "proved" by records that have disappeared, "witnesses" whose stories were suppressed; evidence is suspect, nonevidence is exalted. Typical of this strand are the stories that the Japanese Carrier Striking Force, Kido Butai, was detected on its route to Hawaii, but Hawaii was not told. A Dutch officer claims to have seen Naval Intelligence officers in Washington calmly tracking Kido Butai on December 2. A radio operator on the liner *Lurline* claims to have heard the Japanese fleet "blasting away" on the radio

for hours, northwest of Hawaii on December 1–2, only to have the report he made in Honolulu on December 3 repressed and destroyed.

Kido Butai was indeed stealthily north of Hawaii—but all the warships kept strict radio silence from the moment they steamed east from the Kure naval base on the Inland Sea of Japan in mid-November. This is what frustrated the tracking efforts of Commander Joseph Rochefort in Pearl Harbor. On December 1, the Imperial Navy changed its radio call signals for the second time in two months. On December 2, Rochefort could not pick up any of the Japanese carriers, or the new 1st Air Fleet, which launched the raid.

Layton told Kimmel about the missing carrier fleet. "Do you mean to say," said the commander, half joking, "that they could be rounding Diamond Head and you wouldn't know it?" Like everyone else, he presumed that the "lost" carriers were probably moving south to threaten the Malay Peninsula and the Philippines.

The cornerstone of all the conspiracy theories is the famous "Winds Code" message. On November 19, 1941, Tokyo advised its diplomats that if international communications were cut off they should listen for a coded message to be repeated twice in the daily Japanese-language shortwave news broadcast. The words "east wind, rain" would mean an imminent breakdown of relations with the United States, and they should destroy all their codes and code machines. The message setting up the Winds Code was decoded and translated in the Washington office of Captain Laurence Safford, a brilliant young naval cryptographer, who alerted all Navy intercept stations. He became convinced that on either December 3 or 4 the Japanese used the code to transmit an "east wind, rain" alert.

It was Safford's conviction, and the fact that the supposed warning was never passed on to Pearl Harbor or found in the Navy files, that would in turn convince Kimmel he was the victim of a cover-up. Some eight other Army and Navy officers testified that they, too, had seen a winds execute message. But two of the men com-

GENERAL SHORT: He had tears in his eyes when he testified that he felt betrayed by his friend Chief of Staff Marshall, who did not, he insisted, tell him all he knew. "My conscience is clear." He took the censure more quietly than Kimmel, spending his last days tending roses in Dallas. His ordeal contributed to his death at the age of 69.

ADMIRAL STARK: In the shake-up after Pearl Harbor, Stark was demoted from Chief of Naval Operations, and sent to London as commander of U.S. Naval Forces in Europe. He asked FDR to go easy on Kimmel, but later testified: "I certainly would have had my planes out." He advised Kimmel not to fret and to trust "Old Father Time."

ADMIRAL KIMMEL: For the rest of his long life after Pearl Harbor he fought to clear his name. The first inquiry found him guilty of dereliction of duty. Admiral William Halsey said Kimmel and Short were "the greatest military martyrs this country has ever produced." The majority report of the final congressional investigation, in 1946, decided the failures were "errors of judgment and not derelictions of duty."

REAR ADMIRAL THEODORE WILKINSON: The head of Naval Intelligence did not realize the significance of either the "bomb plot" intercept or Japan's final diplomatic message. But his authority had been emasculated by the fiery Admiral Richmond Kelly Turner, director of the War Plans Division, who refused to allow him to evaluate intelligence and make predictions.

pletely reversed their original testimony, and the others turned out to have only vague recollections. They had not seen the translation, or had only been told about it by some underling.

Many false alarms were reported to the Navy by intelligence officers, who misunderstood the precise nature of the coded message, but whatever the explanations, the Winds Code saga is poor material for a plot. First, Japanese officials told General MacArthur after the war that no "winds" signal was ever sent relating to the United States. This is buttressed by the testimony of Commander Rochefort, who was in naval headquarters at Pearl Harbor. On news of the Japanese code strategem, Rochefort set four of his best language officers on a 24-hour monitoring of Japanese shortwave radio. Not one of them ever intercepted any such message.

Secondly, as events transpired, the Japanese had no need for a news broadcast code. Ordinary commercial communication was available to Japan right up to the December 7 attack. They sent three cables on December 1 and 2, using the purple diplomatic code, ordering diplomats around the world to destroy codes. That was a signal of war in any language. On December 3 the Navy Department alerted Kimmel to what was happening. Kimmel did not take it seriously, nor did he tell Short.

Perhaps the whole question of warnings should be moot in the light of how frequently the vulnerability of Pearl Harbor was discussed in Japan and America well before 1941. A surprise attack was even played out in the 1932 U.S. Pacific Fleet war game maneuvers. And every college staff taught the Japanese addiction to surprise. In any event, the revisionists' claims that Kimmel and Short did not get enough warning falls to the ground in the light of the information Washington indisputably did send, and what little the commanders did with it. These are the most important alerts:

(i) January 24, 1941. Secretary of the Navy Frank Knox, in a letter to Secretary of War Henry Stimson, says war with Japan "would be initiated by a surprise attack upon the fleet or the naval base at Pearl Harbor." The letter was sent to Hawaii.

(ii) January 27, 1941. Ambassador Joseph Grew reported that if war came the Japanese planned a mass attack on Pearl Harbor. This was relayed to Hawaii on February 1.

(iii) November 27, 1941. Two urgent messages warning that hostile action was possible at any moment were sent to all Pacific commands by Marshall and Navy Chief of Staff Admiral Harold Stark. The second warning began: "This dispatch is to be considered a war warning."

Both men responded lamely. Short instituted only Alert Number One: "a defense against sabotage, espionage, and subversive activities without any threat from the outside." He was obsessed by the threat that Hawaii's Japanese-Americans might pose. This racist preoccupation led him to bunch his planes wing tip to wing tip on the ground, with most of their guns and ammunition tightly locked up. Of the thirty-one Army anti-aircraft batteries, only four were in position on the morning of December 7. Kimmel's preparations were little better; three quarters of the 780 anti-aircraft guns on his warships were unmanned that morning, and he had no anti-torpedo nets around his warships.

Perhaps the gravest failure of the commanders was that they did not follow the advice to carry out reconnaissance. Kimmel had 36 planes for long-range air patrols of the lightly trafficked, vulnerable northwesterly approaches. He did not deploy them. Short had the new wonder of radar at eight stations, but decided to operate them only a few hours each day and night.

In the light of all this, no plot is necessary to explain why Pearl Harbor was surprised. This does not exonerate Washington. Roosevelt had the insight to realize that the last Japanese diplomatic message of December 6 meant war, but in the 16 hours before the attack he failed to galvanize the military or even talk to his chief of staff, Marshall. The performance of the military leadership, when it was apprised that the Japanese had secretly set a deadline for delivering their final diplomatic message of 1 p.m. on December 7 (7:30 a.m. in Pearl Harbor), is lamentable. This ominous news could have reached Hawaii hours before the attack (instead of after it) if Admiral Stark had moved on the Navy side, or if someone in the Army had been willing or able to act.

Most of the mistakes hinged on one basic assumption: that the Japanese could not possibly pull off a major attack on Pearl Harbor, way out in the vast emptiness of the Pacific. Much of this was due to a familiar prejudice. For years, Americans had a stereotype of the Japanese as a short, bandy-legged race, too nearsighted to bomb anything very accurately. In assessing American failure, however, it must be remembered that the attack was a daring and formidable accomplishment, carried out by a highly dedicated, efficient and courageous group of men. It was also, in the end, a failure. It did not give the Japanese the year's free hand they had counted on.

Perhaps the final proof that Pearl Harbor was a colossal blunder—and nothing more—came a few hours later in the Philippines. General MacArthur had word of the attack on Pearl Harbor at 2:30 local time on December 8. He could have struck the Japanese 11th Air Fleet on its Formosan base. He did not. At 12:37 p.m. bombers from that fleet destroyed his air force on the ground: 16 B-17s, 55 P-40 fighters and 30 other planes. That virtually sealed the fate of the Philippines. There is simply no limit to the mistakes that even brilliant, experienced commanders can make in war.

CHAPTER TEN

THE CITADEL OF DEMOCRACY
1941–1945
World War II

The war ended the Great Depression. In 1939 the U.S. had a sluggish peacetime economy with 9.4 million unemployed. By 1943–44 it was fully employed, making one ship a day and one aircraft every five minutes for the 15 million men and women who would end the war in the armed services.

Between 1940 and 1943 output was more than doubled in Germany and Russia, more than trebled in Britain, and quadrupled in Japan, but America produced *25 times* as much ($37.5 billion against $1.5 billion in 1940). Germany, Italy and Japan together could produce only half what the United States was producing. Manufacturing productivity rose 25 percent after averaging an increase of 1.9 percent a year from 1889 to 1939. It is a record of incredible achievement by government planning, business enterprise and labor flexibility—20 million Americans moved to take jobs. But it is also an indictment of the priority given to balanced budgets, low wages and deflation by all respectable opinion in the thirties. The necessary stimulus led to huge deficits, peaking at $53 billion in 1943—yet, thanks to a clever mix of taxes, bond drives and price and wage controls, inflation was contained by the middle of that year, consumer prices rose at less than 2 percent in the next two years and the war was on the way to being won. At no period before or since has there been anything to equal the 15 percent rise a year in general industrial expansion created by the war and the vitality of a free people given a chance to show what they could do.

ALL FALL IN: "I, James Maitland Stewart, do solemnly swear . . ." Jimmy Stewart, who had just won the 1940 Oscar for *The Philadelphia Story,* is inducted into the Army with 18 other less well-known young men in Los Angeles, March 23, 1941. He was the first of many big stars to join, over eight months before Pearl Harbor, and he actually fought. Hollywood went to war with brio. The women stars sold billions in bonds; Clark Gable went into the Air Force still mourning the loss of his wife, Carole Lombard, in a plane crash on her way back from a bond drive.

WINNING THE WAR: THE LIMITS OF IDEALISM

Abraham Lincoln told the Union Army at Gettysburg that they had fought so "that government of the people, by the people, for the people, shall not perish from the earth." It was a tall claim for the American Civil War, but prophetically apt rhetoric for the stakes in World War II and for the ideals that then inspired America. However grim the secession of the Confederacy might have been, the break-up of the Union would have been a bagatelle by comparison with the consequences of an Axis victory. Slavery itself would probably not have endured many more years when an independent South tried to make its own way in a world that was more and more finding the practice repellent.

The loss of World War II, on the other hand, would have bequeathed the planet to a genocidal totalitarianism. The Nazi extermination of the Jews, Gypsies, Slavs and Poles, and Japan's more or less systematic decimation of the Chinese, Filipino and Korean peoples, were grim portents for the African, Arabic and Indian nations. Their peoples were even more despised by the Axis's racial supremacists. Sustained by slave labor and murder, by sophisticated modern weaponry, by the technologies of surveillance, and possessed of the moral sensibilities of a tapeworm, the New Order would have perpetuated a long dark night of the soul. One need only look at the rigid social systems, the bombastic ceremonies, the flaccid and constricted art that the dictators so relentlessly promoted, to glimpse what would have been built on the ashes of Western civilization.

The paradox is that if the Union soldiers of 1863 were fighting for the real preservation of the United States and the symbolic preservation of the democratic system of government everywhere, American soldiers 80 years later were asked to dedicate their lives to a reverse order of priorities. The continental U.S. was never in much danger during World War II; human liberty around the world *was*. The forces of freedom triumphed and American democracy itself was enhanced—but, by Lincoln's standard, American aims for the world were only imperfectly realized. The achievement was momentous, but disillusion followed the idealism that sustained four years of war. China did not emerge as the mass democracy of Roo-

sevelt's dreams. The Red Army's penetration to the heart of Europe denied government for the people and by the people to millions in Poland, Czechoslovakia, East Germany, Hungary, Romania, Bulgaria and the Baltic and Balkan states. It was the same story in North Korea. After the war, all these peoples passed into darkness and stayed in it for nearly half a century. The very cause that had impelled Britain to declare war on Germany, the independence of Poland, was lost. FDR's ambitions for colonial peoples were realized, and faster than he imagined possible, but genocide and brutal dictatorship followed all too many of the flag raisings in Asia and Africa. The hallucinatory triumph of communism captivated minds in the emerging Third World, with lamentable consequences. On the one hand, inept indigenous regimes imposed Marxism on societies a stone's throw from feudalism; on the other, Western regimes proved unable to tell the difference between Soviet expansionism and genuine nationalism.

These were ill rewards for so much heroism and sacrifice. The questions that will long be debated are how far they were inevitable and how far the hopes of millions of people were dashed by military and political errors of the Allied, and essentially American, leadership during and after the war. The most important single reason for the disaster must be American isolationism. America entered the war too late and too little prepared for immediate action. In February 1943, having won the decisive battle of Stalingrad, the Red Army was already beginning to roll west at a time when the first American troops to fight the Germans were still tied up in North Africa. The slowness to engage the Germans directly is manifest in the fact that before June 1944 the Allies never fought more than 10 percent of the German Army. The war was being decided on the eastern front; every mile the Red Army advanced cast a lengthening shadow over the destiny of eastern and central Europe. It was the ultimate in hypocrisy after the war for the isolationists who held America back to blame Roosevelt and Eisenhower for losing eastern Europe. Eisenhower's grandson, David, had the perspective right in his *Eisenhower at War: 1943-1945*: "One can see in retrospect that by late 1942 the triumph of the democracies over Hitler had probably become inseparable from the triumph of Russian Communism, an anomaly that was to be a major complicating factor in the conduct of the war and a source of endless troubles to come."

Even with its relatively late start, however, America would have been in a stronger position to enforce its ideals of self-determination if it had stuck to the first strategy it had conceived and agreed with the British early in 1942: a holding operation in the Far East, and a concentration of forces in Europe for an invasion in the spring of 1943. The probability is that the Allies would have succeeded in 1943 in a landing in Europe if Roosevelt and Churchill had assigned the men, landing craft, planes and armor for a concentrated assault. Instead, they dissipated their resources. They committed them first to an invasion of North Africa (Torch) in the fall of 1942. Then logistics compelled them to follow on with the invasion of Italy, where the topography overwhelmingly favored the defenders.

Certainty is not given in these matters. The D-Day landings in 1944 were tough enough, even with a simultaneous offensive by the Russians, and American strength had grown exponentially. But in 1943, the Atlantic Wall was not as formidable as it was in 1944, German war production was less, the Allied preponderance in tanks would have been greater, even at that stage Allied air superiority was assured and the invaders would have faced fewer German divisions. (Even on D-Day, June 6, 1944, it is worth noting, there were 63 German divisions in France and the Low Countries, 25 in Italy. The Russians were then fighting no fewer than 199 German divisions and 63 more from Romania, Hungary, Bulgaria and Finland.) North Africa was a calamitous diversion of resources; as the British historian Clive Ponting has pointed out, it effectively ended the principle of Europe first. In 1943 America had more troops and ships in the Pacific than in Europe and almost as many planes.

Churchill, who later was to make much of the imperative of shaking hands with the Russians as far east as possible, was primarily responsible for the change in the plan for an invasion in 1943. He advocated the North African invasion as a strategy for "closing and tightening the ring around Germany"; in truth he was more concerned to rescue the British forces in North Africa from Rommel, then driving toward Cairo. It was a false alarm. At El Alamein, the British were able to rescue themselves. Churchill also wanted to delay a cross-Channel invasion until the Germans had been worn down by the Russians, and in his heart he probably did not object to the Bolsheviks exhausting themselves. Roosevelt yielded to

Churchill's clever plea that North Africa "affords the sole means by which the U.S. can strike at Hitler in 1942." It might all have been different if Roosevelt had been capable of concerting his military decisions with his Wilsonian rhetoric. It was not in his nature; nor did high strategy of this kind come naturally to Congress, which was obsessed with wreaking vengeance on Japan. Roosevelt at least was sincere in his vision; as Harry Hopkins said, you saw the real Roosevelt when he spoke about the Four Freedoms. They were not merely catch-phrases. He believed them. Nor was he the naive simpleton portrayed by some of his critics. He saw what the Soviet advances might portend. He told Archbishop Francis Spellman in the autumn of 1942, according to the Archbishop's note, that "the European people will simply have to endure" Soviet domination and that "the world will be divided into spheres of influence." He rejected Stalin's bid to share control of a liberated Italy. His concept of the United Nations was more sophisticated than Wilson's League of Nations.

FDR's fireside talks to the American people used Wilson's language—Yalta spelled "the end of the balances of power, and all the other expedients that have been tried for centuries"—but FDR's advocacy of four policemen (America, Britain, the Soviet Union and China) guarding world peace was an attempt at Great Power hegemony, a marriage of Wilson's faith in self-determination and Teddy Roosevelt's ideas on world control exercised by a council of great powers.

The trouble is that FDR never coordinated his flashes of insight with his idealism, or his military and his political decisions. He was never able to see how events he had perceived as separate might dictate a single conclusion. His critical biographer Kenneth Davis sums it up acutely, in a letter to this author: "his was a compartmentalizing, collector's mind." James MacGregor Burns, a more sympathetic biographer, concluded that FDR failed to work out the ends and means necessary to accomplish his lofty purposes partly because of his disbelief in planning far ahead, partly because he elevated short-run goals over long-run and always because of his opportunistic temperament.

Roosevelt was a brilliant leader of the Allied coalition; without him, it would probably have fallen apart. He was crucial to winning the war against the Nazis, and he might have won the peace if he had not died in April 1945. His genius for walking with the devil might have limited, at least, the speed and scale of the descent into the Cold War in Europe and in Asia. Death robbed him of the chance to vindicate his faith in human possibility. The consequences of Roosevelt's habits of mind were nonetheless significant. It was all very well for the President to insist that substantive decisions about the shape of the postwar world should wait until the Axis had been defeated. But they could not wait; the shape was setting as hard as concrete. At the wartime summits, Stalin indulged FDR in his ideas of world government and the rights of man, but to Stalin they were fluff; all that counted was power on the ground. The gesture that summed up the extent of his faith in self-determination was revealed in a postwar meeting with Yugoslavia's Communist leaders in the Kremlin. He gathered up the fingers of his right hand and brought them to his mouth in a swallowing motion: "You ought to swallow Albania—the sooner the better." Stalin's consistent aim was to create a buffer zone of "friendly" states on his western borders. That was why at Teheran he blew off FDR's brief flirtation with the British strategy of moving from Italy into the Balkans; Stalin advocated that after the capture of Rome the Mediterranean forces should be switched to landings in southern France (Anvil). That would ensure a Red Army monopoly in the Balkans.

The Red Army was Stalin's chief negotiator, but he was ready to make deals, especially when the Red Army was not doing so well in 1942–43. He expected the British and Americans to drive a hard bargain. On the eve of the Allied landings in Normandy, he waved his hand in front of a map in which Soviet gains were colored in red, and told Yugoslavia's number-two leader, Milovan Djilas: "They will never accept the idea that so great a space should be red, never, never!" Even as late as October 1944 Churchill, visiting Moscow, found Stalin willing to put a large blue tick on Churchill's half-sheet of paper tabulating the postwar "spheres of influence": a 90 percent predominance for Britain in Greece, in accord with the U.S.; 90 percent for the Soviet Union in Romania, and 75 percent in Hungary, with Bulgaria and Yugoslavia divided 50–50. In 1943 FDR and Secretary of State Cordell Hull strongly objected to Churchill and Foreign Secretary Anthony Eden's exploring with Stalin what the dictator might concede in return for Anglo-American recognition of the Soviets' 1941 border with Poland, the fruits of the Nazi-Soviet pact. Henry Kissinger, in his book *Diplomacy* (1994), says that "with 20–20 historical hindsight," Stalin at this time might have been willing to trade the border for recognition of the Eastern European governments in exile, which he had not then challenged. It is a plausible judgment. But this kind of power politics was anathema to the American mind. It smacked of predators carving up the world. American opinion regarded World

War I as a consequence of balance-of-power politics, rather than of ineptness in application of the principle.

Clearly, one cannot make too much of hypothetical paper deals. Would Stalin have kept his word? Did the Allies have the strength to enforce compliance?

Stalin's strategy was confided at a boozy dinner in his Moscow villa for Yugoslavia's Communist leaders, including Djilas: "This war is not as in the past; whoever occupies a territory also imposes on it his own social system. Everyone imposes his own system as far as his army can reach. It cannot be otherwise." Churchill's historic ears were attuned to this realpolitik frequency. It was why he pressed Supreme Commander Dwight Eisenhower to march into Berlin, Prague and Vienna before the Red Army, why he was so angry when in March 1945 Eisenhower consulted Stalin directly on Allied plans for the final stages of the war, why he spent so much more time than FDR on the internal affairs of friendly and formerly enemy countries in Europe. Roosevelt's priorities were emphatically expressed in the letter he wrote to Churchill where he concluded that "the political considerations you mention are important factors, but military operations based thereupon must be definitely secondary to the primary operations of striking at the heart of Germany." America's military leaders, notably Eisenhower and George Marshall, were tuned only to the din of battle. American policy was in separate boxes. First, win the war; then have

Allied invasion of North Africa (November 1942)

PORTUGAL

SPAIN

ATLANTIC OCEAN

From the United States

Or

Casablanca

Safi MOROCCO

ALGERIA

men of goodwill sort out the world in a United Nations. They regarded Churchill's concern with the postwar balances of power not so much with skepticism as distaste. They had a job to do; they were not going to play politics. But they were playing politics by default. The vacuum of political power was going to be filled. Of course, it has to be said in their defense that they were conscious of the weakness of their military hand; and they were entitled to misgivings about the military notions of the architect of the Gallipoli disaster. Churchill's record of uncanny political foresight entitled him to respect, but he, too, must have known that he spoke as much for the record as for any hope of having immediate effect: he was a

prophet but also a champion grandstander. It would be overdoing it to credit Churchill with the omniscience that permeates his war history. For all his insights, he was shackled by his sense of British weakness and the idea that he could hold on to the Empire. He was blind, or affected to be, to the mass movements in Asia and Africa that Roosevelt admired. His unwillingness to strike at the heart of Germany, except by bombing, could have been fatal to postwar Europe. The editors of his correspondence with FDR, published in 1975, conclude that neither man "developed a coherent political strategy to match their highly successful grand military strategy." But Churchill, at least, was

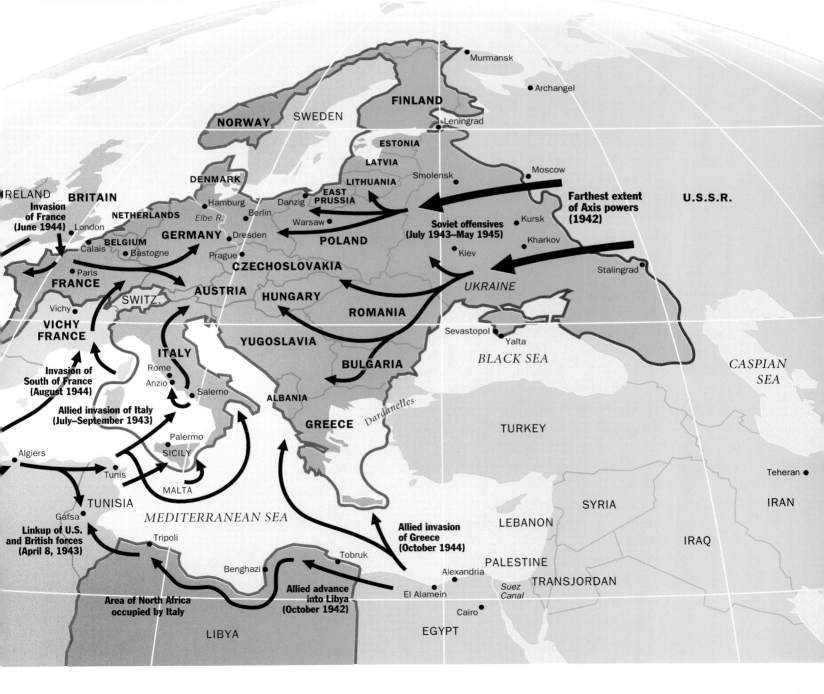

alive earlier to the Soviet menace, and, for all his misjudgment in 1942, fully seized the political relevance of troops on the ground.

Roosevelt himself was not always as unsympathetic to Churchill's geopolitical chess as he sounded in his fireside chats, but the President's insistent priorities, evident at Teheran and Yalta, lay in gaining Stalin's military cooperation: he wanted it for an Allied invasion of France in 1944 and for making war on Japan. On the way to Teheran, George Marshall worried that the Soviets might make a separate peace with Germany, or, still worse, go all the way to the English Channel. For a Soviet commitment to enter the war against Japan, while preserving an independent China, Roosevelt was prepared to give Stalin real estate in Manchuria, Sakhalin and the Kuriles. His anxiety was the opposite of Churchill's: he worried that military action with political overtones might incite more distrust. Stalin took FDR's gifts with a rough geniality. He was adroit in exploiting Roosevelt's disagreements with Churchill. FDR's suspicion of British imperialism colored his attitude to Churchill. At the same time, his sublime confidence in his own ability to outwit people led him to underestimate Stalin's cynical determination to hold on to every bit of territory he could.

A battlefield strategy with an eye to politics and an earlier concern for the shape of the postwar world might well have circumscribed the Soviet Union in eastern and central Europe and in the Far East. These two flawed features of the Allied posture were compounded by a third, the policy of demanding unconditional surrender of the Axis powers, which FDR sprang on Churchill at Casablanca in January 1943. It reassured Stalin that the Allies would not do to him what he did to them in 1939 by carving up Poland with Hitler. It fully expressed the repugnance of the Allied peoples, something of a necessity after the Allies foolishly let Vichy French leaders maintain their Fascist power for a while in liberated North Africa. But it cut the ground out from under the significant number of anti-Nazi German generals who despaired of Hitler. As early as 1942 they had let it be known to the Allies that, given the chance of a fair peace, they would try to ditch Hitler and set up a democratic government. The doctrine of unconditional surrender was also the obstacle that thwarted the peace party in Japan.

America, for all these reasons, fell somewhat short of its sublime goals in World War II—but the war was a vindication of the strength of democracy and its appeal. The new ideologies, of the Fascist right and the Communist left, had pro-

claimed that the democracies were effete, their notions of sovereignty a sham and a delusion, their capitalist business cycles out of sync with the fast, powerful, efficient Age of the Machine. The thirties seemed to confirm all this. The new Fascist states recovered more quickly from the Depression. Germany reforged an extensive welfare state well ahead of Britain and the United States. The Soviet Union trumpeted achievement of its Five-Year plans. The punctuality of Italian trains was exalted to legend. The capitalist democracies seemed confused, moribund and hypocritical.

When the world was "lit by lightning," as Tennessee Williams put it, the totalitarian right seemed more realistic. Mass armies could be summoned, labor and capital conscripted to make the guns of war, public opinion mobilized and focused, demoralizing news suppressed, enemy nations ruthlessly subdued. These were the demands of total war, and an argumentative democracy seemed not up to the task. And yet, like Lincoln's Union, it was.

It would be pleasing to say the Allies won simply because men fought harder for freedom than they did for fascism or communism; but that would be self-delusion. The annals of war gleam with Britain's crucial lone stand in 1940–1942, the spirit of the American garrisons at Wake Island and Bastogne and the heart-stopping assault on the Atlantic Wall, but right up to the end of the war, German and Japanese soldiers fought with valor, and civilians endured ordeals for Hitler and Tōjō (and for Stalin). The Red Army did more than any other single force to crush Hitler—in the service of a dictator every bit as murderous. The scale of the Russian effort is shown in historian John Ellis's calculation that the German Army and the SS spent 7,146 divisional combat months on the eastern front but only 1,121 in Africa, Italy and northwest Europe.

The democracies prevailed against the Fascists for many reasons, but the most striking thing is that some of the greatest triumphs were achieved in the very areas where the totalitarian states were supposed to be innately superior. "In the final enumeration of Hitler's mistakes in waging the Second World War," as military historian John Keegan writes, "his decision to contest the issue with the power of the American economy may well come to stand first." The United States all but outproduced the entire rest of the world. The Red Army marched in American boots, 13 million of them; two thirds of its drivers were in American vehicles. America sent 5 million tons of food, enough for half a pound of concentrated rations for every Soviet soldier for every day of the war. The peace-loving peoples, once roused, learned to be as adept as their martial opponents in the hellish arts of war. The Germans invented the V-1 and V-2 rockets; the Americans, the atomic bomb: succeeding generations lie under the profane shadow of that marriage of terror. Germany maintained superiority in land weaponry and developed a jet fighter, but, by the end of the war, the Allies were producing the most unsinkable battleships, the largest carriers, the farthest ranging submarines, the fastest fighter planes, the most formidable bombers. The Allies cracked the key Axis codes, built the first effective radar systems, mass-produced the most vital wonder drugs. Contrary to the stereotypes, they also produced the deadliest spy networks. Their propaganda in print, movies and billboard was a match for anything Joseph Goebbels could turn out. It oiled the mobilization of tens of millions more men and women for the factories and the civil defense units.

All the statistics and battle stories, though, only beg the question. How did America do it? The answer to this is perhaps the most miraculous part of the whole war: Americans did it the way they had always done things. Consider: throughout the war, no elections on any level were canceled or postponed within the United States. No coalition governments were formed.

Two hard-fought presidential elections were played out. The constitutionally elected chief executive of the United States continued to make all key military and civilian appointments, and they were confirmed or denied by the constitutionally elected Congress. There emerged some of the most able men to serve any government anywhere at any time in history: George C. Marshall, Dwight D. Eisenhower, Douglas MacArthur, Chester Nimitz, Henry Kaiser, Harry Hopkins, Robert Oppenheimer and countless others. Albert Speer, in his postwar interrogation by Paul Nitze, attributed Germany's defeat to the softness and incompetence of the men around Hitler—Göring, Bormann, Himmler, Sauckel—and their insatiable thirst for wine, women and song. In Hitler's court they were spared the scrutiny of a democratic press. None of Roosevelt's men ever plotted to overthrow him or placed a bomb under his briefing table. And he, in turn, did not try to direct their battles for them or have a private secret service spy on and denounce them for disloyalty. The maximum leader's enormous picture was not hung over innumerable public buildings. For the general population, civil liberties were hardly curtailed. Newspapers of all opinions continued to publish; small dissident parties continued to dissent. Churches stayed open; unions were organized. Despite unprecedented controls over the production and allotment of goods and resources, and the absence of some popular consumer items, Americans remained nearly as free as before the war to do and say what they wanted, write what they wanted, join whatever organizations they wanted.

For all the racism displayed in the war and after toward blacks, the Nisei and even Jews in the United States, it may also be that America's relative dedication to the proposition that all men are created equal was a factor in the victory. Millions of loyal Germans perished in concentration camps. Without their absurd racial theories, the Nazis would have retained some of the top atomic scientists in the world, who might have encouraged Hitler to go down the nuclear track. A more tolerant Japan might have rallied legions of Filipinos, Chinese, Malaysians, Indonesians, Vietnamese, Koreans, Indians, Burmese and others to the banner of the rising sun. Instead, the depredations the Axis practiced in all the lands they occupied made them millions of enemies who fought desperately for the Allies when they could because they had no other choice. The great black American boxing champion Joe Louis gave us the right perspective. "There's a lot wrong with America. Hitler ain't the answer."

To be sure, it is possible to take the idea of American exceptionalism too far. For one thing, it was easier to maintain a semblance of normality when the continental United States was never invaded or ever really attacked. Yet this only underlines the uniqueness of the American mission. Just as the Civil War saw the Union ranks filled with men fighting for a principle from which they expected no personal material gain, so did the forces of American democracy fight to preserve the principles of freedom and human dignity around the globe as much as they did to meet any threat to their country's immediate well-being. This moral precept for the most part pervaded the democracies' conduct on the battlefields; there were acts of individual brutality and wrongdoing, but the Western Allied soldiers did not supervise the mass slaughter of women and children. There was no Auschwitz, no Lidice, no barbarous experiments on human beings for the sake of biological warfare (like those the Japanese practiced at Unit 731 at Pingfan), no massacres of disarmed soldiers, no Katyn, no Malmédy, no Manila, no Bataan, no Palawan—nothing where the might of the state was organized for atrocity. The rule of law and the conventions of war were respected.

Except. Except. Except for the war from the air, where the democracies talked themselves into what they had regarded as unthinkable at the beginning of the war: the mass murder of civilians under the guise of strategic bombing. In 1939, such was the sensitivity to opinion in America that RAF bombers unloading propaganda leaflets over German cities were ordered to untie the strings on the bundles so that no one on the ground could be hurt. Prime Minister Neville Chamberlain declared: "Whatever the lengths to which others may go, His Majesty's Government will never resort to the deliberate attack on women and children and other civilians for the purpose of terrorism."

FDR was of the same mind. But the "inhuman barbarism" of bombing that, in his words in 1939, "profoundly shocked the conscience of humanity" became a daily habit, first for the British, and later for the Americans.

The British, of course, were provoked by Hitler's night bombing "Blitz." The decisive event was in November 1940, when the Germans

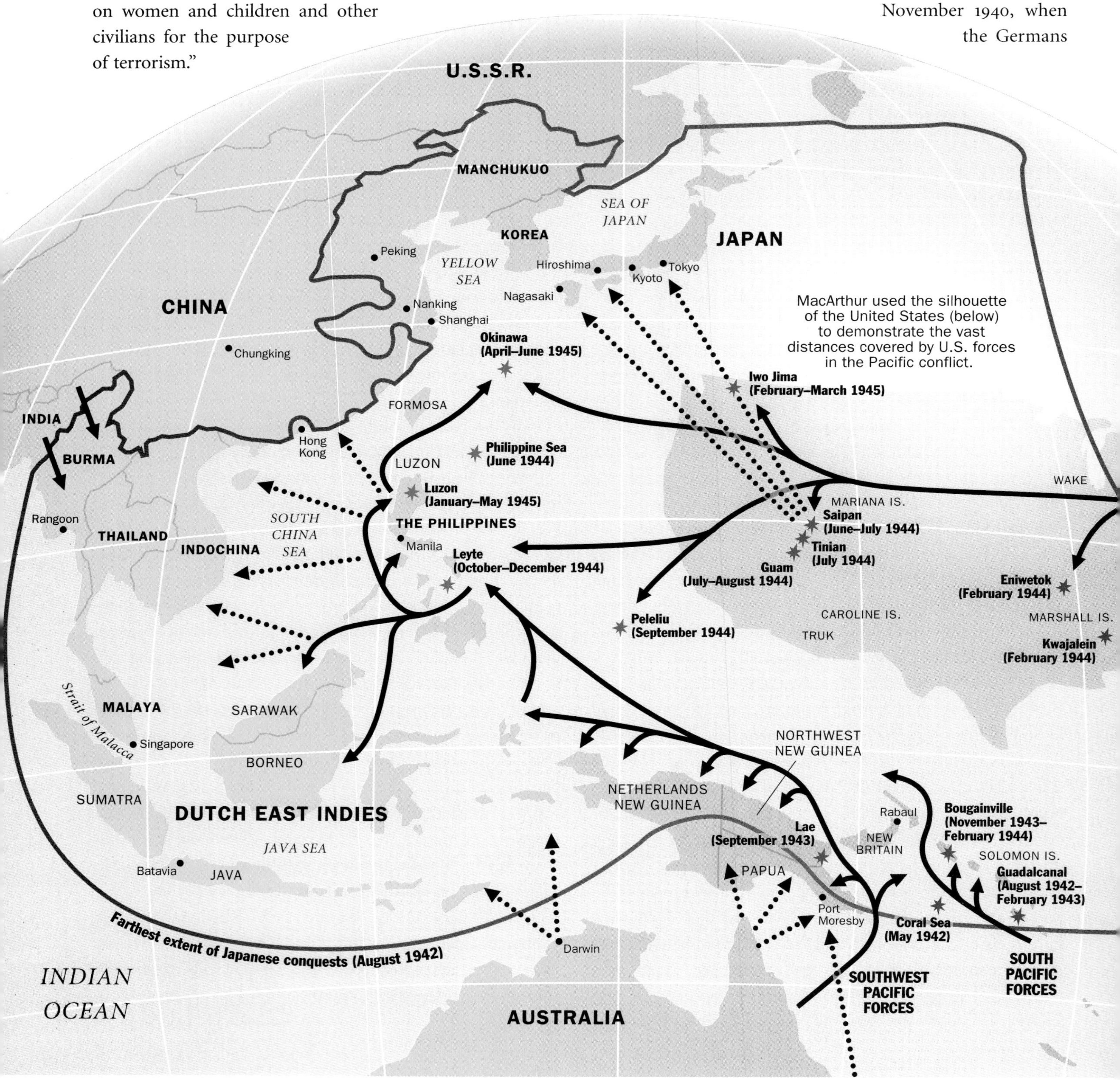

U.S.S.R.

MANCHUKUO

SEA OF JAPAN

KOREA

JAPAN

YELLOW SEA

Peking

Hiroshima

Tokyo

Kyoto

CHINA

Nanking

Nagasaki

Shanghai

Chungking

Okinawa (April–June 1945)

MacArthur used the silhouette of the United States (below) to demonstrate the vast distances covered by U.S. forces in the Pacific conflict.

Iwo Jima (February–March 1945)

FORMOSA

Hong Kong

Philippine Sea (June 1944)

LUZON

Luzon (January–May 1945)

WAKE

INDIA

BURMA

THE PHILIPPINES

Manila

MARIANA IS.

Saipan (June–July 1944)

Rangoon

SOUTH CHINA SEA

Leyte (October–December 1944)

Tinian (July 1944)

THAILAND

INDOCHINA

Guam (July–August 1944)

Eniwetok (February 1944)

MARSHALL IS.

CAROLINE IS.

Peleliu (September 1944)

TRUK

Kwajalein (February 1944)

Strait of Malacca

MALAYA

SARAWAK

Singapore

BORNEO

NORTHWEST NEW GUINEA

SUMATRA

NETHERLANDS NEW GUINEA

Rabaul

Bougainville (November 1943– February 1944)

DUTCH EAST INDIES

Lae (September 1943)

NEW BRITAIN

SOLOMON IS.

JAVA SEA

PAPUA

Guadalcanal (August 1942– February 1943)

Batavia

JAVA

Port Moresby

Coral Sea (May 1942)

Farthest extent of Japanese conquests (August 1942)

Darwin

SOUTHWEST PACIFIC FORCES

SOUTH PACIFIC FORCES

INDIAN OCEAN

AUSTRALIA

killed 568 people in Coventry and destroyed the Cathedral. The next month, for the first time, the RAF aimed at fires lit by incendiaries dropped on the center of Mannheim. It was, as the RAF official history says, the end of "the fiction that the bombers were attacking 'military objectives' in towns." German cities were called "industrial centers," but given the notorious wildness of night bombing, the campaign begun in earnest in February 1942 could not be anything but indiscriminate. By the time of the Casablanca conference in January 1943 the Allied air forces were quite specifically directed to "undermine the morale of the German people," as well as destroy military, industrial and economic systems. In Europe the Americans were for three years fairly faithful to what General Marshall described as "the historic American policy of avoiding terror bombing." The U.S. Air Force concentrated on strategic daytime bombing of military targets. It was involved only minimally in the RAF firebombing of Hamburg in 1943 and of Dresden in February 1945, and Generals Jimmy Doolittle and Nathan Twining, commanders of the 8th and 15th Air Forces, were expressing the general feelings of the Air Force when that same February they protested "morale bombing."

There was no such scruple or pretense of restraint in the war with Japan. On February 22, 1945, after Dresden, Secretary of War Henry Stimson said, "Our policy never has been to inflict terror bombing on a civilian population." The next month, General Curtis LeMay started the systematic firebombing by B-29s of Tokyo, Nagoya, Osaka and Kobe. These were cities of flimsy wooden buildings with a population density of 128,000 to a square mile. The people were incinerated in the greatest man-made fires in history. The loss of life in Tokyo

was comparable to Hiroshima and Nagasaki and three years of British terror bombing in Europe. That was the intention; it was successful, and it undoubtedly had an element of racial vengeance in it. The nature of the change in warfare and the extent of civilian deaths were carefully played down, though it is likely that if the full effects had been known they would have been cheered by the American people as a fitting punishment for the horrors the Japanese had instigated and as a justified means of ending the war quickly. As the writer Eric J. Sundquist has pointed out, by this time the "Jap" had come to be regarded as not human at all. What with kamikaze pilots, ritual disembowelments, beheadings of prisoners and suicidal banzai attacks, war propaganda had a lot of hate material. By 1945 up to 15 percent of Americans were ready to "exterminate" the entire Japanese race. The firebombing was nonetheless a new and more cruel form of warfare.

The crescendo of this campaign, the dropping of two atomic bombs in the space of three days, opened a precarious new era for mankind. In the arms race that followed there was now a possibility that had never existed before in the worst of times: that the human race could wipe itself out. Roosevelt, and his atomic partner, Churchill, had left the question open even while Germany was still in the war. Meeting at Hyde Park on September 19, 1944, they had agreed that when a bomb was available "it might perhaps, after mature consideration, be used against the Japanese, who would be warned that this bombardment will be repeated until they surrender." Nothing like that occurred. When Hiroshima was vaporized on August 6, 1945, without explicit warning, Truman practically ran around the decks of the *Augusta*, on the way back from Potsdam, telling everyone joyously: "This is the greatest thing in history." His exultation can be understood as the release of tremendous anxieties. The end of a grievous war was in sight. But Truman knew that the massacre contravened every law of war, and he was decent enough to lie about his reaction a couple of days later. A Democratic national committeeman telegrammed him to protest the apparent callousness. Truman wrote back at once explaining that his jubilation was on hearing the news that Russia had declared war on Japan; in fact, he heard that news two days after his seaboard jig. It was a minor fib, appealing in its indication of his embarrassment, but it was a portent. Over succeeding decades, the reporting and discussion of the bomb came to be characterized by a lack of candor, from Truman and others, and frequently by deception, evasion and suppression. It oversimplifies and overdramatizes a complex process to describe

Midway
(June 4–7, 1942)

CENTRAL
PACIFIC
FORCES

HAWAIIAN
ISLANDS

Pearl Harbor
(December 7, 1941)

Tarawa
(November 1943)

LBERT IS.

PACIFIC
OCEAN

ELLICE
IS.

BATTLES
ADVANCE OF ALLIED FORCES
ALLIED AIR ATTACKS

FIJI IS.

SAMOA IS.

what happened as a "cover-up," but the political fallout from the Hiroshima monster was a Hiroshima myth: that without atomic bombing the war would have gone on; that the decision to drop the two bombs emerged after prayerful thought from a shared conviction among the military and political leadership; that without them a million American lives would have been sacrificed in an unavoidable invasion of Japan; in short, that there was no alternative. In McGeorge Bundy's phrase, the decision was "historically almost predestined."

There is little doubt now that the war could have been ended without atomic bombing or American invasion (though with the serious consequences we will discuss). The United States Strategic Bombing Survey concluded in 1946: "Certainly prior to December 31, 1945, and in all probability prior to November 1, 1945, Japan would have surrendered, even if the atomic bombs had not been dropped, even if Russia had not entered the war, and even if no invasion had been planned or contemplated." And again: "The Hiroshima and Nagasaki bombs did not defeat Japan, nor by the testimony of enemy leaders who ended the war did they persuade Japan to accept unconditional surrender." A classified 1946 study by the War Department Military Intelligence Division, first disclosed in 1989, also judged that the bombs had been unnecessary to end the war. Russia's entry into the war on August 8, 1945, would alone "almost certainly" have brought surrender. These are retrospective judgments. The authors had the benefit of postwar interviews and observation. What did Truman and his advisers know and when did they know it? The Pacific generals MacArthur and LeMay, were sure at the time that no invasion would be necessary, and MacArthur expected a surrender before September 1. Japan was defeated. It was cut off from oil. Its skies and seas were open. Its fleet was crippled, its air force limited to kamikaze missions. Millions were hungry and homeless. Research over five decades has confirmed that Truman and his civilian advisers knew enough early enough to appreciate that a siege strategy of sea blockade and non-atomic bombing had a prospect, though not a certainty, of ending the war before the November date set for Operation Olympic, the invasion of Kyushu.

The state of knowledge was summarized in a historiographical review in *Diplomatic History* (Spring 1995) by J. Samuel Walker: "The consensus among scholars is that the bomb was not needed to avoid an invasion of Japan and to end the war within a relatively short time. It is clear that alternatives to the bomb existed and that Truman and his advisers knew it." It is clear, too, that this last fact is the one there has

been the most effort to fudge. The myth of Hiroshima the unavoidable seems to have embedded itself in the American psyche in a remarkable manner. It has survived for five decades in high school and college textbooks and in popular journalism. In the publications and television programs on the fiftieth anniversary of Hiroshima and Nagasaki there was an emotional aversion to acknowledging the summation of research. Critical historians were denounced as "diabolical revisionists," as if history were not a continual process of discovery and revision. The most dramatic manifestation of the attitude was the response to an exhibition planned for the Smithsonian National Air and Space Museum in Washington in 1995. The exhibit, focused on the *Enola Gay* B-29, intended to highlight all aspects of the bombing, including pictures of the victims. It was canceled because of a hue and cry, led by the American Legion and then taken up by sections of Congress, that to discuss the bombing was unpatriotic, pro-Japanese and a dishonor to American servicemen. This is curious. It is not as if the servicemen had anything to do with the decision to drop the bombs. The Smithsonian's mistake may have been to confuse a simple commemoration of the sacrifices made by American servicemen with an attempt at dramatizing a complex history, to offer a seminar instead of a salute. But what was striking about the responses was the eruption of hostility to presenting any fact—anywhere at any time—that does not conform with the official version of the events of 1945.

The emotions may have their root in the suspicion, albeit unmerited, that critics of Hiroshima would rather have sacrificed American soldiers than Japanese citizens. Or they may be cathartic, a way of exorcising a sense of guilt. Nobody who was alive at the time can forget the joy when the Japanese surrendered; it is uncomfortable to remember how little thought one had for the Hiroshima and Nagasaki victims, disconcerting to realize how simplistic were our notions of cause and effect, how ignorant we were of what really went on. It is not surprising that 85 percent of the American people endorsed the use of the bomb at the time, with particularly vehement support among left-wing and liberal opinion (*The Nation, The New Republic, PM*). To the public then, the only alternative prospect seemed to be an invasion even more horrific than Okinawa; the fanaticism of the Japanese in that battle made a marked impression. And perhaps it is not surprising that those most intimately involved in the decision, who knew better, have gone to such lengths to preserve our perceptions of 1945. Truman; General Leslie Groves, in charge of the Manhattan Project; Henry Stimson and Secretary of State James Byrnes all tampered with the record.

Truman was at pains to conceal that in July 1945 the Emperor himself had been seeking peace. He never acknowledged that leading cabinet members, including Stimson, and military men repeatedly advised him from May onward that letting the Japanese know they could keep the Emperor might bring an early surrender—and failing to make the gesture would help the intransigent militarists. He never explained why he deleted the crucial ameliorative paragraph 12 from Stimson's draft of the Potsdam Declaration. Of course, the Japanese might have rejected such an overture. Herbert P. Bix, an authority on the imperial system, believes that the Emperor would not have surrendered without the twin psychological shocks of the first bomb and the Soviet entry. This may be so. But if the alternative was as unviable as Bix suggests, why was Truman at pains never to acknowledge what he might so easily have dismissed?

The reason seems to be that he neither organized nor conducted any serious deliberations before making the most controversial decision of his presidency. He has said that it was a "purely military decision," but the military commanders were not brought into any thorough examination with the civilian leadership. When General Eisenhower was asked about it by Stimson in the summer of 1945, it was more of a casual conversation than a consultation with the victorious Supreme Commander. Even so, in 1963 Eisenhower claimed that he had told Stimson he was against using the bomb on two counts: "First, the Japanese were ready to surrender and it wasn't necessary to hit them with the awful thing. Second, I hated to see our country be the first to use such a weapon." Truman's chairman of the Joint Chiefs of Staff, Admiral William Leahy, commented after the war that the United States "had adopted an ethical standard common to the barbarians of the Dark Ages." The discussions of the so-called Interim Committee, contrary to a common perception, were certainly not a sustained examination of the principle of nuclear warfare. Nor was use of the bomb on the agenda at Truman's decisive White House war conference on June 18 with Stimson, Assistant Secretary of War John J. McCloy, Secretary of the Navy James Forrestal, Marshall and the Joint Chiefs. That discussion was confined to Marshall's presentation of the plans for invasion. Truman approved the November landings, but deferred approval of the follow-up landings on the Tokyo plain, Operation Coronet, projected for March 1, 1946. Secrecy was one reason the principle of using the bomb was not on any

agenda. McCloy shocked everyone by the merest mention of the supersecret bomb at the end of the meeting. Truman felt he had to be seen to be taking swift, firm decisions, and the presumption that the bomb was being made to be used had a momentum of its own. General Groves, as diplomatic journalist John Newhouse remarks, was a black-belt bureaucrat, and he was shrewd in his suggestion to Truman that failure to use the bomb would "cast a lot of reflection on Mr. Roosevelt."

Truman was not a heartless man. He was shaken by Hiroshima, which makes it all the more curious that he allowed the second bomb to be dropped, on Nagasaki on August 9—before the Japanese had had time even to realize properly what had happened at Hiroshima, before another demand for surrender was made. The reason seems to be, again, that he had not thought through what he had sanctioned, and the eager Groves had already set the mechanism in place so as to give no time for reflection. In any event, on the day of the Nagasaki bombing, Truman rejected the urging of Senator Richard B. Russell to drop more bombs: "The thought of wiping out another 100,000 people was too horrible." For the rest of his life he closed his mind to his self-deception that the target was "a purely military one."

The bomb was similar in its killing effect to the mass fire-bombing, but it bore an incubus of peculiar evil: radioactive fallout that could play havoc with the very nature of man. This dimension of the bomb seems never to have been properly understood by Truman, though it was well-known to the scientists. The effects of radiation at Hiroshima and Nagasaki—and the Trinity test site—were continually suppressed or distorted by Groves. He dismissed Japanese reports of death from radiation after Hiroshima as "hoax or propaganda" and told Congress that doctors had assured him radiation sickness "is a very pleasant way to die." In his successful efforts to minimize concern, Groves went so far as secretly to hire William L. Laurence, a science reporter with the *New York Times*, whose reports thereafter, unknown to the readers, were themselves not much more than propaganda. Another of his little tricks was to pigeonhole a petition to the president from Leo Szilard and 69 scientists in Chicago warning of the danger of an arms race. It was the beginning of a long, unnecessary and tragic secrecy about radiation that betrayed the people.

Perhaps the saddest part of the rewriting of history is the role of Henry Stimson. In 1945, Stimson was 77 years old, a conservative Republican grandee who had served presidents from the dawn of America as a world power. When Harry Truman was a bank clerk, Stimson was a trust-busting lawyer for

Teddy Roosevelt; when Truman was fixing roads in Missouri, Stimson was President Hoover's secretary of state, fixing the size of the big-power navies. Colonel Stimson, as he preferred to be called, was an austere Christian of immense moral rectitude. He rebuked General "Hap" Arnold, chief of the Army Air Force, for incinerating thousands of civilians in Tokyo. Stimson's figure and language conveyed Olympian authority, and it made a major and lasting impact on public opinion in February 1947, when his name appeared over an article in *Harper's* magazine, testifying that the bomb had been the only alternative to an invasion that would have likely cost the United States a million casualties (i.e., dead, wounded and missing). The article, presented as scholarly history by a distinguished leading participant, was special pleading, and a disservice to the ailing man whose name it carried. The genesis of it has been tracked by James G. Hershberg, the biographer of James B. Conant, the president of Harvard and a leading figure in the Manhattan Project. Conant was alarmed at the "sentimentalist" disquiet aroused by John Hersey's depiction in *The New Yorker* of the civilian sufferings at Hiroshima. Hersey was followed by Admiral Bill Halsey, commander of the 3rd Fleet, who reflected a common Navy view in publicly describing the bomb as "an unnecessary experiment," and Norman Cousins in the *Saturday Review of Literature* called it a "crime." Conant arranged for a counterblast to be researched and written by the young McGeorge Bundy with the help of his father, Harvey Bundy, an assistant of Stimson's, and General Groves and others, but with only Stimson on the byline. Conant secretly edited the article, and the extraordinary fact is that he edited it to suppress discussion of the central argument Stimson himself had advanced in the summer of 1945—that the Japanese might well surrender if they could keep the Emperor. Stimson's war diary was cited as the basis for many of the assertions. But only the entries that supported the thesis were quoted. Vital diary entries on varying the surrender terms and on the shock of Russian entry were neither quoted nor referred to. Stimson wrote in his diary: "When the Potsdam conditions were drawn and left my office where they originated, they contained a provision which permitted the continuance of the dynasty with certain conditions. The President and Byrnes struck that out." And so did Conant.

Stimson's casualty figures for the projected invasion passed into folklore. They had no foundation in fact. It is symptomatic of the history of the atomic bomb that even in 1992 David McCullough's admired biography of Truman still gave credence to inflated estimates that had been independently eviscerated by the scholars Barton Bernstein, Rufus E. Miles, Jr., and John Ray Skates. No military estimate remotely near Stimson's emerged in the reviews of the Joint Chiefs in 1945. Truman, as president, claimed that the bomb saved the lives of around a quarter of a million men, a staggering figure when one considers that 307,000 American lives were lost in all theaters of war in four years of fighting. In his memoir of 1975, Truman went further. He put the number at "half a million American lives." It was a piece of sloppy work by his researchers, who took a figure of 250,000 *casualties* (50,000 to 62,000 lives), converted the casualties into deaths and then, with his approval, doubled the number they first thought of so as not to be in conflict with Stimson's fantasy figure. Of such blunders are myths compounded. But Truman approved the estimate and later spoke of saving "millions." Truman claimed Marshall as the source for the half-million estimate, but the figure Marshall gave Truman at the meeting on June 18 was a Joint War Plan Committee estimate of 31,000 casualties (7,000 to 8,000 deaths) for the first 30 days of Olympic. The estimate for the unlikely two-stage assault of Olympic-Coronet was 40,000 dead (plus 150,000 wounded and 3,500 missing).

Perhaps that's an unrealistically low estimate, but given the dehumanization of the Japanese by 1945, and the sacrifices already made, it was not necessary for Truman, Stimson and Groves (and Churchill) to put wild figures into circulation. Americans would have regarded it as outrageous if Truman had thought of risking a few thousand American lives in preference to using the bomb. But argument about the figures is a diversion. The choice of strategy in the summer of 1945 was wider than invasion or atomic bombing. That is a false antithesis. The choice was atomic bombing or diplomacy backed up by the siege strategy. "Diplomacy" includes a mix of variables: most important, the timely clarification of surrender terms to preserve the Emperor; a warning of an imminent Russian entry into the war, which could have been achieved by inviting Stalin to sign the Potsdam Declaration; and a noncombat demonstration of the bomb, with an explicit warning, which could have been achieved, as McGeorge Bundy has suggested, by inviting an international delegation of great reputation and persuasiveness to the Alamogordo test.

Truman and his closest advisers knew of Japan's desperate plight, and they knew of the Emperor's desire for peace, though Truman did not acknowledge this in his memoir. We now also know what Truman concealed for years—that he thought it possible the Japanese would fold when the Russians attacked. In his Potsdam journal, sections of which became available only in 1979, Truman wrote on July 17: "He [Stalin] will be in Jap War on August 15. Japs fini when that comes about." This is the heart of the matter. Once the Soviet armies moved, Japan would certainly be finished, without U.S. atomic bombing, and in all likelihood before the first stage of the U.S. invasion set for November. Truman's choice—at the beginning of August—was thus not between atomic bombing and invasion. It was between atomic bombing and the prospect of a daily-increasing Soviet presence on the ground that would complicate the peace process. James Forrestal records in his diary of July 28, 1945: "Talked with Byrnes . . . Byrnes said he was most anxious to get the Japanese affair over with before the Russians got in, with particular reference to Darien and Port Arthur. Once in there, he felt, it would not be easy to get them out." In the event, the Soviets did not stop with the cease-fire in August. They drove forward until the official surrender on September 2, capturing Darien on August 22, most of Manchuria, half of Korea and southern Sakhalin—and with newly released Soviet documents from the period, we now know Stalin was ready to take the northern island of Hokkaido, which was not part of the deal at Yalta. Japanese Prime Minister Kantarō Suzuki knew the score. In pressing for a surrender, he argued on August 13: "If we don't act now, the Russians will penetrate not only Manchuria and Korea, but northern Japan as well. If that happens our country is finished. We must act now, while our chief adversary is still the United States."

The best defense for the atomic bombing is therefore not that it avoided the bloody invasion scenario so relentlessly propagated, but that it was a contributing factor in ending the war quickly and so forestalling a rerun of eastern Europe. That argument has appeal. The swift ending also saved hundreds of thousands, if not millions, of Japanese who would have fallen before the Soviet war machine: as it was 2.7 million Japanese nationals fell into Soviet hands and 300,000 "disappeared." But this makes it all the odder that Truman and Byrnes let things get to this point. Why did they not take the opportunity to try for peace in May, June or July, by acknowledging the special position of the Emperor? Why in late July, or early August, did they not contrive to combine this carrot with the very big stick of an impending Soviet declaration of war? There is a strong likelihood, if not a certainty, that they could have ended the war without the bomb and without the risks they ran once the Red Army rolled. Byrnes, perhaps, had complex motives for wanting the bomb to go off. He told Leo Szilard's scientific deputation not that it was necessary to use the bomb to win the war, but that "our possessing and demon-

strating the bomb would make Russia more manageable in Europe." This reinforces the impression from Truman's memoirs, where he says Byrnes told him "the bomb might well put us in a position to dictate our own terms at the end of the war." On that account, Hiroshima, in the words of Nobel Prize–winner P. M. S. Blackett, was "not so much the last military act of the Second World War as the first major operation in the cold diplomatic war." Byrnes may indeed have had cause to be the first practitioner of atomic diplomacy. He was a hostage to Russian behavior in Europe. FDR had used Byrnes at Yalta to draft the Declaration on Liberated Europe (with Alger Hiss) and then sent him to sell it to Congress and the public. It was very much in Byrnes's personal interest to manage the Russians.

There is, in the end, no gainsaying that the massacres at Hiroshima and Nagasaki clouded the heroic triumphs and glorious promise of "the last, best hope of earth." They were not the product of evil minds. They were tragic miscalculations—first and foremost miscalculations by the Japanese. The deceptions that have followed the decision and the popular resentment of their exposure remain troubling for an open society supposedly ruled by reason. In the fevered summer of 1945 when the first atomic bomb was exploded over a crowded city, it would maybe have taken the exalted moral vision and inspired leadership of an Abraham Lincoln for America to have favored any other course.

Once the war was won—and under the same president who dropped the bomb—America recovered the better angels of its nature, reaching out to friends and enemies alike with malice toward none and charity for all. The spirit of moral expediency was not entirely extinguished. In the Cold War, it became embodied in a bloated national security apparatus, the misplaced power of the military-industrial complex rightly identified by President Eisenhower in his farewell address as a threat to the values of the Republic. But the United States has always represented a struggle for the reconciliation of selfless ideals and vested interests. It was never some democratic equivalent of the assorted static utopias claimed by the rising sun, the workers' paradise or the thousand-year Reich. It was and would remain a democracy, and as such promises not the final perfection of man but the freedom to pursue that vision. This was what America had learned after the Civil War—that so long as liberty is preserved, there remains a hope of redeeming even the worst crimes committed in its name. This is what was finally won in 1945, and it was no small triumph.

When America entered the war, the battlegrounds in the West were the Atlantic Ocean, the Libyan desert and the Russian steppes. The Germans had overrun most of Europe, including Greece, and had been fighting in the Soviet Union since June. Armies of millions of Germans and Russians were locked in combat along a 1,800-mile front from the Arctic to the Black Sea. The Wehrmacht had penetrated hundreds of miles into the Soviet Union, besieged Leningrad in the north and Sevastopol in the Crimea, and committed 90 percent of its army. The Red Army halted the invaders within 15 miles of the Kremlin. The Germans had taken 2 million prisoners, but the blitzkrieg had fallen short of Hitler's objectives. The advance was slowed by several factors: by the shortage of tracked vehicles—the famed Panzer units were 90 percent wheeled vehicles and Russia was stunningly short of good roads; by the sacrifice of millions of Russian soldiers; by Russia's capacity to grow new armies; by the quality of its T-34 tank; and by General Winter.

In the Libyan desert, 118,000 British, South African, Indian, New Zealand and Australian troops had by February 1941 defeated the Italians but were now engaged in a seesaw campaign for Libya and Egypt against a combined Axis force of 113,000, led by the newly formed German Afrika Korps under General Erwin Rommel, the Desert Fox.

1941

Jan. 6: FDR appeals to Congress for support of nations fighting for the Four Freedoms—freedom of speech, freedom of religion, freedom from want, freedom from fear.

April 6–23: Germany invades and subdues both Greece and Yugoslavia.

June 22: Germany, with Finnish and Romanian allies, invades the Soviet Union along a 1,800-mile front from the Arctic to the Black Sea. Stalin, ignoring warnings from Britain and his own spy in Germany's Tokyo embassy, is stunned by Hitler's breach of their nonaggression pact. Britain and America both offer aid. By war's end, the Soviet Union had received $11 billion in Lend-Lease.

July 24: Japanese occupy French Indochina.

Aug. 14: British and other Allied ships secretly allowed to join American convoys.

Aug. 25: British and Soviet troops preemptively occupy Iran.

Oct. 31: U.S. destroyer *Reuben James* sunk by U-boat.

Nov. 7–13: The Senate (50–37) and House (212–94) loosen the 1939 Neutrality Act so that U.S. merchant ships can be armed and carry cargo to Britain.

Dec. 5: Germans driven back from Moscow.

Dec. 7: Pearl Harbor.

Dec. 8: The Nazi Final Solution, the mass gassing of Jews, begins as an experiment in the woods of Chełmno, Poland. In September 33,000 Jews had been machine-gunned in the ravine at Babi Yar, Kiev. Now Jews are taken from villages in vans whose exhaust fumes, leaked into the sealed interior, convert them into mobile gas chambers. In the next few months, 360,000 Jews from 200 communities are murdered in this way.

Dec. 11: Germany and Italy declare war on the U.S. and the U.S. responds likewise.

Dec. 22: Washington FDR-Churchill summit, code-named Arcadia, agrees to pool resources under common command and give war in Europe priority.

1942

Jan. 1–2: British break five crucial keys of Germany's Enigma code machine.

Jan. 11: Soviets breach siege of starving Leningrad.

Jan. 13: FDR and Churchill agree to commit 90,000 troops each for 1942 landings in French North Africa, despite opposition of War Secretary Stimson and Army Chief of Staff Marshall, who prefer attack across the English Channel.

Jan. 20: SS leader Reinhard Heydrich, obeying a "Führer order," summons leading Nazis to Berlin suburb of Wannsee to plot "the final solution to the Jewish question"—how to dispose of all 11 million Jews in Europe. Disturbed by growing reluctance of regular German troops to shoot civilians, the group opts for mass gassings in camps served by rail. SS man Adolf Eichmann is named organizer.

Jan. 26: Iowa infantrymen, the first GIs in Europe, arrive to relieve British troops in Belfast.

March 1: Ensign William Tepuni, USNR, flying Lockheed-Hudson off Cape Race, Newfoundland, scores first U.S. sinking of U-boat (U-656).

March 28: British Air Marshal Arthur "Bomber" Harris launches 234-bomber strike against German port and medieval city of Lübeck with express intent of destroying it by fire. Some 312 civilians killed, 15,000 homeless.

April 1: First Arctic convoy, PQ-13, sets sail from Iceland with Allied supplies for Russia. Five of 19 ships sunk.

April 8–14: FDR's aide Harry Hopkins and Chief of Staff Marshall in London press for a cross-Channel invasion in spring of 1943 (Operation Round Up) and try to persuade skeptical British to mount large-scale raid in 1942 (Sledgehammer) if Russians appear near collapse.

April 24: Germans retaliate for Lübeck bombing by "Baedeker Raids" on historic Norwich, York and Bath, killing 938 British civilians over five nights.

May 27: Heydrich, aged 38, is ambushed by British-trained Czech nationals near Prague. He dies of his wounds on June 4.

May 31: The 21 German U-boats operating off the southeastern American coast have sunk a total of 505 Allied merchantmen, many within sight of Florida beaches.

May 31: Germans trap five Soviet armies in pincer movement, capturing 241,000.

June 10: In retaliation for assassination of Heydrich, Germans annihilate village of Lidice. All 199 male villagers are shot. The women and children die in concentration camps.

June 10–20: FDR and Churchill at Hyde Park agree to work together on "Tube Alloys" project—the atomic bomb.

June 21: Rommel, sweeping into Egypt, captures Tobruk and 33,000 British Commonwealth soldiers. "Gentlemen," Rommel tells them, "you have fought like lions and been led by donkeys." Churchill, with FDR in Washington, is devastated: "Defeat is one thing, disgrace is another." FDR promises 300 Sherman tanks for desert war.

July 3: General Claude Auchinleck checks Rommel advance on Cairo in first battle of El Alamein.

—In Yugoslavia, Germans kill thousands of civilians in campaign against partisans. Forty years later the reprisals are to tarnish one of the Wehrmacht officers decorated in the campaign, Austrian Lieutenant Kurt Waldheim, fourth secretary general of the United Nations, 1972–1982.

July 4: Massacre or British PQ-17 convoy, carrying tanks and planes to Arctic Russia. Of 37 ships, 24 are lost.

July 18: Key London war summit opens. Marshall and Admiral Ernest King, having failed to persuade FDR to reverse priorities in favor of all-out drive in Pacific, now argue for 1942 landings in Europe.

July 25: British reject 1942 landings, saying they would be suicidal, since landing craft available only for one division. General Dwight Eisenhower calls it "blackest day in history" (but in postwar memoir says he was wrong). October set as date for Torch, invasion of Morocco and Algeria, held by Vichy French.

Aug. 13: Churchill sacks Auchinleck, who deserves better, and puts General Bernard L. Montgomery in charge of Commonwealth forces in Egypt.

Aug. 17: Brigadier General Ira C. Eaker, the 46-year-old commander of USAAF Bomber Command, leads 12 Flying Fortresses of U.S. 8th Air Force on first European mission, bombing Rouen railway marshaling yards.

Aug. 19: Some 6,000 British and Canadian soldiers, 50 American Rangers and 24 Free French troops launch raid on German U-boat pens in Dieppe, France. Over a thousand men are killed, another 2,000 taken prisoner, and all their equipment lost, as against only 345 German fatalities. Among the dead is Lieutenant Edwin V. Loustalot—the first American fatality in France. The raid's disastrous results are seen to justify British refusal to open second front in 1942.

Sept. 14–18: Room-to-room fighting in Stalingrad, buildings changing hands four or five times a day.

Oct. 23–Nov. 4: In second battle of El Alamein, Montgomery—with 195,000 men, 1,000 tanks, good intelligence intercepts and deceptive tactics—routs Axis army of 104,000 men and 242 tanks. Rommel, returning from sick leave on second day, saves his army in long retreat into Libya.

Nov. 8: In first Anglo-American assault, Allies begin Operation Torch to occupy Vichy French North Africa—delayed for a month by the hostility of Admiral King. (Eisenhower in his diary writes: "One thing that might help win this war is to get someone to shoot King.") Eisenhower in overall command of landings at Casablanca in Morocco, and Oran and Algiers in Algeria, by 107,000 troops, three quarters American, one quarter British, with British directing air and sea forces. Eisenhower strikes deal with reactionary Vichy Admiral Jean Darlan so as to secure French cooperation for Torch. This infuriates supporters of General Charles de Gaulle, leader of Free French, who had set up government in exile September 1941.

Nov. 9: Germans pour into Tunisia in bid to frustrate Torch linkup with Montgomery.

Nov. 11: Germans occupy Vichy France.

Nov. 16: Pushing east from Torch landings, Lieutenant General Kenneth Anderson's 1st Army of 10,000 American and 23,000 British troops are 80 miles from Tunis, having captured the eastern Algerian ports of Bougie, Djidjelli, Philippeville and Bône.

Nov. 23: Marshal Georgi Zhukov traps 250,000 Germans in 25-by-13-mile box around Stalingrad.

Nov. 27: Germans enter Toulon, but French Admiral Jean de Laborde scuttles his 57 warships there.

Dec. 17: Washington, Moscow and London issue denunciations of the Holocaust, and warn that culprits will be tried as war criminals.

Dec. 31: Allied merchant shipping losses for the year add up higher than 1941—1,664 ships totaling 7,790,697 tons. For every U-boat sunk, 60,000 tons of shipping have been lost.

1 9 4 3

Jan. 14: FDR and Churchill meet at newly won Casablanca. Stalin refuses to come, critical of lack of second front. Roosevelt rejects Marshall's argument for a Channel crossing within the year and accepts the British plan to invade Sicily next.

Jan. 31: Germans in Stalingrad surrender—23 generals and 107,000 men, most of whom perish in captivity in Siberia. Cost to Germans since August: 160,000 dead, 50,000 wounded. Russian losses, including civilians, exceed a million.

Feb. 14–20: At Kasserine Pass in Tunisia, in first major land battle for U.S. troops, Rommel routs American II Corps of Allied 1st Army. One of the most humiliating American defeats of the war costs nearly 1,000 dead.

March 16–19: In biggest U-boat battle of the North Atlantic, more than 90 U-boats attack convoys HX 229 and SC 122, totaling 90 merchantmen, at Torpedo Junction, southeast of Greenland. Twenty-two ships with 161,000 tons of cargo go down. Two U-boats sunk, 14 damaged.

April 8: On patrol near Gafsa in Tunisia, Private Perry Searcy of U.S. II Corps shakes hands with Sergeant William Brown of British 12th Lancers—the linkup of Allied armies from west and east.

April 17: In Katyn forest, near Smolensk, Germans uncover mass graves of 4,254 Polish officers murdered by Soviet secret police in 1940. Polish leaders in London call for Red Cross investigation. Stalin accuses them of colluding in Nazi propaganda. (Stalin's guilt is admitted by Mikhail Gorbachev in 1989.)

April 19: In Warsaw ghetto, 1,200 Jewish resistance fighters with only 17 rifles attack 2,100 SS soldiers and hold them off for three weeks. Over 7,000 Jews are killed, another 7,000 transported to Treblinka.

This is the Enemy

WINNER R. HOE & CO., INC. AWARD — NATIONAL WAR POSTER COMPETITION
HELD UNDER AUSPICES OF ARTISTS FOR VICTORY, INC.—COUNCIL FOR GERMENCE—MUSEUM OF MODERN ART

The winning poster in a competition sponsored by U.S. Artists for Victory.

May 13: Victory in North Africa. Cut off in the "Tunisia tip," 238,243 Germans and Italians surrender.

July 5–14: Germans fling 900,000 men into Operation Zitadelle, their third and last summer offensive on Russian front against 1,300,000 Russians in a salient at Kursk. It develops into greatest tank battle in history—altogether 6,000 tanks and 4,000 planes. Germans lose 70,000 dead, 2,950 tanks and 1,400 aircraft and with that, end their initiative on the eastern front.

July 9: In preinvasion glider landings in Sicily, 5,000 American and British paratroopers suffer 27 and 23 percent casualties, respectively—mainly from mix-ups, drownings and "friendly" anti-aircraft fire.

July 10: More than 150,000 British and Americans land in Sicily, with 320,000 to follow, against 315,000 Italians and 90,000 Germans. A personal feud between General George S. Patton, leading the U.S. 7th Army, and Montgomery, leading British 8th, develops in two-track race for Messina.

July 25: Mussolini, back from visit to Hitler, is arrested when he calls on King Victor Emmanuel.

July 27: Hitler sends German troops into Italy, content to hold the north at first, but when Allies do not take the opportunity by land or air he decides to hold line south of Naples.

Aug. 1: U.S. 8th and 9th Air Force B-24s from Libyan bases begin bombing of Ploesti oil refinery in Romania, source of half of Germany's petroleum. Fifty-four planes lost and five Medals of Honor awarded.

Aug. 17: Patton, coming from the west, reaches steps of Messina's town hall at 10:15 a.m., two hours ahead of Montgomery, advancing from the south. Both are too late to prevent 60,000 German and Italian soldiers escaping to Italian mainland.

Aug. 17–24: At Quadrant conference in Quebec, Admiral King clashes bitterly on Europe-first strategy with Britain's military chief, Field Marshal Sir Alan Brooke, who wants Eisenhower given ships and planes for quick invasion of Italy. FDR and Churchill maintain European priority, with invasion of northern and southern France planned for May 1944.

Aug. 29: German Army reoccupies Copenhagen and disarms Danish Army after uprisings in which Danes scuttle their own navy, blow up factories, derail trains, parade and strike in support of the Allies.

Sept. 3: British and Canadians land on toe of Italy to welcome by Italian people. The Italian government secretly surrenders to General Bedell Smith in a mess tent in Sicily.

Sept. 8: As Italy's surrender made known, 400,000 German soldiers now in place disarm a million Italians, ultimately transporting 268,000 back to Germany as forced labor.

Sept. 9: Second Allied landing in Italy. U.S. General Mark Clark commands 69,000 men of 16 nationalities who go ashore at Salerno—X Corps of mainly British and Canadians to the north of the river Sele and U.S. VI Corps of less experienced Americans to the south.

Sept. 12: Mussolini rescued from his Abruzzi mountain prison in daring raid by German airborne troops led by Colonel Otto Skorzeny.

Sept. 13: Panzer attack on U.S. VI Corps nearly pushes them into the sea at Salerno. Clark flings everyone, cooks, clerks, drivers and bandsmen, into the line and 82nd Airborne comes to rescue with day and night drops of 4,000 parachutists. Only on this fifth day does Clark's armor start unloading, delayed by the shortage of shipping.

Sept. 15: Advance units of Montgomery's 8th Army link up with hard-pressed U.S. 5th Army near the Salerno beachhead.

Sept. 24: Allies begin slog up mountainous Italian peninsula, to be consistently out-generaled by defensive Germans.

Oct. 12: Fifth and 8th Armies establish 120-mile line across Italy, with 18 Allied divisions facing 13 German.

Oct. 13: Italy declares war on Germany.

Nov. 14: U.S. Air Force begins flying daytime raids over Germany with fighter protection.

Nov. 23: Churchill and Eisenhower shaken in Cairo conference by U.S. Chiefs' plan for major invasion of Burma. It would deprive the cross-Channel invasion, now known as Operation Overlord, of landing craft, shipping and warships.

Nov. 28–Dec. 1: FDR and Churchill travel from Cairo to summit with Stalin in Teheran. Stalin emphasizes invasion of France is better way of striking at Germany than campaign in Italy or Balkans. He promises to mount offensive around D-Day and to join war on Japan as soon as European war is won.

IN ACTION IN THE ATLANTIC:
U.S. Coast Guard cutter *Spencer*.

THE LONG, GRUELING BATTLE OF THE ATLANTIC

This is a view of the battle of the Atlantic at a turning point in April 1943. We are on the deck of the U.S. Coast Guard cutter *Spencer* in midocean. It has just thrown depth charges at U-175, one of 114 German subs prowling the ocean at this time. U-175 had got within torpedo range of Convoy 233, 57 ships in 11 columns heading east. *Spencer* was one of two Coast Guard cutters in an international escort unit. The damaged U-175 escaped to 38 fathoms and reemerged, 48 minutes later, a mile away at the rear of the convoy. Both U.S. cutters raced back, firing all guns. The U-boat shot back, killing one of *Spencer*'s crew, then it surrendered. The *Spencer* picked up 41 survivors—though many a U-boat, on

Admiral Karl Dönitz's orders, had shot Allied survivors in the sea.

In March, when 22 ships were sunk at the cost of only one U-boat, it looked as if Dönitz might be on his way to severing the New World from the Old (as he nearly had in 1942), a catastrophe that would have ruled out an American invasion of Europe and put Britain's survival in jeopardy. America was slow to fight the U-boat war. Lights blazed along the East Coast until April 1942, silhouetting ships for U-boats to sink in full view of people on shore; the German commanders called it the American turkey run. Admiral King was negligent, too. The British had proved that a weak convoy escort was better than none. King,

Dec. 4–6: Second Cairo conference. Combined Chiefs with [...] and Churchill commit to O[...] lord and invasion of south[...] France (Anvil) in 1944. Only [...] ter much argument and [...] sonal appeal by Churchill to [...] do U.S. Chiefs postpone i[...] sion of Burma and yield up l[...] ing craft for one extra divisi[...]

Dec. 24: Eisenhower appoin[...] to command Overlord.

Dec. 30–31: In Italy, Bri[...] General Harold Alexander ta[...] over top command of ma[...] American and British troops [...] also Canadians, New Zealand[...] Poles, Brazilians, Senegale[...] Nepalese Gurkhas, Indians, [...] estinian Jews, French nationa[...] Moroccans and Algerians. [...] Oliver Leese takes over 8[...] Army on the Adriatic Sea [...] Mark Clark the 5th on t[...] Tyrrhenian Sea.

1944

Jan. 6: Red Army enters Polan[...] having advanced 400 mi[...] since opening of campaign [...] July.

Jan. 20: Texans in 36th Infan[...] Division, II Corps, slaughtered [...] ill-conceived attempt to cro[...] the Rapido River in Italy (lat[...] the subject of a congression[...] inquiry).

Jan. 22: Germans surprised [...] amphibious landings at Anz[...] behind Gustav line. Son[...] 50,000 American and Britis[...] troops in VI Corps get ashore u[...] opposed, only 32 miles alon[...] open road to Rome. But Gener[...] Clark allows U.S. commande[...] Major General John Lucas, [...] squander the opportunity [...] spending eight days consolida[...] ing the bridgehead instead of a[...] tacking. German Field Marsh[...] Albert von Kesselring has time [...] move in major forces, whic[...] nearly push VI Corps into sea. [...] is the beginning of a bloody fou[...] month Allied struggle to surviv[...]

Jan. 27: Leningrad is relieve[...] after 872-day siege in which 1.[...] million Russians die, 80 percer[...] of them civilians.

Feb. 20: Launch of Anglo[...] American week of raids on ba[...] bearing and aircraft factorie[...] Thirteen attacks by 1,00[...] bombers escorted throughou[...] by 900 long-range Mustan[...] fighters. Losses light but raid[...] do not succeed in slowing pro[...] duction, casting further doub[...]

partly out of Anglophobia, insisted that weak escorts were useless. Six disastrous months proved him wrong. In June 1942, Marshall warned him that losses "now threaten our entire war effort." King made good on his mistakes, but it took time to catch up and the Pacific was always his priority. It was not until April 1943 that the kill-ratios changed. Between April 29 and May 7 three "wolf packs," totaling 60 U-boats, attacked a westbound ONS-5 convoy of 42 ships. They sank 13 ships but lost 7 of their own, a kill-ratio Dönitz described as "intolerable." On May 23 Dönitz withdrew from the central Atlantic. By September, 62 convoys had crossed without loss.

The Allied tactical success was due to interlocking convoys; detection devices, particularly radar in aircraft; more air cover, notably from long-range B-24 Liberators reluctantly assigned by King; Henry Kaiser's light escort carriers; and a British success in breaking the new German naval code. The strategic

equation also changed dramatically in 1943. By July more ships were being built than sunk. By the end of the year, shipping losses totaled 3.2 million tons, but the United States built 13 million tons. Dönitz tried a comeback in 1944–45 with the snorkel subs that could cruise continuously submerged, but for every advance the Allies found an answer.

At the end of the war, the Germans had lost 781 U-boats. Some 32,000 submariners lost their lives. Serving on a U-boat was the riskiest of all wartime combat; two out of three men died. The Germans sank 2,828 merchantmen totaling nearly 15 million tons. Something like 40,000 died on the Allied side. One of the most remarkable successes was the movement of hundreds of thousands of American soldiers to the battlefront. They were shuttled across aboard the unescorted ocean liners *Queen Elizabeth* and *Queen Mary,* escaping interception by a speed of 28 knots, secrecy and cunning. And luck.

laim that strategic bombing
e will end the war.

22: Lucas replaced at
o by U.S. Major General Lu-
K. Truscott, Jr.

ch 4: Berlin raided for first
e by American aircraft.

ch 18: Admiral Miklós Hor-
dictator of Hungary, is
ed to allow German occupa-
and the deportation of
,000 Hungarian Jews to
th camps.

il 29: Overlord night training
rcise ends disastrously when
man motor torpedo boats
three landing craft in Chan-
, with loss of more than 600
ericans.

y 11–26: Alexander's Opera-
Diadem opens with aim of
aking stalemate and encir-
g German 10th Army south
Rome. Pincers are almost
sed when 8th British Army
aks Gustav line and drives
link up with breakout of
,000 U.S. and British troops
m Anzio (May 25), but Gen-
al Mark Clark modifies the
n. He turns most of his forces
rthwest so that Americans
n have the glory of taking
me, saying he will fire on the
Army if it tries to advance on
capital. The weakened pin-
r arm enables Kesselring to
cape to form Gothic line.

ay 13: Rommel completes two
es of 517,000 underwater
stacles, off the Normandy
ast.

ne 4: Americans in 5th Army
der Clark enter Rome, de-
ared open city by Kesselring.
lian campaign of 275 days has
st 5th Army 20,389 dead,
,292 of them Americans.

ne 6: D-Day landings on five
eachheads.

ne 10: Linkup of Allied beach-
eads with 326,000 men and
4,000 vehicles. Road and rail
ks between Carentan and
herbourg are cut.

ine 13: First German V-1 flying
ombs strike Britain (Britons
all them doodlebugs). Four of
en launched reach London,
lling six people.

ine 17: Free French forces re-
ke Elba—and de Gaulle, hav-
g outlasted Henri Giraud as
rench leader, sets symbolic
oot on French soil in Normandy
fter four-year exile.

FRONT-LINE DISPATCH
by Ernie Pyle
January 10, 1944, Italy

In this war I have known a lot of officers who were loved and respected by the soldiers under them. But never have I crossed the trail of any man as beloved as Captain Henry W. Waskow of Belton, Tex. Captain Waskow was a company commander in the 36th Division. He had been in this company since before he left the States. He was very young, only in his middle twenties, but he carried in him a sincerity and gentleness that made people want to be guided by him.

"After my own father, he comes next," a sergeant told me.

"He always looked after us," a soldier said. "He'd go to bat for us every time."

"I've never known him to do anything unkind," another one said.

I was at the foot of the mule train the night they brought Capt. Waskow down. The moon was nearly full, and you could see far up the trail, and even part way across the valley. Soldiers made shadows as they walked.

Dead men have been coming down the mountain all evening, lashed onto the back of mules.

They came lying belly down across the wooden packsaddle, their heads hanging down on the left side of the mule, their stiffened legs sticking awkwardly from the other side, bobbing up and down as the mule walked.

The Italian mule skinners were afraid to walk beside dead men, so Americans had to lead the mules down that night. Even the Americans were reluctant to unlash and lift off the bodies, when they got to the bottom, so an officer had to do it himself and ask others to help him.

The first one came early in the morning. They slid him down from the mule, and stood him up on his feet for a moment. In the half light he might have been merely a sick man standing there leaning on the other. Then they laid him on the ground in the shadow of the stone wall alongside the road.

I don't know who that first one was. You feel small in the presence of dead men, and you don't ask silly questions.

We left him there beside the road, that first one, and we all went back into the cowshed and sat on water cans or lay on the straw, waiting for the next batch of new ones.

Somebody said the dead soldier had been dead for four days, and then nobody said anything more about him. We talked for an hour or more. The dead man lay all alone, outside in the shadow of the wall. Then a soldier came into the cowshed and said there were some more bodies outside. We went out into the road. Four mules stood there in the moonlight in the road where the trail came down off the mountain. The soldiers who led them stood there waiting.

"This one is Capt. Waskow," one of them said quickly.

Two men unlashed his body from the mule and lifted it off and laid it in the shadow beside the stone wall. Other men took the other bodies off. Finally there were five lying end to end in a long row. You don't cover up dead men in the combat zones. They just lie there in the shadows until somebody else comes after them.

The uncertain mules moved off to their olive groves. The men in the road seemed reluctant to leave. They stood around and gradually I could sense them moving, one by one, close to Capt. Waskow's body. Not so much to look, I think, as to say something in finality to him and to themselves. I stood close by and I could hear.

One soldier came and looked down and he said out loud:

"God damn it!"

That's all he said and then he walked away.

Another one came, and he said, "God damn it to hell anyway." He looked down for a last few moments and left.

Another man came. I think he was an officer. It was hard to tell officers from men in the dim light, for everybody was grimy and dirty. The man looked down into the dead captain's face and then spoke directly to him, as though he were alive:

"I'm sorry, old man."

Then a soldier came and stood beside the officer and bent over and he too spoke to his dead captain, not in a whisper but awfully tenderly, and he said:

"I am sure sorry, sir."

Then the first man squatted down and he reached down and took the captain's hand and he sat there for a full five minutes holding the dead hand in his own and looking intently into the dead face. And never never uttered a sound all the time he sat there.

Finally he put the hand down. He reached up and gently straightened the points of the captain's shirt collar, and then he sort of rearranged the tattered edges of his uniform around the wound, and then he got up and walked away down the road in the moonlight, all alone.

After that the rest of us went back into the cowshed, leaving the five dead men lying in a line end to end in the shadow of the low stone wall. We lay down on the straw in the cowshed and pretty soon we were all asleep.

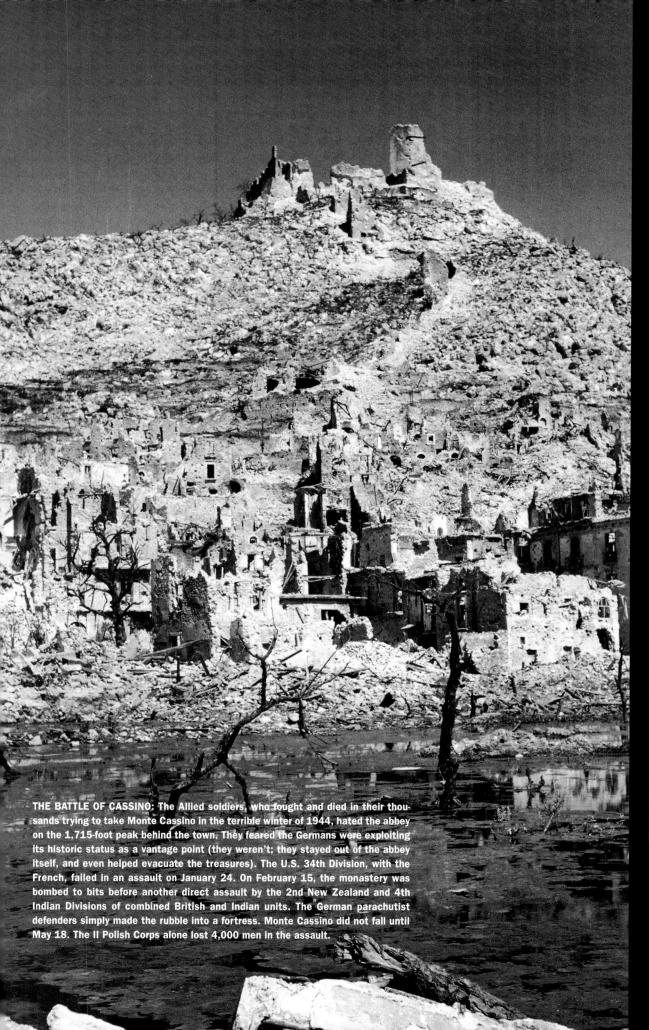

June 18: U.S. 9th Infantry an[d]
82nd Airborne, driven hard b[y]
Major General J. Lawton "Ligh[t]
nin' Joe" Collins, reach Barnevill[e]
on Cotentin Peninsula, cutting o[f]
key port of Cherbourg.

June 20: Allied forces in Franc[e]
exceed half a million.

June 22: On third anniversar[y]
of German invasion, Soviet[s]
launch attack on 400,000 Ger[-]
mans in Byelorussia with 1.[?]
million men, 2,715 tank[s]
24,000 artillery pieces an[d]
6,000 planes.

June 24: The British Air Ministr[y]
and American Assistant Secre[-]
tary of War John J. McCloy rejec[t]
Jewish appeals to bomb rai[l]
lines to concentration camps.

July 5: Evacuations of mother[s]
and children from London[,]
where V-1 attacks have killed[?]
1,700 in two weeks.

July 18: Major British attac[k]
(Operation Goodwood) on Ger[-]
man strongholds south of Caen[,]
designed to precede breakou[t]
attempt (Cobra) by Genera[l]
Omar Bradley's American 1s[t]
Army Group. It fails to achieve[?]
all its objectives, and 400 tank[s]
are lost, but it does induce Ger[-]
mans to divert to Caen tw[o]
Panzer divisions from America[n]
sector. The American and the[?]
British air forces accuse Mont[-]
gomery of being too cautious[,]
but he insists that by holdin[g]

DESERT VICTIM

The American bomber *Lady Be[?]
Good* did not return to its Libya[n]
base in 1943 after a bombing rai[d]
on southern Italy. It was not foun[d]
until 1958, lying in the Sahar[a]
with the skeletons of five of it[s]
crew nearby, and a diary by Lieu[-]
tenant Robert Toner describin[g]
their last days.

THE BATTLE OF CASSINO: The Allied soldiers, who fought and died in their thousands trying to take Monte Cassino in the terrible winter of 1944, hated the abbey on the 1,715-foot peak behind the town. They feared the Germans were exploiting its historic status as a vantage point (they weren't; they stayed out of the abbey itself, and even helped evacuate the treasures). The U.S. 34th Division, with the French, failed in an assault on January 24. On February 15, the monastery was bombed to bits before another direct assault by the 2nd New Zealand and 4th Indian Divisions of combined British and Indian units. The German parachutist defenders simply made the rubble into a fortress. Monte Cassino did not fall until May 18. The II Polish Corps alone lost 4,000 men in the assault.

Patton receives the French Legion of Honor in March 1945—and the traditional "accolade" from General Alphonse Juin, the French Chief of Staff.

**GEORGE SMITH PATTON, JR.
(1885–1945)
"In case of doubt, attack!"**

A swashbuckling cavalryman, crack pistoleer and iron disciplinarian with a war philosophy of "blood and guts," Patton was always testing himself against his Confederate heroes and his belief that centuries earlier he had been a warrior in the legions of Julius Caesar. At West Point he stood up in front of the firing range targets to ensure he could remain calm under fire. He fought in Mexico, World War I, North Africa, Sicily and Europe. He spoiled a brilliant Sicily campaign in two visits to a field hospital. In the first he slapped a battle-shocked GI with his gloves, in the second he pulled out his pistol in a rage, yelling, "You're just a goddamned coward, you yellow son of a bitch. I ought to shoot you myself right now, goddamn you." Eisenhower rebuked him and he apologized. He spent a year in obscurity, then Eisenhower gave him command of the U.S. 3rd Army in Europe as four-star general. By August 1944, his 3rd Army had advanced faster than any army in history. He broke his neck in a freak road accident in December 1945.

There was no reason, beyond national pride, to expect America's amateur soldiers to fight as superbly as they did. In Europe and North Africa they were up against a seasoned army and the German genius for warfare. Colonel Trevor Dupuy has demonstrated that man-for-man the German ground soldiers consistently inflicted casualties at about a 50 percent higher rate than they incurred from American or British troops. This was true in all circumstances, whether they were outnumbered, as they usually were, whether they had numerical superiority, whether they won or whether they lost.

The German soldier had better weapons. America had nothing to match the German 88 mm gun, lethal against planes, tanks and soldiers. The undergunned Sherman tank was a firetrap, no match in firepower and armor for the Panther, still less the Tiger. The German soldier was given a better light machine gun, a hand grenade with a handle that could be hurled farther than the American grenade. When an American soldier fired his rifle, the flash and smoke gave away his position, which German ammunition hardly ever did. The German Army also made better use of its manpower. Its fighting units had more natural cohesion, organized in regional formations, and man-for-man they had more teeth. In June 1944, fighting soldiers made up 54.35 percent of the German Army, against 38 percent in the American Army. The length of the American tail— the units that provided food and transport and backup—was extraordinary. Eighteen soldiers in supply kept one rifleman firing in the U.S. Army; the other Western armies had about an eight-to-one ratio, and the Japanese closer to one-to-one. This meant, of course, that the American soldier was incomparably better looked after, especially by the medical services, but the individual infantryman was overburdened. He carried up to 132 pounds, double the weight carried by a Japanese soldier.

The brunt of the fighting was borne by relatively few of the millions of Americans drafted. Of the 11 million in the Army, only 2 million were in the 90 combat divisions, and of these fewer than 700,000 were at the really sharp end in the infantry. These were the men who suffered ordeals of fear and pain "beyond the limits of hope itself." A March 1944 report said the infantry, 6 percent of the Army, were suffering 53 percent of its battle casualties. These men really did fight. The canard has entered a number of military history books that only 15 to 25 percent of riflemen used their weapons in any given action. The historian Frederic Smoler has exposed, in *American Heritage* magazine in March 1989, that the legend of riflemen who did not fire originated with the military historian Colonel Samuel Lyman

"Th' hell this ain't th' most important hole in th' world. I'm in it," by Bill Mauldin.

"Slam" Marshall, author of *Men Against Fire,* who had no basis at all for his "findings." They were all too uncritically accepted because of the quality of his other work interviewing front-line troops.

The vast mass of the population of America, roused by brilliant morale-building ventures and without experience of any of the bombing or ground fighting known to European civilians, had no idea of the insensate savagery and unrelenting foulness endured by their husbands, sons and brothers in the corpse-filled foxholes and putrescent jungle bivouacs. The combat soldiers did not merely see their comrades die. They saw them eviscerated, decapitated, dismembered, and they saw it so often they knew in their souls it was their turn next. More than 80 percent of the riflemen in 11 infantry divisions were wounded or killed in northwest Europe. In the 83rd Division, 19.2 percent died, and 62.5 percent were wounded in 11 months of combat. This was grim—though not as grim as being in a German U-boat, where the death rate was 63 percent, or an RAF bomber crew (47 percent), a much worse risk than being in the trenches throughout World War I (a death rate of 25 percent).

What kept the individuals going? William Manchester, a Marine sergeant himself, badly wounded at Okinawa, spoke a comradely truth: "Men do not fight for flag or country, for the Marine Corps or glory or any other abstraction. They fight for one another."

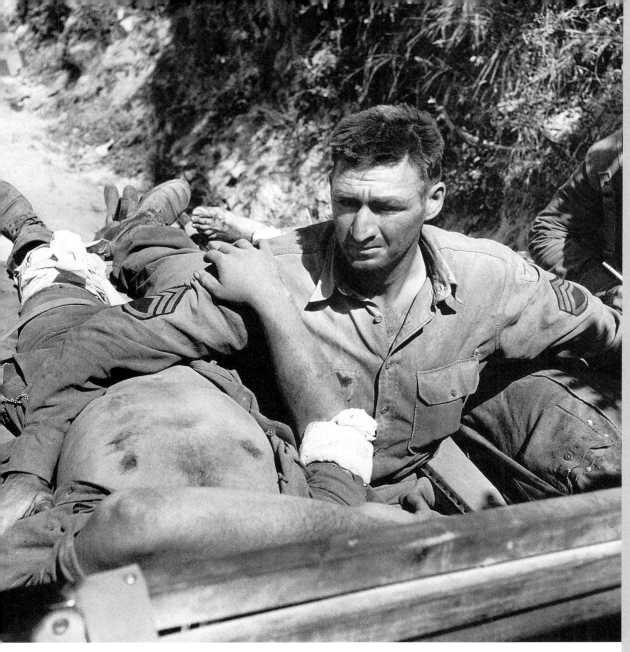

COMRADELY LOVE: Robert Capa's photograph of wounded men being taken to a field hospital was made in Sicily in 1943.

"I THOUGHT MY SHOES WOULD FILL WITH BLOOD"

"I was in the first wave to hit the beach. My particular company landed on a mined area and proceeded to cross to our objective. My C.O. was killed at the same time I got hit thru both legs in the thigh region, in the guts and in both shoulders. There was no pain to it and the wounds bled very little. . . . I finally got thru the minefield and made a path for the men to follow and got them thru. We continued on our objective with me leading, a pistol in one hand and my other holding my guts. I kept thinking that if I was hit very bad I would feel my shoes fill up with blood but felt no signs so kept going. . . . I

looked and was surprised to find a big gob of guts sticking out about two inches above my peter so I sprinkled sulfa drugs on it, and took the internal pills and put on a bandage—at that time I didn't know about the holes in my legs. Half an hour later the squads returned with some prisoners so I took them to the prisoner enclosure and proceeded to the medical dressing station where I was evacuated to a ship."

—Letter from Lieutenant Randall Harris, Pocahontas, Iowa, who landed at Gela, Sicily, with the 1st Rangers, July 10, 1943

GEORGE CATLETT MARSHALL (1880–1959)
"Leadership in conference, even with subordinates, is as important as leadership on the battlefield."

FDR liked his plain speaking and made him Chief of Staff the day Germany invaded Poland. By war's end, the "father" of the modern U.S. Army had 8.5 million men under his command in nine theaters of war. He was aloof, formal and patrician but a master handler of soldiers and civilians. He never allowed himself to be drawn into the White House/New Deal "set." He declined all invitations for weekend visits to Hyde Park. He insisted on being called General Marshall and chose not to laugh at the President's jokes.

He made a name as a cool organizer in World War I when he was chief of operations of the 1st Division in the St.-Mihiel offensive. General Pershing picked him as his aide after the war. The modern American Army took shape from his five years' teaching at the infantry school at Fort Benning (1927–1932). He kept a "little black book" of talent and handpicked the General Staff from 160 of the officers he had seen pass through Benning. Eisenhower was his pick. He convinced FDR of the urgent need for a draft and a bigger budget in 1940. When war began he worked well with the fierce Admiral King but even better with the British Chief of Staff in Washington, Sir John Dill. He backed the Europe-first strategy, but he was often at loggerheads with Churchill, and with FDR when the President was under Churchill's spell. In 1945, he backed Eisenhower's reluctance to drive for Berlin and Prague. With his service after the war as Truman's secretary of state, he merited Harvard's honorary degree commendation as "a soldier and statesman whose ability and character brook only one comparison in the history of the nation."

even Panzer divisions he is holding the hinge of the door so that Bradley, facing only two Panzer divisions, can push it open in the west.

July 20: Hitler narrowly escapes when bomb planted by dissident officers explodes at his HQ in Prussia.

July 25-31: Operation Cobra gets off to bad start with U.S. planes bombing their own men and killing 136, including a U.S. commander, Lieutenant General Lesley McNair. But Cobra is triumph for Bradley as Collins's VII Corps armored spearheads gain momentum, bypassing Germans, racing through cheering villages. The 4th Armored advances 25 miles in 36 hours, reaching Avranches on July 30.

July 30: The way is open for General Patton's 3rd Army to break out of boscage terrain, but instead of turning east to help roll up Germans in Normandy, it controversially races virtually unopposed through open country in Brittany.

Aug. 1: Polish resistance in Warsaw rises. Some 42,500 men and women seize two thirds of the city.

Aug. 3: Bradley orders Patton to swing eastward.

Aug. 4: Anne Frank and her family are betrayed in Amsterdam and deported to a death camp.

Aug. 7: XV Corps, advancing 75 miles in four days, cuts into rear of German armies. Hitler countermands Field Marshal Günther von Kluge plan for withdrawal toward Seine and orders Panzers moved from British front to lunge at Americans from Mortain, in effort to reach sea at Avranches and so cut off Patton and Normandy beachhead. Kluge, under suspicion in Hitler bomb plot, obeys orders he knows will destroy his 7th Army. Bradley destroys the Panzers with help of Thunderbolts and RAF Typhoons.

Aug. 15: Operation Dragoon. U.S. 7th Army, led by General Alexander Patch, with French and Canadian support, opens second front by invading southern France.

—Canadian II Corps in north take Falaise, within 15 miles of U.S. 3rd Army, nearly enveloping two German armies. Polish 1st Armored Division struggles to close this Falaise "pocket."

HARRISON SUMMERS, of West Virginia, was a paratroop staff sergeant who dropped on Utah Beach, in Normandy. He was given 15 men he did not know and assigned the task of neutralizing more than 100 German artillerymen. They were barracked in a series of stone farm buildings, strung out along 700 yards of the road to the beach. Summers ran to the first farmhouse, and discovered he was on his own. His squad was head-down in a ditch. Summers kicked open the door and shot 4 of the enemy with his tommy gun. Now, with supporting fire from one of his squad, he ran 50 yards to another farmhouse, zigzagging to avoid the defenders' fire, shot up the interior and killed 6 Germans. A captain joined him, saying, "I will go with you," and was shot through the heart before he could move. Summers went on alone to empty another building and handed over a bunch of prisoners to his squad. Two others in the squad joined him, and the three of them cleared more buildings along the road, killing 30 Germans. Summers surprised 15 at breakfast in the mess hall and killed them all. Finally, with a squad of three, he shot up the remainder of the barracks. Fifty defenders died and 31 surrendered. An exhausted Summers, asked how he felt, replied, "Not very good. It was all kind of crazy." He was commissioned and awarded a Distinguished Service Cross.

STEVE HALL, an OSS (Office of Strategic Services) captain, expert skier and linguist, parachuted into the Alps on the Austrian-Italian border, on a self-invented mission with the partisans, in August 1944. He backpacked for days, climbing thousands of feet, slipping past patrols in his flier's uniform, sleeping with a cocked pistol at his right hand. He linked up with partisans and rigged up a system for backpacking arms and explosives across the mountains. In a letter that reached home, he wrote: "Even if it hasn't been as much as many, many others have done in this war, I've done something. In my last report by radio to Rome, I was able to say: 'Have organized 6 battalions and 4 intelligence units. Have blown 14 highway bridges and 3 railroad bridges. Have organized 1600 square miles of Alps, and distributed arms therein. Have led 3 attacks. Have sent over 300 intelligence reports.'" On the night of January 25, 1945, in a heavy snowstorm, he set out alone to blow up the hydroelectric plant at Cortina d'Ampezzo. A game warden found him unconscious in the forest with both feet frozen and betrayed him to the SS. They tortured him for two weeks to try to get information, then hanged him. Captain Hall was posthumously awarded the Legion of Merit and Croix de Guerre avec Palme.

DOUGLAS A. MUNRO, from Vancouver, British Columbia, and Cle Elum, Washington, was in charge of a flotilla of nine landing craft at Guadalcanal as a signalman 1st Class in the U.S. Coast Guard. Ordered to evacuate 500 Marines trapped on shore, he did a solo reconnaissance with his own boat, hazarding Japanese machine gun fire to rescue 30 wounded men. He then took three boats back to the beach, and placed his own as a shield against the gunfire. As the rescue boats pulled away, one grounded on the coral. Munro took his vessel alongside, pulled the other free, and covered the retreat by jumping to his own machine guns with signalman Raymond Evans. They silenced the Japanese guns, but Munro was fatally hit. His last words: "Did we get them all off?" He was the only coastguardsman to be awarded the Medal of Honor.

JOHN J. POWERS, from New York, was a U.S. Navy lieutenant pilot who pushed dive bombing to its limits. Leading three Dauntless dive-bombers against the Japanese carrier *Shoho* in the Coral Sea in May 1942, he hazardously maintained his dive to below 1,000 feet so as to be sure of hitting the target. It was one of these bombs that sank the *Shoho* within ten minutes, the first Japanese carrier loss, and it produced the exultant Navy message "Scratch one flattop!" Powers was the squadron gunnery officer on the *Yorktown,* and that night he briefed the pilots on his technique and its risks: longer exposure to anti-aircraft fire, and the danger of being caught by the dive-bomber's own blast. The next day, with the carrier *Shokaku* targeted, Powers announced, "I am going to get a hit if I have to lay it on their flight deck." And he did. He dived through fire and Zeke fighters nearly to the deck. His direct hit stopped the *Shokaku* from launching planes, but at 200 feet the blast from Powers's bomb consumed his own plane. Lieutenant Powers was awarded a posthumous Medal of Honor.

RICHARD N. ANTRIM, from Peru, Indiana, was the executive officer of the USS *Pope,* an old World War I destroyer, sunk in the Java Sea on March 1, 1942. Antrim helped organize the survivors in a week on the open sea until they were picked up by the Japanese and imprisoned at Macassar on Celebes. It was a cruel camp. The guards, showing contempt for men who had surrendered, beat and tortured them for petty infractions. A Navy officer failed to bow low enough to a guard, who started to beat him unconscious. Antrim, taking his life in his hands, stepped forward. "Stop!" he commanded. The astonished guard did as he was told. Antrim argued for the officer in front of the 2,700 Allied prisoners and the

Maynard H. Smith receiving the Medal of Honor from Secretary of War Henry Stimson, July 15, 1943.

entire Japanese force. The camp commandant intervened—only to order 50 lashes for the prostrate naval officer. After 15, Antrim stepped forward again. "I'll take the rest of the lashes." The prisoners cheered. The commandant relented, with a slight bow to Antrim. The camp remained an ordeal, but the senseless beatings were ended. Antrim was awarded the Medal of Honor in 1947.

MAYNARD H. SMITH, from Caro, Michigan, went on his first mission as a B-17 ball-turret gunner on May 1, 1943. On the way to bomb the submarine base at St.-Nazaire, his plane was struck by an anti-aircraft shell, killing the radio and setting the interior on fire. The radio operator jumped out of the plane without a parachute. Smith struggled to get into the body of the blazing plane. He found the second waist gunner trapped by his parachute harness. He released him and helped him jump. Then he put out the fires. Fighters sprang on the lone plane struggling to get back to England. Smith beat them off with the two waist guns, and went into the cockpit to find both pilot and copilot wounded. He treated them, took the pilot's place at the controls and with the copilot's coaching landed, bumpily but safely, at an RAF base. Smith flew 12 more combat missions and was presented with the Medal of Honor in July 1943.

AUDIE L. MURPHY, the most decorated American soldier of the war, was the seventh of twelve children in a poor sharecropper's family that settled in Celeste, Texas. In his most celebrated exploit, the 21-year-old Lieutenant Murphy was ordered to hold a position in the Colmar "pocket" in Alsace-Lorraine.

He had 18 enlisted men, whose commander had been wounded, and two tank destroyers. On the afternoon of January 25, 1945, six Mark VI Tiger tanks and 200 German infantrymen came at them. One of Murphy's tanks ran into a ditch, the other caught fire from a direct hit. Murphy ordered his men back to a finger of woods. From his forward foxhole, he called in supporting artillery and fired on the advancing infantry until he ran out of ammunition. Then he rushed to the burning tank, with his phone lines, and raked the advancing troops with the abandoned tank's 50 mm machine gun. As the tanks kept coming, he kept ordering artillery corrections. "Drop 50," he said. "That's awfully close to you," artillery responded. "Fire!" said Murphy. Now, just 50 yards from him, with its infantry pulverized, the enemy tanks began to pull back. Murphy called in another correction. "That's right on your position," he was warned. "Let her go," said Murphy, "I'm leaving." He leapt from the burning tank and moments later it exploded. He had saved the position and his company, and then, despite a leg wound, he went on the attack.

VERNON BAKER, from Cheyenne, Wyoming, was an infantry lieutenant in Italy in April 1945 who took his 25-man platoon on a predawn assault on a German mountain stronghold at Castle Aghinolfi. He crawled to a German bunker and killed its two defenders, then attacked a camouflaged machine-gun nest and killed two more.

When his company commander was hit on his helmet by a grenade that failed to explode, Baker killed the grenade thrower and then went on alone. He blasted open another concealed bunker, and shot up the enemy inside with a submachine gun he had picked up. Only 7 of Baker's platoon survived, but they killed 26 of the enemy, destroying six machine-gun nests, two observer posts and four dugouts. He won a Distinguished Service Cross. In 1996, a Pentagon investigation of black military honors commended him and six others for its top decoration, the Medal of Honor, never before conferred on a black serviceman. Baker, at 76, was the only one of the seven heroes still alive to receive the award from President Clinton.

Aug. 16: Stalin rejects Anglo-American appeals for Soviets to help the "reckless" Polish Home Army uprising, refuses use of Russian airfields.

Aug. 17: Red Army reaches East Prussia.

Aug. 19: Patton's 3rd Army throws bridgehead across the Seine 40 miles from Paris. Paris rises against Germans; 1,500 Parisians die in street fighting.

Aug. 21: Allies finally close the Falaise "pocket." American 80th Division secures Argentan in linkup with Canadian, Polish and British from north, Americans from south. Some 30,000 Germans escape, taking along key officers, but 50,000 taken prisoner, 10,000 killed and 344 tanks and self-propelled guns captured. Eisenhower visits battlefield and writes: "It was literally possible to walk for hundreds of yards at a time stepping on nothing but dead and decaying flesh."

Aug. 23: Jews from Palestine join the Allied armies as a separate Jewish Brigade Group, flying what would become the flag of the Israeli state.

Aug. 25: Allied troops, officially led by General Jacques Leclerc's French 2nd Armored Division, liberate Paris.

Aug. 26: De Gaulle returns to Paris.

—Eighth Army in Italy breaks through Gothic line.

Aug. 28: French liberate Toulon and Marseilles.

Sept. 1: Eisenhower takes top command of the armies in the field from Montgomery, assigning Montgomery the north and Bradley the center and south. Now 20 U.S. divisions in Europe, 12 British, 3 Canadian, 1 French, 1 Polish. Eisenhower announces Allies will advance into Germany on three broad fronts, rejecting advice of his "great and personal friend . . . and great soldier" Montgomery, who advocates single concentrated thrust.

Sept. 2: British cross into Belgium. Canadians enter Dieppe and Rouen.

Sept. 3: British, Poles and Canadians in 2nd Army liberate Brussels.

Sept. 8: Germans launch V-2 rockets on London.

GENERAL CURTIS LEMAY
(1906–1990)

Before 1940 he was an obscure Army Air Force lieutenant who had never commanded so much as a squadron. He was born into a poor Midwest family, and got into the Army Air in 1929 by way of Ohio State University's ROTC program.

He had an icy manner. His men called him Iron Ass, but respected his relentless perfectionism, his insistence on flying the planes they were given and his readiness to listen to ideas. He learned every nuance of his B-17s, frequently flying his 305th Bombardment Group over Germany. He did that so often at high altitudes he was afflicted with Bell's palsy. He concealed a drooping lower lip by constantly chewing a cigar stub. Assigned to introduce the B-29s to the Pacific theater, he found that high winds wrecked the high-altitude bombing perfected over Germany. His typically innovative and ruthless solution was to send the bombers in at only 5,000 to 6,000 feet, packed with napalm and jellied gasoline. By June 1945 they had wiped out 105 square miles of the leading Japanese cities as surely as an atomic bomb: he thought the A–bomb was unnecessary.

After the war, LeMay built the Strategic Air Command, backbone of the nation's nuclear defense in the fifties. Like the character Jack D. Ripper in the movie *Dr. Strangelove,* his vision was as confined as a bombsight. He argued for a preemptive nuclear strike on the Soviet Union. In the Korean war, he told a Joint Chiefs of Staff meeting, "We ought to nuke the Chinks." His 1965 ghosted autobiography had him saying that the solution in Vietnam was "to bomb them back to the Stone Age." He repudiated the quote, but it was a true indication of his wildness. He ended his public career running for vice president on George Wallace's American Independent party ticket in 1968.

ROUND-THE-CLOCK BOMBING

"Are we beasts? Are we taking this too far?" Thus Winston Churchill in June 1943 while watching film of British bombs raining down on the Ruhr in 43 major raids. But within a month, in the first combined offensive by the British and American air forces, the Allies were to wreak a terror beyond imagination. In the early hours of July 24, in Operation Gomorrah, 791 RAF bombers hit the center of Hamburg with incendiaries and high explosives, creating the war's first firestorm. People in shelters were turned to ashes; others were sucked into the flames by the gale-force winds following the escalation of temperatures to 1500 degrees Farenheit (815 Celsius).

The next day Boeing B-17 Flying Fortresses of the U.S. 8th Air Force followed the mass raid with attacks on the shipyards, and again on July 26. Then on the night of July 27, the British bombers came back again. The RAF dropped a stupendous 8,344 tons. About 50,000 people died, and 580 factories were wiped out. It was a successful example of area bombing, but this kind of attack, pressed relentlessly against German cities by Britain's Air Marshal Arthur "Bomber" Harris, did not bring Germany to her knees as he kept telling Churchill it would. The daylight precision bombing of strategic targets favored by the U.S. Army Air Force was more effective—once the Americans learned how the ability, with the Norden bombsight, to "drop a bomb into a pickle barrel from 20,000 feet" could be less dearly exploited. On August 17, 1943, 376 Flying Fortresses attacked aircraft and ball-bearing factories at Regensburg and Schweinfurt. Sixty planes did not come back, and when they tried again in October 65 were destroyed and 599 airmen lost their lives. At that rate there would soon be no 8th Air Force. The long-distance daylight raids were abandoned pending the creation of a long-distance fighter.

Hermann Göring told Hitler to relax; it was impossible to produce such a plane soon enough. But the Americans already had just the thing in the North American Company's P-51 Mustang. It had been prematurely rejected by the AAF in 1940. The reject had been taken up by the RAF, and once it was fitted with long-range drop tanks and a Rolls-Royce Merlin engine it proved able to protect the Flying Fortresses on long missions into eastern Europe.

From the spring of 1944, the American daylight bombing of oil targets and the combined Allied bombing of transport systems made a real contribution to winning the war. It might well have been shortened by several months if "Bomber" Harris had concentrated on the oil and transport raids he foolishly called "panaceas." Instead, more than half of the British bombs fell on towns. It was a revival of faith in terror, and on February 13, 1945, the terror reached a climax that did no credit to its planners. Operation Thunderclap was supposed to frighten the Germans into surrender. The American Air Force leaders did not believe in the practical effect of terror bombing and had moral doubts, but in the end the U.S. 8th Air Force went along with Thunderclap. The beautiful city of Dresden was targeted, though it had half a million refugees and its center had no industrial or military significance. The RAF dropped 2,660 tons, including 1,182 tons of incendiaries, creating a firestorm in which 40,000 to 50,000 died. Flying Fortresses followed up by bombing the marshaling yards. It is odd that Churchill, who had fretted over the industrial Ruhr, was the principal proponent of the destruction of Dresden. He wanted to impress the advancing Russians.

VICTIMS: Germans? British? Japanese? Cremated by incendiary bombing, these civilian victims speak of a universal horror. They happen to be British, killed in the seminal raid on Coventry in November 1940. It was the beginning of the escalation of the air war into mass killing.

HAMBURG: Astonishingly, war production recovered and thousands returned to make their homes in the rubble.

Arnold (left) walks a French beachhead with General Omar Bradley.

HENRY "HAP" ARNOLD (1886–1950)

The creator of the Army Air Force and its chief throughout the war learned to fly in a four-hour course with a Wright brothers' mechanic. A near-death dive in a Wright-C airplane scared him off flying for four years. The man who got him to fly again, Billy Mitchell, became his idol. Arnold enraged Army brass in 1925 by campaigning for Mitchell and an independent air service.

Arnold was close also to Donald Douglas and the other leading plane makers. As air chief, he gambled that they could make engines to carry the giant B-29 and other heavy long-distance bombers he and his buddy Carl "Toby" Spaatz (1891–1974) dreamed up. The gamble was one of his war-winning decisions. He favored hitting specific military targets, rather than the area bombing practiced by the British. It was the alliance of his energy and toughness with the administrative skills of Assistant Secretary of War Robert Lovett that made the AAF so formidable.

OMAR BRADLEY (1893–1981)

"Every G.I. to me was the son I never had."

Stable, discreet, Bradley was admired by his men and by West Point classmate Eisenhower, who thought him "the master tactician" in North Africa and Europe. A poor farm boy from Missouri, Bradley was in the Army 32 years, graduating from West Point in 1915. He first saw combat in Tunisia in 1943. At the height of the battle of Normandy he had 1.3 million men under his command.

Sept. 9: Stalin finally agrees to send air support to Warsaw insurgents and to let Allies do the same.

Sept. 11: At 6:05 p.m. Staff Sergeant Warner W. Holzinger of 5th Armored Division leads men of 2nd Platoon, Troop B, across the shallow Our River near the village of Wallendorf, the first American fighting man to set foot on German soil in World War II.

Sept. 17: With Allies stalled, Montgomery launches radical plan (Operation Market Garden) to strike at Germany north through Holland, outflanking the Siegfried line and threatening Ruhr. Parachutists of U.S. 101st and 82nd divisions and British airborne division are dropped to seize main bridges in 60-mile corridor to Arnhem, with the aim of securing them for armored columns racing north from Belgium. It is greatest airborne operation ever.

Sept. 18: British Guards Armored Division cuts through to U.S. 101st paratroopers holding bridge at Eindhoven. British drop at Arnhem too scattered and too far from bridge, 9th SS Panzer Division unexpectedly in area and British plans found by Germans on body of an American parachute officer. Colonel John Frost's 2nd Parachute Battalion with 600 men fights through to hold northern end of Arnhem road bridge, but cut off from rest of British paras in defensive box at Oosterbeek.

Sept. 20: British tanks, linking with American paras, cross Nijmegen Bridge, take road to Arnhem. But Frost down to 140 men at Arnhem and German tanks finally get across the bridge.

Sept. 22: Arnhem toll is put at 1,200 dead and 6,450 taken prisoner; 2,163 escape. Eight of nine bridges taken but the "bridge too far" frustrates strategy. This failure puts final nail in coffin of Montgomery's campaign for single concentrated attack on Germany rather than attack on broad front preferred by Eisenhower.

Sept. 27: Polish insurgents in Warsaw surrender after loss of 15,000. In reprisal another 200,000 civilians are killed.

BREACHING THE ATLANTIC WALL

The assault on the Atlantic Wall began twenty minutes after midnight on June 6, 1944, six hours before the H-Hour of landings from the sea. The first of 15,000 American and 8,000 British parachutists, men with faces blackened and their body harnesses festooned with guns and grenades, began to drop into the darkened French countryside.

The drop was a lethal lottery. Weaving through high winds and cloud banks, and dodging German flak, some green Allied Dakota pilots flew bumpily and erratically, to the fury of the paratroopers, who in some instances waved guns to persuade pilots to risk staying on course. U.S. paratrooper John Steele landed on the church steeple of Ste.-Mère-Eglise. The Germans took him prisoner, but by 4:30 a.m. the village was in the hands of the 82nd, and the 101st

Airborne had captured enough points to provide a thin screen for the men fighting their way inland from Utah Beach.

At dawn that day the greatest armada ever assembled lay off the Normandy beaches: 6,500 warships and transport craft in 75 convoys. Protected by 12,000 aircraft, which dominated the skies, the invasion fleet began landing the first wave of 154,000 troops, including 75,215 British and Canadians and 57,000 Americans. Twenty-one of the 47 divisions marked for the invasion were American, the rest British, Canadian and Polish. Brilliant deception tactics had persuaded the Germans that the invasion would be in Pas-de-Calais. Hitler, believing the landing was a feint, held back the main German armor.

HELL ON OMAHA: Robert Capa's icon of H-Hour on Omaha, a lone soldier in the surf under murderous fire unaware that Capa has made him immortal. It was learned after the war that the soldier was 22-year-old Edward K. Regan from Pennsylvania. He survived to recall being reduced to immobility by the chaos. Capa said his own hands trembled with fear, but this image gains its effect by accidental heat blur on the negatives. Of Capa's 72 images, 61 were ruined in the darkroom.

British and Canadian troops at Gold, Juno and Sword beaches and Americans at Utah secured their beachheads. It was only at the bloody Omaha beachhead that the issue was in doubt all day. The V Corps plan was very American. It envisaged a storming frontal assault, victory by force of will. The U.S. Navy made it even more hazardous. It insisted on launching assault craft far out to sea—12 miles, in contrast to the British "lowering areas" of 8 miles or less. Most of the amphibious tanks and guns were swamped and sank in heavy seas. Hundreds of men were drowned, hundreds landed in the wrong places. Men had to run through minefields and intersecting machine gun fire to secure five vital beach exits—defended by eight enemy battalions, not the four expected. Only 62 Rangers of 130 deposited in front of a strong point made it to the safety of the sea wall. Under fire for the first time, men of the 29th Division hugged the beach. The day was saved only by a

gradual accumulation of isolated acts of heroism and leadership. More Rangers followed when Staff Sergeant William Courtney and Private First Class William Braher scaled the 100-foot Pointe du Hoc cliffs to the west of the beachhead at 8:30 a.m. Sergeant Julius Belcher single-handedly seized a pillbox. Men of the 1st Division, "the Big Red One," responded to the challenge of Colonel G. A. Taylor: "Two kinds of people are staying on this beach, the dead and those who are going to die—now let's get the hell out of here."

There were 3,000 casualties at Omaha, ten times the rate on other beaches. By nightfall, 33,000 men had been landed, tenuously holding a beachhead six miles wide and no more than two miles deep. But D-Day was altogether a striking victory. The Wall had been breached along a 50-mile front, at a cost of fewer than 2,500 Allied lives. By June 10, the five beachheads had joined together.

Oct. 21: Aachen falls to General Courtney Hodges's 1st Army, first German city occupied by Allies.

Oct. 24: The Dumbarton Oaks conference, which began in Washington in August, attended by 39 nations, agrees to create the United Nations.

Nov. 18: Patton's 3rd Army enters Germany.

Dec. 16: Hitler stuns Allies by unleashing two Panzer armies, 250,000 men and 950 tanks, in counterattack in forests of Ardennes against 80,000 men and 420 tanks. Operation Autumn Mist is meant to slice Allied armies in two, cross the Meuse and recapture Antwerp, 100 miles distant. General Bradley misreads what develops as battle of the Bulge as a local "spoiling attack" and is slow to react. At Schnee Eifel, nearly 9,000 Americans will surrender, the largest in U.S. history after Bataan.

Dec. 18: At dusk, 10th Armored Division under Brigadier General Anthony C. McAuliffe reaches Bastogne, identified by Eisenhower as key to battle, followed by 101st Armored Division. Bastogne is the only organized center of resistance on a 25-mile front.

Dec. 20: Eisenhower decides that Bradley, with his armies split, cannot control battle on the northern flank of the Bulge and takes unpopular decision of giving Montgomery command of all Allied armies in the north. Bradley is furious. Ike tells him, "Well, Brad, those are my orders."

Dec. 21: U.S. troops in Bastogne encircled.

Dec. 22: McAuliffe in Bastogne sends a written reply to the demand for surrender: "To the German commander. Nuts! The American commander." Patton has fulfilled boast that to help relieve Bastogne he could in 24 hours disengage from Saar battle and wheel at right angles northward over a 60- to 70-mile front, one of the war's most amazing operations. One of his armored columns gets within 5 miles of Bastogne perimeter.

Dec. 26: Patton gets relief column into Bastogne by narrow corridor, but main supply is via air: 800,000 tons dropped between December 23 and 27.

EISENHOWER'S GIFT TO THE ALLIANCE

This is a photograph of a great alliance in strain. On the eve of the triumphant Anglo-American crossing of the Rhine at Wesel, in March 1945, two British generals, Chief of Staff Alan Brooke (left) and Army commander Bernard Montgomery have Supreme Commander Eisenhower in a British sandwich while three American generals stand apart—Omar Bradley (far right), Artillery General Charles C. Brown (behind) and Corps commander John Anderson (left). The Americans were constantly worried that Eisenhower was being seduced by the British. They were irritated from the start that subordinate land, sea and air commands for Overlord were given to three Englishmen—with another Englishman, Air Chief Marshal Sir Arthur Tedder, as Deputy Supreme Commander to Eisenhower. At D-Day there was rough equality in the Anglo-American national contributions, but by 1945 the Americans were providing the preponderance of troops and wanted the preponderance of leadership.

Montgomery himself thought the photograph revealing. "From the look on Bradley's face," he wrote a few days later, "there is obviously trouble ahead!" There was; it was heading straight for Montgomery. At this stage of the war Bradley loathed Montgomery. When the Germans cleaved through the American front in the Ardennes in December 1944, Eisenhower had transferred command of the 9th and 1st U.S. armies in the north from Bradley's 12th Army Group to Montgomery's 21st Army Group. It was a sensible emergency measure, and Montgomery built a wall that helped to break the German attack. Losing his command would have been hard enough for Bradley to swallow, but Montgomery rubbed it in during a personal meeting and an indiscreet press conference. He was too vain and insensitive not to crow; privately, he referred to the Ardennes as "a most awful bloody nose" for the Americans. "I doubt," Eisenhower wrote later, "that Montgomery ever came to realize how deeply resentful some American commanders were. They believed he had deliberately belittled them—

and they were not slow to voice their reciprocal scorn and contempt."

Montgomery was still in command of the 9th for its Rhine crossing when this photograph was taken, ready to begin a great Anglo-American sweep from the north side of the Ruhr and across the plains to Berlin. But three days later he got a bloody nose himself. "For Field Marshal Montgomery's eyes only from Eisenhower," said the top-secret signal.

Eisenhower not only announced he was giving the 9th back to Bradley; he also said he had "coordinated with Stalin" that after the Rhine crossing the Allied armies would mop up on the Ruhr, and then join hands with the Soviets in the Dresden area. It

meant he was leaving Berlin to the Russians. The decision, and the unprecedented direct liaison with Stalin, produced a controversy that lasted well into the war that followed—the Cold War. Did Eisenhower give too much away? Churchill protested in a stream of messages to Eisenhower and the failing Roosevelt. But he and FDR and Stalin had already at Yalta agreed how Germany should be divided into occupation zones; Berlin, though subject to joint rule, was clearly in the Russian zone. Were the political and psychological rewards of taking the capital worth American lives and the risks of colliding with the Russians on the battlefield? Bradley was right to argue in his memoirs that to capture Berlin, at a

cost of perhaps the 100,000 Soviet casualties, then to resign the prize, would have been "a pretty stiff price to pay for a prestige objective." However, there was nothing like the same justification for Eisenhower's decision to halt Patton's 3rd Army when it could have taken Prague.

For all the feuding, the Anglo-American military alliance held together, and it was crucial for victory. Americans put their lives in the trust of Englishmen, and Englishmen took orders from Americans. The friendship of Churchill and Roosevelt was the arch of the temple, but the Samson holding it up was the Supreme Commander, Dwight Eisenhower. None of his best generals—Bradley, Patton, Montgomery—thought he was gifted as a battlefield commander, and he lacked the geopolitical vision of Churchill. But Eisenhower had his own genius. It was his lead-ership, and his alone, that kept 3 million men in the Allied armies fighting together on a line from the Baltic to the Alps. It was his severest critic, Mont-gomery, who concluded, "No one else could have done it." He had a generosity of spirit and integrity that put nationalist jealousies to shame. He had a spiritual power that infused the men at the front with a sense of decency and purpose. But he could not have conciliated prima donnas like Patton, Montgomery and de Gaulle simply by wearing a halo. He had to be clever, even cunning, endlessly re-sourceful, psychic in his understanding of personal-ities. His style was manifest in a story he allowed to circulate about his relief of an American officer of his command for abusing an ally. It was all right, Eisenhower is said to have remarked, to call someone a son of a bitch, but not a British son of a bitch.

Jan. 3: Montgomery's 21st Army Group launches counterattacks north to flatten the Bulge.

Jan. 8: Hitler reluctantly sancions a pullback from Ardennes Bulge and retreats later in the month to his Führerbunker, on grounds of Reich Chancellery in Berlin. Ardennes cost for Germans: 30,000 dead, 40,000 wounded, 30,000 taken prisoner. Total Allied casualties: 76,000, and six weeks lost on drive into Germany. On all fronts total American casualties exceed 138,000; Commonwealth losses are more than 250,000.

Jan. 25: Two million Germans flee Red Army advance of killing, pillage and rape. Sea evacuation from Baltic ports, largest in history, severs East Prussia from the Reich.

Jan. 27: Soviet troops find 7,600 survivors in Auschwitz, death camp for a minimum of 2 million Jews and 2 million Soviet prisoners of war.

Feb. 8: Eisenhower launches three-prong assault to clear Germans west of Rhine with British, Canadian and U.S. 9th Army leading off in north.

Feb. 11: In Yalta, FDR, Stalin and Churchill issue a joint declaration guaranteeing democracy for freed Europeans, but accept Soviet puppet government in Poland until free elections—which Stalin promises in a month.

Feb. 13: RAF and U.S. 8th Air Force destroy Dresden.

Feb. 15: FDR and Churchill meet for last time, on American cruiser *Quincy* off Alexandria.

Feb. 15–17: FDR meets on *Quincy* with King Farouk of Egypt, Emperor Haile Selassie of Ethiopia and King Ibn Saud of Saudi Arabia. Saud rejects FDR's plea for a Zionist state of Palestine.

March 2: FDR, addressing Congress on Yalta, speaks from sitting position, for the first time in public life fully acknowledging the extent of his affliction.

A HISTORIC PHOTOGRAPH: APRIL 25, 1945

IGOR BELOUSOVITCH'S PHOTOGRAPH

Across the top of these pages is the first photograph of the historic linkup—Russian cavalry as spotted by an American patrol on the late afternoon of April 25, 1945, near Clanzschwitz by the Elbe. The photograph was taken by 23-year-old PFC Igor Belousovitch (above), who snatched up a single roll of film, eight shots, as he was called out on one of the three 69th Division patrols.

It is an irony of history, redolent of the romance of America, that Belousovitch might easily have been one of the Russian cavalrymen who wheeled right and galloped toward the Americans. His mother and father were Russians who fled from the Bolshevik revolution to Shanghai, where Belousovitch was born in 1922, a year before they were admitted to America. When the horsemen—and bicyclists—reached the American patrol, Belousovitch said: "I greet you in the name of the American Army and our commanders on this historic occasion. It is a privilege and an honor to be here." The Russian commander replied in kind. A GI climbed on one of the Russian horses and fooled around. Then, after three minutes of excited mingling, both patrols went their separate ways. Belousovitch settled down in Alexandria, Virginia, and in 1996 gave us permission to publish his blurred but unique moment of truth, which he had kept all these years in a desk drawer.

ALBERT KOTZEBUE'S REWARD FOR DISOBEYING

Lieutenant Albert L. Kotzebue disobeyed his orders on April 25, 1945. He was in Company G, the U.S. 273rd Infantry Regiment, 69th Division, part of the 1st Army, which had been impatiently marking time for a week on the banks of the Mulde. General Eisenhower had halted his armies there for fear of running into the Red Army advancing on the Elbe, 25 miles to the east of the Mulde. On April 25, Colonel C. M. Adams sent 21-year-old "Buck" Kotzebue on a strictly limited patrol, one of three patrols that day. Kotzebue and his 35 men, in seven Jeeps, were supposed to go no more than five miles, but after a night out Kotzebue pressed farther east, staying ahead of his radio Jeep in case a summons should come for him to return to camp. At 11:30 a.m., he spotted a horseman in a fur hat in the middle of a bunch of refugees in the village of Leckwitz. He was a Soviet cavalryman, Aitkali Alibekov, from Kazakhstan, who waved the Americans farther eastward. Just before noon, Kotzebue and his men reached the Elbe, near the deserted village of Strehla. He scanned the opposite bank with his field glasses. A group of men in brown shirts came into view. He recalled: "I knew they were Russians, because someone had once told me that Russians wore their medals into battle. Medals on the brown shirts were reflecting sunlight. Yes, these were Russians. The time was 12:05 p.m."

Kotzebue launched two green flares, the prearranged recognition signal. The figures on the other side just stared at them. "Americansky!" shouted Kotzebue's party. "Americansky!" No response. Kotzebue went down to the water's edge and found four shallow boats. No oars. He launched himself into the river with six men, and they paddled across with rifle butts and boards. The brown shirts came down the steep bank on the other side, and now there was an explosion of good feeling, much grinning and backslapping and a series of formal salutes from the Russians—Sergeant Alexander Olshansky and riflemen under Major Grigory Goloborodko. Later, while back west Colonel Adams and his division general fumed about the eager Kotzebue, there

AN AMERICAN PATROL SIGHTS THE RUSSIAN CAVALRY

Rifleman Joe Polowsky—standing on the Jeep amid Russian and American soldiers—never forgot the oath for peace he made on the Elbe, and he never let the world forget. In 1947 he left his studies in botany at the University of Chicago to work for international peace. In later years, when he was a Chicago taxi driver, he stood every April 25 on Chicago's Michigan Avenue Bridge, urging passersby to renew the Oath of the Elbe and end the nuclear arms race. He died in 1983, after unsuccessfully lobbying the United Nations to have April 25 recognized as Elbe Day. He was buried at Torgau, the site of the second linkup that day.

was a party at the farmhouse headquarters of General Vladimir Rusakov. A multitude of vodka toasts were drunk to Roosevelt, Truman, Stalin and Churchill. But it was something that happened in those first awkward moments of the linkup that lingers in one's imagination. Kotzebue was moved by the meeting and by the mounds of dead civilians on the riverbanks who had been trapped in bombardments. He suggested through a rifleman named Joe Polowsky, who spoke German, that the two groups of soldiers should swear an oath for peace, and they all did.

Hours after Kotzebue's meeting and 20 miles north of his first crossing, Second Lieutenant Bill Robertson of the 1st Battalion reached Torgau to a less friendly reception. The Russians on the other side of the Elbe opened fire. Robertson devised a crude Amer-

ican flag by breaking into a store for a sheet and red and blue paint and he waved it from a tower of the city's castle. An antitank shell nearly took him out. Finally, after much shouting and waving and the help of a just liberated Russian prisoner, Robertson clambered out onto the twisted wreckage of the Torgau road bridge to shake hands with the Red Army's Sergeant Nikolai Andreyev. Robertson recalled: "Neither understood the other's words, but the commonality of feeling was unmistakable. We were all soldiers, comrades in arms. We had vanquished a common enemy. The war was over, peace was near. All of us would live another hour, another day." The following day, the press caught up with the action and photographer Allan Jackson set up his famous picture of the handshake across the broken bridge.

Polowsky demonstrates for peace and disarmament at Chicago's Civic Center Plaza, September 4, 1974.

March 7: Ninth U.S. Armored Division of 1st Army finds Hitler's order to blow up all Rhine bridges has not yet been carried out at the Remagen rail bridge. Lieutenant Karl Timmerman races his company toward this last hurdle in the west even as enemy blows, but does not destroy, the bridge. First time an invader has crossed the Rhine into Germany since Napoleon.

March 23: At 9 p.m., more than a million British, Canadian and American troops in Montgomery's 21st Army Group begin crossing of Rhine at ten points on a 20-mile front between Xanten and Rees, preceded by raids by nearly 200 Lancasters and 23 Mosquitoes.

March 24: In the war's most successful parachute operation, U.S. 17th and British 6th Airborne Divisions drop on German positions at Wesel, link up with U.S. 9th and British 2nd armies. By nightfall, Allies are six miles east of Rhine.

March 30: British Chiefs of Staff, and later Churchill, protest Eisenhower's decision to stop Allied forces at the Elbe and urge him to race for Berlin.

April 11: U.S. 9th Army spearheads reach Elbe near Magdeburg after advancing 75 miles in a day.

—Americans liberate slave-labor camp at Buchenwald.

April 12: President Roosevelt dies.

April 13: Red Army occupies Vienna.

April 15: British reach Belsen, where estimated 50,000 Jews died, including Anne Frank. They find 30,000 inmates, 10,000 dead of starvation, and 1,500 Hungarian camp guards still carrying out executions.

April 16: Red armies of 2.5 million men, under Marshal Zhukov in the center and Marshal Ivan Konev in the south, open belated drive for Berlin, held by a ragtag assortment of about a million German fighting men.

April 21: In greatest capitulation, 325,000 Germans trapped in Ruhr "pocket" surrender. Field Marshal Walther Model shoots himself.

They never stopped, day or night, in the Kaiser Shipyards in Portland, Oregon.

THE ARSENAL OF DEMOCRACY

Reichsmarschall Hermann Göring, commander of the Luftwaffe and head of German industry, was scornful of America's war capacity. When Rommel reported that British planes equipped with a new American 40 mm shell were shooting up his tanks in the desert, Göring retorted: "That's completely impossible. The Americans only know how to make razor blades." Nor did he see it as anything more than boasting when FDR told Congress America would build 45,000 warplanes in 1942. Greater Germany's target was 15,556. Germany itself did manage 40,600 planes in 1944, but by then America had doubled its 1942 target. In the five years after the fall of France, America built 296,429 warplanes.

At sea, the U-boats were defeated as much by shipyard know-how as gallantry at sea. A total of 5,600 merchant ships were built in the war with a deadweight tonnage of 56.4 million. By 1943 Henry Kaiser was producing one Liberty ship every 12 hours. At Chrysler they built one Swedish Bofors naval anti-aircraft gun in 10 hours; it had taken 450 hours to make one by hand in Sweden. Pontiac re-duced the time of making the Swiss Oerliken anti-aircraft gun from 428 hours to 346 and cut the cost by 23 percent. In March 1942, General Motors' Saginaw plant produced 28,728 Browning machine guns—and in the process lowered the price from $667 to $141.44. Ford's Willow Run plant, set up to mass-produce bombers, took a long time to rev up, and its high labor turnover was not helped by Henry Ford's veto on employing blacks and women; but by August 1944, when 40 percent of the workforce was women, Ford's grandson was turning out 550 B-24s a month. The Office of Scientific Research and Development, headed by Dr. Vannevar Bush, had $1 billion in funding and made breakthroughs in radar, sonar, fuses, rocketry, amphibious vehicles, flame throwers, blood plasma, penicillin, synthetic drugs, jets, plane cabins, pesticides and atomic fission.

Stalin had a better appreciation than Göring. At the Teheran summit in 1943 he proposed a toast: "To American production, without which this war would have been lost."

Henry John Kaiser had had enough of Washington. At 60, he was a successful dam builder. Yet for days in the wake of Pearl Harbor he had hung around and gotten nowhere in pushing his radical new ideas for mass-producing ships. The Navy had afforded him all of 18 minutes to make his presentation—and then turned him down flat. "I'm licked. I'm going home. I'm catching the afternoon train to California," he told *Washington Post* publisher Eugene Meyer.

Meyer persuaded him to stick around for a few more days and got hold of presidential aide Wayne Coy. Soon Kaiser was being ushered in to see FDR. He left the President's office with an order to build the first 50 of what became known as the Liberty ships. It was a typical bold, snap decision by FDR, but he was probably familiar with Kaiser from his work on public projects in the thirties. Kaiser had left school at 13, and become a major road builder on the West Coast and in Canada and Cuba. He worked on the Hoover, Bonneville, Shasta and Grand Coulee dams and built the piers of the seminal San Francisco–Oakland bridge.

A Liberty cargo ship of British design took 200 days to launch before Kaiser got involved in his shipyards in California and Oregon with prefabrication, welding and assembly-line methods. The average soon fell to 40 days. In September 1942 he built the *John Fitch* in 24 hours after laying the keel. By 1942 the U.S. had launched 646 new freighters—597 of them from Kaiser's yards. He built 118 escort carriers with antisubmarine aircraft, having again convinced FDR, against Navy skepticism, that they could play a vital role in protecting convoys. He also found the energy to fight the American Medical Association and establish the country's biggest prepaid medical plan for his workers.

PAUL ROBESON: The great black singer and actor leads workers in the national anthem in the Oakland Docks, September 1942. His own faith in the war's ideals was to be cruelly shattered.

April 22: U.S. 7th and French 1st armies cross the Danube.

April 24: Himmler, on own initiative, puts out peace feelers to Western allies, with idea of continuing war against USSR. Churchill and Truman insist any surrender must be unconditional and made to Soviets as well.

April 25: American and Russian soldiers link up.

April 26: Half a million Russian troops break into center of Berlin.

April 28: Mussolini, his mistress and staff are captured and executed by Italian partisans.

April 29: Americans liberate Dachau death camp, with 33,000 barely alive survivors, mostly non-Jewish. Angered by piles of corpses, U.S. soldiers summarily shoot hundreds of SS guards.

—German armies in Italy surrender unconditionally.

—In his Berlin bunker, 55 feet below ground, Hitler, just into his 57th year, marries his mistress of 12 years, Eva Braun. He appoints Admiral Karl Dönitz as Supreme Commander.

April 30: With Russians fighting inside the Reichstag just over 200 yards away, Eva takes poison and Hitler shoots himself.

—Eisenhower stops American troops at Linz, short of Czech border. Churchill urges him to continue to Prague.

Women chippers in shipyard, 1942.

WOMEN AT WAR

Of all the countries at war, only the Soviet Union allowed women to take part in combat, but American women did almost everything else. The 1,200 Wasps (Women's Airforce Service Pilots) flew every kind of plane up to the B-29, ferrying them from the factories, testing repaired planes, towing targets, teaching strafing and bombing. Their accident record was better than male pilots, but 38 died. Some 200,000 women altogether served in the auxiliary services of the Army and Navy (Wacs and Waves). And 7 million women war workers joined the 12 million women already at work in 1941.

Women welded, riveted, cut steel, assembled bombers and tanks. Half of them were married, and one in five had a husband away in the armed services. Every second worker in ordnance and electrical manufacturing plants and every third worker in aircraft factories was a woman. Women were thought to be better than men for welding in tight corners and fiddling with fuses because of their smaller fingers. They made the fuses for most of the bombs.

War work doubled the pay of a waitress or clerk moving into munitions. Black women found they

The woman on the right (identified only as Mrs. Hartl) is helping to pull through the propeller of a B-24 Liberator bomber that had been converted into a flying laboratory.

May 2: British General Miles Dempsey, reinforced by American paratroopers of General Matthew Ridgway's XVIII Airborne Corps, wins race to seal off Danish peninsula—24 hours ahead of Red Army.

May 4: Montgomery at Lüneberg Heath receives surrender of all German forces in northwest Germany, Denmark and Holland.

—Third Army enters Austria and Czechoslovakia, but Eisenhower orders it not to move beyond the line of Karlsbad-Pilsen-Budějovice suggested by Stalin.

May 7: At Eisenhower's schoolhouse HQ in Rheims, General Alfred Jodl and Admiral Hans von Friedeburg, acting for Dönitz, agree to unconditional surrender of German forces on all fronts one minute past midnight German time on May 9. In this interval, 1.8 million troops on eastern front escape from Red Army to Western sector. Eisenhower signals U.S. and British chiefs of staff: "The mission of this Allied Force was fulfilled at 0241, local time, May 7, 1945."

ELEANOR AT THE FRONT

Eleanor Roosevelt, with Navy officers at Pearl Harbor in September 1943. Her visits to the battlefront, in the uniform of the Red Cross, were resisted by top brass, attacked as "gallivanting" by Republicans, but warmly welcomed by the soldiers and seamen. In Europe, picking up on complaints about a shortage of socks, she prodded Eisenhower and they found 2 million pairs stuck in a warehouse. It was Eleanor's backing for the ideas of the dashing aviators Jacqueline Cochran and Nancy Harkness Love that induced General Arnold to engage female pilots.

could escape confinement in farm and domestic work. But, for all the advances, the war did not bring universal equality of pay or opportunity. In a popular song serenading Rosie the Riveter, a verse said, "That little frail can do/more than a male can do." Sixty percent of plant managers polled agreed. Yet on average Rosie earned only 60 percent of the male wage. Women pilots got 20 percent less than men of the same grade. The intent of the War Labor Board's injunction that there should be equal pay for equal work was thwarted by employers' segregating comparable work by sex and by discriminating in other ways.

Nor did the influx of women transform social attitudes. Women were hissed in some workplaces where men feared they would be taking their work. They were told they must not wear sweaters, "for moral reasons." Most of the unions were misogynistic. They regarded the women workers as temporary, and they failed to support nurseries in factories or maternity leave. Congress persisted in refusing to give servicewomen treatment comparable to men. It took until 1977 for former Wasps to receive military benefits and the Victory Medal.

The working women helped to win the war, but they had no effective champion for their social concerns. The middle-class women's organizations were preoccupied with more general civic issues rather than Rosie the Riveter's problems in being worker, wife, mother and housekeeper.

AMERICANS SENT TO INTERNMENT CAMPS

Seventy thousand bewildered American citizens found themselves interned in their own country's concentration camps in the spring of 1942. They had done nothing wrong. It was their antecedents, not their actions, that led to their long ordeal. They were American citizens of Japanese descent. Their loyalty to the United States counted for nothing; nor did the Bill of Rights. All together, 120,000 men, women and children were rounded up and interned: the 70,000 were "Nisei," citizens by birth to first-generation immigrants, or "Issei." (The Supreme Court had ruled in 1922 [*Ozawa v. United States*] that Issei, being neither white nor black, could not qualify for citizenship.) They were all forced to leave behind what they could not carry. Most sold their homes and businesses in panic sales; the state of California cheated scores of them out of their farms; and such work as they could get in the camps was ill paid.

The day after Pearl Harbor the FBI swiftly arrested 2,000 male Japanese "bad risks." This was a justified and entirely different process. The 2,000 were all entitled to individual review. The 120,000 were not. Anyone who had as little as one-sixteenth Japanese blood and lived in California or certain areas of Oregon, Arizona or Washington was simply swept up by the Army and shipped out to ten desolate camps. The families were confined behind barbed wire and military guard in bleak tar-papered barrack rooms no more than 20 by 24 feet, and most of them were kept there until 1945. Some bureaucrat tried to call the camps "residence control centers."

The internment was an outrage. As a 1982 investigative commission concluded, it was not justified by any military necessity and it ran counter to a basic premise on which the American nation of immigrants is built—that loyalty to the United States is not determined by ties to an ancestral country. How did it ever happen? The origin is in the racial antagonism felt for "the Jap" as someone of barbaric habit who could never be assimilated, a prejudice inflamed into wild hatred by Pearl Harbor and the fear aroused by the image of a "Jap" with a bayonet unstoppably on the rampage. Even President Roosevelt

was receptive to the advice he got from Smithsonian curator Dr. Aleš Hrdlička that Japanese perfidy and cruelty had a specific racial basis measurable in things like skull size.

National security was the excuse, and the blame is normally laid on the aging Lieutenant General John De Witt, who had responsibility for West Coast defenses. He was a bigot. He wrote that the Japanese race was "an enemy race and while many second and third generation Japanese born on United States soil have become Americanized, the racial strains are undiluted." But De Witt was not at first in favor of mass evacuation. He adopted it as his goal only after being scared by fearmongers, led by the Hearst press, and two men who should have known better: the Californian with the clearest duty to defend the Constitution, its Attorney General, Earl Warren (later Chief Justice Warren), and John J. McCloy, the assistant secretary of war, who was advised by Colonel Karl Bendetsen. Warren, who was gearing up to run for governor, enriched the annals of paranoia: "It is quite significant that in this great state of ours we have had no fifth column activities and no sabotage reported. . . . That was the story of Pearl Harbor. I can't help believing that something is planned for us." Throughout the entire war, no single case was recorded of sabotage, subversion or espionage by any Japanese American.

The Justice Department staff did not believe there was evidence of sabotage, but the attorney general, the aristocratic Francis Biddle, wilted before War Secretary Henry Stimson. Stimson knew internment of American citizens would "make an awful hole in our constitutional system," but, as biographer Godfrey Hodgson says, he saw the constitutional principle as a difficulty to be got around, not as an imperative to be vindicated. He was also too ready to let McCloy call the shots. "You are putting a Wall Street lawyer in a helluva box," said McCloy, "but if it is a question of the safety of the country or the Constitution of the U.S., why, the Constitution is just a scrap of paper to me."

Initially, many whites in the American West were sympathetic to the vulnerable

minority, but the local agitation was given national impetus by journalists such as Damon Runyon, John B. Hughes, Westbrook Pegler and, most influentially, Walter Lippmann. There was a decisive event on January 25, 1942. Justice Owen Roberts released his commission's report on Pearl Harbor. It was a catalytic reminder of that treachery, and opinion changed abruptly. President Roosevelt, without holding any cabinet meetings, called Stimson on the phone on February 19 and said he was signing Executive Order 9066 for internment. "Be as reasonable as you can," he said. The order did not specify Japanese Americans, but there was no question of a mass evacuation of people of German or Italian blood, and Japanese Americans went unmolested in Hawaii. "I don't care

A VISIT FROM THE FBI: By 6:03 a.m. on December 8, 1941, the FBI had arrested 733 Japanese nationals previously identified as potential risks. But FBI Director J. Edgar Hoover objected to the 1942 mass evacuation because it implied his Bureau had failed to grab all the potential spies and saboteurs. The 1942 roundup was based, he said, primarily on public hysteria rather than factual data used in the FBI's earlier roundup.

about the Italians," FDR told Biddle. "They're a lot of opera singers."

The Supreme Court fell into line. In two different cases the Court upheld Order 9066 on grounds of military need and wartime urgency. The Court had a mixed record during the war in protecting the rights of other unpopular groups, but the legal historian Peter Irons showed in 1983 that in the case of the Nisei it was presented with tainted evidence. Two Justice Department lawyers, Edward J. Ennis and John L. Burling, checked with the FBI and the Federal Communications Commission and found De Witt's claims of espionage and sabotage by Japanese Americans to be false. They thought the Supreme Court should know this. McCloy intervened with

Solicitor General Charles Fahy to suppress the information. McCloy had already got De Witt to doctor his report so as to conceal De Witt's opinion that the evacuation was based on race, not military urgency. Nevertheless, one of the three dissenting Supreme Court justices in 1944 called the decision a "legalization of racism."

It took nearly half a century for some sort of justice to emerge. In 1986 a federal court found that the U.S. had lied to the Supreme Court. It overturned the 1942 conviction of Gordon Hirabayashi, who had defied the relocation order. In 1988 Congress voted an apology to all the Nisei and Issei and a payment of $20,000 to each of the 60,000 surviving internees.

THE PATRIOTS

Many of the Japanese-American internees surprised their guards by raising the Stars and Stripes every morning; maybe that was partly out of traditional respect for authority, but no cavils can be allowed about the patriotism of the 33,000 Japanese Americans who joined the U.S. armed services as soon as they were allowed to, in January 1943. Thousands in internment camps at once volunteered to fight for the country that put them there. Their all-Nisei units, the 442nd Infantry and the 100th Infantry, were among the most highly decorated units in the war.

Daniel Inouye (above), who was elected to the U.S. Senate in 1962, volunteered from Hawaii. He lost his right arm in action in Italy. He came home a captain with a Distinguished Service Cross, a Bronze Star and a Purple Heart—and, though in full uniform, was refused a haircut in San Francisco.

SELF-DEFENSE

A Japanese-American grocer in Oakland, California, was wise to proclaim his allegiance. By March 1942, there had been 36 anti-Japanese crimes in the U.S., including 7 murders; some of the victims were actually of Chinese descent.

ASSAULT: A Detroit mob pulls a black motorman from a streetcar in hate riots, June 21–22, 1943, yelling, "Here's some fresh meat!" Fighting between whites and blacks over housing had led to whites seizing one of the few public housing complexes set aside for blacks, and blacks beating up 50 white workers on a streetcar. Nine whites and 25 blacks died in the riots, 17 shot by police; 800 people were injured.

A WAR FOR EQUALITY

Mississippi's Senator James Eastland was an arch reactionary, but at the start of the war he spoke for a common prejudice against blacks when he said: "They are an inferior race. They will not work. They will not fight." Cut to Iwo Jima, March 1945. The fight for the island is supposed to be finished, but in the predawn stillness 300 Japanese coming from nowhere are in among the rear American tents bayoneting sleeping men. Bill D. Ross reports: "First Lieutenant Harry L. Martin of Bucyrus, Ohio, threw up a scrimmage line manned largely by black troops, who coolly beat back one attack, then another, by screaming Japanese firing wildly. The attack was beaten back in furious fighting." Cut to bloody Peleliu in September 1944 and Frank Hough: "The Negro Marines of the 16th Field Depot distinguished themselves throughout as stretcher bearers, working under the heaviest fire and most difficult conditions with courage, cheerfulness, and patience notable in the hardened First Division. Volunteers all of them, this outfit had the reputation of being the 'volunteeringest' in the Marine Corps." Cut to the skies over

Italy in 1943 as B-17 pilot John Muirhead's 5th Bomb Wing flies into flak and his fighters pray their own escort will arrive: "When they joined us, precisely at the time they were supposed to, it was a spectacular rendezvous . . . suddenly the air was full of P-47s, diving and whirling through our formations. They never left us. They showed no inclination to turn away from the flak rising up ahead. I couldn't believe it. They flew through the clouds of bursting shells with deliberate aplomb. It was a grand gesture." The fighters were the all-black 332nd Fighter Group, commanded by Captain Benjamin O. Davis, Jr., the son of America's first black general. The 332nd was later to claim that not one bomber it escorted was lost to fighters. The point is not that black pilots were superior to whites, but that they could do as well when given a proper chance.

Blacks were not taken in the segregated armed forces in large numbers until casualties began to mount in 1944, when even Southern congressmen insisted. The Navy, Air Force and Marines all lagged behind the Army, which was quick to integrate PXs,

AWARD: Black privates driving furiously in the Red Ball Express shuttle kept supply lines open in the 1944 battle of the Bulge. First Army Lieutenant F. N. Patterson of New York receives the Bronze Star for his role. But black heroes were regularly overlooked in the award of honors. No black was awarded the Medal of Honor until 50 years after the war, when the Pentagon recommended seven men (six of whom had since died) to Congress and the White House.

recreation and troop trains and ships and even experimented with putting black and white platoons next to each other in Europe. The Marines accorded its 20,000 blacks second-class status, but eventually broke its own policy to use them in combat. The elitist Navy also gradually worked blacks into combat posts, even commissioning 58 black officers. But it was all along a struggle for blacks to be accepted. In the Air Force, most commanders did not want a black squadron. The announcement of an all-black 477th Bomber Group in January 1944 provoked protests and demonstrations, and it never got overseas.

Blacks had to fight similar prejudices in war work at home. Four hundred thousand blacks moved from the rural South to work in the urban South and in Northern steelworks, shipyards and factories. They doubled the $566 a year they could earn in the cotton and tobacco fields, but white pay rates were nearly double *that*. Ford was among the companies rejecting all blacks. The CIO campaigned for a multiracial workforce in industrial unions, but most unions discriminated against them by rule or practice. When blacks did advance in the workplace, they drew hostility from white workmates. At Packard, 3,000 white workers walked out, encour-

aged by the management, when 3 blacks had jobs upgraded.

There were race riots in 47 cities, the worst in Detroit. Combustion was guaranteed when 60,000 blacks from the South moved in looking for war work along with 440,000 white Southerners whose virulent racism only further inflamed the prejudices of Detroit's largely ethnic white population. In Los Angeles, pitched battles, usually over women, were fought between sailors and gangs of *pachucos* in exaggerated zoot suits from the growing Mexican-American ghetto. The city council made it a crime to wear a zoot suit.

The best thing that happened in the war years was the emergence of the first entirely black civil rights movement, mobilizing the masses for direct action rather than the middle classes for legal redress. It grew out of the campaigning efforts of A. Philip Randolph. FDR signed Executive Order 8802 on June 25, 1941, directing defense contractors and federal agencies to enforce equality. In July, he set up the Fair Employment Practices Committee to hear testimony and bully laggard employers. Order 8802 was the first use of an executive order on race relations since Lincoln signed the Emancipation Proclamation.

FIFTY SCAPEGOATS

Pamphlet published in 1945.

Just after 10:18 p.m. on July 17, 1944, the Port Chicago Naval Magazine in California's San Francisco Bay Area was blasted by an explosion of the same magnitude as that to be produced by the atomic bomb. It obliterated a Liberty ship, hurtled a train thousands of feet into the air and leveled much of the nearby town. Some 323 people were killed, more than two thirds of them black.

Only black men were assigned, untrained, to the perilous work of loading ammunition for the Pacific. They worked at breakneck speed, seven hours a day, under white officers who made bets on which "mule team" could load fastest. The Coast Guard had criticized the Navy's safety standards. But it was the black sailors, not the base commanders or the captain of the port, who got the blame in a Navy court of inquiry, where only white officers testified. Unsurprisingly, black sailors saw things differently. When ordered to resume munitions loading, 258 refused. They were threatened with a firing squad for mutiny. This was a stunner. Theirs was a passive work stoppage, brought on by fear, not an active revolt with the intent of seizing command. The men all expressed their eagerness to fight at sea.

The next day 208 gave in. The other 50 were put on trial. All 50 received 15-year sentences; with postwar clemency, they were in prison for 16 months. An outcry led by the NAACP, Eleanor Roosevelt and Harold Stassen induced the Navy to also assign whites to ammunition loading and to eliminate racial barriers by February 1946. In 1991 Bay Area Congress members forced the Navy to reopen the case. The Navy's conclusion: racial discrimination did play a part in the assignment of blacks to load ammunition, but "there was nothing unfair or unjust in the final outcome of any of the Port Chicago courts martial."

It took all FDR's guile and Churchill's bullying to get the rival French leaders Henri Giraud and Charles de Gaulle to pose together at Casablanca in January 1943.

FDR never got over his dislike and distrust of de Gaulle. When they met, Americans with guns in hand waited outside, ready to spring in case of trouble. FDR had a happy time at Casablanca. He drove to Rabat to picnic on ham and sweet potatoes with 20,000 of the U.S. 5th Army while a band played "Alexander's Ragtime Band"; then, with his closest adviser, Harry Hopkins, he celebrated his sixty-first birthday on the plane home.

CHINA-LOVER
Cairo 1943

FDR made a big fuss over Generalissimo Chiang Kai-shek and his redoubtable wife when they came to his summit meeting with Churchill in Cairo on November 22–26, 1943. America had sent Chiang's Nationalist forces money and guns and military adviser Major General Joseph W. Stilwell. Now FDR promised China membership in "the Big Four" in the United Nations, with a great-power veto, and a major operation in the Andaman Sea off Burma. The latter idea was abandoned at Teheran, on the insistence of the British, who had a low opinion of Chiang's efforts.

DEALING WITH UNCLE JOE AND WINSTON

FDR was sure he could charm Uncle Joe, as he and Winston Churchill called the brutally unavuncular Marshal Joseph Stalin. When Ambassador William Bullitt warned him not to trust the Russians, FDR replied: "Bill, I don't dispute the logic of your reasoning. I just have a hunch that Stalin is not that kind of man. . . . I think that if I give everything I possibly can and ask nothing in return, noblesse oblige, he won't try to annex anything and will work with me for a world of democracy and peace." Bullitt countered that Stalin was "a Caucasian bandit whose only thought when he got something for nothing was that the other fellow was an ass." FDR, irritated, closed the subject. "It's my responsibility and not yours; I'm going to play my hunch."

Bullitt's account may have been self-serving, but throughout the Teheran summit, FDR was at pains to distance himself from Churchill. He said he did not want Stalin to think they had stacked the cards. He refused to caucus with Churchill before the formal sessions. He teased him, in front of Stalin, about John Bull and his Britishness. He turned him down for lunch and closeted himself with Stalin and Foreign Minister Vyacheslav Molotov. He told Churchill: "Stalin hates the guts of all your top people. He thinks he likes me better and I hope he will continue to do so." Churchill, filled with forebodings about Soviet ambitions, was in a black dog of a depression.

FDR got what he wanted at Teheran: a pledge that once Germany was beaten Russia would enter the war against Japan; and endorsement of his idea that four policemen—the U.S., Britain, China and Russia—would deal with threats to peace in a global postwar

THE DYING MAN: A haggard FDR, and Churchill, linger, alone at the Yalta conference table, February 1945. The President had only two months to live. Roosevelt's mind was still intact at Yalta, but his physical deterioration led to enduring rumors that Stalin had bamboozled a mentally enfeebled man.

security system, the embryo of the U.N. Security Council. A return to interwar unilateralism and even isolationism remained a danger in America. FDR had no desire to alarm public opinion before he had the structure he wanted. He was determined to exorcise the ghost of Woodrow Wilson and the overly idealistic League of Nations.

Stalin got what he wanted, too: control of Outer Mongolia and partial control of Manchuria, and an Allied commitment to make a second front in Europe the priority in 1944. He was successful in spiking Churchill's desire to focus on the Balkans, the area of Soviet aspirations. And he put the first nail in the coffin of a democratic Poland. FDR and Churchill hoped that they might yet save Poland, and fought for days at the Yalta conference in February 1945.

This most controversial of the Big Three summits was held amid an oversupply of bedbugs and a dearth of toilets in Czar Nicholas II's Livadia palace overlooking the Black Sea. FDR and Churchill, playing with matchsticks at Teheran, had already accepted the idea of moving 1939 Poland bodily to the west, to give Stalin the territory once occupied by the czars, with the Poles compensated by German territory to the west. At Yalta, they in the end accepted Stalin's fait accompli of a government based around the pro-Soviet Lublin Poles. The Red Army called the shots there. But they finally got what they presented as a genuine Soviet commitment to free and unfettered elections as soon as possible. These elections, said FDR, should be "like Caesar's wife. 'I did not know her but they said she was pure.'" Stalin replied enigmatically, "But in fact she had sins."

Malaya, Singapore, Hong Kong, the Dutch East Indies, southern Burma, the Philippines, northern New Guinea . . . the Japanese seemed unstoppable. In four months they routed the British, the Dutch and the Americans to gain all the land for their Greater East Asia Co-Prosperity Sphere with the loss of only 15,000 men, 380 aircraft and four destroyers. By February 1942 they menaced northern Australia. General Douglas MacArthur, arriving in Australia in March to take command of American and Australian forces, had few resources for defense, and still less for the counterattack he mounted. He had to do battle over a huge area of sea and coral islands and in pestilential jungle where disease might claim two or three times the number of casualties as the enemy. Large areas of the battleground of sea and land were uncharted. He had few ships, no long-range bombers.

And the American effort was divided. MacArthur had command of land, sea and air forces in the southwest Pacific; Admiral Chester Nimitz had charge of all the forces in the central and northern Pacific. MacArthur condemned the division of power as the worst decision of the war: "It resulted in divided effort, the waste of diffusion and duplication of force, and undue extension of war with added casualties and cost." The tactics of the two commanders could not have been more different. Nimitz was the head-down American footballer, MacArthur the Japanese judo artist. Nimitz subdued islands by the force of dogged and costly frontal assaults. MacArthur, with generally numerically inferior but faster moving forces, turned the enemy's strength against him by the tactic of bypassing and isolating strongholds: "Hit 'em where they ain't and let 'em die on the vine."

Apart from a superb fighter plane in the Zero, the Japanese had a massive technological inferiority: late and weak radar for ships and ground-warning, none for planes; underweight in artillery and tanks, and so deficient in antitank weapons they were reduced to using human mines, suicide soldiers who waited in holes to detonate bombs. What they did not lack was courage.

1 9 4 1

Dec. 7: Pearl Harbor.

Dec. 8: Japanese troops, landing on Thailand's Kra Isthmus, strike south in Malaya toward the British garrison of Singapore. Thailand surrenders. Japanese troops in southern China besiege Hong Kong.

—Thirty-six Japanese bombers hit strategic Wake Island, and 108 bombers destroy half of MacArthur's air force on Clark Field in the Philippines.

Dec. 10: In the space of two hours 96 Japanese shore-based planes sink the last effective Allied battleships in the Pacific, the brand-new British *Prince of Wales,* and the battle cruiser *Repulse.*

—The American and native garrison on Guam numbering a few hundred succumb to a Japanese force of 5,000.

Dec. 22: General Masaharu Homma lands 57,000 men on northern Luzon against MacArthur's force of 30,000 Americans and Filipino Scouts and 110,000 Filipino reservists.

Dec. 23: Wake's Marine garrison and civilian volunteers, vastly outnumbered, surrender. A U.S. naval relief force turns back, controversially. Some 470 servicemen and 1,146 civilians are taken prisoner. Several are executed for having resisted so tenaciously.

Dec. 25: The British, Canadian and Indian defenders of Hong Kong finally surrender. Days of mass rape and slaughter of the wounded follow.

1 9 4 2

Jan. 1: Japanese occupy Manila, capital of the Philippines, abandoned by MacArthur.

Jan. 10: Kuala Lumpur falls.

Jan. 11: Japan secures oil supplies by landings in Dutch East Indies islands of Borneo and Celebes.

Feb. 4: Australia yields island chains of New Britain and New Ireland with loss of Rabaul air base.

Feb. 15: The blackest day in British military history. General Arthur Percival, commander of the island garrison of Singapore, walks out with a white flag to surrender 130,000 troops to General Tomoyuki Yamashita, who had conquered Malaya in 54 days. The British, Australian and Indian troops outnumbered the attackers at least two to one, but they had bad generalship and no air cover. And Churchill had not taken heed of American advice that Singapore was in danger if he did not give it priority over North Africa.

Feb. 19: The north Australian port of Darwin is bombed by 188 Japanese planes.

Feb. 27: A Dutch, British, Australian and American fleet is destroyed by a Japanese fleet of comparable size in the battle of Java Sea.

March 8: Outnumbered five to one, Dutch, Australian and British troops surrender the strategic Dutch East Indies island of Java.

March 8–10: Unopposed invasion of northern New Guinea, under British and Australian rule. Japan's farthest southern conquest.

March 11: MacArthur smuggled out of besieged Corregidor.

April 9: Epic four-month struggle to hold Bataan peninsula ends with General Edward King's surrender of his half-starved garrison of some 11,600 American and 65,000 Filipino soldiers. Malaria had crippled the Japanese, too, but Homma had been reinforced in March with 22,000 fresh troops, more guns and planes.

April 15: Eighty-two men in 16 carrier-based B-25s, led by Lieutenant Colonel James Doolittle, fly to bomb Tokyo, Kobe and Osaka without enough fuel to return. Seventy survive after crash and parachute landings in China and Siberia. The raid does little damage but is a boost for American morale, provokes Japan to keep four fighter groups at home and precipitates the attack on Midway in June.

April 29: Japanese capture Lashio, cutting terminus of "Burma Road" and thereby isolating Chinese Nationalists.

May 6: Corregidor island fortress with 15,000 men, surrendered by General Jonathan Wainwright. Several hundred American and Filipino troops continue guerrilla fighting on other Philippine islands —until MacArthur's return.

May 7–8: Battle of Coral Sea, first fought by planes from out-of-sight carriers, frustrates Japanese plans for seaborne landings at Port Moresby, New Guinea. Using their "Magic" interception and decryption of Japanese code, U.S. Pacific Fleet fights larger force to standstill. U.S. loses carrier *Lexington* and *Yorktown* is damaged. Japanese light carrier *Shoho* is sunk and *Shokaku* badly damaged.

May 19: Burma falls.

June 4–6: U.S. triumph in battle of Midway reverses course of war in Pacific.

June 7: *Chicago Tribune* reveals that U.S. code-breaking is central to Midway victory. Tokyo misses the story.

June 8: Japanese army engineers land on fevered jungle island of Guadalcanal to build an air base, part of a plan to seize Port Moresby, New Guinea, and sea off Australia.

Aug. 7–8: In first U.S. amphibious operation since 1898, and first Pacific offensive, U.S. 1st Marine Division chases off a Japanese garrison of 2,200 men on Guadalcanal, seizes the unfinished airstrip and names it Henderson Field for a Marine pilot killed at Midway. Landing marks opening of Guadalcanal campaign in which Japanese land troops at night by "Tokyo Express" convoys, and U.S. Navy tries to stop them to keep control of what campaign's promoter Admiral Ernest King calls the main road to Tokyo—off Queensland.

Aug. 9: Night battle off Savo Island. Vice Admiral Gun'ichi Mikawa sinks four U.S. cruisers but misses U.S. transports unloading troops.

Aug. 20–21: On Guadalcanal, U.S. Marines wipe out 815 men of chhiki Detachment, ending myth of invincibility of Japanese jungle-fighter.

Aug. 24: Battle of Eastern Solomons. Japanese land 1,000 men, but lose carrier, cruiser, destroyer and 70 planes. On and, Marines beat back desperate attempts to take "Bloody Ridge" commanding Henderson Field.

Sept. 17: Japanese advance on Port Moresby halted 30 miles away, at Imita Ridge.

Sept. 18: 4,200 Marines get ashore at Guadalcanal.

Oct. 26: Marines repulse drive on Henderson Field. Offshore, in battle of Santa Cruz, U.S. suffers sinking of new *Hornet* carrier.

Nov. 2: Australians retake Kokoda airstrip, New Guinea.

Nov. 12–15: First major duel of battleships since World War I's battle of Jutland. Americans suffer six ships sunk or crippled off Guadalcanal, including the *Juneau* with 700 men lost. Among them are the five Sullivan brothers. Japanese lose two battleships and land only 4,000 of 12,000 reinforcements.

Nov. 30: Japanese naval force trying to supply starving Japanese on Guadalcanal mauls U.S. in battle of Tassafaronga, but does not get through.

Dec. 1: MacArthur puts General Robert Eichelberger in charge of Australian-American attack on Papuan beachhead of Buna: "Bob, take Buna or don't come back alive."

1 9 4 3

Jan. 1: American troops in Pacific reach 460,000—60,000 more than in European theater.

Jan. 2: Eichelberger takes Buna.

Jan. 16: Japanese make last-ditch stand at Sanananda, last Papuan outpost. Losses: 12,000 dead out of 20,000. Out of 60,000 committed, Australia loses 2,000 dead and U.S. 980, plus 37,000 sick from tropical diseases.

Feb. 9: End of organized Japanese resistance on Guadalcanal.

---

campaign cost 25,000 Imperial soldiers killed by battle or disease out of 36,000. American dead: 1,592 of 60,000 committed. Japanese stragglers live on in jungle: last known survivor surrenders October 1947.

March 2–3: In battle of Bismarck Sea, General George Kenney's land-based Flying Fortresses, flying low, knock out four destroyers and many transports, ruining Japanese attempt to reinforce key northeast New Guinea outpost at Lae. More than 300 Allied planes machine-gun men struggling in the water.

April 18: Admiral Yamamoto, architect of Pearl Harbor, killed on inspection tour after Admiral Halsey learns of itinerary from code breakers. Sixteen American P-38 Lightning fighters from Henderson Field jump Yamamoto's cortege with approval of Admiral Nimitz and FDR.

A poster issued by the Oldsmobile division of General Motors. More than a third of the nation's arms production was centered in Detroit.

June 30: Start of Operation Cartwheel: south Pacific thrust under MacArthur, central Pacific thrust under Nimitz and Raymond Spruance, to cut off Japan from its new empire. Admiral Halsey opens MacArthur's campaign by island-hopping Marine and Army forces northwest from Guadalcanal along the Solomons chain to New Georgia. They take Munda airfield and subdue the island by mid-August, leading the Japanese to abandon their other garrisons in the Solomons.

Sept.: Japan suffers a one-month record of 172,982 gross tons of shipping lost to American submarines.

Sept. 16: Australian and American troops recapture Lae, New Guinea.

Nov. 3: Japanese 18th Division surrounds three of Stilwell's Chinese battalions in Hukawng Valley in northern Burma, where American engineers are building Ledo Road through jungles in southern slopes of Himalayas, one of war's most ambitious engineering efforts. Stilwell flies in to rescue his troops.

Nov. 15: Admiral Lord Louis Mountbatten given new Allied Southeast Asia Command to regain Burma and reopen supply lines to Chiang in China. Soon after, British begin advance into Arakan region of Burma, in conjunction with operations behind enemy lines by 3,000 American volunteers organized in a provisional unit code-named Galahad, later known as Merrill's Marauders for their short-term commander, Brigadier General Frank Merrill.

Nov. 20: Nimitz begins central Pacific thrust for Japan with landings on Makin Atoll and Tarawa in the Gilbert Islands. Makin is easily taken, but Tarawa is one of bloodiest battle in Marine Corps history, with 1,000 dead in six days. Of Japanese garrison of 4,836, only 17 survive. The atolls provide base for assault on the Marshall Islands.

Nov. 21: Marines and GIs establish beachhead on Bougainville with aim of building airfield for bombing of stronghold of Rabaul on New Britain.

Dec. 15: First Marine Division lands at Cape Gloucester, New Britain.

Dec. 26: Airfield at Cape Gloucester secured for daily bombing raids on Rabaul, isolated for rest of war.

1 9 4 4

Jan. 31: Japan loses first national territory, undefended atoll of Majuro in Marshalls.

Feb. 1: U.S. continues assault on Japan's outer defense perimeter

---

in the central Pacific, landing on Kwajalein in the Marshalls after a 36,000-shell bombardment. It falls within a week.

Feb. 17–21: Rear Admiral Marc Mitscher's lightning carrier-based raids on Truk, headquarters of Japanese Combined Fleet, destroy 275 planes and sink 39 merchantmen and warships.

Feb. 18: Marines land on Eniwetok Atoll, where brilliantly concealed Japanese put up suicidal fight. Atoll secured by Feb. 23 with 2,677 Japanese and 339 American dead.

Feb. 29–March 18: MacArthur himself lands with armored cavalry on Admiralty Islands, supposedly evacuated but still held by 4,000 Japanese. With reinforcements and 7th Fleet, islands secure by April 3, providing fine harbor.

March 8: Japanese in Burma halt British and Chinese advances and invade India with 150,000 men.

April 22: MacArthur leapfrogs along New Guinea coast, surprising the 14,000-man Hollandia garrison, who have no air cover and soon give in. Kill-ratio of 51:1 with 4,441 Japanese dead for 87 Americans.

May 17: The Galahads and part of Stilwell's 30th Chinese Division having hazarded steep mountain trails, seize Myitkyina airfield in surprise attack. Exhausted Galahads, who had been promised only three months in Burma, are down to 900 men. Stilwell forces sick and wounded out of evacuation hospitals to begin grueling siege of Myitkyina town on route of Ledo Road.

May 27: First assault on Biak Island defended by 10,000 holed up in caves. Fight goes on to June 21, with 524 American and 5,093 Japanese dead.

June 13–19: Spruance assembles a great flotilla of 535 ships off Saipan in the Marianas, defended by 32,500 Japanese. U.S. raids destroy over 100 Japanese planes on the ground. On June 15, 71,000 Marines begin to land under Lieutenant General Holland "Howlin' Mad" Smith. It is so tough he puts in his reserve 27th (former National Guard) Division.

e 15: Forty-seven B-29 nbers from China airfields nb Japanese steel city of ata.

e 19–20: Greatest carrier tle of the war (three times ger than Midway). Admiral Jis-aro Ozawa sets out to destroy . Pacific Fleet with nine-rier fleet, 473 sea-based nes and more on Guam. Ad-al Spruance, with Vice Admi-Mitscher, has 15 carriers, 6 planes and more experi-ced pilots in new Grumman F (Hellcat), which outperforms e Zero. Spruance also has de-pts of Japanese battle plan. e battle of the Philippine Sea, Great Marianas Turkey Shoot, pilots call it, smashes Japa-se airpower: 480 planes are t along with three carriers, in-ding Ozawa's flagship. Total herican losses are 130 planes, ly 76 aviators. Signs begin to pear openly in Japanese naval ices calling for Tōjō's death.

ne 22: After 80-day siege, In-an city of Imphal relieved by Al-d troops. Japanese 15th Army gins retreat to Burma in early ly. Only 20,000 of its 85,000 en are still alive, with half the sses due to disease and mine. Much of Indian National my dissolves under mistreat-ent by Japanese commanders.

ne 24: On Saipan, Holland nith, outraged by slowness of 7th Division in Death Valley, asks ruance to relieve 27th's com-ander, General Ralph Smith. An my General being sacked by an dmiral at the request of a Marine oduces epic interservice row.

uly 6: On Saipan, Admiral huichi Nagumo (of Pearl Harbor nd Midway) and General Yoshi-sugu Saito commit hara-kiri to ncourage final banzai charges y surviving 3,000 troops.

uly 9: Saipan officially secure, vith 26,000 Japanese soldiers ead. U.S. suffers 3,500 dead nd 13,000 wounded or sick. Of he island's civilian population, 2,000 perish. Thousands com-nit suicide, with hundreds jump-ng off sea cliffs.

uly 18: Disasters produce res-gnation of General Hideki Tōjō, eplaced by General Kuniaki Koiso, rightist nationalist in-olved in Mukden Incident in 1931.

uly 21: Marines land on Guam.

GUTS, AND GENIUS, EXPOSE THE JAPANESE HEARTLAND TO THE ULTIMATE BLOW

Admiral Yamamoto, who knew America better than his peers, had predicted that after six months or a year of running wild Japan would be overwhelmed by "the automobile factories in Detroit and the oil-fields in Texas." The only hope was that the swift "lib-eration" of Malaya, Singapore, Hong Kong, the East Indies and the Philippines, and the destruction of the U.S. Pacific Fleet, would give Japan so much strength in space and resources that the Americans would tire of the bloodshed and agree to a peace that would leave Japan master of the Pacific. Japanese strategy was based on this wishful estimation of American re-solve. Until November 1943, there seemed to be merit in it. The Japanese, anchored in Rabaul, held on to their defensive perimeter of islands in the central and southwest Pacific. But thereafter they were in perpet-ual retreat before a vast expansion of U.S. naval and air power: Japan launched 5 carriers between 1941 and 1944, America 21.

The basic American strategy was to conduct holding operations in Burma and China, with the British and the Chinese Nationalists, and to attack Japan from the southwest by air and sea. This meant ejecting the enemy from small fortress islands and

major islands (New Guinea, the Philippines), using them as stepping-stones for the bombing and invasion of Japan itself. Command was divided between the Navy and the Army. MacArthur was to thrust from New Guinea to the Philippines and then to Japan. Nimitz planned to island-hop westward from Hawaii through the Marianas to Formosa and Japan. The two-prong strategy has been defended as keeping the Japanese off balance, but it was due more to interservice rivalry and the clash of powerful personalities.

It was a war of distances. The Pacific occupies one third of the earth's surface. In the southwest Pacific alone, MacArthur contended for atolls and fetid islands scattered over an area as large as mainland America. He superimposed a sketch of the United States on his huge chart of the southwest Pacific, to

remind everyone that moving men and matériel from the Solomons to the Philippines was akin to moving them from Miami to Seattle. Even to reach this theater, America had to project its power 6,000 miles from the mainland. Five men and their supplies could be got to Europe for the merchant tonnage required to put two into the defense of Australia and the retaking of the Philippines. But Yamamoto's prophecies were fulfilled. By 1945, Japan's defense perimeter had been lost, its navy shattered, its air force confined to kamikazes. It lay exposed to total destruction from the air.

TOUGH TERRAIN: The Japanese typically dug into rock and sand and fought to the last man. In W. Eugene Smith's photograph, Marines blast the enemy from a cave on Hill 382, Iwo Jima.

July 25–26: Suicidal banzai charge by 5,000 Japanese on Guam; 3,200 die.

July 26: Roosevelt, MacArthur and Nimitz confer at Pearl Harbor. Nimitz wants attack on Formosa, MacArthur on Philippines. MacArthur wins.

Aug. 1: Small island of Tinian in Marianas falls, giving U.S. bombers access to Japanese main islands—eventual takeoff point for atomic bomb missions.

Aug. 3: Japanese evacuate Myitkyina, making way for Ledo Road builders.

Aug. 11: Guam is secure, with loss of 1,744 American dead. Small groups of Japanese stay in jungles for decades.

Sept. 15: Nimitz rejects Halsey's proposal to bypass the Palau Islands, but they are more heavily defended than realized. Marines begin assault on Peleliu, held by 10,500 Japanese in caves. For every Japanese soldier killed, 1,589 rounds of ammunition expended. First Marine Regiment wins eight Medals of Honor—and suffers 53.7 percent casualties. Marine and Army cost: 1,950 lives.

Oct. 17: Assault on vast Philippines archipelago opens with U.S. Army Rangers securing islands of Homonhon, Suluan and Dinagat off Leyte.

Oct. 20: MacArthur wades ashore on Leyte. "People of the Philippines, I have returned!" Two U.S. corps land from 420 transports, backed by 157 warships.

Oct. 23–25: Three Japanese fleets of 63 major warships converge on Leyte Gulf for climactic air-sea battles. Halsey falls for Japanese decoy and takes his 98 combat vessels and 1,000 aircraft northward in pursuit of Ozawa's force, which is almost empty of planes. This leaves Thomas Kinkaid's 7th Fleet, protecting MacArthur landings, exposed to pincer movement from fleets led by Admirals Takeo Kurita and Shoji Nishimura. But fight by U.S. rear guard and confusion induce Kurita to retire when he has landing fleet at his mercy in Leyte Gulf. Japanese lose four carriers, three battleships, six heavy cruisers, three light cruisers and ten destroyers, against U.S. losses of only one light carrier, two escort carriers and three destroyers.

REUNION: MacArthur embraces Wainwright (left) at the Japanese surrender ceremony in 1945.

GENERAL DOUGLAS MACARTHUR (1880–1964)

The Allied commander of the southwest Pacific area was an American Caesar, an authentic military genius and egomaniac. The son of a Spanish-American War general, he graduated from West Point with its third highest grade in history (98.14, against Robert E. Lee's 98.33). A lifelong hatred of Washington's unbloodied bureaucrats began when they denied him a congressional Medal of Honor for bravery in the Vera Cruz expedition. He won fame as the youngest divisional commander of World War I, dubbed "the d'Artagnan of the Western Front" for his flamboyance and daring. Then he went back to West Point as superintendent and swept away the outdated curriculum. In 1936 he opposed FDR's budget cuts and took a job as field marshal of the Philippine Army. Washington put him on the retired list in 1937, but FDR recalled him at age 61.

The valiant six-month stand on the Bataan peninsula and the rocks of Corregidor seemed like good news after all the defeats, and it upset the Japanese timetable. MacArthur himself was daringly and reluctantly rescued from the siege by submarine in March. "Hold out until I come for you," he said on handing over command to General Jonathan Wainwright. "I shall return." He was furious when Wainwright surrendered in May, and tried to deny him a decoration. It took 2½ years for MacArthur to return, all of which time Wainwright endured a Japanese prison camp, but the MacArthur campaign in the Pacific was brilliant in concept and execution. He fought his way from Australia back to the Philippines with 27,684 casualties—the Anzio campaign in Italy alone cost double that number of casualties.

UNIT 731—AND OTHER CRIMES IN A TRAIL OF ATROCITIES

We know now—after years of cover-up by both the Japanese and the U.S.—that five years before the rape of Nanking in 1937 Japanese doctors and technicians in Manchuria began carrying out agonizing war experiments on thousands of victims and fomented plagues of cholera, anthrax and paratyphoid in parts of China. "Unit 731," one of a network of biological warfare centers, was a horrific agency. It dissected prisoners without anesthetics, inserted knives into organs to see which produced the quickest death, drilled skulls, subjected victims to pressure changes until their bodies exploded, removed entrails from live bodies. Some 200,000 Chinese died in these experiments. In the war, American and British prisoners were tortured with infections. But as shocking as this savagery is, at the end of the war

the United States excused the leading criminals and recruited them into American studies of bacteriological warfare.

Throughout the Pacific war, Japanese soldiery committed atrocity after atrocity when they were not well commanded. Hundreds of American, British and Australian prisoners were bayoneted and beheaded and obscenely mutilated; nuns were raped, then murdered; civilians were lined up for mass machine-gunning. Conditions in the prisoner-of-war camps were execrable; starvation, disease and random brutality made death part of the daily schedule. Reports in 1941–42 of what the invaders had done in Southeast Asia understandably inflamed Allied sentiment. The Japanese samurai code was said to have instilled the idea that those who surren-

General Tomoyuki Yamashita (1885–1946) at his war-crimes trial after the war. He was hanged on February 23, 1946, for the murder of Filipinos in Manila. General Masaharu Homma (1887–1946) went before a firing squad on April 3, 1946, for the Bataan Death March.

These were injustices that stained the record of General MacArthur, who ordered the trials. In the words of his biographer, William Manchester, MacArthur's chief wartime adversaries were "tried and convicted by kangaroo courts which flouted justice with the Supreme Commander's approval and probably at his urging."

Yamashita had withdrawn from Manila and declared it an open city. The crimes in Manila were the work of Vice Admiral Sanji Iwabuchi, who had 15,000 sailors and marines under his command, and did not recognize Yamashita's authority. The blood of Bataan was on the hands of Colonel Masanobu Tsuji. Homma was considered too kind by the Japanese High Command; he was relieved of his command on June 9, 1940, and spent the rest of the war in Japan. Tsuji escaped to become an adviser to Chiang Kai-shek until 1949, when he went home to Japan. Homma and Yamashita had not ordered or condoned the atrocities. They were found guilty because they had "command responsibility"— but by that reasoning so did Emperor Hirohito.

dered were dishonored, but that had no relevance to the defenseless women and children who were massacred. The worst incident was in 1945, in Manila, where Japanese sailors and marines murdered 100,000 Filipinos.

The most notorious ill treatment of American soldiers followed the 1942 surrender of Bataan, though it did not become known until 1945. The survivors, many already sick and starving, numbered 76,600—11,600 Americans and 65,000 Filipinos. Some 400 Filipino officers and NCOs were at once hacked to death by sword. About half the prisoners were taken to prison camp by truck. The rest had 12 days of horror, dragging themselves more than 60 miles without much food or water, terrorized by the guards. In the walking groups of 500 to 1,000 some were well treated, but in others the weak were bayoneted, run over by trucks, exposed to the sun without water and then buried alive. About 25,000 died, including 5,200 Americans. It was well described as a "death march." The novel and movie *The Bridge over the River Kwai* dramatized the beatings, neglect and malnutrition that killed 12,568 of the 60,000 American, British and Australian prisoners, and 87,500 Asians, forced to build a railway from Burma into Thailand.

A high proportion of prisoners in Japanese hands did not survive—as many as 40 percent of the Americans held in Japan. In German or Italian hands, an Allied prisoner was fairly certain to survive, with a death rate below 4 percent. (But the Germans were systematic about killing Russians. Some 60 percent of the Soviet prisoners taken by the Nazis died in captivity—double the death rate of Germans held by the Soviets.) The Allies brought war-crimes charges against 5,700 Japanese, including fourteen Japanese generals, three admirals, five career diplomats and three bureaucrats. The trials were a shambles by comparison with Nuremberg. Seven Japanese leaders were hanged, including Prime Minister Tōjō and Iwane Matsui, who was in command in China at the time of the rape of Nanking.

SHOWDOWN AT MIDWAY

Five minutes on the beautiful morning of June 4, 1942, were fatal for Japan's ambitions for a Pacific empire. It took only that long to decide a battle in which the Japanese committed their entire fleet to annihilating the very much weaker American Pacific Fleet. Victory would have given the Japanese dominance of the Pacific and an impregnable island defense chain from the north to the south Pacific. Hawaii, the Fijis and Port Moresby would have been exposed. America's West Coast would have been vulnerable to bombing raids.

The Japanese plan was to lure what was left of the Pacific Fleet north from its Pearl Harbor lair by attacks on the Aleutian Islands, strung out between Alaska and Siberia, and on Midway Island, the "sentry" coral atoll 1,100 miles northwest of Hawaii. With luck, the Americans would split their fleet, some decoyed to the Aleutians on June 3, the rest surely drawn to Midway by an invasion on June 5. The mightiest battle fleet the world had ever seen would be there waiting to pounce. Admiral Isoroku Yamamoto led a combined fleet of 11 battleships, 8 carriers, 22 cruisers and 43 destroyers—162 warships in all, with more than 400 carrier planes, plus the bombers Japan expected to be flying from Midway by then. U.S. Pacific Fleet Commander Admiral Chester Nimitz had only three carriers.

The Americans might well have fallen into Yamamoto's trap, but for the code breakers on Hawaii and in Melbourne, the faith Nimitz had in them and, in particular, in the inspired Pearl Harbor cryptanalyst Commander Joe Rochefort. The Navy commander in chief, Admiral Ernest King, did not like or trust Rochefort, and Washington Naval Intelligence and the Joint Intelligence Committee thought the Japanese were going to attack in the south. It was only on May 17, with new information from Melbourne, that King came around to Nimitz's judgment that Midway was the anvil. Nimitz boldly ordered his three carriers, *Enterprise, Hornet* and *Yorktown,* to take up positions northeast of Midway. He acted quickly enough to have them on station before the Japanese submarine screen arrived. At dawn on June 4, American and

Bursts of anti-aircraft fire from the *Yorktown* and escorts, noon, June 4, 1942. Wildcats had already brought down half the force of eighteen Val dive-bombers. Anti-aircraft fire got two more, but six bombers got through the fire and made three hits. At 2:42 ten Kate torpedo planes attacked, and two torpedoes hit. The *Yorktown* was abandoned, but 2,270 men were saved and the carrier stayed afloat. It would have been saved to fight again, but three days later it was sunk by a Japanese submarine.

Japanese battle fleets were converging unseen on each other.

Yamamoto had placed in the vanguard the commander of the carrier force at Pearl Harbor, Admiral Chuichi Nagumo, who was on his flagship, the carrier *Akagi,* with three other carriers, *Kaga, Hiryu* and *Soryu.* Yamamoto steamed in reserve a few hundred miles west of Nagumo, with seven battleships, two seaplane carriers and a light carrier. Nagumo launched 108 bombers against Midway from 215 miles out. He was still in ignorance of the American warships, but as a precaution kept back 93 planes armed with torpedoes. Ten minutes before his first wave struck Midway, at 6:30 a.m., Nagumo's carriers were spotted by a Catalina search plane. Midway sent 15 Superfortresses, four Army Marauders, and six Avenger torpedo planes

against the carriers. They scored no hits on any of them, and 17 planes were lost, but the attacks were not fruitless. They convinced Nagumo that he must destroy Midway's airfield with a second strike.

At 7:15 a.m., he ordered the 93 bombers off the flight deck, to be stripped of torpedoes and reequipped with bombs, an hour's work. At 7:28 a.m., one of his spotter planes vaguely reported "ten American ships" 210 miles northeast of Midway, where none were supposed to be. Nagumo was thrown. His brilliant Pearl Harbor air planner, Commander Minoru Genda, was not on the bridge with him; he was down with a fever. At 7:45 a.m., Nagumo changed his mind about bombing Midway. He ordered that those planes still with torpedoes should keep them, so as to be able to attack warships. And in the middle

of the frantic turmoil he had created, he had to clear all the flight decks to recover the first wave of returning Midway bombers.

Admiral Raymond "Electric Brain" Spruance, commander of *Enterprise* and *Hornet*, was making good use of Nagumo's second thoughts. On hearing of the raid on Midway, Spruance and his intelligence officer, Captain Miles Browning, worked out that if they took the risk of launching planes early, dangerously at the edge of their 175-mile combat radius, they might catch the Japanese carrier groups while they were refueling and rearming. Just after 7 a.m.—15 minutes before Nagumo's order to change the bombers' weapons—Spruance sent off every bomber from both *Enterprise* and *Hornet* (67 Dauntless dive-bombers, 29 Devastator torpedo bombers) with Wildcat fighter escorts. On *Yorktown*, Admiral Frank Fletcher followed up 98 minutes later with 17 dive-bombers and 12 torpedo bombers.

The American pilots had first to find the enemy. *Hornet*'s 35 dive-bombers failed; their fighter escorts ran out of fuel and ditched in the sea. *Hornet*'s 15-plane Torpedo Squadron Eight under Lieutenant Commander John Waldron was the first to spot the carriers, but the squadron had become separated from its high-flying fighter escort. It was an act of supreme heroism for Waldron and his pilots to hurl their slow old Devastators into wave-level attack without protection against swarms of Zero fighters. Only one of 30 Americans survived. None of their obsolete torpedoes hit. Fourteen Devastators from *Enterprise*'s Torpedo Six tried next. They, too, failed and 10 of them were shot down. At 10 a.m., *Yorktown*'s Torpedo Three arrived. Eleven of the 13 planes were destroyed making their runs at sea level, again without the bravery yielding a single hit. It must have seemed to Admiral Nagumo that the Americans had shot their bolt with a last do-or-die raid.

By this time, Nagumo had been told the American "ships" included carriers, and he knew they were an hour's flying time east. There was nothing to prevent him from destroying them. As soon as the last Devastator had been shot down, at 10:24, Nagumo gave the order for the killer blow. Within five minutes he would have 93 superior bombers in the air with torpedoes. Out of the blue at the exact same moment, Commander Mitsuo Fuchida on *Akagi* noted: "A lookout screamed, 'Hell-divers.' I looked up to see three black enemy planes plummeting towards our ship."

The planes were Dauntless dive-bombers from *Enterprise*, led by Lieutenant Commander Clarence W. McClusky, and there were 37 of them, screaming down in a 70-degree dive at 280 knots. There were no deadly Zero fighters to stop them; the torpedo pilots who had sacrificed themselves minutes before had drawn the Zeros to sea level, and the Zero pilots had no time to regain altitude. In minutes Dauntless bombs devastated both the *Akagi* and *Kaga* carriers, their decks packed with loaded bombers, explosives and fuel lines. Nagumo had to be dragged off his blazing flagship. Between 10:25 and 10:28 a separate force of 17 dive-bombers from *Yorktown* under Lieutenant Commander Maxwell F. Leslie scored three direct hits on the *Soryu*. The fourth carrier, *Hiryu*, managed to get off 40 bombers and fighters. At 12:20 p.m. they disabled the *Yorktown*. It was *Hiryu*'s last strike. The *Enterprise*'s Lieutenant W. E. Gallagher found *Hiryu* and broke through her screen of fighters with 24 dive-bombers. Four direct hits finished the *Hiryu*.

June 4 at Midway was a brilliant victory of American naval intelligence, calculation and courage that Fuchida called "dauntless." Washington stole the credit from Rochefort; he was twice denied the Distinguished Service Medal recommended by Nimitz. Spruance was disparaged by underlings for failing to pursue the rest of the Japanese fleet. That would have been disastrous. Yamamoto was waiting with his battleships, hoping America's unprotected carriers would blunder into them. Commander Genda had a better summing up: "We goofed!" Japan lost all four of its large fast carriers; about 100 pilots—a year's output—330 aircraft and 3,500 seamen. A despairing Yamamoto retreated with his battle fleet. It was the end of Japanese expansion in the Pacific.

Oct. 25: First kamikaze ("di wind") suicide dives on U.S. ships by 24 volunteer pilots one escort carrier and dam others in Leyte Gulf.

Nov. 24: In first raid on To since Doolittle's, 110 B-29s t off from Saipan.

Dec. 2: General Sir Will Slim's troops take city of Kale in new Burma drive.

1945

Jan. 9: The U.S. 6th Army inva Luzon at Lingayen, initially land 67,000 and building to 175,0 General Yamashita has 262,0 men, but only 200 planes and navy.

Jan. 12: Resistance on Leyte c lapses. All but 5,000 of the or inal 70,000 defenders kille Americans lose only 3,500 250,000 invading army.

Jan. 27: Counterattacking C nese forces finally reopen Burr Road.

Jan. 31: All major airfields on L zon in U.S. hands.

Feb. 3: First Cavalry penetrat into Manila.

Feb. 16: U.S. Paratroops mal surprise landing on rocks of Cc regidor.

Feb. 19: Armada of 435 shi lands some 30,000 Marines Iwo Jima, 660 miles from Japa Three days of war's heaviest a sea bombardment destroys few than 200 of 915 defense posts caves and rock, and 4,574 Ame icans are killed or wounded.

MIDWAY VICTOR

Admiral Raymond Ames Spruance (1886–1969): Unsurpassed as battle commander, bold bu calculating.

. 23: Stars and Stripes raised
Mount Suribachi, Iwo Jima,
famously photographed.

rch 4: Manila liberated at
t of 1,000 U.S. and 100,000
lian dead, some civilians held
tage and shot by Japanese.

rch 9: LeMay stages first in-
diary bombing raid on Tokyo.
m bases in Mariana Islands,
9 B-29 Superfortresses cre-
a fireball that reaches tem-
atures of 18,000 degrees,
ns out 16 square miles of
wntown and kills between
,000 and 130,000 people,
h loss of only 14 planes. In
xt nine days, cities of Nagoya,
aka, and Kobe firebombed,
ing hundreds of thousands
re civilians.

rch 17: Nimitz declares Iwo
ma secure at cost of 4,189
ad and 19,938 wounded in 26
ys, costliest battle in 168
ars of Marine Corps. Fighting
es on for another 10 days and
724 casualties. Nearly all
,000 defenders killed.

ril 1: Assault on Okinawa. Sup-
rted by some 1,300 warships
d transports, first 60,000 of
sault force of 183,000 lands.
itish Royal Navy joins in with
st carrier force of 22 ships and
44 planes.

pril 5: General Koiso resigns as
ime minister, replaced by mod-
ate Admiral Kantarō Suzuki.

pril 6: Blitz by 355 kamikazes
d 341 conventional bombers
nks three destroyers, transport,
vo munitions ships, off Okinawa.
By July nearly 2,000 kamikazes
nk or damage 263 ships.)

–Great new battleship *Yamato*
teams out of Inland Sea in sui-
idal attempt to reach Okinawa.
estroyed by U.S. bombers. Last
ortie by Imperial Navy.

April 16: Seventy-seventh Divi-
ion lands on Ie Shima off Okinawa. Ernie Pyle, famous war
orrespondent, killed by sniper.

May 3: British and Indian troops
narch into Rangoon.

May 12: Japanese Supreme
Council for the Conduct of the
War openly discusses surrender
or first time.

May 23: Two B-29 raids of over
500 planes drop more than 6,000
incendiaries on Tokyo. Over half
the city, more than 50 square
miles, now a smoking ruin. Over

INVISIBLE ENEMIES

The Pacific naval war was dominated by aircraft carriers and their dive-bombers and torpedo planes. The
Japanese gained early control of the seas, though they
were not the first to exploit the capacity of the carrier
to sink battleships a couple of hundred miles away.
Pearl Harbor was inspired by a British triumph in
November 1940, when 21 flimsy Swordfish torpedo
bombers wreaked havoc on Italy's navy in Taranto,
flying from an unseen carrier 170 miles away.

At the beginning of the war, America had three
fast fleet carriers in the Pacific; the Japanese had six.
The U.S. Navy had four times as many planes as the
Japanese 1,250, but its Wildcat fighters were inferior
to the Japanese Zero, which had a combat radius of
1,160 miles, nearly 400 miles more than the Wildcat.
And American torpedoes were duds.

There were compensations for these initial Japa-

nese advantages. In Admirals King and Nimitz,
America had leaders of strategic vision and organizing genius, and in Admirals Spruance and Halsey redoubtable sea commanders. The Americans had
superior eyes and ears: they knew what the Japanese
were going to do. From 1940, the "Magic" code machine read the Japanese "Purple" diplomatic code,
and by April 1942 the U.S. code breakers were also
deciphering about a third of any message transmitted in the Japanese naval code—a key factor in the
turning-point battle of Midway that June. Secondly,
the Americans were ahead on radar, which the
Japanese had neglected. American battle triumphs
in the central Pacific owed much to radar for air and
surface search, gunfire control, identification of aircraft and navigation.

And the Japanese were continually amazed by

FAMOUS DECK: A Curtis Helldiver returning, 1945, to the USS *Hornet*, one of the victors of Midway, and the launchpad for the 16 B-25s under Colonel Jimmy Doolittle that bombed Tokyo on April 18, 1942.

GENERALS STILWELL
AND CHENNAULT

America's leaders in the China-Burma-India theater were General Joseph Stilwell (1883–1946) (left) and General Claire Chennault (1890–1958). They clashed. "Vinegar Joe" Stilwell, in command of U.S. Army forces and chief of staff to Chiang Kai-shek from January 1942, controlled Lend-Lease supplies and insisted on priority for men and arms on the ground. He was scornful of Chennault's conviction that given just 350 fighters and 150 bombers he could beat the Japanese almost on his own.

Chennault had quit the Air Corps in 1937, a bronchitic from eight packs of cigarettes a day and an isolated fighters-first man among the big-bomber advocates. He wheedled 100 obsolescent P-40s for Chiang and early in 1941 recruited American volunteers to fly them (for $600 to $750 a month and a $500 bonus for every kill). These "Flying Tigers," with a tiger shark's teeth painted on the nose, claimed to have shot down 299 enemy planes, with the loss of only 13 pilots in the six months from December 20, 1941, to July 4, 1942, when a handful were inducted into the AAF. A more plausible kill-rate is just under two to one, similar to the RAF's in the battle of Britain, still a spectacular achievement. Chennault—with a link to FDR through his press officer, Joe Alsop, the President's cousin—was a better operator than Stilwell and kept sweet with Chiang. Chiang, angered by Stilwell's charges of corruption and his campaign that Nationalists should join forces with the Communists, forced Vinegar Joe's recall in October 1944. He was replaced by Major General Albert C. Wedemeyer.

American energy. They never expected the aircraft carrier *Yorktown* to appear at Midway. In the battle of the Coral Sea in May she had been shattered with a direct hit by an 800-pound bomb. The repairs would normally have taken three months. An astonishing effort by 1,400 men in the Pearl Harbor Navy Yard had her back at sea in two days.

In the end, America simply overwhelmed the Japanese. By the end of the war, Japan could barely put up 1,000 planes against America's 22,000. The Japanese began with fine pilots but failed in a system for replacing the dead. After Midway, their pilots were in combat within a few months of their first flight. The American pilots they came up against had two years' training, and from the late summer of 1943 they were in the Hellcat, which could outperform the Zero.

PILOT DEBRIEFING: In the ready room of the new *Yorktown*, a pilot describes dive-bombing mission over Wake Island, October 1943. The first *Yorktown* was sunk by a Japanese submarine just after the battle of Midway.

THE LAST GREAT BATTLES:
IWO JIMA AND OKINAWA

America paid dearly to plant the Stars and Stripes on Japanese soil. Iwo Jima, 8 square miles of volcanic rock, 660 miles from the main islands of Japan, cost 6,821 lives, most of them Marines, in five weeks. Twenty thousand were wounded. Nearly all 21,000 defenders perished. Okinawa, 500 miles from the homeland, was even bloodier. Sixty-seven miles long and fortified with a concrete honeycomb of tunnels and caves, it was for three months the scene of the greatest combined land-air-sea battle in history.

The Japanese knew Okinawa was their last chance to forestall invasion of the homeland. Kamikaze pilots flew more than 1,900 missions, badly damaging 13 carriers, 10 battleships and 5 cruisers, and sinking 21 other ships. To the kamikazes were added *shinto* (crash boats), *koryu* and *kairyu* (midget submarines), *kaiten* (manned torpedoes) and *ohka,* a sort of manned rocket launched from planes. On the island itself, Japanese soldiers carrying packs of explosives flung themselves against tanks.

Two great armies, in William Manchester's phrase, were locked together in unimaginable agony. The American forces dominated sea and air and had a massive superiority in firepower, but for all that, possession of Okinawa came down to the heroism of individual men running uphill against streams of bullets. The terrain, the tenacity of the defenders and the lack of imagination displayed by the American commanding general, Simon Bolivar Buckner, Jr., imposed an ordeal of months of close combat in a no-man's-land as hideous as any in World War I. Day after day, Marines charged up a notorious position called Sugar Loaf Hill, to be caught in interlocking fire from camouflaged openings concealing machine gunners and antitank guns. Those who reached the summit were flung back by hundreds of defenders pouring out of hidden caves and tunnels. Entire Marine rifle companies of 240 men were frequently reduced to no more than a dozen survivors. At night, they had to bivouac in exposed forward positions,

MASS DURING BATTLE: A Marine in midbattle on Iwo Jima receives the communion wafer, at a mass on top of Mount Suribachi. Catholic, Protestant and Jewish services drew men of all faiths—and none.

next two weeks LeMay's bombers devastate Yokohama, Osaka and Kobe, killing 260,000 people and leaving 13 million homeless.

June 22: General Roy Geiger raises U.S. flag at Kadena airfield, marking virtual end of Okinawa campaign.

July 24: Cruiser *Indianapolis* delivers an atomic bomb to Tinian Island. Ship torpedoed on return with scandalous loss of almost 900 to sea and sharks because of communication blunder.

July 25: Incendiary raids destroy a total of 60 percent of the ground area of Japan's 60 largest cities and towns. Food ration reduced below 1,500 calories daily. Aviation fuel being distilled from pine roots, dug up by a million dragooned civilians.

July 26: Atomic bomb detonated in New Mexico.

—The United States broadcasts Potsdam Declaration, demanding unconditional surrender, but promising free and autonomous status for Japan.

Aug. 6: *Enola Gay* drops atomic bomb on Hiroshima.

Aug. 8: Soviet Union repudiates 1942 nonaggression treaty with Japan and declares war.

Aug. 9: Atomic bomb dropped on Nagasaki. Three mechanized Soviet armies of 1.6 million men attack Japan's Kwantung Army in Manchuria.

Aug. 13: Soviet armies envelop large portions of Kwantung Army.

Aug. 15: Emperor's broadcast accepts U.S. surrender terms.

huddling together in pairs in 18-inch-deep pestilent foxholes. Rain poured down unceasingly. The enemy slipped in with knife and grenade. It was impossible to sleep. Death putrefied the air.

By the time the U.S. flag was raised at Kadena airfield on June 22, at least 110,000 Japanese soldiers had been killed. Both battlefield commanders were dead, Buckner by shrapnel on June 18, his enemy General Mitsuru Ushijima by hara-kiri four days later. One third of the civilian population of 475,000 was dead. The U.S. 10th Army lost 7,613 killed and 31,800 wounded; the Navy 4,900 sailors and 4,800 wounded.

George Feifer's book *Tennozan* is a horrifying and moving account of Okinawa. This is a glimpse of what it was like for one American soldier. Melvin Heckt's machine gun section joined an attack on a mountain ridge on May 21, and he later recalled:

"Donvito was first to be hit. Shrapnel in the hip. Dunham was next. He received a concussion and possible broken collarbone. . . . Next Ward Bowers was killed by Nip artillery. . . . We were in a couple of bomb craters. Cullen was passing by with a piece of shrapnel in his back. Andriola was helping him walk back when a Nambu [machine gun] opened up and wounded Andriola in buttocks and Cullen in leg. . . . Hassell . . . ran out to drag them in out of the fire and was hit in nose, mouth and arm. McGee and Congdon ran out and drug Cullen, Hassell and Andriola to safe positions. The artillery and mortar fire became heavier and more intense so I took my section and ran across the open field to Baumhard's 3rd platoon. It is lucky we moved out for Congdon was killed in the location from which we came and probably more of us would have been killed had we not moved. Maritato was hit in buttocks and testicle. Acuna was hit. I placed machine guns in and had the men get in a ditch. . . . Supposedly, this was the safest position anywhere. But the Nips lobbed a mortar right in the ditch and killed three of my men. Jennings, Albett and McGee. Simmons was sitting with the other three and received shrapnel in the leg, arms and side . . . that makes 6 men killed out of my squad. Too damn many boys to lose for any damn land. Poor Red McGee was blown all over the side of the hill. Only his red hair and scalp remained where he had been sitting."

aThree of the six Iwo Jima flag raisers in Joe Rosenthal's famous picture were killed, one was wounded, and two who survived unscathed died alcoholics.

NAVY COMMANDERS

Nimitz, King and Halsey.

CHESTER WILLIAM NIMITZ
(1885–1966)

The commander in chief of the Pacific Fleet, the master of more military power than wielded by all commanders in all previous wars, was court-martialed as a 22-year-old ensign for running a destroyer aground in the Philippines. He was reprimanded, but rose above it by his excellent record—seventh out of 114 at Annapolis—and his demeanor. He was German by descent, a Texan by birth and a gentleman by habit of character. He became a submariner and at 26 commanded a division and invented a new system of refueling at sea.

He was courteous, calm and self-effacing, the opposite of MacArthur, his Army rival in the South Pacific, and of his boss, Admiral King. He was FDR's persona choice to succeed Admiral Kimmel after Pearl Harbor, jumping over 28 more senior admirals. He restored morale by forgoing a purge and listening to his staff. He lived up to the principles printed on a card on his wartime desk: Objective, Offensive, Superiority of Force at Point of Contact, Simplicity, Security, Movement, Economy of Force, Cooperation.

On his desk he also kept a photograph of MacArthur, to discourage interservice rivalry. He forbade Marine General Holland Smith from attending the Japanese surrender ceremony, because Smith had sacked two Army generals. Smith was the only three-star officer missing.

Nimitz's island-by-island assault lost more men than MacArthur's campaign. Nimitz was ruthless enough to plot the shooting down in 1943 of his opposite number, Admiral Yamamoto, but unlike many he resisted the impulse to indulge in racial hatred of the Japanese—or the Germans.

DOGFIGHT TRIUMPH

A pilot of the Navy's VF-17 squadron on Bougainville, Ensign Andy Jagger exults over the results of an air battle over Rabaul, New Britain, in March 1944. The idea of leapfrogging the stronghold was General Marshall's (MacArthur was not at first in favor) and it saved lives and time. The Allies neutralized Rabaul's airpower, flying more than 29,000 land- and carrier-based planes against the island. Even then the Japanese outpost did not give up until September 6, three weeks after Tokyo's surrender.

NAVY COMMANDERS

ERNEST KING
(1878–1956)

Everybody hated King. He became chief of naval operations and commander in chief when he was 63, in 1942, and was in as much of a hurry as he had been as a midshipman fighting the Spanish-American War. He was, said one of his six daughters, "the most even-tempered man in the Navy: he is always in a rage." He was rude, abrupt, autocratic, humorless. He had his own hates: the British, the press, ditherers, toadies and anyone who got in the way of the U.S. Navy. He was a man of granite integrity but he was not a puritan. "You ought to be very suspicious," he once said, "of anyone who won't take a drink or doesn't like women." He was also a naval manager of genius with a rare grasp of overall military strategy. He saw the futility of the North African campaign and backed Marshall on striking at Europe, but he fought and won his case for counter-offensives in the Pacific to keep the Japanese off balance. It was his willpower, insight and sense of timing that gave America the chance to gain Guadalcanal. He made mistakes—his delay in escorting convoys, his failure to make the sinking of Japanese oil tankers a priority until 1944. But King chose the men, designed the strategy and built up the carrier forces that brought victory to the Pacific.

WILLIAM F. ("BULL") HALSEY
(1882–1959)

A fighter like Patton, his message to his fleet was "Kill Japs. Kill Japs. Kill more Japs." MacArthur called him "the greatest fighting admiral" of the war.

Halsey had been a destroyer commander in World War I, and was 53 when he won his naval aviator's wings in 1935 and took command of the carrier *Saratoga*. As commander of the South Pacific fleet from 1942, he led the leapfrogging campaign in the central Pacific. His impulsive aggressiveness was important to Allied victory, though it was sometimes hazardous. In chasing after a decoy in the battle of Leyte Gulf (October 1944) he left the U.S. invasion force open to destruction and was saved only by the quick thinking of Admiral Thomas Kincaid.

Halsey was honored with a fifth star, as were King and Nimitz.

Americans old enough to be cognizant long remembered where they were and what they were doing when they heard the news in the late afternoon of Thursday, April 12, 1945, that President Roosevelt had died suddenly at Warm Springs, Georgia. Not since the murder of President Lincoln—nor again until the assassination of John Kennedy—had an event so arrested the heart of the Republic. It was choked by fear: the lights had suddenly gone out on the real hopes for a brave new world. It was numbed by shock: for twelve turbulent years, four years longer than any other president, the happy warrior had always been there to comfort, galvanize, inspire. In his faith, courage and vitality, he was America. Some FDR-haters lit bonfires, and the children at a school in New Hampshire danced around a flagpole, but an overwhelming number of people from all walks of life considered that they had lost a member of the family in this Hudson Valley patrician. The newspapers and the radio at the time reported it; it was manifest in the tears that watered the path of the casket and a poignant sense of it is palpable in the archives at Hyde Park. The tributes began to arrive the day after the President's death, and were still arriving 15 years later. They include an extraordinary number of privately printed poems and eulogies, often elaborately decorated. They reveal a depth of feeling toward an American leader that is all but unimaginable today. The phenomenon is not explained by political economy. It truly is a family matter. As historian Geoffrey Ward puts it, FDR made even the most rejected feel they were somehow important to the American commonwealth.

FDR had been utterly exhausted when he arrived by train at Warm Springs on Good Friday, March 30. He perked up after a couple of days in the sun. His blood pressure, varying worryingly between $170/88$ and $240/130$, was not helped by ugly messages from a paranoid Stalin fearful that the Anglo-Americans might be about to make a separate peace. FDR had already begun to doubt whether Stalin would keep his word at Yalta on free elections in Poland and eastern Europe. He cabled Churchill on April 12 that "we must be firm," but suggested they minimize the Soviet problem for the time being. On this last day of his life, he was due to appear at a barbecue on Pine Mountain in the late afternoon. In the morning, in bed in the Little White House, he read the *Atlanta Constitution* reports of a Superfortress raid on Tokyo and American troops advancing to within 57 miles of Berlin. Later, he sat in his leather armchair at a card table in the living room, signing papers and bantering with his cousins, Margaret Suckley, who was crocheting, and Laura Delano, who was fixing flowers; and with a beautiful woman facing him: Mrs. Lucy Rutherford, the former Lucy Mercer. Their romance had blossomed again clandestinely sometime around Pearl Harbor; his biographer James MacGregor Burns believes it was by this time "essentially temperamental rather than physical." Mrs. Rutherford had commissioned Elizabeth Shoumatoff to paint a watercolor portrait of the President and he had put on the double-breasted gray suit and Harvard tie she requested. The painter arrived at noon and found him "cheerful and full of pep." She was struck by his "exceptionally good color." At 1 p.m. the President lit a cigarette in his holder and told her: "We have 15 minutes more to work." She recalled later: "Suddenly he raised his hand and passed it over his forehead several times in a strange, jerky way, without emitting a sound, his head bent slightly forward." Miss Suckley reported that he murmured to her, "I have a terrific headache." He never recovered consciousness. At 3:55 p.m. (Warm Springs time, 4:55 p.m. in Washington) he was pronounced dead from a cerebral hemorrhage.

Eleanor Roosevelt was in Washington. She flew down to Warm Springs, arriving near midnight. Her cousin Laura at once told her that Mrs. Rutherford had been present. It was the brutal act of a woman jealous of Eleanor's success. Eleanor heard Laura out, then went into the bedroom to view her husband's body and stayed there, alone, for five minutes. She kept her composure. The next day she joined the presidential train bringing FDR back to Washington. On the long, memorable journey through the South, FDR lay in a flag-draped coffin on a crude catafalque of Georgia pine, a military escort of four from the Army, Navy, Marines and Coast Guard at attention at his side. The lights stayed on all night in his rear car, the blinds up. Solemn knots of people gathered at depots and crossings, in their hundreds at some points. Near Gainesville, Georgia, black women in a cotton field fell to their knees. At Greenville, South Carolina, a Boy Scout troop started singing "Onward, Christian Soldiers," and hundreds along the track picked it up. Someone passed into the funeral car a wreath that had been given to a mother whose son had been killed in the war.

In Washington, six white horses pulled the caisson to the White House, and the coffin was placed in the East Room with an honor guard. Eleanor asked to have the casket opened, and to be left alone. Standing guard at the door, White House usher J. B. West observed her gaze down at her husband and tenderly place a gold ring from her finger on his hand. The whole country was wrapped in a great moment of silence on the Sunday FDR was carried by train to Hyde Park. FDR had jotted down instructions for his burial and funeral as far back as December 26, 1937. He had stuck the note in an envelope in his bedroom safe at the White House and it was not opened until after he was buried in his mother's rose garden at Hyde Park—as he wished.

THE ENEMIES

Hitler's hopes were raised by Roosevelt's death. Goebbels had read him a passage from Thomas Carlyle's *History of Frederick the Great*, describing how in the Seven Years' War, the Prussian king's fortunes had miraculously changed on a single day with the death of the Russian czarina. Goebbels had commissioned a horoscope of Hitler. It predicted a great success for Germany in April, followed by peace in August. Goebbels put out an "In Memoriam" propaganda leaflet saying "We wish to expresss our condolences—across the fronts. . . . Franklin D. Roosevelt has crossed to the Great Beyond and it is not proper to talk about the deeds of a deceased leader at this moment."

In Japan, newspapers exulted in the death. The *Mainichi* called it "Heaven's punishment." But Prime Minister Suzuki made a broadcast expressing "profound sympathy" to the American people, and Radio Tokyo played a special program of music to honor "the passing of a great man." Suzuki's words were for Americans only; they were not heard by the Japanese or reported in their newspapers.

"PLEASE PRAY FOR ME"

Just after five o'clock, Eastern War Time, on April 12, 1945, Vice President Harry Truman, aged 60, was running between a line of statues in the deserted marble halls of Congress, heading out of the door for a car that would take him to the White House. Come "quickly and quietly" was all he had been told on the phone at House Speaker Sam Rayburn's office, where he had dropped in for a drink. At the White House, Mrs. Roosevelt was waiting for him on the second floor. "Harry," she said,

putting her arm on his shoulder, "the President is dead." He could not speak. Finally, he asked, "Is there anything I can do for you?" She replied: "Is there anything we can do for you? You are the one who is in trouble now."

By 7 p.m. that evening, Truman sat looking "absolutely dazed" as a group gathered in the Cabinet Room at the White House for the swearing-in ceremony: his tearful wife, Bess; his daughter, Margaret; most of his inherited cabinet;

Wallace with FDR in 1940.

IT MIGHT HAVE BEEN ME: Henry Wallace, displaced in 1944 as Roosevelt's running mate, was among the witnesses at the swearing in—fifth from left. The others (left to right): Leo Crowley, Chairman of the Federal Deposit Insurance Corporation; Secretary of Labor Frances Perkins; unidentified; Secretary of War Henry Stimson; Wallace; War Production Board administrator Julius A. Krug; Secretary of the Navy James V. Forrestal; Secretary of Agriculture Claude Wickard; War Manpower Commission Deputy Chairman Francis L. McNamee; Attorney General Francis Biddle; Secretary of the Treasury Henry Morgenthau (behind Truman); Truman; Secretary of State Edward Stettinius, Jr.; Mrs. Truman; Secretary of Interior Harold Ickes; Margaret Truman (obscured behind Stone); Chief Justice Harlan Stone; Speaker of the House Sam Rayburn. Also present were Director of the Office of War Mobilization Fred M. Vinson; Minority Leader of the House Joseph W. Martin, Jr.; House Majority Whip Robert Ramspeck; and House Majority Leader John W. McCormack.

the Chief Justice of the United States; congressional leaders from both parties and a handful of newsmen. Howell Crim, a White House usher, found a Gideon Bible in a desk drawer, dusted it off and put it on the table before Truman and Chief Justice Harlan Stone. At 7:09, under the portrait of Woodrow Wilson, 3 hours and 14 minutes after Roosevelt had died,

Truman held the Bible and declared: "I, Harry S Truman, do solemnly swear that I will faithfully execute the office of the President of the United States, and will to the best of my ability preserve, protect and defend the Constitution of the United States. . . . So help me God." He suddenly, fervently, kissed the Bible. "The whole weight of the moon and stars fell

on me," he told the press later. "Please pray for me." The whole ceremony lasted less than a minute. He was back in his modest apartment at 4701 Connecticut Avenue by 9:30 for a turkey sandwich and a glass of milk. He called his mother to tell her not to worry, and went right to sleep.

HARRY S TRUMAN
33rd President (Democrat), 1945–1953

BORN: May 8, 1884, Lamar, Missouri

DIED: December 26, 1972, Kansas City, Missouri

POLITICAL CAREER: Eastern Judge, Jackson County, Missouri, 1922–1924; Presiding Judge, Jackson County, 1926–1934; U.S. Senator from Missouri, 1935–1945; Vice President for 82 days, 1945; President by succession, 1945–1949; President by election, 1949–1953

FIRSTS: First and only president of twentieth century without formal college education. First president to make televised address to nation. First president to address National Association for the Advancement of Colored People (NAACP).

CHARACTER SNAPSHOT: "He stood for common sense, common decency. He spoke the common tongue."
—Biographer David McCullough

"The tension of becoming something he wasn't strengthened him in many ways, but it also left scars: an inordinate touchiness, a quick temper, and an insatiable demand for recognition that stayed with him throughout his life."
—Biographer Alonzo L. Hamby

OMNIVORE: At 12 he had read all of Mark Twain, and the Bible twice. He loved history, Dickens, James Fenimore Cooper, George Eliot. He was inspired to great dreams by his tenth birthday gift of four volumes, *Great Men* and *Famous Women*. He mopped up in a drugstore before high school lessons. At 16, when this photograph was taken, he was living with railway labor gangs as a construction time-keeper; at 18, he was a Kansas City bank clerk. In 1906 he answered his father's call to help run Grandpa Young's farm, and when his father died in 1914 he took over the farm altogether until he enlisted in the Army in 1917.

FARM BOY: He had an idyllic childhood here at Grandview Farm, beloved by his large, clannish, if quarrelsome, family. "Mamma," Martha Ellen Truman (left with her mother, Harriet Young), used the large print in the family Bible to teach him to read before he was 5. He once had to hold a lamp over her in the farmhouse while a local doctor performed an operation without anesthetic. The family moved to Independence to improve his schooling, but his father, a feisty farmer and livestock trader who backed William Jennings Bryan against William McKinley, went broke trading wheat futures in 1901. College was out. So were the lessons in classical piano, where Harry had shown promise.

CAPTAIN TRUMAN: World War I put him back on the road of the great men he had long envisioned for himself. Hoping to make sergeant in his National Guard unit, he was instead elected a first lieutenant by his men—his first victory in any election. He talked his way around an Army eyesight exam, with 20/50 in the right eye and 20/400 in the left. Before going to war, he bought six pairs of pince-nez—like Teddy Roosevelt. Given command of a bunch of Irish American toughs in Battery D, he transformed it from the worst to one of the best units by no-nonsense leadership. In his first action, a shell burst knocked him off his horse, hurling him into a muddy crater. He got out and restored order to his command. Later his unit knocked out a German battery in the Meuse-Argonne offensive.

BESS: With his wife, Bess (Elizabeth) Wallace, and their ten-year-old daughter, Margaret, in 1934. He met Bess when he was 6 in Sunday school and married her 29 years later when he was 35, she 34. Bess was an athletic girl from one of the wealthiest families in Independence. Her father committed suicide, and her possessive and snobbish mother, Madge, told her: "You don't want to marry that farmer boy, he is not going to make it anywhere." The roughest time in their lifelong bliss was early in his presidency, when she felt excluded from his decisions. She was angry not to have been consulted about the atomic bomb. But by 1946 they were political partners again.

THE HABERDASHER: In 1919 Captain Truman teamed up with his battlefront friend Sergeant Edward Jacobson (not pictured), "the Jew in charge of the canteen," to open a men's clothes store just across from Kansas City's leading hotel. They did well the first year, but the Wilson-Mellon depression of 1920–1923 sank them in 1922. Over the next 15 years they insisted on paying back their creditors in full. Jacobson stayed a lifelong friend and played a key part in Truman's decision to recognize Israel.

THE BOSS AND HARRY: Truman with his patron, Tom Pendergast. He owed his entry into politics in 1922 to the Democratic machine controlled in Kansas City and much of Missouri by the Pendergast brothers, Tom and Mike. Lieutenant Truman had saved Mike's son, Jim, from an Army court-martial. Mike rewarded Truman with the chance to run for a county judgeship. The "judges" did not sit in court. They controlled spending on roads and awarded contracts. Big Boss Tom was shocked to find he could not force his crooked contractors on Truman. He cursed him for "the contrariest cuss in Missouri," though Truman in his diary admitted compromises. To get a road system voted, "I had to let a former saloon keeper and murderer, a friend of the Big Boss, steal about $10,000." And again: "I wonder if I did right to put a lot of no account sons of bitches on the payroll in order to satisfy the political powers." Judge Truman was so honest himself that when one of his new roads sliced 11 acres off the family Grandview Farm, he denied his mother the normal compensation. His worst mistake: In the hunt for votes, he naively let his name go forward to join the Ku Klux Klan. He withdrew when they made it clear he would be expected never to hire Catholics.

As senator, he lived down the sneers that he was the senator from Pendergast by humility and hard work as a New Deal liberal (though he erred in putting Bess on the Senate payroll). He defended his old boss even when a federal investigation landed him in jail. He backed antilynching laws, voted to abolish the poll tax, attacked entrenched rail interests. He made his name investigating war production, exposing waste, stopping the production of faulty steel. His office was the birthplace, in 1943, of the historic bipartisan resolution committing the U.S. to lead in the formation of the United Nations.

THE VICE PRESIDENT: In 1944 he was a pawn in byzantine party maneuvers. Factions pressured FDR to dump his vice president, the mystical Henry Wallace, in favor of War Mobilization Director James F. Byrnes or Supreme Court Justice William O. Douglas. FDR encouraged both Wallace and Byrnes, but was warned Byrnes would alienate blacks and labor. Then Truman-promoter Robert Hannegan emerged from meeting FDR in his railcar in Chicago with a letter expressing the President's willingness to run with "either" Truman or Douglas—named in that order. Truman demurred. Bess was opposed. On Wednesday, July 19, he was called to a meeting of party bosses to hear FDR's voice boom out from the telephone: "Well, you tell the senator that if he wants to break up the Democratic Party in the middle of the war, that's his responsibility." That—and the thought of how pleased his mother would be—brought him around.

He saw little of FDR. One of the few times was this sardines-on-toast lunch in the White House Rose Garden on August 18, 1944. "The President looked fine," Truman told the press, but he was shaken that FDR's hand trembled so much he put more of the cream for his coffee in the saucer than the cup. Truman was never fond of FDR. The President was too devious for his taste.

HOW AMERICA NEARLY MISSED THE MOMENT

The action Roosevelt promised after receiving Einstein's letter (below) was soon belied. Two scornful Army and Navy ordnance experts met with Szilard, Teller, Wigner and Sachs under the chairmanship of Lyman J. Briggs, a soil physicist who was head of the Bureau of Standards. This quarrelsome Uranium Committee ended up asking only for $6,000 to buy graphite for Enrico Fermi's work on neutron absorption—and in November FDR simply filed the request. Seven months later, in June 1940, he focused more closely on what science might do in war, naming the Carnegie Institution's Vannevar Bush to head the National Defense Research Committee. Bush brought in the 47-year-old president of Harvard, James Conant, to oversee the Uranium Committee. Both men thought atomic bomb research unrealistic and irrelevant.

The whole American program might well have been aborted had it not been for two other refugees—the Germans Otto Frisch and Rudolf Peierls, who had been welcomed into Britain's University of Birmingham by the Australian Mark Oliphant. In March 1940, Frisch and Peierls made theoretical calculations about the explosive chain reaction potential of pure uranium 235 unalloyed with U-238. Their theory electrified the British, whose scientists had secretly concluded by June 1941 that it was indeed possible to separate the uranium isotopes in the necessary quantities and so build a "practically irresistible"

superbomb of 1,800 tons of TNT from a mere 25 pounds of uranium.

Bush and Conant were apprised of the findings, but nothing happened that summer. Szilard fumed. Mark Oliphant was "amazed and distressed" when he arrived in America in August to find that Briggs had put the Maud draft in his safe and shown it to nobody. Oliphant stirred up the Nobel Prize–winner Ernest Lawrence of Berkeley; he fired up Arthur Compton of Chicago; and, finally, yet another refugee, the Ukrainian chemist George Kistakowsky, convinced Conant. Still, it was October 1941 before Bush presented FDR with the British findings. As Richard Rhodes puts it, America's initial inertia was proportional to its juggernaut of scientific, engineering and industrial might; and acceleration now overcame inertia. The velocity was supplied by General Leslie R. Groves, the hefty, hard-driving Army engineer. Groves was horrified by the mess he found when, in September 1942, he was put in charge of building a bomb (the Manhattan Project). Everybody had been waiting for the chain reaction to be proved. Groves never waited for anything. Within days, he commandeered the uranium ore, he acquired land, and within three weeks he found the scientist he wanted, a 38-year-old Berkeley professor of physics, J. Robert Oppenheimer, decided he was a genius and overrode all objections that he was too left-wing and not a Nobel laureate. He asked him to turn

J. Robert Oppenheimer (1904–1967). "Oppie," director of the Los Alamos laboratory in New Mexico, had a mind of swift, dazzling catholicity. He swept through Harvard, won a Ph.D. at Göttingen for quantum theory discoveries, read the literature of many languages, including Sanskrit, and was a professor at 32. He was a lifelong chain-smoker, skinny and intense, given to self-loathing. "I hardly took an action," he said in 1963, "that did not arouse in me a very great sense of revulsion and of wrong."

an equation into a deliverable bomb. On December 2, 1942, Fermi's team justified Groves's gamble. Working in a former squash court under the stands of Stagg Field, the University of Chicago football stadium, they achieved the first manmade, self-sustaining nuclear chain reaction. Oppenheimer gave Groves his bomb minutes before dawn on July 16, 1945, at Alamogordo, New Mexico: an enormous ball of fire followed by a mushroom cloud towering 30,000 feet over the desert.

EINSTEIN'S WARNING REACHES FDR

Albert Einstein
Old Grove Rd.
Nassau Point
Peconic, Long Island

August 2nd, 1939

F.D. Roosevelt,
President of the United States,
White House
Washington, D.C.

Sir:

Some recent work by E.Fermi and L. Szilard, which has been communicated to me in manuscript, leads me to expect that the element uranium may be turned into a new and important source of energy in the immediate future. Certain aspects of the situation which has arisen seem to call for watchfulness and, if necessary, quick action on the part of the Administration. I believe therefore that it is my duty to bring to your attention the following facts and recommendations:

Three Hungarian refugees began the chain reaction of political decisions that led America to make the atomic bomb. Leo Szilard, by then at Columbia, Eugene Wigner of Princeton and Edward Teller of Columbia combined brilliance in physics with passionate concern that Hitler might build an atomic weapon. On two Sundays in July 1939, they drove out to Peconic Bay on Long Island to see Albert Einstein, winner of the 1921 Nobel Prize.

Alexander Sachs, a Russian émigré economist, persuaded them that the draft letter they worked up with Einstein was best addressed to President Roosevelt, whom he knew. The outbreak of war in Europe kept FDR too busy to see Sachs until October 11. Sachs read FDR an 800-word summary report and handed him Einstein's letter. It referred to the work of Enrico Fermi and Szilard that showed "it may be possible to set up a nuclear chain reaction in a large mass of uranium by which vast amounts of power . . . would be generated." FDR responded: "Alex, what you are after is to see that the Nazis don't blow us up." He called in an aide: "This requires action."

THE GRAY EMINENCE: Truman and Secretary of State James Byrnes on the deck of USS *Augusta* on the way to meet Stalin and Churchill. Byrnes persuaded Truman to embrace his hard-line terms for the Japanese, which made Hiroshima inevitable. Truman looked up to Byrnes, who had shown him the ropes in his early days in the Senate.

JIMMY BYRNES'S BOMB

Two weeks after Truman was sworn in, Secretary of War Henry Stimson smuggled General Leslie Groves into the White House and presented the new president with a typed memorandum. "Within four months," Truman read, "we shall in all probability have completed the most terrible weapon in human history. . . ."

Attempts were made to persuade Truman that he might win an early peace by telling Japan that America did not intend to remove the Emperor. Truman seemed to go along when this was argued on May 28 by Joe Grew, the ambassador to Tokyo for ten years and acting secretary of state, and by Herbert Hoover. On June 12, Stimson, Grew and Navy Secretary James Forrestal recommended that the new terms should be promulgated on the fall of Okinawa, which happened on June 21.

Truman turned this opportunity aside. He postponed an initiative to his meeting with Stalin and Churchill at Potsdam (July 17–August 2), already delayed to allow time for the Alamogordo bomb test. It is now clear, as it was not for 40 years, that Truman succumbed to the persuasions of his old Senate crony, Jimmy Byrnes, former Supreme Court justice and FDR's "assistant president." Byrnes was not sworn in as secretary of state until early July, but Truman made Byrnes his personal representative on Stimson's famous Interim Committee of eight civilians. Byrnes, not the ailing and often absent Stimson, dominated the committee. It was Byrnes who formulated the recommendation that "the bomb should be used against Japan as soon as possible; that it be used on a war plant surrounded by workers' homes; and that it be used without prior warning." It was Byrnes who quashed Marshall's ideas of a demonstration on a military installation and of inviting the Russians to see the test. All Truman's advisers found that Byrnes called the shots. When on June 18 John J. McCloy, Stimson's assistant secretary, sketched how tolerance for the Emperor might end the war quickly, Truman said: "That's exactly what I've been wanting to explore. . . . You go down to Jimmy Byrnes and talk to him about it." McCloy got nowhere with Byrnes.

On July 2, just before Truman left for Potsdam, Stimson presented the draft of an ultimatum. Paragraph 12 said a peacefully inclined Japanese government "may include a constitutional monarchy under the present dynasty." On the voyage, Byrnes got Truman to delete this. It stayed deleted despite the momentous news they received on July 12–13, in mid-Atlantic, from U.S. code breakers, that Tokyo had cabled the Japanese ambassador in Moscow emphasizing the Emperor's "heart's desire" for peace, but adding that demands for unconditional surrender would force Japan to fight on.

Byrnes redrafted the July 26 ultimatum. Out went the explicit assurance on the Emperor. In came a sentence that could be conceived as a threat to him: "There must be eliminated for all time the authority and influence of those who have deceived and misled the people of Japan." The language all but guaranteed Japanese rejection. But when the Japanese did surrender, on August 10, a day after the Russian invasion, Byrnes and Truman accepted that the Emperor would stay. Had they tried that in June, the war might have ended then.

Readying Fat Man for delivery.

FAT MAN

...monster that burst over Nagasaki at 11:02 a.m. on August 9, 1945. Named with Winston Churchill in mind, it was 10 feet 8 inches long, 5 feet in diameter and weighed 10,000 pounds, so heavy that a modified B-29 was the only bomber that could carry it. It was a plutonium bomb, its critical chain reaction set off by a conventional explosive charge crushing two spheres of plutonium together. The Little Boy bomb dropped on Hiroshima was about as long, but much slimmer at 29 inches in diameter. Its chain reaction came from firing a uranium 235 bullet at a uranium 235 target.

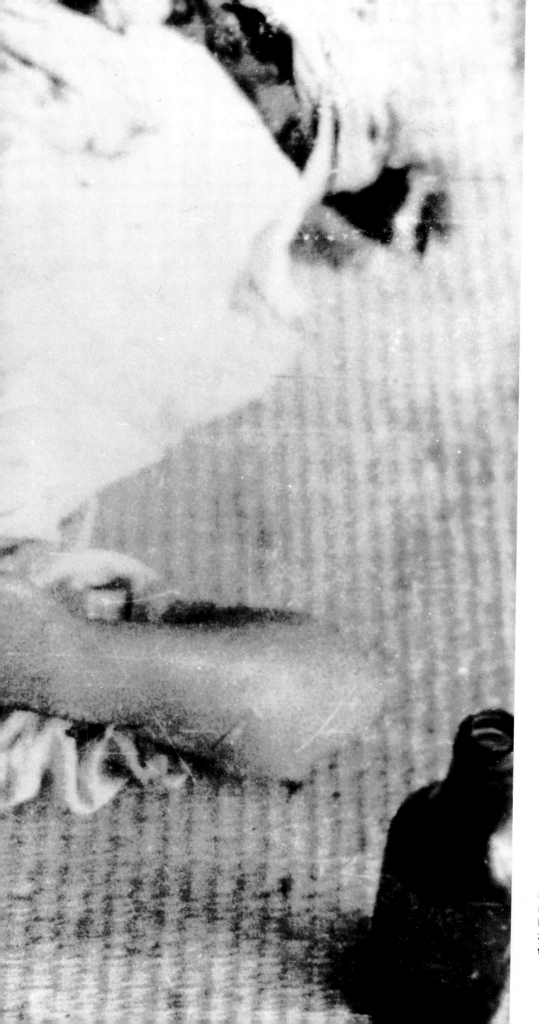

THE MOST HORRIFYING MINUTE IN HISTORY

Hiroshima's streets were teeming with people when the first atomic bomb, Little Boy, exploded 1,900 feet above the courtyard of Shima Hospital at 8:16 a.m. on a beautiful cloudless day, August 6. As a Japanese historian put it, the bomb changed everything into nothing. Some 150,000 who were within a kilometer of the hypocenter, or ground zero, were vaporized in the 5400-degree flash. Thousands of small black bundles of charred flesh stuck to the sidewalks; they were cremated humans. People who had been alive one second were silhouettes on walls the next.

The city and its life and culture vanished in an instant. By the end of the year more than half the population of some 280,000 civilians and 43,000 soldiers had died. Of 76,000 buildings, 70,000 were damaged or destroyed, 48,000 turned into rubble and ash. This is a stupefying percentage. By comparison, the horrendous March 19 firebombing of Tokyo killed 100,000, or 10 percent of 1 million total casualties, in a city of millions. By 1950, radiation deaths related to the bombing had reached 200,000, and people were still dying 40 years later from cancers attributable to the radiation.

Three days after Hiroshima, a B-29 called Bock's Car by its commander, Frederick Bock, flattened Nagasaki with a different type of atomic bomb, called Fat Man. It obliterated 44 percent of the city, with 54 percent of the people. A U.S. Navy officer visiting the city more than a month after the bombing wrote, "A smell of death and corruption pervades the city.... [There is] the absolute essence of death in the sense of finality without hope of resurrection."

REPROACH: She was a student. She lies on a straw mat at the Red Cross Hospital of Hiroshima. She continually cried, "Water . . . water," until she died on the fourth day, August 10. Victims had little hope of early medical aid. Of the city's 300 physicians, only 28 were still able to function and only 3 of 55 hospitals could offer care.

THE EMPEROR BREAKS THE DEADLOCK

The doomsday clock ticked away for Japan in the summer of 1945. The military men tried not to hear it. Emperor Hirohito heard it, but he had to work within the Japanese system of consensus. In the third week of June, with Okinawa lost, he summoned the Big Six to his underground bunker complex in the Imperial Garden: the 78-year-old prime minister, Admiral Kantarō Suzuki; Foreign Minister Shigenori Togo; and the four military chiefs. Urged on by his Privy Seal, Marquis Kido, the Emperor asked them to study "concrete means" for ending the war.

The military men lived under the illusion that the Soviet Union, not at war with Japan, would mediate a settlement—though in April Moscow had said it would not renew the neutrality treaty due to expire in 1946. Nothing came of the feelers put out in Moscow. On July 7 a haggard and exasperated Emperor asked former Prime Minister Prince Fumimaro Konoe to fly to Moscow. The Russians stalled on receiving Konoe. They were eager to gnaw the bones of a prostrate Japan.

When Truman approved the Potsdam ultimatum, as edited by Byrnes to exclude any hope the Emperor might be retained, he left the peace party in Tokyo vulnerable. In Tokyo, the military pressed for immediate rejection of the ultimatum; the civilians dithered. All the ostriches had their heads in the same Soviet sand. The muddy compromise that emerged was to wait and see, neither reject nor accept, and to discourage press comment. But circumspection could not flourish amid Tokyo's feuds. *Mainichi Shimbun,* no doubt egged on by the military, headlined the ultimatum story "Laughable Matter." Then Prime Minister Suzuki told the press on July 28 that most of the government wanted to "*mokusatsu*" the declaration. The word means "kill with silence." Thus was Hiroshima doomed. It had nine days to live.

The last illusion was exploded two days after Hiroshima. The Japanese finally got an answer from Moscow. It was a Soviet

declaration of war. Two hours later Soviet armies knifed into Manchuria, advancing 100 miles before the end of August 9.

That same morning, Nagasaki was obliterated just as the Big Six were meeting. The civilians were ready to accept Potsdam if America would recognize the lawful status of the Emperor. The military chiefs were bent on national suicide. The full cabinet met in the afternoon and could not resolve the deadlock. Suzuki and Togo, for the first time in Japanese history, asked for an imperial conference, to report a dispute.

The fateful debate of the Big Six, their secretaries and the sage Baron Hiranuma, president of the Privy Council, began around midnight in the Emperor's gloomy and fetid bunker, the civilians sweltering in the court dress of black morning coats and striped trousers, the Emperor wearing white gloves and sitting on a dais. War Minister General Korechika Anami spoke for the military: "Our hundred million people are ready to die for honor, glorifying the deeds of the Japanese race in recorded history." It was after 2 a.m. when Hiranuma asked the Emperor himself to decide. Speaking through the sobbing among the men around him, the anguished Emperor

HIROSHIMA: Emperor Hirohito and his wife arriving at Hiroshima in 1951, their first official visit outside Tokyo. The American press called his walkabouts "ah so desuka" visits because he responded to most things by saying "Indeed," "Is that so," or "How interesting." They made fun of his remark at Hiroshima: "There seems to have been considerable damage here."

gave his sanction to Togo's formula for accepting the Potsdam terms. This made surrender conditional on the prerogatives of the Emperor's being respected. On August 11 Secretary of State Byrnes cabled that "from the moment of surrender the authority of the Emperor . . . shall be subject to the Supreme Commander of the Allied Powers," referring to General MacArthur. The ultimate form of government would be "established by the freely expressed will of the Japanese people."

Hirohito bowed serenely to that. "It would be useless if the people did not want an emperor." The military diehards were plunged into a vortex, torn by shame and pride, and by loyalty to the Emperor. General Anami drove a dagger deep into his abdomen and throat in the disembowelment ritual of seppuku. Groups of younger hotheads staged an insurrection. The coup found its focus in the improbable figure of a hysterical War Ministry officer on a bicycle, Major Kenji Hatanaka, cycling furiously in the heat of August 14 to incite Army commanders. When General Takeshi Mori hesitated, Hatanaka shot him dead; another rebel officer beheaded a colonel who tried to protect Mori. Using the general's seal, Hatanaka had 1,000 Imperial Guardsmen cordon off the palace grounds. Inside, an unsuspecting Hirohito was recording a broadcast, scheduled for the next day, to announce surrender. Hatanaka's men ransacked the palace trying to find the tape, then he took control of the radio station at gunpoint. A wily engineer frustrated him.

Time ran out for Hatanaka, as it had run out for Japan. The Army leadership discovered the false orders and quashed the rebellion. At 11:20 a.m. on August 15 Hatanaka went to the front of the Imperial Palace and shot himself. At noon, the Emperor broke the precedent of imperial silence; the war situation, he said, "has developed not necessarily to Japan's advantage." To the people he blamed the "new and cruel bomb"; to the Japanese forces he justified the surrender as averting Russia's threat to the very foundation of the empire. Outside the palace, thousands bowed to the ground chanting: "Forgive us, O Emperor, our efforts are not enough."

BOWED HEAD (left): A Japanese prisoner on Guam hears Emperor Hirohito's surrender broadcast.

MACARTHUR SETS THE TONE FOR PEACE

Two bullet-marked Mitsubishi bombers heading for the island of Ie Shima on August 19, 1945, were swiftly surrounded by American planes. The Japanese pilots radioed "Bataan, Bataan." The password was acknowledged by the interceptors: "We are Bataan's watchdogs. Follow us." On board the white-painted bombers were 16 Japanese soldiers and diplomats designated to work out the surrender of their armed forces with General MacArthur's staff in Manila. They were apprehensive; GIs who gave them orange juice and a box lunch on the transfer at Ie Shima to a C-54 were bemused to be tipped $10 each. The Japanese were even more astonished to be treated with respect by their conquerors. The instrument of surrender handed to them in Manila City Hall began: "I, Hirohito, Emperor of Japan. . . ." MacArthur's chief translator, Colonel Sidney Mashbir, saw that the language gave offense. "They were dying right there in their chairs." He told them they could draw up the document in the customary imperial language, using the royal "we." The Americans also agreed to postpone the landing of U.S. occupying forces for three days, to August 28. On the way back to Tokyo, a trip enlivened by a crash landing on the edge of the sea, General Torashiro Kawabe reflected that he had just had contact with "a truly great cultural nation."

The surrender ceremonies took place in Tokyo Bay on Sunday, September 2, amid a vast pageant of American power. As far as the eye could see stretched lines of warships, and riding majestically at anchor was the newest of them all, the *Missouri*. From its flagstaff flew the Stars and Stripes that had hung over the Capitol the day the Japanese attacked Pearl Harbor, and draped on a rear gun turret was the flag of 31 stars that Commodore Matthew Perry had flown when he sailed into Tokyo Bay to open Japan to the West 92 years before. Every deck was packed; groups of sailors in white straddled every gun. At 8:55 a.m. an excited silence descended. Painfully, slowly, a figure in a tall silk hat and cutaway and ascot pulled himself up the starboard gangway from a launch and across the quarterdeck to a ladder leading to the ceremony deck. Mamoru Shige-mitsu, the new Japanese foreign minister, who was leading the delegation of 11, had lost a leg to an assassin in Shanghai years before, and he was getting no help from the stone-faced Chief of the Imperial General Staff who followed him, Yoshijiro Umezu. To Umezu, Shigemitsu was a detestable appeaser; only a personal entreaty from Hirohito had induced Umezu to attend.

The delegation stood stiffly in its allotted place facing the signing table, hearing "The Star Spangled Banner" on the amplifiers, waiting for MacArthur to arrive. "A million eyes seemed to beat on us with the million shafts of a rattling storm of arrows barbed with fire," recalled Toshikazu Kazu of the Foreign Ministry. He winced to see the Rising Sun "kills" painted on a bulkhead. But Kazu, Admiral Sadatoshi Tomioka and General Yatsuji Nagai later recorded how dazzled and moved they were when MacArthur began to speak: "The issues, involving divergent ideals and ideologies, have been determined on the battlefields of the world and hence are not for our discussion or our debate," said MacArthur. "Nor is it for us here to meet . . . in a spirit of distrust, malice or hatred. But rather it is for us, both victors and vanquished, to rise to that higher dignity which alone benefits the sacred purposes we are about to serve. . . . It is the hope of all mankind that from this solemn occasion a better world shall emerge out of the blood and carnage of the past, a world founded upon faith and understanding, a world dedicated to the dignity of man and the fulfillment of his most cherished wish for freedom, tolerance and justice." Kazu later told the Emperor that MacArthur was "a man of light. Radiantly, the gathering rays of his magnificent soul embrace the earth."

The signings were over at 9:25. The sun broke through and everyone looked to the sky. Nearly 2,000 war planes swept in salute over the armada.

Not all were so accepting of a New Age. Kamikaze bomber and fighter pilots, enraged by the surrender, had lined up their planes at the Atsugi airfield with the intention of dive-bombing the *Missouri*. They were dissuaded at the last minute only by the arrival of the Emperor's younger brother, Prince Takamatsu.

THE SIGNING

Hard-liner General Umezu bends over to sign for Japan, following Foreign Minister Shigemitsu (top hat, front row). MacArthur and Fleet Admiral Nimitz signed for the U.S. The other signatories:
CHINA: General Hsu Yung-chang
BRITAIN: Admiral Sir Bruce Fraser
SOVIET UNION: Lieutenant General K. Derevyanko
AUSTRALIA: General Sir Thomas Blamey
CANADA: Colonel L. Moore-Cosgrove
FRANCE: General Jacques Leclerc
NETHERLANDS: Admiral Conrad Helfrich
NEW ZEALAND: Air Vice Marshal Sir L. M. Isitt
MacArthur gave a place of honor at his side to General Jonathan Wainwright, who had surrendered the Philippines in 1942, and General Sir Arthur Percival, who had surrendered Singapore, both of whom had survived POW camps.

THE COST TO AMERICA—AND THE WORLD

The war cost America 292,131 dead in battle, out of armed forces totaling 16,353,659. It is impossible to be precise about the global total, but the orders of magnitude are indicated by the following figures:

UNITED STATES
U.S. Army, including Army Air Forces
(total serving: 11,260,000)   234,874
U.S. Navy (4,183,466)   36,950
U.S. Marines (669,100)   19,733
Coast Guard (241,093)   574
Civilians   Under 10

BRITISH COMMONWEALTH
544,596 killed or missing of 8,077,700 under arms
Britain   397,762
Canada   39,319
Australia   29,395

New Zealand   12,262
South Africa   8,681
India   36,092
Other   21,085
British civilian toll   70,000

SOVIET UNION
Military 14,500,000 of 20,000,000 under arms
Civilian   7,700,000

FRANCE
Military   210,671
Civilian   173,260

CHINA (1937–1945)
Military   2,200,000 of 5,000,000 under arms
Civilian   c. 10,000,000

AXIS POWERS
Germany
Military 2,850,000 of 10,000,000 under arms
Civilians   2,300,000

Italy
Military   279,820 of 4,500,000 under arms
Civilian   93,000

Japan (1937–1945)
Military 1,506,000 of 6,000,000 under arms
Civilian   672,000

THE FATE OF PRISONERS
Some 58 percent of Soviet prisoners held by the Germans died in captivity. The rate for British and Americans in Nazi camps was only 4 percent. The death rate of German prisoners held by Soviets was 30 percent. Comparison: death rate on Burma railway, 26 percent; 14 percent on the Bataan march.

AMERICA LEADS
1945–1956

Onset of the Cold War

Franklin D. Roosevelt's wartime dream of one world living in peace and prosperity, its quarrels settled in a United Nations led by America, Russia, Britain, France and China, did not survive the peace. The war left the United States and the Soviet Union the two dominant powers. They did wrangle their way to a charter for the United Nations, unanimously adopted by 51 nations in San Francisco on June 25, 1945, but within five years they had divided the world into two armed camps in a Cold War that would last nearly 50 years.

The two superpowers had mutually reinforcing fears. America saw a Soviet Union denying freedom to the liberated countries of Eastern Europe, menacing neighbors on its vast periphery, creating havoc in the West through subversive Communist parties, masterminding the Communist takeover of China. America read all these happenings as a plan for world domination. The Soviet Union, for its part, saw America, with a monopoly on the atomic bomb, insisting on the restoration of the former enemies of Germany and Japan, and encircling it with a hostile capitalist alliance.

America's assumption of leadership was dramatic. By 1950, America had committed itself to a global role unimaginable even three years before. It financed the rebuilding of Europe and Japan. It led in the creation of a new German state and a new Japan. It committed itself in NATO to the first peacetime military alliance in its history (though it shied away from the term "alliance"). And in a stroke at 6:11 p.m. (EST) on May 14, 1948, it transformed the Middle East by announcing that it would recognize the new Jewish state of Israel proclaimed in Palestine. The price for all this was the long hard years of the Cold War.

BELEAGUERED BUT DEFIANT: We are looking down from the roof of the Reichstag on some 300,000 Berliners. On September 9, 1948, in the middle of the Soviet blockade of the divided city, they packed into the Reichstag Square in the British Zone, just across the line from the Soviet Zone: the Soviet war memorial rises in the distance. It was a rally for freedom, addressed by Mayor Ernst Reuter and others, days after Communist gangs prevented members of the city assembly from meeting in the city offices, which happened to be in the Soviet sector. At the rally, a handful of youths rushed to the Brandenburg Gate and pulled down the Soviet flag. Soviet Zone police and Soviet troops fired on them. Three months later, on December 5, the single city government split in two when the Soviets blocked East Berliners from voting in new city elections. Reuter, a Social Democrat and defector from the Communist Party in 1921, became mayor again in West Berlin. He had won in the first Berlin elections, but a Soviet veto had invalidated the result and kept him out of office. Photograph by Henry Ries.

THE CRUSADE WITH A COST

Halfway through the American Century, the prophecy Henry Luce made in 1941 seemed to have been realized. The country was "at the summit of the world," in Winston Churchill's phrase. Alone among the warring nations, it emerged with its territory inviolate, its people whole, its farms bountiful, its industries able to satisfy every material want, its treasuries replete, its confidence in itself unbounding. It alone possessed the atomic bomb.

Many Americans, said Averell Harriman, just wanted to "go to the movies and drink Coke." And who could blame them? Everyone wanted to get back to Main Street. What were they saying before they were so rudely interrupted? Rioting GIs, impatient with shipping delays, yelled, "We wanna go home." One debt of honor was paid. On Independence Day in 1946, the Stars and Stripes came down over the Philippine Islands, granted their long-promised independence 48 years after Admiral Dewey sailed into Manila Bay. But as yet American leadership was not commensurate with the desperation of most of the world. Congress and the public were in a mean mood. The polls were consistent: Get back every cent we lent during the war. Roosevelt had given the impression that Lend-Lease would be converted to postwar reconstruction. Truman, on bad advice, abruptly ended the program. Ships carrying supplies to Britain, still fighting the last battle in Asia alongside America, and to Russia, were turned around at sea. In a postwar loan negotiation with its prostrate British ally, the U.S. exacted "all the conditions the traffic would bear," in the words of the State Department's Will Clayton, and even then Congress took six months to pass the bill. The U.S. pressed to end discrimination in trade, but retained a high tariff wall against imports. A Russian application for credit was deliberately lost in Secretary of State Byrnes's "Forget File."

But 1945 was not a rerun of 1919. The isolationism that had kept America out of the League of Nations was pronounced dead and buried on January 10, 1945, by Arthur Vandenberg, the florid Republican senator from Michigan who had long been the symbol and leader of the philosophy that the world could go hang itself. Joining the United Nations had the backing of 80 to 90 percent of the people, according to the polls. At Bretton Woods, the United States, with Britain, cosponsored the International Monetary Fund to minimize currency disruptions, and also to provide capital for the International Bank for Reconstruction and Development (the World Bank). These were farsighted creations, the fruit of Roosevelt's vision, but the landscape was everywhere infinitely bleaker than after World War I. The disruption this time was global. Germany had not been invaded in 1919; now it was a battlefield split four ways among the occupying powers. France and Italy had large Communist parties at their throats. Britain was bankrupt. Much of industrial Japan was a cinder. And the shadow of the Red Army lay across the Eurasian mass.

It was the specter of international communism on the march that galvanized America. The perception was skewed, and the progression to world leadership was often alarming, but before we retrace America's postwar career it is fair and right to examine the view from the mountaintop. No victorious power has treated its vanquished enemies as America came to treat Germany and Japan, two nations that had cost the lives of hundreds of thousands of American servicemen. The fates of the peoples conquered by the Soviet Union and America could not have been more different. The 20 million Germans in the Soviet Zone (later East Germany) exchanged one yoke for another. The 40 million in the west found restored in full measure the freedom they had lost in 1933, and America gave to the Japanese a freedom they had never known. The Soviets seized factories and exported skilled workers. Their claims for reparations (from all zones) were not unreasonable considering the damage they had suffered; but in both Germany and Japan the Americans were net givers, not takers. The Germans lucky enough to be under Allied occupation got the Marshall Plan; with the impetus of the Korean war, the Japanese got about as many dollars. American experts taught their ex-enemies the techniques of mass production that had assisted in their defeat. The Soviets everywhere installed secret police. In Japan, almost the first

THE NEW JAPAN: Supreme Commander Douglas MacArthur took a liking to Emperor Hirohito (right). At this meeting in the American embassy in Tokyo in 1945, Hirohito had yet to become an ordinary mortal, but he did on January 1, 1946. In a "declaration of humanity" he formally renounced the "false conception that the Emperor is divine and that the Japanese people are superior to other races of the world." MacArthur was right in his judgment that as a constitutional monarch Hirohito would make a good anchor for the new democratic Japan.

action of General Douglas MacArthur, the Supreme Commander of the Allied Powers, was to dismantle the secret police. The Soviets jailed opponents of communism—and executed uncooperative Communist leaders. In Japan, the arch-conservative MacArthur freed Communists and socialists from prison. The Soviets rigged elections and controlled the press and trade unions. In Germany, having purged the Nazis, America swiftly restored democracy and free speech from the ground up. In Japan, the new constitution America introduced within a six-day span gave the people a bill of rights, including freedom of the press and of assembly, an independent judiciary and freedom to bargain collectively for wages. The constitution also guaranteed equal rights for women—a clause still absent from the constitution of the United States itself.

The argument of various leftists at home and abroad is that all this, in Europe and Asia, was done cynically to provide customers for America's market-hungry industries. Of course, it is true that by pressing for free trade, and restoring the world economy, America was pursuing its enlightened self-interest. And why not? But that is not all there was to America's new role. The insistence of successive administrations on greater European cooperation was not to America's obvious advantage, nor was the rebuilding of Japanese steel, shipping and automobile industries. The criticism altogether ignores the force of moral idealism in America. It ran deep among the increasingly prosperous American taxpayers who paid the bills. A more salient misgiving must be that American idealism led to dark and dangerous diversions in the Cold War that began to seem inescapable in 1946.

It is not possible to date precisely the conversion of wartime allies into peacetime enemies. Since 1917 there had always been a substantial body of anti-Soviet opinion in the U.S. It had been a significant element in prewar isolationism, and the Democrats, even more than Vandenberg, had always to keep one ear cocked for the Catholic vote concentrated in the large cities. But in the summer of 1945 more than half the American people, according to a Gallup poll, believed that the Soviet Union would continue its wartime cooperation. The warmth the American people felt for the Russians was not shared by most of the officials around Truman. In April 1945, even as millions thrilled to the sight of American and Russian troops shaking hands on the Elbe, Soviet Foreign Minister Molotov was leaving Washington in a fury. Truman, briefed by advisers who had never liked Roosevelt's willingness to postpone tough bargaining until the war was won, had peremptorily demanded that the Soviet Union deliver on its Yalta agreements for free elections in Eastern Europe. An ashen Molotov said he had never been spoken to like that in his life, to which Truman had famously bitten back, "Carry out your agreements, and you won't get talked to like that." Harriman, who had been ambassador in Moscow since 1943, had come to Washington that month to alert the new president to Stalin's determination to dominate the Eastern European states. Harriman judged what had happened in Romania in February, while Roosevelt was alive, as a taste of things to come. Pounding his fist on the table, Andrei Vyshinsky, the Soviet deputy foreign minister, had demanded that King Michael dismiss his government, a coalition of genuine democratic parties with Communists, and replace it with one that represented "the truly democratic forces of the country," i.e., one with a predominance of Communists. Didn't the Yalta Declaration on Liberated Europe, asked the King, guarantee free elections? An angry Vyshinsky looked at his watch. "You have just two hours and five minutes to announce the new government." Then he walked out and slammed the door so hard the plaster cracked.

Truman was outraged by what Harriman told him, but as biographer Alonzo Hamby has shown, he was more ambivalent than his bluster suggested. He recognized that getting Soviet cooperation in setting up the United Nations was a more realistic objective than freeing Eastern Europe without war, and he found the Yalta agreements hazy; on his calendar he wrote of "purported" agreements. So he was prepared to deal. There was also, as Walter Lippmann pointed out, a certain hypocrisy in the U.S. position. America objected to the seating of the Polish Communist delegation at the United Nations on the grounds that the government was not democratic, while at the same time steamrolling Latin American states to vote for the admission of the no less democratic and pro-Nazi Perónist regime of Argentina. Truman sent the dying Harry Hopkins to Moscow in May to break the deadlock on the U.N. Charter by reassuring Stalin that "Poland, Romania, Bulgaria, Czechoslovakia, Austria, Yugoslavia, Latvia, Lithuania, Estonia et al. make no difference to U.S. interests." The roadblocks to the U.N. were removed and there was some window dressing of the Polish government. Truman was elated. His ambivalence persisted for nearly a year. Plagued with domestic distractions and divisions among his counselors, he could not decide whether, in Stalin, he was dealing with Tom Pendergast or the devil. Was the man just a tough political boss simply determined to hold on to his gains, or did he have evil designs on the whole world? In the early postwar days, Truman's secretary of commerce, former Vice President Henry Wallace, was not as isolated as he later became in his attitude toward the Soviet Union. Both he and Senator Vandenberg on the right believed British imperialism a bigger menace and both, if in differing degrees, thought Soviet fears of a revived Germany reasonable. In his January 1945 conversion to collective security Vandenberg talked not of the soon-to-be-demonized Kremlin intent on taking on the world, but of the war-ravaged Mother Russia of the scorched steppes, ruined cities and 20 million dead, seeking a buffer of small states for its own security. Even as late as a foreign ministers' conference in Moscow in December 1945, after a sterile meeting in London in September, Secretary of State Byrnes was nestling up to the Russians. He gave them a paper on atomic energy he had not shared with America's atomic partners, Britain and Canada. The poker-faced Molotov, a Russian cigarette dangling from his mouth, could barely contain his glee at the Western disunity.

THE RED ARMY: Colonel Sukhovarov leads armored units in Moscow's May Day parade in 1951. He was a war hero who helped rid Europe of the Nazis. What the West noted was that wherever the Red Army had been, Communist dictatorship followed. That was correct, but much of the postwar fear of a Soviet invasion of the West was based on exaggeration of Soviet strength. Demobilization of the Red Army had been almost as swift as that of the U.S. Army. The commonly cited figure of 208 divisions was wrong. They had 175, all of them only three-quarters the size of an American division and only one third at full strength. Only 30 were in Eastern Europe. In reality, they had 700,000 to 800,000 men to send against an estimated 800,000 Western European troops, hardly enough to attempt an offensive.

Having spent an unenviable Christmas with Stalin, Byrnes returned jubilantly, with an agreement of some democratic participation in the Romanian and Bulgarian regimes in return for U.S. diplomatic recognition of them. But compromises with Stalin now offended two constituencies: the moralists, who despised any "deals" in balance-of-power politics, and the pragmatists, a growing number of State Department officials and congressmen fed up with Molotov's *nyets* and the Soviet vetoes in the United Nations. Truman rebuked Byrnes in person and by a letter dated January 5, 1946. The encounter is remembered for Truman's expostulation, "I'm tired of babying the Soviets," but the real significance was the text, which suggested Russia should everywhere be confronted "with an iron fist." Truman reneged on the deal over Romania and Bulgaria. Public opinion was on his side. By February 1946 only some 35 percent of the American people believed the Soviet Union was helping to rebuild the postwar world.

Truman's suspicions were inflamed that month, when Stalin spoke in Moscow on the eve of elections to the Supreme Soviet. Stalin was no doubt resentful of what he saw as impediments to Soviet recovery, principally the American and British resistance to his demands on Germany for reparations. His speech turned out to be a stock denunciation of capitalism as the creator of crises and armed conflict in the competition for resources and markets. In a jumpy America, it was construed in the press and on Capitol Hill as predicting conflict between Russia and the West. Justice William Douglas dubbed it "the declaration of World War Three." It was nothing of the sort. Stalin's baleful analysis did not envisage conflict with the United States. It was confined to "the splitting of the capitalist world into two hostile camps and war between them." Nerves were still on edge when Winston Churchill came to Fulton, Missouri, on March 5, 1946, but his magnificently brooding presence on a platform with President Truman provoked a more complex response than is generally acknowledged. Everyone knows Churchill's growling tocsin that "from Stettin in the Baltic to Trieste in the Adriatic, an Iron Curtain has descended across the Continent," but the speech was not the turning point everyone remembers. It was widely attacked as an old warrior's premature call to arms. Truman's White House Counsel Clark Clifford recalls that what the crowd clapped for was Churchill's statement "I do not believe that Soviet Russia wants war. . . ." What they signally did not applaud was the Iron Curtain passage. Walter Lippmann called Fulton a "catastrophic blunder"; and the *Wall Street Journal* was enraged at the idea of an Anglo-Saxon alliance against the Soviet Union. Truman was worried enough to pretend he had not read the speech in advance. He wrote to Stalin to say he would be pleased if he, too, would come to Fulton. His administration was hostile to the Soviet Union, but it had not made up its mind whether Stalin was obsessed by national security or international revolution.

The threat of imminent Soviet aggression, as it turned out, was not what it was perceived to be by a developing majority in 1946–47, but it is easy to see why America got nervous—and how its anxieties became self-fulfilling. America's reaction to the fear of communism was perceived by the Soviet Union as a threat to its own security, and it responded in ways that served only to reinforce American anxiety. This spiral is the classic "security dilemma," to use historian Herbert Butterfield's term. Just before World War I, Lord Grey, the British foreign secretary, came up with a prescient definition: "Fear begets suspicion and distrust and evil imaginings of all sorts, till each Government feels it would be criminal and a betrayal of its own country not to take every precaution, while every Government regards every precaution of every other Government as evidence of hostile intent." The catch-22 prevailed even when America made peaceful gestures of the loftiest morality. The Marshall Plan was idealistic even if only halfheartedly offered to the Soviet Union, but in Stalin's mind it raised new phantoms of capitalist penetration, provoking, in turn, a tighter grip in Eastern Europe and still more anxiety in America. The dynamic circularity of U.S.-Soviet relations gained in velocity. Even statesmen of goodwill and imagination may attribute evil motives to an opponent while at the same time finding it hard, if not impossible, to recognize that their own actions might be seen as menacing. Truman had the goodwill, but not the imagination; and the odious Stalin had neither. He was truculent, ruthless, suspicious, mendacious and xenophobic. Whether in these circumstances the cold peace could have been prolonged, and the Cold War avoided, will long be a matter of dispute. In the early postwar years, for all Churchill's rhetoric, Stalin had not yet forged an orbit of Soviet satellites under Communist dictatorship, encouraged revolutions, established the Cominform and the Warsaw Pact or altogether buckled down to a Cold War. He did all these things, as the historian Melvyn Leffler has pointed out, only after the Truman administration prepared to embrace its traditional enemies of Germany and Japan and implant American power on the borders of the Soviet Union. Meanwhile, Czechoslovakia, a liberated ally, and Hungary enjoyed free elections, yielding non-Communist governments. Stalin allowed Finland, an ex-enemy, a measure of independence and abandoned the Greek Communists. Much is made in Cold War histories of the way the Soviets pressed their postwar strategic claims on Iran and Turkey. Neither move should have been surprising. Iran was on the Soviet border and the Russians had shared wartime occupation with the British. The British controlled the oilfields. When the Americans entered a postwar claim to a share, it was natural that the Russians should say "us, too." With Turkey, again, it was not outrageous for the Soviets to ask, as the fruits of war, for joint control of the Dardanelles, the strait between the Black Sea and the Mediterranean that provided Russia's only access to the ports of southern Europe and North Africa. Turkey had closed the straits to the Allies in the war and opened the waters to the Nazis. Washington suggested a United

Nations agency should control the straits, with U.S. representation, but the Russians noted that nothing similar was proposed for Panama and Suez, two waterways that were controlled by the West. Little of this complexity survived the propaganda wars. In both cases, Stalin-as-Pendergast retreated when America put on a show of force. It was a satisfying result, but the Soviet attempt to advance its national interest was fed into the gathering suspicion of a plot to conquer the world. Within two years America had committed itself in Europe to the historic NATO alliance. It had also dedicated itself to an armed ideological crusade that was unimaginable in 1945, one unique in its history.

The tradition and temperament of American policy makers lead them to justify actions by reference to some universal standard rather than by acting case by case with specific solutions to specific problems. The habit may be rooted in a preference for a government of laws, and in the practical necessity of explaining policy to a vast, scattered, heterogeneous population of insular disposition; and perhaps it is reinforced in the business mind by the success of systems. In any event, the tendency is to reduce complexity to a clear definition: Who are the good guys and who are the bad? The either/or cast of American thought and the temper of public discussion rate self-critical analysis as dubious patriotism.

The natural disinclination to see whether the bad guys' behavior can be explained by anything the good guys may have done to provoke it was exemplified in the conflicts over Iran and Turkey. The Western media, with official encouragement, reduced the conflicts of interest to a matter of Communist imperialism versus American benevolence. The demonology paid a double bonus. It obscured the fact that America was behaving like an old-fashioned big power out to defend its interests just like the Russians; and it diverted attention from the unpalatable truth that the regimes the West supported in the name of anticommunism were anything but democratic.

On the desk of Under Secretary of State Dean Acheson the day Churchill's Iron Curtain speech made the headlines was a telegram of 5,450 words that, for good and for ill, was to determine American policy in the universal mode over the next decades. It was from George Kennan, the 42-year-old minister-counselor who was deputizing in Moscow for Ambassador Harriman. Nursing a cold and toothache in the American embassy overlooking Red Square, Kennan was also stricken by inspiration born out of frustration with what he saw as Washington's deafness. Asked by the Treasury Department to explain why the Soviets were pulling out of talks on the International Monetary Fund, Kennan lay in his bedroom dictating

GEORGE POLK: THE PRICE OF TRUTH

George Polk, the archetypal all-American boy. He served in the Navy force at Guadalcanal. He was naive perhaps, but married meticulous accuracy in his reporting with the ideals of the man who recruited him to CBS, Edward R. Murrow. His name is commemorated by a prize in journalism.

"George Polk is the first casualty of the Cold War." —I. F. Stone

On May 16, 1948, the body of CBS correspondent George Polk (left) was dredged out of the Gulf of Salonika. He had been bound, blindfolded and shot once in the head at close range. The Royalist Greek government was quick to blame the Communist guerrillas they were fighting in a civil war. Polk had, it is true, investigated an odious Communist practice of separating families, but he had also just confronted Foreign Minister Constantine Tsaldaris with a tip from an employee of Chase National Bank in New York that Tsaldaris had deposited $25,000 in a secret account. Politician and reporter had a row, with Polk threatening, "I'm going to blow this story sky-high when I get home." In her investigative book *The Polk Conspiracy*, Kati Marton concludes that his killing was organized by Major Nicholas Mouscoundis, chief of security in the region. The CIA and British intelligence assisted in a cover-up because Britain, with American support, had cast the right-wing government as the defender of democratic values against the menace of communism. Walter Lippmann was formally in charge of an inquiry, but it was run by General William J. Donovan, founder of the OSS, who concealed evidence implicating rightists gathered by his own agent, Jim Kellis. Lippmann's biographer Ronald Stone says Lippmann "privately recognized that discrepancies in the evidence pointed damningly toward the Greek government and the CIA."

The incident is not on the scale of other Cold War cruelties, and the Communists were at least as ruthless as the Royalists. Yet the cynicism of murder and cover-up made a mockery of the idealism of the Cold War. Democracy was late in coming to Greece (and elsewhere), and the Polks who tried to tell the truth were often the first victims.

an analysis of Soviet psychology. It was futile for America to believe that gestures of goodwill had any effect in the Soviet Union. The Kremlin was too suspicious of the outside world. Marxism was not the origin of this neurosis; it was merely the fig leaf by which the rulers tried to justify their actions. The real source of Russia's hostility was a traditional and instinctive sense of insecurity. Russia had never known a friendly neighbor. It had always feared direct contact with the Western world, now expressed as fear of "capitalist encirclement." It had learned to seek security only in the patient but deadly struggle for total destruction of rival power, never in compacts and compromises with it. The Russians were impervious to logic but highly sensitive to the logic of force. They would withdraw when they encountered strong resistance at any point from an adversary who made clear his readiness to reply.

Kennan's telegram, received on George Washington's birthday, caused a sensation in the capital. It particularly excited James Forrestal, the former Wall Street deal maker, secretary of the Navy and soon-to-be first secretary of defense, who was trying hard to get Truman to increase defense spending (later he became depressed, and in February 1949, harshly dismissed by Truman, jumped to his death). Forrestal was a brooding anti-Soviet hawk who believed Marxism impelled the Soviet leaders toward all-out war against the West. This was not what Kennan had said or believed, but Forrestal became the patron of the young official. He circulated the so-called Long Telegram, and he got Kennan a job at the National War College, then commissioned him to write a policy paper. He saw to it that this document entered public consciousness as official policy by sanctioning Kennan to write it up as an article for the magazine *Foreign Affairs,* and then confirming to Arthur Krock of the *New York Times* that the author "X" was Kennan. "The main element of any United States policy," the article argued, "must be that of a long-term, patient but firm and vigilant containment of Russian expansive tendencies . . . by the adroit and vigilant application of counterforce at a series of constantly shifting geographical and political points corresponding to the shifts and maneuvers of Soviet policy." America, in short, should draw a line: this far and no farther!

Where and how—and against whom precisely—it should draw a line was to become critically important. In Kennan's mind the areas to be "defended" were Britain, the Rhine Valley and Japan, "where the sinews of modern military strength could be produced in quantity." But he did not say so in the Long Telegram or the X article. He did not limit the geo-

GEORGE KENNAN (b. 1904) THE ROMANTIC LONER WHO CHANGED HISTORY

The father of containment was a romantic loner. After his mother died when he was two months old, his 52-year-old father was emotionally unable to give him much affection. He became a shy, insecure boy with a "dolorous," "diffident," hypochondriac personality. Shipped off to St. John's Military Academy outside his native Milwaukee, he fell in love with the idea of Princeton University after reading F. Scott Fitzgerald's *This Side of Paradise.* He was middle-class, but more snobbish than most of his wealthier colleagues and an elitist. Women, whom he considered essentially frivolous, and blacks should be made wards of the state. He stumbled diffidently through Princeton, and landed in the diplomatic corps, in good part because he did not have the money to go to law school. Once there, he proved a brilliant analyst and persuasive writer, working up through the ranks of the foreign service and coming to know Russia and Eastern Europe like few Americans before or since. He was a contrarian, and in two important instances his thoughts produced results contrary to his intentions. The containment he had thought of as political became militarized; and he was dismayed when the CIA's Office of Special Projects, which he had suggested in 1948, became a promiscuous sponsor of covert action.

graphical scope of his principle or define "force." He became a victim of Murphy's law of diplomacy: that ambiguous passages will always be read upside down. He was appalled when Walter Lippmann's column accused him of dispersing American power around the world "in the service of a heterogeneous collection of unstable governments and of contending powers which happen to be opposed to the Soviet Union." Forrestal's biographers, Townsend Hoopes and Douglas Brinkley, make a persuasive case that the ambiguities were Kennan's way of accommodating Forrestal's harder line, but that later Kennan chose to admit "egregious error" rather than admit the influence of the apocalyptic Forrestal. Kennan ever after maintained that the "containment" he advocated was the political response to a political threat. The "containment" that emerged was the response by military means to military threat. He believed the Russians did not want to invade anywhere. Alas, he was understood to say they were set to invade everywhere. The first thing he meant by "resistance" was being robust in the face of internal subversion and Soviet truculence. The last thing he wanted was rearmament, which would divert resources from economic recovery; but this was the first thing Forrestal wanted. Kennan hoped that if the realities were understood there would be "far less hysterical anti-Sovietism." There was more. Kennan spent years trying to undo the misinterpretations. Once he cornered Lippmann on the parlor car from Washington to New York and talked nonstop, explaining that containment did not mean accepting the perpetual division of Europe.

Some six months after Kennan's article appeared, Clark Clifford and his aide, George Elsey, delivered a document to the President that intimates how the most hawkish opinion had emerged from Kennan's delicate intuitions. Having interviewed senior policy advisers, they denounced the idea, supported by Wallace and a few others, that hopes for peace lay in trying to reach mutual understanding. Soviet foreign policy, they said, was "designed to prepare the Soviet Union for war with the leading capitalist nations of the world." To restrain the Soviet Union, "the United States must be prepared to wage atomic and biological warfare. Any discussion on the limitation of armaments should be pursued slowly and carefully with the knowledge constantly in mind that proposals on outlawing atomic warfare and long-range offensive weapons would greatly limit United States strength while only moderately affecting the Soviet Union." Truman took every copy of the report from Clifford, who never saw it again. "It is very valuable to me," said Truman, "but if it leaked it would blow the roof off the White House, it would blow the roof off the Kremlin." Alonzo Hamby reasonably believes Truman had still not given up hope of a general accord with the Soviets, especially if he could deal directly with Stalin.

The call to arms was not heeded yet, but a few months later, crises in Greece and Turkey incited the United States to transmute Kennan's conception way beyond the needs of the hour.

It was an appropriately rain-dank Friday on February 21, 1947, when the British ambassador's office alerted the State Department that they were sending over a "blue piece of paper," diplomatic shorthand for an important message. They sent two blues. Acheson chose to describe them in his memoir as "shockers." In six weeks, near-bankrupt Britain would stop assisting Greece and Turkey. Greece was riven by a civil war,

Turkey vulnerable to Soviet pressure. Acheson, given free rein by Secretary of State Marshall, seized the occasion now not simply to plug the hole left by the British but to advance a sweeping new American policy.

"I knew we were met at Armageddon," he wrote of the White House meeting with congressional leaders six days later. The Republicans were newly in the ascendant in Congress, determined on cutting taxes, not on "plucking Britain's chestnuts out of the fire." They had just thrown out requests by Marshall and Forrestal for more money for aid and defense. Marshall's appeal on Greece and Turkey, emphasizing humanitarianism as much as communism, fell flat. Acheson had not so long before ribbed Paul Nitze, the new head of the Policy Planning staff at the State Department, that he was "seeing mirages" when Nitze had fretted about Soviet expansion. Now, having absorbed and exaggerated Kennan's apprehensions, Acheson had the fervor of a convert. Three continents lay exposed to Soviet domination! They stood at a bridge of history! Washington and Moscow were Athens and Sparta, Rome and Carthage! In his memoirs, Acheson recalled what he said: "Like apples in a barrel infected by one rotten one, the corruption of Greece would infect Iran and all to the east. It would also carry infection to Africa through Asia Minor and Egypt, and to Europe through Italy and France, already threatened by the strongest Communist parties in Europe." The congressmen were stunned. If Truman would say such things to Congress they would support him. He had to "scare the hell out of the country." Truman did—but once again there was an escalation of the stakes. No longer was America committing itself merely to rescuing Greece and Turkey in the name of anticommunism. On March 12, 1947, President Truman uttered a ringing declaration to a numbed joint session of Congress: "It must be the policy of the United States to support free peoples who are resisting attempted subjugation by armed minorities or by outside pressure."

This was containment with a halo—and a sword. The sweeping rhetoric, soon christened the Truman Doctrine but adopted by successive Republican and Democratic presidents, underlined once again the American taste for moral absolutes. It is as if there is a subliminal sense of shame about the exercise of power in the national interest so that the nakedness of specific action for a specific problem has to be clothed in an elevating generality endorsed by all mankind. Such moral ardor can be utterly inspiring. It was how the Republic began. In the Cold War, it was no doubt necessary from time to time to justify the sacrifices and the risks this way. It was by playing on the fear of a Soviet breakout, after the coup in Czechoslovakia in 1948, that the administration finally got the Marshall Plan through Congress. The American political system, with its checks and balances, seems always to require melodrama for momentum, with a messy afterbirth. Walter Isaacson and Evan Thomas, students of "the wise men" who determined American policy in the postwar years, suggest that in selling the need for NATO and other military commitments, internationalists like Dean Acheson purposely overstated the threat they perceived, then eventually began to internalize and accept their own rhetoric as a foundation for policy. In any event, what they thought of as prudent defensive alliances looked aggressive to the isolated leaders in the Kremlin. They might well ask, as Kennan suggested, what ulterior motive America had for justifying its policies by accusing them of "the one thing they had not done, which was to plan, as yet, to conduct an overt and unprovoked invasion of Western Europe."

By 1948, Kennan himself had less influence than the perversion of his own doctrine. The emotional reaction he feared came about when the Communists staged their coup in Czechoslovakia that February and the Russians began on April 1 to try to force the Allies out of Berlin. The events fitted the thesis of a master plan to take over the world, but as Kennan wrote, they were more sensibly understood as defensive reactions to the initial success of the Marshall Plan, the signing of the Brussels Defense Pact (the progenitor of NATO) and the preparations to set up a separate German government in western Germany. He had warned Secretary Marshall in the fall of 1947 that cool heads would be needed when the ever suspicious Soviets responded. They would, in Trotsky's phrase, "slam the door so that all Europe would shake." Kennan argued that the West should respond with quiet firmness, as it did with the Berlin Airlift, and then be ready to talk with Stalin about the future of Europe once he had got the message that expansionism did not pay. That moment arrived when Stalin did call off the Berlin blockade and indicated he was ready for serious negotiation to forestall the Soviet nightmare of a rearmed Germany. It was, said Kennan in 1994, one of "the great disappointments of my life" that at this moment the United States and the Western allies held out for Stalin's "unconditional surrender." If it was a propitious moment, it was soon clouded by Russia's explosion of an atomic bomb in 1949 and the Korean war in 1950. Only after these events did the military element of

BERLIN: Henry Ries made only this one exposure of the children of Berlin ready to catch candy thrown from the U.S. relief planes.

THE GREAT BERLIN AIRLIFT

It looked like a sentence of death or servitude for the 2.5 million people in the western sectors of Berlin when at 6 a.m. on June 24, 1948, the Soviet Union stopped all road, rail and water traffic crossing its zone. They cut off electricity from their sector, too, so West Berliners had only a few hours' supply a day, and coal for only 45 days. The Soviet squeeze play was a retaliation for the decision of the Western occupying powers to create a separate, capitalist West Germany, with the Deutschmark as its new currency.

The Berliners needed a minimum of 4,000 tons of coal a day to stay alive, 8,000 tons a day to stay in work. The U.S. Air Force and the Royal Air Force immediately started flying cargo around the clock. But the planes were too small. In June and July, the airlift averaged an unviable 1,147 tons a day. The American commander, General Lucius Clay, got bigger C-54s. Pilots were sent to Montana to fly a duplicate run of the twenty-mile-wide air corridors and approaches and to fly on instruments in all weathers. Two new airstrips were built. By December, the young American, British and French pilots—55 of whom died—were bringing in 4,500 tons; by February 1949, 5,500; and by April the magical 8,000 tons. Factories had closed and there was electricity for cooking only two hours a day, but Berlin had made it. The Soviets ended the blockade on May 12, 1949.

How close was war? The Soviets avoided a showdown. A little-known fact of the airlift is that Soviet air-control towers cooperated throughout. General Clay wanted to smash the blockade with an armed convoy. He never stopped believing the Russians would have yielded. But Truman's judgment was sounder. In 1989, Henry Kissinger asked retired Soviet Foreign Minister Andrei Gromyko why they had risked war in the face of America's nuclear monopoly. Stalin, said Gromyko, had told his advisers the Americans would never use nuclear weapons to defend Berlin; if they attempted to push through a convoy, the Red Army was to resist; and if the United States seemed about to attack along the whole front, Stalin reserved the final judgment to himself. "That," concluded Kissinger, "was the point at which he would presumably have settled."

The Berlin Airlift was more than a triumph; it was an inspiration. The West responded to the courage of the Berliners, and the world warmed to the spirit of the rescuers. A young Air Force lieutenant named Carl S. Halverson epitomized America at its best. Out of his own pocket, he started dropping candy to the children watching the landings. The thought caught on with all the other fliers. In Operation Santa Claus in December 1948, thousands of tiny parachutes floated down gifts from America.

containment get out of hand: American defense spending was stable from 1947 to 1950 at around $13 billion; by 1953 it was $53 billion.

The concept that began as a strategically judicious containment of the Soviet Union on its perimeter was transformed into a perverse Wilsonianism, a crusade that was to cost America blood and tears down the Cold War decades from Korea to Vietnam. Something like a million troops were deployed for 25 years on 4,000 bases in 39 countries. American carrier fleets were in the Mediterranean and South China seas, its nuclear bombers and submarines on 24-hour watch. Succeeding presidents outdid one another in rhetoric. President Kennedy bet the bank: "Let every nation know, whether it wishes us ill or well, that we shall pay any price, bear any burden, meet any hardship, support any friend, oppose any foe, to assure the survival and success of liberty." But it was the less eloquent Eisenhower who gave containment its most dangerous metaphor. "You have a row of dominoes all set up, you knock over the first one and what will happen to the last one is a certainty." Acheson had scared the congressmen in 1947 with his metaphor of bad apples. Eisenhower's was more alarming for two reasons: First, it was artificial and mechanistic. Countries are not inorganic raw material but living complexities of history, politics, race, religion, geography and leadership in dynamic relationships with other countries. To ignore all these elements in Vietnam was to guarantee incomprehension and ultimately disaster. Eisenhower shrewdly sidestepped his own logic, but his successors bought it and paid for it. Second, Eisenhower had already laid it down that if a domino fell there would be "massive [nuclear] retaliation . . . instantly by means and at places of our choosing." The European powers' elaborate timetables for mobilization

gave us World War I; Eisenhower's elementary mechanics threatened Armageddon. The words were those of his secretary of state from 1953 to 1959, John Foster Dulles; the thought was Eisenhower's. The President was determined to balance the budget by cutting defense spending and relying on the nuclear deterrent. The man of peace and the brinksman did an effective good cop/bad cop routine. It worked well enough because of Eisenhower's patient good judgment, but the ascent of the devout Presbyterian Dulles gave an extra intellectual spin to the moralistic-legalistic approach that was now firmly the American style. Dulles's bedtime reading was Stalin's *The Problems of Leninism* and *Dialectical and Historical Materialism;* he kept an underlined copy of each on his desk. He became convinced that the Soviet Union was an empire whose ideology demanded conquest. He had even less appreciation than Acheson of the interactive quality of international relations. He was right that America was not an aggressor and did not threaten the security of the Soviet Union, but utterly wrong to conclude "Khrushchev does not need to be convinced of our good intentions."

Dulles made as many enemies for America as Eisenhower made friends. Dulles's insistence that neutrality was an "immoral and short-sighted conception" alienated developing countries, which resented being told they had to choose between good and evil. Dulles felt the same way about "containment." It was, he wrote in the 1952 Republican policy statement, "negative, futile, and immoral." Republicans would abandon containment in favor of liberating the countless human beings condemned to "despotism and godless terrorism." President Eisenhower had to remind his secretary of state to emphasize that it was "peaceful" liberation they had in mind, not war. It was loose talk that cost lives. Not even a peaceful finger was lifted to help the East Germans who

revolted in June 1953, nor the Poles and Hungarians in 1956: too bad they got a different impression from America's Radio Free Europe. Eisenhower restrained Dulles's wilder impulses for a holy war against atheistic communism. He ended the Korean war without giving the Chinese "one hell of a licking" with the atomic bomb, as Dulles had recommended. He refrained from going to the rescue of the French outpost in Vietnam at Dien Bien Phu. But Ike let Dulles set the tone, and the world was more frightening and more dangerous as a result: his belligerent language stiffened the Soviet and Chinese military in their demands for more weapons.

Ike had a passionate desire for détente that his secretary of state did not share. Dulles, as historian and biographer Piers Brendon observed, was of a mind to suspect that Stalin arranged to die on March 5, 1953, only to make it more difficult for the new administration to detect which way the Soviets would jump. In April Ike made his celebrated "Cross of Iron" speech, which gave hope that the world was at a turning point. "Every gun that is fired, every warship launched, every rocket fired signifies, in the final sense, a theft from those who hunger and are not fed, those who are cold and are not clothed. . . ." Ike saw "under the cloud of threatening war . . . humanity hanging from a cross of iron." But Dulles whittled away at Eisenhower's initiative. He killed Churchill's plea for a summit with the new Soviet leaders. There would be no negotiation. That there had been room for maneuver was demonstrated by the surprising Soviet offer of independence for a neutralized Austria, consummated in 1955 despite Dulles's suspicions. Europe meanwhile stayed divided, poised for obliteration if the thermonuclear game plans went awry.

But it was in Asia that the consequences of an undiscriminating "anti-Communist" containment exacted its harshest penalty.

Three days in September 1949 created in America a crisis of confidence that took decades to overcome. In Beijing, on September 21, 1949, Mao Zedong declared the People's Republic of China, claiming Communist control of one third of the world's population and one quarter of its land space. Two days later Truman announced: "We have evidence an atomic explosion occurred in the USSR." The events fused in the public mind as the march of a single conspiracy. The judgment that Mao was his own man seemed eccentric, even though Yugoslavia's Marshal Tito had finally split with Stalin in June 1948. The bipartisan foreign policy of 1945–1948 broke down in Republican bitterness over Truman's reelection. It became the liturgy of the Republicans that traitors in America had given Stalin the bomb and fellow travelers in the State Department had allowed his puppet Mao to defeat Chiang Kai-shek's Nationalists. America had saved Western Europe. Why had it lost China?

Of course, the United States never had China to lose. Nothing more could have been done to save Chiang. But after more than a century of cautious isolationism, the American people had been persuaded almost overnight that they held absolute power to determine the fates of peoples around the globe. The disillusion was traumatic, the kind of shock that some individuals can tolerate only by finding scapegoats, the "them" whose hand can be seen in every reverse, as Richard Hofstadter suggested in his work *The Paranoid Style in American Politics*. That China should have slipped back into "barbarism" was a particular exasperation. America had since the last century cast itself in a missionary role, regarding the Chinese as a people qualified for salvation by America's direct line to God and its political and social know-how. Senator Kenneth Wherry, an undertaker from Nebraska, expressed the spirit perfectly in his cry, "We shall lift Shanghai up, up forever, until it is just like Kansas City!" These feelings were pow-

THE CHINA LOBBY

The "China Lobby," which had gradually been picking up steam since the 1930s, was an odd assortment of old missionaries, businessmen, Republicans and media tycoons whose belief in the Nationalist Chinese regime, in the words of the journalist Henry Brandon, "surpassed their American patriotism." At the top was *Time*'s Henry Luce, prophet of the American Century, born in China of Presbyterian missionaries; his ostentatiously Catholic wife, Clare; the Hearst press, the McCormick press and *U.S. News & World Report;* Joe McCarthy's ghostwriter, Forrest A. Davis, a former editorial writer for the *Cincinnati Enquirer;* columnists George Sokolsky, J. B. Matthews and Fulton Lewis, Jr., of the Mutual Radio Network; the famous leader of the Flying Tigers, Claire Chennault; and, to a considerable extent, Douglas MacArthur. The conservatives had some strange bedfellows—Harry Hopkins, who had become friends with Chiang's brother-in-law, T. V. Soong; the old New Dealer Tom Corcoran; the former Democratic strategist Jim Farley; AFL leader Matthew Woll; and even the International Ladies' Garment Workers Union leader David Dubinsky.

Much of the lobby was funded directly by Chiang from American aid and indirectly from the narcotics trade. Roy Cohn, who was George Sokolsky's executor, told editor and publisher Jason Epstein that he had seen "boxes" of money Sokolsky received from Mme. Chiang. It went to the lobby's vociferous Alfred Kohlberg, who ran several publications from his office in the garment district. Kohlberg, known as the Handkerchief King, had made a modest fortune producing and exporting lacework from China. He was a classic crank, an itinerant conspiracy theorist who reveled in the aggressive anti-intellectualism that became a trademark of the American right.

THE CHIANGS: Chiang Kai-shek and his alluring, scheming wife, the former Mei-ling Soong, with General Marshall. Chiang and his wife were presented to America as saviors of a united, democratic China. Journalist Theodore White, a onetime admirer, concluded that they were "a corrupt political clique that combines some of the worst features of Tammany Hall with the Spanish Inquisition."

erfully exploited by the China Lobby. The United States would not recognize Communist China until 1979.

Striving for so long to keep a de facto government out of the United Nations was Wilsonianism at its most self-righteous. The United Nations was not an alliance, nor was it conceived as one. It was the opposite of an alliance. It was an arena where enemies as well as friends might recognize and reconcile conflicting interests. To deny its universality was to deny the only reason for its existence. The level of emotion the subject of China's admission aroused is suggested by the reaction of Dulles, then assisting Truman, when George Kennan proposed that the U.S. might merely compromise and abstain. Dulles leaked that he used to think highly of Kennan, but had now concluded that he was "a very dangerous man."

The Chinese Communists did not seem to care about winning friends and influencing people. They seized American consular premises and harassed American citizens. They menaced the Nationalist refugees on Taiwan. They peddled a tedious line about capitalist hyenas. They displayed their faith in equality by treating countries that recognized them as badly as countries that did not. But the unpalatable reality was that they controlled the Chinese

mainland and this entitled them to recognition and the seat on the United Nations Security Council held by Chiang's Nationalists. A large part of Palestine had been recognized as the contentious new state of Israel on the very day of its proclamation on May 14, 1948. China was recognized by Britain and India. Support for the same practical response from the U.S. was not lacking among American missionaries and businessmen in China; many newspapers not in the Hearst, McCormick or Scripps-Howard chains; and scholars. But the increasingly frenetic China Lobby prevailed. By 1950, Henry Luce's Time-Life publications were suggesting that general war with communism was probably inevitable and perhaps better sooner than later.

The lobby was not simply the progenitor of a sterile policy. It would evolve into something heretofore unknown in American political life: an ideological, activist, radical right wing. The closest thing to an antecedent this new right had was the Republican "Old Guard," which had developed such a virulent hatred for Roosevelt in the thirties. As Stephen Ambrose puts it, "the Old Guardsmen were a strange breed of isolationists—they wanted to get out of Western Europe, liberate Eastern Europe, and fight all out in Asia." The U.S.

had certainly seen plenty of powerful conservative movements before; indeed, America's basic political inclination is conservative. But what developed in the confusion of the Cold War was something altogether different. This was an ideology that went beyond a general adherence to laissez-faire economics and a distrust of big government. The creators of the China Lobby operated much more like a traditional European Fascist movement, complete with a campaign to drive dissenters out of public life and control the means of information. They had only a nominal devotion to democracy, specialized in the big lie and traced their heritage to a mythic act: Roosevelt's "betrayal" at Yalta. Roosevelt had made a conscious pragmatic decision at Yalta to give up what were some relatively small Asian potatoes in exchange for Russian entry into the war to spare thousands of American lives in what promised then to be a bloody assault of the Japanese homeland. Pat Hurley, FDR's flamboyantly unstable envoy to China, would build an entirely new political career out of claiming that these provisions had been secretly written in by State Department traitors and concealed from Chiang's Nationalists. Hurley's own papers negate his claim, and the Sino-Soviet treaty endorsing the Yalta agreements was signed on August 14, 1945, by a "satisfied" Chiang. But Hurley's lurid thesis was given momentum by the fallout from an FBI raid on the offices of the small left-wing magazine *Amerasia* in June 1945. *Amerasia* had 1,700 government documents, including some written by the State Department's John Stewart Service, who had clashed with Hurley in China. To the China Lobby, the six people associated with the magazine who were arrested were spies who had helped undermine Chiang. That the six were not prosecuted for espionage was "evidence" of a pro-Communist group high in the Truman administration.

The thesis was reiterated by the Republican aspirant for the presidency, Senator Robert Taft of Ohio. The honest but prickly Taft was an unredeemed isolationist. But two young congressmen from Massachusetts and California, John Kennedy and Richard Nixon, agreed with him. Kennedy declared: "What our young men saved, our diplomats and our president have frittered away." Nixon, who labeled the Democrats "the party of treason," coined the staple of the 1952 Republican campaign, that Truman was responsible for the loss of 100 million people a year to communism.

The clamor of the China Lobby, and later the complicity of John Foster Dulles, drove out of office a group of talented Foreign Service officials who had been stationed in China during much of the war. The purges left the U.S. flying blind. John Service, John Paton Davies, Raymond Ludden and Kenneth Emerson, among others, suffered in loyalty investigations because the loyalty being tested was not to the United States but to Chiang. The China hands were one by one vindicated, but the purges left the U.S. policy makers poorly briefed at a critical moment. The transforming event was the Korean war in June 1950.

Dean Acheson, who succeeded Marshall as Truman's secretary of state in January 1949, was the chief policy maker, aided by Philip Jessup and Dean Rusk. One should say Acheson and Acheson made the policies. Acheson 1 was the studiously pragmatic diplomat who could contemplate recognizing Communist China once the dust had settled, but he had differences with Acheson 2, the cold warrior who sought to contain China by announcing military aid for Thailand and Indochina in March 1950. It was Acheson 1 who gave Mao a free hand to take Taiwan, carrying the Joint Chiefs and Truman with him in rejecting the demand for a naval screen from Senators William Knowland and Taft and former President Hoover. Truman restated the position on January 5, 1950: "The United States will not pursue a course which will lead to involvement in the civil conflict in China." Acheson 1 and Acheson 2 suffered a crisis of identity in the first six months of 1950. Policy planners under Paul Nitze, who wrote the seminal National Security Council Paper known as NSC 68, advocated massive rearmament because they were convinced the Kremlin gave orders to every Communist Party, in the service of a master military design for world domination. The Soviet experts disagreed. They thought Stalin put the survival of his regime and "communism in one country" ahead of world revolution. Acheson the cold warrior sided with the planners at the same time that the conciliatory Acheson entertained the possibility of divisions in the supposed Communist monolith. It was Acheson 1 who made a speech at the National Press Club on January 12, 1950, that is remembered because it seemed to put Korea—and Taiwan—outside the Far East "strategic defense crescent" from Japan through Southeast Asia to India, thereby allegedly inviting the North Koreans to invade the South. The defense line Acheson articulated was no more than a restatement of the line described by MacArthur on March 1, 1949, and Acheson did go on to say countries outside the defense line could look to the United Nations, "which so far has not proved a weak reed." It was, all the same, a mistake in the context of the much advertised "containment" policy. We now know that Acheson's speech was used by North Korea's Kim Il Sung to bolster his case with Stalin for support for an invasion. But if Acheson's gratuitous foray into geopolitics was in error, it was not this that caused congressional conservatives and their allies in the press to call for his head. What incensed the China bloc was the implication in the speech that the U.S. might accept Mao's victory. Acheson spoke while Mao was in Moscow negotiating with Stalin what proved to be the Sino-Soviet treaty of February 14, 1950. Acheson 1 cast a discreet, if belated, long-distance lure toward Mao by dwelling on the long history of American philanthropy—and Russian perfidy—in Asia. Asking the right wing to consider the possibility that another Communist country might not be totally under the Soviet thumb, that it might be coaxed back into neutrality or even friendship with the U.S., was asking them to gaze on the Gorgon sisters. Such a rapprochement would have turned to stone the best political issue they had in 20 years. The irony is that as punishment for the speech the House China Lobby and Southern Democrats blocked money for Korea on January 19. Far from exercising the foresight on Communist intentions they were to claim later, the congressional China bloc gave not a thought to Korea.

In his memoir, Acheson belittles this "attack of the primitives." It is certainly nonsense to say that if the Republicans had not been hammering on Truman, he would never have gone into Korea. Truman and his advisers did not need any persuasion. Their points of reference were the Rhineland, Munich and Pearl Harbor, not Capitol Hill. They acted out of moral indignation, not political cowardice. What is true is that Truman's admirable resolve was accompanied by a fatal misreading of the relationships between Korea, China and the Soviet Union, for which Acheson bears the prime responsibility. The Sino-Soviet treaty that winter was a cautious document. It committed the Soviet Union to help Mao only in the event of an attack by or through an already disarmed Japan; Mao was not even guaranteed support in a war to take Taiwan, even if the U.S. helped Chiang. But Acheson 1, who in January had counseled seeing things from China's viewpoint, was now supplanted by Acheson 2, who denounced this cautious document as "an evil omen of imperialistic domination." Acheson 2 swiftly jettisoned the possibility that the Chinese might have different agendas from the Russians.

For all his kite flying in January, Acheson 1 had little idea of how deeply Mao and Stalin hated each other. It was only years later that the significance of Mao's long stay in Moscow was revealed to be insult rather than intimacy. Stalin kept Mao cooling his heels for two months, until he threatened to go home; Mao told his personal physician, Dr. Li Zhisui, that his distrust of Stalin went back to the civil war, when Stalin gave them no help, "not even a fart." But when the North Koreans invaded the South on June 25, 1950, Acheson 1's intuitions were overwhelmed by Acheson 2's indignation. A classic "security dilemma" scenario ensued. China and Russia were seen as integral to the aggression. On June 27, Truman ordered the U.S. 7th Fleet into the Taiwan Strait "to prevent any attack." It was a repudiation of the statement he had made on January 5 forswearing any American involvement in the Chinese civil war. Mao regarded the move as a threat to China itself. He responded with an angry speech on June 28, directed to a Washington audience. The Indian government urged Washington not to take the Chinese reaction lightly. But Washington, persuaded that it was facing a monolithic Communist aggression, was incapable of focusing on signals from China. These Communists, they all looked alike.

We have the benefit today of previously unavailable Chinese and Russian sources, notably in *Uncertain Partners*, by a trio of Russian, American and Chinese scholars, Sergei N. Goncharov, John W. Lewis and Xue Litai. Their researches led them to emphasize the divergent interests of Stalin and Mao. It was Stalin, not Mao, who approved Kim Il Sung's attack. Mao was kept largely in the dark and did not send Kim any substantial help from June to October 1950. Penetrating the labyrinth of Stalin's mind is not given to mortals. No doubt he would have seen America's decision to exclude the Russians from a peace treaty with Japan as provocative. Goncharov and co. suggest that he was pursuing goals on several levels: "to expand the buffer zone along his border, to create a springboard against Japan that could be used during a future global conflict, to test the American resolve, to intensify the hostility between Peking and Washington, and, finally and foremost, to draw U.S. power away from Europe." Stalin certainly succeeded in burying any danger of accommodation between the U.S. and China.

Wilderness walkers who make a small error in a compass reading end up miles from where they think they are. This was the way with Truman and his advisers in the fall of 1950. They reached a summit of success with the expulsion of the North Koreans from the South. The valley beyond promised to lead to a unified, independent and democratic Korea, a prospect of strategic and moral allure. To Acheson, the 38th Parallel was no more than "a surveyor's line." At the end of September, he contrived to have a vague resolution passed in the United Nations General Assembly (where there was no Soviet veto) and Truman authorized MacArthur to cross the parallel ostensibly for "the destruction of the North Korean forces." Whom the gods wish to destroy they first disorient. The decision was a blunder of the first magnitude but Truman, Acheson, Marshall, Jessup, Rusk and Asia specialist John Allison, with their eyes on Moscow, had been walking off course since the spring. They had ignored the Chinese protests then about the 7th Fleet. They had ignored Chinese troop movements in Manchuria. They ignored Chinese warnings in the fall. They disregarded advice from Kennan and Sovietologist Charles "Chip" Bohlen. They proceeded throughout on a calculation of risks preponderantly of what the Soviets might do. They were right that Stalin wanted to stay out of a war with the United States, but the misperceptions about the unity of a Communist design caught up with them in a calamitous manner when the Chinese entered the war independently on October 25.

Dean Acheson's persuasive and elegant memoir *Present at the Creation*, published in 1969, collapses when he looks back on the fall of 1950. Of the advice given to Truman by the secretaries of defense (Marshall) and state (Acheson himself) and the Joint Chiefs of Staff, led by General Omar Bradley, he writes: "I have an unhappy conviction that none of us, myself prominently included, served him as he was entitled to be served." It is an honorable admission, but even then, 19 years after the events, Acheson is incapable of expressing little more than bewilderment. He was writing in the middle of the Cold War, with Communist China still a dark and mysterious force. He found it as hard then as he had in the summer of 1950 to see the Chinese as a separate entity and to imagine how they might feel to have their tenuous revolution menaced by American armies advancing to their borders accompanied by blood-curdling yells from the China Lobby for "unleashing" Chiang Kai-shek's Nationalist forces on Taiwan. Joe Alsop's 1992 memoir describes "the casual arrogance" of Acheson and most of Washington after MacArthur's stunning victory in the South. The Chinese at that point were using the Indian ambassador to Beijing, K. M. Panikkar, to relay their warnings, and Alsop writes: "I still remember Dean Acheson at a dinner he was hosting then, in his most archly aristocratic form, referring dismissively to the Indian diplomat as 'Panicker.'" Panic would have been an appropriate response to what Panikkar had to say, because on October 3 he was communicating the resolve of the Chinese Politburo's meeting the day

before: If U.S. troops crossed the 38th Parallel, "we cannot stand idly by and remain indifferent. We will intervene." Acheson's memoir dismisses this explicit message as "not an authoritative statement of policy." The Chinese could hardly have been less inscrutable. Having no ambassador of their own, they had to use an intermediary. They uttered clear private and public warnings and when they attacked MacArthur's armies it was in stages to give the Americans time to realize what they were getting into. The massive ambushes that began on October 25 were called off on November 5.

It was here that the adventurism of MacArthur played its part. He could have regrouped his armies to defend the narrow waistline of the peninsula from P'yŏngyang to Wŏnsan and done that with South Korean troops alone. Instead, on November 24, without telling Washington, he launched a full-scale general offensive for the Yalu River. He overrode the Joint Chiefs' prohibition against using other than South Korean troops near the Chinese border—Zhou Enlai's public statement of September 30 had pointedly left a loophole, objecting to "foreign" (i.e., non-Korean) troops crossing the parallel. In that last-chance lull in November, MacArthur also brushed aside a cautionary cable from the Chiefs of Staff to stop on the high ground commanding the Yalu. And he bombed so recklessly near the border that U.S. planes assaulted an airfield 100 kilometers inside Soviet territory. The response of Truman-Acheson and the Joint Chiefs to MacArthur's acts of defiance was pathetic. They tut-tutted and did nothing. MacArthur was vainly reckless, but for all his flagrant abuse of power the blame for what happened lies, on the American side, squarely with Truman and his team.

Mao, too, was guilty of grave misjudgments that were costly in Chinese lives and Chinese isolation. He was convinced America wanted to invade China itself. If the U.S. and China had been on speaking terms—one of the penalties of nonrecognition is that they were not—it is conceivable the war could have been averted as late as November, conceivable that North Korea could have been reclaimed up to its P'yŏngyang waist. *Uncertain Partners* gives a clearer idea of what was happening in Beijing in the crisis period.

As MacArthur's armies advanced into North Korea, Mao asked Russia to help. But when Zhou met Stalin at his Black Sea villa on October 10, Stalin refused to risk war with the United States and for three days, October 11–14, also refused any military aid. Mao wavered for a sleepless 70 hours, but nothing he heard from the U.S. or saw in Korea disabused him of his fear that MacArthur would cross the Yalu. Mao told Stalin on October 13 he was going ahead on his own. He would rather fight on Korean soil than Chinese. Only then, on October 14, did Stalin promise covertly to send 16 air regiments of Soviet fighter planes. This was the day, even so, when Mao told Zhou he would delay attacking the United Nations forces for at least six months if they stopped at the P'yŏngyang-Wŏnsan line. This, clearly, is what MacArthur should have been ordered to do after the Chinese warning of October 3. But nobody in Washington listened to the Chinese. Perhaps they had listened for too long to the fulminations of the China Lobby; perhaps the prospect of upstaging that crowd was its own fatal temptation.

The Korean war ensured, as Stalin wished, that there would be no reconciliation between China and the U.S., but it also provided the final impetus for NSC 68's militarization of the Cold War that the Soviet Union, in the end, could not afford. But if America was to emerge triumphant it was also to endure much in the fallout from the war. It was in this period of heightened fear of communism that the supposedly anticolonial United States became enmeshed in supporting the French against Ho Chi Minh's nationalist Communists in Indochina. Korea might have suggested that Vietnamese nationalism was more relevant than international communism, but that consideration was again obscured by moral absolutism. America learned nothing from Korea and was condemned to repeat history as tragedy.

In his discussion of containment, George Kennan wrote: "The greatest danger that can befall us in coping with this problem of Soviet communism is that we shall allow ourselves to become like those with whom we are coping." Not even in the worst days of McCarthyism in the early fifties did America begin to approximate the excesses of Stalinism, but it was prescient of Kennan to adjure America to defend its values with its faith rather than sacrifice them to its fears. The identification of "communism" as the enemy led domestically to an abridgement of traditional American rights in a Red scare that was graver than the Red scare of 1919-20. Four million federal employees were subjected to tests of their loyalty; thousands were judged bad risks, not because of their acts but because of ideas or motives attributed to them by administrative, rather than judicial, boards. The 70-odd thousand members of the now mostly toothless Communist Party lost their First Amendment rights to free speech. Beginning in 1948, more than 100 Communists were sent to prison under the provisions of the 1940 Smith Act, which targeted advocates of revolution. The crime of which the Communists were convicted was the dissemination of Marxist-Leninist doctrine, rather than any specific acts of violence, as Justice William O. Douglas pointed out in his strong dissenting opinion when the Supreme Court upheld the convictions.

It was a regressive judgment, but this second Red scare was based on more reality than the Palmer-Hoover shenanigans of 1919-20. Americans were entitled to be rattled when Russia's first atomic bomb test was accompanied by the discovery and conviction of spies within the British, Canadian and American governments. Truman has been charged with fomenting anti-Communist hysteria by his initiation of the Loyalty Program. In fact, Truman did his best to keep things cool, despite feverish pressure from Catholic organizations, the U.S. Chamber of Commerce, the American Legion and Congress and a whisper campaign by J. Edgar Hoover at the FBI. Truman was undermined by the Republican rabble-rousing victories in the 1946 congressional elections, but even after Whittaker Chambers had exposed Alger Hiss, and Elizabeth Bentley had named Harry Dexter White and more than 40 other officials as sources for Soviet espionage, Truman boldly vetoed a harsh anti-Communist law. Senator Pat McCarran's Internal Security Act denied passports to Communists, ordered their registration with the Attorney General and provided for their internment during national emergencies. "We need not fear the expression of ideas," said Truman, "we do need to fear their suppression." Both houses overrode the President. From this compost, Senator Joe McCarthy soon emerged to accuse Truman of treason.

We now know from the Venona code-breaking program, and from Russian archives opened in the nineties, that leaders of the Communist Party USA did indeed take money and orders from Moscow. There was a Communist underground in the United States in the fifties, as well as in the thirties and forties, with loyalty to America's most dangerous enemy. A judicious national security program was justified. What was not justified was the cruel and cynically partisan way the extreme right exploited legitimate anxiety to pillory innocent individuals and smear the New Deal and liberalism with the taint of communism. The attempt by McCarthy to destroy faith in the patriotism of great Americans like Franklin Roosevelt, Harry Truman, George Marshall, Robert Oppenheimer and numerous others was more subversive than anything the witch-hunters discovered.

The Cold War lasted nearly 50 years. It ended in victory for the West. The Soviet system collapsed, exactly as Kennan had predicted in 1947 when he wrote that if anything were ever to occur to disrupt the iron discipline of the Communist Party, "Soviet Russia might be changed overnight from one of the strongest to one of the weakest and most pitiable of national societies." The Communist Party in the United States died of its own inanities in marching to Moscow's orders, the remnants of their idealism irretrievably betrayed by the suppressions of Hungarian uprising in 1956 and Khrushchev's condemnation the same year of Stalin's crimes.

Kennan assessed the cost of the victory of containment in an article in 1995: "We paid with 40 years of enormous and otherwise unnecessary military expenditures. We paid through the cultivation of nuclear weaponry to the point where the vast and useless nuclear arsenals had become (and remain today) a danger to the very environment of the planet. And we paid with 40 years of Communist control in Eastern Germany, Czechoslovakia, and Hungary, the damages of which to the structure of civilization in those countries we are only now beginning to observe. We paid all this because we were too timid to negotiate." But America did not, in the end, pay for the Cold War by sacrificing its civil rights, as Kennan feared it might. The omens had not been bright. By 1955, more than half the American people polled were ready to jail all admitted Communists. Many individuals suffered assaults on their careers and their sanity. A number took their own lives. Discourse was stultified. The colleges were demoralized. But through all the years of repression there was a sustained, constructive and imaginative opposition that drew strength from the Constitution and succeeded in redeeming the losses—and more. The movement has been underreported, as Allen Weinstein has pointed out. It was not pro-Communist. It was pro-America. It was not an alliance. It was a spontaneous resistance to a new despotism that included many disparate individuals and groups: the thousands who faced and fought loyalty hearings and won 90 percent of the time; the judges who built new case law ruling in their favor; the *New York Times,* the *Washington Post,* the *Milwaukee Journal, The New Yorker,* Ed Murrow of CBS, I. F. Stone and a few others set a brave standard for the generally inept and timid newspapers, broadcasters and wire services; liberal anti-Communist lobbies such as Americans for Democratic Action, the American Veterans Committee, the Anti-Defamation League, the NAACP; the major newsweeklies and liberal journals of opinion; the American Civil Liberties Union. Judge Learned Hand gave eloquent expression to the sickness of a society "where each man begins to eye his neighbor as a possible enemy." In the Supreme Court, Justice John Marshall Harlan restored full freedom of speech for Communists and dissenters by restricting unprotected speech to actual incitement to lawless action. Observing the reaction against the new Red scare, David Lilienthal, the liberal New Dealer who had become chairman of the Atomic Energy Commission, concluded in 1954 that McCarthyism "has invigorated the counterforces of decency and fairness, like the antibodies in the blood stream that a minor illness activates, so that when a major threat to health comes along the antibodies are prepared to do their work." He was right. When the Vietnam war divided America, the dissenters could stand on the barricades built by McCarthy's opponents. Tina Rosenberg was reporting on post-Communist Eastern Europe when she wrote: "The opposite of communism is not anti-communism, which at times resembles it greatly. The opposite is tolerance and the rule of law." It was a truth that America embraced again with the dedication of those who have been through fire.

"Just a Little 'Dirty Business,'" by Daniel Fitzpatrick.

NYET! THAT MEANS NO, SAYS STALIN

Truman, meeting Stalin for the first time at the Potsdam conference in July 1945, judged him "honest—but smart as hell." He was delighted to get confirmation that Russia would soon enter the war against Japan. "I can deal with Stalin," he said. At a private dinner on July 21, he "laid it on thick" that America was on the level in wanting peace with neighborliness and friendship. "I think he believes me and I meant every word of it." Stalin's judgment, confided to Nikita Khrushchev, was that Truman was worthless.

The two leaders were trains rushing past each other in opposite directions. Stalin had no comprehension of the Wilsonian precepts that led America to regard sphere-of-influence politics as immoral. He was suspicious of goodwill. Truman's attempt at their first meeting to be genial about "Uncle Joe" fell flat. Only the balance of power interested Stalin. "How many divisions has the Pope?" he asked, when the rights of Catholics in Poland came up at the sixth session. The Red Army was in Poland. That, and not the Yalta pledge to free elections, settled the question of Poland's future and of Poland's borders, pushed farther west into historic Germany at Stalin's diktat. When Churchill protested that the restrictions in Soviet-occupied Eastern Europe amounted to an Iron Curtain, Stalin retorted, "All fairy tales!" and he did not budge an inch. This was the man who had liquidated 20 million of his own people, whom the U.S. Ambassador Joseph E. Davies thought "wise and gentle" and Eisenhower, after visiting Moscow in the late summer of 1945, called "benign and fatherly." Stalin had cultivated a great poker face. When Truman took him aside on July 24 and whispered that America had perfected "a very powerful explosive," he showed barely a flicker of interest, but he already knew it was an atomic bomb. He knew about the atomic bomb even before Truman because of the espionage of Britain's Klaus Fuchs and Donald McLean. That same evening he cabled Lavrenty Beria to speed up the work on the USSR's own atomic bomb.

By the end of Potsdam, Truman had a sourer view of "Uncle Joe." He made a personal appeal for Stalin to agree to his pet proposal for unrestricted navigation on the international rivers of Europe. Even as Charles Bohlen was translating, Stalin interjected, "Nyet!" and, speaking English for the first time, added with vehemence, "No, I say, no!" Truman flushed: "I cannot understand that man." Years later Truman acknowledged that he had been "an innocent idealist" in these early dealings. He never met Stalin again.

Stalin did not get all his own way. He had to give up on his demand for $20 billion in reparations from Germany, a matter that Roosevelt (but not Churchill) had agreed to at Yalta. Secretary of State Byrnes shrewdly argued that Russia could not expect to take a bite out of German territory as well. They settled for reparations from their own zone.

UP THE GARDEN PATH: The gap between Truman and Stalin is symbolic as they walk to the garden of Potsdam Palace, outside Berlin, in July 1945. Truman was surprised that Stalin (at five foot five) was "a little bit of a squirt."

THE UNITED NATIONS: The name, originally for the Allies fighting the Axis, had come to FDR in the middle of the night in the dark Christmas of 1941. The organization came to life on June 26, 1945, when the delegate from China took a bamboo brush and became the first of envoys from 50 countries to sign the charter. Ralph Bunche (mediating in Palestine, left) was a leading American diplomat, and later won the Nobel Peace Prize for his work. Truman named Eleanor Roosevelt (right) to America's delegation in 1945. She played a central role in getting the U.N. Universal Declaration of Human Rights ratified. President Eisenhower sacked her in 1953 because he thought she had gossiped about his wife's alcoholism. President Kennedy put her back in 1961.

THE WISE MEN WHO MADE THE POSTWAR WORLD

America's destiny as a world power was decided in the postwar years by a small, pragmatic group of like-minded lawyers, bankers and diplomats who have become known as "the wise men," or, as George Ball later called them only half in jest, "the usual suspects." The names of the most notable who came to prominence in the Truman presidency: Dean Acheson, Averell Harriman, George Kennan, Robert Lovett, John McCloy, Paul Nitze, Paul Hoffman, Clark Clifford, Charles Bohlen, Will Clayton and Ball himself. They had all been fired by the follies of appeasing Hitler and Mussolini and resolved that it would never happen again. Between them they constituted almost a caricature of America's Eastern establishment. Most had mutual friends from prep school and the Ivy League, places on the same corporate boards, Wall Street law firms, exclusive clubs. Their spiritual godfathers were Elihu

Root and Henry Stimson, the old Wall Street lawyers and secretaries of war and state, as Walter Isaacson and Evan Thomas trace in their fine study, *The Wise Men*.

They were, of course, all men—not to mention mostly white Protestant men of English descent. They were internationalists, determined America would not sink back into isolationism. They were also intelligent, dedicated, visionary, hardworking and always serenely convinced that they were right. They knew one another, liked one another, worked closely together right from the start. They also shared a common affliction. They were all targets of the politics of resentment—the "Ivy Leaguers born with a silver spoon in their mouths" whom Joe McCarthy demonized for the benefit of the Irish, Italian and German Catholics who bulked large among his supporters.

In the Eisenhower years, the Dulles

family constituted a considerable foreign policy power bloc of a different kind. They, too, were white semiaristocratic Anglo-Saxons from the Eastern seaboard, but the brothers tended to lack the broadness of mind, foresight and selflessness of their Truman counterparts. John Foster had been an isolationist almost up to the first bombs on Pearl Harbor; his law firm, Sullivan and Cromwell, had unseemly ties with the Nazi regime right up to the war. Acheson made him a high-level consultant in his effort to make postwar foreign policy truly bipartisan, but Foster Dulles had gone along only so far as it suited his own interests, and later disavowed key policies he had backed so as to curry favor with the troglodyte Republicans in Congress. He regarded his job as saving the West for Christianity. Even the cold warriors around Eisenhower found Dulles's sanctimony hard to take.

ROBERT LOVETT (1895–1986)

The dapper young Lovett left Yale to become a bomber pilot in World War I and was too bored to finish Harvard Law School. He went right into banking, the air industry and the high life. His father was chief counsel to the railway robber baron E. H. Harriman. He met Harriman's son Averell as a boy, when their fathers' private railcars were hitched together. Lovett was brought to Washington by War Secretary Henry Stimson and helped build the nation's strategic bombing force. Officially a Republican, he served ably as Marshall's deputy at the State Department. Paul Nitze credits Lovett with saving the Marshall Plan from being sabotaged by "Honest" John Tabor, the near-isolationist chairman of the House committee that had to approve the money. Tabor refused to let Nitze bring in experts to say why the U.S. needed to send Austria 25,000 pulse seeds, a type of bean. Why couldn't they grow the beans themselves? Without expert support, every item in the aid program could be so denied. Lovett's answer was to take Tabor aside and ask him, "How many rivets are there on a B-29 wing?" Tabor protested that Lovett would know better because he had been assistant secretary of war for air in World War II. Lovett took the opening: "Well, that's just the point. Some people are more knowledgeable about certain matters. . . . So why don't you let Nitze have his experts to answer technical questions?" And before Tabor could answer, Lovett asked him another: "If it takes eight yards of pink crepe paper to go around an elephant's leg, how long does it take to kill a fly with a flyswatter?" Tabor said it was a nonsensical question, which gave Lovett his clincher: "Of course! Now why don't you stop asking Nitze nonsensical questions?" And Tabor did.

PAUL NITZE (b. 1907)

The cool and incisive Nitze, the ultimate Washington insider, first arrived in the capital in 1940. It was supposed to be a temporary job but the "Silver Fox" was still there in the eighties, a strategic thinker and adviser to Reagan on the more tortuous aspects of nuclear arms control. He was even in Moscow in 1988 for the Gorbachev-Reagan summit. Of German-American ancestry, Nitze had backed Lindbergh's "America First" campaign but became a leading internationalist. He helped push the Marshall Plan, which cost him an Eisenhower Defense Department appointment when the McCarthyites howled. During the Truman administration, he headed Acheson's Policy Planning staff, where he wrote NSC 68, the containment policy with teeth, and argued for the hydrogen bomb. In the Kennedy-Johnson era he ran the Navy, and as early as 1964 he came back from Vietnam to tell Defense Secretary Robert McNamara the U.S. should withdraw. He was a stickler for principle. He quit the Democrats when FDR tried to pack the Supreme Court. He quit the Republicans when Eisenhower failed to back General Marshall. He quit as assistant defense secretary over Watergate. During Jimmy Carter's presidency he founded the Committee on the Present Danger to arouse public awareness of America's strategic disadvantage, which gave him headlines as a hard-liner. But he played a big role in the Anti-Ballistic Missile Treaty and nearly made a breakthrough on missile cutbacks when he went on a famous "walk in the woods" outside Geneva in July 1982 with his Soviet opposite number. His memoir, *From Hiroshima to Glasnost*, is a classic insight into the perspective of the wise men.

DEAN ACHESON (1893–1971)

Acheson was the pen and the lance of the Truman Doctrine and NATO. He was in public office for twelve years, from 1941 to 1953, the last four as Truman's secretary of state. He nurtured the Marshall Plan, created an independent West German state and had a crucial vote on making the hydrogen bomb. It says something for the politics of the time that Richard Nixon jibed at "Dean Acheson's College of Cowardly Communist Containment." Acheson's father was an English Episcopalian bishop, his mother the daughter of a Canadian whisky distiller and bank president. Every May his parents would run up the Union Jack at their Middletown, Connecticut, home and serve claret to celebrate Queen Victoria's birthday. The legacy of this upbringing was both a firm commitment to America's transatlantic allies and a frosty British reserve and arrogance that made him an inordinate number of enemies in Congress. They resented his tweeds and his clipped moustache as much as his cutting wit. He wrote as elegantly as he dressed. It was Acheson who said of the mother country that it had lost an empire and had yet to find a role. His sense of honor got him into trouble. "I do not intend to turn my back on Alger Hiss," he said, then quoting Matthew 25:36. It was a gift to the right, more evidence against the "Red Dean," an absurd epithet for someone so hostile to communism. In later life, he became a hawk on Vietnam and was invited to advise his old adversary Richard Nixon.

ACHESON: The "Red Dean," by David Levine.

JOHN McCLOY (1895–1989)

He was the ultimate éminence grise, a shadowy figure compared to the luminaries, but well identified as the Chairman of the Board of the American Establishment. He was a lifelong Republican who did his best work for Democratic presidents: in a long life he was friend and adviser to nine chief executives. Kennedy thought he was so tough he called him to deal with the Russians at the U.N. in the Cuban missile crisis. No member of the "establishment" came from closer to the wrong side of the tracks. His father's early death left his ambitious mother to bring him up in a working-class Philadelphia neighborhood. She used her wealthy hairdressing clients to get him work tutoring and teaching tennis, an instrument of social entry he exploited ever after, a poor boy volleying at the nets of the rich. He got through college waiting tables and teaching handball and squash, and graduated from Harvard Law School. He was first recruited by Secretary Stimson after serving as an artilleryman in France at the end of World War I, and then worked helping Lovett build the Pentagon. At his lesser prep school, he had come to idolize Periclean Athens and adopted the motto "run with the swift," which he took to mean "work with people who were better than I." This came to entail making and carrying out some of the more dubious policies. He was central to the decision to intern the Nisei, then later made out he was only following orders. From 1943 to 1945 he obstructed a plan to bomb the railways to the Nazi death camps: he was not convinced the Jews were being systematically exterminated, and he said bombing was a waste of resources. But he did have the nerve to question dropping the atomic bomb, and after the war he worked hard to aid displaced Jews and win German reparations for them. As head of the World Bank and U.S. high commissioner for Germany, he helped produce the German miracle, but again his pragmatism invited attack when he abetted the early release of convicted Nazi war criminals, including Alfred Krupp, so they could help with reconstruction and Cold War espionage. Most fatally, along with Robert Lovett and Dean Acheson, he did not sufficiently press on Lyndon Johnson his grave doubts about LBJ's decision to expand the war in Vietnam. It was this equivocation, as much as anything else, that brought about the end of the old Eastern establishment.

AVERELL HARRIMAN (1891–1986)

Harriman was nicknamed "the crocodile," for the way in which his "dull demeanor" would suddenly give way to a "snap of action." His father was one of the richest men in America. Averell first encountered Acheson at Groton, where he taught the cheeky younger boy how to row and become "a good oar" socially as well. Their friendship spanned some 66 years. Harriman's relationship with the Soviet Union was even longer: he crossed the Bering Strait into Siberia as a boy of 7 with his family, and his last visit was in 1983, three years before he died at 95. In between he negotiated with nearly every major Soviet leader from Trotsky to Stalin and Nikita Khrushchev. He was FDR's "special envoy" to first Churchill and then Stalin in the war and became ambassador to the USSR in 1945. He was happiest in foreign affairs. His career detoured into an unsuccessful quest for the Democratic presidential nomination and a lackluster term as governor of New York in the fifties. His perceptive, undogmatic approach to foreign policy made him a valued adviser to presidents. It was his pragmatism that allowed him to be among the first of the wise men to see the futility of America's involvement in Vietnam.

HOW MUCH DID THEY KNOW? A German mother shields the eyes of her son. She was among the German civilians ordered by American officers of the U.S. 9th Army to look at the exhumed corpses of 57 Russian men, women and a baby murdered by the SS.

CONVICTED OUT OF THEIR OWN MOUTHS

Churchill wanted to shoot the Nazi leaders. Truman insisted on trials and so did Stalin. Their crimes finally caught up with 21 Nazi leaders in November 1945, in Nuremberg, the German city where they had exulted in Hitler's massive torchlit rallies. Eight judges, two each from America, Britain, France and the Soviet Union, convicted 18 of them, after a ten-month trial, on charges of waging aggressive war and for crimes against humanity. The worst were convicted out of their own mad mouths. The documents the Nazis had meticulously maintained gave the prosecutors, led by Supreme Court Justice Robert H. Jackson, overwhelming evidence of the Holocaust, mass murder, slave labor and torture.

The Nazis argued what became the classic defense—that, as subjects of the German state or as military officers who had sworn an oath of allegiance, they had simply done their duty to carry out Hitler's orders. They all protested their repugnance when shown films of Dachau, Buchenwald and the Bergen-Belsen camps. Sauckel shook for hours afterward. Frank cried and bemoaned, "To think we lived like kings and believed in that beast. Don't let anybody tell you they had no idea! . . . May God have mercy on our souls!" Fritzsche wept in his cell, and prophesied: "No power in heaven or earth will erase this shame from my country—not in generations, not in centuries!" Göring tried to stay cool. After the films, he told his attorney: "It was such a good afternoon, too, and then they showed that awful film, and it just spoiled everything!"

Sixty-one witnesses were called for the defense. There were 12 other international tribunals in Nuremberg, another in Tokyo and many hundreds of other trials and denazification tribunals, but it was the Nuremberg group trial that caught the world's imagination and won popular acclaim.

Even so, there was disquiet at the idea of the vanquished being tried by the victors. Senator Robert Taft condemned the trials. They could not be impartial, he said, no matter how hedged about with the forms of justice. U.S. Chief Justice Harlan Stone later refused to swear in the principal U.S. judge at Nuremberg, Francis Biddle, or his alternate, calling them part of "Jackson's high grade lynching party."

THE HENCHMEN: In the dock at Nuremberg. Front row (left to right): Göring had kicked his morphine habit while in custody and was smoothly defiant. Hess stared into space most of the time. Ribbentrop was shattered by films of Dachau and Buchenwald. Field Marshal Keitel notoriously defended the murder of Russian civilians with the declaration "Any act of mercy is a crime against the German people." Rear row: Dönitz, Raeder, von Schirach, Sauckel, Jodl, and von Papen.

The inclusion of the Soviets as judges was controversial. Stalin sustained misgivings with a massive display of hypocrisy. He had the trial delayed so that Germans could be indicted for the deaths of 4,254 Polish officer prisoners found buried at the infamous Katyn Forest site. The Soviets went on to pursue the charge at the trial, though the evidence indicated their own guilt. The failure to pin the blame on the Germans led the Russian prosecutor, N. D. Zorya, to take his own life.

THE FATES OF THE EIGHTEEN FOUND GUILTY

Shortly after midnight in the early hours of October 16, 1946, in the Nuremberg prison gymnasium, American Master Sergeant John C. Woods carried out sentences of hanging on ten Nazis. The hangings were botched; they died of slow strangulation, their necks grotesquely elongated; with Keitel, Woods had to go below the shrouded scaffold and pull on the man's feet. Göring escaped the rope by swallowing a concealed cyanide capsule two hours before he was due on the gallows. It was thought to have been given him by U.S. Lieutenant Jack George "Tex" Wheelis, with whom he had become friendly while in prison.

Hanged: Foreign Minister Joachim von Ribbentrop; Field Marshal Wilhelm Keitel, who had authorized mass murders in Russia in 1941–42; Hans Frank, the governor of Poland, who sent 85 percent of Polish Jews to death camps; Julius Streicher, the odious Jew baiter; Ernst Kaltenbrunner, who had run the concentration camp system; Interior Minister Wilhelm Frick; Alfred Rosenberg, boss of the occupied eastern territories; Arthur Seyss-Inquart, Austria's Quisling and governor of the Netherlands; Fritz Sauckel, director of slave labor; and General Alfred Jodl, Hitler's senior military adviser. Martin Bormann was sentenced to death in absentia and officially declared dead in 1973 upon recovery of his jawbone during Berlin street construction.

Imprisoned: Rudolf Hess (life, died in Spandau Prison in 1987, the only one to serve his full life sentence); Walther Funk, president of Reichsbank (life, released because of illness in 1957, died 1960); Grand Admiral Erich Raeder (life, released for sickness in September 1955, died 1960); Grand Admiral Karl Dönitz, U-boat chief (10 years, died 1980); Albert Speer, arms minister (20 years, died 1981); Baldur von Schirach, head of the Hitler Youth (20 years, died 1974); Constantin von Neurath, Hitler's first foreign minister and governor of Bohemia-Moravia to 1941 (15 years, released for sickness in 1952, died 1956).

Acquitted: Hjalmar Horace Greeley Schacht. The brilliant American-born financier, formerly president of the Reichsbank, had broken with Hitler in 1938 over economics and the planning for war, plotted against him during the war, and ended up in a concentration camp after the July 1944 plot. Even so, a German denazification court after Nuremberg sentenced him to eight years, and he did not succeed in winning his appeals until 1950.

Hans Fritzsche, press chief. Later sentenced to nine years' hard labor by denazification court; pardoned 1950, died 1953.

Franz von Papen, vice chancellor, ambassador to Austria and Turkey, former spy in the United States. After Nuremberg, he spent two years in labor camp hospitals, where he was badly beaten by a crazed fellow inmate. Released by denazification courts in 1949, but deprived of civil rights. Died 1969.

GALLOPING TO THE RESCUE OF EUROPE

The square-jawed, six-foot-six American diplomat hunched up in the airplane seat on his way back to Washington from Europe seethed with a conviction. He was writing most of the way, and as soon as he reached his office on the afternoon of May 19, 1947, he dictated a conclusion. Will Clayton, who was then 67 and assistant secretary of state for economic affairs, was a courteous, soft-spoken southerner, but there was nothing muted about his memorandum. He had a vision of millions of people dying in chaos and bloodshed if America did not come to the rescue of Europe. "It is now obvious," he wrote, "that we have grossly underestimated the destruction to the European economy by the war." The physical facts of the war's destruction were manifest, but Clayton, who had grown up amid the Mississippi cotton fields, had noted something more sinister. While millions in the cities went hungry, the European farmers were hoarding food and feeding grain to cattle because the cities had nothing to sell in return. The complex industrial society of Europe was on the point of disintegration. Its only hope of recovery from this economic, political, social and psychological devastation was a concerted European plan, and he spelled out how America should get one going with money and supplies.

Clayton rushed his memorandum to Under Secretary of State Acheson and asked for a meeting with Secretary of State George Marshall. "Doing something" to help Europe was by then a common aspiration of the foreign policy elite. Truman

was sympathetic, waiting on Marshall, who had been in the job only a few months. Marshall himself, on returning from Europe in April, had given the intellectually fertile George Kennan ten days to get a program out of a Policy Planning staff that had as of then no staff and no office. On May 8 the elegant Acheson had taken off his jacket and rolled up his sleeves in a hot, crowded gymnasium at Delta State Teachers' College in Cleveland, Mississippi, and gone public with the duty lying on America to help Europe. When Kennan handed in his report, written under intense pressure that once reduced him to tears, he emphasized the difficulties and dangers of American intervention while the Soviet Union was in its surly mood. As Marshall observed, "The patient is sinking while the doctors deliberate."

It was Clayton's destiny to be the catalyst. In a meeting in Marshall's office on May 28, attended by Acheson, Kennan, counselor Ben Cohen and Charles Bohlen, Clayton argued self-interest and altruism, and Marshall resolved to act at once. He asked Bohlen to take the Clayton and Kennan reports and draft a speech inviting Europe to seek American help, and in the middle of the afternoon of June 5, standing on the steps of Memorial Church in Harvard Yard under the shade of great elm trees, the secretary crisply dedicated the New World to the rescue of the Old. It was, in the words of Winston Churchill, "the most unsordid act in history."

Acheson had advised Marshall that a Harvard commencement speech was a poor forum. Commencement speeches were "a ritual to be endured without hearing." He was right. The *New York Times* printed only a modest headline. But the adroit Acheson had worked behind the scenes, asking three British correspondents to ensure that Foreign Secretary Ernest Bevin realized the urgency of galloping off on the gift horse Marshall was offering before Congress hobbled it. By July 3, the British and French had called a conference of 22 other European nations

to devise a recovery plan—and Stalin had forbidden Soviet participation. On December 17 Truman asked for $17 billion in grants and loans over four years for the European Recovery Program, which everyone called the Marshall Plan.

The plan ran into opposition from the full spectrum of American politics. On the left, the Communists and Henry Wallace's nascent Progressives howled that it was American imperialism. To the right, it was foreign entanglement and spendthrift socialism. But then two men laid their bodies across the chasms: Senator Arthur Vandenberg and Robert Lovett, who knew how to appease or shame congressmen. The Communist coup in Prague in February 1948 and the apparent murder of Foreign Minister Jan Masaryk finally galvanized the querulous right wing. On April 2, the plan passed the Senate 69–17, and the House 329–74. Within days, the freighter *John H. Quick* sailed from Galveston with 9,000 tons of wheat, and before long an armada, 150 ships at any one moment, was shuttling tractors, fishing nets, cotton, tobacco, tires, synthetic resin, borax, sulfur, flour, aircraft parts, oil, farm machinery— and $20 million worth of horsemeat. In 1949, America lent or gave 2.4 percent of its gross national product. By the end of the program in 1952, Marshall aid added up to $13 billion (the equivalent of some $90 billion dollars in 1990).

Acheson had depicted the task as "just a bit less formidable than that described in the first chapter of Genesis. That was to create a world out of chaos; ours, to create half a world, a free half, out of the same material." Western Europe seized the chance to mobilize its skills and plant. By the summer of 1951, its industrial production was 43 percent above prewar levels, farm production 10 percent above. Out of chaos, prosperity and freedom.

THE WRECKAGE: The man is a Jewish refugee, reunited in Berlin with a friend after ten years' exile in Shanghai. Millions of refugees wandered over Europe. By 1946 there were still 4 million of them in western zones of Germany. Photographer Henry Ries, a German-Jewish refugee himself, had just taken this picture when he saw a friend he had not seen since before the war and did not know was still alive. His eyes filled with tears. "I could no longer work then."

AT REST: Having saved Europe, George Marshall takes a break in Capri on October 1, 1952. Back home, Eisenhower was deleting his name from a speech in deference to Joe McCarthy.

CLASS WARFARE: John L. Lewis never minded the hostile stares of the rich and powerful. Pat Candido of the *New York Daily News* caught such a moment in 1949. Despite his defeat by Truman, Lewis remained as irascible and regal as ever. When a busload of tourists gawked at the sight of the great John L. tying his shoe on a Washington street, he remarked, "Even the posterior of a great man is not without interest."

A LION AT BAY

John L. Lewis (1880–1969) fitted to perfection the role he played in the forties as the most hated man in America. He had the look of a vaudeville villain, with dark, baleful eyes under shaggy eyebrows, and a cavernous voice. His scowl, as writer Cabell Phillips observed, was of Olympian ferocity. He wore it most of the time. In the thirties he had been a brilliantly creative labor leader. A former miner himself, he had rebuilt the United Mine Workers' Union, won many reforms in pay and conditions and broken with the AFL to organize mass-production workers in the Congress of Industrial Organizations (CIO). But during the war, he enraged almost everyone by repeatedly leading half a million miners out on strike. He was a passionate isolationist. The media demonized him as a dictator and Nazi.

By the postwar era, his power was flagging, and he had lost control of the CIO to men like David Dubinsky, Sidney Hillman, and his old protégé, Philip Murray.

His mistake in 1946 was to take on Harry Truman. In the small hours of Sunday, November 17, 1946, five men in dinner jackets, meeting in Truman's White House study, broke up after a long, acrid wrangle on what to do about the latest Lewis outrage.

In May, when the owners reneged on a health and welfare fund, the President had averted a strike by seizing the mines and offering to work out a lasting settlement before handing them back. Truman's men and Lewis agreed on a deal, but on October 21 Lewis stunned the country by demanding a renegotiation on pain of a national stoppage. He had thrown down the gauntlet on the eve of the midterm elections. It was an insult to Truman. Lewis's biographers, Melvyn Dubofsky and Warren Van Tine, suggest that his behavior may have been due to a "small" stroke he suffered on September 15, one that was covered up as appendicitis.

Truman's mediator, John Steelman, wanted to appease Lewis, as Roosevelt had sometimes done. Clark Clifford, just out of the Navy and a rising star as an aide in the White House, urged the opposite: "Mr. President," said Clifford, "you have to take him on!" Steelman was angry when Truman announced, "It's a fight to the finish." Truman told Attorney General Tom Clark to charge Lewis with violating the Smith-Connally Act, which banned strikes against government-held plants, then he boarded the presidential plane, *Sacred Cow*, for a vacation in Key West.

The next day, U.S. District Judge T. Alan Goldsborough ordered Lewis not to strike. Lewis persisted, and paid a former FBI agent $16,000 to try to dig up dirt on the judge. On November 25, Lewis was called to court and found guilty of contempt. The union was fined $3.5 million (later reduced to $700,000), and Lewis was fined $10,000, with the union's fine increasing by $250,000 every further day they stayed out.

Lewis tried to call the White House directly. Truman refused to speak to him. "The White House," he said, "is open to anybody with legitimate business, but not to that son of a bitch." On December 7, Lewis gave up. He had met his match. His hell-raising days were all but over.

FRIENDS FOR NOW: James Byrnes, Truman and Henry Wallace wait for FDR's funeral train. Truman dropped both men. Both had nearly become president in his stead.

THE FIRING OF HENRY WALLACE

Henry Wallace, the man who might have been the 33rd president, did not survive long as the last New Dealer in Truman's cabinet. He was a sincere and decent idealist. When FDR and the party bosses removed him from the vice presidential slot in 1944, he bit the bullet and stayed on as secretary of commerce. In the postwar years, it was his misfortune to be at odds with the temper of his times, trapped in a time warp in his view of the Soviet Union. He had a mystical streak. "I sometimes got the impression," wrote Clark Clifford, "[that] his mind had wandered off and left his body behind."

On September 10, 1946, Wallace called on Truman with a speech he was to make. He took Truman through it "page by page." Truman approved; later he said he had only skimmed it, "trusting Henry to play square with me." He might have been more alert; in July, Wallace had startled Truman with a private 12-page letter criticizing America's warlike posture toward the Soviet Union. It included the charge that unnamed members of the U.S. high command had backed the idea of a "preventive war" before the Soviet Union had the bomb: it was true. When he spoke at Madison Square Garden, Wallace told the crowd of 20,000 that America "has no more business in the political affairs of Eastern Europe than Russia has in the political affairs of Latin America." And then added: "And just two days ago, when President Truman read these words, he said they represented the policy of the administration."

Truman had told puzzled reporters, who saw the text in advance, that he had approved it as an expression of policy. In the uproar that followed its delivery, he tried a clumsy lie—that he was only saying he had approved the secretary's right to deliver a speech. Then, in a misunderstanding, Wallace's "red" July letter was released. An enraged Secretary of State James Byrnes insisted that Truman choose between him and Wallace. Finally, on September 20, at 9:30 a.m., Truman fired Wallace by telephone. He was so nice, Truman told his wife, "that I almost backed out. I just don't understand the man and he doesn't either."

Wallace put his passion into a new Progressive party, launched on December 29, 1947, with him as its presidential candidate. He called it a Gideon's army, small in number, powerful in conviction. But too many of the convinced few were Communists. Wallace campaigned valiantly, braving racist crowds in the South. When he lost he went back to breeding corn—and to many of his former views. He backed U.S. intervention in Korea, and eventually voiced regret at his manipulation by the Communists.

TRUMAN GIVES 'EM HELL

Harry Truman had become a national joke as the midterm elections loomed in the fall of 1946. "To err is Truman" was everybody's quip. The *Chicago Tribune* mocked "Little Truman Fauntleroy" in doggerel:

Look at little Truman now,
Muddy, battered, bruised—and how!

His approval ratings, which had peaked at 80 percent in his first hectic months in office, reached a new low of 32 percent. Business was booming and there was almost no unemployment, but inflation was up 6.5 points for the year. Frustrating shortages persisted in housing, cars, refrigerators, stockings, sugar, coffee and, above all, meat. And in 1946, a record 4.6 million of the employed, one in ten of the labor force, went on strike. It did not seem to matter that Truman had beaten a national rail strike in May—or that, in a dramatic moment, the rail leaders gave in just when Truman was telling Congress he was drafting into the Army "all workers who are on strike against their government."

It was a miserable summer for Truman. His wife and daughter fled the Washington heat for Independence. Alone, overworked, depressed, Truman took to calling the White House "the great white jail."

The Republicans came up with the slogan "Had enough?" for what some would call "the beefsteak election" in the fall. Truman was devastated by the

Dewey was better than his speeches.

results. Republicans won the House for the first time since 1930 and by a wide margin, 246–188. They took back the Senate as well and achieved a majority of state governorships. The paradox is that the Republican Congress did not foreshadow Truman's doom, but his resurrection. He was to use it brilliantly as a scapegoat and exploit its attacks on the New Deal. Senator Robert Taft pushed through the Taft-Hartley Act, which outlawed the closed shop, made unions liable for breach of contract, prohibited union contributions to election funds, required union financial reports and stipulated that union leaders had to take non-Communist loyalty oaths. Truman vetoed it. He had risked his bridges to

organized labor by fighting the endless strikes. When the Republicans overrode Truman's veto in the summer of 1947 to pass the Taft-Hartley Act, they were inadvertently restoring a key piece of the fractured New Deal coalition in time for the 1948 presidential election. Labor threw itself on Truman's side with money and manpower.

Truman's more immediate problem was fission in his own party. Panicky New Dealers, including FDR's son, Congressman James Roosevelt, and big city bosses, wanted to dump him in favor of Eisenhower. They kept trying to persuade Ike to run, right up to the doors of the Democratic convention in Philadelphia in July. Nibbling away on the far left was the sacked Henry Wallace at the head of his new Progressive party. And, most menacing of all, was a revolt on the right. The solid South was about to break up. The Roosevelt administration had dragged its feet on civil rights. Truman was pretty much a son of the South. He freely used the word "nigger" in conversation. But the atmosphere of racism he had been brought up in had eroded by 1948. His private correspondence reveals a deepening revulsion with Jim Crow rule. He appointed a Civil Rights Commission, and it spelled out the ongoing persecution of American blacks and the remedies. On February 2, 1948, without previous consultation, he called on Congress to enact at once an antilynching law and an anti–poll tax law, to outlaw discrimination by employers and unions and to prohibit segregation on interstate trains, buses and planes, and in the military. It inflamed the southerners more than Truman had bargained for. He tried to patch things up by diluting his civil rights program at the hot and rowdy Democratic convention, but Hubert Humphrey, the inspired young mayor of Minneapolis, persuaded the convention to reject the fudge: "The time has arrived for the Democratic party to get out of the shadow of states' rights and walk forthrightly in the bright sunlight of human rights." Handy Ellis of Alabama led 13 members of his delegation and the entire Mississippi contingent out the door. The Dixiecrats, as the Southern rebels called themselves, then flew the Confederate flag for Governor J. Strom Thurmond of South

THE *CHICAGO TRIBUNE*'S FAMOUS GAFFE

The paper, hit by a strike, had had to go to press at midday for some morning editions and took its cue from its Washington bureau chief. The headline was the foregone conclusion everyone predicted. No poll, no commentator or reporter, no newspaper, called the election right. The pollsters' blunders:

- They did too little late polling. They presumed that votes did not change after Labor Day because they had not changed in FDR's elections.
- They failed to catch the significance of a large undecided vote.
- They failed to determine who was really intent on voting—13 percent of Dewey "voters" in October stayed at home in November.

When *Newsweek* predicted a landslide after finding not one vote for Truman in a poll of fifty leading political writers, Clark Clifford tried to hide the magazine. Truman insisted on reading it and remarked: "I know every one of these fifty fellows. There isn't one of them who has enough sense to pound sand in a rat hole."

On one occasion when Truman played ragtime, Lauren Bacall jumped on top of the piano. Ben Shahn's satirical drawing replaced her with an ineffective Dewey.

state tax rates by 50 percent. And in the Republican primaries he had stood out bravely against anti-Communist hysteria.

Truman had three weapons against the impressive Dewey. He had found his true voice, the pungent and breezy style of the man who had said, "If you can't stand the heat, get out of the kitchen." In April bored newspaper editors were startled when, at the end of a typically droning speech from a prepared text, he answered questions off the cuff for 30 vivid minutes. He had been urged to try this by his White House staff and he experimented more on a first 9,500-mile whistle-stop excursion in June. The impromptu Truman proved to be warm, homey, relaxed and spirited. He was 64, but the cockiness and energy he displayed on the epic 21,928-mile whistle-stop tour he began on September 17 made him appear young and vital alongside the stiffly formal man 18 years his junior: Dewey, said actress Ethel Barrymore, looked like the little man on top of the wedding cake. At rallies, said commentator Richard Rovere, "he comes out like a man who has been mounted on casters and given a tremendous shove from behind."

Secondly, Truman made the Republican Congress a scapegoat. He recalled it for a special session on July 26, "which out in Missouri we call Turnip Day." Taft, angry at being brought back to a steamy Washington, duly fell into the Truman trap. He led a massacre of Truman's Turnip Day proposals, and the huge crowds at every whistle stop in the campaign heard Truman, from the back of his railcar, gleefully blaming everything on the "do nothing" 80th Congress. The cry "Give 'em hell, Harry!" began to arise, and the delighted President would reply: "I never give anybody hell. I just tell the truth and they think it's hell."

Truman, with 49.5 percent of the vote, carried 28 states and held Dewey to 45.1, a smaller percentage of the vote than he had achieved against FDR in 1944 (popular vote: Truman, 24,105,812; Dewey, 21,970,065; Thurmond, 1,169,063; Wallace, 1,157,172; Norman Thomas, 139,414). Truman had 303 electoral votes, Dewey 189, and Thurmond 39.

For all that, Truman's vote margin was the closest of any winner since 1916. FDR had won by margins averaging 14.75 percent; Truman's was only 4.4 percent.

Carolina, getting him on the ballot in 16 states and even usurping the Democratic line from Truman in Alabama.

It looked hopeless for Truman when the Republicans nominated New York Governor Thomas Dewey. The former gangbusting special prosecutor and district attorney was a reformer and a wizard. In his six years in Albany, he had cleared slums, extended clinics and hospitals, cleaned up mental institutions, outlawed racial discrimination in the workplace, made vast additions to the state's infrastructure and yet had still been able to cut

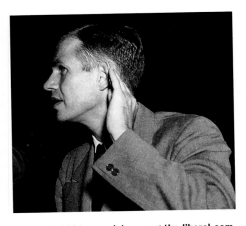

CONFRONTATION: Chambers and Hiss testify. Chambers died in 1961, a pariah among the liberal community, a hero of the right and of such apostate Communists as Arthur Koestler, André Malraux and Czesław Miłosz. President Reagan posthumously awarded him a Medal of Freedom.

THE PUMPKIN FILE

The honor of carrying the United Nations Charter back to Washington in a special plane from the 1945 San Francisco founding conference was given to its organizer, a debonair State Department aide who dryly remarked later that the ride made him understand his true importance: the charter was given a parachute and he wasn't. The aide was Alger Hiss, who was to come crashing down to earth just three years later. His ascent had been marked by reflected glory: protégé of Felix Frankfurter at Harvard; clerk to the great Supreme Court Justice Oliver Wendell Holmes; State Department note taker at Yalta; president of the Carnegie Endowment for International Peace at the behest of his predecessor, John Foster Dulles. He was at Carnegie on Tuesday, August 3, 1948, when his orderly world began to fall apart, dividing America by the darkest thought of the Cold War: Had it been betrayed by its privileged elite?

The national trauma was triggered by Whittaker Chambers, a brooding 47-year-old editor at *Time*. Summoned to the House Un-American Activities Committee (HUAC), he testified that he had been a member of a Communist cell in Washington from 1931 until he quit in 1938. Hiss, he said, had been one of the cell's seven members from 1934 to 1937. None of them had spied. Their aim had been to infiltrate the American government, with espionage as an "eventual" objective.

Hiss unequivocally denied ever being a Communist or knowing somebody called Whittaker Chambers. By comparison with his rumpled accuser, Hiss was crisp and convincing, and Truman slammed the spy scare as "a red herring." The Republican-controlled committee was in "a virtual state of shock." The man who made that observation was Richard Nixon, a 35-year-old freshman from California. Only Nixon's suspicions of Hiss kept the case alive. Scenting headlines for himself, he did not then or years later reveal that he knew the contents of a suggestive, if inconclusive, FBI file on Hiss. Two days later Nixon grilled Chambers in a private session. The man seemed to be uncannily familiar with the intimate details of the private lives of "Hilly" (Alger) and wife "Prossy" (Priscilla). He told of driving their old Ford roadster. He recalled the couple's excitement on seeing a rare bird called a prothonotary warbler. The trap was set for Hiss. Called back before the committee, he exhibited an oddly uneven memory about his life in the thirties, but he ingenuously confirmed details given by the man he was not supposed to know. Yes, he was interested in birds; he had once seen a prothonotary warbler on the Potomac.

Hiss had denied knowing someone called Chambers—but Chambers had been a man of many aliases. One of them was George Crosley. And Hiss eventually conceded that he had befriended someone by that name. On August 17, Nixon brought them together in room 1400 at the Commodore Hotel. "Are you George Crosley?" asked Hiss. "Not to my knowledge," said Chambers. "You are Alger Hiss, I believe." Hiss, after examining Chambers from several angles, even checking his dental work, identified him as Crosley. Then, advancing on his tormentor with clenched fists, he angrily challenged him to make his accusations in public where he could be sued.

THE OUTSIDER: The headlines helped Nixon win a Senate seat in 1950, but earned him the enmity of many who saw his pursuit as no more than an attempt to discredit the New Deal and liberal Democrats. Nixon resented Hiss, but his handling of the case was fair.

Chambers obliged on *Meet the Press:* "Alger Hiss was a Communist and may be one now." Hiss did not respond at once. It was only a month later that he sued. The stage was set for a bizarre showdown.

Chambers went to a relative's house in Brooklyn and from the shaft of a disused dumbwaiter extracted an envelope clotted with cobwebs and the dust of a decade. Inside were 65 typewritten copies or summaries of State Department documents, three cylinders of undeveloped microfilm, two strips of developed film, papers and four notes scribbled by Hiss. All this, Chambers was to say, came to him as the courier for the Hisses, who were Soviet spies. He had hoped not to have to reveal the darker secret of espionage out of a feeling for the Hisses and others; it was out of a feeling for himself, too, since it was an admission he was guilty of espionage and perjury. His story was that every week or ten days between early 1937 and April 1938, Hiss brought home classified State Department cables, which he, Chambers, took away for microfilming. Later, Priscilla would retype what Hiss brought home, ready for Chambers's next pickup.

Chambers yielded the typed pages to the Justice Department. But he kept the microfilms and hid them in his Maryland farmhouse. He wrote in his book *Witness* (1952) that he was in a stupor of distress that the microfilms would ruin other lives besides the Hisses'. He was so anguished he thought of destroying both the films and himself. Then he went for a walk in a wood and in that sylvan setting he had a vision of a Russian revolutionist prisoner burning himself to death as a witness against the flogging of his fellow prison-

ers. The witness! Chambers, too, realized he was called by God to an act of witness. On the night of December 2, when two HUAC investigators arrived at the farm with a subpoena, he took them to a patch of pumpkins in his yard and out of the shadows produced a pumpkin with a hollowed center. The microfilms were inside. Three cables on film, dealing with the Sino-Japanese War, of urgent interest to Moscow, had been initialed by Hiss.

The Justice Department was hesitating as late as December 10 about whether to prosecute Hiss or Chambers. But as the grand jury heard both men Chambers made the better impression and it was Hiss they indicted for perjury. It was hard for him to explain away the proof that personal letters by Priscilla had been typed on the same Woodstock N230099 typewriter used for copying the State Department papers Chambers had produced. Hiss was forced to pose an elaborate frame-up. He did his best to portray Chambers as disturbed. Theories flitted like bats through the gothic psychopathology of Chambers's supposed instabilities. Paranoid revenge for some rejection in the thirties. Transfers of guilt for his brother's suicide. Frustration arising from homosexual urges. It all demeaned the genuine agony Chambers endured in his betrayal of the betrayer.

At the trial in July 1949, four of the jury of twelve gave Hiss the benefit of the doubt. But on January 21, 1950, a new jury found Hiss guilty. Exposure of Nixon's Watergate cover-up in 1972 helped convince many that Hiss was framed, but Allen Weinstein, a meticulous analyst of the case, concluded in *Perjury* in 1978 and again in 1997 that Hiss was guilty as charged.

FLASH FORWARD: 1990S

THE MAN WHO WENT TO YALTA

Hiss at 87, embraced by his second wife, Isabel, in October 1992, when he had good news. Colonel General Dmitri Antonovich Volkogonov, the chairman of Boris Yeltsin's commission on the KGB, announced that he had found no evidence in KGB archives that Hiss was ever a Soviet agent. "Tell Mr. Hiss that the heavy weight should be lifted from his heart." But Volkogonov later acknowledged that he had not searched the archives of military intelligence, known as GRU. And Whittaker Chambers always said they spied for GRU. In 1996 the Hiss roller coaster went downhill fast. The National Security Archive released more decrypted wartime Soviet cables and claimed that "Ales" in a Washington-to-Moscow cable of March 30, 1945, was "probably Alger Hiss." Hiss at once denied it. The cable refers to the agent working with President Roosevelt at Yalta, then flying to Moscow. Hiss was one of four Americans who did that.

Hiss goes to jail, handcuffed to another prisoner.

AMBASSADOR OF PARANOIA

Who lost China? The idea that it was given away by Communists in the State Department tormented American life for two decades. Senator Joe McCarthy exploited the suspicion in the fifties, but what historian Barbara Tuchman called "the dark yeast" of fear, vindictiveness and ambition had been fermenting for five years before Mao Zedong's final triumph over Chiang Kai-shek's Kuomintang regime in September 1949. The man who did much to feed the frenzied brew was a former Oklahoma cowboy and oil speculator given to venting ear-splitting Choctaw Indian war whoops: Patrick J. Hurley, a Republican chosen by FDR to be ambassador to China

in 1944. He was a brave man, a major general wounded in action against the Japanese, but he was vain, reckless and paranoid. Dean Acheson observed that trouble moved with him like a cloud of flies around a steer. As Herbert Hoover's secretary of war, he had colluded with MacArthur's direct disobedience of the President's orders on the Bonus Army. The job FDR gave him in China in 1944–45 was to induce Chiang Kai-shek and the Communists to form a coalition and avert a civil war. It would have challenged a diplomatic genius. The profane and irascible Hurley, with no knowledge of China, did not impress Mao, who called him The

Clown; Hurley's nickname for Mao was Moose Dung. Hurley was charmed by Chiang's circle. Once he had failed to unite Chiang and Mao, he threw all his weight behind Chiang. He backed Chiang's demand for the recall of his vehement critic General Joseph Stilwell. He was livid when the anguished foreign service officers on his staff, behind his back, sent an unprecedented joint telegram to Washington urging that America get tough with Chiang and hold out a hand to Mao, who was gaining strength. Hurley succeeded in getting Mao and Chiang together in September 1945 and predicted a true peace. Truman called him to the White House in

HURLEY'S SUMMIT: The American ambassador induced Mao Zedong (center) to leave Yenan and take his first-ever plane trip to meet Chiang Kai-shek in his mountain lair of Chungking in September 1945. Zhou Enlai and Hurley seem pleased in this photograph. Mao's look justifies Khrushchev's description of him as "a master of concealing his true thoughts and intentions."

THE GOLD WENT WITH CHIANG

A Shanghai policeman shoots an alleged Communist agent in China's civil war in May 1949—about the time Chiang Kai-shek and Nationalist troops cordoned off several blocks of Shanghai near the docks. Coolies carried to a waiting freighter an estimated 3 million ounces of gold—China's last reserve. Chiang, who had officially resigned as president of China on January 21, 1949, took the gold with him to Taiwan. U.S. General Albert Wedemeyer reported that the Nationalists had "ruthlessly, corruptly and avariciously imposed their regime upon a happy and amenable population." Demonstrations brought a violent crackdown, largely unreported in the U.S. press. According to various sources, between 20,000 and 30,000 inhabitants were killed before Taiwan was subdued.

October to congratulate him, but armed clashes broke out even as he was there. Hurley was too thin-skinned to take the newspaper criticism. He began to see himself as the target of another conspiracy, this time by Secretary of State James Byrnes and Under Secretary Acheson. On November 27 he agreed to return at once to Chungking, but the next day, without telling the President, he dramatically resigned. His efforts had been wrecked, he said, by a conspiracy of Communists in the State Department.

Hurley's Choctaw war whoop had a long echo. In three runs for the Senate between 1946 and 1952 he made much of "a shocking secret protocol to the Yalta agreements" that was "the blueprint for Communist conquest of China." Thus the myth of Yalta was born. The day Hurley quit, Truman tapped General Marshall and sent him to China in a vain yearlong effort to patch up peace. Marshall did as well as any man could, but he made a mistake with a report from General Albert Wedemeyer. It denounced the Nationalists, but proposed $2 billion in aid and a five-power trusteeship over Manchuria. Marshall suppressed the whole report, perhaps because he did not want to give the Soviets a chance to get back into Manchuria. It added another twist to the conspiracy theories.

TWO POLICE STATES

Koreans had been virtually enslaved by the Japanese for 35 years. Roosevelt and Truman's agitation for Stalin to join the war against Japan led to Soviet troops entering Korea in August 1945. The U.S. proposed dividing the occupation, and to Washington's surprise Stalin agreed. Dean Rusk was one of two young colonels given half an hour to find a place to cut Korea in half. They suggested the 38th Parallel, which put a rural 21 million people, and the capital of Seoul, in the U.S.-occupied South, and 9 million people and the industry in the North.

Fearing communism, the U.S. backed 70-year-old rightist Syngman Rhee, who had lived in the U.S. since 1910. The Soviets handed North Korea to a Moscow-trained Communist, 33-year-old Kim Il Sung. Both developed police states. The U.S. was uncomfortable with Rhee's dictatorship but rated security against communism ahead of democratic liberties. The Soviets withdrew troops at the end of 1948 and the U.S. six months later.

Many South Koreans, disgusted by Rhee's regime, at first greeted the Communists, but the tune soon changed. Between June and September 1950, the Communists executed 26,000 civilians purging "reactionaries," which meant people who happened to be intellectuals or teachers. The atrocities had a convulsive effect on opinion in the South.

A COMMUNIST GAMBLE ON AMERICA'S LACK OF RESOLVE

What John Foster Dulles did not know, staring into Communist North Korea from the ramparts of a bunker on the border, was that Stalin had finally agreed that the North Korean dictator, Kim Il Sung, could "liberate" the South. In just eight days the bunker would be overwhelmed by Kim's troops, and T-34 tanks supplied by the Soviets would have the South Korean Army (ROK) on the run everywhere. The invasion was seen to vindicate the almost universal perception that there was a monolithic conspiracy to communize the world, with Stalin pulling the strings of Kim and Mao Zedong, newly triumphant master of China. The Democratic secretary of state, Dean Acheson, who had brought in the Republican Dulles as a ges-

ture to a bipartisan foreign policy, was sure that North Korea's attack on the South was only a feint for a main Soviet thrust in Europe or the Middle East.

Cataclysmic events flowed from this perception that Communists everywhere marched to Stalin's drum, but the reality was more subtle and complex. The trio of Russian, American and Chinese scholars, Sergei N. Goncharov, John W. Lewis and Xue Litai, who in 1993 reported on major new documentary sources and interviews with participants, concluded that Stalin, Mao and Kim were not operating as Marxist-Leninist allies in a plot for world domination. They were nationalists playing their own Machiavellian games, concealing facts and motives from one another

On the 38th Parallel, South Korea, June 17, 1950. John Foster Dulles, in his capitalist homburg, stands at a pivotal point in the Cold War.

Darrigo on his special pass.

AN AMERICAN AT THE 38TH

America's encounter with the invaders began with a lone Army officer jumping out of bed around 4 a.m. on June 25, 1950, pulling on his trousers and running outside, shirtless, to find out that the screechings overhead were North Korean shells. Thirty-year-old Joseph R. Darrigo, a military trainer billeted apart from the front-line units, was the only American Army officer at the 38th Parallel. He told the author in 1995: "I knew immediately I heard the barrage that the North Koreans had been trained by the Russians." Following orders, he did not hang about. Within minutes, he was in his Jeep, foot hard on the pedal, swerving south down the dark mountain road to Seoul. When he skidded into Kaesŏng, he had another awakening. A long train had pulled into the station and an enemy infantry regiment was clambering off it. The previous month the North Koreans had puzzled everyone by tearing up the railway track between Kaesŏng and North Korea's P'yŏngyang. They had relaid it in the night and, arriving now in the middle of Kaesŏng, neatly outflanked the defenders at the border. "The 12th Division I had been adviser to was wiped out. Not one of the 15,000 men survived." The invaders spotted Darrigo. "Once they'd fired four or five bullets and I still hadn't been shot, I figured God was steering them away from me." Darrigo fought with the ROK 17th Regiment until invalided out of service in April 1951.

in "reckless war making of the worst kind." It was Kim Il Sung who badgered Stalin for the weapons and advisers to make war. He argued that there would be a popular uprising and no American intervention. He bolstered his case by playing up Dean Acheson's famous speech of January 12, 1950, ostensibly excluding Korea from the U.S. Far East defense perimeter. When Kim finally got what he wanted in late March 1950, it was with Stalin's warning: "If you should get kicked in the teeth, I shall not lift a finger. You have to ask Mao for help."

Stalin was anxious to exclude the possibility of a U.S.-Soviet clash in Korea, but saw a Soviet advantage in fouling up China's relations with the West at a time when the U.S. was implying it might recognize Mao. Acheson's January speech, emphasizing the history of Russia's imperial appetites in Asia, was meant as a friendly warning whisper to Mao, who was then negotiating his seminal treaty with Stalin. President Truman, too, on January 5, 1950, had made a statement distancing America from Formosa.

Mao, for his part, was trapped. He tried to discourage Kim when the Korean visited Mao and his Politburo in Beijing from May 13 to 16. He feared the U.S. would intervene. But when Stalin had asked Mao in January if the U.S. would indeed intervene, Mao had had to downplay the risks because he was at the same time telling Stalin there was no risk of American intervention if the Soviets sold Mao the war matériel to attack Formosa. We do not know how the conversations between Stalin, Mao and Kim played out in detail and nuance, but the North Koreans and the Soviets did keep the Chinese in the dark about their military preparations.

Kim's illusion that he could have a war of his own was a grave misunderstanding of America's resolve and its commitment to the rule of law, but it was only the first of misunderstandings by all the parties to a great tragedy.

SUMMER WAR COUNCIL: President Truman—whose back, Acheson remarked, is eloquent of the man—holds an impromptu meeting of cabinet members on the grounds of the White House on June 27, 1950. This was the day Truman ordered U.S. air and sea forces into the fighting. *Left to right:* Secretary of Agriculture Charles Brannan, Postmaster General Jesse Donaldson, Acheson, Secretary of the Interior Oscar Chapman and the forever-plotting Secretary of Defense Louis Johnson. Photograph by George Tames.

TRUMAN READY FOR A SHOWDOWN

"By God," said Truman, "I'm going to let them have it." He was weekending at home in Independence, Missouri, on Saturday, June 24, 1950, when Secretary of State Dean Acheson phoned with news of North Korea's invasion, but he had made up his mind to fight even before returning to Washington the next day. Acheson had acted swiftly and toughly, asking for an emergency meeting of the U.N. Security Council, which Truman approved.

When Acheson met Truman at the airport that Sunday afternoon, he was able to report that the council had voted 9–0 for North Korea to withdraw its forces to the 38th Parallel, the prewar border. The Soviets could have vetoed that resolution and others, but to the relief of the U.S. the Soviets' Jacob Malik continued the boycott he had begun on January 13, to protest the refusal to seat the Chinese Communist government. At the time it seemed a lucky break, freeing the U.N. to act. But the evidence now suggests the Soviet absence was not chance but a typically malevolent design by Stalin to embroil the U.S. in a potential clash with China; certainly Stalin wanted to keep China isolated and at odds with the U.S.

That evening, over a fried chicken dinner at Blair House (his temporary quarters while the White House was being renovated), Truman and his 13 advisers saw the Soviets as slicing the salami: Poland, the Czech coup, the Berlin blockade and now Korea. America would draw a line. The commitment of air and sea forces was agreed at another Blair House dinner on June 26. On June 27 the Security Council voted 7–1 to join the war on South Korea's side—the first attempt by the world organization to uphold international law by force of arms. Sixteen nations fought together. The U.S. was to contribute the bulk of the forces, followed by South Korea, Britain, Canada, Turkey and Australia. Truman had congressional support but he did not, as the Constitution requires, ask Congress to declare war.

A TRAGEDY IN FOUR ACTS

The fighting, which lasted from June 25, 1950, to July 27, 1953, was divided into four phases. In the first, the North Koreans almost swept the South Korean and U.S. armies into the sea. The capital of Seoul was abandoned on June 27. Seventy-year-old General MacArthur flew in from Tokyo on June 29, drove eight hours to the Han River against the tide of humanity fleeing south and got Washington's approval to fling in the American ground troops from Japan. They were in retreat until September 15, when a brilliant amphibious landing at Inchon, 200 miles in the enemy's rear, allowed the 8th Army in the Pusan perimeter to break out and pursue a broken enemy north. In the second phase, Truman approved orders for MacArthur to cross the 38th Parallel into North Korea on September 30, turning a "police action" into a war of national liber-

As the Marines retreat, in temperatures below zero, the Chinese are in the hills along the icy road from the Chosin Reservoir. David Douglas Duncan immortalized the ordeal in his book *This Is War!* He asked one Marine: "If I were God, what would you want for Christmas?" The answer: "Give me tomorrow."

ation. In the third phase, beginning in earnest on November 27, the Chinese Communist armies joined the war—the scene in the photograph above features the grim retreat from the Chosin Reservoir. The Chinese reached their maximum southern position below the 38th Parallel at the end of January. Then they, too, were repelled and a long war of attrition began. Talks commenced on July 10, 1951, but the fighting went on for over two more years. At least 2 million noncombatant men, women and children were killed. American military deaths are put at 54,246 (33,629 on the battlefield), South Korean at 47,000, North Korean at about 215,000. The most conservative estimate of Chinese deaths is 401,000; others range from 1 to 3 million. And at the end of it all a ravaged Korea remained divided between a Communist North and a capitalist South.

A David Douglas Duncan photograph. He knew the feeling: he had been a Marine himself.

TASK FORCE SMITH
MAKES A STAND

On the cold rainy morning of July 5, 1950, Task Force Smith, a regiment of 406 officers and men flown in from Japan, tried to stop the North Korean steamroller. Led by Lieutenant Colonel Charles B. (Brad) Smith, with 134 artillerymen under Colonel Miller Perry, they stood alone on the hills above the Suwon-Osan road against 5,000 North Koreans advancing behind 33 Soviet T-34 tanks, probably the best tank of World War II. A third of Smith's officers had fought in World War

II, but most of the men were green teenagers and they were ill equipped.

Perry's 105 mm guns opened up first, at a mile. The huge T-34s did not pause. At 700 yards, Smith's 75 mm recoilless rifle teams scored direct hits. The monsters kept coming. Smith's bazooka teams waited until the tanks were right on top of them and scored direct hits at 15 yards. The 2.36-inch rockets bounced off the armor. It had been known since 1945 that the small bazooka was not good enough, but

budget cuts had deprived MacArthur's army of the effective 3.5-inch rockets. All that was left to stop the tanks was one 105 mm gun with armor-piercing HEAT shells. But Perry had only six shells. All but four of the T-34s rolled on down the road to Osan. Smith's men were cut off to face the waves of infantry. They held the passage for three hours, then they were outflanked and finally collapsed into a stumbling cross-country retreat. Task Force Smith lost nearly half its men.

Worse followed. Despite many acts of heroism, particularly by officers, the GIs wrenched out of Japan were not emotionally equipped for the ordeal. Undertrained and undergunned, demoralized units repeatedly threw away their guns and ran. "Bug out fever" became endemic. The retreating U.S. Army dug in at the southeast port of Pusan with its back to the sea behind a 75-mile perimeter. The stage was set for MacArthur's masterstroke.

An amphibious landing at Seoul's seaport of Inchon, 200 miles behind the back of the enemy, was not an original conception by MacArthur. The Pentagon's Colonel Donald McB. Curtis included an Inchon landing in war plan SL-17, a routine piece of contingency planning he happened to finish in early June. MacArthur asked urgently for 50 copies during the week of June 26. What MacArthur brought to Inchon was the vision to see that it was the right plan and the experience to overcome objections. On August 23 in Tokyo, puffing on his corncob pipe, he heard out the "nervous Nellies," as General Omar Bradley later characterized himself and the high brass of Army, Navy and Marines. Then he stood and delivered a spellbinding 45 minutes of emotional blackmail. "I never thought the day would come," he said with a tear in his eye, "when the Navy would be unable to support the Army in its operations." He ended in a theatrical near whisper. "I can almost hear the ticking of the second hand of destiny. . . . We must act now or we will die. . . . We shall land at Inchon and I shall crush them." And so he did.

After the triumphant landing by the 1st Marine Division on September 15, against little opposition, they retook Seoul street by street, and on September 29 a weeping MacArthur presided at a ceremony turning the capital back to Syngman Rhee.

THE FATAL MARCH
TO THE YALU

The ejection of the invaders of South Korea, for which 6,000 American soldiers gave their lives, was an intoxicating event. North Korea lay open to General MacArthur's armies. MacArthur took the risk of splitting his U.N. force of around 250,000 men into two commands. In the east, the South Koreans set off on September 30, 1950, ahead of General Edward Almond's X Corps of Marine and Army divisions. In the west, Walton Walker's 8th Army began to advance into North Korea on October 9.

Three weeks later, when leading American, South Korean and Australian units approached China's border at the Yalu River, scores of thousands of Chinese Communist troops, who had been hiding in North Korea's canyons and desolate valleys, struck them on all sides with devastating speed and surprise. They would come eerily in the night, wave after wave of massed humanity, blowing bugles, horns and whistles (their signaling system) and shooting flares. Their dead would pile up three deep, and still they would come. But it was not just a question of numbers. The clever ambushes, envelopments and roadblocks, mostly concentrated against the 8th Army, destroyed South Korean regiments and forced the battered Americans to retreat south across the Chongchon River. The 8th Army unit that had made the deepest penetration, to within 18 miles of the Yalu, was the 1st Battalion of the 21st Infantry—the very same battalion, led by Lieutenant Colonel Charles Smith, that had made the stand at Osan on July 5. In the east, in the Chosin Reservoir area, the Chinese swarmed all night in hand-to-hand combat with the 7th Marines on November 3, but at dawn, when the Marines could call on close air support and artillery, they retreated. Then it was all over. Mysteriously, on November 6, the Chinese vanished.

Almond kept advancing, but with his forces fatally scattered on the east side of the central spine of mountains. West of the spine, Walker paused for supplies. At 8 p.m. the next night, in subzero weather under a full moon, the first of a series of massive Chinese attacks overwhelmed 8th Army positions. The longest retreat in American history began with terrible losses, as exhausted men ran gauntlets of fire. By mid-December the 8th Army had fallen back more than 120 miles and was dug in below the 38th Parallel. In the east, X Corps forces were cut off and surrounded in the mountains near the Chosin Reservoir. The breakout of 10,000 men of the 5th and 7th Marines from Yudam-ni to Hagaru, and then the fighting withdrawal to the coast of the whole force of Marines and soldiers, gripped America's imagination. The unflappable General Oliver Smith's magnificent reply to a question about the retreat entered Marine Corps legend: "Gentlemen, we're not retreating," said Smith. "We are just advancing in a different direction." And technically he was right: there was no rear. On the precipitous, twisting icy mountain road enfiladed on all sides by Chinese machine guns and mortars, it took two weeks of combat day and night for the Marine column of 1,500 vehicles to get through to the embarkation port of Hŭngnam. There was no "bug out" here. The men advanced in the different direction as a coherent force intact with their heavy equipment, and with the frozen corpses of their fallen comrades. Valor was served by know-how. At Funchilin Pass the column came to a halt at a chasm where the Chinese had blown up a bridge. The answer came floating from heaven: eight bridge sections gently parachuted down by Marine pilots. The chasm was bridged under fire.

Red China pushed MacArthur's forces down below the 38th Parallel, then demanded that the U.S. leave Korea and Taiwan. Once again American resolve was underestimated. When General Walker was killed in a road accident, his successor was one of the best combat generals of World War II, Matthew B. Ridgway, the 82nd Airborne leader who liked to lead from the hottest part of the battlefield with a grenade clipped to his shirt. In the early months of 1951 Ridgway's canny use of firepower hurled the Chinese back above the 38th Parallel. The war of attrition that followed ground on to July 27, 1953, World War I style, with many a headline written in the blood of Heartbreak Ridge, Old Baldy and Porkchop Hill.

On November 24, the day set for the new 8th Army offensive, MacArthur flew in from Tokyo for the jump-off, and, on impulse, told his pilot to fly along the Yalu at 5,000 feet so that he could see the entire area in detail. "All that spread before our eyes," he wrote, "was an endless expanse of utterly barren countryside, jagged hills, yawning crevices, and the black waters of the Yalu locked in the silent death grip of snow and ice. It was a merciless wasteland." MacArthur saw no signs of his destiny: the 300,000 Chinese who were waiting to pounce.

Marine dead in the Chosin Reservoir area. The Marines carried them all home. Chinese infiltrators stripped clothing from some of the bodies.

TRUMAN FIRES MACARTHUR

The brown envelope, brought by a Signal Corps courier at lunchtime on April 12, 1951, was red-stamped "Action for MacArthur." He read the message at home with his wife, Jean, at his side: "I deeply regret that it becomes my duty as President and Commander-in-Chief of the United States military forces to replace you as Supreme Commander, Allied Powers; commander-in-chief of the United Nations command; commander-in-chief Far East; commanding general, U.S. Army, Far East. . . ."

It was signed by the president.

MacArthur was calm. "Jeannie," he said, "we're going home at last." A radio news flash had beaten the official letter to his Tokyo home. The news had leaked because Truman had been indiscreet at a morning staff meeting about the so-and-so double-crosser MacArthur. It was careless of Truman, and he was callous in his manner of ending 52 years of military service, but the recall was overdue. MacArthur had waged a private and public campaign against the Truman administration for total war on Communist China. He asked for 26 atomic bombs to be dropped on North Korea and China. He favored reinstating the corrupt and incompetent regime of Chiang Kai-shek. His conviction was so intense, his ambition so vaulting, that he committed numerous acts of insubordination, amounting to the gravest challenge to civilian control of the military in the history of the Republic.

• On October 24, 1950, he had disobeyed the Joint Chiefs' directive that only South Korean troops could approach the Chinese border. He ordered his commanders to drive forward with all speed.

• On November 5 he overrode the directive that there should be no bombing within five miles of the border. He ordered the Air Force to destroy the bridges over the Yalu.

• On November 25 he rejected the advice of the Chiefs to halt his attack on the high ground commanding the Yalu valley.

• From November 28 to December 4, he gave a series of press interviews protesting the order banning strikes across China's border. Truman put out a gag order.

• On March 15, 1951, he defied the President's gag order. He told the Associated Press that stopping the Army at the 38th Parallel was contrary to the mission of unifying Korea—which he had been told "over and over again" (to quote Acheson) was not his mission.

• On March 24 he sabotaged a major U.S. initiative for peace agreed on by all the U.N. allies by preempting it with an insulting ultimatum to the Chinese to surrender.

• On April 5 House Minority leader Joseph Martin, one of that chamber's worst reactionaries and red-baiters, read out on the House floor a letter from MacArthur commenting on a speech Martin had made. Martin had said that if Truman was not going all out for total victory he should be indicted for "the murder of thousands of American boys." MacArthur's reply backed Martin's call to "unleash" Chiang's Nationalist troops on

Eisenhower on hearing the news. "I am going to maintain silence," he said, "in every language known to man." The two men were public admirers, private enemies. MacArthur described Ike as the apotheosis of mediocrity, the best clerk he ever had. Ike told his diary MacArthur was a big baby who liked "boot lickers" and would probably be ruined by his "love of the limelight."

Korea and concluded by ridiculing the concept of a limited war: "There is no substitute for victory."

MacArthur was not only disloyal. He was derelict in exposing his army. He was terrifyingly reckless in his readiness—

eagerness, even—to risk global nuclear war. He created such a Wagnerian drama out of it all that he is commonly thought responsible for the war with China. He was not. The ultimate blame for that lies with Truman, Dean Acheson and George Marshall, who kept giving in to him.

MacArthur made an emotional departure from Tokyo. Nearly a quarter of a million Japanese stood ten deep on the roads to the airport, many with heads bowed. In San Francisco half a million people came out on the streets. His 34-minute address to a joint session of Congress—later declared by Truman to be "nothing but a bunch of damn bullshit"—called for bombing Manchuria and blockading China. His oracular rhetoric was broken by paroxysms of cheering and 30 wild standing ovations, climaxing in a pandemonium of tears and shouted acclaim. Work stopped all over the country and 20 million people saw his moving peroration on their grainy new televisions: "But I still remember the refrain of one of the most popular barrack ballads of that day, which proclaimed, most proudly, that 'Old soldiers never die. They just fade away.' And like the soldier of the ballad, I now close my military career and just fade away—an old soldier who tried to do his duty as God gave him the light to see that duty. . . . Goodbye."

An important part of the delirium was an explosion of the pent-up frustrations of a people longing to hear that the most intractable problems were still susceptible to the exercise of America's moral will. It did not last. A Gallup poll found that 69 percent of the people backed him, but only 30 percent of the country was willing to go to a wider war with China. At a congressional inquiry, the military chiefs, led by George Marshall, discredited MacArthur's strategy. In June 1952, Robert Taft asked him to be his running mate, but MacArthur, who was by now attracting only small audiences, lost his chance because the Republicans turned aside from Taft in favor of another general, who had once been MacArthur's assistant. Taft lost the nomination narrowly. Had he run and won, MacArthur would have been president for at least three years: Taft died of cancer in 1953.

Seven million people cheered MacArthur at New York's ticker tape parade, twice the number who had turned out for Ike on his return from Europe in 1945. The novelist William Styron wrote that MacArthur's eyes were "like those of a man whose thoughts had turned inward upon some Caesarean dream magnificent beyond compare."

THE DIRTIEST CAMPAIGN

A woman who had just heard Adlai Stevenson speak in the 1952 presidential campaign rushed up to him: "Mr. Stevenson, you have captured the vote of every thinking person in America!" To which Stevenson replied: "Ma'am, we need a majority!" Possibly, the story is apocryphal, but it is vintage Stevenson: cool, witty, modest to a fault. He knew he could not beat Eisenhower, the American hero. "Who did I think I was," he remarked later in defeat, "running against George Washington?"

Eisenhower was not much of a Washington in the campaign itself. He assigned some of the dirty work to his running mate, Richard Nixon, who fomented hysteria on the chemical formula of C_2K_1—communism, corruption and Korea—but Ike's performance throughout was feckless. In the words of his former companion in arms, General Omar Bradley, he went about the country "hypocritically calling into question policies he himself had helped formulate or approved or had carried out." He repudiated Yalta. He ran away from his willingness in 1945, as Supreme Commander, to let the Russians take Berlin, saying it was the political decision of Roosevelt and Truman and he had "no personal responsibility." He condemned Truman for withdrawing U.S. forces from Korea, a decision he was a party to as Army Chief of Staff. He tried to have it all ways on Korea. One minute he blamed Truman for being soft, the next for making a stand: "The Democrats could purchase full employment only at the price of dead and mangled bodies of young Americans." And then he seemed to favor widening the war: "I have always stood behind General MacArthur in bombing those bases on the Yalu from which fighter planes are coming." That statement, too, was false, but the ultimate ignominy was in what he did not say.

No man was more beholden to General George Marshall than Ike. Marshall had plucked him from obscurity to lead the U.S. armies. In 1952 Marshall was under vituperative attack by Republicans for "losing China." Senators William Jenner and Joe McCarthy point-blank accused him of treachery. Ike did not come to the

"NAUGHTY NAUGHTY"

President-elect Eisenhower, on the Korean front in December, had a pork chop lunch with his old outfit, the 15th Regiment of the 3rd Division.

MADLY FOR ADLAI: Stevenson (1900–1965) was an internationalist in the isolationist Midwest, who became governor with an unprecedented half-million plurality. He rooted out corruption in the state police, was thrifty with the public's money, doubled spending on education and vetoed a loyalty oath. He advocated early forms of Peace Corps and Medicare. Unbothered by the "egghead" label, pinned on him for intellectualism, he paraphrased Marx: "Eggheads of the world unite, you have nothing to lose but your yolks."

rescue. He angrily told an inquiring reporter in August there was "nothing of disloyalty in Marshall's soul," but then he went on to endorse the political assassins, shaking their hands and speaking for their campaigns.

There was a moment when his better self seemed about to prevail. On October 2 he left his campaign train for a few hours' rest in Peoria, Illinois. He summoned McCarthy to his hotel room and exploded in "white hot anger" at his tricks. And in the draft of a speech he was to give in Milwaukee in McCarthy's home state, he had a paragraph praising Marshall's "profoundest patriotism." Wisconsin Governor Walter Kohler persuaded Ike's chief of staff, Sherman Adams, that the paragraph should be dropped. Adams went to Ike. "Are you telling me the paragraph is out of place?" Ike asked Adams. "Yes, sir," said Adams. "Then take it out." To make matters worse, he picked up McCarthy's theme. Infiltration of the Democratic administration "meant—in its most ugly triumph—treason itself."

There was a wave of public and press criticism. Senator Wayne Morse of Oregon quit the GOP in disgust; Omar Bradley said, "It turned my stomach." Stevenson was genuinely shocked and saddened, but he could not resist a quip. "My opponent has been worrying about my funnybone. I'm worrying about his backbone." He continued in his graceful overdiffident way, making sound speeches that gained an extra golden haze in the light of the squalid opposition. He assailed McCarthyism in McCarthy's home state. He refused the United Auto Workers a denunciation of the Taft-Hartley Act. He told Virginians racial prejudice was a revolting spectacle.

Stevenson's campaign gained momentum (one convert was Henry Kissinger). But the newspapers were heavily aligned against him (993 dailies to 201) and he had undervalued television. In 1948 there were 345,000 sets, in 1952 there were 17 million. Then, on October 24, Eisenhower played a master card. He promised to concentrate on ending the Korean war. "That requires a personal visit. I shall go to Korea." An unprecedented number of Americans voted—over 61.5 million, or more than 63 percent of eligible voters. Eisenhower won by about 55 to 44 percent and swept the electoral college, 442 to 89.

"I don't believe I ought to quit because I'm not a quitter. And, incidentally, Pat's not a quitter. . . ."

"It isn't easy to come before a nationwide audience and air your life as I've done. . . ."

THE CHECKERS SPEECH

James Wechsler, the liberal editor of the *New York Post,* was gleeful as he wrote the Thursday, September 18, splash headline on Richard Nixon. "This should blow that moralizing, unscrupulous, double-dealing son of a bitch out of the water," he said in the newsroom. Wechsler's headline was:

**SECRET NIXON FUND
SECRET RICH MEN'S TRUST FUND
KEEPS NIXON IN STYLE
BEYOND HIS SALARY**

The new California senator did have a fund of $18,150, contributed in maximum amounts of $500 by Republican businessmen. But it was not secret and it was used legitimately for mailing speeches and political travel. And Adlai Stevenson, it transpired, had a similar fund. Republicans around Eisenhower panicked all the same. They wanted to dump Nixon at once. Nixon, on a whistle-stop tour of the West, was left to sweat it out for two days before Eisenhower called him. Tell the public, said Ike, about any money you have ever received. There followed a memorable exchange.

Nixon: General, do you think after the television program that an announcement could then be made one way or another?

Ike: Maybe.

Nixon: There comes a time in matters like this when you've either got to shit or get off the pot.

In his book *Six Crises,* Nixon recorded his injunction as "time to fish or cut bait," but put the real words in his memoirs, where he wrote, with obvious relish, that "Ike was certainly not used to being talked to in that manner." Less than an hour before the keyed-up Nixon was to go on national television, Ike struck again—from behind the arras. Thomas Dewey called to say all the general's top advisers had concluded Nixon must resign at the end of the

PARTNERS AGAIN: "Let there be no doubt about it," said Ike, "America has taken Dick Nixon to its heart. He is vindicated as a man of courage and honor."

broadcast. Nixon stalled. He was on the edge of tears when he appealed to the 60 million viewers, with Pat at his side, from a studio got up as a homey GI den. It was a masterly performance at two levels. People wept (or writhed) as he bared his soul; only the insiders appreciated the coolness and agility of the coded messages to the leadership. Nixon did not merely itemize all he earned and owned— "Every dime that we've got is honestly ours. Pat doesn't have a mink coat. But she does have a respectable Republican cloth coat." He challenged all candidates to make a similar clean breast. Watching in Cleveland, Eisenhower, who was included by inference, was so startled he jabbed a pencil right through his legal pad. And at the end Nixon put his life in the hands of the Republican National Committee, not of Eisenhower and the Eastern establishment. Eisenhower jabbed his pad again.

Nixon's pitch to the grass roots was perfect in its sentiment and schmaltz. Oh, yes, he should tell them all "we did get something, a gift. . . . It was a little cocker spaniel dog, in a crate, that [was] sent all the way from Texas—black and white, spotted, and our little girl Tricia, the six-year-old—named it Checkers. And you know, the kids, like all kids, loved the dog, and I just want to say this right now, that regardless of what they say about it, we're going to keep it."

The switchboard lit up. Telegrams ran 350–1 in Nixon's favor. Money poured in. When Nixon flew into Wheeling, West Virginia (below), Eisenhower rushed up the steps with his hand outstretched. "You're my boy!"

DWIGHT DAVID EISENHOWER
34th President (Republican), 1953–1961

THE GREAT QUESTION: Vicky, the British cartoonist, speculates on the role Ike would play as president.

ADVENTURES: Ike at 16 (foreground) as "president of the roughnecks." All his life he looked to find in backwoods adventures the virtues of enterprise, resourcefulness and bravery he associated with the romanticized Western frontier of his youth. He believed in luck. He carried three lucky coins—a silver dollar, a guinea gold piece and a French franc. Later in the Army he was so lucky at poker that he had to give it up because his winning created too much resentment among his fellow officers.

BORN: October 14, 1890, Denison, Texas   DIED: March 28, 1969, Washington, D.C.

POLITICAL CAREER: Aide to General Douglas MacArthur, Chief of Staff, U.S. Army, 1932–1935; Senior Military Assistant to General MacArthur advising the Philippines, 1935–1939; Chief of Staff to 3rd Army, San Antonio, Texas, 1941–1942; Commander, American forces in Britain, 1942–1943; Supreme Allied Commander, Europe, 1943–1944; Chief of Staff of U.S. Army, 1945–1948; President, Columbia University, 1948–1950; Supreme Commander, North Atlantic Treaty Organization in Europe, 1950–1952; President, 1953–1961

FIRSTS: First president to preside over 50 states. First professional soldier elected since Ulysses S. Grant in 1868. First man elected president in his first try for elective office since Grant.

CHARACTER SNAPSHOT: "He had the charisma of a film star yet he exuded self-effacing moderation and natural good sense. Ike was the epitome of the common man. And he managed to convey his ordinariness in an extraordinary manner . . . by the projection of human warmth."
                                                                —Biographer Piers Brendon

SIX BOYS: Ike had five brothers. His father, David, and his mother, Ida Stover, were strict puritans, pacifist Mennonites whose families had fled religious persecution in Europe. The family prayed on their knees morning and night. David's store in Hope, Kansas, went belly up when the wheat market collapsed in 1888 and his partner absconded. He was a taciturn $10-a-week railroad hand in Texas when Ike was born. In Ike's infancy, they moved to Abilene, Kansas, and a shack with no running water, no inside lavatory and no electricity. Little Ike (left, at 12) and Big Ike (Edgar, 13, next to him) were adventurous barefoot urchins, like Tom Sawyer and Huck Finn, who wrestled and got into scrapes for which their father beat them mercilessly. The brothers (left to right) are Dwight, Edgar, Earl, Arthur and Roy; baby Milton is in front.

TWENTY-FOUR YEARS ON: At high school, Ike hauled ice and fed the furnace and still got As, and won a place at West Point in 1911 (causing his pacifist mother to weep). He was a notable smoking and swearing rebel and ended up 125th for discipline. He might have done better than 61st out of 164 in his class, but got "a bad case of the blue devils" when a knee injury ended his obsessive dreams of being a football star. When the family got together in 1926, all his brothers, as banker, lawyer, pharmacist, engineer and bureaucrat, were making more money than Dwight, an obscure major who had not even managed to see action in World War I.

THE SUPREMO: As well as the smile, there was a profane vocabulary and a volcanic temper that Ike himself feared. As NATO Supreme Commander in 1951, he got angry with the Europeans for the petty jealousies that complicated a quick buildup of troops and with right-wing attempts in Congress to block the dispatch of American troops to Europe. His ally in this effort, Truman's secretary of state, Dean Acheson, was merely catching a side wind. In November 1951 Truman renewed his past offer to get Ike the Democratic nomination, only to be told flat out: "You can't join a party just to run for office. What reason have you to think I can ever be a Democrat? You know I have been a Republican all my life." It was disingenuous, considering the efforts he had made to obscure his political sympathies. A letter he wrote on October 14, 1951, declaring himself "an adherent to the Republican party and to liberal Republican principles," was kept secret for years. He gave up his NATO post in the spring of 1952 to win the Republican nomination. He rejected a White House invitation to a foreign affairs briefing. A furious Truman wrote him: "I am extremely sorry that you have allowed a bunch of screwballs to come between us."

MAMIE: Ike was 25 when he married Mamie (Mary) Geneva Doud, a "saucy" 19-year-old daughter of a well-off meat packer. She was hopeless about the house, but made happy homes of endless dreary Army housing. Their first son, Doud Dwight (Icky), died from scarlet fever when he was four, and for the rest of his life Ike sent Mamie flowers on the boy's birthday. He wrote 319 loving letters to her while overseas in World War II. At that time, he did have some kind of liaison with Kay Summersby, an Irish divorcee half his age who was promoted from his driver to secretary-aide, but he extricated himself at the end of the war, writing a stiff letter of thanks and goodbye. He affected not to have read her discreet memoir, *Eisenhower Was My Boss* (1948).

COLUMBIA: Ike left the Army at age 57 in 1947, wrote his memoirs, *Crusade in Europe* (1948), in three months, turned corporate offers aside and nearly became head of the Boy Scouts. He rejected the first Democratic and Republican invitations to run for president, and became president of Columbia University instead for $25,000 a year. On July 13, 1948, he admitted political ambitions to General Robert L. Schultz, who kept the secret. One of Ike's first acts at Columbia was persuading football coach Lou Little not to leave for Yale. Ike was not easy among academics, but he left a solid legacy of a better-funded and -organized university. He worked to educate himself politically and by 1949 was lobbying wealthy audiences with increasingly conservative speeches about the need to defend America and the pitfalls of the welfare state.

STILL TOGETHER: Good times with the brothers in 1948—one of them has just found a missing fishhook. They shared a love of hunting, fishing and playing poker around a campfire.

TWO TERMS: At 64, during the night of September 23, 1955, after 27 holes of golf and a hamburger, he woke with a coronary thrombosis. While he convalesced—here in Denver in October—he kept the world guessing whether he would run for a second term. The answer came, in typically confusing language, on February 29, 1956. It added up to a "yes." In June, when he was rushed to the hospital with a blocked intestine, his uniquely detailed medical bulletins were headlines again.

THE NEW
MIDDLE CLASS

President Eisenhower at a family Thanksgiving in 1953 that epitomized the good times.

Even the American taste for superlatives was stretched by the nature of the good times in the fifties. There had been nothing like it before in the history of the world. National output doubled between 1946 and 1956 and would double again by 1970. With the exception of the elderly on fixed incomes, the mass of people enjoyed spectacular increases in their spending power. Personal incomes nearly tripled between 1940 and 1955. A whole new middle class, made up of 60 percent of all American families, was created. What they did with their new wealth is glimpsed in the multiplication tables. Some 13 million new homes were bought in the decade after 1948; 83 percent of American homes had a television; the number of two-car families doubled between 1951 and 1958; and the consumption of hot dogs went from 750 million in 1950 to 2 billion in 1960. America, with 6 percent of the world's population, was consuming one third of the world's goods and services. But that same 6 percent was making no less than two thirds of the world's manufactures.

A typical family in 1951 ate two and a half tons of food: 699 bottles of milk, 578 pounds of meat, 131 dozen eggs, 1,190 pounds of vegetables and 440 pounds of fresh fruit, plus sugar, flour, bread and cereal. It is not just a question of quantity. The American family in 1900 had plenty to eat, but for the masses it was mostly starches and smoked meat. They did not have the choices of green vegetables, frozen foods and fresh meat, and they paid proportionately much more for what they had. The results were all around to see. Children in 1950 were two or three inches taller than they were in 1900. The 1950 woman could expect to live to 71, 20 years longer than the 1900 woman. Male life expectancy rose from 48 to 65. The country got younger. With 40 million births from 1950 to 1960, some 40 percent of the population was under 20 by 1964.

Steve Czekalinski, a Du Pont worker, and his family and their food for a year. Cost in 1951: $1,300.

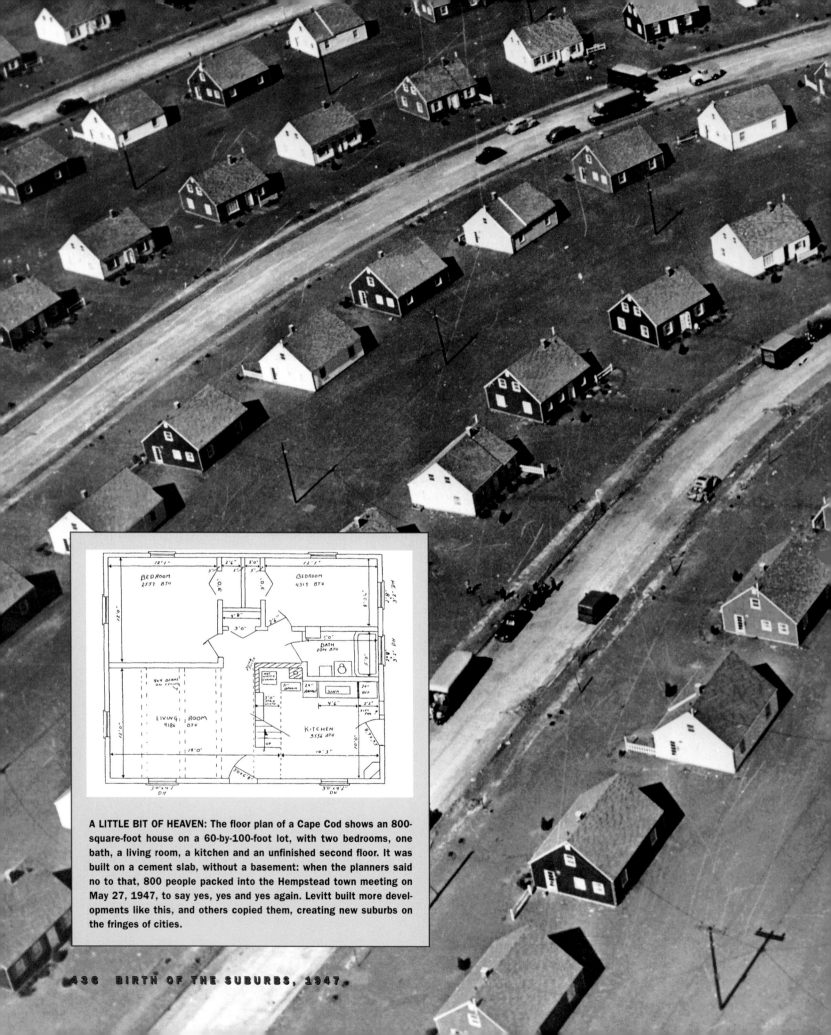

A LITTLE BIT OF HEAVEN: The floor plan of a Cape Cod shows an 800-square-foot house on a 60-by-100-foot lot, with two bedrooms, one bath, a living room, a kitchen and an unfinished second floor. It was built on a cement slab, without a basement: when the planners said no to that, 800 people packed into the Hempstead town meeting on May 27, 1947, to say yes, yes and yes again. Levitt built more developments like this, and others copied them, creating new suburbs on the fringes of cities.

THE MAN WHO CHANGED THE FACE OF AMERICA

As a Seabee on embattled Pacific islands, Bill Levitt drove himself hard all day, racing to build jungle airstrips for the Navy. He dreamed a little, too. About a flat stretch of potato fields on Long Island, just 20 miles out of Manhattan, where he planned to do something revolutionary. He would build middle-class houses more quickly and cheaply than they had ever been built before; build them by the thousands with central heating, GE refrigerators, electric ranges and Bendix washing machines; and build them around a vision of a community with schools, churches, synagogues, swimming pools and baseball fields, and "village greens" full of shops.

At night in the jungle, he talked with the other young builders and craftsmen in the Seabees about how he could extrapolate from the experiment he and his father and brother had tried in 1941, when they won a government contract to build 1,600 row houses for shipyard workers in Norfolk, Virginia. Frustrated by union rules and organizing a myriad of crafts, they had beaten the clock by dividing the building process into 27 separate steps and training 27 teams of workers to carry them out. Those who worked fastest earned the most. It was Henry Ford's mass-production idea all over again, with the difference that in Levitt's scheme it was not the assembly line that moved but the workers.

Levitt was 38 when he came home. Two years later, when Levitt and Sons said they would build 2,000 houses for veterans outside Hempstead, they were besieged. The rising curve of the birthrate had collided with the falling curve of housing starts. Millions of Americans in the richest country in the world were living in garages, coal sheds, chicken coops, toolsheds, granaries, smokehouses, old trolley buses, Army Quonset huts. It was joyous, incredible news that Levitt could offer a two-bedroom home for $6,900 with no down payment for veterans—with the crucial help of a federal housing bill that guaranteed mortgages. Levittown, the name that soon replaced "Island Trees," grew in four years to 17,447 houses on 6,000 acres. It was a neighborly community of 82,000 people, just as Bill Levitt had

MASTER BUILDER: Bill Levitt (1907–1994) came of Russian-Jewish immigrant parents.

dreamed. It was the new surburbia that would thereafter lure millions of Americans out of the cities.

There were critics. Levitt's rules invited attack. No blacks. No fences. No laundry on lines. No shrubs more than four feet high along property lines. Lewis Mumford mocked the monotony. Social experts predicted the development would be a slum in 20 years. Fifty years later Levittown belied the criticism, in all except its racial mix (though the policy was officially abandoned in 1949). There had been, in Leslie Bennett's words, "an explosive assertion of individuality that would have stunned Levittown's early detractors. Almost no two houses look alike." Rooms, bays, dormers, patios and porches had been added; yards landscaped; trees planted. By 1990, the $7,000 box on a slab was selling for $135,000 to $150,000.

All those peasants from Ireland, Russia, Italy and elsewhere, who had spent generations dreaming of a bit of green to call their own, at last achieved it through Levitt and a federal government far more active than after World War I. Levitt sold his company to the International Telephone and Telegraph Company for $92 million in 1968, then lost $34 million in Iran when the Ayatollah Khomeini reneged on a housing deal.

He had to sell his big house and his big yacht. But he stayed adventurous to the end of his life. "I'm not here just to build and sell houses," he said. "To be perfectly frank, I'm looking for a little glory, too."

EMPEROR OF THE CITY

Robert Moses bestrode America's greatest city like a Colossus. With one hand of steel, he tied the metropolis of Manhattan to its suburbs, flinging up seven soaring bridges, ramming six arterial expressways through city areas. With the other, more sensitive hand, he laced 16 elegant parkways through the woods and pastures of Westchester and Long Island, and created at Jones Beach what is arguably America's finest oceanfront park. And with the third hand, for he was a magical man, he gave New York City a gratuity of 658 playgrounds, 15 indoor swimming pools, 17 miles of beaches, 416 miles of parkways and 15,000 acres of new shoreline plucked from the waters. There is something of Robert Moses, good and bad, in the landscape of every American city.

To say he was a master builder is to say Beethoven could play the piano. No single opus of steel and concrete defined him. His significance lay in the vastness of his vision, and in the very simple fact that he got done the impossible things that he always dreamed of doing while a young man at Yale and Oxford. He was never elected to anything, yet he held power through the administrations of six governors and five mayors. In the legislation he cunningly drafted, his authorities, uninhibited by the vagaries of electoral politics, acquired powers and revenues that eventually made Moses the emperor of a sovereign state; in the sixties the surplus on his Triborough Bridge and Tunnel Authority alone ran to $30 million a year.

Moses was not at all democratic. To use the title of Robert Caro's magisterial biography, he was the Power Broker. Personally honest, he procured acquiescence from the dishonest and the greedy with fees and retainers. In the thirties and fifties, he smeared critics as "Pinkos," and he was not above blackmail. At the height of his power, he was ruthless, vindictive, racist, unscrupulous. He built the granite overpasses on Long Island parkways just low enough to prevent buses from traveling on them. He did not want his beautiful beaches open to blacks, whom he presumed would not own cars. The straight line of the Northern State Parkway plunges three miles south because a robber baron secretly gave Moses $10,000 for mapping, but he would not move it four hundred feet to save a score of modest farmers.

The urban consequences of his autocracy were documented by Caro and Jane Jacobs. He erased vibrant communities. He decanted the poor into new slums. He raised such a civic fury, in the end, that one of his legacies was a patchwork of regulatory watchdogs making an ordeal of any and all future projects in New York. His contempt for zoning and mass transit are the mother and father of Long Island's unlovely suburban sprawl and its stupefying traffic jams. Sorting all that out would take a genius. It would take another Robert Moses.

Arnold Newman's portrait of Robert Moses was taken in 1959 on Welfare (now Roosevelt) Island.

DICK TRACYS TO A MAN: Republican members of the House Un-American Activities Committee in 1948 with counsel Robert Stripling (second from right). Richard Nixon (far right) was the fairest and most scrupulous of a vindictive bunch. Chairman J. Parnell Thomas (second from left) was jailed for fraud.

THE HOLLYWOOD TEN

It was B-movie stuff. An underground of Red (and Jewish) writers, stars and directors, in league with New Deal bureaucrats, was bent on making films that subverted America. Such was the scenario the House Un-American Activities Committee (HUAC) hoped to prove in October 1947 when it turned its loopy eye on Hollywood. As critic Walter Goodman wrote, its premise was asinine, its methods gross and its intentions despicable.

The plot never made first cut. Only three movies were cited, all fashioned as propaganda for a wartime ally, so Chairman J. Parnell Thomas went on a witch-hunt. He incited a bunch of friendly witnesses, studio heads like Walt Disney, Jack Warner and Louis B. Mayer, to recklessly "name names" of Communists, without any evidence at all, then summoned 19 of the named and began the hectoring: "Are you now or have you ever been a member of the Communist party?" Ten of the witnesses cited the First Amendment as a prohibition on HUAC's right to ask the question. For four days there was much hollering, mutual name calling and pounding of the chairman's gavel, then the Hollywood Ten, as they came to be called, were held in contempt and jailed for up to a year. They were Alvah Bessie, Herbert Biberman, Lester Cole, Edward Dmytryk, Ring Lardner, Jr., John Howard Lawson, Albert Maltz, Samuel Ornitz, Adrian Scott and Dalton Trumbo.

The *Los Angeles Times* applauded: "Bad as it is to debauch people's minds with filth, it is vastly worse to corrupt and de-

bauch their patriotism." The Hearst press called for censorship. The *New York Times, Washington Post* and *Detroit Free Press* criticized the hearings, but the studio heads trembled and the moneymen in New York panicked. Fifty film executives argued in secret for two days at the Waldorf-Astoria, then declared that none of the "Unfriendly Ten" or any other unrepenting Communist would get work in the movies again.

There was a flurry of rebellion by the creative community. The biggest talents assembled at Ira Gershwin's house. Led by directors John Huston and William Wyler, they organized a Committee for the First Amendment. Five hundred signed, not so much in favor of the Ten as protest of hearings that were "disloyal to the spirit and the letter of our Constitution." The young Lauren Bacall, there with Humphrey Bogart, was the pithiest: "I couldn't believe what was going on—that jerk sitting up there had the power to put these men in jail!" The talent launched a radio campaign called Hollywood Fights Back, and Washington was treated to the sight of the braver stars walking into the Capitol to protest. Thomas hated the criticisms by the likes of Bogie, Spencer Tracy, Katharine Hepburn, Myrna Loy, Gregory Peck, Danny Kaye, Gene Kelly, Judy Garland, James Stewart, Rita Hayworth, Ava Gardner and Frank Sinatra. In her memoirs, Bacall said "we didn't realize until much later that we were being used to some degree by the Unfriendly Ten, in that our focus was altered to defending them individually and collectively."

STARS PROTEST: Humphrey Bogart and Lauren Bacall arrive at the Capitol to attend the hearings, with Richard Conte, June Havoc, John Huston, Paul Henreid, Evelyn Keyes, Danny Kaye, Jane Wyatt and others. Howard Hughes lent them a plane. Not until they were on it did they see his little joke. He had called it *Star of the Red Sea*.

The studios, TV networks and record companies stuck to their odious discrimination. Hundreds of artists were blacklisted for years, among them Zero Mostel, John Garfield, Pete Seeger, Kim Hunter, Sidney Buchman and Clifford Odets. The president of the Screen Actors Guild informed on his fellow actors as Agent T-10 for the FBI. Years later he acknowledged: "Many fine people were accused wrongly of being Communists simply because they were liberals. . . . I was all for kicking Communists out of Hollywood, but some members of the . . . Committee, ignoring standards of truth and fair play, ganged up on innocent people" (Ronald Reagan, *An American Life*, 1990).

THE THOUGHT POLICE

"Investigate *them?* Heck, that's mah possee," by Bill Mauldin.

Bill Mauldin's cartoon attack on HUAC went straight into a dossier J. Edgar Hoover's FBI kept on him from 1946. Mauldin, holder of a Purple Heart himself, was a hero of the GIs in World War II as the creator of Willie and Joe, the mordantly weary riflemen. He was in good company in the thought police lineup. In his *Dangerous Dossiers* (1988), Herbert Mitgang published the files of a glittering array of artists whom the FBI had kept under surveillance. The writings of six Nobel laureates had excited suspicion—Sinclair Lewis, Pearl S. Buck, William Faulkner, Ernest Hemingway, John Steinbeck, Thomas Mann. Others in the spyglass included Robert Frost, Dashiell Hammett, Irwin Shaw, Truman Capote, E. B. White, Carl Sandburg, Theodore Dreiser, Thornton Wilder, Nelson Algren, A. J. Liebling and publisher Alfred Knopf. What triggered a file was in almost all cases some manifestation of social concern. The Faulkner dossier was started for his stand on civil rights, Hemingway's because he was sympathetic to the Spanish Republicans, Buck's for an attack on race prejudice. Steinbeck's poignant novel about the Okies, *The Grapes of Wrath,* was deemed un-American. Mitgang's revelations, and more by Natalie Robins (*Alien Ink,* 1992), were a stunning indictment of the primitive values of the compilers, who were often comic in their misapprehensions. John Kenneth Galbraith was called "doctrinaire" by an informant. "Doctrinaire" got misheard as "Doctorware" so Galbraith was perpetuated as a follower of a sinister subversive called Dr. Ware. The consequences were often not comic at all. Steinbeck was barred from service in the Army. Lies proved hard to purge.

THE GUILT OF JULIUS ROSENBERG

Julius Rosenberg and his wife, Ethel, went to the electric chair in Sing Sing, New York, on June 19, 1953, movingly proclaiming their love and their innocence of the charges of espionage. Of their love, there is no doubt. Several hundred poignant letters they wrote each other from separate cells testify to their mutual devotion. But, after decades of controversy, there is now also no doubt about the guilt of Julius and the complicity of Ethel in a Soviet conspiracy to steal American atomic secrets. Decoded wartime Venona cables from the Soviet consulate in New York to the KGB in Moscow, made public only in July 1995, give us a mental picture of Julius in a New York apartment photographing documents and diagrams brought to him by a small ring—mostly young fellow Communists he met at City College of New York.

None of the intercepts mentioning Julius was in evidence at the trial in March 1951. The U.S. did not want the Soviets to know it had cracked enough of an "unbreakable" code to have proof of a vast espionage effort. It involved leaders of the U.S. Communist Party and as many as 220 spies, many still unidentified. The Rosenbergs were convicted on the evidence of Ethel's bombastic brother, David Greenglass, and his wife, Ruth. David was a young soldier working in a machine shop at Los Alamos, New Mexico, where he picked up information on the design of the plutonium device later dropped on Nagasaki. He gave some crude sketches to Julius and passed on more through Harry Gold, a zany Philadelphia chemist turned Soviet courier. Gold turned up at the Greenglass apartment in Albuquerque, identifying himself with a Jell-O box whose irregularly cut edge matched a portion Julius had given David.

Conviction was not in doubt, but the sentence was. Judge Irving R. Kaufman, Jewish like the accused and the prosecutors, was portrayed in the press as having gone to a synagogue for divine guidance. Roy Cohn, later chief counsel to Joe McCarthy, was on the prosecution team. He was a friend of the judge, and years later told editor Jason Epstein that "the nearest Irving got to a synagogue was the phone booth outside the courthouse. It was not God that concerned him. He asked me how a double death sentence would play in the *New York Times.*" Cohn urged the chair for both Rosenbergs to demonstrate that Jews put country before religion.

The sentences provoked outcry around the world. Executing Ethel, against whom little evidence was produced, and orphaning the couple's young sons, struck many as a cruel and panicky result of the anti-Communist hysteria. Eisenhower was so anxious to speed the Rosenbergs to the chair that his Attorney General, Herbert Brownell, had a secret and improper meeting with Chief Justice Fred Vinson. Brownell asked the Chief Justice to recall the Supreme Court from vacation if Justice William O. Douglas, then sitting alone, ordered a stay of execution. Douglas did. He wanted the lower court to consider the argument that Kaufman did not have a jury vote on the death sentence, as required by the Atomic Energy Act of 1946.

Thanks to the Brownell-Vinson plan, the justices were called back on Friday, June 19. They nullified Justice Douglas's order 6–3. The Rosenbergs were taken to the electric chair just hours later. Julius died at 8:06 p.m., Ethel at 8:15 p.m. Sobbing demonstrators prayed in the moonlight at the White House fence; rival rowdies in Lafayette Park jeered at them with such placards as "Two Fried Rosenbergers Coming Right Up."

THE ORPHANS: Michael was seven and Robert three when their parents were arrested. They were adopted in 1953 by Abel and Anne Meeropol. Robert became a tax lawyer and Michael a college economics professor. Their 1975 autobiography, *We Are Your Sons,* continued a fight to prove their parents innocent.

THE ROSENBERGS: A carefree picture from FBI files. Julius and Ethel were born into Jewish immigrant families on New York's Lower East Side. In their two years on death row, they were only 100 feet apart but saw each other only during weekly visits and meetings with their attorneys.

THE RISE OF A DEMAGOGUE

Joe McCarthy may have been only a "ten-cent Robespierre," but from 1950 to 1954 he held many Americans in the grip of a fear it is difficult to comprehend 45 years later: individual fear of denunciation, collective fear of Communist subversion. He was a bully and a liar who belched in the face of the Bill of Rights. For all the tumult of his investigations, his greatest coup was to expose the menace to national security of a pink army dentist. He did not unmask a single Communist in government. But America was ready to jump out of its skin in 1950. Russia had just got the atomic bomb, the Reds had won in China, American soldiers were fighting Communist invaders in North Korea and Elizabeth Bentley and Whittaker Chambers had testified to a Communist conspiracy. McCarthy exploited the anxiety with intuitive brilliance. No American politician before or since had, as Richard Rovere put it, "a surer, swifter access to the dark places of the American mind." Only once, in 1954, did he garner more than a 50 percent approval rating in the polls, but his unscrupulous, swaggering genius paralyzed the Truman administration, cowed President Eisenhower, mesmerized most of the press, lethally warped foreign policy for a decade, frightened academia, turned friend against friend, wrecked countless careers and moved millions to suspicion of fellow citizens guilty of nothing more than perhaps a subscription to a leftist publication or the courage to stand up to the demagogue. The sinister syllogism McCarthy continually deployed was that he was against communism, therefore anyone who criticized him must be in favor of it.

McCarthy had many personal qualities that have been obscured by his notoriety. He was popular as a profane good-time Charlie; he was warm, funny and generous with his friends. Born into an Irish-Catholic family on a dairy farm near Appleton, Wisconsin, he showed his mettle by leaving school at 14 to start a chicken farm with $65 in savings. He boxed as "Smilin' Joe," and raised on poor hands at poker and invariably won. In less than six years his energy and quick wits took him from a grocery counter to a law office. He

was a judge at 31, the youngest U.S. senator when he was 38. His career showed other tendencies. He was censured by the Wisconsin Supreme Court for destroying evidence. He was not wounded as a tail gunner in the Pacific, as he claimed. The commendation signed by Admiral Nimitz was one McCarthy wrote and submitted himself by forging the signature of his commanding officer. And in 1950 it looked as if his first term in the Senate might be his last: his chiseling and lobbying for special interests—he was known as the Pepsi-Cola Kid—was not playing well in Wisconsin.

McCarthy might have made a tame speech when he went to Wheeling, West Virginia, on February 9, 1950, on a Lincoln's Birthday speaking tour. His office had given him one draft on housing, another on Communists in government. He left the choice to the local Republican who met him at the airport. He was as surprised as everyone when a few of his words transformed American politics. What he said was: "I cannot take the time to name all the men in the State Department who have been named as active members of the

Communist Party and members of a spy ring. I have here in my hand a list of 205—a list of names that were made known to the Secretary of State as being members of the Communist Party and who nevertheless are still working and shaping policy in the State Department."

He had nothing: no names, no Communists, no spies. All he had was a four-year-old letter that was on the public record anyway. The then Secretary of State James Byrnes had written to Congressman Adolph Sabath to say that of 3,000 people screened in State, 285 had not been recommended for permanent employment and, at that date, 79 had been "separated from the service," leaving 206 (not 205). No assertion that the 206 were Communists. At the Denver airport the next day, McCarthy had to deal with State's request for the names. He was sorry, he told reporters, the "list" of "207 bad risks" was in a suit he had left on the plane. By the time he reached Salt Lake City that evening, he had leapt from one melting ice floe to another. Now he claimed that in Wheeling he had said he had the names of 57 "card-carrying members of the Com-

JUST GOOD ENEMIES: McCarthy grins at the discomfiture of Dean Acheson, eyes popping, teeth clenched, to find himself in a Senate office building elevator with his traducer. McCarthy accused Acheson and George Marshall of having been part of "a conspiracy on a scale so immense as to dwarf any previous such venture in the history of man. A conspiracy of infamy so black that, when it is finally exposed, its principals shall be forever deserving of the maledictions of all honest men." McCarthy was numb to the outrage he produced in others, a pathology that led to his downfall. He cheerily stuck out his hand, said, "Hello, Dean," and thought it unfriendly of Acheson to freeze.

THE VISUAL LIE

McCarthy sought revenge on Senator Millard Tydings by helping to defeat him in the 1952 elections. He organized a dirty tricks brigade to go into Maryland. But it was his future wife, not McCarthy, who endorsed the lower photograph, published in half a million copies of a vicious campaign tabloid. The caption had Tydings saying "Oh, thank you, sir" to the man apparently at his side, the former Communist leader Earl Browder. The conversation never occurred and the photograph was never taken. Browder's picture was simply pasted on one of Tydings and rephotographed. The caption referred to "this composite picture," but most people were unfamiliar with the word and were taken in by the seamless visual lie.

munist Party." This time his invention had its tenuous connection to a House report by Robert E. Lee, an ex–FBI agent who had examined hundreds of State's loyalty files before Truman closed them. Lee found no Communists, but put question marks against 57. More than half of the 57 had been investigated and cleared by the FBI; 22 were still under review at that date. Again, McCarthy could identify no Communists. Again, he had no names. Lee's report identified people by number, not name.

But when he took his bulging briefcase into the Senate on February 20, he had decided on a big bluff. In a blustering five-hour speech, he presented the unidentified Lee case histories as if they were freshly fed to him by informants, switching the numbers to conceal his source, twisting the

descriptions for sinister effect. Challenged by skeptical Democrats, he lowered his head, bellowed and charged. Hard-line right-wing Republicans, who had thought of him as a nobody, came to his support for an investigation.

From March to July, McCarthy ran riot. He targeted ten individuals as Communists or dupes. He most venomously indicted Owen Lattimore, a specialist on Mongolia, as "the top Russian spy." All the accused were cleared by the Senate investigation headed by Millard Tydings, a patrician Democrat. His July 17 report condemned McCarthy's charges and methods as "a fraud and hoax." The misuse of the Lee and Sabath documents was laid bare. But with the midterm elections looming, Tydings's report was swamped by ugly party brawling. William Jenner

called the report a "brazen whitewash of treasonable conspiracy in our history."

McCarthy became chairman of an apparently minor Senate committee after the election that put Eisenhower in the White House, but he laid his hands on its permanent investigating committee and turned the apparently obscure into the sensationally obnoxious.

MCCARTHY MEETS HIS MATCH

McCarthy quickly sharpened his subcommittee into an instrument of personal and political terror. In January 1953 he hired as chief counsel a young interrogator with a photographic memory who soon achieved a comparable notoriety. Roy Cohn was only 25, with a pouting baby face, but he was well blooded as a Red hunter, fresh from helping to send the Rosenbergs to the electric chair.

The pair reveled in humiliating witnesses. One was accused of "a close association" with his brother who had "attended a rally at Yankee Stadium in 1948 at which Paul Robeson spoke." Any ex-Communist who was unwilling to inform on past associates became a "Fifth Amendment Communist," smeared thereafter by McCarthy as a Red, a traitor, a spy. The marble caucus room in the Senate Office Building where he conducted his relentless flood-lit inquisitions "stank," said journalist William S. White, "with the odor of fear and the odor of monstrous silliness."

The *Washington Post, Milwaukee Journal* and *New York Times* set an example of scrupulous reporting for generally timid or inept newspaper and wire services, but it was hard for anyone to keep track of McCarthy's kaleidoscopic lies. There was no leadership from the White House. Ike's excuse was that if he repudiated McCarthy it would give a demagogue the

"Have a care, sir!" by Herblock.

Joseph Welch to McCarthy at the Army hearing: "I like to think that I am a gentle man but your forgiveness will have to come from someone other than me."

publicity he wanted: "I just will not—I refuse—to get down into the gutter with that guy." Ike had another reason. He felt personally vulnerable for his wartime decisions not to take Berlin and Prague and for approving some civil appointments of people who turned out to be Communists.

But there was a worm in McCarthy's apple. To please Cohn he agreed to let him hire a rich young man with blond good looks, 26-year-old David Schine, who had written a thin anti-Communist pamphlet for his father's hotel chain. In April 1953, with McCarthy's blessing, they took themselves off to European capitals on a hectic 18-day jaunt to look for librarians they could cross-examine for having books by "Communists, fellow travelers, et cetera." The State Department panicked and banned 418 writers. It was ludicrous and shameful, but the turning point was a private abuse. That summer, when the Army draft reached out for Schine, Cohn pulled strings for a direct commission and exemption from boot camp. He failed and turned on the Army. McCarthy piled into the Army for "coddling" Communists. The two of them went after a non-existent "spy ring" at the Army Signal Corps at Fort Monmouth, New Jersey. Even McCarthyites were sickened when McCarthy blasted Annie Lee Moss, a frail, black middle-aged cafeteria worker turned teletype attendant, obviously sincere and inarticulate, who was clearly

bewildered that she had been mistaken for Mata Hari.

In January 1954 the Army counsel told Cohn it looked as if Private Schine would be posted overseas. Cohn exploded. He would "ruin" Army Secretary Robert T. Stevens. The enraged Army had a weapon. Defense Secretary Charles Wilson invited McCarthy to the Pentagon on March 10, 1954, for an indigestible lunch—an ultimatum that the Army would release a 34-page account of Cohn's scandalous efforts for Schine unless McCarthy fired Cohn. McCarthy refused. He thought Schine was a pest, but he needed Cohn. He had his back to the wall. The newspapers that day were full of the double hit he had sustained on March 9. In the afternoon, the Republican senator from Vermont, 73-year-old Ralph Flanders, denounced him on the floor of the Senate. In the evening, Ed Murrow was devastating on his CBS show *See It Now*. It was the first time a television program had taken on McCarthyism. It was almost all reruns of a swarthy McCarthy hanging himself on his own words, with a minimalist commentary by Murrow that coolly appealed to America's better self: "Cassius was right: 'The fault, dear Brutus, is not in our stars, but in ourselves.'"

The ides of March were upon McCarthy. When the Schine story hit the headlines on March 11, he dug himself a deeper hole. He worked late into the night with Cohn concocting a transparent cover-up. They fabricated 11 back-dated interoffice memos suggesting that the Army was using Schine as a hostage for curtailing investigations. On March 16, McCarthy's subcommittee deserted him. They voted unanimously to conduct a full inquiry. The Army-McCarthy hearings were watched by 80 million over 36 days, utterly absorbed by the capework of the Army's counsel, Joseph Welch, a 63-year-old Boston lawyer who skewered McCarthy and Cohn in a courtly manner. A climax came on June 9, when McCarthy ignored Cohn's entreaties to honor an understanding with Welch. McCarthy insisted on smearing a young lawyer who worked on Welch's staff. He was stunned when the audience burst into applause at Welch's rebuke:

"Let us not assassinate this lad further, Senator. You have done enough. Have you no sense of decency, sir? At long last have you no sense of decency?"

The hearings convinced most people that the persecution of the Army was vindictiveness over Schine, but it was the sight of McCarthy out of control that was ruinous. In attempts to comment on witnesses, he broke into the hearings so frequently with "Point of order . . . point of order" that his menacing monotone became a national joke.

Five and a half months later the Senate voted 67 to 22 to "condemn" McCarthy for "conduct contrary to the senatorial traditions." McCarthy collapsed. He no longer got headlines. His colleagues did not listen to him. He died of acute alcoholism on May 2, 1957. He was 48 years old.

CABAL: In McCarthy's hearings, Roy Cohn (left) was always at his side, a tanned, abrasive Iago with slicked-back hair. He was only 25 when he became McCarthy's chief counsel, to the chagrin of Robert F. Kennedy, who wanted the job himself. On the right, investigator Don Surine, a former FBI agent.

ROY COHN'S SECOND SCANDALOUS CAREER

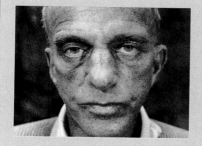

Roy Cohn was 59 when on August 2, 1986, he died in New York of the AIDS he persistently denied he had. He was a gay man who attacked gay rights, and a lawyer with a contempt for the law. Of his sickness, he said, "I can fix anything but I can't fix this." It was as a fixer and favor broker that he thrived in the 30 years after McCarthy.

The famous and the infamous came to him to make celebrity contacts, fight their lawsuits with searing ferocity, get hot sports tickets, easy entry into Studio 54 disco and a quick way out of jail. He was the lawyer for mob bosses, but also for Francis Cardinal Spellman, the Roman Catholic Archdiocese of New York and Donald Trump. His friends included President Reagan, Barbara Walters, Norman Mailer, Rupert Murdoch, William Safire, George Steinbren-

ner, Si Newhouse, Jr., Estée Lauder and scores of politicians and judges. He was tried and acquitted for fraud, bribery, conspiracy and corporate manipulations in 1964, 1969 and 1971, the result, he said, of vendettas by Robert Kennedy and U.S. District Attorney Robert Morgenthau, and he was at constant war with the IRS, which audited him more than 20 years in a row. But his friends stayed loyal to him. William F. Buckley, Jr., was among those who testified for him when he was accused of getting a nearly comatose multimillionaire to name him the executor of his will. He was disbarred from the practice of law two months before he died. The verdict, said Cohn, was the result of a smear campaign engineered by "a bunch of yo-yos."

THE ORDEAL OF ROBERT OPPENHEIMER

Robert Oppenheimer, the genius of the atomic bomb, did not want America to build the hydrogen bomb. Nor did James Conant, the president of Harvard, who had administered the Manhattan Project. Nor indeed did any of the eight members of the Atomic Energy Commission's advisory committee. Two of the members, Enrico Fermi and I. I. Rabi, made their opposition conditional on the Soviet Union also renouncing the potential superweapon. None of them suffered for their judgments as Oppenheimer was made to suffer.

Conant, not Oppenheimer, set the tone when the group met on Saturday, October 29, 1949. He had already said the bomb would be built "over my dead body." Oppenheimer, as chairman, did not show his hand until everyone had spoken. They talked about the technology of a fusion bomb, and they heard the Joint Chiefs say they needed it to stop Russia taking over Europe, but that long, secret Saturday, there was more soul-searching than science. To the moral argument, Conant's principal contribution, Oppenheimer added the strategic point that Americans, living in large cities, were more vulnerable in a thermonuclear arms race than the scattered Russians. And if America did not build the superweapon, it was "less likely" that Russia would attempt to do so and less likely that they would succeed.

Truman did not take the advice of Oppenheimer's committee or the Atomic Energy Commission, then under the chairmanship of David Lilienthal, or George Kennan's Policy Planning staff. In a seven-minute meeting, he asked, "Can the Russians do it?" Heads nodded. "In that case," he said, "we have no choice." On March 10, 1950, Truman ordered the crash program so feverishly sought by the nuclear physicist Edward Teller, the Air Force, Senator Brien McMahon, and Atomic Energy Commissioner Lewis Strauss. On November 1, 1952, three days before Eisenhower was elected president, America tested a device ("Mike") a thousand times more powerful than Hiroshima's Little Boy. It vaporized the Pacific island of Elugelab. Nine months later the Russians tested a smaller device. The U.S. tested a deliverable bomb at Bikini on March 1, 1954, and the Soviets on November 23, 1954.

Oppenheimer was wrong about the Russians. In his 1990 memoir, Andrei Sakharov, creator of the Soviet H-bomb, wrote that in 1949 Stalin and Lavrenty Beria already understood the potential. "Any U.S. move toward abandoning or suspending work on a thermonuclear weapon would have been perceived either as a cunning, deceitful maneuver or as evidence of stupidity or weakness." Sakharov says he felt deeply for Oppenheimer. They shared, he suggests, a similar fate. Sakharov was exiled to Gorky for criticizing the regime. Oppenheimer was humiliated in a security hearing that had elements

ZEALOTS FOR THE HYDROGEN BOMB

Edward Teller (above) and AEC Chairman Lewis Strauss (below) worked together against Oppenheimer. After testifying, Teller approached Oppenheimer with an outstretched hand: "I'm sorry." Oppenheimer took it, saying: "After what you've just said, I don't know what you mean." Teller was a volatile Hungarian refugee who was distracted on the atomic bomb project at Los Alamos by his obsession with a fusion bomb. For his testimony against "Oppie," he became a pariah in the nuclear community.

Strauss was a self-made man. He left school at 16 and hit the road selling shoes. Then he became an aide to Herbert Hoover, helping his relief work, and later an investment banker. He was an admiral when chairman of the War Munitions Board in 1944. He was one of the commissioners who had approved Oppenheimer's security clearance in 1947. But by 1954 Strauss, now chairman of the AEC, had political and personal grudges. The AEC was his last public office. In 1959, when he was nominated for secretary of commerce, he lied under oath while being grilled by a Senate committee. He never got over his 49–46 rejection.

THE LOSER: The normally ebullient "Oppie" was a shadow of himself at the security hearings. Oppenheimer's lawyer recalled that the hearing was more like a murder trial. "Robert was in the most overwrought state imaginable—so was Kitty [his wife]. . . . He would pace his bedroom floor at night . . . he was just an anguished man." Oppenheimer quietly resumed his work as head of the Institute for Advanced Study at Princeton. In 1962, President Kennedy invited him to the White House, and the next year President Johnson presented him with the AEC's highest honor, the Fermi Award. He died in 1967, at 62.

of a Communist show trial. His nemesis was Lewis Strauss. As campaigner for the superweapon, he had been appalled by Oppenheimer's contrary vote; as a vain, insecure man, he hated the way Oppenheimer made him seem ignorant in a row over the export of isotopes; and he was worried by rumors that McCarthy was eyeing Oppenheimer.

Strauss got his chance in November 1953 when William Borden, a former staff aide to Senator McMahon, wrote to him and FBI Director Hoover saying that "more probably than not, J. Robert Oppenheimer is an agent of the Soviet Union." The charge was a mishmash of Oppenheimer's much pawed-over security files; the Communist associations of his wife, Kitty, and brother Frank; and his wartime report to the authorities on an indirect approach by Soviet espionage agents. There was nothing new and nothing new surfaced at the hearing. But Strauss had been busy. He had hired a tough prosecutor, Roger Robb; he had got the FBI wiretappers to listen in to Oppen-

heimer's talks with his lawyer; and he had sought out witnesses who distrusted Oppenheimer's H-bomb vote. Oppenheimer and his too gentlemanly lawyer fared poorly. Robb had files he did not share. It allowed him to give the appearance of deception to Oppenheimer's occasional errors of memory. Forty great names, including General Groves, Conant and John McCloy, vouched for Oppenheimer. But the crucial testimony was from Edward Teller, who (with Stanislaw Ulam) had succeeded in designing an H-bomb. Teller said he believed Oppenheimer was loyal to the United States, but he found him confused and complicated. "If it is a question of wisdom and judgment, as demonstrated by his actions since 1945, then I would say one would be wiser not to grant clearance."

The three-man panel rejected the allegation that Oppenheimer was a spy. They confirmed his loyalty. They praised his ability to keep secrets. But by 2–1 they voted him a security risk, and it was clear it was Oppenheimer's reservations about the

H-bomb that made the difference. Strauss's commissioners voted 4–1 to end Oppenheimer's consultancy because of "fundamental defects in his character." It was now up to Eisenhower, but it was an Eisenhower briefed by Strauss on three weeks of secret testimony. Strauss led Eisenhower to believe the board had not been prejudiced by Oppenhimer's attitude to the H-bomb. But there were hundreds of pages of testimony to the contrary. McGeorge Bundy's study *Danger and Survival* best summed up what happened. "The president of the United States, in the matter of J. Robert Oppenheimer, became the easy captive of Lewis Strauss, and in consequence he was decisively misled."

In 1994, an 87-year-old Stalinist KGB general, Pavel Sudoplatov, whose specialty had been murder and sabotage, claimed that Oppenheimer (and Niels Bohr, Enrico Fermi and Leo Szilard!) had spied for him. His memoir was splashed in *Newsweek,* but it was immediately discredited by scholars for errors and inconsistencies.

THE "LIBERATORS": The CIA's man, Castillo Armas, enters Guatemala City with his moustachioed junta. He had been working in Honduras as a furniture salesman. Castillo Armas sits in front of the Jeep next to his CIA driver. The others are regular Army officers.

THE COUP IN GUATEMALA

Eisenhower approved CIA plans to topple the government of Guatemala over Sunday brunch with John Foster and Allen Dulles at their sister Eleanor's. Only a handful were in the know, though Ike was so proud of the coup he had a hard time keeping quiet about it. He convinced himself he had "averted a Soviet bridgehead" in the Western Hemisphere.

Guatemala's leader, Colonel Jacobo Arbenz, 41, a moody, recovered alcoholic, had won power in 1950 in the country's freest elections in history. He was a Social Democrat, running a revolution based quite consciously on FDR's New Deal. He set out to wean Guatemala from its unhealthy dependence on the Boston-based United Fruit Company, which owned nearly half of Guatemala. Known throughout Central America as El Pulpo, "the Octopus that strangled all it touched," United Fruit provided above-average housing, pay and education, but it was determined Guatemala would stay in its thrall as a banana republic. Arbenz expropriated 400,000 acres of land United Fruit owned, but did not plant, and gave it to 100,000 landless Mayans to grow beans and maize. He offered compensation of $1.2 million, the valuation in the company's tax returns. United Fruit was outraged. It now valued the land at $15.9 million. The CIA leadership tried every trick to portray Arbenz as a tool of the Kremlin. They parachuted Russian-made arms into Guatemala. Then they organized a "spontaneous" rebellion, paying some of Guatemala's discontented military to do nothing to oppose a force of 150 paid "liberators" who would march in from Honduras under Carlos Castillo Armas, an exiled colonel.

Castillo Armas crossed the border on June 18, 1954. He advanced only six miles, but Arbenz panicked (and hit the bottle) when the CIA radio station in Honduras broadcast constant reports of invading "armies of liberation." The only effective action was when four P-47 Thunderbolts, flown by U.S. contract pilots, "lightly" bombed Guatemala City. There was still no popular uprising, and Armas remained stuck in the jungle. Allen Dulles rushed to the White House to beg Eisenhower to commit more bombers. He did (and concealed the fact in his memoir). On June 27, a beleaguered Arbenz fled to Mexico.

Armas ran a brutal police state. Nine thousand liberal leftist "suspects," mostly Indians, were rounded up and hundreds shot. The peasants lost the land they had been given and the vote. The long, bloody night of Guatemala was just beginning. Some 150,000 to 200,000 Guatemalans died over the next 35 years, the vast majority of them Mayan peasants terrorized by the Army and rightist death squads.

MOSADDEQ'S TRIAL: The deposed 70-year-old Premier Mosaddeq, accused of rebellion, challenges the military tribunal, "Kill me." He was jailed for three years.

MOSADDEQ'S NEMESIS: The Shah, more firmly on the peacock throne thanks to Eisenhower's coup, welcomes his savior to Teheran in 1959.

THE COUP IN IRAN

Over cocktails in the Oval Office in 1953 Eisenhower gave his secretary of state, John Foster Dulles, the nod that doomed Mohammad Mosaddeq, Iran's nationalist premier. The "royalist coup" that later gave the young Mohammed Reza Pahlavi absolute power as Shah was the work of the CIA and British intelligence. The CIA's man, Kermit ("Kim") Roosevelt, a 37-year-old grandson of Teddy, revealed in 1979 that the British had wanted to strike in November 1952, but he and his boss, CIA chief Allen Dulles, kept the plot on the back burner because there was little chance of approval from Truman. As soon as he was president, Eisenhower let the CIA off the leash, and on June 25, 1953, Roosevelt was in the CIA headquarters at 2430 E Street to present Britain's 22-page plot, code-named Ajax, to a group that included both Dulles brothers. Foster thumbed through the document. "So this," he said, "is how we get rid of that madman Mosaddeq."

Mosaddeq, an excitable pixie with a beak nose and bald head, was not crazy. Nor was he a Communist. He was just angry with the British, whose Anglo-Iranian Oil Company gave Iran 20 percent of its oil revenues. He saw that American oil companies had blessed Saudi Arabia with a full 50 percent share in their postwar deal. In 1951 Mosaddeq seized the company, then later that year expelled the British. During 1952, the Truman administration tried to broker a deal, but neither the British nor Mosaddeq would compromise. In February 1953, Mosaddeq started campaigning for the eviction of the Shah, and Eisenhower was led to believe Iran was on a downhill course to communism.

Roosevelt paid street mobs to harass Mosaddeq. More dollars and pounds went to army officers. Teheran was torn by rival mobs in August while Roosevelt's CIA plotters lay around the pool in a mountain villa, waiting for the Shah's bodyguard to come back from his hideaway with the *firman*s (royal decrees) dismissing Mosaddeq and installing General Fazlollah Zahedi. They drank vodkas with lime, and played over and over the record from the Broadway hit *Guys and Dolls*. When the *firman*s were ready for delivery, says Kim, "we went 'rolling down the mountain,' as another old song has it, full of hope and hilarity, singing 'Luck Be a Lady Tonight.'" The coup stalled. When the Shah's bodyguard commander called on Mosaddeq with a *firman* ordering him to resign, Mosaddeq arrested the messenger.

The plotters sat in an embassy house, pounding out more *firman*s on a Persian typewriter and hastening them to army units and pro-Shah crowds. Pro-Shah army units took to the streets. Mosaddeq escaped a night riot outside his house by climbing over his garden wall in his pink pajamas. He quit rather than fight a civil war. The reward for America was sharing 80 percent of Iran's oil with Britain, but with it came a legacy of hatred.

CHAPTER TWELVE

THE DAWN OF A NEW FREEDOM

1954–1965

Civil Rights

The descendants of the slaves, who were themselves still only half-free, came striding out of the shadows in the mid-1950s to claim their rightful place in the American sun. In the second hundred years of the Republic, all the great reform movements had passed over race or been forced to leave it behind: Populism and Progressivism, the women's movement, the struggle for rights for working men and women, and even the New Deal had done little to rescue blacks from oppression in the South and supposedly benign neglect in the North.

Thoughtful Americans often speculated on what, if anything, could be done about the apartheid of the South, a way of life and a rule of law. Almost no one anticipated that blacks would do it for themselves. Extraordinary leaders emerged from the "talented tenth" of the community, as W. E. B. Du Bois had foreseen. They had no new revolutionary doctrine, only the old ones enshrined in the Constitution and the Bible, and the dedication to peaceful change.

All the great freedom movements that swept the United States after the Civil War had required action on three fronts: in the courts, at the ballot box and for the hearts and minds of the American people. Blacks fought on all three fronts with bravery, dignity and intelligence. The system they challenged was deeply entrenched and ferociously defended. It was unable to endure against the standards of freedom and fairness the nation had set for itself. American democracy was triumphantly vindicated.

MARSHALL ON THE MARCH: Thurgood Marshall—great-grandson of a slave named Thoroughgood—heads for the U.S. District Court in Birmingham, Alabama, where he will argue and win the case of 26-year-old Autherine Lucy (on his right). Three days of rioting at Tuscaloosa followed her attempt to enroll at the University of Alabama, in February 1956. The university suspended her, not the rioters. In court, Marshall won her reinstatement. Then the university expelled her. The University of Alabama now has an endowed scholarship in her name.

THE INVISIBLE MAN REBELS

America was living a lie for most of the twentieth century. The ideals that were supposed to define the nation were betrayed every hour, every day, for the one tenth of the population that was Negro—or black, as came to be the preferred usage (followed by African American). The oppression was, of course, starkly worse in the South, an area whose cherished "way of life" was little different from South Africa's apartheid system. The iconic photograph of "Colored" and "White" drinking fountains was the least of it. Schools, colleges, hospitals, churches, parks, swimming pools, restaurants, rest rooms, waiting rooms, elevators, buses and streetcars, theaters, cinemas, libraries, beauty parlors, bowling alleys, bars, prisons, cemeteries and most labor unions were all segregated in the South and border states, which meant in practice that Negroes had access only to degraded services and employment in all these areas. They had no political muscle; they were prevented from voting in a one-party dictatorship dedicated to white supremacy. They were excluded from juries and certain of being convicted of anything a white man alleged against them. It took a Supreme Court ruling in 1934 (*Brown v. Mississippi*) to prohibit prosecutors from offering, and state courts from accepting, "confessions" extracted by torture. Injustice was not confined to the South. For decades the spirit of Jim Crow was pervasive everywhere, as law in the South and as custom in the North, where blacks were excluded from the best hotels, the best restaurants, the best schools and jobs and neighborhoods. Even the jewel of FDR's New Deal liberalism, the Civilian Conservation Corps, had segregated camps.

Decade after decade, most white Americans never gave the injustices a moment's thought. They did not "see" the national predicament of the Negro when they hailed a graying "boy" for their bags at a hotel, had their shoes shined at the street corner, prayed for mankind in a church of white-only faces, rooted from the bleachers for major league baseball teams devoid until 1947 of a single black player. John Egerton, the author of *Speak Now Against the Day* (1994), a revealing account of the reformers before the civil rights movement, recalls: "Segregation didn't restrict me in any way, so it was easy to accept things the way they were, to take my freedom for granted and not worry about anyone else's." In 26 years the liberal columnist Walter Lippmann wrote a mere ten times about segregation and in the complacent spirit of Dr. Pangloss. Ralph Ellison's introspective novel *Invisible Man* (1952) described what it was like to be on the other side, to be looked through, as transparent as air: "You ache with the need to convince yourself that you do exist in the real world, that you're part of all the sound and anguish." The Negro community's struggle for identity was all but invisible, too, and so were its achievements in the arts and sciences. The textbooks and teaching in schools, white and black, underplayed or ignored altogether the contributions of people like Dr. Daniel Hale Williams (open heart surgery), George Washington Carver (botany) and others, a situation the black historian Carter Woodson tried so hard to remedy by his formation of the Association for the Study of Negro Life and History in 1915 and his creation of Negro History Week in 1926, now celebrated for all of February. In all this time, no attempt to stir the popular imagination to something different was made by newspapers, magazines or radio; and Hollywood for the most part peddled *Gone With the Wind* stereotypes. The press, of course, was as lily-white as any of the institutions it reported on, including the American Bar Association, for whom the Bill of Rights might as well have been written in Sanskrit. The Democratic party, at least until 1948, was not prepared to do anything that would disturb the Solid South. The unions in the AFL (though not the CIO) excluded blacks. The church and the academy, North and South, were for long inert. Individual preachers sometimes spoke out, but as institutions the churches, black and white, confined their visions of the good

TOP: James Meredith, shot by sniper in Mississippi, 1966. MIDDLE ROW (left to right): Battered "Freedom Rider" James Zwerg, Montgomery, Alabama, 1961; downtown shopper Christine Stovall clubbed, Montgomery, 1960; state troopers use clubs, Selma, Alabama, 1965. BOTTOM LEFT: William Gadsden attacked by police dogs, Birmingham, Alabama, 1963. BOTTOM RIGHT: Birmingham hoses, 1963; state police limber up to prevent James Meredith from enrolling at the University of Mississippi, 1962.

THE MAN WHO KILLED JIM CROW

Charles Hamilton Houston (1895–1950), the grandson of fugitive slaves, was born twelve months before the *Plessy* decision gave legal birth to the Jim Crow laws. He grew up to be "one of the most important lawyers of the twentieth century," in the words of Harvard's Randall Kennedy, when he dedicated his life to reversing *Plessy*. Worn out by his efforts, he died four years before the Supreme Court killed Jim Crow in the *Brown* case in 1954, but it was very much his triumph as an educator and NAACP advocate. He saw that litigation could do more than settle a case; it could shape society. A lawyer, he said, "is either a social engineer or he is a parasite on society." As the exacting dean of the Howard University Law School from 1929, so tough he was nicknamed Cement Pants, he trained a body of black lawyers who could more than hold their own with white lawyers in the fight against racism. One of them was Thurgood Marshall. Of his triumph in the Supreme Court in 1954, Marshall remarked: "We were just carrying [Houston's] bags, that's all." Of Houston's significance for the civil rights movement, Court of Appeals Judge William Hastie, Jr., observed: "He was truly the Moses of that journey."

life to the hereafter. E. Franklin Frazier, a student of the Negro church, suggests that before the fifties the black church, by offering comfort, actually helped the Negro to adjust to an inferior status.

It would be wrong to suggest that blacks were entirely passive in the decades before the civil rights movement. There were brave individuals and there were some organized protests: from 1900 to 1906, 50 years before the seminal boycott in Montgomery, boycotts took place in at least 25 Southern cities against segregated streetcars. Black immigration to the North led to the election of the first black congressman since Reconstruction, Oscar DePriest, a Republican from Chicago's First District, in 1926. And then his replacement, Arthur W. Mitchell, a Democrat and active supporter of the New Deal from 1934 to 1944. But in all the prewar years, consistent organized action against white supremacy was left almost entirely to the lawyers of the NAACP and the National Urban League. It says something for the durability of white resistance and the persistence of the black community that the seed which eventually flowered in *Brown v. Board of Education* in 1954 was planted in 1922. A 21-year-old Harvard student named Charles Garland gave away his inherited $1.3 million, declaring: "I am placing my life on a Christian basis." Garland's foundation awarded $100,000 to the NAACP to mount a legal campaign for equality of education, and Nathan Ross Margold, a Romanian-Jewish immigrant, set it on course to challenge not simply a school district here and there but the whole constitutional validity of segregation.

The South of the old Confederacy, 11 states with 9 million Negroes and 21 million whites, had always been convinced it was the last bastion of civility and honor. It was the least democratic, most backward and brutalized part of the coun-try, and had been from well before the Civil War, but it enjoyed a talent for romantic self-deception brilliantly analyzed in Wilbur Cash's 1941 classic *The Mind of the South*. It was a feudal society, where everyone knew his or her place, and it was abjectly poor, but Southern whites felt superior to the crass outside world, united in the resentful pride of the much misunderstood. Their superiority to their black neighbors was, of course, reassuringly manifest every day in the Jim Crow laws. Altogether, 17 Southern and border states enforced Jim Crow. Unsurprisingly, the least tolerant were the Deep South states of Alabama, Georgia, South Carolina, Mississippi and Louisiana, where there was a much higher proportion of black Americans—near equivalence for many years in Mississippi. Within these states, the worst areas of repression were the Mississippi Delta, southwestern Georgia and Alabama's Black Belt. In Mississippi only 5 percent of voting-age Negroes had been allowed to register by the fifties, and the state held the record for lynchings—539 recorded since Reconstruction.

The poor whites and poor blacks of the region should have been natural allies against their common exploitation in the still largely rural, sharecropping economy, but the power elites and the reigning Democratic party bosses were literally ready to kill to stop that from happening. Murder, house burnings and mass evictions were the response to the Southern Tenant Farmers Union (STFU) when it was founded in 1934 in Tyronza, Arkansas, as a union of black and white sharecroppers (one third of the 30,000 members in six states were black). It was easy enough, in any event, for the demagogues to prey on the prejudices of the working-class whites, tenant farmers and sharecroppers, shopkeepers and cotton mill hands who had been brought up believing that their livelihoods and the safety of their daughters depended on keeping "the nigger" in his place, segregated and subservient from cradle to grave. Their social betters in the towns and plantations prided themselves on treating their "Nigras" as kindly and firmly as they would a recalcitrant child. Liberal visitors enjoying Southern hospitality experienced cognitive dissonance. Surely these nice people could not be the same bigots who countenanced the cruelties of segregation? A visitor who raised an eyebrow was told in all sincerity, "Negroes are happiest among themselves." But the courteous masters of the South tolerated and often encouraged the lynch mobs when anything like the STFU seemed to threaten the natural hierarchy they perceived as essential to public order and the communal good: white supremacy maintained by violence was the Savage Ideal, to use Cash's phrase.

A passion for scientific truth was hardly strong among southerners; the idea was bred in their bones that the poverty and ignorance of the Negro was due to an immutable genetic inferiority ordained by God. The races had to be kept apart because mixing the bloods, the ultimate but frequently transgressed taboo, would imperil the white race. If they read *Huckleberry Finn* or *Pudd'nhead Wilson* they missed the point of Mark Twain's satires on racial pretensions as readily as do the politically correct suppressors of our times. Genetic inferiority was a notion, supported by solemn measurements of assorted craniums, that was a commonplace of teaching in colleges North and South until well after World War I. The fact that hundreds of years of interbreeding had made the whole idea of race genetically meaningless in the South, or that the human species had not existed long enough for any significant differences to emerge even had the Negro race remained on the African continent, could not derail this pseudo-intellectual dogma. There could be no hope for black people until that cranky scholarship was thoroughly repudiated. The process, traced by Richard Kluger in his impressive *Simple Justice,* took more than 30 years, longer than it took for the South to tolerate the teaching of Darwinian evolution. As early as 1911, Franz Boas, a German immigrant physicist who became a professor of anthropology at Columbia, demonstrated in his seminal *The Mind of Primitive Man,* based on studies of 17,000 immigrants and their children, that an individual was molded more by culture than by racial inheritance. By the forties, a body of psychological and sociological work had set out the evidence that black inferiority was unquestionably a product of the environment. A notable irony was the devastating 1936 indictment entitled *Southern Regions of the United States,* prepared at the University of North Carolina

ROBESON, PICKETER: "Mr. Truman take Jim Crow off the American dollar."

THE PERSECUTION OF PAUL ROBESON 1898–1976

Two decades before the civil rights movement, Paul Robeson, the gifted singer and actor, pitted his innocent soul to fight the cruelties to his fellow blacks. Persecuted by the white establishment, and ostracized by the black, he sacrificed his life, his career, his wealth and his happiness.

He was born to heroism. His father was a slave in North Carolina who escaped through the Underground Railroad in 1860, and became a Presbyterian minister in Princeton, New Jersey. Socialism was the second great influence, not as economics but as ethics. Paul Robeson's lifelong faith was the brotherhood of man. It was betrayed by Stalinism. He took as gospel the vision in Sidney and Beatrice Webb's 1935 book, *Soviet Communism: A New Civilization,* and the Soviets tried not to disillusion him on his theatrical visits. He said that there he was not treated like a Negro but with the full dignity of mankind. He was never a member of the Communist Party, but sentiments like these and his support for the Loyalists in the Spanish Civil War excited suspicions. By 1941 he was under surveillance by J. Edgar Hoover. He never equivocated.

In Washington, on September 23, 1946, he and W. E. B. DuBois launched an antilynching crusade and Robeson led a delegation to see Truman. He irritated Truman by attacking British colonialism, and was in turn angered by Truman's argument that the timing was not right for an antilynch law. In that case, said Robeson, blacks would have to defend themselves. Truman ended the interview.

At a peak point of Cold War hysteria, speaking of white workers and blacks, he declared: "Our will to fight for peace is strong. We shall not make war on anyone. We shall not make war on the Soviet Union." The words were instantly misrepresented as treason. Without waiting to learn what Robeson had actually said, the leaders of every black organization felt they had to distance themselves to prove their loyalty. He was grilled by the House Committee on Un-American Activities. Rioters led by the KKK and the American Legion broke up a concert in Peekskill, New York. NBC banned him from appearing on television with Eleanor Roosevelt, and she acquiesced. Stores would no longer stock his records. All major concert halls were closed to him. Then, in August 1950, Truman's State Department made him a prisoner in his own country. It canceled his passport on the grounds that the treatment of blacks in the United States was a "family affair," not to be aired in foreign countries.

He endured eight years of isolation, branded as an outcast. It took until June 1958 for the Supreme Court, in a related case, to rule 5 to 4 that no citizen could lose his passport for political beliefs. He resumed his international career to great acclaim, but his health was broken. The treatment of this "great and gentle warrior" was one of the most shameful episodes in our history.

under the leadership of a white Georgian, Howard Washington Odum; his declaration that "inequalities of opportunity everywhere strike at the heart of any working democracy" was a long journey from his 1910 Columbia dissertation, which aped the general racist thought at that university at the time. The many years of research were crowned in 1944 by the two-volume masterpiece *An American Dilemma,* compiled over six years by the Swedish economist Gunnar Myrdal with a team of black and white scholars, including Myrdal's wife, Alva; Odum; Otto Klineberg; Guy Johnson and Ralph Bunche. The NAACP had been saying as much for years, but Myrdal decisively documented the ever raging conflict between the egalitarian American Creed and the inequitable reality of black life in America. He dramatized the long history of white exploitation that lay at the heart of "the vicious circle of cumulative causation." Denied basic police protection, black communities tended to become more crime-ridden; denied proper sanitary services, they tended to become dirtier; denied decent schools and opportunity, they tended to have higher rates of illiteracy. In 1946, an estimated one quarter of the entire black population was functionally illiterate. How could such people be entrusted with the vote? The Southern Regional Council, a body of civic-minded white and black southerners, was formed the year Myrdal published to try to improve race relations. It became an important fount of enlightenment. Enforcement of the Constitution was another matter. In all the Jim Crow states, social policy, like the Mississippi, rolled on regardless.

The NAACP succeeded in 1944 in building a little dam. Since the 1920s it had been pursuing a masterly, tenacious, long-term strategy to demolish "legal" racial barriers in electoral politics, public accommodations and, above all, education. In the electoral realm, it had been contesting Texas's all-white Democratic primary since 1927. After each NAACP victory the "segs" would escape down some muddy legal tributary. In *Smith v. Allwright* (1944), Thurgood Marshall and William H. Hastie, Jr., won a decisive 8–1 Supreme Court ruling that all such escapes were unconstitutional. The primary, which in most parts of the one-party South amounted to a general election, could not be restricted to one race. The upper South grudgingly complied, at least on paper. The Deep South, with booming Atlanta something of an exception, found still more ways to maintain all-white voting. And it maintained its grip on daily life by the old-fashioned way of terror.

Returning black World War II veterans, as in 1919, increased the pressure for civil rights. The Army had taken these men out of a Jim Crow U.S.A. and set them on the unsegregated shores of Europe. The veterans had been treated as heroes there and presumed that their uniforms entitled them to a measure of respect at home as well. They did succeed at first in registering to vote in surprising numbers—an increase spread variably in Southern states from 3 percent in 1940, very much as it was in 1900, to 12 percent by 1947, but the trend was not to last. The white supremacists exploited the fears aroused by the scent of reform and the return of these more confident black veterans. In the immediate postwar years, there were scores of murders and hundreds of acts of violence. The point was not so much the number of the foul deeds as their official blessing. Coming home from the Pacific, Sgt. Isaac Woodward, who had a row with a bus driver, was blinded by a billy club wielded by a South Carolina police chief. In Walton County, Georgia, two young men and their common-law wives were taken into the woods and shot to death after one of the Negroes, a veteran, had a scuffle with a planter's son. Nobody was punished for these crimes because all too often they were committed with the assistance of law enforcement officers.

The going was almost as dispiriting in the legal fight for equal education. The Supreme Court, from Chief Justice Hughes in the 1930s, was ready to strike down segregation in state institutions of higher learning, but compliance was slow; in 1950, it ruled that Heman M. Sweatt, a veteran and mailman who wanted to be a lawyer, had to be admitted to Texas Law School because the separate, makeshift black school was not equal. But there was hardly a graduate school a black could attend throughout the South. In Mississippi, as late as 1958, Clennon King, a black college teacher, was committed to a mental asylum simply for applying for admission to the University of Mississippi. Another black was framed and run off to prison for the same offense.

As the lower courts, the press, public agencies and Congress continued to fail it, the Negro community looked more and more to the presidency to fulfill the ideals of the Constitution. Truman was the first president since Lincoln to offer national leadership on civil rights. Progressively repelled by Jim Crow, he set up a Civil Rights Committee that came out in 1948 with a strong antidiscrimination report called "To Secure These Rights." The Southern bloc in Congress, in control of key committee chairmanships, made sure the rights were not secured. By Executive Order 19981 Truman decreed "equality of treatment and opportunity" in the U.S. armed forces. It was a candle in the dark. But candles were being snuffed out all over the South. The few politicians who stood for decency, like Georgia's Governor Ellis Arnall, were one after another defeated by right-wing extremists. The liberal organizations in the region were too fractious to unite for a common campaign. The Dixiecrats campaigning for white supremacy against Truman in 1948 lost by two to one in the South as a whole, but once again, rejoicing was premature. "I'd rather die fighting for states' rights than live on Truman Boulevard in nigger heaven," said Alabama's Horace Wilkinson. The Dixiecrats liked nothing better than a lost cause, but it was not such a lost cause when the rump of defeated Dixiecrats and the rump of right-wing Republicans came to form an alliance in Congress. In the Senate 20 southerners and 15 Republicans could block everything and they did. Bills against lynching and the poll tax, and bills for fair employment and national health insurance, were all filibustered to death. The right-wing Republicans, obsessed by communism, affected to see the Red hand behind black demands for equality; and the Dixiecrats were only too ready to foment the suspicion. They in turn supported the McCarthyite witch-hunts. It was all fraudulent. Communists did espouse social equality and had some notable campaigns against injustice, but they were never much of a force in the South. Their atheism was unappealing to an intensely religious people and, as Cash put it, the Marxist vision of a dull and unvarying proletarian order, created by solemn German and Russian brains, did not at all fit with the Negro's "vast humorousness, his restless casualness, his supreme hedonism and love of the spectacular and dramatic, and his individualism." Racism had run into another of its endless self-contradictions. Blacks were feckless children, but they were also dedicated Commie-cadres—the nonsense rolled on. Communism was the new snake oil of Southern politics. Anyone suggesting blacks had constitutional rights was obviously a Commie, right?

STATE OF EDUCATION, BLACK AND WHITE

On average, Southern states spent half as much educating a black child as they spent educating a white. Investment in white school plant was four times higher, white teachers' salaries 30 percent higher.

Seventeen segregating states spent $42 million busing white children—less than $1 million on blacks.

Median years of schooling in segregating states and Washington, D.C.: whites—8.4; blacks—5.1. The percent of whites finishing school was four times that of blacks.

Segregating states spent $86 million on white colleges, $5 million on black ones. There was 1 accredited medical school for blacks, 29 for whites; 1 accredited black school for pharmacology, 40 for whites; 1 law school for blacks, 40 for whites. There was no engineering school for blacks, 36 for whites.

In 1946, an estimated one quarter of the entire black population was functionally illiterate.

By the fifties, full citizenship for black people in the Deep South seemed as remote as ever. Short of federal intervention, the few well-disposed white leaders in the South could vaguely hope only that a more prosperous, better-educated Dixie would gradually shed its complex of fears and hates in favor of offering some modest emancipation. Famously liberal editors of goodwill like Ralph McGill in Atlanta and Hodding Carter in Greenville, Mississippi, were not integrationists and certainly opposed any pressure from Washington. William Faulkner, the most original and perceptive voice of Southern literature, insisted that change would have to be brought about by Southern whites themselves without any carping from northerners. What he, and few others, ever imagined was that the decisive momentum for change after generations of stalemate and regression would come not from the president or Congress or the North or white liberals in the South, but from blacks themselves. It may be true that blacks who made the difference in the civil rights movement were a minority, but they were from all classes. It may be true that powerful assistance came from a few whites and Northern philanthropists and in the sixties from students, but it was essentially a black movement. It may be true that, in the end, all turned on the Supreme Court and stronger federal laws, but the federal government itself, now so often portrayed as the rescuing cavalry, as in the fanciful 1988 movie *Mississippi Burning,* closed its ears in the presidencies of both Eisenhower and Kennedy to many a bugle call.

The first breakthrough was, of course, by the Supreme Court, and it was produced by supposedly inferior Negroes.

Despite the privations of segregated education, a formidable new leadership had emerged. Mordecai Johnson, Charles Houston and William Hastie at tiny Howard University managed to turn out the impressive black legal team that in 1954 finally demolished legal segregation: Thurgood Marshall, James Nabritt, Robert Carter, Spottswood Robinson, Oliver Hill and Louis Redding, who were joined by the likes of Jack Greenberg, Constance Baker Motley and the rest of the NAACP's Legal Defense Fund.

And then there was the Rev. Dr. Martin Luther King.

The establishment of a national holiday honoring King and an editing process in the media have left the impression that the black leadership was King, King, King. Fred Powledge, in his admirable history *Free at Last,* reports resentment about this among veterans of the movement. Meeting separately in 1988, former members of the Student Nonviolent Coordinating Committee (SNCC) and of the Congress of Racial Equality (CORE) "spoke of their admiration for Dr. King, but also expressed their determination that the rest of the Movement be remembered as well." That is proper. The sit-in movement sprang from the students and the Student Nonviolent Coordinating Committee, the Freedom Rides from the Congress of Racial Equality. The individual roll of honor is long. High in it would be the clergymen, notably Vernon Johns, Fred Shuttlesworth, Ralph Abernathy, Wyatt Tee Walker, James Bevel, Jesse Jackson; the students, notably James Lawson, Bob Moses, Marion Barry, Diane Nash, John Lewis, Julian Bond; the activists, notably E. D. Nixon, Amzie Moore, Jim Farmer, Ella Baker, Septima Clark, Medgar Evers, Roy Wilkins, Bayard Rustin, A. Philip Randolph, Andrew Young, Marian Wright Edelman, Fannie Lou Hamer; and the celebrities, notably Paul Robeson, Muhammad Ali, Harry Belafonte, Dick Gregory, Eartha Kitt.

But from 1955 the transcendent figure *was* Martin Luther King. In perseverance, in purity of motive and action, in faith and inspiration, in courage and sheer good-heartedness, he qualifies as one of the greatest Americans. His reputation has become, if anything, underinflated through the years. This was the man who shaped the philosophy of the movement, then gave it a heroic voice. At Crozer Theological Seminary he absorbed Reinhold Niebuhr's *Moral Man and Immoral Society* (1932), an incisive critique of the view of John Dewey and the Social Gospel that evil would be eradicated by education—by preaching. Individual whites might wish to treat Negroes justly, said Niebuhr, but white society would respond only to pressure.

King passionately synthesized Niebuhr with the Gandhian tactics of nonviolence. "The aftermath of nonviolence," he said in 1957, "is the creation of the beloved community, while the aftermath of violence is tragic bitterness." His critics have a point that the nonviolent movement's success came to depend on evoking violence from racists, which would in turn outrage public opinion. King was the first of a cautious leadership, black and white, to endorse the students who started to seek out nonviolent confrontation, to present their heads to the billy clubs. It was a paradox but it was hardly hypocrisy. As King said in 1964, instead of submitting to surreptitious cruelty in thousands of dark jail cells and on countless shadowed streets, he was forcing his oppressor "to commit his brutality openly—in the light of day—with the rest of the world looking on." In his words, to condemn the peaceful Freedom Riders on the grounds that they precipitated violence was like condemning a robbed man because his possession of money had precipitated the evil act of robbery. King and his allies went more than halfway to take any proffered hand of brotherhood. They continually implored blacks to remain in a spirit of conciliation, to love and forgive their persecutors. The unclouded face of Christianity in action should not suffer wrong. Of course, it would be misleading to suggest that all the followers of King practiced pacifist nonviolence. In the more murderous places, blacks kept a shotgun handy for self-defense. Hartman Turnbow, a 70-year-old Mississippi farmer who fought off shooters and firebombers at his home after registering to vote, told Howell Raines (*My Soul Is Rested,* 1977) of meeting King shortly afterward: "Dr. King said to me right there he'd never 'prove of violence. And then I replied to him, I said, 'This nonviolent stuff ain't no good. It'll get ya killed.'"

And King himself had his share of human frailty. He preached Christian morality while engaged in extramarital sex. We now know from Taylor Branch's second volume of his biography that he was capable, in private, of an offensive bitterness. One of the surreptitious FBI tapes catches him making sexually obscene remarks as he watches Mrs. Kennedy beside the coffin of her husband on television. But King endured much. J. Edgar Hoover, the pathological director of the FBI, hated King for more than his indiscretions. He hated the whole idea of a civil rights movement, and when King was awarded the Nobel Peace Prize, Hoover goaded him to kill himself rather than accept it. Hoover had his assistant director, William Sullivan, anonymously send King an audiotape of King's sexual dalliances gleaned from FBI buggings—the sounds of sex in a hotel bedroom and King's bawdy remarks in telephone conversations. "There is but one way out for you," said the accompanying note. "You better take it before your filthy, abnormal, fraudulent self is bared to the nation." King did no such thing, of course, though the constant barrage of criticism, condescension, slander, extortion and mockery he received from friends and foes alike would have been enough to drive many men to suicide. Adam Clayton Powell, Jr., the roguish black congressman from Harlem, once threatened to tell the press the bald-faced lie that King was having an affair with his homosexual adviser, Bayard Rustin, unless Powell received a large cash payoff. White publishers regularly patronized King in print and wondered when his power would fade—though, to their eternal credit, Southern newspaper editors refused to print the FBI's sexual smears. He was jailed in Birmingham, beaten in Montgomery, stoned in Cicero, Illinois. Other civil rights leaders were perpetually jealous, fighting King for funds and needling him in private and in public. Young black activists mocked him as "De Lawd" whenever they felt he was not being militant enough, and black nationalists such as Malcolm X scorned his entire effort as futile.

The personal metamorphosis of the man originally known as Malcolm Little is a moving one, a compelling indictment of American racism and a tribute to human perseverance. Yet politically Malcolm has been distorted out of all perspective by the left's wish fulfillment. The Nation of Islam's ideas of black nationalism were inherently unworkable, narrow-minded and mysogynistic. Founded on a bizarre racial mythology, it was unable to attract more than a handful of followers in even the most downtrodden black communities.

Even after death King was derided by certain blacks and whites alike for his nonviolence, his belief in an integrated color-blind society, for his moderation and for his militancy. Various accusations arose that he had lifted parts of his thrilling oratory from the vast black preacher tradition— a charge King would never have attempted to deny—or that he was a plagiarist, for improperly footnoting parts of his dissertation. His closest associates would add memoirs detailing his sexual liaisons, and every other flaw of a lonely, besieged man constantly and stressfully on the road. Even as he signed the national holiday honoring King into law, Ronald Reagan casually voiced the suspicion that he might have been a Communist provocateur. But King had never stopped fighting for the basic rights of blacks, of the poor of all races, of all the disinherited of American society. He was everywhere—cajoling, teasing, inspiring, reconciling, fighting, never too proud to question his own methods or his motives, never too proud to accept criticism.

THE GENTLE MOSES

Once, arrested in Atlanta for being on a picket line, Robert Moses was asked how he heard of it. He replied truthfully that he had heard while attending a lecture on "Ramifications of Gödel's Theorem." Harlem-born, Harvard-educated, the gentle Moses was a master of metaphysical philosophy, pursuing his doctorate when he threw himself behind SNCC. His self-effacing style and devotion to principle and humility soon made him a legend.

By July 1961 Moses was at work in McComb, Mississippi, leading a team of 12, on the first voter registration project in the Delta. He took 16 local blacks to register in the county courthouse in Magnolia. On August 29, he tried to do the same in the more rural Amite County, infuriating the state representative, E. W. Hurst, a fierce segregationist. Hurst had his nephew, Billy Jack Caston, beat up Moses at the courthouse. To the astonishment of the county prosecutor, Moses insisted on bringing a case. Enraged whites, many with shotguns, poured into Liberty for the trial. Moses walked calmly through the mob. Caston went free, but Moses' courage had made a deep impression on the black community.

Legislator Hurst struck again in late September. He chased and shot to death Herbert Lee, a father of nine who seemed to have done nothing more than occasionally lend his car to Moses. The sheriff occupied his time threatening a poor black epileptic sawmill hand into saying he had seen Lee threaten Hurst with a tire iron. The witness, Louis Allen, soon recanted, telling Moses, "I didn't want to tell no story about the dead, because you can't ask the dead for forgiveness." He said he would tell the grand jury the truth if he got protection. The Justice Department decided not to make a federal case of it. In the hermetic, incestuous world of rural Mississippi, it soon became known that Louis Allen had talked. He fled town, but came back briefly in 1964 and was murdered on his front lawn.

Moses had been campaigning in other Mississippi towns, notably Greenwood, in the face of more arrests, police dogs, beatings and murders. He blamed himself for Allen's death: "We can't protect our own people." He formulated a plan to bring some 1,000 Northern volunteers—many of them white—to Mississippi in the summer of 1964. Like the children who marched in the crucial Birmingham movement in 1963, it would become their fight, too. And like the four girls blown up in Birmingham's Sixteenth Street Baptist Church, some of them would also make the ultimate sacrifice.

FLASH FORWARD: 1982–1993
After coming out against the war in Vietnam, Moses was drafted and fled the country. By 1982 he was a professor of mathematics at the University of Massachusetts. Trying to help his own children with math, he developed a new system rooted in everyday life that won him a MacArthur "genius" award. By 1993, the Moses Algebra Project had been picked up in schools across the country—and particularly in Mississippi.

His work was not done. He had all but vanquished Jim Crow, but his murder robbed the country of a voice of conciliation, of a vision of intensive social reform for the benefit of all underprivileged Americans. If he had lived, he would certainly have tried to guide the civil rights movement away from the quest for racial spoils—for the quotas for broad groups of "minorities" in employment, college education and government-contracting that in the seventies and eighties became so divisive, frequently unfair and sometimes corrupt. He would have seen the claims, as he saw "black power" in 1966, as "racism in reverse."

Taylor Branch has eloquently and sensitively commemorated King in his masterpiece *Parting the Waters*. But for all the excellence of a number of histories and the enterprise of the television documentary *Eyes on the Prize*, the civil rights movement, as inspired by King, has not had its due as a sacrament to American democracy. It was the black people who were foremost in defending the Constitution, not congressmen or federal agencies or presidents. Until Lyndon Johnson came along, the record of the presidents is middling. Dwight D. Eisenhower aroused expectations, a war hero of manifest decency who was not beholden to the South for white votes. In his second term, he enforced the law at Little Rock, appointed two attorneys general who were sympathetic to black rights, and named federal judges who turned out to be invaluable allies of the movement. But Ike's heart was not in the cause. He liked to pontificate that you can't legislate morality, apparently unwilling or unable to comprehend King's rejoinder that "a law may not make a man love me, but it can stop him from lynching me." It can also stop a drive-in hamburger joint from refusing you service. Beyond the grand theatricality of John Kennedy's brilliant inaugural speech dedicated to freedom, one sees a tired soldier back from Vietnam being told one night in Georgia he can eat only if he sneaks round the back. Captain Colin Powell, destined to be chairman of the Joint Chiefs, went hungry.

Kennedy's stirring words did not, after all, directly promise much for the likes of Powell. "The torch," said JFK, " is passed to a new generation, born in this century, tempered by war, disciplined by a hard and bitter peace, proud of our ancient heritage . . . granted the role of defending freedom in its hour of maximum danger." Yet what was this "ancient heritage"? Race, a central theme of America's history, was alluded to only vaguely in two words. The country, he said, was unwilling to see the slow undoing of human rights "at home" and around the world. JFK in time compiled a better civil rights record than any president who had gone before him. His nationally televised speeches were rousing. At the time of his death, he was backing unprecedented civil rights legislation. Yet Kennedy and his brother at the Justice Department had had to be pushed very hard indeed to respond in the spirit of the inaugural. JFK was hobbled in part by the fear Eisenhower shared, that while federal troops might be able to force admittance of black students to white schools, they could not very well teach the classes if the promised "massive resistance" became a reality. This was not an unreasonable fear, but JFK never seems to have regarded it so much as a burning moral issue, of vital importance to the nation, as an embarrassing distraction from his foreign-policy endeavors. The Cold War, Cuba, the missile crisis and nuclear testing were certainly grave distractions, but there was little, if any, evidence of intrinsic feeling on the President's part for the dramatic fight for freedom being played out in front of him. Bobby Kennedy developed a deeper sense of sympathy, but both brothers rarely thought of the struggle in terms other than how it might help or hinder their own ambitions. They kept at arm's length aides who most favored civil rights and social reform —Harris Wofford, Russell Davis, Louis Martin, Sargent Shriver. The Justice Department effort to assist black voters to register was unprecedented but it was still tiny. It came down to the valiant John Doar in the field and the skeptical Burke Marshall in Washington. John Seigenthaler showed considerable courage, and Nicholas Katzenbach was uncommonly skillful in dealing with George Wallace. But such men were few and far between. The main table at Camelot was reserved for political pros wholly indifferent to civil rights, such as Byron "Whizzer" White, who became Kennedy's first and worst appointment to the Supreme Court. Most of JFK's Southern judicial appointments were devout segregationists who had to be overruled time and again in the higher courts. And he and his brother maintained in Hoover a bigoted persecutor of black people as director of the FBI. They authorized Hoover's illegal wiretaps for the phones, offices and homes of not just King but most of the civil rights leaders. The Kennedys despised Hoover and contemplated replacing him during JFK's second term, but their hand was stayed for the time being by Hoover's immense, carefully orchestrated personality cult—and possibly the fact that Hoover had discovered Kennedy's foolish affair with a Mafia moll, pimped to him by Frank Sinatra. It was a grotesque Faustian bargain. The Kennedys forced King to fire valuable advisers—Bayard Rustin, Jack O'Dell and Stanley Levison—because Hoover told them these men were active agents for the Soviet government. (It is regrettable that as of 1996 the FBI's original informant reports on Levison, the most important case, are still withheld from historians. Short of those documents, Taylor Branch and David Garrow have concluded that "without significant doubt" Levison was a man of good character who made a vital contribution to the movement.)

All the more splendid, then, after all the dazzling equivocations and dirty work, was the day Lyndon Johnson unfurled the civil rights banner on Capitol Hill. Soon after taking office he vowed "no deal" with the racists in Congress and pushed through the Civil Rights Act barring discrimination. Then, four months after being elected in his own right, he walked to the rostrum before a joint session of Congress and national television and radio and pledged his presidency to sweeping legislation with the words of the civil rights battle cry: "We shall overcome!" He spoke not as one yielding a concession but as one demanding a right. "We have already waited 100 years and more and the time for waiting is gone. . . ." He invoked the national destiny in the manner of his old hero Franklin Roosevelt: "At times history and fate meet in a single time in a single place to shape a turning point in man's unending search for freedom. So it was at Lexington and Concord. So it was a century ago at Appomattox. So it was last week in Selma, Alabama."

Johnson won the Voting Rights Act he wanted, but he knew that the battle was but entering a new phase. "All of us," he said, reflecting his own experience as a southerner, "must overcome the crippling legacy of bigotry and injustice." The

THE RIGHT TO CRITICIZE

Paradoxically, the South's hostility to the Yankee press in the civil rights struggle ended up enlarging the practical freedoms of print and broadcast media and of all Americans. In March 1960 Montgomery's police commissioner, L. B. Sullivan, followed by the governor and a host of Alabama state and local officials, filed a $500,000 libel suit against the *New York Times* and four SCLC ministers. They claimed they had been defamed by a full-page advertisement, signed by among others Eleanor Roosevelt, Nat King Cole and Jackie Robinson. The advertisement described the officials who broke up demonstrations as "violators of the Constitution." The case wound its way up through a series of expensive findings against the *Times,* which, splendidly, decided to risk all. Finally, it won a seminal Supreme Court victory justifying the right to criticize public officials. In his study of the case, *Make No Law* (1991), the leading First Amendment scholar Anthony Lewis underlines the significance of the decision: "It treated free speech not just as an individual right, but as a political necessity."

persecution and violence continued. The struggle of the black generation of the 1950s and 1960s was not a mild and inevitable hiccup in the march of American progress, as it is remembered today, but a long and heroic ordeal. The bigotry had a long life and illustrious patrons. It is often forgotten that an entire succession of future presidents—Ronald Reagan and George Bush vigorously and Richard Nixon and Gerald Ford ambiguously—had opposed part or all of the three major bills of the period: the 1964 Civil Rights Act, the 1965 Voting Rights Act and the 1968 Fair Housing Act, measures which only enforced black Americans' most basic constitutional rights. Civil rights were hardly mentioned during any of those presidents' campaigns. A convenient statute of limitations seems to have been placed on civil rights cowardice, though even the hoariest, most dubious Red-baiting charges could still be leveled against Bill Clinton as late as 1992. The hardest men of the time, George Wallace and Strom Thurmond and others, have also put a gloss on their incitements. Thurmond's survival into his nineties is judged sufficient achievement to atone for his years of ill-doing. And their crimes, too, have become abstractions, occasional incidents rather than a campaign of terror. Aside from the 40 or so activists who were murdered because of their nonviolent protest, there were many others—blacks as well as a number of sympathetic whites—who were routinely bankrupted, run out of town, beaten, gassed, hosed, clubbed, mutilated. Time and again the supposed guardians of law and order betrayed their oaths of office with impunity. When James Farmer, founder of the nonviolent Congress of Racial Equality (CORE) tried to lead a voter registration drive in Plaquemines Parish, Louisiana, masked state troopers cut off the tiny hamlet from the rest of the world, wrecked the church local blacks were meeting in and rampaged through the black community, torturing and beating citizens to reveal where Farmer was hiding. He finally had to be smuggled out of town in a hearse. One can still see the rotting camp, slowly settling into the marsh outside Plaquemines's appropriately named Port Sulphur, where Leander Perez, the local dictator, planned to incarcerate a mass of local blacks. Perez was so noxious a racist he was eventually excommunicated by the Catholic Church, but it did not seem to dim his luster for Louisiana's white voters. In Mississippi, Bob Zellner, a white activist student from Alabama, tried to pray on the steps of McComb's City Hall. Police and FBI watched as he was attacked by a dozen white thugs. This is his account, as given in the oral history *Voices of Freedom,* by Henry Hampton and Steve Fayer:

They had just every kind of weapon you can imagine: baseball bats, pipes, wrenches. They started shouting to the men who were beating me . . . "Bring him here, we'll kill him!" They were screaming just absolutely like animals. I was holding this Bible and they started dragging me out in the street and I realized that if they got me in the street, no matter what the cops did, nothing was gonna stop that mob from killing me. So I put the Bible down and grabbed ahold of the railing that went down the City Hall steps. . . . My hands were on the railing and they got two, three guys on each leg. They held me around the belt. And they would all pull. And I would hold on.

And then they got even more excited and they started trying to hit my hands with the objects they had: pipes and so forth. . . . Then one of the guys got behind me, got very hysterical and came over the top of my head. This is a very grisly part, but he started putting his fingers into my eye sockets and he would actually work my eyeball out of my eye socket and sort of down on my cheekbone. And I remember being amazed that it would stretch that far. He was trying to get my eyeball between his thumb and his index finger so that he could get a grip on it and really pull it out. He intended to gouge my eye out. So what I would do is, I would wait until he had maneuvered it into a good

THE MARCH ON WASHINGTON

Martin Luther King's speech at the March on Washington was the climax of a day the like of which America had never seen. For the first time the whole nation got a sense of the transcendent spiritual buoyancy that had sustained the civil rights movement through nine long years of scorn and terror. To Mrs. Coretta King, to the thousands at the Lincoln Memorial, and to millions watching on television, the exalted cadences of Martin Luther King that late afternoon of August 28, 1963, seemed to flow through him from Heaven. His dream of an America without hate carried him away beyond the words of his seven-minute text, and the vast swaying audience soared with him.

The March was one of those rare moments that seemed to gather together almost everyone in the movement—even if not all of them approved. Malcolm X was there, belittling the whole event as "the Farce on Washington." A bevy of celebrities, black and white, were on hand. So were J. Edgar Hoover's agents, who bugged King's hotel room. Congress had been scared to death at the prospect of 100,000 black men and women assembling in Washington. The majority white press was hostile. The white clergy participating asked SNCC's John Lewis to tone down his speech after reading a draft that promised to march through Dixie "the way Sherman did." President Kennedy, having failed to get the event called off, had 4,000 troops hidden in the suburbs, and his men were ready to shut off the public address system if any speaker went haywire.

The dignity and joyfulness of the pilgrims put such fears to shame. They burst from the trains and bus convoys in full song: "Woke up this morning with my mind set on freedom/Hallelu, hallelu, hallelujah!" They

crammed together good-naturedly, 200,000 blacks and 50,000 whites. They applauded "The Star-Spangled Banner," sung by Camilla Williams, and Bob Dylan singing his ballad for Medgar Evers. They stood in reverence for W. E. B. Du Bois, dead in Ghana at 95, just the night before. And they cheered a black stewardess, incredibly in 1963 the first in the job. There was no trouble of any kind. And when night fell serenely on the reflecting pool there was nothing but the sigh of a breeze across the water: Bayard Rustin, the flamboyant organizer of the March, was able to report to A. Philip Randolph, the chairman for the day, that their 500-man cleanup squad had left "not one piece of paper, not a cup, nothing." The 73-year-old Randolph was in tears. The March was his idea, a revival of the march he had planned in 1941 only to be dissuaded by President Roosevelt.

It was Randolph who anointed King, speaking last, as "the moral leader of our nation." If it was in doubt, the speech confirmed the accolade. They chanted his name. "Tell 'em about the dream, Martin!" shouted the singer Mahalia Jackson from behind, referring to passages he had been working into speeches earlier that summer; and in an impromptu peroration he did:

"I say to you, my friends, that in spite of the difficulties and frustrations of the moment, I still have a dream. It is a dream deeply rooted in the American dream. I have a dream that one day this nation will rise up and live out the true meaning of its creed: We hold these truths to be self-evident, that all men are created equal. I have a dream that one day on the red hills of Georgia the sons of former slaves and the sons of former slave

owners will be able to sit down together at the table of brotherhood. I have a dream that one day even the state of Mississippi, a state sweltering with the heat of injustice, sweltering with the heat of oppression, will be transformed into an oasis of freedom and justice. I have a dream that my four little children will one day live in a nation where they will not be judged by the color of their skin but the content of their character. . . ."

And on to the final exultant cry that if America were to be a great nation, it must let freedom ring: "When we allow freedom to ring, when we let it ring from every village and every hamlet, from every state and every city, we will be able to speed up that day when all of God's children, black men and white men, Jews and gentiles, Protestants and Catholics, will be able to join hands and sing in the words of the old Negro spiritual, 'Free at last!' Free at last! Thank God Almighty, we are free at last!"

The pilgrims were mightily refreshed, but the journey was not over. Kennedy's civil rights bill was stalled by a Southern filibuster. Eighteen days after the speech, a 50-year-old Klansman named "Dynamite" Bob Chambliss blew up the Sixteenth Street Baptist Church in Birmingham, the focal point of the Birmingham Movement. Four Sunday school children were killed: Addie Mae Collins, Denise McNair, Carole Robertson and Cynthia Wesley. The face of Christ was knocked cleanly out of the only stained-glass window. Local whites reacted not with compassion, but, their blood lust up, stormed the grief-stricken black neighborhood and arbitrarily shot two black bystanders to death. Birmingham, and America, was not there yet.

place and before he could clamp down, I would move my head in such a way that it would make him lose his grip. And my eyeball would slip between his fingers and pop back in my head, with a thunk.

The full fury of the white reaction in the South has been gradually diminished in the popular mind. It is probably fair to say that the average German today experiences more shame over the Hitler years than most white Americans do over how they tolerated a cruel persecution of their fellow citizens. To spell it out: the white response to the movement was nearly always indifferent when it wasn't hostile; petty when it wasn't cruel; vicious when it wasn't murderous. Again and again the supposedly "best elements" of the region, the wealthy and the well-educated, acted with a primitive meanness of spirit. The burghers of Charleston, South Carolina, ostracized federal Judge Julius Waties Waring because he ruled that the Democratic primary should be open to blacks. P. D. East, the satirizing editor of the *Petal Paper* in Hattiesburg, Mississippi, had his business ruined; when I visited him in 1956, he was wondering how to make fun of the bomb flung at his home the night before. Nearly the only part of the Southern white community that sought repeatedly to find a peaceful and fair reconciliation was white businessmen. Many were cajoled and dragooned into joining the White Citizens Council, "the Klan in a clean white collar," but many also became mild reformers when they realized that all the violence would wreck the growing economic vitality of the region.

The Southern press was almost universally hostile. It is a measure of their attitude to Negroes that it was regarded as extraordinary in the fifties when Hazel Brannon Smith in her Hattiesburg newspaper began according Negroes the prefix Mr. or Mrs., and Ralph McGill at the *Atlanta Constitution* capitalized the word "Negro."

Nationally, with the exception of a few brave correspondents, the most respected, relatively liberal organs like the *New York Times, Newsweek, Time,* the *New York Herald Tribune* and the *Washington Post* for years lackadaisically portrayed the deadly struggle for rights as one more mildly amusing political game, with regular winners, losers, leaders and trailers. The 1955 murder of Emmett Till had its big headlines, but two months later a white Mississippi cotton-gin manager, Elmer Kimbell, shot to death a gas attendant, Clinton Melton, and David Halberstam was almost alone in reporting Kimbell's acquittal after a sham of a trial. "There's open season on the Negroes now," a local told Halberstam. "Any peckerwood who wants to can go shoot himself one and we'll free him." The press attitude began to change only after the March on Washington and the Birmingham bombing in 1963. There was for years a schizophrenia that would be repeated in Vietnam: the editors and publishers at home steadfastly refused to believe what their reporters in the field were telling them. Editorials warned constantly against "extremism," on both sides, equating nonviolent activists and the white mob. The leading powers of America's vaunted free press seemed in a constant state of fret that their fellow citizens were demanding rights they had always taken for granted as the air they breathed. Hence the *Times* warned against extending the Freedom Rides in the summer of 1961: "They are challenging not only long-held customs but passionately held feelings. Nonviolence that deliberately provokes violence is a logical contradiction"— putting on a level of moral equivalency this time the wielder of the lead pipe and the recipient of the blow.

This was not an eccentric view. In that first summer of the Freedom Rides, some 63 percent of all Americans were polled as opposing the nonviolent protest actions. When young black men and women went on offending "passionately held feelings," the *Times* imitated its Southern counterparts by simply refusing to give the Freedom Rides more than token coverage for a time. Similarly, when the movement was stalemated in Albany, Georgia, by the segregationists' more subtle tactics, the *New York Herald Tribune* called it a "devastating loss of face" for King—as opposed, say, to a loss for every American professing to love freedom. Similarly, Taylor Branch records, "most reporters took a sportswriter's approach and billed the week's events as Segregation 1, King 0." *Time* magazine called the movement a "confused crusade" and sought out every black leader willing to criticize the involvement of SNCC.

The fight for civil rights was on an altogether different plane from the pettiness of the press. It was the noblest ever waged in America. At the end of it, when President Lyndon Johnson swung the full weight of the federal government behind the movement, people of all kinds began at last to enjoy fairly equal treatment before the law. The memory ought never to be lost of those people who made it happen, who in the face of terror marched singing out of their churches and from their campuses—and won their rights. Martin Luther King said it best: "One day the South will know that when these disinherited children of God sat down at lunch counters, they were in reality standing up for what is best in the American dream and for the most sacred values of our Judeo-Christian heritage."

MARTIN LUTHER KING, JR.: "In the process of gaining our rightful place we must not be guilty of wrongful deeds. Let us not seek to satisfy our thirst for freedom by drinking from the cup of bitterness and hatred. . . . The marvelous new militancy which has engulfed the Negro community must not lead us to a distrust of all white people. . . ." Speaking at the March on Washington, August 28, 1963. Photograph by Charles Moore.

THE KLAN: The four young girls who died in the Klan bombing at the Sixteenth Street Baptist Church in Birmingham "weren't children," according to Connie Lynch, Klanswoman. "Children are little people, little human beings, and that means white people. . . . They're just niggers . . . and if there's four less niggers tonight, then I say 'Good for whoever planted the bomb!'" This photograph by Charles Moore is of the Grand Dragon of North Carolina, James R. (Bob) Jones, with two unidentified Klanswomen.

MARSHALL'S GREAT VICTORY

Harry Briggs, a Navy veteran, and his wife, Liza, thought their five children should not have to walk to school when the white children rode in buses. Their rural South Carolina county had 30 school buses, but none for blacks. Gardner Bishop, a barber in Washington, D.C., was angry that his daughter's school was so crowded it had to have double sessions, while the nearby white junior high had several hundred open places. Oliver Brown, a welder and war vet in Topeka, Kansas, worried every day that his daughter would get killed crossing a railway switching yard that was the only route to a distant all-black school; she was denied entry to a nearby all-white school. Sixteen-year-old Barbara Rose Johns in Virginia didn't see why her high school should remain a drafty tar-paper shack.

The seminal Supreme Court case that became known as *Brown v. Board of Education of Topeka,* headed by five plaintiffs, was actually the climax of scores of cases like these. The originating conscience, too often overlooked, was a quiet, slender black Episcopalian minister and schoolteacher, the Rev. Joseph A. DeLaine of Summerton in Clarendon County, South Carolina, who began mildly protesting in the summer of 1947. On the advice of Thurgood Marshall and the local NAACP, he rounded up a score of plaintiffs who would challenge the lack of school buses for blacks. Harry Briggs was one of them. They were all victimized. Those who were farmers were denied credit and ruined. Briggs was fired from a garage job, Liza from a motel; they ended up in the Bronx. DeLaine was fired from his teaching job, as were his wife, two sisters and a niece. His house and church were burned down, he was assaulted at night by shotgun assailants and finally run out of South Carolina by a combination of threats and trumped-up legal charges and suits.

But DeLaine had started something. The cases he organized led to a landmark ruling from the federal bench in 1951. "Segregation in education can never produce equality. . . . Segregation is per se inequality," said Judge Julius Waties Waring in Charleston. He was bravely in a minority, and he received death threats. His two fellow judges did order the county to intro-

duce real equality, and that seemed the best blacks could hope for when the cases reached the Supreme Court on September 9, 1952.

It was a gamble for the NAACP to ask for desegregation rather than the more easily attainable promise of equal funding: on average Southern states spent half as much educating a black child as they spent educating a white.

The conduct of the case itself was a test of racist theory. The segregationist states employed John W. Davis, the 80-year-old Wall Street lawyer and Democratic presidential nominee in 1924. He looked with condescension on his opponent, Thurgood Marshall, who led a fine legal team, nearly all black, mostly educated at all-black Howard University. Marshall, who would go to an outstanding term of 24 years on the Supreme Court, appointed by Lyndon Johnson in 1967, was put in the ironic position of arguing his own equality. He struck home to a basic purpose of the U.S. Constitution: the protection of minority rights against the will of an unreasoning majority:

"But to all this the plea of necessity is urged; and of the existence of that necessity we are told the state alone is to judge. Where is this to land us? Is it not asserting the right in each state to throw off the federal Constitution at its will and pleasure? If it can be done as to any particular article it may be done to all; and, like the old confederation, the Union becomes a mere rope of sand."

Davis responded that the states were in the process of equalizing their schools and the right to segregate them was not impeded by the Fourteenth Amendment.

The hearings took two days; the consideration took eighteen months. Among the justices, the conflict boiled down to one between four intellectual heavyweights: William O. Douglas and Hugo Black (a former Klansman), who were all for overturning *Plessy v. Ferguson* at once; and Felix Frankfurter and Robert Jackson, who were sympathetic to black rights but had reservations. Frankfurter felt boxed in because in the New Deal cases he had argued that nine old men should not stand in the way of a legislature. How would the federal government cope if there was massive

resistance? The long delay proved a boon to the NAACP. Chief Justice Fred Vinson died and President Eisenhower had to name a new Chief Justice. He chose Earl Warren, the popular three-term governor of California—a man whose name would soon become an epithet throughout the white South. Warren seemed an unlikely angel of the civil rights movement. He had pressed for the despicable relocation of the Nisei in 1942; but, like his new colleague Hugo Black, he was one of those individuals whose life seemed to incorporate his nation's progress. After a second round of *Davis v. Marshall,* rearguing the case in

On the third anniversary of *Brown,* in May 1957, Martin Luther King led 25,000 in the first black protest march on Washington. His speech, "Give us the ballot," established him as the informal leader of the civil rights move- ment and he met Vice President Nixon: Ike would not see him. Photograph by Henri Cartier-Bresson.

December 1953, he used his conciliatory skills to press for a unanimous decision. On May 17, 1954, at 12:52 p.m., Earl Warren coolly and even casually began to read the obituary of *Plessy:*

"To separate [Negro children] from others of similar age and qualifications solely because of their race generates a feeling of inferiority as to their status in the community that may affect their hearts and minds in a way never to be undone. . . ."

The Court invited the South's participation in drawing up plans for desegregation "with all deliberate speed." The answer was a raspberry. Southern white politicians pledged their full resistance to the law of the land. President Eisenhower refused to endorse the ruling until much later. Privately he said Warren's appointment was "the biggest damn fool mistake I ever made." He had invited him to dinner at the White House while the Court was considering the case and sat him next to "a great American"—John W. Davis. Ralph Bunche, the black under secretary to the United Nations, told Thurgood Marshall that he heard Eisenhower appealing to Warren for an understanding of the Southern whites. Warren, said Bunche, told Ike: "I thought I would never have to say this to you, but I now find it necessary to say specifically: You mind your business and I'll mind mine."

THE DAY MOSE WRIGHT
DEFIED MISSISSIPPI'S TERROR

Emmett "Bobo" Till, just graduated from a school on Chicago's South Side at the age of 14, was excited at the idea of a summer break with family in the Mississippi Delta. His mother, Mamie Bradley, kissed him good-bye on August 20, 1955, and he took the long train ride south. The terrestrial journey was short by comparison with the psychic transition from the swinging South Side to the serfdom of Mississippi. Emmett was a perky boy, despite a speech impediment from nonparalytic polio, and his mother cautioned her only child about her home state's attitude toward blacks: "If you have to get on your knees and bow when a white person goes past, do it willingly." The next time she saw him he was a disfigured corpse in a pine box, his face battered to a pulp by defenders of the Southern way of life.

The boys went to stay with his cousin Curtis Jones's grandfather, Mose Wright, a sharecropper and preacher living near the dusty crossroads of Money (population 50) on the Tallahatchie River. On August 24, Till and seven other teenagers borrowed Wright's raggedy '41 Ford and drove to a little country store owned by Roy and Carolyn Bryant. Till, fooling around with local black youngsters, produced a photograph of a white girl he claimed was a friend back home. One of the locals challenged: "Hey, there's a white girl in that store there. I bet you won't go in and talk to her."

Carolyn Bryant later said Till squeezed her hand, asked, "How about a date, baby?" When she withdrew, she said, he jumped between two counters, blocked her path, put his hands around her waist and told her, "Don't be afraid of me, baby. I ain't gonna hurt you. I been with white girls before." She ran to get a pistol and he gave her a wolf whistle and sauntered out. Mrs. Bryant's uncorroborated account invites suspicion. Till was not familiar with the Delta's racial mores, but such behavior might well have got him killed in the Chicago of 1955, or today, and to claim that he remained calm and insulting even when she had a gun is to credit Till with a cool rare even on the battlefield. His mother had another explanation: She said

THE KILLERS: Grins from Bryant (left) and Milam after their acquittal. Later, for $4,000, they told the story of the murder to William Bradford Huie. Milam, by his own account, baited Till with lines such as: "Nigger, you still as good as I am?" and "You still done it to white girls and you gonna keep on doing it?"

he stuttered on *b*'s and *m*'s and she had taught him to "blow it out. . . . I can see him trying to say 'bubble gum' and blowing or whistling."

Roy Bryant was away trucking shrimp with his half brother, J. W. Milam, a six-two, 235-pound decorated veteran of World War II. When her husband got home three days later, Mrs. Bryant did not tell him about the incident. He heard about it from a local black. In the small hours that night Bryant and Milam banged on the door of Mose Wright's cabin and demanded he hand over "that boy who done the talkin'." They dragged Till into their car. They tortured him until dawn; two or more other white men may have joined in the beatings, which gouged out an eye and crushed his forehead. A black sharecropper heard screams coming from a barn, and then "Mama, Lord have mercy, Lord have mercy." The bludgeoned Till was taken to the edge of the Talla-hatchie River and ordered to strip. Milam shot the boy in the head with his .45. They lashed a 75-pound cotton gin fan to his neck with barbed wire and flung the body in the river.

Wright kept quiet, as the kidnappers had ordered. It was Curtis Jones who reported the abduction. Three days later, dredging of the river yielded the body, so

badly disfigured the sheriff wanted an immediate burial. Bradley insisted on her son being shipped home, to display "what they did to my boy." Thousands walked by the open casket, shocked by what they saw; more saw the shocking picture of Till in the black weekly *Jet* (inset).

In Mississippi there was an initial wave of revulsion over the crime. As the defense lawyer told the all-white jury, "Your ancestors will turn over in their graves [if Milam and Bryant] are found guilty, and I'm sure every last Anglo-Saxon of you has the courage to free these men in the face of that [outside] pressure." The key question was whether Mose Wright would skip town or dare to take the witness stand against two white men. It was a historic moment when the old man climbed into the box and pointed to Milam: "Dar he!" Wright recalled, "I wasn't exactly brave and I wasn't scared. I just wanted to see justice done." It wasn't. On September 23, 1955, the 166th anniversary of the signing of the Bill of Rights, the jury acquitted. The federal government failed to bring a civil rights case and Eisenhower kept quiet. But Wright's accusing finger had pointed beyond the hot courtroom in Sumner. It had pointed to America and slowly the country took heed.

ACCUSER: Mose Wright points out the kidnappers and killers. "I could feel the blood boil in the hundreds of white people as they sat glaring in the courtroom." He had been told he would be killed if he testified.

THE EMERGENCE OF MARTIN LUTHER KING

The received mythology is that late on the afternoon of December 1, 1955, a simple seamstress in Montgomery, Alabama, refused to give up her bus seat to a white man because she was too tired, and unknowingly sparked the historic confrontation of the Montgomery bus boycott. The real story is more complex—and more inspiring.

No doubt Rosa Parks's feet were tired, but her own accounts stress her rights more than her arches. "Why do you push us around?" she asked the arresting policeman, making a statement for all the 50,000 blacks of Montgomery condemned to menial work and the daily indignities of segregation. She knew what she was doing challenging Alabama's Jim Crow laws. She did work as a seamstress, but she was also the secretary of the Montgomery chapter of the NAACP and its head, the Rev. E. D. Nixon, a fearless 56-year-old Pullman car porter. Since the Supreme Court's ruling on schools, Nixon had been looking for a good witness for a court fight over bus segregation. Rosa Parks was perfect, a 43-year-old married, churchgoing Methodist of dignified humility and intelligence. Nixon rushed down to her cell in the police station with a white lawyer no less valiant in the fight for social justice—the old New Dealer Clifford Durr. They bailed her out and that night asked her to let them make her a federal case. By a historic tactical blunder, she had been charged under a segregation ordinance, opening the way for a federal court to rule on Jim Crow laws. She agreed "if it will mean something to Montgomery." Her mother and her husband, Raymond, were appalled. "The white folks will kill you, Rosa," said Raymond Parks.

Nobody had mentioned a boycott at this stage. That idea was born in the small hours after midnight on the campus of Alabama State, an all-black college. Jo Ann Robinson, a professor of English, was head of the NAACP's Women's Political Council, an organization of black professional women, mainly teachers. She gathered a number of them in the college under the guise of grading papers, and they stayed up all night churning out 35,000 petitions. "We are asking every Negro to stay off the buses on Monday. . . ." Nixon, who had

VICTORY: Rosa Parks waiting to board a bus in Montgomery on December 21, 1956, the day the city buses were legally integrated. She continued her civil rights work in Detroit, starting her own charitable foundation and working for 20 years on the staff of Congressman John Conyers.

been thinking on the same lines, had meanwhile been working the telephones. By morning, before he put on his white coat and porter's cap for duty on the morning train to Atlanta, he had enlisted about 50 black ministers in a campaigning body that became the Montgomery Improvement Association (MIA). Among them were Ralph Abernathy at the First Baptist Brick a Day Church and a new 26-year-old reverend at the Dexter Avenue Baptist Church named Martin Luther King, Jr.

Monday morning came and the boycott organizers were relieved. The buses

were empty. That afternoon the ministers prepared for a mass meeting to gauge support for continuing the boycott. Some of the ministers were so fearful they wanted to keep their names secret; Rosa Parks had been convicted that morning. A boiling mad Nixon rebuked them: "You ministers have lived off these washwomen for the last hundred years and ain't never done nothing for them." Nobody contested the nomination of King for the exposed position of MIA president.

The church could not hold the 10,000 to 15,000 who turned up to hear King a few hours later; they spilled into the acres outside. They were silent as he began in a slow deep voice. Then he spoke to their anguish: "And you know, my friends," he cried, "there comes a time when people get tired of being trampled over by the iron feet of oppression. . . ." The yesses coalesced into a roar, thousands of stomping feet made thunder, and soon the church and the grounds were trembling. When he could make himself heard again he quietly insisted: "Now let us say we are not here advocating violence. We have overcome that. I want it to be known throughout Montgomery and throughout this nation that we are Christian people. The only weapon we have in our hands this evening is the weapon of protest." Like so many leaders of protest of this country and this century, like so many who loved this country so well and had to fight it so fiercely, King invoked the promise of American life: "But the great glory of American democracy is the right to protest for right. There will be no crosses burned at any bus stops in Montgomery. There will be no white persons pulled out of homes and taken out on some distant road and murdered. There will be nobody among us who will stand up and defy the Constitution of the nation." He closed by speaking of Christian love and justice and rocked the exultant crowd in the rhythm of his peroration. "We are not wrong in what we are doing. If we are wrong—the Supreme Court of this nation is wrong. If we are wrong—God Almighty is wrong! If we are wrong—Jesus of Nazareth was merely a utopian dreamer and never came down to earth! If we are wrong—justice is a lie."

FREE AGAIN: Martin Luther King in fedora and tan suit on the street soon after his release from jail. Photographs above and below by Charles Moore.

The fire that King sparked that night had to be kept lit by the physical and moral courage of the blacks of Montgomery for a whole long year. The MIA set up a car pool that impressively carried 20,000 of the 30,000 to 40,000 daily fares of the boycotted bus company, but the laborers and the cleaners and the teachers walked countless miles in all weathers, they endured the harassment of a hostile police force and the threats and terrorism of white extremists, and never did they lose their unity or their spirit. A woman called Mother Pollard spoke for them when she told King: "My feets is tired, but my soul is rested." King was arrested twice. His home was firebombed. He calmed an angry crowd of several hundred on the brink of rioting: "Don't get panicky. Don't get your weapons. We want to love our enemies."

Eleven months into the siege, the city was on the verge of winning an injunction banning the car pool when King, sitting glumly in the Montgomery courthouse, was handed an Associated Press news wire from Washington: They had

won! The Supreme Court had affirmed that Alabama's bus segregation laws were unconstitutional.

The white backlash was short but severe. Churches and homes were bombed. Shots were fired at integrated buses. Seven

bombers or snipers were acquitted. But the civil rights movement now had the backing of the streets to give momentum to the NAACP's herculean legal efforts, and in King it had found an orator of celestial eloquence.

FROG MARCH: In pain with one hand twisted behind his back, King uses the other to gesture to black bystanders not to interfere with the police. He was arrested and flung into a Montgomery cell for lingering at the door of the courthouse on September 3, 1958, where Ralph Abernathy was giving evidence in a case of domestic violence. The next morning King was sentenced to a fine of $14 or 14 days in jail. As a gesture of defiance, he elected to serve the time, and the MIA planned a 14-day vigil outside the city jail. Before it could begin, someone paid the fine and King was released: the someone turned out to be Police Commissioner Clyde Sellers. His motive, he said, was to deny King publicity for the book he had just published, *Stride Toward Freedom*. It was in New York, signing the book at a Harlem store on September 17, that King nearly lost his life. A crazy woman plunged a knife into his chest. The knife grazed his aorta and it took four suspenseful hours to extract; doctors said a sneeze would have killed him.

THE BATTLE OF LITTLE ROCK

National Guardsmen with fixed bayonets seized Central High School in Little Rock, Arkansas, on the night of September 2, 1957. They were under orders from Governor Orval Faubus (1910–1994) to repel an invasion the next morning—of nine black children. Earlier that day Faubus had been told by a federal judge he must let the nine enroll in the all-white school. His defiance took Little Rock by surprise. Arkansas had not been in the front line of resistance to the school desegregation decreed by the Supreme Court in 1954. Faubus, a wily populist of 47 who had worked as a teacher and a migrant farmer and risen to an Army major in the war, had beaten a white supremacist to win his second term in 1956. He had abetted equality for blacks on the state's buses and trains. In July he had rejected demands that he use his police power to stop school desegregation. "Everyone knows," he said, "no state's laws supersede a federal law." He changed his mind in August because he was harassed by die-hard Deep South politicians and threatened with a racist campaign when he ran for reelection. For the public, he invented the excuse of an incipient riot; the FBI found no evidence for that.

President Eisenhower, golfing in Newport, Rhode Island, came up with an idea to uphold the law but save face for Faubus. He thought he had sold it to him when the two men met for 20 minutes in Ike's tiny vacation office on September 14. Faubus would not withdraw the National Guard. He would simply change its orders to "keep the peace" while he obeyed the court's ruling. Faubus reneged. On September 20, his lawyers showed up before the U.S. District Court and announced that Faubus would "not concede that the United States in this court or anywhere else can question his discretion and judgment." Then they walked out. Faubus explained breaking his promise: "Just because I said it, doesn't make it so."

Faubus did withdraw the National Guard that night, and went off to Georgia. But he had made arrangements for school opening on Monday, September 23. His friend Jimmy "the Flash" Karam, who was head of the Arkansas State Athletic Com-

Central High was desegregated under federal bayonets—but Governor Faubus fought on. A federal judge, responding to the school board, agreed to suspend the desegregation plan for two and a half

years. When the Supreme Court overruled him, Faubus closed the high school for the 1958–59 academic year on the grounds that he was preventing violence.

KEEP OUT! Elizabeth Eckford, aged 15, endures abuse on her way to Central High School. In 1997, the young woman yelling asked for forgiveness.

mission, had a bunch of thugs waiting at Central High. "Here come the niggers," they yelled as four blacks approached. They beat them up. The four were journalists, not students, but the diversion enabled the nine to walk into school. The white students were calm, but the frenzied crowd outside surged through the police cordon vowing to "lynch the niggers." The mayor had the nine removed under police protection and made a frantic appeal to Eisenhower.

Eisenhower was loath to send in troops. He brooded over the proclamation on his sunporch and went to bed without signing it. The next morning the mob was out of control. At 12:08 p.m. Eisenhower gave the order. Crack paratroopers of the 101st Airborne Division joined the federalized National Guard. The following day when the mob tried to get at the nine black students, the troops pushed the rioters back at bayonet point. One of them grabbed a soldier's rifle. He was clubbed with a rifle butt. It was all over quite soon.

Little Rock was not the massive race riot of popular imagination. Nobody, black or white, was seriously hurt. The troops were withdrawn by November and no other major racial incident occurred at the gradually desegregated school. Eisenhower had reluctantly done what he had to do, but the sight of federal troops in a Southern capital evoked all the resentment and rage the region had fostered since the Civil War. Reckless, demagogic defiance became the rule for ambitious Southern politicians. Faubus became a six-term governor.

THE HERO: The graceful and charming Yuri Gagarin became an international hero after he orbited the earth in 1 hour and 48 minutes on April 12, 1961.

THE ONE-WATT SHOCK THAT MADE AMERICA JUMP

Millions of Americans were dismayed—and enchanted—by the sound coming from their radios and televisions in October 1957: beep, beep, beep in A-flat. The signal, picked up between 20 and 40 megacycles, emanated from several hundred miles above the Earth, from a 184.3-pound aluminum sphere the size of a beach ball. It circled the globe every 92 minutes at a velocity of 18,000 miles an hour. The power of the signal itself was only 1 watt, emitted by a battery that died in a few weeks, but the shock it gave America was cataclysmic. The first space satellite, *Sputnik I,* was Russian, and its mocking orbit suggested communism was mastering the universe. Eisenhower was unmoved. "One small ball in the air," he said, "is something which does not raise my apprehensions, not one iota." He was more alarmed that public hysteria would feed the appetite of the military-industrial complex for uncontrolled spending on missiles.

In November, the half-ton *Sputnik II* carried a dog, Laika, into space. In December, the U.S. invited the world to watch it

launch a 3.25-pound satellite on the Navy's Vanguard rocket. It rose a few inches from the pad, then disintegrated in flames. "Kaputnik!" "Flopnik!" "Stayputnik!" were among the headlines, and the reaction launched Senate Majority Leader Lyndon Johnson on a congressional inquisition. A procession of indignant witnesses testified to America's incompetence and vulnerability. The lamentations were overdone, though there had been blunders. Wernher von Braun, the German rocket scientist who had launched the first successful ballistic missile, the V-2, at London, had brought 127 of his team with him to America after the war. They could have had a satellite up early in 1957, using their Army Redstone rocket, but in 1955 the Pentagon, calamitously advised by a civilian committee, had put all its money on the Navy's Vanguard. When von Braun was finally allowed to try in January 1958 he put *Explorer I* in space with a rocket little different from the one the Pentagon had rejected three years before. *Explorer I* contributed a genuine scientific discovery:

the radiation belts outside the atmosphere.

In April 1958, Eisenhower made the brave and crucial decision to put space exploration under civilian control in the National Aeronautics and Space Agency (later Administration). But he had no enthusiasm for putting a man in space. He did not believe that it was the way to win prestige, and he was certain that the moon scientifically was not worth two cents. Perhaps he would have kept cool on April 12, 1961, when Soviet cosmonaut Yuri Gagarin became the first man in space and the first to orbit the Earth. But the man in the White House then had a competitive passion and an appetite for drama. President Kennedy was beside himself. "If somebody can just tell me how to catch up. Let's find somebody—anybody. I don't care if it's the janitor over there." On May 25, 1961, he went before Congress and made a solemn dedication: "I believe this nation should commit itself to achieving the goal, before this decade is out, of landing a man on the moon and returning him safely to the earth." It had the air of fantasy.

SEVEN WITH THE RIGHT STUFF

All seven test pilots in the Mercury space program, immortalized in Tom Wolfe's *The Right Stuff* (and later in the movie), were white Protestants in their thirties from small-town America. From the left:

VIRGIL (GUS) GRISSOM: Born April 3, 1926, grew up in Michigan. A Korean war combat pilot, he was the second American to make a suborbital flight, in July 1961. He almost drowned when the hatch of his capsule blew off after splashdown. On January 27, 1967, in a ground rehearsal, fire in the cockpit of his capsule asphyxiated Grissom and two other astronauts: Ed White, the first American to walk in space, in June 1965, and Roger Chaffee.

DEKE SLAYTON: Born March 1, 1924, grew up in Wisconsin. A fierce Air Force fighter pilot, Slayton was grounded with a heart murmur and made director of flight-crew operations for the Apollo moon program. He died of a brain tumor in 1993.

GORDON COOPER: Born March 6, 1927, grew up reading *Buck Rogers* in Oklahoma and Kentucky. Flew 22 orbits, more than any astronaut before him and in August 1965 was eight days in space in the two-man *Gemini* spacecraft, then a record. Retired from NASA

in 1970 to head his own aviation consulting firm in California. In 1975 he became vice president of research and development for Disney.

JOHN GLENN: Born July 18, 1921, grew up in Ohio, became a fighter ace in World War II and Korea. The first American astronaut to orbit the Earth; he went round three times in February 1962, to the chagrin of his rival Alan Shepard. Glenn was the first astronaut to leave for business, becoming president of a soft drinks company. He was elected to the U.S. Senate in 1974 and ran for president in 1984. But in October 1998, at the age of 77, he was set to be launched into orbit again on a 10-day space-shuttle flight.

M. SCOTT CARPENTER: Born May 1, 1925, grew up in Colorado. On his three-orbit flight in May 1962 he became preoccupied by the spectacular views, used too much fuel and landed 250 miles from the scheduled spot in the ocean. "I only wished," he said, "I could get up the next morning and go through the whole thing again. I wanted the weightlessness again, and to see the sunsets and sunrises and watch the stars drop through the luminous layer." But his next adventure was 200 feet down on the ocean bed: he left

space and joined the Navy's SeaLab II, testing the effect of water pressure.

ALAN B. SHEPARD, JR. (1923–1998): The first American in space made a 15-minute suborbital flight on May 5, 1961. He was grounded throughout the sixties with an inner-ear affliction, but recovered to command *Apollo 14* in 1970. He walked the surface for 33 hours, and celebrated with a world-record golfing drive. He hit balls with an improvised 6-iron and in low lunar gravity they went, he said, for "miles and miles and miles."

WALTER SCHIRRA, JR.: Born March 12, 1923, grew up in New Jersey, flew in the Korean war. Achieved six orbits. He retired from NASA in 1969 to serve as a space commentator on the Apollo missions for CBS. He helped to found the Florida-based Give Kids the World organization and worked in public relations.

QUOTE: "Through it all we remained good friends. We have dug postholes for each other's fences. Our wives are all warm friends. And, like all pilots, we feel a strong sense of responsibility for each other. If one of us were to go down somewhere in a plane one dark night, you would find all six of us spending the entire night out there," said Schirra.

MR. KHRUSHCHEV COMES TO TOWN

President Eisenhower and Nikita Khrushchev had this in common in 1959: they both thought their personal diplomacy could thaw the Cold War. America did not know what to make of the earthy, mercurial Khrushchev. Ousting his rivals after Stalin's death in 1953, he had gone globetrotting for peace with Nikolay Bulganin, buried the hatchet with Yugoslavia's Tito, pulled out of Austria and, in 1956, sensationally denounced Stalin's crimes. But in the same year he brutally suppressed revolts in East Germany, Poland and Hungary, threatened Britain and France with rockets if they did not abandon their war to regain control of the Suez Canal, and followed up in 1958 by giving the Western powers an ultimatum to get out of Berlin. "It's the testicles of the West," he typically said. "Each time I give them a yank, they holler." He was stunned and delighted in July 1959 to get an invitation from Eisenhower to come to the United States for ten days. The invitation was a goof. Eisenhower had told his advisers he would agree to a summit only if Khrushchev broke the stalemate in the foreign ministers' talks at Geneva, and the talks were still stuck. Ike blew up, but relented. He wanted to go down in history as a man who made peace. He was fed up with the Pentagon's constant demands for more weapons. He was no longer restrained by Secretary of State John Foster Dulles, who had died in May.

So it was that Ike in a sporty gray-blue Stetson stood on the red carpet at Andrews Air Force Base on September 15 to greet Khrushchev with a 21-gun salute and the Soviet and American anthems. Khrushchev, his nerves "strained with excitement," as he later put it, reflected that it was a classier reception than Moscow's "proletarian way," but he disguised his insecurity with proud boasts of the Soviet lead in space.

Ike was eager to show off, too. From the White House, he whisked his guest into a helicopter to see the fine homes in the suburbs and the sweeping highways, a glimpse of the 41,000 miles of roads he had spent $76 billion building. To his chagrin, Khrushchev kept a poker face. The Soviet people, he told Ike, did not need to waste so much on cars, roads and houses. They preferred to live close together, and in apartments, unlike restless Americans "who do not seem to like the place where they live and always want to be on the move going someplace." But for all that, he was impressed. He had simply not believed it when Richard Nixon had told him there were 60 million cars in America.

Khrushchev, accompanied by family and some hundred Russian writers, artists and scientists, spent nearly a week traversing the continent like a presidential candidate. He worked the crowds, kissed babies, pinned hammer-and-sickle badges on children, laid a wreath at FDR's grave, insisted on touring Harlem's slums. His pungent, salty speeches went down well. In Pittsburgh, given the key to the city, he told the mayor: "And I promise you that this key will never be used without the host's permission." He had a hard time understanding democratic ways. He debated with the United Automobile Workers' Walter Reuther and his six vice presidents and concluded they were "agents for capitalists." He ran into hostile newsmen and pickets and raged that they

"Do you call a C-minus catching up with the Russians?" Cartoon by Alan Dunn.

The launching of the Soviet *Sputnik* spooked America into a generation of intensified science and math courses.

were plants, but by the time he reached San Francisco he seemed to get the picture: "Poor Eisenhower, I am just beginning to understand what his problems are."

In Hollywood, he was upset to be told he could not tour Disneyland because they could not guarantee his security. He affected to be offended by what he saw of the filming of *Can-Can*. He turned his back on reporters, flipped up his coat in imitation of the dance: "This is what you call freedom—freedom for the girls to show their backsides. To us, it's pornography. . . . It's capitalism that makes girls that way."

In two final days at Camp David and Ike's Gettysburg farm, Khrushchev's moods were volatile. He distrusted his hosts, restricting his discussions with his foreign minister, Andrei Gromyko, to excursions outside his quarters. His hosts, meanwhile, were busy trying to assess his health by collecting samples from his bathroom. But he and Eisenhower began to get along in their private talks. Ike became convinced he was sincere about abating the arms race. On the last day, on a private walk in the woods, Khrushchev agreed to lift his ultimatum on Berlin and stop the jamming of Voice of America. Ike agreed to recommend a Big Four summit meeting and accepted an invitation to Moscow. Back home, Khrushchev praised Ike's statesmanship, courage and valor and threw himself into plans "like a Soviet Ziegfeld." The Big Thaw seemed a real possibility.

The grandmotherly Madame Khrushchev in Hollywood, with Bob Hope and Frank Sinatra. She was a hit.

FARMER TO FARMER: In Coon Rapids, Iowa, Khrushchev called on Roswell Garst, a leading hybrid corn grower. They had corresponded about corn and live-stock. Khrushchev considered Garst a "class enemy," but said he enjoyed his willingness to "trade secrets with others—even with us."

THE KITCHEN DEBATE: Vice President Nixon was the host to Khrushchev at the first-ever U.S. exhibition in Moscow, but he wanted to score points. So did Khrushchev. They volleyed more insults than thoughts, jabbing each other with a finger in the chest to prove that America was superior to the Soviet Union or vice versa. They stand at a kitchen of a model house, which Nixon said any steelworker or veteran could buy for $14,000 over 25 to 30 years. Khrushchev scoffed and exaggerated wildly that "all newly built Russian houses will have this equipment. . . . If an American citizen does not have dollars, he has the right to sleep on the pavement at night." Photograph by William Safire.

EISENHOWER'S DREAM CRASHES IN A PLOWED FIELD

President Eisenhower was skeet shooting out at his Camp David retreat on Sunday morning, May 1, 1960, when he got the news he had been dreading for the past four years. One of his U-2 spy planes was missing from a secret mission photographing a possible Soviet rocket site. Nikita Khrushchev was on top of the Lenin mausoleum reviewing the gargantuan May Day parade when a Soviet air chief climbed up to whisper that an intruder had been shot down. "Wonderful news," he responded. The Russians had been seething at their inability to stop some dozens of U-2 overflights, too high at 70,000 feet to be vulnerable to fighters or ground fire. But for Khrushchev, as for Ike, it was a malign piece of timing. Both had exalted hopes for a summit meeting in Paris in two weeks. Khrushchev, struggling to spend more on consumers and less on soldiers, had pinned his political fortunes on his faith in Eisenhower. Eisenhower thought he could negotiate a permanent ban on nuclear tests, which were poisoning the world.

Who knows what might have happened if the summit had taken place as scheduled. It had been delayed for eight months because President de Gaulle had insisted on waiting until France had tested its own atomic bomb. Eisenhower had not sanctioned any overflights in that period of hope. The program had given him what he wanted: proof of his intuition that the "sanctimonious, hypocritical bastards" in the Pentagon, and their congressional allies, were not justified in demands for panic spending to meet a "bomber gap" and a "missile gap." He agonized when the CIA's Richard Bissell, who managed the U-2 program, and his chief, Allen Dulles, appealed for one more flight. He risked one on April 9, and then one more, emboldened by Khrushchev's silence and the repeated assurances from Bissell and Dulles that no U-2 plane or pilot could ever fall into Soviet hands.

They had three reasons for confidence. The U-2 was a flimsy, glorified glider with a turbojet engine that would disintegrate if it took a hit. Pilots who risked surviving a bailout were ordered first to trigger an explosive charge under the seat and told they would then have 70 seconds to escape. And they were all "exhorted but not ordered" to prefer suicide to capture and possible torture. They were provided with the means: a silver dollar that split open to offer instant death from a tiny pin inside primed with a shellfish toxin the CIA had developed. Francis Gary Powers took the dollar with him when he took off from Pakistan on May 1. He was 30, the son of a poor Appalachian coal miner turned cobbler. Approaching Sverdlovsk, 1,300 miles inside the Soviet Union, his plane pitched nose up. The autopilot had failed. He decided to go on, but in switching to manual he may have lost vital altitude. He heard a "thump" and an orange flash lit the cockpit. The wings fell off. He undid the cockpit canopy and, as he later recalled, found himself flung half out of the plane, unable to reach down to the destructor switches. He broke free of the oxygen hoses and his parachute carried him into a plowed field. As he shivered to earth, he threw away the two halves of his silver dollar but kept the poison pin in his pocket. (The Russians tried it out on a dog; it died within 90 seconds.)

These adventures were unknown to Washington. On May 3, NASA said it had lost a "weather" plane over Turkey. It was the first of five conflicting statements over seven days. On May 5, the Russians announced they had shot down a spy plane. Khrushchev tried to save the summit by blaming Pentagon "militarists," not Ike.

And the next day, the American ambassador in Moscow, Llewellyn Thompson, was allowed to overhear a Soviet diplomat at a party refer to their having "the pilot." Thompson's urgent cable arrived four minutes too late to prevent the U.S. from publishing a more elaborate version of the original lie, all based on the assumption that Powers had not lived to tell the tale.

On May 7, Khrushchev went before the Supreme Soviet to announce: "Comrades, we also have the pilot, who is quite alive and kicking." He offered Ike one more out: "I am quite willing to grant that the President knew nothing. . . ." Ike's attempt to take it—by admitting the U-2 flight but adding that it had not been authorized—did not play in Washington. Who was running the shop? Eisenhower was stung by the suggestion that he was not doing his job, so he issued yet another statement. This time he took responsibility, practically blaming the incursions on the Soviets and reserving the right to continue them. Khrushchev was beside himself. He took Thompson into a side room at a party and begged him: "This U-2 thing has put me in a terrible spot. You have got to get me off it." It was too late for Thompson or anyone else.

At the summit in Paris that May, Khrushchev walked out when Eisenhower would not apologize. The summit's collapse was a prelude to some of the grimmest years of the Cold War, and a bitter disappointment to Eisenhower. Shortly before he died, he told a friend: "I had

Above: "Just between us fellows, who was at the controls?" Ike, Secretary of State Christian Herter and CIA chief Allen Dulles, pricked by Mauldin in the *St. Louis Post-Dispatch.*

Left: Gary Powers in the defendant's box at his Moscow trial, August 1960. Sentenced to ten years in jail, he was exchanged in February 1962 for Soviet spy Rudolf Abel. He was killed in August 1977 when his helicopter crashed while he was covering a fire for KNBC-TV in Los Angeles. His last act was to guide the falling machine away from a field of boys playing baseball.

longed to give the United States and the world a lasting peace. I was able only to contribute to a stalemate." Khrushchev hung on in the Kremlin, but his prestige had been undermined. He was forced out of power in October 1964.

THE SECRET AIR WAR

This spy plane crew was shot down over the Sea of Japan on July 29, 1953. Only one (John Roche) survived.

Gary Powers was but one player in a vast secret espionage effort against the Soviet Union and China. Throughout the 1950s and 1960s thousands of airmen in a variety of planes, but notably RB reconnaissance jets, flew unarmed "ferret" missions for the Air Force, Navy and CIA, often penetrating the international three-mile limit to flush out electronic and radar defenses. They also took photographs of harbors, factories, shipyards and military bases. An incredible weakness in Soviet defense was discovered. There was no early warning radar on the northern border in the fifties and there were only spotty defenses in the sixties, a temptation to the hawks like Air Force Chief General Curtis LeMay, who horrified Eisenhower by arguing for a preemptive nuclear attack across the polar icecap. An investigation by *U.S. News & World Report* in 1993 suggests that at least 252 American airmen were shot down between 1950 and 1970; 24 lost their lives, 90 survived and 138 remain unaccounted for.

LBJ TO THE RESCUE: Kennedy makes a gesture of restraining his running mate, Lyndon Johnson, who is trying to get a nearby plane to shut down its motor. Lady Bird Johnson is in the foreground. LBJ, the disappointed rival for the nomination, saved Texas and much of the South for Kennedy. Photograph by Richard Pipes.

PRESIDENT KENNEDY, BY A HAIRSBREADTH

John Kennedy had the telegenic good looks, the dazzle of his brothers, Bobby and Teddy, the beauty and pregnancy of his wife, Jacqueline—and his father's money. "What's a hundred million," asked Joseph Kennedy, "if it will help Jack?"

Richard Nixon had the experience of high office, a Republican record of eight years of peace and prosperity and the endorsement of a superior father figure, the enormously popular Eisenhower. At least he did when Ike campaigned in the closing stages. In August, Eisenhower let him down badly. Pressed by a reporter to give an example of an idea of the vice president's that he had adopted, Ike snapped. "If you give me a week I might think of one. I don't remember." Ike thought Nixon the better candidate and apologized for the gaffe. In later years he told his editor, Sam Vaughan, that Nixon "lacked star quality."

Nixon, the perennial loner, had other political baggage. His self-pity played badly with the working press, and he made a deliberate decision to snub them. His pre-occupation with politics made him appear callously indifferent to his wife, faithfully trailing in his wake. But there was no personal scandal waiting to explode. It was Kennedy who had skeletons in his cupboard. He was a womanizer. He had won the West Virginia primary in part, according to later FBI wiretaps, because his father tapped Mafia money to bribe officials. He had falsely claimed sole authorship of the Pulitzer Prize–winning book *Profiles in Courage*. He was not as healthy as his campaign insisted he was. He had chronic bouts of venereal disease. A victim of Addison's disease, he was dependent on steroid shots. On at least four occasions he had received the last rites of the Catholic Church.

Nixon did not try to make any of these skeletons dance, at least at first. Later he hired William Casey, a World War II spy and future head of the CIA, to investigate JFK. It was probably no coincidence that someone broke into the offices of both of Kennedy's New York doctors in the fall of 1960. They might have found a great deal—if the doctors had not kept JFK's files under false names. Kennedy's biggest perceived problem was his religion. Would a believing Catholic president be loyal first to Rome or

to the Constitution of the United States? The question, evocative of the campaign that had ruined Al Smith 32 years before, was put not by Nixon but by the Rev. Norman Vincent Peale, the self-appointed pope of conservative Protestantism, speaking on behalf of 150 ministers and laypeople.

Kennedy astutely confined his response to a single powerful speech to 300 Protestant ministers in Houston on September 12, 1960. "If the time should ever come—and I do not concede any conflict to be remotely possible—when my office would require me to either violate my conscience or violate the national interest, then I would resign the office." He ticked off the names of the men who died at the Alamo: ". . . Fuertes and McCafferty and Bailey and Bedillo and Carey—but no one knows whether they were Catholics or not. For there was no religious test there."

In political philosophy there was nothing to choose between the two young men. What moved them was what won votes. Both were cold warriors, but Kennedy was more alarmist. He ran a scare campaign he knew was false on the fiction of a "missile gap" between the Soviet Union and America. Both men were committed to faster progress on civil rights. But neither had sought any deeper understanding of this war rending the country.

It was Kennedy's good fortune that on October 19 Martin Luther King, Jr., was arrested for joining an Atlanta student sit-in. After six days in jail for trespass, he was moved to reactionary De Kalb County and sentenced to four months on the state chain gang. Kennedy aide Harris Wofford had the idea that JFK should make a sympathetic phone call to Mrs. Coretta King. "What the hell," said JFK. "That's a decent thing to do." When Bobby heard the call had been made, he raged that it would cost three Southern states, but he changed his mind the next day. Without telling his brother, he called the judge himself to secure King's release. Nixon could not be persuaded to do anything. Those phone calls may have decided the election. The black vote tipped the scales in big Northern states.

Another element that may have contributed to the hairsbreadth edge was television. On Monday, September 26,

STILL TALKING: Post-debate chat. After he won, Kennedy invited himself to Key Biscayne for an hour with Nixon. Mrs. Nixon and daughter Julie berated Nixon for receiving his political enemy, provoking him to write later that "women find it much harder to lose than do men." Nixon urged his policies on JFK, who later remarked to friends: "It is just as well for all of us he didn't win."

70 million watched the first of four debates. Radio listeners, including Lyndon Johnson, scored that first duel for Nixon. On television, however, voters saw in Nixon someone they wouldn't buy a used car from. He was haggard and in pain. Just before the broadcast, he agonizingly banged a recently infected knee. He refused most makeup, limiting himself to daubing his heavy bluebeard with Lazy Shave pancake powder. On camera, journalist Teddy White wrote, "his eyes [were] exaggerated hollows of blackness, his jaws, jowls and face drooping with strain."

It proved the closest race of the century. Kennedy won by just under 119,450 votes out of more than 68.8 million cast. A switch of 4,500 votes in Illinois plus 23,500 in Texas would have elected Nixon. There is little doubt that Chicago's mayor, Richard Daley, spurred by Joe Kennedy's money, voted the graveyards in such numbers as to deny Illinois to Nixon. But Illinois was not the deciding state of folklore. Even deducting the 27 electoral votes of Illinois, Kennedy would still have had 276, or a majority out of 538. By the time Illinois's suspiciously heavy late returns came in, Michigan's voters had already made Kennedy the 35th president.

JOHN FITZGERALD KENNEDY
35th President (Democrat), 1961–1963

Caricature by Sorel.

BORN: May 29, 1917, Brookline, Massachusetts

DIED: November 22, 1963, Dallas, Texas

POLITICAL CAREER: Member, House of Representatives, from Massachusetts, 1947–1953; U.S. Senator from Massachusetts, 1953–1961; President, 1961–1963

FIRSTS: First president born in the twentieth century. First Roman Catholic elected president. First to hold televised press conferences.

CHARACTER SNAPSHOT: "He was intelligent, detached, curious, candid, not always honest, and he was careless and dangerously disorganized. He was also very impatient, addicted to excitement, living his life as if it were a race against boredom. He was a man of soaring charm who believed that one-on-one he would always prevail."

—Richard Reeves

Caricature by David Levine.

THE DYNASTY: He sprang from two families who in the middle of famine in Ireland around 1850 took the priest's blessing and the boat to Boston. In 100 years they rose from poverty to wealth, and obscurity to fame. Great-grandfather Patrick Kennedy, a cooper, was the first to arrive in 1848. He died of cholera, at 35 in 1858, on the portentous date of November 22. Grandfather P.J. got the family into the liquor trade and politics, and JFK's father, Joseph, used that as a base to build a fortune worth $250 million in banking, movies and real estate (especially the Merchandise Mart in Chicago) and unethical but legal stock market maneuvers. JFK's mother, Rose, was the daughter of John "Honey Fitz" Fitzgerald, twice mayor of Boston, a sunny character but one who let a friend go to jail for his own graft. The original Fitzgerald immigrant, Thomas, was a street fish peddler.

THE HERO: He volunteered for the patrol torpedo (PT) boats, suicidally small, lightly armed and inflammable craft, and was given command of *PT-109*. It had no radar, and unknown to JFK his lookout man was night-blind. On the pitch-black night of August 1, 1943, when *PT-109* was one of fifteen assigned to disrupt "Tokyo Express" convoys, the 2,000-ton destroyer *Amagiri* came out of the blackness and smashed into their starboard side, almost certainly unintentionally. The PT's fuel tank exploded, the crew were flung into water ablaze with gasoline. Two died. JFK hauled stragglers back to the boat's hulk. At dawn he swam ahead to a deserted island, saving a badly burned crewman by swimming for four hours with the straps of the sailor's life jacket between his teeth. His will and spirits kept the starving survivors alive for six days. He swam around to other islands looking for help, and at nights floated for hours by the coral reef holding a signal lamp. Finally his activity brought forth two natives. JFK scratched on the husk of a coconut a message they carried to rescuers: NAURO ISL. NATIVE KNOWS POSIT HE CAN PILOT 11 ALIVE NEED SMALL BOAT KENNEDY. JFK won Navy and Marine Corps medals for heroism. The survivors were devoted to him.

BOYHOOD: He was brought up in a big family where the father goaded them to compete with each other and the mother was a martinet devoted to Catholic ritual and myriad rules. He had so many illnesses his brothers joked that a mosquito took a big risk biting him. He often lay in hospital beds for weeks at a time without a visit from either parent. His father's decision to move from Boston to escape anti-Irish snobbery disrupted his schooling, but he did well at first at Riverdale Country Day School in New York. At Choate prep school he was faulted for being a prankster, and finished 64th of 112 students, but he was popular. He was voted "most likely to succeed" in an election he manipulated as a prank.

YOUNG MAN IN A HURRY: Originally an indifferent government major at Harvard (1936–1940), he was galvanized by the European crisis. He took advantage of his father's appointment as ambassador to the Court of St. James (1937–1940) to work there briefly and at the Paris embassy and to tour Europe. In Germany, he was spat on by Nazis in Nuremberg; in Munich, storm troopers, thinking he was English, hurled rocks at his car. He chased girls a lot, but by his senior year he was working night and day on an honors thesis that became a best-selling study of Britain's slowness to rearm: *Why England Slept* (1940). It quietly cast off his father's knee-jerk isolationism and hostility to all things English.

HIS FIRST CAMPAIGN: On June 17, 1946, the eve of the Democratic primary in Boston, a gaunt, sick JFK leads a parade of fellow members of a Veterans of Foreign Wars post named for his golden elder brother, Joe, who died in 1944 when his bomber blew up over England. JFK collapsed after the march. The nine other candidates for the Eleventh District House seat, which included some of the city's poorest areas, ridiculed his wealth and presumption, but he topped them with 42 percent of the vote, won the general election and was reelected twice. His father had given James Michael Curley the money to vacate the seat and run for a fourth term as mayor, but Joe's money counted less in the race than JFK's charm and energy and the help of the Kennedy women and friends from college and the Navy. He shook hands outside a shipyard, climbed endless tenement stairs, listened well to his working-class aides. In Congress, he lashed the American Legion for opposing low-cost housing and voted against the Taft-Hartley bill, but he joined the Republican attacks on Truman for "losing" China to communism.

THE SENATOR: He beat the formidable incumbent, Henry Cabot Lodge, by 70,000 votes for the Senate, bucking the national swing to the Republicans on Eisenhower's coattails. Here he is in a huddle at the 1956 Democratic convention in a bid for the vice presidential nomination: he lost to Senator Estes Kefauver. He was reelected in 1958 with a state record vote of 73.6 percent. He was pro-labor, anti-Communist—when he bothered to vote. He was in the hospital for the Senate censure of Joe McCarthy, a friend of his father and brother, and was the only Democratic senator who did not attempt to vote or pair his vote with a Republican.

JACKIE: Jacqueline L. Bouvier was a Long Island and Newport socialite from a wealthy but troubled family. Her father, "Black Jack" Bouvier, was a dapper, alcoholic Wall Street trader who separated from her mother when Jackie was 7. Jackie, 21, and Jack, 34, met at a 1951 dinner party in Washington. They were alike in their names; their peripatetic, affection-starved youth; their emotional detachment, wit, curiosity, physical beauty, poise, love of gossip. She had graduated from George Washington University after two years at Vassar and one at the Sorbonne in Paris. "It was a very spasmodic courtship," said Jackie, "conducted mainly at long distance with a great clanking of coins in dozens of phone booths." He proposed by telegram while she was in England photographing the coronation of Queen Elizabeth II for the *Washington Times-Herald*. They married on September 12, 1953. Jackie's divorced father was so drunk that her stepfather, Hugh Auchincloss, had to escort the bride down the aisle. A daughter, Caroline, was born in 1957, and a son, John, Jr., in 1960.

They seemed to have forged a genuine bond of affection, though Jackie was rattled by his intense family attachments and the realization that he had no intention of letting marriage curb his compulsive womanizing. He had affairs with many, including Marilyn Monroe and Judith Campbell (later Exner), a mistress of Mafia chief Sam Giancana. It was not uncommon at parties for Jackie to find herself abruptly alone while Jack disappeared with his latest conquest.

KENNEDY'S BLUNDER

John Kennedy took the first step to humiliation around the swimming pool at his father's winter home in Palm Beach, just 19 days after his election. On November 27, 1960, the avuncular CIA Director Allen Dulles and his deputy, Richard Bissell, laid out maps and charts on a table by the pool to brief the president-elect on Bissell's plot to bring down Fidel Castro's new Communist regime in Cuba. Eisenhower had approved Track One of Operation Pluto (later Zapata). It seemed simple. Slip in a few dozen armed Cuban exiles to stir people to revolt, then watch Castro run in terror, as Jacobo Arbenz had in Guatemala in 1954. By November, with Castro's grip more secure, Bissell had changed the plan. Infiltration had escalated to an amphibious invasion by several hundred Cubans even then being trained by the CIA on a Guatemalan banana plantation. Bissell, mastermind of the U-2 spy planes and the Guatemalan coup, called himself a "man-eating shark." He was a brainy WASP cavalier out of Groton, Yale and the London School of Economics, a daring sailor, a darling of the Georgetown salons and, in Joe Alsop's words, "a terrific dominator." The CIA men went back from Palm Beach with approval to plan an invasion. They also felt authorized to continue Track Two, the assassination of Castro. This was Bissell's idea. In the summer of 1960 he had begun trying to kill Castro and two other foreign leaders: Patrice Lumumba of the Belgian Congo and Rafael Trujillo of the Dominican Republic. Before he died in 1994 he conceded to biographer Evan Thomas that these were "bad judgments" because the demagogues were not as dangerous as he thought, but they were not, he insisted, "bad morality."

How much Eisenhower knew of these assassination plots is unclear, but there is now convincing circumstantial evidence that Kennedy knew and approved. It may have been one of the reasons he kept postponing the invasion. With Castro dead, the invaders had a better chance of the popular rising Bissell counted on.

By the time Kennedy was installed in the White House, in January 1961, Castro knew that the CIA was training an invasion force. He had only to read the American press. The Cuban exile community was talking and the CIA was careless. Kennedy's response to the leaks was not to cancel the invasion, but to mute American involvement so as to be able to deny it altogether. The CIA plan was formally presented to Kennedy, the Joint Chiefs, National Security Adviser McGeorge Bundy, Defense Secretary Robert McNamara, Secretary of State Dean Rusk and others on March 11. It envisaged landing Brigade 2506, 750 men, on the south coast of Cuba near the port of Trinidad, preceded by the destruction on the ground of Castro's air force of around 12 planes. Sixteen elderly B-26 bombers piloted by Cuban nationals were to fly about 40 sorties from Nicaragua. Kennedy objected. "It sounds like D-Day. You have to reduce the noise level of this thing." Bissell could fly only six B-26s, and Trinidad was out. Bissell's people came up with a "quieter" new site about 100 miles to the west, at the Bay of Pigs. Bissell did not remind Kennedy, flying by the seat of his pants, that this doomed the fallback plan: invaders defeated on the beach at the Bay of Pigs would have no chance of hunkering down in the mountains for a long-term Castro-style guerrilla war. Eighty miles of roadless swamps now lay across their escape route.

The decisive meeting was on April 4. To the dismay of his other top advisers, Kennedy ushered in Senator William Fulbright, the chairman of the Senate Foreign Relations Committee. Fulbright had written Kennedy a memo denouncing the hypocrisy and cynicism of the plot. Why, he asked the meeting, did they fear competition from an unshaven megalomaniac? The moralizing irritated the others. The mood was stand-up-and-be-counted. Kennedy was impatient. He had come back in a more bullish mood after an Easter with his father at Palm Beach. He did not finish going round the table for arguments. He wanted a quick yes or no. Paul Nitze had misgivings on the practicality of Zapata but suppressed them to defend the invasion as morally right. Afterward, Arthur Schlesinger, Jr., gave the President a memo opposing the invasion and was told by Robert Kennedy, "Once the President has made up his mind, we support him and we keep our mouths shut." Dean Rusk suppressed another critical memo from his under secretary, Chester Bowles. "I know," said Kennedy to Ted Sorensen, "everyone is grabbing for their nuts on this."

The invasion, as edited by Kennedy, was a disaster. On the morning of April 15, 48 hours before the landings, the six B-26 bombers managed to destroy part of Castro's air force. But Dean Rusk, concerned at the row in the United Nations, where Adlai Stevenson was unknowingly telling lies, persuaded Kennedy to veto the planned second strike timed for the landings. The CIA guerrilla trainer with the invaders was aghast. It was, he said, like "finding out that Superman is a fairy."

Castro was well prepared. There was a hot reception for the members of Brigade 2506, now numbering 1,543, when at dawn on April 17 their five rusty freighters and two landing craft, the *Rio Escondo* and the *Houston,* trolled into the Bay of Pigs. At 6:30 a.m. one of Castro's Sea Furies sank the *Houston* with a rocket. At 9:30 a.m. the *Rio Escondo* exploded. Things got worse. Castro had deployed 20,000 troops and tanks. There was no popular uprising, no place to run. The men trapped on the beach were soon begging for help. This was the moment Bissell had calculated Kennedy would do as Eisenhower had done in Guatemala—relent on American participation.

Kennedy was at a white-tie-and-tails White House reception. That afternoon he had allowed some more B-26 sorties from Nicaragua, which Bissell, defying orders, allowed Americans to fly: four died. At midnight in the Cabinet Room an emotional Bissell, supported by Admiral Arleigh Burke, Navy chief of staff, tried to convince the President and his top men that he should send in six Navy fighters to cover the B-26s on another raid. At 2 a.m.

Kennedy agreed to this direct American involvement. Then the CIA forgot that Nicaragua's time zone was one hour different from Cuba's, so the U.S. jets were still on the deck when the bombers arrived an hour "early" with no cover. Two of them were shot down.

That was it. At 2:32 a.m. the commander of Brigade 2506, Pepe San Roman, radioed his final message to his CIA handler: "I am taking to the swamps. I can't wait for you. And, you, sir, are a son of a bitch."

Kennedy was in tears the next day. Of the invaders, 114 had died and 1,189 were taken prisoner.

In December 1962 he paid a ransom of $53 million in food and medical supplies for their release. He shook up the CIA. "If this were the British parliamentary government, I would resign and you, being a civil servant, would remain," he told Bissell. "But in our government, you and Allen [Dulles] have to go and I have to remain."

THE TARGET: CIA plots to remove Castro, begun in Eisenhower's presidency, included an exploding cigar, a poison pen and the Bay of Pigs invasion. But Castro, born August 13, 1926, to a middle-class plantation owner, was still in power 39 years after deposing Fulgencio Batista's "brutal, bloody and despotic dictatorship"—the words of John Kennedy (caricature, opposite) in 1960.

DAREDEVIL: Bissell at Berlin's Checkpoint Charlie. He knew how to appeal to Kennedy's anti-Communist virility and his fascination with James Bond derring-do.

THE NUCLEAR BLUFFING GAME

Chill winds rattled the windowpanes. Rain lashed the garden. The prospect outside the American residence in Vienna was as bleak on the Saturday morning of June 3, 1961, as it was inside the music room, where President Kennedy and Chairman Khrushchev tried to take each other's mettle at their first and only summit. Kennedy hoped to relax tensions. Khrushchev turned it into a showdown.

The transcripts, released only in 1990, show Kennedy losing control in dialectical turbulence. Khrushchev demolished his opening appeal that for the sake of peace the two great nuclear powers should agree not to upset the complex balances of power around the world. The Soviet Union could not and would not stop people choosing communism if they wanted. It would support wars of national revolution. Kennedy, he taunted, was trying to stop the spread of ideas. The Spanish Inquisition burned people who disagreed with it, but the ideas did not burn. Once the United States was a leader in the fight for freedom. Now it was on the wrong side of history, opposing the will of the people, the sponsor of dictators and the colonial powers. Kennedy's protests were swept aside. In the varied judgment of his advisers he was "shattered" (Averell Harriman); "tongue-tied" (George Kennan); "out of his depth" (Charles Bohlen). All JFK was doing, said Paul Nitze, was "dancing." Kennedy was pale and dazed when he came out of the music room. He paced the floor of his room at the residence, cursing Khrushchev. "He treated me like a little boy."

The crunch came next day over what Khrushchev called "the bone in my throat": Berlin. West Berlin, surrounded on all sides by the Soviet-controlled German Democratic Republic (GDR), was the back door to the West by which 2.5 million East Germans had fled the Communist paradise since 1945. Khrushchev wanted West Berlin and insisted he was going to get it by signing a peace treaty with the GDR no later than December. That would end the Russian nightmare of a united, rearmed Germany. It would also end the West's rights of access and close the Berlin door. Faced with this direct threat, Kennedy stuck out his jaw. He was more

uncompromising than Eisenhower had been. He would not deal on Berlin. It was "out of the question" to give East Germany power over Allied access. Khrushchev slammed his hand on the table. "I want peace. But if you want war that is your problem." Signing the treaty in December was irrevocable. "If that is true," Kennedy said coolly, "then, Mr. Chairman, there will be war. It will be a cold winter." The Berlin crisis had begun.

That hot, frightening summer the two men played atomic chicken. Khrushchev invited the British ambassador to his box at the Bolshoi to tell him six Soviet hydrogen bombs would take care of Britain. Kennedy

called the nation to arms on July 25: "I hear it said that West Berlin is militarily untenable. And so was Bastogne. And so, in fact, was Stalingrad. Any dangerous spot is tenable if men—brave men—will make it so." Attorney General Robert Kennedy used a Soviet secret agent, Georgi Bolshakov, to get the word back to Khrushchev that the death-before-surrender talk was real. Treachery helped. There was a Soviet spy in the Joint Chiefs, U.S. Army Lieutenant William H. Whalen. His reports persuaded Khrushchev of JFK's increasingly grim determination. But unknown to the American people JFK was at the same time giving Khrushchev an escape route.

LEFT TO DIE: East German Peter Fechter, aged 18, was shot in the stomach making a dash to escape on August 17, 1962. The White House ordered a patrol to the scene, but not to cross the border. As Fechter bled to death, hundreds of West Berliners shouted that the East Berliners were murderers and the Americans cowards.

Between 1961 and the fall of the wall in 1989 there were 1,700 shooting incidents. At least 600 people died.

THE WALL: President Kennedy knew it was coming. "There's not a damn thing we can do about it," he said to Walt Rostow in August 1961, a few days before Khrushchev told the East Germans they could build a barrier at the border—"but not a millimeter more." Barbed wire was followed by concrete—102 miles of it, with 189 watchtowers. The USSR called it the Anti-Fascist Protective Rampart. It turned out to be a perfect propaganda target for the West.

JFK was raising his fist over "West Berlin," not "Berlin." The language was a signal to Moscow: Kennedy would tolerate East Berlin's being sealed off from West Berlin. "East Germany is hemorrhaging to death," he told Walt Rostow. "The entire East bloc is in danger. He has to do something to stop this. Perhaps a wall." When Senators William Fulbright and Mike Mansfield publicly floated the idea of closing the border in Berlin, Kennedy did not disavow them. A Ralph Kramden situation developed: Kennedy knew that Khrushchev knew that Kennedy knew that a sealed border was a live option—and Khrushchev knew it.

At 1 a.m. on August 13, 1961, 50,000 East German police surrounded West Berlin and began laying barbed wire. Kennedy kept silent himself for eight days. Khrushchev withdrew the ultimatum for a peace treaty. The road from West Germany stayed open. "A wall," Kennedy said privately, "is a hell of a lot better than a war."

The tensions were relaxed, not ended. In October, Soviet and ten U.S. tanks faced each other from 30 yards away at Berlin's Checkpoint Charlie in a test of nerves, the only confrontation of its kind in the Cold War. Through his brother Robert, Kennedy sent a message to Khrushchev: Pull back your tanks in the next 24 hours and mine will be gone 30 minutes later. It worked. The crisis began over the right of an American diplomat to attend the opera in East Berlin—another reminder of how mindlessly Cold War flashpoints could be rekindled.

THE LAST DAYS OF DIEM

In the third year of his presidency Kennedy gave the nod that doomed Ngo Dinh Diem, the leader of South Vietnam. A despotic mandarin in a sharkskin suit, Diem had been installed as president in 1954 by the CIA's legendary Edward Lansdale, the prototype for "Colonel Hillandale," the missionary of American democracy in *The Ugly American* by William J. Lederer and Eugene Burdick. It was Lansdale's protégé, Colonel Lucien Conein, a burly French-born adventurer raised in Kansas City, who conspired with rebel generals to get rid of Diem in 1963. He was the link between the buccaneering new American ambassador, Henry Cabot Lodge, Jr., and the plotters led by Major General Duong Van Minh—Big Minh, as he was called.

Diem had been a disaster. A celibate bachelor, he had come to live a fantasy life in Norodum palace, separated from the people, in the words of Graham Greene, by "cardinals and police cars with wailing sirens." Meanwhile his country was terrorized by his younger brother, Ngo Dinh Nhu, who was a heavy opium smoker, and Nhu's venomous wife, a lacquered beauty in skintight silks dubbed the Dragon Lady. They were all anti-Communist, but they were better at molesting the majority Buddhists than the Communist guerrillas in the countryside.

Kennedy wavered in the summer weeks when he heard that the generals were ready to depose Diem and Nhu provided they had U.S. support. He gave the first go-ahead over a holiday weekend in a cable of August 24. This angered those advisers who believed, in reporter Homer Bigart's doggerel, "we have to sink or swim with Ngo Dinh Diem." Kennedy's military adviser, General Maxwell Taylor, and his man on the spot, General Paul Harkins, regarded Diem as the best of the bunch in Saigon. Lodge in Saigon and Averell Harriman in Washington pressed the campaign for a coup and won. Kennedy wanted to be sure a coup would succeed—and that it could not be traced back to him. From October 29 on, he insisted on vetting every word between Washington and Saigon. It was to be a coup run from the White House, not the CIA.

On November 1, a heavily armed Lucien Conein was in the rebel headquarters near Tan Son Nhut airport, with $42,000 in contingency escape money for the generals. He had a special CIA radio telephone to send the White House a running commentary in "flash" messages (messages "essential to national survival"). The coup began at 1:30 p.m. Three hours later the beleaguered Diem phoned Lodge from the palace to find out the U.S. attitude. Lodge told him: "If there is anything I can do for your physical safety, please call me." The next morning the brothers were seized at a church in Cholon. On their way to Saigon in an armored personnel carrier they were shot and bayoneted; Madame Nhu was in America and survived.

All the observers agree Kennedy blanched and rushed out of the room at the news. He had secretly sent his friend Torbert MacDonald to Saigon to say: "They're going to kill you. You've got to get out of there temporarily to seek sanctuary in the American embassy and you must get rid of your sister-in-law and your brother." Diem did not listen. JFK could have made saving Diem's life a condition of the coup, but he did not. Lodge at the time was more ebullient. "What would we have done with them if they had lived?" he said to David Halberstam. "Every Colonel Blimp in the world would have made use of them." Within the next 20 months, Diem's death did not bring stability. There were more coups and more elaborate efforts to cover up America's responsibility.

THE FIRST MARTYR: The AP's Malcolm Browne took the shattering photograph of Thich Quang Duc. The 73-year-old monk immolated himself on June 11, 1963, in protest at the persecution of Buddhism, the preeminent religion in South Vietnam. Four more monks burned themselves. Madame Nhu's response: "I clap my hands when they barbecue a *bonze*." On November 2, 1965, Norman R. Morrison, an American Quaker, burned himself to death within 40 feet of Defense Secretary Robert McNamara's Pentagon window.

REPORTERS UNDER SIEGE

Early in Vietnam, when America first planted its foot in the quagmire, a handful of print reporters, mostly in their twenties, wrote what they saw: The "nice little war" against the Vietcong guerrillas was going badly, America was supporting an unpopular and brutal regime and the U.S. military brass was allowing itself to be deluded and in turn deluding Washington. The reporters were not "antiwar." They were as keen as anyone to save South Vietnam from the Communists; they loved the country. They were just appalled by the official lies being fed to the American people. For this they were denounced by their own government as Communists and traitors,

RIVALS FOR TRUTH: David Halberstam, *New York Times;* Malcolm Browne, Associated Press; and Neil Sheehan, UPI, between lifts in the Mekong Delta in 1963.

menaced and beaten by Diem's thugs and often harassed by their own skeptical offices in New York, as William Prochnau vividly documents in *Once Upon a Distant War* (1995). Kennedy was most furious with David Halberstam, the abrasive, relentlessly probing 28-year-old *New York Times* man. In October 1963, at his first meeting with publisher Arthur O. (Punch) Sulzberger, Kennedy made it clear he would be happy if Sulzberger replaced Halberstam. At *Time* magazine, managing editor Otto Fuerbringer, the "Iron Chancellor," routinely had Charley Mohr's dispatches rewritten, often reversing the meaning so as to fit the official line.

BETRAYED: South Vietnam's president Ngo Dinh Diem (left) reviews a parade on October 26, 1963, his eighth anniversary in power. He has only days to live, and the uniformed man behind him on the right, General Duong Van Minh, will order his execution and take power himself. Two weeks after that, Kennedy would be dead, too.

FEELING THE HEAT: Henry Cabot Lodge, Jr. (left), was Kennedy's opponent for the Senate in 1952, and ran against him on Nixon's ticket in 1960, but he accepted Kennedy's call to serve as ambassador in 1963. McNamara admired his bipartisan spirit but found him "patrician and self-confident to the point of arrogance."

THE OPTIMIST: After visiting Vietnam in January 1963, Army chief of staff General Earle G. "Bus" Wheeler returned to Washington imbued with the false optimism of his companion, General Paul D. Harkins (right), commander of U.S. Military Assistance Command. Harkins was a protégé of General George Patton, but he stayed remote from the battlegrounds, preferring to see Vietnam from the air. He was happiest totaling body counts fictitiously reported from the field for McNamara's computers.

PALS: Khrushchev and Castro leaving the Hotel Theresa in Harlem, September 21, 1960, after they both attended a session of the U.N.

EXPOSING THE SOVIET DECEPTION

The countdown that took the world close to nuclear destruction began on Monday, October 15, 1962, in a squalid downtown building at 5th and K streets in Washington, D.C. The CIA's Arthur Lundahl had taken good care to mask the activities of his National Photographic Interpretation Center; they were on the fourth to seventh floors over a car dealership, and that morning he was put out when the efforts to disguise the importance of the building were nullified by a commotion in 5th Street: armed Marines were guarding a double-parked U.S. Navy truck, holding up traffic, as an armed Navy officer and an enlisted man carried a box into the building.

The box held eight cans of film, the fruits of a flight 13 miles high over Cuba by U-2 pilot Major Richard S. Heyser. Around 10 a.m., six photo analysts in three teams of two apiece began to examine the hundreds of frames in Heyser's haul.

Throughout August the new CIA director, John McCone, had aired his anxieties that Khrushchev was installing nuclear missiles in Cuba. He had no direct evidence. Defense Secretary Robert McNamara and Secretary of State Dean Rusk were skeptical. President Kennedy, too, was unconvinced, though on August 23 he had ordered contingency planning. A week later Soviet surface-to-air missile batteries (SAMs) were spotted in Cuba, but four full photo mosaics of the island had failed to confirm McCone's suspicions of surface-to-surface missiles and McCone, in an angry confrontation, had been unable to elicit the source of Senator Kenneth Keating's sensational statement in the Senate on August 31 that there were "rocket installations" in Cuba.

That October morning Gene Lydon, a CIA interpreter, and Jim Holmes, an Air Force interpreter, spotted more military vehicles and tents in the Sierra del Rosario mountains near the town of Los Palacios. It looked just like another part of the surface-to-air missile defense system. Lydon and Holmes looked hard for the usual SA-2 radar set and launchers. They

could not find them. What they did detect around noon were six objects, covered in canvas, that seemed twice the length of a SAM. In the afternoon, the missile back-up team pored over the photography. The CIA team leader, Vince diRenzo, called in missile specialists Dino A. Brugioni and Jay Quantrill and they flipped through their black book containing hundreds of photographs taken at Moscow parades. DiRenzo stopped in the SS-4 book: "That sure looks like it." The SS-4 was a medium-range ballistic missile (MRBM); one of them with a nuclear warhead could obliterate New York. Near 5:30 p.m., Lundahl turned to each man and asked solemnly if he, personally, agreed with the group analysis. Then he called Ray Cline, the CIA's deputy director for intelligence. "You know," said Cline, "all the shit is going to hit the fan when you tell him that."

"Him" was Kennedy. As the congressional elections approached, he had been under ferocious attack from the Republicans for "doing nothing" about Cuba. After the Bay of Pigs fiasco, Kennedy had embargoed trade with Cuba and engineered its exclusion from the Organization of American States (only Mexico dissenting). But these were only the diplomatic front teeth of a mordant obsession. JFK put his brother Bobby in charge of removing Castro and his government. "All else is secondary. No time, money, effort or manpower is to be spared," Bobby told Richard Helms, the CIA's deputy director for plans. The result was Operation Mongoose, directed from Washington by RFK and General Edward Lansdale, one of the most vicious—and ludicrous—operations in CIA history. Its Task Force "W," run from the University of Miami campus, had 300–400 American operatives and anywhere from 2,000 to 12,000 Cubans. By parachute and boat, they sneaked into Cuba to contaminate sugar fields and damage oil refineries and copper mines. They exploded bombs in department stores and set factories on fire. JFK asked for plans "to deliberately seek to provoke a full-scale revolt against Castro that might require U.S. intervention to succeed." Lansdale's original Mongoose timetable scheduled an invasion by October backed by the U.S. military.

These were the circumstances, not divulged during the crisis, that in May–August 1962 led Castro to accept Khrushchev's offer of Soviet-controlled missiles.

On September 4, the day he released the news about the SAM batteries, Kennedy warned that "the gravest issues would arise" if offensive surface-to-surface missiles were installed. This happened to be the day Anatoly Dobrynin, the Soviet ambassador, passed on a message from Khrushchev: No surface-to-surface or "offensive" weapons would be placed in Cuba. Dobrynin was being used as a stooge. On September 8 the Soviet freighter *Omsk* slipped into Havana and unloaded the first cargo of MRBMs under cover of darkness. Atomic warheads for 20 missiles arrived at Mariel on October 4.

Khrushchev had an old Bolshevik's romantic wish to defend Castro's revolution, but he had a strategic motive, too, for his dangerous adventure. Kennedy had unwittingly ignited it. Contrary to his 1960 campaign, the only missile gap was one favorable to the U.S. It had at least a 4:1 missile advantage and in warheads an overwhelming lead of approximately 17:1—more than 5,000 warheads

to around 300. In 1961–62 Kennedy decided to make a point of this superiority in the hope it might make Khrushchev more amenable to reducing the tensions of the Cold War. Kennedy and his team went about this educational task with the sympathy and tact of *Oliver Twist*'s Beadle. The nadir of a clumsily menacing campaign was JFK's article in the *Saturday Evening Post* of March 31, 1962, where, referring to the use of atomic weapons in a European war, he stated that "in some circumstances we might have to take the initiative." Khrushchev read this as a U.S. claim to be "entitled to strike the first atomic blow." In June McNamara inflamed the fears by saying that in a war "military" targets, not cities, would be the major objectives. It was simply not feasible to contain thermonuclear war this way, and to the Soviets it sounded all the more like a screen for a first strike: with a 17:1 superiority any even exchange against "military" targets would leave the USSR all but disarmed against several thousand U.S. warheads. As historian Michael Beschloss argues, Kennedy had almost no understanding of the extent to which he had made Khrushchev feel trapped and deeply insecure. When the Soviet leader went to relax at his dacha on the Black Sea, he could never forget that newly installed U.S. nuclear missiles were minutes away across the water in Turkey. Far from being chastened by Kennedy's cam-

paign, Khrushchev felt impelled to look around for a quick and painless way to redress the balance.

Kennedy did not learn of Khrushchev's missiles the day they were discovered. The next morning, Tuesday, October 16, he was eating breakfast from a tray in his room, still dressed in his nightshirt and slippers, when National Security Adviser McGeorge Bundy gave him the news at 8:45 a.m. Bundy had decided that a quiet evening and a night of sleep were the best preparation for what the President would face in the next few days.

One of the reconnaissance photographs that brought on the crisis.

EYEBALL TO EYEBALL

Three hours after Bundy walked into Kennedy's bedroom on Tuesday, October 16, with the damning Cuban missile photographs, 14 men who would hold the fate of the world in their hands began assembling in the Cabinet Room. George Washington looked down on them, in a portrait by Gilbert Stuart, and microphones secretly placed behind the curtains by Kennedy recorded most of what they said, on the presumption there was going to be a posterity. The men were the core of an ad hoc executive committee of the National Security Council, ever after known as the "ExCom"; others were brought in on occasion over the 13 days of continual, free-wheeling, ultrasecret, deliberations.

ExCom grappled with chilling uncertainties. Sixteen missiles had been identified, but there was "no evidence whatsoever" of nuclear warheads. Were nukes on the way in Soviet ships? How long would it be before the missiles were operational? And what was Khrushchev up to? Was he simply trying to redress the strategic balance? Or was he playing a hot game of nuclear chess, plotting to convert his Cuban pawn into a queen he would then swap for the white queen of Berlin? Would the U.S. be risking a ground counterattack in Europe or possibly nuclear war if it killed Russians—and how many?—in a preemptive air strike against the bases in Cuba?

The odds were worse than ExCom knew. In 1989 Russian participants in a seminar in Moscow testified that 20 nuclear warheads were already in Cuba in October 1962, with 21 rockets. Another 20 warheads and missiles were aboard ships heading for Cuba. And there were 42,000 Soviet soldiers and airmen, four times as many as the CIA estimated, with tactical nuclear weapons. The SS-4 warheads were never mated with the rockets, but it was not merely bombast when Khrushchev wrote in his 1970 memoir, "We had installed enough missiles already to destroy New York, Chicago, and the other huge industrial cities, not to mention a little village like Washington." An immediate surprise air attack on Cuba was urged on JFK by the military, supported by Secretary of State Dean Rusk, National Security

Adviser McGeorge Bundy, the CIA's McCone and, most vociferously, Dean Acheson. Bobby Kennedy scribbled a note to his brother: "I now know how Tojo felt when he was planning Pearl Harbor." Bobby took an early stand against bombing. He backed an alternative first move advocated by Defense Secretary Robert McNamara: a blockade of Soviet ships carrying missiles or warheads to Cuba. The idea was lobbied back and forth until the afternoon of Saturday, October 20, when Kennedy ruled that the first response would be the "quarantining" of Cuba, which he would announce on Monday, October 22, at 7 p.m.

Even as Kennedy spoke to the nation, U.S. forces around the world raised their alert level from the normal Defense Condition (DefCon) 5 to DefCon 3, DefCon 1 being reserved for full-scale war. Some 54 Strategic Air Command bombers, each carrying as many as 4 thermonuclear bombs, scrambled into the air, quadrupling the permanent picket line of 12. Polaris submarines put to sea. Some 579 warplanes went on standby to pound the missile bases. The Navy was ready to land 100,000 GIs and 40,000 Marines. And 156 intercontinental missiles were armed for launching against the Soviet Union.

When the quarantine began at 10 a.m. on Wednesday, nerves were taut in ExCom as two Soviet ships approached the line. McNamara reported that a submarine had joined them. Washington signaled the USS *Essex* to order the sub to surface. If it didn't, the *Essex* was to force it up with depth charges. ExCom waited. The President held one hand over his mouth, the other opening and closing into a fist. He and his brother stared across the table at each other, and Bobby remembered that his thoughts were affectionate, almost nostalgic. "It was almost as though no one else was there, and he was no longer the president. . . . I thought of when he was ill and almost died; when he lost his child; when we learned that our oldest brother had been killed. . . ."

At 10:25 a.m. a courier gave McCone a message. "Mr. President," McCone announced, "we have a preliminary report which seems to indicate that some of the Russian ships have stopped dead in the water." The Soviet submarine had surfaced. One by one the 23 freighters stopped or turned away. This was the

Kennedy and McNamara at the White House, October 29. Both men worried that the military was trigger-happy. Even when the crisis was resolved, Air Force General Curtis LeMay wanted to "go in and make a strike anyway." McNamara had a blazing row in the Navy's command center with Admiral George Anderson, chief of naval operations. He began questioning Anderson's orders for the ships at sea and was briskly told, "This is none of your goddamn business, Mr. Secretary." McNamara retorted: "You're not to fire a single shot at anything without my express permission, is that clear?"

moment Dean Rusk exulted quietly to Bundy: "We're eyeball to eyeball and I think the other fellow just blinked."

He had, but danger remained. Work on the missile sites seemed to be speeding up. That same Wednesday the Joint Chiefs ordered SAC to go to DefCon 2; on his own, its hawkish commander, General Thomas Power, transmitted the order in the open so that the Soviets could pick it up. The Joint Chiefs pressed for an invasion no later than Monday morning. That seemed inescapable, but for three hours from 6 p.m. on Friday evening State began to take agonizingly slow receipt of a long and emotional letter from Khrushchev. If the U.S. promised not to invade Cuba, he concluded, "the necessity of the presence of our military specialists in Cuba will disappear." The letter had taken 12 hours to come from the U.S. embassy in Moscow, transmitted by commercial cable, the same way Soviet ambassador Dobrynin sent his messages from Washington. "Usually," writes Dobrynin in his memoir, "it was the same young black man who came to the embassy on his bicycle. We could only pray that he would take it to the Western Union office without delay and not stop to chat on the way with some girl!" It seems likely that if Kennedy had received Khrushchev's letter promptly, he would have accepted it. Instead the crisis went racing on into its final roller-coaster weekend.

Khrushchev spent Saturday morning the 27th in a Kremlin briefing led by his defense minister, Marshal Rodion Malinovsky. At least as painted in his memoirs, Krushchev had a rough time with his military. He warned that holding fast might result in the death of 500 million human beings. "They looked at me as though I was out of my mind, or what was worse, a traitor." The pressure on Khrushchev showed up, to Washington's confusion, on Saturday in a second, tougher message from him with the extra demand for removing U.S. missiles from Turkey.

To most of ExCom, in session all day, this was unacceptable. They did not know that the Kennedy brothers had already intimated that they were ready to trade. Robert Kennedy had let Dobrynin know this in one of a series of clandestine meetings. He had been sneaking into the Soviet embassy between 1 a.m. and 3 a.m.; Mrs. Dobrynin left them a coffee tray. All Saturday, ExCom debated what to do about the two letters. It was Bobby who came up with the ploy of accepting the offer in the

One hour before Kennedy speaks to the nation on October 22, Soviet Ambassador Dobrynin (in glasses, center) arrives at the State Department for a copy of the speech. Dean Rusk said later: "He aged ten years right in front of my eyes." This was the day the Soviets arrested Colonel Oleg Penkovsky for spying for the U.S. and Britain. In his last message, Penkovsky had warned his CIA handlers a Soviet nuclear attack was imminent—a false and monstrous incitement.

first letter and ignoring the second. At 8:05 p.m. JFK publicly agreed not to invade Cuba, but made no mention of missiles in Turkey. That was left to his brother to convey late that night, when Dobrynin sneaked into the Justice Department.

Bobby told him that if Russia removed its missiles, the U.S. would pull its own missiles from Turkey—provided all this was kept secret. They must have an explicit answer the next day; otherwise, military action would begin against Cuba.

JFK stayed up late watching Audrey Hepburn in *Roman Holiday*. He had a happy awakening. At 9 a.m. Sunday, Radio Moscow announced the dismantling and crating of the missiles: it was the first time the Russian people had heard about them. By the end of the year they had all gone, to Castro's fury.

Khrushchev's willingness to accept a private promise on the Turkish missiles made the deal look more one-sided than it was. Both he and Kennedy showed restraint. Khrushchev did not react when at the height of the crisis a U-2 strayed over Soviet air space, nor when the U.S. test-fired a missile over the Pacific, reckless and potentially catastrophic provocations by a U.S. military command eager for war. Kennedy did not retaliate when a U-2 was shot down over Cuba and the pilot killed. But the big question remains the one put by Walter Lippmann at the time and most stingingly by Garry Wills in 1982 (*The Kennedy Imprisonment*): Why did Kennedy risk everything on Khrushchev's willingness to suffer a public humiliation? The answer of Wills is "macho appearance, not true security." He calls it "surely the most

reckless American act since the end of World War II." Histories of the crisis have stressed the semijudicial calmness of the way ExCom examined all the options, but peaceful diplomacy, open or private, was never discussed. Ambassador Adlai Stevenson exposed Soviet hypocrisy brilliantly at the U.N., but Kennedy resented his persistent advocacy of diplomacy and of a trade for the obsolete U.S. missiles in Turkey—even though, before the crisis, JFK himself had asked for their removal.

Kennedy turned aside from an opening for personal diplomacy when Soviet Foreign Minister Andrei Gromyko arrived in the Oval Office for a previously scheduled meeting on the afternoon of October 18. Bundy says Kennedy kept quiet for fear Khrushchev would rush to the U.N. to defend what he had done. But what Khrushchev had done was provocative and seen to be so by world opinion. Kennedy could have said to Gromyko: "Tell your chairman I am giving him 48 hours to begin pulling out the missiles. If he does, we will say nothing and in a few months we will pull our missiles out of Turkey. If he does not accept this trade, I reserve our freedom to act. And if this offer becomes public I will invade Cuba at once."

The history of the JFK-Khrushchev relationship gives no certainty that such a private ultimatum would have worked. The certainty is there were too many gambles all round. In three post–Cold War international inquests, American, Cuban and Russian participants all agreed that the judgments on all sides were distorted by misinformation, misconception and mistrust.

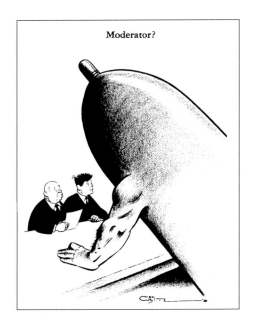

Moderator?

KENNEDY'S "SHAFT OF LIGHT"

One drizzling day in 1961, as Kennedy looked out of his office window, his science adviser Jerome Wiesner reminded him that the rain was washing radioactive debris from the clouds to earth. "You mean that stuff is in the rain out there?" said Kennedy grimly. There was, Arthur Schlesinger, Jr., writes, a deep sadness on his face and it was several minutes before he spoke again: "We test and then they test and we have to test again. And you build up until somebody uses them."

America and Russia had conducted no nuclear tests in the atmosphere since Khrushchev announced a cessation in March 1958 and Eisenhower followed in October. But the truce was shaky. Talks at Geneva to convert the moratorium into a binding treaty had deadlocked. The Russians rejected American insistence that both parties should admit 20 inspection teams a year to verify that seismic disturbances did not represent secret underground testing. And Eisenhower, under pressure from the military, had announced on December 29, 1959, that the U.S. no longer considered itself bound by the moratorium. Kennedy, under similar pressure in 1961, hoped that at the Vienna summit in June he could push Khrushchev closer to a treaty. Playing on Soviet anxieties about China, he stressed that without a ban there might in a few years be 10 or 15 nuclear powers. All he got from Khrushchev was a glum promise: "We will never be the first to break the moratorium. You will break it, and that will force us to resume testing."

Khrushchev's "never" turned out to be three months. On August 30, with the Berlin crisis on the boil, he announced that Russia would conduct one atmospheric test every two days for the next two months, yielding more megatons of explosive power than in all their previous tests combined. And more radioactive debris. It was a terrible contamination that incensed the creator of the Soviet hydrogen bomb, Andrei Sakharov. In his 1992 memoir he says that by 1961 he had calculated that the radiation from every one-megaton test cost ten thousand human lives. He protested the end of the moratorium. Khrushchev denounced him in front of a group of atomic scientists and party officials, shouting that the Americans had conducted many more tests.

Kennedy responded immediately to the new Soviet tests by joining with British Prime Minister Harold Macmillan to offer a ban on atmospheric tests. Khrushchev's answer was a 30-megaton bomb on October 23 and one of at least 50 megatons on October 16—2,500 times larger than the Hiroshima bomb. Kennedy held off renewed American testing until April 1962. None of the tests exceeded 20 megatons, in all one tenth of the yield of the Soviet detonations. They were over by November 1962. In the spring of 1963, Kennedy and Macmillan tried again for a comprehensive ban. Kennedy surpassed him-

POLARIS: A month after having the Limited Test-Ban Treaty ratified, Kennedy watches an unarmed Polaris test-fired from a submarine off Cape Canaveral. It could travel 1,700 miles in less than 30 minutes.

self. On June 10, 1963, he made what Khrushchev was to describe as "the best speech by any president since Roosevelt." JFK broke free of Cold War rhetoric to repudiate the nuclear arms race. Americans detested communism, but they should think of the Soviet people in a friendly spirit, appreciate their unique sacrifices in World War II and reflect how both communities might live in mutual tolerance. On "this small planet, we all breathe the same air. We all cherish our children's future. And we are all mortal." When a single nuclear weapon contained almost ten times the explosive force delivered by all the Allied air forces in the Second World War, peace was "the necessary rational end of rational men." And then Kennedy made a pledge: America would explode no more nuclear weapons in the atmosphere "so long as other states do not do so."

It was an inspiring overture for test-ban talks that began in Moscow on July 15. Averell Harriman, Kennedy's imaginative negotiator, impressed the Russians by clearing points immediately with a telephone call from Spirindonovka Palace to the President in the White House. On July 25, Harriman for the U.S., Andrei Gromyko for the USSR, and Lord Hailsham for Britain, initialed a treaty banning tests of nuclear weapons in the atmosphere, outer space and underwater. Within two years 90 nations, excluding France and China, had taken the pledge. Banning underground tests—which can leak radioactivity into the atmosphere—fell foul of the argument on inspections. In December 1962 Khrushchev had offered three a year, the West had come down to eight, and then Khrushchev's hard-liners had forced him to withdraw inspections altogether. Given the improved seismic techniques, the December 1962 offer was a missed opportunity.

Kennedy threw himself into the campaign to get the two-thirds Senate majority for ratification over the objections of Senator Barry Goldwater, the CIA's John McCone, Edward Teller and sections of the military. On September 24 he had a margin of 14 for consent, 80 votes to 19.

The Test-Ban Treaty was limited—underground testing was in fact expanded—but the ban was, as Kennedy put it, "a shaft of light cut into the darkness."

Three students from all-black Tougaloo College risked sitting down at a Woolworth's lunch counter in Jackson, Mississippi, on May 28, 1961. Memphis Norman is not in the picture because while police watched he was knocked to the floor by a former police officer named Benny Oliver and kicked in the head. The unconscious Norman was then dragged off to jail, accused of disorderly conduct. The two black women—Pearlene Lewis and Ann Moody—were joined at the counter by two white activists, in the foreground—John Salter and Joan Trumpauer. The older man at left is the vicious racist and local bootlegger G. W. "Red" Hydrick, who two months earlier had pistol-whipped both Medgar Evers and a black photographer in front of the police.

SIT-INS SHAKE THE SOUTH

Customers in the downtown Woolworth's in Greensboro, North Carolina, could not believe what they were seeing at 4:30 p.m. on Monday, February 1, 1960. Four young black men were taking seats at a lunch counter where blacks had never sat before. A black worker behind the counter was aghast. "Fellows like you," she said, "make our race look bad." The young men were only 18, freshmen from North Carolina Agricultural and Technical College named Ezell Blair, Jr., Franklin McCain, David Richmond and Joseph McNeil. They had been moved by the youngsters of Little Rock, and they had talked over what they themselves might do with a local white clothing merchant, Ralph Johns, a flamboyant son of Syrian immigrants with a passion for integration. They had no program, or the backing of any organization, and sit-ins during the fifties in 16 Southern and border cities had fizzled, but the

Greensboro four created a shock wave that, as Taylor Branch put it, "helped define the new decade." The hydra-headed civil rights movement was taking another sudden, daring and completely unanticipated jump into the unknown. With the movement's early legal momentum stalled, its official boycott tactic at a standstill, there now erupted almost spontaneous street challenges to the iceberg of white supremacy.

Ezell Blair, Jr., did not get the cup of coffee he asked for. "We don't serve Negroes," the white waitress told them, and they were still sitting unserved when the store closed. The next morning 23 male and female students showed up at the lunch counter. They brought their textbooks for the long, strange wait, and they sat in shifts to avoid missing classes. Before the week had passed more than 400 students were taking part. The sit-in

protests spread to shopping centers, drugstores and drive-ins, then around the state to Raleigh, Durham, Winston-Salem, High Point. By the end of the month thousands of mainly black students in seven states and 31 communities were engaged; there were read-ins at public libraries, stand-ins at theaters, paint-ins at public art galleries, wade-ins at segregated public beaches, kneel-ins at white churches.

The most significant reaction was in Nashville, Tennessee, like Greensboro a center of black education. The Nashville students had been training in workshops on nonviolent protest set up by an affiliate of Martin Luther King's Southern Christian Leadership Conference (SCLC) and run by a black theology student at Vanderbilt, James Lawson, and the white Rev. Glenn E. Smiley. Lawson, a 30-year-old disciple of King, was the son of a Northern Methodist minister. He had gone to prison during the Korean war as a conscientious objector, and then taken himself to India to study the methods of Mahatma Gandhi. Lawson thought the Nashville students needed more training, but a mass meeting on Friday, February 5, brimmed over with eagerness to move. On Saturday, 500 polite, well-dressed students began the Nashville sit-ins. In Woolworth's on February 27 a group of white hoodlums yelling "Nigger" and "chicken" pressed lighted cigarettes on the backs and in the hair of the sitters, singling out women. The police arrested the victims. Vanderbilt expelled Lawson—and then backed down when 400 teachers threatened to resign.

The climax came in mid-April. Racists blew up the home of Alexander Looby, a black city councilman and attorney. Four thousand outraged residents, black and white, marched spontaneously to City Hall. Mayor Ben West, who had been trying to find a compromise, came out to meet them. "We are all Christians together. Let us pray together," said West. A student called out: "How about eating together?" Then another student, Diane Nash, a midwesterner who was 22 years old, was inspired to ask a simple question: Did he as a human being feel it was wrong to discriminate against anyone solely on the basis of race or color? "Well, in my heart," said Mayor West, "I have to say that I think it is wrong. . . . I appeal to all citizens to end discrimination, to have no bigotry, no bias, no hatred." It was at the time an amazing statement for a white public official to make.

Mayor West years later said it was a question he had to answer "as a man and not a politician." The marchers broke into cheers. Lunch counters were desegregated three weeks later. Theaters, hotels and restaurants followed.

Many of the older civil rights campaigners feared that the sit-in movement was too provocative. But Martin Luther King, the most prominent embodiment of black protest in America, backed the students. It was at a conference called by his SCLC in August that the various student groups came together to form the Student Nonviolent Coordinating Committee (SNCC). SNCC provided the shock troops for the movement over the next five years, and they were inspired by a speech from the SCLC's "very regal" executive director, Ella Baker, a woman who had devoted her whole life to civil rights even when the cause seemed hopeless. The movement, she said, had to produce "more than a hamburger."

STANDING IN THE SCHOOLHOUSE DOOR: Alabama Governor George Wallace vowed at his inauguration, "Segregation now—segregation tomorrow—segregation forever!" He played the same charade as his counterpart Barnett in Mississippi, but more skillfully. In June 1963 he stood in the schoolhouse door of the University of Alabama to deny admission to Vivian Malone and James Hood, the first black students. But he had ringed the university with police and warned off the thugs. He reasoned, rightly, that peaceful defiance was wiser and more likely to build a permanent sense of white grievance that he could exploit. After the moment of glory, he yielded to the federalized National Guard and stepped aside. Malone and Hood walked through the door to a round of applause. That night both were welcomed by white student leaders.

JAMES MEREDITH'S VIOLENT ENTRY INTO "OLE MISS"

NO GO: Chief U.S. Marshal James McShane (center) tried to push his way past Lieutenant Governor Paul Johnson, who, backed by state troopers, barred the admission of James Meredith to Ole Miss. John Doar, the Justice Department agent, has a calming hand on Meredith's shoulder.

James Meredith was a short, wiry and emotionally tough man of 29 who had served in the Air Force and studied at Mississippi's all-black Jackson State. Four times in a week in September 1962, Governor Ross Barnett defied the Supreme Court by interposing himself between Meredith and registration at the University of Mississippi (Ole Miss). Barnett was a tool of the burgeoning White Citizens Councils and lethally stupid. He stirred up mobs from all over the Deep South. Never would he give in, he said, while knowing he would, and secretly trying to write a script that would make him appear a gallant victim in a phony confrontation. He asked Attorney General Bobby Kennedy to have 24 federal marshals threaten him: "They must all draw their guns. Then they could point their guns at us and then we could step aside." On Sunday, September 30, facing indefinite jail for contempt of court unless Meredith was admitted by Tuesday, October 2, Barnett promised police protection for him, then reneged. At dusk on that Tuesday, Meredith and 300 marshals were exposed to a mob of more than 2,000 (at its peak). All night the rioters hurled rocks, lead pipe and Molotov cocktails and tried to get at Meredith and the marshals. Later there was gunfire directed at the marshals, who never fired back. A reporter and a bystander were shot dead. The marshals threw tear gas. An amazing 166 of them were wounded, 28 by bullets. Kennedy was slow to order in troops. They did not arrive until 4 a.m.

Meredith was registered the next day. Kennedy pumped a total of 23,000 troops into Oxford, three times the town's population. Meredith graduated on August 18, 1963, and went on to pick up a law degree at Columbia. In June 1966, he set out to walk from Memphis to Jackson to encourage black voter registration. Ten miles out, a white man emerged with a shotgun and left Meredith screaming on the road with over a hundred pellets in him. He recovered, but he eventually grew so disillusioned he joined the staff of one of the South's most mean-spirited and unreconstructed racists, Senator Jesse Helms of North Carolina.

THE MOB TAKES OVER
WHILE THE POLICE LOOK ON

It was Mother's Day in Alabama, May 14, 1961. A mob of white men armed with clubs, iron pipes and knives tried to get at nine black and white passengers inside a bus at the Greyhound station at Anniston. Unrestrained by watching police, they were intent on attacking the nine for exercising rights declared sacrosanct by the Supreme Court. The Court had banned segregation on interstate buses and trains in 1946 (*Morgan v. Virginia*), and in 1960 (*Boynton v. Virginia*) it had ruled that the rest rooms, waiting rooms and lunch counters at terminals should be open to everyone. But the South wasn't listening. The nine hazarding their lives on the bus were the first of the Freedom Riders, pitting their nonviolent beliefs against the mobs in the hope that the crisis would provoke the federal government to do what it had conspicuously failed to do so far: enforce the law.

The Freedom Rides were the latest shift in the movement's strategy to dramatize the humiliations of Jim Crow and challenge the South's power structure directly. They had been planned by CORE's James Farmer, who had publicly asked for volunteers, whites who would use black facilities and blacks who would try to use the white facilities. On May 4, two bus groups set off from Washington. They hoped to pick up others and reach New Orleans by May 17, the seventh anniversary of *Brown*. They never made it. The bus escaped from Anniston back onto Highway 78, but in a scene out of *The Road Warrior* it was followed by 200 screaming white men in cars. At the terminal, they had slashed the tires of the bus and the driver had to pull off the highway. The mob smashed the bus windows with bricks and axes and hurled a firebomb inside. They held the doors shut so those inside would be overcome by the fire. They would have surely died but for the foresight of Alabama's director of public safety, Floyd Mann, one of the few Southern officials who tried to uphold the law. Concerned to protect the riders from ambush, he had secretly put an agent on the bus at Atlanta, "Eli" Cowling, who had eavesdropping equipment so that he could report what the Freedom Riders planned to do. Cowling pulled out a revolver and got the mob to fall back until

Alabama state troopers chased them off.

The smashed, burning bus on the side of the road, an image quickly mounted on a poster by Farmer, became a worldwide symbol of America's racial strife. The second group of Freedom Riders fared even worse. They managed to buy sandwiches at the "whites only" cafeteria, but six Klansmen got on the bus. They beat up two blacks at the front, then attacked two white men, the pacifist Jim Peck and 61-year-old Walter Bergman, a retired professor from Michigan. At Birmingham, a mob clubbed Peck: he needed 35 stitches to close six open head wounds. Bergman, beaten even as he tried to crawl away on hands and knees, suffered permanent brain damage. The injured were denied shelter in all-white hospitals and had to be rescued from the reassembling mob by courageous black families. The violence seemed to have worked. All the Freedom Riders had been stopped. But the white South once again underestimated the determination of the obscure men and women who made up the civil rights movement. CORE's new sister movement in direct action, the Student Nonviolent Coordinating Committee, decided to pick up the Freedom Ride where it had stopped. The driving spirits were Diane Nash, a fiery, elegant black Chicagoan from a middle-class background, and her soon-to-be husband, James Bevel, a young black minister from the tiny town of Itta Bena, Mississippi, who liked to describe himself only half-jokingly as "a chicken-eating, liquor-drinking, woman-chasing Baptist preacher." The heroic Rev. Fred Shuttlesworth of Montgomery, who had helped to rescue the first two groups of riders, was against the idea, but Nash was adamant: "If they stop us with violence, the movement is dead. We're coming."

By now both the Kennedy brothers were engaged, furious with Alabama Governor John Patterson, who would not come to the phone. Bobby Kennedy dispatched his aide John Seigenthaler, a crusading former editor of the *Tennessean,* who was subjected to a table-pounding lecture on a governor's duty to defend segregation against outside agitators. But when Floyd Mann said he could protect travelers from city limits to city limits,

Seigenthaler got what he had come for, a statement by Patterson that he read over the phone to Bobby: "The state of Alabama has the will, the force, the men and the equipment to give full protection to everyone in Alabama, on the highways and elsewhere." Bobby asked: "Does he mean it?" Patterson hollered behind Seigenthaler: "I've given my word as governor of Alabama."

The Freedom Riders set out again on Saturday morning, May 20, now with state escorts to the city limits of Montgomery, where Police Commissioner L. B. Sullivan would take over. Sullivan assured Mann he had the police ready; Mann distrusted him and kept 75 state troopers on call. The Montgomery terminal was empty of police when the Freedom Riders got off the bus. Hundreds of whites materialized with baseball bats, bottles and lead pipes, and assaulted everyone in sight—riders, reporters, passersby. Seigenthaler tried to

ESCAPE: Inside the heavily escorted Freedom Riders' bus, Montgomery, Alabama, after the all-night siege at Ralph Abernathy's church. Photograph by Bruce Davidson.

pull two women into a cab. "One guy grabbed me by the arm, wheeled me around, and said, 'Who the hell are you?' And I said, 'Get back, I'm a federal man.' I turned back and the lights went out. I was hit with a pipe over one ear." Mann and his assistants drew their guns. "I put my pistol to the head of one or two of those folks that was using baseball bats and told them if they swung it just one more time I'd kill them." The arrival of the state troopers saved many lives; some 22 people were hurt, 5 were hospitalized.

Martin Luther King had no part in organizing the Freedom Rides, though his SCLC had provided sanctuary. On Sunday evening a white mob of 3,000 surrounded the church where King was speaking to an estimated 1,500 blacks and some of the Freedom Riders. As the congregation sang "Love Lifted Me" and "We Shall Overcome," the mob hurled rocks, burned cars and got to the church doors through a thin line of brave federal marshals armed with nightsticks, some of Mann's state police and a few local police. Governor Patterson refused to come to the rescue. Bobby Kennedy was still hesitating hours later about ordering in federal troops when Patterson's nerve broke. Patterson sent in 100 National Guardsmen.

Bobby Kennedy wanted to shift the focus to voting rights. He did a deal that civil rights historian Taylor Branch rightly characterizes as extraordinary. The United States would stand aside if Freedom Riders were arrested for breaking local segregation laws on condition that the states protect riders from mobs. Some 200 went cheerfully into Mississippi's brutal jails.

They were mostly black, and men; the whites predominantly Quakers and Jews. They stayed 40 days and 40 nights. "We sang 'We Shall Overcome' at the top of our lungs," wrote James Farmer, "as though shouting to straining ears in cotton fields and shacks on plantations in the far reaches of the state."

The emphasis shifted from the Freedom Rides, but they had galvanized the federal government. Robert Kennedy did put the arm on the Interstate Commerce Commission and on November 1 interstate carriers were forced to at least integrate bus terminals. James Farmer, who had lost 22 pounds in jail, remembered: "Not one of the men and women who shared the Freedom Ride could ever be the same. . . . A Promethean spark somehow had been infused into the soul of each of us."

MISSISSIPPI, THE HEART OF DARKNESS

For ten baleful years in the darkening state of Mississippi, Medgar Evers almost single-handedly kept alive the idea of racial justice. Meeting him in his cluttered green office, an interviewer wrote that "he was made of optimism and he needed it." By 1963 he was exhibiting the same morbid clairvoyance that came to Martin Luther King and Malcolm X. "Freedom," he said at a rally, "has never been free. I love my children and I love my wife with all my heart. And I would die, gladly die, if that would make a better life for them." Two days later, when his brother Charles called from Chicago to say he would see him in July, Evers only replied: "I hope so." As Mary-anne Vollers writes in *Ghosts of Mississippi*, it was the way he said it that bothered Charles. When they hung up, both of these fearless men found themselves crying.

Medgar Evers loved Mississippi. "If everything got straight here," he said on one of his dangerous trips across the Delta, "it would be the best place in the world to live." It was a love of immediate country—a true patriotism—felt so deeply that it came to supersede his heartfelt ambitions of material wealth and even his desire to be with his beloved wife and children.

The conviction that he should do something to put things straight came to him on his return from World War II, where he took part in the liberation of France.

Medgar, Charles and three of their childhood buddies walked over to the county courthouse in Decatur to register to vote. They were turned back by angry men. For a brief moment, inspired by Jomo Kenyatta, he thought of starting a black guerrilla war across the Delta—a sort of Mississippi Mau Mau. Instead, he turned again to his religion. "It didn't take much reading of the Bible," he told an *Ebony* magazine interviewer in 1958, "to

convince me that two wrongs would not make the situation any different and that I couldn't hate the white man and at the same time hope to convert him." He put himself through the all-black Alcorn A & M College near Natchez, with outstanding grades, then took a job in the tiny all-black community of Mound Bayou from a local black businessman and mild civil rights leader named Dr. Theodore Roosevelt Mason "T.R.M." Howard. They sold cheap medical and funeral insurance to the black sharecroppers on the feudal plantations and something more: the story of blacks in America. He would pull a George Washington Carver silver half-dollar from his pocket and say, "This is a colored man." He joined the brave few—Amzie Moore, Aaron Henry, Ruby Hurley among them—trying to make something of the NAACP. He chalked up endless miles in beat-up old cars, organizing, recruiting, investigating

Medgar Evers's bier. By order of President Kennedy, he was buried at Arlington National Cemetery with full military honors. Photograph by Flip Schulke.

and publicizing racial atrocities. It was a daily risk. Blacks who joined the NAACP often lost their jobs or saw their homes and property foreclosed. In the single year of 1955, the Rev. George Lee, who insisted on registering to vote, was murdered by shotgun; 60-year-old Lamar Smith, a black farmer who had actually managed to vote in a primary, was shot dead in a downtown shopping street in Brookhaven; and Gus Courts, a stubborn, semiliterate president of an NAACP chapter, was shot in the arm and abdomen and had his business wrecked. Courts escaped to Chicago, as did Medgar's brother Charles. Many followed. Medgar Evers stayed on.

Evers's faraway superiors disliked direct action but were slow to train their justifiably vaunted legal cannons on Mississippi. Evers himself tested the public accommodation laws in 1958 by taking a front seat

on a bus. He was beaten up for it. Not until March 1963 was school segregation challenged, when Evers himself filed a lawsuit on behalf of his eight-year-old daughter, Rena. He kept a vital link with the students at Jackson's all-black Tougaloo College who were arrested for trying to read in a "whites only" public library. When he turned up at the courthouse in March 1961, one cop remarked loudly, "There he is. We ought to kill him." The racist bootlegger G. W. "Red" Hydrick hit him hard on the back of the head with his .38. When he didn't fall, two cops whacked him from behind with their billy clubs.

By February 1962 Evers was shrugging off the restraints of the NAACP's head office. He worked with Bob Moses and Dave Dennis to set up an alliance with SNCC and CORE. The Jackson movement of sit-ins and shopping boycotts gathered steam. With the help of the Federal Communications Commission, he won television time on May 20, 1963, unprecedented for a black leader in Mississippi, so that he could respond to Mayor Allen Thompson's depiction of Jackson as a racial paradise where trouble was caused only by outside agitators.

June 11 was an unforgettable night. President Kennedy, in the most fervent of his speeches, committed himself (rhetorically) to the civil rights cause. Evers and others watched with elation. Myrlie Evers and the three children had waited up to share the excitement. When they heard the sound of the car door slamming, the kids clamored, "There's Daddy!" In the same instant they heard a shot. A bullet from a .30/06 Enfield rifle hurtled Evers onto the driveway, his keys and a pile of NAACP T-shirts in his hand. He died in the early morning of June 12. He was 37.

Unlike the murder of Emmett Till, the killing was not simply swept behind a white wall of racial solidarity. The police did a credible job. They found the Enfield. With the aid of the FBI, they uncovered a fresh, full fingerprint. It belonged to Byron De La Beckwith, 42, an eccentric, wife-beating, gun-nut fertilizer salesman known as "Delay." He had been orphaned by the age of 12. At 23, he had gone on shore at Tarawa with his Marine unit and displayed surpassing courage. He was wounded and returned a changed man, obsessed by race through three turbulent marriages to the same woman, and was diagnosed as schizo-

FLASH FORWARD: 1994

JUSTICE CATCHES UP

Beckwith waiting for the verdict in New Orleans, 1974.

"DELAY" BECKWITH

"Delay" Beckwith bragged for years about "killing that uppity nigger." He used his notoriety to run for governor. An FBI informant heard him tell a Klan convocation in 1965: "Killing that nigger gave me no more inner discomfort than our wives endure when they give birth to our children." In 1973 he was caught transporting a time bomb into New Orleans to blow up a Jewish anti-Klan activist. Sent to Louisiana's Angola prison farm in 1974, he bragged again. In all, six witnesses appeared at a new trial in 1994. A jury made up of men and women, black and white, most of them working-class, found him guilty of murder. He was sentenced to life in prison and would not be eligible for parole for ten years, when he would be 84 years of age.

phrenic. He was earnestly prosecuted by a populist D.A. and future governor named Bill Waller. But Beckwith had allies. The defense was able to present enough high-level alibi witnesses to bitterly divide first one, then a second jury. Demoralizing as the hung juries were, Waller had got 11 out of a total of 24 Mississippi white men to vote another Mississippi white man guilty of a capital offense against a black race activist.

A DAUGHTER'S QUESTION: King in his dining room with his daughter Yoki (Yolanda Denise) in 1962. He was speaking of personal experience when, in his "Letter from Birmingham Jail," he elaborated on a father's feelings "when you suddenly find your tongue twisted and your speech stammering as you seek to explain to your six-year-old daughter why she can't go to the public amusement park that has just been advertised on television." Photograph by James Karales.

THE CHILDREN'S CRUSADE SAVES THE DAY

Martin Luther King laid siege to Birmingham, Alabama, on April 3, 1963, and on Good Friday, nine days later, he seemed to have lost. The biggest, baddest city in the South, in the words of the Rev. Wyatt Tee Walker, his right-hand man, Birmingham had looked a good target for a campaign in the centennial year of Lincoln's declaration freeing the slaves. It was notorious for the brutal racism of its police chief, Theophilus Eugene "Bull" Connor, and for police ties to the Klan. Dynamite had been the answer to every black assertion of a constitutional right. In the years since *Brown,* around 40 bombs had been set off in Alabama, most of them in "Bombingham."

Blacks still did not have equal access to lunch counters, rest rooms and drinking fountains; they constituted 40 percent of the population, but there were no black clerks in the stores, no black policemen or firemen. The city had responded to a 1962 federal court desegregation order by closing down more than a hundred playgrounds, swimming pools and parks; rather than accept interracial sports, it lost its minor league baseball team.

King's strategy was born of a fear that the movement, frustrated by a decade of terror in the South and indifference in the North, might slip into violence. He stretched that concept to its limit in design-

ing this latest campaign. He wanted to awaken the moral conscience of America, and the aloof Kennedy administration, by provoking a violent reaction to a nonviolent shopping boycott and sit-ins. But by the time the campaign started, Birmingham was in transition. Sidney Smyer, the president of the Chamber of Commerce, was no liberal but he had organized a revolt against Connor and two allied city leaders. In April a more moderate city government, under mayor-elect Albert Boutwell, was poised to take over. Connor and his crew refused to leave office, pending a court ruling, but there was a new optimism in the city—and King was accused of wrecking everything by ill-timed racial confrontation. Black business leaders were opposed to a King campaign; young blacks and movement radicals decried it as too little too late. The national press was critical. The sit-ins fizzled when stores simply shut down. The number of protesters willing to risk jail dwindled. Money for bail dried up. And on April 10 Birmingham officials won a sweeping emergency injunction banning any further protest.

King's men were in low spirits when they sat in Room 30 of the Gaston Motel arguing until the early hours of Good Friday morning. Martin Luther King, Sr., the stern minister of Atlanta's most prominent black congregation, urged his son to obey the injunction, stay out of jail and raise money. King said nothing. At length, he went silently into the bedroom and emerged in a work shirt, blue jeans and "clodhopper" walking shoes. He was ready for jail. "There he goes. Just like Jesus," cried black onlookers as he led a small group down Birmingham's Fifth Avenue. Police manhandled him into a paddy wagon. Ralph Abernathy and 50 others were arrested, but King was put in solitary in "the hole." Lying on his metal bed, the only light a ray of spring sun filtering through prison bars far above, King was "in a nightmare of despair." On April 16, his despair turned to anger. In a newspaper smuggled into jail, he read a denunciation of him and his movement by eight white clergymen, led by Episcopal Bishop C. C. Jones Carpenter. They condemned him as an outside agitator, his campaign as unwise and untimely and civil disobedience as unjustified because it incited hatred and violence. King began writing furiously, in the margins all over the newspaper, what would become the 20-page "Letter from Birmingham Jail," one of the enduring documents of the American black experience, modern Christianity and freedom movements everywhere.

King was bailed out after nine days. His letter, for all its later fame, received little immediate attention. The Rev. James Bevel argued that the only option left was a mass march. He and his wife, Diane, had an army ready—the thousands of junior high and elementary school students whom they had trained in nonviolence. The children's crusade began on the afternoon of May 2. Some 900 of them were jailed. The next day another 2,500 marchers came

out. Bull Connor ordered his firemen to assault them with high-pressure hoses capable of knocking bricks out of a wall. When another group appeared, he had them attacked by German shepherd dogs. Perhaps the ultimate fleeting triumph of nonviolence came on Sunday, May 5, when a prayer pilgrimage to the city jail of some 3,000 mostly young people was ordered to disperse. They knelt in prayer. An apoplectic Connor ordered his men to turn on the fire hoses at point-blank range. The crowd went quiet. The firemen seemed paralyzed at their pumps. Connor repeated, "Dammit! Turn on the hoses!" Still nothing happened. The white firemen stood motionless, some of them crying. In a tense silence, the Rev. Walker came over to suggest the marchers should be allowed through the police line to kneel in prayer in a blacks-only park. More than 1,000 were jailed before the march ended, but with the jails full and business at a standstill, President Kennedy summoned business leader Smyer to Washington for a secret meeting. Unless Birmingham responded, he would send in federal troops. Smyer recoiled from this "black eye" and summoned 70 of Birmingham

and Alabama's "Big Mules," the business elite of the state. They met Burke Marshall, Kennedy's assistant attorney general, at the Chamber of Commerce. The strains of "We Shall Overcome" blasted into their meetings from 3,000 demonstrators. The negotiations were about jobs and lunch counters, not even voting rights or schools, but President Kennedy became continually and personally involved. On May 10 a desegregation settlement was announced. The sitting and dressing rooms in the downtown stores would be integrated at once. Rest rooms and water fountains would be integrated within 30 days, lunch counters in 60 days. More black clerks would be hired and promoted. The demonstrators would be released.

The next day 1,000 Klansmen rallied to denounce the businessmen. Bombs went off at the parsonage of King's minister brother, A.D., and at the Gaston Motel, and an angry crowd gathered. When Colonel Al Lingo arrived with 250 of his state troopers, a full-scale riot ensued. The Kennedys discerned the none-too-subtle hand of George Wallace reaching out to foil the settlement. It was certainly a poor end to a spectacular victory.

LETTER FROM BIRMINGHAM JAIL

King's answer to critical white clergy was smuggled out of his cell. He dealt swiftly with the charge of being an outside agitator: "Injustice anywhere is a threat to justice everywhere." He mocked the notion that nonviolence was wrong if it provoked violence. "Isn't it like condemning a robbed man because his possession of money precipitated the evil act of robbery?" He was at his most scorching in answering the call for patience. Blacks had waited more than 340 years for their constitutional and God-given rights. It was easy for those who had never felt the stinging darts of segregation to say, "Wait." And then, in a magnificent passage, he spelled out what the black man had to endure while he waited: "But when you have seen vicious mobs lynch your mothers and fathers at will

Martin Luther King in Birmingham.
Photograph by Flip Schulke.

and drown your sisters and brothers at whim; when you have seen hate-filled policemen curse, kick and even kill your black brothers and sisters; when you see the vast majority of your twenty million Negro brothers smothering in an airtight cage of poverty in the midst of an affluent society; when you are harried by day and haunted by night by the fact that you are a Negro, living constantly at a tip-toe stance, never quite knowing what to expect next, and plagued with inner fears and outer resentments; when you are forever fighting a degenerating sense of 'nobodiness'; then you will understand why we find it difficult to wait."

THREE DAYS IN DALLAS

The last words John Kennedy heard in his life were at 12:29 p.m. on Friday, November 22, 1963: "You can't say Dallas doesn't love you, Mr. President." His presidential motorcade had just emerged from a canyon of cheers in Houston Street and was making a slow 120-degree turn into Elm Street across from a redbrick building called the Texas School Book Depository. He sat in an open-top car in the glaring sun, the First Lady at his side in a pink wool two-piece suit and matching pillbox hat, and a bunch of red roses between them. He smiled back at Nellie Connally, who had twisted around from the jump seat where she sat with her husband, John, the Texas governor.

The Connallys were relieved. Dallas was the strong-hold of John Birchers, Dixiecrats and ultra-right Republicans, whose extremists had manhandled Adlai Stevenson and Lyndon Johnson in separate trips over the last three years. Kennedy's trip was meant to put a public patch on a war in the state Democratic party between Connally's right-wingers and Senator Ralph Yarborough's liberals, and none of the Democratic feuders could afford to embroil the President in a nasty scene. The triumphant motorcade had ridden over the ugliness of the day's beginning, when the President opened the *Dallas Morning News* to an inflammatory full-page advertisement in black borders accusing him of being a Communist tool. It was signed "Bernard Weissman, chairman of the American Fact-Finding Committee." That was a fictitious organization, nothing more than a handful of extreme rightists, including Nelson Bunker Hunt of the oil-rich Dallas family and Weissman, a 26-year-old salesman just discharged from the U.S. Army, but it had made Jackie feel sick. Kennedy remarked, "We're heading into nut country today," and then he teased her: "You know last night would have been a hell of a night to assassinate a President. There was the rain, and the night and we were getting jostled." He formed his fingers as if they were crooked to fire a gun. "Sup-

pose a man had a pistol in a briefcase. Then he could have dropped the gun and the briefcase and melted away in the crowd." He had whirled about acting the role of assassin.

The motorcade was in Elm Street, a few minutes from luncheon at the Trade Mart. Kennedy was waving. Nellie Connally had barely turned back when, 88 yards behind them, Lee Harvey Oswald, at a window on

WELCOME: JFK and First Lady Jackie in Dallas, hotbed of John Birchers. "This trip," he said, "is turning out to be terrific."

the sixth floor of the Depository, lined up the slow moving car in the 4x telescopic sight of his rifle. He pulled the trigger. Everyone heard the sharp crack. The bullet struck no one, almost certainly deflected by the branch of an intervening oak tree. He worked the bolt and lined up Kennedy again, now in clear view. This second 6.5 mm bullet, with a muzzle velocity of 2,000 feet per second, penetrated Kennedy's back, exited at his throat, entered Connally's back, exited his chest and struck his wrist bone. It was not a fatal wound for either man. Howard Brennan, a bystander, looked up and saw Oswald taking aim again. One. Two. Three. Four. Five. . . . In those five seconds of dumbfounded immobility on the ground, Kennedy lost his life. The third bullet tore off the right side of his head. He was pronounced dead at Parkland Hospital at 1 p.m.

Johnson, fearing the shooting might be part of an evolving conspiracy, rushed off to the airport. Jacqueline insisted, "I'm not going to leave here without Jack." She slipped her wedding ring on his finger and sat on a folding chair outside the trauma room while he was prepared for the casket. JFK's staff somehow shielded her from a grotesque row over the body. Dr. Earl Rose, the medical examiner of Dallas County, ruled that it could not be taken away without an autopsy. That was the law of Texas and he was white-hot determined to enforce it with the backing of Dallas policemen. JFK's staff yelled at him. A county judge, brought in to overrule Rose, wilted. "As far as I'm concerned, it's just another homicide case." Two groups, some 40 sweating, angry men, confronted each other at the exit. Kenneth O'Donnell, JFK's closest companion, boiled over. "Get the hell out of the way," he yelled. "We're leaving." O'Donnell and the Secret Servicemen shoved the outraged Rose aside; the police backed away and the cortege raced to Air Force One at Love Field.

Johnson had not taken off. He was waiting for a Dallas judge, Sarah Hughes, to administer the oath of office. At 2:37 p.m. in Air Force One's sweltering cabin, with Kennedy in a casket in the rear of the plane, and a bloodstained Jacqueline at his side, he took John Kennedy's Bible in his hand and became the 36th president.

Oswald hid his rifle and walked coolly downstairs from his sniper's nest. Within three minutes of the shooting, he was on the street, making his way through the pandemonium to his rooming house. He picked up a pistol and changed his jacket. At 1:15 p.m., Patrolman J. D. Tippit spotted him walking along a bus route. Tippit got out of his car, his gun in its holster. Oswald shot him dead. He ran off, pistol in the air, and ducked into a movie house. It was there that police arrested him shortly before 2. On Sunday, November 24, at 11:21 a.m. the whole world saw him shot to death in police headquarters.

Oswald, in dark glasses, something of a celebrity in Minsk, poses with co-workers at the radio and television factory.

THE ASSASSIN

He wrote his own error-laden biographical note: "Lee Harvey Oswald was born in Oct 1939 in New Orleans, L. the son of insuraen Salesman whose early death left a far mean streak of indepence brought on by negleck." His domineering, erratically indulgent mother was always on the move. He was in an orphanage and 12 schools, diagnosed as having a potential for "explosive, aggressive acting out."

The life fulfilled the analysis. At 17, he joined the Marines. He hated being hazed as "Ozzie Rabbit," was court-martialed for fighting and firing a derringer. Obsessed with Marxism, he traveled to the Soviet Union, tried to defect and cut his wrists when he was initially refused.

The KGB reluctantly relocated him to Minsk. He slacked at the factory where he worked, wrote political tracts at night. The KGB tapes of his bugged apartment give a bleak portrait of his disillusion with the workers' paradise and of his marriage to a pharmacology student named Marina Prusakova. The shock of coming home to the U.S. with his wife and daughter in June 1962 was immense. He was pestered by the FBI. He campaigned for fair play for Castro's Cuba, but could not hold a job and started to beat his wife. He was a nobody in a rage. His solution to reconciling his grandiose self-image with reality was to kill "an enemy of the people." He bought a mail-order rifle for $12.78 and on the night of April 10, 1963, took a shot at right-wing General Edwin Walker sitting in his Dallas home. The bullet just grazed Walker's head. Ozzie Rabbit looked about for another target.

THIRTY-FIVE YEARS OF PLOT AND COUNTERPLOT

Rumor is a pipe,
Blown by surmises, jealousies, conjectures,
And of so easy and so plain a stop,
That the blunt monster with uncounted heads,
The still-discordant wavering multitude,
Can play upon it.
—*Henry IV, Part 2*

A week afterward, only 29 percent of the American people believed that Lee Harvey Oswald, acting alone, had killed President Kennedy. It was the beginning of an efflorescence of rumor and surmise, of speculation and hypothesis, of falsehood and distortion, of fantasy and fabrication, whose hallucinogenic colors began to fade only after 35 dizzy years.

It was altogether natural that there should be suspicion. The killer was an ex-Marine who had defected to Russia, a self-proclaimed pro-Castro Marxist; his killer in turn a minor thug with ties to the Mafia. The elements of the mystery could hardly have been richer.

President Johnson acted quickly to find the truth. He set up a seven-man commission of inquiry on Friday, November 29, headed by Supreme Court Chief Justice Earl Warren, and including Allen Dulles, John McCloy and future president Gerald Ford. In September 1964 it concluded there was no evidence that either Oswald or Ruby was part of any conspiracy, domestic or foreign: the Russians and Cubans were not involved. It was a sound conclusion on the evidence then available, but the Warren Commission accidentally set the bats flying by a series of omissions, errors and contradictions; it underplayed Ruby's links with the mob and also his mental fragility. The reluctance of the FBI and CIA to disclose anything was their natural bureaucratic mind-set, but it was interpreted as the government's having something more sinister to hide than a series of mistakes. So was the secrecy of the autopsy—which was botched anyway. In 1978, anxiety was regenerated by another investigation by the House Select Committee on Assassinations. It debunked many theories, corrected the misleading autopsy, then added mischief of its own. In a hasty revision written after the final draft, it concluded there was a second gunman because audio experts examining a recording from the open microphone on a police motorcycle in Dealey Plaza had discovered "impulse patterns" suggestive of four shots, not three. The committee then pointed the finger at the Mafia. Alas, the "impulse patterns" turned out not to be gunfire and the motorcycle was not even in Dealey Plaza at the time.

By 1993, several hundred books and still more self-published tomes and manuals piled up from these confusions, an incremental Tower of Pisa leaning ever more crazily toward the ground. Oswald's body was exhumed in 1981 to check the theory that when he was in Russia the New Orleans boy had been switched with an identical imposter, a KGB assassin.

The common feature of the conspiracy theories was that Oswald did not act alone. The plotters and their motives were variously identified: Lyndon Johnson, with or without Lady Bird Johnson (to gain the presidency); Nikita Khrushchev (to avenge his Cuban missile defeat); Fidel Castro (to pay back Kennedy's attempts to remove him); and anti-Castro activists (for JFK's failure at the Bay of Pigs); the Mafia doing it either for Russian-Cuban gold or to punish the Kennedys for investigations of Jimmy Hoffa. In the most lurid scenarios, which took life with Jim Garrison, the district attorney in New Orleans, there were, at one time or another, 16 marksmen in Dealey Plaza, working for either a homosexual ring that wanted a thrill or a sinister group in the military-industrial complex frightened that Kennedy would end the war in Vietnam and hence their profits. Oliver Stone's 1991 movie, *JFK*, gave currency to this fantasy and new life to the conspiracists.

Bureaucratic bungling, paranoia and greed supplied adrenaline for some of the efforts to prove that the killing was by anyone but a lone misfit, yet the rash of theories was an acknowledgment of something deeper. They provided psychological balm for the national trauma. As William Manchester remarked, they invested the President's death with meaning, endowing him with martyrdom. He died for something.

TWO KILLERS: As he fired, Ruby yelled, "You killed my President, you rat!" Born Jacob Rubenstein in Chicago, March 25, 1911, Ruby was variously a gambler, tipster, brawler, union organizer, record and boxing promoter, peddler of pizza crusts, liquid vitamins and razor blades, and finally a strip club owner. He moved to Dallas in 1947 after serving in the Air Force, and changed his name to Ruby. He had a mental breakdown in 1952. He was hot-headed, arrested nine times for obscene shows, liquor violations, assault and concealing a weapon: he habitually carried a .38 pistol. He liked to hang around police headquarters, shooting the breeze with cops, pressmen and petty criminals. Roughly tackled by police after he shot Oswald, he cried: "I'm Jack Ruby—you know me." The assassination obsessed him. "Gee," he said everywhere, "his poor children and Mrs. Kennedy, what a terrible thing to happen."

THE SECOND SHOOTER AND OTHER MYTHS

In 1993, the investigative journalist and lawyer Gerald Posner did much to expose the central myths. His book *Case Closed* has not been effectively challenged.

THE SECOND SHOOTER

1. THE HEAD: Abe Zapruder's famous 8-mm home movie seemed to show Kennedy's head jerking backward, feeding speculation that a bullet came from the grassy knoll in front. Computer enhancement shows that Kennedy's head did initially jerk forward 2.3 inches. When it then jerked backward, this was not because of force from the front. It was the result of two pressures: a neuromuscular contraction of the muscles of the back and neck and a "jet effect" calculated by Nobel Prize laureate Dr. Luis Alvarez: on a launching pad, the rocket's fuel is ejected downward, but the rocket goes up. With JFK, the explosion of blood and brain tissue out of the right side of the head provided more momentum than the bullet itself, causing the head to thrust in the opposite direction—backward and to the left. Shooting tests with dummy heads confirmed the Alvarez hypothesis.

2. THE MARKSMAN: But did Oswald alone have time to fire three shots? Yes. Matching the speed of Zapruder's film to the images shows that the shooter had 8 to 8.4 seconds to fire, the first bullet already being in the chamber. Even a mediocre rifleman can do this. Oswald had a Marine sharpshooter qualification.

3. THE "MAGIC" BULLET: JFK was hit twice and Governor Connally once. Doesn't this prove there

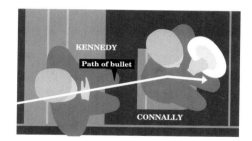

was a second shooter since Oswald had no time to shoot JFK twice and then refire to shoot Connally? Connally himself thought so, but the bullet that wounded him was the same one (bullet No. 2) that hit Kennedy in the back. It needed no magic to go through Kennedy first, penetrate Connally's back and, with a slight deflection from the rib, strike his wrist. A 1978 test showed that the fragments of metal found came from only two bullets. In a meticulous re-creation of the scene in Dealey Plaza, Failure Analysis Associates, a firm specializing in computer reconstruction for lawsuits, reported that the path of the bullet through two men was entirely credible.

THE MYTH OF A PLOT

How did Oswald get into the perfect sniper's position? On October 14, Ruth Paine, a Quaker friend of the family, had coffee with Mrs. Marina Oswald and two other young mothers. One of the women, Linnie Mae Rendle, mentioned that her younger brother had found work at the Texas School Book Depository. Marina asked Ruth to call the manager, Roy Truly. On October 15, Truly gave Oswald a job. Impressed by a quiet ex-Marine who called him sir, he did not bother to check references. The "plotters" would also have had to be clairvoyant. No luncheon site and no route to it had been proposed at this time. The Secret Service and Dallas police did not confirm the route until November 18; it was not public knowledge until November 19.

WAS RUBY A MAFIA HIT MAN?

It is a tantalizing idea that Oswald was a fall guy for the mob, who had him killed by Ruby because he knew too much. Ruby, a minor thug, did have ties to the underworld. One wonders why the masterminds of the mob did not take Oswald for a ride when he left the Depository instead of staging a risky theatrical execution in a room full of armed policemen. In any event, Ruby could not have been planning to kill Oswald on Sunday at 11:21 a.m. Oswald's transfer was due to have taken place an hour earlier. Ruby was then at home lounging in his underwear and might well have stayed there but for a call at 10:19 a.m. from one of his strippers, who asked him for $25, which meant he had to go downtown to send it by Western Union. The police interrogation ended late, at a few minutes after 11. Oswald asked to change his clothes. He put on a beige sweater, then took it off in favor of a black one. If he had not delayed these five minutes, he would have been in and out of the basement while Ruby was still at Western Union, patiently filling in forms. Ruby was able to saunter unchallenged into the basement at 11:20 a.m. only because a policeman on guard stepped away for a moment to stop traffic for a police car trying to get out.

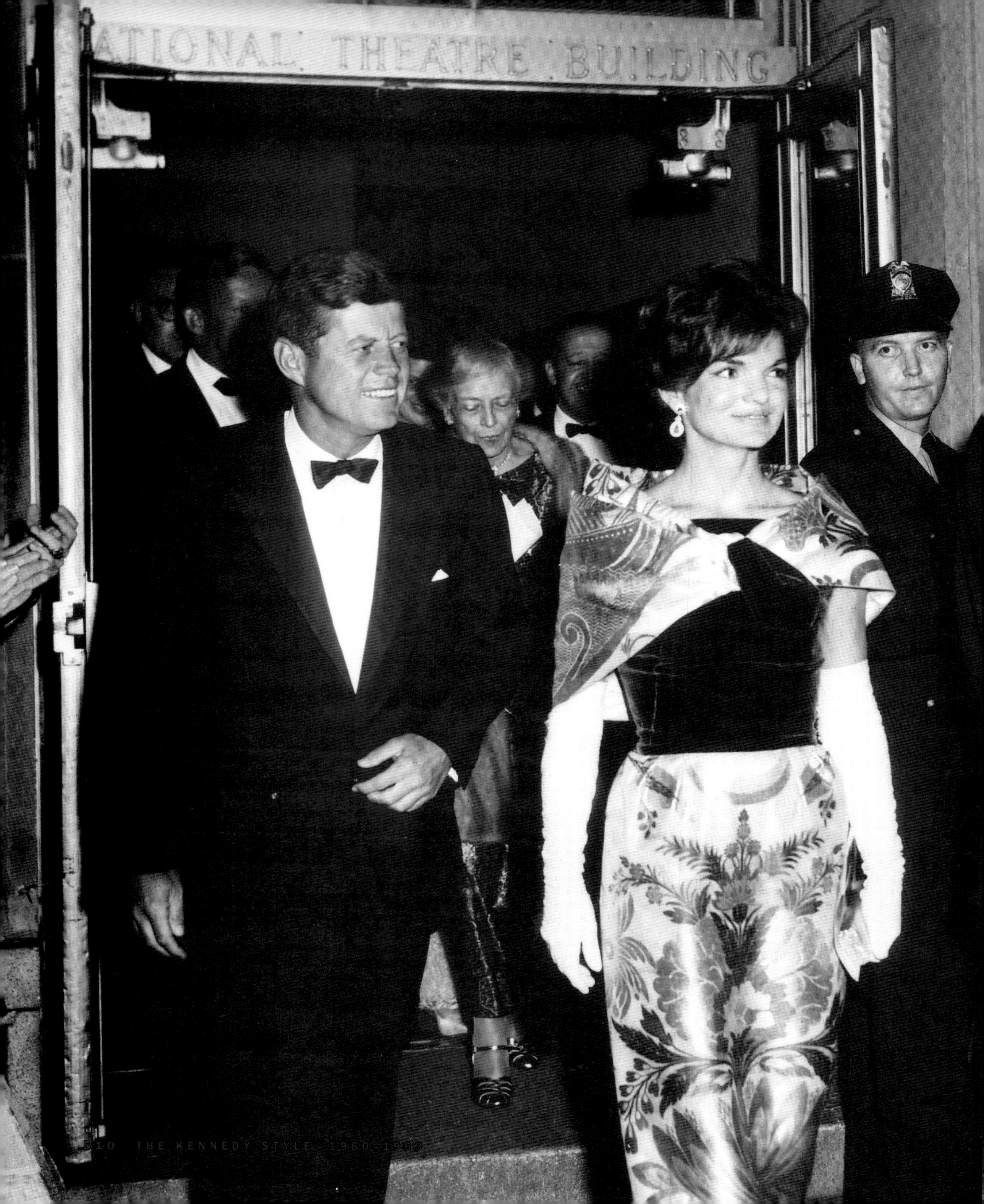
ATIONAL THEATRE BUILDING

THE ROMANCE OF CAMELOT

Jacqueline Kennedy, mourning in Hyannis Port in December, gave life to legend as surely as she lighted the eternal flame over her husband's grave on a hillside in Virginia. A friend, the *Life* magazine writer Theodore White, came to see her and she reminisced how "Jack," before going to sleep, liked to play a song from the end of a popular musical. The lines he loved to hear commanded us never to forget that for "one brief shining moment" there had been a chivalrous kingdom known as Camelot. She had a picture in her mind of little boy Jack, sick most of the time, lying in bed reading history, reading about the Knights of the Round Table, reading Marlborough. "For Jack, history was full of heroes."

The romance of Camelot, of youthful gallantry and love, came to exert a strong hold on the public imagination. It would be fanciful, one must guess, to suppose this has had much to do with politics. It is more likely that "Camelot" has prevailed as a metaphor for the glittering style the Kennedys brought to the White House and the sense of exhilarating possibility in his two years, ten months, and two days in the presidency. Jacqueline, who had no appetite for politics, put her energies and taste into making the White House the first house in the land. Bullying wealthy friends and begging, she transformed the dowdy public rooms with the best in American art and history and showed off their beauty on a television tour for the people. The White House became a theater of the arts and intellect, the stilted state dinners made into cheerful and elegant parties. The zenith perhaps was in April 1962, when the Kennedys honored 49 Western Hemisphere Nobel Prize winners. It was vintage Kennedy to welcome them as "the most extraordinary collection of talent, of human knowledge, that has ever been gathered together in the White House, with the possible exception of when Thomas Jefferson dined alone." Jacqueline's cultivated taste was the inspiration for these parties. Kennedy invested Camelot with his vitality, his relish for social gaiety, his preference for excellence, his conviction that the arts were central to a nation's purpose, his enjoyment of the needle of debate, his courage in pain and his ironic wit and laconic self-depreciation. Told the Republican National Committee had passed a resolution condemning him as a failure, he said he was sure the vote was unanimous. He rejoiced in his wife's knowledge of French culture and the fluency that so impressed General de Gaulle on a state visit to France. He meant it when he said, "I am proud to have been the man who accompanied Jacqueline Kennedy to Paris."

The physical attractiveness and informality of the Kennedys attracted ecstatic crowds. Here they leave a musical comedy, *Mr. President.* JFK's taste ran more to musical comedy and romantic ballads than to ballet or opera.

LYNDON BAINES JOHNSON
36th President (Democrat), 1963–1969

"A Senator Fulbright to see you, Sire. Seems he can't reconcile himself to your infallibility."
Cartoon by Paul Szep, 1967.

BORN: August 27, 1908, near Stonewall, Texas

DIED: January 22, 1973, San Antonio, Texas

POLITICAL CAREER: Member, U.S. House of Representatives, 10th Congressional District of Texas, 1937–1949; U.S. Senator, 1949–1961; Democratic Whip, 1951; Minority Leader, 1953–1955; Majority Leader, 1955–1961; Vice President, 1961–1963; President, 1963–1969.

FIRST: First Southern Democrat elected president since James K. Polk (counting Wilson a New Jerseyan).

CHARACTER SNAPSHOT: "A restless, extravagantly self-centered, brutishly expansive, manipulative, teasing and sly man, he was also genuinely, passionately interested in making life easier and more honorable for millions of terribly hard-pressed working men and women."
—Joseph Califano

THE DEFIANT ONE: He was born of pioneering English-Scotch and German blood in a three-room shack isolated on the Pedernales River in the Hill Country of Texas, and brought up in gritty Johnson City (pop. 323). His mother, Rebekah, a gentle, educated daughter of a ruined attorney, taught Lyndon the alphabet at two; she had been an elocution teacher in Fredericksburg and a "stringer" for the Austin newspaper. He imitated his father and at ten sat at his feet in the Texas legislature: the boisterous "Mr. Sam" was a Populist idealist who refused every bribe in his eight years in the House (1905–1908 and 1918–1923). He went broke farming cotton and had to take work on a road gang. Biographer Robert Caro dates his failure and years of poverty to the beginning of troubles with Lyndon. The town sneered at the family's downfall. A shamefaced Lyndon had to ride to school on a donkey.

REBEL AND HERO: Teenage Lyndon, the troublemaker of the five children, was a self-pitying coarse big-mouth who defied his father's shouts and his mother's pleas. He graduated high school in 1924, but refused to go to college, wrecked his father's car, got into wild escapades with dynamite and ran away twice. Beaten up for trying to steal a girl, he at last conceded he would try for a degree, and in 1927 went to a small teachers' college at San Marcos, Southwest Texas. It was the making of him. He disliked his mother's beloved books, and his overall average was only B minus, but he staged a coup in student politics and shone as a temporary teacher: he was a hero to the Mexican children when he taught in Cotulla for nine months. They educated him about hard-core poverty and prejudice in the United States.

NEWLYWEDS: He was 26 when he married Claudia Alta "Lady Bird" Taylor, aged 21, on November 21, 1934. She was the shy, clever daughter of a wealthy trader. LBJ proposed on their first date, a breakfast, and rushed the wedding with a $2.50 ring. Her nickname came from a nurse who exclaimed, "She's purty as a ladybird." She sustained him loyally, though he treated her like a hired hand and had affairs with a politically savvy Alice Glass and others. Two daughters were born, in 1944 and 1947.

LBJ knew Washington inside out when he showed Lady Bird around her new home in 1934 (right), where he had for three years been secretary to the wealthy Democratic Representative Richard M. Kleberg. When Kleberg said he would vote against New Deal laws to help the farmers, LBJ made him change his mind by threatening to quit.

THE CAMPAIGNER: At college he boasted he would be president of the United States. He was known as Bull(shit) Johnson. But he began to deliver. At 28, as director of the Texas state National Youth Administration, he was a whirlwind success, getting more than 20,000 youths into work or back to school. In 1937 he

won a seat in Congress because it was thought his Washington knowledge would enable him to untie the red tape holding up a dam. It did. Then he campaigned in the capital and the Hill Country for electric power for the Pedernales. When the lights went on in November 1939, people began christening their sons Lyndon.

Reelected five times, he was narrowly defeated for the Senate in 1941. In 1948 he beat Dixiecrat Governor Coke Stevenson by 87 votes out of 988,000. Stevenson charged LBJ with ballot stuffing. The election board decided for LBJ by one vote. Stevenson took the case all the way to the Supreme Court. The Court decided it had no jurisdiction. Both sides cheated, but there is little doubt that the decisive 203 Johnson "votes" in Ballot Box 13 from South Texas were fraudulent. Installed in the Senate, he contrived to acquire a rich broadcasting franchise for Lady Bird.

THE FIXER: The kiss on the bald head of the powerful Speaker Sam Rayburn (another "Mr. Sam") was habitual: Sam was a friend of his father and "a daddy to me." When the Democrats won the Senate in 1955, LBJ, at 46, became the youngest majority leader. Felled by a heart attack in July—he weighed 225 pounds and smoked three packs a day—he recovered to become the most effective leader the Senate had ever seen. He diluted the seniority system and masterminded progressive compromises with the conservatives. He moved from voting with the South. He was one of only three senators from the states of the Confederacy who refused to sign the 1954 Southern Manifesto defying the Supreme Court on *Brown*. In crafty footwork with and against Dixiecrat Richard Russell of Georgia and Mr. Sam, he beat a conservative coalition to pass the Civil Rights Act of 1957.

He pushed for the creation of the National Aeronautics and Space Administration (NASA) after *Sputnik*, got the minimum wage increased and sponsored Hawaii's admission as the 50th state.

He thought he would win the 1960 nomination for president on the first ballot but lost 806–409 to Kennedy. He became JFK's running mate only reluctantly and after deviousness on both sides. Bobby Kennedy and JFK's team were hostile, and LBJ, as vice president, sulked in the undemanding job. He was all but ignored by the White House.

A RARE DEFEAT: The man being subjected to the Johnson Lean is Abe Fortas, a longtime adviser. He was the first person LBJ called after the Dallas shooting and the lawyer who persuaded the Supreme Court that it had no jurisdiction to open the ballot box that made LBJ a senator. He reluctantly became an associate justice of the Supreme Court, tricked by LBJ into appearing at a presidential press conference. But two years later LBJ had to withdraw his nomination to be Chief Justice. He could not find a way around opposition from Senate conservatives. Then exposure of financial indiscretions forced Fortas to resign his seat.

FOLK HERO: The cocky bantamweight George Corley Wallace (b. 1919), who had been a Golden Gloves boxer, ran four times for president, in 1964, 1968, 1972 and 1976. In 1966, when state law prevented him from running again for governor, he put up his sweet wife, Lurleen, though she had undergone surgery for the cancer that was to kill her in 1968. She was a political neophyte, but she won; and Wallace ran the state again.

GEORGE WALLACE PLAYS HIS DARK HUNCH

American politics changed forever at the community center of the St. Sava Serbian Orthodox Church in Milwaukee, Wisconsin, on the night of April 1, 1964. Governor George Wallace, impertinently up from Alabama to campaign for the Democratic presidential nomination in the heart of enemy territory, confirmed his instinct that there were Northern counterparts to the rednecks who made up his base back home. The Slavic plant workers and shop girls and waitresses had packed the church to sway merrily to polka versions of "Dixie" and "Way Down Upon the Swanee River" and root and holler for Wallace's thinly disguised racist pitch. Few blacks lived in Milwaukee at the time, things were booming and there was little crime, yet somehow local whites were convinced blacks were out to steal their money, their homes and their livelihoods.

Wallace entered primaries in Maryland and Indiana as well as Wisconsin. The experts thought he might get 10 percent of the vote. His average was a stunning 35.4 percent. He did not come close to upsetting Johnson, who was running in those states only through surrogates, but Wallace had discovered a vital link in the emerging conservative majority in the North and South. He exploited the white backlash with a raw, visceral genius. He had not always been a racist demagogue. When Wal-

lace lost the governor's election in 1958 he swore, "John Patterson out-nigguhed me. And boys, I'm not to be out-nigguhed again." He began to speak in public with more restraint than in private ("'Course, the U.N.'s just a cannibal club," he told his biographer Marshall Frady, "but I couldn't be going and saying that on TV, you know"). But the voters understood his coded assaults on the civil rights bill and "pointy-headed intellectuals" in Washing-

ton. He created a coalition of frustration from white- and blue-collar workers who had formed the core of the prevailing liberal coalition and suburban white-collar small businessmen. It was as if, wrote TV journalist George Kiker, "Wallace had been awakened by a white blinding vision: they all hate black people, all of them. They're all afraid of them. Great God! That's it! They're all Southern. The whole United States is Southern!"

FLASH FORWARD: 1966–1987

GUNNED DOWN

Badly wounded, he is embraced by his second wife, Cornelia Ellis Snively, a niece of Big Jim Folsom. They had a spectacular breakup in 1977.

Twenty-four hours before his triumph in Maryland and Michigan on May 21, 1972, George Wallace was gunned down in the parking lot of a Laurel, Maryland, shopping center and paralyzed for life. The shooter was 21-year-old Arthur Herman Bremmer, a Milwaukee loner. In 1976, fighting from a wheelchair, Wallace was thrashed by Jimmy Carter, but he won his way back to the governor's mansion from 1983–1987—with the bulk of the black vote. Wallace had repented for his racism. He appointed more blacks than anyone in Alabama's history. He crowned the black homecoming queen of the University of Alabama, where ten years earlier he had stood in the doorway to bar black entry. And when the Rev. Jesse Jackson called on him he implored him, "I'd like you to pray for me," and Jackson did, invoking God's "mercy and healing power."

ALL THE WAY WITH LBJ

In the 1964 presidential campaign, Senator Barry Goldwater, the apocalyptic prophet from Arizona, came galloping out of the desert to tilt his shining lance at Lyndon Johnson and "morally decadent" liberalism. He never struck even a glancing blow. He scared so many people, as he veered wildly to the right, that he was constantly issuing clarifications and denials.

When he said he would end the Cold War by lobbing a grenade into the men's room at the Kremlin, it was only an antic expression of his deepest beliefs. He was a romantic libertarian with about-equal anathema for communism and labor unions. He promised that as president he would drop an atomic bomb on the "Chinese supply lines in North Vietnam"; resume dirty nuclear tests; break off with Russia; give ground "commanders" in Europe discretion to fire tactical nuclear weapons; sell off TVA; and privatize Social Security. He embroidered it all on his banner: "Extremism in the defense of liberty is no vice! And moderation in the pursuit of justice is no virtue." He would have certainly ended the civil rights reforms. He was one of only six Republicans in the Senate to vote against Johnson's landmark Civil Rights Act.

For all that, Barry Goldwater was seen as a nice guy with a zany style. His house on an Arizona mesa was a hodgepodge of devices: a bedroom microphone that picked up the sound of running water from a stream; a flag that automatically raised itself at sunrise and lowered itself at sunset to the boom of an automatic cannon. He loved to fly, following war service of ferrying bombers across the Himalayas. During the roll call that nailed his nomination in San Francisco he was high above the Cow Palace convention, swooping back and forth in a jet.

Goldwater won the Republican nomination because there was an interregnum in American politics between the old power brokers and the new primary system, and a small coterie of right-wing operators took advantage of it. Clifton White, a wartime bomber pilot and public relations consultant, was the key figure. On October 8, 1961, he secretly called 22 of his party friends to Chicago. The old pros

The first major candidate known to be of ethnic Jewish origin, Goldwater used to joke that only half of him could join an exclusive country club. He was the grandson of an early frontiersman, "Big Mike" Goldwasser, from Poland, who founded a trading post that grew into a chain of department stores. Goldwater made a name fighting organized corruption after he was elected to the Phoenix City Council.

The Democratic ads left Goldwater twisting slowly in the wind. A girl plucking daisy petals counted down to the oblivion of an atomic bomb explosion. The film did not mention Goldwater or the Republicans, but the shriek of indignation acknowledged that the point went home. Goldwater's slogan, "In your heart, you know he's right" was translated by Democrats to read, "In your heart, you know he might."

would have thought it absurdly early to plot the unknowable, but by the spring of 1962, the jaunty White had Goldwater lobbyists in nine regions. They worked so subtly at ward and precinct levels that they did not register on the radar of the other candidates from the Eastern liberal wing: Governor Nelson Rockefeller of New York, Governor William Scranton of Pennsylvania, Governor George Romney of Michigan and former senator Henry Cabot Lodge III.

White's group, a convergence of ideologues and party loyalists, attracted the jingoists of the John Birch Society. Founded by an aged Texas oil millionaire, H. L. Hunt, and a wealthy Massachusetts candy manufacturer, Robert Welch, the Birchers were a fringe but they had money and they worked hard; they also tended to be anti-Semitic, racists, prigs and conspiracy theorists. There were more than a hundred of them as delegates at the Republican Convention and they howled when Rockefeller defended moderation; his recent divorce and remarriage excited screams of "Lover, lover!" It took him 15 minutes to get through his 5-minute speech, waiting for the boos and catcalls—plenty of time to leave the Republican party divided and dead for 1964.

Johnson was not without embarrassment at his coronation at the Democratic Convention. Civil rights activists in Mississippi founded a left-liberal multiracial coalition, the Mississippi Freedom Democratic Party (MFDP), and sent 68 delegates to challenge the all-white delegation. Fannie Lou Hamer captivated a live TV audience by describing the way she had been beaten in Winona, Mississippi. Hubert Humphrey brokered a deal for Johnson, who worried about white backlash: MFDP would get two delegates, the rest would be seated as honored guests, and segregated delegations would not be accepted in future years. Fannie, and most of the 68, would not budge.

Probably none of the Republican candidates had a prayer against Johnson, but in state after state Republicans shunned Goldwater. Nobody, not even FDR or Warren Harding, matched LBJ's percentages: 43 million (61 percent) to Goldwater's 27 million (39 percent), 486 to 52 electoral votes. Goldwater carried only the five Deep South states and (barely) his own Arizona.

JOHNSON'S HISTORIC ACHIEVEMENT

Richard Goodwin, summoned to the White House swimming pool, marveled at the massive presidential flesh floating naked in the water, "a sun-bleached atoll breaching the passing sea, passing gently. . . . Moby Dick, I thought." It was April 1964 and Lyndon Johnson was in a hurry to get something down on paper about his vision of what America could become—the Great Society, where the exalted promise would be realized for everyone. Goodwin, a leftover Kennedy aide, first in his class at Harvard Law, recalls that LBJ wanted him to write a statement of national purpose almost prophetic in dimension that would bind citizens in a "great experiment" to achieve abundance, justice and liberty for all; that would satisfy the desire for beauty and the hunger for community and altogether advance the quality of American civilization.

It was a noble conception, first made public by a black-gowned LBJ in a commencement address at Ann Arbor, Michigan, on May 22, 1964. And he delivered. Through the first ten months of 1964, an awesome 90 of his 115 legislative recommendations were signed into law. "Get those coonskins up on the wall," he would tell people around him. It was the last great social-political reform movement of the American century. Even including the Progessive era, and the New Deal, it is not possible to find in American history a swifter and more thoroughly successful articulation of the ideal in the reforms put together by Johnson and his randomly accumulated brain trust of former Kennedy administrators, academics and congressmen. It is also not possible to find an idea or movement in American history that has been as thoroughly demonized in the popular imagination.

Johnson predicted that the wolves would come "tearing at every joint." The attack from the right wing has left the impression that the Great Society was a concoction of wasteful, misguided, ineffectual social work projects that served only to encourage sloth and theft and squandered enormous amounts of taxpayers' money. Most of this is myth. First, none of the Great Society programs included a "dole." Johnson was insistent

on this point. According to Nicholas Lemann, in his groundbreaking work *The Promised Land: The Great Black Migration and How It Changed America,* economist Lester Thurow was given the task of going through the Economic Report of the President and removing anything that could be construed as putting cash in the hands of poor people. All the Great Society social service monies were disbursed for education, legal aid, job training, urban renewal and the health care of the aged and needy—in other words, all of what are now deemed the only worthy areas for investment in social welfare. The language of the Great Society was strikingly similar to the nineties language of "reform," stressing self-help and personal responsibility.

Second, it was not the Great Society that ran a phenomenally rich country into the red. It was the Vietnam war that did that. In Johnson's entire term of office, social welfare spending went from $67 million to $127 billion, including local and state spending. The war cost $842–$885 billion in 1969 dollars. The much maligned

Office of Economic Opportunity budget, including the eminently successful Head Start, Job Corps, Teacher Corps and Volunteers in Service to America (VISTA) programs, doubled from 1965 to 1968, but still only reached a total of $1.7 billion—a good day's bombing in Vietnam. The wider argument can be made that the Great Society caused a long-term budget problem by adding two more popular entitlements to social security, in Medicare and Medicaid. These do take up a significant portion of the federal budget today, but they did not in Johnson's time. Any solution to their cost burden must be predicated on a more general overhaul of the national health care system. A related shibboleth is that the Great Society created a vast new government, run amok. It did create a bevy of new jobs and offices, but other economies were enough to hold the increase in federal employment to 1.3 million nonmilitary workers from 1.1 million. The budget was still balanced in 1969.

Finally, the Great Society did not set off the urban riots of the late sixties that so traumatized America. The chronology of

EMANCIPATION: Kennedy began it, but Johnson finished it: On July 2, 1964, watched by civil rights leaders, the cabinet and congressmen, he signed the Civil Rights Act banning discrimination in public accommodations and employment. In twenty months, 430,000 blacks were added to the voting rolls. Julian Bond was elected to the Georgia House of Representatives, and Jim Clark was thrown out in Selma. Robert Kennedy, who resented Johnson's accession, is the solitary seated figure on the left.

THE JOHNSON TREATMENT

Being lobbied by LBJ was a startling experience. He grabbed people by both lapels, a habit he picked up from his father, and leaned his 6 feet 5 inches on them, talking nose to nose. Picture after picture (see page 513) captures the Johnson treatment. He has the victim by the elbow or the shoulder, poking a finger in the chest. If they are seated, he has drawn himself right up to the subject's chair and once again the long Johnson arm is grappling with an elbow or a knee, the presidential mouth usually agape in some semblance of friendliness—a laugh or a leer or a piece of mimicry—but seemingly more intent on devouring the subject at hand.

His vice president, Hubert Humphrey, said: "He'd come on just like a tidal wave sweeping all over the place. He went through walls. He'd come through a door, and he'd take the whole room over. Just like that. Everything." The long suffering Humphrey would sometimes show the scars where LBJ, releasing his grip, had kicked him on the shin as he ordered, "Get going!" Governor George Wallace had the wind knocked out of him in a White House meeting in March 1965. Johnson put his great arms around him, gripped him by the knee and spoke to him as one populist to another: "Why don't you let the niggers vote?" When Wallace mumbled something about the authority of the

Swimming pool conference with Jack Valenti and Lloyd Hand, August 1965.

county registrars, Johnson flared, "Don't you shit me, George Wallace!"

Of course, LBJ's legislative genius was more than a matter of theatrics. He knew the personal interest of every member of the Senate. He reconciled people with diametrically opposing views by advancing inch by inch on what they could agree on, or trade. He had the quickest of minds and instant recall of detail. He knew where the bodies were buried; he pulled in one key vote on civil rights by appealing to a congressman's black mistress. He

stopped only for four or five hours of nightly rest. One of his aides, Joe Califano, says: "All but a handful of hundreds of memos I sent him for night reading were acted on and returned the following morning." Aides would have to follow him into the bathroom; he talked through the shower and on the toilet, a stream of injunctions coming from the open door. And LBJ had one of the best staffs and one of the best cabinets in presidential history. Their only blind spot, like his, was Vietnam.

---

events inveighs against this calumny. The first of the serious riots took place in Rochester, New York, in the summer of 1963—before Johnson had become president. Rioting recurred in Rochester in 1964 and spread to New York and several other cities before Johnson had even proposed most of the Great Society to Congress. The Watts riot in Los Angeles, one of the worst conflagrations of the decade, took place when Johnson was working the Great Society through Congress. The always unlikely argument that disappointed expectations in the Great Society set off the riots is thus rendered absurd. Johnson's programs had not even begun. Are we supposed to believe that people rioted out of hope? In fact, the riots began to die down around the time that Great Society money and programs were providing jobs and education. Johnson remarked, "If we've had [the riots] with it [the Great Society], you can imagine what we'd have had if we had continued to sit on that

dynamite keg." The point is persuasive but not conclusive. The overwhelming evidence is that most of the riots, perhaps all, took place because of local frustrations as the middle-class white populations and inner-city jobs followed Eisenhower's gleaming new highways to the suburbs and many upwardly mobile blacks joined them, further destabilizing poor black neighborhoods.

Just what did Johnson achieve? Medicare and Medicaid that protected the health of the old and most of the poor. He nearly wiped out elderly poverty at a stroke. Civil rights laws that empowered black Americans as never before, accompanied by the first black appointments to the Cabinet and the Supreme Court. Funds for preschool, elementary, secondary and higher education. Head Start to bring underprivileged children into the mainstream. Cleaner air and water standards that 30 years of backlash have not destroyed. For the working poor, a hike in

the minimum wage and food stamps. For every consumer, a score of protective laws. Cultural enrichment through the National Endowments for the Arts and Humanities, the John F. Kennedy Center for the Performing Arts, the Corporation for Public Broadcasting. Some of these have come under fire for controversial grants, but the majority of their contributions have kept the best traditions of Western culture alive throughout the country. The most ambitious additions in a generation to national parks and other preserved lands. And a nice big tax cut for everyone.

All of the programs bequeathed at least some net, tangible benefit to American society. They were brought about in the best tradition: carefully tailored to a human scale, to specific programs; engineered with the help of leading minds in Congress and society at large; conceived on a national basis but largely administered locally; and sold to the public through sincere and open advocacy.

JOKING MATTER: Neshoba Deputy Sheriff Cecil Ray Price (left) and Sheriff Lawrence Rainey face indictment without a qualm. It is four years since the murders and they expect the jury will acquit them, as Mississippi juries had always acquitted whites accused of crimes against black people or civil rights workers. Photograph by Bill Reed.

THE THREE MARTYRS OF NESHOBA

Cornelius Steele was eager to exercise his right to vote. He was one of the elders of the Mount Zion Methodist Church in the tiny all-black community of Longdale, isolated in the red clay hills of Neshoba County, east central Mississippi. No Negro had been allowed to register in Neshoba since 1935 and he was pleased when early in 1964 two young men drove in to offer help to the citizens of Longdale. They introduced themselves as Michael "Mickey" Schwerner and James Chaney from Meridian, 35 miles away, where they worked in a community center funded by the Congress of Racial Equality (CORE).

Schwerner, who sported a goatee, was a gregarious, 23-year-old white social worker from New York whose wife, Rita, taught a sewing class as part of the Freedom Summer program of voter registration and social work; his inseparable partner, Chaney, nicknamed "Bear," was a quiet black 20-year-old volunteer from Meridian who did most of the driving on their eerie forays along Mississippi's dark, desolate highways. On Memorial Day they spoke to the congregation. On the night of June 16, members leaving church were beaten by a gang of white Klansmen looking for Schwerner. They burned the church to the ground.

Schwerner and Chaney heard the news when they were in Oxford, Ohio, helping to train the first 100 of 600 students who had volunteered for the Mississippi Freedom Summer project. One of them, an aspiring actor who was adept at playing the role of a raging redneck in mock scenarios, was Andrew Goodman, 20, the son of liberal parents from Manhattan's Upper West Side. He accepted Schwerner's invitation to join the Meridian office. On Sunday morn-

ing, June 21, when the trio drove from Meridian to Longdale, they had only three days to live. Schwerner, the first white civil rights worker to venture outside the state capital, had already been marked for "elimination" by Sam Bowers, the owner of a jukebox business with a passion for swastikas and the imperial wizard of the White Knights, a Klan spin-off.

The Klan did what it liked in Neshoba County. Sheriff Lawrence Rainey, 44, and his deputy, Cecil Ray Price, 26, were Klansmen. Rainey had an explosive history of violence against blacks; Price was a race baiter.

Schwerner and his two companions spent less than two hours in Longdale, taking statements from the beaten members of Mount Zion; around 3 p.m. they began the 45-minute drive back. They headed their 1963 blue Ford station wagon down High-

The three disappeared on June 21. Until their bodies were found on August 4, the local attitude was that it was all a publicity stunt. "They're around somewhere laughing at the commotion they've stirred up," said Sheriff Rainey.

THE CHANEYS: Ben, Sr.; Ben, Jr.; and "Mama," Fannie Lee Chaney, at a memorial service for James in August 1964. The Schwerners and Goodmans wanted their sons buried with Chaney. They were forbidden by Mississippi law, which mandated segregated cemeteries. Photograph by Vernon Merritt III.

way 16. Price, on watch near the county seat of Philadelphia, had a full description of their car and license plate, courtesy of the state's secret Sovereignty Commission, a blatantly unconstitutional body set up by the legislature in 1956 "to do and perform any and all acts" to protect "sovereignty." With the help of two state patrolmen, Harry Wiggs and E. R. Poe, Price stopped the Ford and arrested the three civil rights workers for "speeding" and also made them suspects in the Mount Zion arson: arresting civil rights workers for crimes against them passed for humor in the South.

Price locked up his prisoners in the Philadelphia jail. He kept them there on the false pretext there was nobody to handle the case. They were not allowed to make a phone call. The CORE office in Meridian, alarmed by their absence, began calling every jail and hospital starting at 5 p.m. The Philadelphia jailers, an old couple, apparently played dumb. The three were kept locked up until 10 p.m., when they were asked to pay a $20 fine and set free. Price and Rainey had needed those six hours. The Klan had to get its killers together, find a place to dispose of the bodies, and arrange alibis.

Chaney set off in the dark down Highway 19 with his companions. Two cars of armed Klansmen were somewhere behind them. The plan was for the state patrolmen, Wiggs and Poe, to stop the Ford as it passed a gas station. They declined, which gave the unsuspecting Chaney more of a lead on the Klansmen. Price then put himself at the head of the Klan cars in a furious effort to catch Chaney's Ford. It was within ten miles of the county border when Price's headlights showed up in the mirror. His souped-up Chevy, siren screaming, gained on the Ford. Chaney put his foot down, standard procedure for civil rights workers pursued at night in Mississippi by lawmen or any other whites. Then he tried to lose Price by suddenly cutting off at an exit to narrow Highway 492. Price caught up and Chaney stopped.

Price ordered Chaney, Goodman and Schwerner into his car and with the Klansmen following drove up a wooded, unmarked sunken road. There, at the edge of a ditch in the glare of the headlights, the three were swiftly murdered. Wayne Roberts, a 26-year-old Meridian ex–high school football player, who had been dishonorably discharged from the Marines for fighting, drunkenness and absence without leave, said to Schwerner: "Are you that nigger lover?" "Sir," Schwerner responded, still clinging to his faith in reason, "I know just how you feel." Roberts shot him in the heart. Then he killed Goodman. James Jordan shot Chaney in the abdomen, Roberts shot him in the head. The bodies were buried in an earthen farm dam.

Everyone maintained they knew nothing about the "missing" three. Governor Paul Johnson said it was all a hoax and joked publicly about the disappearances with visiting Governor George Wallace. The county and the state did nothing. The FBI, on previous form, would have done nothing, too. But President Johnson was committed to civil rights and he knew how to pressure J. Edgar Hoover. A small army of FBI agents moved in. With the help of a Mafia enforcer and a large reward, they got some Klansmen and others to talk. On August 4, agents dug up the bodies.

Rainey, Price and 17 of their Klan cohorts were charged with conspiracy to deprive the CORE trio of their civil rights. The trial was stalled for years, largely through the help of Southern officials in the federal court system. The federal judge, Harold Cox, was notoriously prejudiced; he called Negroes "chimpanzees." Alibis, notably Rainey's, and real doubt led to hung juries or acquittals for most of the defendants. John Doar, the assistant attorney general, persisted. In his last case, he got his men. On December 29, 1967, an all-white jury convicted Price and six others. Roberts and Sam Bowers were sentenced to ten years in federal prison. Jordan, who cooperated, got four years. Price got six years, as did another Klansman. Three others got three years, apiece.

"They killed one nigger, one Jew, and a white man," Judge Cox later confided. "I gave them what I thought they deserved."

JIM CLARK DELIVERS THE VOTES

Ten years into the civil rights movement, the battle of the lunch counters and bus seats had been more or less won. But for all the eloquence and bloodshed none of the campaigners had made much headway on the right to vote. President Johnson felt he could not so soon follow up the 1964 Civil Rights Act with a Voting Rights Act. His heart was for it, but his head was counting the Southern votes he needed for his Great Society.

King and the SCLC decided that the anvil for political equity should be Selma, Alabama, a decaying Faulknerian town of 29,000 on the muddy banks of the Alabama River that had long played a pivotal role in the politics of the Black Belt. Blacks were terrified of registering, but they were terrified in other places. The attraction of Selma was in the character of James G. Clark, Jr., the Dallas County sheriff. He was a beefy racist with a Mussolini jaw and a hair-trigger temper, a made-for-television bully. If Clark were to be provoked to show what blacks face, public opinion might be galvanized and LBJ would have to act.

Selma was scary. Bernard and Colia Layfayette had scouted the town in 1962–63 for a SNCC campaign, and Bernard had been lucky to escape with his life when two white thugs beat him over the head with a gun on June 12, 1963, the day after Kennedy's great speech and the murder of Medgar Evers. The Layfayettes were joined in September 1963 by SNCC's Diane Nash Bevel and James Bevel— James was also clubbed and jailed—and by John Lewis. Despite all their efforts, by November 1964 only 2.1 percent of eligible blacks were registered.

King arrived in January 1965, trailing clouds of glory as a Nobel Peace Prize winner. To Joe Smitherman, the young mayor, he was still "Martin Luther Coon," but Smitherman and his director of public safety, Wilson Baker, wanted to play it cool. When King led 400 to the courthouse to register, Baker opened "guest books" where applicants could sign and go home to await the unlikely news that they could come back and register. Clark upset the plan. He jailed scores who refused to use a back alley "colored" entrance. He manhandled a revered figure, Mrs. Amelia Boynton, widow of a county agent. The assault on

her provoked 100 black teachers, who had been loath to endanger their relative privilege. Risking their jobs, they marched in silent, bitter protest. When their leader, the Rev. Frederick D. Reese, mounted the courthouse steps, a nearly hysterical Clark jabbed him hard in the stomach with his billy club. Clark then got into a fight with a rugged Mrs. Annie Lee Cooper when she announced, "There ain't nobody scared around here." On February 1 he arrested and jailed King and 960 others. By February 5, some 3,000 blacks were in jail, spilling out into improvised prison camps. On February 10, a posse of thugs Clark had deputized ran out of town nearly 200 protesting high school and junior high students. The deputies jabbed them with electric cattle prods, relenting only three miles out when the students collapsed in exhaustion and terror. On February 16, Clark punched the Rev. C. T. Vivian.

Baker and Smitherman had lost control. Fifty miles down the road in Montgomery, Governor Wallace was ruminating over how he could exploit it all for political advantage. A less cool observer was his director of public safety, the pill-popping Colonel Al Lingo. His poorly disciplined men began to seep into Dallas County. On February 18, they ambushed an ill-advised night march. Jimmy Lee Jackson, a 26-year-old lay preacher who had never been in trouble in his life, tried desperately to protect his mother and his 82-year-old grandfather, who had already been beaten bloody. A trooper clubbed him in the face, another, named Fowler, shot him in the stomach.

Jackson's insufficiently noted death was the origin of the famous march to Montgomery. Bevel proposed they confront Wallace with Jackson's coffin. This proved impractical, but after much dispute between SNCC and SCLC it was decided to go with a petition and defy a Wallace order against marching. King was not there when an impatient 600 set out on foot on the overcast afternoon of Sunday, March 7; he was in Atlanta, on his way back from seeing President Johnson, and was forever after in an "agony of conscience" when he heard what he missed. At 4:15 p.m., 50 of Lingo's helmeted and masked state troopers, lined up across the Edmund Pettus

Bridge, gave the walkers a 90-second warning, then ran at them with billy clubs, tear gas and bullwhips. A posse of Clark's deputies charged, flailing wildly. "Get those goddamned niggers!" Clark bellowed. "And get those goddamned white niggers!" Seventy were hospitalized. John Lewis, a future congressman, fell with a fractured skull. Amelia Boynton was gassed and clubbed. Troopers ran into a church, picked up a teenage boy and hurled him through a stained-glass window depicting Jesus as the good shepherd.

"Bloody Sunday" evoked national outrage. ABC interrupted *Judgment at Nuremberg,* a film about Nazi racism, to show the price of a vote in Alabama. Nearly 400 clergy were among those who answered

The Selma march was like a liberating army to the desperately poor blacks of the Alabama backwoods who poured out to see. It was as if a dam had been broken through which flowed the final pieces of civil rights legislation the movement had been pursuing since 1954. Photograph by James Karales.

King's call to march on Tuesday, March 9 —ministers, rabbis, priests, students and others, many of them white. One of them paid with his life. Such was the ugliness of Selma in 1965, that three unknown, white clergymen walking down a street were assumed to be enemies. Four thugs jumped them, yelling, "Niggers!" The Rev. James Reeb was clubbed to death. As in Philadelphia, Mississippi, the summer before, the death of a white man seemed to make more of a splash than the murder of a black one, embittering some of the radical members of SNCC.

King was in a dilemma. He had gone to court to ask the fair-minded U.S. District Court Judge Frank Johnson to lift Wallace's ban. Johnson could not even hold a hearing until Thursday, March 11. To SNCC's militants that was irrelevant. But, as Andrew Young explained, King distinguished between federal and state judges: "He said that from 1954 the only ally we've had has been the federal courts. And we have to respect the federal courts, even when we disagree." King's compromise, worked out privately with federal mediators and known only to a few, was to lead a token march but turn back at the bridge on the understanding they would not be attacked. He was somewhat disingenuous about it. Just before they all set out, he told

an expectant throng: "Nothing will stop us, even the threat of death itself." When they did turn back, the SNCC activists were furious. They called it Turnaround Tuesday.

But King's was a wise decision. On March 18, Judge Johnson revoked Wallace's ban. On March 21, King led 3,200 marchers on the first leg of a triumphant three-day march buoyed up by the knowledge that they had won not just a battle but the war. President Johnson had already told Attorney General Nicholas Katzenbach: "I want you to write the goddamnedest toughest Voting Rights Act you can devise."

CHAPTER THIRTEEN

THE WAR OF LOST ILLUSIONS 1963–1975

The Watershed of Vietnam

The sky has darkened behind the smiling generals in their summer whites. It is 1967 in Vietnam. Somewhere out there in the rice fields and mountain jungles nearly half a million American combat troops are trying to save South Vietnam from communism (troop strength will peak at 536,000 by the end of 1968). By the end of the Johnson presidency in January 1969, 35,000 of those Americans will have come home in body bags. By the time peace is declared in January 1973, in the Nixon presidency, some 58,174 Americans will have died. By 1975, for all the sacrifice, South Vietnam will be absorbed into the Communist state of Vietnam.

It was the longest war in America's history, in the end the most unpopular war, and the first modern war America lost. Vietnam was a watershed. It ended the liberal consensus that America had a duty to fight everywhere abroad for freedom. It destroyed the illusion of American omnipotence. It demoralized the armed forces. It polarized the country as nothing had since the Civil War. It gave the right a new issue, the lack of patriotism of the flag burners among the dissenting left. It diverted billions of dollars from education, health and welfare. It left a legacy of inflation: the $150 billion spent on the war between 1950 and 1975 was not covered by raising taxes. And it shattered everyone's faith in the honesty and credibility of government, since every administration involved systematically deceived the people.

MORE, PLEASE: Armed Forces Day in South Vietnam, 1967. Commanding General William Westmoreland (center) was telling Washington he was on the verge of winning the war but needed another 200,000 troops to raise the total to 670,000. He did not get them. In Philip Jones Griffiths's photograph, Westmoreland is at a South Vietnamese military cemetery near Saigon with Lieutenant General Chae Myung Shin, commander of South Korean forces in Vietnam, and Lieutenant General Nguyen Huu Co, South Vietnamese premier, who would soon be dismissed on charges of corruption.

THE "NOBLE CAUSE" AMERICA CANNOT FORGET

America fought the war in Vietnam, it has been said, to stop Hitler from taking Czechoslovakia. Four presidents were impaled on that epigram. In the minds of Eisenhower, Kennedy, Johnson and Nixon, Southeast Asia in midcentury looked like Europe in 1938—or so they said by way of justifying a war that none of them wanted. If they allowed the Communists to take South Vietnam, as Neville Chamberlain had allowed Hitler to take Czechoslovakia, then Thailand, Burma, Malaysia, Indonesia and perhaps even India would go red, just as Poland, France, Belgium, Holland, Norway and Denmark had gone Nazi black. In Asia, the falling "dominoes" would topple America's island defense chain of Japan, Taiwan and the Philippines and then on southward across the equator, the hot breath of bolshevism menacing Australia and New Zealand. Lyndon Johnson even asserted that if America lost Vietnam it would find itself defending the beaches of Waikiki.

None of the policy makers in Washington mistook Hanoi's sly Ho Chi Minh (1890–1969) for the ranter of Munich, but in the eyes of the presidents and their bureaucracies, the demons that drove Hitler were matched by the colder imperial ambitions of Uncle Ho's supposed masters in Beijing and Beijing's supposed masters in Moscow. In the Cold War, every challenge to the settled order was assumed until proved otherwise (and even then) to be part of a global ideological conspiracy requiring the same tough response in Saigon as in Salonika or Seoul. It became a reflex. Reality was more complex; and reality changed with the passage of time.

The notion of Indochina as part of a global Communist plot—conventional wisdom in Washington after Mao entered Beijing in 1949 and Kim Il Sung struck out for Seoul in 1950—ought to have at least leaked a little of its air in 1954. Days after the red flag was run up over the French redoubt at Dien Bien Phu, Vyacheslav Molotov and Zhou Enlai lowered it a notch or two at the Geneva peace conference by wringing concessions out of the intransigent Vietminh. China's historic resentment of Vietnamese ambitions manifested itself in Zhou's willingness to pressure the Vietminh to withdraw their battalions from Laos and Cambodia (while two French bases were allowed in Laos). Molotov leaned on the Vietminh to accept a north-south partition at the 17th Parallel, instead of the united Vietnam the battlefield victories had put within their grasp. The Vietminh had to withdraw 100,000 soldiers from the South, and they were obliged to wait two years for the national elections they wanted within six months. Britain's Anthony Eden, cochairing the conference with Molotov, remarked on differences between the Communist participants. Eisenhower's secretary of state, John Foster Dulles, there to scowl but not sign, was too busy trying not to shake hands with Zhou for any of this to make a dent in his vision of monolithic communism. No doubt Moscow relished the illusion of omnipotence, but Molotov was telling the truth when he confessed to Eden that he could not deliver the Chinese. They were "very much their own masters." So were the Vietminh.

Indochina, as part of the Asian mainland, was not originally seen as being on the ramparts of containment, at least not in the eyes of the author of the doctrine, George Kennan, who became an outspoken critic of the war. But even before containment was codified, a simpler anticommunism had begun to override America's historic anticolonialism. The Atlantic Charter and the Truman Doctrine, pledging support for "free peoples resisting subjugation by . . . outside pressures," should have nudged America toward the side of the Vietnamese revolutionaries against the postwar presumptions of the French, who had colonized Cambodia, Laos and Vietnam in the late nineteenth century and been kept on as front men by the wartime Japanese occupiers. Ho, unlike many other nationalists in Southeast Asia, repulsed Japanese efforts to recruit him to their team. The Vietminh, the broad front coalition he formed in 1941, aligned itself with the Allies, pledging to fight both Imperial Japan and Vichy France. American officials encouraged the Vietminh's hopes of postwar independence, and FDR seemed inclined to support them. The Office of Strategic Services (OSS), the precursor of the CIA, trained Vietminh guerrillas, and the OSS Deer team, parachuting into a jungle camp early in 1945, saved Ho's life; Washington's future tormentor was wasting away, "a pile of bones covered with dry yellow skin." Ho acknowledged his benefactors by declaring Vietnamese independence, in Hanoi, on September 2, 1945, with an explicit, unmistakable reference to 1776: "We hold the truth that all men are created equal, that they are endowed by their Creator with certain unalienable rights, among them, life, liberty and the pursuit of happiness." The Soviet Union did not recognize Ho then, or for five years. It showed no interest at all in Indochina, and in his early actions Ho behaved less like a party-line apparatchik than a radical reformer. In the words of a 1947 State Department report, he established himself "as the symbol of nationalism and the struggle for freedom to the overwhelming majority of the population."

He was a Moscow-trained Communist, but he was a fair bet to become the Asian version of Yugoslavia's Marshal Tito. In fact, Ho risked Soviet wrath in 1950 by asking for recognition of his regime from Tito, by then the pariah of the Soviet bloc. As early as May 1945, however, President Truman favored France. It was not that Truman feared Ho's communism; rather, he just had too much on his mind to weigh biography against big-power politics. Indochina was a sideshow. The communism that preoccupied Truman then was in Europe. If the French were thwarted, they might well retaliate by refusing to go along with America's wish to rearm West Germany in the embryonic Atlantic alliance. In the face of apparently limitless Soviet appetites, letting the French resume consumption of their little Asian delicacy seemed a small price for keeping them in an agreeable mood. As for the aspirations of the Vietnamese, the diner was encouraged to leave a gratuity of pious hopes for progress toward independence.

The Far East division of the State Department, as yet unpurged by McCarthyism, had warned that same May 1945 that reimposing French rule would bring "bloodshed and unrest for many years." They lost out to the European desk, but they had it right. Truman took the first blind step into the quagmire in September 1950 when, in the wake of North Korea's attack on South Korea, he approved a military assistance program. By the end of his presidency, America was paying 40 percent of the cost of the war between France and the Vietminh—later pejoratively labeled the Vietcong (Vietnamese Communists, or VC). A little more than a year into the Eisenhower presidency America was paying 80 percent. Having forged a Korean truce, Ike warned against another land war in Asia, and, brushing aside the advice of his vice

LBJ'S DOMINOES: Anything to take his mind off the war, even Ike's metaphor for the threat, at his ranch in January 1968. In Washington, sleepless and in his bathrobe, he would go to the Situation Room and read teletypes to see how many of "his boys" had been lost. He did have a personal stake; his son-in-law Charles "Chuck" Robb was a Marine officer in Vietnam.

Here, military advisers have just told LBJ something big is brewing. They think it is an attack on Khe Sanh, which will be valorously defended; it turns out to be the Tet offensive at the end of the month, a military victory for the U.S., but a political disaster. Photograph by Yoichi Okamoto.

president, he refused to rescue the French at Dien Bien Phu. Yet, as he prepared to hand the White House to Kennedy, he tried to make the president-elect's flesh crawl with visions of the disaster that would ensue if Laos were allowed to fall to communism. In office, Kennedy settled for a tenuously neutral Laos, but was eager to test counterinsurgency doctrines in the fledgling South Vietnam. By the time of his assassination, 16,000 Americans, military and civilian, were advising the Saigon government of Premier Ngo Dinh Diem.

As America took over from the French, after Geneva split the country in two, domestic political calculations added impetus to foreign-policy ones, more perhaps than we have generally realized. Every president knew, as State Department adviser James C. Thomson, Jr., put it, that he was the last domino in line. Joe McCarthy's ghost lingered. No politician

of any party, least of all a Democrat, was willing to expose a flank to the "Who lost China?" witch-hunters. In the 1964 presidential campaign, when there ought to have been a real debate on how deeply America should get involved, Johnson was very happy to embrace a proposal from his right-wing opponent, Barry Goldwater, for a secret pact to preserve national unity by not attacking each other over Vietnam (or civil rights). Goldwater regretted later that he did not force Johnson to "square off" on the issue, though the one who truly should have regretted it was Johnson. A public disavowal of another land war, just a decade after Korea, might have saved him from the slippery slope; his margin of victory was so huge it could have withstood some erosion. But Johnson's style, bred in smoky caucuses, was to obtain a consensus from a tightly knit group of power brokers, and then to sell the public the most palatable version. His determination to avoid wide public discussion and congressional scrutiny only became more intense the more the Vietnamese war became an American war.

In the movie *JFK,* which suggested that Kennedy was killed so that the militarists could have their way, director Oliver Stone makes much of an LBJ remark to a group of service chiefs at a White House reception on Christmas Eve 1963: "Just let me get elected, and then you can have your war." Chilling! It sounds as if his mind was made up. But it wasn't; he was simply telling them what they wanted to hear. Stanley Karnow, the author of the indispensable *Vietnam: A History,* points out that Johnson, like most politicians, often said very different things to different people. A more reliable guide to his thinking—and his despair—became available in 1997, when the Johnson

Library released tapes of some of his private telephone conversations. In one of May 1964, nearly a year before he committed U.S. combat troops, Johnson can be heard confessing a surprising skepticism about Vietnam. "I don't think it's worth fighting for and I don't think we can get out," he lamented to his old mentor Senator Richard B. Russell, the Georgia Democrat. "I don't see that we can ever hope to get out of there once we are committed. It's just the biggest damn mess." This was not a sentiment he dared express in public. He believed that public opinion was already against the conflict—it wasn't, yet—but he worried about Congress. "They'd impeach a president, though, that would run out, wouldn't they?" he asked Russell. Johnson had his own special reason for not offending the fervently anticommunist senators from the South: he needed their votes for his Great Society legislation.

An even more elemental instinct than political gamesmanship was at work through the years both of escalation and of retreat. No president wanted to be the patsy. Nixon said he would rather be a one-term president than permit America to become "a second-rate power." All the presidents believed that for the most exultantly powerful nation in the world to be humbled by barefoot peasants in black pajamas in a "damn little pissant country," as Johnson put it, would be to incite a rash of troublemakers everywhere, petty dictators and subversives as well as supposed Red pawns. That was a rational fear. But for Johnson, and to a lesser extent for Nixon, the Vietcong became as much a personal affront as a strategic challenge. They can't do this to LBJ! They can't do this to RN! Every night when he fell asleep, Johnson told Doris Kearns Goodwin, he could see himself tied to the ground in the middle of a long open space

R. Pryor

and in the distance hear the voices of thousands of people running at him, shouting, "Coward! Traitor! Weakling!"

Clark Clifford, who advised both Kennedy and Johnson, and who himself oscillated from dove to hawk and back to dove again, suggests in *Counsel to the President* (1991) that for all Kennedy's proclaimed anticommunism, his emotional detachment would have kept him from Johnson's fatal course. The scholar John M. Newman concluded, in *JFK and Vietnam* (1992), that while publicly proclaiming a continuing commitment (to appease the right) and modest goals (to appease the left), Kennedy was secretly planning to withdraw as soon as he was reelected. On the other hand, Richard Helms, who was then a high-ranking CIA official, and later director, told the author he was convinced that Kennedy would have fought on because he so hated to lose anything. This is tenable. JFK's closest adviser, Bobby, remained a hawk until 1967. Either way, much more important than the parlor game of what Kennedy would have done is the Kennedy Effect. That was real. Kennedy's ghost was always tugging Johnson's sleeve. Ridiculed as a hayseed, sidelined as a vice president, LBJ yearned to be acclaimed a fit successor to the young martyred president, so gallantly mounted and caparisoned to save the free world. In the anguish of deciding his priorities between "the woman I really loved—the Great Society" and "that bitch of a war," LBJ could always hear echoes of the cheers from the ranks of the elite that crisp sunny morning in 1961 when Kennedy pledged the nation to "bear any burden." The men in Kennedy's cabinet—"the best and the brightest," in David Halberstam's memorably ironic phrase—were there every day to remind Johnson of JFK's commitment. He was impressed

by them, too. It was understandable. Robert McNamara, Dean Rusk, McGeorge Bundy, Walt Rostow and the bookish chairman of the Joint Chiefs of Staff, General Maxwell Taylor, were brainy and assertive New Frontiersmen. McNamara and Bundy were the sharpest blades, trailing glory from the Cuban missile crisis. America's youngest Defense Secretary at 44 in 1961, McNamara was, in Johnson's phrase, "a can-do fellow." He was the epitome of American know-how, of slide rules, systems and brusque logic, plucked from the presidency of the Ford Motor Company after only seven weeks in the job. He had first made his reputation as a wartime whiz kid who had found new techniques for managing the U.S. Air Force. He looked machine-polished, lean and taut in rimless glasses with not a hair out of place—Johnson told the reporter Tom Wicker "that man with the Stay-Comb in his hair is the smartest of the lot." McGeorge Bundy, who became Johnson's National Security Adviser, was a Boston Brahmin, streaking from Groton and Yale and Skull and Bones to be a Harvard dean in his early thirties. He was a determined man; to get into the Army, where he rose from private to a war-planning captain, he concealed his myopia by memorizing the eye tables.

HOW LBJ GOT HIS BLANK CHECK FOR WAR

The picture as Johnson painted it was bound to inflame people in America. Sailing peacefully at night in the Gulf of Tonkin on August 4, 1964, two U.S. destroyers had been attacked by 22 torpedoes launched from North Vietnamese patrol boats. It was the second "unprovoked" attack in two days. It was time to teach them a lesson! Johnson went on national television on August 4 and said the "repeated" acts of violence required the reply that was being given as he spoke. At 10:43 p.m. U.S. naval aircraft began 64 sorties against patrol boat bases and oil storage depots in North Vietnam. The next day Congress gave Johnson, as president and commander in chief, discretion "to take all necessary measures, including the use of armed force," against North Vietnam. Only 16,000 U.S. forces were in Vietnam at the time.

The Gulf of Tonkin Resolution, which had been prepared months earlier, was the justification for a vast expansion: 550,000 troops came to be committed without further consultation. The Constitution gives Congress alone the power to declare war. Johnson and, in turn, Nixon never asked for a declaration of war; and Congress never demanded the right to debate one. No war could have better illustrated the constitutional mandate for a declaration. No one in the House voted against Tonkin and only two senators did: Oregon's Wayne Morse (1900–1974) and Alaska's Ernest Gruening (1887–1974). The senators regarded Morse as a sanctimonious old bore. Hardly anybody was in the chamber when he declared they had been misled.

Morse was right. The battle of August 4 never took place. On a wild night in the gulf, jumpy sailors shot at shadows, misread sonar. The commander of one ship, the *Maddox*, Captain John J. Herrick, had grave doubts. He was harried out of them by Admiral Ulysses Grant Sharp, Jr., commander of the Pacific Fleet in Honolulu, and an impatient McNamara in Washington.

Official and unofficial investigations had by 1984 concluded that there was no attack on August 4. Despite the overwhelming evidence, McNamara balked at admitting error. When he circulated the manuscript of his book *In Retrospect* for comment before its 1995 publication, Karnow pointed out to him that everyone from the CIA and a Senate investigating committee to Admiral James Stockdale, who was flying over the area at the time, concluded that August 4 never was. In his book McNamara stubbornly concluded: "The second attack appears probable but not certain." A second edition was published the next year. In this, McNamara wrote: "On November 9, 1995, as the second

edition was going to press, I learned in a meeting with General Vo Nguyen Giap, North Vietnam's Defense Minister during the war, that the presumed attack on August 4 did not occur." That is all. It was a chilling echo of the intransigence he displayed in the war years.

Nor was the first attack unprovoked. The U.S. warships sailed in disputed waters. And they had been gathering electronic intelligence in the wake of clandestine attacks by South Vietnamese forces on North Vietnamese bases. The attacks originated not with Saigon but with the secret 303 Committee in Washington. In 1964 when Morse suggested the U.S. knew of these "Plan 34A" raids, McNamara retorted: "Our navy played absolutely no part in, was not associated with, was not aware of, any South Vietnamese actions, if there were any. I say this flatly. This is a fact."

It wasn't a fact. McNamara was playing word games—and worse. The 34A operations were administered by the CIA, not the Navy, but Captain Herrick knew all about 34A and the South Vietnamese raids. In *In Retrospect,* McNamara says he had learned "later" of the Navy's involvement: "My statement was honest but wrong." It was wrong and dishonest. The Pentagon Papers include a schedule of 34A attacks approved in McNamara's department ahead of time. He knew all about the 34A raids and must have known the Navy knew. In any event, his reply to Morse was meant to deceive by the pretense that he and the administration knew nothing about the raids. Note his words "if there were any."

McNamara rejects the charge that the administration deliberately provoked the attacks to justify an escalation of the war. The truth is more subtle. The first attack was unexpected. The Pentagon never thought that the North Vietnamese would dare attack a U.S. warship in the vicinity of a 34A raid—but Johnson and his men did try to provoke the second attack by sending warships back. They were so eager to have the ships attacked they probably mistook whatever did occur and used the emotional moment to manipulate Congress and the news media. LBJ had not decided on war, but he remembered well how Truman had suffered politically by going to war in Korea without a congressional declaration. He wanted a blank check in case he needed it, and he got it with the connivance of McNamara, Dean Rusk, Bill Bundy (McGeorge's brother) and others. The effect was to grant the presidency an enormous expansion of power that Congress never intended and the public barely realized until it was too late.

Johnson wanted more than the advice of these Kennedy men; he wanted their respect. And so he listened to them, willing himself to be impressed, hoping a consensus would emerge. It did. They were all hawks, they were all incisive and they all had the lethal gift of certitude. The voices of the Kennedy knights were amplified by the Chiefs and, offstage, by ex-president Eisenhower, who never ceased urging the direct military action from which he himself had recoiled in office. They had no scruple about referring to JFK. On one of the Johnson tapes, Mac Bundy teases: "Also, Mr. President, you can do what I think Kennedy did at least once. . . ." For a year after his accidental accession, Johnson Agonistes held to a middle ground,

resisting the arguments for disengagement advanced by Under Secretary of State George Ball and Senate Majority Leader Mike Mansfield, but again and again rejecting demands for a bombing campaign against North Vietnam. He rejected one after an attack against the Bienhoa air base on October 30, 1964; he rejected another when a barracks in Saigon was blown up on Christmas Eve. The Chiefs had to be content with tough talk. As Minority Leader in 1954, Johnson had heard all the secret arguments about bombing Dien Bien Phu in 1954—arguments finally squashed by President Eisenhower.

But Johnson was vulnerable to his desire for consensus in the club of the powerful. McNamara and McGeorge Bundy learned how to play on his insecurity to get the military action they and the Chiefs thought necessary. The turning point came just one week after LBJ's inauguration, on January 27, 1965, when Bundy and McNamara presented him with what McNamara, in his memoir, calls "our fork-in-the-road memo." The memo edged close to touching the nerve of cowardice. It did so by retailing criticism from Saigon: "Our best friends have been somewhat discouraged by our own inactivity in the face of major attacks on our own installations . . . they see the enormous power of the United States withheld. . . . They feel that we are unwilling to take serious risks." Johnson's "passive policy" could lead only to "disastrous defeat" or a "humiliating" pullout. Then they squeezed the bureaucrats' pincers. He had only two choices: he could decide to fight or he could salvage what little he could by negotiation. "Bob and I tend to favor the first course," Bundy wrote.

Bad luck removed any possibility that Bundy's more prudent instincts might resurface. Dispatched to Vietnam after his memo, he was in Saigon on the night of February 6, when the Vietcong mortared the air base at Pleiku. They killed eight Americans and wounded more than a hundred. Bundy visited the wounded in the hospital. He was appalled and angry. In Washington, Johnson, urged on by McNamara, approved Operation Flaming Dart, a single retaliatory bombing strike against a North Vietnamese army camp. Then, flying back across the Pacific, Bundy, with the help of McNamara's right-hand man, John McNaughton, put the finishing touches to a memorandum that was finally to transform a Vietnamese conflict into an American war. It made the case for "reprisal" raids that would add up to a sustained bombing campaign: there would be "reprisal" raids even if there had been no specific outrage calling for a response. There was no other way, Bundy told Johnson. "Any negotiated withdrawal today would mean surrender on the installment plan." He added the pacifier that the campaign "would in no sense represent any intent to wage war."

The doublespeak runs like a silken thread through the decision making. The ploy of disguising an air war as a series of spontaneous one-time reprisal raids seemed to satisfy Johnson's nervous insistence on doing something—but not something that would crack his domestic support. When the Bundy plan was presented to a National Security Council meeting on February 8, attended by congressional leaders, Johnson said it would be a way of responding to aggression "without escalating the war." Vice President Hubert Humphrey saw through the conceit and, along with Senator Mansfield, said so; he was promptly excluded from a year's NSC

meetings. Johnson gave the bombing go-ahead on February 17, rejecting Bundy's advice to announce it and explain it. Operation Rolling Thunder began on March 2. Only six days later the first U.S. Marine infantry battalion arrived at Da Nang. By the end of the year, 181,000 American fighting men were in Vietnam. They would have been intrigued to learn their presence in no sense represented any intent to wage war.

In the light of Johnson's constant misrepresentation, subterfuge and Texas-size fudging, it is not surprising that the origins of this swift and secret escalation have been cloudy. Clark Clifford, who succeeded McNamara as Defense Secretary, suggests that the military tricked the president into war on the installment plan. It "unanimously" endorsed the air war without telling Johnson that it would necessarily entail sending ground troops to defend the air bases—and that those troops could then be redeployed into offense. It was, says Clifford, "the greatest failure in the entire decision-making process." It was also the birth of the "credibility gap."

Clifford has a point. There was no consensus on combat troops, and none on whether the objective of bombing was military interdiction or political pressure. The Army leadership in Washington and Vietnam had little faith in bombing. They believed only troops would make a difference. But Bundy, author of the air war, was vehemently opposed to committing and so was General Maxwell Taylor, who had become ambassador to Saigon. General Earle Wheeler, who had succeeded Taylor as chairman of the Joint Chiefs, persuaded the divided military leaders that they would have more freedom to maneuver if they kept their misgivings to themselves and unanimously endorsed the air war. They did. And it is true that somehow or other, then, neither McNamara nor the Chiefs told Johnson that approving the air war meant approving the simultaneous dispatch of troops.

The suspicion naturally arises that Johnson was edged along. McNamara denies there was any attempt to deceive. "All of us should have anticipated the need for U.S. ground forces when the first combat aircraft went to South Vietnam—but we did not. The problem lay in a signal and costly failure to foresee the implications of our actions. Had we done so, we might have acted differently." The Chiefs knew the truth; if McNamara is to be believed, they withheld it from their civilian supporters. They had already planned the troop deployments before the air war decision was made. When the Marines went in, the public was told in official statements that they were going simply to defend the air bases. Within three weeks, Westmoreland asked Johnson to allow these defensive

BETRAYAL: Senator J. William Fulbright (1905–1995), the Democratic senator from Arkansas, felt betrayed by his friend Johnson. As chair of the Senate Foreign Relations Committee in 1964, Fulbright got LBJ the power to wage war, in the Gulf of Tonkin Resolution, then became horrified by what he did with it. LBJ picked up Truman's epithet, calling him Senator Halfbright, but Fulbright's Senate hearings, starting in February 1966, were a brave focus of crusading dissent. Photograph by Yoichi Okamoto.

troops to go on the attack; and Johnson agreed, in secrecy, over Taylor's objections.

If Johnson was indeed conned into all this, why did he agree as readily as he did? The answer must be that he deceived himself, or allowed himself to be deceived, as he deceived Congress and the public. He was playing it by ear, unwilling to face either the reality of what he was doing or a public outcry. His mastery of compromise had lifted him to power and now he was once again practicing that fine art, or so he imagined. He was going to war more slowly than the Joint Chiefs wanted, but much faster than the public realized. In July, when he announced a decision to send 175,000 troops by the end of 1965, he followed what an aide called his "policy of minimum candor." They would not be in harm's way; the South Vietnamese would still bear the brunt of offensive operations.

The monumental scale of all the decisions was matched only by the monumental shiftiness of the deciders. But within the military Johnson made no secret of his belligerence. The ferocity of Johnson's response shook the Marine General Victor Krulak, a battle veteran of World War II, when Krulak

briefed him in 1966 on how hard it was for the Marines to find and engage the Vietcong. Johnson, his face flushed with anger, got up from his chair and pounded the desk with his fist: "Kill the goddam bastards, kill 'em, kill 'em, kill 'em!" He had climbed the red-mud parapets of the Alamo.

America was waist deep in "the big muddy" for two decades at high cost to human life and to its self-esteem. Four reasons for the disaster have been suggested here: containment ideology (and idealism); domestic political calculation; fear of humiliation (the Munich syndrome); and individual personality, all compounded by arrogance, bureaucratic ambition and ignorance of Vietnamese history and culture. The mix of motives was as volatile as the U.S. aims. As the war went badly, the abstraction of preserving American prestige and credibility replaced the specific of establishing a free and independent South Vietnam. Altruism was low in John McNaughton's 1965 Pentagon calculus of U.S. aims—"70 percent to avoid a humiliating defeat (to our reputation as guarantor), 20 percent to keep SVN [South Vietnam] (and the adjacent territory) from Chinese hands, 10 percent—to permit the people of SVN to enjoy a better, freer way of life." Strategy came to be designed less to win territory or allegiance than to impel Hanoi toward negotiation by killing as many of the enemy as possible. The "decent interval" that Nixon and Kissinger thought they had bought for South Vietnam to preserve its own independence turned out to be neither decent nor much of an interval, and ended in vast suffering and recrimination.

Vietnam has not ceased to torment America. It has attracted a large body of scholarship and journalism, but reconciliation is elusive. Illuminating as the documents and memoirs are from the American side, we know as yet too little about the decision making on the other side to assess why a settlement remained so hard to achieve through the presidencies of Johnson and Nixon. Hanoi was at least consistent to the end that they would not settle for less than American withdrawal. When America did pull out, none of the dominoes fell with South Vietnam and its auxiliary battlefields, Laos and Cambodia. Hong Kong's peaceful transfer to Communist China had nothing to do with Vietnam. Walt Rostow and others have invited us to take consolation in the fact that the leadership groups in Malaysia, Hong Kong, South Korea and Thailand tell visiting Americans they believe the U.S. stand bought them time in the formative years of 1963 to 1973 to strengthen their societies and transform themselves from vulnerable kittens into fierce little tigers. It is an appealing theory, but that is all it is. Beyond it, there is nothing to show for the sacrifices and the devastation of Indochina.

What went wrong? Almost everything. Who was to blame? Almost everybody.

Through the fifties and most of the sixties, a broad consensus in both parties in Congress, in business and the labor unions, in the prestige press and in the public, vigorously endorsed the domino theory. David Halberstam and Neil Sheehan exposed the corruptions of South Vietnam and the fabrications of the U.S. military, but until 1967 even they backed the war's objectives, and argued against withdrawal. Like almost everyone else, including the rest of the press corps in Vietnam, they wanted their country to stay and win. Even when the expansion of the war was in full swing in February 1966, only five senators were ready to vote to repeal the Gulf of Tonkin Resolution. The only two senators who had voted against the original resolution—Wayne Morse and Ernest Gruening— were turned out by the voters in 1968. Just before the Tet offensive began on January 30, 1968, the Americans who classified themselves as hawks (56 percent) still far outnumbered the doves (28 percent). The early advocates of pulling out were few—and brave. It is peculiarly hard, as suggested earlier in this book, to go against a common sentiment in America. The political and social pressures are for conformity. The first teach-in about the war was held at the University of Michigan at Ann Arbor, in March 1965. It was not until after Tet three years later that the broadcaster Walter Cronkite, "the most trusted man in America," made his famous prediction on the *CBS Evening News* that America was at best facing a stalemate. This was a turning point for the public, but it was no more than a reflection of what the more morose opinion makers were saying in the White House and Pentagon. Earlier skeptics risked being ostracized, or smeared as unpatriotic or Red. Johnson asked

the FBI to investigate Morse's supporters in Oregon. Government spokesmen and their allies in Congress and the media often portrayed antiwar protesters as "hippie" freaks. In fact, the great majority of them were not notably radical. It took years for "negotiation now" to become demands for "immediate withdrawal." Nor was the press a hotbed of pacifist opinion. The editorials in the *Washington Post* were so supportive, until 1968, that Johnson liked to say they were worth 50 divisions. Neil Sheehan told the author that he believes he and David Halberstam would have been fired by the *New York Times* if they had seen the truth earlier and stressed the futility of the strategy of attrition. Henry Luce's *Time* matched William Randolph Hearst's jingoism in the Spanish-American War. The country's leading newsmagazine rewrote reports from Saigon exposing official lies to conform to official optimism, then in its own pages denounced skeptical battlefield reporters for inventions. When the press became more critical after Tet, it was only reflecting divisions in the government, catching a fast-moving train of opinion.

A certain forgetfulness came to prevail later. In 1996, the *New York Times* commented bitterly on McNamara's belated

DOUBLE DEPRESSION: And things got worse. McNamara and his deputy, Cyrus Vance, in May 1965, invigilated by a bust of the president who began it all. Johnson discussed Vietnam at a Tuesday lunch. At this one, the news is that Hanoi is not responding to a bombing pause. By spring of 1967, McNamara was disillusioned. But he bottled up his feelings. He could not bear to share his distress with his wife and children, not even on the day a young Quaker, Norman Morrison, burned himself to death within 40 feet of his Pentagon window. One evening Jackie Kennedy, in a passionate outburst, beat him on the chest, pleading that he "do something to stop the slaughter." The stress got to him. Johnson feared he would take his life, as James Forrestal, Truman's Defense Secretary, had done. On November 1, 1967, a very lucid McNamara sent LBJ a blockbuster of a memorandum for phasing down the war and making peace. He never got a reply. In February 1968, LBJ eased him out to be chairman of the World Bank. Photograph by Yoichi Okamoto.

confession. In every quiet and prosperous moment, it wrote, he must surely still hear "the ceaseless whispers of those poor boys in the infantry, dying in the tall grass, platoon by platoon, for no purpose." But what the *Times* called the "ghosts of those unlived lives" must also circle close around all the mainstream editorial writers of McNamara's day, including those of the *Times* itself.

In the end, it was not McNamara's or Johnson's war; it was America's war.

There were justifications, more or less, for some of the official and popular misperceptions of containment. The official ideology of every Communist Party on earth did, after all, envision the worldwide triumph of communism as a historic inevitability; and that ideology was taken seriously by some who abhorred it as well as by some who embraced it. When Khrushchev said "We will bury you," he meant "We will outlive you," not "We will kill you"—but the message was unsettling all the same. Khrushchev did call wars of national liberation a sacred cause, North Korea did invade South Korea with Soviet complicity, Castro did provide a base for nuclear missiles, Hanoi did get war supplies from China and the Soviets. And the endless flow of optimism from the military led the public to expect another triumph of American arms. "It's silly talking about how many years we will have to spend in the jungles of Vietnam when we could pave the whole country and put parking stripes on it and still be home by Christmas," was the way it was put in October 1965 by a gubernatorial hopeful in California named Ronald Reagan. The main responsibility for the debacle must remain, of course, with the three successive administrations; they all tried to conceal from the people the extent and nature of the war—not for sinister purposes but for a quieter life amid other turmoils. But underlying and affecting both the decision-making process and public opinion in the crucial years was a psychological attitude more important than any of the "mistakes": the mostly unspoken conviction, almost an instinct, that compared with foreign countries America ultimately could do no wrong and had the power to put everything right. In a word, hubris. Walter Lippmann, writing critically in 1965, called it "a visceral feeling. . . . If therefore we are agreed among ourselves, none can withstand us because none should withstand us and we shall and must prevail." Invincible ignorance was the perverse flip side of American optimism and American generosity. The anti-Communist chauvinism of the fifties and early sixties was expressed in simplistic moral terms. Societies unlike America were more or less deficient in virtue and competence; the Western democracies were in the family, but in the role of

genially eccentric uncles and grasping aunts. (It was symptomatic that George Ball's paper of 1964 advocating negotiations was dismissed as "Eurocentric.") Beyond the democracies, there were the primitive states and the Marxist untouchables. There was no penumbra for the complexities of Vietnam.

The Vietnamese had retained their sense of nationhood and cultural continuity against the armies of the Mongol emperor Kublai Khan; they had resisted assimilation by successive Chinese dynasties; in 70 years as French subjects they had taken some that was good from French culture and some that was bad (such as a curiously Cartesian form of Communist romanticism), and rejected most of the rest. Yet it was hardly appreciated that they might not be just another domino with different dots. America, Jonathan Schell noted, was attempting to impose an American fantasy on a Vietnamese reality. It had no comprehension of a society where authority was defined by the clan, the village and the traditionalist sect; where the peasantry regarded great wealth as antisocial; and where leaving one's land under an anti-Communist resettlement program, for example, was tantamount to abandoning one's identity. When American officials made a belated attempt to fit such knowledge into their planning, it was, in the words of Frances FitzGerald in *Fire in the Lake* (1972), "something like the effort of the seventeenth-century astronomers to fit their observations of the planets into the Ptolemaic theory of the universe."

Having reexamined the record of his meetings for his memoir, McNamara stands frankly baffled at how little the best and the brightest knew of Vietnam, and how often they failed to consider basic questions. It was just assumed, he says, that North Vietnam was under the thumb of Moscow, that the fall of South Vietnam would trigger the fall of all Southeast Asia, and that the Vietnamese Communists therefore constituted a grave threat to the West's security: "Such ill-founded judgments were accepted without debate." And even in McNamara's mea culpa there is no glimmer of recognition of what America became in its well-meant ascent up the volcano of assumptions. It became a colonizing power. From 1954, the U.S. merely replaced the French, employing a superior killing machine to deny victory to a national liberation movement led by Communists. The hero of Neil Sheehan's shocking masterpiece *A Bright Shining Lie,* Lieutenant Colonel John Paul Vann, summarized the situation in a 1965 memo: "A popular political base for the Government of South Vietnam does not now exist. . . . The existing government is oriented toward the exploitation of the rural and lower class urban populations. It is, in fact, a continuation of the French colonial system with the upper class (Catholic) Vietnamese replacing the French. . . . The dissatisfaction of the agrarian population is expressed largely through alliance with the [National Liberation Front]."

Is the ignorance McNamara admits excusable? They were "flying blind," he says, because the McCarthy purges of the fifties deprived the Kennedy and Johnson administrations of East Asian and China experts. The loss of the China hands hurt, but it does not explain, still less justify, the vast carelessness. There was information—on Vietnamese society, on the real state of the war, on the roles of Moscow and Beijing. It was available—in the academy, years before the teach-ins; in the middle echelons of the bureaucracy; in journals like *The New Yorker*, *The New Republic* and *The New York Review of Books*; and it was available at the time of the crucial decisions. Early critics like John Kenneth Galbraith, I. F. Stone, Noam Chomsky, C. Wright Mills and George Kahin might have been disregarded as "radical," but there on file was the 1954 report of Army Chief of Staff Matthew Ridgway to Eisenhower that air-naval superiority would be indecisive and intervention would risk a costly air-land war. And there was the French experience. Nobody could read Jean Lacouture, François Sully or Jacques Chaffard and remain sanguine. "Anti-Communism will be a useless tool unless the problem of nationalism is resolved," was the warning General Jacques Leclerc had brought back from Vietnam as early as 1947, and everything during the next two decades simply underlined that truth.

Advice was not sought and it was not welcome. When the Army Chief of Staff George Decker told President Kennedy and Defense Secretary McNamara that the U.S. could not win a conventional war in Southeast Asia, they fired him. McNamara and Rusk had no time for State and CIA experts who had doubts. Johnson ventilated his considerable talent for vilification on Walter Lippmann and Charles de Gaulle when they each started to suggest that Vietnam was not so relevant to America's security and well-being that it merited fighting a land war, one where no lasting military victory was possible. Criticism slid off the gloss of a dazzling self-assurance—long before President Reagan, the warmakers were Teflon men. One of the notable cold warriors, Paul Nitze, then Navy Secretary, has written in his memoirs a description of how McNamara eviscerated dissent. Nitze, having visited Vietnam in the spring of 1965, suggested that sending another 200,000 troops would be futile and it was time to call it quits. "He bore down on me with his piercing black eyes," writes Nitze. The subject was closed as soon as it was opened. The hostility to anything

but the party line radiated from all levels of the leadership. Vann saw very early on in the sixties that the Army he loved was heading down a path of murder and delusion at the service of corrupt and incompetent regimes in Saigon without popular support. He could not get a hearing. The CIA's best experts fared no better when they tried to topple the Humpty Dumpty of the domino theory. In June 1964 Johnson asked his "working group" of eight State, Pentagon and CIA officials, reporting to a superior group headed by Rusk, McNamara, McGeorge Bundy and Taylor, whether the theory was still true. The CIA's Board of National Estimates reported that it wasn't: "With the possible exception of Cambodia it is likely that no nation in the area would quickly succumb to communism as a result of the fall of Laos and South Vietnam. Furthermore a continuation of the spread of communism in the area would not be inexorable, and any spread which did take place would take time—time in which the total situation might change by any number of ways unfavorable to the communist cause." Sensible, but heretical. The working group's report to Johnson put Humpty together again: "the so-called domino theory is oversimplified. . . . Nevertheless Communist control of South Vietnam would almost immediately make Laos extremely hard to hold, have Cambodia bending sharply to the Communist side, put great pressure on Thailand . . . and embolden Indonesia to increase its pressure on Malaysia." The process "could easily, over time, tend to unravel the whole Pacific and South Asian defense structures." The loss of Vietnam "would almost certainly" provoke a major conflict "and perhaps the risk of nuclear war." Would sight of the original CIA report have affected Johnson's thinking? Three years later, on September 12, 1967, the head of the CIA, Richard Helms, sent Johnson a 33-page analysis which concluded that if the U.S. quit Vietnam "the risks are probably more limited and controllable than most previous argument has indicated." Johnson, so far as is known, showed it to nobody.

The policy makers did not have immoral or imperial intentions, as the more radical protesters claimed. The documents show they were not naive enough to think they had much chance of real democracy in South Vietnam. As Johnson said of Diem, echoing FDR on Nicaragua's Anastasio Somoza, he was "our sonofabitch." But they did for years believe they were threatening international communism, and Johnson was imbued with the spirit of the New Deal (or pork barrel politics) when, in 1966, he offered aid that would turn the Mekong Delta into a Tennessee Valley if the Vietcong would stop fighting. In the later stages, the rhetoric of the policy makers may

PACIFIERS: Daniel Ellsberg (right) was a superhawk when he got to know John Vann (center), the T. E. Lawrence of Vietnam, photographed with a village official in remote Hau Nghia in 1965. Ellsberg, a Harvard-educated ex-Marine, was a crusader for Vann's strategy of stealing the social revolution from the Communists. Back in Washington, he had a change of heart. Assigned to work on McNamara's secret project to collate policy documents from 1954 to 1968—the Pentagon Papers—he leaked them to Neil Sheehan at the *New York Times*. The friendship with Vann just about survived, but Vann was killed in a helicopter crash before he had to testify at Ellsberg's trial.

have simply been a way of rationalizing a disaster from which they could not extricate themselves, but at the beginning saving South Vietnam and Southeast Asia, the "noble cause" of President Reagan's later valediction, was a genuine aspiration. The grim consequences for the Vietnamese of falling under totalitarian rule suggest a certain vindication of the effort. The creditable motives of the policy makers, however, hardly justify the deceptions they practiced—beginning with Kennedy right through to Kissinger. Very early in Vietnam, the lies became so complex, as William Prochnau documents in *Once Upon a Distant War* (1995), that American officials became accustomed to lying to themselves. After all, they had to conceal the fact that JFK's noncombatant "advisers" were in combat, and that the thousands who came in were not really there

because that would have violated the Geneva accords prohibiting foreign troops. This is not to suggest Americans had a monopoly here. Hanoi maintained throughout the 1972 peace talks that Saigon faced only a popular insurrection, not an invasion. But major elements of the North Vietnamese Army (NVA) were certainly assembling in the South by the spring of 1965, despite the success of the Vietcong guerrillas.

It might have been a noble cause to defend South Vietnam against "outside" aggression if the South had been a viable state, with some degree of social cohesion, some degree of leadership, some degree of loyalty to the people—in short, some few of the qualities that gave a degree of political legitimacy to South Korea and Malaysia. Hanoi was a repressive regime, and the Vietcong were capable of great brutality. Malcolm Browne is still haunted by what he saw at the village of Dam Doi: the deliberate burning to death of dozens of women and children. In the most conspicuous atrocity of the war, the Vietcong executed 3,000 Saigon government sympathizers in Hue in the Tet offensive. Nearly a million people had fled Communist rule in 1954, mostly Catholics who had backed the French—and tens of thousands more "boat people" did so in 1975. "Uncle" Ho's men were by no means the Khmer Rouge, but neither could they be counted on to be the gentle idealists of some liberal imaginations. Still, it was quixotic of the U.S. to think it could build a nation on the political swamp of Saigon. The 1st Air Cavalry Division and the 3rd Marine Amphibious Force, as Neil Sheehan remarked, could not inspire the loyalty of the Vietnamese peasantry, and General Motors could not manufacture decent non-Communist Vietnamese leadership. Only Vietnamese could do that, and the Vietnamese leadership America had chosen to support proved again and again it could not. To paraphrase Metternich, the Saigon politicians mistook endless bloody intrigue for government. In private, American officials fumed about Saigon's incompetence; in public they talked as if South Vietnam were a model Swiss democracy. They conveniently forgot the awkward fact that the U.S. had encouraged its despotic client not to honor the Geneva pledge for national elections in 1956. Nixon and others later argued that Ho would have rigged the voting in the North, but that is a feeble excuse. The anxiety shared by Ike and his successors was that Ho would have won, even in a free vote. The absence of any semblance of a democratic mandate in the South continually weakened America's moral claim to be fighting for democracy. It helped to seed distrust and cynicism, the credibility gap that Johnson created and Nixon widened. So did the nature of a war in which the Army was trapped between banks of Pentagon computers on one side and a population in which foe was indistinguishable from friend on the other.

If the cause was noble, it was ignobly served by the means of execution. The heroism of the grunt crawling through a minefield to rescue a dying buddy was one thing; there was bravery in combat and innumerable acts of compassion for the Vietnamese. But all was overwhelmed by a conceptual cruelty, the unleashing on a peasant society of the most technologically advanced military machine ever known. The machine was blind. Surplus firepower was its only strategy, the body count its only measure of success. The killing and destruction were bound to be indiscriminate. Four million tons of bombs and 18 million gallons of poisonous chemicals are not instruments of surgical precision. Uprooting 3 million people from their ancestral homes is a form of pacification only to a fantasist. The machine was supposed to be calibrated to exert graduated pressure, on the theory that at some point the enemy would recognize his investment was too expensive. But the enemy was fighting a war of national liberation, not a Pentagon war game. The Americans never knew their enemy. They assumed that superior firepower would break morale. They judged from the body count that they were succeeding. Such cost accountancy was meaningless to the other side, which saw the war as the continuation of two thousand years of resistance to foreign rule. Ho Chi Minh was not indulging in hyperbole when he warned the French in 1946, "You can kill ten of my men for every one I kill of yours, but even at these odds you will lose and I will win."

The machine could never hope to win hearts and minds; it could only destroy buildings and bodies. "Every time the U.S. doubles the effort in Vietnam," said Sir Robert Thompson, the British guerrilla warfare expert, "she squares the error." But was America denied a good old-fashioned military victory by political meddling and panic in the media? It is a conviction that survives to the end of the century, a lingering misconception accepted now even by many who concede that the war was a bad idea. The feeling is understandable. A nation that had won every war by investing whatever it took was frustrated by what Bundy called "an all-out limited war." The difficulty lay in the very conception of the enterprise. If Vietnam was simply a civil war, America had no business being there. It was only the perception of Vietnam as a proxy for a Sino-Soviet drive for hegemony in Southeast Asia that justified intervention. But if it was then imperative to contain the expansion, it was also imperative to do so in a way that would

not provoke the patrons to turn the proxy fight into a super-power showdown. Invading North Vietnam or threatening the use of nuclear weapons would probably have done that. Nobody could be sure. Vietnam, as Churchill said of Russia once, was a riddle wrapped in a mystery inside an enigma. The dynamics among North Vietnam, China and Russia—or those between North Vietnam and the Vietcong—were opaque. In the circumstances, the civilian restraint of the military was the minimum required by common prudence.

The Stennis Senate Subcommittee, sitting in executive session in 1967, condemned McNamara for refusing to expand the air war at the behest of the Chiefs. McNamara made a plausible response. Saturation bombing, far exceeding the levels of World War II though mainly of jungle, had failed to have a decisive effect on men and supplies or Hanoi's will; on the contrary, it seemed to have stiffened resistance. Of 359 fixed targets that the military identified, McNamara had approved 302; 25 had too much pilot risk; 5 were too close to China; and the rest had limited value. Should McNamara have mined North Vietnam's ports as Nixon would in 1972? That would have hurt Hanoi more than bombing the Ho Chi Minh trail—Barry Goldwater, who flew over the trail himself, was right that the jungle canopy made it a poor target. But by the time Nixon bombed the North the circumstances were different. The North Vietnamese Army had sent 120,000 troops across the Demilitarized Zone (DMZ), and Nixon could impose on a Soviet Union eagerness for détente.

Others in the military and the Senate argued that the "mistake" lay in not invading North Vietnam, seizing Haiphong and Hanoi. Maybe Congress, the press and the public would have understood and supported that early on. But what would invasion and occupation have achieved? Barry Goldwater dismisses the idea that the Chinese would have intervened; he cites the high mountains, a barrier that did not exist in Korea, and their historic dislike of the Vietnamese—a dislike that actually is just as likely to have induced them to move in. When McNamara visited Hanoi's leadership in 1996, he asked whether they had had any pledges from the Chinese. He got no clear answer. But even without a rerun of Korea, taking the war into North Vietnam would have been reckless. If not a rerun of Korea, the result would have been a souped-up rerun of South Vietnam—or of Afghanistan, where the Soviets followed the same logic. The Americans would have had to kill hundreds of thousands more Vietnamese, perhaps millions. The idea that not enough was done, or that the press sabotaged victory, becomes ludicrous when one considers that more bombs were dropped by the U.S. on Vietnam—South and North—than in all of World War II; that the U.S. deployed such massive firepower it killed over 1 million enemy combatants; that America fought in Vietnam longer than in all the rest of its twentieth-century wars combined; and that the American public endured ten years and more of false promises. It was not press or public opinion that betrayed the military. The military compounded the political miscalculation with a blindness all its own. General Westmoreland kept getting the troops he asked for, if more slowly than the Joint Chiefs would have liked. They were dispatched on his and their assurance that through the strategy of attrition he could win the war. McNamara came belatedly to see attrition was a fantasy; LBJ sacked him in 1968 for his resistance to sending still more troops, only to find he had sacked the wrong man. But when the disillusioned president relieved Westmoreland after the Tet offensive of 1968 it was too late. Tet was effectively the end of the Vietnam war for America—not because it was reported in a panicky way, as is so often alleged, but because it exposed the futility of the whole strategy. Lieutenant General William De Puy, who wrote the original papers advocating attrition, admitted as much in an interview before he died.

The overture to Tet was a trip to the United States by Westmoreland. He used the occasion to predict that victory was in view. The Communists had been defeated; they were no longer capable of mounting large-scale operations inside South Vietnam. His words of good cheer could not have come at a better time for American public opinion—or a worse time, it transpired, for him. More than 20,000 Americans had been killed by this point, with 50,000 wounded. More than 900,000 men had been drafted and the taking of the sons of the middle class had begun to convulse the campuses. Inflation was on the rise. Not to worry, said Westmoreland, it had all been in a good cause.

Then Tet exploded.

The supposedly defeated enemy was fighting everywhere. The Vietcong and the NVA attacked 36 cities with 84,000 troops. It is true they were defeated. They were not able to hold on to a single city. With this attack, and another in May, the Vietcong in the South was virtually wiped out, suffering 32,000 dead against 2,800 Army of the Republic of Vietnam (ARVN) and some 1,000 American dead. The popular uprising on which the attackers had counted failed to materialize. But 15 guerrillas penetrated the grounds of the U.S. embassy in Saigon, and the symbolism of that stunned a Congress, bureaucracy, press and public that had just heard Westmore-

land say that American withdrawals would begin in 1969. Henry Grunwald, then a hawk editing *Time* magazine, has written how the picture of the hole in the American embassy's massive wall shocked him more than any other photograph from the war, more even than Eddie Adams's photograph of the summary street execution of a VC with a bullet to the head. If the very core of American power could be invaded by guerrillas, things could not be going as well as the public had been told.

The disillusion was strong because the illusion had been so well promoted. The transformation of public opinion that followed Tet—for the first time doves (42 percent) outnumbered hawks (41 percent)—was not the fault of press and television for focusing on the beleaguered embassy. The cathartic event was the sight of the imperturbable General Westmoreland beckoning the young men of America into an unending dark tunnel of death: his delusions intact, he followed Tet by appealing for another 200,000 men.

The fact is there was no way to "win" the war in Vietnam. America could have sent in another million men, invaded the North, fought a war with China there, possibly called on nuclear weapons, but to what purpose and with what domestic consequences? We would still be occupying Vietnam.

When Johnson threw in his hand on March 31, 1968, it was clear that America was not willing to shed more blood and hazard more of its social well-being for a chimera. The hawks were migrating south. Johnson was abandoned by key figures among "the wise men," Dean Acheson, McGeorge Bundy, Douglas Dillon and Henry Cabot Lodge, who only five months before had urged him to hold fast. His new Defense Secretary, Clark Clifford, had become a dove, pressing to speed the negotiations that began in Paris in May. By the time Nixon was inaugurated in January 1969, the plurality in the polls against going on with the war represented a fusion of two very different disaffections. Crudely put, what Nixon was to call "the silent majority" coalesced with the vociferous cheerleaders of the liberal ideology, the shorthairs with the long. The white working class, the Wallace voters and the youth in the less fashionable colleges were pragmatic in their objections. They despised the moralizing of the elites. The war was a mistake rather than a crime. A popular bumper sticker summed up the feelings of ordinary people: "Let's win or get out."

It took four years, mass demonstrations the like of which had never been seen in a Western democracy, and 20,522 more American dead, before peace was finally agreed in Paris on January 23, 1973. It became a tenet of liberal faith that Nixon and Henry Kissinger, his National Security Adviser, could have saved those lives, that the same settlement could have been achieved within months of coming to power if they had not been so concerned with American "credibility," as if they had been as clear in their priorities as De Gaulle in withdrawing from Algeria. Many points of agreement in 1972 were indeed similar to the ten-point plan Hanoi put on the table in Paris in May 1969. The U.S. rejected then what it accepted three bloody years later: the continued presence of North Vietnamese troops in the South after a cease-fire and American withdrawal. The defense is that not until October 1972, with Nixon's reelection in the offing, did Kissinger's "implacable" opposite number, Le Duc Tho, stop insisting on a central political condition—the replacement of Nguyen Van Thieu's Saigon government by a Communist-approved "coalition." Many of the millions who participated in the quiet candlelight processions and mass moratoriums in 1969 would have readily sacrificed Thieu, though that would have been repugnant to other sections of American opinion. The sacrifice of Thieu and company was not demanded even by the minority dove platform espoused by Senators Eugene McCarthy, Ted Kennedy and George McGovern and rejected by the Democratic National Convention. And the disengagement that had been the progressive cry of the hour was mutual withdrawal of forces, not the unilateral withdrawal Nixon carried out.

Nixon and Kissinger, it can be said, did bring the boys home. The tragedy is that it was done so slowly and much that was done by them heightened rancor, with disastrous consequences in Indochina and America alike. An obsessive secrecy, a cynical contempt for Congress, a hatred of "peaceniks," and an unerring talent for aggravation undid the prospect of unity for a common national purpose as the troops came home and the peace talks dragged on. The fault lines were there long before the spiral of Watergate. The military judgment that the sanctuaries in Cambodia were intolerable was correct. It was the political judgment that was flawed. Anything that seemed to extend the war was bound to be anathema. Congress behaved irresponsibly when it cut off aid to Indochina, but it was sorely provoked.

Nixon's announcement on June 8, 1969, that 25,000 U.S. troops were being withdrawn was a defining moment in modern American history. It marked the first recognition of a limit to American power, the first retreat from the role America had shouldered since World War II. The shadow of Vietnam has lain on foreign-policy crises ever since, discouraging intervention except where the goals were clear and the victory assured. President Reagan intervened in Grenada, but was

PRISONERS: American pilots at Gia Lam Airport, Hanoi, on their way home. They were among the 591 prisoners released by Hanoi between February and April 1973. North Vietnam had signed the Geneva Convention of 1949 but tortured, misused and abused captives to force them to "confess" to war crimes. For years after the end of the war, families whose sons had been reported missing in action (MIA) believed they were still being held prisoner. Hanoi repatriated more than 100 sets of remains, but there was never any credible evidence that they were holding live captives. The family anxieties were cruelly exploited by propaganda groups in the U.S.

forced to bring back the Marines from Lebanon and stay out of Nicaragua, except covertly. President Bush intervened, but with overwhelming force, in Panama and again in the Gulf War of 1991. President Clinton withdrew from nation building in Somalia, hesitated before committing American troops to Haiti and refused for two years to do so in Bosnia until genocide had shamed the West.

A soldier who was wounded as an Army captain in Vietnam had a critical say in many of these decisions. General Colin Powell, a National Security Adviser to Reagan and Bush, and a chairman of the Joint Chiefs for Bush and Clinton, offers an insight in his autobiography, *My American Journey:* "Many of my generation, the career captains, majors and lieutenant colonels seasoned in that war, vowed that when our turn came to call the shots, we would not quietly acquiesce in halfhearted warfare for half-baked reasons that the American people could not understand or support. If we could make good on that promise to ourselves, to the civilian leadership, and to the country, then the sacrifices of Vietnam would not have been in vain."

The brilliant Larry Burrows, who took this picture, was one of 135 photographers to die or disappear in the war in Indo-China. He was killed when a helicopter took a direct hit.

ZAPPING THE CONG

The *whup-whup-whup* of the Huey helicopter gunships took the air out of the living rooms of America. They'd fly over suspected VC ground. If they drew much sniper fire, they'd call in fighter bombers or artillery, and then swoop in. The riflemen would jump out of the quivering bird, firing from the hip, rushing into an empty village where there'd be only a woman and an old man and a booby trap to blow off a leg.

The Americans had the air and the day; Charlie, as the Vietcong were called, had the night and most of the ground. The Americans had mobility and firepower; the VC had surprise and spies. Charlie always seemed to know when they were coming; that chopper noise for one thing, and the barrages. On big operations, the "ass in the grass" troops would be directed by officers stacked above them in hierarchical layers, urging them to get themselves more VC. General James F. Hollingsworth, of the Big Red One, the Army's 1st Airborne Division, called it "zapping" the Cong. "There's no better way to fight than goin' out to shoot VCs. An' there's nothing I love better than killin' Cong. No sir," he told reporter Nicholas Tomalin. But when he shot a running guerrilla with his own M16 rifle he picked the man up for life-saving surgery.

In the dank mangrove swamps and rice fields of the Mekong Delta, it was hard to tell foe from friend, hard for GI Joe to find Charlie. Most of the time Charlie came at him first. Fully three quarters of all combat was initiated by the enemy who seemed to be swallowed up by the ground; a vast network of tunnels, it transpired, ran through the plantation country just north of Saigon, and up the Ho Chi Minh trail into Laos.

The other kind of fighting, which came to prevail in the ravined jungles of the north, was the set-piece battle against the regular NVA. At Landing Zone X-Ray in the Ia Drang Valley in October 1965, 450 men of the 1st Battalion of the 7th Cavalry—Custer's regiment at Little Bighorn—dropped by helicopter in the path of an NVA regiment. In a brilliant action, surrounded by 2,000 NVA soldiers, they repulsed the enemy, calling in thousands of rounds of artillery, hundreds of air strikes and, for the first time, B-52 bombers. A second 7th Cav battalion was not so fortunate. It was destroyed, ambushed just like Custer.

The Marines under siege at Khe Sanh had great spirit. Michael Herr, in his vivid *Dispatches,* tells of an NVA soldier in a spider hole who was driving them crazy by popping off with a .50 caliber machine gun from just 200 meters away. The Marines bombarded him with mortars and recoilless rifles; he came up again. Gunships rained rockets on him; when they'd gone he emerged firing. Then they called in a napalm strike; the hole was lost in black and orange flame. "When all of it cleared," writes Herr, "the sniper popped up and fired off a single round, and the Marines in the trenches cheered. They called him Luke the Gook, and after that no one wanted anything to happen to him."

THE UNFURLED FLAGS

There was never any great homecoming for the men and women who served in Vietnam, no parades, no period even of national mourning for those who had sacrificed their lives. They felt forgotten by all but their families. Collections of their letters, notably *Dear America* edited by Bernard Edelman, give a remarkable glimpse of their physical, spiritual and emotional ordeals. Michael Davis O'Donnell (above), a 24-year-old helicopter pilot from Springfield, Illinois, wrote a poem that serves well as a testament for those who went away and those who never came back.

If you are able,
have for them a place
inside of you
and save one backward glance
when you are leaving
for the places they can
no longer go.
Be not ashamed to say
you loved them,
though you may
or may not have always.
Take what they have left
and what they have taught you
with their dying
and keep it with your own.
And in that time
when men decide and feel safe
to call the war insane
take one moment to embrace
those gentle heroes
you left behind.

Less than three months after writing this poem in Dak To, Major O'Donnell and his crew of three were shot down, on March 24, and killed, on a mission to rescue eight soldiers trapped by enemy fire. He was originally listed as missing in action and officially declared dead only in 1978.

THE FACE OF "CHARLIE"

The American patrol has caught a man in an automatic ambush and Philip Jones Griffiths was there for the encounter (above). The suspect produced a *chieu hoi* (safe-conduct pass) to identify himself as a "rallyer" to the South Vietnam side. It may well have been a ruse. Infiltrators streamed down through the jungles from North Vietnam.

They, too, wrote home and kept diaries. Ceo Van Thi's diary records: "For the first time, I infiltrated into the South (B5) at 1330 hours on 19 June 1966. The blue color of the forest and mountain still stands out against the surface of the Ben Hai River. Oh! Dear little Ben Hai . . . it is no more than 30 meters wide but it causes great division between the two Vietnams. I have long dreamed of admiring this stream and

today my dream comes true. I was standing there with my heels in fresh water."

January 6, 1967: "I have returned to B5. Eight months ago the trees were green. Now they look like a burnt forest. If one 'weak spirited' man saw the scene he would not stay here because there are many fields of B-52 bomb craters which are several kilometers long. What would I be like under fire and bombardment?

"Because of the shortage of rice, I have to prepare soup in two cookers [for his group] while over my head enemy helicopters are flying. They look like black buffaloes. There was no smoke while cooking because I used Hoang Canh's cooking system."

Another day: "With a heavy canvas bag of rice on one shoulder I was so tired I

THE FRONT-LINE NURSE

The nurse in the picture is unidentified, but Lynda Van Devanter has given a moving account of her work as an Army nurse with evacuation hospitals at Pleiku and Qui Nhon in her book *Home Before Morning*. Here is a Christmas letter home:

Hi all,

I got wrapped up in several patients, one of whom I scrubbed on when we repaired an artery in his leg. It eventually clotted, and we did another procedure on him to clear out the artery—all this to save his leg. Well, in my free time, I had been working post-op and took care of him. I came in for duty Christmas Eve and was handed an OR slip—above-knee amputation. He had developed gas gangrene. The sad thing was the artery was pumping away beautifully. Merry Christmas, kid, we have to cut your leg off to save your life. We also had three other GIs die that night. Kids, every one. I'm sick of facing every day a new bunch of children ripped to pieces. They're just kids—eighteen, nineteen year olds! It stinks! Whole lives ahead of them—cut off.

Peace, Lynda, December 29, 1969

"A BABY IS NOBODY'S ENEMY"

Specialist Fourth-Class George Olsen, a Ranger who was killed in action March 3, 1970, wrote home in November 1969:

The mission before last we set up next to a waterfall in a 360 degree perimeter, making a hell of a racket doing it, I might add. It would appear that the noise of the water killed our noise because when one of our men looked over the boulders we were in, into a hollow next to us, there was Victor in blissful and fatal ignorance. We had all the time in the world to get ready, and the surprise was total. After a short and

Frank Lawrence (center) and friends just out of three months in the jungle, 1969. They are smoking marijuana. They all came home.

absolutely one-sided firefight we lit out 800 meters to an LZ (landing zone) with one Victoria Charlie and her three month old baby as POWs. We'd just made her a widow and with all the steel flying in that hollow she was lucky to have escaped unscathed. But I will say that there wasn't a man among us who wasn't glad the child wasn't hit as nobody'd seen either of them during the fight. We'd shoot a female out there without blinking an eye as a woman with a rifle can kill you just as dead as any slant-eyed Hector or Ulysses. But a baby is nobody's enemy, and, as I said, it made us feel better that it hadn't been hurt.

Specialist Fifth-Class Thomas Pellaton with the 101st Airborne Division wrote home on July 28, 1970:

There is no reason to be here—and there is even less reason to see Americans dying here. Many of the rear-echelon troops [higher-ranking officers and enlisted men] seem to be immune to their death. It makes me limp with rage—overcome with sorrow! There seem to be so many people that are insensitive to this killing, even many of the political left who called the American GI "animal," etc.

There are so few things here that keep you sane. . . . I went to a village clinic as security and got to help treat some of the children. We played games with them, went for a walk to the beach, took pictures, in general just loved them up. They stole my watch but really it didn't matter, because just before leaving I sang for them (the "Largo al Factotum" from *The Barber of Seville*—you know "Figaro, Figaro"). They loved it, laughed. But what was most gratifying, they started singing part of it back to each other. I was overwhelmed. They called me "Beethoven."

Thomas came home safely; he became maitre d' at the Carlyle Hotel in New York.

wanted to cry. I tied my hammock to tree branches, but about twelve o'clock I had to get up because the B-52s dropped bombs 500 meters from our location. I moved to the base of a big tree. The next night at 2000 hours I saw about 20 B-52 bombers. I was so frightened that I could not get in the shelter even though it was only a meter from me. I was between life and death but ten minutes later my nerves became calm. Then a second series of bombs fell. In the shelter my body was being shaken by the pressure of the bombs. I covered my ears and felt dizzy. A third series of bombs dropped about 15 meters from my shelter. Their fragments flew very fast over my head and cut my hammock. I was afraid and doing lots of thinking. I thought of my native village, parents, brothers and sisters. I remember that when I was a little boy I usually asked my mother for some piasters to buy firecrackers when the new year day came. Dear mother! I felt at this time you missed me and you always thought of me. I did not hear the firecrackers, but the explosion of enemy shells which caused the trembling of mountains and forests. The war makes everybody angry. Let's avenge this."

MAXIMUM DEMOS: Antiwar gathering in San Francisco. A chant developed: "Hey, hey, LBJ, how many kids did you kill today?" It never failed to wound and enrage the President. Later, even more gigantic crowds came out when Nixon did not get an immediate peace—in November 1969 nearly 700,000 marched in Washington, D.C., the largest single demonstration in American history. Photograph by Robert Altman.

A CAMPUS REBELLION CATCHES FIRE

Jack Weinberg, fresh from risking his life in CORE's Mississippi Freedom Summer, led a few others in setting up a civil rights information table on the campus of the University of California at Berkeley on October 1, 1964. A few weeks before, students had picketed the *Oakland Tribune* for its racial discrimination, and the university, embarrassed by a complaint from the newspaper, had banned on-campus political activity—to protests from left and right, including Youth for Goldwater.

Weinberg was soon confronted by two deans and a cop and arrested. He went limp on them. Before they could drag him off to jail several hundred students, swelling to 4,000, surrounded the car, shouting, "Take us all!" Mario Savio, a Mississippi volunteer who had been beaten by rednecks, jumped on top of the trapped car and blew a rhetorical bugle for what came to be known as the Free Speech Movement: "There is a time when the operation of the machine becomes so odious, makes you so sick at heart, that you can't take part; you can't even passively take part and you've got to put your bodies upon the gears and upon the wheels, upon the levers, upon all the apparatus and you've got to make it stop."

The students won their free-speech demands after months of rallies, sit-ins, strikes and mass arrests, but this was only a beginning. Berkeley was the spur for nearly a decade of unrest. Rebellion was everywhere, organized by the Students for a Democratic Society (SDS), which soon had 100,000 members in more than 400 chapters. Everywhere the students won, though with many a scuffle and showdown. And as important as the geographical spread of the movement was its transmutation. The "machine" Mario Savio condemned came to be not simply heavy-handed university administrators treating students like children on an assembly line, dictating where they lived, what they wore, how they grew their hair, what time they went to bed. It came to be America itself—or "Amerika," in the radical caricature of a Nazified society. The unprecedented number of young Americans who came to college in the sixties were not, most of them, radicals. Of the 27,500 enrolled at Berkeley, never more than half were engaged in the Free Speech Movement. They were more like disillusioned patriots; they had been steeped in the greatness of America, the exceptionalism of their country, and they suddenly found it wanting, first in civil liberties and then in the Vietnam war.

The war was not the issue in the early rebellions, but when they won their local battles they were, in Godfrey Hodgson's phrase, "an army in being for the antiwar movement." They were also a cause in themselves—for the rapidly developing new right. Ronald Reagan, running for governor of California in 1966, was always ready to answer a question about "those bastards at Berkeley" and their indulgence, as he liked to put it, in "sex, drugs and treason."

BATTLE LINES: Two thousand students, mainly athletes and business and engineering majors, opposed the takeover and shutdown of Columbia by SDS radicals. Here they try to prevent supplies from reaching the occupiers. In the end, the rebels won. The university promised not to build the gym they had planned in a beautiful public park in a mostly black area with access to be largely denied to the neighborhood. It ended its links with the Institute for Defense Analysis, and liberalized the campus. President Kirk resigned. Photographs (top and bottom) by Gerald Upham.

"MY COUNTER-ATTACK AT PRINCETON SHOULD RELIEVE THE PRESSURE FROM THE IVY LEAGUE ENOUGH TO ALLOW ME TO DEAL SHARPLY WITH THE WEST COAST GUERRILLA ACTIVITY."

— VIETNAM WAR —
U.S. INTELLECTUALS' ATTACKS

Student protests spread to every major campus as the sixties wore on. Fischetti's cartoon was in the *New York Herald Tribune*.

TAKEOVER: It's Dr. Grayson Kirk's cigar but the smoker is one of the rebel students who took over the office of the hard-line Columbia University president in New York in April 1968. Telephone callers were told, "We are sorry, but Dr. Kirk will not be in today because Columbia is under new management." The joke was not appreciated. Cops evicted the occupiers. A hundred students were injured, 700 arrested.

THE MARTYRDOM OF MALCOLM X

In 1965, the mesmerizing Malcolm X guessed that he would soon be dead and that he would be more important in death than in life. He was right on both counts. He knew that Elijah Muhammad, the leader of the Nation of Islam movement, had sanctioned his execution. Muhammad, living in style in Phoenix, had become jealous of Malcolm's celebrity and Malcolm had failed to keep to himself his genuine shock on discovering that the keeper of the faith was an old billy goat who had taken advantage of seven young secretaries and fathered at least thirteen illegitimate children.

On Sunday afternoon, February 21, 1965, when Malcolm was about to speak to a few hundred of his breakaway followers at the Audubon Ballroom at 165th Street and Broadway in New York, he brushed aside the anxieties of his friend Charles Kenyatta. "You've lost your faith in Allah," Malcolm told him. A fracas broke out in the crowd, prearranged by his assassins, and Malcolm raised his arms, a tall, erect figure on the platform: "Let's cool it, brothers." He was dead a few seconds later, blasted backward by a burst from Talmadge Hayer's sawed-off double-barreled 12-gauge shotgun, blasted again as he lay in his own blood, and riddled by bullets from two other Muslims with handguns. He was 39.

"He was lonely," said Kenyatta. "That's why he wanted to die. He wanted to be a martyr. He knew."

Malcolm was a fading light, then, in the constellation of civil rights leaders. He had been all but eclipsed by the established stars and such rising young firebrands of black power as the frothy Stokely Carmichael. In a 1963 *Newsweek* poll, he had ranked last when blacks were asked to name their most influential leaders. He had no achievements in public policy to compare with Charles Houston's or Thurgood Marshall's or Adam Clayton Powell, Jr.'s. He had courage but he was not famous—like Martin Luther King, Jr., or James Farmer, or thousands of black and white civil rights demonstrators—for personal, physical stands against the brutality of white racism. He was an incandescent speaker, but not an organizer of the caliber of A. Philip Randolph. He left no intellectual accomplishment of the order of W. E. B. Du Bois or Dr. Kenneth Clark. His *Autobiography*, dictated to Alex Haley in the last two, chaotic years of his crowded life when he slept only three or four hours a night, is revealing and passionate, but it is also misogynistic, odiously anti-Semitic, unquestioning of the dictatorial, totalitarian Third World regimes he embraced and full of myths—which Spike Lee's workmanlike 1992 film took on face value. Yet within a decade of his death Malcolm was beatified as the purest, the most visionary of all African-American leaders.

There is ambiguity in this appeal. It may lie in his personification of a radical new consciousness of pride and self-respect among the several million blacks who had fled the South only to coagulate in the cities as a vast underclass. For years little of the sunshine of the civil rights reforms filtered through the murk of the ghettos, where many blacks were trapped in the cycle of discrimination, unemployment, poverty, family instability, crime and addiction. For others, Malcolm's enduring appeal may lie not in his fiercely antiwhite separatism, but in his tentative latter-day attempts to reconcile black nationalism with racial brotherhood. And there is certainly inspiration in Malcolm's own redemption, the ghetto criminal who became a disciplined ascetic of immense moral stature. He was always growing.

The living Malcolm would surely have disputed it, but his was a very American story—as much a story of a man caught between the shoals of black and white life as one of black nationalism. He had known all the misery that the black experience in America could offer. His grandfather was white. His father, Earl Little, a laborer and

Malcolm Little, aged 18, at the time of a 1944 Boston arrest for larceny. He got a three-month suspended sentence.

part-time Baptist minister in East Lansing, Michigan, was a zealot for Marcus Garvey. Malcolm was only six when Earl was found dead, dismembered by a trolley car. Ever after, Malcolm swore he had been a victim of white vigilantes. His mother went mad. His own quality showed in his junior high school graduation at the top of his class and his election as class president by his white peers. But he never got a chance. "You've got to be realistic about being a nigger," a teacher told him when he said he aspired to being a lawyer. He dropped out of school, became, by his own account, a shoeshine boy, pimp, hustler, drug dealer and burglar. He was lucky to be caught. In prison for seven years, he discovered books, learning, his mind—and the Nation of Islam. Led by an asthmatic

Malcolm X focuses on a bow-tied Muhammad Ali in a Miami restaurant after Ali had won the heavyweight championship from Sonny Liston on February 26, 1964. He was Ali's guide to the Muslim faith, but two months later when Malcolm split with Elijah Muhammad, Ali stayed with Elijah. In May, back from Africa, Malcolm X was now El-Haji Malik El-Shabazz, but hated by the Black Muslims. "Such a man as Malcolm is worthy of death," wrote his protégé and betrayer, a handsome former track star and calypso singer by the name of Louis Farrakhan. Photograph by Bob Gomel.

semiliterate migrant Georgia sharecropper, a prosaic Elijah Poole who had metamorphosed into the Honorable Elijah Muhammad, the Nation was a hybrid of the current American zeitgeist: an apocalyptic self-improvement course built around the central premise that the white man is a blue-eyed devil, created thousands of years ago by a mad scientist and temporarily predominant only by the leave of Allah and the peculiarly white science of "tricknology."

To Malcolm X—the X representing his long-lost African name—the Nation explained all the torments of his life. Anointed a missionary by Elijah, he lit up dense street rallies with his sardonic eloquence. He never called for any specific violence, but he mocked Martin Luther King's nonviolence as suicidal, and his speeches were rich in the imagery of anti-white mayhem. Du Bois had famously written that the blacks must strive for their rights "by every civilized and peaceful method." Malcolm made that "by any means necessary."

He began to change after his break with Elijah in 1963. He returned from a pilgrim-age to Mecca acknowledging that Islam embraced all colors and the Black Muslims were in error. He never gave up on the idea of a separate black state somewhere in North America but he began to speak enthusiastically of the power of the ballot and dreamed of forming an all-black political party. He was trapped somewhere between his utopian black nationalism with its ties to Mother Africa, and the competing chimera of Martin Luther King's completely integrated, beloved community, and the conflict would tear him apart before it made him a saint.

REVOLUTION IN A BLACK BERET

The Black Panthers came swaggering out of the Oakland ghettos with an attitude white people had never seen before. There were only around 2,000 full-time members, according to *The Shadow of the Panther,* the comprehensive study by Hugh Pearson, but they made an impact out of all proportion to their numbers. They did it by the violence of their speech and the violence of their actions, and by iconography. They wore black leather, sunglasses and berets; they carried guns and cartridge belts; they raised their clenched fists in a revolutionary "black power" salute. There could not have been a starker symbol of the polarization between King's integrationists and the separatists.

The party was launched on October 15, 1966, by Huey Newton and Bobby Seale, college-educated friends doing community work in Lyndon Johnson's antipoverty campaign—a fact that soon helped to stigmatize the party's programs. The two men stole the name from SNCC's Stokely Carmichael, originator of the slogan "black power," who had formed a short-lived Black Panthers' Party in Lowndes County, Alabama. On January 1, 1967, Newton and Seale spent their government paychecks opening up the first BP office in a vacant storefront at 56th and Grove streets in north Oakland. Recruits—and weapons—soon began to drift in. The public relations wizard Eldridge Cleaver, author of *Soul on Ice,* completed the troika when he got parole from doing time in California's Soledad Prison on an attempted murder rap.

There was at first undeniable support for the Panthers in the ghettos across the country. They started free-breakfast programs, a learning center, jobs programs and free health clinics. Their manifesto was a concoction of the laudable and the risible: better housing and full employment coupled with the release of "all black men" held in jail, the exemption of all blacks from military service and "an end to the robbery of the capitalists of our black community." But the Panthers' demand for "an end to police terrorism" was popular, it was justified, and it was dramatically followed up by having armed Panthers patrol the streets to protect blacks from harassment. In the inevitable clashes that followed between 1967 and 1969, nine policemen and ten Panthers were killed. Many if not most of the fights were initiated by police, who suffered no consequences for killing Panthers under dubious circumstances. The FBI's role in

Newton won a university doctorate. "My foes have called me bum, hoodlum, criminal. Some have even called me nigger. I imagine now they'll have to call me Dr. Nigger."

assigning criminals as spies and agents provocateurs was also covered up for years. (In 1982 the families of Panthers Fred Hampton and Mark Clark were paid $1.85 million compensation for their deaths in a 1969 police-FBI raid in Chicago that was virtually a planned execution.)

That said, the Panthers were no angels. For most of their existence, the leadership operated more as a criminal gang than dedicated revolutionaries. They betrayed the worthy efforts of the people who ran the slum programs. The three celebrity leaders of fast-dwindling SNCC—Carmichael, James Forman and H. Rap Brown ("violence is as American as cherry pie")—no sooner joined the party than they left in a hurry. The cause was one afternoon when, over a petty quarrel, Cleaver, Seale and a few others walked into Forman's New York office, stuck a pistol in his mouth and pulled the trigger three times. The gun was unloaded but Forman, who had stood up to the most brutal Southern sheriffs, checked himself into a psychiatric ward. In *Soul on Ice,* Cleaver claimed that he raped white women as a revolutionary act (having practiced first, of course, on black women). He plotted the ambush of an Oakland policeman, jumped bail, fled to Algeria and came back in the mid-1970s to do time for that and subsequent burglaries.

The handsome, eloquent Newton was a drug addict and alcoholic. Jailed in a confused shooting incident in which a policeman died, he became a radical cause célèbre with "Free Huey" buttons everywhere. It was in this period that Leonard Bernstein and white sympathizers threw a chichi fundraiser, memorably lampooned by Tom Wolfe as "radical chic." Newton got out of prison on a technicality after three years, and later confided that he did the shooting. More and more of the Panther funds began to disappear up his nose. He expelled Seale from the party, beating him with a bullwhip and wreaking a violent sodomy on his old best friend. The remaining staff members were in terror of Newton. He beat them up for the smallest reason. He was a habitual rapist. A Panther in Connecticut was tortured to death on suspicion of being an FBI informer. In a few days in 1974, he shot a prostitute on the street for calling him "baby" and nearly bludgeoned his tailor to death for the same mistake.

By the fall of 1982 the Panthers were defunct. Huey Newton wandered the streets of Oakland, committing petty crimes and pathetically trading on his past reputation to feed his crack addiction. "What I keep wondering is why someone hasn't put a bullet in my head yet," he said out loud. In the early morning of August 22, 1989, someone did—a 25-year-old petty drug dealer who shot him three times in the head and walked off through the Oakland slums. It is hard to visualize a more useless end to the Panthers and black nationalism.

BURN, BABY, BURN!: Michigan National Guardsmen with fixed bayonets push rioters away from a burning building on Detroit's west side, July 23, 1967. It was frightening work for ill-trained, suburban young men, some of whom had opted for the Guard to avoid service in Vietnam. In the heat of the moment there was a tendency to see snipers everywhere and respond by raking whole buildings with machine gun fire.

THE LONG HOT SUMMERS IN THE CITIES

In the midsixties it was a commonplace to see helmeted National Guardsmen, and even regular Army troops, armed with loaded automatic weapons, bayonets, and armored personnel carriers and tanks, patrolling the burnt-out ghettos and downtowns of some of America's biggest cities. More than 200 people died in over 100 city riots; more than 4,000 were wounded. The riots seemed to come out of nowhere. A traffic violation. The arrest of a cabdriver. A raid on an illegal after-hours bar. Rumors of somebody, somewhere, beaten or killed by a white cop. Within hours, crowds of thousands would be surging through the streets, torching and looting their own neighborhoods.

The riots occurred in nearly every large city, but the worst ones, the ones that permanently seared the American psyche, took place in the Watts section of Los Angeles, in August 1965, and in Newark, New Jersey, and Detroit within days of each other in July 1967. More than 30,000 blacks were probably rioters in Watts; 34 people died. Detroit's terrible five days, July 23–27, constituted the single bloodiest, costliest and most tragic American riot of the century. It left 43 dead, 1,200 injured, 7,231 arrested, 5,000 homeless.

Over 1,300 buildings were destroyed. The city has never recovered.

"White racism is essentially responsible for the explosive mixture," reported the Kerner Commission to President Johnson in 1968. The country was caught in a fury of analysis. Why should there be all this violence during a decade in which blacks had made more progress than in the previous 300 years?

There was virtually no evidence for the right-wing conclusion that there was a national conspiracy of Communist agitators supported by criminal black snipers. Black thieves and thugs did exploit the riots, but they were not organized. Nearly all of those who died were black and those who shot them were panicky white police and National Guardsmen. John Hersey's investigation of the "Algiers Motel Incident" found that police cold-bloodedly executed three innocent young men during one bad night in the Detroit riots.

Liberal analysis, typified by Kerner, blamed social deprivation—lack of work, bad housing, discrimination, the breakup of the black family. It was plausible, but the riots were not the outgrowth of conventional civil rights protests. Victims were often black store owners. Detroit was

a relatively progressive city where blacks had decent, well-paying jobs in the auto industry, many owned their homes and more than three quarters of the households had male heads. Most of the arrested looters were not poor but solid members of the working class. In Detroit, as elsewhere, the trigger was more the hatred of a bigoted, understaffed and nearly all-white police force. In America's still overwhelmingly segregated cities, police were then the only official white authority figures whom blacks had regular contact with. The resentment of the police, and through them the white population, was not just a question of police brutality. At least as significant was the conviction among the decent black communities that police indifference denied blacks the legal protections that whites, in their communities, enjoyed against criminal violence.

All this should have argued for more integration, but such arguments had little sway among suburban whites or black nationalists. The riots confirmed white fears that violence was innate among blacks, and convinced blacks that they could get no justice from whites. Anyone who could—black and white—kept fleeing to the suburbs.

ROBERT KENNEDY:
THE IMPOSSIBLE DREAM

In the crazy, horrible year of 1968, when first Martin Luther King and then Robert Kennedy were shot to death, people were reading a book Kennedy had just written, *Toward a New World.* He had been inspired by an epigraph from Tennyson's "Ulysses":

The lights begin to twinkle from the rocks:
The long day wanes: the slow moon
*   climbs: the deep*
Moans round with many voices. Come,
*   my friends,*
'Tis not too late to seek a newer world.

It was no affectation. A poetic vision lay deep within the "ruthless brat" his enemies saw (not without justification early on). He was at a rally in a predominately black slum in Indianapolis when he had to announce to his unknowing audience that King had just been assassinated. He improvised a prayer for the country, appealing to them to uphold King's legacy, and he did it by recalling a fragment from Aeschylus that had helped him after his brother's murder: "In our sleep, pain which cannot forget falls drop by drop upon the heart until, in our own despair, against our will, comes wisdom through the awful grace of God."

Half a romantic who admired Che Guevara, half a political realist—Norman Mailer said he was a sheriff who could have been an outlaw—Bobby Kennedy had a wisdom that lay in learning to commune with the better angels of his nature. He had a real, visceral disgust for cruelty and oppression, but it was not a sensibility that was nurtured much on the lawns of Hyannis Port or his Senate inquisitions of labor rackets and the mob. He had first to see and feel what it was like to be a coal miner's family in a derelict West Virginian township, when he campaigned for his brother; he had to look into the eyes of a girl in a Brooklyn tenement whose face had been mangled by rats and ask himself, "How could it happen in the richest city on earth?"; he especially had to endure the traumatic experience of May 24, 1963, when he heard how much his presence "nauseated" black activists at a time when he thought he and his brother were doing all they reasonably could. He was Attorney General then and might have stood on his dignity, but for three hours, getting redder and redder, he endured humiliating vituperation led by Jerome Smith and James Baldwin among a group of black artists and academics he had invited to his New York apartment for a discussion of ideas.

He knew the facts well enough; what he absorbed from his tormentors, and gradually made his own, was the depth of black anguish. By the early summer of 1968, millions in America believed that Bobby Kennedy was the only politician who could lead them to a newer world. Critics had become admirers. He had won all but one of the presidential primaries he entered. In the California primary on June 4 he effectively ended the run of Senator Eugene McCarthy and crushed Hubert Humphrey's slate. In the 85 frenzied days of Kennedy's campaign—its theme The Impossible Dream—thousands flocked to him in the inner cities, trying to touch his slight frame, run hands through his tousled hair. Unlike both Humphrey and Nixon, he had a huge following among the young, even those who insisted that traditional politics was dead and revolution was necessary.

The standard commentary is that he could not have won the nomination or the race. That judgment may underrate the force of personality in American politics. Humphrey had locked up many of the clubhouse-ridden state delegations, but Kennedy had the backing of Chicago's Mayor Richard Daley. The hero of the West could have come thundering into Chicago, beaten the Hump, and gone on to defeat Richard Nixon, psychologically scarred by having a rerun of his 1960 nightmare race.

It was indeed an impossible dream. He was assassinated in the kitchen of the Los Angeles Ambassador Hotel by Sirhan Bishara Sirhan, a 24-year-old Jordanian immigrant and busboy who was convinced that Kennedy was somehow a symbol of Zionism. Biographer and reporter Jack Newfield best summed up the wrenching loss as he watched the funeral train travel through New Jersey on the way to Arlington Cemetery on Saturday, June 8, 1968. On one side of the track he saw tens of thousands of poor blacks waving good-bye, and on the other side tens of

Seven days to live . . . Frustrated by a delay, he was taking a walk on an airstrip in Bakers Field, Oregon, with his dog, Freckles. Burton Berinsky's panoramic photograph memorializes the romantic appeal of Bobby.

thousands of almost-poor whites, waving American flags, standing at attention, hands over their hearts, tears running down their faces: "To this day I keep searching for one more leader who might reconcile and reunite those two injured classes, still trapped on separate sides of the railroad tracks that run through the American Dream."

THE MYSTERIES OF KING'S MURDER

Just after 6 p.m. on April 4, 1968, Martin Luther King, Jr., stepped out on the balcony of the Lorraine Motel in Memphis, Tennessee, and was shot dead by James Earl Ray, a 39-year-old career criminal who had escaped a Missouri prison. There is no doubt Ray was the trigger man, despite skepticism from the King family in 1997, but this is one case in American history where a conspiracy is conceivable. Why should a bank robber on the lam interest himself in such a crime? How was he able to afford the Remington rifle, binoculars, boardinghouse room and car that were instrumental in the plot? Who told him the details of King's movements? How was he able to avoid the police in three countries and get all the way to England and almost to Rhodesia before he was caught two months later?

The last two years of King's life had been a trying mental and spiri-tual journey. He had broken with many conservative black leaders and his most powerful white supporter by announcing his formal opposition to "the madness of Vietnam." He had just started to put together a mul-tiracial class-based coalition to demand social justice in America, and to move beyond identity politics.

On April 3, the day before he was killed, King delivered an eerily clair-voyant speech. "Like anybody, I would like to live a long life. Longevity has its place. But I'm not concerned about that now. I just want to do God's will. And He's allowed me to go up to the mountain and I've looked over, and I've seen the promised land. I may not get there with you. But I want you to know that we, as a people, will get to the promised land. And so I'm happy tonight. I'm not worried about anything. I'm not fear-ing any man. Mine eyes have seen the glory of the coming of the Lord."

MAYOR DALEY'S IRON FIST

DALEY'S YELL: Senator Abraham Ribicoff, nominating George McGovern from the podium, looked directly in the eye of Mayor Richard Daley with the Illinois delegation just below: "If George McGovern were president of the United States we wouldn't have Gestapo tactics in the streets of Chicago." Daley's yell reflected the ugliness of the moment. Television sound did not pick it up, but Ribicoff did: "Fuck you, you Jew sonofabitch." Ribicoff paused and shouted back: "How hard is it to accept the truth?"

Vice President Hubert Humphrey burst into tears in his Washington apartment on March 31, 1968, as he did what Lyndon Johnson had just requested. LBJ had fished a piece of paper from his breast pocket and asked Humphrey to read aloud a few words he had put down as a way of ending his presidential address on Vietnam that evening. "Accordingly," mouthed a thunderstruck Humphrey, "I shall not seek, and I will not accept, the nomination of my party for another term as your president." LBJ's first ending, which he was still considering, was simply an appeal for national unity. Humphrey had judged that first ending "beautiful, just beautiful," but LBJ knew better: "Yes, Hubert, but they won't believe me."

Johnson smelled humiliation. His popularity rating was 35 percent. He had come close to losing the New Hampshire primary to Senator Eugene McCarthy, the aloof Catholic and scholar-poet whose moral denunciations of "Johnson's war" had reaped from the campuses and college towns a vast army of students and young wives, unpaid earnest amateurs all of them but formidable in number and dedication. And then there was Senator Robert Kennedy, perhaps even now buckling on the armor of Camelot. At 9:35 p.m., broadcasting to 85 million Americans, LBJ raised his right arm in a prearranged signal and the TelePrompTer scrolled up the second, "resignation," ending.

Johnson was on his way out, but his would-be successor Humphrey was still his prisoner. He entered few primaries, badly lost those he did, and relied on LBJ and the old Democratic bosses for his support. The vice presidency was the tragedy of Hubert H. Humphrey (1911–1978), the incubator for the presidency in which he lost his political identity. HHH—the Hump—had been the hero of the left, a young reforming mayor of Minneapolis blazing with ideas and idealism. He had been the first to propose the Peace Corps and the Food for Peace program; he had hammered civil rights into the platform at the 1948 Dixiecrat convention, piloted the 1964 Civil Rights Act through the Senate. And then he had begun to march to LBJ's drum. He was a warmly impulsive man suborned from his pacific instincts by personal loyalty and political ambition. The antiwar activists had given up on him. His attempts at political denial made him seem slightly deranged. Declaring his candidacy three weeks after the assassination of Martin Luther King and nationwide rioting, he proclaimed, in his chatty style, "the politics of joy." In 1968, the agony of the Hump was that any hint he gave of changing course on Vietnam would cost him LBJ's support, yet a hard line destroyed any chance of picking up doves attached to Gene McCarthy or RFK successor Senator George McGovern—and might have also cost him the election. "I was in the garden of Gethsemane," was the way he put it to this author.

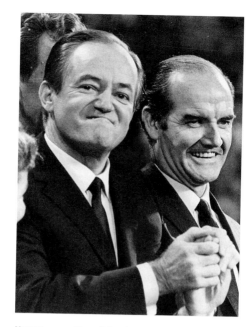

Humphrey aglow, joined on the podium by his defeated rival George McGovern.

Humphrey stuck with LBJ and LBJ delivered. The delegates to the Democratic convention, held in August in a sweltering Chicago, made him the nominee on the first ballot at 11:47 p.m. on Wednesday. They also rejected a peace plank, even though in the primaries antiwar candidates had picked up 80 percent of the vote.

Humphrey's Republican rival, Richard Nixon, watched television from his Florida vacation home with unusual pleasure that evening. Outside the Conrad Hilton Hotel antiwar demonstrators, assembling to march to the convention hall, were set upon by Mayor Richard Daley's police gone berserk. They yelled, "Kill, kill, kill," and clubbed indiscriminately anyone in range, including passing citizens and doctors and nurses who tried to help the injured—a spectacle never to be forgotten by the millions who saw it live on television. A London *Sunday Times* reporter noted, "The kids screamed and were beaten to the ground, rapped in the genitals by cops swinging billies. I saw one girl surrounded by cops, screaming, 'Please God, help me. Help me.'" A young man who tried to help got his head bloodied by a flailing club. Some of the demonstrators were thrown against a window of the hotel and pushed through it.

The sadistic romp was just one incident in a week of screams and bloodshed. Day after day crowds, legally assembled or not, were clubbed and gassed. Cops broke up

scuffles on the convention floor, hitting delegates and newsmen, including Dan Rather of CBS. The climax was at 4 a.m., Friday. Empty beer cans were supposedly thrown down from the Conrad Hilton's room 1506A, the McCarthy headquarters floor. Cops used it as a pretext to invade other rooms on the fifteenth floor, ejecting the sleeping occupants and beating up a number of them.

Daley rushed out a whitewashing report. He portrayed Chicago as beset by a "a lawless violent group of terrorists menacing the lives of millions of our people." He suppressed the scale of injuries to civilians to conceal the fact that more than five demonstrators were injured for each policeman. Mike Royko, a Chicago columnist, noted that a large proportion of police injuries were to hands. A lot of dastardly citizens, he concluded, had been going round smashing policemen's knuckles with their faces.

But Daley's mishmash won the day. Humphrey backed it; so did the *Chicago Tribune* and gradually most of the national press. HHH seemed still to be on another planet. He gleefully accepted the support of the most reactionary Southern delegates, threatened to investigate the networks for daring to show the violence and told CBS's Roger Mudd: "I think we ought to quit pretending that Mayor Daley did anything wrong. He didn't. . . ." The truth that Chicago was an organized police riot had to await the Walker Report to the National Commission on the Causes and Prevention of Violence, which deployed 212 investigators to examine 3,500 eyewitnesses. Daley's violence was hypocritical. He personally opposed the war and had shielded his two sons from it in a National Guard unit.

The early September polls had HHH losing in a landslide to a play-safe Nixon. George Wallace was breathing down his neck from his Deep South base, pitching law and order, anti-busing and victory in Vietnam to blue-collar voters. Humphrey woke up at the end of September. He promised to consider a bombing pause: "The President has not made me his slave, and I am not his humble servant." Now it was true. It may have been just too late. Humphrey's recovery was spectacular. He lost to Nixon by less than 1 percent in the popular vote (43.4 to 42.7). Nearly 10 million (13.5 percent) voted for Wallace.

FORT DALEY: The yippies chanted, "Peace now," "Hell no, we won't go," "Dump the Hump," and they abused Daley's cops: "Fuck the pigs. Pigs are whores." They nominated a pig for president. The scholar and Vietnam veteran Terry Anderson estimates in his study *The Movement* that among the maximum total of 10,000 demonstrators there were 200 or 300 street fighters. Daley deployed 20,000 armed police and soldiers. Photograph by Duane Hall.

RICHARD MILHOUS NIXON
37th President (Republican), 1969–1974

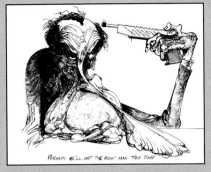

Caricature by Gerald Scarfe.

BORN: January 9, 1913, in Yorba Linda, California

DIED: April 22, 1994, New York, New York

POLITICAL CAREER: Member, House of Representatives from California, 1947–1951; U.S. Senator from California, 1951–1953; Vice President, 1953–1961; President, 1969–1974

FIRSTS: First president to avoid impeachment by resigning. First president to visit China while in office.

CHARACTER SNAPSHOT: "He was heroic, admirable, and inspiring while simultaneously being dishonorable, despicable, and a horrible example. It was a role only Richard Nixon could have invented or played."

—Stephen E. Ambrose

MARKET BOY: When RN was nine, his father gave up on lemons and moved to Hannah's hometown of Whittier (above). He borrowed $5,000 and opened a thriving gas station, then a store. Richard got up at 4 a.m. to bargain in the market for fruits and vegetables.

TOP BOY: He was a star at all his schools in Whittier. He was a champion debater, a classical scholar, top of his class, and a student leader, despite being dubbed Gloomy Gus. The Harvard Club of California judged him the state's best all-around student and offered a tuition scholarship, but the family could not afford his room and board bills so he entered Whittier College, with good grace, in September 1930. His political triumph there was to win the student presidency by promising to get around the ban on college dances. He won and delivered on the promise, outflanking the college president and appealing to the trustees. One of them, a Quaker banker named Herman Perry, was later to nominate him as a congressman. At Whittier, RN also wrestled with his soul in 12 precocious essays entitled "What Can I Believe?" and concluded: "I have as my ideal the life of Jesus." He graduated 2nd of 85 students in Whittier's class of 1934, won a scholarship to Duke Law School and graduated 3rd of 25.

A SEVERE FATHER: He was born of Irish stock in a one-story timber frame house made from an $800 kit by his odd-job father, Frank. He was the second of five children, four of them boys—Richard is at right in the early family group with brother Harold at left and Donald in the middle. The Nixons had a 12-acre lemon grove in Yorba Linda, 30 miles from Los Angeles, but could not make it pay. His gentle Quaker mother, Hannah, taught him to read before he went to school at six. She wanted him to be a missionary. Listening to the steam trains, he dreamed of being a railroad engineer, but he picked up a passion for politics from his father. He said he could remember his father berating his mother for having voted for Woodrow Wilson in 1916. Hannah gave food to beggars in the Depression; Frank railed against "bums." He was a loving father but had fits of temper and shouting. He strapped the boys when they misbehaved.

LOSSES: He was devastated by the deaths of his brother Arthur (right) at seven, three years after this 1922 picture, and then Harold in 1933. His mother later said: "From that time on it seemed that Richard was trying to be three sons in one." The boys died of tuberculosis, very probably victims of their father's insistence on drinking raw milk. RN (at left, standing) is nine, Donald (in tire) is seven.

FOOTBALL LESSON: His father encouraged him to play football at Whittier College, though he was 50 pounds lighter than regular team players and not very nimble. He got knocked about a lot, but he valued his football days, he said later, because of the lesson from the Native American coach "Chief" Wallace Newman: "He drilled into me a competitive spirit and the determination to come back after you have been knocked down or after you lose."

THE RISE OF "TRICKY DICK": The vice president spruces up—only nine years after entering politics. In 1946, former Lieutenant Commander Nixon had staked his life's savings in a "hopeless" run for the House in the 12th District of California. His opponent, five-termer Jerry Voorhis, was a principled social gospeler, one of the few to protest the wartime internment of Japanese Americans. Nixon won an upset victory by portraying Voorhis as soft on communism and the strike-happy unions. By the time Nixon ran for the Senate in 1950 the Hiss case had made him famous. JFK gave him $1,000 from his father, Joseph, for his "Red menace" campaign race against the progressive Congresswoman Helen Gahagan Douglas, the wife of the star Melvyn Douglas (and a lover of young Senator Lyndon Johnson) and a friend of Eleanor Roosevelt. The Korean war erupted just in time; and Truman gave only lukewarm support to Douglas. Nixon smeared her shamelessly: "She's pink right down to her underwear." He put out half a million flyers on pink paper that falsely suggested she was a backer of New York Communist apologist Vito Marcantonio. With the help of a slanted press—87-year-old William Randolph Hearst's *San Francisco Examiner* was hysterical—he won a disgraceful campaign by 680,000 votes, but Douglas landed him with a lifelong epithet, Tricky Dick. Losing to JFK in 1960 and to Pat Brown for the California governorship in 1962 wounded him so much he lost his temper with the reporters: "Just think how much you're going to be missing. You won't have Nixon to kick around anymore, because, gentlemen, this is my last press conference." Everyone thought he was finished.

THE SUITOR (right): He fell in love at first sight of the beautiful redhead Patricia Ryan, on January 16, 1938, when they tried out for amateur parts in a Whittier play. He was a lawyer, she was in her second year teaching high school. She fended him off. She was shy and self-reliant, brought up in poverty on a small farm. Her violent Irish father and German mother died when she was a teenager. It took Nixon two years to win her. They were both 27 when they married on June 21, 1940. In the photograph they take the air in Washington with their baby Patricia (Tricia) soon after his election to Congress. In 1968, their second daughter, Julie, married David Eisenhower, the grandson of President Eisenhower.

POPULAR OFFICER: His decision to join the Navy in August 1942 pained his Quaker family. Lieutenant Nixon earned the respect of his crews in the Solomon Islands in 1943, sweating with them as he loaded aircraft with weapons and casualties. He landed on Green Island (above) in April 1944, just after the first wave of Marines, and helped evacuate the wounded. He was popular. He opened a beer and hamburger stand (Nick's Snack Shack), won a lot of poker pots and made incessant notes of anything he could find to read. In 14 months away, he never failed to write a daily love letter to his new wife.

DEADLY MISSION: The Nixons narrowly escaped being torn apart on May 13, 1958, in Caracas, Venezuela. They were on a goodwill tour to counter perceptions of America as a rich, exploitative bully and backer of dictators. They had a friendly passage in Uruguay, Colombia, Argentina, Paraguay, Bolivia and Ecuador, but the crowds were hostile in Peru, and Venezuela became a nightmare. On the wild drive in from the airport, the motorcade was ambushed with Nixon in one car and Pat in another. They were blocked in for a hellish 12 minutes by a barricade of trucks and cars. A mob rushed at Nixon's car with rocks, iron pipes and clubs, yelling, "Muera Nixon!" The mob began to rock the car to turn it over and set it afire. The Secret Servicemen drew their pistols. Nixon thought he was going to die, but he coolly ordered them not to shoot. "Once a gun went off," he reflected, "the crowd would go berserk and that would be the end of us." Nobody is sure how the motorcade got moving again. On the Nixons' return to Washington airport, Ike and a crowd of 15,000 gave them a heroes' welcome.

GOOD MORNING: From lunar orbit, earthrise is seen for the first time by the human eye. This is a digital scan of the original NASA image made by Michael Light in 1997, from the 70-mm Hasselblad negative created by astronauts Frank Borman, James Lovell and William Anders on the *Apollo 8* mission, December 21–27, 1968.

MOON TO EARTH: THE EAGLE HAS LANDED

On a hot midsummer evening, Americans were joined by some 600 million people around the world to watch in awe as Neil A. Armstrong, aged 38, from Wapakoneta, Ohio, gingerly lowered his left foot into the soft dust of the moon's surface. "That's one small step for man . . . one giant leap for mankind." The *Apollo 11* landing was on July 20, 1969, eight years and 56 days since President Kennedy had promised to land a man on the moon "before the end of the decade." "Man on the moon" was not quite the right expression. The determination all along was to land an American on the moon. Congress had apoplexy at the suggestion that the flag of the U.N.,

or any other symbol of humankind, might supplant the emblem of American power. It was Old Glory that Armstrong and his copilot Edwin "Buzz" Aldrin, age 39, from Montclair, New Jersey, struggled to emplant in the rock and dust of the Sea of Tranquillity, the Stars and Stripes stiffened with wire so that in the airless world of the moon it would seem to fly as heroically as the flag on Iwo Jima.

America could not claim the moon. There was an international agreement on that, so Armstrong and Aldrin enriched the bleak environment with a platitude engraved on the abandoned base of their landing craft: "Here men from the planet

earth first set foot upon the moon July 1969, A.D. We came in peace for all mankind." The wording was a gesture. They set foot on the moon for America, for American prestige, for an America driven not by humanitarianism or science or economic profit but by the simple fear the Russians would get there first. The race for the moon was a myth. It was never a Russian priority. The landing, for all that, was one of America's greatest triumphs— 43 years after Robert Goddard successfully flew the first liquid-fueled rocket at Auburn, Massachusetts, 24 years after Wernher von Braun and his V-2 rocket team from Peenemünde were captured by

"CHEESE": Charles "Pete" Conrad, reflected in the moon helmet, photographs astronaut Alan Bean during the *Apollo 12* mission, November 14–24, 1969. Bean, the Hasselblad on his chest, holds the "long can," a vacuum-sealed container that now holds a sample of moon soil. Bean's cuff checklist is legible on his left sleeve in this print from a digital scan made by Michael Light in 1997.

the American Army in the Bavarian Alps and brought to Texas.

Eight years was an incredibly short time for fulfilling Kennedy's pledge, but a long time for sustaining an effort of national will at a cost of $25 billion. It was an exhilarating demonstration of the American genius for optimism as well as for the American capacity for organization, for concentrated teamwork of the highest quality at the edge of industrial and scientific technology.

Everything for the launch, the four-day flight and the landing in the spidery Eagle was planned and tracked on 450 computer consoles, but cool nerves counted too when on the fourth day of the mission it came time to leave the mother module, Columbia, and power down to the vast unknown in the landing craft Eagle. None

of the watching millions knew that computer alarms kept threatening to abort the landing or that Armstrong had to take over manually when the weird and flimsy Eagle headed for a crater strewn with boulders. Or that when Armstrong sent the magic signal "Houston, Tranquillity Base here. The Eagle has landed," he had but 20 seconds of fuel left.

Armstrong and Aldrin spent 22 hours on the moon, collecting rock, taking pictures, setting up experiments and talking with President Nixon. While they did, the lonely Michael Collins, aged 38, flew Columbia through sunlight and total blackness wondering if his buddies would make it back from somewhere 69 miles below. He wrote later: "My secret terror for the last six months has been leaving

them on the moon and returning to earth alone; now I am within minutes of finding the truth of the matter. If they fail to rise from the surface, or crash back into it, I am not going to commit suicide; I am coming home, forthwith, but I will be a marked man for life and I know. Almost better not to have the option I enjoy." But the single-rocket engine worked and just after midnight on July 22 the trio were on their way home.

Before the program ended with *Apollo 17* in December 1972, ten other men walked on the surface: Charles Conrad, Jr.; Alan L. Bean; Edgar D. Mitchell; James J. Irwin; David R. Scott; Charles M. Duke, Jr.; John W. Young; Eugene A. Cernan; Harrison H. "Jack" Schmitt; and Alan Shepard.

Americans, all.

What Kissinger and Nixon called the "incursion" has been on a month. An exhausted GI lies on the ground and drinks water from his canteen at Tasvos, Cambodia. His company was pinned down by sniper fire.

NIXON'S BIG GAMBLE SETS THE COUNTRY ALIGHT

Over and over again in April 1970, President Nixon sat in the dark in the White House watching World War II General George Patton rousing his troops to combat readiness—swashbuckling "Old Blood and Guts" Patton, as played by George C. Scott in the movie. Nixon felt embattled. He was steeling himself to see through one of the most controversial decisions of his presidency, with never any illusions about the enraging effect it would have on the antiwar movement in America: the decision to invade Cambodia.

Henry Kissinger, in his memoir, describes Nixon variously as "somewhat overwrought," "beside himself," "increasingly agitated," "in a monumental rage" and privately as being "a basket case." Kissinger added: "It does not alter the fact that his analysis was essentially right."

The trigger for the crisis was a coup in Cambodia on March 18. The popular head of state, Prince Norodom Sihanouk, a champion tightrope walker, had kept Cambodia out of the war. He had appeased the North Vietnamese Army (NVA) and Vietcong by tolerating their bases on his border with South Vietnam; and he had

appeased the Americans by turning a blind eye to 3,630 secret B-52 raids on their "sanctuaries." Sihanouk's premier, General Lon Nol, took power while Sihanouk was in Moscow to ask for help in reducing North Vietnam's growing pressure—45,000 troops were now in the sanctuaries.

Here Nixon and Kissinger made an error that was to prove lethal to Cambodia. They did not call for the restoration of Sihanouk. Lon Nol set about trying to eject the NVA himself, with U.S. encouragement. His troops and civilian mobs killed thousands of ethnic Vietnamese civilians, but did so badly against the NVA, breaking out of their bases, that the capital, Phnom Penh, was soon cut off.

At a National Security Council meeting on April 21, Defense Secretary Melvin Laird and Secretary of State William Rogers argued for doing nothing. Nixon and Kissinger saw an opportunity to clean out the sanctuaries using South Vietnamese troops in the Fish Hook region. Nixon was then upstaged by Vice President Spiro Agnew. It was "pussyfooting," said Agnew, not to use Americans and attack the Parrot's Beak sanctuaries as well.

Nixon simmered. Sitting up late into the night in the Lincoln Bedroom, he made up his mind to strike with American troops. He called Kissinger "at least ten times" to "bark an order and immediately hang up." Kissinger remarked to an aide, "Our peerless leader has flipped out."

That was irritation at the velocity of the calls. It was not his considered judgment. "The final decision to proceed was not a maniacal eruption of irrationality," writes Kissinger. "It was taken carefully by a man who had to discipline his nerves almost daily to face his associates and to overcome the partially subconscious, partly deliberate procrastination of his executive departments." Indeed, Nixon agonized four more days. He argued with Rogers and Laird. He asked the opinion of Ambassador to Saigon Ellsworth Bunker and Westmoreland's successor, General Creighton Abrams in Saigon. Only late on Tuesday, April 28, was the die cast. According to Walter Isaacson, a biographer of Kissinger, Nixon's stress was so intense that on Friday night, April 24, the President rang from Camp David "slurring obscenities." He was there with his Miami business pal

WHAT IS IT, HAIG?

SIR, IT'S ABOUT THE HOUSE HEARINGS ON THE SECRET CAMBODIAN BOMBINGS...

WE NEED TO KNOW MORE ABOUT THE RAIDS, SIR. THEY SAY NOBODY BUT YOU KNEW ABOUT THEM.

IT'S NOT TRUE! I TOLD EVERYBODY WHO HAD A NEED OR RIGHT TO KNOW!

YES, SIR, BUT WHO? YOU'VE GOT TO BE MORE SPECIFIC.

WELL, LET ME SEE... THE PILOTS, OF COURSE...

YES, GO ON...

Doonesbury by Garry Trudeau.

Bebe Rebozo, who came on the line to say: "The President wants you to know, Henry, that if this doesn't work, it's your ass."

Militarily, it worked fairly well. On May 1, some 31,000 American and 43,000 South Vietnamese troops crossed the border. The enemy scattered. Two big supply dumps were found but not the VC headquarters. It was there, the Cambodian Communists admitted eight years later. Politically, the invasion was a disaster. Just before Nixon spoke on television, he briefed the bipartisan congressional leadership, doves as well as hawks. They stood and clapped. It was an extraordinary moment. But the defiant speech reignited the antiwar movement, and it was fanned to white heat by two events. The morning after his speech Nixon was walking through the Pentagon lobby when he met the wife of a soldier serving in Vietnam. He told her how much he admired men like her husband. "I have seen them. They are the greatest. You see these bums, you know, blowing up the campuses. Listen, the boys that are on the college campuses today are the luckiest people in the world . . . and here they are burning up the books."

Nixon's gibe was clearly aimed not at all students or even all student protesters but at arsonists who had burned books and set off bombs at Berkeley, Yale and Stanford. The headlines did not distinguish. It was too late to try after May 4. At Kent State University, Ohio, where protesters had torched the ROTC building, panicky National Guardsmen fired on a mass demonstration. Two women walking to class were killed, as were two nonradical students, including an ROTC cadet. Campuses exploded everywhere. More than 400 shut down. Two million students went on strike. Almost overlooked in the may-

hem, Mississippi state police killed two protesting black students at Jackson State College, and wounded eleven others.

A Gallup poll found half of America backed the invasion, 35 percent disapproved. The not-so-silent majority cheered when 200 hard-hat construction workers in New York roughed up a peaceful crowd commemorating the victims at Kent. President Nixon later accepted an honorary hard hat as a symbol of "freedom and patriotism to our beloved country."

His feelings were more complex than this. He affected to hang tough, but he was wounded by the hatred he attracted. On the night of May 8–9, when Washington was besieged by 100,000 demonstrators, he could not sleep. He placed 51 phone calls between 10:35 p.m. and 3:50 a.m.

Dramatic coupling of "campus bum" and John Filo's photograph of victim Jeffrey Miller in the London *Daily Mirror*. The distraught woman is a 14-year-old runaway, Mary Vecchio.

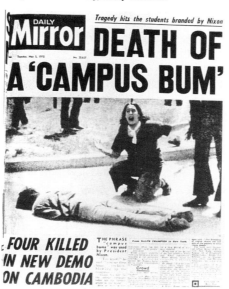

Around four he put on a record of Rachmaninoff's Second Piano Concerto. Through a White House rear window he noticed young people moving toward the Lincoln Memorial and impulsively offered to take his manservant Manolo Sanchez to see it, "the most beautiful sight in Washington." The Secret Service was petrified as Nixon climbed the steps of the Memorial and started talking among groups of students kitted out in protest gear of combat fatigues, long hair, peace badges, and hairbands. "I know that most of you think I'm an SOB," he told them, shaking hands, "but I want you to know that I understand just how you feel." He spoke of his pacifist youth, his support of Chamberlain at Munich, which he came to realize was wrong. He tried to express his love of America, his despair at the gulf between black and white, the "spiritual hunger which all of us have." White House aide Egil "Bud" Krogh, Jr.—a future Watergate plumber—saw a compassionate and profoundly misunderstood man "seeking and giving spiritual refreshment." The judgment of Nixon's chief of staff H. R. Haldeman for his diary was that it was all "very weird." A hostile press took the same view.

Nixon and Kissinger maintained that the "incursion" saved lives and delayed the Communist assault on Saigon. It did nothing for Cambodia. An angry Congress forced American troops out by the end of June. The North Vietnamese built up the Cambodian Communists, the genocidal Khmer Rouge led by Pol Pot. Phnom Penh fell to that madman on April 17, 1975. It was the beginning of a nightmare. By 1979 more than a million people had been starved to death and murdered in Cambodia's killing fields.

AN AMERICAN ATROCITY

Officially, it was a stunning battle victory against the Vietcong. "U.S. Troops Surround Reds, Kill 128" was the headline in the Army newspaper *Stars and Stripes*. General Westmoreland congratulated the 11th Infantry Brigade commander, Colonel Oran K. Henderson. Medals were handed out. The "battle" was a lie, the most grotesque of many in the Vietnam war. What happened on March 16, 1968, was the murder of defenseless Vietnamese women, children and old men in two northern hamlets, My Lai and My Khe, in the sprawling village of Son My, Quang Ngai Province. The atrocity was covered up for 18 months.

The GIs who did the killing were barely out of high school, good American boys from ordinary towns, flung into the swampy floodplains along the South China Sea to fight an invisible enemy. Their average age was 19, and they were evenly divided between white and black. They had arrived only in December 1967 and were assigned to Charlie Company, 1st Battalion, 20th Infantry Brigade, commanded by Captain Ernest "Mad Dog" Medina. In three months, they were never in a firefight, but they saw twenty-eight of their buddies maimed and blinded by booby traps, mines and sniper fire; five died. They became furious that the villagers never warned them. Soon they came to regard every peasant working a rice paddy as a dispensable "dink," "slope" or "gook." The epithets were hardly surprising; President Johnson had urged Army officers to "pin a coonskin to the wall."

On March 15, the day after a popular sergeant was blown to pieces, Medina was summoned to a briefing for a strike force under the 11th Brigade's Lieutenant Colonel Frank Barker. Two recklessly ill-informed intelligence captains, Eugene Kotouc and Robert Ramsdell, reported that the 48th VC Battalion of more than 200 men had been located in My Lai. By 7 a.m., they said, bona fide civilians would have gone to market and everyone in the village would be VC. Barker's orders from Colonel Henderson, running his first combat command, were to destroy the village with all its livestock. He did not specify what should be done with civilians who had not "gone to market." What Barker told Medina and what Medina told the 105 men left in Charlie Com-

DEAD WITHIN MINUTES: One of Ron Haeberle's damning photographs.

pany is disputed. Twenty-one of them, and most of the senior NCOs, later testified that Medina ordered everybody in the village killed. Greg Olsen denied there was any such order. Michael Bernhardt says "he stopped just short of saying that." Charles Hall said he ordered them to "waste anybody that ran from us or fired on us." The follow-up briefing to the 1st Platoon from Lieutenant William "Rusty" Calley, 24, allowed no discretion. "He said not to hesitate to kill anything that moves," recalled Denis Conti. To Calley, children were nothing more than future VC.

The VC battalion was not in My Lai when "Barker's Bastards" were helicoptered in at 0725 the next day. There was no resistance of any kind, but most of the youngsters in both Charlie and B companies began a frenzy of burning and killing. They blew families apart with fragmentation grenades, mowed them down with automatic fire. A handful refused to join in the slaughter, but for some of the berserk GIs, killing was not enough. Peasants were beheaded, women raped and mutilated, then shot. Varnado Simpson says his mind "just went" when he obeyed an order from Calley to shoot a mother and baby. "I killed another 20 to 25, cut their throats, scalped 'em. I did it. A lot of people were doing it."

Conti and Paul Meadlo rounded up a group of about 60 villagers, 20 or so of them old men and women, the rest children of all ages from babies to teenagers. Calley arrived and bawled: "I thought I told you to take care of them." He meant kill them. He ordered his men to open fire. Conti demurred. A sobbing Meadlo stood alongside Calley and at ten feet they emptied magazine after magazine into the group. Later, Calley herded peasants into an irrigation ditch. A monk tried to say there were no Vietcong. Calley shot him, then he ordered Robert Maples: "Load your machine gun and shoot these people." Maples, a black, refused. Calley threatened him with his M16. Maples's buddies turned their rifles on Calley. He backed off, but another soldier obeyed the order, raking the huddled mass with a machine gun. Calley joined in the killing. Mothers and fathers threw themselves sacrificially on top of their children.

Helicopter pilot Warrant Officer Hugh Thompson, hopping over My Lai with a couple of gunships, was horrified by what he saw on the ground. He was adept at hunting VC, but he was a cool and decent man. He caught sight of Medina shooting an injured woman in the head, and then of Calley's bloody ditch. He landed and had a furious argument with Calley. Taking off again, he saw another group of ten civilians running in terror from 2nd Platoon riflemen. He landed between the peasants and the soldiers and confronted the lieutenant in charge, Stephen Brooks. When Brooks

Hugh Thompson, humanitarian. He was decorated for his rescue work.

was unyielding, Thompson shouted to his crewmen that he was going in to rescue the peasants and his crew was to fire on the Americans if they tried to kill them. Thompson got the ten villagers—two men, two women and six children—safely aboard one of his gunships.

Thompson's report at base was relayed to Colonel Barker's helicopter over My Lai. He ordered Medina: "These killings have got to stop."

The murders stopped but the cover-up began. The divisional commander, Major General Samuel Koster, made the fateful decision to let Henderson investigate his own command. Henderson chose to believe the lie of Barker and Medina that it was artillery fire that had accidentally killed "sixty-nine." He ignored proliferating evidence of mass slaughter, and he deceived General Westmoreland with a fictitious account of a military triumph.

Despite Thompson's gallantry and the revulsion felt by a number of men who did not join the killing—Henry Stanley, Dennis Bunning, Herbert Carver, George Garza, Leonard Gonzalez, John Dursi, Thomas Partsch—the cover-up nearly worked. Nobody went public. It was left to Ronald Ridenhour, a 21-year-old helicopter door-gunner, to do what the generals should have done. He heard rumors about mass killings and he followed them up. Four months after his discharge, on April 2, 1969, he set out the evidence in letters to President Nixon, cabinet officers, the Army and Arizona Congressman Morris Udall. Nixon's response work set up an undercover investigation of Ridenhour. But Udall was effective and so now was General Westmoreland, who overrode Nixon's resistance to an inquiry. Lieutenant General William Peers, a veteran of guerrilla wars, cut through the lies and half-truths. He identified a second massacre of 90 peasants in Co Luy by Bravo Company, led by Lieutenant Thomas Willingham. For their part in the cover-up, Peers recommended action against two generals, four full colonels, four majors, six captains and eight lieutenants. In a separate criminal inquiry, Warrant Officer Andre Feher found evidence to charge 30 with major crimes.

The inquiries were in secret. On September 6, the Army briefly announced that William Calley had been charged with murder. Television and newspapers barely noticed. The horror of what had happened did not strike America until a free-lance journalist, Sy Hersh, dug up the gist of the story two months later and Ronald L. Haeberle, a former combat photographer, released the confirming pictures of dead babies and pitiful villagers in the last moments of their lives.

The integrity of the Army's investigators was betrayed by the military justice system. Of all the officers in the cover-up, only Henderson came before a military court and he was acquitted. The criminal charges were dropped against all those who had left the service. Indictments were brought against only four officers—Calley, Medina, Willingham and Kotouc—and nine enlisted men. And only Calley, in the end, was found guilty. He was both war criminal and scapegoat. On trial for four months, he used the Nazi Nuremberg defense that he had no choice but to obey an order from a superior officer. Barker was not there to challenge him, having died in a helicopter crash three months after My Lai. Medina

Calley awaits the verdict. He was a well-behaved prisoner who built model airplanes and stocked an aquarium.

denied any knowledge of the massacre, and was acquitted by a jury of his military peers. Months later he confessed he had suppressed evidence and lied.

Calley was found guilty of premeditated murder of 22 of the villagers. The sentence was hard labor for the rest of his natural life, reduced on appeal to twenty years. But he served only three years and spent most of that time under house arrest in Fort Benning, on the orders of Nixon. In April 1974, Nixon's Secretary of the Army, Howard Calloway, cut the sentence to ten years on the grounds that Calley may have sincerely believed he was acting under orders. He was released on parole in November and went to work in his father-in-law's jewelers' shop in Columbus, Georgia, selling pretty brooches and engagement rings.

RALPH NADER, THE GOOD CITIZEN IN ACTION

A joke about Ralph Nader (1934–) is that if he went to a porn movie—ludicrous prospect—he would come out complaining that the mattress was made of flammable material. Nader takes the jokes in the very long stride of his gaunt six-foot-four-inch frame. They are a recognition of his status as a legend in his own time, the founder and prophet of the modern consumer movement—and more. His campaigns have saved hundreds of thousands of lives, and enhanced more, but his ambitions have soared beyond protecting consumers from exploitation by big business and betrayal by big government. He has come to seek nothing less than the creation of a "countervailing force," a new active citizenry that will make self-governance the reality rather than the romantic gloss of American democracy.

Nader guards his privacy zealously, but it seems he imbibed his instinct for outrage very early in lively evenings at the family dinner table in Winsted, Connecticut, where his father owned a restaurant. His parents were civic-minded immigrants from Lebanon and he was the youngest of four children. Listening to excitable talk about what the authoritarian "they" were doing and what "they" ought to do led Ralph to the books by the muckrakers—Lincoln Steffens, Ida Tarbell, Upton Sinclair, George Seldes. He read them all before he was 14. He was stirred, but as he noted later, "they stopped with exposure. They didn't follow through by politically mobilizing a concerned constituency."

This was a seminal perception. At Harvard Law School, which he found morally complacent, he had a transforming insight over the jurist Sir Henry Maine's dictum that progress to a modern society was to be measured by a subject's advance from the limited fixed rights of status (as serf, vassal or lord) to the citizen's multiple

A SECULAR MONK: The consumer champion does not own a car or much else. He lives frugally in rooms in Washington. He arrived by hitchhiking from Hartford in 1963, at the age of 29, and has never stopped since. Unmarried, he manages on five hours' sleep. In 1996 he ran for president for the Greens and spent less than $5,000 to get 682,000 votes. Photograph by Mark Godfrey.

and variable rights through social and commercial contract. On the contrary, Nader concluded, in area after area of contract—insurance, loans, transport, home-owning, automobile purchase—the buyer was no more than a serf at the mercy of the seller's fine print. The citizen had regressed from multiple rights to status. Nader's paradox powered three decades of investigation and campaigning, most famously beginning with his book *Unsafe at Any Speed* (1965), an indictment of the auto industry for failing to offer the consumer safer cars. General Motors, whose sporty Corvair he most condemned, could not believe that all this public service passion could come spontaneously to an individual. Must be a crank. Must be a plot. Must be a Red. It hired private detectives to stake out Nader, dig through his past and attempt to compromise him with attractive women. When one private eye tailing him in the Senate Office Building mixed up Nader with a *Washington Post* reporter, the story broke, the book catapulted to the top of the best-seller lists, GM President James Roche had to apologize and Nader won $425,000 for invasion of privacy. The money went where all Nader's income goes: into seeding more public interest groups, which were staffed initially by task forces of crusading students—Nader's Raiders, they were dubbed to his initial distaste.

America owes more than it may ever realize to Nader and his Johnny Appleseed research and advocacy groups: Safer cars. Airbags. Medicines that are safe, effective and cheaper. Tractors that don't roll over. Scam-free hearing aids. Decent nursing homes. Fairer credit and insurance. Cleaner water. Safer factories. Smoke-free air travel. Nader and his groups have played a critical role in all these changes and thousands more. Nader is not invulnerable to criticism; he might perhaps too readily assume all producers are wrong, all consumers right. He has had his failures and setbacks, and he certainly has critics, irritated by his piety, and enemies, frightened by his effectiveness. Yet few have achieved more for the American citizen than Ralph Nader and his selfless crusade over the past 30 years.

RACHEL CARSON'S REVERENCE FOR LIFE

A strange stillness overtook the town Rachel Carson described so poetically at the beginning of *Silent Spring*. The robin, the dove and the jay sang no more. No chicks hatched; no trout lay in the shady pools; the apple trees bore no fruit and everywhere, among the families of the farmers as well as in their fields, there was a shadow of death.

The town did not exist, but every one of the disasters she described in her parable had happened somewhere. She documented the disappearance of robins on the campus of Michigan State University, the annihilation of 27 species of fish in the Colorado River below Austin, the rise in the incidence of leukemia in people, and she traced it all to pesticides. She called them the elixirs of death. She was not opposed to chemicals as such, but she showed how their soaring and indiscriminate use was doing subtle, long-term damage to plants, animals and humans.

Rachel Carson was born in May 1907 in a five-room farmhouse (now a national historic landmark) in Springdale in the lower Allegheny Valley of Pennsylvania. She was a quiet, happy child, scribbling essays about her walks through the woodlands and fields. She wanted to be a writer. At the Pennsylvania College for Women (now Chatham College), there occurred one of those incidental persuasions that transform a life and the life affects the world. A talented science teacher, Mary Scott Skinner, convinced her to change her major from English to zoology, the subject of her subsequent honors degree from Johns Hopkins University. When the great moment in her life came along in January 1958, in a letter from a friend, she was superbly equipped to respond. She had the scientific training, she had the reverence for life in all its forms and she had the literary ability to make the subject readable, having already written an acclaimed trilogy about the sea. The letter from her friend Mrs. Olga Owens Huckins moved

Carson by describing the devastation uninvited aerial spraying with DDT had brought to Mrs. Huckins's small bird sanctuary. Encouraged by William Shawn, the editor of *The New Yorker*, Carson embarked on her great work. Two years into it, stricken by cancer, she knew it would be her last. She felt bound, she told a friend, by a solemn obligation. "The beauty of the world I was trying to save has always been uppermost in my mind—that, and anger at the senseless, brutish things that were being done . . . if I didn't at least try I could never again be happy in nature."

It was a valiant struggle. In 1961 she wrote that life "had burned down to a very tiny flame that might so easily flicker out." She lived long enough to enjoy the triumph when the articles first appeared in *The New Yorker* in June 1962, followed by the book in September. The chemical industry did its best to defame her, but DDT was banned and the modern ecological movement took wing.

JIMMY HOFFA PAYS THE PRICE

Jimmy Hoffa, mobsters like to say, is now a hubcap. The longtime leader of the International Brotherhood of Teamsters was abducted and murdered on July 30, 1975, his body most likely disposed of in a car compactor.

All that is known is that he went to the parking lot of the Machus Red Fox restaurant in a suburb of Detroit to bury the hatchet with a pair of gangland brothers, Anthony and Vito Giacalone, and that sometime later he called his wife to ask, "Where the hell is Tony Giacalone? I'm being stood up." The most widely held theory within the FBI is that the killing was arranged by the Giacalones and Tony Provenzano, a psychopathic New Jersey mobster, on the orders of mobster Russell Bufalino and with the knowledge, but not complicity, of Frank Fitzsimmons. "Fitz," a pudgy mediocrity, had taken over as general president while Hoffa served 4½ years in Lewisburg penitentiary for pension fund fraud and jury tampering.

In 1971, Hoffa had been pardoned by President Nixon, a recipient of Teamster election money, on the condition that he did not try to become president again. But he did try and the gangsters, who had found Fitz easier to manipulate than Hoffa, set out to stop him. A war of bombings and shootings started in Detroit. In a 1974 poll Hoffa had the support of 83 percent of the drivers, store clerks, brewery and department store workers among the 1.7 million members. They had warm memories of his ten years as president (1957–1967). He knit the union together and had the respect of the employers because he bargained intelligently, trading efficiencies for benefits. He was generous and a straight talker. He had no racial prejudice. He was a doting father and husband.

He was also fatally close to the mob throughout his career. He put millions in pension funds into mob-backed investments. He turned whole locals over to hoods. Hoffa took bribes and blatantly offered them, but it was ten years from his first arrest on March 13, 1957, to his entry into prison on March 7, 1967. Bobby Kennedy tried for years to get him. The hatred was mutual. On the day JFK was killed, Hoffa stopped the union flag from being lowered. "I'm no hypocrite," he said. "I hope the worms eat his eyes out."

THE SAINT

Miners' leader Jock Yablonski had the nerve to challenge the crooked election that made the vain and corrupt W. A. "Tony" Boyle president again of the United Mine Workers' union. On January 5, 1970, Yablonski and his wife and daughter were found shot dead at their isolated home in Clarksville, Pennsylvania. Boyle, whose minions hired the hit men, went to jail.

It was yet another blow to the labor movement. The popular idea of a labor leader became Lee J. Cobb's Johnny Friendly, the bluff, deadly longshoreman boss in *On the Waterfront*. Gangsters had indeed penetrated many unions for a time—and many businesses—but the stereotype was overstated. Forgotten was the fact that Budd Schulberg's screenplay was based on the real New York water-front, where it was union activists themselves, aided by leftist priests, who drove out the mobsters. A more apt criticism was that unions had become as stodgy and cautious as George Meany, the phlegmatic president of the AFL-CIO (the two unions had merged in 1955). But there were labor leaders of vision—Walter Reuther, A. Philip Randolph, Joseph Rauh. And Cesar Chavez (1927–1993).

Chavez, a second-generation American of Mexican descent, spent his childhood shuttling with his family between farm labor camps; the whole family often earned only a dollar for a day's fruit picking. He went barefoot and could barely read when, at 14, he left the last of his 40 schools. Yet it was the self-taught, frail and shy Chavez who succeeded where every-one else—Wobblies, Communists and the AFL-CIO—had come up short. He organized California's migrant farm workers—and he inspired them. His Farm Workers' Association, started on September 30, 1962, was more than a union. It was La Causa, a broad social movement that enhanced the dignity, pride and well-being of the migrants. Chavez learned tactics from the social activist Saul Alinsky, but it was his spiritual fire that made the difference. He was inspired by his Catholicism and Martin Luther King's example of Christianity in action.

In 1965, his organization—now the United Farm Workers (UFW)—joined Filipino grape pickers on strike in the San Joaquin Valley town of Delano. It was the start of a remarkable ten years of La Huelga (the strike), in which some of the poorest people in America refused to be crushed by powerful growers, industrialists, right-wing politicians and, for a time, the Teamsters, who brought in goons and made sweet-heart deals to squeeze the UFW. Chavez attracted national support. Thousands of idealistic college kids joined him, and 17 million people stopped buying grapes after he called for a boycott in 1968. When violence broke out on both sides, he went on a Gandhian hunger strike. It lasted 25 days. One by one enormous companies gave in. By 1975, the UFW had 50,000 members, wages had tripled and California's Governor Edmund G. "Jerry" Brown had enacted continental America's first collective bargaining right for farm workers.

Yet Chavez was never able to realize his ambition of well-paid farm workers united in a national union. His health gave way and squabbles broke out around him; and the factors that had always frustrated organizers—the seasonal and unskilled nature of the work, the immigrants' lack of political muscle—proved more intractable than had been thought. He died on April 23, 1993, at 66. He had sacrificed himself for La Causa.

A PRODIGIOUS HANDSHAKE
IN BEIJING

Henry Kissinger picked up a celebrated bug on his travels in Asia in July 1971. He described it as stomachache. At a dinner in his honor in Pakistan's steaming capital of Islamabad, everyone had a favorite remedy for the grimacing National Security Adviser, but it was Pakistan's president, Yahya Khan, who prevailed. Kissinger would recover quickly, Yahya insisted, if he spent a couple of days at the presidential rest house in the cool hill station of Nathiagali. At 8 a.m. the next day, July 9, all of Islamabad saw Kissinger's motorcade and its motorcycle escort move off into the mountains, sirens wailing, and the flags of Pakistan and the U.S. trailing in the breeze.

It was all a sham. In the dead of night Kissinger, incongruously decked out in hat and sunglasses, was spirited away to Beijing on a Boeing flown by Yahya's pilot. The stomachache–Nathiagali pantomime, devised by Kissinger with Yahya's boyish enthusiasm, was to keep the world in the dark long enough for Kissinger to fly in for an epochal secret meeting with Chinese Prime Minister Zhou Enlai. Even their first handshake had resonance: at Geneva in 1954 John Foster Dulles had slighted Zhou by declining his outstretched hand. Kissinger offered more practical proof of U.S. sympathies. He showed the Chinese satellite photographs of Soviet military facilities along the border with China.

In the afternoon of July 11, a glowing Kissinger reappeared in Islamabad, as if from the hill station, and by cable Nixon got the single code word he had been dying for: "Eureka!" Four days later, on July 15, in a seven-minute speech disclosing Kissinger's trip, he told the world what it meant. He was accepting an official invitation to visit Beijing. The prospect of the U.S. ending a quarter of a century of angry repudiation of Communist China shook the world, as Zhou Enlai predicted it would. For the initiative to come from the

hottest Red China scaremonger of the fifties and sixties was to make an art form of apostasy.

Nixon's opportunism had never served him, or America, better. He was quick to note signs of rising Sino-Soviet tension in the wake of the Soviet invasion of Czechoslovakia in 1968 and the Brezhnev Doctrine, which insisted on the Kremlin's right to intervene militarily if any Communist country deviated from the true path. The Chinese were scared and resentful and Nixon sensed it. One of his first acts as president, on February 1, 1969, was to dictate into a small tape recorder a memo for Kissinger urging him to explore the chances of opening a door to China. It was prescient. Within a few weeks, the Russians and Chinese were exchanging shots in small-scale border clashes.

Nixon did not spell it out in the memo, but he saw his move primarily as a way of gaining leverage over the Soviets and secondarily of disquieting his North Vietnamese enemies, presumed even then to be puppets of the Chinese. Kissinger was to develop a subtler view of triangular diplomacy, but he was skeptical of their chances. "This crazy guy really does want to normalize our relations with China," he told his deputy, Colonel Alexander Haig, in one of many moments of frustration in the two years between 1969 and 1971. Success turned on the happy marriage of Nixon's willpower and Kissinger's genius for maneuver. In the absence of formal channels, with the State Department dragging its feet and with uncertain signals from Beijing, which had its own factional disputes, dialogue was hard to achieve. The soft service Zhou Enlai popped into Nixon's court in April 1971, an invitation for the American table tennis team to play in China that Nixon immediately approved, was simply one of the more scrutable exchanges.

All the secrecy was justified. Nixon risked much: a humiliating public rebuff from Mao Zedong, alienating the Republican right and especially the friends of Taiwan in Congress, angering the Soviets. One of the best-kept secrets was that even as he landed at Beijing airport on Monday, February 21, 1972, to a Communist military band belting out "The Star-Spangled Banner," Nixon had no appointment with Mao. Zhou had made no commitment. The old man was bedridden, recovering from the complications of a stroke. It was a high moment when he dragged himself

from bed for an hour's badinage. There-after the toasts flowed with great mutual enthusiasm. The reconciliation changed the bipolar balance of power, and changed it in favor of the more flexible West. It broke the American obsession with anti-Communist ideology that since 1949 had excited so much miscalculation and cost so much in blood and intellectual and political freedom. Nor did it sacrifice Tai-wan; Nixon proved right in his judgment that China would not risk the new American friendship to conquer the island. It was Nixon's finest hour.

CHOPSTICKS FOR TWO: Nixon had practiced hard not to eat like a barbarian when served shark's fin and spongy bamboo shoots at the Chinese banquets. His dinner companion, Prime Minister Zhou Enlai, talked to him about Lincoln as one of the few great figures in history.

U.N. FOR ONE: America ended 22 years of stonewalling when it announced it would support China's membership in the U.N. on August 2, 1971, but held out for keeping Taiwan in too. It was outvoted, without a single NATO ally on the U.S. side, and on October 25, 1971, Taiwan was expelled. Beijing's Deputy Foreign Minister Chiao Kuan-Hua and its permanent delegate, Huang-Hua, led the general jubilation, gleeful scenes that outraged Nixon and both liberal and conservative congressmen.

CHAPTER FOURTEEN

THE IMPERIAL PRESIDENCY
1972–1980

Watergate

In the first American century, the great test of the Constitution was the Civil War. In the second century, it was the criminal conspiracy known as Watergate. The scandals were demeaning to American democracy. A president lying to Congress and the people. Bugging and burglary as routine political warfare. And bribery of uncommon boldness, parades of corporate lawyers carrying suitcases stuffed with dollar bills right into cabinet offices.

Watergate was all these things, but the significance of the attempt to cover up the "third-rate burglary" was its dramatization of President Nixon's attempt to withdraw power to an exalted presidency—away from the elected Congress, away from the courts, away from the people. The one sentence that sums it up was spoken by the chief actor after the crisis had passed: "If the President does it, it's legal."

Arthur Schlesinger, Jr., coined the phrase "the imperial presidency" principally to note the way Congress had relinquished its war-making authority, first to Truman and then to Johnson. Nixon's drive was to usurp domestic authority and to replace or circumvent leadership institutions he saw as paralyzed by self-doubt and second thoughts.

The ambitions were frustrated because all the institutions worked as they were meant to work. President Gerald Ford was able to declare "the long national nightmare" over in good time for the celebrations marking the 200th birthday on July 4, 1976, of the most splendidly successful democracy on earth.

"I'LL DRINK TO THAT!" There was no doubt that $200,000 in $100 bills from the fugitive financier Robert Vesco had been handed over to Maurice Stans, former commerce secretary and Nixon's chief fund-raiser. The question a New York jury took four days to answer in 1974 was whether it was illegal and whether John Mitchell, Nixon's 1972 campaign director, and former Attorney General, had then tried to block a Securities and Exchange Commission in-vestigation of Vesco. On April 28, both men were acquitted. Was Mitchell sur-prised? "No way, baby, no way," he said and went to get happily drunk in his hotel room with the legal team Edward O'Connell (left), Walter Bonner (Stans's lawyer, embracing Mitchell), and John Sprizo. In mock deference to the Scottish origins of photographer Harry Benson, they responded to his camera by bursting into rousingly incoherent renditions of Harry Lauder songs.

CONSEQUENCES OF CHARACTER OR THE LACK THEREOF

Richard Nixon, sequestered with his family in the Lincoln Sitting Room on November 7, 1972, was already loudly playing a recording of "Victory at Sea," when a telegram arrived from George McGovern. It conceded at 11:40 p.m. what was already in prospect, that Nixon had won his greatest electoral triumph. In two presidential elections, he had endured suspense to the very last moment, the bitter defeat of 1960, the heart-stopping squeaker of a less-than-one-percent win in 1968. Now, before the night was over, every state in the union was his except Massachusetts. He was to win 60.7 percent of the vote, the greatest ever given a Republican candidate, more popular votes than any previous presidential candidate (47 million) and a stunning triumph in the electoral college of 521–17. It was a round of applause for the diplomatic superman of the Moscow and Beijing summits and a vote of thanks for a buoyant economy: the inflation he inherited down to 2.7 percent, federal taxes for an average family cut 20 percent since he took office. It was not just a victory for 1972. He had redrawn the political map. He was the first Republican to win big among blue-collar workers, union families, traditionally Democratic ethnics and Catholics.

Around midnight the champion took himself off to his office in the empty Executive Office Building, the "wedding cake" building opposite the West Wing of the White House. There, from 1:30 a.m. to near dawn, he was alone with two of his closest aides, special counsel Charles "Chuck" Colson and chief of staff H. (Harry) R. (Robbins)—"Bob"—Haldeman. For any other politician, this would have been a night to savor. It was a fairy tale finale to a tumultuous quarter century in the political arena, yet as his vote soared through the small hours, Nixon grew ever more morose. Colson, the faithful hit man for Nixon's covert political stunts, recalled what it was like: "I couldn't feel any sense of jubilation," he said in a PBS documentary 20 years later. "The attitude was sort of, 'Well, we showed 'em, we got even with our enemies, we beat 'em.' Instead of 'We've been given a wonderful mandate to rule over the next four years.'"

National Security Adviser Henry Kissinger had found that

DIRTY TRICKS: Stressed by smears and lies, Senator Edmund Muskie, Democratic front-runner, breaks down in the snowy New Hampshire primary. A month later, he withdrew and threw his support to George McGovern, Nixon's preferred opponent.

BURGLARS: Howard Hunt (above), served for thirty-three months in jail, James McCord (left) four. Both men were ex-CIA, both blew the Watergate connection to the White House. Hunt did it by leaving evidence in a hotel room and by blackmail ("your cheapest commodity available is money"). McCord wrote a confessional letter to Federal District Judge John J. Sirica, who had threatened maximum sentences. Was there a CIA plot to expose Nixon? Haldeman thought so.

BINGO! Triumphant *Washington Post* quintet, left to right: owner Katharine Graham, intrepid reporting partners Carl Bernstein and Bob Woodward, managing editor Howard Simons, and editor Ben Bradlee. "Deep Throat," the phantom source Woodward met in an underground garage at 2 a.m., has been identified only as someone holding an extremely sensitive position in the executive branch. The *Post* was the first to expose the scandal by relentless reporting and brave editing.

BERLIN WALL: Crew-cut Bob Haldeman, chief of staff, spent hours alone with Nixon discussing permutations of the cover-up. Few got through the man Nixon called his lord high executioner. Haldeman protected Nixon from the personal confrontations he hated.

MARTHA THE MOUTH: John Mitchell's volatile wife, Martha, stirred Watergate mysteries. She made hysterical phone calls saying her husband was involved in Watergate—when he was strenuously denying it—and claimed she was being kept a political prisoner.

NIXON'S NEMESIS (right): Senator Sam J. Ervin, Jr., the North Carolina Democrat, headed the Senate inquiry. He is flanked by Republican Senator Howard Baker, left, and Sam Dash, chief counsel. Professor Arthur Miller is standing.

NIXON'S FBI (left): Nixon loyalist L. Patrick Gray III, acting director of the FBI after J. Edgar Hoover died, was prevailed on to stall the investigation on grounds of national security. John Dean gave him two files of incriminating evidence from Howard Hunt's safe. Reading between the lines, he burned them with his Christmas wrapping paper. The Senate refused to confirm his appointment and he narrowly escaped criminal indictment.

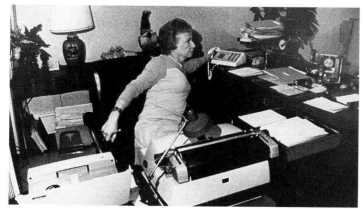

ROSE MARY WOODS'S STRETCH: Rose Mary Woods, Nixon's secretary, said she must have accidentally erased 18 minutes from a key White House tape when typing a transcript. She guessed she pushed a wrong button on the tape machine (left) when stretching to reach a phone. Others guessed the heavy hand was Nixon's.

MO AND JOHN: Waiting to betray his boss, the flashy John W. Dean III, Nixon's counsel, with his wife, Maureen ("Mo"). In 1991 *Silent Coup* by Len Colodny and Robert Gettlin suggested Dean instigated the break-in to gather information on a call-girl ring servicing Democrats. Dean served four months after doing a deal with the prosecutors.

"as his hour of triumph approached, Nixon withdrew ever more, even from his close advisers. His resentments, usually so well controlled, came increasingly to the surface. It was as if victory was not an occasion for reconciliation, but an opportunity to settle the scores of a lifetime."

The secret diary Haldeman dictated every day over four years, published in 1994, confirms Kissinger's insight. The election entries reflect the President's vengeful preoccupations. "He wants total discipline on the press, they're to be used as enemies, not played for help" (November 8). "He wants to be sure the IRS covers all major Democratic contributors and all backers of the new senators" (November 11). A White House tape captures his rage at the bureaucracy, even the loyalists, as he instructs Haldeman what words to use in obtaining the official resignation of every White House staff member and the entire cabinet, each of whom would be allowed to stay on only after presidential scrutiny: Tell them, said Nixon, "You've got one week to plan your holidays now. You're out, you're finished, you're done, done, finished."

Success seemed perversely to heighten his insecurity. On May 19, 1971, flushed with the good news that an arms agreement with the Soviets could be expected by the end of the year, he had taken Kissinger, Haldeman, chief domestic policy adviser John Ehrlichman and Colson for a balmy evening sail on the Potomac aboard the presidential yacht *Sequoia*. Talk of leaks, according to Colson in his book *Born Again,* changed the mood. "The President's finger circled the top of his wineglass slowly. 'One day we will get them—we'll get them on the ground where we want them. And we'll stick our heels in, step on them hard and twist—right, Chuck, right?' Then his eyes darted to Kissinger. 'Henry knows what I mean—just like you do it in negotiations, Henry—get them on the floor and step on them, crush them, show no mercy.'"

On the Sunday before the 1972 election, Nixon gave a glimpse of his second-term domestic agenda in an interview with Garnett Horner of the *Washington Star.* Americans, Nixon asserted, had become too used to a "soft life." What they needed was an end to the "whole era of permissiveness" and "a new feeling of responsibility, a new feeling of self-discipline." Or as he decoded it for John Ehrlichman: "Flush Model Cities and Great Society along with it. It's failed." The lament for Norman Rockwell's sturdier, simpler America was not exceptional in the aftermath of the counterculture sixties. The notable thing was his fixation on the source of the malaise he perceived—the "American leadership classes," as he put it in a memo to Haldeman. His loathing of the Eastern elite was

dinned into Haldeman. "None of them in the cabinet, you understand. None of those Harvard bastards."

On the surface, the talk about the bloated federal budget and the ills of the Great Society sounded as if Nixon had finally become the conservative the Republican right wing had always dreamed of. He did fantasize vaguely of a new party based on what Kevin Phillips had first pegged as the "emerging Republican majority," but he was too egocentric and opportunistic to owe much allegiance to any party, any coalition, any ideology—anything much larger than his desire to consolidate power in his person. In his second term, he attempted to usurp the authority of Congress by refusing to spend funds it had specifically appropriated. He defied the legislature and the courts by his doctrine of unreviewable executive privilege. He reduced the cabinet to an anonymous blob. He had always been a loyal campaigner for other Republicans, but for the most pragmatic reason of piling up reciprocal favors. He had never been comfortable with either wing of the party, nor they with him. He didn't trust big business. His desire to gut the Great Society programs stemmed less from ideological conviction than his perception that his enemies—particularly wealthy, privileged liberals, old New Deal bureaucrats and the elite press—favored them. They were the crowd, in his imagination, who had sneered at the Checkers speech, stuck up for Alger Hiss, sniggered at his California defeat, closed an eye to Kennedy family misconduct, pilloried him for seeking an honorable end to a war the Democrats had blundered into. The depth of his bitterness was such that just before his death more than two decades later, when he had effectively made himself over as an elder statesman, he was still liable to blow a fuse in private about "the corrupt goddamned leadership class" or "goddamned intellectual elitists" or Senator Edward Kennedy's 1969 accident, when late at night he drunkenly drove a car into the water at Chappaquiddick, left a drowned Mary Jo Kopechne and, instead of calling the police at once, concocted a scheme to cover up his part in the affair. "You know, the police didn't even investigate Chappaquiddick for three days," Nixon complained to his editorial assistant Monica Crowley, who published her recollections in 1998 (*Nixon in Winter*). "A cover-up! Everyone including [former Defense Secretary Robert] McNamara was involved in that cover-up. And there the guy sits, still in the Senate, a hero to the women's groups. And they love him because he's a lib; never mind that he has destroyed more women's lives than can be counted."

The roots of the abuse of power in the series of scandals known as Watergate, the most pervasive corruption in the history of the presidency, are here in Nixon's insidious insecurities and unquenchable self-pity. If he was caught in some abuse, he was only protecting himself against his enemies, who did worse to him but were never criticized. In his memoir, *RN*, published five years after his resignation, what begins as a disarming confession typically ends as an accusation. He admits he "sometimes" ordered a tail on an opponent and "sometimes" urged federal departments to check on such opponents, but he attempted this as self-defense: "I told my staff that we should come up with the kind of imaginative dirty tricks that our Democratic opponents used against us and others so effectively in previous campaigns." In private, he was prepared to go much further. He told Haldeman: "Every time we have a leak in our organization we should charge that we're being bugged. Even if you plant one and discover it."

Nixon had undoubtedly been harassed. The bureaucracy was recalcitrant. Johnson bugged his campaign plane in 1968. His tax returns had been leaked in 1952. He was probably right to believe his tax audits in 1961 and 1963 were politically motivated and that Bobby Kennedy, as Attorney General, had considered indicting his mother, Hannah, and brother, Don, over a favorable loan from Howard Hughes in 1960. Still, tit for tat is hardly an adequate description of the baroque edifice of Watergate, or a justification for its blueprint, a basic contempt for the democratic processes of debate, persuasion, compromise and conciliation.

One of the most persistent puzzles of the Watergate break-in then and now—and one sometimes used by his apologists to claim he could not possibly have been the perpetrator—is why Nixon and his aides felt the need to risk dirty tricks. Nixon could not have lost, as George Reedy put it, had the Democratic National Committee been awarded an exclusive contract to count the ballots. George McGovern, a liberal two-term senator from South Dakota, was a decent, thoughtful public servant who had served his country as a bomber pilot in World War II, but he was easily caricatured by Nixon as an advocate of "amnesty, acid and abortion." And the Democrats ran a hopeless campaign, epitomized by the debacle over McGovern's initial choice for running mate, Missouri Senator Thomas Eagleton. When it was revealed that the senator had been hospitalized for depression and undergone shock treatment McGovern pledged to stand behind his veep-in-waiting "one thousand percent," then promptly dropped him for Sargent Shriver.

To ask why the Nixon campaign should have felt compelled to sabotage such a doomed effort is to miss the main point.

THE ENEMIES LIST

On January 25, 1971, Nixon speechwriter and Haldeman aide Tom Huston put together a list of groups of people judged unfriendly. His idea was to torment them by every federal agency that could be persuaded to act. By midyear, Charles Colson and John Dean had expanded the list into the hundreds. When Dean revealed its existence at the Senate hearings on June 25, 1973, the White House said it was merely intended as a social guide. But a large percentage of the "enemies" claimed to have been subject to tax audits and other federal harassment. Some were known political critics and opponents—Edward Kennedy, Walter Mondale, John Kenneth Galbraith, John Lindsay, Theodore Sorensen, Jane Fonda, Ramsey Clark, Dick Gregory, Leonard Woodcock. But much of the list was mainstream America—the presidents of Yale, the Harvard Law School, MIT, the Ford Foundation; 57 newspaper and television people; actors Gregory Peck, Carol Channing, Steve McQueen, Bill Cosby, Barbra Streisand, Paul Newman—and Joe Namath of the New York Jets. It was a sloppy piece of work: Professor Hans Morgenthau was on the list because he was confused with Robert Morgenthau, the U.S. attorney in New York sacked by Nixon; Clark Clifford was "Gifford." The inefficiency should be no solace, remarked Jonathan Schell in *The New Yorker*: "In our country, as elsewhere, once the police break down your door . . . it isn't any help that they can't spell your name."

Watergate did not proceed out of any rational political calculation, but directly—and inevitably—from the twisted, paranoid psyche of Richard Nixon. That was not all there was to Nixon. His supporters, to take Haldeman's metaphor, saw a brighter side of the multifaceted quartz crystal: a man of high intelligence and original mind, gifted with strategic vision, industrious, a friend of the arts, protective of those he loved, a man with the fortitude to stand up for America and the coolest of judgments in a crisis; in October 1973 at the nadir of his struggle over the tapes he mediated in the Yom Kippur war with daring foresight.

But in Watergate it was the dark side of the crystal that caught the light.

The details of the mystery famously encapsulated in Senator Howard Baker's hammerlock question "What did the President know and when did he know it?" are in an important sense irrelevant. Nixon probably did not know that soon after midnight on June 17, 1972, four Cubans and an ex–CIA man wearing sunglasses and surgical gloves were going to break into the headquarters of the Democratic National Committee (DNC) at the Watergate hotel complex. But Nixon had set these and other malefactors in motion as certainly as if he had wound up a set of clockwork soldiers. His churning emotions, his habits of isolation, his appetite for the covert, his impatience with "bureaucratic" procedures and, above all, his choice of the men around him guaranteed gross legal and ethical transgressions. In the vernacular of political warfare, the attempt to replant a bug on the phone of Lawrence O'Brien, the DNC chairman, was among the lesser games. Nixon knew firsthand of the major offenses that came before the botched break-in—the "White House horrors," in the phrase of his Attorney General John Mitchell. The program of illegal wiretapping, the burglary at the offices of Daniel Ellsberg's psychiatrist, the political manipulation of the IRS, the corrupt pressure on corporate executives and labor leaders for millions of dollars in campaign money in return for executive favors, all transcend the incident at the Watergate. And it is possible, anyway, that the break-in derived from Nixon's personal obsession with O'Brien's financial connection to Howard Hughes, and not at all from his campaign's desire to know what the floundering Democrats were up to.

It was Nixon's misfortune, but also a reflection of his character, that there was never close to him a strong personality like Senator Sam Ervin who could have banged the table and said, "Mr. President, I can't let you do that, it would be unconstitutional." Or the sinuously charming Clark Clifford who could have lifted his sights from his petty domestic spites instead of feeding them. It would not have been easy. Early in the second administration, a leading conservative supporter of Nixon's tried to raise Nixon's sights. Newbold Noyes, the editor and part owner of the *Washington Star,* became distressed by the nastiness of the atmosphere. He wrote Nixon a long reasonable letter, asking him to improve the moral tone of his new administration and make some commitment to fight social ills: "Mr. President, do you really mean to convey the impression that to your mind the main thing this country needs is a more responsible attitude on the parts of its disadvantaged citizens?" All Noyes got was a harangue. Inside the White House and the new administration there was nobody like Noyes. John Ehrlichman, with his eye on his domestic programs, did persuade Nixon to see Noyes, but he was eager to compete in machismo. Bob Haldeman, the advertising man, encouraged Nixon's belief that his problems were merely p.r. John Mitchell was too enamored of his own tough guy image, too partisan to understand the role of Attorney General. Charles Colson, commander in chief of the crazies, played to Nixon's worst instincts for ill will and intrigue. And then there was the young right-wing ideologue lawyer from Indiana, Tom Huston, the originator of the idea of an enemies list, who came along in 1970 with a plan that turned out to be the DNA of Watergate.

Huston was only 28 when he joined the White House in 1969, reporting to Haldeman as a speechwriter. He had worked for Nixon's campaign while still in Army intelligence. He was a passionate states' rights man, a rather affected admirer of Cato the Younger, Jefferson and John C. Calhoun. He had founded a chapter of William Buckley's Young Americans for Freedom while at Indiana University, and then created the World Youth Crusade for Freedom to back the war in Vietnam. Somewhere along the way, he constructed a neat libertarian theory to justify illiberal acts. "The real threat to internal security—in any society—is repression. A handful of people can't frontally overthrow the government; but if they can engender enough fear, they can generate an atmosphere that will bring out of the woodwork every repressive demagogue in the country." Hence government would be justified in suppressing dissent for fear of backlash. No longer was the threat to the Republic a conspiracy, real or imagined. On Huston's theory, any protest could be construed as a threat because it might bring out a reactionary right-wing dictator. The left wing had to be saved from itself.

A like-minded Nixon wanted to bend the awkwardly independent intelligence agencies to his will to conduct a secret war on the domestic dissenters, the leakers, the radicals and revolutionaries—they were all much of a muchness to him. Emergency "national security" authority intended for use against foreign enemies was turned against American citizens. On June 5, 1970, he called in the intelligence chiefs—FBI, CIA, NSA (National Security Agency) and DIA (Defense Intelligence Agency)—and got them to appoint Huston as the staff director of an ad hoc committee of deputies to coordinate domestic intelligence. But coordination was a cover word to appease the agencies and give Huston a free hand. What Huston proposed, in J. Anthony Lukas's summary, was (1) intensified electronic surveillance of both "domestic security threats" and foreign diplomats, (2) the monitoring of American citizens using international communication facilities; (3) a relaxation of the restrictions on illegal opening and reading of mail; (4) recruiting more informants on college campuses; (5) lifting restrictions on surreptitious entry, the so-called "black bag jobs" the ordinary world knows as burglary. "Use of this technique is clearly illegal," Huston admitted. "However, it is also the most fruitful tool and can produce a type of intelligence which cannot be obtained in any other fashion."

On July 14, 1970, Nixon approved Huston's top-secret plan, and it was with his blessing that Huston told the first meeting of the working group of agency deputies that "everything is valid, everything is possible."

Nixon, in *RN*, defends Huston's "techniques" as no threat to "legitimate dissent." His plan was directed at terrorism. The times, to be sure, were turbulent. Nixon had cause to be concerned at the failure of the FBI to stop the bombing and arson associated with the Weathermen, a crazy fringe of the antiwar movement. They were a violent offshoot of the disintegrating Students for a Democratic Society, their name adapted from a Bob Dylan refrain "You don't need a weatherman to know which way the wind blows." They thought the wind was blowing for revolution. It wasn't, and they soon blew themselves away, but more than 40 people died in violent incidents between January 1969 and April 1970. Nixon cites 174 major bombings and bombing attempts on campus in the school year 1969–70. He saw the Weathermen and the Black Panthers as enemies of the democratic system, and he was right. He saw them also as part of a conspiracy funded by the likes of Cuba and Algeria, and he was wrong. The FBI and CIA could not establish a conspiracy, but Nixon kept believing it anyway.

The question confronting Nixon and his intelligence chiefs was one of principle and proportion. Was this threat grave enough, was any threat grave enough, to justify unconstitutional measures and conceal them from any kind of independent scrutiny? What was to prevent newly authorized bugging and burglaries being carried out not against putative bombers but against nonviolent dissenters? How could the civil liberties of the people at large be protected from secret police power? The record shows that the list of perceived enemies, vulnerable to illegal assault, came to include political opponents and critics who were completely nonviolent and democratic. In his memoir, Nixon argues that it would be against the national interest to limit a president "to the mechanical functions of executing the precise letter of the law, because laws cannot foresee every circumstance." That is a naked claim to arbitrary power.

J. Edgar Hoover killed the Huston plan, as much out of prudence and bureaucratic jealousy as out of principles he had often sacrificed. He insisted on the President's signature for anything that might be illegal, whereupon Nixon retreated. But the plan did not die in his mind. If he could not get the FBI to direct the police-state apparatus of bugging, break-in and spying, it could be done from the White House.

———————

It was always Halloween in the Nixon White House. They were continually spooked by leaks. The conviction that the national interest may require secrecy, and that on occasion it justifies misleading the public, has been common to every holder of the nation's highest office. Nixon had just cause for secrecy in the delicate opening of China, the Soviet summit and the peace talks with the North Vietnamese—more justification certainly than Johnson had for his deceptive escalations of the war in Vietnam. The seemingly exponential growth in leakages on defense and foreign policy Nixon suffered would have been grave for any administration. For Nixon they were catastrophic. Secrecy on matters great and small was a way of life for the Nixonians; they did so much in secrecy that they were acutely exposed to death by a thousand leaks. The leaks were so pervasive they hardened the suspicion that they might well be coordinated, rather than the routine untidy business of democracy. They might be the work of an enemy of the United States; or they might be the work of enemies at home, concerned not so much with policy debate as destroying Nixon's grip on power. Which of the two motives predominated was important, but a man who feels he has two barrels of a shotgun pointed at him is not much concerned to distinguish between them.

Three features characterized the administration: the nature of what they felt they needed to keep secret, the compulsive interest in other people's presumed secrets and the indiscriminate response directed at anyone who spilled the beans—or was remotely suspected of doing so. The list of suspects grew with every leak, so that fewer and fewer people were allowed to participate in policy making (on Vietnam, the number got down to seven, none of them in the cabinet). The secrecy invited penetration. Those on the outside inevitably wanted to look in. Perhaps that was all there was to the mysterious affair of Navy Yeoman Charles Radford. It was discovered in 1971 that Radford, a link between Kissinger's National Security Council and the Pentagon, had been filching highly sensitive documents from Kissinger's briefcase. He had been copying them—not for the Soviets but for the chairman of the Joint Chiefs of Staff, Admiral Thomas Moorer. It never became clear why the Chiefs thought it necessary to spy on the NSC. They resented Nixon's attempts to curb defense spending, worried about the China opening and arms talks with the Soviets. Whatever the motive, the spying from within aggravated the feeling that nobody was to be trusted.

Even before the leaks proliferated, Nixon was suspicious. One of the first things he did upon taking office was to order the FBI to bug the phones of 37 people. He had already planned a wiretapping program with Hoover, in April 1969, and Kissinger had already supplied a number of names, when the *New York Times* shook the White House on May 9, 1970. It revealed that the administration had been secretly bombing Cambodia since March 18. The intensified wiretapping program that followed was the top of the slippery slope. Kissinger ever after regretted his part in it. He was one of the few to emerge unstained from the Watergate cover-up—Nixon kept everybody in "need to know" compartments—but he was nonetheless caught up in the emotional whirlpool. His furious concern that leaks could damage his talks with the North Vietnamese and U.S. credibility with the Soviets and Chinese (they didn't) only goes some way to explain his leading role in the campaign of eavesdropping. It was an initiation ceremony. The new boy in the grossly anti-Semitic Nixon political family was an immigrant who had to prove that his loyalty had not been suborned by Harvard, a Jewish background and friendships in Georgetown. Nixon was always needling him that leaks came from the doves and Democrats he had appointed to his NSC staff. How Nixon nursed his grudges! In retirement, he told Walter Isaacson, a Kissinger biographer, that he might have been spared a lot of his troubles if Kissinger had hired a more loyally conservative staff. He blamed too much on Kissinger. In May 1973, when he had a new inner circle, tapes released in 1997 reveal him telling his press secretary, Ronald Ziegler: "Henry ordered the whole goddamn thing. He ordered it all, believe me. He was the one who was in my office jumping up and down. I said, 'All right, investigate the sons of bitches.'" Nixon's voice rose to a shout: "And he read every one of those tapes. He reveled in it, he groveled in it, he wallowed in it." In fact, Nixon had taken Kissinger off the transcript distribution list in May 1970. On July 17, 1974, Nixon accepted full responsibility for the bugging in written testimony to the Senate Foreign Relations Committee. Still, there is no doubt that Kissinger felt the pressure to join the club. Hoover recorded him fuming on the phone: "We'll destroy whoever did this if we can find him." Seventeen wiretaps, without court orders, were placed between May 1969 and February 1971, on members of Kissinger's NSC staff and other officials, and four more were placed on newsmen. The numbers were not exceptional; the subjects were. Some of the taps were clearly political—and all of them were later ruled illegal. And the leak they were initially looking for wasn't a leak at all. The bombing information in the *New York Times* came from a correspondent in Cambodia.

Kissinger felt especially vulnerable on June 13, 1971. The *New York Times* began publishing the biggest leak of all, extracts from the 40-volume compilation of documents that became known as the Pentagon Papers. They were a history of the Vietnam war under Kennedy and Johnson, sorting out decisions made by Defense, State, the CIA, the White House and the Joint Chiefs, and as such they were damaging to the Democrats. On that score, Nixon was relaxed, but the fact of yet another leak was combustible material. Kissinger guessed at once that the leaker was Daniel J. Ellsberg. He had employed Ellsberg as a consultant in 1969, and had once taken him for lunch in Nixon's compound at San Clemente. He felt personally betrayed, politically exposed and professionally sabotaged at a time when his clandestine maneuvers with the Chinese were at a critical point. Plausibly enough, Kissinger told Nixon that world leaders would never join in secret negotiations if they felt the U.S. could not control leaks: "It shows you're a weakling, Mr. President." He also portrayed Ellsberg as just the kind of long-haired promiscuous weirdo Nixon hated. Haldeman, Ehrlichman and Colson criticize Kissinger for stirring him up to indict Ellsberg for espionage, theft and conspiracy, and to take legal action enjoining the *New York Times* from publishing any more documents. Haldeman writes: "Henry got Nixon cranked up and then they started cranking each other up until they were both in a frenzy."

Nixon never needed much cranking. How little became even more glaring in 1997. Just when we might be forgiving and forgetting, another batch of profane Oval Office tape transcripts always seems to emerge from the darkness. In *Abuse of Power*, the Watergate historian Stanley I. Kutler published 201 hours of tapes that, among much else, show a president obsessed by three vendettas—getting Ellsberg, getting leakers and smearing the Democrat "establishment" for starting Vietnam, or in Nixonese, getting the "goddamn leakers," the "sons of bitches," the "cocksuckers," the "rich Jews." He tells Haldeman and Colson: "We're up against an enemy, a conspiracy. They're using any means. We are going to use any means. Is that clear?" Any means included for starters a presidentially inspired raid on the Brookings Institution (a Washington think tank)—not for national security but for political warfare against those Democrats who had got America into the morass in the first place. Some Johnson aides had given Brookings a classified Pentagon report on the 1968 bombing halt that Nixon felt had nearly cost him the close election. He was understandably furious to be told that the report could not be obtained by his aides. It had been known that Huston in 1969, then Colson in July 1971, had Brookings in their sights.

Colson's notion was to firebomb the place and then go in disguised as firemen. But the Kutler-edited tapes dramatize Nixon's central role. "Don't discuss it here. You talk to [E. Howard] Hunt. I want the break-in. Hell, they do that. You're to break into the place, rifle the files and bring them in. . . . Just go in and take it. Go in around eight or nine o'clock." And these are lines from another June conversation in an Oval Office meeting with Haldeman, Ehrlichman and Kissinger:

Kissinger: Brookings has no right to have classified documents.
Nixon: I want it implemented. Goddamnit, get in and get those files. Blow the safe and get it.
Haldeman: They may very well have cleaned them by now. . . .
Kissinger: I wouldn't be surprised if Brookings had the files.

Ehrlichman later quietly managed to squash the Brookings adventures. But it was the first of a series of meetings where Nixon thrashed around for someone frankly unscrupulous who would find and spread smears on the Democrats about Vietnam, the Cuban missile crisis, the Bay of Pigs, Korea. His old favorite Tom Huston, now thought less pliable, was dismissed as an "arrogant little bastard." At the same time, Nixon was lambasting the cabinet about the traitors on their staffs. "We've checked and found that 96 percent of the bureaucracy are against us; they're bastards who are here to screw us." Someone set out to prove him right by leaking to the *New York Times* the U.S. fallback positions in the strategic arms talks with the Russians. When the administration's Pentagon Papers case against the *New York Times*—the first government attempt at prior restraint in the history of the Republic—was thrown out 6–3 by the Supreme Court on June 30, 1971, Nixon went into overdrive. Frustrated by what he saw as FBI foot-dragging, he made a fateful decision. He ordered Ehrlichman to form a top-secret White House Special Investigations Unit to work on the Ellsberg "conspiracy" and trace leaks: the Plumbers. David Young, a lawyer on Kissinger's staff, and Egil "Bud" Krogh, an Ehrlichman aide, were separately summoned and put in charge. In turn, they recruited John Mitchell's man G. Gordon Liddy and Colson's protégé E. Howard Hunt. Just at the moment when Nixon had reached a pinnacle of world acclaim, having announced Beijing's invitation to him on July 15, he put his fate in the hands of as odd a pair of operators, in Liddy and Hunt, as have ever been perceived in the kaleidoscope of American politics.

Colson called them "good healthy right-wing exuberants." Howard Hunt was a James Bond with butterfingers, whose blunders and blackmailing helped to doom Nixon. He had been a CIA spy for 23 years and lived the life of his 46 thrillers (under six pen names). He had been one of the CIA's men in the Guatemala coup. The Cubans in the Watergate break-in were men he got to know when he was "Eduardo," a CIA organizer of the Bay of Pigs invasion. He was supposedly a "burnt-out case" who may or may not have been forced out of the CIA when his old chum Colson recruited him for the Plumbers. Hunt promptly equipped himself at a CIA safe house with a red toupee, false glasses, devices to give him a limp and a driver's license and Social Security card in the name of Edward Joseph Warren. He kept his burglary tools, and a gun, in a safe in the White House. He forged a cable to implicate President Kennedy in the murder of South Vietnam's Diem and succeeded in having the smear aired on NBC.

Liddy was a kamikaze ideologue dismayed by the permissive sixties. He was a spellbinder who liked to demonstrate his willpower by scorching his left hand and forearm—but never the right hand. He said he needed that for gunplay. He was a former FBI agent and Jesuit-trained lawyer who had been advising Mitchell on policy about narcotics, bombing and guns. He was a gun nut. As an assistant district attorney in Poughkeepsie, New York, he had once made a point in court by firing a pistol at the ceiling. When Watergate blew, he volunteered to stand on a street corner to be shot for his blunders as a soldier, remarking that it was a pity he was the only person "available to the White House for a domestic sanctioned killing." He was the only Watergate underling who didn't trade his knowledge for leniency.

The notable feature in what followed is how much their political masters tolerated the Plumbers by way of crimes cheerfully admitted. On September 4, 1971, Los Angeles police were called to the Beverly Hills offices of a psychiatrist, Dr. Lewis Fielding, which had been forcibly entered and ransacked. Its file cabinets had been jimmied open. Pills lay among the debris. The cops put it down to a "druggie rip-off raid," as they were intended to. It was, of course, a bag job by Liddy and Hunt and a trio of Bay of Pigs Cuban exiles, one of them Bernard Barker, who was later apprehended in the Watergate break-in. Their assignment from Krogh and Young was to photograph all the medical files relating to one of Dr. Fielding's patients—the "traitor" Ellsberg. Liddy had gone along, with a CIA special camera concealed in a tobacco pouch; they had also fitted him with disguises and a new identity as "George Leonard," courtesy of his buddy Hunt.

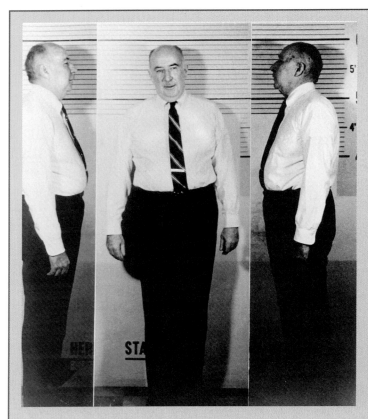

JOHN MITCHELL (1913–1988)

The "big enchilada" in Ehrlichman's words, Mitchell was the first Attorney General (1969–1972) to go to prison, for 19 months. He lied about directing the secret fund held by the Committee to Re-Elect the President (CREEP) and approving Gordon Liddy's program of sabotage, but admitted his own role in the cover-up with surprising stoicism. Mitchell was a bluff cynic who first made his name as a bond lawyer with a magical touch for raising money. He believed passionately that Nixon was a great president, and Nixon had an affection for him. But in 1973, Nixon, Ehrlichman and Haldeman talked about getting Mitchell to take the rap. Nixon thought he would be "a great stone face" as a witness. It was not known until 1994, when it was revealed in Fred Emery's book *Watergate,* that in August 1973 Mitchell did in fact go to the prosecutors and offer to be the fall guy if they would give up the pursuit of Nixon.

WATERGATE QUOTE: Questioned by Carl Bernstein of the *Washington Post,* he threatened the *Post*'s TV franchises in Florida with the remark: "Kate Graham is going to get her tit caught in a big fat wringer. . . ."

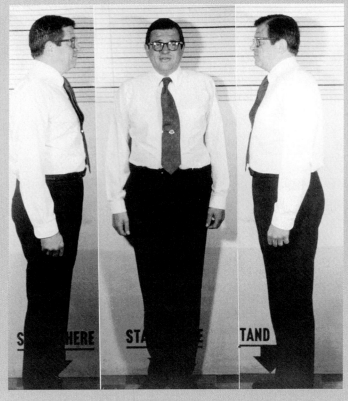

CHUCK COLSON (b. 1931)

Special counsel, or Nixon's alter ego. He served seven months for trying to smear Ellsberg as a treasonous conspirator. His office was next to Nixon's hideaway in the Executive Office Building, and eventually he commanded a staff of 23. He spent hours with Nixon dreaming up dirty trick scenarios, indulging his hate for the Kennedy clan, seared into Colson's soul in fights as a Massachusetts Republican. To Haldeman he was a living end run. An ex-Marine who went to night school to qualify as a lawyer, he kept a Green Beret motto on his wall: "If you've got 'em by the balls, the hearts and minds will follow." He was also a brilliant strategist. William Safire credits him with dreaming up the election-winning "new majority" by pitching to the self-interest of voting groups of ethnics and blue collars rather than to any coalition based on new ideas. He cemented the Teamsters to Nixon in 1972. In the Watergate turmoil, he became a born-again Christian. One of his first acts was to ask forgiveness of Federal Reserve Chairman Arthur Burns for smearing him when Nixon wanted to curb the Fed. After jail, he became a lay minister and chairman of the Prison Fellowship Ministries.

WATERGATE QUOTE: "I never once even remotely thought that my conduct might trespass upon the Constitution or anyone's rights under it."

Young and Krogh had approval from Ehrlichman for this covert operation provided "that it is not traceable." Young told the author he and Krogh were concerned to find out if Ellsberg was part of a conspiracy, not to discredit him for psychiatric reasons. That may well have been their motive—the Pentagon Papers had turned up in Moscow—but Nixon himself was obsessed with exposure. Pacing in front of the doors to the Rose Garden, he told Colson: "We're going to let the country know what kind of hero Mr. Ellsberg is." And it was

for disseminating derogatory information about Ellsberg that a court sentenced Colson to jail.

Young and Krogh were horrified when shown photographs of the ransacked office, and Krogh says Ehrlichman was shocked. The Kutler-edited tapes have Ehrlichman reporting to Nixon on September 8: "We had one little operation. It's been aborted out in Angeles which, I think, it's better that you don't know about." In his memoir, Nixon wrote: "Given the temper of those times and the peril I perceived, I cannot say that had

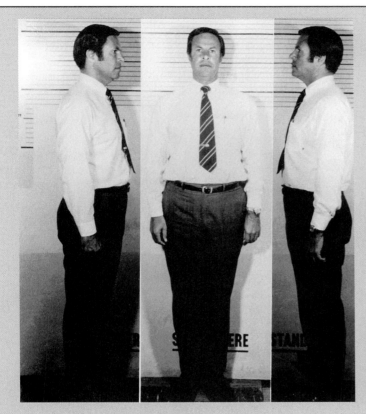

BOB HALDEMAN (1926–1993)
Chief of Staff, served 18 months in jail. His mantra was: "Every President needs a son-of-a-bitch and I'm Nixon's. I'm his buffer and his bastard." A stream of tough memos flowed from their round-the-clock exchanges. He let some of Nixon's wilder orders die, but was active in cover-up scheming. His voice was the other one on the 18.5 minutes of erased tape. He believes they talked about how the trail could lead to Nixon through Colson. Nixon tried to make Haldeman a fall guy when, with red-rimmed eyes, he fired him at Camp David on April 29, 1973. Haldeman later reflected that Nixon was "the weirdest man who ever lived in the White House," but he stayed remarkably loyal. He had quit a top job with J. Walter Thompson Advertising to join him after admiring the Checkers speech. He was a teetotal Christian Scientist and devoted family man. His legacy to history was a daily diary of his years with Nixon, published posthumously in 1994, with the full 750,000 words on a CD-ROM. The historian Stephen E. Ambrose judges it "a priceless document."

GUESS AS TO IDENTITY OF DEEP THROAT: Fred Fielding, John Dean's staff assistant.

WATERGATE QUOTE: "There is no excuse for Watergate. It is inexcusable in every phase and aspect."

JOHN EHRLICHMAN (b. 1925)
Nixon's abrasively bright domestic adviser spent 18 months in jail for conspiracy. He approved the Ellsberg operation, then tried to cover it up. While Ellsberg was on trial, Ehrlichman met twice with U.S. Judge Matt Byrne, once in a Santa Monica park, once at San Clemente, and dangled the prospect of Byrne becoming director of the FBI. Ehrlichman was, like Haldeman, an Eagle Scout, UCLA graduate and Christian Scientist; he didn't drink or smoke. He flew 26 missions as a lead navigator in World War II for the 8th Air Force, tutored a Hearst grandchild, fought zoning cases in Seattle. His tongue lasered the inept, got him hated by Congress and enriched the Watergate syntax. Of FBI Director Gray's stalled nomination, he said, "Let him hang there, let him twist slowly, slowly in the wind." He described one Nixon stalling tactic as "a modified limited hang out." And he advised Dean to "deep six" evidence: to dump it in the Potomac on his way home at night. Out of jail, with his marriage broken, he worked for a time with the Pueblo Indians in New Mexico, and wrote best-selling thrillers.

DEEP THROAT GUESS: Henry Petersen, assistant attorney general in charge of prosecutions.

WATERGATE QUOTE: "The President *is* the government."

I been informed of it beforehand, I would have automatically considered it unprecedented, unwarranted or unthinkable." The justification put up by Ehrlichman also was that it was a "terribly important" national security investigation.

Liddy, far from being rebuked, was promoted. He was taken into the heart of Nixon's campaign on December 6, 1971, when Attorney General Mitchell, about to become director of the Committee to Re-Elect the President (commonly known as CREEP), appointed him campaign committee counsel.

Liddy took Hunt with him. The grand moment that epitomized the Nixon era was on January 27, 1972, when Mitchell, still the chief law officer of the United States, sat puffing his pipe in his office in the Department of Justice, entertaining the idea of financing a vast law-breaking enterprise—on behalf of the President, who had sworn to uphold the Constitution. Liddy made the pitch to Mitchell; the President's counsel, John W. Dean III; and Jeb Magruder, a former cosmetics marketer who was deputy to Mitchell at CREEP. With the help

A photostat is all that remains of G. Gordon Liddy's picture of Howard Hunt on the Daniel Ellsberg mission.

of elaborate charts from a friendly CIA artist, the incomparable Liddy set out a $1 million program he called Gemstone. It envisaged kidnapping hostile demonstrators at the Republican convention, drugging them and dumping them over the border in Mexico; sabotaging air conditioning at the Democratic convention; hiring call girls to entrap Democrats, whose pillow talk would be bugged; staging faked demonstrations; and conducting electronic surveillance of Democratic campaign offices. As Attorney General, Mitchell ought to have arrested Liddy on the spot. Later he claimed to have been appalled, but his main problem with Gemstone seems to have been Liddy's million-dollar price tag. Liddy was allowed to go away and come back with a cheaper plan. In a meeting at Key Biscayne, Florida, on March 30, 1972, Magruder presented Liddy's final plan, which included the kidnappings and the bugging of the Democrats' Watergate headquarters and their main convention hotel, the Fontainebleau in Miami Beach. Mitchell would always deny approving this. But there was clearly pressure from Haldeman and Nixon himself to approve it, and according to Magruder, Mitchell finally said, "Okay, if they say do it, go ahead." By April 1972, according to Haldeman's own records, "Gordon Liddy's intelligence operation proposal ($300[,000]) has been approved."

Break-ins at the DNC offices, supervised by Liddy and Hunt, failed farcically on May 26 and May 27, but late at night on May 28 their team succeeded. Eugenio Martinez and Bernard Barker photographed documents and James McCord and Virgilio Gonzalez planted wiretaps on the phones. It was on a return visit on June 17, to improve the sound quality, that McCord's telltale tape on a door lock led to the detection and arrest of the burglars at 2 a.m. Hunt and Liddy fled their command room in the Howard Johnson motel across the street, leaving behind them a trail of clues that suggested it was more than "a third-rate burglary," as Nixon's press secretary, Ron Ziegler, promptly made out. The clues were soon followed to the White House by the tough trial judge, John J. Sirica, chief judge of the U.S. District Court, and brilliant reporting in the *Washington Post.* But the burglars also left enduring mysteries in which the shadows of CIA spymasters and double agents, call-girl rings, stool pigeons, blackmailers, Greek colonels, Howard Hughes, an informant still known only as Deep Throat and the enigmatic figure of the 37th president mocked the seekers of a cleansing single truth.

In the words of Haldeman in his 1978 memoir, Nixon was involved in the cover-up from day one. That is an understatement. He took over personal direction of it in March 1973, but he was its driving force throughout as the press, the courts and Congress tried to unravel the implications of what the President's men had wrought. He continued the cover-up of his own role through his own memoirs and to the end of his life—and beyond. By his legal actions, thousands of hours of White House tapes and thousands of documents have remained out of the reach of scholars. What is in the unpublished material will darken or relieve the shadows; but what we know is conclusive about Nixon's active and relentless determination to obstruct justice. Nixon partisans have found this as hard to admit as he did. His talk-out was that Haldeman and Ehrlichman ordered John Dean and others to protect the wrongdoers and that when he learned all the facts he insisted on a full investigation and prosecutions. If the cover-up touched him at all, it was out of his loyalty to subordinates. Paul Johnson, the conservative author, in his 1983 book *Modern Times,* portrays Nixon as the victim of a media putsch to overturn the electoral verdict of 1972, the "imperial press" replacing the "imperial presidency." Johnson writes: "Whether Nixon was actually guilty of an attempt to interfere with the course of justice, as alleged, and whether such an attempt, if made, was covered by a legitimate interpretation of raison d'etat, was never established." In fact, Nixon operated every possible stratagem to derail the investigation. He coached grand jury witnesses in perjury about what he and his staff knew. "I don't give a shit what happens, I want you all to stonewall it, let them plead the Fifth Amendment, cover up or anything else, if it'll save it—save the plan." He doctored transcripts of such tapes, not only to remove expletives, but to change their meaning. He raised hush money for the burglars. He lied and lied about his own knowledge. He cited reports clearing the White House staff that never existed; all previous statements were "inoperative." He refused to honor subpoenas for evidence. He suppressed and altered evidence. He ordered Assistant Attorney General Henry Petersen not to investigate the Ellsberg break-in: "Keep the hell out of it!" In the "Saturday night massacre" of October 1973, he fired Archibald Cox, the special prosecutor, over the objections of Attorney General Elliott Richardson and his deputy, William Ruckelshaus, who both resigned; Cox had insisted on having tapes of White House conversations. Decisive proof of Nixon's intent was there in his own words in a taped conversation released on August 5, 1974. In this "smoking gun" tape of June 23, 1972, six days after the break-in, he conspired with Haldeman to use the CIA to back the FBI off the investigation on the false grounds that it involved national security having to do with Cuba. The 42 tapes released by the House Judiciary Committee in April 1974, the Haldeman secret diary published posthumously in 1994, the Kutler-edited tapes of 1997 and the testimony of participants give a cumulative and corroborative picture of Nixon obsessed with the cover-up. In the famous conversation of March 21, 1973, in which his counsel John Dean warns him that there's a cancer close to the presidency—the cancer of blackmail and perjury—Nixon reiterates no fewer than 13 times the importance of paying off Hunt because he knows of too many seamy things. Dean says it might need $1 million to pay off everyone. "You could get a million dollars," Nixon replies. "You could get it in cash. I know where it could be gotten." Nixon has in mind Thomas Pappas, a Greek with ties to the fascist regime of colonels who had asked him to keep a sympathetic ambassador in place. Later, Nixon and others attempted to suggest he did not really mean to pay hush money. Although Nixon did murmur, "It's wrong for sure," at the end of the March conversation, it is also clear on the tape that this is a reference to promising clemency to the malefactors. He specifically approves hush money. That night, through Mitchell, an unmarked envelope containing $75,000 was delivered to Hunt's lawyers.

The sympathetic biographer Jonathan Aitken tap-dances through all this. He concedes Nixon was "less than helpful" in assisting the course of justice, but portrays him as trapped by his treacherous counsel Dean into believing he had to do what he did to protect Mitchell. Dean was certainly a malign figure,

but the person Nixon was concerned to protect was himself. Leonard Garment, Nixon's former law partner and presidential counsel in 1973, remarks in *Crazy Rhythm* (1997) that the transition from bungled break-in to cover-up took place "without even the whisper of gears shifting" precisely because Nixon's sense of personal jeopardy was so great. The break-in could have been admitted as the inspiration of overzealous campaign workers. What had to be concealed were "the other things," in Nixon's parlance, the collection of dirty tricks and illegalities he sponsored through Ehrlichman, Colson and Hunt.

Memory telescopes the events of what Kutler calls the Age of Watergate. The roots were in the divisive dramas of the sixties. The cover-up itself lasted more than two years—from June 1972 to Nixon's resignation under fire on August 9, 1974. It might have worked. By July 1973 a great deal of damaging information had come out. But the dirty water seemed to be receding from the White House. Senator Sam Ervin's committee was running out of steam. Haldeman, Mitchell, Ehrlichman had gone. Nixon had a bushy-tailed new chief of staff in General Alexander Haig. Dean's testimony implicating Nixon in the cover-up for eight months had been damning, but it was the President's word against someone characterized by Senator Howard Baker as "a sleazy lying little sonofabitch," a stool pigeon trying to save his own skin. Nixon was in for censure from the Watergate committee, but once again he was going to survive, perhaps compensate with another dazzling coup in foreign policy. Only the chance exposure of the White House taping system by Alexander Butterfield on Monday, July 16, 1973, precipitated the President's downfall. And even then it was not assured. The hearsay case against Nixon could not have proceeded to the point of a bipartisan vote for three articles of impeachment, as it did the following summer, without the tapes themselves. He might have burned all the tapes between July 16 and July 24, 1974, when the Supreme Court rejected the argument of executive privilege and ordered him to surrender 64 conversations; and he did briefly contemplate defiance. He did not destroy the tapes, he told Monica Crowley 20 years later, because he believed there was enough on them to clear him. Knowing what he did now, would he have destroyed them? she asked. "He lowered his eyes and simply nodded his head, yes." He spared America the final act of obstruction of justice, and there was a poetic justice in the act; the wiretapper had fatally eavesdropped on himself.

Was Watergate just another scandal? Decades after the fact the question is more than a matter of historical curiosity. Like so

FAMILY MAN: Spiro Agnew (right) with Pamela, Susan, Kim, Randy and his wife Judy at his inauguration in Annapolis, Maryland, January 1967.

NIXON'S INSURANCE: SPIRO T. AGNEW

Nixon liked to say he was safe from an assassin's bullet because who would want Vice President Spiro T. Agnew (1918–1996) as president? Nixon came to hope he was also his insurance against impeachment.

Agnew was a Greek American who loved to rub the raw edges of ethnic and class conflict, referring to "Polacks" and, once, to a "fat Jap." His record on civil rights as governor of Maryland was respectable, though he made enemies by summoning black leaders who had failed to stop riots in Baltimore and telling them to their face they were "circuit riding, Hanoi visiting, riot inciting, burn-America-down type of leaders." He became the darling of the right, supported by Ronald Reagan, and maddened Nixon by attacking the China policy.

In spring 1973 it became clear Agnew was on the take, continuing the happy habits of soliciting bribes for public contracts and evading taxes he had perfected as governor. He was stubborn about accepting the scenario in which he quietly resigned to be succeeded by Representative Gerald Ford. As Ehrlichman said, you could not program Agnew to leave a burning building. He gave in on October 10, accepting a sentence of three years' unsupervised probation and a $100,000 fine. He is mainly remembered for his politically incorrect bon mots, such as, "To some extent if you've seen one city slum, you've seen them all," and for Warren Harding–style alliterations in attacking the press—nattering nabobs of negativism; pusillanimous pussyfooters; hopeless, hysterical hypochondriacs of history. They were written for him by Pat Buchanan and William Safire, but delivered with gusto. He never spoke to Nixon after leaving office, but went to Nixon's funeral: "I decided after 20 years of resentment to put it all aside." Not long before his own he had the satisfaction of seeing his head as one of the marble busts in the Capitol statuary corridor. Friends had criticized his 20-year exclusion: "If Aaron Burr's statue is there, why not Spiro Agnew's?"

then? Are the ideals expressed in the Constitution a convenient fiction, always doomed to betrayal by human frailty? Isn't it wiser to tolerate a measure of misconduct than to hold political leaders to impossible standards, hazarding national cohesion and faith in our system for every small crime and misdemeanor? In the dichotomy between cynic and idealist, more is at stake than the historical ranking of a single president. "They all do it" became for a time the predominant, self-fulfilling vision of American politics left and right. For the New Left, already dead though it wasn't aware of the fact, the notion that liberal American democracy was irredeemably corrupt made the case for revolution. For the right, if government was corrupt, the solution was always to get rid of government. It was a rallying cry, summoning the faithful to restore an Arcadian America that never existed. "They all do it" ignores the rational proposition that corrupt "systems" are made corrupt by individuals—such as Richard Nixon—and that it remains in the power of honest men and women to correct them. They are not some inevitable consequence of modern times, or the military-industrial complex, or something demanded or welcomed by the American people. To refute this is to argue against democracy—and to see the world through Nixon's own contorted vision.

The chief apologists have drawn from the arsenal of "historical perspective." Victor Lasky's best-selling book was called *It Didn't Start with Watergate.* Son-in-law David Eisenhower opined as early as September 1974 that "fifteen years hence the offense is going to look pretty small" since Nixon "simply acquiesced in the non-prosecution of aides who covered up a little operation into the opposition's political headquarters, which is a practice that was fairly established in Washington for a long time and that no one took seriously." To William Safire, "the greatest cover-up of all" was "the suppression of truth about Democratic precedents to Watergate on the grounds that it might ameliorate the hatred being focused on Richard Nixon." Robert Bork wrote in 1997 that if Nixon deserved impeachment, President Clinton merited it more for presiding over the "sleaziest administration in history"; Bork was, of course, the Solicitor General who accepted the onus of firing Archibald Cox when Attorney General Elliot Richardson was sacked for refusing Nixon's order. To the columnists Pat Buchanan and James Kilpatrick, the collection of scandals was just business as usual in the highest echelons of American politics—perhaps justified by a virulent and irresponsible opposition. Henry Kissinger also suggested that the animosities of the President and opposition fed on each other. "And if

much else in the American century, the answer has everything to do with how we perceive our democracy today. Does history suggest we can expect no better, more or less, than we got

one lesson of Watergate is the abuse of presidential power, another is that if a democracy is to function, opposition must be restrained by its own sense of civility and limits, by the abiding values of the nation, and by the knowledge that a blanket assault on institutions and motives can paralyze the nation's capacity to govern itself." Even some of the liberal left have been less than convinced by the unique gravity of Watergate. "Nixon's defenders do have a point," said Noam Chomsky, citing illegal FBI operations under Kennedy and Johnson. Nicholas von Hoffman suggested that "the break-ins, the tapping, snooping and harassment have been routine government activities for a generation at least."

There are grains of truth here. Election violence and vote fraud had been endemic for generations. In terms of public money, Watergate does not come close to Teapot Dome, or the gold swindle and other shenanigans under President Grant—or the savings and loan debacles of the eighties. Presidents from all major parties, from at least the 1840s, have raised campaign funds through highly dubious methods. Franklin Roosevelt, Lyndon Johnson and John Kennedy all surreptitiously taped conversations in their offices. Johnson and Kennedy frequently used the FBI for unethical or illegal purposes. FDR used the IRS to hound Huey Long.

One could go on, but the caveats cannot bridge the abyss. Watergate was unique. It did, and still does, constitute a pervasive and unparalleled abuse of power by an American president. John Doar, the Justice Department hero of the civil rights battles in the Kennedy-Johnson era, was the counsel to the House Judiciary Committee. He patiently established a "pattern of conduct . . . designed not to take care that the laws be faithfully executed but to impede their faithful execution" that went beyond what any other administration had attempted. No other president has run a school for perjurers. No other president has, either explicitly or implicitly, so eagerly abetted the efforts of so many top aides in illegally disrupting the campaigns of opponents. No other president has attempted to cover up crime by pitting the CIA against the FBI. No other president, as far as we know, has ever attempted to cover up crime by bribing the criminals. And in the two administrations generally termed more corrupt than Nixon's—Grant's and Harding's—the presidents were stunned to learn what was going on and moved swiftly to put a stop to it.

Many of the apologists' arguments are disingenuous. Watergate was not simply Nixon secretly taping people in his office. What mattered was the felonies the tapes revealed. They rose naturally out of manifest contempt for the law and the Constitution, for the rights of others, for truth. It was incidental that they should also be mean-spirited and vindictive, almost comical in their impeccable cynicism. Nixon, in 1974, was the second president within six years more or less thrown out of office. Disillusion with political leaders was deepening. Senator Kennedy's Chappaquiddick tragedy was a blight on Camelot, and it was followed by revelations about his late brothers' sexual and wiretapping excursions that would set the castle to burning over the course of the seventies. Then there was the Church Committee's stunning exposé of CIA misdeeds, the unmasking of that nearly Shakespearean villain J. Edgar Hoover and, strangest of all, the House investigation in 1978 of the JFK and King assassinations. The special committee blundered to the astounding conclusion that both Martin Luther King, Jr., and President Kennedy had been murdered by conspirators, leaving the average American to believe that our destinies were written by coven and cabal.

Such efforts helped to obscure the real lessons of Watergate and the other scandals. It spoke well of the American democracy that it could withstand such assaults, coming as they did after a decade of war, protest, riot and social turmoil, and right on the heels of the 1973–74 oil embargo's harbinger of economic disaster. Nearly every real scandal saw the wrongdoers uncovered and punished. In the aftermath of Watergate, Congress even passed landmark campaign finance reform. The heart of it was subsequently cut out by a dubious Supreme Court decision, *Buckley v. Valeo* (1976), which equated monetary contribution with free expression—thereby, if logically extended, legalizing bribery.

Yet the point remains. The "system" is reformable, and by America's representatives under its Constitution. Here was President Nixon's historic offense, the blow to the American people's faith in the idea of their country as a government of laws, not men, and one dedicated to certain moral principles. President Nixon broke the law, but he also infringed the moral code implicit in the articles of the Constitution. The Constitution, as the scholar Richard B. Bernstein has eloquently written, is an expression of American national character. In other nations, identity may lie in a common ethnic or linguistic heritage or a single religious tradition. America's identity lies in diverse peoples coming together with shared political values in a system of government that divides power between institutions and cherishes individual rights. Watergate, striking at those central principles, struck at the soul of America. How marvelous it was that in the end the Constitution came to the rescue of the republic it defines.

THE DICK AND HENRY SHOW

The first American president ever to visit Moscow was lying naked on a massage table in the ornate palace of the Czars' Apartments in the Kremlin when he was asked to make one of the crucial decisions of the Cold War. It was around two in the morning of Thursday, May 25, 1972, on the fourth day of the U.S.-Soviet summit. Richard Nixon was exhausted by a day of tricky bargaining on nuclear missiles and a hectic evening. General Secretary Leonid Brezhnev had hijacked him for a 56-mile-an-hour hydrofoil ride on the Moskva River, then sandbagged him in his dacha with three hours of invective on Vietnam. A troika of Soviet leaders yelled at Nixon for the "barbaric," "Nazi-like" mining of Haiphong harbor, which had killed two Soviet sailors. Nixon kept cool. At one point, he stalled the assault, quietly asking, "Are you threatening here?" Then suddenly the tirade dissolved into a jovial, backslapping dinner.

Kissinger reflected later that the rant was probably all a charade to enable the Soviets to send a tough transcript to Hanoi. There was no pretense in the arguments about missiles. After three years of strategic arms limitation talks (SALT), both sides had agreed to freeze the number of launchers. In dispute were the size of missiles to be permitted and the capacity of silos. Kissinger had run through all the esoteric permutations with Nixon. Yet at 2 a.m., after the boisterous night at the dacha, the national security adviser found himself sandwiched between Soviet backsliding and second thoughts from the Pentagon, rather gleefully transmitted from Washington by Kissinger's deputy, Alexander Haig. It was here that Nixon showed his mettle. Consulted by Kissinger as his doctor pummeled his back, Nixon made what Kissinger describes as "one of the most courageous decisions of his Presidency." He told Kissinger not to yield to the Soviets, even if it meant no treaty, and not to change the American position to appease the Joint Chiefs. It was the right call. Two days later the Soviets broke the deadlock by accepting the final American terms.

The world hailed the Moscow summit. The antiballistic missile treaty stopped a defensive arms race that would have upset

"Metternissinger," by Tim.

Henry Kissinger was the first naturalized secretary of state. His glittering diplomatic career from 1969 to 1977 won him various sobriquets—Super K, Secretary of the World, Dr. Strangelove—and the Nobel Peace Prize. He did not collect that award in person; and he gave the money for scholarships for children of servicemen killed in Vietnam. Tim's "Metternissinger" was a play on the subject of Kissinger's Harvard thesis, the Austrian Prince Metternich, the conservative statesman who stifled liberal revolutions to create a stable new order in post-Napoleonic Europe.

the equilibrium of mutual deterrence and cost billions. The SALT agreement had critics. In the end, it was less effective because both sides added multiple warheads to missiles. But Nixon and Kissinger had opened an atmosphere of coexistence as opposed to confrontation that came to be called détente. Cooperative agreements were signed on the peaceful use of space, the environment, incidents at sea and medicine and public health.

Moscow, after Beijing, was the second triumph of the Dick and Henry show. They kept everyone else in the dark, excluding and deceiving Secretary of State William Rogers, a loyal old friend of Nixon. RN and HK were an odd couple, Nixon the gauche lonely brooder, Kissinger the adroit social charmer. But they were both men with original minds who had thought long about foreign policy; when they exchanged geopolitical re-

flections they were like facing mirrors yielding perspectives of liberating depth. They were as determined as anyone to protect American interests—their whole approach was hardheaded rather than sentimental—but they saw beyond the sterile ideological confrontations of the Cold War. The triangular diplomacy they created enabled America to ease tensions with Russia and China and multiplied U.S. options with both. Their concept of linkage, creating a network of incentives and penalties for the foreign other, encouraged friendly behavior on broader fronts. They unashamedly embraced balance-of-power politics. The goal was not to create a brave new world, but to preserve order in the one we have. They rejected the crusading moralisms of Woodrow Wilson, John Foster Dulles and Jack Kennedy as more dangerous and delusional than a tough-minded determination to defend the national interest. American idealism was one factor, not an exclusive one. Typically, Kissinger said of Tibet's Dalai Lama: "You see a holy man, I see a cunning monk." But just as limits came to be defined for Wilson idealism, so they did for Nixon-Kissinger pragmatism in the disastrous sequels to "realistic" deals with the likes of the Shah of Iran and Cambodia's Lon Nol.

Nixon's audacity and resolution were well matched to Kissinger's genius for negotiation, on display at its best in the Middle East. In the wake of the Yom Kippur war of 1973, Nixon was embroiled in Watergate, distraught by the threat of impeachment. Brezhnev threatened to send troops to Egypt to enforce the cease-fire. Without waking the President, Kissinger and a small group of the cabinet met in the early hours of October 25 and put American nuclear forces on a higher state of alert. The ploy worked. Kissinger was free to attempt a miracle in the desert, the disengagement of Israeli and Egyptian forces on the west bank of Suez, and then, in the spring of 1974, an Israeli retreat from part of the Golan Heights annexed from Syria.

Shuttling incessantly between the Middle East capitals in a blue-and-white Boeing 707, with a captive press party of 14, Kissinger pulled it off. He was a hero in the

Arab capitals and Jerusalem alike. It could not have been achieved by mere charm or eloquence—nor by crass duplicity. Kissinger did emphasize different things in the sleepless nights in Damascus going over everything ad nauseam with Hafez al-Assad, or embracing his "brother" Anwar Sadat in Cairo, or in Jerusalem persuading Golda Meir that, though no longer a practicing Jew, he was not anti-Semitic. He played to the characters as he accurately divined them. His intuitive sense is manifest in the character sketches of his memoirs. "Sadat had an uncanny discernment," he writes. "He handled each of the four American presidents he knew with consummate skill. He treated Nixon as a great statesman, Ford as the living manifestation of goodwill, Carter as a missionary almost too decent for this world, and Reagan as the benevolent leader of a popular revolution, subtly appealing to each man's conception of himself and gaining the confidence of each." Kissinger did the same thing. Creative ambiguity was an imperative. If there was a single secret, it was, as he wrote of Metternich, the art of defining a moral framework that made concessions appear not as surrenders but as sacrifices for a common cause.

Kissinger is as complex as they come: vain but generous, gregarious but given to melancholy, ingratiating but suspicious, intellectually brilliant but thin-skinned, secretive but a congenital celebrity, a virtuoso flatterer but abusive of subordinates, highly patriotic but distrustful of the openness of American democracy. The most attractive characteristic he deploys is the capacity for self-mockery, lugubriously delivered in a rumbling accented baritone. Of a proposition he advanced, he said once, "It has the added advantage of being true." Asked if he preferred to be called Mr. Secretary or Dr. Secretary, he said, straight-faced, "I do not stand on protocol. If you just call me Excellency, it will be okay." And again: "Vanity can never be completely disassociated in high office from the perception of national interest." After the Moscow summit, he went to Teheran, where he was caught and photographed with a belly dancer in his lap. He escaped with the remark, "I spent some time telling Nadia how you convert the SLBMs on a D-class submarine into Y-class submarines. I want to make the world safe for Nadia."

CHESS PARTNERS: Nixon and Kissinger inside the Kremlin, May 1972.

FINAL HOURS: There was rejoicing in the White House when a junta led by General Pinochet (seated, opposite) overthrew President Allende of Chile. Above, Allende (center) enters the courtyard of the besieged Moneda presidential palace on the day of the coup. Under gunfire, with the palace in flames and rocketed by fighter jets, he broadcast continuously until around 2 p.m. Then he killed himself with his rifle, a gift from Fidel Castro.

AMERICA'S UNSEEN HAND IN CHILE

In 1975, the public learned some curious things about what the CIA had been doing with its tax dollars: spying on Americans was one of them. Anyone thought to be subversive, like those protesting the war in Vietnam, had his name in a computer. There were 1.5 million such people and the CIA opened their mail. Some people had their homes broken into and their phones bugged.

The Agency had monitored every cable in and out of the U.S. from 1947. In the fifties, it had tested hallucinogenic drugs on 149 hapless subjects, luring them into CIA houses in New York and San Francisco for observation through two-way mirrors; 2 died. It had also attempted to assassinate Fidel Castro and Patrice Lumumba of the Belgian Congo. The spymasters, with semantic drollery, called such murders "termination with extreme prejudice," and they were authorized by the CIA's "Health Alteration Committee."

The revelations came when the CIA was put through the wringer by three separate inquiries. Stung by revelations in the *New York Times* by Seymour Hersh, President Ford set up a commission; and the House and Senate each launched its own investigation. The CIA's new director, William Colby, decided to answer them honestly. In the wake of Watergate, his predecessor, James Schlesinger, had compiled a list of the Agency's illegal actions and these "family jewels" filled 683 pages.

Colby did not display them all at once, but his gift for candor was such that Henry Kissinger, among others, began to wonder if he was a KGB mole.

Colby was even ready to admit that in the bloody coup in Chile in 1973, in which thousands died, America was "responsible to some degree for the final outcome."

Through the Johnson and Nixon presidencies, the Agency spent millions to defeat Salvador Allende Gossens, a Marxist socialist with ties to the Soviet Union and Castro. In 1970, Nixon and Kissinger were alarmed that a three-way race gave Allende a chance. At a meeting on June 27, Kissinger said: "I don't see why we need to stand by and watch a country go Communist due to the irresponsibility of its people." Millions more anti-Allende dollars were spent. On September 4, he squeaked in with 36.3 percent.

On Nixon's orders the CIA tried to create the climate for a military coup. Thomas Karamessines, the agent in charge of this Track II program, described it as "propaganda, disinformation and terrorist activities." And Nixon himself set about making the economy scream by a financial war and a cutback on exports to a country 40 percent dependent on the U.S. for food and machinery. Allende did his part. Over the next two years, he cannoned between the two extremes of his coalition. He recklessly nationalized hundreds of foreign and domestic companies. He tried to bypass his

Congress. He scared capital, and angered the middle class. Strikes and occasional terrorism had the country in chaos. After the coup on September 11, 1973, Chile was in the hands of General Augusto Pinochet. For the next 16 years he held it in a grip of terror. More than 45,000 Chileans were rounded up. Many vanished overnight— the "disappeared." Twenty-five Americans were in the first mass arrests, and some never returned. Estimates of the executions run from 3,000 to 20,000. Torture was commonplace.

What was America's role? The Senate's Church Committee said it found no evidence that the U.S. was directly involved, covertly, in the coup. And indirectly? Kissinger and Haig testified that Track II had been cancelled in October 1970. Karamessines contradicted them: "Track II really never ended." Kissinger said the U.S. gave money to sustain the democratic parties and that was all. But suspicions lingered. The U.S. did have foreknowledge of the coup, and it did not warn Allende. And it restored economic aid to Pinochet on the grounds that he was better than another Castro.

Ambassador Nathaniel Davis provided an intriguing postcript. On the weekend of May 13–15, 1972, the Chilean embassy in Washington was burgled, files jimmied open. Davis said there was "little doubt" it was the work of the men who a month later broke into the Watergate.

SILENT MAJORITY: August 8, the 16-minute resignation speech. A Louis Harris poll found that the percentage of Americans who favored impeachment had risen sharply from 27 percent to 66 percent. Michael O'Brien's picture was taken in a bar in Miami.

THE PRAYER IN THE LINCOLN BEDROOM

Rose Mary Woods was the first to hear. Nixon buzzed for her toward the end of Tuesday, August 6, and asked her to tell his family he was going to resign. He stayed in his office scribbling on his yellow pad. That night there was a tearful "Dear Daddy" note on his pillow from his absent daughter Julie: "Please wait a week or even ten days. Go through the fire just a little bit longer. You are strong! Millions support you."

But the tide against him was overwhelming. The day had begun with a weird cabinet meeting where he had rehearsed the reasons for staying on. George Bush, there as chairman of the Republican National Committee, joined with Attorney General William Saxbe in saying Watergate had to be ended. It was as good as saying, Quit! Kissinger comments: "It was cruel. And it was necessary." As soon as the meeting broke up, Kissinger slipped into the Oval Office to urge resignation.

Late that hot afternoon, Nixon called in his chief of staff, Alexander Haig, and press secretary, Ron Ziegler. "Well, I screwed up good, real good, didn't I?" He told them he would announce his resignation on Thursday night. Or would he? According to Haig, he then launched into a two-hour diatribe in which he would "run it out" to a criminal trial and jail. It was vintage Nixon, testing positions. "You know, Al," he said at one point, "you soldiers have the best way of dealing with a situation like this. . . . You just leave a man alone in a room with a loaded pistol."

The next three days were a torment for everyone. On the Wednesday, there was a silent, tearful dinner with Pat, daughter Tricia and his sons-in-law—Ed Cox and David Eisenhower. Cox was later quoted as saying that a drunken Nixon had taken to roaming the White House corridors making speeches to pictures of former presidents hung on the walls. At 9 p.m. he called Kissinger to the Lincoln Sitting Room. His agony was visible, says Kissinger. He was anxious to know what history would say of him. The two of them, colleagues but never friends, sat in the shadows reminiscing; Nixon brought out the brandy bottle they'd opened to toast the invitation to Beijing three years earlier. When Kissinger was leaving, Nixon impulsively guided him into the Lincoln Bedroom. Every night, he said, he would kneel there, following his Mother's Quaker custom of silent prayer. Wouldn't Kissinger join him, an unorthodox Quaker and an unorthodox Jew? Kissinger with misgivings knelt on the carpet as his president prayed for "help, rest, peace and love." According to Woodward and Bernstein (*The Final Days*), a sobbing Nixon, curled on the carpet like a child, began striking his fist on the floor, crying, "What have I done? What has happened?" and Kissinger held him in a consoling grip. Kissinger puts a different gloss on the scene. The President was "shattered," "deeply distraught," but in control of himself.

When Kissinger got back to the White House, he received another call from

Nixon, asking him, "Henry, please don't tell anyone that I cried, and that I was not strong." It was too late. Kissinger had already told his aides Lawrence Eagleburger and Brent Scowcroft. But he destroyed the tape of the call.

Not until 11 a.m. on Thursday, August 8, did Nixon inform Jerry Ford. On his last full day as president he spared Ford the odium of vetoing an "inflationary" farm bill, and he appointed three federal judges. At 9:01 p.m. from the Oval Office, he spoke calmly to an international television audience of 110 million people and another 40 million radio listeners. He admitted mistakes, but not guilt. He was resigning because he no longer had a strong enough political base in Congress. "I have never been a quitter. To leave office before my term is completed is opposed to every instinct in my body. But as president I must put the interests of America first."

It was as dignified and honest a farewell as Dick Nixon was capable of. He could not keep it up. At 9:30 a.m. the next morning, to the sound of "Hail to the Chief," he entered an East Room packed with staff and cabinet with Mrs. Nixon at his side and delivered a rambling, maudlin, self-pitying speech that dredged up all the resentments, real and imaginary, over wealth and status and power, that had dogged his entire career. "The anguish on the platform engulfed us all," Kissinger wrote. And then it was out to the South Lawn helicopter through the cheers and the sobs and the last salute by a guard of honor.

So ended what General Haig in 1979 called "one of the most dangerous periods in American history." He was referring gnomically to rumors at the time that Nixon, as commander in chief, might stage a military coup. Defense Secretary James Schlesinger stirred it up by telling the Joint Chiefs that any orders to the military from the White House must be referred to him.

The transfer of power could not have been more peaceful. Nixon was over Missouri at 12:03 p.m. when Gerald Ford became the 38th president.

THE LAST ACT: Behind the jaunty waves, a broken man. In deep depression and stricken again with phlebitis, he nearly lost his life. He was not lifted at all by President Ford's proclamation on September 8 of a "full, free and absolute pardon." He was fighting desperately to keep his tapes and archives.

THE WATERGATE FOLLIES

Cartoonists mourned the resignation of Richard Nixon. President Ford's stumbles (much exaggerated) were no match for the 37th president's ski-slope nose, the clandestine tapes and the loopy cast of characters with crew cuts and jutting jaws.

TONY AUTH/*Philadelphia Inquirer*

Robert Grossman

YOU KNOW NOTHING ABOUT WATERGATE. WHICH GROUP WOULD YOU MOST LIKELY SUSPECT OF BURGLARY, THEFT, BREAKING AND ENTERING, WIRETAPPING, ELECTION LAW VIOLATIONS AND CONSPIRACY?

YOUR SET DOES NOT NEED ADJUSTING. THESE THINGS HAVE REALLY BEEN HAPPENING IN THE UNITED STATES.

NEW DISCLOSURES Watergate And The White House

©1973 HERBLOCK

WELL, FIRST LET ME EMPHASIZE MY COMPLETE FAITH IN JUDGE SIR (PAUSE) A GREAT JURIST (CLICK).... WHY, GOOD MORNING, BEBE (PAUS I WAS JUST SITTING HERE THINKING WHAT A (CLICK) GREAT GUY (CLICK) THAT OLD (CLICK) JUDGE SIRICA IS (CLICK) (PAUSE).... ER, WH YES, RICHARD, A WONDERFUL HUMAN BEING, I ALWAYS SAID (PAUSE)....

OLIPHANT
THE DENVER POST
©1973 THE LOS ANGELES TIMES SYNDICATE

© 1974 HERBLOCK

"ALAS, POOR AGNEW, MITCHELL, STANS, EHRLICHMAN, HALDEMAN, DEAN, KALMBACH, LA RUE, MARDIAN, STRACHAN, M'CORD, LIDDY, CHAPIN, HUNT, COLSON, KROGH, MAGRUDER, YOUNG—I KNEW THEM..."

CONRAD © THE LOS ANGELES TIMES, 1973

"Snow White's still at large"

THE WHITE HOUSE
WASHINGTON

August 9, 1974

Dear Mr. Secretary:

I hereby resign the Office of President of the United States.

Sincerely,

Richard Nixon

The Honorable Henry A. Kissinger
The Secretary of State
Washington, D.C. 20520

The Boston Globe

"Happy anniversary."

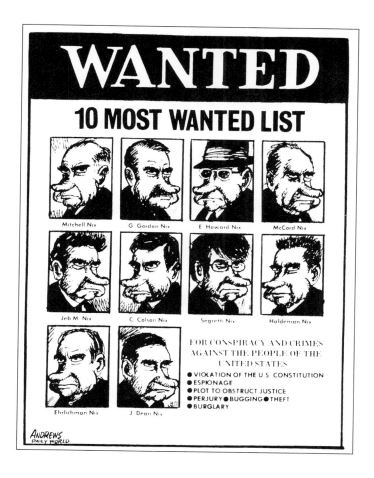

WANTED
10 MOST WANTED LIST

Mitchell Nix — G. Gordon Nix — E. Howard Nix — McCord Nix

Jeb M. Nix — C. Colson Nix — Segretti Nix — Haldeman Nix

Ehrlichman Nix — J. Dean Nix

FOR CONSPIRACY AND CRIMES
AGAINST THE PEOPLE OF THE
UNITED STATES

● VIOLATION OF THE U.S. CONSTITUTION
● ESPIONAGE
● PLOT TO OBSTRUCT JUSTICE
● PERJURY ● BUGGING ● THEFT
● BURGLARY

ANDREWS
DAILY WORLD

GERALD RUDOLPH FORD, JR.
38th President (Republican), 1974–1977

BORN: July 14, 1913, in Omaha, Nebraska

POLITICAL CAREER: U.S. Representative 1949–1973; Minority Leader, 1965–1973; Vice President, [December] 1973–[August] 1974, President, 1974–1977

FIRSTS: First vice president to be appointed under the procedures specified by the 25th Amendment. First president to assume office upon the resignation of his predecessor. First president to issue a pardon to a former president.

Caricature by Robert Osborn.

MR. KING: He was born Leslie Lynch King, Jr., but his father, a wool dealer, often beat his wife, Dorothy, and they were divorced. When he was three (left) she married a paint salesman, Gerald Rudolph Ford, in Grand Rapids, Michigan, and Jerry was brought up with his three half brothers and did not learn until his teens that Gerald Ford, Sr. (in the photograph to the right), was their father but not his. He developed a stutter and a curious ambidexterity—left-handed sitting down, right standing up. While in high school, he took a lunchtime job in a diner flipping hamburgers and washing dishes. One day he noticed a man watching him. Finally, the man said, "I'm Leslie King, your father. Can I take you to lunch?" His father had his new wife with him. When they left after lunch, his father gave him $25, and that night Ford cried himself to sleep.

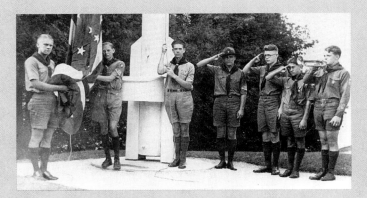

THE STAR: He was an Eagle Scout (far left) and a star athlete (right). His football record helped to win him a scholarship to the University of Michigan in 1931. He paid his way by washing dishes for his Delta Kappa Epsilon fraternity, won the Michigan Wolverines most valuable player award, played in the Shrine Crippled Children's Fund all-star game and declined a professional contract with the Green Bay Packers. In 1935, with a B.A. in economics and political science, he went to Yale to coach boxing and football. Summers he was a Yellowstone Park Ranger. By doggedness, he got a place in the Yale law program in 1938 and finished in the top third in 1941. In 1940, he campaigned for Wendell Willkie.

POINT MAN: World War II put paid to his plans to specialize as a labor lawyer. He enlisted in the Navy three months after Pearl Harbor. They assigned him physical fitness training for aviators, but he pleaded for a billet on a ship, and in spring 1943 joined the aircraft carrier *Monterey* as both physical education director and gunnery division officer. (He's the shirtless man on the left jumping for the tip.) When the *Monterey* attacked Japanese bases in November, his job was to stand on the fantail while the Japanese planes came at them and direct the crew firing the 40-mm anti-aircraft gun. He became an assistant navigator, took part in "the Great Marianas Turkey Shoot" and survived a Japanese attack in the Philippine Sea. On his discharge in 1946 he had the reserve rank of lieutenant commander and ten battle stars.

THE HAWK: Lyndon Johnson's wisecrack that Ford "played football without a helmet and couldn't walk a straight line and chew gum at the same time" did not impede his steady rise as an amiable, honest-to-God conservative Congressman. He was House minority leader from 1965 to 1973. Jerald terHorst, his first press secretary as president, best summed up Ford's politics: If he saw a school kid who needed clothing, "he'd give him the shirt off his back, literally. Then he'd go right into the White House and veto a school-lunch bill."

He supported the harsh McCarran Immigration Bill, opposed a rise in the minimum wage and repeal of the anti-union Taft-Hartley Act, and voted against Medicare and Johnson's "war on poverty." He also went along with all those supporting Joe McCarthy's Communist witch-hunt; later he said this was his biggest regret. He was a superhawk on Vietnam. As a member of the Warren Commission, and its longest survivor, he was steadfast that Oswald killed Kennedy.

LOYALIST: He became a Nixon loyalist, voting for Nixon bills like federal wage and price controls that he disliked. When two Nixon Supreme Court conservative nominees were rejected, he tried to impeach Justice William O. Douglas, the most liberal justice. He stood by Nixon in Watergate until the end, believing Nixon was telling him the truth, even declining Nixon's invitation to listen to the tapes. The Senate approved his nomination as vice president after the resignation of Spiro Agnew 92–3, the House 387–35. Here he is at his swearing-in, giving Betty a kiss—on the advice of Nixon (clapping, right). He nominated liberal Governor Nelson Rockefeller as his vice president, but under pressure from the right dropped him for the 1976 campaign. He only narrowly beat Ronald Reagan for the nomination, dogged by a press image as a klutz who stumbled on staircases and ski slopes. With Kansas Senator Bob Dole as his running mate against Jimmy Carter and Walter Mondale, he lost to Carter in 1976. In 1980 there were moves to make him running mate to Reagan, but they collapsed with his insistence on being virtually copresident.

Few citizens could follow the mind-numbing intricacies of trying to reconcile Russian and American weapons systems. They just knew the world was a very dangerous place.

FORD EYEBALLS BREZHNEV

It is below zero in the port of Vladivostok in November 1974. In the picture opposite, by David Hume Kennerly, the man in the fur hat, looking out, is the new president of the United States, Gerald Ford, on his first foreign mission, an arms-control summit with Brezhnev. The hat, a classic Russian *chapka,* was an impulsive gift of Anatoly Dobrynin, the Soviet ambassador in Washington, who was horrified that the new president naively intended to go hatless into Siberia. In a huddle with his advisers, including Kissinger, Ford has come out of his warm cottage because he fears the Russians have them all bugged.

The dark scene is emblematic of what was happening to détente—because of reactions in America. Brezhnev, who had been chummy with Nixon, liked the new man well enough to tease him with the gift of "a small packet of missiles"—a pipe rack with four pipes for Ford's smoky cogitations. With Kissinger's fretful monitoring, the conclusion of these second SALT talks was an acceptable compromise, which held that until 1995 the two sides would each limit their strategic arms carriers to 2,400. This far exceeded Ford's ex-

pectations, but he was in for what he describes as his biggest disappointment as president. Back home, the anti-Soviet ideologues were riding high in a tacit coalition of right wingers concerned with power and liberals concerned with human rights. They united in a moral crusade against the Soviet Union. Democratic Senator Henry "Scoop" Jackson provided the bridge between the two alien groups, and across it marched the saboteurs of SALT II who rejected any idea of parity with the Soviets.

Jackson had opened the attack on détente in Nixon's time by insisting on tying American trade to the number of Soviet Jews allowed to emigrate. The administration had been effective in quiet diplomacy. The number allowed to leave had gone up from 400 in 1968 to 35,000 in 1973, and there was a private promise to make it 50,000 a year. But Jackson crowed about the deal in public, and the Soviets felt humiliated. They reduced emigration in 1975 to 40 percent of 1973. To Kissinger, the misapplied linkage was an example of the futility of moral posturing. The Jews suffered; undermining SALT II did not im-

prove the military equation; and Soviet expansion continued.

The 1975 agreements known as the Helsinki baskets crystallized American ambivalence between deal making and idealism. One of the three baskets gave the Soviets what they had longed for—recognition of the postwar borders in Europe and mutual U.S.-Soviet promises to keep out of each other's internal affairs. The

second basket liberalized trade, travel and science. The third endorsed human rights. The exiled Russian writer Aleksandr Solzhenitsyn came to Washington to condemn any dealings with Satan. Ford thought he was "a goddamned horse's ass" and wouldn't meet him. The right erupted against Ford's planned attendance at the Helsinki signings. "Jerry Don't Go" was a typical headline in the *Wall Street Journal*.

But Ford did go. He confronted Brezhnev on the third basket: "To my country, they are not clichés or empty phrases. It is important that you recognize the deep devotion of the American people and their government to human rights and fundamental freedoms." Brezhnev was unblinking. He agreed with Americans right and left who howled that basket three was all hot air. Ford and Kissinger

were skewered for trading something for nothing. But the seeds sown in Helsinki germinated, if slowly. Helsinki "watch groups" and dissident democrats in Eastern Europe held the Soviets to the Helsinki language. Human rights was one of the solvents in 1989–90 when the Eastern Europe Brezhnev thought he had glued together began to come apart.

WHO LOST VIET NAM?

"NOT I," SAID IKE. "I JUST SENT MONEY."

"NOT I," SAID JACK. "I JUST SENT ADVISORS."

"NOT I," SAID LYNDON. "I JUST FOLLOWED JACK."

"NOT I," SAID DICK. "I JUST HONORED JACK AND LYNDON'S COMMITMENTS."

"NOT I," SAID JERRY. "WHAT WAS THE QUESTION?"

"YOU LOST VIETNAM," SAID HENRY, "BECAUSE YOU DIDN'T TRUST YOUR LEADERS."

THE EXODUS

The end in Indochina was piteous and shameful. When the last American troops pulled out in March 1973, Saigon had 1.1 million men under arms and a huge air force. This was at least a two-to-one superiority over North Vietnam. And President Thieu thought he had a cast-iron guarantee that America would respond "with full force" if North Vietnam violated the peace. The pledge was given to him, before he accepted the peace agreement, in two secret letters drafted by Henry Kissinger and signed by President Nixon on November 14, 1972, and January 5, 1973.

Yet by May 1975 South Vietnam had vanished, Cambodia had fallen to the Communist Khmer Rouge and Laos to the Pathet Lao.

Nixon was not there to honor his pledge. He had resigned on August 9, 1974. And Congress, when it learned of the promise in April 1975, as Saigon was falling, was furious that it had never been allowed to advise, still less consent. In March, nearly 80 percent of the public opposed any further aid. President Gerald Ford could not even get a vote on emergency assistance.

Saigon's army at first fought well in places, but Thieu conducted a disastrous strategy of withdrawal. Millions of refugees fled the northerly cities. Crazed soldiers randomly shot thousands of their own countrymen. Jan Wollett, a flight attendant on the last flight out of Da Nang, described a typically horrific scene as thousands screamed and clawed to get on the air stairs. "A family of five was running a few feet from me, a mother and a father and two children and a baby in the mother's arms. . . . I reached back to grab the mother's hand, but before I could get it a man running behind them shot all five of them, and they fell and were trampled by the crowd." The soldier who shot them jumped on the air stair and ran into the plane. A plane supposed to carry 133 landed in Saigon with 358—8 of them clinging on in the wheel wells.

In Saigon, Ambassador Graham Anderson Martin had delayed to the very last days evacuation of the 6,000 Americans and 100,000 Vietnamese who had worked for American agencies. On the morning of April 28, with the North Vietnamese Army at the gates of Saigon, the American radio station began playing its prearranged code: Bing Crosby crooning "I'm dreaming of a white Christmas." It was the signal that the final frantic pullout had begun. In the next 18 hours of Operation Frequent Wind, 81 Marine helicopters operating from a besieged airfield and the embassy shuttled 2,312 Americans and 6,422 non-Americans to offshore aircraft carriers. Night landings on the embassy roof were perilous until one of the staff rigged up a 35-mm slide projector to illuminate a rectangle of white light. While the lucky ones were whisked to safety, mobs swarmed the embassy walls. The last Marines were lifted out after dawn, a few hours before NVA tanks rolled through the gates of the presidential palace.

THE LAST PLANE: A man tries to board an American evacuation plane at Nha Trang airport, April 1, 1975. An American punches him in the face in an effort to break his grip on a plane already overloaded with refugees. Nha Trang was overrun by Communist troops the next day.

MS. AMERICA TAKES TO THE STREETS

BUSTS FOR DUSTING: Busy with a duster, the woman who led the wives of America from the parlor to the political arena. Betty Friedan had just published *The Feminine Mystique* when photographed by Steve Shapiro in 1963. She had bought the plaster Lincoln at an auction. "Lincoln is my oldest hero, partly because I'm from Illinois where nobody can grow up without being aware of him, partly because I'm passionate about any kind of emancipation."

BRAS FOR BURNING: To an appreciative audience of mostly males, a San Francisco secretary on a platform in front of a department store displays the bra she has divested. It was antibra day in the city in August 1969, when women all over the world were invited to send their bras to San Francisco for burning.

The 1968 Miss America pageant in Atlantic City attracted 200 women who hated the whole idea. They marched around, denouncing the contest as sexist and racist. "Atlantic City is a town with class," they sang. "They raise your morals and they judge your ass." The women threw into a "freedom trash can" the girdles, bras, hair curlers and false eyelashes they regarded as symbols of enslavement, along with copies of women's magazines. The *New York Times* reported: "The demonstrators belong to what they called the Women's Liberation Movement."

Indeed.

"Women's lib" came to be the shorthand for every kind of gender protest in the late sixties and seventies. But the radicals in Atlantic City represented only one strand of the complex double helix that was to transform the lives of women. Their strand emphasized sexual and reproductive exploitation across races and classes. These were the women who disrupted bridal parties, staged zap-action protests and guerrilla theater to dramatize women's experiences of botched or denied abortions, rape and wife abuse—and women's subordination to men. Kate Millett's *Sexual Politics* examined the patriarchal family as a foundation of male domination. The more radical of these women, big on "consciousness raising," came to be caricatured as antimale harpies. The more practical built a web of community centers to help battered wives and rape victims, and ran "wet-ins" for child care.

The other strand of the double helix was concerned with political and economic equality, firmly within the tradition of Susan B. Anthony and of the first wave of feminism after World War I, which climaxed in constitutional amendments on suffrage and temperance. It did not reject men so much as demand legal equality with them. Both strands had validity. They were in a fractious coalition, different elements of an ongoing, often confusing struggle. Both strands protested the sexist nature of the times, neatly epitomized in the National Airlines wink-wink advertisement: "I'm Cheryl. Fly me." It was circulating when women attendants were fired as soon as they married or reached 32. Congresswoman Martha Griffiths had a question for the managers: "You are asking that a stewardess be young, attractive and single. What are you running, an airline or a whorehouse?"

The mother of the political movement was a suburban housewife and mother of three who was reaching her forty-second birthday when she published *The Feminine Mystique* in 1963. Nowhere in the book did Betty Friedan use the word "feminism," but she brilliantly articulated what she called "the problem that has no name"—the yearning of women to be something more than moms and homemakers. Of the American woman at midcentury she wrote: "As she made the beds, shopped for groceries, matched slipcover material, ate peanut butter sandwiches with her children, chauffeured Cub Scouts and Brownies, lay beside her husband at night, she was afraid to ask even of herself the silent question: 'Is this all?'"

The emotional and intellectual appeal of *The Feminine Mystique* fell on a nagging sense of injustice well documented by Terry H. Anderson in *The Movement and the Sixties.* Women were confined to work ghettos in secretarial pools, teaching, publishing, waitressing and a few other positions deemed acceptable for women—while they waited to get married. By the end of the sixties, women on the average earned little more than half the salaries of men—even when they did the same work or were better qualified. Formal and informal quotas limited the percentage of women engineers to 1 percent, dentists to 2, lawyers to 4, doctors to 7. Title VII of the Civil Rights Act banned workplace discrimination by sex as well as by race, but the provision had been treated as a joke since its passage in 1964.

Betty Friedan did more than theorize. At a lunch on June 29, 1966, she scribbled on cocktail napkins the outline for a new organization, NOW—the National Organization for Women. Others had a hand in the founding, but Friedan was the flame. On August 26, 1970, NOW took to the streets. In a national women's strike for equality, thousands marched under the banner "Don't Iron While the Strike Is Hot." The bolder deposited children on their husband's desks.

The campaign of agitation and legal suits worked. By 1971, NOW had secured $30 million in back pay for women. In 1972 the Supreme Court ruled unanimously that the "equal protection" clause of the Fourteenth Amendment applied to women. The Equal Employment Opportunity Commission began to take enforcement seriously. "Ms." was recognized as a title by the government printing office. Congress overwhelmingly voted for the Equal Rights Amendment (ERA): "Equality of rights under the law shall not be denied or abridged by the United States or any state on account of sex."

Yet there was the inevitable backlash. Various movements popped up, advocating returns to "traditional" femininity. Phyllis Schlafly, a longtime right-wing activist, organized a group called STOP ERA. Her efforts were well funded, and myth multiplied. If the ERA were passed, pregnant women would be sent to the front lines. Alimony and child support would end. All bathrooms would be unisex. ERA campaigns were greeted by jeering men, and some women. Mrs. Saul Schary of the National Council of Women of the U.S. sniffed that there was "no discrimination against women like they say there is and many of them are just so unattractive. I wonder if they're completely well."

Some 63 percent of the people were unshaken in support of ERA. Yet Schlafly knew where to squeeze. She concentrated on a few powerful legislators in a handful of mostly conservative states. In June 1982, the ERA expired, 3 states short of the 38 needed for ratification. It was a symbolic defeat and a curious one. Feminists had lost the battle, but women had won the war.

"And now our guest speaker—Phyllis Schlafly, Harvard grad, TV star and radio commentator, whose distinguished career has taken her all over the country during the past three years fighting for the need for women to stay in the home where they belong!" Cartoon by Paul Szep, 1975.

"First Dollar, First 59 Cents." Cartoon by Doug Marlette, 1982.

"Look guys, why don't we just say that all men are created equal . . . and let the little ladies look out for themselves?" Cartoon by Mike Peters, 1982.

BARBARA JORDAN (1936–1996)

"Notwithstanding the past, my presence here before you is one additional bit of evidence that the American dream need not forever be deferred."

Thus asserted Barbara Jordan in a slow, grave voice at the Democratic national convention in New York in 1976. She was, in journalist Myra MacPherson's phrase, the first black woman everything—the symbolic orator from the South with the stained-glass voice. She was the first black keynoter to address the Democratic convention in the 144 years of its existence. Her pride was a typical sentiment for a woman who would later say, "I can still get goosebumps when I hear 'The Star-Spangled Banner.'" In 1972, she and Andrew Young were the first blacks elected to the House of Representatives from the South since Reconstruction—and she was the first black woman ever elected from the region. She had burst on the national scene in 1974, telling the television audience glued to the House Judiciary Committee's Watergate hearings, "My faith in the Constitution is whole, it is complete, it is total, and I am not going to sit here and be an idle spectator to the diminution, the subversion, the destruction, of the Constitution."

She was born in Houston, the youngest of three daughters of a part-time Baptist minister. She attended a segregated high school and all-black Texas Southern University. She graduated from Boston University's law school, the only woman in her class, unsure she would ever be able to work in her state. Her first law office was the family dining-room table. In 1966, she became the first black woman elected to the Texas State Senate and proved stunningly effective in wheeling and dealing with the all-white, all-male state senators on behalf of the poor and beaten down.

Jordan was one of a remarkable group of women elected to the House—Shirley Chisholm, who had preceded her in 1968 as the first black woman elected to Congress; Bella Abzug (1970); and Elizabeth Holtzman (1972) (all three from New York); and Pat Schroeder (1972) of Colorado, who announced: "I have a brain and a uterus. I intend to use both."

GLORIA STEINEM (b. 1934)

"If men could menstruate, abortion would be a sacrament."

Somehow, although she came relatively late to the movement, she became its diva, the mass media's all-purpose icon of feminism, the sneer on male chauvinist lips: Tell it to Gloria Steinem. In part, it was charm and personality. She defied many of the worst feminist caricatures. She was anything but shrill; she was glamorous in tinted aviators' glasses, miniskirts and backless blouses; she was not a lesbian, she could have any man she wanted—she was even, well, beautiful. In part, it was her gutsy, probing intellect, the drive that led her to "go undercover" and explore what life was like as a Playboy Club waitress, or in January 1972 to launch the magazine she called *Ms.* The name, drawn from a 1930s secretarial handbook that prescribed Ms. as the proper form of address if one was unaware of a woman's marital status, came to be the most common title for all women throughout the United States.

She had a gift for conciliation. She seemed able to find common ground with almost any other woman. She was the reasonable revolutionary. Steinem's childhood trials were invaluable training for the combat of the women's movement, the constant taunts of chauvinist men, the reproaches of holier-than-thou radical women. Born in 1934 in a dysfunctional, downwardly mobile Midwest household, she had to look after her divorced and increasingly disturbed mother in half of a dilapidated, rat-infested house in Toledo, Ohio. She kept her chin up, learning, reinventing herself, keeping up the tap dancing that took her to Ted Mack's *Amateur Hour*. When the downstairs neighbors demanded to know what the racket was all about, Gloria told them, "Someday I'm going to be a big star. And big stars have to practice." She worked to roll back New York's archaic abortion laws, got involved with the McGovern campaign in 1972 and eventually led a friendly rival to NOW, the Women's Action Alliance. She was the human bridge between the radicals and NOW.

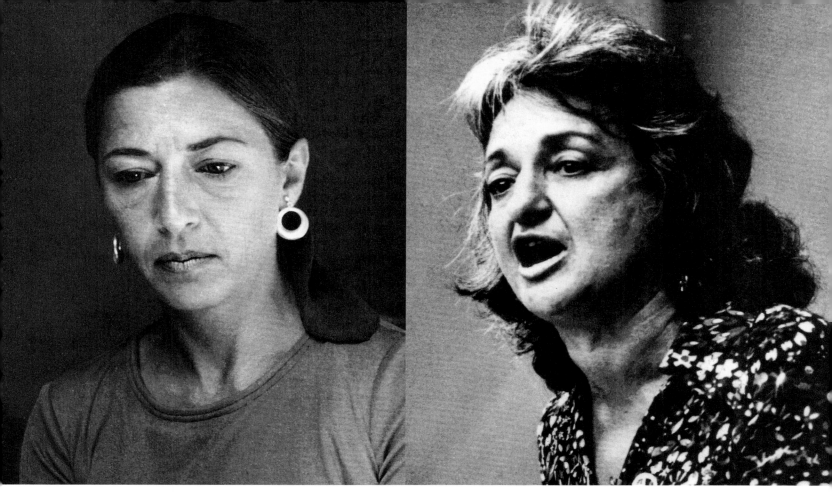

RUTH BADER GINSBURG (b. 1933)

*"Generalizations about the way women are, estimates of
what is appropriate for most women, no longer justify denying
opportunity to women whose talent and capacity place
them outside the average description."*

The young law grad applying for a Supreme Court clerkship with Justice Felix Frankfurter seemed to have all the right qualifications. First in her undergraduate class at Harvard, then with an outstanding record at Columbia Law School. There was only one problem—she was a she. Frankfurter, a dedicated liberal and one of the most influential thinkers in American life, would have none of it: "I can't stand girls in pants." Ginsburg—who in fact would become perhaps the best-dressed justice in court history—would go on to establish a career as the Thurgood Marshall of the women's rights movement, in the words of President Clinton when he nominated her for the Supreme Court from her judgeship on the District of Columbia Court of Appeals. She would also be one of the first women of the modern feminist era to "have it all," reaching the top of her profession while maintaining a strong marriage for more than 40 years and raising two children. It helped, she admits, that her tax lawyer husband is a splendid cook who wouldn't let her in the kitchen.

When Frankfurter said no, she was taken on as an assistant professor at Rutgers Law School in Newark, where she concealed her pregnancy with baggy clothing. (Pregnancy was a firing offense.) She became the first tenured woman at the law school and began a 17-year career teaching civil procedure. She argued six briefs before the Supreme Court and won five. One winning strategy was to present cases of men denied benefits guaranteed to women under the law. Radical feminists attacked the approach as "phallocentric" but it proved highly successful before a then all-male Supreme Court. *The New Republic* columnist Leon Wieseltier said she impressed the judges because "she was as much an aggrieved rationalist as an aggrieved woman."

BETTY FRIEDAN (b. 1921)

*"I'm nasty, I'm bitchy, I get mad,
but by God I'm absorbed in what I am doing."*

Betty Naomi Goldstein Friedan, a brilliant scholar from Peoria, Illinois, abandoned training as a psychologist to marry and raise three children in a pretty Victorian house in Sneden's Landing up in New York's Rockland County. Ten years later, in 1957, she went to her fifteenth reunion at the all-female Smith College in Northampton, Massachusetts, and discovered that her classmates shared with her a frustration that they could not simply live through their children and husbands. She wrote up her findings every day on the dining room table while the children were in school and after they went to bed. Six years later *The Feminine Mystique* lit a million lightbulbs and became one of the most influential—if not *the* most influential—in an era of groundbreaking books.

The National Organization for Women (NOW), which she launched, flourishes with hundreds of thousands of members and a budget of millions. She was accused of concentrating on its white middle-class membership, but she was not elitist. She had always fought for welfare, day care and antipoverty programs. She was resolutely pro-integration, antiracist, antiwar, pro—abortion rights. She had personally experienced one of the worst indignities any woman has to fear, being repeatedly battered by her husband before she ended their 22-year marriage in 1969. Militants in bodies like WITCH, Redstockings, Bread and Roses and Coyote distrusted her respect for marriage and "family values," her slowness to champion political lesbianism. She responded by denouncing "the pseudoradical cop-out which talks about test-tube babies, eliminating men and the one-sex society. Men can't be the enemy. They're here to stay." Her hot temper and merciless tongue led her into a needless feud with Gloria Steinem, who shared much of her viewpoint.

THE LIFE AND TIMES OF HARVEY MILK

HARVEY MILK IN 1976: "If I turned around every time someone called me a faggot, I'd be walking backward." Photograph by Daniel Nicoletta.

Of all the liberation movements that rocked America in the late sixties and early seventies, none was more shocking than gay liberation. Americans who had gone to jail for civil rights and marched for equality for women often still felt a revulsion for male homosexuality. Lesbianism was somewhat less vilified, if only because many people, like Queen Victoria, could not really believe that such a thing happened.

The stirrings of protest against discrimination began in the midsixties. *The Advocate* newspaper was started in 1967 out of Los Angeles. Gays asserted themselves in New York in 1969, staging a two-

day riot when police cracked down on a gay bar in Greenwich Village, the Stonewall. In 1977, the commissioners of Dade County, Florida, banned antigay discrimination. Anita Bryant, a former beauty queen and cheery spokeswoman for orange juice, forced a referendum, and on June 7 the Dade County voters repealed the antidiscrimination ordinance by better than 2–1. The stunning rebuke galvanized the gay community across America, nowhere more than in its unofficial capital of San Francisco. A rising gay leader, soon to be elected to the Board of Supervisors, helped to organize an anti-Bryant rally. His name was Harvey Milk.

Milk defied categorization. In his midforties, he was a transplanted Wall Street broker who liked to dress up as a clown. He had been a supporter of Barry Goldwater and had volunteered for the Navy to stop the Communists from seizing Asia. He had put together a fine record as a deep-sea diver and chief petty officer on a carrier, but suffered the ignominy of a dishonorable discharge when his homosexuality was discovered. In San Francisco, he became known as the mayor of Castro Street, the colorful enclave where many of the estimated 100,000 gays and lesbians in the city of 700,000 congregated. His vision for the city was to enhance such neighborhoods, marrying Fiorello La Guardia–style progressivism with the community ideals spelled out in Jane Jacobs's *Death and Life of American Cities*.

In 1978, he pushed a citywide gay rights ordinance through the board with one dissenting vote. It was from Dan White, an Irish-American supervisor from one of the city's more conservative white-ethnic neighborhoods. White had an all-American résumé—high school sports star, Vietnam, a cop, a fireman. He was a swing vote between the socially liberal, economically conservative members, led by Dianne Feinstein, and the "radicals," led by Milk. But something went wrong with Dan White. He quit the board in a fit of pique, then wanted to "unresign." George Moscone, the liberal mayor, was inclined to relent. Milk was not. He wanted Moscone to appoint a more liberal supervisor to swing the balance of power his way.

When White's ouster became final on

Ford survived two attempts on his life. In the second incident (right), Bill Sipple puts both hands forward, deflecting a shot from the disturbed Sara Jane Moore (behind the woman in the foreground).

November 27, 1978, he dressed in his best suit, but entered City Hall by climbing through a basement window. He was packing a .38 caliber Smith and Wesson revolver and wanted to evade the front door's metal detector. He barged into Moscone's office and shot him in the chest at point-blank range. Then he stood over him and fired twice into the back of the mayor's head. He reloaded and ran down the hall to Milk's office. "Oh, no" was all Milk had time to shout. White shot him five times—again firing the last two shots into the brain.

The following spring White's lawyers got him off with convictions only for voluntary manslaughter, good for seven years and eight months in jail. They pleaded depression, aggravated by a "broad spectrum of social, political and ethical issues" and, most infamously, "the Twinkie defense"— White's constant consumption of Coke, Twinkies and potato chips. The Twinkie defense made headlines, but it was the social argument that hit a raw nerve with people. The way White's attorney put it, White was an exemplar of American values, family and home, frustrated by the way he saw the city deteriorating as a place for decent people. The implication was clear: Gay people were inherently offensive and their lives could be held cheaply.

Immediately after the deaths, some 25,000 San Franciscans, gay and straight, held a peaceful mourning vigil. Then some 3,000 to 5,000 enraged gay men and women marched on City Hall. Most of their animosity was directed at the city cops, many of whom had vociferously expressed their support for White's murderous rampage. In the "White Night Riot," 11 police cars were torched.

Milk had left a more uplifting message. He had tape-recorded a political will in which he presciently declared: "If a bullet should enter my brain, let that bullet destroy every closet door." He urged every gay lawyer, every gay architect to "come out, stand up and let the world know. Only that way will we start to achieve our rights." More elected officials came out. Wisconsin, followed by Massachusetts, was the first to enact a statewide antidiscrimination law. Just what the rights of homosexuals and lesbians were to be in America would remain a point of political contention well into the 1990s, but the closet doors were off their hinges.

THE HEROISM OF BILL SIPPLE

Oliver "Bill" Sipple, a paunchy former Marine and high school football star, aged 33, was walking past San Francisco's St. Francis Hotel on September 22, 1975, when President Ford emerged. Just three weeks before in Sacramento, Lynette "Squeaky" Fromme, a deranged acolyte of the murderous cult leader Charles Manson, had got within a few yards of the President with a loaded gun. She had failed to get a shot off, but now the Secret Service was watching a small crowd of protesters across the street.

Sipple moved toward the front of the crowd to see his president. He saw him all right—as well as a gray-haired woman by his side, pulling a revolver out of her blue raincoat. Sipple grabbed her arm. Her shot missed the President by a few feet. Sipple wrestled her to the ground, and prevented her from getting off a second shot by shoving his hand into the firing mechanism.

Sipple shunned publicity. He was gay and he had never told his straitlaced Baptist mother. But Harvey Milk knew. "That guy saved the President's life. It shows that we do good things, not just all that ca-ca about molesting children and hanging out in bathrooms." It was Milk, according to the respected journalist Randy Shilts, in his biography *The Mayor of Castro Street,* who outed Sipple by an item dropped in Herb Caen's gossip column. A despairing Sipple told reporters: "I want you to know that my mother told me today she can't walk out of her front door because of the press stories." He insisted: "My sexual orientation has nothing to do with saving the President's life." Apparently President Ford thought it did. There was no invitation to the White House for Sipple, not even a commendation. Milk made a fuss about that. Finally, weeks later, Sipple received a brief note of thanks.

Exposure was too much for Sipple. Already listless, he drifted into alcoholism and drug dependency, finally taking his own life. It was a sorry end to a heroic act—and the beginning of an issue that would roil the gay community and identity politics in the decades to come. Did anyone have a right to "out" someone else?

Ford ducked a bullet, Sipple the publicity.

JAMES (JIMMY) EARL CARTER, JR.
39th President (Democrat), 1977–1981

BORN: October 1, 1924, Plains, Georgia

POLITICAL CAREER: Sumter County Board of Education, 1956–1962; Georgia State Senate, 1963–1967; Governor of Georgia, 1971–1975; President, 1977–1981

FIRST: First president from the Deep South since Andrew Jackson.

CHARACTER SNAPSHOT: "Jimmy Carter is a saint. . . . Being a saint isn't all kindness and sweetness and compassion. . . . Saints can be hard on people around them. They can be blind to ordinary human feelings and ordinary human failings, including their own."
—Hendrik Hertzberg

"Well, I've often seen a cat without a grin," thought Alice, "but a grin without a cat! That's the most curious thing I ever saw!" Cartoon by Paul Conrad.

HUCK FINN: His mother, Lillian Gordy Carter—with Jimmy at about eight and sister Gloria—was "eccentric," meaning she was an early advocate of racial equality. A trained nurse, she joined the Peace Corps when she was 68. His father, Earl, would not come into the house when Lillian entertained black neighbors in her parlor. Earl, of English origin, owned a store and 4,000 acres near Plains, which had more than 200 black tenant farmers. Most of Jimmy's playmates were black. The family home at Archery, near Plains, was a small clapboard house with no electricity or running water. Jimmy, the eldest of four, pumped water, carried slop to the hogs, cut wood; in summer he tramped his father's fields without shirt or shoes, fished for eel and catfish and sold peanuts on the streets of Plains. Earl whipped him six times, once for stealing a penny from the collection plate in their Baptist church. At nine, Earl gave him an acre. Jimmy saved up enough to buy five bales of cotton, waited four years and sold them for three times the price he paid. He rolled the money into five shacks, collected $16.50 a month in rent from the black tenants until he left Plains in 1943.

SIX GOOD HABITS: At school, small for his age, he began the practice of a lifetime, walking up to other boys with a grin and hand extended, "Hi, I'm Jimmy Carter!" In eighth grade, he wrote six rules for "good mental habits" in his scrapbook, Ben Franklin style. The climax: "A person who wants to build good mental habits should avoid the idle daydream; should give up worry and anger; hatred and envy; should neither fear nor be ashamed of anything that is honest and purposeful." At 13, he read *War and Peace* and was reinforced in the populist view that great events were ultimately determined not by the leaders but by the common people.

IN THE NAVY NOW: As a cadet at the U.S. Naval Academy in Annapolis from 1943, he got a beating for refusing to sing General Sherman's battle hymn, "Marching Through Georgia." In 1948 he finished third out of 52 seamen in the Navy's submarine program. Assigned to the nuclear sub *Sea Wolf,* he was one of the volunteers the U.S. sent to dismantle a berserk Canadian reactor, and was exposed to 89 seconds of radiation as a member of one of the teams entering the reactor.

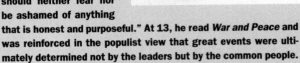

In 1953, on his father's death, he resigned his commission to rescue the family farm and peanut brokerage. He consoled himself that "God did not intend for me to spend my life working on instruments of destruction to kill people." When the Supreme Court ruled for school integration, the White Citizens Council invited him to join the fight. He refused. They offered to pay his $5 dues. "I would as soon," he said, "flush $5 down the toilet." His businesses were boycotted and the family was kicked out of the country club.

ROSALYNN: Rosalynn Smith was his sister Ruth's best friend. As a girl, she had bought ice cream from Jimmy's stand. She liked the way he had grown up when Ruth showed her a photograph of him in Navy uniform. While he was on leave in July 1945, they went to a picnic, saw a movie, and in the rumble seat of the car on the way home she let herself be kissed—the first time on a first date. Soon after his graduation from Annapolis they were married, on July 7, 1946. The couple moved around the country, following Jimmy's Navy postings. Some of her experiences were eye-openers. "It was shocking to me," Rosalynn wrote. "In Plains, I had never seen a white woman doing yard labor or housework for a white person."

GOVERNOR: In tears after his defeat in the 1966 gubernatorial primary by the racist Lester Maddox, he went back to Plains, broke, and began to reexamine his life. With the spiritual guidance of his sister Ruth, he experienced an epiphany and spent the next four years campaigning as a born-again Christian. He and Rosalynn reckoned to have shaken 600,000 hands in 600 communities. Wags said he took his initials too seriously. The piety did not inhibit his running a tough personal campaign against "Cufflinks Carl" Sanders, a former governor, and he was more cunning on race. He opposed busing to achieve racial balance in schools and had racist Governor George Wallace campaign for him. It cost him black votes in the primary, but they came back for the general election. Then he surprised Georgians with an inaugural declaration: "I say to you quite frankly, the time for racial discrimination is over." He put blacks on state boards—up from 3 to 53 in his term—and increased the state's employment of blacks by 40 percent. And he sang "We Shall Overcome," holding hands with civil rights leaders, while Martin Luther King's portrait went up in the state capitol gallery.

DEFEAT OF FORD: The nationally unknown Carter worked the new primary system to tie up the Democratic nomination on the first ballot in 1976 with Walter Mondale of Minnesota as his running mate. He did it the same way he had become governor, starting years ahead, working the hustings of Iowa and New Hampshire one vote at a time. He squeaked past a divided field of liberals and humbled George Wallace, destroying the racist wing of the party in the South. President Ford quickly fell 30 points behind, hurt by his pardon of Nixon, Carter's campaign for moral regeneration and a TV-debate stumble implying the Soviet Union did not "dominate" Eastern Europe. Carter's own blunder was what he added when he thought a *Playboy* interview was over. Was he going to be a holier-than-thou president? "I try not to commit a deliberate sin. I recognize that I'm going to do it anyhow, because I'm human. . . . And Christ set some almost impossible standards for us . . . I've looked on a lot of women with lust. I've committed adultery in my heart many times." Carter, with the South, white ethnic and black votes just made it: 40.8 million votes to Ford's 39.1 million, 297 electoral votes to 240.

COURTROOM TURNING POINT: Quitman County's boss Joe Hurst wanted the well-respected Homer Moore in the State Senate in 1962, and Joe always got his way even if he had to burn down the house of anyone so foolish as to argue. Carter, running against Moore in the primary, saw Joe at work casting ballots for the dead and intimidating Carter voters. By day's end in Georgetown, 333 people had voted 420 ballots and Carter was out. Or was he? He hired an Atlanta attorney, Charles Kirbo, and interested the *Atlanta Journal*. At the trial (above), Carter brought witnesses to testify they had been turned away at polling stations. Carter's heart was in his mouth when Judge Carl Crow ordered the ballot box opened. There were now even more votes for Moore, and voting records were missing. Judge Crow said that, since legal and illegal votes could not be distinguished, none of Georgetown's votes would be allowed. Moore still carried Quitman, but without Georgetown he lost by 65 votes to Carter. In the general election, after more legal maneuvers, Carter won by almost a thousand votes.

EX-PRESIDENT: Building houses for the homeless with his own hands.

THE EASY TIMES FIZZLE OUT

In the midseventies, the American century seemed to be collapsing. People began to sit around and mope about one foreign insult after another and, most of all, about the apparent end of the good times: runaway prices, the devalued dollar no longer pegged to gold, bankrupt cities, labor rackets, American televisions and automobiles that didn't work, and much more.

Through the late forties, fifties and sixties Americans had taken it for granted that their country was invulnerable and their own prosperity sweeter every year. The ever more outrageous fins on Detroit's gas guzzlers perfectly expressed the reckless flamboyance of the nation. For the majority who considered themselves middle class, the good times were a fact. Median family income increased annually by 2.7 percent between 1947 and 1973. It was all downhill from there, especially for the bottom two thirds of the workforce. Family income fell and kept falling right into the early eighties. And, unthinkably, America ran out of gas.

The watershed was the oil embargo imposed by the Arabs in the Yom Kippur war of October 1973. Americans fumed in endless lines for gasoline (which had zoomed in price from 35 to 45 cents a gallon), shook their fists at the multinational oil companies, whose profits soared, and shivered in underheated homes and offices. The embargo ended in March 1974, whereupon people and Congress rapidly forgot about the whole thing. Nixon and Ford tried price controls, lower speed limits, slashed airline schedules, stimulation for solar and nuclear energy, but little was achieved. The country had been self-sufficient in energy in 1950. By 1973 it was importing 35 percent of its oil—and when Carter was inaugurated in 1977 it was importing nearly 50 percent. He declared "the moral equivalent of war" on energy, emphasizing conservation. To demonstrate his sincerity, he lowered the thermostats in the White House and in February devoted his first "fireside chat" to energy, sitting by an open fire in the White House library in a cardigan sweater. It was tough going against a cynical public and a Democratic Senate dominated by energy interests.

Two years into Carter's presidency, the producers' cartel, the Organization of Petroleum Exporting Countries (OPEC), delivered the second oil shock. Egged on by the Shah of Iran, they doubled prices overnight, and then some. Oil that had been $1.50 a barrel in 1970 was now on the way to $32 a barrel. Billions of dollars were sucked out of the Western economies and the poorer countries were devastated. In America, all the benevolent indexes fell: real wages, savings, investment. Inflation went over 10 percent in 1979–80. Carter's new chairman of the Federal Reserve, Paul Volcker, jacked up interest rates to more than 20 percent. Unemployment was in double digits in some areas. A new word defined the misery: stagflation.

ENERGY CRISIS: When times were slack at this gas station in Carter's hometown of Plains, Georgia, the "good ole boys" would sit around and shoot the breeze, drink beer and shoot craps, according to the owner, Billy Carter, the President's happy-go-lucky younger brother. Billy, imbibing in the photograph, would become an even greater embarrassment when he became an official agent for Muammar Qaddafi. A slice of seventies America photographed by George Tames.

CAMP DAVID: Carter is the meat in the sandwich of Begin and Sadat.

CARTER'S COUP FOR PEACE

On April 4, 1977, Jimmy Carter wrote, "a shining light burst on the Middle East for me." He had met the Egyptian president Anwar Sadat and the two men formed a spiritual rapport. He hurried to Rosalynn and told her he had had his best day as president. A few months later he met Prime Minister Menachem Begin of Israel and thought he could work with him. In November, Sadat surprised the world, risking Arab wrath to accept Begin's historic invitation to speak to the Knesset; and Begin visited Egypt. But then everything went cold.

Carter's inspiration was to invite both men to the wooded retreat of Camp David in Maryland. When they accepted, he spent days studying copious intelligence briefings. He wanted to know the depth of these men's souls. They arrived on September 4, 1978, with retinues large enough for them to run their governments from Camp David. Cooks trained to make Egyptian and kosher food were brought in. Carter clamped down on security. He

warned everyone to utter not a word. He need not have worried. Both the Israelis and the Egyptians were discreet because they erroneously assumed he had bugged their phones (wrong president).

Sadat began by producing a document with unreasonably tough demands. The tension mounted as Begin read it in disbelief. "Why don't you sign it?" asked Carter. "It would save us all a lot of time." The joke broke the ice, but the next day both men were screaming at each other. Carter met with them separately, trying to explain what the other was facing. Begin had not understood that Sadat was in many ways trying to represent the whole Arab world. As an autocrat, Sadat hadn't grasped the intricate demands of a democracy.

Day after day Carter worked into the small hours shuttling sentences between the two men. Begin was so slow and stubborn about West Bank settlements and the status of Jerusalem that Sadat on the eighth day and again on the eleventh said he was going home. Carter persuaded him

to stay, promising that if any side rejected any part of the final agreement, then none of the proposals would stay in effect. It helped when one day he took the two leaders around the nearby Gettysburg battlefield. Sadat felt that Carter, a southerner, understood the pain of his nation's defeat in the 1973 Yom Kippur war.

Success came on Sunday, September 17. Israel would begin withdrawing troops from Sinai. Egypt would revoke the 1956 ban on Israel using the Suez Canal. A second agreement envisaged moves to self-government for the Palestinians in the Israeli-occupied West Bank and Gaza. Carter was relentless. When the treaty seemed in doubt again in March, he took a politically risky trip to Egypt and Israel to sort it out. He got the peace process back on track.

On March 26, 1979, Begin and Sadat came to Washington. A historic treaty signed in a huge tent on the White House lawn ended 30 years of war.

444 DAYS OF SHAME AND RAGE

"He knows how to draw a crowd," President Carter wryly remarked of his guest standing with him on the South Lawn of the White House on November 15, 1977. The crowd was hostile—Iranian exiles outside the White House protesting the visit of the Shah of Iran, Mohammad Reza Pahlavi. Tear gas fired by police drifted into the eyes of Carter and the welcoming party, an omen of real tears to come. Undeterred, Carter went to Iran on New Year's Eve. His Majesty, he said, was beloved by his people for maintaining an island of stability in one of the more troubled areas of the world.

Carter's prize entry in Famous Last Words was a product of American history, his character and political expediency. When he won the White House he inherited the ignominious past of U.S.-Iran relations: The CIA had put the Shah on the throne to shield rich supplies of oil from the eddies of nationalism, but his regime survived only on American arms and the ferocious secret police, Savak. Carter's regard for human rights called for him to abandon the Shah, but he had a sense of loyalty to an ally, and the congressional Republicans would have lynched him. His idea of integrity took him down a fatal middle road. He remonstrated, but he did not sell out the Shah, and he did not back him completely when the crunch came.

On January 16, 1979, nudged by the U.S., the Shah fled his country, which was disintegrating in mutiny and riot. On February 1, the messianic Shiite leader Ayatollah Ruhollah Khomeini, landed from exile in Paris to tumultuous acclaim. Possibly, a letter then from Carter apologizing for past U.S. interference might have appeased Khomeini, who blamed Savak and ultimately the U.S. for the deaths of both his father and his son. Little understood outside the country was how real and explosive was Iranian resentment of generations of exploitation by one foreign power or another, and how much the Shiite Muslim clergy detested the infiltration of Western cultural values on everything from the status of women to rock 'n' roll.

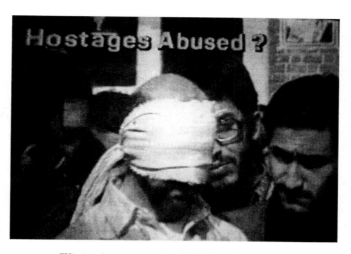

Fifty-two hostages endured 444 days in captivity. The fifty-third hostage was President Jimmy Carter.

The Khomeini revolution was a nightmare of anarchy, assassinations and daily executions. Americans in Iran, down to 10,000 from 25,000, were clearly in danger. Millions of Iranians were on the streets. Stirred up by the Ayatollah's indictment of "foreign devils," waves of militants beat regularly against the iron gates of the embassy chanting for the death of Carter and the Shah. The embassy, renamed Fort Apache, was a 27-acre parkland compound stretching 20 city blocks, a mile-long wall sealing off the chancery, offices, houses and the absent ambassador's residence. In the White House Carter asked a group of advisers: "Does someone have the answer as to what we do if the diplomats in our embassy are taken hostage?" Nobody answered. "I gather not," said Carter. "On that day, we will sit here with long, drawn, white faces and realize that we've been had."

The day came on a gray, drizzly Sunday in Teheran, November 4. Eleven days before, Carter had relented on his refusal to give asylum to the Shah, who had ended up in Mexico, stricken with lymphoma. Pressed for an act of mercy and encouraged by the Iranians to believe there would be no reprisals, he had let the Shah enter the U.S. on October 23 for treatment in New York.

There were 66 people scattered about the compound on Hostage Sunday. The guard of 19 Marines had orders not to shoot, but to delay the mob with tear gas. The walls were breached at 10:30 a.m. Surrender came around 1 p.m. But a group of diplomats destroying documents behind the steel doors of a vault in the chancery went undetected until around 3 p.m. A militant held a knife to the throat of a hostage and threatened to kill him unless the vault was opened. When it was, and the document-shredding discovered, the group inside was beaten. Another hostage, Frederick L. Kupke, 34, was held down with a knife blade against his eye, threatened with blinding unless he remembered a safe combination number that had been shredded. All the hostages were blindfolded, hands bound with tape and led outside to face a terrifying mob— and television cameras, which were to be more significant than the screamers.

Every day in the first few weeks was a turn of the thumbscrew for an America inchoate with rage and impotence. The mobs were in American living rooms, burning the Stars and Stripes, yelling abuse, intensifying fears for the lives of the hostages. Richard Morefield, 51, of San Diego, the consul general, was tortured by three mock executions. A secretary, Elizabeth Montagne, 41, had a gun with one bullet put to her heart by a militant. She "died" five times as he pulled the trigger. Then he relented. Many of the captives in the early days had their hands tied day and night, were confined in semidarkened rooms and were forbidden to speak to other hostages. On November 19, eight "oppressed" blacks and five women secretaries were freed, but the remainder lived for 14 months in a cycle of fear, hope and despair.

The hostages were pawns in Iran's internal power struggles. In the U.S., a group led by Brzezinski argued for force, another led by Secretary of State Cyrus Vance for patience and diplomacy. Carter put the lives of the hostages ahead of retaliation. The student captors had said they would "destroy all the hostages immediately" if there was "even the smallest military action." In April the Ayatollah vetoed a secret deal between Carter and Iranian President Abolhassan Bani-Sadr. It was then that Carter finally gave the approval, in Brzezinski's words, to "lance the boil."

OPERATION EAGLE CLAW

Before dawn, U.S. time, on the day the hostages were seized, the Pentagon summoned Colonel Charles "Chargin' Charlie" Beckwith to rescue them. Beckwith, a veteran of Korea and Vietnam, had been asked in 1977 to train a counterterrorist unit and demanded two years to do it. "I wanted a bunch of red-blooded American soldiers who lived together, ate together, worked together, screwed together and if necessary died together. You can get together a half-assed team in six weeks, but I wasn't going to lead a half-assed team." Carter's aide Hamilton Jordan described him as a large-framed raspy-voiced Georgian whose blue eyes would squint hard when he wanted to make a point. He did not hesitate a second in assessing the probability of success: "Zero, sir."

Back at Fort Bragg, North Carolina, Beckwith and two generals, Air Force Lieutenant General Philip Gast and Army Major General James Vaught, built a model of the Teheran embassy, then figured out how to infiltrate 118 Delta force commandos at night. Six Hercules C-130s would fly them from Egypt to Desert One, an uninhabited spot about 250 miles southeast of Teheran. There they would rendezvous with eight large RH-53D Sea Stallion helicopters performing a 600-mile hop from the carrier *Nimitz* in the Gulf of Oman. The choppers would refuel and fly the commandos to Desert Two, a mountain hideout 50 miles southeast of Teheran. They would arrive just before daylight and rest. That night they would drive to the embassy walls in trucks bought by CIA agents and disguised with Iranian Army markings. They would know, from U.S. satellite photographs, about any change in the general disposition of guards; the satellite could identify every truck and car entering the compound. One commando group would scale the compound to neutralize the guards. Another group would collect the hostages. They would lead them to sites in the compound where helicopters from Desert Two would descend to lift them to an abandoned airstrip near the city. Two transport planes would take them out.

In eight night rehearsals in the Arizona desert, Beckwith's men practiced scaling walls, blowing doors, scanning pitch-dark rooms with infrared glasses, firing live rounds into dummies of guards. They had memorized 53 faces, made allowance for the growth of beards. There was concern that the commandos might accidentally hit an American sitting next to a guard. Beckwith reassured the White House it wouldn't happen. It turned out later that in every drill Beckwith and some of his officers had sat in the darkened room in place of the American dummies, each time in a different place, waiting quietly for the commandos' aim to be as good as they said it was.

When the raid was approved in April 1980, Secretary of State Cyrus Vance was alone in opposing it. He believed it was "a damn complex operation." It might inflame the Soviets. It might hazard the 300 or so Americans still voluntarily residing in Teheran. Jordan wrote later that he thought "Cy was going to feel like a damn fool when the helicopters landed on the South Lawn and our hostages climbed out." On April 21 Vance secretly resigned, an act he agreed to make public only after the raid, successful or not.

Operation Eagle Claw began when the Sea Stallions lifted off from the *Nimitz* at dusk on Thursday, April 24, for the supposed three-hour flight. All the C-130s landed on schedule. Almost at once a bus loomed up out of the darkness on a seldom used dirt road. The commandos, with the approval of Carter over the satellite, invited the astonished 44 passengers to board a C-130 for "a nice long trip" to Egypt. Next, a pickup and a fuel truck came down the road. The commandos, firing at the headlights, ignited the fuel truck. The driver jumped out and escaped in the pickup. Beckwith believed they were gasoline smugglers who thought they had run into police and would not sound the alarm.

The helicopters were in trouble. Soon after takeoff, one was abandoned with a cracked rotor blade. Then a violent sandstorm blew up. The gyroscope vital for blind flying failed on another helicopter, forcing the pilot back to the *Nimitz*. The six remaining choppers struggled to Desert One, the last one landing at 1:40 a.m. Iranian time, almost three hours late. A pilot now reported failed hydraulics, reducing the number of choppers to five.

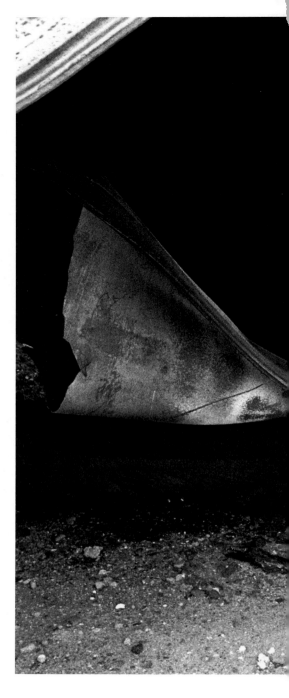

SACRIFICE: The failed rescue mission had to leave the desert too quickly to recover the charred bodies of the men who died, three Marines, four Air Force officers and an Air Force enlisted man. The Iranians took them back to Teheran and displayed the coffins in the embassy compound. Later, the remains were returned to the U.S. through the Red Cross. Photograph by Abbas.

Beckwith and General Vaught, who was in Egypt in overall command, calculated they would lose three in the raid. They decided against leaving Desert One with fewer than six. Carter deliberated and prayed for several minutes, then he approved their recommendation to withdraw Eagle Claw.

At 2:10 a.m. Delta began transferring gear from the helicopters back to the transports. One of the Sea Stallion pilots nudged his craft about 20 feet in the air to go around a C-130. The whipped-up dust clouded his view. A rotor blade slashed into the C-130 and the two aircraft exploded in flames. Eight men died. They, and the helicopters, were abandoned in the rush to escape before daybreak.

Back in the U.S. Carter met the Delta team at a secret location. Beckwith and he, fellow Georgians, embraced and wept in each other's arms. Carter had to endure a stream of false news reports that he had cut back Delta's resources and ended the

mission out of cowardice when Delta wanted to continue. Dirt storms were flying in a presidential election year.

Diplomatic negotiations picked up speed after the Shah died in Egypt on July 27, stalled again when Iraq invaded Iran on September 22. Just two days before the voters decided between Jimmy Carter and Ronald Reagan, Carter received the text of an Iranian agreement to release the prisoners that a less scrupulous man might have acclaimed as a victory. He considered it needed refinement and merely announced a "constructive step." On November 4 Ronald Reagan won in a landslide.

Carter was robbed of the joy of the fi-

nal deal he made on January 16, with the help of Algeria, whereby Iran released the hostages in return for its gold and frozen assets worth nearly $12 billion. All through the night and small hours of January 19–20, as the clock ticked toward the noon inauguration of Reagan, Carter stayed up in the White House, trying to push the financial jigsaw to completion in hectic international calls between Algiers, Teheran and London. In Teheran, the hostages were moved near the airport. Buses stood by to take them to the planes. At 10:45 a.m. Carter was dragged away by Rosalynn to put on his rented morning clothes and greet the Reagans.

CARTER'S ENDLESS RUN OF BAD LUCK

Carter had begun his presidency by walking back to the White House from his bitter-cold inauguration ceremony, stunning the thousands along the parade route by stepping out of the armored car with his family. He wanted to symbolize the end of the imperial presidency. He stopped bands playing "Hail to the Chief." He would be the president who trusted the people, the captive of no business lobby or cabal of liberal ideologues. He would be the president who would never knowingly tell a lie, a president so frugal with public money that he would carry his own suitbag, sell the presidential yacht *Sequoia*, order television sets removed from staff offices, cut salaries by 10 percent—and bill White House guests for their breakfast. In the first six months he personally reviewed all requests to use the White House tennis court. He was the anti-Washington outsider, come to cleanse the temples.

But the time was out of joint for him. He was unlucky with the oil crisis, with the phenomenon of "stagflation," with Iran. He was unlucky in the disjunction of his character and the politics of the time. He was more a moral than a political leader. His abiding sense of right and wrong, a rare enough quality in a president, played well in his courageous diplomacy. Unim-

peded by Congress, he balanced the advice of the conciliator Cyrus Vance and the cold warrior Zbigniew Brzezinski, and followed his own instincts in the fight for human rights, the Panama Canal treaty and the Camp David accords. His policies freed numerous Latin American dissidents and helped the emergence of democracy throughout the region.

His moral sense would have been the salvation of America in the civil rights confrontations and the Vietnam War. In the judgment of Hendrik Hertzberg, one of his speechwriters, Carter in these circumstances would have been one of the great presidents, and the argument is suggestive. Certainly, it has been his moral example as a house builder to the poor and a tireless community leader that has made even his critics hail him as one of the greatest ex-presidents in American history. Out of a vacuum, virtue.

But the domestic problems that preoccupied America in the late seventies were managerial and political: energy, inflation, welfare, city finance, transport, health insurance, banking, weapons systems. Carter could master the complexities. He would stay up half the night pondering 300-page position papers. He used his own slide rule before he decided to cancel

the B-1 bomber. Nobody could fool him about the design failure in the cooling system in reactor 2 at the Three Mile Island nuclear power plant in Pennsylvania. But deciding what was right on the basis of merit, case by case in a communion with one's intellect and soul, was one thing. Other people had ideas, which was tolerable; what was hard for him to bear in domestic policy was that they had interests. His behavior seemed arrogant, but it was a function of idealism, not pomposity. He knew he was right and he was often correct in his assessment. But it was politically ruinous. Carter himself said it: "I am pretty rigid. It's been very difficult for me to compromise when I believe in something deeply. I generally prefer to take it to the public, to fight it out to the last vote, and if I go down, I go down in flames." When Carter made his big speech on energy, Speaker of the House Tip O'Neill ("all politics is local") gave him a list of congressmen he should call to keep up the pressure. Carter recoiled. He wouldn't dream of it. The American people would know he was right. O'Neill confessed: "I could have slugged him."

Carter and the unsophisticated Georgians in the White House, notably his chief aide, Hamilton Jordan, were soon at war

Voting was only weeks away when Carter ran in a ten-kilometer race near Camp David. Halfway through, he collapsed. It was an unhappy metaphor for the end of his presidency. Photograph by Phil Stewart.

with Senator Edward Kennedy, who led the liberal wing of the party in Congress, and with his bustling cabinet star, HEW Secretary Joe Califano, Jr., and even with his loyal vice president, Walter Mondale. They were passionately attached to social programs Carter could not fit into the balanced budget he had promised the people, but they also represented a way of doing things, of compromise and coalition building by giving here and taking there, that he found repugnant. "The worst thing you could say to Carter," Mondale told Carter biographer Peter Bourne, "was that it was politically the best thing to do." The bustling Califano saw himself representing a constituency without representation, the poor. To Carter, even so deserving a sectional interest corrupted his ideal of staying above politics.

He was attempting an act of impossible levitation. To adapt the words of the writer Esmond Wright, he wore his rectitude like a banner, and stopped too often to salute it. How would an economically feasible welfare package be made politically acceptable to the 119 congressional committees and subcommittees that had a say? It was not just a Democratic party problem. The whole of Congress was bent on reasserting itself after the erosion of power in the Nixon years. And when Carter did bend, such as funding ten of the nineteen water projects he had vetoed, it did him

little good with the disappointed suppliants and none at all with his image as a strong new leader. What would have been routine trading for another president was, for Carter, a question of credibility. The facts justified his support of his friend Bert Lance, the astute budget director, who came under exaggerated attack for banking practices before his appointment, but he had to go. Carter had excited an irredeemable public expectation and kept on doing so. The perceptual gap combined with the endless economic troubles all too soon produced a mood of despair.

The climax and epitome came in the summer of 1979. He was troubled by having to make a fifth speech on energy. Pat Caddell, his young pollster, told him he would put people to sleep. "America is a nation deep in crisis," Caddell wrote. Americans had lost faith in their institutions, in the economy, in their future. Carter took himself off for meditation in Camp David. He invited nearly 150 people from all walks of life to come and commune with him. Privately, he met with small groups of citizens in homes in Pennsylvania and West Virginia, listening to their anxieties and ideas. Once more, he was "born again." And on July 15, he invited the country to repent and be born again. It was derided as his "malaise" speech by his critics—he never used the word—but it was a spectacular success.

His ratings jumped 11 points, albeit only to 37 percent. Then he blew it. He asked the entire cabinet and White House staff to resign. It gave the appearance of crisis, of passing the buck and of personal politics when he sacked Cabinet secretaries who were competent but critical and retained loyal incompetents.

Carter did have some early successes with the help of Tip O'Neill. He created the departments of Energy and Education, deregulated the airlines (and trucking in 1980), banned the dumping of raw sewage in the ocean, controlled strip mining, reformed the civil service. In his last year, he tried to guard his flank on the right. He raised the defense budget and cut social spending. He responded to the Soviet invasion of Afghanistan with a boycott of the Olympic Games and, despite its unpopularity, by reinstituting draft legislation. He put Paul Volcker in as chairman of the Federal Reserve and endured a recession. He might just still have won if the Iranian hostages had come home in a blaze of glory. But the Ayatollah delivered the final blow, delaying their release. In November 1980, Ronald Reagan became the 40th president, with just under 51 percent of the popular vote. It was Carter's luck that a third-party "good government" candidate, John Anderson, helped Reagan take the electoral votes in 44 states.

PUT OUT MORE FLAGS
1980-1989

The Reagan Revolution

At the end of the seventies, America simmered with accumulated fears and frustrations. The country seemed ripe for political revolution. Middle-class families were already worried about rising unemployment and street crime, permissiveness and race relations. Then double-digit inflation and 15 percent interest rates had been added to the brew, pushing even modest earners into higher tax brackets and foreclosing many dreams of home ownership. Every April in millions of households vile things were wished on the apparent perpetrator of the misery, big government and especially liberal Democrats, who were perceived as having lost touch with the working masses and identified with the counterculture. Anxiety levels were high from mid-1974, according to the polls, and they were higher still in the watershed election of 1980, when the new right wing of the Republican party put up against the fretful Jimmy Carter a confident, sunny, cultural populist and tax cutter who seemed to have a cheerful answer for everything. His favorite aphorism was "Government isn't the answer. It's the problem."

Ronald Reagan's victory ushered in a Gilded Age of wealth and display. It was the third Republican "capitalist heyday," to use the term of political analyst Kevin Phillips, after the first Gilded Age (mid-1870s to 1890s) and the Roaring Twenties. The consequences were not all that the middle classes expected.

STARSTRUCK: Nancy led the ecstatic reception for her Ronnie at the Republican party's Dallas convention in 1984. A year before she had been against his running for a second term. The brittle, direct and elegant Nancy was always an unabashed protector of his image and his health, unforgiving of anyone who put him at risk. She thought CIA Director William Casey and Chief of Staff Donald Regan had done that. The bruisingly tough Regan resigned in tears not long after being caught in Nancy's laser. He retaliated in his 1988 memoir by revealing that the White House schedulers had been driven crazy by her insistence on manipulating engagements around Reagan's good and bad days as divined by an astrologist in San Francisco. Her most prominent public position was a campaign against drugs ("Just Say No"); her most significant was her private persuasion for Ronnie to try to make peace with the Soviets. Photograph by Wally McNamee.

PUT OUT MORE FLAGS

On the night of January 20, 1981, the nation's new president, 17 days short of his seventieth birthday, and First Lady danced their feet off at ten different inaugural balls in the capital. Washington was aglow with celebration as festive conservatives streamed from gala to gala. They were overjoyed at having finally come in from the cold, 16 years after the Goldwater disaster. The triumph they were celebrating was the improbable ascension of Ronald Wilson Reagan, the "dumb actor" who had been so easy to underrate. He hung in the Cabinet Room of the West Wing a portrait of a Republican president he thought had also been underrated: Calvin Coolidge. Reagan, in fact, was the first "missionary" conservative elected president since Silent Cal; the intervening Republican presidents, Hoover, Eisenhower and Nixon, having run and governed as moderates. And November 4, 1980, was only the opening night of an eight-year run.

Reagan barely cleared 50 percent of the popular vote, but he took one traditional Democratic bastion after another. Where Goldwater had not carried a state outside the Deep South and his native Arizona, Reagan won California, Illinois, Michigan, Pennsylvania, New Jersey; Texas and Florida from Carter's native South—even New York, thanks to the independent John Anderson's splitting the vote. There was more going on than the victory of an optimist over an exhausted incumbent. All over the country, capable, articulate and powerful Democratic senators were going down. Often they were defeated by political unknowns—"right-wing, nihilistic, counterreformationist" conservatives, as Elizabeth Drew described them, who "do not play by the old rules of the club." Before the night was over the Republicans controlled the Senate for the first time since 1952, when Eisenhower brought them in. The Democrats had ostensibly kept the House, but there were enough conservative Democrats from the South to give the Republicans a working majority on many issues. These Southern "Boll Weevils" shared the values of the conservative Republican social agenda: anti-abortion, anti-ERA, antigay, antiwelfare, anti–racial quotas, antiregulation.

Reagan's victory, and the victory of so many Republicans over incumbent senators, representatives and governors, had many sources. Carter was not able to welcome the Iranian hostages home in time for the election, but he was able to land himself in a recession. Just like Hoover, the only other twentieth-century president to do it, he put himself up for reelection when the national income was shrinking. Ask yourself, said Reagan to millions of viewers at the climax of his television debate with Carter, "Are you better off now than you were four years ago?" Nor was Carter able to give anyone, even himself, much hope that he would do much better in a second term. Reagan and Carter both grasped that people were weary, sickened by two decades of scandal and crisis; but only Reagan understood how much they hated the defeatist suggestion that the American dream was no longer realizable for everyone. Reagan was firmly in the saddle of American exceptionalism. He promised a "morning in America" and through eight years, two of them economically grim, his good nature transformed the national mood. Though he could be startlingly indifferent to his children and his aides, he was never personally mean. He remained good-humored, confident of his and America's higher destiny, personally modest but never forgetful of the proud symbolism of the presidency. His attention deficit disorders were marked—but they were concealed by the most ingenious marketers ever to inhabit the White House. Nobody knew at the time, for instance, that as president he went into his first Big Seven summit without having even opened the thick briefing book prepared by James Baker. "Well, Jim," he explained, "*The Sound of Music* was on last night." His imaginative powers were strong but selective. He could not imagine people struggling at the receiving end of Social Darwinism; but he was so effective at imagining himself in dramatic situations that he seemed to believe that he really had filmed the Nazi death camps in World War II (in fact, he never left the country). For all that, he had the qualities required of any successful president. As the historian Alan Brinkley notes, "He was highly effective in his most important task: establishing broad themes for his administration and keeping his subordinates focused on them." In this and his unflappability, he was very much like his political hero, Franklin Roosevelt. One of Reagan's aides later

Reagan was not as consistent as the popular view of him portrayed.

IN '64 I VOTED FOR JOHNSON BECAUSE HE PROMISED PEACE.

BUT HE BETRAYED ME. HE ESCALATED THE WAR!

IN '68 I VOTED FOR NIXON BECAUSE HE PROMISED AN END TO BIG GOVERNMENT.

BUT I WAS FOOLED AGAIN. HE BUGGED PHONES, OPENED MAIL AND DOUBLED THE WHITE HOUSE STAFF.

IN '76 I VOTED FOR CARTER BECAUSE HE PROMISED TO CUT MILITARY EXPENDITURES.

BUT INSTEAD HE KEPT RAISING THE MILITARY BUDGET YEAR AFTER YEAR!

FINALLY I FIGURED IT OUT! I REALIZED THAT POLITICIANS ALWAYS DO THE OPPOSITE OF WHAT THEY PROMISE.

SO I VOTED FOR REAGAN.

BUT HE'S DOING EXACTLY WHAT HE SAID HE'D DO!!

recalled: "It was striking how often we on the staff would become highly agitated by the latest news bulletins. Reagan saw the same events as nothing more than a bump on the road; things would get better tomorrow. His horizons were just not the same as ours." There was scandal and crisis in full measure during the Reagan administration, but more often than not he floated over them with a smile, a wisecrack and a hearty wave from beneath the roaring blades of the presidential helicopter. In his two terms, Reagan was often more popular than his policies: in Congresswoman Pat Schroeder's exasperated epithet, he was the Teflon president.

The 1980 election was a triumph for Reagan, but less a triumph for conservatism per se than an expression of dissatisfaction with the status quo. That dissatisfaction was global. In the wake of the oil shocks and economic stresses of the late seventies, electorates throughout the democratic world were seizing their first opportunity to chuck out whoever was in charge. In France and Spain, the Socialist parties of François Mitterrand and Felipe Gonzalez benefited from the anti-incumbent mood; in Britain and West Germany, right-of-center parties swept to victory. Reagan won in 1980 more in spite of his right-wing ideology than because of it. Before the voters would accept him as a safe choice, he had to convince them that even though he might have some cranky ideas, he was not the sort of fellow who would be likely to blow up the world or abolish social security. Conservatism didn't put Reagan in the White House. But once he was installed in it, he brilliantly used its bully pulpit to reshape the entire political spectrum in his own image. Unlike the Republican victories of 1952, 1956, 1968 and 1972, therefore, the elections of 1980, 1984 and 1988 marked an ascendancy of conservative political doctrine. The intellectual focus of political debate changed sharply from public to private initiatives. But the full right-wing agenda was never enacted, nor was there a permanent political realignment comparable to the realignment after 1932. The country was disenchanted with Democratic management of social programs and ached to restore national prestige. It liked putting out more flags. But it was unwilling to renounce the New Deal welfare state and liberalism as much as New Right rhetoric suggested. The much hailed "turn to the right" requires qualification.

The Reagan era was the coming of age of a new conservative coalition, a fragile reconciliation between the fading, pragmatic, old-style "moderate" or traditional "establishment" Republicans and the ideological Goldwater wing, which had licked its wounds and surged back. Among the activists there were also new overlapping constituencies, roughly:

- Economic libertarian conservatives, among them aggressive new entrepreneurs from the Sun Belt who had no personal memory of the Great Depression. Their priority was to dismantle government and slash taxes.
- Social conservatives identified by Kevin Phillips in 1975 as a major component of the "New Right" who were reacting against permissiveness, single mothers on welfare, the more strident of the women's and gay groups, violence on television and pornographic display.
- "Evangelicals"—militantly religious groups, mostly Protestant but some Catholics, agitated principally by an IRS threat to the charitable status of their independent schools, but also by legalized abortion, the banning of school prayer and sex education.
- Racist right-wing populists who scapegoated federal bureaucrats, "pointy-headed" intellectuals, and metropolitan elites, the code word for clever liberal Jews. Their bastions, wrote Kevin Phillips, were "a combination of lower-middle-class Archie Bunker country at the end of the big city subway lines, commuter country and small towns almost anywhere, and new look-alike suburbs backhoed and bulldozed out of red Georgia clay, Florida mangrove swamp, East Texas piney woods and the fringe of California desert."
- A small but vocal praetorian guard of former liberal and leftist intellectuals offended by the excesses of the New Left. Michael Harrington, the democratic socialist writer and activist, scornfully dubbed them "neoconservatives"; like Quakers and contras, they adopted the title and wore it with pride. In the words of Irving Kristol, the ex-Trotskyist who became their most prominent networker, neoconservatives were liberals who had been mugged by reality. They included Irving Kristol and his wife, the social historian Gertrude Himmelfarb; Norman Podhoretz of *Commentary*, and his journalist wife, Midge Decter; Nathan Glazer, co-author of *Beyond the Melting Pot* (and, briefly, his collaborator, Daniel Patrick Moynihan); and, on the not quite neoconservative fringe, Martin Peretz, owner of *The New Republic*. The move from left to right endowed them with a patina of open-mindedness while enhancing the aura of general liberal decay.

It was an unstable coalition. Economic libertarians and social conservatives are uneasy allies. If individuals have liberty in the marketplace, why not in their moral choices? Of course, the left has the problem in reverse: How can liberty in social conduct be reconciled with control in economic conduct? But all the conservative groups were at least united in demonizing "big government," its taxes and intrusions, and they were all hostile to the least accommodation with godless communism. Perhaps their founding father was the heir to an oil fortune, a cultivated Catholic intellectual brought up on his family's 47-acre Connecticut estate and its South Carolina getaway, educated at English and American prep schools and at Yale, and the precocious author of a book attacking Yale as insufficiently "Christian" and another enthusiastically defending Joe McCarthy. This was William F. Buckley, Jr. As a fluent and perceptive young man, he founded *National Review* in 1955 with the mission, as he put it, "to stand athwart history yelling Stop!" To borrow a word from his taste for scavenging Greek linguistic shipwrecks, he was eristical, which is to say he liked to argue. Through *National Review* and Young Americans for Freedom, the conservative youth organization he founded in 1960, Buckley was the St. Paul of a movement that, for the first time, became a coherent political force. Despite his defense of McCarthy and other youthful indiscretions, Buckley helped make conservatism respectable by driving out of the new right-wing paradise all the old isolationists, the worst John Birch extremists, the most vocal atheists and most of the anti-Semites, in order to unite the movement around a crusading anticommunism. The movement had many voices. The platoon leaders were the televangelists, supported by mortar fire from the emerging radio talk show hosts, and the heavy artillery of the Heritage Foundation, the midseventies creation of Paul Weyrich, a young activist who was backed by the beer money of Joseph Coors. Meanwhile, some measure of emancipation from reliance on big business was afforded by a young clerk in a Houston oil company, Richard Viguerie, who had worked as a fund-raiser for Buckley. He struck gold by devising computerized direct mail appeals to frustrated subgroups. The money they donated was useful, but the names also represented a reserve army of foot soldiers, ready to be mobilized in various right-wing causes. Viguerie was one of the people—Howard E. Phillips and Weyrich were others—who persuaded the televangelists to become their political allies. The IRS provided the clincher in 1978 by trying to deny charitable status to independent Christian schools, and hence tax exemption, on the grounds that they had insignificant numbers of minority students. (The IRS had a point: many of the schools had started as "seg academies," founded to get around the Supreme Court's 1954 school desegregation decision.) Here was a cause to which Viguerie's

mailing lists eagerly responded. With the blooming also of right-wing radio talk shows, the Republicans acquired their own grassroots momentum, co-opting great numbers of disappointed former Democrats. They were no longer a party of Eastern elites.

But how did all these disparate interests fit a conservative program? And what did the Republicans' electoral success say about the country?

The search for a single definition to describe a political movement is seductive, but it has been, and will continue to be, a treacherous pursuit. For a start, the terms "liberal" and "conservative" are a philosophical spaghetti. The labels mean different things in different political democracies—in Europe, a liberal is an apostle of free markets. And liberal and conservative have meant different things at different times in American history. They are often used disingenuously by politicians. Reagan's massive and popular defense buildup was hailed as a classic conservative response to communism, but the men who created NATO and the Marshall Plan to defend Europe from Soviet expansion regarded themselves as liberals, while many of the conservative politicians at the time, such as Robert A. Taft, shied away from foreign commitments. But Vietnam and the countercultural upheavals of the sixties shattered the liberals' self-confidence and splintered the constituencies—labor, intellectuals, blacks, blue-collar workers—on which their power had been based. By the end of the seventies, the word "liberal" carried such overtones of licentiousness and complacency about Soviet expansion that a politician would rather walk naked down Pennsylvania Avenue than wear the label. In the eighties, the conservatives, stressing order over liberty, were able to caricature a liberal as a coked-up loony-left radical who would open the jails, destroy business and sell out to the Reds. Michael Dukakis's handlers were so worried about this, in his election contest with George Bush in 1988, that they put a helmet on his head and stuffed him into the cockpit of a tank—where, alas, he looked more like Snoopy than Patton. It may not be possible for American domestic dialogue to give the term "liberal" anything more than a decent funeral. Many liberal-left survivors now announce they are "progressives."

The term "conservative" has been corrupted in another direction. Nobody with an interest in preserving his mental equilibrium can answer the editor and publisher Jason Epstein's question: "How do Plato and Augustine fit with Joe McCarthy and Ralph Reed, or Burke, Gibbon, and Dr. Johnson with Jesse Helms, Pat Buchanan and Irving Kristol, or original sin with free market theory, or the Ten Commandments with selling machine guns?" Conservatives, priding themselves on respect for the wisdom of long experience, used to cherish tradition and reject change of a radical nature. Their case, in Edmund Burke's phrase, was that custom reconciles us to everything, that society should be regarded as an organic union of the living and the dead. Burke would have had apoplexy to hear that people calling themselves conservatives were preparing to discard 200 years of civilized discourse about the United States Constitution for the sake of what Robert H. Bork, Reagan's 1987 rejected nominee for the Supreme Court, called the doctrine of original intent. Burke would have been equally puzzled to find that conservation had become a dirty word to conservatives. James G. Watt, Reagan's Interior Secretary, was at the extreme in his shrill determination to consume any public land or resource that could be drilled, mined, flooded, developed or shipped to Japan, but even less rabid conservatives were anti-environment in ways that would have sent Teddy Roosevelt reaching for his Winchester. How could the ransacking of public lands be squared with conservatism? How could the capitalist emphasis on individual gain be reconciled with conservative duty to family and community?

An answer of sorts is that American conservatives had accepted the doctrines of a pair of Austrian economists: Ludwig von Mies (*Omnipotent Government,* 1949), a European liberal in the old sense of the word who found refuge in America from the Nazis, and his laissez-faire protégé, Friedrich A. von Hayek (*The Road to Serfdom,* 1943), who moved to the University of Chicago and held lively Wednesday night salons with a brilliant variety of scholars, including Milton Friedman. Conservation implies regulation, and von Hayek, von Mies and later Friedman articulated the nascent conservative credo that regulation impedes economic freedom, which in turn is the foundation of liberty. Like the Marxists they scorned, the new free-market conservatives were economic determinists. Wrote von Mies, "All the other principles of liberalism [read conservatism!]—democracy, personal freedom of the individual, freedom of choice, freedom of speech and of the press, religious tolerance, peace among nations—are consequences of this basic postulate." In due course, Friedman came up with a practical economic theory to justify the philosophical repudiation of government. For thirty years since the Great Depression, liberal ideas had prevailed on the conduct of the economy. It was Nixon who said, "We're all Keynesians

now." But if some Republicans had come to recognize that Keynes was not the Antichrist, the body of the party still twitched at the name. It was all too painful a reminder of the impotence of Republican policymakers in the face of Great Depression job lines, all too much a justification of government economic engineering. In the stagflation of the seventies, the conservatives lost their inferiority complex by adopting as received truth Friedman's laissez-faire monetarist teachings, which were basically a repudiation of New Deal pump-priming. There was a "natural" level of unemployment. Trying to increase demand and jobs by manipulating the money supply would produce high and accelerating inflation that would destroy the whole economy. The party rank and file may not have followed the algebra, but they absorbed Friedman's libertarian political message that life would be better if market forces prevailed.

The monetarist preference for restraining prices over providing jobs appealed to those on fixed incomes and to some business puritans, but how would it play in Peoria? Friedman's theories hardly offered enough to tempt voters to eject the welfare-state Democrats who had dominated Congress for almost 50 years. A more dazzling seduction was required, and myth has it that one day in 1975 the economist Arthur Laffer captured it like a pretty butterfly while lunching at the Two Continents restaurant near the Treasury: it was a beautifully symmetrical curve drawn on a napkin. Laffer disclaims the anecdote, but he did draw a curve that was treated for a while as reverently as $E = mc^2$ because it was a panacea that offered a way out of the prudent old Republican economics of "no free lunch." Laffer's optimism chimed perfectly with Reagan's ever sunny temperament. Conservatives could offer tax cuts without risk of budget deficits! How? Laffer's curve affected to prove that since high tax rates on incremental income may discourage higher earners from earning even more, low taxes should have the opposite effect. Low rates, according to Laffer, would so encourage investment, savings and enterprise that the result would be not lesser, but greater federal revenues. The precision of the curve was a joke. The serious point (which Keynes himself had countenanced) was that if the government cut taxes at the margin, it might not lose much, if any, revenue because businesses and people would work harder, and the higher earnings would yield more tax revenues. This "supply side" argument for rewarding the suppliers of wealth, rather than the consumers, was seized by the journalist Jude Wanniski, who sold it to the *Wall Street Journal;* by Irving Kristol; and by jolly Jack Kemp, a former quarterback for the Buffalo Bills and a presidential aspirant. Congressman Kemp joined with Senator William Roth of Delaware in drafting a bill to cut federal income taxes by 30 percent over three years. Kemp-Roth was the core of Reagan's first budget.

The ideology of minimal government had been widely popularized a generation earlier through the literary skill of a volatile young Russian émigré named Alice Rosenbaum, who hammered together her pseudonym—Ayn Rand—from the names of a favorite actress and a typewriter and became one of the best-selling writers in the history of the English language. Her epic novels *The Fountainhead* (1943) and *Atlas Shrugged* (1957) dramatized heroes who embodied her philosophy of rational self-interest. She liked to call it objectivism. We should all be faithful to our own drives and to the moral values they imply, and reject all moral, religious or spiritual obligations to others. There was no such thing as the common good, Rand taught, foreshadowing Margaret Thatcher's scoff, "There is no such thing as society." Ayn Rand was not an anarchist. She allowed for an army, a police force and a judicial system to protect individual rights—but that was about all. Public responsibility for employment or wages was sloppy altruism, bound to be perverted into totalitarian communism or fascism. Rand's atheism disqualified her for movement membership in the eyes of many conservative thinkers, notably Buckley, but her romantic individualism appealed to some powerful people. They included Ronald Reagan; her old acolyte Alan Greenspan, who became chairman of the Federal Reserve; Martin Anderson, Reagan's first domestic policy adviser; and his senior associate counselor, Christopher Cox (later a California legislator).

The central question of individualism is one that goes to the heart of the continuing argument of the American century. American conservatives and American liberals both claim to represent the tradition of American individualism, but neither successfully relates the rights of the individual to the concessions and duties required by community life. America has never had a robust socialist or collective tradition, and what little it had was certainly all but defunct by 1980. The question for both liberals and conservatives is what constitutes grounds for intervention—and on whose side? For conservatives the American dream has meant minimizing state intervention against the power of big business, even when that power deprives the individual of his liberties. Republicans are split between their libertarians and their corporatists as well as between their libertarians and their social conservatives. Within reason, these are all tenable positions. But when they ossify into ideologies, their internal contradictions are no longer just a verbal, theoretical problem but a practical political one. Liberalism has its own paradoxes. The liberal intellectual tradition espoused by Thomas Jefferson (the darling of the new conservatives) embraces the theory that rights are natural to man and not endowments from authority. Jeffersonian liberalism defends the individual, his personal inalienable rights and his property against the intrusions of the state, and also those of the corporation, the church and demons of populism like the railroads and the Eastern banks. Jefferson is a father of American populism. But Jeffersonian liberalism, in contrast to the skeptical "realism" of conservative doctrine, has also been infused with the Enlightenment notion that human reason can improve the environment and so justifies pragmatic experiments by government to reconcile liberty and equality. It was Jefferson, the defender of liberty, who argued, in one of his letters to James Madison, for "silently lessening the inequality of property" by progressive taxation.

To achieve the American dream, liberals have been ready to restrict individual liberty for the sake of social justice. Try anything and see if it works was FDR's creed. Progressive taxation and the redistribution of income downward have been the norm, but in the seventies liberals did a double backward somersault from their base in individual rights. Pushed by the academy, public interest law firms, civil lobbies and foundations—especially Ford and Rockefeller—Democratic congresses sponsored legislation promoting group rights, the antithesis of individualism. In the guilty confusions of the post–civil rights era, they promoted the multiculturalist concept of America as a heterogeneous nation divided into five "minorities" (American Indians or Alaskan Natives, Asians, Blacks, women and Hispanics), and then endorsed the notion that all these groups were entitled to preference in employment, education and government contracts and to their own ethnic blocs in legislatures produced by gerrymandering. Such interventions gave conservatives a chance to capture the citadel of liberalism by taking over its high ground of individualism and natural rights—even if the conservative programmatic agenda still effectively valued property rights over the rights of individuals. Republican presidents from Nixon to Bush inveighed against racial quotas but supported minority "set-aside" programs that encouraged entrepreneurship.

Liberalism, in the sense of faith in the positive power of government intervention, succeeded brilliantly for the four decades beginning in 1932. At home it created a large prosperous middle class, upheld justice and extended fundamental freedoms; in the greater world it crushed fascism and stopped communism in its tracks. For those 40 years, federal government was seen as benefactor. It sent the check to get you through the hard times or old age, it provided new jobs building a local school or bridge, it helped with college tuition, and with a loan to save the family homestead; and after 1965, through Medicaid and Medicare, it assured a minimum level of health care, too. Economic growth for years absorbed the rising costs of these programs, as it also enlarged personal opportunities, but growth faltered in the seventies following the oil crises and the credit crunches of 1973 to 1975 and again in 1979. Thereafter control of inflation was given a higher priority than full employment. Stagflation halted the sustained rise in median family income from World War II and with it the long decline in the numbers of Americans officially classified as poor. Especially after the happy surfing in the prosperous sixties, the shock of being dumped on a rocky shore was severe. Exceptional America was no longer exceptional. Its people were no longer the richest in the world. They had fallen behind the Swiss, the West Germans, the Belgians and the Scandinavians. By the end of the seventies, inflation was pushing millions of middle-class Americans into marginal tax brackets that two decades earlier had been intended only for the rich. Godfrey Hodgson's study of the conservative ascent, *The World Turned Right Side Up* (1996), illuminates what happened in the sixties. In 1961, nine out of ten Americans were paying a flat federal income tax rate of 22 percent (though the rates for the highest brackets ranged up to 91 percent). Two decades later that had changed significantly; 45 percent of all taxpayers were now paying higher marginal rates. Liberal administrations had failed to keep taxes from increasing, often in disproportionate percentages for the working and middle class. The average family of 1980 was taxed twice as much as the family of 1950. Meanwhile, the share borne by corporations fell year after year.

California was the first to rebel when it voted to limit the tax on property. Californians had not objected when most high-value property was owned by the wealthiest citizens, but inflation and prosperity had changed that. Among the traditional Democratic constituencies, people on fixed incomes and black homeowners were particularly hard hit by rising property taxes, but it was too late for liberals to do more than wring their hands. Howard Jarvis, an eccentric former semi-pro baseball player and professional boxer turned home appli-

ance magnate, led that first tax revolt in 1978. His proposal to fix the tax at 1 percent of actual value envisaged saving homeowners $2 billion and business $3.5 million. Jarvis and Richard Viguerie orchestrated the old progressive device of a direct referendum with computer-assisted direct mailings. They scared individual taxpayers with straight-line projections of their own future taxes. Proposition 13 passed overwhelmingly. It cut revenues by 23 percent, permanently beggared many local schools and libraries, and retarded industrial development in unexpected ways. A dozen other states copied California—even liberal Massachusetts.

The tax rebellion should have set off alarm bells in liberal caucuses and think tanks from Berkeley to Cambridge. That it did not suggested that they had become fatally complacent. Except for four scattered years during the Eisenhower administration, Democrats had controlled both houses of Congress from 1933 to 1981. Many individual Democrats cozied up to monied interests instead of doing the hard organizing work needed to widen their electorate by voter registration drives and galvanizing populist coalitions on issues that touch people's everyday lives. They allowed one of the most reliable pillars of their party, the unions, to become bogged down by a bureaucratic elite, ignoring such upstarts as Cesar Chavez's farm workers. And they adopted new procedures, sponsored by Senator George McGovern, after Carter's loss of the presidency, that increased the power of middle-class doctrinaires and cultural elites in the party. These elements sponsored a "rights revolution" that sounded splendid except that it benefited almost every conceivable group except male voters in the South and in northern cities who were a key element in the traditional Democratic coalition.

Conservatives proved adept at maximizing these gifts. The theme was that Washington did nothing for the common man, personified by Kevin Phillips as someone driving a two-year-old Pontiac, grumbling about welfare chiselers, and pondering a move to suburbia to get away from the city's poor schools and high crime rates. All Washington did was take the hard-earned dollars of working people and give them to the undeserving poor. This conservative appeal was addressed to one half of America's split political personality. Lloyd A. Free and Hadley Cantril in *The Political Beliefs of Americans* (1967) showed that ideologically Americans are conservative, believers in small government, but operationally they are liberal, supporters of a wide range of spending programs and government regulation of big business. In the seventies and eighties, the conservative personality prevailed. Benjamin I. Page and

Robert Y. Shapiro in their detailed study of fifty years of public opinion, *The Rational Public* (1992), suggest that was in part because the public was misled by "a massive and misleading public relations campaign" to blame inflation and rising taxes on "vast increases" in public spending. If not quite a campaign, there was informal consensus to this effect and it did oversimplify the relationship between deficits and inflation. Spending in these years was stable as a percentage of GNP and it was low in relation to the proportions in other industrial countries. All the same, the fallacies were absorbed into the conventional wisdom. The apparent endorsement in the 1980 elections then led many commentators and revisionist Democrats to agree that the electorate had once and for all repudiated the New Deal welfare state and the most important components of the Great Society. That is not what happened. It is an extrapolation too far.

Thomas Ferguson and Joel Rogers examined a variety of polling data for their book *Right Turn: The Decline of the Democrats and the Future of American Politics* (1986) and foreshadowed Page and Shapiro. A high and generally stable level of support persisted for government action on social security, education (especially), jobs, medical care, the cities, the environment and consumer safety, coupled with a surprising willingness to pay taxes for these purposes. By early 1983 a CBS/*New York Times* poll reported that 74 percent favored a public jobs program even if it meant increasing the federal deficit. Even after Reagan's landslide reelection in 1984, only 35 percent of Americans favored reducing the deficit by substantial cuts in social programs. The shift in public policy was not matched, therefore, by a shift in public opinion. This was little consolation for the battered Democrats. Though reluctant to abandon New Deal policies, voters were disenchanted by Democratic management of the economy. Reagan, after all, brought inflation down with a bump and did so without dismantling the major liberal programs. Harvard's Hugh Heclo suggests that much as FDR and the New Deal had the effect of preserving capitalism, "so Reaganism will eventually be seen to have helped preserve a predominantly status quo, middle-class welfare state."

On the social side, the evidence suggests that America tilted right on questions of law and order, including drugs, capital punishment, school prayer, pornography and the flag. Support for harsher penalties for criminals increased in the seventies and eighties, but again the scrutineers of the polls concur that in other ways public opinion remained steadfastly liberal. "Religion, feminism, civil liberties, abortion and race

relations are the policy areas in which the public has shown the sharpest increase in liberalism since World War II. The rate of increase has slowed during the post-1973 period, but at no time has the public actually become more conservative on these issues" (Ferguson and Rogers). Recent studies, including Alan Wolfe's *One Nation After All* (1998), have confirmed this impression of an American public broadly more tolerant than ever before in American history.

The conservative electoral ascension was, of course, real enough, even if generalizations about the rightist mood of the country were oversimplified. But there was this other reason for Reagan's success: a politics of resentment whose modern impresario was neither an Austrian economist nor a Connecticut country squire, but George C. Wallace. It was Wallace, taking a leaf from the Southern Bourbons against the turn-of-the-century Populists, who showed in 1964 and 1968 how white working- and middle-class men and women could be turned into what would later be called "Reagan Democrats" through appeals to their antiblack sentiments. It was Wallace who gave the Republicans a clear winning strategy by shifting the South nearly as solidly into the GOP's column after 1976 as it had once been in the Democratic camp. It was Wallace who had first ranted against "pointy-headed" bureaucrats and intellectuals, a theme that Reagan brilliantly exploited—albeit in a more gentle, anecdotal, less obviously racial style. "Southerners saw in him," wrote Wayne Greenshaw in *Elephants in the Cotton Fields,* "something they had seen in the former Golden Gloves champion George C. Wallace. Perhaps Ronald Reagan never stated his position as strongly, but they knew exactly what he meant when he spilled out his own brand of rhetoric." Nor was it simply that southerners could be persuaded to vote Republican. Northerners, too, could be persuaded to vote on the basis of race. Kevin Phillips had grasped the point years earlier in his seminal work *The Emerging Republican Majority* (1967). Politics was all about whom you hate—"that is the secret."

There was overwhelming national acceptance of the ideal, enshrined in the Civil Rights Act of 1964, that no individual should suffer in applying for a job or a college place because of race, color, religion, sex or national origin. It was also widely accepted that for a time affirmative action was justified to recruit among disadvantaged minorities as a remedy for historical injustice. But the identity politics of ethnic grievance encouraged by the liberal elites distorted these original good intentions. By the end of the seventies, great offense had been caused by the system of quotas, which penalized the white male. The first key decision was the Supreme Court ruling in 1971 in *Griggs v. Duke Power Company*. It exposed employers to prosecution if "disparate impact analysis" could demonstrate that the racial composition of a workforce did not match the racial balance in the surrounding community. There was no need to prove intent to discriminate. If his presence disturbed the numerical ratios, a white male who was more qualified for a job or a college place would lose the equal protection of the Fourteenth Amendment and the specific protection of the Civil Rights Act. This was dangerous ground.

Allan Paul Bakke, 38, was a Vietnam vet and NASA engineer who decided to go to medical school. Despite high test scores, he was judged old to launch such a career, and he had trouble gaining admittance. When the University of California at Davis seemed inclined to turn him down, Bakke sued, noting that he had higher qualifications than any of the 16 minority members guaranteed acceptance in places reserved for "disadvantaged" students. The Supreme Court (*Regents of the University of California v. Bakke*) fudged a ruling in 1978. It decided 5–4 that state universities could not set aside a fixed quota of seats in each class for minority group members. Bakke should be admitted. At the same time, the Court also ruled that the Fourteenth Amendment did not bar colleges from considering race as one factor in achieving diversity in a student body. "Diversity" thus replaced equality of opportunity and color-blind antidiscrimination policies.

The case was trickier than conservatives made it out to be. Colleges already had preferences that perpetuated the white majority, notably the preferments for "legacies" (the children of alumni) or athletes—practices that continue today. Nor were there any complaints when veterans received extra "points" toward college admissions and civil service jobs. Davis routinely used geography to assure a diverse student body. If a university could admit someone because he came from Montana, why not admit someone to right a historical wrong? Just what, after all, was so sacred about the SAT and related exams? Affirmative action advocates would note in years to follow that Allan Bakke ended up in a part-time practice in cosmetic surgery while the black man chosen "instead" of him became a dedicated general practitioner serving a low-income neighborhood. Still, there was no escaping the public support for Bakke. It was hard to defend settling historical scores on the backs of living people, however infrequently it happened. Some millions of white people seemed to know a friend of a brother or a cousin who

had been passed up for a job or a college slot or training program for an obviously less well qualified black or Hispanic. Multiculturalism, as it was developed in the 1970s and 1980s, was a wrong turning for the Democrats. It was unfair—and it broke up the New Deal coalition between blacks and white ethnics. A better alternative to the tokenism of preferences would have been a renewal of money and programs to attack individual discrimination and raise all members of the underclass. But that would have been expensive, and it would have required more determination, energy and unity of vision than liberals then possessed.

Busing was more explosive still. It led to an ugly, years-long siege in and around the dilapidated Irish ethnic neighborhood of South Boston and a few other white enclaves. The issue nationally was how to give black children an equal education when most of the white children and the money had fled to the suburbs, leaving inner-city schools predominantly black and poor. A study by the University of Chicago's James S. Coleman reported that the students' family background, not the school budget, was the main determinant of success. But Coleman also showed that black children seemed to do better when mixed with whites. Liberals went to the courts to achieve integration by busing. It was an issue that smoldered without flame in Boston until Judge W. Arthur Garrity ruled on May 10, 1975, that the number of students bused had to be increased from 14,900 to 25,000. Then riots erupted. In his balanced, soul-searching study of the Boston crisis, *Common Ground,* J. Anthony Lukas concluded that "solutions" like busing could work only if they were perceived as fair by a substantial constituency and implemented by skilled managers. Otherwise, they could produce consequences the opposite of what the reformers intended—such as increased white flight from city schools. Since Boston, better answers have emerged to keep middle-class white students in public schools. Many parents have welcomed the chance to enroll their children in "magnet schools" of high quality where the racial mix is balanced. But here, again, the liberal imagination faltered when it was most needed.

In the seventies, when tensions were high, Reagan and his advisers saw how vulnerable the Democrats had become and sent appropriate signals to flag down the Southern votes in particular. Reagan was not a bigot himself, but he agreed to open his 1980 campaign in the obscure Southern town of Philadelphia, Mississippi, where civil rights workers James Chaney, Andrew Goodman and Michael Schwerner had been murdered 16 years before. The symbolism was unmistakable. His speech made no mention of their names, or of civil rights. It was the same strategy that had taken him in 1979 to a Dallas meeting of Moral Majority, a group formed in the wake of the IRS ruling on Christian schools. "I know you can't endorse me," he told them, "but I want you to know that I endorse you and what you are doing." The efforts of Reagan (and later Bush) to reverse the trend in affirmative action away from number-oriented hiring and admission was one thing, and defensible, but racial populism was the dark side of the nostalgia for the good old days. Given Reagan's character, it can only be explained—like so much in his presidency—by his capacity for innocent self-deception. The man who made his career telling anecdotes of government excess and waste did nothing to curb either in his two terms. On the contrary, the national debt rose from $908.5 billion to nearly $2.7 *trillion* in his administration. The number of federal employees increased by over 200,000. The trade deficit soared fourfold to $137.3 billion. It was not only big government, it was often bad government playing fast and loose with the public money in financial scandals of a scale unmatched in Washington since the Harding administration. It was almost as if Reagan wanted to prove how corrupt big government could be, presiding over major scandals in Housing and Urban Development, the Environmental Protection Agency, Pentagon procurement and the S&L balloon. This was a president who spoke constantly of his deep religious devotion but rarely attended church; a president who pledged his wholehearted support to the right-to-life movement, then never made a serious attempt to push an anti-abortion bill through Congress; a candidate who had specifically pledged to shut down the Energy and Education departments and left them with their biggest budgets yet. Under Reagan the normal creative tension of democratic politics often seemed like a set of parallel lines, doomed never to meet, wandering out into cognitive dissonance.

Reaganism turned out to be something new in American politics: a form of state capitalism in which the services of a large federal government were put behind the wealthiest and most powerful private interests in the country. Reagan's income tax cuts proved illusory for all except the rich. In fact, a sharp increase in the regressive social security tax in 1983 and higher state and local taxes actually increased the total tax burden on the average family in the conservative eighties. Poor children were badly affected. Income for the

ALL MY OWN WORK: Ben Sargent's *Texas Monthly* cartoon of Reagan the proud rooster.

bottom 10 percent of families fell by 10.5 percent from 1977 to 1987, Lou Cannon reported in *Role of a Lifetime*. The top 10 percent gained 24.4 percent and the top 1 percent some 74.2 percent.

Reagan left office in the glow of his meetings with the last Soviet leader Mikhail Gorbachev, with high ratings and the warm affection of the American people. But the disparities he left behind created deeper divisions in American life, just as the more divisive conservative rhetoric that accompanied his tenure helped erode the idea of a common polity, a common good. And the end of the Soviet threat dissolved much of the glue of the conservative coalition. After Reagan himself had gone, the stasis of his era soon broke up into a search for new answers, however inchoate, spurred on by the onset of an extended recession. The quest threw up such characters as Jack Kemp, Steve Forbes, Pat Buchanan, Ross Perot (the incarnation of "none of the above")—and, of course, Bill Clinton—suggesting superficially at least that American politics was fragmenting, as in the 1910s, 1950s and 1960s, when there were at least two wings to each major party and several nascent third-party movements. Buchanan and his socially conservative isolationists opposed Bush's New World Order and Kemp's free-trade libertarians. Wealthy Clinton social liberals opposed blue-collar protectionist Democrats. The religious right despaired of remaking the Republican party in its image and threatened to go it alone. But the ferment reflected a search for solutions within the traditional limits of democratic politics, and therein suggested that America was thriving as the new century approached.

RONALD WILSON REAGAN
40th President (Republican), 1981–1989

"In other news today, 89 percent of the workforce is not unemployed."
Cartoon by Paul Conrad.

BORN: February 6, 1911, Tampico, Illinois

POLITICAL CAREER: Governor of California, 1967–1975; President, 1981–1989

FIRSTS: First president to have been divorced. First to have been a lifetime member of an AFL-CIO union. First elected when he was over 70.

CHARACTER SNAPSHOTS: "The actor in him loved applause, but he saw these as testimonials to his performance, rather than approval of his personality. Of the larger conceits that plague most politicians—the craving for credit, the thrill of power for power's sake—he had none at all. Never was so much id combined with so little ego."
—Biographer Edmund Morris

"Reagan does not argue for American values. He embodies them."   —Garry Wills

SAVING LIVES: His parents moved ten times. From the age of nine he lived happily in the small town of Dixon, Illinois. For the rest of his life he was true to the words he wrote below his picture in the high school yearbook: "Life is just one grand sweet song, so start the music." He hiked the hills, canoed the Rock River, watched the bird life, drew cartoons, played right guard in football, became a champion swimmer, fed elephants at 4 a.m. as a circus roustabout, and at 15 talked himself into a summer job as a lifeguard at Lowell Park on the Rock River. He notched a stick for every life he saved and ended up with 77. Even after falling victim to Alzheimer's disease in the 1990s, he could still recall what he did on the banks of the river waiting for a rescue call. At Eureka (Illinois) College from 1928 to 1932 he waited on tables to earn his way, barely got passing grades in economics and sociology. But he was a popular figure, chosen in freshman year as the spokesman for students in a strike against academic cutbacks and dancing that led to the resignation of the college president.

MAKING STORIES: For five years, from 1932 to 1937, he was into make-believe as a sportscaster. First at Davenport, Iowa, and then Des Moines, he gave the listener an exciting description of a major league baseball or Big Ten football game he could not see. He visualized it for the unsuspecting listener from telegraph copy. Once, when the wire went dead in the ninth inning, he extemporized for six minutes and forty-five seconds describing nonexistent action. He became a regional celebrity: this is a promotional postcard featuring the nonsmoking Reagan with pipe and dog to please the tobacco sponsor.

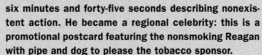

JOKES AND PRAYER: A whopping ten pounds at birth in a rented flat over a bank in tiny Tampico, he is two here, with his older brother, Neil, his Irish Catholic father, Jack, and mother, Nelle, in 1913. His nickname "Dutch" came from Jack's boasts about his "fat little Dutchman." Jack was a natty, wisecracking small-town shoe salesman with dreams of owning his own store, and an open-minded FDR Democrat who spoke out when he encountered racial or religious bigotry. He was also a sporadic drunk. Dutch was Momma's boy. Unlike his brother, he stayed with his mother's church, the Disciples of Christ. She was a true believer and faith healer who visited prisons and mental hospitals, but she was also a frustrated actress, given to zesty dramatic readings. Dutch, pushed by her into church skits, discovered he loved applause. She had taught him to read by the time he was five and he lost himself in boys' adventure stories. He did well at grade school. A photographic memory helped him cope with undiagnosed myopia.

THE GIPPER: Warner Brothers was so impressed with his 1937 screen test they gave him a seven-year contract at $200 a week, a big boost from Des Moines. He was to appear in some 54 movies over 27 years. He became a star in quick, low-budget movies, a reliable supporting player in the more ambitious productions, and only once, uneasily, as a bad guy. He came to notice first in *Knute Rockne—All American* (1940) playing Notre Dame tailback George Gipp, who on his deathbed tells the coach, "Maybe you can ask the boys to go in there and win just one for the Gipper." In between takes of another movie, *Brother Rat and a Baby* (1940), he proposed to actress Jane Wyman. They were married on January 26, 1940—with him here with their daughter, Maureen, on his way to report for duty as a second lieutenant in the Army Reserve. Barred from combat by his eyesight, he spent the war in California making war propaganda and training films. The heroic stories made such an impression on his mind he could never thereafter acknowledge they were fantasy. He was fond of saying that the heroic act of a Negro kitchen hand at Pearl Harbor, cradling a machine gun in his arms, ended segregation in the armed services. The fact that it didn't happen and segregation persisted until 1948 made no difference to him.

MODEL MAN: In 1940, he is 29, newly married, a rising movie star and the choice model of the art students at the University of Southern California. Professor Merrel Gage's class saw still pictures of him in the role of George Gipp and chose him for their portrait of a twentieth-century Adonis possessing the most nearly perfect male figure. Reagan had a 32-inch waist and a 41-inch chest, stood six-foot-one and weighed 180 pounds.

NANCY: Jane Wyman pained him by winning a divorce in 1948. "Me and you, Ronnie," she said, "we ran out of gas." In court papers, she complained that he talked about politics at every meal. She blamed his preoccupation with the Screen Actors Guild: he was twice president and a good negotiator. In 1949 he met actress Nancy Davis, stepdaughter of a conservative surgeon, and began a long, happy marriage on March 4, 1952. He was already beyond his father's instinctive hostility to big business and appalled by strike violence at the Warner gates. Having campaigned for Harry Truman in 1948, he abandoned Helen Douglas in midcampaign in her 1950 Senate race and worked surreptitiously for Nixon. He said later he was sickened by the attempted Communist takeover of movies, "which a lot of my liberal friends refused to admit ever happened." He secretly gave names for the FBI to investigate and supported the blacklist.

GE'S MAN: From 1954, he was for 8 years host and occasional actor in the General Electric Theater on Sunday-night television. Soon he took up the sword for capitalism (the still is him as George Custer in *The Santa Fe Trail*). He visited all 139 GE plants, making 9,000 speeches. The grumbles he heard about regulation and high taxes fell on the sympathetic ears of a high taxpayer. His stock speech became more and more a crusade for the free enterprise system against big government and communism: he was still making McCarthyite speeches years after McCarthy's disgrace. The "near hopeless hemophiliac liberal" Democrat who "bled for causes" became a vehement spokesman for the New Right. He still idolized FDR, but argued he would not have let the bureaucracy grow after the war. In 1960, Dutch was a Democrat for Nixon against Kennedy, but he was closer to the Goldwater wing. He joined the Republican party in 1962.

CITIZEN GOVERNOR: On October 27, 1964, he had liftoff from a single electrifying speech on conservative values, called "A Time for Choosing." Commentator David Broder judged it the most successful debut since William Jennings Bryan's 1896 "Cross of Gold" speech. It attracted record contributions for Barry Goldwater, running against Johnson, but with Goldwater's defeat Reagan was the new hero of the right. In 1966, he beat incumbent Pat Brown by a million votes to become governor of California. "How will I do as governor? Dunno. Never played governor before." He sent National Guardsmen to put down rioting on the campuses of the University of California, fired its president, lowered faculty salaries, talked with protesters, vetoed bills to decriminalize small amounts of marijuana. He found the state was broke and fixed it by raising taxes and cutting welfare rolls by 200,000. His rhetoric was fiercer than his record. Over the course of two terms, he bargained well with the Democratic legislature. The cut-and-slash campaigner ended with a doubled state budget (and doubled state taxes) and 5 percent more staff. He increased all education spending, signed a liberal abortion law, granted conjugal visiting rights to prisoners, helped defeat a ban on homosexual teachers in public schools, backed Redwood National Park and advanced more Mexicans and blacks than any of his predecessors. In 1976, he nearly took the Republican presidential nomination from President Ford. In the photograph (left) he waves to spectators lining the streets in East Los Angeles during a parade commemorating the 157th anniversary of Mexican independence from Spanish rule.

LIGHT FANTASTIC: The Reagans fox-trotting at the White House, said *Vanity Fair,* had Fred-and-Gingered up the social life of America. Harry Benson took the special set-up photograph in May 1985 on the night of a state dinner.

JOKERS: It was ever thus. The president has pulled another joke out of the hat and Diana Walker's photograph confirms another winner. Everyone there remembers the moment, but nobody in the picture was willing to repeat the joke so that it could be shared with posterity. The laugh-in was at a White House champagne party for Walter Cronkite after his final appearance as the CBS news anchor. Left to right: President Reagan; Cronkite; Press Secre-

DID YOU HEAR THE ONE ABOUT THE DEFICIT?

He had a joke for everything. In the election, he said: "A recession is when your neighbor loses his job. A depression is when you lose yours. And recovery is when Jimmy Carter loses his." It did not work out that way. By the end of 1981, Ronald Reagan was presiding over the deepest recession since the Great Depression. He had promised a balanced budget by 1984 and never in eight years submitted a single one. When his fiscal policy produced a record imbalance, first doubling then tripling the national debt, he managed a rueful grin: "I'm not worried about the deficit—it's big enough to take care of itself." He blamed Congress anyway. "Presidents don't create deficits; Congress does." Some of the one-liners were borrowed chestnuts made tolerable on repe-

tition by his delight in the telling, but he had a spontaneous wit and amazing resilience. With an assassin's bullet in his lung less than an inch from his heart, he looked up at the doctors about to operate and murmured, "I hope you're all Republicans." In the recovery room, when he had a tube in his throat, he blitzed the nurses with scribbled notes: "I'd like to do this scene again—starting at the hotel." And: "Send me to L.A. where I can see the air I'm breathing." Another pink-paper note paraphrased W. C. Fields dodging Sioux arrows: "All in all, I'd rather be in Philadelphia."

It was easy not to take him seriously. One of the few unions to endorse Reagan, PATCO, the air traffic control union, made that mistake within months of his

election. Thirteen thousand of the 17,000 federal air traffic controllers in the powerful union walked out on August 3, 1981, for more money than they had been offered. This broke a law passed by Congress and a no-strike pledge signed by every member of the union. Reagan gave them 48 hours to go back to work. Then he fired them all. He drafted military controllers. It took two years to train new controllers, but flying was not disrupted, PATCO was dead and the union movement had suffered its worst setback in decades. "I would have been just as forceful," he wrote later, "if I thought management had been wrong in that dispute."

His next trick was to present a dramatic budget, cutting personal and corporate taxes by 30 percent over three years and

tary Jim Brady (obscured); Director of Communications David Gergen; Attorney General Ed Meese; Vice President George Bush; Chief of Staff Jim Baker; and in the foreground CBS producer Ben Benjamin.

HONEY, I FORGOT TO DUCK: Grace under pressure. The words were originally Jack Dempsey's, explaining to his wife why he lost a big fight. Reagan conjured them up again when he opened his eyes in the hospital to see Nancy, shortly after he was wounded by one of John Hinckley, Jr.'s bullets on March 30, 1981. Reagan did not know he had been hit. Leaving the Hilton Hotel (right), he heard a small, fluttery *pop-pop-pop,* and found himself bundled into the limo by Jerry Parr, the head of the Secret Service unit. He might well have died, and the slowness of his recovery was concealed from the public. Press Secretary James S. Brady suffered permanent brain damage. His wife launched a gun-control crusade that Reagan later supported. Of Hinckley, he wrote in 1990: "I asked the Lord to heal him, and I still do." The immediate political fallout was a setback for Alexander Haig, the secretary of state. In a well-meaning intrusion to answer a press conference question within the confused first hour, he declared: "As of now I am in control, here in the White House, pending return of the vice president [who was in the air] and in close touch with him. If something came up, I would check with him of course."

It was unexceptional, but the frenzied way he said it made waves. "I'm in control here" became a national joke.

Photographs by Ron Edmonds.

adding billions to military spending. The Democratic leadership just knew he would be hopeless in the cut and thrust of detail. But Reagan said what he meant and meant what he said. With the help of Southern "Boll Weevil" Democrats, he got the budget through the Democratic House more or less unchanged: taxes were cut 25 percent over three years, the largest in American history, with most of the gains going to the better off. His polished and pragmatic chief of staff, James Baker, worked 16-hour days massaging Congress and press, but that spring the notoriously indolent Reagan himself—"They say hard work never killed anyone, but I figure why risk it?"—had 69 meetings jawboning 467 members of Congress. They said they saw more of him in four months than of Carter in four years.

Reagan's grasp of the details was minimal. In November 1981, his budget director David Stockman, 35, dropped a bomb in the pages of the *Atlantic.* He told William Greider he had changed the Office of Management and Budget computers to reflect the optimistic assumptions of Reagan's budget he did not really share. The budget was really a "Trojan horse" to reduce the top tax rate from 70 to 50 percent. And the deficit? It was all a mystery: "None of us really understands what's going on with all these numbers."

Reagan found it hard to fire mavericks. Stockman stayed on and when he finally resigned wrote a devastating critique of Reaganomics. Reagan remained loyal to James G. Watt, his wild interior secretary, who called environmentalists "Nazis" but that was only a warm-up for a series of tongue lashings. He was finally forced out by a storm over his remark about the membership of one of his commissions: "I have a black, I have a woman, two Jews and a cripple."

Once the budget battle was over, Reagan stayed aloof from day-to-day management, almost always passively accepting the promptings of his kitchen cabinet— Baker, Ed Meese and Michael Deaver (with Nancy whispering in his ear). Al Haig, whose thin skin finally cost him his job as secretary of state in 1982, summed up the atmosphere this way in his memoir, ghosted by Charles McCarry: "To me the White House was as mysterious as a ghost ship; you heard the creak of the rigging and the groan of the timber, and sometimes even glimpsed the crew on deck. But which of the crew had the helm? Was it Meese, was it Baker, was it someone else? It was impossible to know for sure."

In the end, it was Captain Reagan.

THE RISE OF THE RELIGIOUS RIGHT

When Sandra Day O'Connor, a conservative appeals court judge in Arizona, was named by President Reagan in July 1981 as the first woman justice on the Supreme Court, there was a loud raspberry from a new political movement in American politics. It called itself the Moral Majority. Its president, the latest in muscular Christianity, was a fundamentalist preacher by the name of the Rev. Jerry Falwell. It was offensive, Falwell declared, for Reagan to nominate someone who as a state senator had backed legislation to propagate medically approved family planning methods. All "good Christians" should object to such a libertine on the highest court in the land. Barry Goldwater, O'Connor's sponsor, responded: "Every good Christian ought to kick Falwell right in the ass."

It was a typically forthright response from Goldwater, and brave in the circumstances. Moral Majority was just over two years old but it had made itself felt since the night that Falwell, flying back to his flock in Lynchburg, Virginia, got a call through the darkness from the Lord God. Falwell, who had condemned Martin Luther King in the decade before for the whole idea of mixing politics and religion, was now apparently divinely instructed to do just that, in particular to bring "the good people of America" together in a Christian crusade to fight the pollution of America's public schools by "pornography, obscenity, vulgarity, and profanity under the guise of sex education and 'values clarification.' " Actually, the stimulus was an IRS ruling that exposed private Christian (segregated) schools to taxation.

The organization's name was the brainchild of the conservative activist Paul Weyrich. It was a shrewd stroke, combining intimations of Reagan triumphalism with the old Nixonian resentments of the Silent Majority. The right wing had been trying for years to harness the souls and dollars of religious conservatives, and it was rewarded in 1980 when Moral Majority came out of the gate running. It worked to elect Reagan and targeted major liberal senators—George McGovern of South Dakota, Frank Church of Idaho, Birch Bayh of Indiana, Gaylord Nelson of Wisconsin, John Culver of Iowa, Warren Magnuson of Washington and Alan Cranston of California. Only Cranston survived.

Moral Majority was notorious for taking more than its share of the credit in any right-wing victory. The Democrats suffered mostly from weakness at the top of the ticket and the general confusion of liberalism. Still, Moral Majority's effect was real. Four-term Senator Church's defeat by fewer than 4,000 votes was in good part due to a door-to-door campaign run by a zealous Baptist minister, Buddy Hoffman. Ronald Reagan was so eager to have Moral Majority's support in 1980 that he expressed skepticism about evolution and came close to repudiating the historic separation of church and state.

The Rev. Jerry Falwell by the baptismal waterslide in Heritage Park, South Carolina, in 1987. Falwell built his congregation from a handful of Christians meeting in a bottling plant to a church with 18,000 members and a Liberty University with 1,500 students. His "Old-Time Gospel Hour" on Liberty Broadcasting Network reached 1.5 million subscribers. In 1997 he used it to propagate the fantasy that President Clinton plotted to murder White House counsel Vincent Foster. Photograph by Rob Nelson.

Many of the Christians making a noise on the right were Southern fundamentalists, descendants of the crowd at the Scopes trial who believed in the literal word-for-word truth of the Bible. Others were conservative evangelicals and Catholics united in concern over the 1962 Supreme Court ruling (*Engel v. Vitale*) striking down all oral prayers and Bible readings in public classrooms, and by the 1973 abortion ruling. They did not speak for the entire body of Christians. Congregations in the multi-ethnic north generally evolved into what Martin E. Marty calls the "four-faith pluralism" of liberal Protestantism, Catholicism, Judaism and secular humanism. They were more tolerant and more intellectually curious than they had ever been. They supported civil rights, lobbied government on behalf of the poor, questioned militarism and nuclear strategy. Some endorsed aspects of women's liberation, even aspects of gay liberation.

The fundamentalists and their allies recoiled from such free thinking. They felt besieged by every touch of modernism. They saw the undeniable flood of drugs, prostitution, violent crime, pornographic display and violence in schools as a consequence of moral dissolution. And Southern fundamentalists still smoldered over the *Brown* ruling. In the words of Alabama Congressman George Andrews, "They put Negroes in the schools and now they're driving God out." The frustrations showed in the figures. While "mainstream" church membership dropped several million between 1965 and 1980, the numbers for the Southern Baptist convention rose from 10.8 million to 13.6 million.

The anger was at first inchoate. Ironically, it was the media of the hated modern world that gave the fundamentalists a focus and political clout. The Federal Communications Commission decided in the early 1970s for the first time that the religious hours it stipulated could be filled by paid religious advertising. By 1980, 90 percent of all religion on television was commercial and almost all of it was controlled by conservative evangelicals with a far more political message than the early televangelists Billy Graham and Rex Humbard. In 1978, some 25 Christian ministries were broadcasting regularly on television. By 1989 there were 336—and 36 of them were being audited by the IRS.

Many of the new televangelists fell easily into the eighties penchant for luxury, not to mention hypocrisy. The first lapses came in the spring of 1987. They performed as sinners in sex-and-money cliches, as if Elmer Gantry had traded in the Chautauqua circuit for an electronic pulpit. South Carolina's Rev. Jim Bakker, who ran a TV ministry called the PTL Club (probably Praise the Lord) and had an annual income of at least $1.6 million, confessed to an affair with a young volunteer—who then posed nude for *Penthouse* magazine and betrayed enough of his business affairs to have him convicted on 24 counts of fraud and conspiracy in 1984. He was sentenced to 45 years in prison. The Rev. Jimmy Swaggart, who borrowed $2 million from his own ministry to build himself three houses, went on TV with his own sobbing jag and confession about an illicit affair with a New Orleans prostitute.

Of more significance than these melodramas was the bigotry of the fundamentalists, harking back to their old nativist origins. "With all due respect to those dear people," said the Rev. Bailey Smith, president of the Southern Baptist Convention, "God does not hear the prayer of a Jew." Falwell said the same thing in the 1980 campaign. In 1994, the Anti-Defamation League reported that Pat Robertson—by this time the leading televangelist—had told a prayer meeting that Jews were "spiritually deaf" and "spiritually blind."

It was only the fingertip of his anti-Semitism. Michael Lind, in an eye-opening article for *The New York Review of Books* on February 2, 1995, found extensive evidence of even hoarier and more insidious hatreds in Robertson's writings, particularly in his 1991 volume, *The New World Order*. It was little more than a glossy, dressed-up, smiley-face version of *The Protocols of the Elders of Zion*, blaming every trouble from the Civil War to the Cold War on a vast conspiracy of Freemasons, Illuminati, and Jewish-American bankers running up "compound interest." His denunciations of usury were bizarre in the light of his own vast financial empire. All this fitted in, Lind pointed out, with an earlier Robertson book (*The New Millennium*, 1990) where he warned "cosmopolitan, liberal secular Jews" of the fate they would suffer for assaulting Christianity with smut and pornography and the murder of the unborn. Again and again, Robertson made it clear just how careful Jews

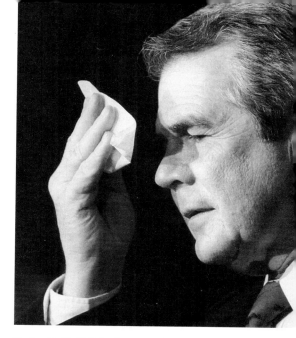

Marion G. "Pat" Robertson was the first major religious leader in American history actively to seek a major party presidential nomination. In 1988, he shook George Bush by coming in first in Iowa, ahead of Bush and just behind Senator Bob Dole. Here he sweats it out for the results of Super Tuesday primaries. They were not so good, but with key aide Ralph Reed the defeated candidate went on to organize the Christian Coalition as a vibrant, tax-exempt successor to Falwell's Moral Majority. He had 33 million subscribers to his Christian Broadcasting Network. The Christian Coalition became adept at highly organized, stealth campaigns at levels of politics as low as school boards. Photograph by Joe Holloway.

should be in America. No leading conservative rushed to denounce Robertson's hate speech, but the Church Martial began to scare Americans in the late eighties. Increasingly, notably outside the South, politicians trumpeted as "born again" began to fall. They had alienated millions of Jewish, Catholic, female and young urban voters who might otherwise have been attracted to their conservative financial policies.

Whether the fundamentalists' missionary zeal will outpace the growing number of non-Christian and Catholic immigrants to the United States is an open question. It seems certain that the religious right will remain a highly motivated group, but the consequences are less clear. The very act of participating in the political process lures people into compromise and even moderation. This is the genius of democracy, American democracy; if the Christian Coalition and its friends evade such lures they will be the first major political participant to do so.

THE RIGHT-TO-LIFE CONFLICTS

In the homey setting of an Austin garage sale, two doctoral students at the University of Texas got into conversation with a brilliant 24-year-old graduate named Sarah Weddington. The students, Judy Smith and Bea Vogel, had started a birth control information center and didn't know how to advise all the women who asked about abortions. Weddington was not sure either and consulted an attorney and friend, Linda Coffee. They decided to challenge the state law that allowed abortion only when a mother's life was in danger. A third lawyer, Henry J. McCluskey, Jr., provided the plaintiff. She was Norma McCorvey, 21, a ticket seller in a traveling carnival, pregnant with a third, unwanted child. She headed for fame with the name she took for privacy: Jane Roe.

On March 3, 1970, Coffee went to the Dallas federal courthouse and filed the complaint *Roe v. Wade* (Wade being the Dallas district attorney) at a cost of $15 from her own pocket.

When the young Texas team eventually came to argue *Roe* before the Supreme Court, they stood on the shoulders of another determined woman, Estelle Trebert Griswold, whose fight against Connecticut's ban on birth control devices or information, traced by David Garrow in *Liberty and Sexuality,* altered the entire American idea of freedom. Griswold, a singer turned medical technologist, described even by her friends as "super-aggressive," teamed up with Dr. Charles Lee Buxton, a professor at Yale Medical School, and they adopted a strategy devised by their attorneys, Fowler Harper and Katie Roraback. Harper was an irascible, maverick law professor at Yale who liked to drink, roll the dice and play poker and had led crusades against McCarthyist prosecutions; Roraback was the daughter of a Congregationalist minister and one of Connecticut's leading Republicans.

This unlikely couple sensed a potential in the Ninth Amendment: "The enumeration in the Constitution of certain rights, shall not be construed to deny or disparage others retained by the people." Surely, they argued, no right could be more intrinsic to the people than the right to the privacy of their bedroom: "There must be a limit to the extent to which the moral scruples of a minority, for that matter a majority, can be enacted into laws which regulate the sex life of all married peoples."

What Harper was after, a right to privacy, was spelled out nowhere in the Constitution. The Supreme Court giants Oliver Wendell Holmes and Louis Brandeis had written of "the right to be left alone," but no Court had quite dared to make it explicit in law. Hammering together aspects of the Fifth, Sixth and Fourteenth Amendments in a breezy opinion from William O. Douglas, the Warren Court determined in 1965 that there was indeed a right to privacy. It ruled for Griswold by 7–2.

VICTIM: Dr. John Bayard Britton, 69, in his bullet-proof vest, photographed by Mary Ellen Mark. He and a clinic escort, James H. Barrett, 74, a retired Air Force lieutenant colonel, were shot dead in 1994 in Pensacola, Florida. It was the third murder of an abortion doctor in Florida. A federal law guaranteeing access to abortion clinics was enacted in May 1994, but the campaign of violence continued—30,000 anti-abortion activists were arrested between 1987 and 1989. They succeeded in limiting the number of abortion doctors and clinics and making legal abortion an impossibility again for millions of American women.

On January 22, 1973, by which time McCorvey had given birth, the Supreme Court accepted Weddington's argument that the "Griswold" right to privacy encompassed a woman's right to do as she chose with her own body—within limits. Did Roe have a right to an abortion? Justice Harry Blackmun, speaking for the 7–2 majority, said that not until the point at which another potential life was at risk could the state "assert interests beyond the protection of the pregnant woman alone." The Court was thereby forced to answer the question: When does life begin? It noted that those trained in the disciplines of medicine, philosophy and religion could not agree when a fetus becomes a person, so it made "viability" its point of definition. In the first two trimesters, a fetus could not be expected to survive outside the womb. Abortion in this period was not taking a life. Only in the last trimester might a state "go so far as to proscribe abortion . . . except when it is necessary to preserve the life or health of the mother." Laws presuming that the fetus becomes a person at conception were invalid because the fetus was not viable. In other words, a woman could do what she wanted with her body up to three months of pregnancy, and maybe beyond, depending on the state law where she lived.

The ruling, misreported as "abortion on demand," nonetheless invalidated the abortion laws in 30 states. It touched off a national right-to-life crusade, united in revulsion but diverse in expression. Protesters prayed and marched, grilled candidates, harassed patients. Dorothy Toth Beasley, an opposing attorney in the related case *Doe v. Bolton* cemented the battle lines. The "real liberty" being sought, she declared, was "the right to destroy a living child without state interference." The child within a woman's body was not part of her and/or her body; from its earliest stage it was already a boy or girl. Did the right to privacy embrace an unlimited freedom "to so invade another's right to privacy that he may be exterminated?"

Despite the more extreme reaction, Blackmun's opinion represented a judicious compromise that was typical of the Court during the Warren and early Burger years. Again and again, the Supreme Court served as a lightning rod taking on and at least partially defusing explosive issues. The question remained: What would happen on the fast-approaching day when medical technology made the *Roe* compromise meaningless?

The rally was called the International Day of Action for Reproductive Rights. Photograph by Ann Chwatsky.

THE
MORAL
MAJORITY
IS
NEITHER

INTERN...
DAY OF
ACTION
FOR
REPRODUC...
RIGHTS

abortion
A Woman's Right
carasa

THE MARINES GO IN AGAIN

INVASION TELECON: Reagan made the decision to invade Grenada while on a golfing weekend in Augusta, Georgia, after he was awakened at 2:45 a.m. on October 22, 1983. The call was from Secretary Shultz and NSC Adviser McFarlane, patching through six Caribbean prime ministers. In his bathrobe and slippers, he talked to Vice President Bush and gave the go-ahead just before dawn. Photograph by Doug Mathieson.

"Send in the Marines!" Reagan seemed to have done it with effect in Lebanon in 1982. At dawn on August 25, 800 Marines joined French and Italian troops in Beirut to oversee a peace based on the expulsion of 10,000 Palestinian Liberation Organization guerrillas who had provoked an Israeli invasion. Reagan had already made his humanitarianism felt. Horrified by television pictures of victims of the Israeli bombing of Beirut, he had put in an impromptu call to Israel's Prime Minister Menachem Begin to denounce the bombing as a "holocaust." Twenty minutes later Begin phoned back. The bombing was over. "I didn't know I had that kind of power," Reagan remarked to Michael Deaver, his public relations counsel.

The trouble lay in the follow-up. In the confusions of a Lebanese civil war with a score of different armed groups the U.S. got drawn into supporting Amin Gemayel's Christian government, which did not have the support of the majority of Muslim factions. The Marines, who had been welcomed as peacekeepers by all sides, came to be seen as enemies, a judgment disastrously reinforced when National Security Adviser Robert McFarlane won approval from Reagan for U.S. warships to shell Muslim positions. Secretary of State George Shultz was convinced the Marines were essential to his diplomatic efforts to maneuver for a more stable peace between Syria, Israel and the Lebanese factions. Defense Secretary Caspar Weinberger and the Joint Chiefs were equally certain the Marine deployment was a grandiose folly. There were too few Marines to fight, too many to die. Time and again Weinberger urged Reagan to pull them out. Reagan backed Shultz and McFarlane. Somehow their optimism survived an April 1983 truck bombing of the U.S. embassy in Beirut, which killed 63, including 17 Americans. The reckoning

came at 6:22 a.m. on Sunday, October 23. Another truck bomber drove into the Marine headquarters, where 346 were asleep: 241 died.

Not until the following January did Reagan agree to a pullout (when it was favored by a majority in the polls). And then he approved of a final barrage, a vindictive act that led to a series of reprisals by a Shiite faction, notably the hijacking of a TWA plane in June 1985.

The Lebanon disaster had an important effect on later calls for intervention. Weinberger's military assistant, Major General Colin Powell, noted that when the State Department argued for a commitment of troops as a presence, a symbol, a signal, it was too often an attempt "to give the appearance of clarity to mud." When Powell was later chairman of the Joint Chiefs under Presidents Bush and Clinton, he ensured that the U.S. employed overwhelming force in the invasion of Panama to oust General Manuel Noriega in 1989 and in the Gulf War in 1991, and he resisted other commitments: "When ancient ethnic hatreds reignited in the former Yugoslavia in 1991, and well-meaning Americans thought we should 'do something,' the shattered bodies of Marines at the Beirut airport were never far from my mind in arguing for caution."

The impact of the Lebanon tragedy on the American public's willingness to commit troops to foreign endeavors was immediately obscured. Days after the bombing the public was applauding Reagan's decision to save democracy on the tiny Caribbean island of Grenada. Cynics saw it as a clever diversion from the humiliation of Beirut but it was a genuine, if overblown, response to an emergency. Reagan had secretly taken the decision to invade Grenada a full day before the Marines were killed. Six thousand Marines and Army troops landed to restore order and "rescue" 800 American medical students caught in anarchy following the murder of the Communist Prime Minister by his even more radical Marxist deputy. Reagan was also concerned that Grenada was an incipient Cuba or Nicaragua:

Cubans were building a suspiciously large airfield.

The invasion, in the judgment of Colin Powell, was "sloppy." Most of the Americans who died were killed by other Americans, notably in helicopter collisions in a raid forced on General H. Norman Schwarzkopf by the chiefs in Washington. Grenada suggested, too, that interservice cooperation had a long way to go. "We don't fly Army soldiers in Marine helicopters," a Marine colonel coolly told Schwarzkopf. Schwarzkopf won the eyeball-to-eyeball encounter with the threat of a court-martial. Powell, too, noted the lessons. The two generals were ready to apply them when ordered to evict Saddam Hussein from Kuwait in 1991.

THE FIRST WOMAN: Geraldine Ferraro was America's first female vice presidential candidate from a major party. She was a cheerfully scrappy four-term congresswoman from Queens who was picked over San Francisco Mayor Dianne Feinstein. Critics charged that she had too little experience to be a heartbeat from the presidency, but she was as qualified as most vice presidents in history and fought a feisty campaign. She held her own in debate with a condescending George Bush, and she rose above Mrs. Bush, who referred to her as "something that rhymes with 'witch,'" but she was unable to shake questions about her realtor husband's business with suspected mob figures or his leases to other unsavory clients (she was later criticized by a congressional ethics inquiry). Photograph by Sylvia Plachy.

TWO HOSTAGES: President Reagan held hostage at his own White House photo op. Jesse Jackson had flown to Damascus on Christmas Day, 1983, and somehow shamed Syrian dictator Assad into releasing Lieutenant Robert O. Goodman, Jr., a Navy bombardier-navigator shot down over Lebanon. White House officials had tried to stop Jackson's mission, but now Reagan was eager to share the glory. His handlers had other ideas—they tried to keep Jackson out of the picture and did not schedule him to say anything at all. Jackson simply reached across and took the mike from Reagan. Photograph by George Tames.

THE GIPPER'S LANDSLIDE

In 1984, at the age of 73, Ronald Reagan, already the oldest man ever to serve as president, scored one of the greatest victories in American political history. His opponent, Walter Mondale, a progressive three-term senator and Carter's vice president, carried only his home state of Minnesota.

Four years later a wistful Mondale blamed defeat on the glossiness of Reagan's campaign. "I tried to get specific and Reagan patted dogs. I should have patted more dogs." It became a commonplace that the political process had become so degraded that it could be decided by a few patriotic images or by a good one-liner in a television debate—pressed on his age, Reagan scored by replying: "I am not going to exploit, for political purposes, my opponent's youth and inexperience." The Gipper, in fact, won his landslide the old-fashioned way. He gave the right rhetorical signals to hold the faithful and drew a decisive majority of uncommitted by virtue of presiding over a country that was both newly prosperous and at peace. If the

election was decided by anything in the campaign, it was the hair shirt waved by Mondale. Having skewered the vaporish newness of his rival Gary Hart with the question "Where's the beef?," he tried a knockout punch on Reagan, too. At the Democratic convention in San Francisco on July 19, 1984, he declared: "I mean business. By the end of my first term, I will cut the deficit by two thirds. Let's tell the truth. Mr. Reagan will raise taxes and so will I. He won't tell you. I just did."

It was bad economics, worse politics. The country was just starting to breathe again after the harshest recession since the thirties. In 1982, one in ten Americans had been out of work. Tax increases of the size Mondale envisaged would have knocked back the sharp recovery produced by belatedly lowered interest rates and a collapse in world oil prices. The voters might not know John Maynard Keynes from Milton Friedman, but they knew that the dour Mondale was promising a dark Nordic noon. They preferred morning in America with the sunny Mr. Reagan.

The first serious challenge by a black man for a major party's presidential nomination was mounted in 1984, and pressed hard in 1988. In crowded, lackluster Democratic fields, the Rev. Jesse Jackson stood out like a diamond in the rough. In 1984, he took 21 percent of the vote in the primaries and caucuses combined. He came even closer in 1988, when Governor Michael Dukakis was the front-runner. On "Super Tuesday"—March 8, 1988—there were 21 primaries and caucuses. Jackson finished first or second in 16 of them. In the South he took 27 percent of the vote. His share of white votes rose as high as 24 percent, nearly three times better than in 1984.

Jackson was another American success story, a boy born into a poor, fractured family in Greenville, South Carolina, who pulled himself up and through little North

THE "PRESIDENT OF BLACK AMERICA" FORMS A RAINBOW COALITION

Carolina A&T, where he starred at quarterback, and then to the ministry and the campaigns of Dr. Martin Luther King, Jr. After King's death, he had gradually shucked off his more radical postures, running showy but moderately effective campaigns in Chicago for economic improvement and justice. He had become the most inspiring orator in American politics, save Mario Cuomo, and he offered an optimistic populist political philosophy in jubilant, playful speeches of rolling cadences and vivid, choppy street metaphors. At the 1984 and 1988 conventions he brought the delegates to tears and then wild applause. This was the way he proclaimed his Rainbow Coalition:

"We must turn to each other and not on each other, and choose higher ground. Our flag is red, white and blue, but our nation is rainbow—red, yellow, brown, black and white, we are all precious in God's sight! Our time has come! Our faith, hope and dreams have prevailed. Our time has come! Weeping has endured for nights, but joy cometh in the morning. Our time has come! No grave can hold our body

down. Our time has come! No lie can live forever. Our time has come! We must leave the racial battleground and come to the economic common ground and the higher moral ground. America, our time has come . . . !"

Jackson ran afoul of a fear of identity politics and a few of his own missteps. He rescued the Navy flier Lieutenant Goodman from Syria, 49 Cubans and Americans from Castro's jails and, most dramatically, three planeloads of Saddam Hussein's hostages on the eve of the Gulf War. The pundits were still sensitive over the more extreme claims of sixties radicals that American minorities owed greater loyalty to the Third World than to the United States, so his admirable mercy missions got a bleak reception. "Contemptible," was the *New York Time*'s verdict. The press was eager to jump on him when in a casual conversation with a pair of black reporters, he referred to New York City as "Hymie town" and its Jewish population as "Hymies." Jackson apologized again and again. It had been a crude and insensitive remark but he had insistently stood

against anti-Semitism. More disturbing than "Hymie town" was his reluctance to dissociate himself from the demagogue and reverse racist Louis Farrakhan.

Yet Jackson got little credit for making the most inclusionary appeal of any figure in any party. He gave heart to ruined farmers in Iowa, white coal miners in Kentucky, destitute oil workers in Texas. He was nearly alone among modern American politicians in his willingness to speak unabashedly of morality in public policy, as opposed to a tendency, in Gore Vidal's phrase, to oscillate between hypocrisy and organized religion. He talked to gang leaders in L.A. and walked them down to the mayor's office to discuss job programs. In Milwaukee, he appeared before a crowd of 5,000 and challenged his audience by going on at length about gay rights. It was a brave act by a man determined to push his constituency beyond provincialism.

Jackson, like King, was always much stronger on inspiration than organization. But the coalition he did assemble, traversing lines of race and class and region, was potentially of major significance.

Roberto D'Aubuisson ordered the murders of Archbishop Romero and the El Salvadoran Attorney General. Photograph by Eli Reed.

WITH FRIENDS LIKE THESE

American nuns raped, murdered and mutilated. Before the Cold War reached Central America, the outrage would have provoked swift punishment. It happened in El Salvador on December 3, 1980. Sisters Ita Ford, Maura Clarke and Dorothy Kazel and lay worker Jean Donovan, from Cleveland, were on missions of mercy, delivering food, clothing and medicine to the homeless. This was regarded as provocative by the right-wing government fighting a civil war. In 1980 alone there were 10,000 victims of political assassination. In March a prominent critic, Archbishop Oscar Romero, was gunned down while he said Mass.

President Carter angrily demanded that the killers of the nuns be brought to

Ambassador Deane Hinton: his report that no evidence could be found to confirm a massacre at El Mozote was translated by the State Department into an outright denial. Photograph by Harry Mattison.

justice. He cut all military aid. But shortly before handing power over to Ronald Reagan in January 1981, the champion of human rights felt obliged to renew the flow of weapons to El Salvador. Five antigovernment guerrilla forces merged into the Farabundo Marti National Liberation Front (FMLN) were winning. Already blamed for the "loss" of Nicaragua to the Cuban-backed Marxist Sandinistas the year before, Carter could not stand to lose El Salvador as well. On President Reagan's accession, the domino theory met the Monroe Doctrine with full force in Nicaragua and El Salvador. Military aid to El Salvador was accelerated and in Nicaragua Reagan gave guns and money to the contra guerrillas trying to overthrow President Daniel Ortega's undemocratic but reformist regime.

The grievances of the peasants were real in the grossly inequitable societies of Central America—14 families owned most of El Salvador—but anything that looked like Communist support for the oppressed persuaded the U.S. to throw its weight behind the repressive alliances of the military and the oligarchies. Reagan's ambassador to the U.N., Jeane Kirkpatrick, who suggested the nuns were killed because they were political activists, argued that the "authoritarian" regimes of the right, which simply kept a rough order, were less obnoxious than "totalitarian" regimes of the left, which claimed the right to run every aspect of life.

Congress responded to the murder of the nuns (for which four National Guardsmen were belatedly convicted) by insisting that military aid be conditional on the administration's certifying progress in human rights. For the next eight years, Reagan ritually certified so before Congress and Congress dutifully increased aid. An early test came in December 1981. Troops of El Salvador's Atlacatl Brigade, trained and equipped by the U.S., entered El Mozote and several neighboring towns in the Morazán region and systematically slaughtered everyone. Most of the 900 or more victims were evangelical Christians

who tended to avoid contact with the rebels. On December 11, some of them sang as they died in the church and in their homes. Mark Danner's painstaking reconstruction for *The New Yorker* in 1993 described how men were decapitated by machete or shot; women were raped and tortured before being killed; children were burned alive. A pregnant woman was sliced open and the fetus removed.

Six weeks after the massacre, Raymond Bonner of the *New York Times,* Alma Guillermoprieto of the *Washington Post* and the photographer Susan Meiselas ventured into FMLN territory and counted some of the decaying bodies. The day after the story hit the front pages of the *Times* and *Post,* President Reagan certified that El Salvador was making "a concerted and significant effort to comply with internationally recognized human rights." The massacre? All got up by the press and the FMLN. There was "no evidence." The provisional president, the moderate José Napoleón Duarte, who was a political captive of the junta, said the massacre was "a guerrilla trick." The *Wall Street Journal* denounced the reporters.

The civil war was settled with U.N. help in 1992. A right-winger was elected president and the FMLN won a large part of the assembly. Excavation then proved that the massacre had taken place exactly as reported by a handful of survivors. Along with the masses of tangled skeletons, investigators found hundreds of used M-16 rifle cartridges, each stamped "manufactured for the United States government at Lake City, Missouri."

The bodies of the murdered nuns were disinterred in the presence of U.S. Ambassador Robert E. White and photographer Susan Meiselas. White was recalled for objecting to the renewal of military aid.

OLLIE NORTH, WITH CAKE AND BIBLE

Oliver Laurence North was brought into the White House in 1981, when he was 38, to carry maps and compile military reports for the National Security Council. He was a lieutenant colonel in the Marines, a genuine decorated war hero who still had in his body the shrapnel absorbed in Vietnam. He brightened his cramped, dilapidated office with symbols of his passionate anticommunism: a red-starred Chinese fur hat from the Chinese People's Liberation Army, a bullet-holed Cuban helmet and a canteen cup shot off his hip in Vietnam. He was a ferocious worker with a million ideas for fighting terrorism. He was also a fantasist, a quality he fatefully shared with his president.

By 1984, the humble chart carrier on $40,900 a year was running a secret military junta with millions of dollars in Swiss bank accounts (wrung out of Arab oil states), dummy companies and its own airplanes, pilots, airfield and ship. The first task of The Enterprise, as he called his operation, was smuggling munitions to the private army of contras trying to upset the leftist Sandinista government of Nicaragua. The CIA's director, Bill Casey, had been doing that, but a querulous Congress was about to cut off all assistance and somebody else had to be found to carry out President Reagan's secret order that "the resistance must be held together body and soul." Casey induced National Security Adviser Robert McFarlane to let North set up his own show. When Congress became suspicious, North assured everyone that he wasn't doing what he energetically was.

Nobody asked questions about the second operation because it was inconceivable. Reagan excoriated Iran, which he considered among the terrorist outlaw states "run by the strangest collection of misfits, Looney Tunes and squalid criminals since the advent of the Third Reich." On July 8, 1985, he described Iran as Murder Incorporated. A few weeks later, upset after meeting families of hostages, he authorized a ransom payment to Murder Incorporated in the form of 96 U.S. antitank missiles, routed through Israel. The deal was that "moderates" in Iran would arrange

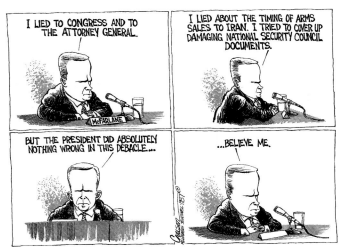

I LIED TO CONGRESS AND TO THE ATTORNEY GENERAL.

I LIED ABOUT THE TIMING OF ARMS SALES TO IRAN. I TRIED TO COVER UP DAMAGING NATIONAL SECURITY COUNCIL DOCUMENTS.

BUT THE PRESIDENT DID ABSOLUTELY NOTHING WRONG IN THIS DEBACLE...

...BELIEVE ME.

Cartoon by Stuart Carlson.

the release of four of the seven Americans being held by pro-Iranian Shiites in Beirut. The missiles were sent on August 20. No hostage was released.

This was to be the pattern over 15 months, the Iranians consistent in their bad faith, the Americans steadfast in their credulity. McFarlane and North put their trust in Manucher Ghorbanifar, an Iranian arms dealer already branded by the CIA as a treacherous liar and fabricator. They took huge personal risks. McFarlane had resigned, but in May 1986 he agreed to fly to Teheran with North to meet the three most powerful Iranian leaders and hand over U.S. weapons for hostages. The pair, traveling on false Irish passports and phony names, might well themselves have been made hostages by the rifle-toting Revolutionary Guards who eventually

showed up at the airport. North had brought a gift set of matching pistols for his hosts and a birthday cake which they wolfed down, and six poison pills for his own team, a gift from Bill Casey.

Only low-level Iranians showed up at the Teheran Hilton, and they haggled for days before offering only two hostages. There were tense moments between North, who wanted to settle, and McFarlane, who aborted the mission. On May 29, he advised Reagan to break off dealing. He did not. In October the President inscribed a Bible for North to take to another bargaining session in Frankfurt, this one approved by McFarlane's successor, Admiral John Poindexter.

By the end of North's efforts only three of the original seven hostages were released and seven more Americans had been kidnapped in Lebanon. North had another motive for his eagerness to trade. It was the "neat idea" of charging the Iranians six times cost and diverting profits to the contras. Through it all, North was confident the public would approve. He wrote in his notebook: "Ultimately on side of angles [sic]."

SECRETS TO THE GRAVE

William Casey, North's secret control, was a bluff Irish-American lawyer whose shambling manner concealed a keen intellect and passion. He was a lower-middle-class boy from Queens who made a fortune in risky investments, didn't care about money and became the champion of the little man as the Nixon-appointed chairman of the Securities and Exchange Commission. He saved Reagan's 1980 campaign, then revitalized the CIA. He had a passion for cloak and dagger from his World War II service with "Wild Bill" Donovan, when he infiltrated 102 secret agents into Nazi Germany. He escaped a grilling by Congress because he had a stroke and brain cancer and died on May 6, 1987, the second day of Joint Senate-House hearings on Iran-Contra. Watergate reporter Bob Woodward reported in his book *Veil* that on his deathbed Casey admitted his role of master planner of Iran-Contra. Photograph by James Nachtwey.

THE TARGETING OF AMERICANS

Terrorists struck hard at America in the eighties, mostly for its support of Israel and for the U.S. shelling of Shiite camps and towns in Lebanon in 1984–85. Of 690 hijackings, shootings, kidnappings and bombings around the world in 1985, 217 were against Americans. Most had their origins in Iran, Lebanon, Libya and the Gaza Strip. In Beirut, Hezbollah (Party of God) guerrillas captured scores of foreign hostages to protest the treatment of Lebanon's Shiite Muslim minority or to spring other terrorists from jail.

The hostages were brutally treated, held blindfolded and shackled for years. William Buckley, the CIA station chief, died from his ill treatment. Terry Anderson, an Associated Press reporter captured on March 16, 1985, was a prisoner nearly seven years.

The calendar of terror included:

June 14, 1985: TWA flight 847 is hijacked in the Middle East. One passenger, a U.S. Navy diver, Robert Dean Stethem, 23, is shot dead as a demonstration, his body thrown onto the tarmac. The hostages are released in return for 700 Shiites held by Israel.

October 7, 1985: The Italian cruise ship *Achille Lauro* is hijacked off Port Said by five Palestine Liberation Front (PLF) terrorists. One of them, Yussef Molqui, puts a bullet in the forehead of Leon Klinghoffer, a partially paralyzed New York shop owner, because he has a Jewish name, then has him tossed overboard while still in his wheelchair.

December 20, 1985: Abu Nidal's Palestinians machine-gun Rome and Vienna airports. Four Americans are among the 14 dead.

President Reagan had marked his accession to power, as the Iranian hostages came home in January 1981, by promising that future terrorists would meet "swift and effective retribution." The *Achille Lauro* outrage provided the first dramatic success in years of frustration. The Egyptians, who accepted the surrender of the PLF men and their leader, Abul Abbas, put them on a plane to Tunisia. At midnight on October 10, two F-14 Tomcats forced the plane down at Sigonella, Sicily, where a U.S. Delta antiterrorist team was in wait. The Delta team arrested the hijackers, but they, in turn, were surrounded by Italian *carabinieri*. It was a tense moment. A shoot-out with Italian police on Italian soil was too much to risk. Abbas and the four were handed over. Abbas, infuriatingly, was freed. The other four were sentenced to terms of 20 to 30 years.

On April 14, 1986, U.S. planes bombed Tripoli and Benghazi and the desert compound of Libya's leader, Qaddafi, condemned by Reagan as a "mad dog" sponsor of terrorism. The raid was in retaliation for Qaddafi's part in the April 5 bombing of a Berlin disco frequented by U.S. military.

THE REWRITING OF HISTORY

The conspirators in the White House did their best to bluff it out after an item in a Lebanese magazine on November 3, 1986, unleashed a storm of outrage over arms for Iran. McFarlane, Poindexter and North wrote a false chronology, with Casey's approval, intended to help everyone involved distance President Reagan from the transactions. The chorus from the President, Vice President Bush, Poindexter, Casey, Chief of Staff Donald Regan and Attorney General Ed Meese was that there had been no swap of arms for hostages. "Utterly false," said Reagan on television. "No foundation."

Secretary of State George Shultz and Defense Secretary Caspar Weinberger knew much of it was lies. Deadly rivals, they had been at one trying to convince Reagan the arms deal was folly. It all became more frantic on November 20, when Meese put himself in charge of finding out what had gone on. North rushed off to shred documents before Meese's investigators arrived. Poindexter tore up a presidential "finding of necessity"—a presidential statement required to legalize covert action—because he reckoned it would embarrass Reagan. Signed by the President on December 5, 1985, it plainly authorized the sale of arms for hostages, and retrospectively at that. Then on November 23, 1986, Meese's men found the evidence that North had diverted arms profits to the contras. It was a diversion in itself from the primary story of a capitulation to terrorists.

Reagan struggled to reconcile the emerging awkward facts with his pride in the three hostages freed and the money flowing to his beloved freedom fighters. He found refuge in what Garry Wills has called "constantly expanding areas of forgetfulness." Was he already suffering from the Alzheimer's disease he reported to the American people in 1994? Not according to the testimony of Marlin Fitzwater, who was close to him for many years as the White House spokesman. Reagan, he said, never had a good memory, but he was in fine mental shape right to the end of his presidency. Reagan lamented: "I told the American people I did not trade arms for hostages. My heart and my best intentions tell me that is true, but the facts and the evidence tell me that it is not."

Independent Counsel Lawrence E. Walsh concluded in 1993 that McFarlane, Poindexter and North were scapegoats, sacrificed to protect the Reagan administration in its final two years. Walsh's 14 indictments included Caspar Weinberger, reinforcing the view of some that the post-Watergate office of independent counsel had a built-in bias for prosecution. Weinberger, like Shultz, had done his best to dissuade Reagan. President Bush pardoned Weinberger and also McFarlane. The convictions of North and Poindexter were set aside on appeal, on the grounds that it had not been fair to use their immunized congressional testimony against them.

THREE ON THE SPOT

ROBERT "BUD" MCFARLANE, National Security Adviser from October 1983 to December 1985, took an overdose of Valium the night before he was to testify before Joint Senate-House hearings in May 1987. "I thought I had failed the country," he wrote in his memoir. He also thought he had been betrayed by his fellow Marine, North, and buried him with adjectives: deceitful, mendacious, treacherous, devious, self-serving, self-aggrandizing. The arms deal originated with an Israeli suggestion to McFarlane that he would be dealing with Iranian "moderates" ready to overthrow the Ayatollah. The only moderates in Iran, observed Defense Secretary Weinberger, were in the cemetery, but McFarlane was moved by a vision that he was opening a dialogue similar to Henry Kissinger's with Communist China.

FAWN HALL, North's secretary, shredded papers, typed fake official documents, and left the office with other papers tucked in her boots and hidden beneath her coat. It wasn't a cover-up, she explained. "I was in a protective mode." Her worst moment before the committee was blurting out, "Sometimes you have to go above the written law." By 1997, she had married, overcome a cocaine addiction and decided that Ollie, who wouldn't return her phone calls, had used her. "I was like a piece of Kleenex to him."

JOHN POINDEXTER, National Security Adviser from December 1985 to his sacking in November 1986, blew smoke at his congressional inquisitors, stoically ready to go to prison for the deniability he had given the President. He was a vice admiral throbbing with brainpower. He graduated first out of 900 in the Annapolis class of 1958 and made computers for fun—but he hadn't a clue how the American system of government worked. He read neither the *Washington Post* nor the *New York Times* and would rather communicate with a colleague next door by pounding his computer than by talking face to face.

THE PREDATORS OF THE GO-GO EIGHTIES

In Frank Capra's Christmastime staple *It's a Wonderful Life,* a guardian angel gives George Bailey (Jimmy Stewart) a nightmare vision of what would happen to the community of little Bedford Falls if the rapacious old banker Mr. Potter (Lionel Barrymore) succeeded in closing rival Bailey's savings and loan (S&L). Instead of the town's savings being pooled to build decent homes for working families making their way up the ladder of the American dream, Potter has put the money into honky-tonk dives and gaudy nightclubs, and Bedford Falls has lost its community spirit to greed and bitterness.

The sentiments of Capra's movie lay at the core of Reaganism, with its nostalgia for small-town life. Yet it was Jimmy Stewart's old pal, Ronald Reagan, and his deregulators, with a lot of help from incompetent professionals, who finally sacrificed the values of the Bedford Falls of America and created the largest and most bizarre banking scandal in history. Americans will be paying for it for decades to come. The total cost to taxpayers may well be over $500 billion. Charles Keating, Jr., one of the most intriguing of the S&L bandits, alone made $2 billion disappear.

The first fix for the troubled S&Ls, effected on Jimmy Carter's watch, was to attract more savings by the government's guaranteeing up to $100,000 of any deposit. The original intent of deposit insurance at $40,000 had been to avert panic runs by small local savers of the kind George Bailey endured. The new rules allowed wealthy individuals and corporations to split their spare millions into packages of $100,000. Fine—but thrifts still could not survive paying risk-free 18 percent interest to investors and collecting 8 percent from home buyers. By 1982 nearly every one of the 4,000 S&Ls was broke.

The "solution" of October 1982—dreamed up by Senator Jake Garn (R-Utah) and Representative Fernand "Freddy" St. Germain (D-R.I.)—was to let thrifts try to compensate for the losses on mortgages by investing 40 percent in other deals. Some state legislatures gave even greater freedom. California-chartered thrifts could invest wherever they liked and it would all be federally in-

sured. Such was the intoxication with "free" markets that, with its full faith and credit on the line, the Reagan administration also, incredibly, weakened the scrutiny of ownership and accounting standards. William Seidman, federal insurer of the regular banks, observed that the new law made the government "full partner in a nationwide casino."

Scores of swindlers and shady, mob-related characters looted thrifts, most of all in Texas and California. They used deposit money to buy themselves yachts, mansions and corporate jets and to throw

Gatsby-style parties. But most S&L owners were honest. It was just that as a breed they were used to lending on single-family houses around the corner from their offices and operating on the 3-6-3 rule: borrowing at 3 percent, lending at 6, and always on the golf course by 3 p.m. They lost millions when they speculated on race horses, windmill farms, exotic financial instruments and chancy real estate ventures. Thousands of accountants and state officials also proved incompetent.

Keating was a man of grander imagination. For a master of every form of bank fraud, he had a curious pedigree. In World War II, he was a carrier-based night fighter pilot. Then he got into combat as a fruit stand owner, haggling at 3 a.m. with wholesalers about the price of oranges. He took a law degree and launched a crusade against pornography and *Hustler* magazine's Larry Flynt in particular. He learned a lot in Cincinnati as counsel to Carl Lind-

ner, one of the earliest takeover artists. In the heady days of 1982, after he had left Lindner, Keating had no trouble picking up Lincoln Savings and Loan, in Irvine, California, despite some earlier trouble with the Securities and Exchange Commission. Junk-bond king Michael Milken at Drexel Burnham Lambert provided the $50 million buy-in. Keating spent it furiously fast. From his headquarters in Phoenix, Arizona, he built landscaped homes at eight a day, but his horizons were unlimited. A hotel in the desert for $300 million. A new city of Estrella, with homes and jobs for 250,000 people. By May of 1988 he had bought about $5 billion—billion!—of brokered deposits. He moved the money around the world so fast, and through subsidiaries so complex, booking notional profits so prolifically, that it took years to catch a glimpse of his heels in the gold dust. It took longer to figure out that the profits he booked—42 percent return on equity—were actually prodigious losses.

Keating was an unpredictable force of nature dispensing money and fear. He liked walking through one of his companies dropping pink slips on executive desks, or firing someone not sweltering in the stipulated dark suit, but he might suddenly hand secretaries $500 in greenbacks on condition they spend it in 20 minutes. Every mother on a Bahamian island who named a son Charles got $100. He gave $6 million to charity (from corporate, not personal, funds) and flew Mother Teresa around in his jet. Biographers Michael Binstein and Charles Bowden see him as a dreamer as much as a thief. He and his family collected $41.5 million in salaries, benefits and perks in the five years he ran Lincoln, but he insisted he did nothing wrong. He saw greed and power as essential motivators of America's success. He had a refreshing candor. When it was suggested his political contributions gave him influence over politicians, he replied, "I certainly hope so." From 1984 to 1988 he gave $2 million to candidates and $1.4 million to his special angels—Senators Alan Cranston (D), John Glenn (D), John McCain (R), Donald Riegle (D) and Dennis DeConcini (D). Senator Pete Wilson (R) qualified as a sixth. They tried to protect him from the regulators.

Many federal and state officials and experts were on the side of people like Keating. As treasury secretary, Donald Regan had refused to approve more regulators. Alan Greenspan, later chairman of the Federal Reserve, was hired by Keating to testify before Congress on behalf of the new S&Ls. Of the 17 he commended, 16 failed and the survivor was not an S&L. Two of the Big Eight accounting firms, Arthur Anderson and Arthur Young, were asleep.

One of the few heroes of the whole saga was Edwin Gray, a public relations flak and mainstream Reaganite who was made chairman of the Federal Home Loan Bank Board. He sounded the alarm. In the House, Speaker Jim Wright, and Texas Democrats J. J. Pickle and Jim Chapman, fought him at every turn. In the Senate he was repeatedly harangued by the Keating Five. By the end of his term, in June 1987, Gray was all in, "like a boxer who had taken too many punches." He was replaced by M. Danny Wall, a dressy banker from Utah who promptly suspended the audit of Keating's Lincoln S&L and set out on junkets round the country telling everyone that 90 percent of S&Ls were healthy—as if the fantasy realm of Reaganism could be infinitely extended and no disconcerting reality ever confronted.

Wall resigned in 1989. President George Bush signed an act setting up the Resolution Trust Corporation to manage and sell the insolvent trusts. Keating was sentenced to 10 years in one trial and 12 years in another.

MICHAEL MILKEN, an amateur magician credited with possessing "an eccentric monster brain," plucked fortunes out of thin air by inventing the high-yielding junk bond. Between 1977 and 1989, the obsessive Milken and his department at Drexel Burnham Lambert raised almost $100 billion for investment in American business, especially for hostile takeovers by raiders. In 1987, Milken received what was considered the world's record W-2 form—$550 million in commissions that year alone. In April 1990, with tears running down his face, he confessed to six felonies. Somewhere along the way he went wrong, rigging the bond market in a thrust for monopoly, pumping up prices by having borrowers invest in his own bonds, and defrauding some of his clients. He served four years for that. But he had revolutionized the corporate structure of America; in a sense he had democratized capital.

CHARLES KEATING, JR., in a Los Angeles courtroom in November 1991. He did not ask for leniency or show remorse: "Someday I hope that I'll be able to tell the full story and I hope that these people who have suffered so will feel a lot different about it."

IVAN BOESKY—"greed is all right . . . everybody should be a little greedy"—leaves federal court in April 1987. He admitted paying for advance knowledge of mergers and takeovers—in the illegal Wall Street practice known as "insider trading"—then wore a wire for the feds to trap others. He went to prison for four and a half years.

644 THE DRUG WARS, 1983–

THE DRUG WARS

Crack pushers dealing openly, with lookouts posted left and right, caught by Angel Franco's camera. The scene is New York, 1986, 42nd Street at Times Square, but it might have been any one of a score of American urban neighborhoods in the eighties—to name a few, the Graveyard in Miami, the War Zone in Dallas, the Wild Western District in Baltimore, Chicago's West Side, the Desire project area in New Orleans, Drake Place in Washington, D.C., East St. Louis, Illinois, or South Central Los Angeles. Murders in New York peaked at 2,000 in the early nineties—before declining to 760 in 1997.

Addictions played havoc with millions of lives in the eighties. Alcohol, heroin and marijuana had long been an escape and a trap for the deprived and unemployed in the decaying inner cities, and cocaine was insidiously in the bloodstream of many high performers in the professional classes. But 1983 was a tipping point that transformed a serious social ill into a national catastrophe. Someone cooked baking soda and water with cocaine to produce crack. It had cost social snorters of coke $100 to $150 for a teaspoonful of powder, good for a "high" for two people for several hours. The equivalent in crack cost $5. The illicit trade in crack exploded, among the poor as well as the strivers, and with it an epidemic of violence shocking even to a country inured to leading the civilized world in murders and prison population.

There was just too much money in crack, produced from smuggled Colombian powder in the derelict public housing projects and mass marketed at downtown street corners. It rapidly became a business generating tens of billions of dollars. Dealers fighting for turf turned areas of major American cities into war zones. Gunfire from automatic weapons shattered the nights and fear ruled by day. The number of individuals sent to prison for drug crimes had by 1990 exceeded the number sent up for property crimes, but the police were hard-pressed just to contain the warfare. With jails bulging and overburdened prosecutors more ready to accept pleas, the police often found that someone arrested at risk of life and limb was out on the streets again in a few weeks. Civil authority and social services broke down. The chemistry was combustible: on the one hand, glittering lifestyles on the television and a get-rich-quick public ethic, and on the other, jobless young people without secure families, living in squalid surroundings with easy money for the take in drug running.

The Center on Addiction and Substance Abuse at Columbia University found alcohol and/or drug abuse implicated in some three fourths of all murders, rapes, child molestations and deaths of babies and children suffering from parental neglect. The center's chairman, Joseph A. Califano, Jr., former HEW Secretary, argues persuasively that prevention and treatment of addiction must be a prime element in attacking the complex social problems of health care, poverty, crime and violence. Residential treatment centers like Phoenix House have shown that in more than half the cases an addict can not merely be cured but turned into a good citizen. Almost all the effort under successive presidents, however, has been on supply, not demand. Interdiction is necessary, and so is shutting down the open-air drug bazaars in the cities, but the enforcing authorities concede that controlling supply cannot be more than a holding action when 5 million Americans find themselves pathetically unable to apply Nancy Reagan's solution of just saying no.

REAGAN AND GORBACHEV: THE BEST OF ENEMIES

Ronald Reagan had a dream of a world free of nuclear weapons. It was easy to ridicule. Many of his associates thought he was unbelievably naive. Détente was dead. At the end of his first term, the arms race was deadlier than ever. America and the Russians had both evaded the SALT limits on launchers by adding multiple warheads to thousands of missiles. Reagan himself, having denounced the "evil empire," had called for more weapons to close a "window of vulnerability" created by the Russian lead in intercontinental missiles. The Soviets, for their part, saw his pledge to build an antimissile defense system as an attempt to gain a first-strike advantage. They installed SS-20 intermediate range missiles to hold Europe hostage. NATO retaliated with midrange Pershing missiles that could destroy Moscow in five minutes.

Alone among the Reagan administration, Secretary of State George Shultz tried to keep the lines open to the Kremlin after the Soviets walked out of arms talks in Geneva. He was reviled for his pains. According to George Bush, the National Security Council staff repeatedly sent Reagan "absolutely vicious memos" contradicting Shultz's own; Shultz wrote in his memoirs, "Apparently my office was bugged by the NSC." His big chance came with the accession of the dynamic reformist Mikhail Gorbachev in March 1985. By the end of the year, Shultz had Gorbachev, 54, and Reagan, 74, tucked away for a cozy fireside chat in the pool house of a lakeside château in wintry Geneva. They hit it off personally, but Washington worried about Reagan's ability to deal with Gorbachev. John Kennedy's 1961 humiliation by Khrushchev in Vienna was every diplomat's scar tissue.

Many of the people around Reagan had little regard for his intelligence or skill in foreign affairs. The hawkish coterie of Defense Secretary Caspar Weinberger, U.N. Ambassador Jeane Kirkpatrick, CIA Director William Casey, several National Security advisers and most of the national security staff had been opposed to negotiations of any kind, but they were convinced it would be a catastrophe when Reagan himself got involved. Shultz had a different view. He believed that beneath

TOURIST TROIKA: Gorbachev joins Reagan and President-elect George Bush on Governors Island, December 7, 1988. Photograph by Paul Hosefros.

Reagan's proclivity to ignore "tedious detail" lay "a bedrock of principle and purpose." He was right. He also believed that the accession of Gorbachev opened a door, and he was right again.

Reagan had little grasp of the stupefying complexities of differentiated American and Russian arsenals. Gorbachev was fluent in throw weights and telemetry. Reagan's memory for facts had always been weak. He preferred telling stories. In one anguished encounter, while he and Gorbachev fretted for the outcome of a last-minute wrangle on wording, he began a tale he had read in *People* magazine about a 1,200-pound man who got stuck in his bathroom doorway. Gorbachev tried to fathom the hidden relevance in Reagan's recital of the man's knee measurements. As Reagan's press secretary, Marlin Fitzwater, tells it, Gorbachev took his ambassador into the men's room to ask

what in the hell this 1,200-pound man was all about.

Reagan's team was always on pins and needles in negotiations when the President drifted into story mode. He was fondest of describing how Americans and Russians would unite to repel invaders of Earth from other planets by laser beams from his fanciful nuclear umbrella, the Strategic Defense Initiative (SDI). "Oh, no," his aides would groan, "here come the little green men again." When Reagan went for his meeting with Gorbachev in Geneva, staff hung a sign from the low underhang of the stairs at the Villa Pometta. "Jerry Ford says watch your head, Mr. President." He laughed and continued laughing all the way to the motorcade. They need not have worried. As General Colin Powell observed, while Gorbachev was clearly superior to Reagan in mastery of the details, there was not a trace of condescension in his manner. He recognized that Reagan was "the embodiment of his people's down-to-earth character, practicality and optimism."

In four Reagan-Gorbachev summits, in Geneva, Reykjavík, Washington and Moscow, Shultz found a way to give form and articulation to Reagan's inchoate longings to be a great peacemaker. The breakthroughs were breathtaking. At Reykjavík on October 11–12, 1986, where Reagan and Gorbachev had 9 hours and 48 minutes of face-to-face meetings, Gorbachev was forthcoming in nearly every area of arms control. He and Reagan astonishingly agreed on a first step to cut strategic nuclear forces in half. Then they got excited about the prospect of eliminating nuclear weapons altogether, including missiles and strategic bombers. "I have a picture," said Reagan, "that after ten years you and I come to Iceland and bring the last two missiles in the world and have the biggest damn celebration of it!"

One word—"one lousy word," said Reagan later—spoiled that picture. Gorbachev insisted on confining SDI to "laboratory" testing. And Reagan would not forsake his pet project. Remarkably, he offered to share it. Gorbachev feared SDI would expose the Soviets to an unanswerable strike. At midnight, haggard from the long day, the two men walked in silence from a supposedly haunted Hofdi House. "Mr. President," said Gorbachev when they reached Reagan's car, "you have missed a unique chance of going down in history as a great president who paved the way for nuclear disarmament." A gloomy Reagan answered: "That applies to both of us."

His hawks were appalled that he had offered to give up all nuclear weapons. They tried to cover it up. "They resembled," wrote Garry Wills, "a crew of absent-minded Frankensteins who had fiddled at separate parts of a monster for benevolent but widely varying purposes, only to see him break the clasps and rear himself up off the table in a weird compulsion to do some monstrous Good Thing that none of them had ever believed possible."

Reagan, beset at the same time by the Iran-contra fiasco, did not lose his nerve. He reaped a rich reward. In February 1987, Gorbachev said he would no longer let SDI stand in the way of a treaty to remove missiles from Europe and Asia. The Intermediate Nuclear Forces Treaty the leaders signed on December 8, 1987, led to the first-ever agreement to destroy nuclear missiles: 859 of America's and 1,836 Soviet missiles with a range of 300 to 3,400 miles. That was only 4 percent of the nuclear arsenal but it was unprecedented and unpredicted, and it was an exhilarating prelude to the end of the Cold War.

RED SQUARE: The ultimate photo op—Reagan at the heart of the evil empire being introduced to a Soviet child as "Grandfather Reagan." The White House image makers balked at the idea of Reagan being photographed at the cynosure of communism, but Shultz and the President loved the idea. The groups they bumped into in Red Square, with or without infants, uncannily turned out to have questions on all the precise topics of the summit—they were KGB plants. Gorbachev had been a hit in Washington when he stopped his car on Connecticut Avenue and went walking among genuine bystanders eager to press the flesh—Gorbymania, it was called. Reagan had the same excited reception from ordinary Muscovites when he and Nancy dropped in on the crowded Arbat shopping mall. Later, Gorbachev stood aside when Reagan met 100 Soviet dissidents; human rights was now firmly on the agenda. A reporter asked Reagan if he still thought the Soviet Union was an evil empire. "No," said Reagan. "I was talking about another time, another era."

POLITICAL MUGGINGS

Reporters pondering why the best speaker in the Democratic party, New York Governor Mario Cuomo, decided not to run for president in 1988 decided he must have some skeleton in his cupboard—probably one in cement overshoes. This was a grotesque ethnic slur against the Italian-American Cuomo, by all evidence an exemplary public servant. The better question would have been why anyone in their right mind would enter the race, considering what a howling circus presidential politics had become; the rising stars Senator Sam Nunn and Senator Bill Bradley both decided to sit it out.

The campaign, begun in 1987, marked the definitive end of privacy. Two scenes epitomized what candidates now risked: a wife made virtually a prisoner in her home, besieged by scores of media; a daughter at college stalked by cameramen. The press was demanding to know how they "felt" about the revelations that husband and father Gary Hart seemed to have had affairs. The former two-term senator from Colorado had made himself the Democratic front runner with thoughtful proposals to cut the deficit and health care costs, break America of its oil dependency and bring in some form of "national service" for young people. But he had also responded recklessly to questions about adultery. He said it was "an issue" if "other campaigns" were spreading rumors about him; and then he made an even worse mistake, telling the *New York Times Magazine:* "Follow me around. I don't care. I'm serious. If anybody wants to put a tail on me, go ahead. They'd be very bored." The *Miami Herald* did and wasn't. Five reporters staked out Hart's Washington house on a May night and reported that he had a compromising woman guest: one Donna Rice. He quit the race.

The Democratic nominee, Michael Dukakis, was the Greek-American governor of Massachusetts, a decent if dry technocrat who had kept taxes down while balancing the state budget. The Atlanta Democratic convention needled Bush. Ted Kennedy led choruses of "Where was George?"—mocking his disingenuous insistence that he was "out of the loop on Iran-contra." Trailing 17 points, Bush went negative with a deadly efficient campaign staff headed by Roger Ailes, the man responsible for effectively packaging Nixon in 1968, and Lee Atwater, a ruthless South Carolina media master. Wild distortions of Dukakis's record followed. The most notorious was the Willie Horton commercial featuring a black convicted murderer who had raped a woman and stabbed her husband while on weekend furlough—a furlough program begun by Dukakis's Republican predecessor. That was low enough, but at least it had something to do with an issue, crime. But the attacks became amazingly vicious and personal. Personal smears were no novelty in American politics, but never had they come so openly and from such a high level, from aides and elected politicians so directly linked to a major candidate. They smeared his fidelity to his Greek Orthodox faith (because he had married a Jewish woman). They suggested he had a history of pscyhiatric problems; he didn't—it was his brother. Reagan referred to him as "an invalid." Idaho Senator Steven Symms falsely asserted that there were pictures of Mrs. Dukakis burning an American flag while she was an antiwar demonstrator. Senator Orrin Hatch called the Democrats "a party of homosexuals." Bush never dissociated himself from any of this. Almost none of the media nailed the spectacular lies. Dukakis stuck to the high—and too often uninspired—road. He badly fumbled a question on the TV debate when he was asked whether he would favor the death penalty if his wife were raped and murdered.

Dukakis lost 54–46 percent and 426–111 in the electoral college. It was the most electoral votes any Democrat had managed since 1976, but the voters were sickened. Fewer turned out to vote than at any time since 1924. Lee Atwater, dying from a brain tumor, apologized after the election to Dukakis and others he had smeared, but the whole process was also out of hand in terms of money and time. The candidates for 1988 had often declared early in 1987. Spending at all campaign levels totaled $2.7 billion—up 50 percent from 1984. Fundraising, as well as defamation, was well on the way to becoming the major activity of American candidates.

Donna Rice — What Really Happened

NATIONAL ENQUIRER

GARY HART ASKED ME TO MARRY HIM

Exclusive Photos of Fun-Filled Weekend in the Bahamas

Vanna to Wed Linda Evans' Ex-Fiance

MONKEY BUSINESS: Michael Dukakis, caught by David Burnett with a little-boy-lost expression at the 1988 Democratic National Convention in Atlanta. He was to endure a relentless campaign of smears, which outdid the ordeal of one-time front runner Gary Hart. Hart was never able to live down either the escapade with a bright blonde, Donna Rice, or the name of the yacht (*Monkey Business*) he and a Louisiana lawyer, Bill Broadhurst, rented for a "fun-filled" trip to Bimini from Turnberry Isle, Florida, with Rice and her friend Lynn Armandt. It was Armandt, owner of a local bikini shop, who tipped off the *Miami Herald* about the Rice-Hart connection, and who used Donna's camera to take the photograph (shown at left), which she sold to the *National Enquirer.*

ABC WIDE WORLD OF NEWS.

YEAH, THIS IS ATWATER OVER AT THE BUSH CAMPAIGN...

I JUST WANTED TO LET YOU KNOW OUR TOPIC-OF-THE-DAY IS ENERGY. THE PHOTO OP IS AT AN OFFSHORE OIL RIG, AND THE LINE-OF-THE-DAY IS "READ MY LIPS: TAX BREAKS FOR OIL COMPANIES!"

AND GUESS WHAT? YOU'RE GOING TO PUT IT **ALL** ON THE NEWS TONIGHT BECAUSE YOU'RE PATSIES AND YOU HAVEN'T A **CLUE** HOW TO TELL THE STORY WITHOUT OUR VISUALS AND SOUND BITES! RIGHT?

UH... RIGHT. BUT YOU'RE PUSHING YOUR LUCK, BUDDY!

YEAH, YEAH. BLOW ME A KISS, PUSSY-CAT!

GEORGE HERBERT WALKER BUSH
41st President (Republican), 1989–1993

BORN: June 12, 1924, Milton, Massachusetts

POLITICAL CAREER: Chairman of Harris County (Houston area) Republican party, 1963–1964; U.S. House of Representatives, 1967–1971; U.S. Ambassador to the United Nations, 1971–1973; Chairman of Republican National Committee, 1973–1974; Chief U.S. Liaison in China, 1974–1975; Director of Central Intelligence, 1976–1977; Vice President of the United States, 1981–1989; President, 1989–1993

FIRST: The first president to have been director of the CIA.

CHARACTER SNAPSHOT: "Bush is the spiritual opposite of Groucho Marx; he never knew a club that he didn't want to be a member of."
—John Podhoretz

"Read My Lips."
Wooden sculpture by
Gary A. Batte.

THE BUSHES: Three generations of Bushes—George is top row, far left. Their forebears from England settled on Cape Cod, Massachusetts, in the mid-1600s. His investment banker father, Prescott S. Bush, was a private in General Pershing's expedition to catch Pancho Villa and a captain in World War I. He was U.S. Senator from Connecticut from 1953 to 1963, a moderate Republican who opposed Joe McCarthy and helped found Planned Parenthood. He was also an expert golfer who advised Eisenhower on his game. Ike thought young George should go into politics. Bush's mother, Dorothy, was a tennis star. From them and his schools—Greenwich Country Day and boarding at Phillips Academy in Andover—he acquired strong feelings about loyalty and fair play. He named his boat *Fidelity*.

BARBARA: He had called his plane *Barbara*. They had fallen in love at first sight at a Christmas dance in 1942, when he was 18 and she was a never-been-kissed high school girl of 16. They were secretly engaged in August 1943 on the eve of his dispatch to the Pacific. Barbara Pierce, 19, and George Bush, 20, were married on January 6, 1945, in Barbara's hometown of Rye, New York. The Japanese surrender saved him from joining a new Navy torpedo bomber group in the invasion of the home islands.

WAR HERO: As soon as he was 18, he enlisted as seaman second class. When he earned his wings, he was the youngest Navy pilot in World War II. Assigned to the VT-51 bomber squadron on board USS *San Jacinto*, he piloted a 3-man Grumman TBM Avenger. He was lucky to survive his 58 combat missions. On June 19, 1944, he had to ditch the Avenger with four depth charges on board and got away just before they blew up. On September 2, his plane was hit while dive-bombing Chichi Jima island. He stayed with the dive, dropped his four bombs on a radio tower, then ordered his crewmates to bail out. When he jumped himself, his parachute was slashed, he cut open his head on the plane's tail and broke his emergency water container. He seemed doomed, drifting in the ocean on his seatback rubber life raft, but ninety minutes later a dozen U.S. submariners were pulling him on board the USS *Finback*. He spent the next month underwater with them as they attacked Japanese ships. He was awarded the Distinguished Flying Cross.

FIRST BASE: At Yale, "Poppy" Bush majored in economics, minored in sociology. He studied hard and did well enough to graduate Phi Beta Kappa and with honors, but his real minor, he said, was baseball. He played first base for Yale, where he was captain and a good field, no hit, for 51 games in his two seasons. He kept his glove in a drawer in the Oval Office. He was a member of the fashionable Delta Kappa Epsilon ("Deke") fraternity and in his senior year was inducted into Yale's secret society, Skull and Bones.

HIS FINEST HOUR: In Diana Walker's euphoric photograph, President Bush tosses souvenir tie clips to U.S. troops in the Saudi Arabian desert on a Thanksgiving visit with Barbara in 1990. Bush had swiftly drawn a line in the sand when the Iraqi dictator, Saddam Hussein, seized Kuwait on August 2, 1990. Within days, U.S. troops were pouring into Saudi Arabia in Operation Desert Shield to prevent further aggression. Bush talked with world leaders for hours on the phone, rallying hesitant Arab leaders and winning United Nations backing for sanctions, without Soviet dissent: All those foreign funerals he had attended as vice president paid off. Then, for Operation Desert Storm in January to February 1991, he stitched together a great international military alliance of 40 nations— ultimately more than 800,000 troops and coordinated navies and air forces—that expelled Hussein from Kuwait after a five-week air-and-sea bombardment and 100 hours of war on land.

The triumph in the desert won Bush a 91 percent approval rating in a Gallup poll, the highest in its history. It was a just reward for inspired leadership from someone never supposedly good on "the vision thing." He had become his own man, having won the Republican nomination in 1988 by passing himself off as Reagan's heir rather than the moderate-to-liberal Republican he had been for most of his career. He chose the young, right-wing James Danforth ("Dan") Quayle as his running mate against Dukakis and Lloyd Bentsen. He made a promise he came to regret: "Read my lips. No new taxes." In 1992 his Democratic challenger, Bill Clinton, made this phrase the centerpiece of his attack. Bush was stunned that his invitation to compare his character with the challenger's was of less concern than the recession. His epitaph was the Clinton campaign slogan "It's the economy, stupid."

STRIKING OIL: His contacts could have landed the 24-year-old graduate an easy job on Wall Street, but he took a chance. He drove his '47 Studebaker to Texas to sell oil drilling equipment, then moved Barbara and their infant son George (the first of six children) into a ramshackle house in Odessa. He learned a lot in two years of travels as a salesman and in 1950 borrowed $350,000 from an uncle to set up an oil development company. In 1954 he founded Zapata Off-Shore, and for the next ten years built offshore platforms for companies on five continents. He sold out for a million dollars in 1966.

TWO DEFEATS: Twice he ran for the Senate and lost, in 1964 to Ralph Yarborough, and in 1970 to Lloyd Bentsen. Here he is dolefully watching returns with his brother and father. In 1964 he ran a right-wing campaign, denouncing Medicare, the Civil Rights Act of 1964 and Kennedy's nuclear test ban treaty. It was against his convictions—he said he hoped never to do it again—and in his successful 1966 run for Congress he played up personal qualities over ideology: "Labels are for cans." He backed Johnson's Fair Housing Act in 1968 and now told his jeering constituents he didn't see why a black soldier coming home from Vietnam should be barred from a decent home. His country club expelled his family, but at one stormy public meeting his courage won a standing ovation and saved his House seat.

NIXON'S MAN: In a huddle with aides at the U.N. in September 1971. Adlai Stevenson III called it "an insult" to the U.N. when Nixon appointed Bush ambassador and the *New York Times* was sharply critical of his lack of knowledge. In his 22 months, his toughest task was trying—and failing—to get the U.N. to let Taiwan stay in the U.N. when the majority favored giving Red China the Security Council seat. It was Nixon's idea that Bush should take over the chairmanship of the Republican party in his second term. On August 7, 1974, in the Watergate climax, it was Bush who had the painful task of telling his benefactor to resign. A poll of congressional Republicans favored Bush 255–181 for vice president but Ford chose New York Governor Nelson Rockefeller and offered Bush the ambassadorship of Britain or France. Bush surprised Ford by asking for China. With Kissinger at State, Bush had little power in secretive Beijing, but he was popular. He gave up his official Chrysler sedan and rode around on a bicycle (with Barbara, right), acquiring yet another nickname: "Busher who rides the bicycle, just as Chinese do." He was popular, too, with the spooks. At Ford's request, he took over a CIA shattered by scandal, cleaned house and restored morale.

THE VICE PRESIDENT: Campaigning for president in 1980, he beat Reagan in the Iowa caucuses and Michigan primaries, deriding Reagan's "voodoo economics," which proposed cutting taxes to increase federal revenues. Then he ran out of money and steam. Conservatives were critical when Reagan picked him as running mate. He soon shed much of his moderate image. In eight years as vice president, he did just a little better than the brother in Mark Twain's story: one went to sea; the other became vice president. Neither was heard from again. . . . Bush led task forces on federal regulations, terrorism and drugs, but he was such a quietly loyal Reaganite that Garry Trudeau, in his *Doonesbury* comic strip, portrayed him as invisible. As president-elect and president, he was initially scared of getting too close to Mikhail Gorbachev.

LET FREEDOM RING

Showmanship comes naturally to the American temperament. The 100th-anniversary party of the Statue of Liberty, in July 1986, would have seemed incomplete without its hundreds of professional Elvis imitators in white capes and rhinestones, its thousands of parading tap dancers, fiddlers and trumpeters, its bevies of movie stars, torch bearers and champion athletes, its flotillas of sailing ships and fireboats and its gigantic, breathtaking, night-into-day fireworks spectacular. In the inky waters of New York Harbor, the aircraft carrier USS *John F. Kennedy* lay anchored at the statue's feet. Standing on the flight deck, the President of the United States, with the President of France at his side, pressed a button and, as a symphony orchestra and a vast choir burst into "America the Beautiful," a thick beam of laser light flashed across the night and lit Liberty anew for all the world to see.

With what extravaganza could the United States be expected to extol the more significant anniversary—three years later, in 1989—of the fulfillment of the second hundred years of the American experiment and the advent of the third century of the oldest democratic republic on earth? Venerability is not something one associates with the United States, but the Scottish historian of America, Denis W. Brogan, did well to remind us that when Americans began their journey in 1789 "the French monarchy still stood; there was a Holy Roman Emperor, a Venetian Republic and a Dutch Republic, an Autocrat in St. Petersburg, a Sultan-Caliph in Constantinople, an Emperor vested with the 'mandate of heaven' in Peking and a Shogun ruling the hermit empire of Japan in the name of a secluded, impotent and almost unknown Mikado." For the bicentennial of President Washington's

FIFTY YEARS ON IN NEW YORK'S UNION SQUARE: Jerome Liebling, whose emblematic 1947 photograph of citizens appears at the front of this book, went back for us in 1997. His new photograph gives a flavor of the changes in the country's ethnic makeup and its style—and the inscription above them completes Jefferson's words: "How little do my countrymen know what precious blessings they are in possession of and which no other people on earth enjoy."

inauguration, on April 29, 1989, President Bush, as I re-marked in the introduction, offered a few words, bereft of marching bands, pyrotechnics or laser beams and with nary a tap dancer in sight. But reality, in that brilliant climactic year of the American century, offered a celebration more thrilling than any theatrical impresario might devise, one not wholly anticipated even in the flushed rhetoric of 1986. It was stun-ning in its surprise, it was beautiful in its simplicity, and it was apt. It was, in a word, freedom. The anthem in 1989 was the sound of sledgehammer striking concrete, as joyful as the solitary trumpet call floating in the air in the final act of Beethoven's *Fidelio*. The 28-mile Berlin Wall encircling the free sectors of the city began to be torn down by eager hands on November 11, 1989. Nobody had choreographed the event. Nobody could have. It was all a little untidy. The happy wreckers were a few months late for the April bicentennial, but in the long arc of history the timing was extraordinary, as uncanny in its way as the peaceful deaths of John Adams and Thomas Jefferson within a few hours of each other on the fiftieth anniversary of American independence. One day the Brandenburg Gate was desolate, the next tens of thousands surged through the checkpoints the failing East Germans opened at midnight. In the exultant darkness everyone wanted a piece of the wall that for 28 years had been a symbol of tyranny. Now it was, as they say, history. The cracks in the Soviet monolith were already apparent as 1989 began, and then, throughout America's anniversary year, tens of millions of men and women in East and Central Europe claimed their freedom, just as the Americans of 1776 had claimed theirs, and succeeding generations have fought for fulfillment of that promise. On June 4, 1989, Poland freely voted for Lech Wałesa's anticommunist Solidarity coalition; and the Red Army did not intervene. On October 7, Hungary renounced communism. On October 18, East Germany's Communist leader Erich Honecker resigned. The banners of free men and women were soon raised in Bulgaria, Czechoslovakia, Roma-nia and the Baltic states. Then dictatorial communism van-ished under—and within—the very walls of the Kremlin, and overnight the coercive Soviet Union itself disintegrated. As the millennium approached, it could not be said, as Henry Adams had said a hundred years before, that America was "drifting in the dead water of the fin de siecle." This global triumph of liberal democracy over Communist totalitarian-ism was the pinnacle of the American century.

How much of a conceit is it to claim the revolution as an American triumph? A little. Many hands tore at the wall,

FREE AT LAST: At the Berlin Wall on November 10, 1989. In Thomas Kien-zle's photograph, ecstatic Berliners dance and sing on top of the wall; the next day they began pulling it down. Guy Le Querrec photographed the

joyous reunification of the two Germanies at the Brandenburg Gate (top). By the end of the year, Czechoslovakia and Romania were free, too.

including those of the European democrats, Pope John Paul II, and the dissidents in the Soviet Union. And emancipation would not have come anywhere near as quickly without the reforming initiatives of the last leader of the Soviet Union, Mikhail Sergeievich Gorbachev, without his willingness to put his country before his party, without his determination to let the Russian people confront the cruel deeds done in their name. Gorbachev's own hammer blow for Eastern Europe was to renounce Brezhnev's imperial doctrine by which the Soviet Union had claimed the right to intervene in defense of its ideology in any Communist country. Gorbachev was a revolutionary, though not in the way he intended. Though he claimed, no doubt sincerely, to be a Leninist, he had more in common with Gandhi than with Lenin. The last Soviet leader, unlike the first, never behaved as if he believed that the ends would justify the means. Gorbachev wanted the Soviet Union to be what he called a "normal" country and he also wanted it to be Communist. It could not, of course, be both. Gorbachev dispelled the pall of fear that alone had kept the party state alive—and once that was done the rest was inevitable. After seven decades of violence, the regime collapsed, messily but peacefully of its own dead weight. George Kennan and Arthur Schlesinger, Jr., had long predicted that this would happen, that political containment would work eventually. The trick, of course, was to contain communism without blowing up the world or, in the name of freedom, destroying freedom at home. This is what the West successfully did for 45 years, led by America under Democratic and Republican administrations alike. There were dangerous passages, as we have noted, but nerves were steadied at critical times. Schlesinger's seminal 1949 book, *The Vital Center*, offered the rallying point of a robust anticommunist liberal position between the fellow-traveling left and the reckless right. The American trade unions, too, deserve a place in any pantheon of liberators. What if Irving Brown of the AFL-CIO had not been down on the docksides in France and Italy in 1949, secretly organizing anticommunist unions and factions? The Red unions might have succeeded in stopping all those Marshall Plan tractors and wheat and steel. Then, goodbye, free Europe! The American union movement led by David Dubinsky, George Meany, Walter Reuther, Jay Lovestone, Lane Kirkland, Albert Shanker, Thomas Donahue and others was also effective in giving material succor and hope to the oppressed workers behind the iron curtain. Out of all this came Poland's Solidarity movement.

The final, critical, American contribution was provided by the puzzling person of Ronald Reagan. It was Reagan who had the vision—William F. Buckley, Jr., calls it the innocent audacity—to recognize that the Soviet Union was not merely a great power to be contained but an "evil empire" to be transformed, and it was Reagan who also defied his conventionally hawkish aides by being willing to negotiate fairly and in good faith. Gorbachev was able to carry his generals with him only because they came to see that they could not win an arms race against Reagan's resurgent America and a resolute Europe. The judgment of Jack Matlock, Jr., who was in and out of the Kremlin from 1987 to 1991 as ambassador for both Reagan and Bush, is that the arms-control establishment, the liberal wing of the Democratic party and the media, who all campaigned for conciliation at any cost, would have deprived Gorbachev of his most powerful weapon against his hardliners. At the same time, the most skeptical Republicans and bureaucrats risked an historic opportunity when they tried to prevent Reagan from talking man-to-man with Gorbachev. If their intransigence had prevailed, as it nearly did in the early fumbling days of the Bush presidency, Gorbachev might have been swept aside by the apparatchiks around him instead of by the ballots cast for Boris Yeltsin. At the end of the American century, there might have been nothing to celebrate.

History will go on unraveling the knot of circumstance, stratagem, chance and personality. In the end it is likely that no single brow will be able to claim the wreath of victory over a dangerous and depressing totalitarianism. But there can be no doubt that it was the American example, in its spiritual as well as its material beneficence, that in the long dark years was the torch of freedom all the world could see.

Capitalism defeated communism. The question for the next century is whether capitalism can triumph over its own contradictions. More or less all the struggles we have explored in *The American Century* cross the bridge with us into the twenty-first century—racism, immigration, poverty, crime, drugs, nuclear weapons, the disparity between rich and poor, greed and corruption, the pillaging of the natural environment, the struggles of labor, the privileges of wealth, the decay of the cities, the dilution of educational standards, the distortions of the mass media, the dilemma of where personal freedom ends and public responsibility begins. Yet Americans enjoy more happiness and more individual liberty under the law than ever dreamt of in 4,000 years of ordered societies. They are, as David Potter phrased it, "a

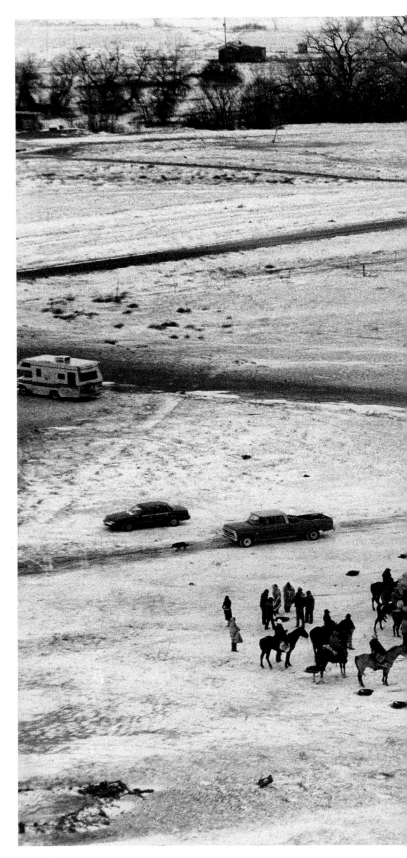

REMEMBRANCE: 100 years is but the flight of a bird in the 500-year history of Native Americans and white invaders. In Guy Le Querrec's photograph, Sioux Indians gather in a circle of prayer in the frozen wastes of South Dakota in 1990. They have paused during a grueling 17-day ride retracing

Big Foot's journey to Wounded Knee, where so many of their tribesmen died. The Indian peoples at the end of the century are in parlous condition despite their status as the only minority in the United States with sovereign territorial rights. Tribes receive hundreds of millions in federal subsidies and earn money from selling casino gambling rights and storing wastes, but a third of their households are on welfare. The tribes are vulnerable, as always, to white exploitation—yet they are restive with their continued status as wards of the white man's government in Washington.

THE PEA PICKER, 1936: Florence Thompson, 32, pregnant and widowed, huddled with three of her five hungry children in a lean-to in Nipomo, California. Dorothea Lange, having finished a month's assignment photographing the migrant labor camps, drove past the sign to the pea-picking camp that bitterly cold March day and then, 20 miles along the highway, responded to an instinct to turn back and take photographs. "She seemed to know that my pictures might help her, and so she helped me. There was a sort of equality about it."

THE PEA PICKER, 1979: Florence Thompson with her daughters Norma Rydiewski (front), Katherine McIntosh and Ruby Sprague at Norma's house in Modesto, California. "I left Oklahoma in 1925 and went to California. The Depression hit just about the time them girls' [her daughters'] dad died." Everything she owned she packed in or on top of the car and went looking for work. "I'd pick four or five hundred pounds of cotton every day. I didn't even weigh a hundred pounds." Living under the bridge at Bakersfield described in Steinbeck's *Grapes of Wrath*, she walked downtown for a 50-cents-a-day restaurant job, and fed the family on the leftovers. During World War II, her daughters worked as shipyard welders and a son went to Guam. Florence worked in a hospital until she was 66. "She kept us together," says Katherine. "We all have good jobs and we all own our own homes. And none of us has ever been in trouble." Photograph by Bill Ganzel.

people of plenty." They have a sense of progress, an intense faith in the opportunity to rise by one's own efforts. There were notable victories along the way—against the trusts that threatened to stifle democracy at the turn of the century; against the organized money that fought the New Deal; against the oppression of women; against Jim Crow, the Slave Power's wicked heir; against secrecy and censorship; against the menace of the totaliarianisms. There were periods when all seemed right. The twenties and the 15 years after World War II were both marked by abundance, social mobility, optimism, patriotism, and confidence, so that despite the inequities there was a high level of trust in the nation's institutions and its traditional values. The emphasis was on social harmony, the efficacy of the melting pot, the attainment of the American dream of individual fulfilment by equal opportunity. The most satisfying expression of Federal will was Franklin Roosevelt's Servicemen's Readjustment Act (1944), better known as the GI Bill of Rights. Elitists ridiculed the notion of millions of ordinary men and women being fit for scholarship, but those veterans, having won the war, won the peace. They helped America soar in the fifties and sixties.

And every time one of them stepped up to receive his diploma, a lightbulb lit up in everyone's mind: What a waste of this country's talent we had endured by limiting higher education to the well-off, what an undemocratic denial of a citizen's potential we had tolerated! The sixties to the eighties, rather like the thirties, saw a reversal of mood on virtually all fronts. Despair supplanted optimism, cynicism eroded faith, the counterculture derided traditional values, certainty of progress was replaced by the conviction that capitalism was incompetent and corrupt, ethnic differences were highlighted. And yet for all the distress and turmoil, the militant movements—for civil rights, peace, the environment and women's rights—left America a fairer, better place before the retreat into the narcissism of the "me decade," fractious identity politics and the culture of victimization so witheringly analyzed in Robert Hughes's polemic, *The Culture of Complaint.*

The British scholar Paul Kennedy, in *The Rise and Fall of*

PLEDGING ALLEGIANCE: "Here individuals of all nations are melted into a new race of men." That was the observation of the French American immigrant J. Hector St. John de Crèvecoeur in 1776. At the end of the second century, worries whether the vision could be sustained were dispelled by the enthusiasm of the new citizens. Photograph by Alon Reininger.

the *Great Powers*, advanced the general thesis that the previous great world powers—China, Spain, France, Great Britain, Russia—all saw their influence decline precipitously when their grasp and ambition too grievously exceeded their resources. He suggested a similar fate for the United States. Another English observer, as I mentioned in the introduction, felt sure America was bound to disintegrate as an epic archipelago of warring tribes. Rudyard Kipling was proved wrong, but the tribes have multiplied in ways he could never have imagined. It is certainly possible that the United States could fall apart, fracturing along its ethnic fault lines or the chilling and increasing disparities between wealthy and poor, between the city and the gated communities of the new suburban pods—suburbs that have grown so fast that now America, uniquely, has more suburbanites than city or rural dwellers. The psychological gap between rich and poor has grown, the rich apparently desiring to "secede" from the rest of society with their private schools and private police forces: There were already more private than public police in 1970; at the end of the American century, reports Robert Kaplan, there were three times as many, and in California four times as many. The gap between rich and poor is the most extreme in Western civilization. The top 1 percent of Americans have more wealth than the bottom 90 per cent. Nearly 40 million people have no health insurance. Crime strikes the poorest most of all. America leads Europe and Japan in beggars, murders, and prisons per capita.

MAN-TO-MEDIA: There were few filters between Theodore Roosevelt and the electorate in the 1912 presidential race—here an expectant crowd and just a couple of reporters. By the end of the century, nobody argued anymore with Marshall McLuhan's 1964 statement that "the medium is the message." *Right:* Richard Ellis's photograph epitomizes the circus. It happens to be of a 1998 press briefing by the independent counsel Kenneth Starr, investigating President Clinton.

Hope lies in a resurgent economy and increasing social mobility rather than in political action from the center. We began the century with politics in thrall to money, and we end it that way. Congressmen seem to spend most of their time raising money to pay for television advertising—which should be free anyway, since the airwaves belong to the public—and then they owe favors to the special interests that put up the dollar. The Supreme Court, though erratically activist, has failed to come to the rescue, unwisely concluding that this form of bribery cannot be outlawed because money is a form of free speech. Money talks! The speed and prolixity of modern communication is stupendous, but politically there is a disconnection. In the polls people say they want radical reform of campaign finance, and simple universal health care, yet on the edge of the millennium neither proposal had been seriously debated in Congress or put to a vote. The parties have become empty vessels. The community groups of the sixties have mostly calcified into shrill single-cause lobbyists. State governments are among the most corrupt and undemocratic of all our institutions. Even in presidential elections, participation and voting has continued to decline

to the point where only half the electorate is involved. Possibly, in its third century, America will evolve new forms of democratic participation. Perhaps well-informed citizens will decide on hundreds of proposals by means of interactive television and the Internet. The frustration with conventional politics is certainly intense. In California, impatience with the party machinery and state bureaucracy has led more and more to citizens using the initiative to force referendums on crucial issues. In 1998, Californians voted overwhelmingly to end bilingual education. Hispanic families recognized, as political activists refused to do, that the system was failing to prepare their children for advancement in an English-speaking society.

Ethnicity seems set to be destiny in the politics of the third century. Immigration ran out of control after the ill-judged 1965 Immigration Reform Act, with more than 1 million a year admitted, compared to 300,000 before. The ethnic mix of the country was transformed. The proportion of the flow from Europe, the primary historic homeland, was cut back sharply. In something like an extended civil-rights gesture to the world's huddled masses, 85 percent of the 16.7 million legal immigrants between 1968 and 1992 were from the Third World—47 percent from Latin America. Another 2 to 3 million illegals come each year from and through Mexico, though a proportion are transient workers. In any event, at the end of the century, 25 million of America's population had been born somewhere else. The cosmopolitan influx

refreshes the uniformity of American culture. In a morning stroll in few blocks of New York you may buy a paper from a Sikh running a newsstand, a bagel from an Egyptian working in a Jewish delicatessen, an apple from a Mexican working in a Korean market, a paperback from an African running a street-corner bookstall. You may lunch at a Greek pizza parlor, spend an hour at an Indian movie theater, take home wine from a Chinese liquor store. That is the bright side. In New York there are also Iranian and Bengali taxi drivers sleeping six to a room. Los Angeles harbors sweatshops full of illegal Mexicans working as slave labor behind barbed wire. Americans of all classes sometimes worry that the Mexican immigrants in particular might be a threat to the national identity because parts of the United States. were once Mexican, and their devotion to their language and culture might well tempt them to separatism. Can they be assimilated? Do they want to be assimilated? Or will America be like Rome, destroyed by its domestic hostilities and the immigration of determined peoples from northern Europe, Asia and North Africa attracted by its economic dynamism? Arthur Schelsinger, Jr., whose best-seller on mulitculturalism bore the disturbing title *The Disuniting of America*, nonetheless concluded with optimism. He predicted that we will remember "that we are members one of another, Americans first and last, tied together, in Martin Luther King's phrase, into 'a single garment of destiny.' " The political scientist Peter Skerry says his research does not support the fear that in the

The 42nd president who took America into the twenty-first century—along with some of those who came before. A *New Yorker* cover by Edward Sorel.

Southwest, America has the makings of its own Quebec. Mexican immigrants want to become part of mainstream America. The reporter Roberto Suro concludes his book *Strangers Among Us:* "The Latino era of immigration will produce its own hot crucible and America will emerge from it with a stronger vision of itself." This seems plausible. Millions of Mexican Americans have resided in former Mexican territory for 150 years now, and never has there been a serious separatist movement. Whole communities, such as the Cubans in Miami, have become conservative Americans. The values deemed traditional flourish in the family and church-oriented Hispanic community. The Asians, if anything, seem more American than Americans, as if they were descended from a branch of eighteenth-century Scotch Presybterians or Dutch burghers who had landed in California. A more substantial concern must lie in the way Latinos are being encouraged to identify themselves not as immigrants facing the difficulties immigrants have faced for decades, but as victims of racial discrimination and therefore deserving of preferential treatment. Today's Hispanic and Asian immigrants have an incentive to stay out of the melting pot because in the system of racial preferences ordained by Congress and sanctified by the Supreme Court they are eligible for the rewards in affirmative action in employment, education, business contracts and gerrymandered voting districts. Intriguingly, the Asian immigrants who regularly score better than Americans on test scores and anchor their financial success around extended-family businesses have actually led fights to end affirmative action in many places because it limits Asian admissions. The most vulnerable community, in fact, may be the African American, in whose name racial preferences were first mandated.

Black Americans, as Professor Henry Louis Gates, Jr., has pointed out, are in a unique position. For them, the country of oppression and the country of liberation are one and the same—and both are the United States of America. African

Lone woman voter: The citizen, by Burt Glinn.

Americans have nowhere to go back to. Their only option—our only option—is to make this country live up to its nominal creed. Most of them did not come to escape tyranny; most of them were brought to America in furtherance of tyranny. Their ancestors were brought here long before the ancestors of the vast majority of other Americans. Over the last 30 years, blacks have made amazing strides in voting, freedom from harassment, educational achievements and standard of living. There are now four times as many black families with incomes of over $50,000 a year as there were in 1968. But if we have enabled the "submerged tenth" to escape the ghetto, those left behind have become more mired in intractable social pathologies. And most black children still go to black schools in black neighborhoods where they are likely to get an inferior education. As in everything else, America is half-way to heaven in solving seemingly unsolvable problems, and still tied to earth.

If the hundred years have taught us anything, however, it must be that the dream of permanent solutions—except of the most dreadful kind—is a delusion. The twentieth century is a junkyard of the broken-down utopias of the millenarians and the Social Darwinists, the fascists and the communists; and it is sure that the "orgiastic future" of Jay Gatsby's dreams will year by year recede before us. Americans will go on stubbornly believing in the future, but the saving grace of the society is its openness and a restless disposition that never quite allows an organic optimism to congeal into self-satisfaction. The most outrageous prophecy is apt to look absurd in the face of American ingenuity, courage, flexibility, pragmatism, avarice, hubris and just plain chutzpah. Americans best understand the paradox that if anything is to be preserved it must change. It is the possibility of reasoned change that gives life to democracy. Rudyard Kipling, that relentless critic, had a line, "What stands if Freedom fall?" In the American adventure, all is possible while freedom lives.

ACKNOWLEDGMENTS

The American Century would have taken me even longer in the writing and organization of illustration without the dedication over an unexpected 12 years of the two principal collaborators I engaged: Gail Buckland and Kevin Baker. Gail, an authority on photography and a distinguished author in her own right, was infinitely resourceful in bringing forward thousands of photographs from which I made the final selection with surprisingly few disagreements. Her integrity, knowledge and imagination played a critical role throughout and without her administrative talents I would never have emerged from all the complications. Kevin was my chief history researcher. He supplemented the work of other researchers and my own readings and interviews with an encyclopedic knowledge of American politics and inexhaustible enthusiasm. It is remarkable that these two gifted individuals stayed the course despite the inevitable interruptions in my writing schedule as I moved my career from magazines to books and back again to magazines and newspapers.

Historical research was also carried out for me by Dr. Delphine Taylor, Lawrence Mirsky, Karen McGuinness, Luke Mitchell, Maggie Lee, Esther Gross, David Lefer, Christopher Spelman, Richard Feeley, and Harkness Fellow Nick Cull. Jack Hitt did research for the dummy of the book way back in 1986. The librarian W. Gregory Gallagher went to great lengths to locate obscure publications. At different periods, I had office assistance from a number of eager hands. It was tragic that Julie Day, who joined me from Harvard and Duke in 1989, died in the middle of her work when she was only in her twenties. She was a brilliant colleague who did much to organize my early drafts. Esther Gross and Elsa Burt rode shotgun on the manuscript.

My first conception for the book, way back in 1985, was executed as a dummy with speed and grace by Alessandro Franchini, who had worked with me on *The Sketchbooks of Picasso* when I was at the Atlantic Monthly Press. When he moved to Chicago, Charles Churchward and David Harris at *Vanity Fair* carried the original concept to fruition. Wendy Byrne was imaginative in marrying the various design contributions into something entirely her own, and ingenious in solving every problem. Merri Ann Morrell was an indefatigable and valiant typesetter. The graphic designers John Grimwade and Gregory Wakabayashi were uncomplaining on the nth revision of the maps. At Knopf, I was sustained by many hands in the course of production. Katherine Hourigan, managing editor, remained uncannily gracious, though firm, as deadlines approached and receded. The quality of the book's production owes a huge amount to the dedication, taste and expertise of Andy Hughes. Dori Carlson and Kevin Bourke were marvelous production editors, and Trent Duffy was a meticulous copy editor and I surely am very much in his debt. Also at Knopf, I want to thank Archie Ferguson, Leyla Aker, Shelley Berg, Vanessa Leander and Richela Fabian, and the fabulous publishing team of Pat Johnson, Bill Loverd, Paul Bogaards, and Jill Morrison.

Shirley Green was the principal picture researcher in Washington and she was knowledgeable and relentless. Tori Egherman, Marianne Fulton, Bronwin Latimer, Suzanne Hodgart, and Annabelle Merullo in London assisted Gail with photo research, and Steve Heller, design director of the *New York Times Book Review*, gave us early help by putting us in contact with James Fraser and Renee Weber Jadushlever, whose knowledge of political cartoons and caricatures was invaluable. I am especially indebted to the Associated Press, its renowned photographic guru, former vice president Hal Buell (who taught me much), the former AP librarian Kevin Kushel and the present director Chuck Zoeller. Brian Deutsch and Charles Merullo at the Hulton Deutsch, now Hulton Getty, were generous of their time and resources, as were Harry and Gigi Benson, Jacques Lowe, Faigi Rosenthal and Eric Meskauskas, Mary Ann Golon, Norman Pearlstine, editor in chief at Time, Inc., Ben Bradlee at the *Washington Post*, James D. Squires at the *Chicago Tribune*, Shelby Coffey at the *Los Angeles Times*, Timothy Leland at the *Boston Globe*, and John Seigenthaler at the Freedom Forum. In the separate list of credits, Gail acknowledges the photographers, photographic libraries and historical societies. Henry J. Stern, New York City Commissioner of Parks and Recreation, and his staff helped us with photography in Union Square.

I am especially grateful to the academic historians, politicians and journalists who have commented on all or part of my manuscript, and who are of course not responsible in any way for the text. Joel Fleischman, then vice chancellor of Duke University, kindly provided a number of these academic introductions. I thank John Kenneth Galbraith at Harvard, William Chafe at Duke University, Arthur Schlesinger, Jr., Edmund Morris, Allen Weinstein, Kenneth B. Davis, Richard B. Frank and Stanley I. Kutler. They were constructive in their criticisms, as were the journalists and editors Jason Epstein, Stanley Karnow, Sidney Blumenthal, Rick Hertzberg, Jim Hoge, Richard Holbrooke, Bob Loomis, Fred Emery, Howell Raines, Peter Prichard, Neil Sheehan, Walter Isaacson, Sam Tannenhaus, Gerald Posner and my dear friend the late Richard Clurman. President Ford and General Colin Powell were good enough to read small portions relevant to their special areas of knowledge.

I began writing this book when I was in Washington as editorial director of *U.S. News & World Report* and editor in chief of the Atlantic Monthly Press, with the encouragement of my agent, Mortimer Janklow. The chairman of those companies, Mortimer B. Zuckerman, was a fellow immigrant in love with the romance of America—he is from Canada—and he more than lived up to the American tradition of welcoming newcomers. He was a stimulating colleague. I am also grateful to his partner, Fred Drasner, who came to the rescue with accommodation in New York when my home was collapsing under the weight of research material. Another immigrant, Alberto Vitale, when he was chairman of Bantam Books, was the first person in book publishing to urge me on, and his editorial colleagues Steve Rubin, Charles Mitchell and Ann Harris made many good suggestions. Sonny Mehta, yet another immigrant, took over the publishing arrangements at Knopf with legendary skill. Finally, I most warmly thank my Knopf editor, Ashbel Green. Of long American heritage, Ash was sagacious and—like everyone else associated with this book—gifted with patience. None, of course, more than my wife, Tina Brown, and our two children. They came to know full well and tolerate the fact that 100 years of American history is a long time. My most fervent hope is that George and Isabel, new Americans, will come to think their father's long confinements—begun before they were born—were all worthwhile.

HAROLD EVANS,
New York, 1998

PHOTOGRAPHIC ACKNOWLEDGMENTS

Harold Evans and I owe an enormous debt of gratitude to every photographer named in the list of picture credits and to the photographic archivists and curators whose collections are cited. In the 12 years since Harry invited me to join him on his book, I have talked to, worked with and shared a conviction with people all across the nation that photography is not only a dynamic means of visual communication but a vital resource in fully comprehending history. The nation's photographs have many caretakers, and I salute them all.

Harry always saw *The American Century* as a marriage of text and photographs, each having equal weight and power. I thank him for his commitment to photography and his respect and support for my passion, and sometimes near obsession, for finding just the right photograph to tell the story that needed to be told and convey the emotion appropriate to the subject.

Many of the individuals providing me with the greatest assistance over the years have already been mentioned in Harry's acknowledgments. The names that follow reflect only a partial list of the hundreds of photographers, historians and librarians who have helped me with my research since 1987.

The audiovisual archivists at the presidential libraries are a remarkable and knowledgeable group of professionals. They are also courteous and patient, especially when my visits and inquiries seemed to have no end. I should like to thank Pat Wildenberg at Hoover, Mark Renovitch at F.D. Roosevelt, Pauline Testerman at Truman, Kathy Struss at Eisenhower, Alan Goodrich at Kennedy, Philip Scott at Johnson, Dick McNeil at the Nixon Project, Ken Hafeli at Ford, Dave Stanhope at Carter and Mary Finch at Bush. Contact sheets by White House photographers during the Reagan administration were shown to me by Carol McKay and Barbara Henckel at the White House Photo Office. Prints from the original negatives of my selections were generously provided.

The photographic archives of presidents who served prior to Hoover are overseen by an enthusiastic group of specialists and I should especially like to thank Sally Donze, former librarian at the McKinley Museum; Wallace Finley Dailey, curator of the Theodore Roosevelt Collection at Harvard; Ella Rayburn, formerly of the Taft National Historic Site; Jean Preston, former curator of manuscripts, Princeton University Library (Woodrow Wilson Collection); Tauni Graham, formerly of the Archives-Library Division, Ohio Historical Society (Warren Harding Collection) and Cyndy Bittinger, executive director of the Calvin Coolidge Memorial Foundation. Sandra Eisert, who was in the White House Photo Office under Ford, made us aware of very special pictures from Ford's presidency.

Many photographers searched for negatives long forgotten and suggested images unknown to me. A few went to extraordinary lengths to be of help: Jerome Liebling, Henry Ries, Flip Schulke, Duane Hall, James Karales, and the late George Tames. To all the photographers—thank you.

Three men, each of whom had extraordinary war experiences, provided rare photographs from their personal collections. History has been enhanced because of their generosity in sharing their stories and their photographs with us. They are: Igor Belousovich, Joseph Darrigo and Walter Karliner.

Fred Pernell of the National Archives made that very large government institution a friendly, welcoming place to do research. Jim Huffman of the Photographs and Prints Division, Schomburg Center for Research in Black Culture, and his predecessor, Deborah Willis, were both a fountain of knowledge on black history. Robert L. Allen, senior editor, *The Black Scholar,* shared his research and collections on the Port Chicago disaster with us. Thomas Featherstone of the Walter P. Reuther Library at Wayne State University provided us with hauntingly powerful pictures of labor's struggles over the years. My good friend Jane Carmichael, keeper of photographs at the Imperial War Museum, London, assisted both Harry and me in our World War I and World War II research; Faigi Rosenthal of the *Daily News* and Laura Rosen of Bridges and Tunnels, Metropolitan Transit Authority, made working in these New York collections an enjoyable and profitable experience.

Alice Grabiner and Shaun O'Sullivan shared their considerable knowledge of photojournalism with me when my office was part of the U.S. News complex.

Renee Weber Jadushlever carried out important research on cartoons and caricatures, especially those done outside the United States. Dr. James Fraser, a prolific author, a scholar and director of the library at Fairleigh Dickinson University, where a world-class collection of political cartoons is housed, was extraordinarily generous with his advice, his research on our behalf and access to his collection.

My relationship with picture agencies has been amiable even though I kept photos out far longer than I care to mention. Among my many helpful colleagues, I should especially like to thank Norman Currie at Corbis-Bettmann; the late Meredith Collins, Brown Brothers; Ben Chapnick and the late Howard Chapnick, Black Star; Robert Pledge and Catherine Pledge, Contact Press; Eliane Laffont, Sygma; Woodfin Camp, Woodfin Camp & Associates; Debra Cohen and Laura Giammarco, Time/Life Syndication; and Carrie Chalmers at Magnum Photos and previous researchers Laura Strauss and Nancy Carrizales. Harry has already thanked the Associated Press staff, but there are not enough thanks possible to express how wonderful and supportive Kevin Kushel, Chuck Zoeller and Ronnie Farley have been over the years under the wise leadership of AP's President and Chief Executive Officer, Lou D. Boccardi.

Three high school students have assisted me. First Juno Turner and then Luisa Capasso intelligently and cheerfully carried out each task I gave them. The third student was only five when this book began, and will soon be going to college. My daughter, Alaina Buckland, is my last, and dearest, assistant on the book.

GAIL BUCKLAND
WESTFIELD, NEW JERSEY, 1998

BIBLIOGRAPHY

The following is a selected bibliography, drawn from the more than 5,000 volumes used to compile *The American Century*. Other sources includes pamphlets, my notes from travels in the fifties, interviews, archival documents and numerous articles drawn from many different newspapers and magazines, both in the United States and abroad.

Most sources are arranged under those chapters in which they were of primary importance. Many were used in more than one chapter; the additional ones are indicated in parentheses after the entry.

GENERAL USE

Allen, Frederick Lewis. *The Big Change: America Transforms Itself, 1900–1950.* New York: Harper. 1952.

Allman, T. D. *Unmanifest Destiny: Mayhem and Illusion in American Foreign Policy—From the Monroe Doctrine to Reagan's War in El Salvador.* Garden City, New York: The Dial Press. 1984.

Bailey, Thomas A. *The Man on the Street: The Impact of American Public Opinion on Foreign Policy.* New York: Macmillan. 1948.

Bailey, Thomas A. *Presidential Greatness: The Image and the Man from George Washington to the Present.* New York: Appleton-Century. 1966.

Bailey, Thomas A. *A Diplomatic History of the American People.* Englewood Cliffs, New Jersey: Prentice-Hall. 1980.

Barber, James David, ed. *Political Leadership in American Government.* Boston: Little, Brown. 1964.

Barber, James David, and Barbara Kellerman, eds. *Women Leaders in American Politics.* Englewood Cliffs, New Jersey: Prentice-Hall. 1986.

Barber, James David. *Politics by Humans: Research on American Leadership.* Durham, North Carolina: Duke University Press. 1988.

Barber, James David. *The Presidential Character: Predicting Performance in the White House.* Englewood Cliffs, New Jersey: Prentice-Hall. 1992.

Bennett, David H. *The Party of Fear: From Nativist Movements to the New Right in American History.* Chapel Hill, North Carolina: University of North Carolina Press. 1988.

Bennett, W. Lance. *Public Opinion in American Politics.* New York: Harcourt Brace Jovanovich. 1980.

Bernstein, Barton J., ed. *Towards a New Past: Dissenting Essays in American History.* New York: Pantheon Books. 1968.

Boorstin, Daniel J. *The Americans: The Democratic Experience.* New York: Vintage Books. 1974.

Boorstin, Daniel J. *America and the Image of Europe: Reflections on American Thought.* Gloucester, Massachusetts: P. Smith. 1976.

Butterfield, Roger. *The American Past: A History of the United States from Concord to the Great Society.* New York: Simon and Schuster. 1966.

Bryce, James. *The American Commonwealth.* New York: Macmillan. 1913.

Chafee, Zachariah, Jr. *Free Speech in the United States.* Cambridge, Massachusetts: Harvard University Press. 1941.

Chafee, Zachariah, Jr. *The Blessings of Liberty.* Philadelphia: Lippincott. 1956.

Chamberlain, John. *Farewell to Reform: The Rise, Life and Decay of the Progressive Mind in America.* Chicago: Quadrangle Books. 1965.

Chamberlain, John. *The Enterprising Americans: A Business History of the United States.* New York: Harper & Row. 1974.

Commager, Henry Steele, and Allan Nevins, eds. *The Heritage of America.* Boston: Little, Brown. 1949.

Commager, Henry Steele. *The American Mind: An Interpretation of American Thought and Character Since the 1880's.* New Haven, Connecticut: Yale University Press. 1950.

Cooper, William, Jr., and Thomas E. Terrill. *The American South: A History.* New York: Alfred A. Knopf. 1990.

Cunliffe, Marcus, and the Editors of American Heritage. *The American Heritage History of the Presidency.* New York: American Heritage Publishing. 1968.

Dallek, Robert. *The American Style of Foreign Policy.* New York: Alfred A. Knopf. 1983.

Dimbleby, David, and David Reynolds. *An Ocean Apart.* New York: Random House. 1987.

Douglas, Paul H. *In Our Time.* New York: Harcourt, Brace & World. 1968.

Eaton, Herbert. *Presidential Timber: A History of Nominating Conventions, 1868–1960.* London: Collier-Macmillan. 1964.

Foner, Eric, and John A. Garraty, eds. *The Reader's Companion to American History.* Boston: Houghton Mifflin. 1991.

Fox, Dixon Ryan, and Arthur M. Schlesinger, eds. *The Cavalcade of America.* Springfield, Massachusetts: Milton Bradley Company. 1937.

Friendly, Fred W. *The Good Guys, the Bad Guys and the First Amendment: Free Speech vs. Fairness in Broadcasting.* New York: Vintage Books, 1976.

Friendly, Fred W., and Martha J. H. Elliott. *The Constitution, That Delicate Balance.* New York: Random House. 1984.

Galbraith, John Kenneth. *Money: Whence It Came, Where It Went.* Boston: Houghton Mifflin. 1975.

Galbraith, John Kenneth. *American Capitalism: The Concept of Countervailing Power.* White Plains, New York: M.E. Sharpe. 1980.

Galbraith, John Kenneth. *A Journey Through Economic Time: A Firsthand View.* New York: Houghton Mifflin. 1994.

Garraty, John A. *Interpreting American History: Conversations with Historians.* 2 vols. New York: Macmillan. 1970.

Garraty, John A. *Quarrels That Have Shaped the Constitution.* New York: Harper & Row. Publishers, 1975.

Garraty, John A., and Robert A. McCaughey. *The American Nation.* New York: Harper & Row. 1987.

Gatell, Frank Otto, and Allen Weinstein, eds. *American Themes: Essays in Historiography.* New York: Oxford University Press. 1968.

Goldstein, Robert Justin. *Political Repression in Modern America.* New York: Schenkman Publishing. 1977.

Greider, William. *Secrets of the Temple.* New York: Simon and Schuster. 1987.

Hamby, Alonzo. *The Imperial Years: The United States Since 1939.* New York: Longman. 1978.

Hobsbawm, E. J. *The Age of Extremes: A History of the World, 1914–1991.* New York: Pantheon Books. 1994.

Hofstadter, Richard, William Millier, and Daniel Aaron. *The American Republic.* Englewood Cliffs, New Jersey: Prentice-Hall. 1970.

Hofstadter, Richard. *The American Political Tradition and the Men Who Made It.* New York: Vintage Books. 1989.

Hughes, Emmet John. *The Living Presidency: The Resources and Dilemmas of the American Presidential Office.* Baltimore: Penguin Books. 1973.

Johnson, Paul. *Modern Times: A History of the Modern World from 1917 to the 1980s.* London: Weidenfeld and Nicolson. 1983.

Johnson, Paul. *A History of the American People.* London: Weidenfeld and Nicolson. 1997.

Keegan, John. *A History of Warfare.* London: Hutchinson. 1993.

Kennedy, Paul. *The Rise and Fall of the Great Powers.* New York: Random House. 1987.

Kindeberger, Charles P. *The World Economy and National Finance in Historical Perspective.* Ann Arbor, Michigan: University of Michigan Press. 1995.

Kindleberger, Charles P. *World Economic Primacy: 1500–1990.* New York: Oxford University Press. 1996.

Kissinger, Henry. *Diplomacy.* New York: Simon and Schuster. 1994.

Kolko, Gabriel. *Main Currents in Modern American History.* New York: Harper & Row. 1976.

Kolko, Gabriel. *Century of War: Politics, Conflicts, and Society Since 1914.* New York: New Press. 1994.

LaFeber, Walter, and Richard Polenberg. *The American Century: A History of the United States Since the 1890s.* New York: Wiley. 1979.

LaFeber, Walter. *The American Age: United States Foreign Policy at Home and Abroad Since 1750.* New York: Norton. 1989.

Lerner, Max. *America as a Civilization.* New York: Simon and Schuster. 1957.

Leuchtenburg, William E., general ed. *The Unfinished Century: America Since 1900.* Boston: Little, Brown. 1973.

Link, Arthur S. *American Epoch.* New York: Alfred A. Knopf. 1963.

Manchester, William. *The Glory and the Dream: A Narrative History of America, 1932–1972.* New York: Little, Brown, and Company. 1974.

Morison, Samuel Eliot. *The Oxford History of the American People.* New York: New American Library. 1972.

Nelson, Daniel. *Shifting Fortunes: The Rise and Decline of American Labor, from the 1820s to the Present.* Chicago: Ivan R. Dee. 1997.

Nevins, Allan, and Henry Steele Commager. *A Short History of the United States.* New York: The Modern Library. 1956.

Oxford Analytica. *America in Perspective.* Boston: Houghton Mifflin. 1986.

Patterson, James T. *America's Struggle Against Poverty, 1900–1985.* Cambridge, Massachusetts: Harvard University Press. 1986.

Patterson, James T. *The Second American Revolution.* New York: Morrow. 1994.

Perret, Geoffrey. *A Country Made by War: From the Revolution to Vietnam —the Story of America's Rise to Power.* New York: Random House. 1989.

Renshaw, Patrick. *American Labor and Consensus Capital, 1935–1990.* Jackson, Mississippi: University Press of Mississippi. 1991.

Schlesinger, Arthur Meier. *Political and Social Growth of the American People, 1865–1940.* New York: Macmillan. 1942.

Schlesinger, Arthur Meier, and Dixon Ryan Fox, eds. *A History of American Life.* 13 vols. New York: Macmillan. 1948.

Schlesinger, Arthur Meier. *The Rise of Modern America, 1865–1951.* New York: Macmillan. 1951.

Schlesinger, Arthur M., Jr. *The Vital Center: The Politics of Freedom.* Boston: Houghton Mifflin. 1962.

Schlesinger, Arthur M., Jr. *The Cycles of American History.* Boston: Houghton Mifflin. 1986.

Schwarz, Jordan A., ed. *The Ordeal of Twentieth-Century America: Interpretative Readings.* Boston: Houghton Mifflin. 1974.

Sowell, Thomas. *Ethnic America: A History.* New York: Basic Books. 1981.

Steel, Ronald. *Walter Lippmann and the American Century.* New York: Random House. 1980.

Stevens, John D. *Shaping the First Amendment: The Development of Free Expression.* Beverly Hills, California: Sage Publications. 1982.

Sullivan, Mark. *Our Times: The United States 1900–1925. Vol. I–VI.* New York: Scribners. 1926.

Taft, John. *American Power: The Rise and Decline of U.S. Globalism, 1918–1988.* New York: Harper. 1989.

Truman, Margaret. *First Ladies.* New York: Random House. 1995.

Weinstein, Allen, and Frank Otto Gatell, eds. *Essays on the National Past.* 2 vols. New York: Random House. 1970.

Weinstein, Allen, and R. Jackson Wilson. *Freedom and Crisis: An American History.* 2 vols. New York: Random House. 1978.

White, Donald W. *The American Century: The Rise and Decline of the United States as a World Power.* New Haven, Connecticut: Yale University Press. 1996.

White, William Allen. *The Old Order Changeth: A View of American Democracy.* New York: Macmillan. 1910.

White, William Allen. *Masks in a Pageant.* New York: Macmillan. 1928.

Williams, William Appleman. *The Tragedy of American Diplomacy.* New York: Dell 1972.

Williams, William Appleman. *Americans in a Changing World: A History of the United States in the Twentieth Century.* New York: Harper & Row. 1978.

Williams, William Appleman. *The Contours of American History.* New York: W.W. Norton. 1988.

Wilson, Edmund. *To the Finland Station: A Study in the Writing and Acting of History.* New York: Farrar, Straus and Giroux. 1972.

Woloch, Nancy. *Women and the American Experience.* New York: Alfred A. Knopf. 1984.

Woodward, C. Vann. *The Old World's New World.* New York: Oxford University Press. 1991.

Zinn, Howard. *A People's History of the United States.* New York: Harper & Row. 1980.

GENERAL REFERENCE

The American Heritage Pictorial History of the Presidents of the United States, Vols. 1–2. New York: American Heritage. 1968.

Bailey, Thomas A., and Stephen M. Dobbs *Voices of America: The Nation's Story in Slogans, Sayings, and Songs.* New York: The Free Press. 1976.

Blake, Lord, and C. S. Nicholls, eds. *The Dictionary of National Biography— The Concise Dictionary, Part II. 1901–1970.* New York: Oxford University Press. 1982.

Blake, Lord, and C. S. Nicholls, eds. *The Dictionary of National Biography, 1971–1980.* New York: Oxford University Press. 1986.

Blake, Lord, and C. S. Nicholls, eds. *The Dictionary of National Biography, 1981–1985.* New York: Oxford University Press. 1990.

Carnes, Mark C. S., and John A. Garraty, with Patrick Williams. *Mapping America's Past: A Historical Atlas.* New York: Henry Holt. 1996.

Chafee, Zechariah, Jr. *Documents on Fundamental Human Rights.* 2 vols. New York: Atheneum. 1963.

Commager, Henry Steele, ed. *Documents of American History.* Englewood Cliffs, New Jersey: Prentice-Hall. 1973.

Current, Richard N., and John A. Garraty, eds. *Words That Made American History: Selected Readings.* 2 vols. Boston: Little, Brown. 1962.

DeGregorio, William A. *The Complete Book of American Presidents.* New York: Wings Books. 1991.

Douglas, Paul H. *Real Wages in the United States, 1890–1926.* New York: Houghton Mifflin. 1930.

Frost, Elizabeth, ed. *The Bully Pulpit: Quotations from America's Presidents.* New York: New England Publishing Associates. 1988.

Garraty, John A., and Robert A. Divine, eds. *Twentieth-Century America: Contemporary Documents and Opinions.* Boston: Little, Brown. 1968.

Garraty, John A., ed. *Encyclopedia of American Biography.* New York: Harper & Row. 1974.

Gelb, Arthur, and A. M. Rosenthal. *Great Lives of the Twentieth Century.* New York: Times Books. 1988.

Glennon, Lorraine, ed. *Our Times. The Illustrated History of the 20th Century.* Atlanta: Turner Publishing. 1995.

Graff, Henry F. *The Presidents: A Reference History.* New York: Scribners. 1996.

Greenspan, Karen. *The Timetable of Women's History.* New York: Simon and Schuster. 1994.

Hofstadter, Richard, and Michael Wallace, eds. *American Violence: A Documentary History.* New York: Alfred A. Knopf. 1970.

Hofstadter, Richard, and Beatrice K. Hofstadter, eds. *Great Issues in American History: From Reconstruction to the Present Day, 1864–1981.* New York: Vintage Books. 1982.

Linton, Calvin D., ed. *The Bicentennial Almanac: 200 Years of America 1776–1976.* Nashville, Tennessee: T. Nelson. 1975.

Linton, Calvin D. *American Headlines.* Nashville, Tennessee: Thomas Nelson. 1985.

The New Encyclopaedia Britannica. Chicago: Encyclopaedia Britannica. 1990.

Nicholls, C. S., ed. Sir Keith Thomas, consulting ed. *The Dictionary of Na-*

WILLIAM HOWARD TAFT, a big baseball fan, initiates the custom of throwing out the first ball on opening day, April 14, 1910, at a game between the Washington Senators and the Philadelphia Athletics in Washington's old Griffith Stadium.

tional Biography, 1986–1990. New York: Oxford University Press. 1996.

Schlesinger, Arthur, Jr. *History of American Presidential Elections, 1789–1968, Vols. I–III.* New York: Chelsea House Publishers with McGraw-Hill. 1971.

Schlesinger, Arthur M., Jr., ed. *History of U.S. Political Parties.* New York: Chelsea House. 1973.

Schlesinger, Arthur M., Jr., and Roger Bruns, eds. *Congress Investigates: A Documented History, 1792–1974.* New York: Chelsea House. 1975.

Sherr, Lynn, and Jurate Kazickas. *The American Woman's Gazetteer.* New York: Bantam Books. 1976.

Stephen, Leslie, and Sidney Lee, eds. *Dictionary of National Biography.* 66 vols. London: Smith, Elder, & Co. 1901.

Wattenberg, Ben J. *The Statistical History of the United States.* New York: Basic Books. 1976.

INTRODUCTION

Adams, Brooks. *The New Empire.* New York: Macmillan. 1903.

Adams, Henry. Ernest Samuels, ed. *The Education of Henry Adams.* Boston: Houghton Mifflin. 1974. (1, 2, 3, 4)

Bellamy, Edward. Cecelia Tichi, ed. *Looking Backward, 2000–1887.* New York: Penguin Books. 1982.

Bok, Edward William. *The Americanization of Edward Bok: The Autobiography of a Dutch Boy Fifty Years After.* New York: Charles Scribner's Sons. 1923.

Bryce, James. *The Study of American History.* New York: Macmillan. 1922.

Carnegie, Andrew. Edward C. Kirkland, ed. *The Gospel of Wealth, and Other Timely Essays.* Cambridge, Massachusetts: Belknap Press of Harvard University Press. 1962. (2)

Carnegie, Andrew. *Triumphant Democracy; or, Fifty Years' March of the Re-*

public. Port Washington, New York: Kennikat Press. 1971.

Dos Passos, John. Donald Pizer, ed. *John Dos Passos: The Major Nonfictional Prose.* Detroit: Wayne State University Press. 1988. (7)

Emerson, Ralph Waldo. Brooks Atkinson, ed. *Complete Essays and Other Writings.* New York: Modern Library. 1950.

Garraty, John A., ed. *The Transformation of American Society, 1870–1890.* New York: Harper & Row. 1968.

Garraty, John A. *The New Commonwealth, 1877–1890.* New York: Harper & Row. 1968.

Hart, Albert Bushnell, ed. *The American Nation: A History.* New York: Harper & Brothers. 1918.

James, Henry. *The American Scene.* New York: Harper & Brothers. 1907.

James, Henry. *The American.* Fairfield, New Jersey: A. M. Kelley. 1976.

James, Henry. *Collected Travel Writings: Great Britain and America.* New York: Library of America. 1993.

Kipling, Rudyard. Arrell Morgan Gibson, ed. *American Notes: Rudyard Kipling's West.* Norman, Oklahoma: University of Oklahoma Press. 1981.

Kobler, John. *Luce: His Time, Life, and Fortune.* Garden City, New York: Doubleday. 1968. (9, 10, 11, 12, 13)

Lowe, David. *Stanford White's New York.* New York: Doubleday. 1992.

Luce, Henry R. *The American Century.* New York: Farrar & Rinehart. 1941. (10, 11)

McCullough, David G. *The Great Bridge.* New York: Simon and Schuster. 1972.

Stevenson, Robert Louis. *Across the Plains.* New York: Scribners. 1916.

Stevenson, Robert Louis. James D. Hart, ed. *From Scotland to Silverado.* Cambridge, Massachusetts: Harvard University Press. 1966.

Tocqueville, Alexis de. John Stone and Stephen Mennell, eds. *Alexis de Tocqueville on Democracy, Revolution, and Society: Selected Writings*. Chicago: University of Chicago Press. 1980.

Tocqueville, Alexis de. J.P. Mayer, ed.; George Lawrence, trans. *Democracy in America*. New York: Harper & Row. 1988.

Turner, Frederick Jackson. *The Frontier in American History*. New York: Holt, Rinehart and Winston. 1962. (1)

Twain, Mark. *Mark Twain's Autobiography*. New York: Harper & Brothers. 1924.

Twain, Mark. *The Innocents Abroad: Or, the New Pilgrim's Progress*. New York: Harper & Row. 1976.

Twain, Mark, and Charles Dudley Warner. Bryant Morey French, ed. *The Gilded Age: A Tale of To-Day*. Indianapolis, Indiana: Bobbs-Merrill. 1977. (3)

Wells, H. G. *Anticipations of the Reaction of Mechanical and Scientific Progress Upon Human Life and Thought*. New York: Harper & Brothers. 1902.

Wells, H. G. *The New America, the New World*. New York: Macmillan. 1935.

Wells, H. G., with Raymond Postgate and G. P. Wells. *The Outline of History, Being a Plain History of Life and Mankind*. Garden City, New York: Doubleday. 1971.

Wells, H. G. *The Future in America*. New York: Arno Press. 1974.

Whitman, Walt. *Complete Poetry and Collected Prose*. New York: Literary Classics of the United States/Viking Press. 1982.

Wilde, Oscar. *Complete Works of Oscar Wilde*. London: Collins. 1966.

CHAPTER ONE

Adams, Alexander B. *Sitting Bull: An Epic of the Plains*. New York: Putnam and Sons. 1973.

American Heritage History of the Great West. New York: American Heritage/McGraw-Hill. 1965.

Anderson, Gary Clayton. *Sitting Bull and the Paradox of Lakota Nationhood*. New York: HarperCollins. 1996.

Andrist, Ralph K. *The Long Death: The Last Days of the Plains Indians*. New York: Collier Books. 1993.

Axelrod, Alan. *Chronicle of the Indian Wars: From Colonial Times to Wounded Knee*. New York: Prentice-Hall. 1993.

Barney, Garold D. *Mormons, Indians, and the Ghost Dance Religion of 1890*. Lanham, Maryland: University Press of America. 1986.

Beasley, Conger. *We Are a People in This World: The Lakota Sioux and the Massacre at Wounded Knee*. Fayetteville, Arkansas: University of Arkansas Press. 1995.

Boas, Diane Doris. *The Mohonk Mountain House: The Role of the Resort Hotel in Late Nineteenth Century America*. Ms. thesis, Columbia University. 1985.

Bolt, Christine. *American Indian Policy and American Reform: Case Studies of the Campaign to Assimilate the American Indians*. Boston: Allen & Unwin. 1987. (7, 8)

Brown, Dee. *Bury My Heart at Wounded Knee*. New York: Holt, Rinehart and Winston. 1970.

Burns, Robert, Andrew Gillespie, and Willing Richardson. *Wyoming's Pioneer Ranches*. Laramie, Wyoming: Top-of-the-World Press, 1955. (Introduction)

Burton, Jeffrey. *Indian Territory and the United States, 1866–1906: Courts, Government, and the Movement for Oklahoma Statehood*. Norman, Oklahoma: University of Oklahoma Press. 1995.

Cadwalader, Sandra L., and Vine Deloria, Jr., eds. *The Aggressions of Civilization: Federal Indian Policy Since the 1880s*. Philadelphia: Temple University Press. 1984. (7, 8)

Coleman, Michael C. *American Indian Children at School, 1850–1930*. Jackson, Mississippi: University Press of Mississippi. 1993. (7, 8)

Costo, Rupert. *Indian Treaties: Two Centuries of Dishonor*. San Francisco: Indian Historian Press. 1977.

Crook, George. Martin F. Schmitt, ed. *General George Crook: His Autobiography*. Norman, Oklahoma: University of Oklahoma Press. 1986.

Debo, Angie. *And Still the Waters Run: The Betrayal of the Five Civilized Tribes*. Princeton, New Jersey: Princeton University Press. 1940.

Debo, Angie. *A History of the Indians of the United States*. Norman, Oklahoma: University of Oklahoma Press. 1970.

Debo, Angie. *Geronimo: The Man, His Time, His Place*. Norman, Oklahoma: University of Oklahoma Press. 1976.

Deloria, Vine, Jr., ed. *American Indian Policy in the Twentieth Century*. Norman, Oklahoma: University of Oklahoma Press. 1985. (7, 8)

Dick, Everett. *The Sod-House Frontier, 1854–1890*. Lincoln, Nebraska: Johnsen Publishing Company. 1954. (2)

Ellis, Clyde. *To Change Them Forever: Indian Education at the Rainy Mountain Boarding School, 1893–1920*. Norman, Oklahoma: University of Oklahoma Press. 1996. (7)

Faulk, Odie B. *The Geronimo Campaign*. New York: Oxford University Press. 1969.

Fuess, Claude Moore. *Carl Schurz, Reformer 1829–1906*. Port Washington, New York: Kennikat Press. 1963.

Geffs, Irving. *The First Eight Months of Oklahoma City*. Oklahoma City: McMaster Printing Co. 1890.

Geronimo. Barrett, S.M., and Frederick W. Turner, III, eds. *Geronimo: His Own Story*. New York: Dutton. 1970.

Gibson, Arrell Morgan. *The History of Oklahoma*. Norman, Oklahoma: University of Oklahoma Press. 1984.

Hagan, William Thomas. *American Indians*. Chicago: University of Chicago Press. 1993.

Hess, Milton Jerome. *The Origin and Implementation of the Dawes Act in the Dakotas, 1865–1914*. Ph.D. thesis, Columbia University. 1982.

Hoxie, Frederick E. *A Final Promise: The Campaign to Assimilate the Indians, 1880–1920*. Lincoln, Nebraska: University of Nebraska Press. 1984. (7)

Jackson, Helen Hunt. *A Century of Dishonor: A Sketch of the United States Government's Dealings with Some of the Indian Tribes*. Minneapolis: Ross & Haines. 1964.

Jensen, Richard E. *Eyewitness at Wounded Knee*. Lincoln, Nebraska: University of Nebraska Press. 1991.

Johnson, Swafford. *History of the U.S. Cavalry*. Bison Books. 1985.

Josephy, Alvin M. *500 Nations: An Illustrated History of North American Indians*. New York: Alfred A. Knopf. 1994.

Lauderdale, John Vance. *After Wounded Knee: Correspondence of Major and Surgeon John Vance Lauderdale While Serving with the Army Occupying the Pine Ridge Indian Reservation, 1890–1891*. East Lansing, Michigan: Michigan State University Press. 1996.

Limerick, Patricia Nelson. *The Legacy of Conquest: The Unbroken Past of the American West*. New York: W.W. Norton. 1987. (7, epilogue)

Lyman, Stanley David. *Wounded Knee 1973: A Personal Account*. Lincoln, Nebraska: University of Nebraska Press. 1991.

Matthiessen, Peter. *In the Spirit of Crazy Horse*. New York: Viking Press. 1980. (8)

McKee, Russell. *The Last West: A History of the Great Plains of North America*. New York: Thomas Y. Crowell Company. 1974.

Means, Russell. *Where White Men Fear to Tread: The Autobiography of Russell Means*. New York: St. Martin's Press. 1995. (Epilogue)

Mercer, A.S. *The Banditti of the Plains*. Norman, Oklahoma: University of Oklahoma Press. 1954.

Miles, Nelson. *Personal Recollections and Observations of General Nelson A. Miles*. New York: The Werner Company, 1896.

Mooney, James. *The Ghost-Dance Religion and the Sioux Outbreak of 1890*. Lincoln, Nebraska: University of Nebraska Press. 1991.

Nies, Judith. *Native American History*. New York: Ballantine Books. 1996. (7, 8)

Olson, James C. *Red Cloud and the Sioux Problem*. Lincoln, Nebraska: University of Nebraska Press. 1965

Parkman, Francis. Mason Wade, ed. *The Journals of Francis Parkman*. New York: Harper. 1947.

Parkman, Francis. John Tebbel, ed. *The Battle for North America*. Garden City, New York: Doubleday. 1948.

Pearce, Roy Harvey. *Savagism and Civilization: A Study of the Indian and the American Mind*. Berkeley, California: University of California Press. 1988. (7, 8)

Potomac Corral of the Westerners. *Great Western Indian Fights*. Lincoln, Nebraska: University of Nebraska Press. 1960.

Prucha, Francis Paul, compiler. *Americanizing the American Indians: Writings by the "Friends of the Indian," 1880–1900*. Cambridge, Massachusetts: Harvard University Press. 1973.

Prucha, Francis Paul. *American Indian Policy in Crisis: Christian Reformers*

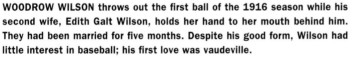

WOODROW WILSON throws out the first ball of the 1916 season while his second wife, Edith Galt Wilson, holds her hand to her mouth behind him. They had been married for five months. Despite his good form, Wilson had little interest in baseball; his first love was vaudeville.

WARREN HARDING shows his form to two members of the Chicago Cubs. Harding was nominated for the presidency in Chicago; his mistress, Nan Britton, later reported that he rode to the convention on the city's famed el that day. Despite such distractions, he spent most of the trip peeking over at another passenger's newspaper, trying to get a glimpse of the Cubs score.

and the Indian, 1865–1900. Norman, Oklahoma: University of Oklahoma Press. 1976.

Prucha, Francis Paul, ed. *Documents of United States Indian Policy.* Lincoln, Nebraska: University of Nebraska Press. 1990. (7, 8)

Rausch, David A., and Blair Schlepp. *Native American Voices.* Grand Rapids, Michigan: Baker Books. 1994. (7, 8)

Roberts, David. *Once They Moved Like the Wind: Cochise, Geronimo, and the Apache Wars.* New York: Simon & Schuster. 1993.

Schaefer, Jack. James C. Work, ed. *Shane: The Critical Edition.* Lincoln, Nebraska: University of Nebraska Press. 1984.

Sievers, Harry Joseph. *Benjamin Harrison.* Chicago: Henry Regnery and Co. 1968.

Slotkin, Richard. *The Fatal Environment: The Myth of the Frontier in the Age of Industrialization, 1800–1890.* New York: Atheneum. 1985.

Slotkin, Richard. *Gunfighter Nation: The Myth of the Frontier in Twentieth-Century America.* New York: Macmillan. 1992. (15)

Smith, Helena Huntington. *The War on Powder River.* Lincoln, Nebraska: University of Nebraska Press. 1966.

Smith, Paul Chaat. *Like a Hurricane: The Indian Movement from Alcatraz to Wounded Knee.* New York: New Press. 1996.

Socolofsky, Homer E., and Allan B. Spetter. *The Presidency of Benjamin Harrison.* Lawrence, Kansas: University Press of Kansas. 1987.

Spier, Leslie. *The Prophet Dance of the Northwest and Its Derivatives: The Source of the Ghost Dance.* New York: AMS Press. 1979.

Thompson, John. *Closing the Frontier: Radical Response in Oklahoma, 1889–1923.* Norman, Oklahoma: University of Oklahoma Press. 1986. (2, 5, 7)

Tolman, Newton F. *The Search for General Miles.* New York: Putnam. 1968.

Turner, C. Frank. *Across the Medicine Line.* Toronto: McClelland and Stewart. 1973.

Utley, Robert Marshall. *The Last Days of the Sioux Nation.* New Haven, Connecticut: Yale University Press. 1963.

Utley, Robert Marshall. *The Indian Frontier of the American West.* Albuquerque, New Mexico: University of New Mexico Press. 1984.

Utley, Robert M. *The Lance and the Shield: The Life and Times of Sitting Bull.* New York: Ballantine. 1994.

Viola, Herman J. *Diplomats in Bucskins: A History of Indian Delegations in Washington City.* Washington, D.C.: Smithsonian Institution Press. 1981.

Webb, Walter Prescott. *The Great Plains.* New York: Grosset and Dunlap. 1931.

Webb, Walter Prescott. *The Great Frontier.* Boston: Houghton Mifflin. 1952.

Webb, Walter Prescott. *Divided We Stand: The Crisis of a Frontierless Democracy.* Westport, Connecticut: Hyperion Press. 1985. (Introduction)

Weeks, Philip. *Farewell, My Nation: The American Indian and the United States, 1820–1890.* Arlington Heights, Illinois: H. Davidson. 1990.

Weems, John Edward. *Death Song: The Last of the Indian Wars.* Garden City, New York: Doubleday. 1976.

Wister, Owen. *The Virginian.* New York: Macmillan. 1960.

Wood, Leonard. Jack C. Lane, ed. *Chasing Geronimo: The Journal of Leonard Wood, May–September, 1886.* Albuquerque, New Mexico: University of New Mexico Press. 1970.

Wooster, Robert Allen. *The Military and United States Indian Policy, 1865–1903.* New Haven, Connecticut: Yale University Press. 1988.

Wooster, Robert Allen. *Nelson A. Miles and the Twilight of the Frontier Army.* Lincoln, Nebraska: University of Nebraska Press. 1993.

CHAPTER TWO

Alger, Horatio. *Ragged Dick and Mark, the Match Boy.* New York: Collier Books. 1962.

Anderson, David D. *Ignatius Donnelly.* Boston: Twayne Publishers. 1980.

Apel, Karl-Otto. John Michael Krois, trans. *Charles S. Peirce: From Pragmatism to Pramaticism.* Amherst, Massachusetts: University of Massachusetts Press. 1981.

Armstrong, William M. *E. L. Godkin: A Biography.* Albany, New York: State University of New York Press. 1978.

Ashby, LeRoy. *William Jennings Bryan: Champion of Democracy.* Boston: Twayne Publishers. 1987. (3, 6, 7)

Bannister, Robert C. *Social Darwinism: Science and Myth in Anglo-American Social Thought.* Philadelphia: Temple University Press. 1988. (3)

Barnard, Harry. *"Eagle Forgotten": The Life of John Peter Altgeld.* Indianapolis, Indiana: Bobbs-Merrill. 1962.

Barnes, Donna A. *Farmers in Rebellion: The Rise and Fall of the Southern Farmers Alliance and People's Party in Texas.* Austin, Texas: University of Texas Press. 1984.

Berton, Pierre. *Klondike: The Last Great Gold Rush, 1896–1899.* Toronto: McClelland and Stewart. 1972.

Berton, Pierre. *The Klondike Quest: A Photographic Essay, 1897–1899.* Boston: Little, Brown and Company. 1983.

Beth, Loren P. *John Marshall Harlan: The Last Whig Justice.* Lexington, Kentucky: University Press of Kentucky. 1992.

Brommel, Bernard J. *Eugene V. Debs: Spokesman for Labor and Socialism.* Chicago: C.H. Kerr Publishing Company. 1978. (5, 6)

Carnegie, Andrew. *Results of the Labor Struggle.* New York: J.J. Little. 1886.

Carnegie, Andrew. *Autobiography of Andrew Carnegie.* Boston: Northeastern University Press. 1986. (3, 5, 6)

Caudill, Edward. *Darwinian Myths: The Legends and Misuses of a Theory.* Knoxville, Tennessee: University of Tennessee Press. 1997. (3)

Cherny, Robert W. *A Righteous Cause: The Life of William Jennings Bryan.* Glenview, Illinois: Scott, Foresman and Company. 1985. (3, 6, 7)

Clanton, Gene. *Populism: The Humane Preference in America, 1890–1900.* Boston: Twayne Publishers. 1991.

Cotkin, George. *William James: Public Philosopher.* Champaign, Illinois: University of Illinois Press. 1994.

Crook, D. P. *Benjamin Kidd: Portrait of a Social Darwinist.* New York: Cambridge University Press. 1984.

Curtis, Bruce. *William Graham Sumner.* Boston: Twayne Publishers. 1981.

Darwin, Charles. *The Origin of Species by Means of Natural Selection, or, The Preservation of Favored Races in the Struggle for Life.* New York: Modern Library. 1993.

Demarest, David P., and Fannia Weingartner, eds. *"The River Ran Red": Homestead, 1892.* Pittsburgh: University of Pittsburgh Press. 1992.

Dewey, John, and James H. Tufts. *Ethics.* New York: Henry Holt. 1908.

Dewey, John. *The Influence of Darwin on Philosophy, and Other Essays in Contemporary Thought.* New York: P. Smith. 1910.

Dewey, John. *Creative Intelligence: Essays in the Pragmatic Attitude.* New York: Henry Holt. 1917.

Dewey, John. *Liberalism and Social Action.* New York: Capricorn Books. 1935.

Dewey, John. Debra Morris and Ian Shapiro, eds. *The Political Writings.* Indianapolis, Indiana: Hackett Publishing Co. 1993.

Dos Passos, John. *The 42nd Parallel.* New York: New American Library. 1979.

DuBois, W. E. B. *The Autobiography of W. E. B. DuBois: A Soliloquy on Viewing My Life from the Last Decade of Its First Century.* New York: International Publishers. 1968. (12)

DuBois, W. E. B., Julius Lester, ed. *The Seventh Son: The Thought and Writings of W. E. B. DuBois, Vol. I & II.* New York: Vintage Books. 1971. (12)

DuBois, W. E. B. *The Emerging Thought of W. E. B. DuBois: Essays and Editorials from* **The Crisis**. New York: Simon and Schuster. 1972.

DuBois, W. E. B. *The Souls of Black Folk.* New York: Vintage Books. 1990.

Faulkner, Harold Underwood. *The Decline of Laissez-Faire, 1897–1917.* New York: Rinehart. 1951. (3, 4, 5)

Franklins, Robert Michael. *Liberating Visions: Human Fulfillment and Social Justice in African-American Thought.* Minneapolis: Fortress Press. 1990. (7, 8, 10, 12)

Friesen, Richard J. *The Chilkoot Pass and the Great Gold Rush of 1898.* Ottawa: National Historic Parks and Sites Branch, Parks Canada, Environment Canada. 1981.

Gallie, W. B. *Peirce and Pragmatism.* Westport, Connecticut: Greenwood Press. 1975.

George, Henry. *Progress and Poverty.* New York: Robert Schalknebach Foundation. 1985.

George, Henry. Kenneth C. Wenzer, ed. *An Anthology of Henry George's Thought.* Rochester, New York: University of Rochester Press. 1997.

Ginger, Ray. *Altgeld's America: The Lincoln Ideal Versus Changing Realities.* Chicago: Quadrangle Books. 1965.

Goodwyn, Lawrence. *Democratic Promise: The Populist Moment in America.* New York: Oxford University Press. 1976.

Gould, Lewis L. *The Presidency of William McKinley.* Lawrence, Kansas: Regents Press of Kansas. 1980.

Gould, Stephen Jay. *The Mismeasure of Man.* New York: Norton. 1981.

Hacker, Louis Morton. *The World of Andrew Carnegie: 1865–1901.* Philadelphia: Lippincott. 1968.

Harlan, Louis R. *Booker T. Washington: The Making of a Black Leader. 1856–1901.* New York: Oxford University Press. 1972.

Harlan, Louis R. *Booker T. Washington: The Wizard of Tuskegee, 1901–1915.* New York: Oxford University Press. 1983.

Hofstadter, Richard. *Social Darwinism in American Thought.* Boston: Beacon Press. 1992.

Kazin, Michael. *The Populist Persuasion: An American History.* New York: Basic Books. 1995. (8)

Kennedy, James Gettier. *Herbert Spencer.* Boston: Twayne Publishers. 1978.

Kirkland, Edward C. *Industry Comes of Age: Business, Labor and Public Policy, 1860–1897.* Chicago: Quadrangle Books. 1967.

Konvitz, Milton R., and Gail Kennedy, eds. *The American Pragmatists.* New York: Meridian Books, 1960. (6)

Krause, Paul. *The Battle for Homestead, 1880–1892: Politics, Culture, and Steel.* Pittsburgh: University of Pittsburgh Press. 1992.

Leech, Margaret. *In the Days of McKinley.* New York: Harper. 1959.

Lewis, David L. *W. E. B. DuBois: Biography of a Race.* New York: Henry Holt. 1993. (12)

Leyendecker, Liston E. *Palace Car Prince: A Biography of George Mortimer Pullman.* Niwot, Colorado: University Press of Colorado. 1992.

Lofgren, Charles A. *The Plessy Case: A Legal-Historical Interpretation.* New York: Oxford University Press. 1987. (12)

Malthus, T. R. *An Essay on Population.* New York: Dutton. 1958.

Marshall, Alfred. J. K. Whitaker, ed. *The Early Economic Writings of Alfred Marshall, 1867–1890.* London: Macmillan. 1975.

Massey, Douglas S. *American Apartheid: Segregation and the Making of the Underclass.* Cambridge, Massachusetts: Harvard University Press. 1993. (7, 8, 12)

McCloskey, Robert G. *American Conservatism in the Age of Enterprise,* 1865–1910: *A Study of William Graham Sumner, Stephen J. Field, and Andrew Carnegie.* New York: Harper & Row. 1964.

McMath, Robert C., Jr. *Populist Vanguard: A Social History, 1877–1898.* New York: Hill and Wang. 1993.

Meier, August. *Negro Thought in America, 1880–1915: Racial Ideologies in the Age of Booker T. Washington.* Ann Arbor, Michigan: University of Michigan Press. 1966.

Miller, Donald L. *City of the Century: The Epic of Chicago and the Making of America.* New York: Simon and Schuster. 1996.

Miller, Joshua I. *Democratic Temperament: The Legacy of William James.* Lawrence, Kansas: University Press of Kansas. 1997.

Nevins, Alan. *Grover Cleveland: A Study in Courage.* New York: Dodd, Mead. 1966.

Palmer, Bruce. *"Man Over Money": The Southern Populist Critique of American Capitalism.* Chapel Hill, North Carolina: University of North Carolina Press. 1980.

Pfeffer, William Alfred. Peter H. Argersinger, ed. *Populism: Its Rise and Fall.* Lawrence, Kansas: University Press of Kansas. 1992.

Ricardo, David. *The Principles of Political Economy and Taxation.* London: Dent. 1984.

Salvatore, Nick. *Eugene V. Debs: Citizen and Socialist.* Urbana, Illinois: University of Illinois Press. 1982. (5, 6)

Scheffler, Israel. *Four Pragmatists: A Critical Introduction to Peirce, James, Mead, and Dewey.* New York: Routledge & Kegan Paul. 1986.

Schreiner, Samuel Agnew, Jr. *Henry Clay Frick: The Gospel of Greed.* New York: St. Martin's Press. 1995.

Serrin, William. *Homestead: The Glory and Tragedy of an American Steel Town.* New York: Times Books. 1992. (8, 11, 15, epilogue)

Smith, Adam. *The Wealth of Nations.* New York: Alfred A. Knopf. 1991. (8, 15)

Smith, Carl S. *Urban Disorder and the Shape of Belief: The Great Chicago Fire, the Haymarket Bomb, and the Model Town of Pullman.* Chicago: University of Chicago Press. 1995.

Spencer, Herbert. *First Principles.* New York: D. Appleton and Company. 1912.

Spencer, Herbert. *The Man Versus the State.* Boston: The Beacon Press. 1950.

Spencer, Herbert. *Social Statistics; or, The Conditions Essential to Human Happiness Specified, and the First of Them Developed.* New York: A.M. Kelley. 1969.

Sullivan, Oscar Matthias. *North Star Sage: The Story of Ignatius Donnelly.* New York: Vantage Press. 1953.

Sumner, William Graham. *Social Darwinism: Selected Essays.* Englewood Cliffs, New Jersey: Prentice-Hall. 1963.

Sumner, William Graham. Murray Polner, ed. *The Conquest of the United States by Spain, and Other Essays.* Chicago: Regnery, 1965

Sumner, William Graham. *What Social Classes Owe to Each Other.* Caldwell, Idaho: Caxton Printers. 1982

Sumner, William Graham. *Folkways.* Salem, New Hampshire: Ayer Company. 1992.

Taylor, Michael, ed. *Herbert Spencer and the Limits of the State: The Late Nineteenth-Century Debate Between Individualism and Collectivism.* Dulles, Virginia: Thoemmes Press. 1996. (15)

Thayer, H. S. *Meaning and Action: A Study of American Pragmatism.* Indianapolis, Indiana: Bobbs-Merrill. 1973.

Thomas, Brook, ed. *Plessy v. Ferguson: A Brief History with Documents.* Boston: Bedford Books. 1997.

Thompson, Mildred I. *Ida B. Wells-Barnett: An Exploratory Study of an American Black Woman, 1893–1930.* Brooklyn: Carlson Publishing. 1990.

Trachtenberg, Alan. *The Incorporation of America: Culture and Society in the Gilded Age.* New York: Hill and Wang. 1982. (3, 4, 5)

Tuchman, Barbara W. *The Proud Tower: A Portrait of the World Before the War, 1890–1914.* New York: Macmillan. 1966. (1, 3, 4, 5)

Tugwell, Rexford Guy. *Grover Cleveland.* New York: Macmillan. 1968.

Veblen, Thorstein. Wesley C. Mitchell, ed. *What Veblen Taught: Selected Writings of Thorstein Veblen.* New York: A.M. Kelley, 1964. (3)

Veblen, Thorstein. *The Theory of the Leisure Class.* New York: A.M. Kelley. 1975. (3)

Ward, Lester Frank. *Outlines of Sociology.* New York: Macmillan. 1898.

Ward, Lester Frank. Henry Steele Commager, ed. *Lester Ward and the Welfare State.* Indianapolis, Indiana: Bobbs-Merrill. 1967. (8)

Warren, Kenneth. *Triumphant Capitalism: Henry Clay Frick and the Industrial Transformation of America.* Pittsburgh: University of Pittsburgh Press. 1996. (3)

Washington, Booker T. *The Story of My Life and Work.* New York: Negro Universities Press. 1969.

Washington, Booker T. *Up from Slavery: An Autobiography.* New York: Carol Publishing Company. 1989.

Webster, Duncan. *Looka Yonder! The Imaginary America of Populist Culture.* New York: Routledge. 1988.

Weiner, Philip Paul. *Evolution and the Founders of Pragmatism.* New York: Harper & Row. 1965.

Welch, Richard E., Jr. *The Presidencies of Grover Cleveland.* Lawrence, Kansas: University Press of Kansas. 1988.

Wells-Barnet, Ida B. Alfreda M. Duster, ed. *Crusade for Justice: The Autobiography of Ida B. Wells.* Chicago: University of Chicago Press. 1970.

Wells-Barnet, Ida B. Jacqueline Jones Royster, ed. *Southern Horrors and Other Writings: The Anti-Lynching Campaign of Ida B. Wells, 1892–1900.* Boston: Bedford Books. 1997.

White, William Allen. Sally Foreman Griffith, ed. *The Autobiography of William Allen White.* Lawrence, Kansas: University Press of Kansas. 1990. (3, 6, 7, 8, 9)

Woodward, C. Vann. *Origins of the New South, 1877–1913.* Baton Rouge, Louisiana: Louisiana State University Press. 1951. (12)

CALVIN COOLIDGE throws out the first ball of the 1924 World Series, the first and only World Series won by the Washington Senators. The running gag was that the Washington franchise was "first in peace, first in war, and last in the American League."

Woodward, C. Vann. *The Strange Career of Jim Crow.* New York: Oxford University Press. 1957 (6, 7, 8, 10, 12)

Woodward, C. Vann. *Tom Watson: Agrarian Rebel.* New York: Oxford University Press. 1963.

Woodward, C. Vann. *The Burden of Southern History.* Baton Rouge, Louisiana: Louisiana State University Press. 1993. (8, 12)

Yarborough, Tinsley E. *Judicial Enigma: The First Justice Harlan.* New York: Oxford University Press. 1995.

CHAPTER THREE

Allen, Douglas. *Frederic Remington and the Spanish-American War.* New York: Crown. 1971.

Bain, David Haward. *Sitting in Darkness: Americans in the Philippines.* Boston: Houghton Mifflin. 1984.

Balfour, Sebastian. *The End of the Spanish Empire, 1898–1923.* New York: Clarendon Press. 1997.

Beale, Howard K. *Theodore Roosevelt and the Rise of America to World Power.* Baltimore: Johns Hopkins University Press. 1984. (4)

Beisner, Robert L. *Twelve Against Empire: The Anti-Imperialists, 1898–1900.* New York: McGraw-Hill. 1968.

Bowle, John. *The Imperial Achievement.* London: Secher and Warburg. 1974.

Bradford, James C., ed. *Crucible of Empire: The Spanish-American War and Its Aftermath.* Annapolis, Maryland: Naval Institute Press. 1993.

Braeman, John. *Albert J. Beveridge: American Nationalist.* Chicago: University of Chicago Press. 1971. (5)

Brands, H. W. *The Reckless Decade: America in the 1890s.* New York: St. Martin's Press. 1995. (2)

Brands, H. W. *T.R.: The Last Romantic.* New York: Basic Books. 1997. (4, 5, 6)

Brown, Charles Henry. *The Correspondents' War: Journalists in the Spanish-American War.* New York: Scribners. 1967.

Chadwick, French Ensor. *The Relations of the United States and Spain: The Spanish-American War.* New York: Russell & Russell. 1968.

Chernow, Ron. *The House of Morgan: An American Banking Dynasty and the Rise of Modern Finance.* New York: Simon & Schuster. 1990. (5, 7, 8, 15)

Chernow, Ron. *Titan: The Life of John D. Rockefeller, Sr.* New York: Random House. 1998. (5)

Chessman, G. Wallace. *Governor Theodore Roosevelt: The Albany Apprenticeship, 1898–1900.* Cambridge, Massachusetts: Harvard University Press. 1965.

Christopher, A. J. *The British Empire at Its Zenith.* Beckenham, England: Croom Helm. 1988.

Clymer, Kenton J. *John Hay: The Gentleman as Diplomat.* Ann Arbor,

Michigan: University of Michigan Press. 1975.

Collins, Michael L. *That Damned Cowboy: Theodore Roosevelt and the American West.* New York: P. Lang. 1989.

Crouch, Thomas W. *A Yankee Guerrillero: Frederick Funston and the Cuban Insurrection, 1896–1897.* Memphis, Tennessee: Memphis State University Press. 1975.

Davies, Marion. Pamela Pfau and Kenneth S. Marx, eds. *The Times We Had: Life with William Randolph Hearst.* Indianapolis, Indiana: Bobbs-Merrill. 1975.

Dewey, George. Eric McAllister Smith, ed. *Autobiography of George Dewey, Admiral of the Navy.* Annapolis, Maryland: Naval Institute Press. 1987.

Dierks, Jack Cameron. *A Leap to Arms: The Cuban Campaign of 1898.* Philadelphia: Lippincott. 1970.

Feuer, A. B. *The Spanish-American War at Sea: Naval Action in the Atlantic.* Westport, Connecticut: Praeger. 1995.

Floud, Roderick, and Donal McCloskey eds. *The Economic History of Britain Since 1700. Vol. 2: 1860 to the 1970s.* New York: Cambridge University Press. 1981. (8, 11)

Flynn, John T. *God's Gold: The Story of Rockefeller and His Times.* New York: Harcourt, Brace. 1932. (4, 5)

Freidel, Frank Burt. *The Splendid Little War.* New York: Bramhall House. 1958.

Gale, Robert L. *John Hay.* Boston: Twayne Publishers. 1978.

Gatewood, Willard B. *Black Americans and the White Man's Burden, 1898–1903.* Urbana, Illinois: University of Illinois Press. 1975.

Gould, Lewis L. *The Spanish-American War and President McKinley.* Lawrence, Kansas: University Press of Kansas. 1982. (2)

Gould, Lewis L. *The Presidency of Theodore Roosevelt.* Lawrence, Kansas: University Press of Kansas. 1991. (4, 5)

Harbaugh, William Henry. *Power and Responsibility: The Life and Times of Theodore Roosevelt.* New York: Farrar, Straus and Cudahy. 1961. (4, 5, 6)

Herner, Charles. *The Arizona Rough Riders.* Tucson, Arizona: University of Arizona Press. 1970.

Hobsbawm, E. J. *The Age of Empire, 1875–1914.* New York: Vintage Books. 1989.

Hobson, J. A. *Imperialism: A Study.* Ann Arbor, Michigan: University of Michigan Press. 1965.

Hofstadter, Richard, ed. *The Progressive Movement, 1900–1915.* Englewood Cliffs, New Jersey: Prentice-Hall. 1963. (4, 5)

Howells, William Dean. *A Hazard of New Fortunes.* Bloomington, Indiana: Indiana University Press. 1976.

Jackson, Stanley. *J. P. Morgan: A Biography.* New York: Stein and Day. 1983. (5)

Jeffers, H. Paul. *Colonel Roosevelt: Theodore Roosevelt Goes to War, 1897–1898.* New York: Wiley. 1996.

Johnson, E. A. *History of Negro Soldiers in the Spanish-American War, and Other Items of Interest.* New York: Johnson Reprint Corporation. 1970.

Josephson, Matthew. *The Robber Barons: The Great American Capitalists, 1861–1901.* New York: Harcourt, Brace. 1934. (2, 5)

Karnow, Stanley. *In Our Image: America's Empire in the Philippines.* New York: Random House. 1989. (9, 10)

Kolko, Gabriel. *The Triumph of Conservatism: A Re-Interpretation of American History, 1900–1916.* New York: Free Press of Glencoe. 1963.

LaFeber, Walter. *The New Empire: An Interpretation of American Expansion, 1860–1898.* Ithaca, New York: Cornell University Press. 1963.

Lorant, Stefan. *The Life and Times of Theodore Roosevelt.* Garden City, New York: Doubleday. 1959. (4, 5, 6)

Mahan, Alfred Thayer. *The Interest of America in Sea Power, Present and Future.* N. Stratford, New Hampshire: Ayer Company. 1970.

Mahan, Alfred Thayer. *The Influence of Sea Power Upon History, 1660–1783.* New York: Dover Publications. 1987.

May, Ernest. *Imperial Democracy: The Emergence of America as a Great Power.* New York: Harcourt, Brace & World. 1961. (4, 5)

McCullough, David. *Mornings on Horseback.* New York: Simon and Schuster. 1981.

Miller, Nathan. *Theodore Roosevelt: A Life.* New York: Morrow. 1992. (4, 5, 6)

Milton, Joyce. *The Yellow Kids: Foreign Correspondents in the Heyday of Yellow Journalism.* New York: Harper & Row. 1989.

Mitchell, John Ames. *The Silent War.* New York: Life Publishing Company. 1906.

Mommsen, Theodor. William Purdie Dickson, trans. *The History of Rome.* New York: Charles Scribner's Sons. 1905.

Morison, Samuel Eliot, Frederick Merk, and Frank Freidel. *Dissent in Three American Wars.* Cambridge, Massachusetts: Harvard University Press. 1970.

Morris, Edmund. *The Rise of Theodore Roosevelt.* New York: Coward, McCann & Geoghegan. 1979.

Morris, James. *Pax Britannica: The Climax of an Empire.* London: Faber and Faber. 1968.

Mowry, George Edwin. *The Era of Theodore Roosevelt and the Birth of Modern America, 1900–1912.* New York: Harper. 1962. (4, 5)

Mugridge, Ian. *The View from Xanadu: William Randolph Hearst and United States Foreign Policy.* Buffalo, New York: McGill-Queen's University Press. 1995. (8, 9, 11)

Musicant, Ivan. *Empire by Default: The Spanish-American War and the Dawn of the American Century.* New York: Henry Holt. 1998.

O'Toole, G. J. A. *The Spanish War: An American Epic.* New York: Norton. 1984.

Phelan, Craig. *Divided Loyalties: The Public and Private Life of Labor*

HERBERT HOOVER prepares to throw out the first ball of the 1929 season at Washington's Griffith Stadium. Grinning just to her husband's right is Lou Hoover; seated to the left is Secretary of the Treasury Andrew Mellon, who had already done more to destroy the Hoover administration than anyone else. Standing to Mellon's left is "the Big Train," Walter Johnson, Washington's manager and one-time pitching immortal, who in his time racked up 416 career victories—second only to Cy Young. Standing next to Johnson is Clark Griffith, the club's notoriously tightfisted owner.

Leader John Mitchell. Albany, New York: State University of New York. 1994.

Puleston, W. D. *Mahan: The Life and Work of Captain Alfred Thayer Mahan.* New Haven, Connecticut: Yale University Press. 1939.

Rickover, Adm. H. G. *How the Battleship Maine Was Destroyed.* Annapolis, Maryland: Naval Institute Press. 1994.

Roosevelt, Theodore. Wayne Andrews, ed. *The Autobiography of Theodore Roosevelt.* New York: Octagon Books. 1975. (5, 6)

Samuels, Peggy, and Harold Samuels. *Remembering the Maine.* Washington, D.C.: Smithsonian Institution Press. 1995.

Samuels, Peggy. *Teddy Roosevelt at San Juan: The Making of a President.* College Station, Texas: Texas A&M University Press. 1997.

Segovia, Lazaro. Frank de Thoma, trans. *The Full Story of Aguinaldo's Capture.* Manila, Philippines: MCS Enterprises. 1969.

Sinclair, Andrew. *Corsair: The Life of J. Pierpont Morgan.* Boston: Little, Brown. 1981. (5)

Smith, Joseph. *The Spanish-American War: Conflict in the Caribbean and the Pacific, 1895–1902.* New York: Longman. 1994.

Spector, Ronald H. *Admiral of the New Empire: The Life and Career of George Dewey.* Columbia, South Carolina: University of South Carolina Press. 1988.

Strong, Josiah. *Expansion Under New-World Conditions.* New York: Garland Publishers. 1971.

Swanberg, W. A. *Citizen Hearst: A Biography of William Randolph Hearst.* New York: Scribners. 1961.

Trask, David F. *The War with Spain in 1898.* New York: Macmillan. 1981.

Traxel, David. *1898: The Birth of the American Century.* New York: Alfred A. Knopf. 1998.

Twain, Mark. *Mark Twain's Weapons of Satire: Anti-Imperialist Writings on the Philippine-American War.* Syracuse, New York: Syracuse University Press. 1992.

Wilkerson, Marcus Stanley. *Public Opinion and the Spanish-American War: A Study in War Propaganda.* New York: Russell & Russell. 1967.

Williams, William Appleman. *The Roots of the Modern American Empire: A Study of the Growth and Shaping of Social Consciousness in a Marketplace Society.* New York: Random House. 1969. (4, 5)

CHAPTER FOUR

Adams, Brooks. *The Law of Civilization and Decay: An Essay on History.* New York: Vintage Books. 1955. (2)

Addams, Jane. James Hurt, ed. *Twenty Years at Hull-House with Autobiographical Notes.* Urbana, Illinois: University of Illinois Press. 1990.

Allen, Oliver E. *The Tiger: The Rise and Fall of Tammany Hall.* Reading, Massachusetts: Addison-Wesley. 1993. (7, 8)

FRANKLIN ROOSEVELT prepares to throw out the first ball of the 1933 World Series, between the New York Giants and the Washington Senators. Steadying FDR by his arm is Joe Cronin, the manager and star shortstop of the Senators, and a future Hall of Famer. Standing to Cronin's left is Bill Terry, the first baseman and manager of the Giants, another Hall of Famer and the last National Leaguer to hit over .400. On the other side of Terry is Washington owner Clark Griffith. Cronin was Griffith's son-in-law—but it would not prevent him from being traded to the Boston Red Sox when Griffith was offered enough money. The Senators would go on to lose the Series, four games to one; they would never see another one.

Amfitheatrof, Erik. *The Children of Columbus: An Informal History of Italians in the New World.* Boston: Little, Brown. 1973. (5, 7, 8)

Anguizola, G. A. *Philippe Bunau-Varilla: The Man Behind the Panama Canal.* Chicago: Nelson-Hall. 1980.

Asbury, Herbert. *The Gangs of New York: An Informal History of the New York Underworld.* New York: Old Town Books. 1928.

Ashford, Bailey K. *A Soldier in Science: The Autobiography of Bailey K. Ashford.* New York: Morrow. 1934.

Bailey, Thomas A. *Theodore Roosevelt and the Japanese-American Crises.* Gloucester, Massachusetts: P. Smith. 1964.

Baker, Ray Stannard. *American Chronicle: The Autobiography of Ray Stannard Baker.* New York: Charles Scribner's Sons. 1945.

Bannister, Robert C., Jr. *Ray Stannard Baker: The Mind and Thought of a Progressive.* New Haven: Yale University Press. 1966. (5)

Bean, William A., M.D. *Walter Reed: A Biography.* Charlottesville, Virginia: University Press of Virginia. 1982.

Beatty, Jack. *The Rascal King: The Life and Times of James Michael Curley (1874–1958).* New York: Addison-Wesley. 1992.

Berkin, Carol Ruth, and Mary Beth Norton. *Women of America: A History.* Boston: Houghton Mifflin. 1979. (5, 7, 8, 10, 14)

Blumberg, Dorothy Rose. *Florence Kelley: The Making of a Social Pioneer.* New York: A.M. Kelley. 1966. (5)

Brady, Kathleen. *Ida Tarbell: Portrait of a Muckraker.* New York: Seaview/Putnam. 1984.

Coffey, Michael, ed., with Terry Golway. *The Irish in America.* New York: Hyperion. 1997.

Cohen, Michael P. *The Pathless Way: John Muir and American Wilderness.* Madison, Wisconsin: University of Wisconsin Press. 1984.

Collin, Richard H. *Theodore Roosevelt's Caribbean: The Panama Canal, the Monroe Doctrine, and the Latin American Context.* Baton Rouge, Louisiana: Louisiana State University Press. 1990.

Connable, Alfred, and Edward Silberfarb. *Tigers of Tammany: Nine Men Who Ran New York.* New York: Holt, Rinehart and Winston. 1967. (5, 7, 8)

Cutright, Paul Russell. *Theodore Roosevelt: The Making of a Conservationist.* Urbana, Illinois: University of Illinois Press. 1985.

De Conde, Alexander. *Half Bitter, Half Sweet: An Excursion into Italian-American History.* New York: Scribners. 1971.

Di Franco, J. Philip. *The Italian American Experience.* New York: T. Doherty Associates. 1988.

Duffy, Francis Patrick. *Father Duffy's Story: A Tale of Humor and Heroism, of Life and Death with the Fighting Sixty-Ninth.* New York: George H. Doran Company. 1919. (6)

Dunne, Finley Peter. Charles Fanning, ed. *Mr. Dooley and the Chicago Irish: The Autobiography of a Nineteenth-Century Ethnic Group.* Washington, D.C.: Catholic University of America Press. 1987.

Epstein, Beryl Williams, and Samuel Epstein. *William Crawford Gorgas: Tropic Fever Fighter.* New York: J. Messner. 1953.

Erie, Steven P. *Rainbow's End: Irish-Americans and the Dilemmas of Urban Machine Politicis, 1840–1985.* Berkeley, California: University of California Press. 1988. (7, 8, 13, 15)

Falk, Candace. *Love, Anarchy, and Emma Goldman.* New York: Holt, Rinehart and Winston. 1984. (6)

Feingold, Henry L. *Zion in America: The Jewish Experience from Colonial Times to the Present.* New York: Hippocrene Books. 1974. (5, 9)

Feldstein, Stanley. *The Land That I Show You: Three Centuries of Jewish Life in America.* Garden City, New York: Anchor Press/Doubleday. 1978. (5, 9)

Filler, Louis. *Voice of the Democracy: A Critical Biography of David Graham Phillips, Journalist, Novelist, Progressive.* University Park, Pennsylvania: Pennsylvania State University Press. 1978.

Finlay, Carlos E. Morton C. Kahn, ed. *Carlos Finlay and Yellow Fever.* New York: Oxford University Press. 1940.

Fox, Stephen R. *John Muir and His Legacy.* Madison, Wisconsin: University of Wisconsin Press. 1985.

Gallo, Patrick J. *Old Bread, New Wine: A Portrait of the Italian-Americans.* Chicago: Nelson Hall. 1981. (5, 7, 8)

Gambino, Richard. *Vendetta: The True Story of the Worst Lynching in America, the Mass Murder of Italian-Americans in New Orleans in 1891.* Garden City, New York: Doubleday. 1977.

Gates, Frederick Taylor. *Chapters in My Life.* New York: Free Press. 1977.

Gibson, John Mendinghall. *Physician to the World: The Life of General William C. Gorgas.* Durham, North Carolina: Duke University Press. 1950.

Glazer, Nathan, and Daniel Patrick Moynihan. *Beyond the Melting Pot: The Negroes, Puerto Ricans, Jews, Italians, and Irish of New York City.* Cambridge, Massachusetts: M.I.T. Press. 1963. (5, 12, 13, 15)

Goldman, Emma. *Living My Life.* New York: Alfred A. Knopf. 1931. (6)

Goldmark, Josephine Clara. *Impatient Crusader: Florence Kelley's Life Story.* Urbana, Illinois: University of Illinois Press. 1953. (2, 5)

Greeley, Andrew M. *That Most Distressful Nation: The Taming of the*

HARRY TRUMAN prepares to throw out the first ball of the 1949 season. Just behind Truman's pitching is the legendary Connie Mack (Cornelius McGillicuddy), the owner and manager of the visiting Philadelphia Athletics for 50 years (1901–1950). Mack was the last manager to wear street clothes in the dugout—and the grandfather of current U.S. senator Connie Mack (R.-Fla.).

American Irish. Chicago: Quadrangle.Books. 1972. (5, 8)

Harris, Leon A. *Upton Sinclair, American Rebel.* New York: Crowell. 1975.

Henderson, Thomas M. *Tammany Hall and the New Immigrants: The Progressive Years.* New York: Arno Press. 1976.

Hennesey, James. *American Catholics: A History of the Roman Catholic Community in the United States.* New York: Oxford University Press. 1981.

Hill, Ralph Nading. *The Doctors Who Conquered Yellow Fever.* New York: Random House. 1957.

Hofstadter, Richard. *The Age of Reform.* New York: Alfred A. Knopf. 1989. (2, 3, 5, 6, 7, 8)

Ignatiew, Noel. *How the Irish Became White.* New York: Routledge. 1995.

Jones, Beverly Washington. *Quest for Equality: The Life and Writings of Mary Eliza Church Terrell, 1863–1954.* Brooklyn, New York: Carlson Publishers. 1990. (2)

Josephson, Matthew. *The Politicos.* New York: Harcourt Brace and World. 1958. (2, 3, 5)

Kaplan, Justin. *Lincoln Steffens: A Biography.* New York: Simon and Schuster. 1974.

Kee, Robert. *The Most Distressful Country.* London: Quartet Books Limited. 1976. (1, 5)

Kelley, Florence, ed. *Hull-House Maps and Papers.* New York: Arno Press. 1970. (5)

Kessner, Thomas. *The Golden Door: Italian and Jewish Immigrant Mobility in New York City, 1880–1915.* New York: Oxford University Press. 1977.

Kochersberger, Robert C., ed. *More Than a Muckraker: Ida Tarbell's Lifetime in Journalism.* Knoxville, Tennessee: University of Tennessee Press. 1994.

Low, Seth. *The Trend of the Century.* New York: T.Y. Crowell & Company. 1899.

Lyon, Peter. *Success Story: The Life and Times of S. S. McClure.* New York: Scribners. 1963.

Mangione, Jerre, and Ben Morreale. *La Storia: Five Centuries of the Italian American Experience.* New York: HarperCollins. 1992.

Marks, Frederick W., III. *Velvet on Iron: The Diplomacy of Theodore Roosevelt.* Lincoln, Nebraska: University of Nebraska Press. 1979. (3, 5)

McCullough, David. *The Path Between the Seas: The Creation of the Panama Canal 1870–1914.* New York: Simon and Schuster. 1977.

McGeary, M. Nelson. *Gifford Pinchot, Forester-Politician.* Princeton, New Jersey: Princeton University Press. 1960. (5)

Mitchell, Greg. *The Campaign of the Century: Upton Sinclair's Race for Governor of California and the Birth of Media Politics.* New York: Random House. 1992. (8)

O'Connor, Edwin. *The Last Hurrah.* New York: Bantam Books. 1962.

O'Gara, Gordon Carpenter. *Theodore Roosevelt and the Rise of the Modern Navy.* New York: Greenwood Press. 1969.

Phillips, David Graham. *The Treason of the Senate.* Chicago: Quadrangle Books. 1964.

Plunkitt, George Washington, as told to William L. Riordon. *Plunkitt of Tammany Hall: A Series of Very Plain Talks on Very Plain Politics.* New York: McClure, Phillipps and Company. 1905 (5)

Ravitz, Abe C. *David Graham Phillips.* New York: Twayne Publishers. 1966.

Reckner, James R. *Teddy Roosevelt's Great White Fleet.* Annapolis, Maryland: Naval Institute Press. 1988.

Riis, Jacob. *How the Other Half Lives: Studies Among the Tenements of New York.* New York: Hill and Wang. 1957. (Introduction, 5)

Santé, Luc. *Low Life: Lures and Snares of Old New York.* New York: Vintage Books. 1991.

Schenkel, Albert F. *The Rich Man and the Kingdom: John D. Rockefeller, Jr., and the Protestant Establish-ment.* Minneapolis: Fortress Press. 1995. (5)

Schlesinger, Arthur Meier. *The Rise of the City, 1878–1898.* New York: Macmillan. 1933. (Introduction, 5)

Shannon, William V. *The American Irish.* Toronto: Macmillan. 1963. (5, 8, 9, 12)

Sherr, Lynn. *Failure Is Impossible: Susan B. Anthony in Her Own Words.* New York: Times Books. 1995. (5)

Simon, Maron J. *The Panama Affair.* New York: Charles Scribner's Sons. 1971.

Sinclair, Upton. *The Jungle.* Urbana, Illinois: University of Illinois Press. 1988.

Sklar, Kathryn Kish. *Florence Kelley and the Nation's Work: The Rise of Women's Political Culture, 1830–1900.* New Haven, Connecticut: Yale University Press. 1995. (5, 6, 7)

Sochen, June. *Movers and Shakers: American Women Thinkers and Activists, 1900–1970.* New York: Times Books. 1973. (3, 4 6, 8, 14)

Steffens, Lincoln. *The Autobiography of Lincoln Steffens.* New York: Harcourt Brace & World. 1958. (6)

Steffens, Lincoln. *The Shame of the Cities.* New York: Hill and Wang. 1988.

Tarbell, Ida M. David M. Chalmers, ed. *The History of the Standard Oil Company.* New York: Harper & Row. 1966.

Taylor, Bob Pepperman. *Our Limits Transgressed: Environmental Political Thought in America.* Lawrence, Kansas: University Press of Kansas. 1992. (5, 13)

Terrell, Mary Church. *A Colored Woman in a White World.* New York: Arno Press. 1980.

Wexler, Alice. *Emma Goldman: An Intimate Life.* New York: Pantheon Books. 1984. (6)

Williams, Greer. *The Plague Killers.* New York: Charles Scribner's Sons. 1969.

Woloch, Nancy. *Muller v. Oregon: A Brief History with Documents.* Boston: Bedford Books/St. Martin's Press. 1996. (5)

Zangwill, Israel. *The Melting-Pot: A Drama in Four Acts.* New York: Arno Press. 1975.

CHAPTER FIVE

Anderson, Judith Icke. *William Howard Taft: An Intimate History.* New York: Norton. 1981. (7)

Baskerville, Stephen W. *Of Laws and Interpretations: An Intellectual Portrait of Louis Dembitz Brandeis.* Rutherford, New Jersey: Fairleigh Dickinson University Press. 1994. (8)

Baxandall, Rosalyn Fraad. *Words on Fire: The Life and Writing of Elizabeth Gurley Flynn.* New Brunswick, New Jersey: Rutgers University Press. 1987.

Bird, Stewart, Dan Georgakas, and Deborah Shaffer, compilers. *Solidarity Forever: An Oral History of the IWW.* Chicago: Lake View Press. 1985. (3, 6)

Bragdon, Henry Wilkinson. *Woodrow Wilson: The Academic Years.* Cambridge, Massachusetts: Belknap Press. 1967.

Burgchardt, Carl R. *Robert M. La Follette, Sr.: The Voice of Conscience.* New York: Greenwood Press. 1992. (6, 7)

Burton, David H. *The Learned Presidency: Theodore Roosevelt, William Howard Taft, Woodrow Wilson.* Rutherford, New Jersey: Fairleigh Dickinson University Press. 1988.

Camp, Helen C. *Iron in Her Soul: Elizabeth Gurley Flynn and the American Left.* Pullman, Washington: Washington State University Press. 1995. (6, 11)

Carlson, Peter. *Roughneck: The Life and Times of Big Bill Haywood.* New York: W.W. Norton. 1983. (3, 6)

Clendenen, Clarence C. *The United States and Pancho Villa: A Study in Unconventional Diplomacy.* Port Washington, New York: Kennikat Press. 1972.

Collier, Peter, and David Horowitz. *The Fords: An American Epic.* New York: Summit Books. 1987. (8, 10)

Cooper, John Milton, Jr. *The Warrior and the Priest: Woodrow Wilson and Theodore Roosevelt.* Cambridge, Massachusetts: Belknap Press. 1983. (6)

Davis, Allen F. *American Heroine: The Life and Legend of Jane Addams.* New York: Oxford University Press. 1973. (6)

Debs, Eugene V. Jean Y. Tussev, ed. *Eugene V. Debs Speaks.* New York: Pathfinder Press. 1972. (2, 6)

Deegan, Mary Jo. *Jane Addams and the Men of the Chicago School, 1892–1918.* New Brunswick, New Jersey: Transaction Books. 1988.

Dubofsky, Melvyn. *We Shall Be All: A History of the Industrial Workers of the World.* Chicago: Quadrangle Books. 1969. (3, 6)

Dubofsky, Melvyn. *"Big Bill" Haywood.* Manchester, England: Manchester University Press. 1987. (3, 6)

Eisenhower, John S. D. *Intervention: The United States Involvement in the Mexican Revolution, 1913–1917.* New York: W.W. Norton. 1993.

Flynn, Elizabeth Gurley. *The Rebel Girl: An Autobiography. My First Life.* New York: International Publishers. 1973. (6)

Foner, Philip S. *Fellow Workers and Friends: I.W.W. Free Speech Fights as Told by Participants.* Westport, Connecticut: Greenwood Press. 1981. (6)

Gable, John Allen. *The Bull Moose Years: Theodore Roosevelt and the Progressive Party.* Port Washington, New York: National University Publications. 1978.

Gardner, Joseph L. *Departing Glory: Theodore Roosevelt as Ex-President.* New York: Scribners. 1973. (6)

Garraty, John A. *Right-Hand Man: The Life of George W. Perkins.* New York: Harper. 1960.

Gilderhus, Mark T. *Diplomacy and Revolution: U.S.-Mexican Relations Under Wilson and Carranza.* Tucson, Arizona: University of Arizona Press. 1977.

Gitelman, H. M. *Legacy of the Ludlow Massacre: A Chapter in American Industrial Relations.* Philadelphia: University of Pennsylvania Press. 1988.

Golin, Steve. *The Fragile Bridge: The Paterson Silk Strike, 1913.* Philadelphia: Temple University Press. 1988.

Green, Martin. *New York 1913: The Armory Show and the Paterson Strike Pageant.* New York: Scribners. 1988.

Grieb, Kenneth J. *The United States and Huerta.* Lincoln, Nebraska: University of Nebraska Press. 1969.

Guzman, Martin Luis. Harriet de Onis, trans. *The Eagle and the Serpent.* Garden City, New York: Dolphin Books. 1965.

Guzman, Martin Luis. Virginia H. Taylor, trans. *Memoirs of Pancho Villa.* Austin, Texas: University of Texas Press. 1965.

Haley, P. Edward. *Revolution and Intervention: The Diplomacy of Taft and Wilson with Mexico, 1910–1917.* Cambridge, Massachusetts: M.I.T. Press. 1970.

Hall, Linda Biesele. *Alvaro Obregon: Power and Revolution in Mexico, 1911–1920.* College Station, Texas: Texas A&M University Press. 1981.

Hampton, Wayne. *Guerrilla Minstrels: John Lennon, Joe Hill, Woody Guthrie, and Bob Dylan.* Knoxville, Tennessee: University of Tennessee Press. 1986.

Haywood, William D. *Bill Haywood's Book: The Autobiography of William D. Haywood.* Westport, Connecticut: Greenwood Press. 1983. (3, 6)

Healy, David. *Gunboat Diplomacy in the Wilson Era: The U.S. Navy in Haiti, 1915–1916.* Madison, Wisconsin: University of Wisconsin Press. 1976.

Heckscher, August. *Woodrow Wilson.* New York: Collier Books. 1991. (6)

Heinl, Robert Debs, Jr., and Nancy Gordon Heinl. *Written in Blood: The Story of the Haitian People, 1492–1971.* Boston: Houghton Mifflin. 1978.

Kelly, Frank K. *The Fight for the White House: The Story of 1912.* New York: Crowell. 1961.

Kornbluh, Joyce L., ed. *Rebel Voices: An IWW Anthology.* Chicago: C.H. Kerr. 1988. (3, 6)

Lacey, Robert. *Ford: The Man and the Machine.* Boston: Little, Brown and Company. 1986. (8, 10)

Lamont, Corliss, ed. *The Trial of Elizabeth Gurley Flynn by the American Civil Liberties Union.* New York: Horizon Press. 1968. (11)

Leyburn, James G. *The Haitian People.* Westport, Connecticut: Greenwood Press. 1980.

Link, Arthur S. *Woodrow Wilson and the Progressive Era, 1910–1917.* New York: Harper & Row. 1963. (6)

Link, Arthur S. *Wilson.* Princeton, New Jersey: University of Princeton Press. 1964. (6)

Manners, William. *TR and Will: A Friendship That Split the Republican Party.* New York: Harcourt, Brace & World. 1969.

McCraw, Thomas K. *Prophets of Regulation: Charles Francis Adams, Louis D. Brandeis, James M. Landis, Alfred E. Kahn.* Cambridge, Massachusetts: Belknap Press. 1984. (8)

Merz, Charles. *And Then Came Ford.* Garden City, New York: Doubleday, Doran. 1929.

Millspaugh, Arthur Chester. *Haiti Under American Control, 1915–1930.* Westport, Connecticut: Negro Universities Press. 1970.

Mowry, George Edwin. *Theodore Roosevelt and the Progressive Movement.* New York: Hill and Wang. 1960.

Mulder, John M. *Woodrow Wilson: The Years of Preparation.* Princeton, New Jersey: Princeton University Press. 1978.

Olin, Spencer C., Jr. *California's Prodigal Sons: Hiram Johnson and the Progressives, 1911–1917.* Berkeley,

California: University of California Press. 1968.

Orleck, Annelise. *Common Sense and a Little Fire: Women and Working-Class Politics in the United States, 1900–1965.* Chapel Hill, North Carolina: The University of North Carolina Press. 1995. (4, 6, 8, 13)

Painter, Nell Irvin. *Standing at Armageddon: The United States, 1877–1919.* New York: W.W. Norton & Company. 1987. (1, 2, 3, 4, 6)

Papanikolas, Zeese. *Buried Unsung: Louis Tikas and the Ludlow Massacre.* Salt Lake City, Utah: University of Utah Press. 1982.

Paper, Lewis J. *Brandeis.* Englewood Cliffs, New Jersey: Prentice-Hall. 1983. (8)

Parkinson, Roger. *Zapata: A Biography.* New York: Stein and Day. 1975.

Penick, James L., Jr. *Progressive Politics and Conservation: The Ballinger-Pinchot Affair.* Chicago: University of Chicago Press. 1968. (4)

Pinchot, Amos. Helene Maxwell Hooker, ed. *History of the Progressive Party, 1912–1916.* New York: New York University Press. 1958.

Plummer, Brenda Gayle. *Haiti and the Great Powers, 1902–1915.* Baton Rouge, Louisiana: Louisiana State University Press. 1988.

Preston, William. *Aliens and Dissenters: Federal Suppression of Radicals, 1903–1933.* New York: Harper & Row. 1966. (6, 7)

Pringle, Henry Fowles. *The Life and Times of William Howard Taft: A Biography.* Hamden, Connecticut: Archon Books. 1964. (7)

Shepherd, Naomi. *A Price Below Rubies: Jewish Women as Rebels and Radicals.* Cambridge, Massachusetts: Harvard University Press. 1993. (4, 7, 8)

Smythe, Donald. *Guerrilla Warrior: The Early Life of John J. Pershing.* New York: Scribners. 1973. (3)

Stein, Leon. *The Triangle Fire.* New York: Carroll & Graf/Quicksilver. 1962.

Stein, Leon, ed. *Out of the Sweatshop: The Struggle for Industrial Democ-*

racy. New York: Quadrangle/New York Times. 1977. (4, 6, 8, 13)

Thelen, David P. *Robert M. La Follette and the Insurgent Spirit.* Boston: Little, Brown. 1976. (6, 7)

Thorsen, Niels. *The Political Thought of Woodrow Wilson, 1875–1910.* Princeton, New Jersey: Princeton University Press. 1988.

Tripp, Anne H. *The I.W.W. and the Paterson Silk Strike of 1913.* Urbana, Illinois: University of Illinois Press. 1987.

Urofsky, Melvin I. *A Mind of One Piece: Brandeis and American Reform.* New York: Scribners. 1971. (8)

Weatherson, Michael A., and Hal W. Bochin. *Hiram Johnson: Political Revivalist.* Lanham, Maryland: University Press of America. 1995. (6, 8, 9)

Wilson, Woodrow. *A History of the American People.* New York: Harper. 1902.

Wilson, Woodrow. *The New Freedom: A Call for the Emancipation of the Generous Energies of a People.* New York: Doubleday, Page and Company. 1921.

Wilson, Woodrow. Edwin Tribble, ed. *A President in Love: The Courtship Letters of Woodrow Wilson and Edith Bolling Galt.* Boston: Houghton Mifflin. 1981. (6)

Winters, Donald E., Jr. *The Soul of the Wobblies: The I.W.W., Religion, and American Culture in the Progressive Era, 1905–1917.* Westport, Connecticut: Greenwood Press. 1985. (3, 4, 6)

Womack, John, Jr. *Zapata and the Mexican Revolution.* New York: Vintage Books. 1970.

DWIGHT D. EISENHOWER rears back to throw out the first ball of the 1958 season. To Ike's left in the last (bottom, right) picture is manager Pinky Higgins of the visiting Boston Red Sox. Within three years, the old Washington Senators would be gone, moved to Minnesota—though they would be immediately replaced by an expansion team with the same name.

JOHN F. KENNEDY maneuvers for a foul ball behind the dugout. The athletic Kennedy's game was football, although he was never healthy or heavy enough to be a starting player at Harvard.

CHAPTER SIX

Asprey, Robert B. *At Belleau Wood.* New York: Putnam. 1965.

Avrich, Paul. *Sacco and Vanzetti: The Anarchist Background.* Princeton, New Jersey: Princeton University Press. 1991. (7)

Bailey, Thomas A. *Woodrow Wilson and the Lost Peace.* Chicago: Quadrangle Books. 1963.

Bailey, Thomas A. *Woodrow Wilson and the Great Betrayal.* Chicago: Quadrangle Books. 1963.

Bailey, Thomas A., and Paul B. Ryan. *The Lusitania Disaster: An Episode in Modern Warfare and Diplomacy.* New York: Free Press. 1975.

Bernstein, Irving. *The Lean Years: A History of the American Worker, 1920–1933.* Baltimore, Maryland: Penguin Books. 1966. (7, 8)

Bickers, Richard Townshend. *The First Great Air War.* London: Hodder & Stoughton. 1988.

Braim, Paul F. *The Test of Battle: The American Expeditionary Forces in the Meuse-Argonne Campaign.* Newark, Delaware: University of Delaware Press. 1987.

Brownrigg, Rear-Admiral Sir Douglas. *Indiscretions of the Naval Censor.* New York: Cassell and Company. 1920. (9)

Burk, Kathleen. *Britain, America and the Sinews of War, 1914–1918.* Boston: G. Allen & Unwin. 1985.

Burton, David H. *Cecil Spring Rice: A Diplomat's Life.* Rutherford, New Jersey: Fairleigh Dickinson University Press. 1990.

Churchill, Sir Winston. *The Great War.* London: G. Newnes. 1934.

Clarkson, Grosvenor B. *Industrial America in the World War: The Strategy Behind the Line 1917–1918.* Englewood, New Jersey: Ozer. 1974.

Clements, Kendrick A. *William Jennings Bryan, Missionary Isolationist.* Knoxville, Tennessee: University of Tennessee Press. 1982. (5)

Coben, Stanley. *A. Mitchell Palmer: Politician.* New York: Columbia University Press. 1963.

Cockfield, Jamie H. *With Snow on Their Boots: The Tragic Odyssey of the Russian Expeditionary Force in France, 1915–1920.* New York: St. Martin's Press. 1998.

Cooke, James J. *Pershing and His Generals: Command and Staff in the AEF.* Westport, Connecticut: Praeger. 1997.

Copeland, Tom. *The Centralia Tragedy of 1919: Elmer Smith and the Wobblies.* Seattle: University of Washington Press. 1993.

Cowley, Robert. *1918: Gamble for Victory; The Greatest Attack of World War I.* New York: Macmillan. 1964.

Cuff, Robert D. *The War Industries Board: Business-Government Relations During World War I.* Baltimore: Johns Hopkins University Press. 1973.

Dallas, Gregor. *At the Heart of a Tiger: Clemenceau and His World 1841–1929.* London: Macmillan. 1993.

Devlin, Patrick. *Too Proud to Fight: Woodrow Wilson's Neutrality.* New York: Oxford University Press. 1975.

Dos Passos, John. *1919.* New York: New American Library. 1979.

Dos Passos, John. *The Big Money.* New York: New American Library. 1979.

Ehrmann, Herbert B. *The Untried Case: The Sacco-Vanzetti Case and the Morelli Gang.* New York: Vanguard Press. 1960.

Ellis, John. *Eye-Deep in Hell: Trench Warfare in World War I.* New York: Pantheon Books. 1976.

Esposito, Vincent J., ed. *A Concise History of World War I.* New York: Praeger. 1964.

Felix, David. *Protest: Sacco-Vanzetti and the Intellectuals.* Bloomington, Indiana: Indiana University Press. 1965.

Fic, Victor M. *The Collapse of American Policy in Russia and Siberia, 1918: Wilson's Decision Not to Intervene.* Boulder, Colorado and New York: East European Monographs/Columbia University Press. 1995.

Frankfurter, Felix. *The Case of Sacco and Vanzetti: A Critical Analysis for Lawyers and Laymen.* Boston: Little, Brown and Company. 1927.

Freud, Sigmund, and William C. Bullitt. *Thomas Woodrow Wilson, Twenty-Eighth President of the United States: A Psychological Study.* Boston: Houghton Mifflin Company. 1967. (5)

Frost, Richard H. *The Mooney Case.* Stanford, California: Stanford University Press. 1968.

Garraty, John Arthur. *Henry Cabot Lodge: A Biography.* New York: Alfred A. Knopf. 1953. (2, 3, 4, 5, 7)

George, Alexander L. and Juliette L. George. *Woodrow Wilson and Colonel House: A Personality Study.* New York: Dover Publications. 1964.

Gies, Joseph. *Crisis, 1918: The Leading Actors, Strategies, and Events in the German Gamble for Total Victory on the Western Front.* New York: Norton. 1974.

Gilbert, Bentley Brinkerhoff. *David Lloyd George: A Political Life.* Columbus, Ohio: Ohio State University Press. 1987.

Gilbert, Martin. *First World War.* London: Weidenfeld and Nicolson. 1994.

Goldhurst, Richard. *Pipe Clay and Drill: John J. Pershing, the Classic American Soldier.* New York: Reader's Digest Press. 1977. (3, 5)

Grayson, Benson Lee. *Russian-American Relations in World War I.* New York: Ungar. 1979.

Grayson, Cary T. *Woodrow Wilson: An Intimate Memoir.* New York: Holt, Rinehart and Winston. 1960. (5)

Hallas, James H. *Squandered Victory: The American First Army at St. Mihiel.* Westport, Connecticut: Praeger. 1995.

Hatch, Alden. *Edith Bolling Wilson, First Lady Extraordinary.* New York: Dodd, Mead. 1961.

Hoover, Herbert. *The Ordeal of Woodrow Wilson.* New York: McGraw-Hill. 1958.

Hudson, James J. *Hostile Skies: A Combat History of the American Air Service in World War I.* Syracuse, New York: Syracuse University Press. 1968.

James, Lawrence. *The Golden Warrior: The Life and Legend of T. E. Lawrence.* London: Weidenfeld and Nicolson. 1990.

Johnson, Claudius O. *Borah of Idaho.* Seattle: University of Washington Press. 1967. (9)

Johnson, Hubert C. *Breakthrough! Tactics, Technology, and the Search for Victory on the Western Front in World War I.* Novato, California: Presidio. 1994.

Johnson, J. H. *Stalemate! The Great Trench Warfare Battles of 1915–1917.* New York: Arms and Armour/Sterling Publishers. 1995.

Johnson, J. H. *1918: The Unexpected Victory.* London: Arms and Armour. 1997.

Keegan, John. *The Face of Battle.* London: Jonathan Cape. 1976.

Kennan, George W. *Russia and the West Under Lenin and Stalin.* New York: Atlantic Monthly Press. 1961. (9, 10, 11)

Keynes, John Maynard. *The Economic Consequences of the Peace.* New York: Penguin Books. 1988. (8)

Klingaman, William K. *1919: The Year Our World Began.* Harper. 1989.

Kocka, Jurgen. Barbara Weinberger, trans. *Facing Total War: German Society, 1914–1918.* Leamington Spa, England: Berg Publishers. 1984.

Kohn, Stephen M. *American Political Prisoners: Prosecutions Under the Espionage and Sedition Acts.* Westport, Connecticut: Praeger. 1994.

Lansing, Robert. *The Peace Negotiations: A Personal Narrative.* Port Washington, New York: Kennikat Press. 1969.

Lawrence, Joseph Douglas. Robert H. Ferrell, ed. *Fighting Soldier: The AEF in 1918.* Boulder, Colorado: Colorado Associated University Press. 1985.

Lawrence, T. E. *Seven Pillars of Wisdom: A Triumph.* New York: Penguin Books. 1979

Liddell Hart, Captain B. H. *The Real War: The Short History of the First World War.* Boston: Atlantic Monthly Press/Little, Brown. 1930.

Link, Arthur S. *Wilson the Diplomatist: A Look at His Major Foreign Policies.* Chicago: Quadrangle. 1965. (5)

Link, Arthur S. *Woodrow Wilson: Revolution, War, and Peace.* Arlington Heights, Illinois: AHM Publishing Corporation. 1979. (5)

Lord, Walter. *The Good Years: From 1900 to the First World War.* New York: Harper. 1960. (3, 4, 5)

Lovell, S. D. *The Presidential Election of 1916.* Carbondale, Illinois: Southern Illinois University Press. 1980.

Lower, Richard Coke. *A Bloc of One: The Political Career of Hiram W. Johnson.* Stanford, California: Stanford University Press. 1993. (5, 7, 8, 9)

MacIntyre, W. Irwin. *Colored Soldiers.* Macon, Georgia: J.W. Burke. 1923.

Maddox, Robert J. *The Unknown War with Russia: Wilson's Siberian Intervention.* San Rafael, California: Presidio Press. 1977.

Mantoux, Paul. Arthur S. Link and Manfred F. Boemeke, eds. and trans. *The Deliberations of the Council of Four (March 24–June 28, 1919): Notes of the Official Interpreter, Paul Mantoux.* Princeton, New Jersey: Princeton University Press. 1992.

May, Ernest R. *The World War and American Isolation, 1914–1917.* Cambridge, Massachusetts: Harvard University Press. 1959.

McKenna, Marian C. *Borah.* Ann Arbor, Michigan: University of Michigan Press. 1961. (9)

Mee, Charles L., Jr. *The End of Order: Versailles, 1919.* New York: Dutton. 1980.

Meigs, Mark. *Optimism at Armageddon: Voices of American Participants in the First World War.* New York: New York University Press. 1997.

Mock, James R. *Censorship, 1917.* Princeton, New Jersey: Princeton University Press. 1941.

Montgomery, Robert H. *Sacco-Vanzetti: The Murder and the Myth.* New York: Devin-Adair Co. 1960.

Newhall, David S. *Clemenceau: A Life at War.* Lewiston, New York: E. Mellen Press. 1991.

O'Connor, Richard. *Black Jack Pershing.* Garden City, New York: Doubleday. 1961. (3, 5)

Pershing, John J. *My Experiences in the World War.* New York: Frederick A. Stokes Company. 1931.

Pipes, Richard. *The Russian Revolution.* New York: Alfred A. Knopf. 1990.

Polenberg, Richard. *Fighting Faiths: The Abrams Case, the Supreme Court, and Free Speech.* New York: Viking. 1987.

Post, Louis Freeland. *The Deportations Delirium of Nineteen-Twenty: A Personal Narrative of an Historic Official Experience.* New York: Da Capo Press. 1970.

Powers, Richard Gid. *Secrecy and Power: The Life of J. Edgar Hoover.* New York: The Free Press. 1988. (8, 10, 11, 12, 13, 14)

Remarque, Erich Maria. A.W. Wheen, trans. *All Quiet on the Western Front.* Boston: Little, Brown. 1975.

Ross, Ishbel. *Power with Grace: The Life Story of Mrs. Woodrow Wilson.* New York: Putnam. 1975. (5)

Russell, Francis. *Tragedy in Dedham: The Story of the Sacco-Vanzetti Case.* New York: McGraw-Hill. 1962.

Sacco, Nicola, and Bartolomeo Vanzetti. Marion Denman Frankfurter and Gardner Jackson, eds. *The Letters of Sacco and Vanzetti.* New York: Penguin Books. 1997.

Shactman, Tom. *Edith & Woodrow: A Presidential Romance.* New York: Putnam. 1981. (5)

Smith, Gene. *When the Cheering Stopped: The Last Years of Woodrow Wilson.* Simon and Schuster. 1968.

Smythe, Donald. *Pershing, General of the Armies.* Bloomington, Indiana: Indiana University Press. 1986.

Stallings, Laurence. *The Doughboys: The Story of the AEF, 1917–1918.* New York: Harper & Row. 1963. (9)

Sweeney, Willaim Allison. *History of the American Negro in the Great World War; His Splendid Record in the Battle Zones of Europe.* New York: Johnson Reprint. 1970.

Toland, John. *No Man's Land: 1918, the Last Year of the Great War.* Garden City, New York: Doubleday. 1980.

Trask, David F. *The AEF and Coalition Warmaking, 1917–1918.* Lawrence, Kansas: University Press of Kansas. 1993.

Tuchman, Barbara. *The Zimmermann Telegram.* New York: Dell Publishing Company. 1958.

Tuchman, Barbara. *The Guns of August.* New York: Bantam Books. 1962. (12)

Tumulty, Joseph P. *Woodrow Wilson as I Know Him.* Garden City, New York: Doubleday, Page & Company. 1921.

Vincent, C. Paul. *The Politics of Hunger: The Allied Blockade of Germany, 1915–1919.* Athens, Ohio: Ohio University Press. 1985.

Walworth, Arthur. *Wilson and His Peacemakers: American Diplomacy at the Paris Peace Conference, 1919.* New York: Norton. 1986.

Ward, Estolv Ethan. *The Gentle Dynamiter: A Biography of Tom Mooney.* Palo Alto, California: Ramparts Press. 1983.

Weinstein, Edwin A. *Woodrow Wilson: A Medical and Psychological Biography.* Princeton, New Jersey: Princeton University Press. 1981. (5)

Widenor, William C. *Henry Cabot Lodge and the Search for an American Foreign Policy.* Berkeley, California: University of California Press. 1980. (3, 4)

Williams, Joyce Grigsby. *Colonel House and Sir Edward Grey: A Study in Anglo-American Diplomacy.* Lanham, Maryland: University Press of America. 1984.

Wilson, Edith Bolling. *My Memoir.* New York: The Bobbs-Merrill Company. 1939. (5)

Witcover, Jules. *Sabotage at Black Tom: Imperial Germany's Secret War in America, 1914–1917.* Chapel Hill, North Carolina: Algonquin Books of Chapel Hill. 1989.

CHAPTER SEVEN

Agawa, Hiroyuki. John Bester, trans. *The Reluctant Admiral: Yamamoto and the Imperial Navy.* New York: Kodansha International. 1979. (8, 9, 10)

Allen, Frederick Lewis. *Only Yesterday: An Informal History of the Nineteen-Twenties.* New York: Harper & Row. 1964.

Allsop, Kenneth. *The Bootleggers: The Story of Chicago's Prohibition Era.* New Rochelle, New York: Arlington House. 1968.

Babbitt, Irving, et al. *Criticism in America: Its Functions and Status.* New York: Harcourt, Brace and Company. 1924.

Baker, Liva. *The Justice from Beacon Hill: The Life and Times of Oliver Wendell Holmes.* New York: HarperCollins. 1991. (5, 6, 8)

Barton, Bruce. *The Man Nobody Knows.* Indianapolis, Indiana: Bobbs-Merrill. 1962.

Behr, Edward. *Prohibition: Thirteen Years That Changed America.* New York: Arcade Publishers. 1996. (8)

Bergreen, Laurence. *Capone: The Man and the Era.* New York: Simon and Schuster. 1994. (8)

Booraem, Hendrik. *The Provincial: Calvin Coolidge and His World, 1885–1895.* Cranbury, New Jersey: Associated University Presses. 1994.

Britton, Nan. *The President's Daughter.* New York: Elizabeth Ann Guild. 1927.

Bruere, Martha Bensley. *Does Prohibition Work?* New York: Harper & Brothers. 1927. (6, 8)

Bukowski, Douglas. *Big Bill Thompson, Chicago, and the Politics of Image.* Urbana, Illinois: University of Illinois Press. 1998.

Burner, David. *Herbert Hoover: A Public Life.* New York: Alfred A. Knopf. 1979. (6, 8)

Carse, Robert. *Rum Row.* New York: Rinehart. 1959.

Chidsey, Donald Barr. *On and Off the Wagon: A Sober Analysis of the Temperance Movement from the Pilgrims through Prohibition.* New York: Cowles Book Company. 1969. (8)

Coffey, Thomas M. *The Long Thirst: Prohibition in America, 1920–1933.* New York: Norton. 1975. (8)

Cohen, Jeremy. *Congress Shall Make No Law: Oliver Wendell Holmes, the First Amendment, and Judicial Decisions-Making.* Ames, Iowa: Iowa State University Press. 1989. (5, 6, 8)

Conot, Robert. *A Streak of Luck.* New York: Seaview/Simon and Schuster. 1979.

Cronon, E. David. *Black Moses: The Story of Marcus Garvey and the Universal Negro Improvement Association.* Madison, Wisconsin: University of Wisconsin Press. 1969.

Davis, Burke. *The Billy Mitchell Affair.* New York: Random House. 1967.

Dixon, Thomas. *The Clansman; An Historical Romance of the Ku Klux Klan.* Ridgewood, New Jersey: Gregg Press. 1967.

Dutton, David. *Austen Chamberlain: Gentleman in Politics.* Bolton, England: Ross Anderson. 1985. (8, 9)

Eddot, Paula. *Governor Alfred E. Smith: The Politician as Reformer.* New York: Garland Publishing. 1983. (4, 5, 8)

Eliot, T. S. *Essays Ancient & Modern.* London: Faber and Faber. 1936.

Eliot, T. S. *Collected Poems, 1909–1962.* New York: Harcourt, Brace & World. 1970.

Ellison, Ralph. John F. Callahan, ed. *The Collected Essays of Ralph Ellison.* New York: Modern Library. 1995. (12, 13)

Fitzgerald, F. Scott. *Tales of the Jazz Age.* New York: Charles Scribner's Sons. 1922.

Fitzgerald, F. Scott. *The Great Gatsby.* New York: Scribners. 1981.

Friendly, Fred. *Minnesota Rag.* New York: Random House. 1981.

Gelfand, Lawrence E., ed. *Herbert Hoover—The Great War and Its Aftermath, 1914–23.* Iowa City, Iowa: University of Iowa Press. 1979. (6)

Grayson, Richard S. *Austen Chamberlain and the Commitment to Europe: British Foreign Policy, 1924–29.* Portland, Oregon: Frank Cass. 1997. (8, 9)

Hobson, Fred. *Mencken: A Life.* New York: Random House. 1994. (6, 8)

Hodgson, Godfrey. *The Colonel: The Life and Wars of Henry Stimson, 1867–1950.* New York: Alfred A. Knopf. 1990. (3, 4, 5, 9, 10)

Hoff-Wilson, Joan. *Herbert Hoover: Forgotten Progressive.* Boston: Little, Brown. 1975. (6, 8)

Hoover, Herbert. *The Memoirs of Herbert Hoover: Years of Adventure 1874–1920.* New York: Macmillan. 1951.

Hurley, Alfred F. *Billy Mitchell, Crusader for Air Power.* Bloomington, Indiana: Indiana University Press. 1975.

Kerber, Linda K., and Jane Sherron De Hart, eds. *Women's America: Refocusing the Past.* New York: Oxford University Press. 1991. (5, 14, 15)

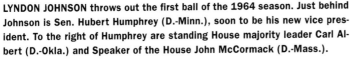

LYNDON JOHNSON throws out the first ball of the 1964 season. Just behind Johnson is Sen. Hubert Humphrey (D.-Minn.), soon to be his new vice president. To the right of Humphrey are standing House majority leader Carl Albert (D.-Okla.) and Speaker of the House John McCormack (D.-Mass.).

RICHARD NIXON makes ready to toss out the first ball of the 1969 season, in a game the Senators would lose to Mel Stottlemyre and the New York Yankees, 8–4. Nixon was probably the biggest baseball fan ever to occupy the Oval Office; later that year he would name his own, all-time all-star team in the *New York Times*, as part of major league baseball's celebration of 100 years of professional play. He later expressed astonishment that Hillary Rodham Clinton had never heard of the 1930s shortstop Arky Vaughn, a Hall of Famer from her adopted state.

Kobler, John. *Capone: The Life and World of Al Capone.* Greenwich, Connecticut: Fawcett Publications. 1971. (8)

Kobler, John. *Ardent Spirits: The Rise and Fall of Prohibition.* New York: Da Capo Press. 1993. (8)

Lacey, Robert. *Little Man: Meyer Lansky and the Gangster Life.* Boston: Little, Brown and Company. 1991. (8)

Lardner, Ring. Maxwell Geismar, ed. *The Ring Lardner Reader.* New York: Scribners. 1963.

Lee, Henry. *How Dry We Were: Prohibition Revisited.* Englewood Cliffs, New Jersey: Prentice-Hall. 1963. (8)

Levine, Lawrence W. *Defender of the Faith: William Jennings Bryan, the Last Decade, 1915–1925.* Cambridge, Massachusetts: Harvard University Press. 1987. (5, 6)

Lewis, Sinclair. *Elmer Gantry.* Cambridge, Massachusetts: R. Bentley. 1979.

Lewis, Sinclair. *Babbitt.* New York: New American Library. 1980.

Lewis, Sinclair. *Main Street.* New York: New American Library. 1980.

Manchester, William. *Disturber of the Peace: The Life of H. L. Mencken.* Amherst, Massachusetts: University of Massachusetts Press. 1986. (8)

Martin, Tony, ed. *African Fundamentalism: A Literary and Cultural Anthology of Garvey's Harlem Renaissance.* Dover, Massachusetts: Majority Press. 1991.

McCoy, Donald. *Calvin Coolidge: The Quiet President.* New York: Macmillan. 1967.

Mencken, H. L. *Notes on Democracy.* New York: Alfred A. Knopf. 1926.

Mencken, H. L. Alistair Cooke, ed. *The Vintage Mencken.* New York: Vintage Books. 1961. (6, 8)

Mencken, H.L. *Heathen Days.* New York: AMS Press. 1987. (8)

Merz, Charles. *The Dry Decade.* Seattle: University of Washington Press. 1969.

Murray, Robert K. *The Harding Era: Warren G. Harding and His Administration.* Minneapolis: University of Minnesota Press. 1969.

Murray, Robert K.: *The Politics of Normalcy: Governmental Theory and Practice in the Harding-Coolidge Era.* New York: Norton. 1973.

Nash, George H. *The Life of Herbert Hoover.* New York: W.W. Norton. 1983. (6, 8)

Novick, Sheldon M. *Honorable Justice: The Life of Oliver Wendell Holmes.* Boston: Little, Brown. 1989. (5, 6, 8)

O'Connor, Richard. *The First Hurrah: A Biography of Alfred E. Smith.* New York: G. P. Putnam's Sons. 1970. (8)

Perrett, Geoffrey. *America in the Twenties: A History.* New York: Simon and Schuster. 1982. (6)

Pohlman, H. L. *Justice Oliver Wendell Holmes: Free Speech and the Living Constitution.* New York: New York University Press. 1991. (6)

Russell, Francis. *The Shadow of Blooming Grove: Warren G. Harding in His Times.* New York: McGraw-Hill. 1968.

Sandino, Augusto Cesar. Sergio Ramirez, ed., and Robert Edgar Conrad, trans. and ed. *Sandino: The Testimony of a Nicaraguan Patriot, 1921–1934.* Princeton, New Jersey: Princeton University Press. 1990. (15)

Sann, Paul. *The Lawless Decade.* New York: Crown Publishers. 1961.

Schickel, Richard. *D. W. Griffith: An American Life.* New York: Simon and Schuster. 1984.

Schmidt, John R. *The Mayor Who Cleaned Up Chicago: A Political Biography of William E. Dever.* Dekalb, Illinois: Northern Illinois University Press. 1989. (8)

Schoenberg, Robert J. *Mr. Capone: The Real—and Complete—Story of Al Capone.* New York: Morrow. 1992. (8)

Sewell, Tony. *Garvey's Children: The Legacy of Marcus Garvey.* Trenton, New Jersey: Africa World Press. 1990.

Shirley, Glenn. *"Hello, Sucker!": The Story of Texas Guinan.* Austin, Texas: Eakin Press. 1989.

Sinclair, Andrew. *Era of Excess: A Social History of the Prohibition Movement.* New York: Harper & Row. 1964.

Smith-Irvin, Jeannette. *Foot Soldiers of the Universal Negro Improvement Association: Their Own Words.* Trenton, New Jersey: Africa World Press. 1989.

Stearns, Harold, ed. *Civilization in the United States: An Inquiry by Thirty Americans.* New York: Harcourt, Brace and Company. 1922.

Tierney, Kevin. *Darrow: A Biography.* New York: Thomas Y. Crowell. 1979. (5)

Timberlake, James H. *Prohibition and the Progressive Movement, 1900–1920.* Cambridge, Massachusetts: Harvard University Press. 1963. (3, 4, 5)

Van Voris, Jacqueline. *Carrie Chapman Catt: A Public Life.* New York: Feminist Press. 1987. (4)

Weinberg, Arthur, and Lila Weinberg. *Clarence Darrow: A Sentimental Rebel.* New York: Putnam. 1980. (5, 8)

Wendt, Lloyd, and Herman Kogan. *Big Bill of Chicago.* Indianapolis, Indiana: Bobbs-Merrill. 1953.

Werner, M. R., and John Starr. *Teapot Dome.* New York: Viking Press. 1959.

White, William Allen. *A Puritan in Babylon: The Story of Calvin Coolidge.* New York: Capricorn Books. 1965.

Wilson, Edmund. *The American Earthquake: A Documentary of the Twenties and Thirties.* New York: Octagon Books. 1971. (6, 8)

CHAPTER EIGHT

Abbott, Philip. *The Exemplary Presidency: Franklin D. Roosevelt and the American Political Tradition.* Amherst, Massachusetts: University of Massachusetts Press. 1990. (9, 10)

Adams, Henry H. *Harry Hopkins: A Biography.* New York: Putnam. 1977 (9, 10)

Agee, James, and Walker Evans. *Let Us Now Praise Famous Men.* Boston: Houghton Mifflin. 1941.

Allen, Frederick Lewis. *Since Yesterday: The Nineteen-Thirties in America, September 3, 1929–September 3, 1939.* Garden City, New York: Blue Ribbon Books. 1943.

Baker, Leonard. *Brandeis and Frankfurter: A Dual Biography.* New York: Harper & Row. 1984.

Barber, William J. *From New Era to New Deal: Herbert Hoover, the Economists, and American Economic Policy, 1921–1933.* New York: Cambridge University Press. 1985. (7)

Bergamini, David. *Japan's Imperial Conspiracy.* New York: Pocket Books. 1972. (9)

Bernstein, Irving. *Turbulent Years: A History of the American Worker, 1933–1941.* Boston: Houghton Mifflin. 1970.

Bernstein, Irving. *A Caring Society: The New Deal, the Worker, and the Great Depression, 1933–1941.* Boston: Houghton Mifflin. 1985.

Bonnifield, Paul. *The Dust Bowl: Men, Dirt and Depression.* Albuquerque, New Mexico: University of New Mexico Press. 1982.

Brinkley, Alan. *Voices of Protest: Huey Long, Father Coughlin, and the Great Depression.* New York: Vintage Books. 1983.

Brown, Robert J. *Manipulating the Ether: The Power of Broadcast Radio in Thirties America.* Jefferson, North Carolina: McFarland. 1997.

Burns, James MacGregor. *Roosevelt: The Lion and the Fox.* New York: Harcourt Brace Jovanovich. 1984. (9, 10)

Caldwell, Erskine, and Margaret Bourke-White. *You Have Seen Their Faces.* New York: Modern Age Books. 1937.

Callahan, North. *TVA: Bridge Over Troubled Waters.* South Brunswick, New Jersey: A.S. Barnes. 1980.

Cashman, Sean Dennis. *America in the Twenties and Thirties: The Olympian Age of Franklin Delano Roosevelt.* New York: New York University Press. 1989. (7)

Clark, Paul F., Peter Gottlieb, and Donal Kennedy, eds. *Forging a Union of Steel: Philip Murray, SWOC, and the United Steelworkers.* Ithaca, New York: ILR Press. 1987.

Clarke, Jeanne Nienaber. *Roosevelt's Warrior: Harold L. Ickes and the New Deal.* Baltimore: Johns Hopkins University Press. 1996. (9, 10)

Conkin, Paul K. *FDR and the Origins of the Welfare State.* New York: Crowell. 1967.

Daniels, Roger. *The Bonus March: An Episode of the Great Depression.* Westport, Connecticut: Greenwood Publishing Company. 1971.

Davis, Kenneth S. *FDR: The Beckoning of Destiny, 1882–1928.* New York: Random House. 1979.

Davis, Kenneth S. *FDR: The New York Years, 1928–1933.* New York: Random House. 1983.

Davis, Kenneth S. *FDR: The New Deal Years, 1933–1937.* New York: Random House. 1986.

Dawson, Nelson Lloyd. *Louis D. Brandeis, Felix Frankfurter, and the New Deal.* Hamden, Connecticut: Archon Books. 1980.

Dewey, Thomas E. Rodney Campbell, ed. *Twenty Against the Underworld.* Garden City, New York: Doubleday. 1974.

Dubinsky, David, and A. H. Raskin. *David Dubinsky: A Life with Labor.* New York: Simon and Schuster. 1977. (11, 12)

Dubofsky, Melvyn, and Warren Van Tine. *John L. Lewis: A Biography.* Urbana, Illinois: University of Illinois Press. 1986. (6, 7, 9, 10, 11)

Eccles, Marriner S. Sidney Hyman, ed. *Beckoning Frontiers: Public and Personal Recollections.* New York: Alfred A. Knopf. 1966.

Ellis, Edward Robb. *A Nation in Torment: The Great American Depression 1929–1940.* New York: Capricorn Books. 1971.

Fraser, Steven. *Labor Will Rule: Sidney Hillman and the Rise of American Labor.* New York: The Free Press. 1991. (5, 6, 10, 13)

Freidel, Frank. *Franklin D. Roosevelt: A Rendez-Vous with Destiny.* Boston: Little, Brown. 1990. (9, 10)

Galbraith, John Kenneth. *The Great Crash 1929.* Boston: Houghton Mifflin. 1988. (7)

Gallagher, Hugh Gregory. *FDR's Splendid Deception.* New York: Dodd, Mead. 1985.

Geisst, Charles R. *Wall Street: A History.* New York: Oxford University Press. 1997. (2, 3, 5, 7, 15)

Girardin, G. Russell, with William J. Helmer. *Dillinger: The Untold Story.* Bloomington, Indiana: Indiana University Press. 1994.

Goodman, James. *Stories of Scottsboro.* New York: Pantheon. 1994.

Guthrie, Woody. *Bound for Glory.* New York: E.P. Dutton. 1968.

Hair, William Ivy. *The Kingfish and His Realm: The Life and Times of Huey P. Long.* Baton Rouge, Louisiana: Louisiana State University Press. 1991.

Harris, William H. *Keeping the Faith: A. Philip Randolph, Milton P. Webster, and the Brotherhood of Sleeping Car Porters, 1925–37.* Urbana, Illinois: University of Illinois Press. 1977. (10)

Heckscher, August. *When La Guardia Was Mayor: New York's Legendary Years.* New York: Norton. 1978.

Hickok, Lorena A. *Reluctant First Lady.* New York: Dodd, Mead. 1962.

Hill, Edwin G. *In the Shadow of the Mountain: The Spirit of the CCC.* Pullman, Washington: Washington State University Press. 1990.

Hockett, Jeffrey D. *New Deal Justice: The Constitutional Jurisprudence of Hugo L. Black, Felix Frankfurter, and Robert H. Jackson.* Lanham, Maryland: Rowman & Littlefield. 1996. (10, 11, 12)

Hoover, Herbert. *The Memoirs of Herbert Hoover: The Cabinet & the Presidency 1920–1933.* New York: Macmillan. 1952. (7)

Hurt, R. Douglas. *The Dust Bowl: An Agricultural and Social History.* Chicago: Nelson-Hall. 1981.

Huthmacher, J. Joseph. *Senator Robert F. Wagner and the Rise of Urban Liberalism.* New York: Atheneum. 1968.

Ickes, Harold L. *The Secret Diaries: The Inside Struggle.* New York: Simon and Schuster. 1954.

Kelly, Lawrence C. *The Assault on Assimilation: John Collier and the Origins of Indian Policy Reform.* Albuquerque, New Mexico: University of New Mexico Press. 1983.

Kessner, Thomas. *Fiorello H. La Guardia and the Making of Modern New York.* New York: McGraw-Hill. 1989.

Keynes, John Maynard. *The General Theory of Employment, Interest, and Money.* New York: Harcourt, Brace & World. 1965. (6)

Kindleberger, Charles P. *The World in Depression, 1929–1939.* Berkeley, California: University of California Press. 1986.

Lange, Dorothea, and Paul Schuster Taylor. *An American Exodus: A Record of Human Erosion.* New York: Reynal & Hitchcock. 1939.

Lange Dorothea. Howard M. Levin and Katherine Northrup, eds. *Dorothea Lange: Farm Security Administration Photographs, 1935–1939.* Glencoe, Illinois: Text-Fiche Press. 1980.

Lash, Joseph P. *Eleanor and Franklin.* New York: W.W. Norton. 1971. (9, 10)

Lash, Joseph P. *Dealers and Dreamers: A New Look at the New Deal.* New York: Doubleday. 1988.

Leuchtenburg, William E. *The FDR Years: On Roosevelt and His Legacy.* New York: Columbia University Press. 1995. (9, 10)

Leuchtenburg, William E. *The Supreme Court Reborn: The Constitutional Revolution in the Age of Roosevelt.* New York: Oxford University Press. 1995. (12)

Lewis, Sinclair. *It Can't Happen Here.* New York: New American Library. 1970.

Lichtenstein, Nelson. *The Most Dangerous Man in Detroit: Walter Reuther and the Fate of American Labor.* New York: HarperCollins. 1995. (12, 13)

Lilienthal, David E. *The Journals of David E. Lilienthal.* 7 vols. New York: Harper & Row. 1983. (10, 11)

Lisio, Donald J. *The President and Protest: Hoover, Conspiracy, and the Bonus Riot.* Columbia, Missouri: University of Missouri Press. 1974.

Long, Huey P. *My First Days in the White House.* Harrisburg, Pennsylvania: The Telegraph Press. 1935.

Lowitt, Richard. *George W. Norris: The Making of a Progressive.* Syracuse, New York: Syracuse University Press. 1963. (5)

Lowitt, Richard. *George W. Norris: The Persistence of a Progressive, 1913–1933.* Urbana, Illinois: University of Illinois Press. 1971. (6, 7)

Lowitt, Richard. *George W. Norris: The Triumph of a Progressive, 1933–1944.* Urbana, Illinois: University of Illinois Press. 1978.

Maney, Patrick J. *"Young Bob" La Follette: A Biography of Robert M. La Follette, Jr. 1895–1953.* Columbia, Missouri: University of Missouri Press. 1978. (9)

Martin, George. *Madam Secretary, Frances Perkins.* Boston: Houghton Mifflin. 1976. (10)

McCraw, Thomas K. *TVA and the Power Fight, 1933–1939.* Philadelphia: Lippincott. 1971.

McElvaine, Robert S. *The Great Depression: America, 1929–1941.* New York: Times Books, 1993.

McJimsey, George. *Harry Hopkins: Ally of the Poor and Defender of Democracy.* Cambridge, Massachusetts: Harvard University Press. 1987. (9, 10)

Meuse, Steve M. *David E. Lilienthal: The Journey of an American Liberal.* Knoxville, Tennessee: University of Tennessee Press. 1996. (10, 11)

Miller, Nathan. *F.D.R.: An Intimate History.* New York: Doubleday. 1983.

Mohr, Lillian Holmen. *Frances Perkins, That Woman in FDR's Cabinet.* Croton-on-Hudson, New York: North River Press. 1979. (10)

Namorato, Michael V. *Rexford G. Tugwell: A Biography.* New York: Praeger. 1988.

Ness, Eliot, with Oscar Fraley. *The Untouchables.* New York: Pocket Books. 1985. (7)

Ohl, John Kennedy. *Hugh S. Johnson and the New Deal.* Dekalb, Illinois: Northern Illinois University Press. 1985.

Owen, A. L. Riesch. *Conservation Under FDR.* New York: Praeger. 1983.

Parrish, Michael E. *Felix Frankfurter and His Times.* New York: The Free Press. 1982. (12)

Philp, Kenneth R. *John Collier's Crusade for Indian Reform, 1920–1954.* Tucson, Arizona: University of Arizona Press. 1977.

Potter, Claire Bond. *War on Crime: Bandits, G-Men, and the Politics of Mass Culture.* New Brunswick, New Jersey: Rutgers University Press. 1998.

Powers, Richard Gid. *G-Men, Hoover's FBI in American Popular Culture.* Carbondale, Illinois: Southern Illinois University Press. 1983.

Pusey, Merlo J. *Charles Evans Hughes.* 2 vols. New York: Macmillan. 1951. (4, 6, 7)

Romasco, Albert U. *The Poverty of Abundance: Hoover, the Nation, the Depression.* New York: Oxford University Press. 1965.

Romasco, Albert U. *The Politics of Recovery: Roosevelt's New Deal.* New York: Oxford University Press. 1983.

Roosevelt, Eleanor. *This I Remember.* New York: Harper. 1949. (9, 10, 11)

Roosevelt, Franklin D. Russell D. Buhite and David W. Levy, eds. *FDR's Fireside Chats.* Norman, Oklahoma: University of Oklahoma Press. 1992. (9, 10)

Salmond, John A. *The Civilian Conservation Corps, 1933–1942: A New Deal Case Study.* Durham, North Carolina: Duke University Press. 1967.

Sandilands, Roger J. *The Life and Political Economy of Lauchlin Currie: New Dealer, Presidential Adviser, and Development Economist.* Durham, North Carolina: Duke University Press. 1990. (10, 11)

Sann, Paul. *Kill the Dutchman!* New York: Popular Library. 1971.

Schapmeiser, Edward L., and Frederick H. Schapmeiser. *Henry A. Wallace of Iowa: The Agrarian Years, 1910–1940.* Ames, Iowa: Iowa State University Press. 1968.

Schlesinger, Arthur M., Jr. *The Age of Roosevelt: The Crisis of the Old Order.* Boston: Houghton Mifflin. 1957. (4, 5, 6, 7)

Schlesinger, Arthur M., Jr. *The Age of Roosevelt: The Coming of the New Deal.* Boston: Houghton Mifflin. 1959.

Schlesinger, Arthur M., Jr. *The Age of Roosevelt: The Politics of Upheaval.* Boston: Houghton Mifflin. 1960.

Schwarz, Jordan A. *The Interregnum of Despair: Hoover, Congress, and the Depression.* Urbana, Illinois: University of Illinois Press. 1970.

Smith, Gene. *The Shattered Dream: Herbert Hoover and the Great Depression.* New York: Morrow. 1970.

Smith, Richard Norton. *An Uncommon Man: The Triumph of Herbert Hoover.* New York: Simon and Schuster. 1984. (6, 7)

Sobel, Robert. *The Great Bull Market: Wall Street in the 1920s.* New York: W.W. Norton. 1968. (7)

Steinbeck, John. *The Grapes of Wrath.* New York: Viking. 1989.

Stolberg, Mary M. *Fighting Organized Crime: Politics, Justice, and the Legacy of Thomas E. Dewey.* Boston: Northeastern University Press. 1995. (10, 11)

Turner, Henry Ashby, Jr. *Hitler's Thirty Days to Power: January 1933.* Reading, Massachusetts: Addison-Wesley. 1996.

Urofsky, Melvin I. *Felix Frankfurter: Judicial Restraint and Individual Liberties.* Boston: Twayne Publishers. 1991. (12)

Ward, Geoffrey C. *Before The Trumpet, Young Franklin Roosevelt 1882–1905.* New York: Harper. 1985.

Ward, Geoffrey C. *A First-Class Temperament: The Emergence of Franklin Roosevelt 1882-1905.* New York: Harper & Row. 1989.

Watkins, T. H. *Righteous Pilgrim: The Life and Times of Harold L. Ickes, 1874–1952.* New York: Henry Holt. 1990. (9, 10, 11)

Williams, T. Harry. *Huey Long.* New York: Vintage Books. 1981.

Wolfskill, George, and John A. Hudson. *All but the People: Franklin D. Roosevelt and His Critics, 1933–39.* New York: Macmillan. 1969.

Worster, Donald. *Dust Bowl: The Southern Plains in the 1930s.* New York: Oxford University Press. 1979.

Zieger, Robert H. *John L. Lewis: Labor Leader.* Boston: Twayne Publishers. 1988. (6, 11)

Zieger, Robert H. *The CIO, 1935–1955.* Chapel Hill, North Carolina: University of North Carolina Press. 1995. (11)

Zucker, Norman L. *George W. Norris: Gentle Knight of American Democracy.* Urbana, Illinois: University of Illinois Press. 1966. (6, 7)

CHAPTER NINE

Bailey, Thomas A., and Paul B. Ryan. *Hitler vs. Roosevelt: The Undeclared Naval War.* New York: The Free Press. 1979. (10)

Beard, Charles. *President Roosevelt and the Coming of the War, 1941: A Study in Appearances and Realities.* New Haven, Connecticut: Yale University Press. 1948.

Beschloss, Michael. *Kennedy and Roosevelt: The Uneasy Alliance.* New York: Norton. 1980. (8, 12)

Brinkley, Douglas, and David R. Facey-Crowther, eds. *The Atlantic Charter.* New York: St. Martin's Press. 1994.

Bullock, Alan. *Hitler and Stalin: Parallel Lives.* New York: Alfred A. Knopf. 1992. (10)

Butow, Robert J. C. *Tojo and the Coming of the War.* Stanford, California: Stanford University Press. 1969. (8)

Carpenter, Ronald H. *Father Charles E. Coughlin: Surrogate Spokesman for the Disaffected.* Westport, Connecticut: Greenwood Press. 1998. (8)

Carroll, Peter N. *The Odyssey of the Abraham Lincoln Brigade: Americans in the Spanish Civil War.* Stanford, California: Stanford University Press. 1994.

Charmley, John. *Chamberlain and the Lost Peace.* London: Hodder & Stoughton. 1989.

Charmley, John. *Churchill's Grand Alliance: The Anglo-American Special Relationship, 1940–57.* New York: Harcourt Brace & Company. 1995. (10, 11)

Chuev, Felix. Albert Resis, ed. *Molotov Remembers: Inside Kremlin Politics.* Chicago: I.R. Dee. 1993. (10, 11)

Churchill, Sir Winston. *The Second World War: The Gathering Storm.* Boston: Houghton Mifflin. 1948.

Churchill, Sir Winston. *The Second World War: Their Finest Hour.* Boston: Houghton Mifflin. 1949.

Churchill, Sir Winston. Robert Rhodes James, ed. *Winston S. Churchill: His Complete Speeches, 1897-1963.* New York: Chelsea House. 1974. (10, 11)

Cole, Wayne S. *Charles A. Lindbergh and the Battle Against American Intervention in World War II.* New York: Harcourt Brace Jovanovich. 1974.

Cole, Wayne S. *Roosevelt and the Isolationists, 1932–45.* Lincoln, Nebraska: University of Nebraska Press. 1983. (8, 10)

Cull, Nicholas John. *Selling War: The British Propaganda Campaign Against American "Neutrality" in World War II.* New York: Oxford University Press. 1995.

Dallek, Robert. *Franklin Roosevelt and American Foreign Policy, 1932–1945.* New York: Oxford University Press. 1979. (10, 11)

Davis, Kenneth S. *The Hero: Charles A. Lindbergh and the American Dream.* Garden City, New York: Doubleday. 1959.

Davis, Kenneth S. *FDR, Into the Storm, 1937–1940: A History.* New York: Random House. 1993. (8)

Deighton, Len. *Fighter: The True Story of the Battle of Britain.* New York: Alfred A. Knopf. 1978.

Dickinson, Matthew J. *Bitter Harvest: FDR, Presidential Power, and the Growth of the Presidential Branch.* New York: Cambridge University Press. 1997. (8, 10)

Dobson, Alan P. *U.S. Wartime Aid to Britain, 1940–1946.* Dover, New Hampshire: Croom Helm. 1980. (10, 11)

Eby, Cecil D. *Between the Bullet and the Lie: American Volunteers in the Spanish Civil War.* New York: Holt, Rinehart and Winston. 1969.

Fehrenbach, T. R. *F.D.R.'s Undeclared War, 1939–1941.* New York: David McKay. 1967.

Feingold, Henry L. *The Politics of Rescue: The Roosevelt Administration and the Holocaust, 1938–1945.* New York: Holocaust Library/Schocken Books. 1980.

Finkelstein, Norman H. *With Heroic Truth: The Life of Edward R. Murrow.* New York: Clarion Books. 1997. (11)

Friedlander, Saul. Aline B. and Alexander Werth, trans. *Prelude to Downfall: Hitler and the United States, 1939–41.* New York: Alfred A. Knopf. 1967.

Friedlander, Saul. *Memory, History, and the Extermination of the Jews of Europe.* Bloomington, Indiana: Indiana University Press. 1993. (10, 11)

Friedman, Saul S. *No Haven for the Oppressed: United States Policy Toward Jewish Refugees, 1938–1945.* Detroit: Wayne State University Press. 1973. (10)

Grew, Joseph. Walter Johnson and Nancy Harvison Hooker, eds. *Turbulent Era: A Diplomatic Record of Forty Years, 1904–1945.* Boston: Houghton Mifflin. 1952. (8, 10)

Heinrichs, Waldo H., Jr. *American Ambassador: Joseph C. Grew and the Development of the United States Diplomatic Tradition.* Boston: Little, Brown. 1966.

Heinrichs, Waldo H. *Threshold of War: Franklin D. Roosevelt and American Entry into World War II.* New York: Oxford University Press. 1988.

Hemingway, Ernest. *For Whom the Bell Tolls.* New York: Charles Scribner's Sons. 1945

Hoyt, Edwin Palmer. *Yamamoto: The Man Who Planned Pearl Harbor.* New York: McGraw-Hill. 1990. (7, 8, 10)

Iriye, Akira. *The Origins of the Second World War in Asia and the Pacific.* New York: Longman. 1987. (8, 10)

Kanawada, Leo V., Jr. *Franklin D. Roosevelt's Diplomacy and American Catholics, Italians, and Jews.* Ann Arbor, Michigan: University of Michigan Research Press. 1982. (8, 10)

Kennedy, John F. *Why England Slept.* Garden City, New York: Doubleday. 1962. (12)

Kimball, Warren F. *The Most Unsordid Act: Lend-Lease, 1939–1941.* Baltimore: Johns Hopkins Press. 1969.

Kinsella, William E., Jr. *Leadership in Isolation: FDR and the Origins of the Second World War.* Boston: G.K. Hall. 1978.

LaFeber, Walter. *The Clash: A History of U.S.-Japan Relations.* New York: W.W. Norton. 1997. (4, 10, 11)

Lash, Joseph P. *Roosevelt and Churchill, 1939–1941: The Partnership That Saved the West.* New York: Norton. 1976.

Lukacs, John. *The Duel: 10 May–31 July 1940: The Eighty-Day Struggle Between Churchill and Hitler.* New York: Ticknor & Fields. 1991.

MacLeish, Archibald. *American Opinion and the War.* New York: Macmillan. 1942.

GERALD FORD throws out the first pitch of the **1976** season in Arlington, Texas, where the second Washington Senators team had moved before the **1972** season to become the Texas Rangers. It was the end of major league baseball in the nation's capital, and that bicentennial year the all-star game would be held in Philadelphia. Ford, despite his mishaps on the golf course and staircases, was probably the best athlete ever to serve as president. He was an All-American center on the University of Michigan's football teams, in the prestigious Big Ten conference. None of that kept Lyndon Johnson from repeating, when Ford was minority leader in the House, that "Gerry Ford played too much football without his helmet on."

JIMMY CARTER connects at the plate, during a softball game in Plains, Georgia, in the summer of 1977. By this time, presidents usually made their way over to the Baltimore Oriole's home field to do the first ball honors.

Madison, James, ed. *Wendell Willkie: Hoosier Internationalist.* Bloomington, Indiana: Indiana University Press. 1992.

Manchester, William. *The Last Lion: Winston Spencer Churchill.* Boston: Little, Brown. 1983. (10, 11)

Marcus, Sheldon. *Father Coughlin: The Tumultuous Life of the Priest of the Little Flower.* Boston: Little, Brown. 1973. (8)

Marks, Frederick W. *Wind Over Sand: The Diplomacy of Franklin Roosevelt.* Athens, Georgia: University of Georgia Press. 1988. (10)

McDonough, Frank. *Chamberlain, Appeasement, and the Road to War.* New York: Manchester University Press. 1998.

Moscow, Warren. *Roosevelt and Willkie.* Englewood Cliffs, New Jersey: Prentice-Hall. 1968.

Neal, Steve. *Dark Horse: A Biography of Wendell Willkie.* Garden City, New York: Doubleday. 1984.

Orwell, George. *Homage to Catalonia.* New York: Harcourt Brace Jovanovich. 1980.

Persico, Joseph E. *Edward R. Murrow: An American Original.* New York: McGraw-Hill. 1988. (11)

Ponting, Clive. *Churchill.* London: Sinclair-Stevenson. 1994. (10, 11)

Prange, Gordon W., in collaboration with Donald M. Goldstein and Katherine V. Dillon. *At Dawn We Slept: The Untold Story of Pearl Harbor.* New York: Penguin Books. 1987.

Read, Anthony, and David Fischer. *The Deadly Embrace: Hitler, Stalin and the Nazi-Soviet Pact 1939–1941.* New York: W.W. Norton. 1988.

Rock, William R. *Chamberlain and Roosevelt: British Foreign Policy and the United States, 1937–1940.* Columbus, Ohio: Ohio State University Press. 1988.

Rubinstein, W. D. *The Myth of Rescue: Why the Democracies Could Not Have Saved More Jews from the Nazis.* New York: Routledge. 1997. (10)

Shirer, William L. *The Rise and Fall of the Third Reich: A History of Nazi Germany.* New York: Simon and Schuster. 1960. (8, 10, 11)

Smith, Richard Norton. *The Colonel: The Life and Legend of Robert R. McCormick, 1880–1975.* Boston: Houghton Mifflin. 1997. (7, 8, 10, 11)

Swanberg, W. A. *Norman Thomas: The Last Idealist.* New York: Scribners. 1976. (8, 11)

Taylor, A. J. P. *The Origins of the Second World War.* New York: Atheneum. 1983.

Thomas, Gordon, and Max Morgan Witts. *Voyage of the Damned.* New York: Stein and Day. 1974.

Toland, John. *Infamy: Pearl Harbor and Its Aftermath.* Garden City, New York: Doubleday. 1982.

Tuttle, Dwight William. *Harry Hopkins and Anglo-American-Soviet Relations, 1941–1945.* New York: Garland Publishing. 1983. (10)

Warren, Donald I. *Radio Priest: Charles Coughlin, the Father of Hate Radio.* New York: The Free Press. 1996. (8)

Watt, Donald Cameron. *How War Came: The Immediate Origins of the Second World War, 1938–1939.* New York: Pantheon Books. 1989.

Welles, Benjamin. *Sumner Welles, FDR's Global Strategist: A Biography.* New York: St. Martin's Press. 1997. (10)

Wetzler, Peter. *Hirohito and War: Imperial Traditions and Military Decision Making in Prewar Japan.* Honolulu, Hawaii: University of Hawaii Press. 1998. (8, 10)

Willkie, Wendell L. *One World.* New York: Simon and Schuster. 1943. (10)

Wilson, Theodore A. *The First Summit: Roosevelt and Churchill at Placentia Bay, 1941.* Lawrence, Kansas: University Press of Kansas. 1991.

Wyden, Peter. *The Passionate War: A Narrative History of the Spanish Civil War, 1936–1939.* New York: Simon and Schuster. 1983.

Wyman, David S. *The Abandonment of the Jews: America and the Holocaust, 1941–1945.* New York: Pantheon Books. 1984.

CHAPTER TEN

Adams, Stephen B. *Mr. Kaiser Goes to Washington: The Rise of a Government Entrepreneur.* Chapel Hill, North Carolina: University of North Carolina Press. 1997.

Alldritt, Keith. *The Greatest of Friends: Franklin D. Roosevelt and Winston Churchill, 1941–1945.* London: Robert Hale. 1995. (9)

Allen, Robert L. *The Port Chicago Mutiny.* New York: Warner Books. 1989.

Alperovitz, Gar. *The Decision to Use the Atomic Bomb.* New York: Alfred A. Knopf. 1995.

Ambrose, Stephen. *Eisenhower and Berlin, 1945: The Decision to Halt at the Elbe.* New York: W.W. Norton. 1967.

Ambrose, Stephen. *The Supreme Commander: The War Years of General Dwight D. Eisenhower.* Garden City, New York: Doubleday. 1970. (11)

Ambrose, Stephen. *D-Day, June 6, 1994: The Climactic Battle of World War II.* New York: Simon and Schuster. 1994.

Anderson, Jervis. *A. Philip Randolph: A Biographical Portrait.* New York: Harcourt Brace Jovanovich. 1974. (12)

Beck, John Jacob. *MacArthur and Wainwright: Sacrifice of the Philippines.* Albuquerque, New Mexico: University of New Mexico Press. 1974.

Berezhkov, Valentin M. Sergei M. Mikheyev, trans. *At Stalin's Side: His Interpreter's Memoirs from the October Revolution to the Fall of the Dictator's Empire.* Secaucus, New Jersey: Carol Publishing Group. 1994. (9, 11)

Bernstein, Barton J., ed. *The Atomic Bomb: The Critical Issues.* Boston: Little, Brown. 1976.

Blumenson, Martin. *Mark Clark.* New York: Congdon & Weed. 1984. (11)

Brackman, Arnold C. *The Other Nuremberg: The Untold Story of the Tokyo War Crimes Trial.* New York: Morrow. 1987.

Bradley, Omar. *A Soldier's Story.* New York: Henry Holt. 1951.

Brandt, Nat. *Harlem at War: The Black Experience in WWII.* Syracuse, New York: Syracuse University Press. 1996.

Breuer, William B. *Storming Hitler's Rhine: The Allied Assault, February–March 1945.* New York: St. Martin's Press. 1985.

Breuer, William B. *Operation Torch: The Allied Gamble to Invade North Africa.* New York: St. Martin's Press. 1986.

Buell, Thomas B. *The Quiet Warrior: A Biography of Admiral Raymond A. Spruance.* Boston: Little, Brown. 1974.

Buell, Thomas B. *Master of Sea Power: A Biography of Fleet Admiral Ernest J. King.* Boston: Little, Brown. 1980.

Burns, James MacGregor. *Roosevelt: The Soldier of Freedom, 1940–1945.* New York: Harcourt, Brace & World. 1970. (9)

Calvocoressi, Peter, Guy Wint, and John Pritchard. *Total War: The Causes and Courses of the Second World War.* New York: Viking. 1989. (9)

Calvocoressi, Peter. *Fall Out: World War II and the Shaping of Postwar Europe.* New York: Longman. 1997. (11)

Capeci, Dominic J., Jr. *The Harlem Riot of 1943.* Philadelphia: Temple University Press. 1977.

Chinnock, Frank W. *Nagasaki: The Forgotten Bomb.* New York: World Publishing Company. 1969.

Churchill, Sir Winston. *The Second World War: The Grand Alliance.* Boston: Houghton Mifflin. 1950. (9)

Churchill, Sir Winston. *The Second World War: The Hinge of Fate.* Boston: Houghton Mifflin. 1950.

Churchill, Sir Winston. *The Second World War: Closing the Ring.* Boston: Houghton Mifflin. 1951.

Churchill, Sir Winston. *The Second World War: Triumph and Tragedy.* Boston: Houghton Mifflin. 1953.

Churchill, Sir Winston, and Franklin D. Roosevelt. Warren F. Kimball, ed. *Churchill and Roosevelt: The Complete Correspondence.* Princeton, New Jersey: Princeton University Press. 1984. (9)

Churchill, Sir Winston, Franklin D. Roosevelt, and Joseph Stalin. *The Secret History of World War II: The Ultra-Secret Wartime Letters and Cables of Roosevelt, Stalin and Churchill.* New York: Richardson & Steirman. 1986.

Conrat, Maisie, and Richard Conrat. *Executive Order 9066: The Internment of 110,000 Japanese Americans.* Los Angeles: University of California, Los Angeles, Asian Studies Center. 1992.

Crane, Conrad C. *Bombs, Cities, and Civilians: American Airpower Strategy in World War II.* Lawrence, Kansas: University Pres of Kansas. 1993.

Crost, Lyn. *Honor by Fire: Japanese Americans at War in Europe and the Pacific.* Novato, California; Presidio. 1994.

Dallek, Robert. *The Roosevelt Diplomacy and World War II.* New York: Holt, Rinehart and Winston. 1970.

Davis, Richard G. *Carl A. Spaatz and the Air War in Europe.* Washington, D.C.: Smithsonian Institution Press. 1992.

Deighton, Len. *Blood, Tears, and Folly: An Objective Look at World War II.* New York: HarperCollins. 1993.

D'Este, Carlo. *Fatal Decision: Anzio and the Battle for Rome.* New York: HarperCollins. 1991.

Djilas, Milovan. *Conversations with Stalin.* New York: Harcourt, Brace. 1952.

Doubler, Michael D. *Closing with the Enemy: How GIs Fought the War in Europe, 1944-1945.* Lawrence, Kansas: University Press of Kansas. 1994.

Dunnigan, James F. *Victory at Sea: World War II in the Pacific.* New York: Morrow. 1995.

Dupuy, Trevor N., David L. Bongard, and Richard C. Anderson, Jr. *Hitler's Last Gamble: The Battle of the Bulge, December 1944–January 1945.* New York: HarperCollins. 1994.

Edgerton, Robert B. *Warriors of the Rising Sun: A History of the Japanese Military.* New York: W.W. Norton. 1997. (8, 9)

Edmonds, Robin. *The Big Three: Churchill, Roosevelt, and Stalin in Peace and War.* New York: W.W. Norton. 1991. (8, 9, 11)

Eisenhower, Dwight. *Crusade in Europe.* Garden City, New York: Doubleday. 1948.

Ellis, John. *The Sharp End: The Fighting Man in World War II.* New York: Scribners. 1980.

Ellis, John. *Brute Force: Allied Strategy and Tactics in the Second World War.* London: Deutsch. 1990.

Erickson, John. *Stalin's War with Germany.* 2 vols. London: Weidenfeld and Nicolson. 1983.

Feifer, George. *Tennozan: The Battle of Okinawa and the Atomic Bomb.* New York: Ticknor & Fields. 1992.

Frank, Richard B. *Guadalcanal: The Definitive Account of the Landmark Battle.* New York: Random House. 1990.

Fussell, Paul. *Wartime: Understanding and Behavior in the Second World War.* New York: Oxford University Press. 1989.

Gailey, Harry A. *Howlin' Mad vs. the Army: Conflict in Command, Saipan, 1945.* Novato, California: Presidio Press. 1986.

Gailey, Harry A. *The War in the Pacific: From Pearl Harbor to Tokyo Bay.* Novato, California: Presidio Press. 1995. (9)

Garfinkel, Herbert. *When Negroes March: The March on Washington Movement in the Organizational Politics for FEPC.* Glencoe, Illinois: Free Press. 1959. (12)

Gelb, Norman. *Ike and Monty: Generals at War.* New York: Morrow. 1994.

Gilbert, Martin. *The Holocaust: A History of the Jews of Europe During the Second World War.* New York: Holt, Rinehart, and Winston. 1986. (9, 11)

Girdner, Audrie, and Anne Loftis. *The Great Betrayal: The Evacuation of the Japanese-Americans During World War II.* Toronto: Macmillan. 1969.

Goodwin, Doris Kearns. *No Ordinary Time: Franklin and Eleanor Roosevelt: The Home Front in World War II.* New York: Simon and Schuster. 1994. (8, 9)

Hamilton, Nigel. *Master of the Battlefield: Monty's War Years, 1942–1944.* New York: McGraw-Hill. 1983.

Harbutt, Fraser J. *The Iron Curtain: Churchill, America, and the Origins of the Cold War.* New York: Oxford University Press. 1986. (11)

Harper, Stephen. *Miracle of Deliverance: The Case for the Bombing of Hiroshima and Nagasaki.* London: Sidgwick & Jackson. 1985.

Harries, Meirion, and Susie Harries. *Soldiers of the Sun: The Rise and Fall of the Imperial Japanese Army.* New York: Random House. 1992.

Harriman, W. Averell, and Elie Abel. *Special Envoy to Churchill and Stalin, 1941–1946.* New York: Random House. 1975.

Hastings, Max. *Overlord: D-Day, June 6, 1944.* New York: Simon and Schuster. 1984.

Hersey, John. *Hiroshima.* New York: Modern Library. 1946.

Hersey, John. *Into the Valley: A Skirmish of the Marines.* New York: Alfred A. Knopf. 1956.

Hershberg, James G. *James B. Conant: Harvard to Hiroshima and the Making of the Nuclear Age.* New York: Alfred A. Knopf. 1993. (11)

Hoopes, Townsend, and Douglas Brinkley. *FDR and the Creation of the U.N.* New Haven, Connecticut: Yale University Press. 1997.

Horne, Alistair, with David Montgomery. *Monty: The Lonely Leader, 1944–1945.* New York: HarperCollins. 1994.

Hoyt, Edwin P. *The U-Boat Wars.* New York: Arbor House. 1984.

Hughes, Terry, and John Costello. *The Battle of the Atlantic.* New York: Joanne Wade/Dial Press. 1977.

Irving, David. *The War Between the Generals.* London: A. Lane. 1981.

Jablonsky, David. *Churchill, the Great Game and Total War.* London: F. Cass. 1991. (6, 9)

Jackson, Robert. *Storm from the Skies: The Strategic Bombing Offensive, 1943–1945.* London: Barker. 1974.

Jackson, W. G. F. *The Battle for Italy.* New York: Harper & Row. 1967.

Keegan, John. *Six Armies in Normandy: From D-Day to the Liberation of Paris.* New York: Penguin Books. 1983.

Keegan, John. *The Mask of Command.* London: Jonathan Cape. 1987. (6)

Keegan, John. *The Price of Admiralty: The Evolution of Naval Warfare.* New York: Viking. 1989. (6)

Keegan, John. *The Second World War.* New York: Viking. 1989. (9, 11)

Kerr, E. Bartlett. *Flames Over Tokyo: The U.S. Army Air Force's Incendiary Campaign Against Japan, 1944–45.* New York: Donald I. Fine. 1991.

Kimball, Warren F. *Forged in War: Roosevelt, Churchill, and the Second World War.* New York: Morrow. 1997. (9)

Knox, Donald. *Death March: The Survivors of Bataan.* New York: Harcourt Brace Jovanovich. 1981.

Laqueur, Walter. *Stalin: The Glasnost Revelations.* New York: Scribners. 1990. (9, 11)

Large, Stephen S. *Emperor Hirohito and Showa Japan: A Political Biography.* London: Routledge. 1992. (7, 8, 9, 11)

Larrabee, Eric. *Commander in Chief: Franklin Delano Roosevelt, His Lieutenants, and Their War.* New York: Harper & Row. 1987. (9)

Lawren, William. *The General and the Bomb: A Biography of General Leslie R. Groves, Director of the Manhattan Project.* New York: Dodd, Mead. 1988.

Leckie, Robert. *Delivered From Evil: The Saga of World War II.* New York: Harper & Row. 1987.

Levine, Alan J. *The Strategic Bombing of Germany, 1940–1945.* New York: Praeger. 1992.

Liddell Hart, Sir Basil Henry. *History of the Second World War.* New York: Putnam. 1971. (9)

Lifton, Robert Jay. *Hiroshima in America: Fifty Years of Denial.* New York: Putnam's Sons. 1995.

Lipsitz, George. *Rainbow at Midnight: Labor and Culture in the 1940s.* Urbana, Illinois: University of Illinois Press. 1994. (11)

Maddox, Robert James. *Weapons for Victory: The Hiroshima Decision Fifty Years Later.* Columbia, Missouri: University of Missouri Press. 1995.

Marshall, S. L. A. *Night Drop: The American Airborne Invasion of Normandy.* Nashville, Tennessee: The Battery Press. 1962.

McKee, Alexander. *Dresden 1945: The Devil's Tinderbox.* London: Souvenir Press. 1982.

Messenger, Charles. *"Bomber" Harris and the Strategic Bombing Offensive, 1939–1945.* London: Arms and Armour. 1984.

Miller, Sally M., and Daniel A. Cornford, eds. *American Labor in the Era of World War II.* Westport, Connecticut: Praeger. 1995.

Mitcham, Samuel W., Jr., and Friedrich von Stauffenberg. *The Battle of Sicily: How the Allies Lost Their Chance for Total Victory.* New York: Orion Books. 1991.

Morison, Samuel Eliot. *History of United States Naval Operations in World War II.* 15 vols. Boston: Atlantic Monthly Press/Little, Brown. 1962.

Morton, Louis. *Germany First: The Basic Concept of Allied Strategy in World War II.* Washington, D.C.: Center of Military History, U.S. Army. 1990.

Muirhead, John. *Those Who Fall.* New York: Random House. 1986.

Nadeau, Remi A. *Stalin, Churchill, and Roosevelt Divide Europe.* New York: Praeger. 1990.

RONALD REAGAN, then governor of California, throws out the first ball of the third game of the 1972 World Series, at Oakland's Alameda County Stadium. To the right, Nancy Reagan clasps her hands, anticipating the throw; just to her right, leaning back, is Charlie Finley, the flamboyant owner of the Oakland Athletics—Connie Mack's Philadelphia Athletics, a couple incarnations later. Finley's "Swingin' A's" would go on to defeat the Cincinnati Reds, four games to three, in one of the most exciting series ever played. Finley became famous—or notorious—for suggesting such never implemented innovations as an orange baseball.

Newman, Robert P. *Truman and the Hiroshima Cult.* East Lansing, Michigan: Michigan State University Press. 1995.

Overy, Richard. *Why the Allies Won.* New York: W.W. Norton. 1996.

Parrish, Thomas. *Roosevelt and Marshall: Partners in Politics and War.* New York: Morrow. 1989. (8)

Perlmutter, Amos. *FDR and Stalin: A Not So Grand Alliance.* Columbia, Missouri: University of Missouri Press. 1993.

Perret, Geoffrey. *Days of Sadness, Years of Triumph: The American People, 1939–1945.* New York: Coward, McCann & Geoghegan. 1973. (9)

Perret, Geoffrey. *There's a War to Be Won: The U.S. Army in World War II.* New York: Random House. 1991.

Pfeffer, Paula F. *A. Philip Randolph, Pioneer of the Civil Rights Movement.* Baton Rouge, Louisiana: Louisiana State University Press. 1990. (12)

Pogue, Forrest C. *George C. Marshall: Organizer of Victory, 1943–45.* New York: Viking. 1973. (11)

Polenberg, Richard. *America at War: The Home Front, 1941–1945.* Englewood Cliffs, New Jersey: Prentice-Hall. 1968.

Polenberg, Richard. *War and Society: The United States, 1941–1945.* Philadelphia: Lippincott. 1972.

Ponting, Clive. *Armageddon: The Reality Behind the Distortions, Myths, Lies and Illusions of World War II.* New York: Random House. 1995.

Pyle, Ernie. David Nichols, ed. *Ernie's War: The Best of Ernie Pyle's World War II Dispatches.* New York: Random House. 1986.

Rhodes, Richard. *The Making of the Atomic Bomb.* New York: Simon and Schuster. 1986. (11)

Ryan, Cornelius. *The Longest Day: June 6, 1944.* New York: Simon and Schuster. 1959.

Ryan, Cornelius. *The Last Battle.* London: Four Square. 1967.

Ryan, Cornelius. *A Bridge Too Far.* New York: Simon and Schuster. 1974.

Sainsbury, Keith. *Churchill and Roosevelt at War: The War they Fought and the Peace They Hoped to Make.* Houndmills, England: Macmillan. 1994.

Schultz, Duane P. *The Maverick War: Chennault and the Flying Tigers.* New York: St. Martin's Press. 1987.

Scott, Mark, and Semyon Krasilshchik, eds. *Yanks Meet Reds: Recollections of U.S. and Soviet Vets from the Linkup in World War II.* Santa Barbara, California: Capra Press. 1988.

Skates, John Ray. *The Invasion of Japan: Alternative to the Bomb.* Columbia, South Carolina: University of South Carolina Press. 1994.

Spector, Ronald H. *Eagle Against the Sun: The American War with Japan.* New York: The Free Press. 1985.

Speer, Albert. Richard and Clara Winston, trans. *Inside the Third Reich: Memoirs.* New York: Collier Books. 1981. (8, 9)

Stimson, Henry L., and McGeorge Bundy. *On Active Service in Peace and War.* New York: Octagon Books. 1971. (4, 6, 7)

Stoler, Mark A. *The Politics of the Second Front: American Military Planning and Diplomacy in Coalition Warfare, 1941–1943.* Westport, Connecticut: Greenwood Press. 1977.

Taylor, Lawrence. *A Trial of Generals: Homma, Yamashita, MacArthur.* South Bend, Indiana: Icarus Press. 1981.

Toland, John. *Battle: The Story of the Bulge.* New York: Random House. 1959.

Toland, John. *But Not in Shame: The Six Months After Pearl Harbor.* New York: Random House. 1961. (9)

Toland, John. *The Rising Sun.* New York: Random House. 1970 (7, 8, 9)

Toland, John. *Adolf Hitler.* 2 vols. Garden City, New York: Doubleday. 1976. (8, 9)

Tregaskis, Richard. *Guadalcanal Diary.* New York: Random House. 1943.

Tuchman, Barbara W. *Stilwell and the American Experience in China, 1911–45.* New York: Macmillan. 1971. (8)

Tusa, Ann, and John Tusa. *The Nuremberg Trial.* New York: Atheneum. 1986.

Walker, J. Samuel. *Prompt and Utter Destruction: Truman and the Use of Atomic Bombs Against Japan.* Chapel Hill, North Carolina: University of North Carolina Press. 1997.

Weigley, Russell F. *Eisenhower's Lieutenants: The Campaign of France and Germany, 1944–1945.* Bloomington, Indiana: Indiana University Press. 1981.

Weinberg, Gerhard L. *A World At Arms.* Cambridge, England: Cambridge University Press. 1994. (9, 11)

Whitman, John W. *Bataan, Our Last Ditch: The Bataan Campaign, 1942.* New York: Hippocrene Books. 1990.

Wyden, Peter. *Day One: Before Hiroshima and After.* New York: Simon and Schuster. 1984. (11)

CHAPTER ELEVEN

Abramson, Rudy. *Spanning the Century: The Life of W. Averell Harriman. 1891–1986.* New York: Morrow. 1992. (10, 12, 13)

Acheson, Dean. *Present at the Creation: My Years in the State Department.* New York: W.W. Norton & Company. 1969.

Albright, Joseph, and Marcia Kunstel. *Bombshell: The Secret Story of America's Unknown Atomic Spy Conspiracy.* New York: Times Books. 1997. (10)

Alsop, Joseph, and Stewart Alsop. *We Accuse! The Story of the Miscarriage of American Justice in the Case of J.*

Robert Oppenheimer. New York: Simon and Schuster. 1954.

Ambrose, Stephen. *Eisenhower.* 2 vols. New York: Simon and Schuster. 1984. (10)

Appleman, Roy E. *Disaster in Korea: The Chinese Confront MacArthur.* College Station, Texas: Texas A & M University Press. 1989.

Baker, Russell. *The Good Times.* New York: Morrow. 1989.

Bayley, Edwin R. *Joe McCarthy and the Press.* Madison, Wisconsin: University of Wisconsin Press. 1981.

Belfrage, Cedric. *The American Inquisition, 1945–1960.* Indianapolis, Indiana: Bobbs-Merrill. 1973.

Beschloss, Michael. *May-Day: Eisenhower, Khrushchev and the U-2 Affair.* New York: Harper. 1986.

Bird, Kai. *The Chairman: John J. McCloy: The Making of the American Establishment.* New York: Simon and Schuster. 1992. (10, 12, 13)

Black, Allida M. *Casting Her Own Shadow: Eleanor Roosevelt and the Shaping of Postwar Liberalism.* New York: Columbia University Press. 1996.

Blair, Clay. *The Forgotten War: America in Korea 1950–1953.* New York: Times Books. 1987.

Bohlen, Charles E. *Witness to History, 1929–1969.* New York: Norton. 1973. (12, 13)

Bowles, Chester. *Promises to Keep: My Years in Public Life, 1941–1969.* New York: Harper. 1971. (10, 12, 13)

Brendon, Piers. *Ike: His Life and Times.* New York: Harper. 1986. (10)

Brinkley, Douglas. *Dean Acheson: The Cold War Years, 1953–1971.* New Haven, Connecticut: Yale University Press. 1992.

Buckley, William, Jr., and L. Brent Bozell. *McCarthy and His Enemies: The Record and Its Meaning.* Chicago: Henry Regnery Company. 1954.

Buhite, Russell D. *Patrick J. Hurley and American Foreign Policy.* Ithaca, New York: Cornell University Press. 1973.

Caro, Robert. *The Power Broker: Robert Moses and the Fall of New York.* New York: Random House. 1974. (15)

Chambers, Whittaker. *Witness.* New York: Random House. 1952.

Churchill, Sir Winston, and Dwight D. Eisenhower. Peter G. Boyle, ed. *The Churchill-Eisenhower Correspondence, 1953–1955.* Chapel Hill, North Carolina: University of North Carolina Press. 1990.

Clay, Lucius D. *Decision in Germany.* Garden City, New York: Doubleday. 1950.

Conot, Robert E. *Justice at Nuremberg.* New York: Carroll & Graf. 1983.

Cook, Fred J. *The Nightmare Decade: The Life and Times of Senator Joe McCarthy.* New York: Random House. 1971.

Cotton, James. *Asian Frontier Nationalism: Owen Lattimore and the American Policy Debate.* Atlantic Highlands, New Jersey: Humanities Press International. 1989.

Crozier, Brian, with Eric Chou. *The Man Who Lost China: The First Full Biography of Chiang Kai-shek.* New York: Scribners. 1976.

Davies, John Paton, Jr. *Foreign and Other Affairs.* New York: Norton. 1966.

Finn, Richard B. *Winners in Peace: MacArthur, Yoshida, and Postwar Japan.* Berkeley, California: University of California Press. 1992. (10)

Fossedal, Gregory A. *Our Finest Hour: Will Clayton, the Marshall Plan, and the Triumph of Democracy.* Stanford, California: Hoover Institution Press. 1993.

Foster, James Caldwell. *The Union Politic: The CIO Political Action Committee.* Columbia, Missouri: University of Missouri Press. 1975. (8, 10)

Fromkin, David. *In the Time of the Americans: The Generation That Changed America's Role in the World.* New York: Alfred A. Knopf. 1995. (10, 12, 15, Epilogue)

Furuya, Keiji, ed. Chun-ming Chang, trans. *Chiang Kai-shek, His Life and Times.* New York: St. John's University Press. 1981. (8, 9, 10)

Goncharov, Sergei N., John W. Lewis, and Xue Litai. *Uncertain Partners: Stalin, Mao, and the Korean War.* Stanford, California: Stanford University Press. 1993.

Goode, James F. *The United States and Iran: In the Shadow of Musaddiq.* New York: St. Martin's Press. 1997. (14, 15)

Goodman, Walter. *The Committee: The Extraordinary Career of the House Committee on Un-American Activities.* New York: Farrar, Straus and Giroux. 1968.

Greenstein, Fred I. *The Hidden-Hand Presidency: Eisenhower as Leader.* New York: Basic Books. 1982.

Griffith, Robert. *The Politics of Fear: Joseph R. McCarthy and the Senate.* Amherst, Massachusetts: University of Massachusetts Press. 1987.

Halberstam, David. *The Fifties.* New York: Villard Books, 1993.

Hamby, Alonzo. *Beyond the New Deal. Harry S Truman and American Liberalism.* New York: Columbia University Press. 1973.

Hamby, Alonzo. *Man of the People: A Life of Harry S Truman.* New York: Oxford University Press. 1995. (10)

Hammel, Eric M. *Chosin: Heroic Ordeal of the Korean War.* New York: Vanguard Press. 1981.

Hiss, Alger. *In the Court of Public Opinion.* New York: Alfred A. Knopf. 1957.

Hiss, Alger. *Recollections of a Life.* New York: Seaver Books/Henry Holt. 1988.

Hoffmann, Stanley, and Charles Maier, eds. *The Marshall Plan: A Retrospec-*

tive. Boulder, Colorado: Westview Press. 1984.

Hofstadter, Richard. *The Paranoid Style in American Politics, and Other Essays.* New York: Alfred A. Knopf. 1965. (6)

Holloway, David. *Stalin and the Bomb: The Soviet Union and Atomic Energy, 1939–1956.* New Haven, Connecticut: Yale University Press. 1994. (10)

Hughes, Emmet John. *The Ordeal of Power: A Political Memoir of the Eisenhower Years.* New York: Atheneum. 1975.

Isaacson, Walter, and Evan Thomas. *The Wise Men: Six Friends and the World They Made.* New York: Simon and Schuster. 1986. (10, 12, 13)

Jackson, Robert. *The Berlin Airlift.* Wellinborough, England: Patrick Stephens. 1988.

James, D. Clayton. *The Years of MacArthur.* 3 vols. Boston: Houghton Mifflin. 1985. (8, 10)

Kahn, Gordon. *Hollywood on Trial: The Story of the Ten Who Were Indicted.* New York: Arno Press. 1972.

Kennan, George. *Sketches from a Life.* New York: Pantheon. 1989.

Khrushchev, Nikita. Strobe Talbott, ed. and trans. *Khrushchev Remembers.* Boston: Little, Brown. 1970. (12)

Kindleberger, Charles P. *Marshall Plan Days.* Boston: Allen & Unwin. 1987.

LaFeber, Walter. *America, Russia, and the Cold War, 1945–1990.* New York: McGraw-Hill. 1991. (10, 12, 13, 14, 15)

Lash, Joseph P. *Eleanor: The Years Alone.* New York: Norton. 1972.

Lattimore, Owen. *Ordeal by Slander.* Boston: Little, Brown. 1950.

Manchester, William. *American Caesar: Douglas MacArthur, 1880–1964.* Boston: Little, Brown and Company. 1978. (6, 7, 8, 9, 10)

Markowitz, Norman D. *The Rise and Fall of the People's Century: Henry A. Wallace and American Liberalism, 1941–1948.* New York: The Free Press. 1973. (10)

Marks, Frederick W., III. *Power and Peace: The Diplomacy of John Foster Dulles.* Westport, Connecticut: Praeger. 1993.

Marton, Kati. *The Polk Conspiracy: Murder and Cover-Up in the Case of CBS News Correspondent George Polk.* New York: Farrar, Straus & Giroux. 1990.

McCullough, David. *Truman.* New York: Simon and Schuster. 1992. (10)

McKeever, Porter. *Adlai Stevenson: His Life and Legacy.* New York: Morrow. 1989. (12)

McShane, Clay. *Down the Asphalt Path: The Automobile and the American City.* New York: Columbia University Press. 1994. (5, 13, 15, Epilogue)

Mee, Charles L., Jr. *Meeting at Potsdam.* New York: M. Evans. 1975.

Mee, Charles L., Jr. *The Marshall Plan: The Launching of the Pax Americana.* New York: Simon and Schuster. 1984.

Messer, Robert L. *The End of an Alliance: James F. Byrnes, Roosevelt, Truman, and the Origins of the Cold War.* Chapel Hill, North Carolina: University of North Carolina Press. 1982. (10)

Mitgang, Herbert. *Dangerous Dossiers: Exposing the Secret War Against America's Greatest Authors.* New York: Donald I. Fine. 1988.

Morwood, William. *Duel for the Middle Kingdom: The Struggle Between Chiang Kai-shek and Mao Tse-Tung for Control of China.* New York: Everest House. 1980.

Mosley, Leonard. *Dulles: A Biography of Eleanor, Allen and John Foster Dulles and Their Family Network.* New York: Dial Press. 1976. (12)

Newman, Robert P. *Owen Lattimore and the "Loss" of China.* Berkeley, California: University of California Press. 1992.

Nitze, Paul H., with Ann M. Smith and Steven L. Rearden. *From Hiroshima to Glasnost: At the Center of Decision: A Memoir.* New York: Grove Weidenfeld. 1989. (10, 12, 13, 14, 15)

Oshinsky, David M. *A Conspiracy So Immense: The World of Joe McCarthy.* New York: The Free Press. 1983.

Perrett Geoffrey. *A Dream of Greatness: The American People, 1945–1963.* New York: Coward, McCann & Geoghegan. 1979. (10, 12)

Pogue, Forrest C. *George C. Marshall: Statesman.* New York: Viking. 1987. (10)

Radosh, Ronald, and Joyce Milton. *The Rosenberg File: A Search for the Truth.* New York: Holt, Rinehart and Winston. 1983.

Raucher, Alan R. *Paul G. Hoffman: Architect of Foreign Aid.* Lexington, Kentucky: University Press of Kentucky. 1985.

Reeves, Thomas C. *The Life and Times of Joe McCarthy.* New York: Stein and Day. 1982.

Rhodes, Richard. *Dark Sun: The Making of the Hydrogen Bomb.* New York: Simon and Schuster. 1995.

Robertson, David. *Sly and Able: A Political Biography of James F. Byrnes.* New York: Norton. 1994. (10, 12)

Robins, Natalie S. *Alien Ink: The FBI's War on Freedom of Expression.* New York: Morrow. 1992.

Roosevelt, Kermit. *Countercoup: The Struggle for the Control of Iran.* New York: McGraw-Hill. 1979. (14, 15)

Rovere, Richard H. *Senator Joe McCarthy.* New York: The World Publishing Company. 1969.

Ruddy, T. Michael. *The Cautious Diplomat: Charles E. Bohlen and the Soviet Union, 1929–1969.* Kent, Ohio: Ohio State University Press. 1986. (12, 13)

Schaffer, Howard B. *Chester Bowles: New Dealer in the Cold War.* Cambridge, Massachusetts: Harvard University Press. 1993.

Schapmeiser, Edward L., and Frederick H. Schapmeiser. *Prophet in Politics: Henry A. Wallace and the War Years, 1940–1965.* Ames, Iowa: Iowa State University Press. 1971. (9, 10)

Schlesinger, Stephen, and Stephen Kinzer. *Bitter Fruit: The Untold Story of the American Coup in Guatemala.* New York: Doubleday. 1984. (15)

Schneir, Walter, and Miriam W. Schneir. *Invitation to an Inquest.* New York: Pantheon. 1983.

Schrecker, Ellen. *Many Are the Crimes: McCarthyism in America.* New York: Little, Brown. 1998.

Schwartz, Thomas Alan. *America's Germany: John J. McCloy and the Federal Republic of Germany.* Cambridge, Massachusetts: Harvard University Press. 1991.

Seagrave, Sterling. *The Soong Dynasty.* New York: Harper & Row. 1986. (8, 9, 10, 12)

Service, John S. *The Amerasia Papers: Some Problems in the History of US-China Relations.* Berkeley, California: Center for Chinese Studies, University of California. 1971.

Smith, Richard Norton. *Thomas E. Dewey and His Times.* New York: Simon and Schuster. 1982. (8, 10)

Stone, I. F. *The Haunted Fifties: A Non-conformist History of Our Times, 1951–63.* Boston: Little, Brown. 1963. (12)

Tannenhaus, Sam. *Whittaker Chambers: A Biography.* New York: Random House. 1997.

Taylor, Telford. *The Anatomy of the Nuremberg Trials: A Personal Memoir.* New York: Alfred A. Knopf. 1992.

Toland, John. *In Mortal Combat: Korea, 1950–1953.* New York: Morrow. 1991.

Urquhart, Brian. *Ralph Bunche: An American Life.* New York: W.W. Norton. 1993.

Vlanton, Elias, with Zak Mettger. *Who Killed George Polk? The Press Covers Up a Death in the Family.* Philadelphia: Temple University Press. 1996.

Von Hoffman, Nicholas. *Citizen Cohn.* New York: Doubleday. 1988.

Walker, Martin. *The Cold War: A History.* New York: Henry Holt, 1994.

Watkins, Arthur V. *Enough Rope: The Inside Story of the Censure of Senator Joe McCarthy by His Colleagues.* Englewood Cliffs, New Jersey: Prentice-Hall. 1969.

Wechsler, James A. *The Age of Suspicion.* New York: Primus/Donald Fine. 1981.

Weinstein, Allen. *Perjury: The Hiss-Chambers Case.* New York: Random House. 1997.

Whelan, Richard. *Drawing the Line: The Korean War, 1950–1953.* Boston: Little, Brown. 1990.

Wilcox, Francis O. *Arthur H. Vandenberg, His Career and Legacy.* Ann Arbor, Michigan: University of Michigan Press. 1975. (9, 10)

GEORGE BUSH meets baseball immortal Babe Ruth in the spring of 1948. Ruth, "the Bambino," "the Sultan of Swat," was and is the greatest baseball player in history: a free spirit of gargantuan appetites who first excelled as a pitcher and then changed the whole nature of the game with his prodigious home runs. The son of a Baltimore bartender, all but abandoned by his parents, he was discovered playing for the team of his Catholic orphanage, where a priest had taught him the game. Honored at Yankee Stadium the same year—"the House that Ruth Built"—his voice reduced to a rasp by throat cancer, he told the packed house with typical, unflinching directness, "I know I sound pretty bad. Well, it feels just as bad." He would be dead before the summer was out, aged 53.

York, Herbert F., with Hans A. Bethe. *The Advisors: Oppenheimer, Teller, and the Superbomb.* Stanford, California: Stanford University Press. 1989.

CHAPTER TWELVE

Albert, Peter J., and Ronald Hoffman, eds. *We Shall Overcome: Martin Luther King and the Black Freedom Struggle.* New York: Pantheon. 1990.

Allyn, Bruce J.; James G. Blight, and David A. Welch, eds. *Back to the Brink: Proceedings of the Moscow Conference on the Cuban Missile Cri-*

sis, January 27–28, 1989. Lanham, Maryland: University Press of America. 1992.

Anderson, Jervis. *Bayard Rustin: Troubles I've Seen: A Biography*. New York: HarperCollins. 1997.

Ashmore, Harry S. *Civil Rights and Wrongs: A Memoir of Race and Politics 1944–1994*. New York: Pantheon. 1994. (10, 13, 15)

Ball, Howard, and Phillip J. Cooper. *Of Power and Right: Hugo Black, William O. Douglas, and America's Constitutional Revolution*. New York: Oxford University Press, 1992. (15)

Belfrage, Sally. *Freedom Summer*. New York: Viking Press. 1965.

Bernstein, Irving. *Guns or Butter: The Presidency of Lyndon Johnson*. New York: Oxford University Press. 1996. (13)

Beschloss, Michael R. *The Crisis Years: Kennedy and Khrushchev, 1960–1963*. New York: HarperCollins Publishers. 1991.

Beschloss, Michael R. *Taking Charge: The Johnson White House Tapes, 1963–1964*. New York: Simon and Schuster. 1997.

Bisell, Richard M., Jr., with Jonathan E. Lewis and Frances T. Pudlo. *Reflections of a Cold Warrior: From Yalta to the Bay of Pigs*. New Haven, Connecticut: Yale University Press. 1996. (11)

Blair, Anne E. *Lodge in Vietnam: A Patriot Abroad*. New Haven, Connecticut: Yale University Press. 1995. (13)

Blight, James G., Bruce J. Allyn, and David A. Welch, eds., with the assistance of David Lewis. *Cuba on the Brink: Castro, the Missile Crisis, and the Soviet Collapse*. New York: Pantheon Books. 1993.

Boas, Franz. *Race, Language, and Culture*. Chicago: University of Chicago Press. 1988.

Branch, Taylor. *Parting the Waters: America in the King Years 1954–63*. New York: Simon and Schuster. 1988.

Branch, Taylor. *Pillar of Fire: America in the King Years 1963–65*. New York: Simon and Schuster. 1998.

Brauer, Carl M. *John F. Kennedy and the Second Reconstruction*. New York: Columbia University Press. 1977.

Brown, Cynthia Stokes, ed. *Ready from Within: Septima Clark and the Civil Rights Movement*. Navarro, California: Wild Trees Press. 1986.

Buckley, William F., Jr., ed. *Did You Ever See a Dream Walking? American Conservative Thought in the Twentieth Century*. New York: Bobbs-Merrill. 1970. (15)

Cagin, Seth, and Philip Dray. *We Are Not Afraid: The Story of Goodman, Schwerner, and Chaney and the Civil Rights Campaign for Mississippi*. New York: Macmillan. 1988.

Caro, Robert. *The Years of Lyndon B. Johnson: The Path to Power*. New York: Alfred A. Knopf. 1982.

Caro, Robert. *The Years of Lyndon B. Johnson: Means of Ascent*. New York: Knopf. 1990.

Carson, Clayborne [et al.] *The Eyes on the Prize Civil Rights Reader*. New York: Penguin. 1991. (13)

Carter, Dan T. *The Politics of Rage: George Wallace, the Origins of the New Conservatism, and the Transformation of American Politics*. New York: Simon and Schuster. 1995. (13, 15)

Cash, W. J. *The Mind of the South*. New York: Alfred A. Knopf. 1957.

Clark, E. Culpepper. *The Schoolhouse Door: Segregation's Last Stand at the University of Alabama*. New York: Oxford University Press. 1993.

Cray, Ed. *Chief Justice: A Biography of Earl Warren*. New York: Simon & Schuster. 1997. (10)

Dallek, Robert. *Lone Star Rising: Lyndon Johnson and His Times 1908–1960*. New York: Oxford University Press. 1991.

Divine, Robert A. *The Sputnik Challenge*. New York: Oxford University Press. 1993.

Dobrynin, Anatoly. *In Confidence*. New York: Times Books. 1995. (10, 11, 13, 14, 15)

Duberman, Martin. *Paul Robeson*. New York: Alfred A. Knopf. 1988. (10, 13)

Dunne, Gerald T. *Hugo Black and the Judicial Revolution*. New York: Simon and Schuster. 1977. (8, 14, 15)

East, P. D. *The Magnolia Jungle*. New York: Simon and Schuster. 1960.

Egerton, John. *Speak Now Against the Day: The Generation Before the Civil Rights Movement in the South*. New York: Alfred A. Knopf. 1994. (10)

Ellison, Ralph. *Invisible Man*. New York: Random House. 1952.

Epstein, Edward Jay. *Deception*. New York: Simon and Schuster. 1989.

Fager, Charles E. *Selma, 1965*. New York: Charles Scribner's Sons. 1974.

Farmer, James. *Lay Bare the Heart: An Autobiography of the Civil Rights Movement*. New York: Arbor House. 1985. (13)

Faulkner, William. *Intruder in the Dust*. New York: Random House. 1948.

Fradkin, Phillip L. *Fallout: An American Nuclear Tragedy*. Tucson, Arizona: University of Arizona Press. 1989.

Frady, Marshall. *Wallace*. New York: Random House. 1976. (13)

Galbraith, John Kenneth. *The Affluent Society*. Boston: Houghton Mifflin. 1958.

Gallagher, Carole. *American Ground Zero: The Secret Nuclear War*. Cambridge, Massachusetts: MIT Press. 1993.

Garrow, David J. *Protest at Selma: Martin Luther King, Jr., and the Voting Rights Act of 1965*. New Haven, Connecticut: Yale University Press. 1978.

Gelb, Norman. *The Berlin Wall*. New York: Times Books. 1986.

Goldberg, Robert Alan. *Barry Goldwater*. New Haven, Connecticut: Yale University Press. 1995. (15)

Goodwin, Doris Kearns. *The Fitzgeralds and the Kennedys: An American Saga*. New York: Simon and Schuster. 1987.

Graham, Hugh Davis, ed. *Civil Rights in the United States*. University Park, Pennsylvania: Pennsylvania State University Press. 1994. (2, 3, 7, 8, 10)

Grant, Joanne. *Ella Baker: Freedom Bound*. New York: Wiley. 1998.

Greenberg, Jack. *Crusaders in the Courts: How a Dedicated Band of Lawyers Fought for the Civil Rights Revolution*. New York: Basic Books. 1994.

Gribkov, General Anatoli I., and General William Y. Smith. *Operation ANADYR: U.S. and Soviet Generals Recount the Cuban Missile Crisis*. Chicago: Edition Q. 1994.

Grose, Peter. *Gentleman Spy: The Life of Allen Dulles*. New York: Houghton Mifflin. 1994. (11)

Halberstam, David. *The Making of a Quagmire*. New York: Random House. 1964. (13)

Halberstam, David. *The Children*. New York: Random House. 1998.

Hamilton, Nigel. *JFK: Reckless Youth*. New York: Random House. 1992.

Hampton, Henry, and Steve Fayer. *Voices of Freedom: An Oral History of the Civil Rights Movement from the 1950s to the 1980s*. New York: Bantam. 1990. (13, 15)

Harrington, Michael. *The Other America: Poverty in the United States*. New York: Macmillan. 1962.

Hodgson, Godfrey. *America in Our Time*. Garden City, New York: Doubleday. 1976. (13, 14)

Irons, Peter, and Stephanie Guitton, eds. *May It Please the Court: The Most Signifcant Oral Arguments Made Before the Supreme Court Since 1955*. New York: The New Press. 1993. (13, 14, 15)

Kennedy, John F. *Profiles in Courage*. New York: Harper. 1956.

Kessler, Ronald. *The Sins of the Father: Joseph P. Kennedy and the Dynasty He Founded*. New York: Warner. 1996. (9, 13)

King, Coretta Scott. *My Life with Martin Luther King*. London: Hodder & Stoughton. 1969. (13)

King, Martin Luther, Jr. *Why We Can't Wait*. New York: New American Library. 1964.

Kluger, Richard. *Simple Justice: The History of Brown v. Board of Education and Black America's Struggle for Justice*. New York: Vintage Books. 1977.

Lemann, Nicholas. *The Promised Land: The Great Black Migration and How It Changed America*. New York: Vintage Books. 1992. (10, 13, 14, 15)

Lewis, Anthony. *Gideon's Trumpet*. New York: Vintage Books. 1989.

Lewis, Anthony. *Make No Law: The Sullivan Case and the First Amendment*. New York: Random House. 1991.

Lodge, Henry Cabot. *As It Was: An Inside View of Politics and Power in the '50s and '60s*. New York: Norton. 1976. (11)

Manchester, William. *The Death of a President: November 20–November 25 1963*. New York: Harper & Row. 1967.

Mann, Robert. *The Walls of Jericho: Lyndon Johnson, Hubert Humphrey, Richard Russell, and the Struggle for Civil Rights*. New York: Harcourt Brace & Company. 1996.

Martin, Ralph G. *Seeds of Destruction: Joe Kennedy and His Sons*. New York: G.P. Putnam's Sons. 1995. (9, 13)

Massengill, Reed. *Portrait of a Racist: The Man Who Killed Medgar Evers?* New York: St. Martin's Press. 1994.

May, Ernest R., and Philp D. Zelikow. *The Kennedy Tapes: Inside the White House During the Cuban Missile Crisis*. Cambridge, Massachusetts: The Belknap Press. 1997.

McAdam, Doug. *Freedom Summer*. New York: Oxford University Press. 1988.

Miller, William J. *Henry Cabot Lodge: A Biography*. New York: Heinemann. 1967. (11, 13)

Millis, Kay. *This Little Light of Mine: The Life of Fannie Lou Hamer*. New York: Dutton. 1993.

Myrdal, Gunnar. *An American Dilemma: The Negro Problem and Modern Democracy*. New York: Harper & Row. 1969.

Nash, George H. *The Conservative Intellectual Movement in America: Since 1945*. New York: Basic Books. 1976. (15)

Navasky, Victor. *Kennedy Justice*. New York: Atheneum. 1971.

Newman, Roger K. *Hugo Black: A Biography*. New York: Pantheon Books. 1994. (8, 14, 15)

Nossiter, Adam. *Of Long Memory: Mississippi and the Murder of Medgar Evers*. New York: Addison-Wesley. 1994.

Oates, Stephen B. *Let the Trumpet Sound: The Life of Martin Luther King, Jr.* New York: Harper & Row. 1982. (13)

O'Neill, Daniel T. *The Firecracker Boys*. New York: St. Martin's Press. 1994. (10, 11)

Payne, Charles M. *I've Got the Light of Freedom: The Organizing Tradition and the Mississippi Freedom Struggle*. Berkeley, California: University of California Press. 1995. (8)

Pollack, Jack Harrison. *Earl Warren: The Judge Who Changed America*. Englewood Cliffs, New Jersey: Prentice-Hall. 1979.

Posner, Gerald L. *Case Closed: Lee Harvey Oswald and the Assassination of JFK*. New York: Random House. 1993.

Reeves, Richard. *President Kennedy: Profile of Power.* New York: Simon and Schuster. 1993.

Reeves, Thomas. *A Question of Character: A Life of John F. Kennedy.* Prima Publishing. 1998.

Raines, Howell. *My Soul Is Rested: Movement Days in the Deep South Remembered.* New York: Putnam. 1977. (13)

Rulon, Philip Reed. *The Compassionate Samaritan: The Life of Lyndon Baines Johnson.* Chicago: Nelson-Hall. 1981. (13)

Salmond, John A. *A Southern Rebel: The Life and Times of Aubrey Willis Williams, 1890–1965.* Chapel Hill, North Carolina: University of North Carolina Press. 1983.

Salmond, John A. *The Conscience of a Lawyer: Clifford J. Durr and American Civil Liberties, 1899–1975.* Tuscaloosa, Alabama: University of Alabama Press. 1990.

Schlesinger, Arthur M., Jr. *A Thousand Days: John F. Kennedy in the White House.* Boston: Houghton Mifflin. 1965.

Schwartz, Bernard. *Super Chief: Earl Warren and His Supreme Court: A Judicial Biography.* New York: New York University Press. 1983. (15)

Sheehan, Neil. *A Bright Shining Lie: John Paul Vann and America in Vietnam.* New York: Random House. 1988. (13)

Silver, James W. *Mississippi: The Closed Society.* New York: Harcourt, Brace and World. 1963.

Stone, I. F. *In a Time of Torment, 1961–1967.* Boston: Little, Brown. 1989. (13)

Stern, Mark. *Calculating Visions: Kennedy, Johnson, and Civil Rights.* New Brunswick, New Jersey: Rutgers University Press. 1992.

Thompson, Robert Smith. *The Missiles of October: The Declassified Story of John F. Kennedy and the Cuban Missile Crisis.* New York: Simon and Schuster. 1992.

Trattner, Walter I. *From Poor Law to Welfare State: A History of Social Welfare in America.* New York: The Free Press. 1984. (8)

Udall, Stewart L. *The Myths of August: A Personal Exploration of Our Tragic Cold War Affair with the Atom.* New York: Pantheon. 1994. (10, 11, 14, 15, Epilogue)

United States Department of Energy. *Human Radiation Experiments: The Department of Energy Road Map to the Story and the Records.* Washington, D.C.: U.S. Department of Energy. 1995.

Vollers, Maryanne. *Ghosts of Mississippi: The Murder of Medgar Evers, the Trials of Byron De La Beckwith, and the Haunting of the New South.* New York: Little, Brown and Company. 1995.

Wallace, Lane E. *Flights of Discovery: 50 Years at the NASA Dryden Flight Re-search Center.* Washington, D.C.: NASA/United States Printing Office. 1996.

Warren, Earl. *The Memoirs of Earl Warren.* Garden City, New York: Doubleday. 1977. (10, 15)

Weaver, John D. *Warren: The Man, the Court, the Era.* Boston: Little, Brown. 1967. (10)

White, F. Clifton, with William J. Gill. *Suite 3505: The Story of the Draft Goldwater Movement.* New Rochelle, New York: Arlington House. 1967.

White, G. Edward. *Earl Warren, A Public Life.* New York: Oxford University Press. 1982. (10)

White, Theodore H. *The Making of the President 1960.* New York: Atheneum. 1961.

Williams, Juan. *Eyes on the Prize: America's Civil Rights Years, 1954–1965.* New York: Viking. 1987.

Wofford, Harris. *Of Kennedys and Kings: Making Sense of the Sixties.* Pittsburgh: University of Pittsburgh Press. 1980. (13)

Wolfe, Tom. *The Right Stuff.* New York: Farrar, Straus, and Giroux. 1983. (13)

Wyden, Peter. *Bay of Pigs.* New York: Simon and Schuster. 1979.

Wyden, Peter. *Wall: The Inside Story of Divided Berlin.* New York: Simon and Schuster. 1989. (Epilogue)

CHAPTER THIRTEEN

Albert, Judith Clavir, and Stewart Edward Albert, eds. *The Sixties Papers: Documents of a Rebellious Decade.* New York: Praeger Publishers. 1984. (12)

Ambrose, Stephen E. *Nixon.* 3 vols. New York: Simon and Schuster. 1991. (11, 12, 14)

Anderson, Terry H. *The Movement and the Sixties: Protest in America from Greensboro to Wounded Knee.* New York: Oxford University Press. 1995. (12)

Armbrister, Trevor. *Act of Vengeance: The Yablonski Murders and Their Solution.* New York: E.P. Dutton. 1975.

Baritz, Loren. *Backfire: A History of How American Culture Led Us into Vietnam and Made Us Fight the Way We Did.* New York: Ballantine Books, 1986. (12)

Califano, Joseph A., Jr. *The Triumph & Tragedy of Lyndon Johnson: The White House Years.* New York: Simon and Schuster. 1991. (12)

Carson, Rachel. *Silent Spring.* Boston: Houghton Mifflin. 1962.

Chafe, William H. *Never Stop Running: Allard Lowenstein and the Struggle to Save American Liberalism.* New York: Basic Books. 1993. (12)

Chester, Lewis, Godfrey Hodgson, and Bruce Page. *An American Melodrama: The Presidential Campaign of 1968.* New York: Viking. 1969.

Cleaver, Eldridge. *Soul on Ice.* New York: Laurel/Dell. 1992.

Clegg, Claude Andrew, III. *An Original Man: The Life and Times of Elijah Muhammad.* New York: St. Martin's Press. 1997.

Collins, Michael. *Carrying the Fire: An Astronaut's Journeys.* New York: Farrar, Straus and Giroux. 1974. (12)

Crowley, Monica. *Nixon in Winter.* New York: Random House. 1998. (14)

Day, Mark. *Forty Acres: Cesar Chavez and the Farm Workers.* New York: Praeger Publishers. 1971.

Dyson, Michael Eric. *Making Malcolm: The Myth and Meaning of Malcolm X.* New York: Oxford University Press. 1995.

Edelman, Bernard, ed. *Dear America: Letters Home from Vietnam.* New York: W.W. Norton. 1985.

Fanon, Frantz. *The Wretched of the Earth.* New York: Grove Press. 1968. (12)

Fine, Sidney. *Violence in the Model City: The Cavanaugh Administration, Race Relations, and the Detroit Riot of 1967.* Ann Arbor, Michigan: The University of Michigan Press. 1989.

FitzGerald, Frances. *Fire in the Lake: The Vietnamese and the Americans in Vietnam.* Boston: Little, Brown. 1972. (12)

Gardner, Lloyd C. *Pay Any Price: Lyndon Johnson and the Wars for Vietnam.* Chicago: I.R. Dee. 1995. (12)

Garretson, Charles Lloyd, III. *Hubert H. Humphrey: The Politics of Joy.* New Brunswick, New Jersey: Transaction Publishers. 1993. (12)

Georgakas, Dan, and Marvin Surkin. *Detroit: I Do Mind Dying: A Study in Urban Revolution.* New York: St. Martin's Press. 1975.

Gitlin, Todd. *The Sixties: Years of Hope, Days of Rage.* New York: Bantam Books, 1987. (12)

Goldman, Peter. *The Death and Life of Malcolm X.* New York: Harper & Row. 1973.

Gordon, Leonard, ed. *A City in Racial Crisis: The Case of Detroit Pre- and Post- the 1967 Riot.* Dubuque, Iowa: Wm. C. Brown Company. 1971

Goulden, Joseph C. *Truth Is the First Casualty: The Gulf of Tonkin Affair, Illusion and Reality.* Chicago: Rand McNally. 1969. (12)

Halberstam, David. *The Best and the Brightest.* New York: Ballantine. 1992. (12)

Hayden, Tom. *Rebellion in Newark: Official Violence and Ghetto Response.* New York: Random House. 1967.

Hersh, Seymour M. *Cover-Up: The Army's Secret Investigation of the Massacre at My Lai 4.* New York: Random House. 1972.

Hoopes, Townsend. *The Limits of Intervention: An Inside Account of How the Johnson Policy of Escalation in Vietnam Was Reversed.* New York: David McKay. 1969.

Jacobs, Jane. *The Death and Life of Great American Cities.* New York: Random House. 1961.

GEORGE BUSH throws out the first pitch at the home opener of the Texas Rangers in 1991. His son, George W. Bush, is one of the owners of the Rangers—and currently governor of Texas and a leading presidential contender for the year 2000. Despite his form here, George, Sr., was a college ball player: captain and starting first baseman for a first-rate Yale nine, following his military service. He was known as a good fielder but a spotty hitter.

James, Ralph C., and Estelle Dinerstein James. *Hoffa and the Teamsters: A Study of Union Power.* New York: Van Nostrand Company. 1965.

Karnow, Stanley. *Vietnam: A History.* New York: Viking Press. 1983. (12)

Kearns, Doris. *Lyndon Johnson and the American Dream.* New York: Harper & Row. 1976. (12)

Kerner Commission. *The Kerner Report.* New York: Pantheon. 1988.

Levy, Jacques E. *Cesar Chavez: Autobiography of La Causa.* New York: W.W. Norton. 1975.

Mailer, Norman. *The Armies of the Night: History as a Novel, the Novel as History.* New York: New American Library. 1968.

McGinniss, Joe. *The Selling of the President, 1968.* New York: Trident Press. 1969.

McKnight, Gerald D. *The Last Crusade: Martin Luther King, Jr., the FBI, and the Poor People's Campaign.* Boulder, Colorado: Westview Press. 1998.

McMaster, H. R. *Dereliction of Duty: Lyndon Johnson, Robert McNamara, the Joint Chiefs, and the Lies That Led to Vietnam.* New York: Harper. 1997. (12)

McNamara, Robert S. *In Retrospect: The Tragedy and Lessons of Vietnam.* New York: Times Books. 1995. (12)

Meister, Dick, and Anne Loftis. *A Long Time Coming: The Struggle to Union-*

ize America's Farm Workers. New York: Macmillan. 1977.

Mitchell, Greg. Tricky Dick and the Pink Lady: Richard Nixon vs. Helen Gahagan Douglas—Sexual Politics and the Red Scare, 1950. New York: Random House. 1998. (11)

Moldea, Dan E. The Hoffa Wars: Teamsters, Rebels, Politicians, and the Mob. New York: Paddington Press Ltd. 1978.

Morgan, Joseph G. The Vietnam Lobby: The American Friends of Vietnam, 1955–1975. Chapel Hill, North Carolina: University of North Carolina Press. 1997.

Moynihan, Daniel P. Maximum Feasible Misunderstanding: Community Action in the War on Poverty. New York: Free Press. 1969. (12, 15)

Moynihan, Daniel P. Miles to Go: A Personal History of Social Policy. Cambridge, Massachusetts: Harvard University Press. 1996. (12, 15, Epilogue)

Mueller, John E. War, Presidents, and Public Opinion. Lanham, Maryland: University Press of America. 1985. (11)

Murray, Bruce C. Journey into Space: The First Three Decades of Space Exploration. New York: Norton. 1989. (12)

Nader, Ralph. Unsafe at Any Speed: The Designed-In Dangers of the American Automobile. New York: Pocket Books. 1966.

Newfield, Jack. Robert Kennedy: A Memoir. New York: New American Library. 1988. (12)

Nixon, Richard. Six Crises. Garden City, New York: Doubleday. 1962. (11, 12)

Oberdorfer, Don. Tet! New York: Doubleday. 1971.

Pearson, Hugh. The Shadow of the Panther: Huey Newton and the Price of Black Power in America. New York: Addison-Wesley. 1994.

Pimlott, John. Vietnam: The Decisive Battles. New York: Macmillan. 1990. (12, 14)

Porambo, Ron. No Cause for Indictment: An Autopsy of Newark. New York: Holt, Rinehart and Winston. 1971.

Posner, Gerald. Killing the Dream: James Earl Ray and the Assassination of Martin Luther King. New York: Random House. 1998.

Powell, Colin, with Joseph E. Persico. My American Journey. New York. Random House. 1995. (15, epilogue)

Prochnau, William. Once Upon a Distant War. New York: Times Books. 1995.

Salisbury, Harrison E. Vietnam Reconsidered: Lessons From a War. New York: Harper & Row. 1984. (12)

Sauter, Van Gordon, and Burleigh Hines. Nightmare in Detroit: A Rebellion and Its Victims. Chicago: Henry Regnery Company. 1968.

Schipper, Martin. Robert Lester, ed. Memos of the Special Assistant for National Security Affairs: McGeorge Bundy to President Johnson, 1963–1966. Frederick, Maryland: University Publications of America. 1985.

Schlesinger, Arthur M., Jr. The Bitter Heritage: Vietnam and American Democracy, 1941–1966. Boston: Houghton Mifflin. 1967. (12)

Schlesinger, Arthur M., Jr. The Crisis of Confidence: Ideas, Power, and Violence in America. Boston: Houghton Mifflin. 1969.

Schlesinger, Arthur M., Jr. Robert Kennedy and His Times. Boston: Houghton Mifflin. 1978. (12)

Schoenbaum, Thomas J. Waging Peace and War: Dean Rusk in the Truman, Kennedy and Johnson Years. New York: Simon and Schuster. 1988.

Sharpley, Deborah. Promise and Power: The Life and Times of Robert McNamara. Boston: Little, Brown. 1993. (12)

Shawcross, William. Sideshow: Kissinger, Nixon and the Destruction of Cambodia. New York: Simon and Schuster. 1979. (14)

Shesol, Jeff. Mutual Contempt: Lyndon Johnson, Robert Kennedy, and the Feud That Defined a Decade. New York: W.W. Norton. 1997. (12)

Sloane, Arthur A. Hoffa. Cambridge, Massachusetts: The MIT Press. 1991.

Smith, John T. Rolling Thunder: The American Strategic Bombing Campaign Against North Vietnam, 1964–68. Walton on Thames, England: Air Research Publications. 1994.

Solberg, Carl. Hubert Humphrey: A Biography. New York: Norton. 1984. (12)

Stone, I. F. The Killings at Kent State: How Murder Went Unpunished. New York: Vintage Books. 1971.

Viorst, Milton. Fire in the Streets: America in the 1960s. New York: Simon and Schuster. 1979. (12)

Walker, Daniel. Rights in Conflict: Chicago's 7 Brutal Days. New York: Grosset & Dunlap. 1968.

Wells, Tom. The War Within: America's Battle Over Vietnam. Berkeley: University of California Press. 1994.

Williams, William Appleman, ed. America in Vietnam: A Documentary History. New York: W.W. Norton. 1989. (12, 14)

Wills, Garry. Nixon Agonistes: The Crisis of the Self-Made Man. New York: New American Library. 1979. (14)

Wolfe, Tom. The Electric Kool-Aid Acid Test. New York: Bantam Books. 1969.

Wolfe, Tom. Radical Chic & Mau-Mauing the Flak Catchers. New York: Farrar, Straus and Giroux. 1970. (12)

X, Malcolm, as told to Alex Haley. The Autobiography of Malcolm X. New York: Ballantine Books. 1990.

Young, Hugo, with Brian Silcock and Peter Dunn. Journey to Tranquility: The Long, Competitive Struggle to Reach the Moon. New York: Doubleday. 1970. (12)

Ambrose, Stephen E. Nixon, Vol. 2: The Triumph of a Politician, 1962–1972. New York: Simon and Schuster. 1989. (13)

Ambrose, Stephen E. Nixon, Vol. 3: Ruin and Recovery 1973–1990. New York: Simon and Schuster. 1991.

Bernstein, Carl, and Bob Woodward. All the President's Men. New York: Simon and Schuster. 1974.

Bourne, Peter G. Jimmy Carter: A Comprehensive Biography from Plains to Post-Presidency. New York: Scribner. 1997.

Brodie, Fawn M. Richard Nixon: The Shaping of His Character. New York: W.W. Norton. 1981.

Brownmiller, Susan. Against Our Will: Men, Women and Rape. New York: Bantam. 1976.

Bundy, McGeorge. Danger and Survival: Choices About the Bomb in the First Fifty Years. New York: Random House. 1988. (10, 11, 12)

Califano, Joseph A., Jr. Governing America. New York: Simon and Schuster. 1981.

Cannon, James. Time and Chance: Gerald Ford's Appointment with History. New York: HarperCollins. 1994.

Cohen, Marcia. The Sisterhood: The True Story of the Women Who Changed the World. New York: Simon and Schuster. 1988.

Colby, William. Honorable Men: My Life in the CIA. New York: Simon and Schuster. 1978. (11, 12, 13)

Colson, Charles W. Born Again. Old Tappan, New Jersey: Chosen Books. 1976.

Commager, Henry Steele. The Defeat of America: Presidential Power and the National Character. New York: Simon and Schuster. 1974.

Davis, Flora. Moving the Mountain: The Women's Movement in America Since 1960. New York: Simon and Schuster. 1991. (15)

Dean, John. Blind Ambition. New York: Simon and Schuster. 1976.

Ehrlichman, John. Witness to Power: The Nixon Years. New York: Simon and Schuster. 1982.

Emery, Fred. Watergate: The Corruption of American Politics and the Fall of Richard Nixon. New York: Times Books. 1994.

Ferguson, Thomas, and Joel Rogers. The Hidden Election: Politics and Economics in the 1980 Presidential Campaign. New York: Pantheon Books. 1980.

Friedan, Betty. The Feminine Mystique. New York: Norton. 1963.

Galbraith, John Kenneth. The Age of Uncertainty. Boston: Houghton Mifflin. 1977. (13, 15)

Galbraith, John Kenneth. Andrea D. Williams, ed. Annals of an Abiding Liberal. Boston: Houghton Mifflin. 1979. (8, 10, 11, 12, 13, 15)

Germond, Jack W., and Jules Witcover. Blue Smoke and Mirrors: How Reagan Won and Why Carter Lost the Election of 1980. New York: Viking. 1981.

Greer, Germaine. The Female Eunuch. New York: Bantam. 1972.

Halberstam, David. The Reckoning. New York: Avon Books. 1987.

Haldeman, H. R., and Joseph diMona. The Ends of Power. New York: New York Times Books. 1978.

Haldeman, H. R. The Haldeman Diaries: Inside the Nixon White House. New York: G.P. Putnam's Sons. 1994.

Hersh, Seymour M. The Price of Power: Kissinger in the Nixon White House. New York: Summit Books. 1983.

Isaacson, Walter. Kissinger. A Biography. New York: Simon and Schuster. 1992.

Jaworski, Leon. The Right and the Power: The Prosecution of Watergate. New York: Reader's Digest Press. 1976.

Jordan, Hamilton. Crisis: The Last Year of the Carter Presidency. New York: Putnam. 1982.

Keith, Ronald C. The Diplomacy of Zhou Enlai. Basingstoke, England: Macmillan. 1989. (11)

Kissinger, Henry. White House Years. Boston: Little, Brown and Company. 1979.

Kissinger, Henry. Years of Upheaval. New York: Little, Brown and Company. 1982. (13)

Kutler, Stanley I. The Wars of Watergate: The Last Crisis of Richard Nixon. New York: Alfred A. Knopf. 1990.

Kutler, Stanley I. Abuse of Power: The New Nixon Tapes. New York: The Free Press. 1997.

Kyle, James H., with John Robert Eidson. The Guts to Try: The Untold Story of the Iran Hostage Resuce Mission by the On-Scene Desert Commander. New York: Orion Books. 1990.

Lang, Gladys Engel, and Kurt Lang. The Battle for Public Opinion: The President, the Press, and the Polls During Watergate. New York: Columbia University Press. 1983.

Lukas, J. Anthony. Nightmare: The Underside of the Nixon Years. New York: The Viking Press. 1975.

Marcus, Eric. Making History: The Struggle for Gay and Lesbian Equal Rights: 1945–1990. New York: HarperCollins. 1992.

McCarthy, Mary. The Mask of State: Watergate Portraits. New York: Harcourt Brace Jovanovich. 1974.

McQuaid, Kim. The Anxious Years: America in the Vietnam-Watergate Era. New York: Basic Books. 1989. (12, 13)

Mezvinsky, Edward, with Kevin McCormally and John Greenya. A Term to Remember. New York: Coward, McCann & Geoghegan. 1977.

Miller, Neil. Out of the Past: Gay and Lesbian History from 1869 to the

BILL CLINTON meets former St. Louis Cardinal legend Stan "the Man" Musial in the Oval Office. Musial, a member of the Hall of Fame, once held the National League record for hits, and was given his nickname by awed Brooklyn Dodger fans.

Present. New York: Vintage Books. 1995.

Millett, Kate. *Sexual Politics.* Garden City, New York: Doubleday. 1970.

The New York Times, Staff of. *The End of a Presidency.* New York: Holt, Rinehart and Winston. 1974.

Newhouse, John. *Cold Dawn: The Story of SALT.* Washington, D.C.: Pergamon-Brassey's. 1989. (12, 15)

Nixon, Richard. Gerald Gold, general ed. *The White House Transcripts.* New York: Viking Press. 1974.

Nixon, Richard. *RN: The Memoirs of Richard Nixon.* 2 vols. New York: Warner Books. 1979. (11, 12, 13)

Nixon, Richard. Bruce Oudes, ed. *From the President: Richard Nixon's Secret Files.* New York: Harper & Row. 1989.

Nixon, Richard. *In the Arena: A Memoir of Victory, Defeat, and Renewal.* New York: Simon and Schuster. 1990. (11, 12, 13)

Olmsted, Kathryn. *Challenging the Secret Government: The Post-Watergate Investigations of the CIA and FBI.* Chapel Hill, North Carolina: University of North Carolina Press. 1996.

Powers, Thomas. *The Man Who Kept the Secrets: Richard Helms and the CIA.* New York: Alfred A. Knopf. 1979. (11, 12, 13)

Ranelagh, James. *The Agency: The Rise and Fall of the CIA.* New York: Simon and Schuster. 1986. (11, 12, 13, 15)

Safire, William. *Before the Fall.* New York: Doubleday. 1975.

Schapmeiser, Edward L. *Gerald R. Ford's Date with Destiny: A Political Biography.* New York: P. Lang. 1989.

Schell, Jonathan. *The Time of Illusion.* New York: Vintage Books. 1976.

Schlesinger, Arthur M., Jr. *The Imperial Presidency.* Boston: Houghton Mifflin. 1973.

Schrag, Peter. *Test of Loyalty: Daniel Ellsberg and the Rituals of Secret Government.* New York: Simon and Schuster. 1974.

Shawcross, William. *The Shah's Last Ride: The Fate of an Ally.* New York: Simon and Schuster. 1988.

Sheehan, Neil, ed. *The Pentagon Papers.* New York: Quadrangle Books. 1971. (13)

Shilts, Randy. *The Mayor of Castro Street: The Life and Times of Harvey Milk.* New York: St. Martin's Press. 1982.

Shilts, Randy. *And the Band Played On: Politics, People, and the AIDS Epidemic.* New York: Penguin Books. 1988

Sick, Gary. *All Fall Down: America's Tragic Encounter with Iran.* New York: Random House. 1985.

Sirica, John. *To Set the Record Straight.* New York: W.W. Norton. 1979.

Smith, Gaddis. *Morality, Reason, and Power: American Diplomacy in the Carter Years.* New York: Hill and Wang. 1986.

Steinem, Gloria. *Outrageous Acts and Everyday Rebellions.* New York: Holt, Rinehart and Winston. 1983.

Talbott, Strobe. *The Master of the Game: Paul Nitze and the Nuclear Peace.* New York: Alfred A. Knopf. 1988. (11, 12, 15)

Thornton, Richard C. *The Carter Years: Toward a New Global Order.* New York: Paragon House. 1991.

Tretick, Stanley, and William V. Shannon. *They Could Not Trust the King: Nixon, Watergate, and the American People.* New York: Macmillan. 1974.

Weiss, Mike. *Double Play: The San Francisco City Hall Killings.* Reading, Massachusetts: Addison-Wesley. 1984.

Wells, Tim. *444 Days: The Hostages Remember.* San Diego: Harcourt Brace Jovanovich. 1985.

White, Theodore H. *Breach of Faith: The Fall of Richard Nixon.* New York: Atheneum. 1975.

Williams, William Appleman. *Empire as a Way of Life: An Essay on the Causes and Character of America's Present Predicament, Along with a Few Thoughts About an Alternative.* New York: Oxford University Press. 1980. (11, 12, 13, 15)

Wise, David, and Thomas B. Ross. *The Invisible Government.* New York: Random House. 1964. (11, 12, 13)

Woodward, Bob, and Carl Bernstein. *The Final Days.* New York: Simon and Schuster. 1976.

Wooten, James T. *Dasher: The Roots and the Rising of Jimmy Carter.* New York: Summit Books. 1978.

Yergin, Daniel. *The Prize: The Epic Quest for Oil, Money, and Power.* New York: Simon and Schuster. 1991.

Zonis, Marvin. *Majestic Failure: The Fall of the Shah.* Chicago: University of Chicago Press. 1991.

CHAPTER FIFTEEN

Anderson, Martin. *Revolution: The Reagan Legacy.* Stanford, California: Hoover Institution Press. 1993.

Balitzer, Alfred, ed. *A Time for Choosing: The Speeches of Ronald Reagan, 1961–1982.* Chicago: Regnery Gateway. 1983.

Ball, Howard, and Phillip J. Cooper. *Of Power and Right: Hugo Black, William O. Douglas, and America's Constitutional Revolution.* New York: Oxford University Press. 1992. (12, 14)

Barber, James David. *The Pulse of Politics: Electing Presidents in the Media Age.* New York: Norton. 1980. (Epilogue)

Barlett, Donald L., and James B. Steele. *America: What Went Wrong?* Kansas City: Andrews and McMeel. 1992. (Epilogue)

Barrett, Laurence I. *Gambling with History: Ronald Reagan in the White House.* Garden City, New York: Doubleday. 1983.

Binstein, Michael, and Charles Bowden. *Trust Me: Charles Keating and the Missing Billions.* New York: Random House. 1993.

Blumenthal, Sidney. *Pledging Allegiance: The Last Campaign of the Cold War.* New York: HarperCollins. 1990.

Bonner, Raymond. *Weakness and Deceit: U.S. Policy and El Salvador.* New York: Times Books. 1984.

Bradlee, Ben, Jr. *Guts and Glory: The Rise and Fall of Oliver North.* New York: Donald I. Fine. 1988.

Buckley, Tom. *Violent Neighbors: El Salvador, Central America and the United States.* New York: Times Books. 1984.

Burns, E. Bradford. *At War in Nicaragua: The Reagan Doctrine and the Politics of Nostalgia.* New York: Harper & Row. 1987.

Callahan, David. *Dangerous Capabilities: Paul Nitze and the Cold War.* New York: HarperCollins. 1990. (11, 12, 13, 14)

Campbell, Colin, and Bert A. Rockman, eds. *The Bush Presidency: First Appraisals.* Chatham, New Jersey: Chatham House Publishers. 1991.

Cannon, Lou. *Reagan.* New York: G.P. Putnam's Sons. 1982. (13, 14)

Cannon, Lou. *President Reagan: The Role of a Lifetime.* New York: Simon and Schuster. 1991. (13, 14)

Chang, Laurence, et al., eds. *The Chronology: The Documented Day-by-Day Account of the Secret Military Assistance to Iran and the Contras.* New York: Warner Books. 1987.

Cockburn, Leslie. *Out of Control: The Story of the Reagan Administration's Secret War in Nicaragua, the Illegal Arms Pipeline and the Contra Drug Connection.* New York: Atlantic Monthly Press. 1987.

Craig, Barbara Hinkson, and David M. O'Brien. *Abortion and American Politics.* Chatham, New Jersey: Chatham House Publishers. 1993. (14)

Cramer, Richard Ben. *What It Takes: The Way to the White House.* New York: Random House. 1992.

Dallek, Robert. *Ronald Reagan: The Politics of Symbolism.* Cambridge, Massachusetts: Harvard University Press. 1984.

Dinges, John. *Our Man in Panama: The Shrewd Rise and Brutal Fall of Manuel Noriega.* New York: Times Books. 1991. (epilogue)

Djilas, Milovan. *The Fall of the New Class: A History of Communism's Self-Destruction.* New York: Alfred A. Knopf. 1988. (Epilogue)

Douglas, William O. *Vern Countryman,* ed. *The Douglas Opinions.* New York: Random House. 1977. (12, 14)

Draper, Theodore. *A Very Thin Line: The Iran-Contra Affairs.* New York: Hill and Wang. 1991.

Dunn, Peter M., and Bruce W. Watson, eds. *American Intervention in Grenada: The Implications of Operation "Urgent Fury."* Boulder, Colorado: Westview Press. 1985.

Edwards, Anne. *Early Reagan: The Rise to Power.* New York: Morrow. 1987.

Egerton, John. *The Americanization of Dixie: The Southernization of America.* New York: Harper's Magazine Press. 1974. (12, 13 14)

Ferguson, Thomas. *Right Turn: The Decline of the Democrats and the Future of American Politics.* New York: Hill and Wang. 1986. (Epilogue)

Fitch, Robert. *The Assassination of New York.* New York: Verso. 1993. (13, Epilogue)

Foege, Alec. *The Empire God Built: Inside Pat Robertson's Media Machine.* New York: John Wiley & Sons. 1996.

Frady, Marshall. *Jesse: The Life and Pilgrimage of Jesse Jackson.* New York: Random House. 1996.

Friedman, Benjamin M. *Day of Reckoning: The Consequence of American Economic Policy Under Reagan and After.* New York: Random House. 1988. (Epilogue)

Galbraith, John Kenneth. *The Culture of Contentment.* Boston: Houghton Mifflin. 1992. (Epilogue)

Garrow, David J. *Liberty and Sexuality: The Right to Privacy and the Making of "Roe v. Wade."* New York: Macmillan. 1994. (14)

Gates, Robert. *From the Shadows.* New York: Simon and Schuster. 1996.

Goldman, Peter, and Tom Mathews. *The Quest for the Presidency 1988.* New York: Simon and Schuster. 1989.

Guillermoprieto, Alma. *The Heart That Bleeds: Latin America Now.* New York: Alfred A. Knopf. 1984.

Haig, Alexander M., Jr. *Caveat: Realism, Reagan and Foreign Policy.* New York: Macmillan. 1984.

Hamby, Alonzo. *Liberalism and Its Challengers: From F.D.R. to Bush.* New York: Oxford University Press. 1992. (8, 11, 12, 13, 14)

Harrington, Michael. *The New American Poverty.* New York: Penguin Books. 1984. (12)

Hertzke, Allen D. *Echoes of Discontent: Jesse Jackson, Pat Robertson, and the Resurgence of Populism.* Washington, D.C.: CQ Press. 1993. (Epilogue)

Hodgson, Godfrey. *The World Turned Right Side Up: A History of the Conservative Ascendancy in America.* New York: Houghton Mifflin Company. 1996. (13, 14)

Hyland, William G. *The Cold War is Over.* New York: Times Books. 1990. (Epilogue)

Johnson, Haynes. *Sleepwalking Through History: America in the Reagan Years.* New York: Anchor Press. 1992.

Kahlenberg, Richard D. *The Remedy: Class, Race, and Affirmative Action.* New York: Basic Books. 1996. (12, 13, Epilogue)

Kindleberger, Charles P. *Keynesianism vs. Monetarism, and Other Essays in Financial History.* Boston: Allen & Unwin. 1985. (8)

Leamer, Laurence. *Make-Believe: The Story of Nancy and Ronald Reagan.* New York: Harper & Row. 1983.

LaFeber, Walter. *The Panama Canal: The Crisis in Historical Perspective.* New York: Oxford University Press. 1978. (4)

LaFeber, Walter. *Inevitable Revolutions: The United States in Central America.* New York: Norton. 1983. (4, 5, 7, 11)

Langston, Thomas S. *Ideologues and Presidents: From the New Deal to the Reagan Revolution.* Baltimore: Johns Hopkins University Press. 1992. (8, 10, 11, 12, 13, 14)

Lukas, J. Anthony. *Common Ground: A Turbulent Decade in the Lives of Three American Families.* New York: Vintage Books. 1986.

Mayer, Jane, and Doyle McManus. *Landslide: The Unmaking of the President, 1984–1988.* Boston: Houghton Mifflin Company. 1989.

McFarlane, Robert, and Zofia Smardz. *Special Trust.* New York: Cadell and Davies. 1994.

Moynihan, Daniel Patrick. *Came the Revolution: Argument in the Reagan Era.* New York: Harcourt Brace Jovanovich. 1988.

Nove, Alec. *Stalinism and After: The Road to Gorbachev.* Boston: Unwin Hyman. 1989. (10, 11, 12, 14, Epilogue)

Parmet, Herbert S. *George Bush: The Life of a Lone Star Yankee.* New York: Scribner. 1997.

Persico, Joseph E. *Casey: The Lives and Secrets of William J. Casey, from the OSS to the CIA.* New York: Viking. 1990.

Phillips, Kevin. *Boiling Point: Republicans, Democrats, and the Decline of Middle-Class Prosperity.* New York: Random House. 1993. (Epilogue)

Pizzo, Stephen, Mary Fricker, and Paul Muolo. *Inside Job: The Looting of America's Savings and Loans.* New York: HarperPerennial. 1991.

Reagan, Ronald. *An American Life.* New York: Simon and Schuster. 1990.

Rubin, Eva R., ed. *The Abortion Controversy: A Documentary History.* Westport, Connecticut: Greenwood Press. 1994. (14)

Ruge, Gerard. *Gorbachev.* London: Chatto and Windus. 1991. (Epilogue)

Sakharov, Andrei. *Memoirs.* New York: Alfred A. Knopf. 1990. (11, 12, 14)

Sandoz, Elliot, and Cecil V. Crabb, Jr., eds. *Election 84: Landslide Without a Mandate?* New York: New American Library. 1985.

Schieffer, Bob, and Gary Paul Gates. *The Acting President: Ronald Reagan and the Supporting Players Who Helped Him Create the Illusion That Held America Spellbound.* New York: E.P. Dutton. 1989.

Schlesinger, Arthur M., Jr. *The Disuniting of America.* New York: W.W. Norton. 1998.

Seidman, William L. *Full Faith and Credit: The Great S&L Debacle and Other Washington Sagas.* New York: Times Books. 1993.

Shultz, George. *Turmoil and Triumph: My Years as Secretary of State.* New York: Scribners. 1993.

Simon, James F. *Independent Journey: The Life of William O. Douglas.* New York: Harper & Row. 1980. (12, 15)

Sklar, Holly. *Washington's War on Nicaragua.* Boston: South End Press. 1988.

Stockman, David. *The Triumph of Politics: Why the Reagan Revolution Failed.* New York: Harper. 1986.

Timberg, Robert. *The Nightingale's Song.* New York: Simon and Schuster. 1995.

Tower, John, Edmund Muskie, and Brent Scowcroft. *The Tower Commission Report.* New York: Bantam Books and Times Books. 1987.

Tribe, Laurence H. *Abortion: The Clash of Absolutes.* New York: W.W. Norton. 1990.

Von Mises, Ludwig. Leland B. Yeager, trans. *Nation, State, and Economy: Contributions to the Politics and History of Our Time.* New York: New York University Press. 1983. (6)

Walker, Thomas W., ed. *Reagan Versus the Sandinistas: The Undeclared War on Nicaragua.* Boulder, Colorado: Westview Press. 1987.

White, Lawrence J. *The S&L Debacle: Public Policy Lessons for Bank and Thrift Regulation.* New York: Oxford University Press. 1991.

Wills, Garry. *Reagan's America: Innocents at Home.* Garden City, New York: Doubleday. 1987.

Woodward, Bob. *The Commanders.* New York: Simon and Schuster. 1991.

AFTERWORD

Auster, Lawrence. *The Path to National Suicide.* Monterey, Virginia: The American Immigration Control Foundation. 1990.

Beschloss, Michael R., and Strobe Talbott. *At the Highest Levels: The Inside Story of the End of the Cold War.* Boston: Little, Brown. 1993. (15)

Bordewich, Fergus M. *Killing the White Man's Indian: Reinventing Native Americans at the End of the 20th Century.* New York: Doubleday. 1996.

Brimelow, Peter. *Alien Nation.* New York: Random House. 1995.

Chafe, William H., and Harvard Stikoff, eds. *A History of Our Time: Readings on Postwar America.* New York: Oxford University Press. 1995.

Entman, Robert. *Democracy Without Citizens: Media and the Decay of American Politics.* New York: Oxford University Press. 1989. (15)

Ferguson, Thomas. *Golden Rule: The Investment Theory of Party Competition and the Logic of Money-Driven Political Systems.* Chicago: University of Chicago Press. 1995. (14, 15)

Galbraith, John Kenneth, and Stanislav Menshikov. *The Good Society: The Humane Agenda.* Boston: Houghton Mifflin. 1996.

Grunwald, Henry. *One Man's America.* New York: Doubleday. 1997.

Hitchens, Christopher. *Prepared for the Worst.* New York: Hill and Wang. 1988. (15)

Hughes, Robert. *The Culture of Complaint.* New York: Oxford University Press. 1993.

Kaplan, Robert D. *An Empire Wilderness.* New York: Random House. 1998.

Kennedy, Paul. *Preparing for the Twenty-First Century.* New York: Random House. 1993.

Leuchtenburg, William E. *In the Shadow of FDR: From Harry Truman to Bill Clinton.* Ithaca, New York: Cornell University Press. 1993. (11, 12, 13, 14, 15)

Lind, Michael. *The Next American Nation.* New York: Free Press. 1995.

Matlock, Jack F., Jr. *Autopsy on an Empire.* New York: Random House. 1995. (15)

Nixon, Richard. *Beyond Peace.* New York: Random House. 1994. (15)

Patterson, James, and Peter Kim. *The Day America Told the Truth: What People Really Believe About Everything That Really Matters.* New York: Prentice-Hall Press. 1991.

Pfatt, William. *Barbarian Sentiments: How the American Century Ends.* New York: Hill & Wang. 1989.

Phillips, Kevin. *The Politics of Rich and Poor: Wealth and the American Electorate in the Reagan Aftermath.* New York: Random House. 1990. (15)

Remnick, David. *Lenin's Tomb: The Last Days of the Soviet Empire.* New York: Vintage Books. 1994. (15)

Rifkin, Jeremy. *The End of Work: The Decline of the Global Labor Force and the Dawn of the Post-Market Era.* New York: G.P. Putnam's Sons. 1995. (15)

Samuelson, Robert J. *The Good Life and Its Discontents: The American Dream in the Age of Entitlement.* New York: Times Books. 1995. (15)

Schwarz, John E. *America's Hidden Success: A Reassessment of Public Policy from Kennedy to Reagan.* New York: W.W. Norton. 1988. (12, 13, 14, 15)

Schwarz, John E. *Illusions of Opportunity: The American Dream in Question.* New York: W.W. Norton. 1997. (15)

Sifry, Micah L., and Christopher Cerf. *The Gulf War Reader: History, Documents, Opinions.* New York: Times Books. 1991.

Simon, Julian L. *Population Matters: People, Resources, Environment, and Immigration.* New Brunswick, New Jersey: Transaction Publishers. 1990.

Suro, Roberto. *Strangers Among Us: How Latino Immigration Is Transforming America.* New York: Alfred A. Knopf. 1998.

Wattenberg, Ben. *The Birth Dearth.* New York: Pharos Books. 1987.

Wilson, Robert, ed. *Character Above All: Ten Presidents from FDR to George Bush.* New York: Simon and Schuster. 1995. (8, 10, 11, 12, 13, 14, 15)

Wolfe, Alan. *One Nation After All.* New York: Viking. 1998.

Woodward, Bob. *The Agenda: Inside the Clinton White House.* New York: Simon and Schuster. 1994.

BASEBALL PHOTO CAPTIONS BY KEVIN BAKER.

Note: Page numbers in *italics* refer to illustrations

Abernathy, Rev. Ralph, 459, 472, 473, 505
abortion, 629, 630, *631*
Abrams, Gen. Creighton, 556
Abzug, Bella, 598
Acheson, Dean, *407, 422, 433, 445,* 536
    and China, 418, 419, 420–21, 428
    and Cold War, 392, 394, 395, 396, 399–401, 420–21
    and containment, 392, 394, 395, 396, 399–401
    and Cuban Missile Crisis, 494
    and Korean war, 400–401, 420–21, 423
    and Marshall Plan, 410
    and NATO, 395, 407
    as secretary of state, 399–401, 406, 407, 420–21, 423, 433
    and Truman Doctrine, 394, 395, 407
    and World War II, 306
Achille Lauro hijacking, 640
ACLU (American Civil Liberties Union), 187, 253, 403
Adams, Brooks, 59
Adams, Col. C. M., 344
Adams, Evangeline, 231
Adams, Henry Brooks, 56, 76, 77, 104
Adams, John, 133
Adams, John Quincy, 104
Adams, Sherman, 431
Adams-Onis Treaty, 56
Addams, Jane, 92, *122, 144,* 149
addictions, 645
Adonis, Joe, 256
affirmative action, 622–23
AFL (American Federation of Labor), 36, 55, 108, 109, 110, 223, 276, 413
African Americans, *see* blacks
Agnew, Spiro T., 556, 580, *580*
Agricultural Adjustment Act (1933), 247, 273
Aguinaldo y Famy, Emilio, 66–67, *66*
Ailes, Roger, 648
Air Force, U.S., 207, 323, 338–39, 348, 352–53, 395
air traffic controllers, 626
Alabama, racial issues in, 456, 462, 463, 464, 465, 467, 472–73, 499–501, 504–5, 514, 520–21, *521*
Alamo, 483
Alaska:
    border dispute of, 98
    gold rush in, *46–47*
    purchase of, 56
Albania, 297, 318
alcohol addiction, 645
Aldrich, Nelson, 20, 95, 116–17, *116*
Aldrin, Edwin "Buzz," 554
Alexander III, Czar, 100
Alger, Horatio, 24, 38
Alger, Russell, 64
Algren, Nelson, 441
Alibekov, Aitkali, 344
Alinsky, Saul, 563
Allende Gossens, Salvador, 584, *584*
Allen, James, 261

Allen, Oscar K. "O.K.," 269
Allison, John, 401
Almond, Gen. Edward, 427
Alsop, Joe, 270, 365, 401
Altgeld, John Peter, *38,* 39, 92
Alvarez, Luis, 509
Amalgamated Association of Iron, Steel and Tin Workers, 36
Amalgamated Clothing Workers, 276
America, *see* Latin America; United States
American Civil Liberties Union (ACLU), 187, 253, 403
American Federation of Labor, *see* AFL
American flag, 18, *18–19*
American Indian Movement, 15
American Liberty League, 227, 271, 276
American Medical Association, 94, 95
American Railway Union, 38
American South:
    "Boll Weevils" (conservative Democrats) from, 614, 627
    cooperative movement in, 25, 28
    and elections, 414, 456, 458, 474, 515, 551, 603, 621–22, 634
    fundamentalists in, 629
    Ku Klux Klan in, 26, 35
    and labor unions, 276
    plantations in, 234
    and politics of resentment, 621–23
    Populist party in, 28
    poverty in, xxi
    race issues in, 28, 34–35, 261, 456–59; *see also* blacks; civil rights
American Steel and Wire, 78
American West:
    contempt for the East in, 5
    cowboys and Indians in, 4–7
    independent spirit in, 5, 25
    Indian wars, 12, 13, 15
    Johnson County cattle war in, 8–9
    land rush into, xxi–xxii, 2–3, *2–3*
    Populism in, 25, 26, 28
    railroads in, 4, 6, 8, 16
    ranches in, *xvi–xvii,* 4–5, 8–9, 248
    survival in, 4
American Woolen Company, 119
Ammons, Elias, 124
Anami, Gen. Korechika, 383
anarchists, 38, 93, 176, 178–79
Anderson, Adm. George, 494
Anderson, John, 342, *343,* 611, 614
Anderson, Marian, 259
Anderson, Martin, 619
Anderson, Maxwell, 286
Anderson, Terry (hostage), 640
Anderson, Terry H., 551, 597
Anderson, William, 190
Andrews, George, 629
Andreyev, Nikolai, 345, *345*
Anglo-Iranian Oil Company, 451
Anthony, Susan B., 92, *92,* 596
Anti-Ballistic Missile Treaty, 406, 582
Anti-Defamation League, 403, 629
Anti-Imperialist League, 54–55
Anti-Saloon League, 211
Antrim, Richard N., 336–37
Arbenz, Col. Jacobo, 450
Argentina, 390
Arizona, statehood of, 56
Armandt, Lynn, 649

Armour, Philip D., 78
Armstrong, Louis, 194
Armstrong, Neil A., 554–55
Army, U.S.:
    and airpower, 206–7
    blacks in, *163,* 352–53, *353,* 458
    and the draft, 156, 334
    in Granada, 633
    and HUAC hearings, 446–47
    and Japanese-American internment, 350–51
    women's auxiliary of, 348
    and World War I, 156, *156–57,* 159–63
    and World War II, *315,* 332, 334–41
    see also Vietnam
Arnall, Ellis, 458
Arnold, Gen. Henry "Hap," 326, 339, *339*
Ashford, Bailey K., 102
Asia:
    boat people from, 534
    Cold War in, 397–407, 490
    and domino theory, 396–97, 524, 530–31, 533
    see also specific nations and wars
Asian-Americans, and entitlement programs, 619, 663
Assad, Hafez al-, 583, 634
Astaire, Fred, 89
Astor, Vincent, 236
Atlantic Charter (1940), 304–5
atomic bombs, 323–27, 376–82, *378–79, 380–81,* 383, 448–49
    and Cold War, 395, 397, 402, 404, 444
    fallout from, 325–26, 480, 497, *497*
    and test-ban treaty, 496–97
    testing of, 448
Atomic Energy Act (1946), 443
Atomic Energy Commission, 248, 448, 497
Atwater, Lee, 648
Augustine, Saint, 618
Australia:
    and Korean war, 423
    and U.S. Navy, 104
    and World War II, 385
Austria:
    and depression, 221
    self-determination of, 169, 397, 478
    and World War II, 297
Austria-Hungary, and World War I, 144, 151, 290
automobiles:
    manufacture of, 112–13
    Model T, 113, *113*
Averell, Jim, 9
Avrich, Paul, 178
Axson, Isaac Stockton, 147

Babbitt (Lewis), 185
Bacall, Lauren, 440, *441*
Bacon, Robert, 78
Baden, Prince Maximilian von, 162
Baer, George F., 80
Bagehof, Walter, 130
Baker, Ella, 458, 459, 499
Baker, Howard, *569,* 570, 579
Baker, James A., 614, 627, *627*
Baker, Newton, 92, 143, 156, 164, 241
Baker, Ray Stannard, *94*
Baker, Vernon, 337, *337*

Baker, Wilson, 520
Bakke, Allan Paul, 622
Bakker, Rev. Jim, 629
Baldwin, James, 548
Baldwin, Roger, 187, 253
Balkan states, and World War II, 316, 318, 355
Ball, George, 406, 528, 532
Ballantine, Joseph W., 309
Ballinger, Richard, 96
Baltic provinces:
    communism abandoned in, 654
    and Russia-Germany agreement, 148
    and World War II, 316
Bani-Sadr, Abolhassan, 607
banking:
    deposit insurance, 133
    emergency closing of, 246
    farmers and, 290
    Federal Reserve, 133, 222, 224, 226, 271
    investment, 78
    national currency, 28
    postal savings bank, 117
barbed wire, 4–5, 8, *8*
Barber, Amos W., 8
Barker, Bernard, 575
Barker, Ernest, 578
Barker, Col. Frank, 558–59
Barnett, Big Mose, 187
Barnett, Ross, 499
Barney, Charles, 133
Barnum, P. T., 229
Barry, Marion, 459
Baruch, Bernard, *217*
Bates, Ruby, 261
Bayh, Birch, 614, 628
Bayonne, N.J., strike in, 124, *125*
Bean, Alan L., 555
Beard, Dewey, 262
Beasley, Dorothy Toth, 630
Beckwith, Col. Charles, 608–9
Begin, Menachem, 606, *606*
Belafonte, Harry, 459
Belcher, Sgt. Julius, 341
Belgium:
    aid to, 217, 236
    and Holocaust, 289
    and Kellogg-Briand Pact, 204
    and World War I, 151
    and World War II, 317
Bell, Alexander Graham, 89
Belousovitch, Igor, 344
Benchley, Robert, 84
Bendetsen, Col. Karl, 350
Benjamin, Ben, 626–27
Bennett, Harry, 280
Bennett, Leslie, 437
Bennion, Capt. Mervyn S., 311
Benson, Harry, 567, 626
Bentley, Elizabeth, 402, 444
Bentsen, Lloyd, 651
Bergman, Walter, 500
Beria, Lavrenty, 404, 448
Berkman, Alexander, 36, 93
Berlin, Germany, 342–43, *386–87,* 395, 395, 423, 478, 488–89
Berlin, Irving, 89, 156
Berlin Wall, 488–49, *488–49, 654–55*
Bernhardt, Michael, 558
Bernstein, Carl, *568,* 576

Bernstein, Irving, 249
Bernstein, Richard B., 581
Beschloss, Michael, 493
Bessarabia, 299
Bessie, Alvah, 440
Bethlehem Steel, 143
Bethmann-Hollweg, Theobald von, 146, 147, 148
Betzinez, Jason, 263
Bevel, Rev. James, 459, 500, 505, 520
Beveridge, Albert, 51, 54, 117
Bevin, Ernest, 410
Biberman, Herbert, 440
Bicknell, George W., 308
Biddle, Francis, 350–51, 373, 408
Bierce, Ambrose, 68
Big Foot, Chief, 15
Big Head, Chief, 10
Big Mane, Chief, 11
Birmingham, Alabama, racial issues in, 454, 455, 460, 461, 464, 465, 467, 504–5
birth control, 123, 630, 631
Bishop, Gardner, 468
Bismarck, Otto von, 104
Bissell, Richard, 480, 486–87, 487
Black, Hugo, 275, 468
Black Coyote, 15
Blackett, P.M.S., 327
Blackmun, Harry A., 630
Black Panthers, 546, 573
black power, 546
blacks:
    and affirmative action, 622
    "back to Africa" movement of, 186, 194–95
    and busing, 622–23
    in cities, 194, 547
    and entitlement programs, 619, 663
    and genetic inferiority, 457
    and Jim Crow laws, 35, 414, 454–58, 472, 500
    in labor unions, 194, 352, 352, 353, 454
    lynching of, 16, 35, 176, 192, 192–93, 200, 289, 456, 457
    in the military, 163, 337, 337, 352–53, 353, 457–58
    and NAACP, see NAACP
    nationalism of, 544–46
    and Nation of Islam, 460, 544–45
    and New Deal, 259, 454
    Niagara movement of, 35
    and politics of resentment, 621–22
    and racism, see racism
    and Rainbow Coalition, 635
    rights of, 16
    Scottsboro Nine, 260, 261
    and segregation, 34–35, 259, 454–65, 468
    and separatism, 460, 544
    in Spanish-American War, 35, 163
    voting rights of, xxi, 35, 454, 456–58, 462–64, 500, 502, 518–21
    war work of, 346, 353
    Watts riot and, 517
    in women's reform movements, 92
    see also civil rights
Black Star Line (BSL), 195
Blaine, James G., 30
Blair, Ezell, Jr., 498
Blanck, Max, 121

Blanquet, Aurellano, 134
Blarney, Gen. Sir Thomas, 384
Bliss, Gen. Tasker H., 167
Bly, Nellie, xxii
Boas, Franz, 457
Bock, Frederick, 381
Boesky, Ivan, 643
Bogart, Humphrey, 440, 441
Bohlen, Charles "Chip," 401, 404, 406, 410
Bohr, Niels, 449
Bolshakov, Georgi, 488
Bond, Julian, 459, 516
Bone, Homer, 288
Bonner, Raymond, 637
Bonner, Walter, 567
Bonus Expeditionary Force (BEF), 239
boomers, land rush of, 2–3, 2–3
Borah, William E., 172, 172, 173, 186, 204, 271, 287, 290
Borden, William, 449
Bork, Robert, 580
Bork, Robert H., 618
Bormann, Martin Ludwig, 321, 409
Bosnia, 537
Bothwell, Albert J., 9
Bourke-White, Margaret, 234
Boutwell, Albert, 504
Bowers, Montgomery, 124
Bowers, Sam, 518, 519
Bowles, Chester, 487
Bowles, Samuel, 55
Box, Herbert P., 325
Boxer Rebellion, 56
Boyd, Frank Sumner, 108
Boyle, W. A. "Tony," 563
Boynton, Amelia, 520
Bradlee, Ben, 568
Bradley, Bill, 648
Bradley, Gen. Omar, 339, 339, 342–43, 343, 401, 426, 430, 431
Brady, Alice, 245
Brady, James S., 626–27, 627
Braher, PFC William, 341
Branch, Taylor, 461, 462, 465, 501
Brandeis, Louis D., 92, 133, 186, 187, 272–73, 273, 274, 274, 630
Brandon, Henry, 398
Brannan, Charles, 422
Bratton, Col. Rufus, 309
Braun, Wernher von, 476, 554
Breckinridge, Henry, 142–43
Breen, John J., 119
Brennan, Howard, 506
Brezhnev, Leonid, 582, 592–93, 655
Brezhnev Doctrine, 564
Briand, Aristide, 204
Bridges, Harry, 258
Briggs, Harry, 468
Briggs, Lyman J., 376
Bright, John, 130
Brighton ranch, Nebraska, 8–9, 8
Bristow, Joseph, 117
Britain, battle of, 294, 300
Britton, John Bayard, 630
Britton, Nan, 201, 201
Brockdorff-Rantzau, Count Ulrich von, 169, 170
Brooke, Alan, 342, 342
Brookings Institution, 574–75
"Brother, Can You Spare a Dime?," 241

Brotherhood of Sleeping Car Porters, 352
Browaski, Hulda, 228
Browder, Earl, 445
Brown, Gen. Charles C., 342, 343
Brown, Edmund G. "Jerry," 563
Brown, H. Rap, 546
Brown, Irving, 655
Brown, Oliver, 468
Brown, Pat, 625
Browne, Malcolm, 490, 534
Brownell, Herbert, 443
Browning, Capt. Miles, 363
Brown v. Board of Education, 456, 468, 469, 500, 504, 513, 629
Brown v. Mississippi, 454
Bruere, Martha Bensley, 245
Brugioni, Dino A., 492
Brüning, Heinrich, 221
Brussels Defense Pact (1948), 395
Bryan, William Jennings, 41, 79, 132, 133, 136, 215
    death of, 197
    and elections, 40, 42, 43, 45, 106, 129
    and foreign policy, 53, 55, 136, 137, 143–46
    and Scopes trial, 196–97, 196, 197
    and silver standard, 40, 46, 625
    and World War I, 143–46
    and World War II, 286
Bryant, Roy and Carolyn, 470, 470
Bryce, James, 84, 86, 96
Brzezinski, Zbigniew, 607, 610
Buchanan, Frank, 9
Buchanan, Pat, 618, 623
Buchenwald concentration camp, 289, 408
Buchman, Sidney, 440
Buck, Pearl S., 441
Buckley, William (hostage), 640
Buckley, William F., Jr., 447, 617, 619, 656
Buckley v. Valeo, 581
Buckner, Gen. Simon Bolivar, Jr., 366–67
Buda, Mario, 179
Bulganin, Nikolay, 478
Bulgaria:
    communism abandoned in, 654
    and World War I, 151
    and World War II, 316, 317, 318
Bull Head, Chief, 10, 11, 12
Bullitt, William, 292, 299, 354
Bull Moose party, 129, 183
Bunau-Varilla, Philippe, 100–101
Bunche, Ralph, 404, 405, 457, 469
Bundy, McGeorge, 324, 326, 449, 486, 493, 494, 495, 527–29, 535, 536
Bunker, Ellsworth, 556
Bureau of Indian Affairs, 15
Burke, Arleigh, 487
Burke, Edmund, 130, 618
Burling, John L., 351
Burma, 299
Burroughs, John, 190
Burrows, Larry, 538
Bush, Barbara, 650, 651
Bush, George, xiii, 586, 623, 627, 646, 650, 651, 654
    and civil rights, 462–63, 623
    and elections, 617, 629, 634, 648
    foreign policy of, 537, 633

    presidency of, 497, 650–51, 656
    and S&L debacle, 643
    as vice president, 632, 640, 651
Bush, Vannevar, 346, 376
business:
    and affirmative action, 622
    antitrust laws, 272–73
    big, 133, 183, 273, 619
    black, 194–95
    competition in, 133, 247
    and Congress, 95, 116–17
    and the economy, see economy
    and elections, 302
    and labor movement, see labor
    laissez-faire in, 180, 186, 236
    in Latin America, 134, 136, 137
    and military-industrial complex, 327
    and New Deal, 247, 249, 271, 276
    and "normalcy," 182–86
    politics of, 42
    and public works, 225
    robber barons in, 20, 24, 76–80, 268
    sexual discrimination in, 349
    and taxation, 620
    and unions, see labor
    and World War I, 288
    and World War II, 285, 287, 288, 299, 314, 320
Butcher, Solomon D., 8
Butler, Pierce, 187, 272–73, 272–73, 274–75
Butterfield, Alexander, 579
Butterfield, Herbert, 391
Buxton, Charles Lee, 630
Byrne, Rev. John, 82, 83
Byrnes, James F., 375, 413, 413
    and Cold War, 388, 390, 404
    and Japan/World War II, 325, 326–27, 377, 383
    as secretary of state, 325, 377, 383, 388, 390, 404, 419, 444

Cagney, Jimmy, 253, 286
Cain, Christopher C., 34
Cakobau, king of Hawaii, 52
Califano, Joseph A., Jr., 517, 611, 645
California:
    acquisition of, 56
    direct referendums in, 620, 661
    EPIC campaign in, 95
    and Japanese-American intern-ment, 350–51
    Muir Woods in, 96
    Reagan as governor of, 625
    S&L debacle in, 642–43
Calley, Lt. William, 558–59, 559
Calloway, Howard, 559
Cambodia, 524, 530, 533, 537, 556–57, 574, 594
Campbell, Hardy Webster, 4
Camp David accords, 606, 606
Canada:
    border dispute of, 98
    and Cold War, 402
    and Korean war, 423
    and World War II, 305, 340–41, 385
Cannon, Joe, 42, 96, 117
Cannon, Lou, 623
Cantril, Hadley, 621
Capa, Robert, 335, 339
capitalism, 20–21

capitalism (continued)
  communism defeated by, 656
  and depressions, 108
  and imperialism, 51–52
  and individualism, 111
  and labor unions, see labor
  laissez-faire philosophy of, 22, 23, 25, 40, 42, 86, 94, 228, 272
  money system in, 27, 28, 40, 133
  welfare, 111
  see also business; economy
Capone, Al, 212, 213, 250, 251
Capone, Mae, 251
Capote, Truman, 441
Capra, Frank, 642
Cardozo, Benjamin N., 273, 274, 274–75
Caribbean, protection of, 59, 98
Carmichael, Stokely, 544, 546
Carnegie, Andrew, xxiii, 16, 22, 36, 37, 55, 75, 78, 89
Carpenter, Rev. C. C. Jones, 505
Carpenter, M. Scott, 477, 477
Carr, R. G., 5
Carranza, Venustiano, 136, 138
Carroll, James, 102, 103
Carson, Rachel, 561, 561
Carter, Billy, 605
Carter, Hodding, 459
Carter, Jimmy, 236, 259, 583, 602, 603
  and Camp David accords, 606, 606
  and elections, 591, 603, 609, 611, 620
  and Latin America, 636
  presidency of, 406, 497, 602–11, 614, 627, 642
Carter, Robert, 459
Carter, Rosalynn, 602, 606
Cartier-Bresson, Henri, 469
Carver, George Washington, 454
Case, Ken, 497, 497
Casey, William, 483, 613, 638, 638, 640, 646
Cash, Wilbur, 456, 457, 458
Castillo Armas, Carlos, 450, 450
Castro, Cipriano, 98
Castro, Fidel, 486–87, 487, 492–95, 492, 532, 584
Catch-the-Bear, 12
Catholic Church:
  and politics, 83, 214, 215
  and prejudice, 185, 193, 252, 291
Catt, Carrie Chapman, 185
cattle:
  and cowboys, 4–5
  mavericks, 8
  ranches, 4–5
  range for, 4, 8, 232
  rustlers of, 8–9
cattle barons, 8–9, 232
Cattle Kate, 9, 9
CCC (Civilian Conservation Corps), 247
Century of Dishonor, A (Jackson), 6
Ceo Van Thi, 540–41
Cermak, Anton, 241
Cernan, Eugene A., 555
Chae Myung Shin, Gen., 522–23
Chaffard, Jacques, 533
Chaffee, Roger, 477
Chaffee, Zechariah, Jr., 176, 186
Chamberlain, Austen, 204

Chamberlain, Neville, 290, 291, 296, 297, 301, 322
Chambers, Whittaker, 402, 416–17, 416, 444
Champion, Nate, 8–9
Chaney, James, 518–19, 623
Chaney, Mayris, 259
Channing, Carol, 571
Chaplin, Charlie, 95, 286
Chapman, Jim, 643
Chapman, Oscar, 422–23
Charger, Chief, 11
Chavez, Cesar, 563, 563, 620
Chennault, Gen. Claire, 365, 365, 398
Chernow, Ron, 79
Cherokee Outlet, land rush into, 2–3
Chiang Kai-shek, 307, 354, 365, 397–401, 398, 418–19, 428
Chiao Kuan-hua, 565
Chicago:
  meat processing scandal in, 95
  mobsters in, 212, 212, 251
  in nineteenth century, xviii
  police riot in, 550–51
  police vs. unions (1937) in, 278–79
Chicago Board of Trade, 94
child labor, 106–7, 110, 258
Chile, 584
China:
  American troops in, 48
  Boxer Rebellion in, 56
  civil war in, 419
  and Cold War, 397–401, 418–19, 418–19, 444, 564–65, 582
  decline of, 660
  and Japan, 104, 266–67, 266, 284, 285, 292, 306–7, 360, 361, 400
  and Korean war, 400–402, 420, 423, 425, 427, 428
  missionaries in, 56
  Mukden Incident, 266–67
  Nixon's visit to, 564–65, 564–65, 575
  Open Door in, 205
  secret treaty of Japan and Russia on, 104
  and Soviet Union, 564
  street fighting in, 266
  and UN membership, 398, 405, 423, 565, 565
  and U.S. Navy, 104
  and Vietnam, 532
  and World War II, 306, 316, 317, 320, 354–55, 385
China Lobby, 398–402
Chisholm, Shirley, 598
Chomsky, Noam, 533, 581
Christian Broadcasting Network, 629
Christian Coalition, 629
Chrysler, Walter, 280
Chrysler Corporation, 280, 281, 346
Church, Frank, 614, 628
Churchill, Winston, 284, 301, 301
  and Cold War, 388, 391, 392, 397, 404
  and FDR, 285, 304–5, 304, 320, 343, 354–55, 370
  and Great Depression, 231
  and League of Nations, 287
  and Lend-Lease, 304–5
  on the Marshall Plan, 410
  in postwar years, 408

at Teheran, 354–55
and Truman, 377
and World War II, 297, 304–5, 307, 317–20, 323, 338, 339
at Yalta, 342, 355, 355, 370
Chwatsky, Anna, 631
CIA (Central Intelligence Agency), 392, 393, 420, 579, 581
  and Kennedy assassination, 508
  and Latin America, 450, 486–87, 492–95, 584, 638
  and Middle East, 451, 607
  and OSS, 392, 524–25
  and U-2s, 480–81, 492, 495
  and Vietnam, 490, 527, 528
CIO (Congress of Industrial Organizations), 111, 276, 279, 280, 353, 413
cities:
  black migration to, 194
  corruption in, 85–87, 94, 256
  diseases in, 84
  drug wars in, 644–45, 645
  immigrants in, 84–87
  organized crime in, 245
  populations in, 84
  race riots in, 547, 547
  self-government in, 84
  skyscrapers in, xviii-xix
  "Tugwell Towns," 249
  unemployment in, 86
  white flight from, 623
  see also specific cities
city commissions, 87
Civilian Conservation Corps (CCC), 247
civilization, human mind and, 25
civil rights, viii, 16, 111, 195, 414, 452–75, 498–505, 514, 544
  and affirmative action, 622–23
  with "all deliberate speed," 469
  as black movement, 459, 461
  boycotts for, 456, 472–73, 504
  "by any means necessary," 545
  children's crusade, 505
  constitution and, 108, 403, 444, 464, 468, 472
  and diversity, 622
  education and, 454, 456–59, 461, 468–69, 472, 474–75, 503, 617, 623
  in employment, 461, 516
  Freedom Riders, 454, 459, 460, 465, 500–501
  and Great Society, 517
  of groups vs. individuals, 619–20
  legislation for, 34, 462–63
  and McCarthyism, 402–3
  March on Washington for, 464, 465, 466, 469
  and National Guard, 474–75, 474–75, 499, 501, 547, 547, 551
  natural, 619–20
  Near v. Minnesota, 187
  nonviolent protests in, 459–60, 465, 498–99, 505, 545
  privacy, 630, 648
  property rights vs., 286, 620
  and "radical chic," 546
  and Red scare, 458
  "rights revolution" and, 620–21
  and secret police power, 573

sit-ins for, 459, 465, 483, 498–99, 498, 503, 504–5
and Supreme Court, 34, 186, 187, 261, 350–51, 402, 403, 454, 456–59, 463, 468–69, 472, 473, 475, 500, 513, 617, 622
in wartime, 291, 350–51, 353, 457–58
see also blacks
Civil Rights Acts: (1875), 34; (1957), 513; (1964), 462–63, 515, 516, 520, 622
Civil Rights Commission, 414, 458
civil service, 30
Civil War, U.S., 16, 44, 316, 321
Civil Works Administration, 248
Clapp, Moses, 117
Clark, Champ, 156
Clarke, Sister Maura, 636
Clark, James G., Jr., 520–21
Clark, Mark, 546
Clark, Ramsey, 571
Clark, Septima, 458, 459
Clark, Thomas, 413
Clark, Walter Appleton, cartoon by, 85
Clay, Gen. Lucius, 395
Clayton, Will, 388, 406, 410
Clayton Antitrust Act (1914), 109, 133
Cleaver, Eldridge, 546
Clemenceau, Georges, 20, 162, 168–69, 168, 170–71
Cleveland, Frances Folsom, 30, 31
Cleveland, Grover, 30, 33, 80, 242
  cabinet of, 30–31
  and gold standard, 40
  and imperialism, 52, 53, 55, 59
  and income tax, 40
  and Indian lands, 6, 10
  and labor unrest, 39
  laissez-faire philosophy of, 22, 224
  second term of, 30
  and tariffs, 16
Cleveland, Oscar Folsom, 31
Cleveland, Ruth, 31
Clifford, Clark M., 391, 394, 406, 413, 527, 529, 536, 571, 572
Cline, Ray, 492
Clinton, Bill, 137, 463, 537, 599, 623, 633, 662
Clinton, Hillary Rodham, 259
Cloud, Henry Roe, 262
Cobden, Richard, 130
Cody, Buffalo Bill, 12
Coffee, Linda, 630
Cohen, Ben, 410
Cohn, Roy, 398, 443, 446–47, 447
Colby, William, 584
Cold War, 293, 327, 386–407, 416–51, 478, 479
  and arms limitation, 582, 592–93
  belligerent language in, 397
  and Berlin, 395, 423, 478, 488–89, 488–89, 654–55
  and China, 397–401, 418–19, 418–19, 444, 564–65, 582
  and containment, 393–99, 402–3, 406, 524, 530, 532, 535
  Cuban missile crisis, 492–95
  and domino effect, 396–97, 524, 530–31, 533
  and elections, 483
  end of, 646–47

espionage in, 402, 404, 416–17, 443–49, 446–51, 480–81, *480–81*, 584
and idealism, 389, 391
and Iron Curtain, 391, 392, 404, 413
and Korean war, 395, 397, 400–402, 420–29, 444, 525, 532
and McCarthyism, 431, 444–47
and Marshall Plan, 410
and nuclear threat, 448–49
and Pumpkin File, 416–17
and radical right wing, 398–400, 402, 403, 410, 444–45
and test-ban treaty, 496–97
and Vietnam, 490, 524–43
Cole, Lester, 440
Coleman, James A., 622
Cole, Nat "King," 463
Collier, John, 262, 263
Collier's, 85, 95
Collins, Addie Mae, 464
Collins, Mary Clementine, 13
Collins, Michael, 555
Colombia:
    and canal, 100, 101
    and drug wars, 645
Colorado, mines in, 124
Colorado, Mangas (Apache leader), 12
Colorado Fuel and Iron Company, 124
Colson, Charles, 568, 570–72, 574–76, *576*, 579
Colt, Samuel, 113
Committee for the First Amendment, 440
communism:
    and big government, 617
    and China, 397–400, 418–19
    and Cold War, *see* Cold War
    collapse of, 654–56
    and concentration camps, 264
    and domino theory, 524, 530–31, 533
    and Korean war, 400, 420
    and middle class, 620
    and Soviet Union, 220, 285, 294, 317, 402–3, 564, 584
    and U.S. moralism, 532, 636
    and Vietnam, 522, 525
    and World War II, 299, 316, 320
Communist party:
    arrests of members of, 119, 402
    between wars, 287, 291, 293
    and depression, 221
    and espionage, 416–17
    FBI and, 252, 253
    and HUAC, 416–17, 440–41
    and labor unions, 176, 276, 280, 655
    and Loyalty Program, 402
    U.S. Red scare, 176, 178–79, 187, 215, 285, 402–3, 443–45, 458, 462, 463
competition:
    and antitrust laws, 39, 80, 272–73
    biological, 25
    in business, 133, 247
    of the marketplace, 23, 291
Compton, Arthur, 376
Conant, James B., 326, 376, 448, 449
concentration camps, 53, 264, 289, 321, 408, 409
Conein, Col. Lucien, 490
Congress, U.S.:
    and armed intervention, 136

and bank closing, 246
business interests in, 95, 116–17
and campaign finance, 581, 648
and child labor, 110
and China, 56, 564
and civil rights, 414, 458, 462–64
and Cold War, 395
and corruption, 198–99
and Democratic party, 620–21
and disease appropriations, 102
election of, 28, 40, 94, 117
and energy conservation, 604
and entitlement programs, 663
and FDR, 246–47, 259, 271, 272, 276, 289, 293
and foreign aid, 636
and Great Depression, *238*, 239, 292
and Great Society, 516–17, 526
and immigration, 91, 289
and imperialism, 53–54
and Indian lands, 262
and Iran-Contra affair, 638, 640–41
and isolationism, 285, 288–90, 92–93
Johnson and, 513, 516, 526, 528, 566
and Kellogg-Briand Pact, 204
and Korean war, 423
and labor, 626
and League of Nations, 168–69, 172–73, 174, 175, 267
and Lend-Lease, 304–5
and Marshall Plan, 395, 410
and Panama Canal, 100, 101
and railroads, *27*
and Reagan, 614, 626, 627
and Republican party, 620
and S&L debacle, 643
and space program, 554
stagnation of, 660
and Supreme Court, 272–75
and taxation, 20, 117
and Truman, 414, 415, 566
and unemployment, 33
and Vietnam, 526, 528–31, 535–37, 594
women elected to, 123, 598, *598*
and World War I, 156, 167, 168–69, 173, 285
and World War II, 285, 288–89, 293, 294, 301, 302, 309, 312, 317, 346, 349
Congress of Industrial Organizations, *see* CIO
Connally, John, 506, 509
Connally, Nellie, 506
Connery, William P., Jr., 276
Connor, Theophilus Eugene "Bull," 504–5
Conrad, Charles "Pete", Jr., *555*
conservatism:
    divisive rhetoric of, 623
    free-market, 618
    and identity politics, 622
    meanings of word, 617–18, 619
    and Moral Majority, 623, 628–29
    as prevalent ideology in U.S., 621
    and Reagan, *see* Reagan, Ronald
Constitution, U.S.:
    1st Amendment, 187, 440
    5th Amendment, 110, 630
    6th Amendment, 630
    9th Amendment, 630

13th Amendment, 34
14th Amendment, 7, 23, 34, 110, 273, 468, 597, 622, 630
15th Amendment, xxi
16th Amendment, 94, 133
17th Amendment, 94
18th Amendment, 184, 211, 245
19th Amendment, 94, 123
21st Amendment, 245
civil rights in, 108, 403, 444, 464, 468, 472
contempt for, 581
and doctrine of original intent, 618
national character expressed in, 581
and Supreme Court, *see* Supreme Court
and war declaration, 528, 633
consumer activism, 560
Consumers' League, 122
Conte, Richard, 440, *441*
Coolidge, Calvin, 22, 184, *202*, *203*, 222, 243
    and business, 182
    and depression, 221, 224, 236
    and labor unions, 276
    presidency of, 183, 186, 190, 202–3, 207–14, 246, 614
Coolidge, Grace Goodhue, *202*, 214
Cooper, Annie Lee, 520
Cooper, Gordon, *476–77*, *477*
cooperative movement, 25, 28
Coors, Joseph, 617
Corcoran, Tom, 273, 398
CORE (Congress of Racial Equality), 459, 463, 500, 503, 518–19
Cornwell, Dean, 102
Cosby, Bill, 571
Cosio y Cisneros, Evangelina, *61*
Cosmopolitan, 94
Costello, Frank, 256
Costigan, Edward, 271
Coué, Emile, 182
Coughlin, "Bathhouse John," 87
Coughlin, Rev. Charles E., 271, 294, *294*
Courtney, Sgt. William, 341
Courts, Gus, 503
Cousins, Norman, 326
Couzens, James, 113
cowboys, 4–7, 8–9
Cowling, Eli, 500
Cox, Archibald, 579, 580
Cox, Christopher, 619
Cox, George, 87
Cox, Harold, 519
Cox, James M., 183, 215, *243*
Coxey, Jacob, 33, *33*
Coxey's army, *32*
Coy, Wayne, 347
crack cocaine, 645
Cramer, Charles, 200, *201*
Cranston, Alan, 628, 642
Cranton, Thomas Benton, 198
Crazy Horse, Chief, 12
Creel, George, 167, 288, 290
Crim, Howell, 373
crime, organized, *see* mobsters
Croker, Richard, 86, 87
Croly, Herbert, 25, 94, 129, 133
Cromwell, William Nelson, 100, 101
Cronkite, Walter, 531, *626*
Crook, Gen. George, 6, 10, 12

Crosby, Bing, 594
Crow Eagle, Chief, *11*
Crow Foot, 12
Crowley, Leo, *372*, 373
Crowley, Monica, 570
Cuba:
    Bay of Pigs, 486–87, 493
    concentration camps in, 53
    independence of, 50, 53, 54, 66
    Marxism exported by, 636
    Soviet missiles in, 407, 492–95
    and Spanish-American War, 48, *48–49*, 50, 51, 52–53, 56, 60, 64, 66
    U.S. intervention in, 137, 486–87
    yellow fever in, 102, *103*
Cudahy, John, 265
culture, popular (1920s), 184
Culver, John, 614, 628
cummings, e. e., 286, 287
Cummings, Homer, 274
Cummins, Albert, 117
Cuomo, Mario, 635, 648
Curley, James Michael, 82, 86, 485
currency:
    and Bretton Woods, 388
    Deutschmark, 395
    national, 28, 40
Curtis, Col. Donald McB., 426
Curtis, Jennie, 38
Custer, Col. George Armstrong, 10, 12, 15
Czechoslovakia:
    Communist control of, 395, 403, 410, 423, 564
    self-determination of, 169, 171, 297, 391, 654
    and World War II, 284, 285, 290, 297, 299, 316
Czekalinski, Steve, *434–35*
Czolgosz, Leon, 68, 69

Dachau concentration camp, 264, 289, 408
Dalai Lama, 582
Daley, Richard, 483, 550–51
Dana, Charles A., 23, 59
Daniel, John, 51
Daniels, Josephus, 35, 147, 206, 243
Danner, Mark, 637
Darrigo, Joseph R., 421, *421*
Darrow, Clarence, 196–97, *196*, 231
Darwin, Charles, 22, 124, 197
Dash, Sam, 569
D'Aubuisson, Roberto, *636*
Daugherty, Harry M., *199*, 200
Daughters of the American Revolution (DAR), 259
Davies, John Paton, 399
Davies, Joseph E., 404
Davis, Capt. Benjamin O., Jr., 352
Davis, Forrest A., 398
Davis, John W., 183, 215, 468, 469
Davis, Joseph E., 248
Davis, Nathaniel, 584
Davis, Norman, *217*
Davis, Russell, 462
Davis v. Marshall, 468–69
Davy, Benjamin, 269
Dawes, Henry L., 6
Dawes General Allotment (Severalty) Act (1887), 6–7, 10, 262

Daws, S. O., 27
Day, Stephen A., 288
Dean, John W. III, *569*, 571, 577–79
Dean, Maureen "Mo," *569*
Deaver, Michael, 627, 632
Debs, Eugene, 38, 39, 111, *128*, 129, *178*, 200, 223, 276, 352
debt, national, 623
Decker, George, 533
DeConcini, Dennis, 642
Decter, Midge, 616
de Gaulle, Charles, 343, *354*, 480, 511, 533
De La Beckwith, Byron, 503, *503*
Delaine, Rev. Joseph A., 468
Delano, Laura, 370
Demarest, Henry Lloyd, 80
democracy:
    and court system, 187
    and equality, 186
    fighting for freedom, 316–17, 320, 321, 327
    and free competition, 291
    and military-industrial complex, 327
    participation in, 661
    and Social Darwinism, 22–25
    survival of, 581, 629
Democratic party:
    "Boll Weevils," 614, 627
    and FDR, 241, 271
    and gold standard, 40
    and liberalism, 628
    and Populists, 5, 28, 40, 621
    and racial issues, 454, 456
    and Reagan revolution, 614, 621, 623
    and "rights revolution," 620–21
    and social welfare, 618
    and Tammany Hall, *see* Tammany Hall
    Wilson and, 132
Dempsey, Jack, 627
Denby, Edwin, 198
Dennis, Dave, 503
Depew, Chauncey, 23
depressions, *see* economy; Great Depression
DePriest, Oscar, 456
Derevyanko, Gen. K., 384
Dernburg, Bernhard, 153
de Sapio, Carmine, 259
Desert Land Act (1877), 5
Detroit, race riots in, 547
Dever, William E., 212
De Voto, Bernard, 184
Dewey, Adm. George, 73
    and Caribbean protection, 98
    and Metropolitan Club, 59
    and Philippines, 52, 56, 64, 66, 388
Dewey, John, 24, 459
Dewey, Thomas E., 228, 245, 255, *255*, 256, 415, *415*
De Witt, Gen. John, 350, 351
Díaz, Porfirio, 134
Dill, Sir John, 335
Dillinger, John, 252, 253, *253*
Dillon, C. Douglas, 536
Dineen, Msgr. Joseph P., *83*
diRenzo, Vince, 492
Disney, Walt, 440
diversity, 622
Dixiecrats, *see* American South

Dixon, Thomas, Jr., 192
Djilas, Milovan, 318
Dmytryk, Edward, 440
Doar, John, 462, *499*, 519, 581
Dobrynin, Anatoly, 493, 495, *495*, 592
Doe v. Bolton, 630
Dog Bear, Chief, *11*
Doheny, Edward, 198–99
Dole, Robert J., 591, 629
Dole, Stanford, 52
Dolliver, Jonathan, 117
Dominican Republic, 48, 137, 142
Donahue, Thomas, 655
Donaldson, Jesse, *422*
Dönitz, Adm. Karl, 330–31, 408, 409, *409*
Donnelly, Ignatius, 27, 29
Donovan, Gen. William J., 392
Donovan, Jean, 636
Doolittle, Gen. Jimmy, 323, 365
Dos Passos, John, 38, 179, 183, 286
Douglas, Helen, 625
Douglas, William O., 375, 391, 402, 443, 468, 630
Dreiser, Theodore, 441
Drew, Elizabeth, 614
Duarte, Jose Napoleon, 637
Dubinsky, David, 223, 276, *276*, 398, 413, 655
Dubofsky, Melvyn, 111, 119
Du Bois, W. E. B., *35*, 194, 352, 452, 464, 545
Duffy, Rev. Francis P., *82*, 83
Dukakis, Michael, 178, 617, 634, 648, *649*
Duke, Charles M., Jr., 555
Dulles, Allen, 397, 450, 451, 480, 486, 487, 508
Dulles, Eleanor, 397
Dulles, John Foster, *420*, 450, 478
    and Cold War, 396–99, 406, 416, 421, 524, 564
    and containment, 396–97
    and isolationism, 291, 294, 406
    and Korean war, 420
    and Middle East, 451
    and World War II, 294
Duncan, David Douglas, 426
Duong Van Minh, Gen., 490, *491*
du Pont family, 236, 276
Du Puy, Gen. William, 536
Durr, Clifford, 458, 472
Dutch East Indies, 306
Duvalier, François "Papa Doc," 137
Dylan, Bob, 464, 573
Dynamic Sociology (Ward), 25

Eagleburger, Lawrence, 587
Eaglehead, Mary, *263*
Eagle Star, Chief, *11*
Eagleton, Thomas, 571
East, P. D., 464
Eastland, James, 458
Ebert, Friedrich, *169*
Eccles, Marriner S., 226, 249
Eckford, Elizabeth, *475*
economics:
    Open Door school of, 51, 56, 399
    Reaganomics, 618–21, 627
    supply-side, 618–19
economy:

and aggregate demand, 224–25
depressions, 33, 38, 40, 108, 133; *see also* Great Depression
and elections, 568, 604, 612, 614, 621, 634, 651
financial panics, 30, 33, 133
global, 616
gold standard, 27, 30, 40, 46, 246–47
grounds for intervention in, 619
hope for future in, 660
and labor, 108–9
and New Deal, *see* New Deal
New Era prosperity, 182–86
prosperity, 434–37, *434*
S&L scandals, 642–43
silver standard, 28, 40, 46
stagflation, 604, 618, 620–21
and tax revolts, 620
and unemployment, *see* unemployment
and war, 53, 54, 225, 226, 286, 291, 314, 522
see also specific presidencies
Edelman, Marian Wright, 459
Eden, Anthony, 318, 524
Edison, Thomas, 89, 190, *191*, 229
education:
    and affirmative action, 622–23
    and busing, 622–23
    government spending for, 25
    and Great Society, 516–17
    and integration, 454, 456–59, 461, 468–69, 472, 474–75, 503, 617, 623
    magnet schools, 623
    school prayers and Bible readings, 629
    seg academies, 617, 623
    tax exemption of, 617, 623, 628
Edwards, William, *263*
EEOC (Equal Employment Opportunity Commission), 597
Egypt:
    and Camp David accords, 606
    slavery in, 51
    and terrorism, 640
    Yom Kippur War (1973), 582
Ehrlichman, John, 570, 572, 574–80, *577*
Einstein, Albert, 89, 95, 376
Einstein, Isadore, 211, *211*
Eisenhower, David, 316–17, 580
Eisenhower, Dwight D., 42, 239, 404, *428*, *432*, *439*, *451*
    and civil rights, 459, 461, 462, 468–70, 474–75
    and Cold War, 396–97, 443, 444, 448, 478, 480–81, 488, 496
    "Cross of Iron" speech of, 397
    and elections, 414, 430–31, *430*, *431*, 433, 483, 614, 620
    family of, *432*, *433*, 435
    and Korean War, 397, 431, 525
    and Latin America, 450, 486–87
    and military-industrial complex, 327
    presidency of, 406, 432–33, 446, 449–51, 452–81
    and space race, 476
    and United Nations, 405
    and Vietnam, 397, 524, 525, 528, 533
    and World War II, 316, 318, 321, 325, 334, 335, 342–43, *342*, 344
Eisenhower, Mamie Doud, *433*

elections:
    campaign funds in, 581, 648
    and conservatism, 616, 621–22
    direct, 28, 94
    and economy, 568, 604, 612, 614, 621, 634, 651
    fraudulent, 16, 128, 129, 581
    media campaigns in, 40, 95, 302, 303, 431, 483, 648, *648–49*, 660
    party control of, 28
    personal disclosures in, 31
    and Rainbow Coalition, 635
    secret ballot in, 16, 28
    Socialist party in, 128, 129, 178, 183
    the South and, 414, 456, 458, 474, 515, 551, 603, 621–22, 634
    steamroller tactics in, 42
    see also voting rights; *specific candidates*
Eliot, George Fielding, 286
Eliot, T. S., 184
Eller, Emmanuel, 212, *212*
Elliott, Pvt. George, Jr., 309
Ellis, Handy, 414
Ellison, Ralph, 194, 454
Ellsberg, Daniel, *534*, 572, 574–76, 579
El Salvador, 636–37
Elsey, George, 394
Emergency Banking Act (1933), 246
Emerson, Kenneth, 399
energy conservation, 604
England:
    moral authority of, 50
    social classes in, 76
    social programs in, 23, 86
    see also Great Britain
Ennis, Edward J., 351
Enola Gay, 324
Epstein, Jason, 618
ERA (Equal Rights Amendment), 597
Erdman Act (1898), 110
Ernst, Morris, 253
Ervin, Sam J., Jr., *569*, 572, 579
espionage:
    and Cold War, 402, 404, 416–17, 443–49, 446–51, 480–81, *480–81*, 492, 495, 584
    internal, 572–78
    U–2 planes, 480–81, *480–81*, 492, 495
    in World War II, 321, *343*, 350–51
    see also CIA
Espionage Act (1942), 294
Estonia, 299
Ethiopia, 287
ethnicity, 661
Ettor, "Smiling Joe," *109*, 119
Europe:
    aid to, 164, 217, 448
    anarchists in, 38
    Cold War in, 386–407
    and depression, 221–22
    imperialism of, 286
    and Kellogg-Briand Pact, 204
    and Latin America, 98, 99, 169
    liberalism in, 617
    lost generation in, 184
    Marshall Plan in, 388, 391, 395, 410
    NATO in, 386, 392, 395, 407, 433
    and Western Hemisphere, 142
    see also specific nations and wars
European Recovery Program (Marshall Plan), 410

Evans, Hiram, *193*, 268
Evans, Raymond, 336
Evans, Walker, 234
Evers, Medgar, 459, 464, 498, 502–3, *502–3*, 520
evolution:
  and Scopes trial, 196–97, 629
  and Social Darwinism, 22–25

Fahy, Charles, 351
Fair Employment Practices Committee (1941), 353
Fair Housing Act (1968), 463
Faisal, Emir, king of Iraq, *168*
Fall, Albert, 175, 198–99, *199*, 200
Falwell, Rev. Jerry, 628, *628*, 629
Farley, Jim, 398
Farmer, James, 459, 463, 500–501
farmers:
  cooperative movement of, 27, 28
  and Great Depression, 222, 223
  incomes of, xxi, 185
  and labor unions, 276, 563
  migrant, 108, *232*, 234, *234–35*, 276
  and New Deal, 247, 249, 290
  Okies, 234, *234–35*
  and Populist party, 27, 28, 290
  sharecroppers, 233, 234, 249, 259, 456
farming:
  and barbed wire, 4, 5
  crop-lien system of, 27
  dry-land, 4
  in Dust Bowl, *219*, 232–33, *232–33*, 249
  and Indian tribal culture, 7, 10, 12
  land available for, *140–41*, 248
  and tariffs, 185
  by tenants, 27, 234, 249
  and windmills, 4, *5*
Farney, Henry, 11
Farrakhan, Louis, 545, 635
fascism, 221, 252, 286, 287, 290–94, 320, 620
Fast Thunder, Chief, *11*
Faubus, Orville, 474–75
Faulkner, William, 286, 441, 459
FBI, 252–53, *252*, *253*
  and antiwar movement, 573
  and civil rights movement, 464, 519, 546
  and communism, 262, 399, 402, 440, 441, 449
  and Japanese-American internment, 350–51, *350–51*
  and Kennedy assassination, 508
  and Nixon administration, 573–75, 579, 581
  and unions, 252, 413
FDR, *see* Roosevelt, Franklin D.
Federal Children's Bureau, 92
Federal Reserve Act (1913), 133
Federal Reserve System, 133, 222, 224, 226, 271, 643
Federal Tort Claims Act (1946), 497
Federal Trade Commission (1914), 133
Feher, Andre, 559
Feifer, George, 367
Feinstein, Dianne, 600, 634
Feldstein, Andrew, 89
feminism, *see* women
Ferguson, Thomas, 621
Fermi, Enrico, 376, 448, 449

Ferraro, Geraldine, *634*, 651
fetus, and personhood, 630
Fields, W. C., 626
Fiji, 52
financial panics: (1893), 30, 33, 133; of (1895), 133; of (1907), 133
fingerprinting, 252
Finland, 299, 317, 391
Finlay, Carlos, 102
Firestone, Harvey, 190, *190*
First Lady, position of, 259
Fish, Hamilton, 288
Fitzgerald, F. Scott, 184, 393
Fitzwater, Marlin, 640
Fiume, 168, 171
Five-Power Naval Treaty (1921), 205
Flanders, Ralph, 446
Flattail, Philip, *263*
Flegenheimer, Arthur (Dutch Schultz), *254*, 255
Fletcher, Adm. Frank, 363
Florida, acquisition of, 56
"Flying Tigers," 365, 398
Flynn, Elizabeth Gurley "Rebel Girl," 119, *119*
Flynn, J. P., 78
Flynt, Larry, 642
FMLN (Farabundo Marti National Liberation Front), 636–37
Foch, Marshal Ferdinand, 162, 204
Fonda, Henry, 234
Fonda, Jane, 571
Foolish Elk, Chief, *10*
Forbes, Col. Charlie, 200
Forbes, Steve, 623
Ford, Betty, *591*
Ford, Edsel, 280
Ford, Gerald R., 580, 583, *590*, *591*, *593*, 651
  assassination attempts on, 601, *601*
  and civil rights, 462–63
  Nixon pardoned by, 566, 587, 603
  and Nixon's resignation, 587
  presidency of, 587, 590–601
  and Warren Commission, 508
Ford, Henry, 112–13, *191*, 246, *280*
  and the economy, 182, 222, 237
  My Life and Work by, 190
  prejudices of, 190, 280, 291
  and World War I, 144
  and World War II, 292, 294, 346
Ford, Sister Ita, 636
Ford, John, 234
Fordney-McCumber Act (1921), 185
Ford Foundation, 619
Ford Motor Company, 112, 346, 353
foreign policy:
  balance of power in, 104, 142, 285, 293, 318, 396
  and Cold War, *see* Cold War
  control of the sea in, 59
  detente in, 646–47
  and empire, 48–57, 59
  and idealism, 57, 633
  interactive quality of, 396
  internationalists in, 406–7
  and international law, 144–47
  intervention, *see* Latin America
  isolationism, 104, 282, 284–94, 299, 302, 316, 388, 397, 398–99, 623
  Lend-Lease, 304–5
  manifest destiny, 50, 52, 54, 57

Marshall Plan, 410
  missionary role for U.S. in, 397
  Monroe Doctrine, 98, 99, 148, 169, 286
  moral absolutes in, 394–95, 397, 400, 402, 428, 487, 532
  moralizing vs. greed in, 53
  neutrality, 285–88, 291–93, 396
  Open Door, 51, 56, 98, 99, 205
  preclusive imperialism in, 56
  and preemption, 56–57
  and pride, 56
  self-determination, 169, 317–18
  shuttle diplomacy, 582–83, 592–93
  tactics and timing in, 57
  territorial integrity, 306
  trade deficit, 623
  see also specific nations and wars
Foreman, John, 55
Forest Service, U.S., 96
"forgotten man, the," 23, 24, 40, 241, 268, 620–21
Forman, James, 546
Formosa, and World War II, 307
Forrestal, James V., 325, 327, *372*, *373*, 377, 393, 394, 531
Forsyth, Col. James W., 15
Fortas, Abe, *513*
France:
  aid to, 217
  atomic weapons of, 480
  colonies of, 50
  Communist party in, 388
  decline of, 660
  depression in, 221, 227
  and Five-Power Naval Treaty, 205
  and Holocaust, 289
  and Indochina, 306, 524–25, 532–33, 535
  and Kellogg-Briand Pact, 204
  and Panama Canal, 100, 101, 102
  and postwar economy, 410
  Socialist party in, 616
  Vichy government in, 289, 306, 320
  and World War I, 144, 151, 159, 160, 162, 168–69, 266
  and World War II, 282–93, 297, 299, 300, 317–18, 320, 340–41, 385
Franco, Gen. Francisco, 287, *287*
Frank, Hans, 408, 409
Frankensteen, Richard, 280, *280*, 281
Frankfurter, Felix, 176, 178, 248, 271, 416, 468, 599
Franz Ferdinand, Archduke, 151, *151*
Fraser, Adm. Sir Bruce, 384
Free, Lloyd A., 621
Frick, Henry Clay, 36, 93, 173
Frick, Wilhelm, 409
Friedan, Betty, 596–97, *596*, 599, *599*
Friedman, Milton, 618
Frisch, Otto, 376
Fritzsche, Hans, 408, 409
Fromme, Lynette "Squeaky," 601
frontier, *see* American West
Frost, Robert, 441
Frye, Will F., 54
Fuchida, Comm. Mitsuo, 309, 310, 363
Fuchikami, Tadao, 309
Fuchs, Klaus, 404
Fuerbringer, Otto, 490
Fulbright, J. William, 486, 489, 530
Fuller, Alvan, 178

Fulton, C. W., 96
fundamentalists, 628–29
Funk, Walther, 409
Funston, Gen. Frederick, 66–67

Gable, Clark, 315
Gadsden, William, 454, *455*
Gadsden Purchase, 56
Gagarin, Yuri, 476, *476*
Galamb, Joseph, 113
Galbraith, John Kenneth, 23, 133, 222, 223, 441, 533, 571
Galeani, Luigi, 179
Gall, Chief, 12, 13
Gallagher, Carole, 497
Gallagher, Lt. W. E., 363
Gallico, Paul, 281
Gambere, Giovanni, 178
Gambetta, Léon, 57
Gandhi, Mohandas K., 460, 499, 563
gangsters, *see* mobsters
Gardner, Ava, 440
Garfield, James A., 16
Garfield, John, 440
Garland, Charles, 456
Garland, Judy, 440
Garner, "Cactus" Jack, 241
Garn, Jake, 642
Garraty, John A., 221
Garrity, W. Arthur, 622
Garrow, David, 462, 630
Garvey, Marcus, 186, 194–95, *194–95*, 352
Gast, Gen. Philip, 608
Gates, Rev. Frederick T., 102, 124
Gates, John Warne "Bet-a-million," 78, 79
Gates, Merrill, 6
gay rights, 600–601
Geiger, Robert, 232
Gemayel, Amin, 632
Genda, Comm. Minoru, 362, 363
General Motors, 280, 281, 285, 346, 560
genetics, 123
George, Henry, 25, 27, 87, 124
George V, king of England, 148, *166*
Georgia, racial issues in, 456, 465
Gerard, James W., 151
Gergen, David, 626, *627*
Germany:
  anti-incumbency in, 616
  Berlin Airlift in, 395, *395*
  Berlin Wall in, 488–89, *488–89*, *654–55*
  concentration camps in, 264, 289, 321, 408, 409
  Deutschmark, 395
  division of, 316, 388, 395, 396–97, 403, 407, 423, 488–89, 525
  economy of, 171, 221, 226–27, 264
  Holocaust in, 284, 289, 316, 321, 408–9
  and imperialism, 56, 59
  and Kellogg-Briand Pact, 204
  Kristallnacht in, 289
  Nazis in, 264–65, *264–65*, 289, 291, 294, 316, 320, 408
  Nuremberg laws in, 265
  Nuremberg trials in, 298, 408–9, *408–9*
  postwar years in, 388–91, 393, 395, 404

Germany (continued)
  and Russo-Japanese War, 99
  social programs in, 23, 86
  and Soviet Union, 291, 298, 299
  Third Reich, 264–65
  threat of, 104
  U-boats of, 144, 146, 147, 148–49, 153,
    288, 299, 304, 305, *330–31*, 346
  and Venezuela, 98
  Weimar Republic of, 171, 227, 264,
    287
  and World War I, 142–49, 151–63,
    167–71, 264
  and World War II, 282–304, 306, 314,
    316–23, 328–44, 346–49, 354, 361,
    385
Geronimo, Chief, 12, 263
Ghorbanifar, Manucher, 638
Ghost Dance, 12, 15
ghost towns, 4
GI Bill of Rights (1944), 658
Gilded Age, The (Twain), 20
Gillam, 88
Ginsburg, Ruth Bader, 599, *599*
Giovannitti, Arturo, 119
Giraud, Henri, *354*
Girdler, Tom, 279
Gladstone, William, 130
Glass, Carter, 215, 221
Glazer, Nathan, 616
Glenn, John, 477, *477*, 642
Glidden, Joseph, 4
global economy, 616
G-men, 252; *see also* FBI
Godkin, E. L., 23, 55
Goebbels, Joseph, *265*, 371
Goebel, William, 68
Gold, Harry, 443
Goldman, Emma, 68, *93*
Goldman, Robert Justin, 111
Goldmark, Josephine, 92
gold rush, *46–47*
Goldsborough, Alan, 413
gold standard, 27, 30, 40, 46, *246–47*
Goldwater, Barry, 497, 515, 526, 535,
  614, 616, 625, 628
Gompers, Samuel, 55, 108, 109–10, *110*,
  111, 203, 223, 276
Goncharov, Sergei N., 400, 420
Gonzalez, Felipe, 616
Gonzalez, Virgilio, 578
Goodman, Andrew, 518, 623
Goodman, Lt. Robert O., Jr., *634–35*
Goodman, Walter, 440
Goodwin, Richard, 516
Goodwyn, Lawrence, 27
Gorbachev, Mikhail S., 623, 646–47,
  646, 647, 651, 655, 656
Gore, Thomas, 146
Gorgas, Maj. William Crawford, 102,
  103
Göring, Hermann, 294, 298, 321, 338,
  346, 408, *408, 409*
Gould, Stephen Jay, 24
government:
  authority of, 80
  as benefactor, 620
  business interests of, 129
  centralized, 273
  corruption in, 187, 198–201, 211
  credibility gap in, 529
  cutbacks in, 616, 619, 621

  demonization of, 617
  do-nothing, 271
  intervention by, 129, 222, 224–27,
    234, 237, 241, 246–49, 619–20
  limits on, 22, 272, 399
  meat inspection by, 95
  and Populist party, 28
  private initiatives vs., 616–17
  and progressives, 302
  public works, *see* New Deal
  social programs of, 23–25, 33, 86,
    109, 258, 616, 618, 621, 633; *see also*
    New Deal
Graham, Billy, 310, 629
Graham, Katharine, *568*, 576
Grand Canyon of the Colorado, 96
Grand Coulee Dam, 96, *246–47*
Grange, defeat of, 27
Grant, Ulysses S., 5, 16, 52, 224, 581
Gray, Spalding, 185
Gray, Edwin, 643
Grayson, Cary T., 132, 136, 173, 174
Great Britain:
  and Atlantic Charter (1940), 305
  and China, 398
  and Cold War, 392, 393, 402, 404,
    478
  decline of, 660
  depression in, 221, 226, 227
  empire of, xxiii, 50, 51, 56–57
  and Five-Power Naval Treaty, 205
  and Hay-Pauncefote Treaty, 100
  and Holocaust, 289
  and Korean war, 423
  and Middle East, 355
  and Mukden Incident, 267
  postwar years in, 388, 391, 394, 410
  Royal Air Force of, 300, 322–23, 334,
    338–39, 395
  Royal Navy of, 286
  and Russia, 164
  slavery abolished in, 50
  and World War I, 144–48, 151, 153,
    155, 156, 159, 160, 162, 168–69, 171,
    266
  and World War II, 282, 284–94, 297,
    299–300, *301*, 302, 304–5, 307, 309,
    314, 317–23, 338–43, 354–55, 385
Great Depression, 77, 218–47
  and democracy, 227
  dust storms and, *219*, 232–34, *232–33,*
    234–35
  and FDR, 224–25, *246–47*
  and financial industry, 222–23, 224,
    224, 226, 228
  and government engineering, 618
  and government spending, 225–26,
    227, 237, 239
  and Hoover, 218, 221–22, 224, 227,
    228, 236–37, 239
  and immigration, 289
  and intervention, 222, 224–27, 237,
    241, 246–47, 292
  speculation and, 220, 222, 223, 231
  suicides in, 228
  Wall Street crash and, 218, 221,
    222–24, 226, 228, 236, *237*
  and war, 221–22, 314
  and wealth distribution, 222, 223
  as worldwide, 221–22, 227
Great Northern Railroad, 38
Great Plains:

  drought in, 4, 10, 249
  and dry-land farming, 4
  Dust Bowl of, *219*, 232–34, *232–33,*
    249
  homesteaders in, 4, 232
  windmill introduced in, 4, *5*
Great Society, 516–17, 520, 526, 621
Greece, 318, 391, 392, 394
Greeley, Andrew, 88
Green, Hetty, *74*
Greenbackers, 133
Greenberg, Jack, 459
Greenglass, David and Ruth, 443
Greenshaw, Wayne, 621
Greenspan, Alan, 619, 643
Gregory, Dick, 459, 571
Greider, William, 133, 627
Grenada, 537, 632, 633
Grew, Joseph, 306–7, *306*, 309, 313, 377
Grey, Sir Edward, 143, 145–46, 147–48
Griffith, D. W., 192
Griggs v. Duke Power Company, 622
Grissom, Virgil "Gus," *476*, 477
Griswold, Estelle Trebert, 630
Gromyko, Andrei, 395, 478, 495, 497
Groves, Gen. Leslie, 324–26, 376, 377,
  449
Gruening, Ernest, 528, 531
Grunwald, Henry, 536
Guadalupe-Hidalgo, Treaty of, 56
Guam, annexation of, 50
Guardipee, Charlie, 262
Guatemala, 450, *450*
Guerrero, Manuel Amador, 101
Guilford, Howard, 187
Guillermoprieto, Alma, 637
Guinan, Texas, *210*
Gulf War (1991), 537, 633, 635, *650–51*
Guthrie, Woody, 227, 234

Haeberle, Ronald L., 559
Haig, Gen. Alexander M., Jr., 564, 579,
  582, 584, 586, 587, 627
Haiti:
  military occupation in, 137
  and preclusive imperialism, 56
  U.S. intervention in, 48, 137, 142, 537
Halberstam, David, 465, 490, 527, 531
Haldeman, H. R. "Bob," 568, *569*,
  570–72, 574–75, 577–79, *577*
Hale, Eugene, 55
Haley, Alex, 544
Hall, Fawn, *641*
Hall, Steve, 336
Halpin, Maria, 31
Halsey, Adm. Bill, 326, 364, *368*, 369
Halverson, Lt. Carl S., 395
Hamaguchi, Osachi, 267
Hamer, Fannie Lou, 459, 515
Hammett, Dashiell, 441
Hampton, Fred, 546
Hand, Learned, 403
Hand, Lloyd, *517*
Hanna, Mark, *43, 44, 45,* 71, 87
  and imperialism, 53, 56, 57
  and McKinley, 42, 43, 44, 45
  and Panama Canal, 100, 101
Hannegan, Robert, 375
Hanneken, Capt. H. H., 137
Hansen, Ib S., 62
Harburg, Yip, 241
Hardin, John Wesley, 198

Harding, Florence Mabel Kling, 189,
  189, 200, 201
Harding, Warren G., *181,* 188–89, *191*
  death of, 190, 201, 203
  and elections, 189, 243
  foreign policy of, 209
  and government scandals, 198–201,
    581
  presidency of, 178, 180, 182–86, 188–89,
    198–201, 221
Harkins, Gen. Paul, 490, *491*
Harlan, John Marshall, 34–35, 403
Harper, Fowler, 630
Harriman, Averell, 388, 389–90, 392,
  406, 407, *407*, 490, 497
Harriman, Edward H., 80
Harrington, Michael, 616
Harris, Isaac, 121
Harris, Lt. Randall, 335
Harrison, Benjamin, xiii, 16, *16,* 17, 59,
  80
  and American flag, 18, *18–19*
  and cattle war, 9
  and conservation, 96
  and Indian lands, 6, 10
Harrison, George, 222
Harrison, William Henry "Tippeca-
  noe," 16
Hart, Gary, 634, 648, *648,* 649
Hart, Capt. Liddell, 162
Hastie, William H., Jr., 457, 459
Hatanaka, Maj. Kenji, 383
Hatch, Orin, 648
Havoc, June, 440
Hawaii:
  and Japan, 56
  Pearl Harbor in, 206, 308–11, *310–11,*
    312
  protection of, 59
  U.S. acquisition of, 51, 52, 59
Hawgood, Johnson, 286
Hawley, Willis, *237*
Hay, John, 44, 54, *56,* 59, 101
Hayek, Friedrich A. von, 618
Hayer, Talmadge, 544
Hayes, Rutherford B., 16, 55
Hay-Pauncefote Treaty (1901), 100
Haywood, William "Big Bill," *109,* 111,
  119, 223, 276
Hayworth, Rita, 440
health:
  and addictions, 645
  government programs of, 25, 102
  and Great Society, 516–17
  Medicare/Medicaid, 516, 517, 620
Hearst, William Randolph, *60–61,* 68,
  94, 104, 106, 215, 241, 245, 271
Hearst press, 398, 440, 531
Heaven's Gate (movie), 9
Heckscher, August, 132
Heckt, Melvin, 367
Heclo, Hugo, 621
Helfrich, Adm. Conrad, 384
Helms, Jesse, 618
Helms, Richard, 493, 527, 533
Hemingway, Ernest, 184, 286, 441
Henderson, Col. Oran K., 558–59
Hennessey, David, 89
Henreid, Paul, 440
Henry, Aaron, 502
Hepburn, Katharine, 440
Heritage Foundation, 617

Herr, Michael, 539
Herrick, Capt. John J., 528
Hersey, John, 326, 547
Hersh, Seymour, 559, 584
Hershberg, James G., 326
Hess, Rudolf, 408, 409, *409*
Hewitt, Abram S., 86
Heyser, Maj. Richard S., 492
Highlander Folk School, 458
Hill, James J., 23, 33, 38, 80, 102
Hill, Joe, 118, *126*
Hill, Oliver, 459
Hillman, Sidney, 223, 276, 413
Himmelfarb, Gertrude, 616
Himmler, Heinrich, 321
Hinckley, John, Jr., 627
Hindenburg, Paul von, 147
Hine, E., 130
Hine, Lewis, 107
Hines, James J., 256, *257*
Hinton, Deane, *636*
Hirabayashi, Gordon, 351
Hirohito, emperor of Japan, *267*, 307,
    308–9, 325, 326–27, 361, 377, 383,
    384, *389*
Hispanics, and entitlement programs,
    619–20, 663
Hiss, Alger, 294, 402, 416–17, *416*, *417*
History of the American People, A
    (Wilson), 88–89
Hitchcock, Ethan Allen, 96
Hitler, Adolf, 24, *264*, 524
    anti-Semitism of, 190, 289
    and the economy, 171, 226, 264
    and World War II, 282–85, 287, 291,
        293, 294, 297–99, 306, 310, 317,
        320–22, 340, 343, 371, 376, 408
Hoar, George, 55, 56
Hobart, Garrett A., 50, 66
Hobson, John, 51
Ho Chi Minh, *169*, 402, 524–25,
    534–35
Hodgson, Godfrey, 543, 620
Hoffa, Jimmy, 276, 562, *562*, 563
Hoffman, Paul, 406
Hoffman, Rev. Buddy, 628
Hoffmann, Heinrich, 265
Hofstadter, Richard, 111, 133
Holland, *see* Netherlands
Hollingsworth, Gen. James F., 539
Holloway, Joe, 629
Hollow Horn Bear, Chief, *10*
Hollywood Ten, 440–41, *440–41*
Holmes, Jim, 492
Holmes, Oliver Wendell, 23, 186, 187,
    272, 273, 416, 630
Holocaust, 284, 289, 316, 321, 408–9
Holtzman, Elizabeth, 598
Homestead Act (1862), 5
homesteaders:
    and cattle war, 9
    on Great Plains, 4, 232
    on Indian lands, 7
    and lynching, 9
    and railroads, 16
Homestead strike (1892), 16, 36
Homma, Gen. Masaharu, 361
homosexuality, 600–601
Honecker, Erich, 654
Hong Kong, 530
Hood, James, 499
hookworm, 102

Hoover, Herbert, 22, 171, 201, *216*, *217*,
    236
    and aid to Europe, 164, 217, 448
    and bank closing, 246
    and China, 267, 399
    and elections, 214, 215, 241, 302, 614
    federal works projects of, 225
    and Great Depression, 218, 221–22,
        224, 227, 228, 236–37, 239
    and Indian lands, 262
    and isolationism, 286, 299
    and labor unions, 276
    presidency of, 216–17, 218–28,
        236–39, 246, 418
    on Prohibition, 245
    and World War II, 377
Hoover, J. Edgar, 252–53, *253*, 351, 402,
    441, 449
    and blacks, 194, 460, 462, 464
    and Bonus Army, 239
    and deportations, 176
    see also FBI
Hoover, Lou Henry, *216*
Hoover Dam, 96
Hope, Bob, *478*
Hopkins, Harry, *248*, 294, 305, *305*, 308,
    317, 321, 354, 390, 398
Hopkins, John P., 39
Horton, Willie, 648
House, Col. Edward, 132, 143, 148, 167,
    169, 175
House of Representatives, *see*
    Congress, U.S.
Houston, Charles Hamilton, 456, *456*,
    459
Howe, Louis, 243
Howells, William Dean, 55
How the Other Half Lives (Riis), 84–85
Hoxsey, Arch, 73
Hsu Yung-chang, Gen., 384
HUAC (House Un-American
    Activities Committee), 416–17,
    440–41, *440–41*, 445–47
Huang-Hua, 565
Huerta, Gen. Victoriano, 134, *134*, 136,
    138
Huff, Edward "Spider," 112
Hughes, Charles Evans, *187*, *272*
    and elections, 146
    as secretary of state, 205
    and Supreme Court, 187, 272–73,
        274–75, *274–75*, 458
Hughes, Howard, 440, 572
Hughes, John B., 350
Hughes, Robert, 658
Hughes, Sarah, 506
Hull, Cordell, 282, 284, 285, 289, 306–9,
    313, 318
Hull House, 92
human rights, 593
Humbard, Rex, 629
Humphrey, Hubert H., 414, 515, 517,
    529, 550–51, *551*
Hungary:
    freedom fighters in, 396–97, 403, 478
    self-determination of, 169, 391, 654
    and World War I, 144, 151
    and World War II, 316, 317, 318
Hunt, E. Howard, *568*, 569, 575, 577–79
Hunt, H. L., 515
Hunt, Nelson Bunker, 506
Hunter, Kim, 440

Hurley, Patrick, 239, 399, 418–19, *419*
Hurley, Ruby, 502
Hurst, E. W., 461
Hussein, Saddam, 168, 633, 635, 651
Huston, John, 440
Huston, Tom, 571–75
Hutton, Graham, 290
Hydrick, G. W. "Red," 498
hydrogen bomb, 406, 407, 448–49

Ickes, Harold, 225, 248, *248*, 262, 271,
    302, 306
idealism, moral force of, 389, 391
immigrants, xxi–xxii, 82, 84–87
    admission of, 6
    assimilation of, 90–91, *90*
    citizenship ceremony of, *659*
    and entitlement programs, 663
    illegal, 258, 661
    and land rush, 2–3
    and loyalty, 350
    mass deportations of, 176
    numbers of, 84
    and politics, 83, 86–87, 661, 663
    prejudice against, 88–89, *88–89*, 104,
        176, 178, 184, 185, 193, 290–91
    and Prohibition, 184
    restriction of, 28, 184, 289
    voting rights of, 84
    workers, 108
Immigration Reform Act (1965), 661
India:
    in British empire, 51
    and China, 398, 401
    famine in, 293
    and Korean war, 400, 401
    and World War II, 299, 385
Indian Reorganization Act (1934), 262
Indian Rights Association, 6
Indians (Native Americans), *262*, *263*,
    656–57
    absorption into society, 6, 7, 10, 12
    arrest/murder of, 12, 13, 15
    broken agreements with, 2, 5–7, 10,
        13
    citizenship for, 7
    communal ownership by, 6, 7
    compensation for, 262
    cowboys and, 4–7
    and entitlement programs, 619–20
    Ghost Dance of, 12, 15
    land taken from, 2–3, 6–7, 10, 13,
        262
    last Apache, *263*
    and Mohonk plan, 6
    reservations of, 5, 6, 10, 263
    self-government for, 262
    visit to Washington by, 6, *7*, 10, *10–11*
    and Wounded Knee, 12, *14–15*, 15,
        262, 657
Indian Territory, 2–3, *2–3*
individualism, 5, 22, 24, 25, 133
    vs. community responsibility, 619
    economic, 111
    and government intervention, 129,
        619–20
    and Populism, 28
    vs. property rights, 620
    and workers' rights, 109, 110, 124
Indochina, 299, 306–7, 399, 402, 524;
    see also Vietnam
Industrial Recovery Act (1933), 247

Influence of Sea Power Upon History,
    The (Mahan), 59
Ingalls, John J., 28
Inouye, Daniel, 351, *351*
Insull, Samuel, *229*
Intermediate Nuclear Forces Treaty
    (1987), 647
Internal Revenue Service (IRS), 133,
    251, 572, 581, 616, 617, 623, 628, 629
Internal Security Act (1946), 402
International Harvester Company, 78,
    80
International Labor Defense (ILD),
    261
International Ladies' Garment Workers
    Union (ILGWU), 120, 276
International Merchant Marine, 78
International Monetary Fund, 388
In the Spirit of Crazy Horse
    (Matthiessen), 15
Iowa, Hoover's birthplace in, *216*
Iran, 391, 392, 604, 607–9, *607*
Iran-Contra affair, 638–41
Iraq, 168, 609
Ireland, 27, 147
Irey, Elmer L., 251
Irish-Americans:
    and politics, 82, 86–87
    and prejudice, 88, 89
IRS, *see* Internal Revenue Service
Irwin, James J., 555
Isaacson, Walter, 395, 406
Isitt, Sir L. M., 384
Israel, 638, 640
    and Camp David accords, 606
    creation of, 168, 386, 398
    and Lebanon, 632
    Yom Kippur War (1973), 582, 604
Isthmian Canal Commission, 100, 102
Italians:
    as immigrants, 89, 90–91, 290
    lynchings of, 89
    money sent home by, 91
Italy:
    Communist party in, 388
    fascism in, 221
    and Fiume, 168, 171
    and Kellogg-Briand Pact, 204
    Monte Cassino in, *333*
    and terrorism, 640
    and World War I, 151, 155, *168*
    and World War II, 284, 297, 299, 314,
        317–18, 320, *333*, 385
Itaya, Comm. Shigeru, 309
Iwabuchi, Adm. Sanji, 361
Iwo Jima, *358–59*, *366–67*
IWW (Industrial Workers of the
    World), 108, 109, 110–11, 119, *126*,
    223, 276, 352

Jackson, Allan, 345
Jackson, Helen Hunt, 6
Jackson, Henry "Scoop," 592
Jackson, Rev. Jesse, 459, 514, 634–35, *635*
Jackson, Jimmy Lee, 520
Jackson, Mahalia, 464
Jackson, Robert H., 408, 468
Jacobson, Edward, 375
James, William, 24, 55
Japan:
    atomic bombs dropped on, 323–27,
        377–82, *380–81*, 383

Japan (continued)
   and Bataan Death March, *360–61,*
    361, 385
   and Bolshevism, 164
   and China, 104, 266–67, *266,* 284,
    292, 306–7, 360, 361, 400
   Double Leaf Society, 266
   and FDR's death, 371
   and Five-Power Naval Treaty, 205
   and Hawaii, 56
   immigration from, 266
   and Indochina, 306–7
   kamikaze pilots of, *366*
   and Korea, 104, 316, 420
   and Mukden Incident, 266–67
   and *Panay,* 292
   and Pearl Harbor, 206, 266, 291, 292,
    301, 308–13, *310–11*
   and Philippines, 104, 316
   postwar years in, 388–89, 391, 393
   rising power of, 52
   Russo-Japanese War, 48, 98–99,
    104
   samurai code of, 360–61
   surrender of, 383, *384–85,* 389
   and U.S. Navy, 104
   and U.S. trade, 307
   and Vietnam, 524
   and World War I, 147, 151, 266
   and World War II, 284–85, 291, 293,
    299, 306–13, 314, 316, 317, 320–27,
    352, 356–69, 377–85
Japanese-Americans, internment of,
   259, 350–51, *350–51,* 407, 468
Jarvis, Howard, 620
Jebb, Sir Gladwin, *423*
Jefferson, Thomas, 130, 511, 619
Jeffersonian liberalism, 22, 619
Jenner, William, 430, 445
Jessup, Philip, 399, 401
Jews:
   and education, 91
   Holocaust and, 284, 289, 316, 321,
    408–9
   immigrants, 89, 90, 259, 410, *411*
   and Kristallnacht, 289
   pogroms of, 91, 265
   prejudice against, 89, 184, 185, 187,
    193, 252, 265, 286, 289, 291, 294,
    616, 629, 635
   relief agencies formed by, 91
   and right-wing coalition, 616
Jim Crow laws, 35, 414, 454–58, 472,
   500
Jodl, Alfred, 408, 409, *409*
John Birch Society, 515
John Grass, Chief, *11*
John Paul II, Pope, 655
Johns, Barbara Rose, 468
Johns, Ralph, 498
Johns, Rev. Vernon, 459
Johnson, Frank, 521
Johnson, Guy, 457
Johnson, Hiram, 172, *172,* 173, 186, 189,
   271, 286, *288,* 290
Johnson, Gen. Hugh, *249,* 258, 286
Johnson, Lady Bird, *482,* 512, *512*
Johnson, Louis, *422–23*
Johnson, Lyndon B., *iv,* vi, 449, *482,*
   512, 513, 517, 525
   and civil rights, 461, 462, 465, 468,
    516–17, *516,* 519–21, 547

   and elections, 513, 514, 515, 526,
    550–51, 571, 625
   and Great Society, 516–17, 520, 526
   and Kennedy assassination, 506, 508
   legislative program of, viii, 133
   presidency of, 512–13, 581, 584
   resignation of, 550
   and space race, 476
   and Vietnam war, 407, 516, 517, 522,
    524–31, 533, 536, 542, 558, 566, 574
Johnson, Mordecai, 459
Johnson, Paul, 185, 226, 499, 519
Johnson, Tom, 87
Johnson County cattle war, 8–9, *8*
Jones, Curtis, 470
Jones, Mother Mary Harris, 109
Jones, Samuel M., 87
Jordan, Barbara, 598, *598*
Jordan, Hamilton, 608, 610
Jordan, James, 519
Joseph, Chief, 13
Josephson, Matthew, 28
Jungle, The (Sinclair), 95
jute trust, 27

Kahin, George, 533
Kaiser, Henry J., 321, 331, 346, 347, *347*
Kaltenbrunner, Ernst, 409
Kamenev, Lev, 164
Kane, Francis Fisher, 176
Kansas:
   cooperative movement in, 28
   guns in the state house in, *28–29*
Kanter, Robert, 280
Karam, Jimmy "the Flash," 474–75
Karamessines, Thomas, 584
Karliner family, 289, *289*
Karnow, Stanley, 66, 526
Katzenbach, Nicholas, 462, 521
Kaufman, Irving R., 443
Kawabe, Gen. Torashiro, 384
Kaye, Danny, 440
Kazel, Sister Dorothy, 636
Kazu, Toshikazu, 384
Kean, Rev. John J., 214
Keating, Charles, Jr., 642–43, *643*
Keating, Kenneth, 492
Kefauver, Estes, 485
Kelley, Florence, 92, *92*
Kelley, William "Pig Iron," 92
Kellis, Jim, 392
Kellogg-Briand Pact (1928), 204, 267
Kelly, Edward, 278–79
Kelly, Gene, 440
Keitel, Wilhelm, 408, 409, *409*
Kemp, Jack, 619, 623
Kennan, George, *393,* 406, 410, 448
   and Cold War, 392–94, 395, 401,
    402–3, 655
   and containment, 393–94, 395,
    402–3, 524
   and UN, 398
Kennedy, Caroline, *iv–v,* vi, 485
Kennedy, Edward M. "Ted," 483, 537,
   570, 571, 581, 610–11, 648
Kennedy, Jacqueline, *iv,* vi, 483, 484,
   485, 506, *510,* 511, 531
Kennedy, J. J., 280
Kennedy, John F., vi, viii, 291, 399,
   449, *482,* 483, 484, 485, *494, 506,*
   510, 511
   assassination of, 370, 506–9, 562, 581

   and Bay of Pigs, 486–87, 493
   and Berlin, 488–89
   and civil rights, 459, 461–62, 464,
    483, 499, 500, 503–5, 520
   and Cuban missile crisis, 407,
    492–95
   and elections, 483, 513
   presidency of, 396, 405, 461–62, 464,
    476, 484–97, 581, 646
   and space race, 476, 555
   and test-ban treaty, 496–97, *496*
   and Vietnam, 490, 524, 525, 527–28,
    533–34, 574
Kennedy, John F., Jr., *vi,* vi, 485
Kennedy, Joseph P., 241, 286, 294, 297,
   300, 483, 484
Kennedy, Paul, 650, 658
Kennedy, Robert F., 513, *516, 549,* 550
   assassination of, 548
   as attorney general, 447, 462,
    488–89, 500–501, 548, 562, 571, 581
   and Berlin, 489
   and civil rights, 462, 483, 500–501,
    548
   and Cuba, 493, 494, 495
   and espionage, 488, 493, 495
   and Vietnam, 527
Kenyatta, Charles, 544
Kenyatta, Jomo, 502
Keppler, Joseph, 16
Kerensky, Alexander, 165
Keyes, Evelyn, 440
Keynes, John Maynard, 171, 217,
   224–27, *225,* 618
Khan, Yahya, 564
Khmer Rouge, 557, 594
Khomeini, Ayatollah Ruhollah, 437,
   607, 611, 641
Khrushchev, Nikita:
   and Cold War, 396, 404, 478, 480–81,
    488–89, 492–97, 532, 646
   ouster of, 481
   Stalin denounced by, 403
   U.S. visits of, 478, *479, 492*
Khrushchev, Nina, *478*
Kido, Marquis, 383
Kilpatrick, James R., 280
Kimbell, Elmer, 465
Kim Il Sung, 399, 400, 420–21, 524
Kimmel, Adm. Husband, 308–9,
   312–13, *312,* 368
Kincaid, Adm. Thomas, 369
Kindelberger, Charles P., 222
King, Adm. Ernest J., 330–31, 335, 362,
   364, 368, *368,* 369
King, Clennon, 458
King, Coretta, 464, 483
King, Rev. Martin Luther, Jr., 458, *504,*
   628
   assassination of, 548, 549, 550, 581
   and civil rights movement, 459–61,
    464, 465, 469, 472–73, *473,* 483,
    498–99, 501, 502, 504–5, 520–21,
    545
   FBI and, 460
   holiday in honor of, 461
   influence of, 461, 520–21, 563, 635
   and March on Washington, 464,
    466, 469
   Nobel Peace Prize to, 460
   and nonviolent protest, 460,
    498–99, 505, 545

   and SCLC, 498, 499, 501, 520
   writings of, 473, 504, 505
Kipling, Rudyard, xv, 57, 132, 660, 663
Kirby, Rollin, 241
Kirkland, Lane, 655
Kirkpatrick, Jeane, 636, 646
Kissinger, Henry A., 104, 169, 395, 431,
   583, 651
   and Cambodia, 556–57
   and China, 564, 641
   and espionage, 573, 584
   and Nixon, 556–57, 568, 570,
    586–87
   Nobel Peace Prize awarded to, 582
   shuttle diplomacy of, 582–83,
    592–93
   and Vietnam, 530, 534, 536–37, 594
   and Watergate, 573–75, 580–81
   writings of, 318
Kissinger, Pvt. John R., 102, *103*
Kistakowsky, George, 376
Kitt, Eartha, 459
Klineberg, Otto, 457
Klinghoffer, Leon, 640
Kluger, Richard, 457
Knights of Labor, 108
Knopf, Alfred, 441
Knowland, William, 399
Knox, Frank, 313
Knox, Philander C., 80
Kohlberg, Alfred, 398
Kohler, Walter, 431
Kolchak, Adm. A. V., 164
Konoe, Fumimaro, 306–7, *307,* 383
Korea:
   and Cold War, 399, 400, 444
   division of (38th parallel), 400–401,
    420, 424–25, 427
   and Japan, 104, 316, 420
   and World War II, 316
Korean-American Treaty (1882), 104
Korean war, 395, 397, 400–402, 420–30,
   431, 444, 525, 528, 532, 566
Koster, Gen. Samuel, 559
Kotouc, Capt. Eugene, 558–59
Kotzebue, Albert L., 344–45
Kramer, Alvin, 308
Kristol, Irving, 616, 618
Krock, Arthur, 393
Krogh, Egil "Bud", Jr., 557, 575–76
Krug, Julius A., *372,* 373
Krulak, Gen. Victor, 530
Krupp, Alfred, 407
Kuhn, Fritz, 290
Ku Klux Klan, 26, 35, 185, 192, 197, 268,
   271, 460, 464, *467,* 504–5, 518–19
Kupke, Frederick L., 607
Kurusu, Saburo, 307, *308,* 309

labor, 106–27, 562
   blacks in unions, 194, 352, *352,* 353,
    454
   bureaucratic elite in, 620
   child labor, *106–7,* 110, 258
   children's crusade, 119
   collective bargaining of, 276
   and Communist threat, 176, 276,
    280, 655
   and Congress, 626
   and cycle of political action, 119
   deportations and, 111
   and the economy, 108–9

farm workers, 276, 563
and FBI, 252, 413
and Great Depression, 223
Homestead strike, 16, 36
legislation about, 28, 106, 108, 109, 110, 117, 120, 279
in mass production, 108
and muckrakers, 94
and New Deal, 36, 247, 249, 271, 276, 302, 352
open shop and, 110
and police brutality, 119, 124, 278–79, *278–79*
and property rights, 109, 115
Pullman strike, 38–39, 109
rights of, 23, 43, 106, 108, 120, 124, 133, 258
sit-down strikes of, 281
and Smith-Connally Act, 413
and Solidarity, 655
strikebreakers, *127*
labor *(continued)*
and strikes against government plants, 413
and strikes against public safety, 203, 626
SWOC picnic, 278–79
and Taft-Hartley Act, 414, 431
in trade unions, 24, 108, 120
Triangle fire, 120, *120–21*
unrest, 31, 36, 38–39, 106, 109, 110, 119, 120, 124, 126, 203, 413, 626
wages of, 106, 108, 109, 113, 115, 119, 349
and women, 119, 276, 349
worker's compensation, 106
and World War II, 314
Lacey, Robert, 280
Lacouture, Jean, 533
Ladd, Edwin, 95
Ladies' Home Journal, 94, 95
Lafayette, Bernard and Colia, 520
LaFeber, Walter, 51
Laffer, Arthur, 618–19
La Follette, Robert M., 110, 117, *117*, 183, 186
La Follette, Robert M., Jr., 271, *288*, 290
La Guardia, Fiorello, 186, 256, *256*, 259
Laird, Melvin R., 556
Lamb, William, 27
land, xvi–xvii, *140–41*
of farmers, 4, 27, 290
mineral and timber rights to, 96
monopolies of, 25
preservation of, 16, 96, 248, 517, 618
public, frauds of, 96
taken from Indians, 2–3, 6–7, 10, 13, 262
tenants on, 27, 234, 249
Landis, Kenesaw Mountain, 111
Landon, Alf, 271, 302
Land Revision Act (1891), 16
land rush, 2–3, *2–3*, 9, *9*
Lange, Dorothea, images by, *234–35*
Langer, William, 56
Lansdale, Edward, 490, 493
Lansing, Robert, 142, 143, 146, 167, 169, 174, 175
Laos, 524, 530, 533, 594
Lardner, Ring, 184
Lardner, Ring, Jr., 440
Lasky, Victor, 580

Last Hurrah, The (O'Connor), 82
Latin America:
Americans murdered in, 636–37, *636–37*
Bay of Pigs, 486–87
business in, 134, 136, 137
CIA in, 450, 486–87, 492–95, 584, 638
Cuban missile crisis, 492–95
dollar diplomacy in, 209
and Good Neighbor Policy, 137
immigration from, 661
and Iran-Contra affair, 638, 640–41
and Monroe Doctrine, 98, 99, 148, 169, 286
Panama Canal, 100–101, 114
political assassinations in, 636
and United Nations, 390
and U.S. imperialism, 54
U.S. intervention in, 48, 136, 137, 138–39, 142, *208*, 209, 450, 486–87, 537, 584, 633
see also specific nations
Lattimore, Owen, 445
Latvia, 299
Lauder, Estée, 447
Laurence, William L., 325
Lavelle, Msgr. Michael Joseph, *83*
Lawrence, Ernest, 376
Lawrence, Mass., strike, 119
Lawrence, Col. T. E., *168*
Lawson, James, 458, 459, 498–99
Lawson, John Howard, 440
Lazear, Jesse William, 102
League of Nations, 204, *204*
achievements necessary for success of, 147, 148
and collective security, 285, 287, 292
and communism, 285, 317
and Congress, 168–69, 172–73, 174, 175, 267
FDR and, 243, 265, 288, 355
and isolationism, 285–88, 290, 292, 388
and Versailles, 168–69, 173, 264
Wilson and, 147, 148, 164, 168–69, 171, 172–73, 174, 243, 288, 317, 355
Leahy, Adm. William, 325
Lease, Mary, 26
Lebanon, 537, 632–33, *632–33*, 634, 638, 640
Leclerc, Gen. Jacques, 384, 533
Le Duc Tho, 537
Lee, Rev. George, 503
Lee, Robert E., 360
Leech, Margaret, 44, 53
Le Hand, Missy, 246
Lehman, Herbert, 236
Leibowitz, Samuel, *260*, 261
LeMay, Gen. Curtis, 323, 324, 338, *338*, 481, 494
Lend-Lease Act (1940), 293, 294, 304–5, 365, 388
Lenin, V. I., 167
Lenroot, Irvine, 186
Leopold, Nathan, 197
Leo XIII, Pope, 114
Leslie, Lt. Maxwell F., 363
Lesseps, Ferdinand de, 100
Leuchtenberg, William E., 292
Levison, Stanley, 462
Levitt, Bill, 437, *437*

Levittown, *436–37*, 437
Lewelling, Lorenzo D., 28, 29
Lewis, Anthony, 463
Lewis, Fulton, Jr., 398
Lewis, John L., 223, 252, 276, *276*, 286, 289, 294, *412*, 413
Lewis, John W., 400, 420, 459, 464, 520
Lewis, Pearlene, 498
Lewis, Sinclair, 180, 184, 185, 441
liberalism:
and Democratic party, 628
and identity politics, 622
Jeffersonian, 22, 619
meanings of word, 617
paradoxes of, 619
prevalence of, 621
in Reagan revolution, 614, 617, 619, 628
Liddy, G. Gordon, 575, 577–78
Liebling, A. J., 441
life, beginning of, 630
Lilienthal, David, *248*, 403, 448
Liliuokalani, queen of Hawaii, 52, 59
Lincoln, Abraham, 18, 132, 286, 316, 320, 353, 370, 458
Lind, Michael, 629
Lindbergh, Charles A., 286, 291, 294, *295*, 406
Linderfelt, Karl, 124
Lindner, Carl, 642
Lindsay, John V., 571
Lingo, Col. Al, 520
Lippmann, Walter:
and civil rights, 454
and Cold War, 390, 391, 392, 393, 495
on FDR, 274
isolationism of, 291
and Polk inquiry, 392
on UN, 390
and Vietnam war, 532, 533
on Wilson, 132, 147, 288
and xenophobia, 184, 350
Lips, Chief, *10*
Lithuania, 299
Little, Frank, 108
Little Bighorn, battle of, 10, 12, 15
Little Rock, Arkansas, racial issues in, 461, 474–75, *474–75*
Li Zhisui, 400
Lloyd George, David, 168–69, *168*, 171
Locarno Pact (1925), 282
Lockard, Pvt. Joseph, 309
Locke, Alain, 194
Lodge, Henry Cabot, 16, 54, 59, 88, 149, 172–73, *173*, 175
Lodge, Henry Cabot, Jr., *423*, 485, 490, *491*, 536
Lodge, Henry Cabot III, 515
Loeb, Richard, 197
Loewe Company, 109
Lombard, Carole, 315
Long, Breckenridge, 289
Long, Huey P., 239, 252, 268, *268*, *269*, 271, 581
Long, John, 73
Longworth, Alice Roosevelt, 200, 291, 302
Lon Nol, Gen., 556
Looby, Alexander, 499
Los Angeles, Watts riots in, 547
lost generation, 184
Louisiana:

Long in, 268
racial issues in, 456, 463
Louisiana Purchase, 56
Louis, Joe, 321
Lovestone, Jay, 655
Lovett, Robert, 406, *406*, 407, 410
Low, Seth, 87
Lowden, Frank, 189
Lowell, A. Lawrence, 178
Loy, Myrna, 440
Luce, Clare Booth, 398
Luce, Henry, xiv, 388, 398, 531
Luciano, Charles "Lucky," 255, 256
Lucy, Autherine, 453
Ludden, Raymond, 399
Ludlow, Colo., mine massacre in, 124
Lukas, J. Anthony, 622
Luks, George, 42–43
Lumumba, Patrice, 486, 584
Lundahl, Arthur, 492
Lundeed, Ernest, 288
Lusitania, 145, 148, *152*, 153, 155
Lydon, Gene, 492

McAdoo, William G., 133, 180, 215, 241, 245
MacArthur, Gen. Arthur, 67, 114
MacArthur, Gen. Douglas, *239*, 368, 424–30, *429*
and Bonus Army, 239, 418
and China Lobby, 398, 402
and FDR, 239
and Hoover, 239, 418
and Japanese surrender, 383, 384, *385*, 389, *389*
and Korean War, 399, 401–2, 424–27, *427*, 428
and Truman, 401–2, 424, 428
Truman's firing of, 428
and World War II, 239, 313, 321, 324, 359, 360, *360*
McCain, Franklin, 498
McCain, John, 642
McCarran, Pat, 402
McCarthy, Eugene, 537, 550
McCarthy, Joseph, 402, 406, 418, 430–31, 443, 444–47, *444*, *447*, 449, 485, 617, 618
McCarthyism, 248, 402–3, 431, 444–47, 458, 625, 630
McCloy, John J., 325, 350, 351, 377, 406, 407, *407*, 449, 508
McCloy, Ens. R. C., 309
McClure, S. S., 94
McClure's, 94
McCluskey, Henry J., Jr., 630
McClusky, Lt. Clarence W., 363
McCone, John, 492, 494, 497
McCord, James, *568*, 578
McCormack, John W., 373
McCormick, Cyrus, 113
McCormick, Joseph Medill, 172
McCormick, Col. Robert, 187, *187*
McCormick, Vance, *217*
McCormick press, 398
McCorvey, Norma, 630
McCullough, David, 101
MacDonald, Jeanette, *244–45*
MacDonald, Ramsay, 221
McDuffie, Irvin, 246
McEnery, Samuel, 57
McFarlane, Robert, 632, 638, 640, *641*

McGill, Ralph, 459, 464
McGillycuddy, Valentine, 12
McGovern, George, 537, 550, *551*, 568, 571, 614, 620, 628
McIntosh, Katherine, *658*
McIntyre, Marvin, 246
Mack, Connie, 236
McKenna, Mike "Hinky Dink," 87
McKinley, William, *42–43, 44, 45, 52,* 61, 129
   assassination of, 68, *68, 69,* 93
   and Civil War, 16
   and conservation, 96
   and elections, 42–43, 45
   and imperialism, 53, 54, 55, 56–57
   presidency of, 42, 44–45, 48–57, 56, 80
   and Spanish-American War, 62, 66, 67
   and tariffs, 20, 42
McLaughlin, James, 12
McLaurin, John, 57
McLean, Donald, 404
MacLeish, Archibald, 300
McLemore, Jeff, 146
McLuhan, Marshall, 660
McMahon, Brien, 448–49
Macmillan, Harold, 496–97
McNair, Denise, 464
McNamara, Robert S., 406, 486, 490–94, *494,* 527–29, 531–36, *531,* 570
McNamee, Francis L., *372,* 373
McNaughton, John, 529, 530
McNeil, Joseph, 498
McQuade, Rev. Bernard, *83*
McQueen, Steve, 571
McReynolds, James C., 187, 273, 274, 275
McShane, James, 499
Macune, Charles W., 27, 28
Mad Bear, Chief, *11*
Madero, Francisco I., 134, *134,* 136
Mafia, *see* mobsters
Magnuson, Warren, 614, 628
Magruder, Jeb, 577–78
Mahan, Adm. Alfred Thayer, 54, *58,* 59, 104
Mailer, Norman, 447
Maine, 53, 62–63, *62–63*
Maine, Sir Henry, 560
Maitland, Frederic, 285
Malaya, 299
Malcolm X, 194, 195, 460, 464, 502, 544–45, *544*
Malik, Jacob, 423
Malinovsky, Rodion, 495
Malone, Michael, 251
Malone, Vivian, 499
Malthus, Thomas Robert, 23
Maltz, Albert, 440
Manchester, William, 334
Manchuria, 266–67, 355, 360, 383, 401, 419, 428
Mangas Colorado (Apache leader), 12
Manhattan Project, 324–26, 376, 448
Mann, Floyd, 500–501
Mann, Thomas, 441
Mansfield, Mike, 489, 528–29
Mao Zedong, 397, 399–402, 418, *418–19,* 420–21, 524, 564
March, William, 286

March of Dimes, 241
Marcy, Helen, 261
Margold, Nathan Ross, 456
Marine Corps, U.S.:
   blacks in, 352–53
   in Grenada, 633
   in Korean war, *424–25, 426, 427, 427*
   in Lebanon, 632–33, *632–33*
   in World War II, 366–67, *366–67*
   see also Vietnam war
market forces, and supply-side theory, 618–19
marketplace, competition of, 23
Markham, Edwin, 108
Marshall, Alfred, 23
Marshall, Burke, 462, 505
Marshall, George C., *335, 398, 410*
   as army chief of staff, 305, 312, 313, 335
   and atomic bomb, 325, 326
   and Cold War, 394, 401, 402, 419, 430, 445
   Eisenhower and, 430–31
   and Korean war, 401, 428
   and Marshall Plan, 410
   and Pearl Harbor, 309, 312, 313
   as secretary of defense, 401
   as secretary of state, 335, 399
   and Truman Doctrine, 394
   and World War I, 335
   and World War II, 309, 312, 313, 318, 320, 321, 323, 325, 326, 331, 335
Marshall, Thomas R., 174
Marshall, Thurgood, *453,* 457, 459, 468–69
Marshall Plan, 388, 391, 395, 406, 407, 410
Marsui, Iwane, 361
Martin, Graham A., 594
Martin, Lt. Harry L., 352
Martin, Joseph W., Jr., 373, 428
Martin, Louis, 462
Martinez, Eugenio, 578
Marty, Martin E., 629
Marx, Karl, 109
Marxism, 316, 636
Masaryk, Jan, 410
Mashbir, Col. Sidney, 384
Matlock, Jack, Jr., 656
Matsuoka, Yosuke, 299, *299*
Matthews, J. B., 398
Matthiessen, Peter, 15
Mauldin, Bill, *334, 441*
mavericks, 8
Mayer, Louis B., 440
Mayo, Adm. Henry T., 136
Meany, George, 276, 655
Meat Inspection Act (1906), 95
media:
   and city politics, 85–86
   and civil rights, 454, 460, 462, 463, 464–65, 520
   and Cold War, 398, 403, 420, 444, 446, 584
   and the Constitution, 187
   and election campaigns, 40, 95, 302, 303, 431, 483, 648, *648–49,* 660
   and FDR, *270,* 274
   financial experts in, 231
   and gay rights, 601
   and hostages, 607
   and imperialism, 53, 55, 60

and isolationism, 288
   and labor unrest, 38, 39, 119, 280
   and Latin America, 486, 637
   muckrakers, 94, *94,* 95, 187, 261, 560
   and Nixon, 570
   press briefing, 660, *661*
   propaganda in, 325–26, 350, 353, 621, 636–37, 640
   public officials vilified by, 68, 249, 259, 271, 303, 305, 383, 635
   and Reagan, 627
   and Scopes trial, 196–97
   and Spanish-American War, 60, 62, 73
   technology and, 217
   televangelists, 617, 628, 629
   and Vietnam, 465, 490, 528, 530, 531, 535–36, 559
   and World War II, 300, 325, 350
   yellow journalism, 60
Medicare and Medicaid, 516, 517, 620
medicine:
   diseases in cities, 84
   hookworm, 102
   yellow fever, 102, *103*
Medina, Capt. Ernest, 558–59
Meese, Edwin 3rd, *626,* 627, 640
Mei-ling Soong (Madame Chiang), *398*
Meir, Golda, 583
Meiselas, Susan, 637
Mellon, Andrew W., 173, *223,* 224
Melton, Clinton, 465
Mencken, H. L., 184, 196, 215, 236
Mercer, Lucy, 243, 370–71
Meredith, James, 454, *455, 499*
Meriam, Lewis, 262
Merriam, Frank "Old Baldy," 95
Merwin, H. C., 77
Merz, Charles, 185
metals, production of, 4
Mexico:
   immigrants from, 661, 663
   and U.S. foreign policy, 134, *134, 135,* 136–39, 142, 209
   and World War I, 147, 149
middle class, 620–21
Middle East:
   and Camp David accords, 606, *606*
   Gulf War in, 537, 633, 635, *650–51*
   hostages in, 607–9, *607,* 635, 638, 640
   Iran-Contra affair, 638, 640–41
   Iran-Iraq war, 609
   oil in, 355, 391, 451, 604, 607
   and shuttle diplomacy, 582–83
   terrorists from, 640
   Yom Kippur War (1973), 582, 604
   see also specific nations
Mies, Ludwig von, 618
Milam, J. W., 470, *470*
Milburn, John G., *68*
Miles, Joshua W., 133
Miles, Gen. Nelson, 11, 12, 15, 64
military-industrial complex, 327, 395–96, 403, 476, 478, 480, 496
Milken, Michael, 642, *643*
Milk, Harvey, 600–601, *600*
Miller, Arthur (professor), 569
Millett, Kate, 596
Millis, Walter, 286
Mills, C. Wright, 533
Mills, Michelson, 236

minerals and mining, 4, *106–7*
   in Mexico, 134
   and strikes, 80, 109, 124, 413
minimum wage legislation, 92, 258, 275
minority groups, 619–20
Mississippi, racial issues in, 456, 463, 464, 470, 502–3, 623
Mitchell, Arthur W., 456
Mitchell, Charles, 228
Mitchell, Edgar D., 555
Mitchell, Greg, 95
Mitchell, John N., 80, *567, 569,* 572, 575–79, *576*
Mitchell, Martha, 569
Mitchell, Gen. William, 206–7, *207*
Mitchell, William D. (attorney general), *272,* 273
Mitgang, Herbert, 441
Mithelstadt, Jacob, family of, 91
Mitterrand, François, 616
mobsters, 187, 212–13, 245, *250,* 251–56, *254, 255, 257,* 276
Mohonk plan, 6
Mohr, Charley, 490
Molotov, Vyacheslav, 285, 354, 389, 390, 524
Mommsen, Theodor, 59
Moncada, José Maria, 209
Mondale, Walter F., 571, 591, 603, 611, 634, 651
money:
   as commodity, 27
   as free speech, 660
money system, 27, 28, 40, 133, 618
monopolies, 20–21, 24, 25, 94
   and prices, 27
   and Sherman Anti-Trust Act, 39, 80
Monroe, James, 275
Monroe, Marilyn, 485
Monroe Doctrine, 98, 99, 148, 169, 286
Montagne, Elizabeth, 607
Montana, metals and mining in, 4
Montgomery, Alabama, racial issues in, 456, 460, 463, 472–73
Montgomery, Bernard, 342–43, *342*
Montgomery, Olen, *260,* 261
Montojo, Adm. Patricio, 64
Moody, Ann, 498
Moody, William Vaughn, 55
Moon, space walks on, 554–55, *554, 555*
Moore, Amzie, 459, 502
Moore, Fred, 179
Moore, Sara Jane, 601
Moore-Cosgrove, Col. L., 384
Moorer, Adm. Thomas, 573
Moral Majority, 623, 628–29
Moran, Bugs, 212
Moran, John J., 102
Morefield, Richard, 607
Morgan, J. P., 78, *79,* 80, 101
   as banker's banker, 133, 228
   and Great Depression, 228, 231
   international investments of, 143
   and world wars, 288, *294*
Morgenthau, Henry, 225, 226, 265, 289, *373*
Morgenthau, Robert, 447, 571
Mori, Gen. Takeshi, 383
Morison, George S., 101
Morley, John, 131
Morocco, U.S. warships to, 104
Morris, Edmund, 72

Morris, Jan, 50
Morrison, Norman R., 490, 531
Morrow, Dwight, 207
Morse, Wayne, 431, 528, 531
Mosaddeq, Mohammad, 451, *451*
Moscone, George, 600–601
Moses, Robert (civil rights), 459, 461, *461*, 503
Moses, Robert (development), 438, *438–39*
Moss, Annie Lee, 446
Mostel, Zero, 440
Motley, Constance Baker, 459
Mouscoundis, Maj. Nicholas, 392
movies:
    antiwar themes in, 286
    and HUAC, 440–41
    patriotic, 302
    propaganda in, 95
Moynihan, Daniel Patrick, 82, 87, 616
muckrakers, 94, *94*, 95, 187, 261, 560
Mudd, Roger, 551
Muhammad, Elijah, 545
Muhammad Ali, 459, *545*
Muir, John, 96, *97*
Muirhead, John, 352
Mukden Incident, 266–67
Muller v. Oregon, 92
multiculturalism, 622
Mumford, Lewis, 437
Munro, Douglas A., 336
Munsey's, 94
Murdoch, Rupert, 447
Murphy, Audie L., 337
Murphy, Charles Francis, 87
Murphy, Frank, 281
Murray, Philip, 279, 413
Murrow, Edward R., 300, *300*, 392, 403, 446
Muskie, Edmund, *568*
Mussolini, Benito, 204, 265, 287, 294, 297, 299
Mutual Films, 138
Myrdal, Gunnar, *An American Dilemma*, 457

NAACP (National Association for the Advancement of Colored People), 35, 92, 122, 194, 353, 403, 456, 457, 459, 468, 472–73, 502–3
Nabritt, James, 459
Nader, Ralph, 560, *560*
Nagai, Gen. Yatsuji, 384
Nagumo, Adm. Chuichi, 308, 362–63
NAM (National Association of Manufacturers), 110
Namath, Joe, 571
Napoleon Bonaparte, Emperor, 50
NASA (National Aeronautics and Space Agency), 476, 477, 513
Nash, Diane (Bevel), 459, 499, 500, 505, 520
Nast, Thomas, 27, 85
Nation, Carry A., 211
National Farmers' Alliance, 27, 28
national forests, preservation of, 16, 618
National Industrial Recovery Act (1933), 276
National Labor Relations Act (1935), 120

National Labor Relations Board, 279, 280
National Municipal League, 84
national park system, 248
National Reclamation Act (1902), 96
National Recovery Administration (NRA), 247, 249, 272–73
National Review, 617
National Urban League, 456
Nation of Islam, 460, 552–53
Native Americans, *see* Indians
nativism, 88–89, *88–89*, 289
NATO, 386, 392, 395, 407, 433
Navy, U.S.:
    around-the-world trip of, 104
    segregation in, 352–53
    and Spanish-American War, 64
    and Vietnam war, 528
    women's auxiliary of, 348
    and World War II, 341, 347, 352, 362–63, *362–63*, 364–65, 368–69
Nazis, *see* Germany
Near, Jay, 187
Near v. Minnesota, 187
Nebraska:
    cattle war in, 8–9, *8*
    farmland in, *140–41*
Negroes, *see* blacks
Nelson, Baby Face, 253
Nelson, Donald, 305
Nelson, Gaylord, 614, 628
Nelson, Knute, 51
neoconservatives, 616
Ness, Eliot, 251, *251*
nesters, 5
Netherlands:
    colonies of, 50
    and Holocaust, 289
    and World War I, 143, 144
    and World War II, 307, 317
Neurath, Constantin von, 409
Neutrality Acts (1935–37), 282, 285–88, 291–93, 299
Newark, New Jersey, 547
New Deal, 246–49, 619
    and big government, 302
    and business, 247, 249, 271, 276
    Congress and, 246–47, 293
    corruption curbed by, 256
    and deficit spending, 225–26, 246
    and elections, 241, 291, 302
    and farmers, 247, 249, 290
    FDR and, *see* Roosevelt, Franklin D.
    and government intervention, 224–25, 234, 241, 248
    Hoover and, 221, 224, 246
    Hopkins and, 305
    idealism and, 40, 302, 413
    and Keynesian economics, 225–26, 227
    and McCarthyism, 402
    repudiation of, 621
    Second, 271, 272
    and segregation, 454
    and Supreme Court, 272–75, 468
    and unemployment, 221, 225–26, 302
    and unions, 36, 247, 249, 271, 276, 302, 352
Newell, Frederick H., 96
New Era, 182–86, 220, 223
Newhouse, Si, Jr., 447

Newman, John M., 527
Newman, Paul, 571
New Mexico, 56
New Panama Canal Company, 100, 101
newspapers, *see* media
Newton, Huey, 546, *546*
New York City:
    Catholic Church in, 83
    drug wars in, *644–45*, 645
    Empire State Building in, 220
    Harlem in, 256
    Henry Street settlement in, 92
    La Guardia in, 256, *256*
    Moses in, 438, *438–39*
    parades in, *xi, xii–xiii*, 429, 653
    Statue of Liberty in, 653
    Tammany Hall in, *see* Tammany Hall
    Tweed Ring in, *85*
    Union Square in, *652–53*
New York Stock Exchange, 78, 94
New York Times, The, 176, 574, 575
New Zealand, and World War II, 385
Ngo Dinh Diem, 490, *491*, 525, 533
Ngo Dinh Nhu, 490
Nguyen Huu Co, Gen., *522–23*
Nguyen Van Thieu, 537, 594
Niagara movement, 35
Nicaragua:
    and canal, 100, 101
    and Iran-Contra affair, 636, 638
    U.S. intervention in, 48, 137, 142, *208*, 209, 537, 636
Nicholas II, czar of Russia, *164–65*, 355
Nicolson, Harold, 168
Niebuhr, Reinhold, 459–60
Niles, David K., 271
Nimitz, Adm. Chester W., 321, 359, 362, 363, 364, 368, *368*, 369, 384
Nine-Power Act (1922), 267
Nininger City, Minnesota, 27
Nitze, Paul, 321, 394, 399, 406, *406*, 487, 533
Nixon, Rev. E. D., 459, 472
Nixon, Patricia Ryan, 431, 483, *553*, 586, 587
Nixon, Richard M., 95, 226, *416, 483, 552, 553, 583*, 592
    and arms limitation, 582–83
    in China, 564–65, *564–65*, 575
    and civil rights, 462–63
    and Cold War, 416–17, 478, *479*, 584
    and dirty tricks, 571, 579
    and elections, 399, 430, *431*, 483, 551, 568, 570, 625, 648
    enemies list of, 571–72
    Ford's pardon of, 587
    and HUAC, *440*
    presidency of, 552–67, 568–89
    resignation of, 579, 586–87, *587*, 594
    and tapes, 569, 574–77, 579, 581, 587
    and Vietnam war, 522, 524, 526, 528, 530, 534–37, 542, 556–59, 594
    and Watergate, 566–81
Nomura, Adm. Kichisaburo, 306, 307, *308*, 309
Noriega, Gen. Manuel, 633
Norman, Memphis, 498
Norris, Clarence, *260*, 261
Norris, George W., 184, 186, *246*, 271, 290

Newman, John M., 527
North, Oliver L., 638–41, *639*
North Africa, in World War II, 317, 320
Northern Pacific Railroad, 80
Northern Securities, 80
North Korea, *see* Korea; Korean war
NOW (National Organization for Women), 597, 599
NRA (National Recovery Administration), 247, 249, 272–73
nuclear warfare:
    and detente, 646–47
    and SALT, 582–83, 592–93, 646–47, 656
    and SDI, 646–47
    threat of, 325, 327, 403, 448–49, 515, 535
Nunn, Sam, 648
Nuremberg trials, 298, 408–9, *408–9*
Nye, Gerald, 186, 288, 290, 291–92, 294

OAS (Organization of American States), 493
O'Bannion, Dion, 212
Obin, Philone, 137
O'Brien, Lawrence, 572
O'Brien, Pat, 83
Ochs, Adolph, 113
O'Connell, Edward, 567
O'Connor, Edwin, 82
O'Connor, James, 269
O'Connor, Sandra Day, 628
O'Dell, Jack, 462
Odets, Clifford, 440
O'Donnell, Kenneth, 506
O'Donnell, Michael Davis, 540
Odum, Howard Washington, 457
oil:
    embargo on, 604
    and global economy, 616
    and market forces, 618
    in Mexico, 134
    in Middle East, 355, 391, 451, 604, 607
    Standard Oil, 74, 78, 80, 92, 124, *125*
Okinawa, 366–67, 377, 383
Oklahoma:
    Indian land taken in, 262
    land rush into, 2–3, *2–3, 9, 9*
    population in, 3
    railroads in, 4
    statehood for, 3
Okumura, Katzuo, 309
Olds, Ransom Eli, 112
Oliphant, Mark, 376
Olney, Richard, *30*, 31, 33, 39
Olsen, George, 541, *541*
Olsen, Greg, 558
Olson, Floyd, 187
Olympic Games, (1936), 282
O'Neill, Tip, 611
OPEC (Organization of Petroleum Exporting Countries), 604
Open Door policy, 51, 56, 98, 99, 205
Oppenheimer, J. Robert, 321, 376, *376*, 402, 448–49, *449*
Oppenheimer, Kitty, 449
Organization of American States (OAS), 493, 633
Origin of Species (Darwin), 22, 124, 197
Orlando, Vittorio, *168*
Ornitz, Samuel, 440
Ortega, Daniel, 636

OSS (Office of Strategic Services), 392, 524–25
Oswald, Lee Harvey, 506, 508–9, *508, 509*
Otis, Gen. Elwell Stephen, 66
Owen, Chandler, 352
Owens, Jesse, 282

Page, Benjamin I., 621
Page, Walter Hines, 102, 143
Pahlavi, Shah Mohammad Reza, 451, *451,* 604, 607, 609
Painter, Nell Irvin, 92
Palestine:
    British control of, 168
    and Israel, 168, 398
    PLF terrorists, 640
    PLO guerrillas, 632
    and Saudi Arabia, 355
Palmer, A. Mitchell, 176, *177*
Panama, 537, 633
Panama Canal:
    construction of, 100–101, *100–101,* 114
    protection of, 59, 142, 392
    and yellow fever, 102
Panama Canal Zone, 50
Panikkar, K. M., 401
Papen, Franz von, 408, 409, *409*
parallels (1890–1990), xx
Parker, Lt. John, 64
Parks, Rosa, 261, 458, 472, *472*
Parnell, Charles, 27
Parr, Jerry, 627
Paterson, N.J., strike, 119
Patterson, Lt. F. N., *353*
Patterson, Haywood, *260,* 261
Patterson, James T., 86, 220
Patterson, John, 500–501, 514
Patton, Gen. George S., Jr., 239, 334, *334,* 343, 491, 556
Paul, Alice, 122–23, *122*
Paul-Boncour, Joseph, 221
Payne, Sereno E., 117
Peabody, Endicott, 242
Peale, Rev. Norman Vincent, 483
Pearl Harbor, 52, 206, 266, 291–94, 301, 308–13, *310–11,* 350, 364, 384
Peck, Gregory, 440, 571
Peck, Jim, 500
Peers, Gen. William, 559
Pegler, Westbrook, 303, 350
Peierls, Rudolf, 376
Pellaton, Thomas, 541, *541*
Pendergast, Tom, *375*
Penkovsky, Col. Oleg, 495
Pennsylvania, steel industry in, *36–37*
Pentagon Papers, 534, 574–76
Peralte, Charlemagne Massena, *137*
Percival, Gen. Sir Arthur, 384
Peretz, Martin, 616
Perkins, Frances, 258–59, *258,* 272, 276, *372,* 373
Perkins, George W., 133
Perot, Ross, 623
Perrett, Geoffrey, 184
Perry, Comm. Matthew, 384
Perry, Col. Miller, 426
Pershing, Gen. John J. "Black Jack," 64
    in Mexico, 138, 139, *139*
    in World War I, *158,* 159, 162, 206
pesticides, banning of, 561

Pétain, Gen. Henri, 162
Petersen, Henry, 579
Pettigrew, Richard, 55
Pfenning, E., 112
Phelps Dodge mining company, 111
Philippines:
    annexation of, 35, 54–57
    and China, 56
    independence of, 55, 57, 114, 388
    and Japan, 104, 316
    protection of, 51, 104
    and Spanish-American War, 48, 50, 51, 52, 53–57, 64, 66–67
    and World War II, 313, 384
Phillips, David Graham, 94
Phillips, Howard E., 617
Phillips, Kevin, 612, 616, 620, 622
Phoenix House, 645
Pickle, J. J., 643
Pierrefeu, Jean de, 162
Pillsbury, Charles A., 78
Pinchot, Gifford, 96, *96*
Pingree, Hazen, 87
Pinkerton detectives, 36, 276
Pinochet, Gen. Augusto, 584, *585*
Pittman, Key, 186, 292
Plato, 618
Platt, Orville H., 51
Platt, Tom, 42, 73
Plessy, Homer Adolph, 34, 35
Plessy v. Ferguson, 16, 34–35, 456, 468–69
Plunkitt, George Washington, 86
Podhoretz, Norman, 616
Poindexter, Adm. John, 638, 640, *641*
Poland:
    Communist control of, 404, 423, 478
    and Russia-Germany agreement, 148
    self-determination of, 169, 171, 355
    Solidarity in, 654, 655
    uprising in, 396–97
    and World War II, 299, 316, 318, 320, 340
Polenberg, Richard, 51
police, training of, 252
politics:
    of business, 42
    in cities, 84, 85–86
    corruption in, 85–87, 94, 96, 198–99
    gerrymandering, 619
    and hatred, 622
    identity, 622
    and labor reform, 119
    parties as empty vessels, 660–61
    personal obligation in, 82, 86–87
    reform movements in, 117
    of resentment, 621–23
    and social change, 87
    see also specific politicians
Polk, George, 392, *392*
Polowsky, Joe, 345, *345*
Pol Pot, 557
polygamy, 16
population figures, 140
populism, racial, 621, 623
Populist party, *26,* 108, 117
    beginnings of, 25, 27
    and credit reform, 40
    and Democratic party, 5, 28, 40, 621
    disillusionment in, 26, 288

in elections, 28, 29, 40, 621
    and farmers, 27, 28, 290
    Jefferson and, 619
    rise of, 38
Posner, Gerald, 509
postal savings bank, 117
Post, Louis, 176
Potsdam conference (1945), 325, 326, 404, *404, 405*
Potter, Henry Codman, 18
Pound, Ezra, 184
poverty:
    and addictions, 645
    and Bonus Army, 239
    and character, 86
    and city slums, 84–85
    gap between wealth and, 660
    and Great Depression, 220–21, 236, 237
    and Great Society, 517
    in nineteenth century, xxi
    and stagflation, 620
    and tax burden, 623
Powderly, Terence V., 108
Powell, Adam Clayton, Jr., 460
Powell, Adam Clayton, Sr., 352
Powell, Gen. Colin, 461, 537, 633, 646
Powell, Ozie, *260,* 261
Power, Gen. Thomas, 494
Powers, Francis Gary, 480–81, *480–81*
Powers, John J., 336
Powledge, Fred, 459
pragmatism, 24, 55
Pratt, E. Spencer, 66
presidents, U.S.:
    Civil War generals as, 16
    leadership powers of, 71, 81, 96, 132, 133
    Supreme Court appointments of, 16, 274–75, 462, 468, 513, 599, 628
    see also specific presidents
press, *see* media
Pressman, Lee, 279
Pretty Boy Floyd, 253
Price, Cecil Ray, 518–19, *518*
Price, Robert S., 62
Price, Victoria, 261
Princeton University, 131
privacy, right to, 630, 648
Prochnau, William, 490, 534
Progressive movement/party, 620
    birth of, 25, 28
    and farmers, 290
    and Marshall Plan, 410
    T. Roosevelt and, 25, 116, 122, 129, 183, 302
    and union movement, 108, 111
    Wallace and, 410, 413, 414, 415
    Wilson and, 25, 129, 132–33
Prohibition, 92, 184, 197, *210,* 211, 212, 215, 244–45, 251
Proposition 13 (California), 620
public accommodations, *see* civil rights
public land:
    exploitation of, 618
    homesteaders on, 4–5
    national park system, 248
    railroads on, 4
    ranches on, 4–5, 248
Public Works Administration (PWA), 247

Puerto Rico:
    Alphonso Guards of, *48–49*
    and Spanish-American War, 50, 51, 53
    and U.S. citizenship, 50
Pulitzer, Joseph, 60, 61, 73, 101
Pullman, George M., *38,* 43
Pullman Company, 352
Pullman strike (1894), 38–39, 109
Pumpkin File, 416–17
Pure Food and Drug Act (1906), 95
Putnam, H. W., 4
Pyle, Ernie, 332

Qaddafi, Col. Muammar el-, 638, 640
Quantrill, Jay, 492
Quayle, James Danforth "Dan," 651
Quay, Matthew, 16
quota system, 622

Rabi, I. I., 448
racial quotas, 622
racism, 252, 259
    and conservative coalition, 616
    global ethnic hatreds, 633
    and immigration, 266
    and imperialism, 54, 55
    and muckrakers, 94
    and *Plessy v. Ferguson,* 34–35
    and Populism, 28, 621, 623
    and Scottsboro case, 261
    in World War II, 313, 316, 321, 323, 350–53
    see also blacks; civil rights; Ku Klux Klan
Radford, Charles, 573
Radiation Exposure Compensation Act (1990), 497
radio, *see* media
Raeder, Erich, 408, 409, *409*
railroads:
    in American West, 4, 6, 8, 16
    and Congress, 27
    financial control of, 78, 80
    government ownership of, 28
    and homesteaders, 16
    and Indians, 10
    and labor demands, 23, 110
    land given to, 4
    in Mexico, 134
    and muckrakers, 94
    Pullman strike, 38–39, 109
    regulation of, 246
Rainbow Coalition, 635
Raines, Howell, 460
Rainey, Lawrence, 518–19, *518*
Ramsay, Francis, 59
Ramsdell, Capt. Robert, 558
Ramspeck, Robert, 373
ranches, *xvi-xvii,* 4–5, 8–9, 248
Rand, Ayn, 619
Randolph, A. Philip, 194, 276, 352, *352,* 353, 459, 464, 563
Randolph, Robert Isham, 251
Rankin, Jeanette, *123*
Raskob, John J., 215, 220, 236, 276
Rather, Dan, 551
rational self-interest, 619
Rauh, Joseph, 563
Raulston, John T., 197
Ray, James Earl, 549

Ray, Nick, 8
Rayburn, Sam, 186, 372, *373, 513,* 527
Reagan, Maureen, *624*
Reagan, Nancy Davis, *612, 613, 614, 625, 626, 627,* 645
Reagan, Ronald, 22, 533, 543, 583, *613, 624, 625, 626, 632, 634–35, 646, 647*
  assassination attempt on, *627*
  and civil rights, 461, 462–63
  and elections, 591, 609, 611, 612–16, 621, 626, 634
  and financial scandals, 623, 642–43
  and foreign policy, 104, 209, 537, 617, 632–33, 636–38, 640, 641, 646–47, 656
  and HUAC, 440, 447
  presidency of, 612–23, 624–47
  self-deception of, 623, 624, 637, 640
  as Teflon president, 616
  and Vietnam, 532, 534
Reagan Democrats, 614, 621, 623, 627
Reagan revolution, 612–47
  conservative social agenda of, 614–23
  liberalism in, 614, 617, 619, 628
Red Cloud, Chief, 6, 13, 15
Redding, Louis, 459
Red Tomahawk, Sgt., 12
Reeb, Rev. James, 521
Reed, James, 156, 172
Reed, John, 109, 112, 138
Reed, Ralph, 629
Reed, Stanley, 274
Reed, Thomas Brackett, 42, 52, 55, 57
Reed, Maj. Walter, 102, *103*
Reese, Rev. Frederick D., 520
Regan, Donald T., 613, 642–43
Regan, Edward K., *340–41*
Reid, Whitelaw, 54
religion:
  animosities of, 28
  and civil rights, 454–55
  evangelicals and, 616, 628–29
  "four-faith pluralism," 629
  and the presidency, 483, 484
  separation of church and state, 628
Remington, Frederic, 60, 61, 64, 73
Remus, George, *211*
Reproductive Rights, 630, *631*
Republican party, 129
  and business politics, 42
  cattle barons in, 8
  and cattle war, 9
  and conservatism, 616–17
  vs. Democrat-Populists, 40
  and entitlement programs, 620
  and isolationists, 302, 398–99
  new breed in, 116, 117
  "Old Guard" of, 116, 117, 398–400
  radical right wing of, 398–400, 402, 403, 410, 444–45
  and Reagan revolution, 612–47
  and Red Scare, 402
Republic Steel, 279
Resolution Trust Corporation, 643
Reuter, Ernst, 387
Reuther, Victor, 276
Reuther, Walter, 276, 280, 478, 563, 655
Reynolds, Robert, 288
Rhee, Syngman, 104, 420, 426
Rhineland, 297

Rhodes, Cecil, 51
Ribbentrop, Count Joachim von, *298, 299,* 408, *409, 409*
Ribicoff, Abraham A., *550*
Ricardo, David, 23
Rice, Donna, 648, *648,* 649
Richardson, Elliott L., 579, 580
Richberg, Donald, 274
Richmond, David, 498
Rickenbacker, Capt. Eddie, *162*
Rickover, Adm. Hyman G., 62–63
Ridenhour, Ronald, 559
Ridgway, Matthew, 533
Riegle, Donald, 642
Ries, Henry, 387, 395, 410
Riis, Jacob, 73, 84–85
Rio Pact, 633
Ripley, William Z., 222
robber barons, 20, 24, 76–80, 268
Robb, Roger, 449
Roberson, Willie, *260,* 261
Roberts, Owen J., 187, 273, *273,* 274–75, *274–75,* 312, 350
Roberts, Wayne, 519
Robertson, Bill, 345, *345*
Robertson, Carole, 464
Robertson, Rev. Marion G. "Pat," 629, *629*
Robeson, Paul, 459
Robins, Natalie, 441
Robinson, Jackie, 463
Robinson, Jo Ann, 472
Robinson, Joseph, 275, *275*
Robinson, Spottswood, 459
Roche, James, 560
Rochefort, Comm. Joseph, 312, 313, 362, 363
Rockefeller, John D., 56, *74,* 78, 94, 102, 124
Rockefeller, John D., Jr., 22, 23, 116, 124, 245
Rockefeller, Nelson A., 515, 591, 651
Rockefeller Foundation, 619
Roerich, Nicholas, 303
Roe v. Wade, 630
Rogers, Joel, 621
Rogers, Will, *207*
Rogers, William P., 556, 582
Röhm, Ernst, 265
Romania:
  communism abandoned in, 654
  and World War I, 151
  and World War II, 316, 317, 318
Romanovs, murder of, 164
Romero, Rev. Oscar, 636
Rommel, Erwin, 317, 346
Romney, George, 515
Roosevelt, Alice, 302
Roosevelt, Eleanor, 243, *243,* 246, *259,* 305
  activism of, 259, 352, 353, 463
  and FDR's death, 371, 372
  and New Deal, 259
  and UN, 405
  and women's rights, 122, 258
Roosevelt, Franklin D., 217, *240, 242–43, 247, 270, 275, 354, 355, 372, 375,* 658
  and airpower, 206
  and atomic bomb, 376
  "brains trust" of, 249
  and China, 267

  and Churchill, 285, 304–5, *304,* 320, 343, 354–55, 370
  and civil rights, 16, 353, 414
  conservative opposition to, 398–99
  death of, 370–71, 372–73
  on the dime, 241
  and elections, 215, 241, 271, 293, 302, 303, 415
  and FBI, 252
  fireside chats of, 246, 275, 292, 299, 317
  first hundred days of, 246–47
  and foreign policy, 209, 284–94, 430
  and the Four Freedoms, 317
  Good Neighbor Policy of, 137
  and Great Depression, 221, 224–27, 239, 292
  and Holocaust, 289
  influence of, 462, 616, 625
  and Korea, 420
  and labor unions, 276, 279, 352, 413
  and League of Nations, 243, 265, 288, 355
  and Lend-Lease, 304
  and New Deal, 221, 224–27, 241, 246–49, 256, 271, 291, 293, 402, 619
  office tapes of, 303
  and polio, 241, 243
  presidency of, 242–43, 246–80, 281–313, 314–69, 581
  quarantine speech of, 292
  and social programs, 23, 36, 133, 241
  and social reform, 87, 120
  and Supreme Court, 272–75
  and TVA, 96
  and United Nations, 405
  and World War II, 282, 284–85, 287–94, 297, 299–300, 302, 304–9, *304,* 312, 313, 316–20, 322, 335, 342–43, 346, 347, 350–51, 386, 389, 404
  at Yalta, 317, 318, 320, 327, 342, *354,* 355, 370, 399, 430
Roosevelt, James, 414
Roosevelt, Kermit "Kim," 451
Roosevelt, Sara Delano, 242, 243
Roosevelt, Theodore, 42, *72–73*
  book by, 59
  and Bull Moose party, 183
  bully pulpit of, 71, *81,* 96
  cabinet of, 56
  and elections, 106, 114, 115, 122, 129, *129,* 242, 243, *660*
  family of, *70–71*
  as hunter, 73, 96
  illness and death of, 172
  and imperialism, 53, 54, 57, 59
  inaugural of, 12
  international mind of, 104, 317
  and labor reform, 110
  and land preservation, 16, 96, *97*
  and McKinley's assassination, 68, 69
  as mediator, 80, 98, *98–99,* 104
  motto of, *57,* 71, 98
  and muckrakers, 94, 95
  and naval power, 104, *105*
  and New Nationalism, 129, 133
  Nobel Peace Prize to, 72, 99
  and Panama Canal, 100–101, 102
  presidency of, xvi, 71–81, 94–101, 104, 106, 110, 114, 117, 224

  and Progressive movement, 25, 116, 122, 129, 183, 302
  and Russo-Japanese War, 48
  and Spanish-American War, 53, 62, *64, 65,* 72–73
  and Square Deal, 241
  and World War I, 142, 146, 149, 153, 156
Roosevelt, Theodore, Jr., 259
Roosevelt Dam, 96
Root, Elihu, 54, 67, 80, 129, 406
Roraback, Katie, 630
Rose, Earl, 506
Rosenbaum, Alice, 619
Rosenberg, Alfred, 409
Rosenberg, Julius and Ethel, *442,* 443
Rosenberg, Tina, 403
Rosenman, Sam, 241, 274
Rostow, Walter, 527, 530
Rothstein, Arthur, 234
Roth, William V., Jr., 619
Royer, Daniel F., 12
Royko, Mike, 551
Ruby, Jack, 508, *509*
Ruckelshaus, William, 579
Runyon, Damon, 350
Rusk, Dean, 399, 401, 420, 486–87, 492, 494, 495, 527–28, 533
Russell, Richard B., 325, 526
Russia:
  Bolshevism in, 164, 165, 167
  Czar's abdication (1917), 148, 165
  and Manchuria, 266
  menace of, 104, 290
  Nicholas II in, 148, *164–65,* 355
  Romanovs murdered in, 164, 165
  and World War I, 148, 151, 160, 162, 168
  and World War II, 284–85, 287, 299, 305, 306, 314, 316–20, 323–27, 339, 342–45, 348, 354–55, 361, 377, 383, 385, 399, 404
  see also Soviet Union
Russo-Japanese War (1906), 48, 98–99, 104
Rustin, Bayard, 459, 462, 464
Ruth, Babe, 223
Rutherford, Lucy Mercer, 370–71
Rydlewski, Norma, 658

S&L debacle, 642–43
Sabath, Adolph, 444
Sacco, Nicola, 178–79, *179,* 261
Sachs, Alexander, 376
Sadat, Anwar, 583, 606, *606*
Safford, Capt. Laurence, 312
Safire, William, 447
St. Germain, Fernand "Freddy," 642
St. John de Crevecoeur, Hector, 659
Sakharov, Andrei, 448, 496
Salomon, Erich, image by, *236*
SALT (strategic arms limitation talks), 582–83, 592–93, 646–47, 656
Salter, John, 498
Samano, Fortino, 134, *135*
Samoa, protection of, 59
Sandburg, Carl, 441
Sandinistas, 636, 638
Sandino, Gen. Augusto, 209, *209*
Sanford, Edward, 187
San Francisco:
  earthquake relief for, 114

San Francisco (continued)
    White Night Riot in, 601
Sanger, Margaret, 123, 185
San Roman, Pepe, 487
Sargent, Ben, 623
Satanta, Chief, 12
Saturday Evening Post, 94
Sauckel, Fritz, 408, 409, 409
Saud, Ibn, king of Saudi Arabia, 355
Saudi Arabia, 355
Savio, Mario, 543
Sawyer, Philetus, 117
Saxbe, William B., 586
Saxton, Ida, 45
Scandinavia, and World War I, 143
Schacht, Hjalmar, 227, 409
Schaefer, Jack, 9
Schechter Poultry case, 272–73, 273
Schell, Jonathan, 532
Schine, David, 446–47
Schirach, Baldur von, 408, 409, 409
Schlafly, Phyllis, 597
Schlesinger, Arthur, Jr., xv, 51, 92, 132,
    259, 487, 496, 566, 655
Schlesinger, James R., 584, 587
Schmitt, Harrison H. "Jack," 555
Schrank, John, 129
Schroeder, Pat, 598, 616
Schulman, Joseph W., 212, 212
Schultz, Dutch, 254, 255, 256
Schurz, Carl, 6, 55
Schwab, Charles, 78, 243
Schwarzkopf, Gen. H. Norman, 633
Schwerner, Michael, 518, 623
Schwieger, Walther, 153
Schwimmer, Rosika, 144
Schwitzgebel, John, 228
Scopes, John Thomas, 196–97
Scopes trial, 196–97, 196–97, 629
Scott, Adrian, 440
Scott, David R., 555
Scott, Dred, 34
Scottsboro Nine, 260, 261
Scowcroft, Brent, 587
SDI (Strategic Defense Initiative),
    646–47
SDS (Students for a Democratic
    Society), 543, 543, 573
Seale, Bobby, 546
Secret Service, 239
Sedition Act (1918), 291
Seeger, Pete, 440
Segovia, Lazaro, 67
segregation, see civil rights
Seidman, William, 642
Seigenthaler, John, 462, 500
Seldes, George, 560
Selective Service Act (1917), 156; (1941),
    293, 302
Sellers, Clyde, 473
Selma, Alabama, racial issues in, 462,
    520–21
Senate, see Congress, U.S.
Service, John Stewart, 399
Servicemen's Readjustment Act (1944),
    658
settlement movement, 92
Severalty Act (1887), 6–7, 10, 262
Seyss-Inquart, Arthur, 409
Shafter, Gen. William, 64
Shahn, Ben, 234, 415
Shaler, Col. James, 101

Shane (movie), 9
Shanker, Albert, 655
Shannon, William, 86
Shapiro, Robert Y., 621
Shapiro, Sam, 187
Sharp, John, 132
Sharp, Adm. Ulysses Grant, Jr., 528
Sharp, William, 267
Shave Head, 12
Shaw, Irwin, 441
Sheehan, "Blue-Eyed" Billy, 242
Sheehan, Neil, 490, 531, 532–34
sheepherders, 5
Shepard, Alan B., Jr., 477, 477, 555
Shepard, James H., 95
Sherman, Gen. William T., 6, 53
Sherman Anti-Trust Act (1890), 39, 80,
    109
Shidehara, Kijuro, 267
Shigemitsu, Mamoru, 384, 385
Shimazaki, Shigezaku, 310
Shipp, Tom, 192, 192–93
Shipstead, Henrik, 290
Shirrah, Walter, Jr., 477, 477
Shonts, Theodore P., 102
Short, Gen. Walter, 308, 309, 312–13, 312
Shoumatoff, Elizabeth, 370–71
Shriver, Sargent, 462, 571
Shultz, George P., 632, 640, 646
Shuttlesworth, Rev. Fred, 459, 500
Sigsbee, Capt. Charles, 62
Sihanouk, Prince Norodom, 556
silent majority, 536, 628
silver standard, 28, 40, 46
Simmons, William Joseph, 193
Simons, Howard, 568
Simon, William E., 618
Simpson, Colin, 153
Simpson, "Sockless" Jerry, 27, 28
Sinatra, Frank, 440, 462, 478
Sinclair, Harry F., 198–99, 198
Sinclair, Upton, 95, 95, 179, 560
Singer, Isaac, 59, 113
Singing Wires (Farney), 11
Sioux Act (1889), 6
Sipple, Oliver "Bill," 601, 601
Sirhan, Sirhan B., 548
Sirica, John J., 568, 578
Sitting Bull, Chief, 6, 10, 11, 12, 12, 13, 13,
    15
Skerry, Peter, 661, 663
Slayton, Deke, 476, 477
Sloan, Alfred, 276, 280, 281, 285
Slotkin, Richard, 5
Smiley, Rev. Glenn E., 498–99
Smiley brothers of Mohonk, 6
Smith, Adam, 6, 23
Smith, Al, 120, 186, 214–15, 214–15, 241,
    258, 271, 483
Smith, Rev. Bailey, 629
Smith, Col. Charles B., 426, 427
Smith, Gen. Jacob, 67
Smith, Hazel Brannon, 464
Smith, Helena Huntington, 9
Smith, Hoke, 31
Smith, Gen. Holland, 366, 366, 368
Smith, Jerome, 548
Smith, Jerry, 30
Smith, Jess, 200, 201, 211
Smith, Judy, 630
Smith, Lamar, 503
Smith, Maynard H., 337, 337

Smith, Moe, 211, 211
Smith, Gen. Oliver, 427
Smith, W. Eugene, 359
Smith Act (1940), 402
Smith-Connally Act, 413
Smitherman, Joe, 520
Smoot, Reed, 237
Smoot-Hawley Tariff (1930), 222, 237
Smuts, Gen. Jan, 171
Smyer, Sidney, 504–5
SNCC (Student Nonviolent
    Coordinating Committee), 459,
    461, 464, 465, 499, 500, 503,
    520–21, 546
Sobel, Robert, 222
Social Darwinism, 5, 22–25, 55, 59, 86,
    87, 114, 197, 294, 614
Socialist party, 95
    and anti-incumbency, 616
    and elections, 128, 129, 178, 183
    and labor reform, 108–9, 111, 119
    and Red scare, 177
social security, 258, 271, 275, 302, 623
Social Statistics (Spencer), 22, 23
social welfare:
    and Democratic party, 618
    drug wars and, 645
    food stamps, 249, 517
    government programs of, 23–25, 33,
        86, 258, 616, 618, 621, 663; see also
        New Deal
    Great Society and, 516–17, 516, 621
    Reagan revolution and, 614–23
    women's reform movements in, 92,
        122, 123, 245
    of workers, 106, 108–11, 124, 248
sodbusters, 5
Sokolsky, George, 398
Somalia, 537
Somoza Garcia, Anastasio, 209
Somoza family, 209
Sooners, land rush of, 2–3
Soong, T. V., 398
Sorensen, Charles "Adonis," 113
Sorensen, Theodore, 487, 571
South, see American South
South Africa, and World War II, 385
South Carolina, racial issues in, 456,
    464, 468–69
Southern Alliance, 27
Southern Regional Council, 457
Southern Tenant Farmers Union
    (STFU), 456, 457
South Korea, see Korea; Korean war
Soviet Union:
    American aid to, 164, 165, 236
    and arms limitation, 582–83, 592–93
    atomic weapons of, 395, 397, 402,
        404, 444, 448–49, 496–97
    and Berlin, 342–43, 387, 395, 430
    and China, 564
    and Cold War, 293, 327, 386–407,
        410, 413, 448, 478, 483, 492–97,
        564, 584, 608, 646–47
    collapse of, 402–3, 623–24, 654–56,
        660
    communism in, 220, 285, 294, 317,
        402–3, 564, 584
    and Cuban missile crisis, 407,
        492–95
    expansionism of, 316
    fascism and, 287

    and Germany, 291, 298, 299
    and Kellogg-Briand Pact, 204
    and Korean war, 400–402, 420–21
    and space race, 476–77, 478
    summit meetings with, 646
    and test-ban treaty, 496–97, 646
    and United Nations, 390, 400, 423
    and Vietnam, 525, 532
    see also Russia
space exploration, 554–55, 554, 555
space race, 476–77, 478
Spain:
    civil war in, 287, 291
    decline of, 660
    fascism in, 287, 287
    Guernica, 287
    Socialist party in, 616
Spanish-American War (1898), 48–49,
    65, 72–73
    and American imperialism, 50–57,
        64–67
    blacks in, 35, 163
    Hearst and, 60, 60
    and the Maine, 62–63, 62–63
    and Treaty of Paris, 66
    and yellow fever, 102
Speer, Albert, 321, 409
Spellman, Francis Cardinal, 317, 447
Spence, Mason, 269
Spencer, Herbert, 22–23, 24
spoils system, 6, 16, 18
Sprague, Ruby, 658
Spreckels, Claus, 52
Sprizo, John, 567
Spruance, Adm. Raymond "Electric
    Brain," 363, 364
Sputnik launchings, 476, 478, 513
Stalin, Joseph, 24, 287
    atrocities of, 220, 403
    and China, 400–402, 421, 423
    and Churchill, 318
    and Cold War, 389, 390–92, 395, 396,
        397, 399–405
    death of, 397
    and FDR, 317, 318, 320, 354–55, 355,
        370
    and Hitler, 285, 299, 320
    and Korean war, 400–402, 420–21,
        423
    and postwar years, 408, 410
    at Potsdam, 404, 405
    at Teheran, 318, 320, 346, 354–55, 355
    and Truman, 390–91, 404
    and World War II, 285, 299, 305, 307,
        317–20, 327, 342, 346
    writings of, 396
    at Yalta, 318, 320, 342, 355, 370
Stallings, Laurence, 286
Standard Oil, 74, 78, 80, 94, 124, 125
Stans, Maurice, 567
Stanton, Elizabeth Cady, 92
Stark, Adm. Harold, 308–9, 312, 313
Starr, Kenneth, 660, 661
Stassen, Harold, 353
states' rights:
    vs. federal laws, 468, 474
    and labor unrest, 39
    and rural interests, 84
    and Supreme Court, 272–73
Statue of Liberty, 653
Stearns, Harold, 184
Stedman, Seymour, 178

Steele, Cornelius, 518
Steele, John, 340
Steelman, John, 413
Steffens, Lincoln, *94*, 560
Steinbeck, John, 234, 441
Steinbrenner, George, 447
Steinem, Gloria, 598, *598*
Steinmetz, Charles Proteus, *89*
Stephenson, David, *193*
Sterling, Col. Edmund, 239
Stethem, Robert Dean, 640
Stettinius, Edward, *373*
Steuer, Max, 121
Stevens, John, 52, 102
Stevenson, Adlai E., 42, 430, *430*, 431, 487, 495, 506
Stevenson, Coke, 513
Stevens, Robert T., 446
Stewart, James, *315*, 440, 642
Stiles, Charles Wardell, 102, *103*
Stilwell, Gen. Joseph W. "Vinegar Joe," 354, 365, *365*, 418
Stimson, Henry, *209*, 246, *372*, 373, 406
  and atomic bomb, 325–26, 377
  Interim Committee of, 377
  and intervention in Latin America, 209
  and Japanese-American internment, 350
  as secretary of state, 209, 267, 326
Stimson, Henry (continued)
  as secretary of war (World War II), 293, 306, 307, 313, 323, 325–26, *337*, 350, 377, 407
Stockdale, Adm. James B., 528
Stockman, David, 627
Stone, Harlan Fiske, *272*, 274, *274–75*, 275
  as Chief Justice, 373, *373*, 408
  and FBI, 252–53
  and Nuremberg trials, 408
  and prior restraint, 187
  and states' rights, 273
Stone, I. F., 403, 533
Stone, William, 146–47
Stoval, Christine, 454, *455*
Straight Head, Chief, *11*
Strange Career of Jim Crow, The (Woodward), 35
Strauss, Lewis, 448–49, *448*
Streicher, Julius, 409
Streisand, Barbra, 571
strikes, *see* labor
Stripling, Robert, *440*
Strong, Rev. Josiah, 54, 88
Students for a Democratic Society (SDS), 551, *551*, 581
suburbs:
  birth of, *436–37*
  growth of, 660
Suckley, Margaret, 370–71
Sudoplatov, Pavel, 449
Suez Canal, 392, 478
suffrage, *see* voting rights
Sukhovarov, Colonel, *390*
Sullivan, L. B., 463, 500
Sullivan, Mark, 116
Sully, François, 533
Sulzberger, Arthur D. "Punch," 490
Summers, Harrison, 336
Sumner, William Graham, 22, 23–24, *23*, 25, 55, 114

supply-side economics, 618–19
Supreme Court, U.S., *272–73*, 660
  and abortion, 629, 630
  and campaign finance, 581
  and civil rights, 34, 186, 187, 261, 350–51, 402, 403, 454, 456–59, 463, 468–69, 472, 473, 475, 500, 513, 617, 622
  and Communist Party, 402, 403
  Dred Scott decision of, 34
  and entitlement programs, 663
  and FDR, 272–75
  and interstate commerce, 272–73
  and Issei citizenship, 350–51
  and labor reform, 23, 109–10, 276, 281
  and Pentagon Papers, 575
  presidential appointments to, 16, 274–75, 462, 468, 513, 599, 628
  and prior restraint, 187
  and progressivism, 186
  and religion, 629
  and Schechter Poultry case, 272–73
  and Sherman Anti-Trust Act, 80, 109
  and Watergate, 579
  women justices of, 599, 628
  and women's rights, 92, 597
  and World War II, 309, 312
Surine, Don, *447*
Suro, Roberto, 663
Sutherland, George, 187, 272–73, *272*, *274–75*
Suzuki, Adm. Kantaro, 383
Swaggart, Rev. Jimmy, 629
Swanson, Gloria, *244–45*
Sweatt, Hemann, 458
Sweeney, Martin L., 288
Swift Bear, Chief, *10*
Swift Bird, Chief, *11*
Swift, Gustavus F., 78
Symms, Steven, 648
Syria, French control of, 168
Szilard, Leo, 325, 327, 376, 449

Tabor, "Honest" John, 406
Taft, Charles, *115*
Taft, Helen (daughter), *115*
Taft, Helen "Nellie" Herron (wife), *115*, 119
Taft, Robert A., *115*, 286, 293, 399, 408, 414, 415, 428, 617
Taft, William Howard, 59, 106, *114*, *115*, *116*
  as Chief Justice, *115*, 187
  and conservation, 96
  death of, 187
  and elections, 106, 114, 115, 129
  and foreign policy, 136, 139, 142, 209
  and labor reform, 110
  and the Philippines, 67, *67*, *114*
  presidency of, 108–11, 114–17, 133, 134
  as secretary of war, 102, 114
Taft-Hartley Act (1946), 414, 431
Taiwan:
  and Chinese civil war, 419
  and Cold War, 399–401, 564–65
Tammany Hall, *85*, 86, 87, 214–15, 242, 243, 256, 259
Tanaka, Baron Glichi, *266*
Tarbell, Ida, *94*, 560

tariffs, 16, 20, *20–21*, 24, 30, 42, 44, 51, 52, 53, 54, 116, 117, 133, 185, 222, 223, 237, 388
taxation:
  and budget deficits, 618
  business and, 620, 626
  and economic growth, 620
  and Great Society, 517
  on income, 23, 28, 40, 94, 102, 117, 133, 251, 619, 623, 626
  on land, 25
  on property, 620
  and Second New Deal, 271
  and social welfare, 621
  see also Internal Revenue Service; tariffs
tax revolts, 620
Taylor, A.J.P., 284
Taylor, Frederick, 113
Taylor, Col. G. A., 341
Taylor, Gen. Maxwell, 490, 527, 529–30
Teapot Dome scandal, 198–99, 259, 581
Teheran summit meeting (1943), 318, 320, 346, 354–55, *355*
television, *see* media
Teller, Edward, 376, 448–49, *448*, 497
Teller, Henry, 54, 57
Tennessee, racial issues in, 498–99
Tennessee Valley Authority (TVA), 96, 246, 247, 248, 275, 290, 302
Terrell, Rev. Mary Church, 92
terrorism, 640
test-ban treaty, 496–97, *496–97*
Texas:
  acquisition of, 56
  cattle industry in, 4
  S&L debacle in, 642
Thacher, Thomas, 273
Thailand, 399
Thatcher, Margaret, 619
Thayer, Webster, 178
Theory of the Leisure Class (Veblen), 76
Thich Quang Duc, 490
Third World:
  and communism, 316
  immigration from, 661
Thomas, Evan, 395, 406
Thomas, J. Parnell, 440, *440*
Thomas, Norman, 291, 415
Thompson, Allen, 503
Thompson, Florence, *658*
Thompson, Hale "Big Bill," 187, 212, *213*
Thompson, Hugh, 558–59, *558*
Thompson, Llewellyn, 481
Thompson, Sir Robert, 535
Thurmond, J. Strom, 414–15, 463
Thurow, Lester, 516
Tikas, Louis, 124
Till, Emmett, 465, 470–71, *471*, 503
Tippit, J. D., 506
Titanic, 78
Tito, Marshal (Josip Broz), 397, 478, 525
Togo, Shigenori, 309, 383
Tojo, Hideki, 266, 307, 320, 361
Tolson, Clyde, *253*
Tomioka, Adm. Sadatoshi, 384
Torrio, John, 212, *213*
Townsend, Francis, 271
Toyoda, Adm. Feijiro, 307
Tracy, Spencer, 440
Trenchard, Hugh, 206

Triangle Shirtwaist fire, 120, *120–21*
Trujillo, Rafael, 486
Truman, Bess, 372, *373*, *374*, 375
Truman, Harry S, *374*, *375*, *377*, *404*, *413*, *422*, 625
  and atomic bombs, 323–27, 377
  and civil rights, 352, 414, 458
  and Eisenhower, 433
  and elections, 414–15, *414*
  and Korea, 104, 401, 420, 423–24, 428, 430, 525, 528, 566
  and labor, 413
  at Potsdam conference, 404, *404*, *405*
  presidency of, 374–75, 389–91, 393–95, 397–407, 413–24, 428, 430, 444, 448, 451, 525
  swearing-in as president, 372–73
  and World War II, 383, 404, 408
Truman, Margaret, 372, *374*
Truman Doctrine, 222, 394–95, 407, 524
Trumbo, Dalton, 286, 440
Trump, Donald, 447
Trumpauer, Joan, *498*
Tsaldaris, Constantine, 392
Tsuji, Col. Masanobu, 361
Tuchman, Barbara, 418
Tugwell, Rexford G., *249*, 259
Tumulty, Joe, 173, *174*
Turkey:
  and Cold War, 391, 392, 394
  and Dardanelles, 391–92
  and Korean war, 423
  U.S. missiles in, 495
  and World War I, 151
Turnbow, Hartman, 460
Turner, Adm. Richmond Kelly, 313
Turner, Frederick Jackson, xv–xvi, 5
TVA (Tennessee Valley Authority), 96, 246, 247, 248, 275, 290, 302
TWA flight 847 hijacking, 640
Twain, Mark, 20, 50, 55, 288, 457
Tweed Ring, New York City, 85
Twining, Gen. Nathan, 323
Twinkie defense, 601
Tydings, Millard, 445, *445*
Tyler, Kermit, 309

Udall, Morris, 559
Udall, Stewart L., 497
Ukraine, 148
Ulam, Stanislaw, 449
Umezu, Yoshijiro, 384
unemployment, 22, *32*, 33, 86, 108, 226, 237, 276, 314, 612, 618, 620
UNIA (Universal Negro Improvement Association), 194
unions, *see* labor
United Automobile Workers (UAW), 280, 281
United Fruit Company, 450
United Hatters' Union, 109
United Hebrew Charities of New York, 89
United Kingdom, *see* Great Britain
United Mine Workers (UMW), 80, 109, 124, 276, 413, 563
United Nations, 172, 317, 319, 354–55, 386, 388, 390, 392, 398, 399, 400, 402, 405, 416, 423, *423*, 427, 487, 495, 565, *565*, 633, 651

United States:
centennial celebration of, 18,
18–19
as melting pot, 91; *see also*
immigrants
New Era in, 182–86, 220, 223
"normalcy" in, 182–86, 200
parallels (1890–1990), xx, 663
social classes in, 76–77, *76*, 106
Social Darwinism in, 22–25
treatment of enemies in postwar
years, 388–89
as world power, xiv–xv, xxii–xxiii,
16, 406; *see also* foreign policy
see also specific programs and wars
United Steelworkers of America, 279
Ushijima, Gen. Mitsuru, 367
USSR, *see* Soviet Union
U.S. Steel, 78, 279

Vachon, John, 234
Valdinoci, Carlo, 179
Valenti, Jack, *517*
Vallee, Rudy, 241
Van Buren, Martin, 224
Vance, Cyrus R., *531*, 607, 608, 610
Vandenberg, Arthur, *288*, 290, 388, 389,
390, 410
Vanderbilt, Cornelius, 78
Vanderbilt family, *75*, 76–77
Van Devanter, Lynda, 541, *541*
Van Devanter, Willis, 187, 272–73,
272–73, 274–75, 275
Van Doren, Irita, 303
Vanity Fair, 237
Vann, John, *534*
Vanzetti, Bartolomeo, 178–79, *179*, 261
Vaught, Gen. James, 608
Veblen, Thorstein, 25, *76*, 77, 226
Venezuela, debts of, 98, 99
Vermont, Coolidge birthplace in, *202*
Versailles, Treaty of (1919), 167–73, *168,*
169, 170–71, 217, 264, 282, 285, 286
Vesco, Robert, 567
Victoria, queen of England, 50, 151
Vidal, Gore, 243, 635
Viereck, George Sylvester, 288
Vietnam, 396, 397, 402, 490
Vietnam war, 522–43
American withdrawal from, 594,
594–95
antiwar demonstrations, *542, 557,*
573
body count in, 535
costs of, 516, 522
and credibility gap, 529, 532–35
and firepower, 535–36, 539
Johnson and, 407, 516, 517, 522,
524–31, 533, 536, 542, 558, 566, 574
and liberalism, 617
media and, 465, 490, 528, 530, 531,
535–36, 559
My Lai atrocity in, 558–59, *558*
and Pentagon Papers, 534, 574–76
POWs and MIAs in, *537*
reasons for failure in, 530
Viguerie, Richard, 617, 620
Villa, Pancho, 136, 138–39, *138–39*
Vinson, Fred M., 373, 443, 468
Virginian, The (Wister), 5, 9
Virgin Islands, 50, 52
Vital Center (Schlesinger), 655

Vivian, Rev. C. T., 520
Vogel, Bea, 630
Volcker, Paul, 604, 611
Volstead Act (1919), 211
Vo Nguyen Giap, Gen., 528
votes, purchase of, 16
voting rights:
of blacks, xxi, 35, 454, 456–58,
462–64, 500, 502, 518–21
of immigrants, 84
and Nineteenth Amendment, 94,
123
of women, 5, 40, 92, 122, 123, 140
of workers, 124
Voting Rights Act (1965), 462–63,
520–21
Vyshinsky, Andrei, 389–90, *423*

Wagner, Robert F., 120, 186, 276, 289
Wainwright, Gen. Jonathan, 360, *360*,
384
Waldron, Lt. John, 363
Wałesa, Lech, 654
Walker, Adm. John, 102
Walker, Gentleman Jimmy, 256
Walker, J. Samuel, 324
Walker, Walton, 427
Walker, Rev. Wyatt Tee, 459, 504–5
Wallace, George C., *499, 514*
and elections, 338, 514, 551, 603
and politics of resentment, 621–22
and racial issues, 261, 462, 463, 499,
505, 514, 517, 519, 520–21
shooting of, 514
Wallace, Henry A., *249*, 271, 303, *372,*
373, 375, 394, 413
and food stamps, 249
and Progressive party, 410, 413, 414,
415
as secretary of agriculture, 249
as secretary of commerce, 390, 413
Truman's firing of, 413
Waller, Bill, 503
Wall, M. Danny, 643
Walsh, Frank, 124
Walsh, Lawrence E., 640
Walsh, Thomas, 186, 199
Walters, Barbara, 447
Walters, Walter W., 239
Wanamaker, John, 16
Wandersee, John, 113
Wanniski, Jude, 619
Ward, Lester Frank, 24–25, *25*
Waring, Julius Waties, 464, 468
War Labor Board, 349
Warner, Jack, 440
War Production Board, 305
Warren, Earl, 350, 468–69, 508
Warren Commission, 508
Washakie, Chief, 10
Washington, Booker T., *34*, 72, 194
Washington, D.C.:
antiwar demonstrations in, 542
cherry trees in, 115
and civil rights, 464, 465, 466, *469*
Washington, George, xiii, 130, 653–54
Washington Post, 568, 576
Waskow, Capt. Henry W., 332
Watergate, 566–81
cover-up attempts in, 578–81
Jordan on, 598
lesson of, 581

and Nixon's resignation, 586–87
roots of, 570–71, 579
and "Saturday Night Massacre," 579
Watson, Ella (Cattle Kate), 9, *9*
Watson, Tom, *26*
Watt, James G., 618, 627
WCTU (Women's Christian
Temperance Union), 92, 211
wealth:
distribution of, xx–xxi, 619, 620–21,
623, 627, 660
global, 620
Weathermen, 573
Weaver, Gen. James, 28
Webb, Walter Prescott, 4
Webster, Chief, *10*
Wechsler, James, 431
Weddington, Sarah, 630
Wedemeyer, Gen. Albert, 419
Weems, Charlie, *260*, 261
Weinberg, Jack, 543
Weinberger, Casper W., 632–33, 640,
641, 646
Weisner, Jerome, 496
Weiss, Carl, *269*
Welch, Joseph, *446*, 447
Welch, Robert, 515
welfare programs, *see* social welfare
Welles, Sumner, 285
Wells, H. G., xvi, 77, 84, 87, 91
Wells, Ida B., 35
West, Ben, 499
Western Federation of Miners, 110–11
Western U.S., *see* American West
Westley, Cynthia, 464
Westmoreland, Gen. William, *523*,
529–30, 536, 558–59
Weyler, Gen. Valeriano "Butcher," 53
Weyrich, Paul, 617, 628
Whalen, Lt. William H., 488
Wheeler, Burton K., 186, 274, 290, 291
Wheeler, Gen. Earle G. "Bus," *491, 529*
Wheeler, Wayne B., 211
Wheelis, Lt. Jack George "Tex," 409
Wherry, Kenneth, 397
White, Byron "Whizzer," 462
White, Clifton, 515
White, Dan, 600–601
White, E. B., 441, 483
White, Ed, 477
White, Harry Dexter, 402
White, Henry, 167
White, Robert E., 637
White, Theodore, 398
White, William Allen, 28, 85, 114, 291
White, William S., 446
White Ghost, Chief, *10*
White Night Riot, 601
White Swan, Chief, *10*
Whitney, Richard, 228, *229*
Whitside, Maj. Samuel, 15
Wickard, Claude, *372, 373*
Wiggin, Albert H., 224
Wigner, Eugene, 376
Wilder, Thornton, 441
Wilhelm II, Kaiser, 98, 99, 104, 146,
147
exile of, 264
and World War I, 59, 146, 147, 148,
151, 162
Wilkerson, James H., 251
Wilkins, Roy, 268, 459

Wilkinson, Adm. Theodore, *313*
Willard, Frances, 92
Williams, Aubrey, 458
Williams, Camilla, 464
Williams, Daniel Hale, 454
Williams, Eugene, *260*, 261
Williams, G. Mennen, 261
Williams, Tennessee, 320
Williamsburg Sugar Plant strike, *126*
Willingham, Lt. Thomas, 559
Willkie, Wendell, 302, *303*
Wilson, Charles, 446
Wilson, Edith Bolling, 131, 146, 166,
168, 173, 174–75, *174*
Wilson, Ellen Louise Axson, *131*, 143,
151
Wilson, Frank, 251
Wilson, Henry Lane, 134, *134*
Wilson, Janet "Jessie," *130*
Wilson, Joseph Ruggles, *130*
Wilson, Margaret, *131*
Wilson, Pete, 642
Wilson, Woodrow, 94, 112, *130*, 131, *132,*
150, 166, 167, 175
disability of, 174–75, 176
and elections, 129, *146*, 147
and foreign policy, 123, 134, 136–39,
142–49, 164, 288, 299, 306, 317, 404
Fourteen Points of, 166–68, 169, 171,
305
and labor troubles, 110, 124, 276
and League of Nations, 147, 148, 164,
168–69, 171, 172–73, 174, 243, 288,
317, 355
moral principles of, 142–44, 173, 174
political evolution of, 142–49
presidency of, 130–33, 136–39,
140–76, 215, 224, 242, 274
and Progressive party, 25, 129, 132–33
and Prohibition, 211
and racism, 130, 192
at Versailles, 168, *168*, 172
and women's rights, 123
and World War I, 142–49, 151, 153,
156, 159, 162
writings of, 88–89, 130
windmills, 4, *5*
Wiseman, Sir William, 143
Wister, Owen, 5, 9
Wizi, Chief, *11*
Wobblies (IWW), 108, 109, 110–11, 119,
126
Wofford, Harris, 462, 483
Wolfe, Alan, 621
Woll, Matthew, 398
Woloch, Nancy, 51
women:
and birth control, 123
in cabinet, 258–59
in Congress, 123, 598, *598*
and entitlement programs, 619–20
firefighters, *311*
and labor reform, 119, 276, 349
in nineteenth century, xxii
and reform movements, 92, 115, *118,*
119, *122, 123*, 245, 596–99
as Supreme Court justices, 599,
628
voting rights to, 5, 40, 92, 122, 123,
140
war work of, *311*, 346, 348–49,
348–49

Women's Trade Union League, 120, 122
Wood, Gen. Leonard, 102, 189
Wood, Robert E., 294
Wood, William, 119
Woodard, Sgt. Isaac, 458
Woodcock, Leonard, 571
Woods, John C., 409
Woods, Rose Mary, *569*, 586
Woodson, Carter, 454
Woodward, Bob, *568*
Woodward, C. Vann, 35
Workman, Charlie "the Bug," 255
World Bank, 388
World Court, 294
World War I:
    aftermath of, 166–73, 221, 222,
      264–65, 266, 285–88, 290
    air power for, 206, 207
    and balance of power, 318, 396
    death rate of, 334
    and labor reform, 110, 111
    preliminaries to, 59, 142–55
    and Prohibition, 211
    spark ignited in, 151
    U.S. entry into, 156–63
    Versailles Treaty, 167–73, 217, 264,
      282, 285, 286
    Wilson's Fourteen Points and,
      166–68, 169, 171, 305
World War II, 314–85; *maps, 318–19,*
    322–23
World War II *(continued)*
    and air power, 286, 300, 305, 309,
      310–11, 321–25, 336–39, 348,
      364–65, *364–65*
    appeasement attempts and, 284–85,
      287
    in the Atlantic, *330–31*
    and Atlantic Charter, 305
    and atomic bombs, 323–27
    and balance of power, 319
    and Bataan Death March, *360–61,*
      361, 385
    codes and codebreakers in, 306, 307,
      308–9, 312–13, 321, 331, 362, 364,
      377
    and collective security, 285, 291–92
    costs of, 385
    D-Day, 317, *340–41*
    death rate of, 334
    Dunkirk in, 300
    and the economy, 221–22
    and Eleanor Roosevelt, 259
    in Europe, calendar of events in,
      328–33, 336–37, 340–41, 344, 346,
      348–49
    Holocaust and, 284, 289
    and idealism, 316–17, 320, 321, 327,
      354
    isolationism and, 282, 284–94, 302,
      304, 316, 355
    and Japanese-American intern-
      ment, 350–51, *350–51*
    and Lend-Lease, 304, 388
    literature of, 286
    and Nuremberg trials, 298, 408–9,
      408–9
    in the Pacific, 306–11, 317, *map,*
      322–23, 323–27, 352; calendar of
      events, 356–59, 363–64, 367
    and Pearl Harbor, 291, 292, 293, 294,
      308–13, *310–11*

postwar years, *see* Cold War
    and Potsdam Declaration, 325, 326
    preliminaries to, 282–313
    U.S. entry into, 123, 310–13
    U.S. productivity in, 320–21, 338,
      346, *346–47*
Wounded Knee massacre, 12, *14–15,* 15,
    262, 657
Wovoka (Paiute), 12
Wright, Andy, *260,* 261
Wright, Daniel T., 109–10
Wright, Jim, 643
Wright, Mose, 470–71, *471*
Wright, Roy, *260,* 261
Wright, Wade, 261
Wright Brothers, 73
Wyatt, Jane, 440
Wyler, William, 440
Wyman, Jane, *624,* 625
Wyoming:
    Cattle Kate lynched in, 9
    Johnson County cattle war in, 8–9
    population in, xvi, 4
    Tweed's Ranch in, *xvi-xvii*

Xue Litai, 400, 420

Yablonski, Jock, 563
Yalta (1945), *354–55,* 389, 390, 404, 419
    Churchill and, 342, 355, *355,* 370
    FDR and, 317, 318, 320, 327, 342, *354,*
      355, 370, 399, 430
    Stalin and, 318, 320, 342, 355, 370
Yamamoto, Adm. Isoroku, *206,* 310,
    358–59, 362, 363, 368
Yamashita, Gen. Tomoyuki, 361, *361*
Yarborough, Ralph, *viii,* 506, 651
Yellow Bird (medicine man), 15
yellow fever, 102, 103
Yellow Hair, Chief, 10, *11*
Yellowstone National Park, 96
Yeltsin, Boris, 656
Yom Kippur War (1973), 582, 604
Yosemite National Park, *97*
Young, Andrew, 459, 521, 598
Young, David, 575–76
Young, John W., 555
Young Americans for Freedom, 617
Yugoslavia:
    and Cold War, 397, 478
    ethnic hatreds in, 633
    self-determination of, 169, 171, 318
    and World War II, 318

Zahedi, Gen. Fazlollah, 451
Zangara, Joe, 241
Zangwill, Israel, 91
Zapata, Emiliano, 136
Zapruder, Abe, 509
Zellner, Bob, 463
Zhou Enlai, 401, *418,* 419, 524, 564–65,
    564–65
Ziegler, Ronald, 574, 578, 586
Zimmermann, Arthur, 147, 151
Zimmermann Plot (1917), 147, 149
Zorya, N. D., 408
Zuta, Jack, 212
Zwerg, James, 454, *455*

ILLUSTRATION CREDITS

ABBREVIATIONS

AP: Associated Press
BB: Brown Brothers
C-B: Corbis-Bettmann
CMP: California Museum of Photography, University of California, Riverside
DDE: Dwight D. Eisenhower Library
FD: Chesler Collection, F-M Campus Library, Fairleigh Dickinson University
FDR: Franklin D. Roosevelt Library
HG: Hulton Getty Picture Collection Limited
HST: Harry S. Truman Library
JFK: John Fitzgerald Kennedy Library
LBJ: Lyndon Baines Johnson Library
LC: Library of Congress
NA: National Archives
NYPL: New York Public Library
NYT: New York Times
NSHS: Solomon D. Butcher Collection, Nebraska State Historical Society
OHS: Ohio Historical Society
PUL: Princeton University Library
RN: Richard Nixon Library and Birthplace Foundation
SCHS: Stark County Historical Society, Canton, Ohio
TR: Theodore Roosevelt Collection, Harvard College Library

The name of the photographer or artist, when known, is listed before the name of collection. Illustrations are courtesy the following individuals and collections:

ENDPAPERS

Harlan A. Marshall/Manchester Historic Association

FRONT MATTER

iv-v George Tames/NYT Pictures; **viii** Russell Lee/Center for American History at the University of Texas, Austin; **xi** Collection of The New-York Historical Society; **xii-xiii** Jerome Liebling; **xvi-xvii** J. E. Stimson/Stimson Collection, Wyoming State Museum; **xviii-xix** BB.

CHAPTER ONE

2-3 Thomas Croft or Phillip A. Miller/ Archives & Manuscripts Division, Oklahoma Historical Society; **5** Solomon D. Butcher/NSHS; **7** LC; **8** Solomon D. Butcher/NSHS; **9** (top) Western History Collections, University of Oklahoma Library, (bottom) American Heritage Center, University of Wyoming; **10-11** C. M. Bell, December 1889/ LC-USZ62-95885; **11** Henry F. Farney, *The Song of the Talking Wire*, 1904, oil on canvas, 22 1/16" x 40". Signed lower right: "H.F. FARNEY.O. 1904." 1931.466 Bequest of Mr. Charles Phelps and Mrs. Anna Sinton Taft, The Taft Museum, Cincinnati, Ohio; **12** NA 111-SC-87268; **13** LC-USZ62-62749; **14-15** George Trager,

January 1, 1891/ LC-USZ62-44458; **15** AP; **16** copyright Mathew Brady/LC-USZ62-792Q; **17** LC-USZ62-32808; **18-19** The President Benjamin Harrison Home, Indianapolis, Indiana.

CHAPTER TWO

20-21 Droughboy, "Strenous Sam and His Tariff Wall," cover, *Life*, December 4, 1902/LC- USZ62-29008; **22** "Economic Darwinism - Right-Thinking Person: 'The visionaries and Socialist demogogues may rant against us, my boy, but they can't alter the divine law of the Survival of the Fattest!'" FD; **23** BB; **25** Brown University Library; **26** (top) Solomon D. Butcher/NSHS, (left) BB, (right) LC-USZ62-36676; **27** Thomas Nast, "The Senatorial Round House"/ LC-USZ62-36918; **28-29** Kansas State Historical Society; **30-31** BB; **31** "Another Voice for Cleveland," lithograph after Frank Beard in *Judge*, September 27, 1884/LC-USZ62-34246; **32** LC-USZ62- 9803Q; **33** (top) BB, (bottom left) LC-USZ62-96180, (bottom right) AP; **34** LC-USZ62-53-T6012; **35** (left) Department of Special Collections, University of Chicago Library, (right) BB; **36-37** stereograph published by H.C. White Co., 1906/Hagley Museum and Library; **37** (inset) BB; **38** (top left) Pullman Research Group, (bottom) BB; **38-39** LC-USZ62-10546Q; **39** LC- Z62-2115Q; **40** "Swallowed (William Jennings Bryan, as Populist Party python, swallowing the Democratic Party)" in *Puck* /LC-USZ62-8425Q; **41** LC-USZ62-53841Q; **42-43** George Luks, *The Verdict*, March 13, 1899; **43** (top) BB, (bottom) SCHS; **44** (top left) Victor, *Judge*, May 3, 1890; (top right) LC-USZ62-28396Q, (bottom right) W. Moller/LC-USZ62- 12949Q; (bottom left) The Western Reserve Historical Society, Cleveland, Ohio; **45** (top) C-B, (bottom) SCHS; **46** The Bancroft Library; **46-47** E. A. Hegg, 1898/The Bancroft Library.

CHAPTER THREE

48-49 (top) NA-111-SC-94538, (bottom) NA-111-SC-113614; **51** LC-USZ62-61459; **52** SCHS; **53** "A Snap Shot" from *Book of Cartoons of Our War with Spain*, 1898/FD; **54** Lt. O'Keefe, Signal Corps, distributed by Universal Photo Art Co., 1898/CMP; **55** C. C. Pierce and Co./California Historical Society, Title Insurance and Trust Photo Collection, Department of Special Collections, University of Southern California Libraries; **56** J. E. Purdy, 1902/ LC-USZ62-96904; **57** Holrymple, "The World's Constable" in *Judge*, January 14, 1905/ LC-USZ62-28092; **58** LC-USZ62-3124; **59** LC-USZ62-22488; **60** BB, **60-61** "The Yellow Peril—William Randolph Hearst" by Oliver Herford in *Life*, August 17, 1922/LC; **61** (bottom) *New York Journal*, (right) BB, (far right) Culver Pictures; **62** Collection of The New-York Historical

Society; **62-63** Department of the Navy, U.S. Naval Academy, The Nimitz Library; **64** (bottom) "Most everbody says this suit looks best on me" from *St. Paul Pioneer Press*, reproduced in *Our Times*, vol. 1, by Mark Sullivan (Scribner's Sons, 1926) (top) TR; **65** W. G. Read © 1898 (detail)/LC-USZ62-135, (inset) *Scotland for Ever!* 1881 by Lady Butler, Leeds Museum and Gallery, City Art Museum; **66** LC-USZ62-36612Q; **67** Frederick W. Nash/William Howard Taft National Historic Site; **68** Robertson and Fowler /SCHS, (inset) LC-USZ62-13856; **69** (top left) LC-USZ62-29317, (top right) LC, (bottom) TR; **70-71** LC-USZ62- 32238; **72** (top left) E. Hine in *Harper's Weekly*, August 17, 1912/FD, (three) TR; **72-73** LC-J698-61365; **73** (bottom left and two top right) TR, (rhino) C-B, (bottom right) LC-USZ62-37925; **74** (left) C-B, (right) BB; **75** (left) Carnegie Library, Pittsburgh, (right) C-B; **76** LC- USZ62-45985; **77** Byron/Museum of the City of New York; **78** Erik Johan Smith, 1923, Collection of the Jonson Gallery of the University Art Musuem, University of New Mexico, Albuquerque; **79** C-B; **81** LC-USZ62-95886.

CHAPTER FOUR

82-83 LC; **85** General Research Division, NYPL, Astor, Lenox and Tilden Foundations; **88** "The Immigrant" by Gillam © 1903 Judge Company of New York/Author's Collection; **89** Harrison D. Horblit Collection; **90** National Photo Co./LC-F801-4509; **91** (both) National Park Service: Statue of Liberty National Monument; **92** (top) C-B, (bottom) Nicholas Kelley Papers, Rare Books and Manuscripts Division, NYPL, Astor, Lenox and Tilden Foundations; **93** Chicago Historical Society (DN-003882, photographer *Chicago Daily News*); **94** (top left) LC-B2-33531, (bottom left) BB, (top right) LC, (bottom right) LC-USZ62-36754; **95** (both) BB; **96** LC-USZ62-8672; **97** LC-F8-34404; **98-99** NA, **99** *Pasquino* (Turin)/FD; **100-101** NA; **102** *Conquerors of Yellow Fever* by Dean Cornwall Otis Historical Archives, National Museum of Health and Medicine, Armed Forces Institute of Pathology; **103** (top and two bottom right) Otis Historical Archives, National Museum of Health and Medicine, Armed Forces Institute of Pathology, (bottom two left) National Library of Medicine; **104** TR; **105** TR.

CHAPTER FIVE

106-107 Lewis Hine/LC-USZ62-23753; **109** (left) BB, (right) Tamiment Institute Library, New York University; **110** (left) LC-USZ62-23725, (right) George Meany Memorial Archives; **112** From the collections of Henry Ford Museum and Greenfield Village (detail from negative P.833.850); **113** Ford Archives, Dearborn, Michigan; **114** (top left) published in *Confessions of a Caricaturist* by Oliver

Herford, 1917, (bottom left) U.S. Army Military History Institute, (top right) OHS, (bottom right) William Howard Taft National Historic Site; **115** (top) Author's Collection, print Courtesy James Danziger Gallery, New York, (center) published in *The American Past* by Roger Butterfied, 1947, (bottom left) LC, (bottom right) LC-USZ62-31541; **116** (top) George Grantham Bain/LC-USZ62-29318, (bottom) Robert Carter, published in *New York World*, reprinted in *The American Past*; **117** State Historical Society of Wisconsin; **118** BB; **119** Magnum Photos Inc. © 1951 Burt Glinn; **120** (inset) BB; **120-121** Tamiment Institute Library, New York University; **122** (left) Jane Addams Memorial Collection, Special Collections, The University Library, University of Illinois at Chicago, (right) C-B; **123** (both) UPI/ C-B; **124** Rockefeller Archive Center; **125** BB; **126** (both) The Archives of Labor and Urban Affairs, Wayne State University; **127** LC-B2-2045-6; **128** unknown source; **129** (all) TR; **130** (top left) E. Hine in *Harper's Weekly*, August 10, 1912/FD, (bottom left) LC-USZ62-46113, (top right) LC-USZ62-10684, (bottom right) PUL; **131** (left) LC-USZ62-10125, (top right) PUL, (bottom right) LC-USZ62- 7633; **132** Weal/ LC-USZ62-34101; **133** AP; **134** (top) and **135** Agustin Victor Casasola/Casasola Archive, Instituto Nacional de Antropología e Historia, Mexico City, **134** (left) from *The Wind That Swept Mexico: The History of the Mexican Revolution of 1910-1942* by Anita Brenner, 1943, (bottom right) LC-USZ62-44272; **135** Agustín Victor Casasola/Casasola Archive, Instituto Nacional de Antropología e Historia, Mexico City; **136** © Keystone Press Agency/photograph courtesy the Photography Collection, Harry Ransom Research Center, The University of Texas at, Austin; **137** (top) from *Simplicissimus*, May 11, 1914/LC-510732, (bottom) NA; **138-139** LC-USZ62-29357; **139** HG.

CHAPTER SIX

140-141 Louis Bostwick from the Bostwick/Frohardt Collection, owned by KMTV, on loan to Western Heritage Museum, Omaha, Nebraska; **144** LC-B2-3443-11; **145** "Dropping the Pilot" from *The Sun*, June 11, 1915/LC-USZ62-34283; **146** "Berlin's Candidate" by Rollin Kirby, published in *New York World*/FD; **150** LC-USZ62-14398Q; **151** (bottom) HG; **152** (inset) AP; **152-153** NA-111-SC-16578; **154-155** NA-111-SC-16568; **156-157** NA-111-SC-16571; **158** AP; **159** *The Daily Mirror* (London) August 16, 1917; **160-161** AP; **162** NA-111-SC-29656; **163** African-American recruits at Camp Meade, Maryland, 1918/NA-111-SC-21000; **164-165** Popperfoto/Archive; **165** NA-111-SC-76083; **166** NA 111-SC-62979; **167** NA-111-SC-61183; **168** (top) NA-111-SC-158966, (bottom) The Trustees of the Imperial War Museum, London; **169** (top) NA-111-SC-61141, (bottom) LC-

USZ62-62808; 170–171 HG; 172 LC-F81-11547; 173 LC-USZ62-96172; 174 LC-USZ62-70151; 175 LC-F8-17266; 176 FD; 177 LC-USZ62-59680; 178 (top) C-B, (bottom) Bancroft Library, University of California, Berkeley; 179 (top) courtesy of the Trustees of the Boston Public Library, (bottom) BB.

CHAPTER SEVEN

180–181 OHS; 182 "End of the Climb" by Rollin Kirby/FD; 183 LC-USZ62-95891; 184 FD; 185 "The Candidate for Reelection" by J. P. Alley in *The Commercial Appeal*, February 8, 1923; 187 (top) Collection of the Supreme Court of the United States, (bottom) Tribune Archives, Robert R. McCormick Research Center, Wheaton, Illinois; 188 (top left) Drawing by David Levine. Reprinted with permission from *The New York Review of Books*. Copyright © 1965 Nyrev, Inc.; 188–189 (all except middle photo on 189) OHS; 189 (middle) LC-USZ62-91607; 190–191 LC-USZ62-32953; 192–193 unknown source; 193 (inset) Museum of Modern Art/Film Stills Archive; 193 (three) AP; 194–195 "Marcus Garvey at Viewing Stand, 1924" by James Van Der Zee/Photograph courtesy Donna Mussenden Van Der Zee; 196–197 AP; 198 (top) AP, (bottom) LC-USZ62-34308; 199 (top) LC-USZ62-51323, (bottom) C-B; 201 (top) OHS, (bottom) AP; 202 (top left) Courtesy VANITY FAIR. Copyright © 1932 (renewed 1960) by the Conde Nast Publications Inc., (top right) Calvin Coolidge Memorial Foundation, (bottom left and center) AP, (bottom right) C-B; 203 (top) LC-USZ62-34526, (insets, left to right) LC-USZ62-29740, LC-USZ62-52536, Calvin Coolidge Memorial Room, Forbes Library, Northampton, Massachusetts, (bottom left) *The Boston Globe*, (bottom right) oil painting by Arthur J. Keller, ca. 1924/The Vermont Divison for Historic Preservation of Montpelier, Vermont; 204 (insets) NA; 204–205 Dr. Erich Salomon/Bildarchiv Preussischer Kulturbesitz, Berlin; 205 (inset) NA 111-SC-80612, (top) LC; 206 (both) C-B; 207 (top) AP, (bottom) LC-F801-35135; 208 FD; 209 (left) NA-127-N-522050, (right) Culver Pictures; 210 C-B; 211 (top) C-B, (bottom) BB; 212 (top) AP, (bottom) *Chicago Tribune*; 213 (top and bottom center) AP; (bottom left) New York *Daily News*, (bottom right) C-B; 214 Gluyas Williams, *Life*, February 15, 1929/LC-USZ62-104548; 214–215 C-B; 216 (all except bottom left) Herbert Hoover Presidential Library, (bottom left) BB; 217 (left) C-B; (top) Bernard M. Baruch Papers, PUL, (middle) LC-USZ62-22160, (bottom) C-B.

CHAPTER EIGHT

218–219 LC-USZ62-35799E; 220 Louisville, Kentucky, 1931/LC-USZ62-34887; 221 FD; 223 published in *The*

American Past by Roger Butterfield, 1947; 224 Arthur Rothstein, Haverhill, Iowa, 1939/LC-USF34-28362; 225 Author's Collection; 227 Bakersfield, California 1940/ LC-USZ62-97686; 228 FD; 229 (top) NA- 306-NT-92795, (bottom) AP; 230–231 LC-USZ62-108456; 232 Dorothea Lange, November 1936/ LC-USF34-16102C; 232-233 Records of the Soil Conservation Service, NA-114-SD-5089; 234–235 LC-12466-F34-9841; 236 Bildarchiv Preussischer Kulturbesitz, Berlin; 237 (left) C-B, (right) courtesy VANITY FAIR. Copyright © 1933 (renewed 1961) by The Condé Nast Publications, Inc.; 238 LC-USZ62-14459; 239 NA-111-SC-97517; 240 AP; 241 NA; 242 (top) Harry Ransom Humanities Research Center, University of Texas, Austin, (bottom, both) FDR 242–243 C-B; 243 (bottom left) FDR, (top) NA-19-N-104, (middle) C-B, (bottom) NA-306-NT-173-825c; 244–245 C-B; 246 AP; 246–247 AP; 248 (top) published in *St. Louis Post-Dispatch*, October 10, 1937, courtesy State Historical Society of Missouri, Columbia, (middle) David E. Lilienthal Papers, PUL, (bottom) LC; 249 (top and left) AP, (right) LC-USZ62-053185; 250 New York *Daily News*; 251 (both) AP; 252 (top) AP, (bottom) NA-65-H-252-5D; 253 NA-65-H-308-1; 254 AP; 255 (published in *Twenty Against the Underworld* by Thomas E. Dewey, 1974, (bottom) C-B; 256 Culver Pictures; 257 AP; 258 NA-208-PU-155Q-38; 259 loaned by Eleanor Roosevelt Foundation, FDR; 260 BB; 261 LC-USF-34-31-245D; 262–263 (top, all) NA, Rocky Mountain Division; 262 (bottom) AP; 263 (bottom) Author's Collection; 264–265 Heinrich Hoffmann Press-Illustationen, copyright Zeitgeschichtliches Bildarchiv, Munich; 265 Popperfoto/Archive; 266 (left) AP, (right) LC-USZ62-70043; 267 (left) C-B, (right) FD; 268 published in *I Remember Distinctly: A Family Album of the American People, 1918–1941* by Agnes Rogers 1947; 269 (top) NA-306-NT-315J-1, (left) *The Shooting of Huey Long*, 1939, by John McCrady, Southern regionalist master (1911–1968)/ Mr. and Mrs. Keith C. Marshall, New Orleans, (right) C-B; 270 drawing by Gluyas Williams © 1942, 1970 *The New Yorker* Magazine, Inc.; 271 FDR; 272–273 (both) C-B; 274–275 (top and bottom) AP; 275 C-B; 276 I.L.G.W.U. Archives, Kheel Center for Labor-Management Documentation and Archives, Cornell University; 277 AP; 278–279 AP; 280 (top) Ford Motor Company; 280–281 (left and center) The Archives of Labor and Urban Affairs, Wayne State University, (right) C-B.

CHAPTER NINE

282–283 Stanley Devon; 284 David Low, February 18, 1938/London *Evening Standard*, Solo Syndication, London; 285 John Mackey/FD; 287 Annabel

Merullo Collection, London; 288 AP; 289 collection Walter Karliner; 294 (left) *New York Journal American* Collection, Harry Ransom Humanities Research Center, University of Texas, Austin, (right) AP; 295 AP; 296 HG; 297 (top) David Low, July 8, 1936/London *Evening Standard*, Solo Syndication, London, 298 (top and bottom) Sovfoto; (inset) *Daily Herald* Picture Library, National Museum of Photography Film and Television, Bradford, England; 299 reproduced in *Signal: Years of Triumph 1940–42* (Hitler's Wartime Picture Magazine), reprinted 1978; 300 C-B; 301 (left) HG, (right) C-B; 302-303 AP; 304–305 FDR; 306 C-B; 307 C-B; 308 AP 310 (left) collection Dr. David Goldstein, (top) NA-80-G19948; 310–311 NA-80-30554; 311 (top left) HG, (top right) NA-80- 32414; 312 (all) AP; 313 C-B.

CHAPTER TEN

314–315 *Los Angeles Times* Photo Archive, Department of Special Collections, University Research Library, UCLA; 329 FD; 330–331 NA-026-G-1517; 333 (left) Carl Mydans/LIFE Magazine © TIME, Inc., (right) published in *The Second World War: A Complete History* by Martin Gilbert, 1989; 334 (left) NA-SC-202321, (right) copyright 1945 Bill Mauldin; 335 (left) Magnum Photos Inc. © 1943 Robert Capa, (right) NA-111-SC-438967; 337 (top) NA 111-SC-185960, (bottom) *U.S. News and World Report*; 338 A. Y. Owen/LIFE Magazine © TIME Inc.; 338–339 C-B; 339 (bottom) Heinrich Hoffmann/HG, (right) Magnum Photos Inc. © 1944 Robert Capa; 342–343 NA-111- SC-202622; 343 The Trustees of the Imperial War Musum, London; 344, 344–345 Igor Belousovitch; 345 (left) HG, (right top and bottom) *Chicago Tribune* photo; used by permission; 346–347 Oregon Historical Society ORH-44544; 347 (bottom) NA-208-NS-3848-2, (right) AP; 348 NA-RGWWT-85-33; 348–349 NA-86-WWT-14-6, 349 FDR; 350–351 AP, 351 (top) U.S. Army Museum of Hawaii, (bottom) NA-210-G2-A35; 352 (left) James Campbell/Photographs and Prints Division, Schomburg Center for Research in Black Culture, NYPL, Astor, Lenox, and Tilden Foundations, (right) AP; 353 (left) NA-111-SC-197376-5, (right) collection Robert Allen; 354 (top) NA-111-SC-152411, (bottom) FDR; 354–355 NA-111-SC-199753; 355 (top) HG, (bottom) NA-111-SC-200376; 357 FD; 358–359 W. Eugene Smith/LIFE Magazine © TIME Inc.; 360 NA-111-SC-377788; 360–361, 361 AP; 362–363 NA-80-G-414423, 363 AP; 364–365 Charles Kerlee/NA-80-G-320999; 365 (bottom) Charles Kerlee /NA-80-432598, (right) AP; 366 (top) AP, (bottom) HG; 366–367 L. R. Burmeister/ NA-127-N-110322; 368 AP; 368–369

Fenno Jacobs/NA-80-G-475024; 370 (top and bottom)Wayne Miller/NA-80-G-377558 and NA-80-G-377559, (center) George Tames/NYT Pictures; 371 Wayne Miller/(top) NA-80-G-377579, (middle) NA-80-G-377568, (bottom) NA-80-G-377554; 372 FDR; 372–373 HST; 374 (all except bottom left) HST, (bottom left) *Kansas City Star*, courtesy HST; 375 (top) C-B, (left) HST, (right) AP; 376 (both) AP; 377 HST; 378 C-B; 378–379 NA-164708; 380-381 Miyatake Hajime/*Asahi Shimbun*, Osaka; 382 NA-80-G-490317; 383 Magnum Photos Inc. © 1951 Werner Bischof; 384–385 Carl Mydans/LIFE Magazine © TIME, Inc.

CHAPTER ELEVEN

386–387 Henry Ries; 389 NA-208-N-46403-FA; 390 Sovfoto; 392 (both) C-B; 393 AP; 395 Henry Ries; 396–397 Vicky/ courtesy The Centre for the Study of Cartoons and Caricature, The University of Kent at Canterbury/copyright London *Evening Standard*, Solo Syndication, London; 398 AP; 403 State Historical Society of Missouri, Columbia; 404 United Nations; 404–405 HG; 405 United Nations; 406 (left) AP, (right) C-B; 407 (right) Drawing by David Levine. Reprinted with permission from *The New York Review of Books*. Copyright © 1970 Nyrev, Inc., (both) AP; 408 NA-111-SC-205629; 408–409 AP; 410 HG; 411 Henry Ries; 412 New York *Daily News*; 413 HST; 414 (both) AP; 415 © Estate of Ben Shahn/ Licensed by VAGA, New York, NY; 416 (all) AP; 417 (both) AP; 418-419 NA-208-PU-207W-2; 419 Popperfoto/ Archive; 420 LC-513-835; 420–421 John Foster Dulles Papers, Public Policy Collections, Department of Rare Books and Special Collections, Princeton University Library; 421 Joseph R. Darrigo; 422–423 George Tames/NYT Pictures; 423 AP; 424–425, 426 From *This Is War!* by David Douglas Duncan. Text and photographs copyright © 1990 by David Douglas Duncan; foreword copyright © 1990 by Harrison E. Salisbury. By permission of Little, Brown and Company; 427 (top) NA-111-SC-352944, (bottom) NA-127-GK-197-A5348; 428 LC-USZ62-14458; 429 C-B; 430 HERBLOCK, October 29, 1952, published in *HERBLOCK Special Report*, W.W. Norton, Inc., 1974; (bottom left) NA-111-SC- 416392; (bottom right) C-B; 431 (top left) AP; (top right) C-B; (bottom) Joe Scherschel LIFE Magazine © 1952 Time Inc.; 432 (top left) Vicky/copyright London *Evening Standard*, Solo Syndication, London; (top right, bottom left and right) DDE; 433 (top) NA-306-PS-52-13171; (middle left) DDE, (middle right) NA-306-PS-53-332, (bottom left) Leland Benfer/*Milwaukee Sentinel*; (bottom right) AP; 434–435 Alex Henderson/Hagley Museum and Library; 435 C-B; 436 Levittown Public Library; 436–437 Photo © 1947 Cliff De

Bear/*Newsday*. Los Angeles Times Syndicate; **438–439** © Arnold Newman; **440** C-B; **440–441** C-B; **441** Bill Mauldin; **442** F.B.I.; **443** AP; **444–445** AP; **445** (top) C-B, (bottom) AP; **446** (top) AP, (bottom) from HERBLOCK's *Here and Now* (Simon & Schuster, 1955); **447** (top and middle) AP, (bottom) detail of portrait by Mary Ellen Mark; **448, 449** (all) C-B; **450** AP; **451** (top) AP, (bottom) Magnum Photos Inc. © 1959 Sergio Larrain.

CHAPTER TWELVE
452–453 AP; **455** (top) AP, (middle row, left to right) C-B, Charles Moore/Black Star, AP; (bottom left) Bill Hudson/AP, (bottom right, top and bottom) AP, Charles Moore/Black Star; **456** C-B; **461** Steve Shapiro/Black Star; **466, 467** Charles Moore/Black Star; **468–469** Magnum Photos Inc. © 1957 Henri Cartier-Bresson; **470, 471** Joe Mignon/ C-B, **472** C-B; **473** (both) Charles Moore/ Black Star; **474–475, 475** C-B; **476** copyright Topham/The Image Works, Woodstock, N.Y.; **476–477** Lee Lockwood/Black Star; **478** (left) Magnum Photos Inc. © 1959 Burt Glinn (detail), (right) Alan Dunn © 1958 from *The New Yorker* Collection. All rights reserved; **479** (top) LC-U93122, (bottom) William Safire/AP; **480** (headline) NYT, (photo) AP; **480–481** SHAPE Radiophoto, Stephen White Collection II; **481** (top) copyright Bill Mauldin, (bottom) *U.S. News and World Report,* March 15, 1993; **482** Richard Pipes; **483** AP; **484** (top left) Edward Sorel, (bottom left) JFK, (center) Drawing by David Levine. Reprinted with permission from *The New York Review of Books.* Copyright © 1987 Nyrev, Inc., (top right) Magnum Photos Inc. © 1961 Elliott Erwitt, (bottom right) Dr. Erich Salomon/Nederlands Photo Archive; **485** (top) JFK, (left) Magnum Photos Inc. © 1956 Burt Glinn (detail), (right) Magnum Photos Inc.; **486** Leslie Illingworth/National Library of Wales/copyright London *Daily Mail,* Solo Syndication; **487** (top) AP, (bottom) Family of Richard Bissell, Jr.; **488–489** Robert Hunt Library, London; **489** copyright Topham/The Image Works, Woodstock, N.Y.; **490** (both) AP; **491** (top) AP, (left) Harry Redl/Black Star, (right) U.S. Army Photo SC-610231; **492** New York *Daily News*; **493** (top) Mike Peters/© Tribune Media Services. All rights reserved. Reprinted with permission, (bottom) JFK; **494** JFK; **495** LC-U9-8655 28-32, (bottom) FD; **496–497** © 1963 Flip Schulke; **497** © Carole Gallagher from *America Ground Zero: The Secret Nuclear War,* M.I.T. Press, 1993; **498** AP; **499** (top) AP, (bottom) © 1962 Flip Schulke; **500–501** Magnum Photos Inc. © 1961 Bruce Davidson; **502–503** © 1963 Flip Schulke, **503** AP; **504** James Karales; **505** Flip Schulke/Black Star; **506,**

507 AP; **508** NA; **509** (top) Bob Jackson, (center) diagram by John Grimwade from *Case Closed: Lee Harvey Oswald and the Assassination of J.F.K.* by Gerald Posner, Random House, 1993; **510–511** NA 79-AR-7494B; **512** (top left) Paul Szep/reprinted courtesy of *The Boston Globe,* (all) LBJ; **513** (left and top) LBJ, (middle) © 1956 *The Washington Post.* Reprinted with permission, (bottom) George Tames/NYT Pictures; **514** (both) AP; **515** (top) NYPL, (bottom) LBJ; **516** reproduced in *The Glorious Burden: The American Presidency* by Stefan Lorant, 1968; **517** Yoichi Okamoto/LBJ; **518** Bill Reed/Black Star; **519** (left) C-B, (right) Vernon Merritt/Black Star; **520–521** James Karales.

CHAPTER THIRTEEN
522–523 Magnum Photos Inc. © 1967 Philip Jones Griffiths; **525** Yoichi Okamoto/LBJ; **526, 527** Robert Pryor; **530, 531** Yoichi Okamoto/LBJ; **534** John Paul Vann segment, Neil Sheehan Papers, Manuscript Division, LC; **535** Tech. Sgt. Eddie P. Boaz/U.S. Army Photo SC-667414; **538–539** Larry Burrows/LIFE Magazine © 1964 Time, Inc.; **540** Sangamon Valley Collection, Lincoln Library, Springfield, Illinois; **540–541** Magnum Photos Inc. © 1970 Philip Jones Griffiths; **541** (both) California Museum of Photography; **542–543** Robert Altman; **543** (top and bottom) Gerald S. Upham, (middle) John Fischetti Collection, Ohio State University, Cartoon Research Library; **544** from *Malcolm X: The Great Photographs,* text by Thuliani Davis, photographs selected by Howard Chapnick, New York: Stewart, Tabori and Chang, 1993; **544–545** Bob Gomel/LIFE Magazine © 1963 Time, Inc.; **546** C-B; **547** C-B; **548–549** courtesy Helene Berinsky; **550** AP; **551** (left) AP, (right) Duane Hall; **552** (top left) Gerald Scarfe, (all) RN; **553** (top) Ollie Atkins/George Mason University, (left center) RN, (right center) Stanley Tretick/RN, (bottom) AP; **554, 555** NASA/print by Michael Light; **556** AP; **557** (top) DOONESBURY © 1973 G. B. Trudeau. Reprinted with permission of UNIVERSAL PRESS SYNDICATE. All rights reserved, (bottom) *The Daily Mirror* (London), May 5, 1970/ photograph by John Filo; **558** (top) Ron Haeberle/ LIFE Magazine, © Time Inc., (bottom) AP; **559** AP; **560** Mark Godfrey; **561** AP; **562–563** George Tames/NYT Pictures; **563** Bob Fitch/Black Star; **564** Tim for *L'Express,* 1969/ FD; **564–565** AP; **565** C-B.

CHAPTER FOURTEEN
566–567 Harry Benson; **568** (top to bottom) AP, © 1973 *The Washington Post.* Reprinted with permission, C-B, Mark Godfrey; **569** (top left) Fred Ward/Black Star, (top right) C-B, (middle left and

bottom right)© 1973 *The Washington Post* Reprinted with permission, (middle right and bottom left) AP; **576–577** published in Fred Emery *Watergate: The Corruption of American Politics and the Fall of Richard Nixon,* Touchstone, 1994; **578** NA; **580** AP; **582** Official White House photo; **583** FD; **584** NYT Pictures; **585** Charles Gerretsen/Gamma-Liaison; **586** Michael O'Brien; **587** AP; **588** (top right) Tony Auth/ *Philadelphia Inquirer,* (top left) Robert Grossman, (middle right) Reprinted with permission, Paul Conrad, *Los Angeles Times* Syndicate, 1973, (bottom left) from *Herblock Special Report,* W. W. Norton, 1984, (bottom right) OLIPHANT copyright UNIVERSAL PRESS SYNDICATE. Reprinted with permission. All rights reserved; **589** (top left) from *Herblock: A Cartoonist's Life,* Lisa Drew Books/Macmillan, 1993, (top right) Reprinted with permission, Paul Conrad, *Los Angeles Times* Syndicate, 1973, (left middle and bottom) Paul Szep. Reprinted courtesy of *The Boston Globe,* (bottom right) Bill Andrews/ *Daily World.* From *Best Editorial Cartoons of the Year 1974,* edited by Charles Brooks, Pelican Publishing Co., 1974; **590** (top left) © Robert Osborn/Eliot and Nic Osborn, (top and middle right, middle left) Gerald R. Ford Library, (bottom right) NA 80-G-417628; **591** (top and bottom) AP, (right) © Tony Spina; **592** John Trever/*Albuquerque Journal*; **593** David Hume Kennerly/ Gerald R. Ford Library; **594** © 1975 Jules Feiffer; **595** C-B; **596** (top) Steve Shapiro, (bottom) AP; **597** (top) Paul Szep. Reprinted courtesy *The Boston Globe,* (middle) Doug Marlette, (bottom) Mike Peters/© Tribune Media Services. All rights reserved. Reprinted with permission; **598** (left) Alan Greth/AP, (right) J. P. Laffont/ Gamma-Liaison; **599** (left) The Supreme Court of the United States, (right) C-B; **600** Daniel Nicoletta; **601** (top left) Gerald R. Ford Library, (top right, bottom left) AP, (bottom right) C-B; **602** (top) Reprinted with permission, Paul Conrad, *Los Angeles Times* Syndicate, 1976, (left, both and bottom right) Jimmy Carter Library, (middle right) Jimmy Carter National Historic Site, United States Department of Interior, National Park Service; **603** (top left) Charles Rafshoon, (top and middle right) Jimmy Carter Library, (bottom) Paul Obregon/Habitat for Humanity International; **604–605** George Tames/NYT Pictures; **606** Jimmy Carter Library; **607** AP; **608–609** © 1980 Abbas/Magnum Photos Inc., **610–611** (all) Phil Stewart/Gamma-Liaison.

CHAPTER FIFTEEN
612–613 Wally McNamee/Newsweek; **615** Edward Sorel; **623** Ben Sargent © 1983 *Austin-Smerican Statesman.* Reprinted with permission of Universal Perss Syndicate. All rights reserved; **624** (top left) Reprinted with permission,

Paul Conrad, *Los Angeles Times* Syndicate, 1983, (top right) AP; **625** (top) C-B, (center left) New York *Daily News,* (center right) publicity photo, General Electric, (bottom) Ben Olender/*Los Angeles Times* Syndicate; **626** photograph by Harry Benson/cover courtesy VANITY FAIR. Copyright © 1985 by the Condé Nast Publications Inc.; **626–627** © 1981 Diana Walker/TIME Magazine; **627** Ron Edmonds/AP; **628** Rob Nelson; **629** Joe Holloway/AP; **630** Mary Ellen Mark; **631** Ann Chwatsky/Black Star; **632** Doug Mathieson/Gamma-Liaison; **632–633** Alan Tannenbaum/Sygma; **634** Sylvia Plachy; **634–635** George Tames/ NYT Pictures; **636** (top) Magnum Photos Inc. © Eli Reed, (bottom) Harry Mattison; **636–637** Magnum Photos Inc. © 1980 Susan Meiselas; **638** (top) Stuart Carlson/*Milwaukee Sentinal,* (bottom) Magnum Photos Inc. © 1984 James Nachtwey; **639** Lana Harris/AP; **640** Eldon Pletcher/© *New Orleans Times Picayune*; **641** (top) J. Scott Applewhite/AP, (bottom left) Lana Harris/AP, (bottom right) Scott Stewart/AP; **642** Reprinted with permission, Paul Conrad, *Los Angeles Times* Syndicate, 1981; **643** Nick Ut/AP, (bottom two) AP; **644–645** © 1986 Angel Franco/Woodfin Camp & Associates. All rights reserved; **646** Paul Hosefros/NYT Pictures; **647** AP; **648** copyright *National Enquirer,* courtesy AP; **648–649** David Burnett/Contact Press Images; **649** DOONESBURY © 1988 G. B. Trudeau. Reprinted with permission of UNIVERSAL PRESS SYNDICATE. All rights reserved; **650** (top) Gary A. Batte/photo courtesy George Bush Presidential Library, (all others) George Bush Presidential Library; **650–651** © 1990 Diana Walker/TIME Magazine; **651** (middle left and right) AP, (bottom left) J. Scott Applewhite/AP, (bottom right) George Bush Presidential Library.

AFTERWORD
652–653 Jerome Liebling; **654–655** (top) Magnum Photos Inc. © 1989 Guy Le Querrec, (bottom) Thomas Kienzle/AP; **656–657** Magnum Photos Inc. © 1990 Guy Le Querrec; **658** Dorothea Lange LC-USF34-9058-C, (right) Bill Ganzel; **659** Alon Reininger/Contact; **600** TR, **601** Richard Ellis/Sygma; **662** Edward Sorel; **663** Magnum Photos Inc. © 1970 Burt Glinn.

BIBLIOGRAPHY
668 C-B; **669** LC-USZ62-9981; **670** OHS; **671** LC-USZ62-23234; **672** LC-USZ62-22163; **673** C-B; **674** James Whitmore/LIFE Magazine © TIME Inc.; **675** AP; **676** National Baseball Hall of Fame; **677** C-B; **678** AP; **680** Gerald R. Ford Library; **681** Karl Schumacher/Jimmy Carter Library; **682** C-B; **684** (both) AP; **686** AP; **688** C-B.

HAROLD EVANS is Editorial Director and Vice Chairman of *U.S. News & World Report, Atlantic Monthly, New York Daily News,* and *Fast Company.* He was President and Publisher of the Random House Trade Group from 1990 to 1997.

Evans was from 1967 to 1981 the prizewinning editor of *The Sunday Times* of London and in 1981–82 editor of *The Times,* which became the subject of his memoir, *Good Times, Bad Times.* He was awarded the European Gold Medal of the Institute of Journalists for his investigation of and campaign for thalidomide children, and he won the Hood Medal of the Royal Photographic Society for his photojournalism.

Evans received an M.A. from Durham University. He won a Harkness Fellowship for study at the University of Chicago and Stanford University and for travel in the United States. He reported from America for the *Manchester Evening News and Guardian* and returned to Britain to edit *The Northern Echo.* In 1984 he moved to the United States as a visiting professor at Duke University. Subsequently he was editor in chief of Atlantic Monthly Press and the founding editor of *Condé Nast Traveler.* He edited the two-volume memoirs of Henry Kissinger, a study of the Soviet Union by Zbigniew Brzezinski, the final book by President Nixon, and the memoir of General Colin Powell.

He lives in New York City with his wife, Tina Brown, and their two children.

GAIL BUCKLAND is Associate Professor of the History of Photography at The Cooper Union. In 1991 she held the Nobel Chair in Art and Cultural History at Sarah Lawrence College and taught there again in 1996. She is the former curator of the Royal Photographic Society of Great Britain and has organized numerous photographic exhibitions on both sides of the Atlantic, including *From Today Painting Is Dead* at the Victoria and Albert Museum, *Fox Talbot and the Invention of Photography* at the Pierpont Morgan Library, and *Visions of Liberty* at the New-York Historical Society. She is the author of eight books on photography and history, including the forthcoming *Making America.*

KEVIN BAKER is the author of the novels *Dreamland* and *Sometimes You See It Coming,* and the forthcoming history *The Rivalry: Boston and New York in the Twentieth Century.* He lives and works in New York City.

A NOTE ON THE TYPE

This book was set in Minion, a typeface produced by the Adobe Corporation specifically for the Macintosh personal computer, and released in 1990. Designed by Robert Slimbach, Minion combines the classic characteristics of old-style faces with the full complement of weights required for modern typesetting.

Halftones prepared by Carolyn Hess, North Market Street Graphics, Lancaster, Pennsylvania
Composed by Precision Graphics, Chester, Connecticut
Printed and bound by Quebecor Printing, Kingsport, Tennessee
Designed by Wendy Byrne